601 SPANISH VERBS

Lori Langer de Ramírez Ed.D.
with
Stephen Kehs M.A.T., Asela Laguna-Mourao M.A.Ed.,
Jim Sarris M.A., Sandy Williamson, M.A.T.

Berlitz Publishing
New York London Singapore

601 Spanish Verbs

Contacting the Editors
Every effort has been made to provide accurate information in this publication, but changes are inevitable. The publisher cannot be responsible for any resulting loss, inconvenience, or injury. We would appreciate it if readers would call our attention to any errors or outdated information; we also welcome your suggestions. Please contact us at: comments@berlitzpublishing.com

2nd Edition: July 2013
Printed in China by CTPS

Head of Language: Kate Drynan
Project Manager/Editor: Nela Navarro
Editorial: Nancy Kelly, Janeth Pataroyo, Alejandra Gritsipis
Production Manager: Vicky Glover
Cover Design: Claudia Petrilli
Interior Design/Art: Claudia Petrilli and Datagrafix, Inc.

Distribution
UK, Ireland and Europe:
Apa Publications (UK) Ltd;
sales@insightguides.com
United States and Canada:
Ingram Publisher Services;
ips@ingramcontent.com
Australia and New Zealand:
Woodslane;
info@woodslane.com.au
Southeast Asia:
Apa Publications (SN) Pte;
singaporeoffice@insightguides.com
Worldwide:
Apa Publications (UK) Ltd;
sales@insightguides.com

Special Sales, Content Licensing and CoPublishing
Insight Guides can be purchased in bulk quantities at discounted prices. We can create special editions, personalised jackets and corporate imprints tailored to your needs.
sales@insightguides.com;
www.insightguides.biz

Contents

About the Authors

Lori Langer de Ramírez, Ed.D.

Lori Langer de Ramírez holds a Master's Degree in Applied Linguistics and a Doctorate in Curriculum and Teaching from Teachers College, Columbia University. She is currently the Chairperson of the ESL and World Language Department for Herricks Public Schools in New Hyde Park, N.Y. Dr. Langer de Ramírez is the author of several Spanish-language books and texts and has contributed to many textbooks and written numerous articles about second language pedagogy and methodology. Her interactive website, www.miscositas.com, offers teachers over 40 virtual picturebooks and other curricular materials for teaching foreign languages.

Stephen Kehs, M.A.T.

Stephen Kehs has a B.A. in Spanish and an M.A.T. from the University of North Carolina at Chapel Hill. He is an upper school Spanish teacher at Saint John's School in Houston, Texas. Over the course of his career, he has taught Spanish I through IV, served as a student advisor, and lead several student trips to Spain.

Asela Laguna-Mourao, M.A.Ed.

Asela Laguna-Mourao has a B.A. in Latin American Studies from Rutgers University and an M.A.Ed. in Supervision from St. Peter's College. She has studied abroad at University of Salamanca, Spain and in Costa Rica. She has taught all levels of Spanish including heritage speakers and she is currently teaching middle and high school Spanish in the Dunellen, N.J. school district.

Jim Sarris, M.A.

Jim Sarris has B.A. in Education from the University of Massachusetts, Amherst and an M.A. in TESOL/Bilingual Ed. from Southern Connecticut State University. He has been teaching all levels of Spanish (from beginner to AP) for 15 years and is currently at Horace Greeley High School in Chappaqua, N.Y. He has also published various books on enhancing memory skills as well as Spanish language learning books.

Sandy Williamson, M.A.T.

Sandy Williamson received her B.A. and M.A.T. from Duke University and has taught Spanish in North Carolina schools since 1974, from levels I through AP. She was a Fulbright Teaching Fellow in Argentina and a Carnegie Mellon Fellow at the University of North Carolina at Chapel Hill. She has traveled extensively with her students throughout the Hispanic world. She has presented at state and national conferences and has been an AP reader since 1996. She is currently teaching at East Chapel Hill High School in Chapel Hill, North Carolina.

Reviewers

Berlitz Publishing is grateful for the valuable comments and suggestions made by the team of teacher and student reviewers during the stages of development. Their contributions, expertise, experience and passion for the Spanish language are clearly reflected in this important project.

¡***Mil gracias***!

Teachers

María Bazarra, Science Park High School, Newark, New Jersey

Ana Medina Burgess, Great Falls Language Academy, Great Falls, Virginia

Sherifa Meguid, Strake Jesuit College Preparatory, Houston, Texas

Ximena Mieles, Fordham University, Bronx, New York

Catalina Nacher, Edgemont High School, Scarsdale, New York

Susan Quintyne, Herricks High School, Herricks, New York

Marta Cabrera-Serrano, Rutgers University-Newark, Newark, New Jersey

Rebecca Spring, North Carolina State University, Raleigh, North Carolina

Danielle Zieser, Glen Ridge High School, Glen Ridge, New Jersey

José Borreguero, Kean University, Union, New Jersey

Nancy Kelly, Chapel Hill-Carrboro City Schools, Chapel Hill, North Carolina

Students

Gerren Crosson, St. John's School, Houston, Texas

Yasmine Kulesza, St. Thomas University, Miami, Florida

Rebecca Lange, East Chapel Hill High School, Chapel Hill, North Carolina

Cody Rapp, St. John's School, Houston, Texas

Ana Rivera Mosquera, Rutgers University-Newark, Newark, New Jersey

Nicole Roscigno, East Chapel Hill High School, Chapel Hill, North Carolina

Yannek Smith, Rutgers University-Newark, Newark, New Jersey

Damian Williams, State University of New York at Albany, Albany, New York

Dear Students,

As with everything in life, if you want to become good at something, you have to practice. Learning Spanish is the same: it is crucial to your growth as budding Spanish speakers that you practice the language in many different contexts. For example:

- *watching Spanish language television*
- *listening to Spanish language radio broadcasts and podcasts*
- *reading Spanish language books, stories, and newspaper magazine articles*
- *and, most importantly: engaging native speakers of Spanish in conversation*

These are all critical ways to expose yourself to the structures and vocabulary of Spanish. Along with this authentic practice is the need for precision – and this is where 601 Spanish Verbs can help you to improve your fluency. When you are through producing a story, an essay, a blog entry or an email in Spanish, consult 601 Spanish Verbs to ensure that your message is being communicated correctly. A good understanding of the verb tenses, their conjugations and their structures will enable you to express yourself freely and correctly. And take some time to work through the activities at the end of 601 Spanish Verbs. They are aimed at assessing your understanding of the use of verbs in real-life contexts such as conversations and short stories.

It is our hope that 601 Spanish Verbs will become an invaluable source of information for you during your years on the road to Spanish fluency.

It is also our hope that your road will be paved with the joy of learning and the wonder of communicating in a new language. ¡Buena suerte!

- Dr. Lori Langer de Ramírez

Dear Teachers,

It is so exhilarating to watch our students grow and thrive in their study of the Spanish language. We watch in awe as they master subject-verb agreement and we smile with delight when they finally grasp the subjunctive mood! But there are also trying times on the road to Spanish proficiency. Understanding the many different tenses and conjugations in Spanish can prove challenging to many students. This is where 601 Spanish Verbs can serve as an important source of support and encouragement for our students.

601 Spanish Verbs is an essential book for your students and you to use as a reference at home, in the classroom or library. We all recall times when a student wants to say or write something in Spanish, but just doesn't have the verb paradigm mastered quite yet. While communication can certainly take place without this precision of language, it is less likely to be successful and can often frustrate students. By having 601 Spanish Verbs handy when students are working in the language, teachers can help scaffold the language that students have already acquired. Students can check their work using the book as well as use it for reference as they create essays, blog entries, original creative writing pieces and other writing or oral productions in the Spanish classroom.

601 Spanish Verbs can help students to feel secure in the language while also providing valuable information and practice that can lead to more advanced proficiency in the language. We all know that a secure student is a student who is open to learning more. It is our hope that 601 Verbs serves as an important support for students as they continue on their road to Spanish proficiency. ¡Buena suerte!

- Dr. Lori Langer de Ramírez

How to Use This Book

Welcome to *601 Spanish Verbs*! This is *the* verb reference book for today's student. This book was created to help you learn the Spanish verb system, not for the sake of studying about Spanish verbs, but so that you can communicate and enjoy speaking Spanish! *601 Spanish Verbs* will help make studying easier and also provide you with opportunities to improve, practice and even have fun *en español*.

Learn to make the most of this book by becoming familiar with the contents. Go back to the Table of Contents (TOC) on Page 3. The TOC will help you navigate and locate the following sections in this book:

About the Authors/Reviewers

You will notice that *601 Spanish Verbs* is written by a team of experienced teachers committed to helping you learn Spanish. The book was reviewed by another team of equally experienced teachers and engaged students from various schools and universities.

Letter to the Student/Letter to the Teacher

Dr. Lori Langer de Ramírez, one of the book's main authors, shares tips to help you practice Spanish in different contexts. Dr. Langer de Ramírez also tells you how *601 Spanish Verbs* will help you improve your overall fluency in Spanish, whether you are writing an essay, a blog, an email, a text-message or prepping for an exam.

Verb Guide

The Verb Guide is a brief, clear, student-friendly overview of all the important parts of the Spanish verb system. The Verb Guide also provides you with practical tips on how to place accents correctly to enhance your writing skills. It also provides useful memory tips to help you understand how important verbs, such as *ser* and *estar*, are used.

Alphabetical Listing of 601 Verbs

601 Spanish Verbs provides an alphabetical listing of 601 of the most commonly-used Spanish verbs in academic, professional and social contexts. Each verb page provides an English translation of the Spanish verb. The verb conjugations have endings that are highlighted for easy reference, which makes learning the conjugations of the different tenses much easier! We have identified 75 of the most useful and common Spanish verbs. These *75 Must Know Verbs* are featured with a blue background for easy reference. In addition author Jim Sarris, who is a memory expert, wrote tips to help you remember key verbs. These verbs are also marked for easy reference.

Verb Activity Pages/Answer Key for Activities

These activity pages provide you with a variety of accessible and practical exercises that help you practice both the conjugation and usage of verbs. There is an answer key on page 686 so that you can check your answers.

Must-know Verbs

You will find a list of Must Know Verbs. These verbs are 75 of the most useful and common Spanish verbs. Remember, these verbs are marked for easy reference in the body of the book. Note: sometimes Must Know Verbs have memory tips, and in this case the page is only marked with the memory tip design.

Tech Verb List

Here you will find a list of verbs commonly used with technology. Now you can send an email, download a podcast, open documents and use search engines in Spanish!

Text Messaging in Spanish Guide

Time to have fun in Spanish! Use this text-messaging guide to text *en español.* You can also use this text-messaging guide when writing emails or when communicating in social networking sites.

Test Prep Guide

The Test Prep Guide offers a quick bulleted list of helpful strategies for test prep for Spanish and for your other classes. These tips will help you before, during and after the exam. On page 677, you will also find a list of 75 Spanish verbs that are likely to be useful in a test. *¡Buena suerte!*

Index of Over 2500 Spanish Verbs Conjugated Like Model Verbs

At the beginning of the index you will find a list of model verbs. We have included these verbs since most other Spanish verbs are conjugated like one of these model forms. We suggest that you study these model verbs; once you know these conjugations you will be able to conjugate most any verb!

The index provides an additional 2500 verbs used in Spanish. Each verb includes an English translation. The English translation is followed by a number, for example: *abalanzar*, to balance, 67. The number 67 refers to the page where you will find the conjugation of the verb *colgar*. The verb abalanzar is conjugated like the model verb *colgar*.

Verb Guide Table of Contents

Verb Guide

Introduction

The purpose of this book is to help you understand and successfully navigate the Spanish verb system. There are three broad concepts that you need to understand to help you do this, and they are the following:

- What is meant by "conjugating" a verb
- What is meant by "tense" and how the Spanish verb tenses work
- What is meant by "mood" and how the indicative, subjunctive, and imperative moods are used in Spanish

In this introduction you will learn about these three concepts and you will see that what appears to be a dauntingly complicated system is really quite simple once you understand the key, which is the use of patterns. Armed with your knowledge of patterns in the Spanish verb system, you will be able to use this book to help you communicate well in Spanish.

List of tenses

English/English explanation	Spanish/Spanish example using "hablar"
present indicative (what you do or are doing)	presente de indicativo (*hablo*)
imperfect indicative (what you used to do/ were doing)	imperfecto de indicativo (*hablaba*)
preterite (what you did)	pretérito (*hablé*)
future (what you will do)	futuro (*hablaré*)
conditional (what you would do)	condicional simple (*hablaría*)
present perfect (what you have done)	perfecto de indicativo (*he hablado*)
past perfect (what you had done)	pluscuamperfecto de indicativo (*había hablado*)
pretéterito anterior	pretérito anterior (*hube hablado*)
future perfect (what you will have done)	futuro perfecto (*habré hablado*)
conditional perfect (what you would have done)	condicional compuesto (*habría hablado*)
present subjunctive*	presente de subjuntivo (*hable*)
imperfect subjunctive*	imperfecto de subjuntivo (*hablara*)
present perfect subjunctive*	perfecto de subjuntivo (*haya hablado*)
past perfect subjunctive*	pluscuamperfecto de subjuntivo (*hubiera hablado*)

*Translation of these tenses will vary with the context. See examples in sections on the uses of the subjunctive mood.

What is conjugation?

Let's start by thinking about what you know about verbs in general. You know that they are sometimes called "action words" and that no sentence is complete without a verb. In English, verbs almost always have a subject or word that does the action of the verb. Without the subject, the sentence seems incomplete. What you will find about Spanish verbs that makes them special is that each verb form gives you more information than its English counterpart. While an English verb form communicates only the action, a Spanish verb form also tells who does the action and when it takes place.

The infinitive

In Spanish, the basic form of a verb that you will see when you look in the dictionary is called an infinitive. This form has no subject because it is unconjugated, but it carries the basic meaning of the verb, the action. In Spanish all infinitives end in "-ar," "-er," or "-ir," and each one of these endings indicates how you will conjugate or change the verb to make it agree with a subject. While there are times when you will leave the verb in the infinitive form, most of the time you will need to change the infinitive ending to agree with a subject and to show a tense. Once you learn the basic pattern that all Spanish verbs follow for conjugation, you will see that changing a subject or a tense is very simple. Even irregular verbs will follow this simple pattern.

When can you leave a verb in the infinitive, or unconjugated, form?

- An infinitive may act like an English gerund. A gerund is a verb form that is used as a noun. In the English sentence "*Running* is good for your health", the subject of the sentence is the gerund "running." In Spanish, however, you use an infinitive to express the same idea: "*Correr* es bueno para la salud."
- An infinitive is frequently used as a complement to a conjugated verb. A complement is a second verb form that completes the meaning of the first verb, as in these examples:

Quiero *practicar* español.	I want *to practice* Spanish.
Tengo que *ir* a la tienda.	I have *to go* to the store.
Voy a *estudiar* mañana.	I am going *to study* tomorrow.

- An infinitive is often used after a preposition in Spanish, where a gerund might be used in English:

antes de *comer*	before *eating*
después de *llegar*	after *arriving*
al *entrar*	upon *entering*

How do I conjugate a verb so that I can use it in a sentence?

In order to master the conjugation pattern that all Spanish verbs follow, you just need to learn the basic format. Here is a simple chart to help you visualize the pattern:

singular forms	**plural forms**
1st person = the one speaking/acting	1st person = the ones speaking/acting
2nd person = the one spoken to	2nd person = the ones spoken to
3rd person = the one spoken about	3rd person = the ones spoken about

In any tense, Spanish verbs always have six forms, and they always follow this pattern. Which form you need to use depends on who or what the subject of the verb is, no matter what tense you are using. You can always use this pattern to help you understand and use verbs in Spanish. It will never change, no matter what the verb or the tense.

Subject pronouns

The first thing you need to learn is the pattern for personal (or subject) pronouns in Spanish, which are the same for all verb conjugations.

1st person singular = yo (I)	1st person plural = nosotros, nosotras (we)
2nd person singular = tú (you, informal)	2nd person plural = vosotros, vosotras (you plural, informal)
3rd person singular = él, ella, usted (he, she, you formal)	3rd person plural = ellos, ellas, ustedes (they, masculine/they, feminine/ you plural, formal)

Notice that while in English there is only one way to say "you," in Spanish there are four variations. That is because in Spanish there is a social distinction between the two ways to address others, depending on how well you know someone. Second person subject pronouns and verb forms are used to indicate familiarity, and third person forms indicate a social distance and are therefore more formal.

In all Spanish-speaking countries, you use the "tú" form of the verb when you are addressing someone with whom you are on a first-name basis, like a friend or family member, especially someone younger. An exception would be when you address an older family member to whom you wish to show respect, like a grandparent. The "usted" form is used with strangers, people you know but with whom you have a more formal relationship, or with older people who deserve your respect, like your teacher. In Spain, this same distinction is made in the plural verb forms, but "vosotros" is not used in other countries. In all other countries, the "ustedes" verb form is used for all plural expressions of "you." In this book, "you" will be used to indicate a singular form ("tú" or "usted"), and "you all" will be used to indicate a plural form ("vosotros" or "ustedes").

In some countries in Central and South America, there is an alternate form for the second person singular, or familiar "you" form, which is the "vos" form. It requires slightly different verb forms, but anyone in the countries where "vos" is commonly used will understand you if you use the "tú" form, so it is really not necessary to learn it. If you spent some time in a country where "vos" is common, you would easily learn the correct usage.

You will also notice that the plural forms of personal pronouns in Spanish (nosotros/nosotras, vosotros/vosotras, ellos/ellas) can generally be masculine or feminine, another concept that is different from English. In Spanish, all nouns have gender and number, and so do these personal pronouns. You will see that the ending "-os" will be used to designate a group of masculine persons or things or a mixed gender group, while the ending "-as" designates a group of feminine persons or things.

The last big difference about personal pronouns used with verbs in Spanish is that you can often omit them, unlike in English. This is because the endings in different verb conjugations will generally tell you who the subject is. Examples will be given later to show you how all these concepts work.

What is meant by "tense" in Spanish?

In any language, the verb's tense indicates the time frame for the action of the verb. In fact, in Spanish the word for "tense" (tiempo) is also the word for "time." So, if you want to talk about what is going on now, you will choose the present tense. If you want to talk about what happened yesterday or last year, you will choose one of the two simple past tenses. If you want to talk about your life in twenty years, you will choose the future tense, and so on. This is the same in Spanish as it is in English. What is different about Spanish is that the verb endings you will learn for each tense convey more information than those in English. They will tell you not only what time period is being referred to, but also who or what the subject of the verb is.

The Present Indicative Tense (el presente de indicativo)

Let's start with the present tense, which can be used to talk about current action or routine action. Verbs whose infinitives end in "-ar" are called first conjugation verbs and are the most common type of verb in Spanish. All "-ar" verbs are conjugated the same way, unless they are irregular. A regular verb is simply one that follows the rules for conjugation, and an irregular verb does not follow those rules. Once you learn the pattern for each conjugation, you can apply it to any regular verb in that category. If a verb is irregular, you will use the same basic pattern, but you will have to memorize the irregular forms.

In order to conjugate a regular verb, you start with the infinitive stem, which is the infinitive minus the "-ar,' "-er," or "-ir." So, for the verb "hablar" (to speak or talk), you remove the "-ar" and get the infinitive stem "habl-." Then you simply add the present tense for "-ar "verbs, which are given below:

-o	-amos
-as	-áis
-a	-an

These endings correspond to the chart of personal pronouns given previously and automatically tell you who the subject is. For example, if a verb ends in "-o," you know right away that the subject is "yo" (I) and that you are using the present tense. If it ends in "-as," the subject can only be "tú" (the informal, singular "you"). Let's look at an example to see how this works. A common regular "-ar" verb in Spanish is "hablar." Here is the chart for the present tense conjugation of this verb:

yo hablo = I speak	nosotros hablamos = we speak
tú hablas = you speak	vosotros habláis = you all speak
él, ella, usted habla = he speaks, she speaks, you speak	ellos, ellas, ustedes hablan = they speak, you all speak

The translation of the present tense in Spanish is pretty flexible. For example, "yo hablo" may mean "I speak, I do speak, or I am speaking," depending on the context. As we saw before, since each verb form in Spanish is directly related to a specific subject, it is perfectly normal to drop the personal pronoun and use only the verb. Consider the following brief interchange:

¿Hablas español? = Do you speak Spanish?
Sí, hablo un poco de español. = Yes, I speak a little Spanish.

Anyone who heard this conversation would know right away who was speaking, simply by the endings used. Only "yo" can be the subject of "hablo," and only "tú" can be the subject of "hablas," so the subject pronouns are not necessary, except for emphasis. This is true for the first and second person plural forms, as well. Third person forms are a bit different, since there is more than one possible subject for this form. Hence, unless you have already made it clear whom you are talking about, it is more likely that a subject will be used with these forms (either a noun or a pronoun). For example, if you hear someone say "*Habla español muy bien*," you have no clue who speaks Spanish well unless the speaker has already mentioned him or her. If the speaker has previously said "*Mi hermano Pablo vive en México*," (My brother Pablo lives in Mexico), then you can assume that the subject of "*Habla español muy bien.*" is "he," even though it is not directly stated.

Second conjugation verbs are those whose infinitives end in "-er," and their present tense endings are slightly different than those of "-ar" verbs. Here is the chart for these verbs:

-o	-emos
-es	-éis
-e	-en

Here is the present tense conjugation the for verb "comer," to eat.

yo como = I eat	nosotros comemos = we eat
tú comes = you eat	vosotros coméis = you all eat
él, ella, usted come = he eats, she eats, you eat	ellos, ellas, ustedes comen = they eat, you all eat

What you notice right away is that these endings use the vowel "e" where "-ar" verbs use the vowel "a." First person, or the "yo" form, is the same for all regular verbs in the present tense, since they all end in "-o."

Third conjugation verbs are those whose infinitives end in "-ir," and the chart for their present tense endings is below:

-o	-imos
-es	-ís
-e	-en

Some of these endings are the same as those used for "-er" verbs, so that means you only have to learn two different endings, those for "nosotros" and "vosotros." Those two endings will always let you know whether the verb is a second or third conjugation verb.

Here is the present tense conjugation of the verb "vivir," to live.

yo vivo = I live	nosotros vivimos = we live
tú vives = you live	vosotros vivís* = you all live
él, ella, usted vive = he lives, she lives, you live	ellos, ellas, ustedes viven = they live, you all live

Notice that for the present tense, only the ending for "vosotros" needs an accent mark to let you know how to pronounce the verb. It's quite easy to remember where to place the accent mark: on the "a" of "-ar" verbs ("-áis"), on the "e" of "-er" verbs ("-éis"), and on the "i" of "-ir" verbs ("-ís"). In the present tense, unaccented verbs are always stressed on the next to the last syllable.

The idea of action that began in the past but continues into the present may also be expressed using several special constructions in the present tense, such as the following:

Hace dos años que vivimos aquí.

Vivimos aquí desde hace dos años.

Llevamos dos años viviendo aquí.

Once you know the present tense endings, all you need to do to switch to a different tense is change the endings. For most tenses you add these endings to the infinitive stem (the infinitive minus the "-ar," "-er," or "-ir.") For some tenses you add the endings directly to the infinitive, as you will see.

Stem changes in the present tense

There is a special group of verbs in Spanish that are called stem-changing verbs. This means that the infinitive stem of the verb has a change in the last vowel in the stem before the present tense endings are added. A stem-changing verb may be from any of the three conjugations (-ar,-er, or -r). The changes occur only in the forms in which the stem is stressed when the verb is pronounced, which includes all forms except for first and second person plural. These verbs are sometimes called "boot" or "shoe" verbs, because the pattern in which the stem changes forms the shape of a boot or shoe. (See chart on next page.) There are three types of change possible: the final vowel in the verb's stem may change from e to ie, from o to ue, or from e to i. (Only in one case does a verb's stem change from u to ue, in the verb "jugar.")

An example of the first of these changes (e→ie), which is the most common of the three possibilities, is the verb "cerrar" (to close.) The infinitive stem is "cerr-". Before conjugating the verb, you will change the e to ie, making the new stem "cierr-." The chart of the present tense conjugation of cerrar is below:

cierro* = I close	cerramos = we close
cierras* = you close	cerráis = you all close
cierra* = he closes, she closes, you close	cierran* = they close, you all close

*Notice that the highlighted forms form a boot. This is the pattern for all stem-changing verbs in the present tense. Notice also that the regular endings for –ar verbs have not changed.

An example of group two stem-changing verbs (o→ue) is the verb "dormir" (to sleep). After the stem-change is made, the infinitive stem changes from "dorm-" to "duerm-" and the regular endings for third conjugation verbs are used.

duermo* = I sleep	dormimos = we sleep
duermes* = you sleep	dormís = you all sleep
duerme* = he sleeps, she sleeps, you sleep	duermen* = they sleep, you all sleep

The third group of stem changes (e→i) may be seen in the verb "repetir" (to repeat). The infinitive stem is "repet-," which changes to "repit-" before being conjugated. This type of stem change occurs only with some of the "-ir" stem-changing verbs.

repito* = I repeat	repetimos = we repeat
repites* = you repeat	repetís = you all repeat
repite* = he repeats, she repeats, you repeat	repiten* = they repeat, you all repeat

When you first learn a new verb, you will know that it is stem-changing when you see the stem change indicated in parentheses after the infinitive. An example is the verb "entender" (ie), to understand. The "ie" lets you know what change to make in the verb's stem before adding present tense endings.

Reflexive verbs in the present tense

Verbs whose subjects and objects are the same are called reflexive verbs, and in order to conjugate these verbs you must add a reflexive pronoun that agrees with the subject pronoun. An example of this in English is seen in the constructions "I hurt myself" and "He saw himself in the mirror."

Below is a chart with all the reflexive pronouns:

me (myself)	nos (ourselves)
te (yourself)	os (yourselves)
se (himself, herself, yourself)*	se (themselves, yourselves)*

*Note that there is only one reflexive pronoun for third person verb forms, whether the verb is singular or plural.

You can see that the reflexive pronouns correspond to the subject pronouns and follow the same pattern. If the subject of a reflexive verb is "yo," then the reflexive pronoun for that verb form must be "me." An example of a common reflexive verb is "bañarse," to bathe/take a bath.

(yo) me baño = I take a bath (I bathe myself)	(nosotros) nos bañamos = we take a bath (we bathe ourselves)
(tú) te bañas = you take a bath (you bathe yourself)	(vosotros) os bañáis = you all take a bath (you all bathe yourselves)
(él, ella, usted) se baña = he takes a bath, she takes a bath, you take a bath (he bathes himself, she bathes herself, you bathe yourself)	(ellos, ellas, ustedes) se bañan = they take a bath, you all take a bath (they bathe themselves, you all bathe yourselves)

*Notice that the appropriate reflexive pronoun will be placed before the conjugated verb form. In the infinitive form of a reflexive verb, the pronoun is often attached to the end, as in the sentence: "*Voy a bañarme.*" (I am going to take a bath/bathe myself.)

In English the reflexive construction is relatively uncommon, but in Spanish it is extremely common. While in English we are more likely to use a possessive adjective (as in the expression "I am washing my hands."), in Spanish that same construction will be reflexive, without the possessive adjective ("*Yo me lavo las manos.*") The use of the reflexive pronoun makes the possessive adjective redundant and unnecessary in Spanish.

Almost any verb may be reflexive in Spanish, under certain conditions. You can recognize a reflexive verb because the infinitive of the verb will have the reflexive pronoun "se" attached to the end, as in "llamarse." The verb "llamar" means to call, but when it is reflexive, it means to call oneself, as in the expression "*¿Cómo te llamas?*" or What is your name? (Literally, this expression means "What do you call yourself?") When you want to say "My name is," you can use this verb and say "*Me llamo. . .*"

There are several reasons why a verb may be reflexive:

- To create a truly reflexive construction, in which the subject and the object are the same:

  Ella se cepilla los dientes. She is brushing her teeth.

- To distinguish between two verbs with different meanings:

  Mi hija duerme mucho. My daughter sleeps a lot.
  Mi hija se duerme a las siete. My daughter falls asleep at seven.

- To express reciprocal action when the subject is plural:

  Los dos amigos se hablan mucho. The two friends talk to each other a lot.

- To express an impersonal situation in the third person:

  ¿Cómo se dice eso? How do you say that?
  ¿Cómo se escribe tu nombre? How do you spell your name?

Irregular forms in the present tense

There are some verbs that are completely irregular in the present tense, and you simply have to memorize their conjugations. Fortunately, most are very common verbs which you will use so frequently that it doesn't take long to remember them. An example of this type of verb is the verb "ir," which means "to go."

yo voy = I go	nosotros vamos = we go
tú vas = you go	vosotros vais* = you all go
él, ella, usted va = he goes, she goes, you go	ellos, ellas, ustedes van = they go, you all go

Notice that the vosotros form, which normally carries an accent mark, has no accent here because it is only one syllable.

There are many verbs in the present tense that are regular in all forms except the "yo" form. For these verbs, you must memorize the irregular "yo" form, but this is easier when you see the patterns involved. For example, there is a group of verbs with an irregular "yo" form that ends in "-go," so we can call them the "go" verbs and know that they all work the same way. Some examples are given below:

Infinitive:	**Irregular "yo" form:**
hacer (to make or do)	*hago*
poner (to put or place)	*pongo*
tener (*ie*)* (to have)	*tengo*
venir (*ie*)* (to come)	*vengo*
caer (to fall)	*caigo*
traer (to bring)	*traigo*
oír (to hear)	*oigo*
decir (*i*)* (to say or tell)	*digo*

*These verbs are also stem-changing in the present tense. They will follow the "boot" pattern, with the exception of the "yo" form, which is irregular.

As you will see, sometimes a verb may be irregular and stem-changing, irregular and reflexive, or reflexive and stem-changing. What you can count on is that the patterns you have learned here will still apply. For example, consider the verb "acostarse" (to lie down/go to bed). It is a group two stem-changing verb (o→ue), and it is also reflexive. This means that when you conjugate this verb in the present tense, you must add the reflexive pronouns, and you must also change the stem before adding the regular present tense endings for an "-ar" verb.

me acuesto = I lie down	nos acostamos = we lie down
te acuestas = you lie down	os acostáis = you all lie down
se acuesta = he lies down, she lies down, you lie down	se acuestan = they lie down, you all lie down

Other common irregularities in the present tense "yo" form include the following:

- Verbs that end in "-cer" and "-cir" generally add a "z" in the "yo" form, as in the verb "conocer" (to know or be familiar with). The "yo" form of conocer is "conozco."
- Verbs that end in "-ger" and "-gir" generally change the "g" to a "j" in the "yo" form , as in the verb escoger (to choose). The "yo" form of "escoger" is "escojo."

- Verbs that end in "-uir" generally add a "y" to the "yo" form, as in the verb construir (to build). The "yo" form of "construir" is "construyo."
- Some verbs follow no pattern and simply must be memorized, like the verb "saber" (to know information). The "yo" form of saber is "sé."

Note that if a verb has an irregular "yo" form, that does not mean that the rest of the verb is irregular. Generally, the rest of the forms follow the normal pattern, but if they do not, you will need to memorize them. An example of this is the verb "oír" (to hear). Not only does it have an irregular "yo" form; it also has other irregular forms that facilitate pronunciation. Here is the chart for this verb in the present tense:

oigo = I hear	oímos* = we hear
oyes = you hear	oís* = you all hear
oye = he hears, she hears, you hear	oyen = they hear, you all hear

The only forms of this verb that are regular in the present tense are those for "nosotros" and "vosotros." Notice that there is an additional accent mark in the "nosotros" form, which separates the weak vowel "i" from the strong vowel "o." This combination of weak and strong vowels that form a single syllable is called a diphthong, and in order to stress the weak vowel in a verb form, you must accent it.

*All these irregularities are included in the verb charts that follow this introduction.

The irregular verbs *ser* and *estar*

There are two very important verbs that are irregular in the present tense that often confuse students, because they seem to mean the same thing. In English, each one is translated "to be." However, once you understand the uses of these two verbs in Spanish, you should be able to keep them straight. Here are the charts for the present tense of these two verbs:

SER

soy = I am	somos = we are
eres = you are	sois = you all are
es = he is, she is, you are	son = they, you all are

ESTAR

estoy = I am	estamos = we are
*estás = you are	*estáis = you all are
*está = he is, she is, you are	*están = they, you all are

Notice the accent marks on these forms. In Spanish, all words that end in a vowel or the letters "n" or "s" receive the spoken stress on the next-to-last syllable. This is the normal stress pattern for the present tense. However, when a word in this category is NOT pronounced that way, then you always need to add an accent mark to indicate which syllable is strongest.

Uses of *ser* and *estar*

The basic difference between these two verbs is that "ser" identifies and describes people and things, while "estar" is used to refer to changeable conditions. For example, "ser" is used to name things, including things that seem to be changeable, like time of day or the date. For example, if you ask in Spanish *¿Qué hora es?* (What time is it?) and your answer is *Son las dos.* (It's two o'clock), you are naming a specific moment, even though that moment is about to change. When you ask *¿Cuál es la fecha?* (What is the date?) or *¿Qué día es?* (What day is it?), even though that date or day will change very soon, you are still identifying a particular moment in time.

"Ser" is used to name the general categories that identify people and things, such as profession, race, religion, political affiliation, relationships, etc., as in these examples:

Mi padre es profesor.	My dad is a teacher.
Mucha gente en España es católica.	Lots of people in Spain are Catholic.

The verb "ser" also describes relationships, whether they are permanent or not:

Él es mi hermano.	He is my brother. (an unchanging relationship)
Él es mi novio.	He is my boyfriend. (subject to change!)

In both of these examples, you are identifying a relationship between two people. At the time of speaking, that is the identity of the person, even though it could change later. Other examples are the following:

¿De quién es el libro? Es de Pablo.	Whose book is it? It's Pablo's. (the relationship between a person and a possession)

¿De dónde es ella? Es de Argentina. Where is she from? She's from Argentina. (the relationship between a person and her origin)

If you want to describe instrinsic qualitites of people or things, you use "ser," as in the following sentences:

Mi hermano es alto y guapo. My brother is tall and handsome.
La clase es difícil, pero es interesante. The class is hard, but it's interesting.

The easiest way to remember the difference between "ser" and "estar" is to learn the three things that "estar" can do. Then you know that all other times when you need the verb "to be" in Spanish, you will use "ser." Here is a list of the three things that the verb "estar" can do in Spanish:

- Location of all concrete objects (people, places, and things, even permanent things like countries or buildings)*

  ¿Dónde está la pelota? Where is the ball?
  ¿Dónde está el maestro? Where is the teacher?
  ¿Dónde está el Museo del Prado? Where is the Prado Museum?

  *"Ser" is used to give the location of events. In this case it be translated "to take place."

  ¿Dónde es el partido? Where is the game (taking place)?

- Changeable conditions, like your health, your feelings, the weather, etc.

  ¿Cómo estás? How are you feeling?
  Mi amiga está triste hoy. My friend is sad today.
  Está muy nublado hoy. It's really cloudy today.

- Progressive action, which by definition is changing and unstable

  Mis amigos están practicando español ahora. My friends are practicing Spanish now.

Some teachers give students mnemonic devices to help them remember some of the most common uses of "ser" and "estar". On the next page are two acronyms that many teachers use:

SER

Description	*Su coche es verde.*
Origin	*Mis abuelos son de Panamá.*
Characteristics	*Carlos es alto y delgado.*
Time/date	*Son las dos de la tarde./Es el once de mayo.*
Occupation	*Mi tío es carpintero.*
Race, religion, relationship*	*Ana y Pedro son hermanos.*

*These are all categories that help identify a person.

ESTAR

Position	*Mi libro está en la mesa.*
Location of all concrete objects*	*El Museo del Prado está en Madrid.*
Action	*Estoy estudiando para el examen.*
Conditions	*Están cansados.*
Emotion	*¿Estás triste?*

*Remember that ser is used for the location of events.

If you understand the overall concept of "ser" versus "estar," then as you learn more rules, they will make sense. For example, there is a series of adjectives in Spanish whose definitions change in English when you change the verb from "ser" to "estar." This makes perfect sense if you remember that "ser" describes qualities and characteristics, while "estar" describes changeable conditions. Here are some examples:

El muchacho está aburrido.	The boy is bored. (He isn't always bored!)
El muchacho es aburrido.	The boy is boring. (He is always dull.)
Ella está alegre ahora.	She's happy now. (This could change!)
Ella es una chica alegre.	She's a cheerful, happy person. (This is the way she is.)

Expressing Past Actions: The Preterite Tense (el pretérito)

In Spanish there are two simple past tenses, the preterite and the imperfect. Each has different uses, so you will need to learn them both. The preterite tense describes completed actions in the past, while the imperfect tense expresses repeated actions, ongoing actions, or conditions in the past. (A chart and examples explaining the different uses of these two tenses follows the section on the formation of both tenses.)

The Preterite Tense (el pretérito)

To talk about completed actions in the past you will use the preterite tense. There are only two sets of endings for regular verbs in this tense, one set for "-ar" verbs and another for "-er" and "-ir" verbs. Here are the "-ar" endings, which you add to the infinitive stem:

Preterite endings for regular "-ar" verbs:

-é	-amos
-aste	-asteis
-ó	-aron

The chart for the preterite of the verb "hablar" is given below:

hablé* = I spoke	hablamos = we spoke
hablaste = you spoke	hablasteis = you all spoke
habló* = he, she, you spoke	hablaron = they, you all spoke

You can see that the first and third person singular endings for this tense have accent marks to indicate that the spoken stress is on the last syllable. These accent marks also help you differentiate these forms from similar forms in the present tense. Hence, "hablo" means "I do speak," and "habló" means "he, she, or you did speak." The accent mark changes both the subject and the time frame of the action.

Regular "-er" and "-ir" verbs share a single set of endings:

-í	-imos
-iste	-isteis
-ió*	-ieron

Notice that the accent mark is on the "-o," not the "-i."

The chart for the "-er" verb "comer" in the preterite is given below:

comí = I ate	comimos = we ate
comiste = you ate	comisteis = you all ate
comió = he, she, you ate	comieron = they, you all ate

Here is the chart for the "-ir" verb "vivir" in the preterite:

viví = I lived	vivimos = we lived
viviste = you lived	vivisteis = you all lived
vivió = he, she, you lived	vivieron = they, you all lived

Spelling changes in the preterite tense

There is a group of verbs whose "yo" form in the preterite has a spelling change, usually to maintain the sound of the consonant preceding the infinitive ending. There are three types of verbs in this group: verbs whose infinitives end in "-car," verbs whose infinitives end in "-gar," and verbs whose infinitives end in "-zar." Here is the pattern these verbs follow:

- Verbs that end in "-car" change the "c" to "qu" before adding the "yo" form ending. The verb "buscar" (to look for) becomes "busqué" in this form.
- Verbs that end in "-gar" change the "g" to "gu" before adding the "yo" form ending. The verb llegar (to arrive) becomes "llegué" in this form.
- Verbs that end in "-zar" change the "z" to "c" before adding the "yo" form ending. The verb "empezar" (to begin) becomes "empecé" in this form.
- Note that these changes occur ONLY in the "yo" form. All other forms are conjugated normally for "-ar" verbs in the preterite.

Here is the chart for the verb "jugar" (to play):

jugué = I played	jugamos = we played
jugaste = you played	jugasteis = you all played
jugó = he, she, you played	jugaron = they, you all played

There is one other group of verbs that have a spelling change in the preterite. These are "-er" and "-ir" verbs whose stems end in a vowel. For these verbs, in the third person singular and plural forms, the "-i" of the preterite endings changes to a "-y" to facilitate pronunciation. Here is a chart to show you this pattern:

leí = I read	leímos* = we read
leíste* = you read	leísteis* = you all read
leyó = he, she, you read	leyeron = they, you all read

Notice that in addition to the accent marks on the first and third person singular endings, you also need accent marks on the other forms to separate the diphthong. This is the case for most other verbs in this category, such as caer, creer, oír, etc.

Stem changes in the preterite

The pattern for stem changes in the preterite is different from the present tense, or boot, pattern. Here is a chart to help you see the difference:

Present tense stem changes:	**Preterite tense stem changes:**
-may occur in any conjugation (-ar, -er, or -ir)	-only occur for -ir verbs*
-may be one of three changes (e→ie, o→ue, e→i)	-only two changes are possible (e→i or o→u)
-only occur in four of the six forms (the "boot")	-only occur in 3rd person forms

*There are NO stem changes for any "-ar" or "-er" verbs in the preterite tense.

An example of this pattern is seen in the preterite of the verb "dormir":

dormí = I slept	dormimos = we slept
dormiste = you slept	dormisteis = you all slept
durmió = he, she, you slept	durmieron = they, you all slept

*Note that the regular endings for "-ir" verbs in the preterite are used. Just as in the present tense, once the stem has been changed, regular conjugation rules apply. Stem changes are NOT irregularities, since these are normal patterns for verbs in Spanish. Third conjugation stem-changing verbs that do not follow this pattern in the preterite are irregular and must be memorized. (An example of this pattern will be given in the next section.) Third conjugation stem-changing verbs are indicated in the dictionary in this way: "dormir" (ue/u) to indicate that there are two possible stem changes, depending on the tense.

Irregular forms in the preterite

While the vast majority of verbs in Spanish are regular in the preterite tense, some of the most commonly used verbs are irregular. The good thing about these irregular verbs is that most of them share a common set of endings. Since some are "-ar" verbs, some are "-er" verbs, and some are "-ir" verbs, these irregular endings are a combination of the endings for all three types of verbs.

-e*	-imos
-iste	-isteis
-o*	-ieron

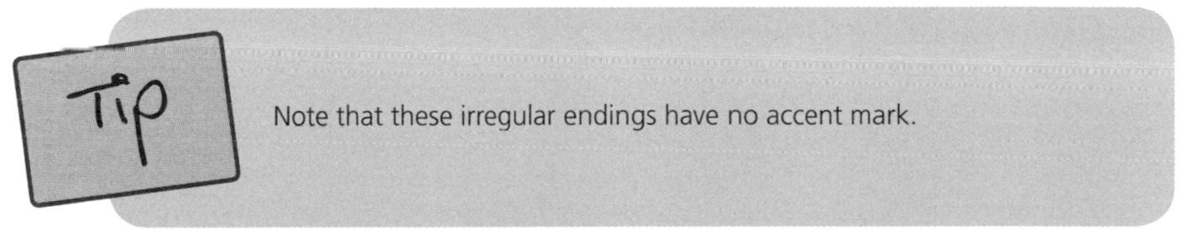

Note that these irregular endings have no accent mark.

Another difference for these verbs is that instead of using the infinitive stem, as you do for regular verbs, you will start with special stems used only for this tense. Here are the most common irregular verbs and their preterite stems:

Infinitive	**Irregular preterite stem**
hacer (to make or do)	*hic-*
querer (to want or love)	*quis-*
venir (to come)	*vin-*
tener (to have)	*tuv-*
estar (to be)	*estuv-*
andar (to walk)	*anduv-*
poder (to be able)	*pud-*
poner (to put or place)	*pus-*
saber (to know)	*sup-*
haber (to have)	*hub-*
caber (to fit)	*cup-*

Here is the chart for the irregular verb "tener" in the preterite:

tuve = I had	tuvimos = we had
tuviste = you had	tuvisteis = you all had
tuvo = he, she, you had	tuvieron = they, you all had

There is a small group of verbs whose irregular preterite forms are slightly different, because the stem ends in j. For these verbs, all the irregular endings are the same, except for third person plural. In this form you will drop the "i" of the ending*. An example of this is the verb "decir" (to say or tell):

dije = I said	dijimos = we said
dijiste = you said	dijisteis = you all said
dijo = he, she, you said	dijeron* = they, you all said

Some of the other verbs in this group are the following:

traer (to bring) *traj-**
conducir (to drive or lead) *conduj-**
producir (to produce) *produj-**
traducir (to translate) *traduj-*

There are only a handful of other verbs in Spanish that are irregular in this tense, and you can easily memorize them. They are the verbs "ir", "ser", and "dar". The first two verbs use the same forms for the preterite tense, but the context in which they are used will always let you know which verb it is.*

Ser and Ir (to be/to go)

fui = I was/I went	fuimos = we were/we went
fuiste = you were/you went	fuisteis = you all were/you all went
fue = he was, she was, you were/he, she, you went	fueron = they, you all were/they, you all went

*Ella *fue* mi amiga. She *was* my friend.
*Ella *fue* a casa. She *went* home.

Dar (to give)

di = I gave	dimos = we gave
diste = you gave	disteis = you all gave
dio = he, she, you gave	dieron = they, you all gave

As for all the other irregular verbs in this tense, there are no accent marks on first and third person forms.

Ver (to see)

vi = I saw	vimos = we saw
viste = you saw	visteis = you all saw
vio = he, she, you saw	vieron = they, you all saw

*Note that "ver" is only considered irregular because it does not have accents on first and third person forms. Otherwise, it is completely regular.

The Imperfect Indicative Tense (el imperfecto de indicativo)

In order to talk about routine past action in Spanish (the way things used to be) or progressive actions (what someone was doing when something else happened), you need to use the imperfect tense. While the preterite tense allows you to describe actions and reactions in the past, the imperfect tense lets you describe past conditions, feelings, and circumstances, as well as routine or progressive actions. This is the most regular of all Spanish tenses. Like the preterite tense, the imperfect has only two sets of endings (one for "-ar" verbs and one for "-er" and "-ir" verbs), but unlike the preterite, there are only three irregular verbs to memorize. To form this tense, you start with the infinitive stem, just as you did for the present and the preterite tenses.

Below are the charts for the regular endings for this tense:

Endings for "-ar" verbs:

-aba	-ábamos*
-abas	-abais
-aba	-aban

The "nosotros" form is the only form that has an accent mark.

Here is the chart for the imperfect of the verb "hablar":

hablaba = I used to speak/I was speaking	hablábamos = we used to speak/we were speaking
hablabas = you used to speak/you were speaking	hablabais = you all used to speak/you all were speaking
hablaba = he, she, you used to speak/he, she was speaking, you were speaking	hablaban = they, you all used to speak/they, you all were speaking

Endings for "-er" and "-ir" verbs:

-ía	-íamos
-ías	-íais
-ía	-ían

Note that all the endings have an accent mark, to separate the diphthong formed by the weak vowel "i" and the strong vowel "a."

Here is the chart for the imperfect of the verb "comer":

comía = I used to eat/was eating	comíamos = we used to eat/were eating
comías = you used to eat/were eating	comíais = you all used to eat/were eating
comía = he, she, you used to eat/he, she was eating, you were eating	comían = they, you all used to eat/were eating

Here is the chart for the imperfect of the verb "vivir":

vivía = I used to live/was living	vivíamos = we used to live/were living
vivías = you used to live/were living	vivíais = you all used to live/were living
vivía = he, she, you used to live/he, she was living, you were living	vivían = they, you all used to live/were living

Irregular forms in the imperfect tense

The only three verbs that are irregular in this tense are "ser", "ir", and "ver". Since these verbs do not follow the pattern for the imperfect tense, you must memorize their forms. Here are their charts:

Ser (to be)

era = I was/used to be	éramos* = we were/used to be
eras = you were/used to be	erais = you all were/used to be
era = he, she was, you were/used to be	eran = they, you all were/used to be

Ir (to go)

iba = I was going/used to go	íbamos* = we were going/used to go
ibas = you were going/used to go	ibais = you all were going/used to go
iba = he, she was going, you were going/used to go	iban = they, you all were going/used to go

Notice that the only accented form for these two irregular verbs is the "nosotros" form.

Ver (to see)

veía = I was seeing/used to see	veíamos = we were seeing/used to see
veías = you used to see/were seeing/ used to see	veíais = you were seeing/used to see
veía = he, she was seeing, you were seeing/used to see	veían = they, you all were seeing/used to see

Also notice that for the verb "ver," the only reason it is irregular is that you don't drop the entire infinitive ending ("-er"), only the "-r," before adding the regular endings for an "-er" verb.

Uses of the preterite and the imperfect

Here is a chart to help you remember the different uses of these two tenses:

Preterite:	**Imperfect:**
-describes completed past actions or events	-describes routine or repeated past actions
-describes reactions to past actions or events	-describes ongoing or progressive past actions
	-describes conditions or circumstances in the past
	-describes background action, as opposed to main action

Here are some examples to help you see the difference in the two tenses:

Ayer hubo un accidente.	Yesterday there was an accident. (an event happened)
Estuve muy asustado.	I was very scared. (my reaction to the event)
Había muchos heridos.	There were many injured people (the resulting condition)
La semana pasada fui al cine.	Last week I went to the movies. (a single event)
Cuando era niño, siempre iba al parque.	When I was a child, I always used to go the park. (condition or circumstance/ repeated past action)
Cenaba cuando sonó el teléfono.	I was eating dinner when the phone rang. (action in progress when main action occurred)

Because they are conditions, time of day and age are always imperfect, but what happened at a certain time or age could be preterite.

Eran las cinco cuando papa llegó.	It was five o'clock when Dad arrived.
Tenía siete años cuando me rompí el brazo.	I was five when I broke my arm.

You can think of the imperfect tense as a long, unbroken line, with no beginning or end. The preterite could be represented by specific points on that line or by a limited segment of that line, a moment framed in time. If you know when an action started, when it ended, or how long it lasted, use the preterite tense.

There are some verbs whose definitions in English change in these two tenses, but this makes sense if you understand the overall concept of preterite versus imperfect. Here are a couple of examples:

Ayer conocí a Fernando.	Yesterday I *met* Fernando. (a specific action)
Cuando era pequeño, no conocía a Raúl.	When I was little, I *did* not *know* Raúl. (an ongoing condition)
No sabía la respuesta correcta.	I *did* not *know* the right answer. (a condition)
La supe luego.	I *found* it *out* later. (a specific action)

The Future and Conditional Tenses (el futuro y el condicional simple)

The future tense is used to say what will happen, and the conditional tense is used to say what would happen under certain conditions. These two tenses are the only simple tenses in Spanish that are not formed by using the infinitive stem. Instead, for all regular verbs, these tenses are based on the entire infinitive form. In addition, for each of these tenses there is only one set of endings, which are used with all verbs, both regular and irregular. And, finally, these two tenses share the same set of irregular stems. So, once you learn the future tense, the conditional tense is really easy.

Here is the chart for future tense endings, which are added directly to the infinitive of regular verbs:

-é	-emos*
-ás	-éis
-á	-án

Note that only the "nosotros" form does NOT carry an accent mark.

These same endings are used for all verbs, both regular and irregular, regardless of the conjugation. All regular "-ar," "-er," and "-ir" verbs work the same way in this tense.

For the verb "hablar," the future tense looks like this:

hablaré = I will speak	hablaremos = we will speak
hablarás = you will speak	hablaréis = you all will speak
hablará = he, she, you will speak	hablarán = they, you all will speak

For the verb "comer," the future tense looks like this:

comeré = I will eat	comeremos = we will eat
comerás = you will eat	comeréis = you all will eat
comerá = he, she, you will eat	comerán = they, you all will eat

For the verb "vivir," the future tense looks like this:

viviré = I will live	viviremos = we will live
vivirás = you will live	viviréis = you all will live
vivirá = he, she, you will live	vivirán = they, you all will live

Uses of the future tense:

- To express predictions in the present, as in the sentence: *Ella dice que llegará a las cinco de la tarde*. (She says that she will arrive at 5:00 P.M.)
- To express conjecture or probability in the present, as in this question and answer: *¿Qué hora será? Serán las ocho*. (I wonder what time it is? It must be 8:00.)

An alternative to the future tense that is used frequently in Spanish is known as the "immediate future," and is expressed with the verb "ir" (to go) + a + an infinitive complement, as in this sentence: *Voy a estudiar esta noche*. (I am going to study tonight.)

Here is the chart for conditional tense endings, which are also added directly to the infinitive of regular verbs:

-ía	-íamos
-ías	-íais
-ía	-ían

Notice that these endings look exactly like the endings for regular "-er" and "-ir" verbs in the imperfect tense, but since you add them to the infinitive, the conjugated verb forms do NOT look the same.

Here is the chart for the verb "hablar" in the conditional tense:

hablaría = I would speak	hablaríamos = we would speak
hablarías = you would speak	hablaríais = you all would speak
hablaría = he, she, you would speak	hablarían = they, you all would speak

For the verb "comer," the conditional tense looks like this:

comería = I would eat	comeríamos = we would eat
comerías = you would eat	comeríais = you all would eat
comería = he, she, you would eat	comerían = they, you all would eat

For the verb "vivir," the conditional tense looks like this;

viviría = I would live	viviríamos = we would live
vivirías = you would live	viviríais = you all would live
viviría = he, she, you would live	vivirían = they, you all would live

Uses of the conditional tense:

- To express predictions in the past, as in this sentence: *Ella dijo que llegaría a las cinco de la tarde*. (She said that she would arrive at 5:00 P.M.)
- To express conjecture or probability in the past, as in the question and answer: *¿Dónde estaría? Estaría en casa*. (Where could he have been? He must have been at home.)
- In past tense "if" clauses that express contrary-to-fact conditions, such as this sentence: *Si pudiera, te ayudaria*. (If I could, I would help you.)

Irregular stems for the future and conditional tenses

Both these tenses use the same irregular stems, which are listed below:

Infinitive:	**Irregular stem:**
hacer	*har-*
decir	*dir-*
querer	*querr-*

poder	*podr-*
salir	*saldr-*
tener	*tendr-*
poner	*pondr-*
venir	*vendr-*
saber	*sabr-*
haber	*habr-*
caber	*cabr-*

Since the irregular stems are the same for both tenses, all you need to learn are the two sets of endings.

Here are the charts for the verb "decir" in these two tenses. Note that the same irregular stem is used for both; only the endings change.

The future of "decir":

diré = I will say/tell	diremos = we will say/tell
dirás = you will say/tell	diréis = you all will say/tell
dirá = he, she, you will say/tell	dirán = they, you all will say/tell

The conditional of "decir":

diría = I would say/tell	diríamos = we would say/tell
dirías = you would say/tell	diríais = you all would say/tell
diría = he, she, you would say/tell	dirían = they, you all would say/tell

The Progressive Forms

The present progressive

The progressive forms of the simple tenses are composed of the helping verb "to be" (estar) and the present participle of the verb, what we know as the gerund or "-ing" form of the verb. "I am eating now" is an example of the present progressive tense in English. There are four progressive tenses in Spanish, which are formed by changing the tense of the verb "estar." The present participle never changes, no matter what the subject or the tense of "estar."

Forming the present participle

- For "-ar" verbs, simply drop the infinitive ending and add "-ando." The present participle of the verb hablar is "hablando."
- For "-er" and "-ir" verbs, drop the infinitive ending and add "-iendo."

For the verb "comer", the present participle is "comiendo," and for "vivir," the present participle is "viviendo."

- Only "-ir" stem-changing verbs have a stem change in this form, and they follow the same pattern as they do in the preterite tense. So, the present participle of the verb "dormir" is "durmiendo," and for "pedir" it is "pidiendo." First and second conjugation verbs have no stem changes in this form.
- Second and third conjugation verbs whose stems end in a vowel also have a spelling change in this form, just as they do in the third person forms of the preterite. For these verbs, the "-i" of the ending will change to "-y." Examples are "leyendo," "oyendo," and "huyendo."
- Reflexive and object pronouns may be attached to the end of a present participle.*

When this happens, you must add an accent mark to maintain the stress pattern, as in this example: *Estoy leyéndolo.* (I am reading it.)

Forming the present participle

- While the translation of the present participle makes it seem like an English gerund, this is not the case. A gerund in English is a verb form that is used as a noun, as in the sentence "Skating is fun." In Spanish a present participle is NEVER used as a noun. (Remember that the Spanish infinitive is the equivalent of the English gerund.)
- The present participle may follow the verb "estar" and a few other verbs in progressive constructions. An example is seen in the sentences "*Ella está hablando.*" (She is talking.) and "*Ella sigue hablando.*" (She is still talking.)
- The present participle may be used as an adverb to modify the action of a verb. An example of this is in the sentence "*Ellos llegaron gritando.*" (They arrived shouting.)
- The present participle is used to express the phrase "by doing something," as in this example: "*Practicando, se aprende.*" (By practicing, one learns.)

Forming the present progressive

To form the present progressive, the helping verb "estar" must be conjugated in the present tense. Here is the chart for the verb "hablar":

estoy hablando = I am talking	estamos hablando = we are talking
estás hablando = you are talking	estáis hablando = you all are talking
está hablando = he, she is talking/you are talking	están hablando = they, you all are talking

In English you can use the present progressive to indicate future intention, as in the sentence "This weekend I am going to the beach." In Spanish this form is NEVER used to express intention. It is used chiefly to emphasize action in progress. In order to express intention in Spanish, you will use the "ir + a + infinitive" construction. An example of this distinction is the sentence "*Ahora estoy trabajando, pero luego voy a descansar.*" (Now I am working, but later I am going to rest.)

The past progressive

To form the past progressive, you will conjugate the helping verb "estar" in the imperfect tense. Here is the chart for the past progressive of the verb comer:

estaba comiendo = I was eating	estábamos comiendo = we were eating
estabas comiendo = you were eating	estabais comiendo = you all were eating
estaba comiendo = he, she was eating/you were eating	estaban comiendo = they, you all were eating

The future and conditional progressive

To form the future progressive, conjugate "estar" in the future tense. Here is the chart for the future progressive of the verb "abrir":

estaré abriendo = I will be opening	estaremos abriendo = we will be opening
estarás abriendo = you will be opening	estaréis abriendo = you all will be opening
estará abriendo = he, she, you will be opening	estarán abriendo = they, you all will be opening

To form the conditional progressive, conjugate "estar" in the conditional tense. Here is the chart for the conditional progressive of the verb "cantar":

estaría cantando = I would be singing	estaríamos cantando = we would be singing
estarías cantando = you would be singing	estaríais cantando = you all would be singing
estaría cantando = he, she, you would be singing	estarían cantando = they, you all would be singing

Simple Versus Compound Tenses

Simple tenses are those that are formed by a single word, and compound tenses, as the name implies, have two parts, like a compound word. The simple tenses you have learned are the present, the preterite, the imperfecT, the future, and the conditional. There are five compound tenses, known as the "perfect tenses," but only four are commonly used.

The perfect tenses use the helping verb "haber" (to have) and the past participle of the verb, or the "-ed" form. "They have not arrived yet" is an example of the present perfect tense. Just as in English, there are also some irregular past participles, which you must memorize.

Forming the past participle

- For "-ar" verbs, drop the infinitive ending and add "-ado." The past participle for the verb "hablar" is "hablado."
- For "-er" and "-ir" verbs, drop the infinitive ending and add "-ido." The past participle for the verb "comer" is "comido" and for the verb "vivir" is "vivido."

Second and third conjugation verbs whose stem ends in a vowel will need an accent on the "-i" of the ending, in order to separate the diphthong. Some examples are traído, leído, and creído.

- There are some irregular past participles, just like in English, and you must memorize them. Here are the most common irregular past participles in Spanish:

Infinitive:	**Irregular past participle:**
hacer (to make or do)	*hecho* (made or done)
decir (to say or tell)	*dicho* (said or told)
poner (to put or place)	*puesto* (put or placed)
ver (to see)	*visto* (seen)
volver (to return, come back)	*vuelto* (returned)
escribir (to write)	*escrito* (written)
romper (to break)	*roto* (broken)
morir (to die)	*muerto* (died)
freír (to fry)	*frito* (fried)
abrir (to open)	*abierto* (opened)
cubrir (to cover)	*cubierto* (covered)

Other verbs based on these verbs are generally conjugated the same as the root verb, including their irregular forms. So, if the past participle of "volver" is "vuelto," the past participle of verbs based on "volver" will have the same irregularity, as in "devolver (devuelto)" and "revolver (revuelto)". Others in this group include "descubrir (descubierto)", "imponer (impuesto)", "describir (descrito)", and "deshacer (deshecho)".

Once you know how to form the past participle, in order to form the four perfect tenses, you merely need to change the tense of the helping verb "haber."

The present perfect tense (el perfecto de indicativo)

The present perfect tense is roughly equivalent to the preterite in terms of the information that it conveys. In fact, in Spain the two tenses are used interchangeably to express completed past actions. For example, if you say either of the following, you will be communicating the same information:

I already ate.	*Ya comí.*	(preterite tense)
I have already eaten.	*Ya he comido.*	(present perfect tense)

However, there are some ideas that the present perfect tense conveys that the preterite does not, such as the following:

Have you ever been to Spain?	*¿Has ido a España alguna vez?*
I have never eaten octopus.	*No he comido el pulpo jamás.*
We have lived here for two years.	*Hemos vivido aquí por dos años.**

To form the present perfect tense, you need to use the present tense of the helping verb "haber," which is irregular in all forms except the "vosotros" form. Here is the chart.

he	hemos
has	habéis
ha	han

Do not confuse this verb with the other Spanish verb that means "to have," the verb "tener." "Tener" is NEVER used as an auxiliary verb.

Here is the present perfect tense of the verb "hablar":

he hablado = I have spoken	hemos hablado = we have spoken
has hablado = you have spoken	habéis hablado = you all have spoken
ha hablado = he, she has spoken/you have spoken	han hablado = they, you all have spoken

Uses of past participles

- The past participle follows the verb "haber" in the perfect tenses, in which case it is invariable and does NOT agree with the subject of the verb. An example of this is the sentence "*Yo he abierto la puerta.*" (I have opened the door.) This sentence describes an action.
- The past participle may be used as an adjective, in which case the ending will change to agree in gender and number with the word being modified. Here is an example of this use: "*La puerta está abierta.*" (The door is open.) This sentence describes the result of an action.
- The past participle may follow the verb "ser" to form the passive voice, and in this case it is also considered an adjective and must agree with the subject of the verb "ser." An example of this is the sentence "*La puerta fue abierta por la profesora.*" (The door was opened by the teacher.) This form of the passive voice is mainly used when the speaker wishes to indicate by whom the action was done. When this is not important, you will most often use the more common form of the passive voice, formed by adding the impersonal "se" to the verb in the third person, as in the following examples:

¿Dónde se venden periódicos?	Where are newspapers sold?
Aquí se habla español.	Spanish is spoken here.

The past perfect tense (el pluscuamperfecto de indicativo)

To form the past perfect tense, also known as the pluperfect, the helping verb "haber" is conjugated in the imperfect tense. Here is the chart for the verb comer in this tense:

había comido = I had eaten	habíamos comido = we had eaten
habías comido = you had eaten	habíais comido = you all had eaten
había comido = he, she, you had eaten	habían comido = they, you all had eaten

The future and conditional perfect tenses (el futuro perfecto y el condicional compuesto)

To form the future perfect tense, "haber" is conjugated in the future tense. Here is the chart for the verb "vivir" in this tense:

habré vivido = I will have lived	habremos vivido = we will have lived
habrás vivido = you will have lived	habréis vivido = you all will have lived
habrá vivido = he, she, you will have lived	habrán vivido = they, you all will have lived

To form the conditional perfect, "haber" is conjugated in the conditional tense. Here is the chart for the verb "escribir" in this tense:

habría escrito = I would have written	habríamos escrito = we would have written
habrías escrito = you would have writ-ten	habríais escrito = you all would have written
habría escrito = he, she, you would have written	habrían escrito = they, you all would have written

The preterite perfect tense (el pretérito anterior)

There is one other compound tense, known as the preterite perfect or anterior preterite, but it is not commonly used in modern Spanish. This tense is translated exactly like the past perfect, or pluperfect, so it is not necessary in everyday speech. However, if you read a lot in Spanish, you will probably see it. Here is the chart for the verb "hacer" in this tense:

hube hecho = I had made/done	hubimos hecho = we had made/done
hubiste hecho = you had made/done	hubisteis hecho = you all had made/done
hubo hecho = he, she, you had made/done	hubieron hecho = they, you all made/done

What is the Subjunctive Mood?

All the verb tenses you have seen so far are the "indicative mood," which must be distinguished from the "subjunctive mood." While "tense" refers to time, "mood" refers to the attitude of the speaker towards the action being described. Because the subjunctive mood is very rarely used in English, it is not a concept English speakers immediately recognize. However, it is extremely common in Spanish, and you must use it in many situations. You will find that there are different tenses in the subjunctive mood, just as in the indicative mood.

Basically, in Spanish you use the indicative mood when you are objectively describing your experience in the world around you, and you use the subjunctive mood when you are reacting subjectively to your experience. Here is a simple chart to help you understand the difference between the indicative and subjunctive moods:

Verbs in the indicative mood:	**Verbs in the subjunctive mood:**
-state objective truth or facts	-give subjective reactions
-imply certainty	-imply doubt
-inform, confirm, or verify	-suggest, question, or deny

Formation of the present subjunctive (el presente de subjuntivo)

Once you are thoroughly familiar with the present indicative, it is easy to form the present subjunctive. Except for six verbs with an irregular present subjunctive, the present subjunctive is based on the "yo" form of the present indicative. This means that whatever happens in the "yo" form is repeated throughout the present subjunctive, except for certain stem-changing verbs.

To form the present subjunctive of the verb "hablar," you will start with the "yo" form (hablo), drop the final "-o," and then add the opposite endings. Instead of using the vowel "-a," as you do in the present indicative, you will use the vowel "-e." (For second and third conjugation verbs, you will switch the vowels "-e" and "-i" to the vowel "-a.")

Here is an example of this pattern for an -ar verb:

hable*	hablemos
hables	habléis
hable*	hablen

*Notice that first and third person singular forms are identical. You will need to use the context or subject pronouns to distinguish them.

Here is the present subjunctive of the verb "comer":

coma	comamos
comas	comáis
coma	coman

Here is a common "-ir" verb in the present subjunctive:

viva	vivamos
vivas	viváis
viva	vivan

Here is a simple way to remember this pattern:

- Start with the "yo" form
- Drop the "-o"
- Add opposite endings ("-a" becomes "-e"/ "-e" and "-i" become "-a")

Translations have not been given for these forms because the present subjunctive has several possible translations in English. Here are some examples:

- The present subjunctive may refer to present or future actions, depending on the context:

  Espero que *no llueva ahora.* — I hope that *it is not raining now.*
  Espero que *no llueva más tarde.* — I hope that *it will not rain later.*

- Although in Spanish the present subjunctive is almost always in a dependent clause following the relative pronoun "que" (that), in English the same construction may be expressed with an infinitive clause:

  Quiero *que ellos me ayuden.* — I want *them to help me.*

Stem changes in the present subjunctive

For first and second conjugation verbs, the present subjunctive follows the same pattern for stem changes as the present indicative, the "boot" pattern. However, for third conjugation stem-changing verbs, the pattern is slightly different. For these verbs, in addition to the regular stem changes, there is also a change in the "nosotros" and the "vosotros" forms, following the same pattern as you saw for these verbs in the preterite tense (e→i and o→u). See the charts below:

Dormir (ue/u)

duerma	durmamos
duermas	durmáis
duerma	duerman

Sentirse (ie/e)

me sienta	nos sintamos
te sientas	os sintáis
se sienta	se sientan

Spelling changes in the present subjunctive

Just as in the preterite, there are some verbs whose stem has a spelling change before the present subjunctive endings are added. Verbs whose stem ends in "-car" change the "-c" to "-qu;" verbs whose stem ends in "-gar" change the "-g" to "-gu;" and verbs whose stem ends in "-zar" change the "-z" to "-c." Unlike the preterite, however, these spelling changes occur in all forms, not just the "yo" form. See the charts below:

Buscar (to look for)

busque*	busquemos
busques	busquéis
busque*	busquen

Note that while these forms look like the first person singular preterite form, the lack of an accent mark lets you know that they are NOT that form. The pronunciation is also different, of course.

Llegar (to arrive)

llegue	lleguemos
llegues	lleguéis
lleguemos	lleguen

Empezar (to begin)

empiece	empecemos*
empieces	empecéis*
empiece	empiecen

*Note that there is no stem change here, because in the present subjunctive only "-ir" stem-changing verbs have a stem change in these two forms.

Verbs with irregular present subjunctive forms

There are only six verbs whose present subjunctive forms are irregular. Because their "yo" forms do not end in "-o," they do not follow the pattern for regular present subjunctive. These verbs are given below:

Ser (to be)

sea	seamos
seas	seáis
sea	sean

Saber (to know)

sepa	sepamos
sepas	sepáis
sepa	sepan

Ir (to go)

vaya	vayamos
vayas	vayáis
vaya	vayan

Haber (to have)

haya	hayamos
hayas	hayáis
haya	hayan

Dar (to give)

dé	demos
des	deis
dé	den

Estar (to be)

esté	estemos
estés	estéis
esté	estén

Uses of the present subjunctive

In general, the subjunctive mood is used in sentences with a dependent clause, when there is an element in the main clause that requires the subjunctive in the dependent clause. Here is what many of these sentences will look like:

Main clause* + que + second subject + dependent clause

*must contain a subjunctive cue

There are four general categories of what we can call "subjunctive cues," or expressions that require the use of the subjunctive mood. These categories are doubt/negation, emotion, opinion, and command/request.

Here are some lists of common subjunctive cues in all four categories:

Doubt/negation

dudar	to doubt	*no estar seguro**	not to be sure
negar	to deny	*no es cierto/verdad**	it is not true
*no creer**	not to believe	*es dudoso*	it is doubtful

*If these expressions drop the "no," they become expressions of certainty and do NOT require the use of the subjunctive mood.

No estoy seguro que vaya a llover.	I'm not sure that it's going to rain.
Estoy seguro que va a llover.	I am sure that it's going to rain.

Emotion*

alegrarse	to be glad	*preocupar*	to worry
lamentar/sentir	to be sorry/to regret	*molestar*	to bother
sorprenderse	to be surprised	*irritar*	to irritate
temer/tener miedo	to fear/be afraid	*gustar*	to please
estar contento, triste, etc.	to be happy, sad, etc.	*esperar*	to hope

*These expressions of emotion require the subjunctive mood whether they are affirmative or negative. Either way, they express your feelings, which are subjective.

Me alegro de que vengas a mi fiesta.	I am glad that you will come to my party.
No me preocupa que ella no esté aquí todavía.	It doesn't worry me that she is not here yet.

Opinion

There are too many expressions of opinion to list here, but here are a few to help you understand the concept. These are most often impersonal expressions that contain adjectives.

Es importante	It's important	*Es imprescindible*	It's crucial
Es necesario	It's necessary	*Es sorprendente*	It's surprising
Es interesante	It's interesting	*Es posible*	It's possible
Es bueno/malo	It's good/bad	*Vale la pena*	It's worth it
Es justo/injusto	It's fair/not fair	*Importa*	It matters

Es posible que ella llegue mañana.	It's possible that she will arrive tomorrow.
Importa que todos salgan a tiempo.	It matters that everyone leave on time.

Command/Request

querer	to want	*sugerir*	to suggest
insistir	to insist	*rogar*	to beg
aconsejar	to advise	*exigir*	to demand
pedir	to request	*recomendar*	to recommend
mandar	to order/command	*decir**	to tell

*The verb "decir" requires the subjunctive only when the sentence implies a request that someone do something. If the statement merely gives information, then "decir" does not require the subjunctive.

Mis padres me dicen que limpie mi cuarto.	My parents tell me to clean up my room.
Mis padres me dicen que soy inteligente.	My parents tell me that I am smart.

Remember that the pattern of these sentences is a main clause with a subjunctive cue followed by a dependent clause that uses the subjunctive. Let's look at another sentence that follows this pattern, contrasted with a similarly constructed sentence that uses the indicative.

Dudo que haya un examen hoy.	I doubt that there is a test today.

The verb "dudar" (to doubt) requires the use of the subjunctive of the verb "haber" in the dependent clause. In contrast to this sentence, if there were no doubt, you would use the indicative of the verb "haber" in the dependent clause:

Sé que hay un examen hoy.	I know that there is a test today.

Since we so often react to the world around us, the subjunctive mood is used extensively in Spanish. If we merely reported information, we would not need to use the subjunctive mood, but since we frequently express our opinions, feelings, and wishes, the subjunctive mood is essential for more sophisticated communication in Spanish.

The following is an example of a statement in which we merely report information:

Mi hermano Pablo está enfermo.	My brother Pablo is sick.

The following is an example of a subjective response to that information:

Es muy triste que tu hermano Pablo esté enfermo.	It is very sad that your brother Pablo is sick.

In this sentence, the verb in the dependent clause is in the subjunctive because the main clause expresses an emotion.

When you give your opinion about something, it is always subjective. For that reason, the subjunctive is used after impersonal expressions of opinion. Here are some examples:

Es bueno que estés aquí.	It's good that you are here.
Es importante que todos se preparen.	It's important that everyone get ready.

However, if the impersonal clause expresses truth or certainty, the indicative is used, as in these examples:

Es cierto que tenemos un examen hoy.	It's true that we have a test today.
Estoy seguro de que no va a llover.	I'm sure that it isn't going to rain.

Another common use of the present subjunctive is in the formation of indirect commands, when we are expressing our wish that someone else do something. Here is an example of that structure:

Recomiendo que todos aprendan el subjuntivo.	I recommend that everyone learn the subjunctive.

The verb "recomendar" (to recommend) in the first clause requires the use of the subjunctive in the second clause.

The subjunctive is also used when there is doubt about when an action will take place, and this is indicated by the use of certain adverbial expressions. Here are some examples:

Cuando llegues, llámame.	When you arrive, call me.
No lo hará hasta que tenga tiempo.	He won't do it until he has time.

Here are two handy lists to help you remember when to use the subjunctive with adverbial expressions:

SIEMPRE SUBJUNTIVO

These expressions ALWAYS require the use of the subjunctive mood, no matter what the tense of the sentence. Just remember **ESCAPA** to know which expressions are in this group.)

En caso de que	in case
S*in que*	without
C*on tal de que*	provided that
A*ntes de que*	before
P*ara que*	so that
***A** menos que*	unless

Pablo limpia su cuarto para que sus padres no se enojen.	Pablo cleans up his room so that his parents won't get mad.
Pablo limpió su cuarto para que sus padres no se enojaran.	Pablo cleaned up his room so that his parents wouldn't get mad.

A VECES SUBJUNTIVO

These expressions only require the use of the subjunctive when the action has not occurred. The key here is the tense of the verb in the main clause. If the verb is future or a command, you will use the subjunctive for the dependent clause because there is some doubt about when or if the action will occur. If the main clause is in the present or the past, you use the indicative because there is no doubt. When you see the **McDEATH** expressions, you know that you need to ask yourself if the action has or has not occurred.

M*ientras*	while
C*uando*	when
D*espués*	after
E*n cuanto*	as soon as
A*unque*	although/even though
T*an pronto como*	as soon as
H*asta que*	until

Ella trabaja hasta que lo termina todo.	She works until she finishes everything. (This is a routine action, so there is no doubt.)
Ella trabajó hasta que lo terminó todo.	She worked until she finished everything. (This is completed action, so there is no doubt.)
Ella trabajará hasta que lo termine todo.	She will work until she finishes everything. (She has not finished yet, and we don't know when that will happen.)
Trabaja hasta que lo termines todo.	Work until you finish it all. (You did not finish yet.)

The subjunctive is used in adjective clauses that refer to an indefinite or negative antecedent. Here are some examples:

Busco un mecánico que pueda reparar mi carro.	I am looking for a mechanic who can fix my car.
No hay nadie que me escuche.	There is no one who will listen to me.

If you are describing something that is definite, you don't need to use the subjunctive:

Tengo un mecánico que siempre repara mi carro.	I have a mechanic who always fixes my car.
Veo a la señora que siempre me escucha.	I see the lady who always listens to me.

Other subjunctive tenses

There are only three other tenses of the subjunctive mood that are commonly used. These are the imperfect subjunctive, the present perfect subjunctive, and the past perfect subjunctive.

Imperfect Subjunctive (el imperfecto de subjuntivo)

To form the imperfect subjunctive, you begin with the third person plural form of the preterite and drop the "-ron." This means that whatever happens in that form (stem-changes, spelling changes, irregularities, etc.) will also occur in all six forms of the imperfect subjunctive. So, once you know the preterite tense well, the imperfect subjunctive is easy to form.

There are two sets of imperfect subjunctive endings used by native speakers of Spanish, but the most commonly used one is the first. Here are the charts for both possible endings:

-ra	-ramos
-ras	-rais
-ra	-ran

Here is the verb "hablar" in the imperfect subjunctive:

hablara	habláramos*
hablaras	hablarais
hablara	hablaran

Notice that this form has an accent mark on the vowel that precedes the ending. Also note that some of these forms resemble the future indicative, but the fact that these forms have no accent marks will help you keep them straight.

Here is a second conjugation verb in this form:

comiera	comiéramos
comieras	comierais
comiera	comieran

Since the preterite endings for first and second conjugation verbs are different, the imperfect subjunctive looks slightly different, as well.

Here is what the irregular verb "tener" (to have) looks like in the imperfect subjunctive:

tuviera	tuviéramos
tuvieras	tuvierais
tuviera	tuvieran

The alternate endings for the imperfect subjunctive are in this chart:

-se	-semos
-ses	-seis
-se	-sen

Here is what the verb "hablar" would look like with these endings:

hablase	hablásemos*
hablases	hablaseis
hablase	hablasen

Notice again that this form has an accent mark on the vowel that precedes the ending.

The Present Perfect Subjunctive (el perfecto de subjuntivo)

To form the perfect tenses of the subjunctive, you merely need to change the helping verb "haber" to the appropriate subjunctive tense. The present perfect subjunctive of "hablar" looks like this:

haya hablado	hayamos hablado
hayas hablado	hayáis hablado
haya hablado	hayan hablado

The Past Perfect Subjunctive (el pluscuamperfecto de subjuntivo)

The past perfect, or pluperfect, subjunctive looks like this:

hubiera* hablado	hubiéramos hablado
hubieras hablado	hubierais hablado
hubiera hablado	hubieran hablado

*If you use the alternate form of the imperfect subjunctive of the helping verb "haber," the first person form will be "hubiese hablado."

Sequence of tenses

Which tense of the subjunctive you choose will depend on the tense of the verb in the main clause. If the main verb is in the present, future, present perfect, or command form, you may choose either the present subjunctive or the present perfect subjunctive, depending on whether the action of the dependent clause has happened. Here is a chart to help you remember which tense to choose:

If the verb in the main clause is:	Use one of these subjunctive tenses:
present indicative future indicative present perfect indicative a command	present subjunctive (to express present or future action) OR present perfect subjunctive (to express possible past action) OR imperfect subjunctive (to express completed past action)

Examples:

Espero que llegues a tiempo. I hope that you do/will arrive on time.

(The dependent clause refers to an action that has not happened yet.)

*Dudo que hayan llegado ya.**	I doubt that they have already arrived.
*Dudo que llegaran ya.**	I doubt that they did arrive already.

(The dependent clauses refer to actions in the past, so you may use either the present perfect subjunctive or the imperfect subjunctive, depending on what you mean to say.)

*Note that these two sentences have slightly different translations in English, but they convey basically the same information. Remember that the present perfect indicative and the preterite are very similar in meaning, so it follows that the two past subjunctive tenses that refer to similar past actions are also interchangeable in some sentences. In years past, the imperfect subjunctive was not accepted in this kind of sentence, but today it is very common and grammatically acceptable.

Llámame cuando llegues.	Call me when you arrive.

(The action of the dependent clause has not happened yet, so you must use the present subjunctive.)

When expressing past actions, there is also a sequence of tenses that you must observe. If the main verb is in any past tense, you may choose either the imperfect subjunctive or the past perfect subjunctive, depending on whether or not the action of the dependent clause has happened.

If the verb in the main clause is:	**Use one of these subjunctive tenses:**
preterite	imperfect subjunctive (to express possible past action)
imperfect	OR
conditional	past perfect subjunctive (to refer to an event further in the past, prior to the action of the main verb)
past perfect	

Examples:

Esperaban que llegaras a tiempo.	They were hoping that you would arrive on time.

(Although both clauses are in the past, the action of the dependent clause has not yet occurred.)

Dudábamos que hubieran llegado ya.	We doubted that they had already arrived.

(The action of the dependent clause is prior to the action of the main clause.)

The Imperative Mood

Another important use of the present subjunctive is to form commands, also known as the "imperative mood" in English. In Spanish, almost all commands are formed by using the present subjunctive. The only exceptions are affirmative "tú" and "vosotros" commands. All formal commands (those for "usted" and "ustedes"), as well as the "we" commands and all negative commands, are formed by using the present subjunctive.

Here are some examples:

Hable usted español.	Speak Spanish.
Coman ustedes más fruta.	Eat more fruit.
Hagamos la tarea ahora.*	Let's do our homework now.
No hagas eso.	Don't do that.

*An alternative to the "we" command expressed by the present subjunctive is the commonly used expression "Vamos a + infinitive." For this example, instead of "hagamos," you can say "vamos a hacer."

The only irregular "nosotros" command is that of the verb "ir" (to go). This is the only verb in Spanish whose "we" command is NOT in the subjunctive mood.

Vamos a casa. Let's go home.

However, since all negative commands are subjunctive, the negative command for "ir" follows the rules and is subjunctive:

No vayamos ahora. Let's not go now.

For affirmative commands, reflexive and object pronouns are attached to the end instead of preceding the verb, as in these examples:

Acuéstense ustedes temprano.* Go to bed early.

Cómpreme el libro, por favor.* Please buy me the book.

Since adding a pronoun to the end of the verb changes the stress pattern, you will need to add an accent mark to indicate that the stressed syllable has not changed.

"Nosotros" commands for reflexive verbs drop the final "s" before adding the reflexive pronoun "nos."

Acostémonos.	Let's go to bed.

In negative commands, the pronoun precedes the command form, as in these examples:

No se preocupe usted.	Don't worry.
No se vayan ustedes.	Don't leave.

The only commands that do not require the subjunctive mood are affirmative "tú" and "vosotros" commands. For regular verbs, the second person singular command form looks just like the third person singular indicative form of the verb, as in these examples:

(*Remember, these same commands in their negative forms will use the subjunctive.)

Habla español.	Speak Spanish.
**No hables inglés.*	Don't speak English.
Come más verduras.	Eat more vegetables.
**No comas comida chatarra.*	Don't eat junk food.

The "vosotros" command, which is used in Spain, is formed by dropping the final "r" of the infinitive form and replacing it with a "d." If the verb is reflexive, the "d" is dropped before the reflexive pronoun is added.

Hablad más despacio, por favor.	Please speak more slowly.
**No habléis tan rápido.*	Don't speak so fast.
Comed más fruta.	Eat more fruit.
**No comáis carne.*	Don't eat meat.
Marchaos ahora mismo.	Leave right now.
No os marchéis hasta más tarde	Don't leave until later.

Here are two charts to help you see how commands work. As you can see, most command forms are in the present subjunctive:

Indicative command forms

	** affirmative vosotros
affirmative "tú" commands: habla, come, abre, márchate	

**Remember that this form is not a present tense form, but a variation of the infinitive: hablad, comed, abrid, marchaos. (The "d" is eliminated when a reflexive pronoun is used).

Subjunctive command forms

	affirmative and negative "nosotros" commands: hablemos, no hablemos/comamos, no comamos/abramos, no abramos/ marchémonos/no nos marchemos
negative "tú" commands: no hables, no comas, no abras, no te marches	negative "vosotros" commands: no habléis, no comáis, no abráis, no os marchéis
affirmative and negative "Ud." commands: hable, no hable/coma, no coma/abra, no abras/márchese, no se marche	affirmative and negative "Uds." commands: hablen, no hablen/coman, no coman/abran, no abran/ márchense, no se marchen

Special Cases

Although each of the 601 verbs in the reference section of conjugated verbs is shown in all tenses and forms, there are some verbs that are not generally used in all tenses and/or forms. These verbs include "gustar" and "costar" (to cost), which are normally used in the third person singular or plural; "llover" (to rain), "nevar" (to snow), and "anochecer" (to grow dark), which are generally used only in the third person singular; and "soler" (to be accustomed to), which is used in most but not all tenses and is followed by the infinitive.

Conclusion

Now that you understand how to conjugate a verb in Spanish, how to form and use the different tenses, and when to use the subjunctive mood, you are ready to start using this knowledge to help you communicate in Spanish. The rest of this book will give you a handy reference to hundreds of common verbs, as well as practice exercises to help you learn and remember how these verbs work in Spanish. Don't be discouraged if it is challenging at first. Learning how to navigate through the Spanish verb system will take time and effort, but it will be worth it when you can read, write, speak, and understand what others say in Spanish.
Remember that *La práctica hace al maestro* (Practice makes perfect), in any language!

Sandy Williamson, M.A.T.
East Chapel Hill High School
Chapel Hill, North Carolina

to abandon, to leave — abandonar

gerundio **abandonando** participio de pasado **abandonado**

presente de indicativo

SINGULAR	PLURAL
abandon**o**	abandon**amos**
abandon**as**	abandon**áis**
abandon**a**	abandon**an**

imperfecto de indicativo

SINGULAR	PLURAL
abandon**aba**	abandon**ábamos**
abandon**abas**	abandon**abais**
abandon**aba**	abandon**aban**

pretérito

SINGULAR	PLURAL
abandon**é**	abandon**amos**
abandon**aste**	abandon**asteis**
abandon**ó**	abandon**aron**

futuro

SINGULAR	PLURAL
abandonar**é**	abandonar**emos**
abandonar**ás**	abandonar**éis**
abandonar**á**	abandonar**án**

condicional simple

SINGULAR	PLURAL
abandonar**ía**	abandonar**íamos**
abandonar**ías**	abandonar**íais**
abandonar**ía**	abandonar**ían**

presente de subjuntivo

SINGULAR	PLURAL
abandon**e**	abandon**emos**
abandon**es**	abandon**éis**
abandon**e**	abandon**en**

imperfecto de subjuntivo

SINGULAR	PLURAL
abandonar**a**	abandonár**amos**
abandonar**as**	abandonar**ais**
abandonar**a**	abandonar**an**
OR	
abandonas**e**	abandonás**emos**
abandonas**es**	abandonas**eis**
abandonas**e**	abandonas**en**

imperativo

SINGULAR	PLURAL
—	abandonemos
abandona; no abandones	abandonad; no abandonéis
abandone	abandonen

perfecto de indicativo

SINGULAR	PLURAL
he abandonado	**hemos** abandonado
has abandonado	**habéis** abandonado
ha abandonado	**han** abandonado

pluscuamperfecto de indicativo

SINGULAR	PLURAL
había abandonado	**habíamos** abandonado
habías abandonado	**habíais** abandonado
había abandonado	**habían** abandonado

pretérito anterior

SINGULAR	PLURAL
hube abandonado	**hubimos** abandonado
hubiste abandonado	**hubisteis** abandonado
hubo abandonado	**hubieron** abandonado

futuro perfecto

SINGULAR	PLURAL
habré abandonado	**habremos** abandonado
habrás abandonado	**habréis** abandonado
habrá abandonado	**habrán** abandonado

condicional compuesto

SINGULAR	PLURAL
habría abandonado	**habríamos** abandonado
habrías abandonado	**habríais** abandonado
habría abandonado	**habrían** abandonado

perfecto de subjuntivo

SINGULAR	PLURAL
haya abandonado	**hayamos** abandonado
hayas abandonado	**hayáis** abandonado
haya abandonado	**hayan** abandonado

pluscuamperfecto de subjuntivo

SINGULAR	PLURAL
hubiera abandonado	**hubiéramos** abandonado
hubieras abandonado	**hubierais** abandonado
hubiera abandonado	**hubieran** abandonado
OR	
hubiese abandonado	**hubiésemos** abandonado
hubieses abandonado	**hubieseis** abandonado
hubiese abandonado	**hubiesen** abandonado

abarcar — to embrace, to encompass

gerundio **abarcando** participio de pasado **abarcado**

SINGULAR	PLURAL	SINGULAR	PLURAL
presente de indicativo		perfecto de indicativo	
abarc**o**	abarc**amos**	**he** abarcado	**hemos** abarcado
abarc**as**	abarc**áis**	**has** abarcado	**habéis** abarcado
abarc**a**	abarc**an**	**ha** abarcado	**han** abarcado
imperfecto de indicativo		pluscuamperfecto de indicativo	
abarc**aba**	abarc**ábamos**	**había** abarcado	**habíamos** abarcado
abarc**abas**	abarc**abais**	**habías** abarcado	**habíais** abarcado
abarc**aba**	abarc**aban**	**había** abarcado	**habían** abarcado
pretérito		pretérito anterior	
abarqu**é**	abarc**amos**	**hube** abarcado	**hubimos** abarcado
abarc**aste**	abarc**asteis**	**hubiste** abarcado	**hubisteis** abarcado
abarc**ó**	abarc**aron**	**hubo** abarcado	**hubieron** abarcado
futuro		futuro perfecto	
abarcar**é**	abarcar**emos**	**habré** abarcado	**habremos** abarcado
abarcar**ás**	abarcar**éis**	**habrás** abarcado	**habréis** abarcado
abarcar**á**	abarcar**án**	**habrá** abarcado	**habrán** abarcado
condicional simple		condicional compuesto	
abarcar**ía**	abarcar**íamos**	**habría** abarcado	**habríamos** abarcado
abarcar**ías**	abarcar**íais**	**habrías** abarcado	**habríais** abarcado
abarcar**ía**	abarcar**ían**	**habría** abarcado	**habrían** abarcado
presente de subjuntivo		perfecto de subjuntivo	
abarqu**e**	abarqu**emos**	**haya** abarcado	**hayamos** abarcado
abarqu**es**	abarqu**éis**	**hayas** abarcado	**hayáis** abarcado
abarqu**e**	abarqu**en**	**haya** abarcado	**hayan** abarcado
imperfecto de subjuntivo		pluscuamperfecto de subjuntivo	
abarcar**a**	abarcár**amos**	**hubiera** abarcado	**hubiéramos** abarcado
abarcar**as**	abarcar**ais**	**hubieras** abarcado	**hubierais** abarcado
abarcar**a**	abarcar**an**	**hubiera** abarcado	**hubieran** abarcado
OR		OR	
abarcas**e**	abarcás**emos**	**hubiese** abarcado	**hubiésemos** abarcado
abarcas**es**	abarcas**eis**	**hubieses** abarcado	**hubieseis** abarcado
abarcas**e**	abarcas**en**	**hubiese** abarcado	**hubiesen** abarcado

imperativo

—	abarquemos
abarca; no abarques	abarcad; no abarquéis
abarque	abarquen

gerundio **abatiendo** participio de pasado **abatido**

SINGULAR	PLURAL	SINGULAR	PLURAL
presente de indicativo		perfecto de indicativo	
abat**o**	abat**imos**	**he** abatido	**hemos** abatido
abat**es**	abat**ís**	**has** abatido	**habéis** abatido
abat**e**	abat**en**	**ha** abatido	**han** abatido
imperfecto de indicativo		pluscamperfecto de indicativo	
abat**ía**	abat**íamos**	**había** abatido	**habíamos** abatido
abat**ías**	abat**íais**	**habías** abatido	**habíais** abatido
abat**ía**	abat**ían**	**había** abatido	**habían** abatido
pretérito		pretérito anterior	
abat**í**	abat**imos**	**hube** abatido	**hubimos** abatido
abat**iste**	abat**isteis**	**hubiste** abatido	**hubisteis** abatido
abat**ió**	abat**ieron**	**hubo** abatido	**hubieron** abatido
futuro		futuro perfecto	
abatir**é**	abatir**emos**	**habré** abatido	**habremos** abatido
abatir**ás**	abatir**éis**	**habrás** abatido	**habréis** abatido
abatir**á**	abatir**án**	**habrá** abatido	**habrán** abatido
condicional simple		condicional compuesto	
abatir**ía**	abatir**íamos**	**habría** abatido	**habríamos** abatido
abatir**ías**	abatir**íais**	**habrías** abatido	**habríais** abatido
abatir**ía**	abatir**ían**	**habría** abatido	**habrían** abatido
presente de subjuntivo		perfecto de subjuntivo	
abat**a**	abat**amos**	**haya** abatido	**hayamos** abatido
abat**as**	abat**áis**	**hayas** abatido	**hayáis** abatido
abat**a**	abat**an**	**haya** abatido	**hayan** abatido
imperfecto de subjuntivo		pluscuamperfecto de subjuntivo	
abatier**a**	abatiér**amos**	**hubiera** abatido	**hubiéramos** abatido
abatier**as**	abatier**ais**	**hubieras** abatido	**hubierais** abatido
abatier**a**	abatier**an**	**hubiera** abatido	**hubieran** abatido
OR		OR	
abaties**e**	abatiés**emos**	**hubiese** abatido	**hubiésemos** abatido
abaties**es**	abaties**eis**	**hubieses** abatido	**hubieseis** abatido
abaties**e**	abaties**en**	**hubiese** abatido	**hubiesen** abatido

imperativo

—	abatamos
abate; no abatas	abatid; no abatáis
abata	abatan

abdicar — to abdicate

gerundio **abdicando** participio de pasado **abdicado**

SINGULAR	PLURAL
presente de indicativo	
abdic**o**	abdic**amos**
abdic**as**	abdic**áis**
abdic**a**	abdic**an**
imperfecto de indicativo	
abdic**aba**	abdic**ábamos**
abdic**abas**	abdic**abais**
abdic**aba**	abdic**aban**
pretérito	
abdiqu**é**	abdic**amos**
abdic**aste**	abdic**asteis**
abdic**ó**	abdic**aron**
futuro	
abdicar**é**	abdicar**emos**
abdicar**ás**	abdicar**éis**
abdicar**á**	abdicar**án**
condicional simple	
abdicar**ía**	abdicar**íamos**
abdicar**ías**	abdicar**íais**
abdicar**ía**	abdicar**ían**
presente de subjuntivo	
abdiqu**e**	abdiqu**emos**
abdiqu**es**	abdiqu**éis**
abdiqu**e**	abdiqu**en**
imperfecto de subjuntivo	
abdicar**a**	abdicár**amos**
abdicar**as**	abdicar**ais**
abdicar**a**	abdicar**an**
OR	
abdicas**e**	abdicás**emos**
abdicas**es**	abdicas**eis**
abdicas**e**	abdicas**en**
imperativo	
—	abdiquemos
abdica; no abdiques	abdicad; no abdiquéis
abdique	abdiquen

SINGULAR	PLURAL
perfecto de indicativo	
he abdicado	**hemos** abdicado
has abdicado	**habéis** abdicado
ha abdicado	**han** abdicado
pluscuamperfecto de indicativo	
había abdicado	**habíamos** abdicado
habías abdicado	**habíais** abdicado
había abdicado	**habían** abdicado
pretérito anterior	
hube abdicado	**hubimos** abdicado
hubiste abdicado	**hubisteis** abdicado
hubo abdicado	**hubieron** abdicado
futuro perfecto	
habré abdicado	**habremos** abdicado
habrás abdicado	**habréis** abdicado
habrá abdicado	**habrán** abdicado
condicional compuesto	
habría abdicado	**habríamos** abdicado
habrías abdicado	**habríais** abdicado
habría abdicado	**habrían** abdicado
perfecto de subjuntivo	
haya abdicado	**hayamos** abdicado
hayas abdicado	**hayáis** abdicado
haya abdicado	**hayan** abdicado
pluscuamperfecto de subjuntivo	
hubiera abdicado	**hubiéramos** abdicado
hubieras abdicado	**hubierais** abdicado
hubiera abdicado	**hubieran** abdicado
OR	
hubiese abdicado	**hubiésemos** abdicado
hubieses abdicado	**hubieseis** abdicado
hubiese abdicado	**hubiesen** abdicado

gerundio **ablandando** participio de pasado **ablandado**

SINGULAR	PLURAL
presente de indicativo	
ablando	ablandamos
ablandas	ablandáis
abland**a**	abland**an**
imperfecto de indicativo	
abland**aba**	abland**ábamos**
abland**abas**	abland**abais**
abland**aba**	abland**aban**
pretérito	
abland**é**	abland**amos**
abland**aste**	abland**asteis**
abland**ó**	abland**aron**
futuro	
ablandar**é**	ablandar**emos**
ablandar**ás**	ablandar**éis**
ablandar**á**	ablandar**án**
condicional simple	
ablandar**ía**	ablandar**íamos**
ablandar**ías**	ablandar**íais**
ablandar**ía**	ablandar**ían**
presente de subjuntivo	
abland**e**	abland**emos**
abland**es**	abland**éis**
abland**e**	abland**en**
imperfecto de subjuntivo	
ablandar**a**	ablandár**amos**
ablandar**as**	ablandar**ais**
ablandar**a**	ablandar**an**
OR	
ablandas**e**	ablandás**emos**
ablandas**es**	ablandas**eis**
ablandas**e**	ablandas**en**
imperativo	
—	ablandemos
ablanda;	ablandad;
no ablandes	no ablandéis
ablande	ablanden

SINGULAR	PLURAL
perfecto de indicativo	
he ablandado	**hemos** ablandado
has ablandado	**habéis** ablandado
ha ablandado	**han** ablandado
pluscuamperfecto de indicativo	
había ablandado	**habíamos** ablandado
habías ablandado	**habíais** ablandado
había ablandado	**habían** ablandado
pretérito anterior	
hube ablandado	**hubimos** ablandado
hubiste ablandado	**hubisteis** ablandado
hubo ablandado	**hubieron** ablandado
futuro perfecto	
habré ablandado	**habremos** ablandado
habrás ablandado	**habréis** ablandado
habrá ablandado	**habrán** ablandado
condicional compuesto	
habría ablandado	**habríamos** ablandado
habrías ablandado	**habríais** ablandado
habría ablandado	**habrían** ablandado
perfecto de subjuntivo	
haya ablandado	**hayamos** ablandado
hayas ablandado	**hayáis** ablandado
haya ablandado	**hayan** ablandado
pluscuamperfecto de subjuntivo	
hubiera ablandado	**hubiéramos** ablandado
hubieras ablandado	**hubierais** ablandado
hubiera ablandado	**hubieran** ablandado
OR	
hubiese ablandado	**hubiésemos** ablandado
hubieses ablandado	**hubieseis** ablandado
hubiese ablandado	**hubiesen** ablandado

gerundio **aborreciendo** | participio de pasado **aborrecido**

SINGULAR	PLURAL	SINGULAR	PLURAL
presente de indicativo		perfecto de indicativo	
aborrezc**o**	aborrec**emos**	**he** aborrecido	**hemos** aborrecido
aborrec**es**	aborrec**éis**	**has** aborrecido	**habéis** aborrecido
aborrec**e**	aborrec**en**	**ha** aborrecido	**han** aborrecido
imperfecto de indicativo		pluscuamperfecto de indicativo	
aborrec**ía**	aborrec**íamos**	**había** aborrecido	**habíamos** aborrecido
aborrec**ías**	aborrec**íais**	**habías** aborrecido	**habíais** aborrecido
aborrec**ía**	aborrec**ían**	**había** aborrecido	**habían** aborrecido
pretérito		pretérito anterior	
aborrec**í**	aborrec**imos**	**hube** aborrecido	**hubimos** aborrecido
aborrec**iste**	aborrec**isteis**	**hubiste** aborrecido	**hubisteis** aborrecido
aborreci**ó**	aborrec**ieron**	**hubo** aborrecido	**hubieron** aborrecido
futuro		futuro perfecto	
aborrecer**é**	aborrecer**emos**	**habré** aborrecido	**habremos** aborrecido
aborrecer**ás**	aborrecer**éis**	**habrás** aborrecido	**habréis** aborrecido
aborrecer**á**	aborrecer**án**	**habrá** aborrecido	**habrán** aborrecido
condicional simple		condicional compuesto	
aborrecer**ía**	aborrecer**íamos**	**habría** aborrecido	**habríamos** aborrecido
aborrecer**ías**	aborrecer**íais**	**habrías** aborrecido	**habríais** aborrecido
aborrecer**ía**	aborrecer**ían**	**habría** aborrecido	**habrían** aborrecido
presente de subjuntivo		perfecto de subjuntivo	
aborrezc**a**	aborrezc**amos**	**haya** aborrecido	**hayamos** aborrecido
aborrezc**as**	aborrezc**áis**	**hayas** aborrecido	**hayáis** aborrecido
aborrezc**a**	aborrezc**an**	**haya** aborrecido	**hayan** aborrecido
imperfecto de subjuntivo		pluscuamperfecto de subjuntivo	
aborrecier**a**	aborreciér**amos**	**hubiera** aborrecido	**hubiéramos** aborrecido
aborrecier**as**	aborrecier**ais**	**hubieras** aborrecido	**hubierais** aborrecido
aborrecier**a**	aborrecier**an**	**hubiera** aborrecido	**hubieran** aborrecido
OR		OR	
aborrecies**e**	aborreciés**emos**	**hubiese** aborrecido	**hubiésemos** aborrecido
aborrecies**es**	aborrecies**eis**	**hubieses** aborrecido	**hubieseis** aborrecido
aborrecies**e**	aborrecies**en**	**hubiese** aborrecido	**hubiesen** aborrecido

imperativo

—	aborrezcamos
aborrece; no aborrezcas	aborreced; no aborrezcáis
aborrezca	aborrezcan

gerundio **abrazando** participio de pasado **abrazado**

SINGULAR	PLURAL	SINGULAR	PLURAL
presente de indicativo		perfecto de indicativo	
abraz**o**	abraz**amos**	**he** abrazado	**hemos** abrazado
abraz**as**	abraz**áis**	**has** abrazado	**habéis** abrazado
abraz**a**	abraz**an**	**ha** abrazado	**han** abrazado
imperfecto de indicativo		pluscuamperfecto de indicativo	
abrazab**a**	abrazáb**amos**	**había** abrazado	**habíamos** abrazado
abrazab**as**	abrazab**ais**	**habías** abrazado	**habíais** abrazado
abrazab**a**	abrazab**an**	**había** abrazado	**habían** abrazado
pretérito		pretérito anterior	
abrac**é**	abraz**amos**	**hube** abrazado	**hubimos** abrazado
abraz**aste**	abraz**asteis**	**hubiste** abrazado	**hubisteis** abrazado
abraz**ó**	abraz**aron**	**hubo** abrazado	**hubieron** abrazado
futuro		futuro perfecto	
abrazar**é**	abrazar**emos**	**habré** abrazado	**habremos** abrazado
abrazar**ás**	abrazar**éis**	**habrás** abrazado	**habréis** abrazado
abrazar**á**	abrazar**án**	**habrá** abrazado	**habrán** abrazado
condicional simple		condicional compuesto	
abrazar**ía**	abrazar**íamos**	**habría** abrazado	**habríamos** abrazado
abrazar**ías**	abrazar**íais**	**habrías** abrazado	**habríais** abrazado
abrazar**ía**	abrazar**ían**	**habría** abrazado	**habrían** abrazado
presente de subjuntivo		perfecto de subjuntivo	
abrac**e**	abrac**emos**	**haya** abrazado	**hayamos** abrazado
abrac**es**	abrac**éis**	**hayas** abrazado	**hayáis** abrazado
abrac**e**	abrac**en**	**haya** abrazado	**hayan** abrazado
imperfecto de subjuntivo		pluscuamperfecto de subjuntivo	
abrazar**a**	abrazár**amos**	**hubiera** abrazado	**hubiéramos** abrazado
abrazar**as**	abrazar**ais**	**hubieras** abrazado	**hubierais** abrazado
abrazar**a**	abrazar**an**	**hubiera** abrazado	**hubieran** abrazado
OR		OR	
abrazas**e**	abrazás**emos**	**hubiese** abrazado	**hubiésemos** abrazado
abrazas**es**	abrazas**eis**	**hubieses** abrazado	**hubieseis** abrazado
abrazas**e**	abrazas**en**	**hubiese** abrazado	**hubiesen** abrazado

imperativo

—	abracemos
abraza; no abraces	abrazad; no abracéis
abrace	abracen

abrir — to open

gerundio **abriendo** participio de pasado **abierto**

SINGULAR	PLURAL	SINGULAR	PLURAL
presente de indicativo		perfecto de indicativo	
abr**o**	abr**imos**	**he** abierto	**hemos** abierto
abr**es**	abr**ís**	**has** abierto	**habéis** abierto
abr**e**	abr**en**	**ha** abierto	**han** abierto
imperfecto de indicativo		pluscuamperfecto de indicativo	
abr**ía**	abr**íamos**	**había** abierto	**habíamos**abierto
abr**ías**	abr**íais**	**habías** abierto	**habíais** abierto
abr**ía**	abr**ían**	**había** abierto	**habían** abierto
pretérito		pretérito anterior	
abr**í**	abr**imos**	**hube** abierto	**hubimos** abierto
abr**iste**	abr**isteis**	**hubiste** abierto	**hubisteis** abierto
abri**ó**	abr**ieron**	**hubo** abierto	**hubieron** abierto
futuro		futuro perfecto	
abrir**é**	abrir**emos**	**habré** abierto	**habremos** abierto
abrir**ás**	abrir**éis**	**habrás** abierto	**habréis** abierto
abrir**á**	abrir**án**	**habrá** abierto	**habrán** abierto
condicional simple		condicional compuesto	
abrir**ía**	abrir**íamos**	**habría** abierto	**habríamos** abierto
abrir**ías**	abrir**íais**	**habrías** abierto	**habríais** abierto
abrir**ía**	abrir**ían**	**habría** abierto	**habrían** abierto
presente de subjuntivo		perfecto de subjuntivo	
abr**a**	abr**amos**	**haya** abierto	**hayamos** abierto
abr**as**	abr**áis**	**hayas** abierto	**hayáis** abierto
abr**a**	abr**an**	**haya** abierto	**hayan** abierto
imperfecto de subjuntivo		pluscuamperfecto de subjuntivo	
abrier**a**	abrié**ramos**	**hubiera** abierto	**hubiéramos** abierto
abrier**as**	abrier**ais**	**hubieras** abierto	**hubierais** abierto
abrier**a**	abrier**an**	**hubiera** abierto	**hubieran** abierto
OR		OR	
abries**e**	abriés**emos**	**hubiese** abierto	**hubiésemos** abierto
abries**es**	abries**eis**	**hubieses** abierto	**hubieseis** abierto
abries**e**	abries**en**	**hubiese** abierto	**hubiesen** abierto

imperativo

—	abramos
abre; no abras	abrid; no abráis
abra	abran

gerundio **absolviendo** participio de pasado **absuelto**

SINGULAR	PLURAL
presente de indicativo	
absuelv**o**	absolv**emos**
absuelv**es**	absolv**éis**
absuelv**e**	absuelv**en**
imperfecto de indicativo	
absolv**ía**	absolv**íamos**
absolv**ías**	absolv**íais**
absolv**ía**	absolv**ían**
pretérito	
absolv**í**	absolv**imos**
absolv**iste**	absolv**isteis**
absolv**ió**	absolv**ieron**
futuro	
absolver**é**	absolver**emos**
absolver**ás**	absolver**éis**
absolver**á**	absolver**án**
condicional simple	
absolver**ía**	absolver**íamos**
absolver**ías**	absolver**íais**
absolver**ía**	absolver**ían**
presente de subjuntivo	
absuelv**a**	absolv**amos**
absuelv**as**	absolv**áis**
absuelv**a**	absuelv**an**
imperfecto de subjuntivo	
absolvier**a**	absolviér**amos**
absolvier**as**	absolvier**ais**
absolvier**a**	absolvier**an**
OR	
absolvies**e**	absolvié**semos**
absolvies**es**	absolvies**eis**
absolvies**e**	absolvies**en**
imperativo	
—	absolvamos
absuelve; no absuelvas	absolved; no absuelváis
absuelva	absuelvan

SINGULAR	PLURAL
perfecto de indicativo	
he absuelto	**hemos** absuelto
has absuelto	**habéis** absuelto
ha absuelto	**han** absuelto
pluscuamperfecto de indicativo	
había absuelto	**habíamos** absuelto
habías absuelto	**habíais** absuelto
había absuelto	**habían** absuelto
pretérito anterior	
hube absuelto	**hubimos** absuelto
hubiste absuelto	**hubisteis** absuelto
hubo absuelto	**hubieron** absuelto
futuro perfecto	
habré absuelto	**habremos** absuelto
habrás absuelto	**habréis** absuelto
habrá absuelto	**habrán** absuelto
condicional compuesto	
habría absuelto	**habríamos** absuelto
habrías absuelto	**habríais** absuelto
habría absuelto	**habrían** absuelto
perfecto de subjuntivo	
haya absuelto	**hayamos** absuelto
hayas absuelto	**hayáis** absuelto
haya absuelto	**hayan** absuelto
pluscuamperfecto de subjuntivo	
hubiera absuelto	**hubiéramos** absuelto
hubieras absuelto	**hubierais** absuelto
hubiera absuelto	**hubieran** absuelto
OR	
hubiese absuelto	**hubiésemos** absuelto
hubieses absuelto	**hubieseis** absuelto
hubiese absuelto	**hubiesen** absuelto

abstenerse — to abstain

gerundio **absteniéndose** participio de pasado **absteniendo**

presente de indicativo

SINGULAR	PLURAL
me absteng**o**	nos absten**emos**
te abstien**es**	os absten**éis**
se abstien**e**	se abstien**en**

imperfecto de indicativo

SINGULAR	PLURAL
me absten**ía**	nos absten**íamos**
te absten**ías**	os absten**íais**
se absten**ía**	se absten**ían**

pretérito

SINGULAR	PLURAL
me abstuv**e**	nos abstuv**imos**
te abstuv**iste**	os abstuv**isteis**
se abstuv**o**	se abstuv**ieron**

futuro

SINGULAR	PLURAL
me abstendr**é**	nos abstendr**emos**
te abstendr**ás**	os abstendr**éis**
se abstendr**á**	se abstendr**án**

condicional simple

SINGULAR	PLURAL
me abstendr**ía**	nos abstendr**íamos**
te abstendr**ías**	os abstendr**íais**
se abstendr**ía**	se abstendr**ían**

presente de subjuntivo

SINGULAR	PLURAL
me absteng**a**	nos absteng**amos**
te absteng**as**	os absteng**áis**
se absteng**a**	se absteng**an**

imperfecto de subjuntivo

SINGULAR	PLURAL
me abstuvier**a**	nos abstuviér**amos**
te abstuvier**as**	os abstuvier**ais**
se abstuvier**a**	se abstuvier**an**
OR	
me abstuvies**e**	nos abstuviés**emos**
te abstuvies**es**	os abstuvies**eis**
se abstuvies**e**	se abstuvies**en**

imperativo

SINGULAR	PLURAL
—	abstengámonos
abstente; no te abstengas	absteneos; no os abstengáis
absténgase	absténganse

perfecto de indicativo

SINGULAR	PLURAL
me he abstenido	**nos hemos** abstenido
te has abstenido	**os habéis** abstenido
se ha abstenido	**se han** abstenido

pluscuamperfecto de indicativo

SINGULAR	PLURAL
me había abstenido	**nos habíamos** abstenido
te habías abstenido	**os habíais** abstenido
se había abstenido	**se habían** abstenido

pretérito anterior

SINGULAR	PLURAL
me hube abstenido	**nos hubimos** abstenido
te hubiste abstenido	**os hubisteis** abstenido
se hubo abstenido	**se hubieron** abstenido

futuro perfecto

SINGULAR	PLURAL
me habré abstenido	**nos habremos** abstenido
te habrás abstenido	**os habréis** abstenido
se habrá abstenido	**se habrán** abstenido

condicional compuesto

SINGULAR	PLURAL
me habría abstenido	**nos habríamos** abstenido
te habrías abstenido	**os habríais** abstenido
se habría abstenido	**se habrían** abstenido

perfecto de subjuntivo

SINGULAR	PLURAL
me haya abstenido	**nos hayamos** abstenido
te hayas abstenido	**os hayáis** abstenido
se haya abstenido	**se hayan** abstenido

pluscuamperfecto de subjuntivo

SINGULAR	PLURAL
me hubiera abstenido	**nos hubiéramos** abstenido
te hubieras abstenido	**os hubierais** abstenido
se hubiera abstenido	**se hubieran** abstenido
OR	
me hubiese abstenido	**nos hubiésemos** abstenido
te hubieses abstenido	**os hubieseis** abstenido
se hubiese abstenido	**se hubiesen** abstenido

to bore — aburrir

gerundio **aburriendo** participio de pasado **aburrido**

SINGULAR	PLURAL
presente de indicativo	
aburr**o**	aburr**imos**
aburr**es**	aburr**ís**
aburr**e**	aburr**en**
imperfecto de indicativo	
aburr**ía**	aburr**íamos**
aburr**ías**	aburr**íais**
aburr**ía**	aburr**ían**
pretérito	
aburr**í**	aburr**imos**
aburr**iste**	aburr**isteis**
aburri**ó**	aburr**ieron**
futuro	
aburrir**é**	aburrir**emos**
aburrir**ás**	aburrir**éis**
aburrir**á**	aburrir**án**
condicional simple	
aburrir**ía**	aburrir**íamos**
aburrir**ías**	aburrir**íais**
aburrir**ía**	aburrir**ían**
presente de subjuntivo	
aburr**a**	aburr**amos**
aburr**as**	aburr**áis**
aburr**a**	aburr**an**
imperfecto de subjuntivo	
aburrier**a**	aburriér**amos**
aburrier**as**	aburrier**ais**
aburrier**a**	aburrier**an**
OR	
aburries**e**	aburriés**emos**
aburries**es**	aburries**eis**
aburries**e**	aburries**en**
imperativo	
—	aburramos
aburre; no aburras	aburrid; no aburráis
aburra	aburran

SINGULAR	PLURAL
perfecto de indicativo	
he aburrido	**hemos** aburrido
has aburrido	**habéis** aburrido
ha aburrido	**han** aburrido
pluscuamperfecto de indicativo	
había aburrido	**habíamos** aburrido
habías aburrido	**habíais** aburrido
había aburrido	**habían** aburrido
pretérito anterior	
hube aburrido	**hubimos** aburrido
hubiste aburrido	**hubisteis** aburrido
hubo aburrido	**hubieron** aburrido
futuro perfecto	
habré aburrido	**habremos** aburrido
habrás aburrido	**habréis** aburrido
habrá aburrido	**habrán** aburrido
condicional compuesto	
habría aburrido	**habríamos** aburrido
habrías aburrido	**habríais** aburrido
habría aburrido	**habrían** aburrido
perfecto de subjuntivo	
haya aburrido	**hayamos** aburrido
hayas aburrido	**hayáis** aburrido
haya aburrido	**hayan** aburrido
pluscuamperfecto de subjuntivo	
hubiera aburrido	**hubiéramos** aburrido
hubieras aburrido	**hubierais** aburrido
hubiera aburrido	**hubieran** aburrido
OR	
hubiese aburrido	**hubiésemos** aburrido
hubieses aburrido	**hubieseis** aburrido
hubiese aburrido	**hubiesen** aburrido

abusar to abuse, to take advantage of

gerundio **abusando** participio de pasado **abusado**

SINGULAR	PLURAL	SINGULAR	PLURAL
presente de indicativo		perfecto de indicativo	
abus**o**	abus**amos**	**he** abusado	**hemos** abusado
abus**as**	abus**áis**	**has** abusado	**habéis** abusado
abus**a**	abus**an**	**ha** abusado	**han** abusado
imperfecto de indicativo		pluscuamperfecto de indicativo	
abus**aba**	abus**ábamos**	**había** abusado	**habíamos** abusado
abus**abas**	abus**abais**	**habías** abusado	**habíais** abusado
abus**aba**	abus**aban**	**había** abusado	**habían** abusado
pretérito		pretérito anterior	
abus**é**	abus**amos**	**hube** abusado	**hubimos** abusado
abus**aste**	abus**asteis**	**hubiste** abusado	**hubisteis** abusado
abus**ó**	abus**aron**	**hubo** abusado	**hubieron** abusado
futuro		futuro perfecto	
abusar**é**	abusar**emos**	**habré** abusado	**habremos** abusado
abusar**ás**	abusar**éis**	**habrás** abusado	**habréis** abusado
abusar**á**	abusar**án**	**habrá** abusado	**habrán** abusado
condicional simple		condicional compuesto	
abusar**ía**	abusar**íamos**	**habría** abusado	**habríamos** abusado
abusar**ías**	abusar**íais**	**habrías** abusado	**habríais** abusado
abusar**ía**	abusar**ían**	**habría** abusado	**habrían** abusado
presente de subjuntivo		perfecto de subjuntivo	
abus**e**	abus**emos**	**haya** abusado	**hayamos** abusado
abus**es**	abus**éis**	**hayas** abusado	**hayáis** abusado
abus**e**	abus**en**	**haya** abusado	**hayan** abusado
imperfecto de subjuntivo		pluscuamperfecto de subjuntivo	
abusar**a**	abusár**amos**	**hubiera** abusado	**hubiéramos** abusado
abusar**as**	abusar**ais**	**hubieras** abusado	**hubierais** abusado
abusar**a**	abusar**an**	**hubiera** abusado	**hubieran** abusado
OR		OR	
abusas**e**	abusás**emos**	**hubiese** abusado	**hubiésemos** abusado
abusas**es**	abusas**eis**	**hubieses** abusado	**hubieseis** abusado
abusas**e**	abusas**en**	**hubiese** abusado	**hubiesen** abusado

imperativo

—	abusemos
abusa; no abuses	abusad; no abuséis
abuse	abusen

to finish, to end, to complete **acabar**

gerundio **acabando** participio de pasado **acabado**

SINGULAR	PLURAL	SINGULAR	PLURAL
presente de indicativo		*perfecto de indicativo*	
acab**o**	acab**amos**	**he** acabado	**hemos** acabado
acab**as**	acab**áis**	**has** acabado	**habéis** acabado
acab**a**	acab**an**	**ha** acabado	**han** acabado
imperfecto de indicativo		*pluscuamperfecto de indicativo*	
acab**aba**	acab**ábamos**	**había** acabado	**habíamos** acabado
acab**abas**	acab**abais**	**habías** acabado	**habíais** acabado
acab**aba**	acab**aban**	**había** acabado	**habían** acabado
pretérito		*pretérito anterior*	
acab**é**	acab**amos**	**hube** acabado	**hubimos** acabado
acab**aste**	acab**asteis**	**hubiste** acabado	**hubisteis** acabado
acab**ó**	acab**aron**	**hubo** acabado	**hubieron** acabado
futuro		*futuro perfecto*	
acabar**é**	acabar**emos**	**habré** acabado	**habremos** acabado
acabar**ás**	acabar**éis**	**habrás** acabado	**habréis** acabado
acabar**á**	acabar**án**	**habrá** acabado	**habrán** acabado
condicional simple		*condicional compuesto*	
acabar**ía**	acabar**íamos**	**habría** acabado	**habríamos** acabado
acabar**ías**	acabar**íais**	**habrías** acabado	**habríais** acabado
acabar**ía**	acabar**ían**	**habría** acabado	**habrían** acabado
presente de subjuntivo		*perfecto de subjuntivo*	
acab**e**	acab**emos**	**haya** acabado	**hayamos** acabado
acab**es**	acab**éis**	**hayas** acabado	**hayáis** acabado
acab**e**	acab**en**	**haya** acabado	**hayan** acabado
imperfecto de subjuntivo		*pluscuamperfecto de subjuntivo*	
acabar**a**	acabár**amos**	**hubiera** acabado	**hubiéramos** acabado
acabar**as**	acabar**ais**	**hubieras** acabado	**hubierais** acabado
acabar**a**	acabar**an**	**hubiera** acabado	**hubieran** acabado
OR		OR	
acabas**e**	acabás**emos**	**hubiese** acabado	**hubiésemos** acabado
acabas**es**	acabas**eis**	**hubieses** acabado	**hubieseis** acabado
acabas**e**	acabas**en**	**hubiese** acabado	**hubiesen** acabado

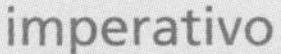

imperativo

—	acabemos
acaba; no acabes	acabad; no acabéis
acabe	acaben

acalorarse — to get hot

gerundio **acalorándose** participio de pasado **acalorado**

SINGULAR	PLURAL	SINGULAR	PLURAL
presente de indicativo		perfecto de indicativo	
me acalor**o**	nos acalor**amos**	**me he** acalorado	**nos hemos** acalorado
te acalor**as**	os acalor**áis**	**te has** acalorado	**os habéis** acalorado
se acalor**a**	se acalor**an**	**se ha** acalorado	**se han** acalorado
imperfecto de indicativo		pluscuamperfecto de indicativo	
me acalor**aba**	nos acalor**ábamos**	**me había** acalorado	**nos habíamos** acalorado
te acalor**abas**	os acalor**abais**	**te habías** acalorado	**os habíais** acalorado
se acalor**aba**	se acalor**aban**	**se había** acalorado	**se habían** acalorado
pretérito		pretérito anterior	
me acalor**é**	nos acalor**amos**	**me hube** acalorado	**nos hubimos** acalorado
te acalor**aste**	os acalor**asteis**	**te hubiste** acalorado	**os hubisteis** acalorado
se acalor**ó**	se acalor**aron**	**se hubo** acalorado	**se hubieron** acalorado
futuro		futuro perfecto	
me acalorar**é**	nos acalorar**emos**	**me habré** acalorado	**nos habremos** acalorado
te acalorar**ás**	os acalorar**éis**	**te habrás** acalorado	**os habréis** acalorado
se acalorar**á**	se acalorar**án**	**se habrá** acalorado	**se habrán** acalorado
condicional simple		condicional compuesto	
me acalorar**ía**	nos acalorar**íamos**	**me habría** acalorado	**nos habríamos** acalorado
te acalorar**ías**	os acalorar**íais**	**te habrías** acalorado	**os habríais** acalorado
se acalorar**ía**	se acalorar**ían**	**se habría** acalorado	**se habrían** acalorado
presente de subjuntivo		perfecto de subjuntivo	
me acalor**e**	nos acalor**emos**	**me haya** acalorado	**nos hayamos** acalorado
te acalor**es**	os acalor**éis**	**te hayas** acalorado	**os hayáis** acalorado
se acalor**e**	se acalor**en**	**se haya** acalorado	**se hayan** acalorado
imperfecto de subjuntivo		pluscuam perfecto de subjuntivo	
me acalorar**a**	nos acalorár**amos**	**me hubiera** acalorado	**nos hubiéramos** acalorado
te acalorar**as**	os acalorar**ais**	**te hubieras** acalorado	**os hubierais** acalorado
se acalorar**a**	se acalorar**an**	**se hubiera** acalorado	**se hubieran** acalorado
OR		OR	
me acaloras**e**	nos acalorás**emos**	**me hubiese** acalorado	**nos hubiésemos** acalorado
te acaloras**es**	os acaloras**eis**	**te hubieses** acalorado	**os hubieseis** acalorado
se acaloras**e**	se acaloras**en**	**se hubiese** acalorado	**se hubiesen** acalorado

imperativo

—	nos acaloremos
acalórate; no te acalores	acaloraos; no os acaloréis
acalórese	acalórense

to caress — acariciar

gerundio **acariciando** participio de pasado **acariciado**

SINGULAR	PLURAL
presente de indicativo	
acarici**o**	acarici**amos**
acarici**as**	acarici**áis**
acarici**a**	acarici**an**
imperfecto de indicativo	
acarici**aba**	acarici**ábamos**
acarici**abas**	acarici**abais**
acarici**aba**	acarici**aban**
pretérito	
acarici**é**	acarici**amos**
acarici**aste**	acarici**asteis**
acarici**ó**	acarici**aron**
futuro	
acariciar**é**	acariciar**emos**
acariciar**ás**	acariciar**éis**
acariciar**á**	acariciar**án**
condicional simple	
acariciar**ía**	acariciar**íamos**
acariciar**ías**	acariciar**íais**
acariciar**ía**	acariciar**ían**
presente de subjuntivo	
acarici**e**	acarici**emos**
acarici**es**	acarici**éis**
acarici**e**	acarici**en**
imperfecto de subjuntivo	
acariciar**a**	acariciár**amos**
acariciar**as**	acariciar**ais**
acariciar**a**	acariciar**an**
OR	
acaricias**e**	acariciás**emos**
acaricias**es**	acaricias**eis**
acaricias**e**	acaricias**en**
imperativo	
—	acariciemos
acaricia; no acaricies	acariciad; no acariciéis
acaricie	acaricien

SINGULAR	PLURAL
perfecto de indicativo	
he acariciado	**hemos** acariciado
has acariciado	**habéis** acariciado
ha acariciado	**han** acariciado
pluscuamperfecto de indicativo	
había acariciado	**habíamos** acariciado
habías acariciado	**habíais** acariciado
había acariciado	**habían** acariciado
pretérito anterior	
hube acariciado	**hubimos** acariciado
hubiste acariciado	**hubisteis** acariciado
hubo acariciado	**hubieron** acariciado
futuro perfecto	
habré acariciado	**habremos** acariciado
habrás acariciado	**habréis** acariciado
habrá acariciado	**habrán** acariciado
condicional compuesto	
habría acariciado	**habríamos** acariciado
habrías acariciado	**habríais** acariciado
habría acariciado	**habrían** acariciado
perfecto de subjuntivo	
haya acariciado	**hayamos** acariciado
hayas acariciado	**hayáis** acariciado
haya acariciado	**hayan** acariciado
pluscuamperfecto de subjuntivo	
hubiera acariciado	**hubiéramos** acariciado
hubieras acariciado	**hubierais** acariciado
hubiera acariciado	**hubieran** acariciado
OR	
hubiese acariciado	**hubiésemos** acariciado
hubieses acariciado	**hubieseis** acariciado
hubiese acariciado	**hubiesen** acariciado

accionar — to activate, to trigger

gerundio **accionando** — participio de pasado **accionado**

SINGULAR	PLURAL
presente de indicativo	
acciono	accionamos
accionas	accionáis
acciona	accionan
imperfecto de indicativo	
accionaba	accionábamos
accionabas	accionabais
accionaba	accionaban
pretérito	
accioné	accionamos
accionaste	accionasteis
accionó	accionaron
futuro	
accionaré	accionaremos
accionarás	accionaréis
accionará	accionarán
condicional simple	
accionaría	accionaríamos
accionarías	accionaríais
accionaría	accionarían
presente de subjuntivo	
accione	accionemos
acciones	accionéis
accione	accionen
imperfecto de subjuntivo	
accionara	accionáramos
accionaras	accionarais
accionara	accionaran
OR	
accionase	accionásemos
accionases	accionaseis
accionase	accionasen
imperativo	
—	accionemos
acciona; no acciones	accionad; no accionéis
accione	accionen

SINGULAR	PLURAL
perfecto de indicativo	
he accionado	hemos accionado
has accionado	habéis accionado
ha accionado	han accionado
pluscuamperfecto de indicativo	
había accionado	habíamos accionado
habías accionado	habíais accionado
había accionado	habían accionado
pretérito anterior	
hube accionado	hubimos accionado
hubiste accionado	hubisteis accionado
hubo accionado	hubieron accionado
futuro perfecto	
habré accionado	habremos accionado
habrás accionado	habréis accionado
habrá accionado	habrán accionado
condicional compuesto	
habría accionado	habríamos accionado
habrías accionado	habríais accionado
habría accionado	habrían accionado
perfecto de subjuntivo	
haya accionado	hayamos accionado
hayas accionado	hayáis accionado
haya accionado	hayan accionado
pluscuamperfecto de subjuntivo	
hubiera accionado	hubiéramos accionado
hubieras accionado	hubierais accionado
hubiera accionado	hubieran accionado
OR	
hubiese accionado	hubiésemos accionado
hubieses accionado	hubieseis accionado
hubiese accionado	hubiesen accionado

gerundio **acelerando** participio de pasado **acelerado**

SINGULAR	PLURAL	SINGULAR	PLURAL
presente de indicativo		perfecto de indicativo	
acelero	aceleramos	**he** acelerado	**hemos** acelerado
aceleras	aceleráis	**has** acelerado	**habéis** acelerado
acelera	aceleran	**ha** acelerado	**han** acelerado
imperfecto de indicativo		pluscuamperfecto de indicativo	
aceleraba	acelerábamos	**había** acelerado	**habíamos** acelerado
acelerabas	acelerabais	**habías** acelerado	**habíais** acelerado
aceleraba	aceleraban	**había** acelerado	**habían** acelerado
pretérito		pretérito anterior	
aceleré	aceleramos	**hube** acelerado	**hubimos** acelerado
aceleraste	acelerasteis	**hubiste** acelerado	**hubisteis** acelerado
aceleró	aceleraron	**hubo** acelerado	**hubieron** acelerado
futuro		futuro perfecto	
aceleraré	aceleraremos	**habré** acelerado	**habremos** acelerado
acelerarás	aceleraréis	**habrás** acelerado	**habréis** acelerado
acelerará	acelerarán	**habrá** acelerado	**habrán** acelerado
condicional simple		condicional compuesto	
aceleraría	aceleraríamos	**habría** acelerado	**habríamos** acelerado
acelerarías	aceleraríais	**habrías** acelerado	**habríais** acelerado
aceleraría	acelerarían	**habría** acelerado	**habrían** acelerado
presente de subjuntivo		perfecto de subjuntivo	
acelere	aceleremos	**haya** acelerado	**hayamos** acelerado
aceleres	aceleréis	**hayas** acelerado	**hayáis** acelerado
acelere	aceleren	**haya** acelerado	**hayan** acelerado
imperfecto de subjuntivo		pluscuamperfecto de subjuntivo	
acelerara	aceleráramos	**hubiera** acelerado	**hubiéramos** acelerado
aceleraras	acelerarais	**hubieras** acelerado	**hubierais** acelerado
acelerara	aceleraran	**hubiera** acelerado	**hubieran** acelerado
OR		OR	
acelerase	acelerásemos	**hubiese** acelerado	**hubiésemos** acelerado
acelerases	aceleraseis	**hubieses** acelerado	**hubieseis** acelerado
acelerase	acelerasen	**hubiese** acelerado	**hubiesen** acelerado

imperativo

SINGULAR	PLURAL
—	aceleremos
acelera; no aceleres	acelerad; no aceleréis
acelere	aceleren

acercar — to approach

gerundio **acercando** — participio de pasado **acercado**

SINGULAR	PLURAL
presente de indicativo	
acerc**o**	acerc**amos**
acerc**as**	acerc**áis**
acerc**a**	acerc**an**
imperfecto de indicativo	
acerc**aba**	acerc**ábamos**
acerc**abas**	acerc**abais**
acerc**aba**	acerc**aban**
pretérito	
acerqu**é**	acerc**amos**
acerc**aste**	acerc**asteis**
acerc**ó**	acerc**aron**
futuro	
acercar**é**	acercar**emos**
acercar**ás**	acercar**éis**
acercar**á**	acercar**án**
condicional simple	
acercar**ía**	acercar**íamos**
acercar**ías**	acercar**íais**
acercar**ía**	acercar**ían**
presente de subjuntivo	
acerqu**e**	acerqu**emos**
acerqu**es**	acerqu**éis**
acerqu**e**	acerqu**en**
imperfecto de subjuntivo	
acercar**a**	acercár**amos**
acercar**as**	acercar**ais**
acercar**a**	acercar**an**
OR	
acercas**e**	acercás**emos**
acercas**es**	acercas**eis**
acercas**e**	acercas**en**
imperativo	
—	acerquemos
acerca; no acerques	acercad; no acerquéis
acerque	acerquen

SINGULAR	PLURAL
perfecto de indicativo	
he acercado	**hemos** acercado
has acercado	**habéis** acercado
ha acercado	**han** acercado
pluscuamperfecto de indicativo	
había acercado	**habíamos** acercado
habías acercado	**habíais** acercado
había acercado	**habían** acercado
pretérito anterior	
hube acercado	**hubimos** acercado
hubiste acercado	**hubisteis** acercado
hubo acercado	**hubieron** acercado
futuro perfecto	
habré acercado	**habremos** acercado
habrás acercado	**habréis** acercado
habrá acercado	**habrán** acercado
condicional compuesto	
habría acercado	**habríamos** acercado
habrías acercado	**habríais** acercado
habría acercado	**habrían** acercado
perfecto de subjuntivo	
haya acercado	**hayamos** acercado
hayas acercado	**hayáis** acercado
haya acercado	**hayan** acercado
pluscuamperfecto de subjuntivo	
hubiera acercado	**hubiéramos** acercado
hubieras acercado	**hubierais** acercado
hubiera acercado	**hubieran** acercado
OR	
hubiese acercado	**hubiésemos** acercado
hubieses acercado	**hubieseis** acercado
hubiese acercado	**hubiesen** acercado

gerundio **acercándose** participio de pasado **acercado**

SINGULAR	PLURAL	SINGULAR	PLURAL
presente de indicativo		perfecto de indicativo	
me acerc**o**	nos acerc**amos**	**me he** acercado	**nos hemos** acercado
te acerc**as**	os acerc**áis**	**te has** acercado	**os habéis** acercado
se acerc**a**	se acerc**an**	**se ha** acercado	**se han** acercado
imperfecto de indicativo		pluscuamperfecto de indicativo	
me acerc**aba**	nos acerc**ábamos**	**me había** acercado	**nos habíamos** acercado
te acerc**abas**	os acerc**abais**	**te habías** acercado	**os habíais** acercado
se acerc**aba**	se acerc**aban**	**se había** acercado	**se habían** acercado
pretérito		pretérito anterior	
me acerqu**é**	nos acerc**amos**	**me hube** acercado	**nos hubimos** acercado
te acerc**aste**	os acerc**asteis**	**te hubiste** acercado	**os hubisteis** acercado
se acerc**ó**	se acerc**aron**	**se hubo** acercado	**se hubieron** acercado
futuro		futuro perfecto	
me acercar**é**	nos acercar**emos**	**me habré** acercado	**nos habremos** acercado
te acercar**ás**	os acercar**éis**	**te habrás** acercado	**os habréis** acercado
se acercar**á**	se acercar**án**	**se habrá** acercado	**se habrán** acercado
condicional simple		condicional compuesto	
me acercar**ía**	nos acercar**íamos**	**me habría** acercado	**nos habríamos** acercado
te acercar**ías**	os acercar**íais**	**te habrías** acercado	**os habríais** acercado
se acercar**ía**	se acercar**ían**	**se habría** acercado	**se habrían** acercado
presente de subjuntivo		perfecto de subjuntivo	
me acerqu**e**	nos acerqu**emos**	**me haya** acercado	**nos hayamos** acercado
te acerqu**es**	os acerqu**éis**	**te hayas** acercado	**os hayáis** acercado
se acerqu**e**	se acerqu**en**	**se haya** acercado	**se hayan** acercado
imperfecto de subjuntivo		pluscuamperfecto de subjuntivo	
me acercar**a**	nos acercár**amos**	**me hubiera** acercado	**nos hubiéramos** acercado
te acercar**as**	os acercar**ais**	**te hubieras** acercado	**os hubierais** acercado
se acercar**a**	se acercar**an**	**se hubiera** acercado	**se hubieran** acercado
OR		OR	
me acercas**e**	nos acercás**emos**	**me hubiese** acercado	**nos hubiésemos** acercado
te acercas**es**	os acercas**eis**	**te hubieses** acercado	**os hubieseis** acercado
se acercas**e**	se acercas**en**	**se hubiese** acercado	**se hubiesen** acercado

imperativo	
—	acerquémonos
acércate;	acercaos;
no te acerques	no os acerquéis
acérquese	acérquense

acertar — to get something right

gerundio **acertando** — participio de pasado **acertado**

presente de indicativo

SINGULAR	PLURAL
aciert**o**	acert**amos**
aciert**as**	acert**áis**
aciert**o**	aciert**an**

imperfecto de indicativo

SINGULAR	PLURAL
acert**aba**	acert**ábamos**
acert**abas**	acert**abais**
acert**aba**	acert**aban**

pretérito

SINGULAR	PLURAL
acert**é**	acert**amos**
acert**aste**	acert**asteis**
acert**ó**	acert**aron**

futuro

SINGULAR	PLURAL
acertar**é**	acertar**emos**
acertar**ás**	acertar**éis**
acertar**á**	acertar**án**

condicional simple

SINGULAR	PLURAL
acertar**ía**	acertar**íamos**
acertar**ías**	acertar**íais**
acertar**ía**	acertar**ían**

presente de subjuntivo

SINGULAR	PLURAL
aciert**e**	acert**emos**
aciert**es**	acert**éis**
aciert**e**	aciert**en**

imperfecto de subjuntivo

SINGULAR	PLURAL
acertar**a**	acertár**amos**
acertar**as**	acertar**ais**
acertar**a**	acertar**an**
OR	
acertas**e**	acertás**emos**
acertas**es**	acertas**eis**
acertas**e**	acertas**en**

imperativo

SINGULAR	PLURAL
—	acertemos
acierta; no aciertes	acertad; no acertéis
acierte	acierten

perfecto de indicativo

SINGULAR	PLURAL
he acertado	**hemos** acertado
has acertado	**habéis** acertado
ha acertado	**han** acertado

pluscuamperfecto de indicativo

SINGULAR	PLURAL
había acertado	**habíamos** acertado
habías acertado	**habíais** acertado
había acertado	**habían** acertado

pretérito anterior

SINGULAR	PLURAL
hube acertado	**hubimos** acertado
hubiste acertado	**hubisteis** acertado
hubo acertado	**hubieron** acertado

futuro perfecto

SINGULAR	PLURAL
habré acertado	**habremos** acertado
habrás acertado	**habréis** acertado
habrá acertado	**habrán** acertado

condicional compuesto

SINGULAR	PLURAL
habría acertado	**habríamos** acertado
habrías acertado	**habríais** acertado
habría acertado	**habrían** acertado

perfecto de subjuntivo

SINGULAR	PLURAL
haya acertado	**hayamos** acertado
hayas acertado	**hayáis** acertado
haya acertado	**hayan** acertado

pluscuamperfecto de subjuntivo

SINGULAR	PLURAL
hubiera acertado	**hubiéramos** acertado
hubieras acertado	**hubierais** acertado
hubiera acertado	**hubieran** acertado
OR	
hubiese acertado	**hubiésemos** acertado
hubieses acertado	**hubieseis** acertado
hubiese acertado	**hubiesen** acertado

gerundio **aclamando** participio de pasado **aclamado**

SINGULAR	PLURAL	SINGULAR	PLURAL
presente de indicativo		perfecto de indicativo	
aclam**o**	aclam**amos**	**he** aclamado	**hemos** aclamado
aclam**as**	aclam**áis**	**has** aclamado	**habéis** aclamado
aclam**a**	aclam**an**	**ha** aclamado	**han** aclamado
imperfecto de indicativo		pluscuamperfecto de indicativo	
aclam**aba**	aclam**ábamos**	**había** aclamado	**habíamos** aclamado
aclam**abas**	aclam**abais**	**habías** aclamado	**habíais** aclamado
aclam**aba**	aclam**aban**	**había** aclamado	**habían** aclamado
pretérito		pretérito anterior	
aclam**é**	aclam**amos**	**hube** aclamado	**hubimos** aclamado
aclam**aste**	aclam**asteis**	**hubiste** aclamado	**hubisteis** aclamado
aclam**ó**	aclam**aron**	**hubo** aclamado	**hubieron** aclamado
futuro		futuro perfecto	
aclamar**é**	aclamar**emos**	**habré** aclamado	**habremos** aclamado
aclamar**ás**	aclamar**éis**	**habrás** aclamado	**habréis** aclamado
aclamar**á**	aclamar**án**	**habrá** aclamado	**habrán** aclamado
condicional simple		condicional compuesto	
aclamar**ía**	aclamar**íamos**	**habría** aclamado	**habríamos** aclamado
aclamar**ías**	aclamar**íais**	**habrías** aclamado	**habríais** aclamado
aclamar**ía**	aclamar**ían**	**habría** aclamado	**habrían** aclamado
presente de subjuntivo		perfecto de subjuntivo	
aclam**e**	aclam**emos**	**haya** aclamado	**hayamos** aclamado
aclam**es**	aclam**éis**	**hayas** aclamado	**hayáis** aclamado
aclam**e**	aclam**en**	**haya** aclamado	**hayan** aclamado
imperfecto de subjuntivo		pluscuamperfecto de subjuntivo	
aclamar**a**	aclamár**amos**	**hubiera** aclamado	**hubiéramos** aclamado
aclamar**as**	aclamar**ais**	**hubieras** aclamado	**hubierais** aclamado
aclamar**a**	aclamar**an**	**hubiera** aclamado	**hubieran** aclamado
OR		OR	
aclamas**e**	aclamás**emos**	**hubiese** aclamado	**hubiésemos** aclamado
aclamas**es**	aclamas**eis**	**hubieses** aclamado	**hubieseis** aclamado
aclamas**e**	aclamas**en**	**hubiese** aclamado	**hubiesen** aclamado

imperativo

—	aclamemos
aclama; no aclames	aclamad; no aclaméis
aclame	aclamen

aclarar — to make clear, to lighten

gerundio **aclarando** participio de pasado **aclarado**

SINGULAR	PLURAL	SINGULAR	PLURAL
presente de indicativo		perfecto de indicativo	
aclar**o**	aclar**amos**	**he** aclarado	**hemos** aclarado
aclar**as**	aclar**áis**	**has** aclarado	**habéis** aclarado
aclar**a**	aclar**an**	**ha** aclarado	**han** aclarado
imperfecto de indicativo		pluscuamperfecto de indicativo	
aclar**aba**	aclar**ábamos**	**había** aclarado	**habíamos** aclarado
aclar**abas**	aclar**abais**	**habías** aclarado	**habíais** aclarado
aclar**aba**	aclar**aban**	**había** aclarado	**habían** aclarado
pretérito		pretérito anterior	
aclar**é**	aclar**amos**	**hube** aclarado	**hubimos** aclarado
aclar**aste**	aclar**asteis**	**hubiste** aclarado	**hubisteis** aclarado
aclar**ó**	aclar**aron**	**hubo** aclarado	**hubieron** aclarado
futuro		futuro perfecto	
aclarar**é**	aclarar**emos**	**habré** aclarado	**habremos** aclarado
aclarar**ás**	aclarar**éis**	**habrás** aclarado	**habréis** aclarado
aclarar**á**	aclarar**án**	**habrá** aclarado	**habrán** aclarado
condicional simple		condicional compuesto	
aclarar**ía**	aclarar**íamos**	**habría** aclarado	**habríamos** aclarado
aclarar**ías**	aclarar**íais**	**habrías** aclarado	**habríais** aclarado
aclarar**ía**	aclarar**ían**	**habría** aclarado	**habrían** aclarado
presente de subjuntivo		perfecto de subjuntivo	
aclar**e**	aclar**emos**	**haya** aclarado	**hayamos** aclarado
aclar**es**	aclar**éis**	**hayas** aclarado	**hayáis** aclarado
aclar**e**	aclar**en**	**haya** aclarado	**hayan** aclarado
imperfecto de subjuntivo		pluscuamperfecto de subjuntivo	
aclarar**a**	aclarár**amos**	**hubiera** aclarado	**hubiéramos** aclarado
aclarar**as**	aclarar**ais**	**hubieras** aclarado	**hubierais** aclarado
aclarar**a**	aclarar**an**	**hubiera** aclarado	**hubieran** aclarado
OR		OR	
aclaras**e**	aclarás**emos**	**hubiese** aclarado	**hubiésemos** aclarado
aclaras**es**	aclaras**eis**	**hubieses** aclarado	**hubieseis** aclarado
aclaras**e**	aclaras**en**	**hubiese** aclarado	**hubiesen** aclarado
imperativo			
—	aclaremos		
aclara; no aclares	aclarad; no aclaréis		
aclare	aclaren		

gerundio **acogiendo** participio de pasado **acogido**

SINGULAR	PLURAL	SINGULAR	PLURAL
presente de indicativo		perfecto de indicativo	
acoj**o**	acog**emos**	**he** acogido	**hemos** acogido
acog**es**	acog**éis**	**has** acogido	**habéis** acogido
acog**e**	acog**en**	**ha** acogido	**han** acogido
imperfecto de indicativo		pluscuamperfecto de indicativo	
acog**ía**	acog**íamos**	**había** acogido	**habíamos** acogido
acog**ías**	acog**íais**	**habías** acogido	**habíais** acogido
acog**ía**	acog**ían**	**había** acogido	**habían** acogido
pretérito		pretérito anterior	
acog**í**	acog**imos**	**hube** acogido	**hubimos** acogido
acog**iste**	acog**isteis**	**hubiste** acogido	**hubisteis** acogido
acog**ió**	acog**ieron**	**hubo** acogido	**hubieron** acogido
futuro		futuro perfecto	
acoger**é**	acoger**emos**	**habré** acogido	**habremos** acogido
acoger**ás**	acoger**éis**	**habrás** acogido	**habréis** acogido
acoger**á**	acoger**án**	**habrá** acogido	**habrán** acogido
condicional simple		condicional compuesto	
acoger**ía**	acoger**íamos**	**habría** acogido	**habríamos** acogido
acoger**ías**	acoger**íais**	**habrías** acogido	**habríais** acogido
acoger**ía**	acoger**ían**	**habría** acogido	**habrían** acogido
presente de subjuntivo		perfecto de subjuntivo	
acoj**a**	acoj**amos**	**haya** acogido	**hayamos** acogido
acoj**as**	acoj**áis**	**hayas** acogido	**hayáis** acogido
acoj**a**	acoj**an**	**haya** acogido	**hayan** acogido
imperfecto de subjuntivo		pluscuamperfecto de subjuntivo	
acogier**a**	acogiér**amos**	**hubiera** acogido	**hubiéramos** acogido
acogier**as**	acogier**ais**	**hubieras** acogido	**hubierais** acogido
acogier**a**	acogier**an**	**hubiera** acogido	**hubieran** acogido
OR		OR	
acogies**e**	acogiés**emos**	**hubiese** acogido	**hubiésemos** acogido
acogies**es**	acogies**eis**	**hubieses** acogido	**hubieseis** acogido
acogies**e**	acogies**en**	**hubiese** acogido	**hubiesen** acogido

imperativo

—	acojamos
acoge; no acojas	acoged; no acojáis
acoja	acojan

A

acometer — to cease, to attack

gerundio **acometiendo** participio de pasado **acometido**

presente de indicativo

SINGULAR	PLURAL
acomet**o**	acomet**emos**
acomet**es**	acomet**éis**
acomet**e**	acomet**en**

imperfecto de indicativo

SINGULAR	PLURAL
acomet**ía**	acomet**íamos**
acomet**ías**	acomet**íais**
acomet**ía**	acomet**ían**

pretérito

SINGULAR	PLURAL
acomet**í**	acomet**imos**
acomet**iste**	acomet**isteis**
acomet**ió**	acomet**ieron**

futuro

SINGULAR	PLURAL
acometer**é**	acometer**emos**
acometer**ás**	acometer**éis**
acometer**á**	acometer**án**

condicional simple

SINGULAR	PLURAL
acometer**ía**	acometer**íamos**
acometer**ías**	acometer**íais**
acometer**ía**	acometer**ían**

presente de subjuntivo

SINGULAR	PLURAL
acomet**a**	acomet**amos**
acomet**as**	acomet**áis**
acomet**a**	acomet**an**

imperfecto de subjuntivo

SINGULAR	PLURAL
acometier**a**	acometiér**amos**
acometier**as**	acometier**ais**
acometier**a**	acometier**an**
OR	
acometies**e**	acometiés**emos**
acometies**es**	acometies**eis**
acometies**e**	acometies**en**

imperativo

SINGULAR	PLURAL
—	acometamos
acomete; no acometas	acometed; no acometáis
acometa	acometan

perfecto de indicativo

SINGULAR	PLURAL
he acometido	**hemos** acometido
has acometido	**habéis** acometido
ha acometido	**han** acometido

pluscuamperfecto de indicativo

SINGULAR	PLURAL
había acometido	**habíamos** acometido
habías acometido	**habíais** acometido
había acometido	**habían** acometido

pretérito anterior

SINGULAR	PLURAL
hube acometido	**hubimos** acometido
hubiste acometido	**hubisteis** acometido
hubo acometido	**hubieron** acometido

futuro perfecto

SINGULAR	PLURAL
habré acometido	**habremos** acometido
habrás acometido	**habréis** acometido
habrá acometido	**habrán** acometido

condicional compuesto

SINGULAR	PLURAL
habría acometido	**habríamos** acometido
habrías acometido	**habríais** acometido
habría acometido	**habrían** acometido

perfecto de subjuntivo

SINGULAR	PLURAL
haya acometido	**hayamos** acometido
hayas acometido	**hayáis** acometido
haya acometido	**hayan** acometido

pluscuamperfecto de subjuntivo

SINGULAR	PLURAL
hubiera acometido	**hubiéramos** acometido
hubieras acometido	**hubierais** acometido
hubiera acometido	**hubieran** acometido
OR	
hubiese acometido	**hubiésemos** acometido
hubieses acometido	**hubieseis** acometido
hubiese acometido	**hubiesen** acometido

gerundio **acompañando** participio de pasado **acompañado**

SINGULAR	PLURAL	SINGULAR	PLURAL
presente de indicativo		perfecto de indicativo	
acompañ**o**	acompañ**amos**	**he** acompañado	**hemos** acompañado
acompañ**as**	acompañ**áis**	**has** acompañado	**habéis** acompañado
acompañ**a**	acompañ**an**	**ha** acompañado	**han** acompañado
imperfecto de indicativo		pluscuamperfecto de indicativo	
acompañ**aba**	acompañ**ábamos**	**había** acompañado	**habíamos** acompañado
acompañ**abas**	acompañ**abais**	**habías** acompañado	**habíais** acompañado
acompañ**aba**	acompañ**aban**	**había** acompañado	**habían** acompañado
pretérito		pretérito anterior	
acompañ**é**	acompañ**amos**	**hube** acompañado	**hubimos** acompañado
acompañ**aste**	acompañ**asteis**	**hubiste** acompañado	**hubisteis** acompañado
acompañ**ó**	acompañ**aron**	**hubo** acompañado	**hubieron** acompañado
futuro		futuro perfecto	
acompañar**é**	acompañar**emos**	**habré** acompañado	**habremos** acompañado
acompañar**ás**	acompañar**éis**	**habrás** acompañado	**habréis** acompañado
acompañar**á**	acompañar**án**	**habrá** acompañado	**habrán** acompañado
condicional simple		condicional compuesto	
acompañar**ía**	acompañar**íamos**	**habría** acompañado	**habríamos** acompañado
acompañar**ías**	acompañar**íais**	**habrías** acompañado	**habríais** acompañado
acompañar**ía**	acompañar**ían**	**habría** acompañado	**habrían** acompañado
presente de subjuntivo		perfecto de subjuntivo	
acompañ**e**	acompañ**emos**	**haya** acompañado	**hayamos** acompañado
acompañ**es**	acompañ**éis**	**hayas** acompañado	**hayáis** acompañado
acompañ**e**	acompañ**en**	**haya** acompañado	**hayan** acompañado
imperfecto de subjuntivo		pluscuamperfecto de subjuntivo	
acompañar**a**	acompañár**amos**	**hubiera** acompañado	**hubiéramos** acompañado
acompañar**as**	acompañar**ais**	**hubieras** acompañado	**hubierais** acompañado
acompañar**a**	acompañar**an**	**hubiera** acompañado	**hubieran** acompañado
OR		OR	
acompañas**e**	acompañás**emos**	**hubiese** acompañado	**hubiésemos** acompañado
acompañas**es**	acompañas**eis**	**hubieses** acompañado	**hubieseis** acompañado
acompañas**e**	acompañas**en**	**hubiese** acompañado	**hubiesen** acompañado

imperativo

—	acompañemos
acompaña; no acompañes	acompañad; no acompañéis
acompañe	acompañen

A

aconsejar — to advise, to counsel

gerundio **aconsejando** — participio de pasado **aconsejado**

presente de indicativo

SINGULAR	PLURAL
aconsej**o**	aconsej**amos**
aconsej**as**	aconsej**áis**
aconsej**a**	aconsej**an**

imperfecto de indicativo

SINGULAR	PLURAL
aconsej**aba**	aconsej**ábamos**
aconsej**abas**	aconsej**abais**
aconsej**aba**	aconsej**aban**

pretérito

SINGULAR	PLURAL
aconsej**é**	aconsej**amos**
aconsej**aste**	aconsej**asteis**
aconsej**ó**	aconsej**aron**

futuro

SINGULAR	PLURAL
aconsejar**é**	aconsejar**emos**
aconsejar**ás**	aconsejar**éis**
aconsejar**á**	aconsejar**án**

condicional simple

SINGULAR	PLURAL
aconsejar**ía**	aconsejar**íamos**
aconsejar**ías**	aconsejar**íais**
aconsejar**ía**	aconsejar**ían**

presente de subjuntivo

SINGULAR	PLURAL
aconsej**e**	aconsej**emos**
aconsej**es**	aconsej**éis**
aconsej**e**	aconsej**en**

imperfecto de subjuntivo

SINGULAR	PLURAL
aconsejar**a**	aconsejár**amos**
aconsejar**as**	aconsejar**ais**
aconsejar**a**	aconsejar**an**
OR	
aconsejas**e**	aconsejás**emos**
aconsejas**es**	aconsejas**eis**
aconsejas**e**	aconsejas**en**

imperativo

SINGULAR	PLURAL
—	aconsejemos
aconseja; no aconsejes	aconsejad; aconsejéis
aconseje	aconsejen

perfecto de indicativo

SINGULAR	PLURAL
he aconsejado	**hemos** aconsejado
has aconsejado	**habéis** aconsejado
ha aconsejado	**han** aconsejado

pluscuamperfecto de indicativo

SINGULAR	PLURAL
había aconsejado	**habíamos** aconsejado
habías aconsejado	**habíais** aconsejado
había aconsejado	**habían** aconsejado

pretérito anterior

SINGULAR	PLURAL
hube aconsejado	**hubimos** aconsejado
hubiste aconsejado	**hubisteis** aconsejado
hubo aconsejado	**hubieron** aconsejado

futuro perfecto

SINGULAR	PLURAL
habré aconsejado	**habremos** aconsejado
habrás aconsejado	**habréis** aconsejado
habrá aconsejado	**habrán** aconsejado

condicional compuesto

SINGULAR	PLURAL
habría aconsejado	**habríamos** aconsejado
habrías aconsejado	**habríais** aconsejado
habría aconsejado	**habrían** aconsejado

perfecto de subjuntivo

SINGULAR	PLURAL
haya aconsejado	**hayamos** aconsejado
hayas aconsejado	**hayáis** aconsejado
haya aconsejado	**hayan** aconsejado

pluscuamperfecto de subjuntivo

SINGULAR	PLURAL
hubiera aconsejado	**hubiéramos** aconsejado
hubieras aconsejado	**hubierais** aconsejado
hubiera aconsejado	**hubieran** aconsejado
OR	
hubiese aconsejado	**hubiésemos** aconsejado
hubieses aconsejado	**hubieseis** aconsejado
hubiese aconsejado	**hubiesen** aconsejado

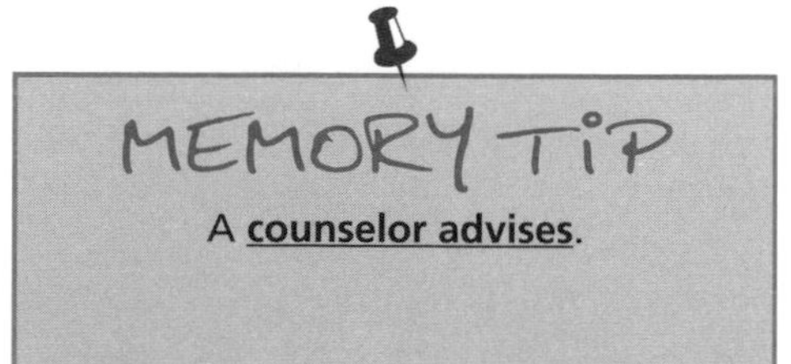

gerundio **acordándose** participio de pasado **acordado**

SINGULAR	PLURAL	SINGULAR	PLURAL
presente de indicativo		perfecto de indicativo	
me acuerd**o**	nos acord**amos**	**me he** acordado	**nos hemos** acordado
te acuerd**as**	os acord**áis**	**te has** acordado	**os habéis** acordado
se acuerd**a**	se acuerd**an**	**se ha** acordado	**se han** acordado
imperfecto de indicativo		pluscuamperfecto de indicativo	
me acord**aba**	nos acord**ábamos**	**me había** acordado	**nos habíamos** acordado
te acord**abas**	os acord**abais**	**te habías** acordado	**os habíais** acordado
se acord**aba**	se acord**aban**	**se había** acordado	**se habían** acordado
pretérito		pretérito anterior	
me acord**é**	nos acord**amos**	**me hube** acordado	**nos hubimos** acordado
te acord**aste**	os acord**asteis**	**te hubiste** acordado	**os hubisteis** acordado
se acord**ó**	se acord**aron**	**se hubo** acordado	**se hubieron** acordado
futuro		futuro perfecto	
me acordar**é**	nos acordar**emos**	**me habré** acordado	**nos habremos** acordado
te acordar**ás**	os acordar**éis**	**te habrás** acordado	**os habréis** acordado
se acordar**á**	se acordar**án**	**se habrá** acordado	**se habrán** acordado
condicional simple		condicional compuesto	
me acordar**ía**	nos acordar**íamos**	**me habría** acordado	**nos habríamos** acordado
te acordar**ías**	os acordar**íais**	**te habrías** acordado	**os habríais** acordado
se acordar**ía**	se acordar**ían**	**se habría** acordado	**se habrían** acordado
presente de subjuntivo		perfecto de subjuntivo	
me acuerd**e**	nos acord**emos**	**me haya** acordado	**nos hayamos** acordado
te acuerd**es**	os acord**éis**	**te hayas** acordado	**os hayáis** acordado
se acuerd**e**	se acuerd**en**	**se haya** acordado	**se hayan** acordado
imperfecto de subjuntivo		pluscuamperfecto de subjuntivo	
me acordar**a**	nos acordár**amos**	**me hubiera** acordado	**nos hubiéramos** acordado
te acordar**as**	os acordar**ais**	**te hubieras** acordado	**os hubierais** acordado
se acordar**a**	se acordar**an**	**se hubiera** acordado	**se hubieran** acordado
OR		OR	
me acordas**e**	nos acordás**emos**	**me hubiese** acordado	**nos hubiésemos** acordado
te acordas**es**	os acordas**eis**	**te hubieses** acordado	**os hubieseis** acordado
se acordas**e**	se acordas**en**	**se hubiese** acordado	**se hubiesen** acordado

imperativo

—	acordémonos
acuérdate; no te acuerdes	acordaos; no os acordéis
acuérdese	acuérdense

A

acostarse — to go to bed, to lie down

gerundio **acostándose** — participio de pasado **acostado**

SINGULAR	PLURAL
presente de indicativo	
me acuest**o**	nos acost**amos**
te acuest**as**	os acost**áis**
se acuest**a**	se acuest**an**
imperfecto de indicativo	
me acost**aba**	nos acost**ábamos**
te acost**abas**	os acost**abais**
se acost**aba**	se acost**aban**
pretérito	
me acost**é**	nos acost**amos**
te acost**aste**	os acost**asteis**
se acost**ó**	se acost**aron**
futuro	
me acostar**é**	nos acostar**emos**
te acostar**ás**	os acostar**éis**
se acostar**á**	se acostar**án**
condicional simple	
me acostar**ía**	nos acostar**íamos**
te acostar**ías**	os acostar**íais**
se acostar**ía**	se acostar**ían**
presente de subjuntivo	
me acuest**e**	nos acost**emos**
te acuest**es**	os acost**éis**
se acuest**e**	se acuest**en**
imperfecto de subjuntivo	
me acostar**a**	nos acostár**amos**
te acostar**as**	os acostar**ais**
se acostar**a**	se acostar**an**
OR	
me acostas**e**	nos acostás**emos**
te acostas**es**	os acostas**eis**
se acostas**e**	se acostas**en**
imperativo	
—	acostémonos
acuéstate; no te acuestes	acostaos; no os acostéis
acuéstese	acuéstense

SINGULAR	PLURAL
perfecto de indicativo	
me he acostado	**nos hemos** acostado
te has acostado	**os habéis** acostado
se ha acostado	**se han** acostado
pluscuamperfecto de indicativo	
me había acostado	**nos habíamos** acostado
te habías acostado	**os habíais** acostado
se había acostado	**se habían** acostado
pretérito anterior	
me hube acostado	**nos hubimos** acostado
te hubiste acostado	**os hubisteis** acostado
se hubo acostado	**se hubieron** acostado
futuro perfecto	
me habré acostado	**nos habremos** acostado
te habrás acostado	**os habréis** acostado
se habrá acostado	**se habrán** acostado
condicional compuesto	
me habría acostado	**nos habríamos** acostado
te habrías acostado	**os habríais** acostado
se habría acostado	**se habrían** acostado
perfecto de subjuntivo	
me haya acostado	**nos hayamos** acostado
te hayas acostado	**os hayáis** acostado
se haya acostado	**se hayan** acostado
pluscuamperfecto de subjuntivo	
me hubiera acostado	**nos hubiéramos** acostado
te hubieras acostado	**os hubierais** acostado
se hubiera acostado	**se hubieran** acostado
OR	
me hubiese acostado	**nos hubiésemos** acostado
te hubieses acostado	**os hubieseis** acostado
se hubiese acostado	**se hubiesen** acostado

SINGULAR	PLURAL
presente de indicativo	
me acostumbr**o**	nos acostumbr**amos**
te acostumbr**as**	os acostumbr**áis**
se acostumbr**a**	se acostumbr**an**
imperfecto de indicativo	
me acostumbr**aba**	nos acostumbr**ábamos**
te acostumbr**abas**	os acostumbr**abais**
se acostumbr**aba**	se acostumbr**aban**
pretérito	
me acostumbr**é**	nos acostumbr**amos**
te acostumbr**aste**	os acostumbr**asteis**
se acostumbr**ó**	se acostumbr**aron**
futuro	
me acostumbrar**é**	nos acostumbrar**emos**
te acostumbrar**ás**	os acostumbrar**éis**
se acostumbrar**á**	se acostumbrar**án**
condicional simple	
me acostumbrar**ía**	nos acostumbrar**íamos**
te acostumbrar**ías**	os acostumbrar**íais**
se acostumbrar**ía**	se acostumbrar**ían**
presente de subjuntivo	
me acostumbr**e**	nos acostumbr**emos**
te acostumbr**es**	os acostumbr**éis**
se acostumbr**e**	se acostumbr**en**
imperfecto de subjuntivo	
me acostumbrar**a**	nos acostumbrár**amos**
te acostumbrar**as**	os acostumbrar**ais**
se acostumbrar**a**	se acostumbrar**an**
OR	
me acostumbras**e**	nos acostumbrás**emos**
te acostumbras**es**	os acostumbras**eis**
se acostumbras**e**	se acostumbras**en**
imperativo	
—	acostumbrémonos
acostúmbrate; no te acostumbres	acostumbraos; no os acostumbréis
acostúmbrese	acostúmbrense

SINGULAR	PLURAL
perfecto de indicativo	
me he acostumbrado	**nos hemos** acostumbrado
te has acostumbrado	**os habéis** acostumbrado
se ha acostumbrado	**se han** acostumbrado
pluscuamperfecto de indicativo	
me había acostumbrado	**nos habíamos** acostumbrado
te habías acostumbrado	**os habíais** acostumbrado
se había acostumbrado	**se habían** acostumbrado
pretérito anterior	
me hube acostumbrado	**nos hubimos** acostumbrado
te hubiste acostumbrado	**os hubisteis** acostumbrado
se hubo acostumbrado	**se hubieron** acostumbrado
futuro perfecto	
me habré acostumbrado	**nos habremos** acostumbrado
te habrás acostumbrado	**os habréis** acostumbrado
se habrá acostumbrado	**se habrán** acostumbrado
condicional compuesto	
me habría acostumbrado	**nos habríamos** acostumbrado
te habrías acostumbrado	**os habríais** acostumbrado
se habría acostumbrado	**se habrían** acostumbrado
perfecto de subjuntivo	
me haya acostumbrado	**nos hayamos** acostumbrado
te hayas acostumbrado	**os hayáis** acostumbrado
se haya acostumbrado	**se hayan** acostumbrado
pluscuamperfecto de subjuntivo	
me hubiera acostumbrado	**nos hubiéramos** acostumbrado
te hubieras acostumbrado	**os hubierais** acostumbrado
se hubiera acostumbrado	**se hubieran** acostumbrado
OR	
me hubiese acostumbrado	**nos hubiésemos** acostumbrado
te hubieses acostumbrado	**os hubieseis** acostumbrado
se hubiese acostumbrado	**se hubiesen** acostumbrado

gerundio **acreditando** participio de pasado **acreditado**

SINGULAR	PLURAL	SINGULAR	PLURAL
presente de indicativo		perfecto de indicativo	
acredit**o**	acredit**amos**	**he** acreditado	**hemos** acreditado
acredit**as**	acredit**áis**	**has** acreditado	**habéis** acreditado
acredit**a**	acredit**an**	**ha** acreditado	**han** acreditado
imperfecto de indicativo		pluscuamperfecto de indicativo	
acredit**aba**	acredit**ábamos**	**había** acreditado	**habíamos** acreditado
acredit**abas**	acredit**abais**	**habías** acreditado	**habíais** acreditado
acredit**aba**	acredit**aban**	**había** acreditado	**habían** acreditado
pretérito		pretérito anterior	
acredit**é**	acredit**amos**	**hube** acreditado	**hubimos** acreditado
acredit**aste**	acredit**asteis**	**hubiste** acreditado	**hubisteis** acreditado
acredit**ó**	acredit**aron**	**hubo** acreditado	**hubieron** acreditado
futuro		futuro perfecto	
acreditar**é**	acreditar**emos**	**habré** acreditado	**habremos** acreditado
acreditar**ás**	acreditar**éis**	**habrás** acreditado	**habréis** acreditado
acreditar**á**	acreditar**án**	**habrá** acreditado	**habrán** acreditado
condicional simple		condicional compuesto	
acreditar**ía**	acreditar**íamos**	**habría** acreditado	**habríamos** acreditado
acreditar**ías**	acreditar**íais**	**habrías** acreditado	**habríais** acreditado
acreditar**ía**	acreditar**ían**	**habría** acreditado	**habrían** acreditado
presente de subjuntivo		perfecto de subjuntivo	
acredit**e**	acredit**emos**	**haya** acreditado	**hayamos** acreditado
acredit**es**	acredit**éis**	**hayas** acreditado	**hayáis** acreditado
acredit**e**	acredit**en**	**haya** acreditado	**hayan** acreditado
imperfecto de subjuntivo		pluscuamperfecto de subjuntivo	
acreditar**a**	acreditár**amos**	**hubiera** acreditado	**hubiéramos** acreditado
acreditar**as**	acreditar**ais**	**hubieras** acreditado	**hubierais** acreditado
acreditar**a**	acreditar**an**	**hubiera** acreditado	**hubieran** acreditado
OR		OR	
acreditas**e**	acreditás**emos**	**hubiese** acreditado	**hubiésemos** acreditado
acreditas**es**	acreditas**eis**	**hubieses** acreditado	**hubieseis** acreditado
acreditas**e**	acreditas**en**	**hubiese** acreditado	**hubiesen** acreditado

imperativo

—	acreditemos
acredita; no acredites	acreditad; no acreditéis
acredite	acrediten

to stimulate, to activate, to trigger **activar**

gerundio **activando** participio de pasado **activado**

SINGULAR	PLURAL
presente de indicativo	
activ**o**	activ**amos**
activ**as**	activ**áis**
activ**a**	activ**an**
imperfecto de indicativo	
activ**aba**	activ**ábamos**
activ**abas**	activ**abais**
activ**aba**	activ**aban**
pretérito	
activ**é**	activ**amos**
activ**aste**	activ**asteis**
activ**ó**	activ**aron**
futuro	
activar**é**	activar**emos**
activar**ás**	activar**éis**
activar**á**	activar**án**
condicional simple	
activar**ía**	activar**íamos**
activar**ías**	activar**íais**
activar**ía**	activar**ían**
presente de subjuntivo	
activ**e**	activ**emos**
activ**es**	activ**éis**
activ**e**	activ**en**
imperfecto de subjuntivo	
activar**a**	activár**amos**
activar**as**	activar**ais**
activar**a**	activar**an**
OR	
activas**e**	activás**emos**
activas**es**	activas**eis**
activas**e**	activas**en**
imperativo	
—	activemos
activa; no actives	activad; no activéis
active	activen

SINGULAR	PLURAL
perfecto de indicativo	
he activado	**hemos** activado
has activado	**habéis** activado
ha activado	**han** activado
pluscuamperfecto de indicativo	
había activado	**habíamos** activado
habías activado	**habíais** activado
había activado	**habían** activado
pretérito anterior	
hube activado	**hubimos** activado
hubiste activado	**hubisteis** activado
hubo activado	**hubieron** activado
futuro perfecto	
habré activado	**habremos** activado
habrás activado	**habréis** activado
habrá activado	**habrán** activado
condicional compuesto	
habría activado	**habríamos** activado
habrías activado	**habríais** activado
habría activado	**habrían** activado
perfecto de subjuntivo	
haya activado	**hayamos** activado
hayas activado	**hayáis** activado
haya activado	**hayan** activado
pluscuamperfecto de subjuntivo	
hubiera activado	**hubiéramos** activado
hubieras activado	**hubierais** activado
hubiera activado	**hubieran** activado
OR	
hubiese activado	**hubiésemos** activado
hubieses activado	**hubieseis** activado
hubiese activado	**hubiesen** activado

actuar — to act, to perform

gerundio **actuando** — participio de pasado **actuado**

SINGULAR	PLURAL
presente de indicativo	
actú**o**	actu**amos**
actú**as**	actu**áis**
actú**a**	actú**an**
imperfecto de indicativo	
actu**aba**	actu**ábamos**
actu**abas**	actu**abais**
actu**aba**	actu**aban**
pretérito	
actu**é**	actu**amos**
actu**aste**	actu**asteis**
actu**ó**	actu**aron**
futuro	
actuar**é**	actuar**emos**
actuar**ás**	actuar**éis**
actuar**á**	actuar**án**
condicional simple	
actuar**ía**	actuar**íamos**
actuar**ías**	actuar**íais**
actuar**ía**	actuar**ían**
presente de subjuntivo	
actú**e**	actu**emos**
actú**es**	actu**éis**
actú**e**	actú**en**
imperfecto de subjuntivo	
actuar**a**	actuár**amos**
actuar**as**	actuar**ais**
actuar**a**	actuar**an**
OR	
actuas**e**	actuás**emos**
actuas**es**	actuas**eis**
actuas**e**	actuas**en**
imperativo	
—	actuemos
actúa; no actúes	actuad; no actuéis
actúe	actúen

SINGULAR	PLURAL
perfecto de indicativo	
he actuado	**hemos** actuado
has actuado	**habéis** actuado
ha actuado	**han** actuado
pluscuamperfecto de indicativo	
había actuado	**habíamos** actuado
habías actuado	**habíais** actuado
había actuado	**habían** actuado
pretérito anterior	
hube actuado	**hubimos** actuado
hubiste actuado	**hubisteis** actuado
hubo actuado	**hubieron** actuado
futuro perfecto	
habré actuado	**habremos** actuado
habrás actuado	**habréis** actuado
habrá actuado	**habrán** actuado
condicional compuesto	
habría actuado	**habríamos** actuado
habrías actuado	**habríais** actuado
habría actuado	**habrían** actuado
perfecto de subjuntivo	
haya actuado	**hayamos** actuado
hayas actuado	**hayáis** actuado
haya actuado	**hayan** actuado
pluscuamperfecto de subjuntivo	
hubiera actuado	**hubiéramos** actuado
hubieras actuado	**hubierais** actuado
hubiera actuado	**hubieran** actuado
OR	
hubiese actuado	**hubiésemos** actuado
hubieses actuado	**hubieseis** actuado
hubiese actuado	**hubiesen** actuado

gerundio **acudiendo** participio de pasado **acudido**

SINGULAR	PLURAL	SINGULAR	PLURAL
presente de indicativo		perfecto de indicativo	
acud**o**	acud**imos**	**he** acudido	**hemos** acudido
acud**es**	acud**ís**	**has** acudido	**habéis** acudido
acud**e**	acud**en**	**ha** acudido	**han** acudido
imperfecto de indicativo		pluscuamperfecto de indicativo	
acud**ía**	acud**íamos**	**había** acudido	**habíamos** acudido
acud**ías**	acud**íais**	**habías** acudido	**habíais** acudido
acud**ía**	acud**ían**	**había** acudido	**habían** acudido
pretérito		pretérito anterior	
acud**í**	acud**imos**	**hube** acudido	**hubimos** acudido
acud**iste**	acud**isteis**	**hubiste** acudido	**hubisteis** acudido
acud**ió**	acud**ieron**	**hubo** acudido	**hubieron** acudido
futuro		futuro perfecto	
acudir**é**	acudir**emos**	**habré** acudido	**habremos** acudido
acudir**ás**	acudir**éis**	**habrás** acudido	**habréis** acudido
acudir**á**	acudir**án**	**habrá** acudido	**habrán** acudido
condicional simple		condicional compuesto	
acudir**ía**	acudir**íamos**	**habría** acudido	**habríamos** acudido
acudir**ías**	acudir**íais**	**habrías** acudido	**habríais** acudido
acudir**ía**	acudir**ían**	**habría** acudido	**habrían** acudido
presente de subjuntivo		perfecto de subjuntivo	
acud**a**	acud**amos**	**haya** acudido	**hayamos** acudido
acud**as**	acud**áis**	**hayas** acudido	**hayáis** acudido
acud**a**	acud**an**	**haya** acudido	**hayan** acudido
imperfecto de subjuntivo		pluscuamperfecto de subjuntivo	
acudier**a**	acudiér**amos**	**hubiera** acudido	**hubiéramos** acudido
acudier**as**	acudier**ais**	**hubieras** acudido	**hubierais** acudido
acudier**a**	acudier**an**	**hubiera** acudido	**hubieran** acudido
OR		OR	
acudies**e**	acudiés**emos**	**hubiese** acudido	**hubiésemos** acudido
acudies**es**	acudies**eis**	**hubieses** acudido	**hubieseis** acudido
acudies**e**	acudies**en**	**hubiese** acudido	**hubiesen** acudido

imperativo

—	acudamos
acude; no acudas	acudid; no acudáis
acuda	acudan

acumular — to accumulate

gerundio **acumulando** participio de pasado **acumulado**

SINGULAR	PLURAL
presente de indicativo	
acumul**o**	acumul**amos**
acumul**as**	acumul**áis**
acumul**a**	acumul**an**
imperfecto de indicativo	
acumul**aba**	acumul**ábamos**
acumul**abas**	acumul**abais**
acumul**aba**	acumul**aban**
pretérito	
acumul**é**	acumul**amos**
acumul**aste**	acumul**asteis**
acumul**ó**	acumul**aron**
futuro	
acumular**é**	acumular**emos**
acumular**ás**	acumular**éis**
acumular**á**	acumular**án**
condicional simple	
acumular**ía**	acumular**íamos**
acumular**ías**	acumular**íais**
acumular**ía**	acumular**ían**
presente de subjuntivo	
acumul**e**	acumul**emos**
acumul**es**	acumul**éis**
acumul**e**	acumul**en**
imperfecto de subjuntivo	
acumular**a**	acumulár**amos**
acumular**as**	acumular**ais**
acumular**a**	acumular**an**
OR	
acumulas**e**	acumulás**emos**
acumulas**es**	acumulas**eis**
acumulas**e**	acumulas**en**
imperativo	
—	acumulemos
acumula; no acumules	acumulad; no acumuléis
acumule	acumulen

SINGULAR	PLURAL
perfecto de indicativo	
he acumulado	**hemos** acumulado
has acumulado	**habéis** acumulado
ha acumulado	**han** acumulado
pluscuamperfecto de indicativo	
había acumulado	**habíamos** acumulado
habías acumulado	**habíais** acumulado
había acumulado	**habían** acumulado
pretérito anterior	
hube acumulado	**hubimos** acumulado
hubiste acumulado	**hubisteis** acumulado
hubo acumulado	**hubieron** acumulado
futuro perfecto	
habré acumulado	**habremos** acumulado
habrás acumulado	**habréis** acumulado
habrá acumulado	**habrán** acumulado
condicional compuesto	
habría acumulado	**habríamos** acumulado
habrías acumulado	**habríais** acumulado
habría acumulado	**habrían** acumulado
perfecto de subjuntivo	
haya acumulado	**hayamos** acumulado
hayas acumulado	**hayáis** acumulado
haya acumulado	**hayan** acumulado
pluscuamperfecto de subjuntivo	
hubiera acumulado	**hubiéramos** acumulado
hubieras acumulado	**hubierais** acumulado
hubiera acumulado	**hubieran** acumulado
OR	
hubiese acumulado	**hubiésemos** acumulado
hubieses acumulado	**hubieseis** acumulado
hubiese acumulado	**hubiesen** acumulado

gerundio **acusando** participio de pasado **acusado**

SINGULAR	PLURAL
presente de indicativo	
acus**o**	acus**amos**
acus**as**	acus**áis**
acus**a**	acus**an**
imperfecto de indicativo	
acus**aba**	acus**ábamos**
acus**abas**	acus**abais**
acus**aba**	acus**aban**
pretérito	
acus**é**	acus**amos**
acus**aste**	acus**asteis**
acus**ó**	acus**aron**
futuro	
acusar**é**	acusar**emos**
acusar**ás**	acusar**éis**
acusar**á**	acusar**án**
condicional simple	
acusar**ía**	acusar**íamos**
acusar**ías**	acusar**íais**
acusar**ía**	acusar**ían**
presente de subjuntivo	
acus**e**	acus**emos**
acus**es**	acus**éis**
acus**e**	acus**en**
imperfecto de subjuntivo	
acusar**a**	acusár**amos**
acusar**as**	acusar**ais**
acusar**a**	acusar**an**
OR	
acusas**e**	acusás**emos**
acusas**es**	acusas**eis**
acusas**e**	acusas**en**
imperativo	
—	acusemos
acusa; no acuses	acusad; no acuséis
acuse	acusen

SINGULAR	PLURAL
perfecto de indicativo	
he acusado	**hemos** acusado
has acusado	**habéis** acusado
ha acusado	**han** acusado
pluscuamperfecto de indicativo	
había acusado	**habíamos** acusado
habías acusado	**habíais** acusado
había acusado	**habían** acusado
pretérito anterior	
hube acusado	**hubimos** acusado
hubiste acusado	**hubisteis** acusado
hubo acusado	**hubieron** acusado
futuro perfecto	
habré acusado	**habremos** acusado
habrás acusado	**habréis** acusado
habrá acusado	**habrán** acusado
condicional compuesto	
habría acusado	**habríamos** acusado
habrías acusado	**habríais** acusado
habría acusado	**habrían** acusado
perfecto de subjuntivo	
haya acusado	**hayamos** acusado
hayas acusado	**hayáis** acusado
haya acusado	**hayan** acusado
pluscuamperfecto de subjuntivo	
hubiera acusado	**hubiéramos** acusado
hubieras acusado	**hubierais** acusado
hubiera acusado	**hubieran** acusado
OR	
hubiese acusado	**hubiésemos** acusado
hubieses acusado	**hubieseis** acusado
hubiese acusado	**hubiesen** acusado

adaptarse — to adapt

gerundio **adaptándose** participio de pasado **adaptado**

presente de indicativo

SINGULAR	PLURAL
me adapt**o**	nos adapt**amos**
te adapt**as**	os adapt**áis**
se adapt**a**	se adapt**an**

imperfecto de indicativo

SINGULAR	PLURAL
me adapt**aba**	nos adapt**ábamos**
te adapt**abas**	os adapt**abais**
se adapt**aba**	se adapt**aban**

pretérito

SINGULAR	PLURAL
me adapt**é**	nos adapt**amos**
te adapt**aste**	os adapt**asteis**
se adapt**ó**	se adapt**aron**

futuro

SINGULAR	PLURAL
me adaptar**é**	nos adaptar**emos**
te adaptar**ás**	os adaptar**éis**
se adaptar**á**	se adaptar**án**

condicional simple

SINGULAR	PLURAL
me adaptar**ía**	nos adaptar**íamos**
te adaptar**ías**	os adaptar**íais**
se adaptar**ía**	se adaptar**ían**

presente de subjuntivo

SINGULAR	PLURAL
me adapt**e**	nos adapt**emos**
te adapt**es**	os adapt**éis**
se adapt**e**	se adapt**en**

imperfecto de subjuntivo

SINGULAR	PLURAL
me adaptar**a**	nos adaptár**amos**
te adaptar**as**	os adaptar**ais**
se adaptar**a**	se adaptar**an**
OR	
me adaptas**e**	nos adaptás**emos**
te adaptas**es**	os adaptas**eis**
se adaptas**e**	se adaptas**en**

imperativo

SINGULAR	PLURAL
—	adaptémonos
adáptate; no te adaptes	adaptaos; no os adaptéis
adáptese	adáptense

perfecto de indicativo

SINGULAR	PLURAL
me he adaptado	**nos hemos** adaptado
te has adaptado	**os habéis** adaptado
se ha adaptado	**se han** adaptado

pluscuamperfecto de indicativo

SINGULAR	PLURAL
me había adaptado	**nos habíamos** adaptado
te habías adaptado	**os habíais** adaptado
se había adaptado	**se habían** adaptado

pretérito anterior

SINGULAR	PLURAL
me hube adaptado	**nos hubimos** adaptado
te hubiste adaptado	**os hubisteis** adaptado
se hubo adaptado	**se hubieron** adaptado

futuro perfecto

SINGULAR	PLURAL
me habré adaptado	**nos habremos** adaptado
te habrás adaptado	**os habréis** adaptado
se habrá adaptado	**se habrán** adaptado

condicional compuesto

SINGULAR	PLURAL
me habría adaptado	**nos habríamos** adaptado
te habrías adaptado	**os habríais** adaptado
se habría adaptado	**se habrían** adaptado

perfecto de subjuntivo

SINGULAR	PLURAL
me haya adaptado	**nos hayamos** adaptado
te hayas adaptado	**os hayáis** adaptado
se haya adaptado	**se hayan** adaptado

pluscuamperfecto de subjuntivo

SINGULAR	PLURAL
me hubiera adaptado	**nos hubiéramos** adaptado
te hubieras adaptado	**os hubierais** adaptado
se hubiera adaptado	**se hubieran** adaptado
OR	
me hubiese adaptado	**nos hubiésemos** adaptado
te hubieses adaptado	**os hubieseis** adaptado
se hubiese adaptado	**se hubiesen** adaptado

to go forward, to advance **adelantar**

gerundio **adelantando** participio de pasado **adelantado**

SINGULAR	PLURAL
presente de indicativo	
adelant**o**	adlenat**amos**
adelant**as**	adelant**áis**
adelant**a**	adelant**an**
imperfecto de indicativo	
adelant**aba**	adelant**ábamos**
adelant**abas**	adelant**abais**
adelant**aba**	adelant**aban**
pretérito	
adelant**é**	adelant**amos**
adelant**aste**	adelant**asteis**
adelant**ó**	adelant**aron**
futuro	
adelantar**é**	adelantar**emos**
adelantar**ás**	adelantar**éis**
adelantar**á**	adelantar**án**
condicional simple	
adelantar**ía**	adelantar**íamos**
adelantar**ías**	adelantar**íais**
adelantar**ía**	adelantar**ían**
presente de subjuntivo	
adelant**e**	adelant**emos**
adelant**es**	adelant**éis**
adelant**e**	adelant**en**
imperfecto de subjuntivo	
adelantar**a**	adelantár**amos**
adelantar**as**	adelantar**ais**
adelantar**a**	adelantar**an**
OR	
adelantas**e**	adelantas**emos**
adelantas**es**	adelantas**eis**
adelantas**e**	adelantas**en**
imperativo	
—	adelantemos
adelanta; no adelantes	adelantad; no adelantéis
adelante	adelanten

SINGULAR	PLURAL
perfecto de indicativo	
he adelantado	**hemos** adelantado
has adelantado	**habéis** adelantado
ha adelantado	**han** adelantado
pluscuamperfecto de indicativo	
había adelantado	**habíamos** adelantado
habías adelantado	**habíais** adelantado
había adelantado	**habían** adelantado
pretérito anterior	
hube adelantado	**hubimos** adelantado
hubiste adelantado	**hubisteis** adelantado
hubo adelantado	**hubieron** adelantado
futuro perfecto	
habré adelantado	**habremos** adelantado
habrás adelantado	**habréis** adelantado
habrá adelantado	**habrán** adelantado
condicional compuesto	
habría adelantado	**habríamos** adelantado
habrías adelantado	**habríais** adelantado
habría adelantado	**habrían** adelantado
perfecto de subjuntivo	
haya adelantado	**hayamos** adelantado
hayas adelantado	**hayáis** adelantado
haya adelantado	**hayan** adelantado
pluscuamperfecto de subjuntivo	
hubiera adelantado	**hubiéramos** adelantado
hubieras adelantado	**hubierais** adelantado
hubiera adelantado	**hubieran** adelantado
OR	
hubiese adelantado	**hubiésemos** adelantado
hubieses adelantado	**hubieseis** adelantado
hubiese adelantado	**hubiesen** adelantado

adelantarse — to go forward, to advance

gerundio **adelantándose** participio de pasado **adelantado**

SINGULAR	PLURAL	SINGULAR	PLURAL
presente de indicativo		perfecto de indicativo	
me adelant**o**	nos adelant**amos**	**me he** adelantado	**nos hemos** adelantado
te adelant**as**	os adelant**áis**	**te has** adelantado	**os habéis** adelantado
se adelant**a**	se adelant**an**	**se ha** adelantado	**se han** adelantado
imperfecto de indicativo		pluscuamperfecto de indicativo	
me adelant**aba**	nos adelant**ábamos**	**me había** adelantado	**nos habíamos** adelantado
te adelant**abas**	os adelant**abais**	**te habías** adelantado	**os habíais** adelantado
se adelant**aba**	se adelant**aban**	**se había** adelantado	**se habían** adelantado
pretérito		pretérito anterior	
me adelant**é**	nos adelant**amos**	**me hube** adelantado	**nos hubimos** adelantado
te adelant**aste**	os adelant**asteis**	**te hubiste** adelantado	**os hubisteis** adelantado
se adelant**ó**	se adelant**aron**	**se hubo** adelantado	**se hubieron** adelantado
futuro		futuro perfecto	
me adelantar**é**	nos adelantar**emos**	**me habré** adelantado	**nos habremos** adelantado
te adelantar**ás**	os adelantar**éis**	**te habrás** adelantado	**os habréis** adelantado
se adelantar**á**	se adelantar**án**	**se habrá** adelantado	**se habrán** adelantado
condicional simple		condicional compuesto	
me adelantar**ía**	nos adelantar**íamos**	**me habría** adelantado	**nos habríamos** adelantado
te adelantar**ías**	os adelantar**íais**	**te habrías** adelantado	**os habríais** adelantado
se adelantar**ía**	se adelantar**ían**	**se habría** adelantado	**se habrían** adelantado
presente de subjuntivo		perfecto de subjuntivo	
me adelant**e**	nos adelant**emos**	**me haya** adelantado	**nos hayamos** adelantado
te adelant**es**	os adelant**éis**	**te hayas** adelantado	**os hayáis** adelantado
se adelant**e**	se adelant**en**	**se haya** adelantado	**se hayan** adelantado
imperfecto de subjuntivo		pluscuamperfecto de subjuntivo	
me adelantar**a**	nos adelantár**amos**	**me hubiera** adelantado	**nos hubiéramos** adelantada
te adelantar**as**	os adelantar**ais**	**te hubieras** adelantado	**os hubierais** adelantado
se adelantar**a**	se adelantar**an**	**se hubiera** adelantado	**se hubieran** adelantado
OR		OR	
me adelantas**e**	nos adelantás**emos**	**me hubiese** adelantado	**nos hubiésemos** adelantado
te adelantas**es**	os adelantas**eis**	**te hubieses** adelantado	**os hubieseis** adelantado
se adelantas**e**	se adelantas**en**	**se hubiese** adelantado	**se hubiesen** adelantado

imperativo

SINGULAR	PLURAL
—	adelantémonos
adelántate; no te adelantes	adelantaos; no os adelantéis
adeléntese	adeléntense

to lose weight — adelgazar

gerundio **adelgazando** participio de pasado **adelgazado**

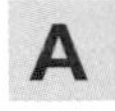

SINGULAR	PLURAL
presente de indicativo	
adelgaz**o**	adelgaz**amos**
adelgaz**as**	adelgaz**áis**
adelgaz**a**	adelgaz**an**
imperfecto de indicativo	
adelgaz**aba**	adelgaz**ábamos**
adelgaz**abas**	adelgaz**abais**
adelgaz**aba**	adelgaz**aban**
pretérito	
adelga**cé**	adelgaz**amos**
adelgaz**aste**	adelgaz**asteis**
adelgaz**ó**	adelgaz**aron**
futuro	
adelgazar**é**	adelgazar**emos**
adelgazar**ás**	adelgazar**éis**
adelgazar**á**	adelgazar**án**
condicional simple	
adelgazar**ía**	adelgazar**íamos**
adelgazar**ías**	adelgazar**íais**
adelgazar**ía**	adelgazar**ían**
presente de subjuntivo	
adelgac**e**	adelgac**emos**
adelgac**es**	adelgac**éis**
adelgac**e**	adelgac**en**
imperfecto de subjuntivo	
adelgazar**a**	adelgazár**amos**
adelgazar**as**	adelgazar**ais**
adelgazar**a**	adelgazar**an**
OR	
adelgazas**e**	adelgazás**emos**
adelgazas**es**	adelgazas**eis**
adelgazas**e**	adelgazas**en**
imperativo	
—	adelgacemos
adelgaza; no adelgaces	adelgazad; no adelgacéis
adelgace	adelgacen

SINGULAR	PLURAL
perfecto de indicativo	
he adelgazado	**hemos** adelgazado
has adelgazado	**habéis** adelgazada
ha adelgazado	**han** adelgazado
pluscuamperfecto de indicativo	
había adelgazado	**habíamos** adelgazado
habías adelgazado	**habíais** adelgazado
había adelgazado	**habían** adelgazado
pretérito anterior	
hube adelgazado	**hubimos** adelgazado
hubiste adelgazado	**hubisteis** adelgazado
hubo adelgazado	**hubieron** adelgazado
futuro perfecto	
habré adelgazado	**habremos** adelgazada
habrás adelgazado	**habréis** adelgazado
habrá adelgazado	**habrán** adelgazado
condicional compuesto	
habría adelgazado	**habríamos** adelgazado
habrías adelgazado	**habríais** adelgazado
habría adelgazado	**habrían** adelgazado
perfecto de subjuntivo	
haya adelgazado	**hayamos** adelgazado
hayas adelgazado	**hayáis** adelgazado
haya adelgazado	**hayan** adelgazado
pluscuamperfecto de subjuntivo	
hubiera adelgazado	**hubiéramos** adelgazado
hubieras adelgazado	**hubierais** adelgazado
hubiera adelgazado	**hubieran** adelgazado
OR	
hubiese adelgazado	**hubiésemos** adelgazado
hubieses adelgazado	**hubieseis** adelgazado
hubiese adelgazado	**hubiesen** adelgazado

adivinar — to guess, to foretell

gerundio **adivinando** — participio de pasado **adivinado**

SINGULAR	PLURAL	SINGULAR	PLURAL
presente de indicativo		perfecto de indicativo	
adivin**o**	adivin**amos**	**he** adivinado	**hemos** adivinado
adivin**as**	adivin**áis**	**has** adivinado	**habéis** adivinado
adivin**a**	adivin**an**	**ha** adivinado	**han** adivinado
imperfecto de indicativo		pluscuamperfecto de indicativo	
adivin**aba**	adivin**ábamos**	**había** adivinado	**habíamos** adivinado
adivin**abas**	adivin**abais**	**habías** adivinado	**habíais** adivinado
adivin**aba**	adivin**aban**	**había** adivinado	**habían** adivinado
pretérito		pretérito anterior	
adivin**é**	adivin**amos**	**hube** adivinado	**hubimos** adivinado
adivin**aste**	adivin**asteis**	**hubiste** adivinado	**hubisteis** adivinado
adivin**ó**	adivin**aron**	**hubo** adivinado	**hubieron** adivinado
futuro		futuro perfecto	
adivinar**é**	adivinar**emos**	**habré** adivinado	**habremos** adivinado
adivinar**ás**	adivinar**éis**	**habrás** adivinado	**habréis** adivinado
adivinar**á**	adivinar**án**	**habrá** adivinado	**habrán** adivinado
condicional simple		condicional compuesto	
adivinar**ía**	adivinar**íamos**	**habría** adivinado	**habríamos** adivinado
adivinar**ías**	adivinar**íais**	**habrías** adivinado	**habríais** adivinado
adivinar**ía**	adivinar**ían**	**habría** adivinado	**habrían** adivinado
presente de subjuntivo		perfecto de subjuntivo	
adivin**e**	adivin**emos**	**haya** adivinado	**hayamos** adivinado
adivin**es**	adivin**éis**	**hayas** adivinado	**hayáis** adivinado
adivin**e**	adivin**en**	**haya** adivinado	**hayan** adivinado
imperfecto de subjuntivo		pluscuamperfecto de subjuntivo	
adivinar**a**	adivinár**amos**	**hubiera** adivinado	**hubiéramos** adivinado
adivinar**as**	adivinar**ais**	**hubieras** adivinado	**hubierais** adivinado
adivinar**a**	adivinar**an**	**hubiera** adivinado	**hubieran** adivinado
OR		OR	
adivinas**e**	adivinás**emos**	**hubiese** adivinado	**hubiésemos** adivinado
adivinas**es**	adivinas**eis**	**hubieses** adivinado	**hubieseis** adivinado
adivinas**e**	adivinas**en**	**hubiese** adivinado	**hubiesen** adivinado

imperativo

—	adivinemos
adivina; no adivines	adivinad; no adivinéis
adivine	adivinen

gerundio **admitiendo** participio de pasado **admitido**

SINGULAR	PLURAL
presente de indicativo	
admit**o**	admit**imos**
admit**es**	admit**ís**
admit**e**	admit**en**
imperfecto de indicativo	
admit**ía**	admit**íamos**
admit**ías**	admit**íais**
admit**ía**	admit**ían**
pretérito	
admit**í**	admit**imos**
admit**iste**	admit**isteis**
admit**ió**	admit**ieron**
futuro	
admitir**é**	admitir**emos**
admitir**ás**	admitir**éis**
admitir**á**	admitir**án**
condicional simple	
admitir**ía**	admitir**íamos**
admitir**ías**	admitir**íais**
admitir**ía**	admitir**ían**
presente de subjuntivo	
admit**a**	admit**amos**
admit**as**	admit**áis**
admit**a**	admit**an**
imperfecto de subjuntivo	
admitier**a**	admitiér**amos**
admitier**as**	admitier**ais**
admitier**a**	admitier**an**
OR	
admities**e**	admitiés**emos**
admities**es**	admities**eis**
admities**e**	admities**en**
imperativo	
—	admitamos
admite; no admitas	admitid; no admitáis
admita	admitan

SINGULAR	PLURAL
perfecto de indicativo	
he admitido	**hemos** admitido
has admitido	**habéis** admitido
ha admitido	**han** admitido
pluscuamperfecto de indicativo	
había admitido	**habíamos** admitido
habías admitido	**habíais** admitido
había admitido	**habían** admitido
pretérito anterior	
hube admitido	**hubimos** admitido
hubiste admitido	**hubisteis** admitido
hubo admitido	**hubieron** admitido
futuro perfecto	
habré admitido	**habremos** admitido
habrás admitido	**habréis** admitido
habrá admitido	**habrán** admitido
condicional compuesto	
habría admitido	**habríamos** admitido
habrías admitido	**habríais** admitido
habría admitido	**habrían** admitido
perfecto de subjuntivo	
haya admitido	**hayamos** admitido
hayas admitido	**hayáis** admitido
haya admitido	**hayan** admitido
pluscuamperfecto de subjuntivo	
hubiera admitido	**hubiéramos** admitido
hubieras admitido	**hubierais** admitido
hubiera admitido	**hubieran** admitido
OR	
hubiese admitido	**hubiésemos** admitido
hubieses admitido	**hubieseis** admitido
hubiese admitido	**hubiesen** admitido

adoptar — to adopt

gerundio **adoptando** — participio de pasado **adoptado**

presente de indicativo

SINGULAR	PLURAL
adopt**o**	adopt**amos**
adopt**as**	adopt**áis**
adopt**a**	adopt**an**

imperfecto de indicativo

SINGULAR	PLURAL
adopt**aba**	adopt**ábamos**
adopt**abas**	adopt**abais**
adapt**aba**	adopt**aban**

pretérito

SINGULAR	PLURAL
adopt**é**	adopt**amos**
adopt**aste**	adopt**asteis**
adopt**ó**	adopt**aron**

futuro

SINGULAR	PLURAL
adoptar**é**	adoptar**emos**
adoptar**ás**	adoptar**éis**
adoptar**á**	adoptar**án**

condicional simple

SINGULAR	PLURAL
adoptar**ía**	adoptar**íamos**
adoptar**ías**	adoptar**íais**
adoptar**ía**	adoptar**ían**

presente de subjuntivo

SINGULAR	PLURAL
adopt**e**	adopt**emos**
adopt**es**	adopt**éis**
adopt**e**	adopt**en**

imperfecto de subjuntivo

SINGULAR	PLURAL
adoptar**a**	adoptár**amos**
adoptar**as**	adoptar**ais**
adoptar**a**	adoptar**an**
OR	
adoptas**e**	adoptás**emos**
adoptas**es**	adoptas**eis**
adoptas**e**	adoptas**en**

imperativo

SINGULAR	PLURAL
—	adoptemos
adopta; no adoptes	adoptad; no adoptéis
adopte	adopten

perfecto de indicativo

SINGULAR	PLURAL
he adoptado	**hemos** adoptado
has adoptado	**habéis** adoptado
ha adoptado	**han** adoptado

pluscuamperfecto de indicativo

SINGULAR	PLURAL
había adoptado	**habíamos** adoptado
habías adoptado	**habíais** adoptado
había adoptado	**habían** adoptado

pretérito anterior

SINGULAR	PLURAL
hube adoptado	**hubimos** adoptado
hubiste adoptado	**hubisteis** adoptado
hubo adoptado	**hubieron** adoptado

futuro perfecto

SINGULAR	PLURAL
habré adoptado	**habremos** adoptado
habrás adoptado	**habréis** adoptado
habrá adoptado	**habrán** adoptado

condicional compuesto

SINGULAR	PLURAL
habría adoptado	**habríamos** adoptado
habrías adoptado	**habríais** adoptado
habría adoptado	**habrían** adoptado

perfecto de subjuntivo

SINGULAR	PLURAL
haya adoptado	**hayamos** adoptado
hayas adoptado	**hayáis** adoptado
haya adoptado	**hayan** adoptado

pluscuamperfecto de subjuntivo

SINGULAR	PLURAL
hubiera adoptado	**hubiéramos** adoptado
hubieras adoptado	**hubierais** adoptado
hubiera adoptado	**hubieran** adoptado
OR	
hubiese adoptado	**hubiésemos** adoptado
hubieses adoptado	**hubieseis** adoptado
hubiese adoptado	**hubiesen** adoptado

gerundio **adorando** participio de pasado **adorado**

SINGULAR	PLURAL	SINGULAR	PLURAL
presente de indicativo		perfecto de indicativo	
ador**o**	ador**amos**	**he** adorado	**hemos** adorado
ador**as**	ador**áis**	**has** adorado	**habéis** adorado
ador**a**	ador**an**	**ha** adorado	**han** adorado
imperfecto de indicativo		pluscuamperfecto de indicativo	
ador**aba**	ador**ábamos**	**había** adorado	**habíamos** adorado
ador**abas**	ador**abais**	**habías** adorado	**habíais** adorado
ador**aba**	ador**aban**	**había** adorado	**habían** adorado
pretérito		pretérito anterior	
ador**é**	ador**amos**	**hube** adorado	**hubimos** adorado
ador**aste**	ador**asteis**	**hubiste** adorado	**hubisteis** adorado
ador**ó**	ador**aron**	**hubo** adorado	**hubieron** adorado
futuro		futuro perfecto	
adorar**é**	adorar**emos**	**habré** adorado	**habremos** adorado
adorar**ás**	adorar**éis**	**habrás** adorado	**habréis** adorado
adorar**á**	adorar**án**	**habrá** adorado	**habrán** adorado
condicional simple		condicional compuesto	
adorar**ía**	adorar**íamos**	**habría** adorado	**habríamos** adorado
adorar**ías**	adorar**íais**	**habrías** adorado	**habríais** adorado
adorar**ía**	adorar**ían**	**habría** adorado	**habrían** adorado
presente de subjuntivo		perfecto de subjuntivo	
ador**e**	ador**emos**	**haya** adorado	**hayamos** adorado
ador**es**	ador**éis**	**hayas** adorado	**hayáis** adorado
ador**e**	ador**en**	**haya** adorado	**hayan** adorado
imperfecto de subjuntivo		pluscuamperfecto de subjuntivo	
adorar**a**	adorár**amos**	**hubiera** adorado	**hubiéramos** adorado
adorar**as**	adorar**ais**	**hubieras** adorado	**hubierais** adorado
adorar**a**	adorar**an**	**hubiera** adorado	**hubieran** adorado
OR		OR	
adoras**e**	adorás**emos**	**hubiese** adorado	**hubiésemos** adorado
adoras**es**	adoras**eis**	**hubieses** adorado	**hubieseis** adorado
adoras**e**	adoras**en**	**hubiese** adorado	**hubiesen** adorado

imperativo

—	adoremos
adora; no adores	adorad; no adoréis
adore	adoren

adquirir — to acquire, to buy

gerundio **adquiriendo** participio de pasado **adquirido**

presente de indicativo

SINGULAR	PLURAL
adquier**o**	adquir**imos**
adquier**es**	adquir**ís**
adquier**e**	adquier**en**

imperfecto de indicativo

SINGULAR	PLURAL
adquir**ía**	adquir**íamos**
adquir**ías**	adquir**íais**
adquir**ía**	adquir**ían**

pretérito

SINGULAR	PLURAL
adquir**í**	adquir**imos**
adquir**iste**	adquir**isteis**
adquir**ió**	adquir**ieron**

futuro

SINGULAR	PLURAL
adquirir**é**	adquirir**emos**
adquirir**ás**	adquirir**éis**
adquirir**á**	adquirir**án**

condicional simple

SINGULAR	PLURAL
adquirir**ía**	adquirir**íamos**
adquirir**ías**	adquirir**íais**
adquirir**ía**	adquirir**ían**

presente de subjuntivo

SINGULAR	PLURAL
adquier**a**	adquir**amos**
adquier**as**	adquir**áis**
adquier**a**	adquier**an**

imperfecto de subjuntivo

SINGULAR	PLURAL
adquirier**a**	adquiriér**amos**
adquirier**as**	adquirier**ais**
adquirier**a**	adquirier**an**
OR	
adquiries**e**	adquiriés**emos**
adquiries**es**	adquiries**eis**
adquiries**e**	adquiries**en**

imperativo

SINGULAR	PLURAL
—	adquiramos
adquiere; no adquieras	adquirid; no adquiráis
adquiera	adquieran

perfecto de indicativo

SINGULAR	PLURAL
he adquirido	**hemos** adquirido
has adquirido	**habéis** adquirido
ha adquirido	**han** adquirido

pluscuamperfecto de indicativo

SINGULAR	PLURAL
había adquirido	**habíamos** adquirido
habías adquirido	**habíais** adquirido
había adquirido	**habían** adquirido

pretérito anterior

SINGULAR	PLURAL
hube adquirido	**hubimos** adquirido
hubiste adquirido	**hubisteis** adquirido
hubo adquirido	**hubieron** adquirido

futuro perfecto

SINGULAR	PLURAL
habré adquirido	**habremos** adquirido
habrás adquirido	**habréis** adquirido
habrá adquirido	**habrán** adquirido

condicional compuesto

SINGULAR	PLURAL
habría adquirido	**habríamos** adquirido
habrías adquirido	**habríais** adquirido
habría adquirido	**habrían** adquirido

perfecto de subjuntivo

SINGULAR	PLURAL
haya adquirido	**hayamos** adquirido
hayas adquirido	**hayáis** adquirido
haya adquirido	**hayan** adquirido

pluscuamperfecto de subjuntivo

SINGULAR	PLURAL
hubiera adquirido	**hubiéramos** adquirido
hubieras adquirido	**hubierais** adquirido
hubiera adquirido	**hubieran** adquirido
OR	
hubiese adquirido	**hubiésemos** adquirido
hubieses adquirido	**hubieseis** adquirido
hubiese adquirido	**hubiesen** adquirido

gerundio **advirtiendo** participio de pasado **advertido**

presente de indicativo

SINGULAR	PLURAL
adviert**o**	advert**imos**
adviert**es**	advert**ís**
adviert**e**	adviert**en**

imperfecto de indicativo

SINGULAR	PLURAL
advert**ía**	advert**íamos**
advert**ías**	advert**íais**
advert**ía**	adven**ían**

pretérito

SINGULAR	PLURAL
advert**í**	advert**imos**
advert**iste**	advert**isteis**
advirti**ó**	advirt**ieron**

futuro

SINGULAR	PLURAL
advertir**é**	advertir**emos**
advertir**ás**	advertir**éis**
advertir**á**	advertir**án**

condicional simple

SINGULAR	PLURAL
advertir**ía**	advertir**íamos**
advertir**ías**	advertir**íais**
advertir**ía**	advertir**ían**

presente de subjuntivo

SINGULAR	PLURAL
adviert**a**	advirt**amos**
adviert**as**	advirt**áis**
adviert**a**	adviert**an**

imperfecto de subjuntivo

SINGULAR	PLURAL
advirtier**a**	advirtiér**amos**
advirtier**as**	advirtier**ais**
advirtier**a**	advirtier**an**
OR	
advirties**e**	advirtiés**emos**
advirties**es**	advirties**eis**
advirties**e**	advirties**en**

imperativo

SINGULAR	PLURAL
—	advirtamos
advierte; no adviertas	advertid; no advirtáis
advierta	adviertan

perfecto de indicativo

SINGULAR	PLURAL
he advertido	**hemos** advertido
has advertido	**habéis** advertido
ha advertido	**han** advertido

pluscuamperfecto de indicativo

SINGULAR	PLURAL
había advertido	**habíamos** advertido
habías advertido	**habíais** advertido
había advertido	**habían** advertido

pretérito anterior

SINGULAR	PLURAL
hube advertido	**hubimos** advertido
hubiste advertido	**hubisteis** advertido
hubo advertido	**hubieron** advertido

futuro perfecto

SINGULAR	PLURAL
habré advertido	**habremos** advertido
habrás advertido	**habréis** advertido
habrá advertido	**habrán** advertido

condicional compuesto

SINGULAR	PLURAL
habría advertido	**habríamos** advertido
habrías advertido	**habríais** advertido
habría advertido	**habrían** advertido

perfecto de subjuntivo

SINGULAR	PLURAL
haya advertido	**hayamos** advertido
hayas advertido	**hayáis** advertido
haya advertido	**hayan** advertido

pluscuamperfecto de subjuntivo

SINGULAR	PLURAL
hubiera advertido	**hubiéramos** advertido
hubieras advertido	**hubierais** advertido
hubiera advertido	**hubieran** advertido
OR	
hubiese advertido	**hubiésemos** advertido
hubieses advertido	**hubieseis** advertido
hubiese advertido	**hubiesen** advertido

afectar — to affect

gerundio **afectando** participio de pasado **afectado**

presente de indicativo

SINGULAR	PLURAL
afect**o**	afect**amos**
afect**as**	afect**áis**
afect**a**	afect**an**

imperfecto de indicativo

SINGULAR	PLURAL
afect**aba**	afect**ábamos**
afect**abas**	afect**abais**
afect**aba**	afect**aban**

pretérito

SINGULAR	PLURAL
afect**é**	afect**amos**
afect**aste**	afect**asteis**
afect**ó**	afect**aron**

futuro

SINGULAR	PLURAL
afectar**é**	afectar**emos**
afectar**ás**	afectar**éis**
afectar**á**	afectar**án**

condicional simple

SINGULAR	PLURAL
afectar**ía**	afectar**íamos**
afectar**ías**	afectar**íais**
afectar**ía**	afectar**ían**

presente de subjuntivo

SINGULAR	PLURAL
afect**e**	afect**emos**
afect**es**	afect**éis**
afect**e**	afect**en**

imperfecto de subjuntivo

SINGULAR	PLURAL
afectar**a**	afectár**amos**
afectar**as**	afectar**ais**
afectar**a**	afectar**an**
OR	
afectas**e**	afectás**emos**
afectas**es**	afectas**eis**
afectas**e**	afectas**en**

imperativo

SINGULAR	PLURAL
—	afectemos
afecta;	afectad;
no afectes	no afectéis
afecte	afecten

perfecto de indicativo

SINGULAR	PLURAL
he afectado	**hemos** afectado
has afectado	**habéis** afectado
ha afectado	**han** afectado

pluscuamperfecto de indicativo

SINGULAR	PLURAL
había afectado	**habíamos** afectado
habías afectado	**habíais** afectado
había afectado	**habían** afectado

pretérito anterior

SINGULAR	PLURAL
hube afectado	**hubimos** afectado
hubiste afectado	**hubisteis** afectado
hubo afectado	**hubieron** afectado

futuro perfecto

SINGULAR	PLURAL
habré afectado	**habremos** afectado
habrás afectado	**habréis** afectado
habrá afectado	**habrán** afectado

condicional compuesto

SINGULAR	PLURAL
habría afectado	**habríamos** afectado
habrías afectado	**habríais** afectado
habría afectado	**habrían** afectado

perfecto de subjuntivo

SINGULAR	PLURAL
haya afectado	**hayamos** afectado
hayas afectado	**hayáis** afectado
haya afectado	**hayan** afectado

pluscuamperfecto de subjuntivo

SINGULAR	PLURAL
hubiera afectado	**hubiéramos** afectado
hubieras afectado	**hubierais** afectado
hubiera afectado	**hubieran** afectado
OR	
hubiese afectado	**hubiésemos** afectado
hubieses afectado	**hubieseis** afectado
hubiese afectado	**hubiesen** afectado

to shave oneself **afeitarse**

gerundio **afeitándose** participio de pasado **afeitado**

presente de indicativo

SINGULAR	PLURAL
me afeit**o**	nos afeit**amos**
te afeit**as**	os afeit**áis**
se afeit**a**	se afeit**an**

imperfecto de indicativo

SINGULAR	PLURAL
me afeit**aba**	nos afeit**ábamos**
te afeit**abas**	os afeit**abais**
se afeit**aba**	se afeit**aban**

pretérito

SINGULAR	PLURAL
me afeit**é**	nos afeit**amos**
té afeit**aste**	os afeit**asteis**
se afeit**ó**	se afeit**aron**

futuro

SINGULAR	PLURAL
me afeitar**é**	nos afeitar**emos**
te afeitar**ás**	os afeitar**éis**
se afeitar**á**	se afeitar**án**

condicional simple

SINGULAR	PLURAL
me afeitar**ía**	nos afeitar**íamos**
te afeitar**ías**	os afeitar**íais**
se afeitar**ía**	se afeitar**ían**

presente de subjuntivo

SINGULAR	PLURAL
me afeit**e**	nos afeit**emos**
te afeit**es**	os afeit**éis**
se afeit**e**	se afeit**en**

imperfecto de subjuntivo

SINGULAR	PLURAL
me afeitar**a**	nos afeitár**amos**
te afeitar**as**	os afeitar**ais**
se afeitar**a**	se afeitar**an**
OR	
me afeitas**e**	nos afeitás**emos**
te afeitas**es**	os afeitas**eis**
se afeitas**e**	se afeitas**en**

imperativo

SINGULAR	PLURAL
—	afeitémonos
afeítate; no te afeites	afeitaos; no os afeitéis
afeítese	afeítense

perfecto de indicativo

SINGULAR	PLURAL
me he afeitado	**nos hemos** afeitado
te has afeitado	**os habéis** afeitado
se ha afeitado	**se han** afeitado

pluscuamperfecto de indicativo

SINGULAR	PLURAL
me había afeitado	**nos habíamos** afeitado
te habías afeitado	**os habíais** afeitado
se había afeitado	**se habían** afeitado

pretérito anterior

SINGULAR	PLURAL
me hube afeitado	**nos hubimos** afeitado
te hubiste afeitado	**os hubisteis** afeitado
se hubo afeitado	**se hubieron** afeitado

futuro perfecto

SINGULAR	PLURAL
me habré afeitado	**nos habremos** afeitado
te habrás afeitado	**os habréis** afeitado
se habrá afeitado	**se habrán** afeitado

condicional compuesto

SINGULAR	PLURAL
me habría afeitado	**nos habríamos** afeitado
te habrías afeitado	**os habríais** afeitado
se habría afeitado	**se habrían** afeitado

perfecto de subjuntivo

SINGULAR	PLURAL
me haya afeitado	**nos hayamos** afeitado
te hayas afeitado	**os hayáis** afeitado
se haya afeitado	**se hayan** afeitado

pluscuamperfecto de subjuntivo

SINGULAR	PLURAL
me hubiera afeitado	**nos hubiéramos** afeitado
te hubieras afeitado	**os hubierais** afeitado
se hubiera afeitado	**se hubieran** afeitado
OR	
me hubiese afeitado	**nos hubiésemos** afeitado
te hubieses afeitado	**os hubieseis** afeitado
se hubiese afeitado	**se hubiesen** afeitado

aficionarse — to be a fan of something

gerundio **aficionándose** participio de pasado **aficionado**

SINGULAR	PLURAL

presente de indicativo

SINGULAR	PLURAL
me aficion**o**	nos aficion**amos**
te aficion**as**	os aficion**áis**
se aficion**a**	se aficion**an**

imperfecto de indicativo

SINGULAR	PLURAL
me aficion**aba**	nos aficion**ábamos**
re aficion**abas**	os aficion**abais**
se aficion**aba**	se aficion**aban**

pretérito

SINGULAR	PLURAL
me aficion**é**	nos aficion**amos**
te aficion**aste**	os aficion**asteis**
se aficion**ó**	se aficion**aron**

futuro

SINGULAR	PLURAL
me aficionar**é**	nos aficionar**emos**
te aficionar**ás**	os aficionar**éis**
se aficionar**á**	se aficionar**án**

condicional simple

SINGULAR	PLURAL
me aficionar**ía**	nos aficionar**íamos**
te aficionar**ías**	os aficionar**íais**
se aficionar**ía**	se aficionar**ían**

presente de subjuntivo

SINGULAR	PLURAL
me aficion**e**	nos aficion**emos**
te aficion**es**	os aficion**éis**
se aficion**e**	se aficion**en**

imperfecto de subjuntivo

SINGULAR	PLURAL
me aficionar**a**	nos aficionár**amos**
te aficionar**as**	os aficionar**ais**
se aficionar**a**	se aficionar**an**
OR	
me aficionas**e**	nos aficionás**emos**
te aficionas**es**	os aficionas**eis**
se aficionas**e**	se aficionas**en**

imperativo

SINGULAR	PLURAL
—	aficionémonos
aficiónate; no te aficiones	aficionaos; no os aficionéis
aficiónese	aficiónense

SINGULAR	PLURAL

perfecto de indicativo

SINGULAR	PLURAL
me he aficionado	**nos hemos** aficionado
te has aficionado	**os habéis** aficionado
se ha aficionado	**se han** aficionado

pluscuamperfecto de indicativo

SINGULAR	PLURAL
me había aficionado	**nos habíamos** aficionado
te habías aficionado	**os habíais** aficionado
se había aficionado	**se habían** aficionado

pretérito anterior

SINGULAR	PLURAL
me hube aficionado	**nos hubimos** aficionado
te hubiste aficionado	**os hubisteis** aficionado
se hubo aficionado	**se hubieron** aficionado

futuro perfecto

SINGULAR	PLURAL
me habré aficionado	**nos habremos** aficionado
te habrás aficionado	**os habréis** aficionado
se habrá aficionado	**se habrán** aficionado

condicional compuesto

SINGULAR	PLURAL
me habría aficionado	**nos habríamos** aficionado
te habrías aficionado	**os habríais** aficionado
se habría aficionado	**se habrían** aficionado

perfecto de subjuntivo

SINGULAR	PLURAL
me haya aficionado	**nos hayamos** aficionado
te hayas aficionado	**os hayáis** aficionado
se haya aficionado	**se hayan** aficionado

pluscuamperfecto de subjuntivo

SINGULAR	PLURAL
me hubiera aficionado	**nos hubiéramos** aficionado
te hubieras aficionado	**os hubierais** aficionado
se hubiera aficionado	**se hubieran** aficionado
OR	
me hubiese aficionado	**nos hubiésemos** aficionado
te hubieses aficionado	**os hubieseis** aficionado
se hubiese aficionado	**se hubiesen** aficionado

gerundio **afligiendo** participio de pasado **afligido**

SINGULAR	PLURAL
presente de indicativo	
aflij**o**	afligi**mos**
aflig**es**	aflig**ís**
aflig**e**	aflig**en**
imperfecto de indicativo	
aflig**ía**	aflig**íamos**
aflig**ías**	aflig**íais**
aflig**ía**	aflig**ían**
pretérito	
aflig**í**	aflig**imos**
aflig**iste**	aflig**isteis**
aflig**ió**	aflig**ieron**
futuro	
afligir**é**	afligir**emos**
afligir**ás**	afligir**éis**
afligir**á**	afligir**án**
condicional simple	
afligir**ía**	afligir**íamos**
afligir**ías**	afligir**íais**
afligir**ía**	afligir**ían**
presente de subjuntivo	
aflij**a**	aflij**amos**
aflij**as**	aflij**áis**
aflij**a**	aflij**an**
imperfecto de subjuntivo	
afligier**a**	afligiér**amos**
afligier**as**	afligier**ais**
afligier**a**	afligier**an**
OR	
afligies**e**	afligiés**emos**
afligies**es**	afligies**eis**
afligies**e**	afligies**en**
imperativo	
—	aflijamos
aflige; no aflijas	afligid; no aflijáis
aflija	aflijan

SINGULAR	PLURAL
perfecto de indicativo	
he afligido	**hemos** afligido
has afligido	**habéis** afligido
ha afligido	**han** afligido
pluscuamperfecto de indicativo	
había afligido	**habíamos** afligido
habías afligido	**habíais** afligido
había afligido	**habían** afligido
pretérito anterior	
hube afligido	**hubimos** afligido
hubiste afligido	**hubisteis** afligido
hubo afligido	**hubieron** afligido
futuro perfecto	
habré afligido	**habremos** afligido
habrás afligido	**habréis** afligido
habrá afligido	**habrán** afligido
condicional compuesto	
habría afligido	**habríamos** afligido
habrías afligido	**habríais** afligido
habría afligido	**habrían** afligido
perfecto de subjuntivo	
haya afligido	**hayamos** afligido
hayas afligido	**hayáis** afligido
haya afligido	**hayan** afligido
pluscuamperfecto de subjuntivo	
hubiera afligido	**hubiéramos** afligido
hubieras afligido	**hubierais** afligido
hubiera afligido	**hubieran** afligido
OR	
hubiese afligido	**hubiésemos** afligido
hubieses afligido	**hubieseis** afligido
hubiese afligido	**hubiesen** afligido

agarrar — to grasp

gerundio **agarrando** — participio de pasado **agarrado**

SINGULAR	PLURAL
presente de indicativo	
agarr**o**	agarr**amos**
agarr**as**	agarr**áis**
agarr**a**	agarr**an**
imperfecto de indicativo	
agarr**aba**	agarr**ábamos**
agarr**abas**	agarr**abais**
agarr**aba**	agarr**aban**
pretérito	
agarr**é**	agarr**amos**
agarr**aste**	agarr**asteis**
agarr**ó**	agarr**aron**
futuro	
agarrar**é**	agarrar**emos**
agarrar**ás**	agarrar**éis**
agarrar**á**	agarrar**án**
condicional simple	
agarrar**ía**	agarrar**íamos**
agarrar**ías**	agarrar**íais**
agarrar**ía**	agarrar**ían**
presente de subjuntivo	
agarr**e**	agarr**emos**
agarr**es**	agarr**éis**
agarr**e**	agarr**en**
imperfecto de subjuntivo	
agarrar**a**	agarrár**amos**
agarrar**as**	agarrar**ais**
agarrar**a**	agarrar**an**
OR	
agarras**e**	agarrás**emos**
agarras**es**	agarras**eis**
agarras**e**	agarras**en**

SINGULAR	PLURAL
perfecto de indicativo	
he agarrado	**hemos** agarrado
has agarrado	**habéis** agarrado
ha agarrado	**han** agarrado
pluscuamperfecto de indicativo	
había agarrado	**habíamos** agarrado
habías agarrado	**habíais** agarrado
había agarrado	**habían** agarrado
pretérito anterior	
hube agarrado	**hubimos** agarrado
hubiste agarrado	**hubisteis** agarrado
hubo agarrado	**hubieron** agarrado
futuro perfecto	
habré agarrado	**habremos** agarrado
habrás agarrado	**habréis** agarrado
habrá agarrado	**habrán** agarrado
condicional compuesto	
habría agarrado	**habríamos** agarrado
habrías agarrado	**habríais** agarrado
habría agarrado	**habrían** agarrado
perfecto de subjuntivo	
haya agarrado	**hayamos** agarrado
hayas agarrado	**hayáis** agarrado
haya agarrado	**hayan** agarrado
pluscuamperfecto de subjuntivo	
hubiera agarrado	**hubiéramos** agarrado
hubieras agarrado	**hubierais** agarrado
hubiera agarrado	**hubieran** agarrado
OR	
hubiese agarrado	**hubiésemos** agarrado
hubieses agarrado	**hubieseis** agarrado
hubiese agarrado	**hubiesen** agarrado

imperativo

—	agarremos
agarra; no agarres	agarrad; no agarréis
agarre	agarren

gerundio **agitando** participio de pasado **agitado**

SINGULAR	PLURAL	SINGULAR	PLURAL
presente de indicativo		perfecto de indicativo	
agit**o**	agit**amos**	**he** agitado	**hemos** agitado
agit**as**	agit**áis**	**has** agitado	**habéis** agitado
agit**a**	agit**an**	**ha** agitado	**han** agitado
imperfecto de indicativo		pluscuamperfecto de indicativo	
agit**aba**	agit**ábamos**	**había** agitado	**habíamos** agitado
agit**abas**	agit**abais**	**habías** agitado	**habíais** agitado
agit**aba**	agit**aban**	**había** agitado	**habían** agitado
pretérito		pretérito anterior	
agit**é**	agit**amos**	**hube** agitado	**hubimos** agitado
agit**aste**	agit**asteis**	**hubiste** agitado	**hubisteis** agitado
agit**ó**	agit**aron**	**hubo** agitado	**hubieron** agitado
futuro		futuro perfecto	
agitar**é**	agitar**emos**	**habré** agitado	**habremos** agitado
agitar**ás**	agitar**éis**	**habrás** agitado	**habréis** agitado
agitar**á**	agitar**án**	**habrá** agitado	**habrán** agitado
condicional simple		condicional compuesto	
agitar**ía**	agitar**íamos**	**habría** agitado	**habríamos** agitado
agitar**ías**	agitar**íais**	**habrías** agitado	**habríais** agitado
agitar**ía**	agitar**ían**	**habría** agitado	**habrían** agitado
presente de subjuntivo		perfecto de subjuntivo	
agit**e**	agit**emos**	**haya** agitado	**hayamos** agitado
agit**es**	agit**éis**	**hayas** agitado	**hayáis** agitado
agit**e**	agit**en**	**haya** agitado	**hayan** agitado
imperfecto de subjuntivo		pluscuamperfecto de subjuntivo	
agitar**a**	agitár**amos**	**hubiera** agitado	**hubiéramos** agitado
agitar**as**	agitar**ais**	**hubieras** agitado	**hubierais** agitado
agitar**a**	agitar**an**	**hubiera** agitado	**hubieran** agitado
OR		OR	
agitas**e**	agitás**emos**	**hubiese** agitado	**hubiésemos** agitado
agitas**es**	agitas**eis**	**hubieses** agitado	**hubieseis** agitado
agitas**e**	agitas**en**	**hubiese** agitado	**hubiesen** agitado

imperativo

—	agitemos
agita; no agites	agitad; no agitéis
agite	agiten

agotar — to use up, to exhaust

gerundio **agotando** — participio de pasado **agotado**

SINGULAR	PLURAL
presente de indicativo	
agot**o**	agot**amos**
agot**as**	agot**áis**
agot**a**	agot**an**
imperfecto de indicativo	
agot**aba**	agot**ábamos**
agot**abas**	agot**abais**
agot**aba**	agot**aban**
pretérito	
agot**é**	agot**amos**
agot**aste**	agot**asteis**
agot**ó**	agot**aron**
futuro	
agotar**é**	agotar**emos**
agotar**ás**	agotar**éis**
agotar**á**	agotar**án**
condicional simple	
agotar**ía**	agotar**íamos**
agotar**ías**	agotar**íais**
agotar**ía**	agotar**ían**
presente de subjuntivo	
agot**e**	agot**emos**
agot**es**	agot**éis**
agot**e**	agot**en**
imperfecto de subjuntivo	
agotar**a**	agotár**amos**
agotar**as**	agotar**ais**
agotar**a**	agotar**an**
OR	
agotas**e**	agotás**emos**
agotas**es**	agotas**eis**
agotas**e**	agotas**en**
imperativo	
—	agotemos
agota;	agotad;
no agotes	no agotéis
agote	agoten

SINGULAR	PLURAL
perfecto de indicativo	
he agotado	**hemos** agotado
has agotado	**habéis** agotado
ha agotado	**han** agotado
pluscuamperfecto de indicativo	
había agotado	**habíamos** agotado
habías agotado	**habíais** agotado
había agotado	**habían** agotado
pretérito anterior	
hube agotado	**hubimos** agotado
hubiste agotado	**hubisteis** agotado
hubo agotado	**hubieron** agotado
futuro perfecto	
habré agotado	**habremos** agotado
habrás agotado	**habréis** agotado
habrá agotado	**habrán** agotado
condicional compuesto	
habría agotado	**habríamos** agotado
habrías agotado	**habríais** agotado
habría agotado	**habrían** agotado
perfecto de subjuntivo	
haya agotado	**hayamos** agotado
hayas agotado	**hayáis** agotado
haya agotado	**hayan** agotado
pluscuamperfecto de subjuntivo	
hubiera agotado	**hubiéramos** agotado
hubieras agotado	**hubierais** agotado
hubiera agotado	**hubieran** agotado
OR	
hubiese agotado	**hubiésemos** agotado
hubieses agotado	**hubieseis** agotado
hubiese agotado	**hubiesen** agotado

gerundio **agradando** participio de pasado **agradado**

SINGULAR	PLURAL	SINGULAR	PLURAL
presente de indicativo		perfecto de indicativo	
agrad**o**	agrad**amos**	**he** agradado	**hemos** agradado
agrad**as**	agrad**áis**	**has** agradado	**habéis** agradado
agrad**a**	agrad**an**	**ha** agradado	**han** agradado
imperfecto de indicativo		pluscuamperfecto de indicativo	
agrad**aba**	agrad**ábamos**	**había** agradado	**habíamos** agradado
agrad**abas**	agrad**abais**	**habías** agradado	**habíais** agradado
agrad**aba**	agrad**aban**	**había** agradado	**habían** agradado
pretérito		pretérito anterior	
agrad**é**	agrad**amos**	**hube** agradado	**hubimos** agradado
agrad**aste**	agrad**asteis**	**hubiste** agradado	**hubisteis** agradado
agrad**ó**	agrad**aron**	**hubo** agradado	**hubieron** agradado
futuro		futuro perfecto	
agradar**é**	agradar**emos**	**habré** agradado	**habremos** agradado
agradar**ás**	agradar**éis**	**habrás** agradado	**habréis** agradado
agradar**á**	agradar**án**	**habrá** agradado	**habrán** agradado
condicional simple		condicional compuesto	
agradar**ía**	agradar**íamos**	**habría** agradado	**habríamos** agradado
agradar**ías**	agradar**íais**	**habrías** agradado	**habríais** agradado
agradar**ía**	agradar**ían**	**habría** agradado	**habrían** agradado
presente de subjuntivo		perfecto de subjuntivo	
agrad**e**	agrad**emos**	**haya** agradado	**hayamos** agradado
agrad**es**	agrad**éis**	**hayas** agradado	**hayáis** agradado
agrad**e**	agrad**en**	**haya** agradado	**hayan** agradado
imperfecto de subjuntivo		pluscuamperfecto de subjuntivo	
agradar**a**	agradár**amos**	**hubiera** agradado	**hubiéramos** agradado
agradar**as**	agradar**ais**	**hubieras** agradado	**hubierais** agradado
agradar**a**	agradar**an**	**hubiera** agradado	**hubieran** agradado
OR		OR	
agradas**e**	agradás**emos**	**hubiese** agradado	**hubiésemos** agradado
agradas**es**	agradas**eis**	**hubieses** agradado	**hubieseis** agradado
agradas**e**	agradas**en**	**hubiese** agradado	**hubiesen** agradado

imperativo

—	agrademos
agrada; no agrades	agradad; no agradéis
agrade	agraden

agradecer — to be grateful, to thank

gerundio **agradeciendo** — participio de pasado **agradecido**

SINGULAR	PLURAL
presente de indicativo	
agradezc**o**	agradec**emos**
agradec**es**	agradec**éis**
agradec**e**	agradec**en**
imperfecto de indicativo	
agradec**ía**	agradec**íamos**
agradec**ías**	agradec**íais**
agradec**ía**	agradec**ían**
pretérito	
agradec**í**	agradec**imos**
agradec**iste**	agradec**isteis**
agradec**ió**	agradec**ieron**
futuro	
agradecer**é**	agradecer**emos**
agradecer**ás**	agradecer**éis**
agradecer**á**	agradecer**án**
condicional simple	
agradecer**ía**	agradecer**íamos**
agradecer**ías**	agradecer**íais**
agradecer**ía**	agradecer**ían**
presente de subjuntivo	
agradezc**a**	agradezc**amos**
agradezc**as**	agradezc**áis**
agradezc**a**	agradezc**an**
imperfecto de subjuntivo	
agradecier**a**	agradeciér**amos**
agradecier**as**	agradecier**ais**
agradecier**a**	agradecier**an**
OR	
agradecies**e**	agradeciés**emos**
agradecies**es**	agradecies**eis**
agradecies**e**	agradecies**en**
imperativo	
—	agradezcamos
agradece; no agradezcas	agradeced; no agradezcáis
agradezca	agradezcan

SINGULAR	PLURAL
perfecto de indicativo	
he agradecido	**hemos** agradecido
has agradecido	**habéis** agradecido
ha agradecido	**han** agradecido
pluscuamperfecto de indicativo	
había agradecido	**habíamos** agradecido
habías agradecido	**habíais** agradecido
había agradecido	**habían** agradecido
pretérito anterior	
hube agradecido	**hubimos** agradecido
hubiste agradecido	**hubisteis** agradecido
hubo agradecido	**hubieron** agradecido
futuro perfecto	
habré agradecido	**habremos** agradecido
habrás agradecido	**habréis** agradecido
habrá agradecido	**habrán** agradecido
condicional compuesto	
habría agradecido	**habríamos** agradecido
habrías agradecido	**habríais** agradecido
habría agradecido	**habrían** agradecido
perfecto de subjuntivo	
haya agradecido	**hayamos** agradecido
hayas agradecido	**hayáis** agradecido
haya agradecido	**hayan** agradecido
pluscuamperfecto de subjuntivo	
hubiera agradecido	**hubiéramos** agradecido
hubieras agradecido	**hubierais** agradecido
hubiera agradecido	**hubieran** agradecido
OR	
hubiese agradecido	**hubiésemos** agradecido
hubieses agradecido	**hubieseis** agradecido
hubiese agradecido	**hubiesen** agradecido

gerundio **agrandando** participio de pasado **agrandado**

SINGULAR	PLURAL	SINGULAR	PLURAL
presente de indicativo		perfecto de indicativo	
agrand**o**	agrand**amos**	**he** agrandado	**hemos** agrandado
agrand**as**	agrand**áis**	**has** agrandado	**habéis** agrandado
agrand**a**	agrand**an**	**ha** agrandado	**han** agrandado
imperfecto de indicativo		pluscuamperfecto de indicativo	
agrand**aba**	agrand**ábamos**	**había** agrandado	**habíamos** agrandado
agrand**abas**	agrand**abais**	**habías** agrandado	**habíais** agrandado
agrand**aba**	agrand**aban**	**había** agrandado	**habían** agrandado
pretérito		pretérito anterior	
agrand**é**	agrand**amos**	**hube** agrandado	**hubimos** agrandado
agrand**aste**	agrand**asteis**	**hubiste** agrandado	**hubisteis** agrandado
agrand**ó**	agrand**aron**	**hubo** agrandado	**hubieron** agrandado
futuro		futuro perfecto	
agrandar**é**	agrandar**emos**	**habré** agrandado	**habremos** agrandado
agrandar**ás**	agrandar**éis**	**habrás** agrandado	**habréis** agrandado
agrandar**á**	agrandar**án**	**habrá** agrandado	**habrán** agrandado
condicional simple		condicional compuesto	
agrandar**ía**	agrandar**íamos**	**habría** agrandado	**habríamos** agrandado
agrandar**ías**	agrandar**íais**	**habrías** agrandado	**habríais** agrandado
agrandar**ía**	agrandar**ían**	**habría** agrandado	**habrían** agrandado
presente de subjuntivo		perfecto de subjuntivo	
agrand**e**	agrand**emos**	**haya** agrandado	**hayamos** agrandado
agrand**es**	agrand**éis**	**hayas** agrandado	**hayáis** agrandado
agrand**e**	agrand**en**	**haya** agrandado	**hayan** agrandado
imperfecto de subjuntivo		pluscuamperfecto de subjuntivo	
agrandar**a**	agrandár**amos**	**hubiera** agrandado	**hubiéramos** agrandado
agrandar**as**	agrandar**ais**	**hubieras** agrandado	**hubierais** agrandado
agrandar**a**	agrandar**an**	**hubiera** agrandado	**hubieran** agrandado
OR		OR	
agrandas**e**	agrandás**emos**	**hubiese** agrandado	**hubiésemos** agrandado
agrandas**es**	agrandas**eis**	**hubieses** agrandado	**hubieseis** agrandado
agrandas**e**	agrandas**en**	**hubiese** agrandado	**hubiesen** agrandado

imperativo

—	agrandemos
agranda;	agrandad;
no agrandes	no agrandéis
agrande	agranden

agravar — to aggravate, to make worse

gerundio **agravando** — participio de pasado **agravado**

SINGULAR	PLURAL
presente de indicativo	
agrav**o**	agrav**amos**
agrav**as**	agrav**áis**
agrav**a**	agrav**an**
imperfecto de indicativo	
agrav**aba**	agrav**ábamos**
agrav**abas**	agrav**abais**
agrav**aba**	agrav**aban**
pretérito	
agrav**é**	agrav**amos**
agrav**aste**	agrav**asteis**
agrav**ó**	agrav**aron**
futuro	
agravar**é**	agravar**emos**
agravar**ás**	agravar**éis**
agravar**á**	agravar**án**
condicional simple	
agravar**ía**	agravar**íamos**
agravar**ías**	agravar**íais**
agravar**ía**	agravar**ían**
presente de subjuntivo	
agrav**e**	agrav**emos**
agrav**es**	agrav**éis**
agrav**e**	agrav**en**
imperfecto de subjuntivo	
agravar**a**	agravár**amos**
agravar**as**	agravar**ais**
agravar**a**	agravar**an**
OR	
agravas**e**	agravás**emos**
agravas**es**	agravas**eis**
agravas**e**	agravas**en**
imperativo	
—	agravemos
agrava; no agraves	agravad; no agravéis
agrave	agraven

SINGULAR	PLURAL
perfecto de indicativo	
he agravado	**hemos** agravado
has agravado	**habéis** agravado
ha agravado	**han** agravado
pluscuamperfecto de indicativo	
había agravado	**habíamos** agravado
habías agravado	**habíais** agravado
había agravado	**habían** agravado
pretérito anterior	
hube agravado	**hubimos** agravado
hubiste agravado	**hubisteis** agravado
hubo agravado	**hubieron** agravado
futuro perfecto	
habré agravado	**habremos** agravado
habrás agravado	**habréis** agravado
habrá agravado	**habrán** agravado
condicional compuesto	
habría agravado	**habríamos** agravado
habrías agravado	**habríais** agravado
habría agravado	**habrían** agravado
perfecto de subjuntivo	
haya agravado	**hayamos** agravado
hayas agravado	**hayáis** agravado
haya agravado	**hayan** agravado
pluscuamperfecto de subjuntivo	
hubiera agravado	**hubiéramos** agravado
hubieras agravado	**hubierais** agravado
hubiera agravado	**hubieran** agravado
OR	
hubiese agravado	**hubiésemos** agravado
hubieses agravado	**hubieseis** agravado
hubiese agravado	**hubiesen** agravado

to add, to aggregate **agregar**

gerundio **agregando** participio de pasado **agregado**

SINGULAR	PLURAL
presente de indicativo	
agreg**o**	agreg**amos**
agreg**as**	agreg**áis**
agreg**a**	agreg**an**
imperfecto de indicativo	
agreg**aba**	agreg**ábamos**
agreg**abas**	agreg**abais**
agreg**aba**	agreg**aban**
pretérito	
agregu**é**	agreg**amos**
agreg**aste**	agreg**asteis**
agreg**ó**	agreg**aron**
futuro	
agregar**é**	agregar**emos**
agregar**ás**	agregar**éis**
agregar**á**	agregar**án**
condicional simple	
agregar**ía**	agregar**íamos**
agregar**ías**	agregar**íais**
agregar**ía**	agregar**ían**
presente de subjuntivo	
agregu**e**	agregu**emos**
agregu**es**	agregu**éis**
agregu**e**	agregu**en**
imperfecto de subjuntivo	
agregar**a**	agregár**amos**
agregar**as**	agregar**ais**
agregar**a**	agregar**an**
OR	
agregas**e**	agregás**emos**
agregas**es**	agregas**eis**
agregas**e**	agregas**en**
imperativo	
—	agreguemos
agrega;	agregad;
no agregues;	no agreguéis
agregue	agreguen

SINGULAR	PLURAL
perfecto de indicativo	
he agregado	**hemos** agregado
has agregado	**habéis** agregado
ha agregado	**han** agregado
pluscuamperfecto de indicativo	
había agregado	**habíamos** agregado
habías agregado	**habíais** agregado
había agregado	**habían** agregado
pretérito anterior	
hube agregado	**hubimos** agregado
hubiste agregado	**hubisteis** agregado
hubo agregado	**hubieron** agregado
futuro perfecto	
habré agregado	**habremos** agregado
habrás agregado	**habréis** agregado
habrá agregado	**habrán** agregado
condicional compuesto	
habría agregado	**habríamos** agregado
habrías agregado	**habríais** agregado
habría agregado	**habrían** agregado
perfecto de subjuntivo	
haya agregado	**hayamos** agregado
hayas agregado	**hayáis** agregado
haya agregado	**hayan** agregado
pluscuamperfecto de subjuntivo	
hubiera agregado	**hubiéramos** agregado
hubieras agregado	**hubierais** agregado
hubiera agregado	**hubieran** agregado
OR	
hubiese agregado	**hubiésemos** agregado
hubieses agregado	**hubieseis** agregado
hubiese agregado	**hubiesen** agregado

agrupar — to group, to form groups

gerundio **agrupando** — participio de pasado **agrupado**

SINGULAR	PLURAL	SINGULAR	PLURAL
presente de indicativo		perfecto de indicativo	
agrup**o**	agrup**amos**	**he** agrupado	**hemos** agrupado
agrup**as**	agrup**áis**	**has** agrupado	**habéis** agrupado
agrup**a**	agrup**an**	**ha** agrupado	**han** agrupado
imperfecto de indicativo		pluscuamperfecto de indicativo	
agrup**aba**	agrup**ábamos**	**había** agrupado	**habíamos** agrupado
agrup**abas**	agrup**abais**	**habías** agrupado	**habíais** agrupado
agrup**aba**	agrup**aban**	**había** agrupado	**habían** agrupado
pretérito		pretérito anterior	
agrup**é**	agrup**amos**	**hube** agrupado	**hubimos** agrupado
agrup**aste**	agrup**asteis**	**hubiste** agrupado	**hubisteis** agrupado
agrup**ó**	agrup**aron**	**hubo** agrupado	**hubieron** agrupado
futuro		futuro perfecto	
agrupar**é**	agrupar**emos**	**habré** agrupado	**habremos** agrupado
agrupar**ás**	agrupar**éis**	**habrás** agrupado	**habréis** agrupado
agrupar**á**	agrupar**án**	**habrá** agrupado	**habrán** agrupado
condicional simple		condicional compuesto	
agrupar**ía**	agrupar**íamos**	**habría** agrupado	**habríamos** agrupado
agrupar**ías**	agrupar**íais**	**habrías** agrupado	**habríais** agrupado
agrupar**ía**	agrupar**ían**	**habría** agrupado	**habrían** agrupado
presente de subjuntivo		perfecto de subjuntivo	
agrup**e**	agrup**emos**	**haya** agrupado	**hayamos** agrupado
agrup**es**	agrup**éis**	**hayas** agrupado	**hayáis** agrupado
agrup**e**	agrup**en**	**haya** agrupado	**hayan** agrupado
imperfecto de subjuntivo		pluscuamperfecto de subjuntivo	
agrupar**a**	agrupár**amos**	**hubiera** agrupado	**hubiéramos** agrupado
agrupar**as**	agrupar**ais**	**hubieras** agrupado	**hubierais** agrupado
agrupar**a**	agrupar**an**	**hubiera** agrupado	**hubieran** agrupado
OR		OR	
agrupas**e**	agrupás**emos**	**hubiese** agrupado	**hubiésemos** agrupado
agrupas**es**	agrupas**eis**	**hubieses** agrupado	**hubieseis** agrupado
agrupas**e**	agrupas**en**	**hubiese** agrupado	**hubiesen** agrupado

imperativo

—	agrupemos
agrupa;	agrupad;
no agrupes;	no agrupéis
agrupe	agrupen

gerundio **aguantando** participio de pasado **aguantado**

SINGULAR	PLURAL
presente de indicativo	
aguanto	aguantamos
aguantas	aguantáis
aguanta	aguantan
imperfecto de indicativo	
aguantaba	aguantábamos
aguantabas	aguantabais
aguantaba	aguantaban
pretérito	
aguanté	aguantamos
aguantaste	aguantasteis
aguantó	aguantaron
futuro	
aguantaré	aguantaremos
aguantarás	aguantaréis
aguantará	aguantarán
condicional simple	
aguantaría	aguantaríamos
aguantarías	aguantaríais
aguantaría	aguantarían
presente de subjuntivo	
aguante	aguantemos
aguantes	aguantéis
aguante	aguanten
imperfecto de subjuntivo	
aguantara	aguantáramos
aguantaras	aguantarais
aguantara	aguantaran
OR	
aguantase	aguantásemos
aguantases	aguantaseis
aguantase	aguantasen
imperativo	
—	aguantemos
aguanta; no aguantes	aguantad; no aguantéis
aguante	aguanten

SINGULAR	PLURAL
perfecto de indicativo	
he aguantado	hemos aguantado
has aguantado	habéis aguantado
ha aguantado	han aguantado
pluscuamperfecto de indicativo	
había aguantado	habíamos aguantado
habías aguantado	habíais aguantado
había aguantado	habían aguantado
pretérito anterior	
hube aguantado	hubimos aguantado
hubiste aguantado	hubisteis aguantado
hubo aguantado	hubieron aguantado
futuro perfecto	
habré aguantado	habremos aguantado
habrás aguantado	habréis aguantado
habrá aguantado	habrán aguantado
condicional compuesto	
habría aguantado	habríamos aguantado
habrías aguantado	habríais aguantado
habría aguantado	habrían aguantado
perfecto de subjuntivo	
haya aguantado	hayamos aguantado
hayas aguantado	hayáis aguantado
haya aguantado	hayan aguantado
pluscuamperfecto de subjuntivo	
hubiera aguantado	hubiéramos aguantado
hubieras aguantado	hubierais aguantado
hubiera aguantado	hubieran aguantado
OR	
hubiese aguantado	hubiésemos aguantado
hubieses aguantado	hubieseis aguantado
hubiese aguantado	hubiesen aguantado

ahorrar — to save, to economize

gerundio **ahorrando** — participio de pasado **ahorrado**

SINGULAR	PLURAL
presente de indicativo	
ahorr**o**	ahorr**amos**
ahorr**as**	ahorr**áis**
ahorr**a**	ahorr**an**
imperfecto de indicativo	
ahorr**aba**	ahorr**ábamos**
ahorr**abas**	ahorr**abais**
ahorr**aba**	ahorr**aban**
pretérito	
ahorr**é**	ahorr**amos**
ahorr**aste**	ahorr**asteis**
ahorr**ó**	ahorr**aron**
futuro	
ahorrar**é**	ahorrar**emos**
ahorrar**ás**	ahorrar**éis**
ahorrar**á**	ahorrar**án**
condicional simple	
ahorrar**ía**	ahorrar**íamos**
ahorrar**ías**	ahorrar**íais**
ahorrar**ía**	ahorrar**ían**
presente de subjuntivo	
ahorr**e**	ahorr**emos**
ahorr**es**	ahorr**éis**
ahorr**e**	ahorr**en**
imperfecto de subjuntivo	
ahorrar**a**	ahorrár**amos**
ahorrar**as**	ahorrar**ais**
ahorrar**a**	ahorrar**an**
OR	
ahorras**e**	ahorrás**emos**
ahorras**es**	ahorras**eis**
ahorras**e**	ahorras**en**
imperativo	
—	ahorremos
ahorra; no ahorres	ahorrad; no ahorréis
ahorre	ahorren

SINGULAR	PLURAL
perfecto de indicativo	
he ahorrado	**hemos** ahorrado
has ahorrado	**habéis** ahorrado
ha ahorrado	**han** ahorrado
pluscuamperfecto de indicativo	
había ahorrado	**habíamos** ahorrado
habías ahorrado	**habíais** ahorrado
había ahorrado	**habían** ahorrado
pretérito anterior	
hube ahorrado	**hubimos** ahorrado
hubiste ahorrado	**hubisteis** ahorrado
hubo ahorrado	**hubieron** ahorrado
futuro perfecto	
habré ahorrado	**habremos** ahorrado
habrás ahorrado	**habréis** ahorrado
habrá ahorrado	**habrán** ahorrado
condicional compuesto	
habría ahorrado	**habríamos** ahorrado
habrías ahorrado	**habríais** ahorrado
habría ahorrado	**habrían** ahorrado
perfecto de subjuntivo	
haya ahorrado	**hayamos** ahorrado
hayas ahorrado	**hayáis** ahorrado
haya ahorrado	**hayan** ahorrado
pluscuamperfecto de subjuntivo	
hubiera ahorrado	**hubiéramos** ahorrado
hubieras ahorrado	**hubierais** ahorrado
hubiera ahorrado	**hubieran** ahorrado
OR	
hubiese ahorrado	**hubiésemos** ahorrado
hubieses ahorrado	**hubieseis** ahorrado
hubiese ahorrado	**hubiesen** ahorrado

to reach, to suffice — alcanzar

gerundio **alcanzando** — participio de pasado **alcanzado**

presente de indicativo

SINGULAR	PLURAL
alcanz**o**	alcanz**amos**
alcanz**as**	alcanz**áis**
alcanz**a**	alcanz**an**

imperfecto de indicativo

SINGULAR	PLURAL
alcanz**aba**	alcanz**ábamos**
alcanz**abas**	alcanz**abais**
alcanz**aba**	alcanz**aban**

pretérito

SINGULAR	PLURAL
alcanc**é**	alcanz**amos**
alcanz**aste**	alcanz**asteis**
alcanz**ó**	alcanz**aron**

futuro

SINGULAR	PLURAL
alcanzar**é**	alcanzar**emos**
alcanzar**ás**	alcanzar**éis**
alcanzar**á**	alcanzar**án**

condicional simple

SINGULAR	PLURAL
alcanzar**ía**	alcanzar**íamos**
alcanzar**ías**	alcanzar**íais**
alcanzar**ía**	alcanzar**ían**

presente de subjuntivo

SINGULAR	PLURAL
alcanc**e**	alcanc**emos**
alcanc**es**	alcanc**éis**
alcanc**e**	alcanc**en**

imperfecto de subjuntivo

SINGULAR	PLURAL
alcanzar**a**	alcanzár**amos**
alcanzar**as**	alcanzar**ais**
alcanzar**a**	alcanzar**an**
OR	
alcanzas**e**	alcanzás**emos**
alcanzas**es**	alcanzas**eis**
alcanzas**e**	alcanzas**en**

imperativo

SINGULAR	PLURAL
—	alcancemos
alcanza; no alcances	alcanzad; no alcancéis
alcance	alcancen

perfecto de indicativo

SINGULAR	PLURAL
he alcanzado	**hemos** alcanzado
has alcanzado	**habéis** alcanzado
ha alcanzado	**han** alcanzado

pluscuamperfecto de indicativo

SINGULAR	PLURAL
había alcanzado	**habíamos** alcanzado
habías alcanzado	**habíais** alcanzado
había alcanzado	**habían** alcanzado

pretérito anterior

SINGULAR	PLURAL
hube alcanzado	**hubimos** alcanzado
hubiste alcanzado	**hubisteis** alcanzado
hubo alcanzado	**hubieron** alcanzado

futuro perfecto

SINGULAR	PLURAL
habré alcanzado	**habremos** alcanzado
habrás alcanzado	**habréis** alcanzado
habrá alcanzado	**habrán** alcanzado

condicional compuesto

SINGULAR	PLURAL
habría alcanzado	**habríamos** alcanzado
habrías alcanzado	**habríais** alcanzado
habría alcanzado	**habrían** alcanzado

perfecto de subjuntivo

SINGULAR	PLURAL
haya alcanzado	**hayamos** alcanzado
hayas alcanzado	**hayáis** alcanzado
haya alcanzado	**hayan** alcanzado

pluscuamperfecto de subjuntivo

SINGULAR	PLURAL
hubiera alcanzado	**hubiéramos** alcanzado
hubieras alcanzado	**hubierais** alcanzado
hubiera alcanzado	**hubieran** alcanzado
OR	
hubiese alcanzado	**hubiésemos** alcanzado
hubieses alcanzado	**hubieseis** alcanzado
hubiese alcanzado	**hubiesen** alcanzado

alegrarse — to be glad

gerundio **alegrándose** participio de pasado **alegrado**

SINGULAR	PLURAL	SINGULAR	PLURAL
presente de indicativo		perfecto de indicativo	
me alegr**o**	nos alegr**amos**	**me he** alegrado	**nos hemos** alegrado
te alegr**as**	os alegr**áis**	**te has** alegrado	**os habéis** alegrado
se alegr**a**	se alegr**an**	**se ha** alegrado	**se han** alegrado
imperfecto de indicativo		pluscuamperfecto de indicativo	
me alegr**aba**	nos alegr**ábamos**	**me había** alegrado	**nos habíamos** alegrado
te alegr**abas**	os alegr**abais**	**te habías** alegrado	**os habíais** alegrado
se alegr**aba**	se alegr**aban**	**se había** alegrado	**se habían** alegrado
pretérito		pretérito anterior	
me alegr**é**	nos alegr**amos**	**me hube** alegrado	**nos hubimos** alegrado
te alegr**aste**	os alegr**asteis**	**te hubiste** alegrado	**os hubisteis** alegrado
se alegr**ó**	se alegr**aron**	**se hubo** alegrado	**se hubieron** alegrado
futuro		futuro perfecto	
me alegrar**é**	nos alegrar**emos**	**me habré** alegrado	**nos habremos** alegrado
te alegrar**ás**	os alegrar**éis**	**te habrás** alegrado	**os habréis** alegrado
se alegrar**á**	se alegrar**án**	**se habrá** alegrado	**se habrán** alegrado
condicional simple		condicional compuesto	
me alegrar**ía**	nos alegrar**íamos**	**me habría** alegrado	**nos habríamos** alegrado
te alegrar**ías**	os alegrar**íais**	**te habrías** alegrado	**os habríais** alegrado
se alegrar**ía**	se alegrar**ían**	**se habría** alegrado	**se habrían** alegrado
presente de subjuntivo		perfecto de subjuntivo	
me alegr**e**	nos alegr**emos**	**me haya** alegrado	**nos hayamos** alegrado
te alegr**es**	os alegr**éis**	**te hayas** alegrado	**os hayáis** alegrado
se alegr**e**	se alegr**en**	**se haya** alegrado	**se hayan** alegrado
imperfecto de subjuntivo		pluscuamperfecto de subjuntivo	
me alegrar**a**	nos alegrár**amos**	**me hubiera** alegrado	**nos hubiéramos** alegrado
te alegrar**as**	os alegrar**ais**	**te hubieras** alegrado	**os hubierais** alegrado
se alegrar**a**	se alegrar**an**	**se hubiera** alegrado	**se hubieran** alegrado
OR		OR	
me alegras**e**	nos alegrás**emos**	**me hubiese** alegrado	**nos hubiésemos** alegrado
te alegras**es**	os alegras**eis**	**te hubieses** alegrado	**os hubieseis** alegrado
se alegras**e**	se alegras**en**	**se hubiese** alegrado	**se hubiesen** alegrado

imperativo

—	alegrémonos
alégrate;	alegraos;
no te alegres	no os alegréis
alégrese	alégrense

gerundio **almorzando** participio de pasado **almorzado**

SINGULAR	PLURAL	SINGULAR	PLURAL
presente de indicativo		perfecto de indicativo	
almuerz**o**	almorz**amos**	**he** almorzado	**hemos** almorzado
almuerz**as**	almorz**áis**	**has** almorzado	**habéis** almorzado
almuerz**a**	almuerz**an**	**ha** almorzado	**han** almorzado
imperfecto de indicativo		pluscuamperfecto de indicativo	
almorz**aba**	almorz**ábamos**	**había** almorzado	**habíamos** almorzado
almorz**abas**	almorz**abais**	**habías** almorzado	**habíais** almorzado
almorz**aba**	almorz**aban**	**había** almorzado	**habían** almorzado
pretérito		pretérito anterior	
almorc**é**	almorz**amos**	**hube** almorzado	**hubimos** almorzado
almorz**aste**	almorz**asteis**	**hubiste** almorzado	**hubisteis** almorzado
almorz**ó**	almorz**aron**	**hubo** almorzado	**hubieron** almorzado
futuro		futuro perfecto	
almorzar**é**	almorzar**emos**	**habré** almorzado	**habremos** almorzado
almorzar**ás**	almorzar**éis**	**habrás** almorzado	**habréis** almorzado
almorzar**á**	almorzar**án**	**habrá** almorzado	**habrán** almorzado
condicional simple		condicional compuesto	
almorzar**ía**	almorzar**íamos**	**habría** almorzado	**habríamos** almorzado
almorzar**ías**	almorzar**íais**	**habrías** almorzado	**habríais** almorzado
almorzar**ía**	almorzar**ían**	**habría** almorzado	**habrían** almorzado
presente de subjuntivo		perfecto de subjuntivo	
almuerc**e**	almorc**emos**	**haya** almorzado	**hayamos** almorzado
almuerc**es**	almorc**éis**	**hayas** almorzado	**hayáis** almorzado
almuerc**e**	almuerc**en**	**haya** almorzado	**hayan** almorzado
imperfecto de subjuntivo		pluscuamperfecto de subjuntivo	
almorzar**a**	almorzár**amos**	**hubiera** almorzado	**hubiéramos** almorzado
almorzar**as**	almorzar**ais**	**hubieras** almorzado	**hubierais** almorzado
almorzar**a**	almorzar**an**	**hubiera** almorzado	**hubieran** almorzado
OR		OR	
almorzas**e**	almorzás**emos**	**hubiese** almorzado	**hubiésemos** almorzado
almorzas**es**	almorzas**eis**	**hubieses** almorzado	**hubieseis** almorzado
almorzas**e**	almorzas**en**	**hubiese** almorzado	**hubiesen** almorzado
imperativo			
—	almorcemos		
almuerza; no almuerces	almorzad; no almorcéis		
almuerce	almuercen		

alquilar — to rent

gerundio **alquilando** participio de pasado **alquilado**

SINGULAR	PLURAL	SINGULAR	PLURAL
presente de indicativo		perfecto de indicativo	
alquil**o**	alquil**amos**	**he** alquilado	**hemos** alquilado
alquil**as**	alquil**áis**	**has** alquilado	**habéis** alquilado
alauil**a**	alquil**an**	**ha** alquilado	**han** alquilado
imperfecto de indicativo		pluscuamperfecto de indicativo	
alquil**aba**	alquil**ábamos**	**había** alquilado	**habíamos** alquilado
alquil**abas**	alquil**abais**	**habías** alquilado	**habíais** alquilado
alquil**aba**	alquil**aban**	**había** alquilado	**habían** alquilado
pretérito		pretérito anterior	
alquil**é**	alquil**amos**	**hube** alquilado	**hubimos** alquilado
alquil**aste**	alquil**asteis**	**hubiste** alquilado	**hubisteis** alquilado
alquil**ó**	alquil**aron**	**hubo** alquilado	**hubieron** alquilado
futuro		futuro perfecto	
alquilar**é**	alquilar**emos**	**habré** alquilado	**habremos** alquilado
alquilar**ás**	alquilar**éis**	**habrás** alquilado	**habréis** alquilado
alquilar**á**	alquilar**án**	**habrá** alquilado	**habrán** alquilado
condicional simple		condicional compuesto	
alquilar**ía**	alquilar**íamos**	**habría** alquilado	**habríamos** alquilado
alquilar**ías**	alquilar**íais**	**habrías** alquilado	**habríais** alquilado
alquilar**ía**	alquilar**ían**	**habría** alquilado	**habrían** alquilado
presente de subjuntivo		perfecto de subjuntivo	
alquil**e**	alquil**emos**	**haya** alquilado	**hayamos** alquilado
alquil**es**	alquil**éis**	**hayas** alquilado	**hayáis** alquilado
alquil**e**	alquil**en**	**haya** alquilado	**hayan** alquilado
imperfecto de subjuntivo		pluscuamperfecto de subjuntivo	
alquilar**a**	alquilár**amos**	**hubiera** alquilado	**hubiéramos** alquilado
alquilar**as**	alquilar**ais**	**hubieras** alquilado	**hubierais** alquilado
alquilar**a**	alquilar**an**	**hubiera** alquilado	**hubieran** alquilado
OR		OR	
alquilas**e**	alquilás**emos**	**hubiese** alquilado	**hubiésemos** alquilado
alquilas**es**	alquilas**eis**	**hubieses** alquilado	**hubieseis** alquilado
alquilas**e**	alquilas**en**	**hubiese** alquilado	**hubiesen** alquilado

imperativo

—	alquilemos
alquila; no alquiles	alquilad; no alquiléis
alquile	alquilen

to illuminate, to light — alumbrar

gerundio **alumbrando** participio de pasado **alumbrado**

SINGULAR	PLURAL
presente de indicativo	
alumbr**o**	alumbr**amos**
alumbr**as**	alumbr**áis**
alumbr**a**	alumbr**an**
imperfecto de indicativo	
alumbr**aba**	alumbr**ábamos**
alumbr**abas**	alumbr**abais**
alumbr**aba**	alumbr**aban**
pretérito	
alumbr**é**	alumbr**amos**
alumbr**aste**	alumbr**asteis**
alumbr**ó**	alumbr**aron**
futuro	
alumbrar**é**	alumbrar**emos**
alumbrar**ás**	alumbrar**éis**
alumbrar**á**	alumbrar**án**
condicional simple	
alumbrar**ía**	alumbrar**íamos**
alumbrar**ías**	alumbrar**íais**
alumbrar**ía**	alumbrar**ían**
presente de subjuntivo	
alumbr**e**	alumbr**emos**
alumbr**es**	alumbr**éis**
alumbr**e**	alumbr**en**
imperfecto de subjuntivo	
alumbrar**a**	alumbrár**amos**
alumbrar**as**	alumbrar**ais**
alumbrar**a**	alumbrar**an**
OR	
alumbras**e**	alumbrás**emos**
alumbras**es**	alumbras**eis**
alumbras**e**	alumbras**en**
imperativo	
—	alumbremos
alumbra; no alumbres	alumbrad; no alumbréis
alumbre	alumbren

SINGULAR	PLURAL
perfecto de indicativo	
he alumbrado	**hemos** alumbrado
has alumbrado	**habéis** alumbrado
ha alumbrado	**han** alumbrado
pluscuamperfecto de indicativo	
había alumbrado	**habíamos** alumbrado
habías alumbrado	**habíais** alumbrado
había alumbrado	**habían** alumbrado
pretérito anterior	
hube alumbrado	**hubimos** alumbrado
hubiste alumbrado	**hubisteis** alumbrado
hubo alumbrado	**hubieron** alumbrado
futuro perfecto	
habré alumbrado	**habremos** alumbrado
habrás alumbrado	**habréis** alumbrado
habrá alumbrado	**habrán** alumbrado
condicional compuesto	
habría alumbrado	**habríamos** alumbrado
habrías alumbrado	**habríais** alumbrado
habría alumbrado	**habrían** alumbrado
perfecto de subjuntivo	
haya alumbrado	**hayamos** alumbrado
hayas alumbrado	**hayáis** alumbrado
haya alumbrado	**hayan** alumbrado
pluscuamperfecto de subjuntivo	
hubiera alumbrado	**hubiéramos** alumbrado
hubieras alumbrado	**hubierais** alumbrado
hubiera alumbrado	**hubieran** alumbrado
OR	
hubiese alumbrado	**hubiésemos** alumbrado
hubieses alumbrado	**hubieseis** alumbrado
hubiese alumbrado	**hubiesen** alumbrado

alzar — to lift, to pick up

gerundio **alzando** participio de pasado **alzado**

SINGULAR	PLURAL
presente de indicativo	
alz**o**	alz**amos**
alz**as**	alz**áis**
alz**a**	alz**an**
imperfecto de indicativo	
alz**aba**	alz**ábamos**
alz**abas**	alz**abais**
alz**aba**	alz**aban**
pretérito	
alc**é**	alz**amos**
alz**aste**	alz**asteis**
alz**ó**	alz**aron**
futuro	
alzar**é**	alzar**emos**
alzar**ás**	alzar**éis**
alzar**á**	alzar**án**
condicional simple	
alzar**ía**	alzar**íamos**
alzar**ías**	alzar**íais**
alzar**ía**	alzar**ían**
presente de subjuntivo	
alc**e**	alc**emos**
alc**es**	alc**éis**
alc**e**	alc**en**
imperfecto de subjuntivo	
alzar**a**	alzár**amos**
alzar**as**	alzar**ais**
alzar**a**	alzar**an**
OR	
alzas**e**	alzás**emos**
alzas**es**	alzas**eis**
alzas**e**	alzas**en**
imperativo	
—	alcemos
alza; no alces	alzad; no alcéis
alce	alcen

SINGULAR	PLURAL
perfecto de indicativo	
he alzado	**hemos** alzado
has alzado	**habéis** alzado
ha alzado	**han** alzado
pluscuamperfecto de indicativo	
había alzado	**habíamos** alzado
habías alzado	**habíais** alzado
había alzado	**habían** alzado
pretérito anterior	
hube alzado	**hubimos** alzado
hubiste alzado	**hubisteis** alzado
hubo alzado	**hubieron** alzado
futuro perfecto	
habré alzado	**habremos** alzado
habrás alzado	**habréis** alzado
habrá alzado	**habrán** alzado
condicional compuesto	
habría alzado	**habríamos** alzado
habrías alzado	**habríais** alzado
habría alzado	**habrían** alzado
perfecto de subjuntivo	
haya alzado	**hayamos** alzado
hayas alzado	**hayáis** alzado
haya alzado	**hayan** alzado
pluscuamperfecto de subjuntivo	
hubiera alzado	**hubiéramos** alzado
hubieras alzado	**hubierais** alzado
hubiera alzado	**hubieran** alzado
OR	
hubiese alzado	**hubiésemos** alzado
hubieses alzado	**hubieseis** alzado
hubiese alzado	**hubiesen** alzado

gerundio **amando** participio de pasado **amado**

SINGULAR	PLURAL	SINGULAR	PLURAL
presente de indicativo		perfecto de indicativo	
am**o**	am**amos**	**he** amado	**hemos** amado
am**as**	am**áis**	**has** amado	**habéis** amado
am**a**	am**an**	**ha** amado	**han** amado
imperfecto de indicativo		pluscuamperfecto de indicativo	
am**aba**	am**ábamos**	**había** amado	**habíamos** amado
am**abas**	am**abais**	**habías** amado	**habíais** amado
am**aba**	am**aban**	**había** amado	**habían** amado
pretérito		pretérito anterior	
am**é**	am**amos**	**hube** amado	**hubimos** amado
am**aste**	am**asteis**	**hubiste** amado	**hubisteis** amado
am**ó**	am**aron**	**hubo** amado	**hubieron** amado
futuro		futuro perfecto	
amar**é**	amar**emos**	**habré** amado	**habremos** amado
amar**ás**	amar**éis**	**habrás** amado	**habréis** amado
amar**á**	amar**án**	**habrá** amado	**habrán** amado
condicional simple		condicional compuesto	
amar**ía**	amar**íamos**	**habría** amado	**habríamos** amado
amar**ías**	amar**íais**	**habrías** amado	**habríais** amado
amar**ía**	amar**ían**	**habría** amado	**habrían** amado
presente de subjuntivo		perfecto de subjuntivo	
am**e**	am**emos**	**haya** amado	**hayamos** amado
am**es**	am**éis**	**hayas** amado	**hayáis** amado
am**e**	am**en**	**haya** amado	**hayan** amado
imperfecto de subjuntivo		pluscuamperfecto de subjuntivo	
amar**a**	amár**amos**	**hubiera** amado	**hubiéramos** amado
amar**as**	amar**ais**	**hubieras** amado	**hubierais** amado
amar**a**	amar**an**	**hubiera** amado	**hubieran** amado
OR		OR	
amas**e**	amás**emos**	**hubiese** amado	**hubiésemos** amado
amas**es**	amas**eis**	**hubieses** amado	**hubieseis** amado
amas**e**	amas**en**	**hubiese** amado	**hubiesen** amado

imperativo

—	amemos
ama; no ames	amad; no améis
ame	amen

A

añadir — to add

gerundio **añadiendo** | participio de pasado **añadido**

SINGULAR	PLURAL	SINGULAR	PLURAL
presente de indicativo		perfecto de indicativo	
añad**o**	añad**imos**	**he** añadido	**hemos** añadido
añad**es**	añad**ís**	**has** añadido	**habéis** añadido
añad**e**	añad**en**	**ha** añadido	**han** añadido
imperfecto de indicativo		pluscuamperfecto de indicativo	
añad**ía**	añad**íamos**	**había** añadido	**habíamos** añadido
añad**ías**	añad**íais**	**habías** añadido	**habíais** añadido
añad**ía**	añad**ían**	**había** añadido	**habían** añadido
pretérito		pretérito anterior	
añad**í**	añad**imos**	**hube** añadido	**hubimos** añadido
añad**iste**	añad**isteis**	**hubiste** añadido	**hubisteis** añadido
añadi**ó**	añad**ieron**	**hubo** añadido	**hubieron** añadido
futuro		futuro perfecto	
añadir**é**	añadir**emos**	**habré** añadido	**habremos** añadido
añadir**ás**	añadir**éis**	**habrás** añadido	**habréis** añadido
añadir**á**	añadir**án**	**habrá** añadido	**habrán** añadido
condicional simple		condicional compuesto	
añadir**ía**	añadir**íamos**	**habría** añadido	**habríamos** añadido
añadir**ías**	añadir**íais**	**habrías** añadido	**habríais** añadido
añadir**ía**	añadir**ían**	**habría** añadido	**habrían** añadido
presente de subjuntivo		perfecto de subjuntivo	
añad**a**	añad**amos**	**haya** añadido	**hayamos** añadido
añad**as**	añad**áis**	**hayas** añadido	**hayáis** añadido
añad**a**	añad**an**	**haya** añadido	**hayan** añadido
imperfecto de subjuntivo		pluscuamperfecto de subjuntivo	
añadier**a**	añadiér**amos**	**hubiera** añadido	**hubiéramos** añadido
añadier**as**	añadier**ais**	**hubieras** añadido	**hubierais** añadido
añadier**a**	añadier**an**	**hubiera** añadido	**hubieran** añadido
OR		OR	
añadies**e**	añadiés**emos**	**hubiese** añadido	**hubiésemos** añadido
añadies**es**	añadies**eis**	**hubieses** añadido	**hubieseis** añadido
añadies**e**	añadies**en**	**hubiese** añadido	**hubiesen** añadido

imperativo

—	añadamos
añade; no añadas	añadid; no añadáis
añada	añadan

SINGULAR	PLURAL
presente de indicativo	
analiz**o**	analiz**amos**
analiz**as**	analiz**áis**
analiz**a**	analiz**an**
imperfecto de indicativo	
analiz**aba**	analiz**ábamos**
analiz**abas**	analiz**abais**
analiz**aba**	analiz**aban**
pretérito	
analic**é**	analiz**amos**
analiz**aste**	analiz**asteis**
analiz**ó**	analiz**aron**
futuro	
analizar**é**	analizar**emos**
analizar**ás**	analizar**éis**
analizar**á**	analizar**án**
condicional simple	
analizar**ía**	analizar**íamos**
analizar**ías**	analizar**íais**
analizar**ía**	analizar**ían**
presente de subjuntivo	
analic**e**	analic**emos**
analic**es**	analic**éis**
analic**e**	analic**en**
imperfecto de subjuntivo	
analizar**a**	analizár**amos**
analizar**as**	analizar**ais**
analizar**a**	analizar**an**
OR	
analizas**e**	analizás**emos**
analizas**es**	analizas**eis**
analizas**e**	analizas**en**
imperativo	
—	analicemos
analiza; no analices	analizad; no analicéis
analice	analicen

SINGULAR	PLURAL
perfecto de indicativo	
he analizado	**hemos** analizado
has analizado	**habéis** analizado
ha analizado	**han** analizado
pluscuamperfecto de indicativo	
había analizado	**habíamos** analizado
habías analizado	**habíais** analizado
había analizado	**habían** analizado
pretérito anterior	
hube analizado	**hubimos** analizado
hubiste analizado	**hubisteis** analizado
hubo analizado	**hubieron** analizado
futuro perfecto	
habré analizado	**habremos** analizado
habrás analizado	**habréis** analizado
habrá analizado	**habrán** analizado
condicional compuesto	
habría analizado	**habríamos** analizado
habrías analizado	**habríais** analizado
habría analizado	**habrían** analizado
perfecto de subjuntivo	
haya analizado	**hayamos** analizado
hayas analizado	**hayáis** analizado
haya analizado	**hayan** analizado
pluscuamperfecto de subjuntivo	
hubiera analizado	**hubiéramos** analizado
hubieras analizado	**hubierais** analizado
hubiera analizado	**hubieran** analizado
OR	
hubiese analizado	**hubiésemos** analizado
hubieses analizado	**hubieseis** analizado
hubiese analizado	**hubiesen** analizado

andar — to walk

gerundio **andando** — participio de pasado **andado**

presente de indicativo

SINGULAR	PLURAL
and**o**	and**amos**
and**as**	and**áis**
and**a**	and**an**

imperfecto de indicativo

SINGULAR	PLURAL
and**aba**	and**ábamos**
and**abas**	and**abais**
and**aba**	and**aban**

pretérito

SINGULAR	PLURAL
anduv**e**	anduv**imos**
anduv**iste**	anduv**isteis**
anduv**o**	anduv**ieron**

futuro

SINGULAR	PLURAL
andar**é**	andar**emos**
andar**ás**	andar**éis**
andar**á**	andar**án**

condicional simple

SINGULAR	PLURAL
andar**ía**	andar**íamos**
andar**ías**	andar**íais**
andar**ía**	andar**ían**

presente de subjuntivo

SINGULAR	PLURAL
and**e**	and**emos**
and**es**	and**éis**
and**e**	and**en**

imperfecto de subjuntivo

SINGULAR	PLURAL
anduvier**a**	anduviér**amos**
anduvier**as**	anduvier**ais**
anduvier**a**	anduvier**an**
OR	
anduvies**e**	anduviés**emos**
anduvies**es**	anduvies**eis**
anduvies**e**	anduvies**en**

imperativo

SINGULAR	PLURAL
—	andemos
anda; no andes	andad; no andéis
ande	anden

perfecto de indicativo

SINGULAR	PLURAL
he andado	**hemos** andado
has andado	**habéis** andado
ha andado	**han** andado

pluscuamperfecto de indicativo

SINGULAR	PLURAL
había andado	**habíamos** andado
habías andado	**habíais** andado
había andado	**habían** andado

pretérito anterior

SINGULAR	PLURAL
hube andado	**hubimos** andado
hubiste andado	**hubisteis** andado
hubo andado	**hubieron** andado

futuro perfecto

SINGULAR	PLURAL
habré andado	**habremos** andado
habrás andado	**habréis** andado
habrá andado	**habrán** andado

condicional compuesto

SINGULAR	PLURAL
habría andado	**habríamos** andado
habrías andado	**habríais** andado
habría andado	**habrían** andado

perfecto de subjuntivo

SINGULAR	PLURAL
haya andado	**hayamos** andado
hayas andado	**hayáis** andado
haya andado	**hayan** andado

pluscuamperfecto de subjuntivo

SINGULAR	PLURAL
hubiera andado	**hubiéramos** andado
hubieras andado	**hubierais** andado
hubiera andado	**hubieran** andado
OR	
hubiese andado	**hubiésemos** andado
hubieses andado	**hubieseis** andado
hubiese andado	**hubiesen** andado

gerundio **anocheciendo** participio de pasado **anochecido**

SINGULAR	PLURAL	SINGULAR	PLURAL
presente de indicativo		perfecto de indicativo	
anochezc**o**	anochec**emos**	**he** anochecido	**hemos** anochecido
anochec**es**	anochec**éis**	**has** anochecido	**habéis** anochecido
anochec**e**	anochec**en**	**ha** anochecido	**han** anochecido
imperfecto de indicativo		pluscuamperfecto de indicativo	
anochec**ía**	anochec**íamos**	**había** anochecido	**habíamos** anochecido
anochec**ías**	anochec**íais**	**habías** anochecido	**habíais** anochecido
anochec**ía**	anochec**ían**	**había** anochecido	**habían** anochecido
pretérito		pretérito anterior	
anochec**í**	anochec**imos**	**hube** anochecido	**hubimos** anochecido
anochec**iste**	anochec**isteis**	**hubiste** anochecido	**hubisteis** anochecido
anocheci**ó**	anochec**ieron**	**hubo** anochecido	**hubieron** anochecido
futuro		futuro perfecto	
anochecer**é**	anochecer**emos**	**habré** anochecido	**habremos** anochecido
anochecer**ás**	anochecer**éis**	**habrás** anochecido	**habréis** anochecido
anochecer**á**	anochecer**án**	**habrá** anochecido	**habrán** anochecido
condicional simple		condicional compuesto	
anochecer**ía**	anochecer**íamos**	**habría** anochecido	**habríamos** anochecido
anochecer**ías**	anochecer**íais**	**habrías** anochecido	**habríais** anochecido
anochecer**ía**	anochecer**ían**	**habría** anochecido	**habrían** anochecido
presente de subjuntivo		perfecto de subjuntivo	
anochezc**a**	anochezc**amos**	**haya** anochecido	**hayamos** anochecido
anochezc**as**	anochezc**áis**	**hayas** anochecido	**hayáis** anochecido
anochezc**a**	anochezc**an**	**haya** anochecido	**hayan** anochecido
imperfecto de subjuntivo		pluscuamperfecto de subjuntivo	
anochecier**a**	anocheciér**amos**	**hubiera** anochecido	**hubiéramos** anochecido
anochecier**as**	anochecier**ais**	**hubieras** anochecido	**hubierais** anochecido
anochecier**a**	anochecier**an**	**hubiera** anochecido	**hubieran** anochecido
OR		OR	
anochecies**e**	anocheciés**emos**	**hubiese** anochecido	**hubiésemos** anochecido
anochecies**es**	anochecies**eis**	**hubieses** anochecido	**hubieseis** anochecido
anochecies**e**	anochecies**en**	**hubiese** anochecido	**hubiesen** anochecido

imperativo

SINGULAR	PLURAL
—	anochezcamos
anochece; no anochezcas	anocheced; no anochezcáis
anochezca	anochezcan

anunciar — to announce, to foretell

gerundio **anunciando** — participio de pasado **anunciado**

SINGULAR	PLURAL
presente de indicativo	
anunci**o**	anunci**amos**
anunci**as**	anunci**áis**
anunci**a**	anunci**an**
imperfecto de indicativo	
anunci**aba**	anunci**ábamos**
anunci**abas**	anunci**abais**
anunci**aba**	anunci**aban**
pretérito	
anunci**é**	anunci**amos**
anunci**aste**	anunci**asteis**
anunci**ó**	anunci**aron**
futuro	
anunciar**é**	anunciar**emos**
anunciar**ás**	anunciar**éis**
anunciar**á**	anunciar**án**
condicional simple	
anunciar**ía**	anunciar**íamos**
anunciar**ías**	anunciar**íais**
anunciar**ía**	anunciar**ían**
presente de subjuntivo	
anunci**e**	anunci**emos**
anunci**es**	anunci**éis**
anunci**e**	anunci**en**
imperfecto de subjuntivo	
anunciar**a**	anunciár**amos**
anunciar**as**	anunciar**ais**
anunciar**a**	anunciar**an**
OR	
anuncias**e**	anunciás**emos**
anuncias**es**	anuncias**eis**
anuncias**e**	anuncias**en**
imperativo	
—	anunciemos
anuncia; no anuncies	anunciad; no anunciéis
anuncie	anuncien

SINGULAR	PLURAL
perfecto de indicativo	
he anunciado	**hemos** anunciado
has anunciado	**habéis** anunciado
ha anunciado	**han** anunciado
pluscuamperfecto de indicativo	
había anunciado	**habíamos** anunciado
habías anunciado	**habíais** anunciado
había anunciado	**habían** anunciado
pretérito anterior	
hube anunciado	**hubimos** anunciado
hubiste anunciado	**hubisteis** anunciado
hubo anunciado	**hubieron** anunciado
futuro perfecto	
habré anunciado	**habremos** anunciado
habrás anunciado	**habréis** anunciado
habrá anunciado	**habrán** anunciado
condicional compuesto	
habría anunciado	**habríamos** anunciado
habrías anunciado	**habríais** anunciado
habría anunciado	**habrían** anunciado
perfecto de subjuntivo	
haya anunciado	**hayamos** anunciado
hayas anunciado	**hayáis** anunciado
haya anunciado	**hayan** anunciado
pluscuamperfecto de subjuntivo	
hubiera anunciado	**hubiéramos** anunciado
hubieras anunciado	**hubierais** anunciado
hubiera anunciado	**hubieran** anunciado
OR	
hubiese anunciado	**hubiésemos** anunciado
hubieses anunciado	**hubieseis** anunciado
hubiese anunciado	**hubiesen** anunciado

to put out, to turn off — apagar

gerundio **apagando** participio de pasado **apagado**

presente de indicativo

SINGULAR	PLURAL
apag**o**	apag**amos**
apag**as**	apag**áis**
apag**a**	apag**an**

imperfecto de indicativo

SINGULAR	PLURAL
apag**aba**	apag**ábamos**
apag**abas**	apag**abais**
apag**aba**	apag**aban**

pretérito

SINGULAR	PLURAL
apagu**é**	apag**amos**
apag**aste**	apag**asteis**
apag**ó**	apag**aron**

futuro

SINGULAR	PLURAL
apagar**é**	apagar**emos**
apagar**ás**	apagar**éis**
apagar**á**	apagar**án**

condicional simple

SINGULAR	PLURAL
apagar**ía**	apagar**íamos**
apagar**ías**	apagar**íais**
apagar**ía**	apagar**ían**

presente de subjuntivo

SINGULAR	PLURAL
apagu**e**	apagu**emos**
apagu**es**	apagu**éis**
apagu**e**	apagu**en**

imperfecto de subjuntivo

SINGULAR	PLURAL
apagar**a**	apagár**amos**
apagar**as**	apagar**ais**
apagar**a**	apagar**an**
OR	
apagas**e**	apagás**emos**
apagas**es**	apagas**eis**
apagas**e**	apagas**en**

imperativo

SINGULAR	PLURAL
—	apaguemos
apaga; no apagues	apagad; no apaguéis
apague	apaguen

perfecto de indicativo

SINGULAR	PLURAL
he apagado	**hemos** apagado
has apagado	**habéis** apagado
ha apagado	**han** apagado

pluscuamperfecto de indicativo

SINGULAR	PLURAL
había apagado	**habíamos** apagado
habías apagado	**habíais** apagado
había apagado	**habían** apagado

pretérito anterior

SINGULAR	PLURAL
hube apagado	**hubimos** apagado
hubiste apagado	**hubisteis** apagado
hubo apagado	**hubieron** apagado

futuro perfecto

SINGULAR	PLURAL
habré apagado	**habremos** apagado
habrás apagado	**habréis** apagado
habrá apagado	**habrán** apagado

condicional compuesto

SINGULAR	PLURAL
habría apagado	**habríamos** apagado
habrías apagado	**habríais** apagado
habría apagado	**habrían** apagado

perfecto de subjuntivo

SINGULAR	PLURAL
haya apagado	**hayamos** apagado
hayas apagado	**hayáis** apagado
haya apagado	**hayan** apagado

pluscuamperfecto de subjuntivo

SINGULAR	PLURAL
hubiera apagado	**hubiéramos** apagado
hubieras apagado	**hubierais** apagado
hubiera apagado	**hubieran** apagado
OR	
hubiese apagado	**hubiésemos** apagado
hubieses apagado	**hubieseis** apagado
hubiese apagado	**hubiesen** apagado

aparecer — to appear, to show up

gerundio **apareciendo** participio de pasado **aparecido**

SINGULAR	PLURAL
presente de indicativo	
aparezc**o**	aparec**emos**
aparec**es**	aparec**éis**
aparec**e**	aparec**en**
imperfecto de indicativo	
aparec**ía**	aparec**íamos**
aparec**ías**	aparec**íais**
aparec**ía**	aparec**ían**
pretérito	
aparec**í**	aparec**imos**
aparec**iste**	aparec**isteis**
aparec**ió**	aparec**ieron**
futuro	
aparecer**é**	aparecer**emos**
aparecer**ás**	aparecer**éis**
aparecer**á**	aparecer**án**
condicional simple	
aparecer**ía**	aparecer**íamos**
aparecer**ías**	aparecer**íais**
aparecer**ía**	aparecer**ían**
presente de subjuntivo	
aparezc**a**	aparezc**amos**
aparezc**as**	aparezc**áis**
aparezc**a**	aparezc**an**
imperfecto de subjuntivo	
apareciera	apareciér**amos**
aparecier**as**	aparecier**ais**
aparecier**a**	aparecier**an**
OR	
aparecies**e**	apareciés**emos**
aparecies**es**	aparecies**eis**
aparecies**e**	aparecies**en**
imperativo	
—	aparezcamos
aparece; no aparezcas	apareced; no aparezcáis
aparezca	aparezcan

SINGULAR	PLURAL
perfecto de indicativo	
he aparecido	**hemos** aparecido
has aparecido	**habéis** aparecido
ha aparecido	**han** aparecido
pluscuamperfecto de indicativo	
había aparecido	**habíamos** aparecido
habías aparecido	**habíais** aparecido
había aparecido	**habían** aparecido
pretérito anterior	
hube aparecido	**hubimos** aparecido
hubiste aparecido	**hubisteis** aparecido
hubo aparecido	**hubieron** aparecido
futuro perfecto	
habré aparecido	**habremos** aparecido
habrás aparecido	**habréis** aparecido
habrá aparecido	**habrán** aparecido
condicional compuesto	
habría aparecido	**habríamos** aparecido
habrías aparecido	**habríais** aparecido
habría aparecido	**habrían** aparecido
perfecto de subjuntivo	
haya aparecido	**hayamos** aparecido
hayas aparecido	**hayáis** aparecido
haya aparecido	**hayan** aparecido
pluscuamperfecto de subjuntivo	
hubiera aparecido	**hubiéramos** aparecido
hubieras aparecido	**hubierais** aparecido
hubiera aparecido	**hubieran** aparecido
OR	
hubiese aparecido	**hubiésemos** aparecido
hubieses aparecido	**hubieseis** aparecido
hubiese aparecido	**hubiesen** aparecido

gerundio **aplaudiendo** participio de pasado **aplaudido**

SINGULAR	PLURAL
presente de indicativo	
aplaud**o**	aplaud**imos**
aplaud**es**	aplaud**ís**
aplaud**e**	aplaud**en**
imperfecto de indicativo	
aplaud**ía**	aplaud**íamos**
aplaud**ías**	aplaud**íais**
aplaud**ía**	aplaud**ían**
pretérito	
aplaud**í**	aplaud**imos**
aplaud**iste**	aplaud**isteis**
aplaud**ió**	aplaud**ieron**
futuro	
aplaudir**é**	aplaudir**emos**
aplaudir**ás**	aplaudir**éis**
aplaudir**á**	aplaudir**án**
condicional simple	
aplaudir**ía**	aplaudir**íamos**
aplaudir**ías**	aplaudir**íais**
aplaudir**ía**	aplaudir**ían**
presente de subjuntivo	
aplaud**a**	aplaud**amos**
aplaud**as**	aplaud**áis**
aplaud**a**	aplaud**an**
imperfecto de subjuntivo	
aplaudier**a**	aplaudiér**amos**
aplaudier**as**	aplaudier**ais**
aplaudier**a**	aplaudier**an**
OR	
aplaudies**e**	aplaudiés**emos**
aplaudies**es**	aplaudies**eis**
aplaudies**e**	aplaudies**en**
imperativo	
—	aplaudamos
aplaude; no aplaudas	aplaudid; no aplaudáis
aplauda	aplaudan

SINGULAR	PLURAL
perfecto de indicativo	
he aplaudido	**hemos** aplaudido
has aplaudido	**habéis** aplaudido
ha aplaudido	**han** aplaudido
pluscuamperfecto de indicativo	
había aplaudido	**habíamos** aplaudido
habías aplaudido	**habíais** aplaudido
había aplaudido	**habían** aplaudido
pretérito anterior	
hube aplaudido	**hubimos** aplaudido
hubiste aplaudido	**hubisteis** aplaudido
hubo aplaudido	**hubieron** aplaudido
futuro perfecto	
habré aplaudido	**habremos** aplaudido
habrás aplaudido	**habréis** aplaudido
habrá aplaudido	**habrán** aplaudido
condicional compuesto	
habría aplaudido	**habríamos** aplaudido
habrías aplaudido	**habríais** aplaudido
habría aplaudido	**habrían** aplaudido
perfecto de subjuntivo	
haya aplaudido	**hayamos** aplaudido
hayas aplaudido	**hayáis** aplaudido
haya aplaudido	**hayan** aplaudido
pluscuamperfecto de subjuntivo	
hubiera aplaudido	**hubiéramos** aplaudido
hubieras aplaudido	**hubierais** aplaudido
hubiera aplaudido	**hubieran** aplaudido
OR	
hubiese aplaudido	**hubiésemos** aplaudido
hubieses aplaudido	**hubieseis** aplaudido
hubiese aplaudido	**hubiesen** aplaudido

apoderarse — to take power

gerundio **apoderándose** — participio de pasado **apoderado**

SINGULAR	PLURAL	SINGULAR	PLURAL
presente de indicativo		perfecto de indicativo	
me apoder**o**	nos apoder**amos**	**me he** apoderado	**nos hemos** apoderado
te apoder**as**	os apoder**áis**	**te has** apoderado	**os habéis** apoderado
se apoder**a**	se apoder**an**	**se ha** apoderado	**se han** apoderado
imperfecto de indicativo		pluscuamperfecto de indicativo	
me apoder**aba**	nos apoder**ábamos**	**me había** apoderado	**nos habíamos** apoderado
te apoder**abas**	os apoder**abais**	**te habías** apoderado	**os habíais** apoderado
se apoder**aba**	se apoder**aban**	**se había** apoderado	**se habían** apoderado
pretérito		pretérito anterior	
me apoder**é**	nos apoder**amos**	**me hube** apoderado	**nos hubimos** apoderado
te apoder**aste**	os apoder**asteis**	**te hubiste** apoderado	**os hubisteis** apoderado
se apoder**ó**	se apoder**aron**	**se hubo** apoderado	**se hubieron** apoderado
futuro		futuro perfecto	
me apoderar**é**	nos apoderar**emos**	**me habré** apoderado	**nos habremos** apoderado
te apoderar**ás**	os apoderar**éis**	**te habrás** apoderado	**os habréis** apoderado
se apoderar**á**	se apoderar**án**	**se habrá** apoderado	**se habrán** apoderado
condicional simple		condicional compuesto	
me apoderar**ía**	nos apoderar**íamos**	**me habría** apoderado	**nos habríamos** apoderado
te apoderar**ías**	os apoderar**íais**	**te habrías** apoderado	**os habríais** apoderado
se apoderar**ía**	se apoderar**ían**	**se habría** apoderado	**se habrían** apoderado
presente de subjuntivo		perfecto de subjuntivo	
me apoder**e**	nos apoder**emos**	**me haya** apoderado	**nos hayamos** apoderado
te apoder**es**	os apoder**éis**	**te hayas** apoderado	**os hayáis** apoderado
se apoder**e**	se apoder**en**	**se haya** apoderado	**se hayan** apoderado
imperfecto de subjuntivo		pluscuamperfecto de subjuntivo	
me apoderar**a**	nos apoderár**amos**	**me hubiera** apoderado	**nos hubiéramos** apoderado
te apoderar**as**	os apoderar**ais**	**te hubieras** apoderado	**os hubierais** apoderado
se apoderar**a**	se apoderar**an**	**se hubiera** apoderado	**se hubieran** apoderado
OR		OR	
me apoderas**e**	nos apoderás**emos**	**me hubiese** apoderado	**nos hubiésemos** apoderado
te apoderas**es**	os apoderas**eis**	**te hubieses** apoderado	**os hubieseis** apoderado
se apoderas**e**	se apoderas**en**	**se hubiese** apoderado	**se hubiesen** apoderado

imperativo

—	apoderémonos
apodérate; no te apoderes	apoderaos; no os apoderéis
apodérese	apodérense

to appreciate — apreciar

gerundio **apreciando** participio de pasado **apreciado**

presente de indicativo

SINGULAR	PLURAL
aprecio**o**	apreci**amos**
apreci**as**	apreci**áis**
apreci**a**	apreci**an**

imperfecto de indicativo

SINGULAR	PLURAL
apreci**aba**	apreci**ábamos**
apreci**abas**	apreci**abais**
apreci**aba**	apreci**aban**

pretérito

SINGULAR	PLURAL
apreci**é**	apreci**amos**
apreci**aste**	apreci**asteis**
apreci**ó**	apreci**aron**

futuro

SINGULAR	PLURAL
apreciar**é**	apreciar**emos**
apreciar**ás**	apreciar**éis**
apreciar**á**	apreciar**án**

condicional simple

SINGULAR	PLURAL
apreciar**ía**	apreciar**íamos**
apreciar**ías**	apreciar**íais**
apreciar**ía**	apreciar**ían**

presente de subjuntivo

SINGULAR	PLURAL
apreci**e**	apreci**emos**
apreci**es**	apreci**éis**
apreci**e**	apreci**en**

imperfecto de subjuntivo

SINGULAR	PLURAL
apreciar**a**	apreciár**amos**
apreciar**as**	apreciar**ais**
apeciar**a**	apreciar**an**
OR	
apreciase	apreciás**emos**
aprecias**es**	aprecias**eis**
aprecias**e**	aprecias**en**

imperativo

SINGULAR	PLURAL
—	apreciemos
aprecia; no aprecies	apreciad; no apreciéis
aprecie	aprecien

perfecto de indicativo

SINGULAR	PLURAL
he apreciado	**hemos** apreciado
has apreciado	**habéis** apreciado
ha apreciado	**han** apreciado

pluscuamperfecto de indicativo

SINGULAR	PLURAL
había apreciado	**habíamos** apreciado
habías apreciado	**habíais** apreciado
había apreciado	**habían** apreciado

pretérito anterior

SINGULAR	PLURAL
hube apreciado	**hubimos** apreciado
hubiste apreciado	**hubisteis** apreciado
hubo apreciado	**hubieron** apreciado

futuro perfecto

SINGULAR	PLURAL
habré apreciado	**habremos** apreciado
habrás apreciado	**habréis** apreciado
habrá apreciado	**habrán** apreciado

condicional compuesto

SINGULAR	PLURAL
habría apreciado	**habríamos** apreciado
habrías apreciado	**habríais** apreciado
habría apreciado	**habrían** apreciado

perfecto de subjuntivo

SINGULAR	PLURAL
haya apreciado	**hayamos** apreciado
hayas apreciado	**hayáis** apreciado
haya apreciado	**hayan** apreciado

pluscuamperfecto de subjuntivo

SINGULAR	PLURAL
hubiera apreciado	**hubiéramos** apreciado
hubieras apreciado	**hubierais** apreciado
hubiera apreciado	**hubieran** apreciado
OR	
hubiese apreciado	**hubiésemos** apreciado
hubieses apreciado	**hubieseis** apreciado
hubiese apreciado	**hubiesen** apreciado

aprender — to learn

gerundio aprendiendo   **participio de pasado** aprendido

SINGULAR	PLURAL
presente de indicativo	
aprend**o**	aprend**emos**
aprend**es**	aprend**éis**
aprend**e**	aprend**en**
imperfecto de indicativo	
aprend**ía**	aprend**íamos**
aprend**ías**	aprend**íais**
aprend**ía**	aprend**ían**
pretérito	
aprend**í**	aprend**imos**
aprend**iste**	aprend**isteis**
aprend**ió**	aprend**ieron**
futuro	
aprender**é**	aprender**emos**
aprender**ás**	aprender**éis**
aprender**á**	aprender**án**
condicional simple	
aprender**ía**	aprender**íamos**
aprender**ías**	aprender**íais**
aprender**ía**	aprender**ían**
presente de subjuntivo	
aprend**a**	aprend**amos**
aprend**as**	aprend**áis**
aprend**a**	aprend**an**
imperfecto de subjuntivo	
aprendier**a**	aprendiér**amos**
aprendier**as**	aprendier**ais**
aprendier**a**	aprendier**an**
OR	
aprendies**e**	aprendiés**emos**
aprendies**es**	aprendies**eis**
aprendies**e**	aprendies**en**
imperativo	
—	aprendamos
aprende; no aprendas	aprended; no aprendáis
aprenda	aprendan

SINGULAR	PLURAL
perfecto de indicativo	
he aprendido	**hemos** aprendido
has aprendido	**habéis** aprendido
ha aprendido	**han** aprendido
pluscuamperfecto de indicativo	
había aprendido	**habíamos** aprendido
habías aprendido	**habíais** aprendido
había aprendido	**habían** aprendido
pretérito anterior	
hube aprendido	**hubimos** aprendido
hubiste aprendido	**hubisteis** aprendido
hubo aprendido	**hubieron** aprendido
futuro perfecto	
habré aprendido	**habremos** aprendido
habrás aprendido	**habréis** aprendido
habrá aprendido	**habrán** aprendido
condicional compuesto	
habría aprendido	**habríamos** aprendido
habrías aprendido	**habríais** aprendido
habría aprendido	**habrían** aprendido
perfecto de subjuntivo	
haya aprendido	**hayamos** aprendido
hayas aprendido	**hayáis** aprendido
haya aprendido	**hayan** aprendido
pluscuamperfecto de subjuntivo	
hubiera aprendido	**hubiéramos** aprendido
hubieras aprendido	**hubierais** aprendido
hubiera aprendido	**hubieran** aprendido
OR	
hubiese aprendido	**hubiésemos** aprendido
hubieses aprendido	**hubieseis** aprendido
hubiese aprendido	**hubiesen** aprendido

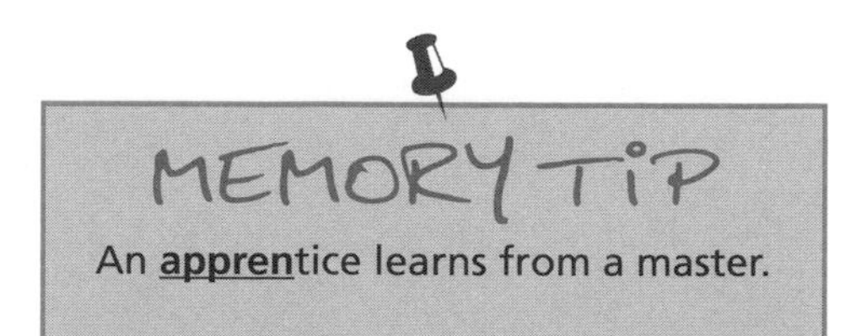

to approve, to pass a test **aprobar**

gerundio **aprobando** participio de pasado **aprobado**

SINGULAR	PLURAL
presente de indicativo	
aprueb**o**	aprob**amos**
aprueb**as**	aprob**áis**
aprueb**a**	aprueb**an**
imperfecto de indicativo	
aprob**aba**	aprob**ábamos**
aprob**abas**	aprob**abais**
aprob**aba**	aprob**aban**
pretérito	
aprob**é**	aprob**amos**
aprob**aste**	aprob**asteis**
aprob**ó**	aprob**aron**
futuro	
aprobar**é**	aprobar**emos**
aprobar**ás**	aprobar**éis**
aprobar**á**	aprobar**án**
condicional simple	
aprobar**ía**	aprobar**íamos**
aprobar**ías**	aprobar**íais**
aproba**ía**	aprobar**ían**
presente de subjuntivo	
aprueb**e**	aprob**emos**
aprueb**es**	aprob**éis**
aprueb**e**	aprueb**en**
imperfecto de subjuntivo	
aprobar**a**	aprobár**amos**
aprobar**as**	aprobar**ais**
aprobar**a**	aprobar**an**
OR	
aprobas**e**	aprobás**emos**
aprobas**es**	aprobas**eis**
aprobas**e**	aprobas**en**
imperativo	
—	aprobemos
aprueba;	aprobad;
no apruebes	no aprobéis
apruebe	aprueben

SINGULAR	PLURAL
perfecto de indicativo	
he aprobado	**hemos** aprobado
has aprobado	**habéis** aprobado
ha aprobado	**han** aprobado
pluscuamperfecto de indicativo	
había aprobado	**habíamos** aprobado
habías aprobado	**habíais** aprobado
había aprobado	**habían** aprobado
pretérito anterior	
hube aprobado	**hubimos** aprobado
hubiste aprobado	**hubisteis** aprobado
hubo aprobado	**hubieron** aprobado
futuro perfecto	
habré aprobado	**habremos** aprobado
habrás aprobado	**habréis** aprobado
habrá aprobado	**habrán** aprobado
condicional compuesto	
habría aprobado	**habríamos** aprobado
habrías aprobado	**habríais** aprobado
habría aprobado	**habrían** aprobado
perfecto de subjuntivo	
haya aprobado	**hayamos** aprobado
hayas aprobado	**hayáis** aprobado
haya aprobado	**hayan** aprobado
pluscuamperfecto de subjuntivo	
hubiera aprobado	**hubiéramos** aprobado
hubieras aprobado	**hubierais** aprobado
hubiera aprobado	**hubieran** aprobado
OR	
hubiese aprobado	**hubiésemos** aprobado
hubieses aprobado	**hubieseis** aprobado
hubiese aprobado	**hubiesen** aprobado

aprovechar — to take advantage of

gerundio **aprovechando** participio de pasado **aprovechado**

SINGULAR	PLURAL	SINGULAR	PLURAL
presente de indicativo		perfecto de indicativo	
aprovech**o**	aprovech**amos**	**he** aprovechado	**hemos** aprovechado
aprovech**as**	aprovech**áis**	**has** aprovechado	**habéis** aprovechado
aprovech**a**	aprovech**an**	**ha** aprovechado	**han** aprovechado
imperfecto de indicativo		pluscuamperfecto de indicativo	
aprovech**aba**	aprovech**ábamos**	**había** aprovechado	**habíamos** aprovechado
aprovech**abas**	aprovech**abais**	**habías** aprovechado	**habíais** aprovechado
aprovech**aba**	aprovech**aban**	**había** aprovechado	**habían** aprovechado
pretérito		pretérito anterior	
aprovech**é**	aprovech**amos**	**hube** aprovechado	**hubimos** aprovechado
aprovech**aste**	aprovech**asteis**	**hubiste** aprovechado	**hubisteis** aprovechado
aprovech**ó**	aprovech**aron**	**hubo** aprovechado	**hubieron** aprovechado
futuro		futuro perfecto	
aprovechar**é**	aprovechar**emos**	**habré** aprovechado	**habremos** aprovechado
aprovechar**ás**	aprovechar**éis**	**habrás** aprovechado	**habréis** aprovechado
aprovechar**á**	aprovechar**án**	**habrá** aprovechado	**habrán** aprovechado
condicional simple		condicional compuesto	
aprovechar**ía**	aprovechar**íamos**	**habría** aprovechado	**habríamos** aprovechado
aprovechar**ías**	aprovechar**íais**	**habrías** aprovechado	**habríais** aprovechado
aprovechar**ía**	aprovechar**ían**	**habría** aprovechado	**habrían** aprovechado
presente de subjuntivo		perfecto de subjuntivo	
aprovech**e**	aprovech**emos**	**haya** aprovechado	**hayamos** aprovechado
aprovech**es**	aprovech**éis**	**hayas** aprovechado	**hayáis** aprovechado
aprovech**e**	aprovech**en**	**haya** aprovechado	**hayan** aprovechado
imperfecto de subjuntivo		pluscuamperfecto de subjuntivo	
aprovechar**a**	aprovechár**amos**	**hubiera** aprovechado	**hubiéramos** aprovechado
aprovechar**as**	aprovechar**ais**	**hubieras** aprovechado	**hubierais** aprovechado
aprovechar**a**	aprovechar**an**	**hubiera** aprovechado	**hubieran** aprovechado
OR		OR	
aprovechas**e**	aprovechás**emos**	**hubiese** aprovechado	**hubiésemos** aprovechado
aprovechas**es**	aprovechas**eis**	**hubieses** aprovechado	**hubieseis** aprovechado
aprovechas**e**	aprovechas**en**	**hubiese** aprovechado	**hubiesen** aprovechado

imperativo

—	aprovechemos
aprovecha;	aprovechad;
no aproveches	no aprovechéis
aproveche	aprovechen

to take advantage of **aprovecharse**

gerundio **aprovechándose** participio de pasado **aprovechado**

presente de indicativo

SINGULAR	PLURAL
me aprovech**o**	nos aprovech**amos**
te aprovech**as**	os aprovech**áis**
se aprovech**a**	se aprovech**an**

imperfecto de indicativo

SINGULAR	PLURAL
me aprovech**aba**	nos aprovech**ábamos**
te aprovech**abas**	os aprovech**abais**
se aprovech**aba**	se aprovech**aban**

pretérito

SINGULAR	PLURAL
me aprovech**é**	nos aprovech**amos**
te aprovech**aste**	os aprovech**asteis**
se aprovech**ó**	se aprovech**aron**

futuro

SINGULAR	PLURAL
me aprovechar**é**	nos aprovechar**emos**
te aprovechar**ás**	os aprovechar**éis**
se aprovechar**á**	se aprovechar**án**

condicional simple

SINGULAR	PLURAL
me aprovechar**ía**	nos aprovechar**íamos**
te aprovechar**ías**	os aprovechar**íais**
se aprovechar**ía**	se aprovechar**ían**

presente de subjuntivo

SINGULAR	PLURAL
me aprovech**e**	nos aprovech**emos**
te aprovech**es**	os aprovech**éis**
se aprovech**e**	se aprovech**en**

imperfecto de subjuntivo

SINGULAR	PLURAL
me aprovechar**a**	nos aprovechár**amos**
te aprovechar**as**	os aprovechar**ais**
se aprovechar**a**	se aprovechar**an**
OR	
me aprovechas**e**	nos aprovechás**emos**
te aprovechas**es**	os aprovechas**eis**
se aprovechas**e**	se aprovechas**en**

imperativo

SINGULAR	PLURAL
—	aprovechémonos
aprovéchate; no te aproveches	aprovechaos; no os aprovechéis
aprovéchese	aprovéchense

perfecto de indicativo

SINGULAR	PLURAL
me he aprovechado	**nos hemos** aprovechado
te has aprovechado	**os habéis** aprovechado
se ha aprovechado	**se han** aprovechado

pluscuamperfecto de indicativo

SINGULAR	PLURAL
me había aprovechado	**nos habíamos** aprovechado
te habías aprovechado	**os habíais** aprovechado
se había aprovechado	**se habían** aprovechado

pretérito anterior

SINGULAR	PLURAL
me hube aprovechado	**nos hubimos** aprovechado
te hubiste aprovechado	**os hubisteis** aprovechado
se hubo aprovechado	**se hubieron** aprovechado

futuro perfecto

SINGULAR	PLURAL
me habré aprovechado	**nos habremos** aprovechado
te habrás aprovechado	**os habréis** aprovechado
se habrá aprovechado	**se habrán** aprovechado

condicional compuesto

SINGULAR	PLURAL
me habría aprovechado	**nos habríamos** aprovechado
te habrías aprovechado	**os habríais** aprovechado
se habría aprovechado	**se habrían** aprovechado

perfecto de subjuntivo

SINGULAR	PLURAL
me haya aprovechado	**nos hayamos** aprovechado
te hayas aprovechado	**os hayáis** aprovechado
se haya aprovechado	**se hayan** aprovechado

pluscuamperfecto de subjuntivo

SINGULAR	PLURAL
me hubiera aprovechado	**nos hubiéramos** aprovechado
te hubieras aprovechado	**os hubierais** aprovechado
se hubiera aprovechado	**se hubieran** aprovechado
OR	
me hubiese aprovechado	**nos hubiésemos** aprovechado
te hubieses aprovechado	**os hubieseis** aprovechado
se hubiese aprovechado	**se hubiesen** aprovechado

apurar — to hurry

gerundio **apurando** — participio de pasado **apurado**

SINGULAR	PLURAL
presente de indicativo	
apur**o**	apur**amos**
apur**as**	apur**áis**
apur**a**	apur**an**
imperfecto de indicativo	
apur**aba**	apur**ábamos**
apur**abas**	apur**abais**
apur**aba**	apur**aban**
pretérito	
apur**é**	apur**amos**
apur**aste**	apur**asteis**
apur**ó**	apur**aron**
futuro	
apurar**é**	apurar**emos**
apurar**ás**	apurar**éis**
apurar**á**	apurar**án**
condicional simple	
apurar**ía**	apurar**íamos**
apurar**ías**	apurar**íais**
apurar**ía**	apurar**ían**
presente de subjuntivo	
apur**e**	apur**emos**
apur**es**	apur**éis**
apur**e**	apur**en**
imperfecto de subjuntivo	
apurar**a**	apurár**amos**
apurar**as**	apurar**ais**
apurar**a**	apurar**an**
OR	
apuras**e**	apurás**emos**
apuras**es**	apuras**eis**
apuras**e**	apuras**en**
imperativo	
—	apuremos
apura;	apurad;
no apures	no apuréis
apure	apuren

SINGULAR	PLURAL
perfecto de indicativo	
he apurado	**hemos** apurado
has apurado	**habéis** apurado
ha apurado	**han** apurado
pluscuamperfecto de indicativo	
había apurado	**habíamos** apurado
habías apurado	**habíais** apurado
había apurado	**habían** apurado
pretérito anterior	
hube apurado	**hubimos** apurado
hubiste apurado	**hubisteis** apurado
hubo apurado	**hubieron** apurado
futuro perfecto	
habré apurado	**habremos** apurado
habrás apurado	**habréis** apurado
habrá apurado	**habrán** apurado
condicional compuesto	
habría apurado	**habríamos** apurado
habrías apurado	**habríais** apurado
habría apurado	**habrían** apurado
perfecto de subjuntivo	
haya apurado	**hayamos** apurado
hayas apurado	**hayáis** apurado
haya apurado	**hayan** apurado
pluscuamperfecto de subjuntivo	
hubiera apurado	**hubiéramos** apurado
hubieras apurado	**hubierais** apurado
hubiera apurado	**hubieran** apurado
OR	
hubiese apurado	**hubiésemos** apurado
hubieses apurado	**hubieseis** apurado
hubiese apurado	**hubiesen** apurado

gerundio **arrancando** participio de pasado **arrancado**

SINGULAR	PLURAL	SINGULAR	PLURAL
presente de indicativo		perfecto de indicativo	
arranc**o**	arranc**amos**	**he** arrancado	**hemos** arrancado
arranc**as**	arranc**áis**	**has** arrancado	**habéis** arrancado
arranc**a**	arranc**an**	**ha** arrancado	**han** arrancado
imperfecto de indicativo		pluscamperfecto de indicativo	
arranc**aba**	arranc**ábamos**	**había** arrancado	**habíamos** arrancado
arranc**abas**	arranc**abais**	**habías** arrancado	**habíais** arrancado
arranc**aba**	arranc**aban**	**había** arrancado	**habían** arrancado
pretérito		pretérito anterior	
arranqu**é**	arranc**amos**	**hube** arrancado	**hubimos** arrancado
arranc**aste**	arenc**asteis**	**hubiste** arrancado	**hubisteis** arrancado
arranc**ó**	arranc**aron**	**hubo** arrancado	**hubieron** arrancado
futuro		futuro perfecto	
arrancar**é**	arrancar**emos**	**habré** arrancado	**habremos** arrancado
arrancar**ás**	arancar**éis**	**habrás** arrancado	**habréis** arrancado
arrancar**á**	arrancar**án**	**habrá** arrancado	**habrán** arrancado
condicional simple		condicional compuesto	
arrancar**ía**	arrancar**íamos**	**habría** arrancado	**habríamos** arrancado
arrancar**ías**	arrancar**íais**	**habrías** arrancado	**habríais** arrancado
arrancar**ía**	arancar**ían**	**habría** arrancado	**habrían** arrancado
presente de subjuntivo		perfecto de subjuntivo	
arranqu**e**	arranqu**emos**	**haya** arrancado	**hayamos** arrancado
arranqu**es**	arranqu**éis**	**hayas** arrancado	**hayáis** arrancado
arranqu**e**	arranqu**en**	**haya** arrancado	**hayan** arrancado
imperfecto de subjuntivo		pluscamperfecto de subjuntivo	
arrancar**a**	arrancár**amos**	**hubiera** arrancado	**hubiéramos** arrancado
arrancar**as**	arrancar**ais**	**hubieras** arrancado	**hubierais** arrancado
arrancar**a**	arancar**an**	**hubiera** arrancado	**hubieran** arrancado
OR		OR	
arrancas**e**	arrancás**emos**	**hubiese** arrancado	**hubiésemos** arrancado
arrancas**es**	arrancas**eis**	**hubieses** arrancado	**hubieseis** arrancado
arrancas**e**	arrancas**en**	**hubiese** arrancado	**hubiesen** arrancado

imperativo

SINGULAR	PLURAL
—	arranquemos
arranca; no arranques	arrancad; no arranquéis
arranque	arranquen

arreglar — to fix, to arrange

gerundio **arreglando** participio de pasado **arreglado**

SINGULAR	PLURAL
presente de indicativo	
arreglo	arreglamos
arreglas	arregláis
arregla	arreglan
imperfecto de indicativo	
arreglaba	arreglábamos
arreglabas	arreglabais
arreglaba	arreglaban
pretérito	
arreglé	arreglamos
arreglaste	arreglasteis
arregló	arreglaron
futuro	
arreglaré	arreglaremos
arreglarás	arreglaréis
arreglará	arreglarán
condicional simple	
arreglaría	arreglaríamos
arreglarías	arreglaríais
arreglaría	arreglarían
presente de subjuntivo	
arregle	arreglemos
arregles	arregléis
arregle	arreglen
imperfecto de subjuntivo	
arreglara	arregláramos
arreglaras	arreglarais
arreglara	arreglaran
OR	
arreglase	arreglásemos
arreglases	arreglaseis
arreglase	arreglasen
imperativo	
—	arreglemos
arregla; no arregles	arreglad; no arregléis
arregle	arreglen

SINGULAR	PLURAL
perfecto de indicativo	
he arreglado	hemos arreglado
has arreglado	habéis arreglado
ha arreglado	han arreglado
pluscamperfecto de indicativo	
había arreglado	habíamos arreglado
habías arreglado	habíais arreglado
había arreglado	habían arreglado
pretérito anterior	
hube arreglado	hubimos arreglado
hubiste arreglado	hubisteis arreglado
hubo arreglado	hubieron arreglado
futuro perfecto	
habré arreglado	habremos arreglado
habrás arreglado	habréis arreglado
habrá arreglado	habrán arreglado
condicional compuesto	
habría arreglado	habríamos arreglado
habrías arreglado	habríais arreglado
habría arreglado	habrían arreglado
perfecto de subjuntivo	
haya arreglado	hayamos arreglado
hayas arreglado	hayáis arreglado
haya arreglado	hayan arreglado
pluscamperfecto de subjuntivo	
hubiera arreglado	hubiéramos arreglado
hubieras arreglado	hubierais arreglado
hubiera arreglado	hubieran arreglado
OR	
hubiese arreglado	hubiésemos arreglado
hubieses arreglado	hubieseis arreglado
hubiese arreglado	hubiesen arreglado

gerundio **arrojando** participio de pasado **arrojado**

SINGULAR	PLURAL	SINGULAR	PLURAL
presente de indicativo		perfecto de indicativo	
arroj**o**	arroj**amos**	**he** arrojado	**hemos** arrojado
arroj**as**	arroj**áis**	**has** arrojado	**habéis** arrojado
arroj**a**	arroj**an**	**ha** arrojado	**han** arrojado
imperfecto de indicativo		pluscuamperfecto de indicativo	
arroj**aba**	arroj**ábamos**	**había** arrojado	**habíamos** arrojado
arroj**abas**	arroj**abais**	**habías** arrojado	**habíais** arrojado
arroj**aba**	arroj**aban**	**había** arrojado	**habían** arrojado
pretérito		pretérito anterior	
arroj**é**	arroj**amos**	**hube** arrojado	**hubimos** arrojado
arroj**aste**	arroj**asteis**	**hubiste** arrojado	**hubisteis** arrojado
arroj**ó**	arroj**aron**	**hubo** arrojado	**hubieron** arrojado
futuro		futuro perfecto	
arrojar**é**	arrojar**emos**	**habré** arrojado	**habremos** arrojado
arrojar**ás**	arrojar**éis**	**habrás** arrojado	**habréis** arrojado
arrojar**á**	arrojar**án**	**habrá** arrojado	**habrán** arrojado
condicional simple		condicional compuesto	
arrojar**ía**	arrojar**íamos**	**habría** arrojado	**habríamos** arrojado
arrojar**ías**	arrojar**íais**	**habrías** arrojado	**habríais** arrojado
arrojar**ía**	arrojar**ían**	**habría** arrojado	**habrían** arrojado
presente de subjuntivo		perfecto de subjuntivo	
arroj**e**	arroj**emos**	**haya** arrojado	**hayamos** arrojado
arroj**es**	arroj**éis**	**hayas** arrojado	**hayáis** arrojado
arroj**e**	arroj**en**	**haya** arrojado	**hayan** arrojado
imperfecto de subjuntivo		pluscuamperfecto de subjuntivo	
arrojar**a**	arrojár**amos**	**hubiera** arrojado	**hubiéramos** arrojado
arrojar**as**	arrojar**ais**	**hubieras** arrojado	**hubierais** arrojado
arrojar**a**	arrojar**an**	**hubiera** arrojado	**hubieran** arrojado
OR		OR	
arrojas**e**	arrojás**emos**	**hubiese** arrojado	**hubiésemos** arrojado
arrojas**es**	arrojas**eis**	**hubieses** arrojado	**hubieseis** arrojado
arrojas**e**	arrojas**en**	**hubiese** arrojado	**hubiesen** arrojado

imperativo

—	arrojemos
arroja; no arrojes	arrojad; no arrojéis
arroje	arrojen

articular — to articulate

gerundio **articulando** participio de pasado **articulado**

SINGULAR	PLURAL	SINGULAR	PLURAL
presente de indicativo		perfecto de indicativo	
articul**o**	articul**amos**	**he** articulado	**hemos** articulado
articul**as**	articul**áis**	**has** articulado	**habéis** articulado
articul**a**	articul**an**	**ha** articulado	**han** articulado
imperfecto de indicativo		pluscamperfecto de indicativo	
articul**aba**	articul**ábamos**	**había** articulado	**habíamos** articulado
articul**abas**	articul**abais**	**habías** articulado	**habíais** articulado
articul**aba**	articul**aban**	**había** articulado	**habían** articulado
pretérito		pretérito anterior	
articul**é**	articul**amos**	**hube** articulado	**hubimos** articulado
articul**aste**	articul**asteis**	**hubiste** articulado	**hubisteis** articulado
articul**ó**	articul**aron**	**hubo** articulado	**hubieron** articulado
futuro		futuro perfecto	
articular**é**	articular**emos**	**habré** articulado	**habremos** articulado
articular**ás**	articular**éis**	**habrás** articulado	**habréis** articulado
articular**á**	articular**án**	**habrá** articulado	**habrán** articulado
condicional simple		condicional compuesto	
articular**ía**	articular**íamos**	**habría** articulado	**habríamos** articulado
articular**ías**	articular**íais**	**habrías** articulado	**habríais** articulado
articular**ía**	articular**ían**	**habría** articulado	**habrían** articulado
presente de subjuntivo		perfecto de subjuntivo	
articul**e**	articul**emos**	**haya** articulado	**hayamos** articulado
articul**es**	articul**éis**	**hayas** articulado	**hayáis** articulado
articul**e**	articul**en**	**haya** articulado	**hayan** articulado
imperfecto de subjuntivo		pluscamperfecto de subjuntivo	
articular**a**	articulár**amos**	**hubiera** articulado	**hubiéramos** articulado
articular**as**	articular**ais**	**hubieras** articulado	**hubierais** articulado
articular**a**	articular**an**	**hubiera** articulado	**hubieran** articulado
OR		OR	
articulas**e**	articulás**emos**	**hubiese** articulado	**hubiésemos** articulado
articulas**es**	articulas**eis**	**hubieses** articulado	**hubieseis** articulado
articulas**e**	articulas**en**	**hubiese** articulado	**hubiesen** articulado

imperativo

—	articulemos
articula; no articules	articulad; no articuléis
articule	articulen

gerundio **asegurando** — participio de pasado **asegurado**

SINGULAR	PLURAL
presente de indicativo	
asegur**o**	asegur**amos**
asegur**as**	asegur**áis**
asegur**a**	asegur**an**
imperfecto de indicativo	
asegur**aba**	asegur**ábamos**
asegur**abas**	asegur**abais**
asegur**aba**	asegur**aban**
pretérito	
asegur**é**	asegur**amos**
asegur**aste**	asegur**asteis**
asegur**ó**	asegur**aron**
futuro	
asegurar**é**	asegurar**emos**
asegurar**ás**	asegurar**éis**
asegurar**á**	asegurar**án**
condicional simple	
asegurar**ía**	asegurar**íamos**
asegurar**ías**	asegurar**íais**
asegurar**ía**	asegurar**ían**
presente de subjuntivo	
asegur**e**	asegur**emos**
asegur**es**	asegur**éis**
asegur**e**	asegur**en**
imperfecto de subjuntivo	
asegurar**a**	asegurár**amos**
asegurar**as**	asegurar**ais**
asegurar**a**	asegurar**an**
OR	
asegurase	asegurás**emos**
asegurase**s**	asegurase**is**
asegurase	asegurase**n**
imperativo	
—	aseguremos
asegura; no asegures	asegurad; no aseguréis
asegure	aseguren

SINGULAR	PLURAL
perfecto de indicativo	
he asegurado	**hemos** asegurado
has asegurado	**habéis** asegurado
ha asegurado	**han** asegurado
pluscamperfecto de indicativo	
había asegurado	**habíamos** asegurado
habías asegurado	**habíais** asegurado
había asegurado	**habían** asegurado
pretérito anterior	
hube asegurado	**hubimos** asegurado
hubiste asegurado	**hubisteis** asegurado
hubo asegurado	**hubieron** asegurado
futuro perfecto	
habré asegurado	**habremos** asegurado
habrás asegurado	**habréis** asegurado
habrá asegurado	**habrán** asegurado
condicional compuesto	
habría asegurado	**habríamos** asegurado
habrías asegurado	**habríais** asegurado
habría asegurado	**habrían** asegurado
perfecto de subjuntivo	
haya asegurado	**hayamos** asegurado
hayas asegurado	**hayáis** asegurado
haya asegurado	**hayan** asegurado
pluscamperfecto de subjuntivo	
hubiera asegurado	**hubiéramos** asegurado
hubieras asegurado	**hubierais** asegurado
hubiera asegurado	**hubieran** asegurado
OR	
hubiese asegurado	**hubiésemos** asegurado
hubieses asegurado	**hubieseis** asegurado
hubiese asegurado	**hubiesen** asegurado

asir — to seize, to grasp

gerundio **asiendo** — participio de pasado **asido**

SINGULAR	PLURAL	SINGULAR	PLURAL
presente de indicativo		perfecto de indicativo	
asg**o**	as**imos**	**he** asido	**hemos** asido
as**es**	as**ís**	**has** asido	**habéis** asido
as**e**	as**en**	**ha** asido	**han** asido
imperfecto de indicativo		pluscamperfecto de indicativo	
as**ía**	as**íamos**	**había** asido	**habíamos** asido
as**ías**	as**íais**	**habías** asido	**habíais** asido
as**ía**	as**ían**	**había** asido	**habían** asido
pretérito		pretérito anterior	
as**í**	as**imos**	**hube** asido	**hubimos** asido
as**iste**	as**isteis**	**hubiste** asido	**hubisteis** asido
as**ió**	as**ieron**	**hubo** asido	**hubieron** asido
futuro		futuro perfecto	
asir**é**	asir**emos**	**habré** asido	**habremos** asido
asir**ás**	asir**éis**	**habrás** asido	**habréis** asido
asir**á**	asir**án**	**habrá** asido	**habrán** asido
condicional simple		condicional compuesto	
asir**ía**	asir**íamos**	**habría** asido	**habríamos** asido
asir**ías**	asir**íais**	**habrías** asido	**habríais** asido
asir**ía**	asir**ían**	**habría** asido	**habrían** asido
presente de subjuntivo		perfecto de subjuntivo	
asg**a**	asg**amos**	**haya** asido	**hayamos** asido
asg**as**	asg**áis**	**hayas** asido	**hayáis** asido
asg**a**	asg**an**	**haya** asido	**hayan** asido
imperfecto de subjuntivo		pluscamperfecto de subjuntivo	
asier**a**	asiér**amos**	**hubiera** asido	**hubiéramos** asido
asier**as**	asier**ais**	**hubieras** asido	**hubierais** asido
asier**a**	asier**an**	**hubiera** asido	**hubieran** asido
OR		OR	
asies**e**	asiés**emos**	**hubiese** asido	**hubiésemos** asido
asies**es**	asies**eis**	**hubieses** asido	**hubieseis** asido
asies**e**	asies**en**	**hubiese** asido	**hubiesen** asido

imperativo

—	asgamos
ase; no asgas	asid; no asgáis
asga	asgan

gerundio **asistiendo** participio de pasado **asistido**

SINGULAR	PLURAL
presente de indicativo	
asist**o**	asist**imos**
asist**es**	asist**ís**
asist**e**	asist**en**
imperfecto de indicativo	
asist**ía**	asist**íamos**
asist**ías**	asist**íais**
asist**ía**	asist**ían**
pretérito	
asist**í**	asist**imos**
asist**iste**	asist**isteis**
asist**ió**	asist**ieron**
futuro	
asistir**é**	asistir**emos**
asistir**ás**	asistir**éis**
asistir**á**	asistir**án**
condicional simple	
asistir**ía**	asistir**íamos**
asistir**ías**	asistir**íais**
asistir**ía**	asistir**ían**
presente de subjuntivo	
asist**a**	asist**amos**
asist**as**	asist**áis**
asist**a**	asist**an**
imperfecto de subjuntivo	
asistier**a**	asistiér**amos**
asistier**as**	asistier**ais**
asistier**a**	asistier**an**
OR	
asisties**e**	asistiés**emos**
asisties**es**	asisties**eis**
asisties**e**	asisties**en**
imperativo	
—	asistamos
asiste;	asistid;
no asistas	no asistáis
asista	asistan

SINGULAR	PLURAL
perfecto de indicativo	
he asistido	**hemos** asistido
has asistido	**habéis** asistido
ha asistido	**han** asistido
pluscuamperfecto de indicativo	
había asistido	**habíamos**asistido
habías asistido	**habíais** asistido
había asistido	**habían** asistido
pretérito anterior	
hube asistido	**hubimos** asistido
hubiste asistido	**hubisteis** asistido
hubo asistido	**hubieron** asistido
futuro perfecto	
habré asistido	**habremos** asistido
habrás asistido	**habréis** asistido
habrá asistido	**habrán** asistido
condicional compuesto	
habría asistido	**habríamos** asistido
habrías asistido	**habríais** asistido
habría asistido	**habrían** asistido
perfecto de subjuntivo	
haya asistido	**hayamos** asistido
hayas asistido	**hayáis** asistido
haya asistido	**hayan** asistido
pluscuamperfecto de subjuntivo	
hubiera asistido	**hubiéramos** asistido
hubieras asistido	**hubierais** asistido
hubiera asistido	**hubieran** asistido
OR	
hubiese asistido	**hubiésemos** asistido
hubieses asistido	**hubieseis** asistido
hubiese asistido	**hubiesen** asistido

asustarse — to be frightened, to be scared

gerundio **asustándose** participio de pasado **asustado**

SINGULAR	PLURAL

presente de indicativo

me asust**o**	nos asust**amos**
te asust**as**	os asust**áis**
se asust**a**	se asust**an**

imperfecto de indicativo

me asust**aba**	nos asust**ábamos**
te asust**abas**	os asust**abais**
se asust**aba**	se asust**aban**

pretérito

me asust**é**	nos asust**amos**
te asust**aste**	os asust**asteis**
se asust**ó**	se asust**aron**

futuro

me asustar**é**	nos asustar**emos**
te asustar**ás**	os asustar**éis**
se asustar**á**	se asustar**án**

condicional simple

me asustar**ía**	nos asustar**íamos**
te asustar**ías**	os asustar**íais**
se asustar**ía**	se asustar**ían**

presente de subjuntivo

me asust**e**	nos asust**emos**
te asust**es**	os asust**éis**
se asust**e**	se asust**en**

imperfecto de subjuntivo

me asustar**a**	nos asustár**amos**
te asustar**as**	os asustar**ais**
se asustar**a**	se asustar**an**
OR	
me asustas**e**	nos asustás**emos**
te asustas**es**	os asustas**eis**
se asustas**e**	se asustas**en**

imperativo

—	asustémonos
asústate;	asustaos;
no te asustes	no os asustéis
asústese	asústense

SINGULAR	PLURAL

perfecto de indicativo

me he asustado	**nos hemos** asustado
te has asustado	**os habéis** asustado
se ha asustado	**se han** asustado

pluscamperfecto de indicativo

me había asustado	**nos habíamos** asustado
te habías asustado	**os habíais** asustado
se había asustado	**se habían** asustado

pretérito anterior

me hube asustado	**nos hubimos** asustado
te hubiste asustado	**os hubisteis** asustado
se hubo asustado	**se hubieron** asustado

futuro perfecto

me habré asustado	**nos habremos** asustado
te habrás asustado	**os habréis** asustado
se habrá asustado	**se habrán** asustado

condicional compuesto

me habría asustado	**nos habríamos** asustado
te habrías asustado	**os habríais** asustado
se habría asustado	**se habrían** asustado

perfecto de subjuntivo

me haya asustado	**nos hayamos** asustado
te hayas asustado	**os hayáis** asustado
se haya asustado	**se hayan** asustado

pluscamperfecto de subjuntivo

me hubiera asustado	**nos hubiéramos** asustado
te hubieras asustado	**os hubierais** asustado
se hubiera asustado	**se hubieran** asustado
OR	
me hubiese asustado	**nos hubiésemos** asustado
te hubieses asustado	**os hubieseis** asustado
se hubiese asustado	**se hubiesen** asustado

SINGULAR	PLURAL
presente de indicativo	
atac**o**	atac**amos**
atac**as**	atac**áis**
atac**a**	atac**an**
imperfecto de indicativo	
atac**aba**	atac**ábamos**
atac**abas**	atac**abais**
atac**aba**	atac**aban**
pretérito	
ataqu**é**	atac**amos**
atac**aste**	atac**asteis**
atac**ó**	atac**aron**
futuro	
atacar**é**	atacar**emos**
atacar**ás**	atacar**éis**
atacar**á**	atacar**án**
condicional simple	
atacar**ía**	atacar**íamos**
atacar**ías**	atacar**íais**
atacar**ía**	atacar**ían**
presente de subjuntivo	
ataqu**e**	ataqu**emos**
ataqu**es**	ataqu**éis**
ataqu**e**	ataqu**en**
imperfecto de subjuntivo	
atacar**a**	atacár**amos**
atacar**as**	atacar**ais**
atacar**a**	atacar**an**
OR	
atacas**e**	atacás**emos**
atacas**es**	atacas**eis**
atacas**e**	atacas**en**
imperativo	
—	ataquemos
ataca; no ataques	atacad; no ataquéis
ataque	ataquen

SINGULAR	PLURAL
perfecto de indicativo	
he atacado	**hemos** atacado
has atacado	**habéis** atacado
ha atacado	**han** atacado
pluscamperfecto de indicativo	
había atacado	**habíamos** atacado
habías atacado	**habíais** atacado
había atacado	**habían** atacado
pretérito anterior	
hube atacado	**hubimos** atacado
hubiste atacado	**hubisteis** atacado
hubo atacado	**hubieron** atacado
futuro perfecto	
habré atacado	**habremos** atacado
habrás atacado	**habréis** atacado
habrá atacado	**habrán** atacado
condicional compuesto	
habría atacado	**habríamos** atacado
habrías atacado	**habríais** atacado
habría atacado	**habrían** atacado
perfecto de subjuntivo	
haya atacado	**hayamos** atacado
hayas atacado	**hayáis** atacado
haya atacado	**hayan** atacado
pluscamperfecto de subjuntivo	
hubiera atacado	**hubiéramos** atacado
hubieras atacado	**hubierais** atacado
hubiera atacado	**hubieran** atacado
OR	
hubiese atacado	**hubiésemos** atacado
hubieses atacado	**hubieseis** atacado
hubiese atacado	**hubiesen** atacado

atenerse — to rely on, to depend on

gerundio **ateniéndose** participio de pasado **atenido**

SINGULAR	PLURAL	SINGULAR	PLURAL
presente de indicativo		perfecto de indicativo	
me ateng**o**	nos aten**emos**	**me he** atenido	**nos hemos** atenido
te atien**es**	os aten**éis**	**te has** atenido	**os habéis** atenido
se atien**e**	se atien**en**	**se ha** atenido	**se han** atenido
imperfecto de indicativo		pluscuamperfecto de indicativo	
me aten**ía**	nos aten**íamos**	**me había** atenido	**nos habíamos** atenido
te aten**ías**	os aten**íais**	**te habías** atenido	**os habíais** atenido
se aten**ía**	se aten**ían**	**se había** atenido	**se habían** atenido
pretérito		pretérito anterior	
me atuv**e**	nos atuv**imos**	**me hube** atenido	**nos hubimos** atenido
te atuv**iste**	os atuv**isteis**	**te hubiste** atenido	**os hubisteis** atenido
se atuv**o**	se atuv**ieron**	**se hubo** atenido	**se hubieron** atenido
futuro		futuro perfecto	
me atendr**é**	nos atendr**emos**	**me habré** atenido	**nos habremos** atenido
te atendr**ás**	os atendr**éis**	**te habrás** atenido	**os habréis** atenido
se atendr**á**	se atendr**án**	**se habrá** atenido	**se habrán** atenido
condicional simple		condicional compuesto	
me atendr**ía**	nos atendr**íamos**	**me habría** atenido	**nos habríamos** atenido
te atendr**ías**	os atendr**íais**	**te habrías** atenido	**os habríais** atenido
se atendr**ía**	se atendr**ían**	**se habría** atenido	**se habrían** atenido
presente de subjuntivo		perfecto de subjuntivo	
me ateng**a**	nos ateng**amos**	**me haya** atenido	**nos hayamos** atenido
te anteng**as**	os ateng**áis**	**te hayas** atenido	**os hayáis** atenido
se ateng**a**	se ateng**an**	**se haya** atenido	**se hayan** atenido
imperfecto de subjuntivo		pluscuamperfecto de subjuntivo	
me atuvier**a**	nos atuvié**ramos**	**me hubiera** atenido	**nos hubiéramos** atenido
te atuvier**as**	os atuvier**ais**	**te hubieras** atenido	**os hubierais** atenido
se atuvier**a**	se atuvier**an**	**se hubiera** atenido	**se hubieran** atenido
OR		OR	
me atuvies**e**	nos atuviés**emos**	**me hubiese** atenido	**nos hubiésemos** atenido
te atuvies**es**	os atuvies**eis**	**te hubieses** atenido	**os hubieseis** atenido
se atuvies**e**	se atuvies**en**	**se hubiese** atenido	**se hubiesen** atenido

imperativo

—	atengámonos
atente;	ateneos;
no te atengas	no os atengáis
aténgase	aténganse

gerundio **atravesando** participio de pasado **atravesado**

SINGULAR	PLURAL
presente de indicativo	
atravies**o**	atraves**amos**
atravies**as**	atraves**áis**
atravies**a**	atravies**an**
imperfecto de indicativo	
atraves**aba**	atraves**ábamos**
atraves**abas**	atraves**abais**
atraves**aba**	atraves**aban**
pretérito	
atraves**é**	atraves**amos**
atraves**aste**	atraves**asteis**
atraves**ó**	atraves**aron**
futuro	
atravesar**é**	atravesar**emos**
atravesar**ás**	atravesar**éis**
atravesar**á**	atravesar**án**
condicional simple	
atravesar**ía**	atravesar**íamos**
atravesar**ías**	atravesar**íais**
atravesar**ía**	atravesar**ían**
presente de subjuntivo	
atravies**e**	atraves**emos**
atravies**es**	atraves**éis**
atravies**e**	atravies**en**
imperfecto de subjuntivo	
atravesar**a**	atravesár**amos**
atravesar**as**	atravesar**ais**
atravesar**a**	atravesar**an**
OR	
atravesas**e**	atravesás**emos**
atravesas**es**	atravesas**eis**
atravesas**e**	atravesas**en**
imperativo	
—	atravesemos
atraviesa;	atravesad;
no atravieses	no atraveséis
atraviese	atraviesen

SINGULAR	PLURAL
perfecto de indicativo	
he atravesado	**hemos** atravesado
has atravesado	**habéis** atravesado
ha atravesado	**han** atravesado
pluscamperfecto de indicativo	
había atravesado	**habíamos** atravesado
habías atravesado	**habíais** atravesado
había atravesado	**habían** atravesado
pretérito anterior	
hube atravesado	**hubimos** atravesado
hubiste atravesado	**hubisteis** atravesado
hubo atravesado	**hubieron** atravesado
futuro perfecto	
habré atravesado	**habremos** atravesado
habrás atravesado	**habréis** atravesado
habrá atravesado	**habrán** atravesado
condicional compuesto	
habría atravesado	**habríamos** atravesado
habrías atravesado	**habríais** atravesado
habría atravesado	**habrían** atravesado
perfecto de subjuntivo	
haya atravesado	**hayamos** atravesado
hayas atravesado	**hayáis** atravesado
haya atravesado	**hayan** atravesado
pluscamperfecto de subjuntivo	
hubiera atravesado	**hubiéramos** atravesado
hubieras atravesado	**hubierais** atravesado
hubiera atravesado	**hubieran** atravesado
OR	
hubiese atravesado	**hubiésemos** atravesado
hubieses atravesado	**hubieseis** atravesado
hubiese atravesado	**hubiesen** atravesado

atreverse — to dare, to venture

gerundio **atreviéndose** participio de pasado **atrevido**

SINGULAR	PLURAL	SINGULAR	PLURAL
presente de indicativo		perfecto de indicativo	
me atrev**o**	nos atrev**emos**	**me he** atrevido	**nos hemos** atrevido
te atrev**es**	os atrev**éis**	**te has** atrevido	**os habéis** atrevido
se atrev**e**	se atrev**en**	**se ha** atrevido	**se han** atrevido
imperfecto de indicativo		pluscamperfecto de indicativo	
me atrev**ía**	nos atrev**íamos**	**me había** atrevido	**nos habíamos** atrevido
te atrev**ías**	os atrev**íais**	**te habías** atrevido	**os habíais** atrevido
se atrev**ía**	se atrev**ían**	**se había** atrevido	**se habían** atrevido
pretérito		pretérito anterior	
me atrev**í**	nos atrev**o**	**me hube** atrevido	**nos hubimos** atrevido
te atrev**iste**	os atrev**isteis**	**te hubiste** atrevido	**os hubisteis** atrevido
se atrev**ió**	se atrev**ieron**	**se hubo** atrevido	**se hubieron** atrevido
futuro		futuro perfecto	
me atrever**é**	nos atrever**emos**	**me habré** atrevido	**nos habremos** atrevido
te atrever**ás**	os atrever**éis**	**te habrás** atrevido	**os habréis** atrevido
se atrever**á**	se atrever**án**	**se habrá** atrevido	**se habrán** atrevido
condicional simple		condicional compuesto	
me atrever**ía**	nos atrever**íamos**	**me habría** atrevido	**nos habríamos** atrevido
te atrever**ías**	os atrever**íais**	**te habrías** atrevido	**os habríais** atrevido
se atrever**ía**	se atrever**ían**	**se habría** atrevido	**se habrían** atrevido
presente de subjuntivo		perfecto de subjuntivo	
me atrev**a**	nos atrev**amos**	**me haya** atrevido	**nos hayamos** atrevido
te atrev**as**	os atrev**áis**	**te hayas** atrevido	**os hayáis** atrevido
se atrev**a**	se atrev**an**	**se haya** atrevido	**se hayan** atrevido
imperfecto de subjuntivo		pluscamperfecto de subjuntivo	
me atrevier**a**	nos atreviér**amos**	**me hubiera** atrevido	**nos hubiéramos** atrevido
te atrevier**as**	os atrevier**ais**	**te hubieras** atrevido	**os hubierais** atrevido
se atrevier**a**	se atrevier**an**	**se hubiera** atrevido	**se hubieran** atrevido
OR		OR	
me atrevies**e**	nos atreviés**emos**	**me hubiese** atrevido	**nos hubiésemos** atrevido
te atrevies**es**	os atrevies**eis**	**te hubieses** atrevido	**os hubieseis** atrevido
se atrevies**e**	se atrevies**en**	**se hubiese** atrevido	**se hubiesen** atrevido

imperativo

—	atrevámonos
atrévete;	atreveos;
no te atrevas	no os atreváis
atrévase	atrévanse

gerundio **avanzando** participio de pasado **avanzado**

SINGULAR	PLURAL	SINGULAR	PLURAL
presente de indicativo		**perfecto de indicativo**	
avanz**o**	avanz**amos**	**he** avanzado	**hemos** avanzado
avanz**as**	avanz**áis**	**has** avanzado	**habéis** avanzado
avanz**a**	avanz**an**	**ha** avanzado	**han** avanzado
imperfecto de indicativo		**pluscamperfecto de indicativo**	
avanz**aba**	avanz**ábamos**	**había** avanzado	**habíamos** avanzado
avanz**abas**	avanz**abais**	**habías** avanzado	**habíais** avanzado
avanz**aba**	avanz**aban**	**había** avanzado	**habían** avanzado
pretérito		**pretérito anterior**	
avanc**é**	avanz**amos**	**hube** avanzado	**hubimos** avanzado
avanz**aste**	avanz**asteis**	**hubiste** avanzado	**hubisteis** avanzado
avanz**ó**	avanz**aron**	**hubo** avanzado	**hubieron** avanzado
futuro		**futuro perfecto**	
avanzar**é**	avanzar**emos**	**habré** avanzado	**habremos** avanzado
avanzar**ás**	avanzar**éis**	**habrás** avanzado	**habréis** avanzado
avanzar**á**	avanzar**án**	**habrá** avanzado	**habrán** avanzado
condicional simple		**condicional compuesto**	
avanzar**ía**	avanzar**íamos**	**habría** avanzado	**habríamos** avanzado
avanzar**ías**	avanzar**íais**	**habrías** avanzado	**habríais** avanzado
avanzar**ía**	avanzar**ían**	**habría** avanzado	**habrían** avanzado
presente de subjuntivo		**perfecto de subjuntivo**	
avanc**e**	avanc**emos**	**haya** avanzado	**hayamos** avanzado
avanc**es**	avanc**éis**	**hayas** avanzado	**hayáis** avanzado
avanc**e**	avanc**en**	**haya** avanzado	**hayan** avanzado
imperfecto de subjuntivo		**pluscamperfecto de subjuntivo**	
avanzar**a**	avanzár**amos**	**hubiera** avanzado	**hubiéramos** avanzado
avanzar**as**	avanzar**ais**	**hubieras** avanzado	**hubierais** avanzado
avanzar**a**	avanzar**an**	**hubiera** avanzado	**hubieran** avanzado
OR		OR	
avanzas**e**	avanzás**emos**	**hubiese** avanzado	**hubiésemos** avanzado
avanzas**es**	avanzas**eis**	**hubieses** avanzado	**hubieseis** avanzado
avanzas**e**	avanzas**en**	**hubiese** avanzado	**hubiesen** avanzado

imperativo

—	avancemos
avanza; no avances	avanzad; no avancéis
avance	avancen

A

gerundio **avergonzando** participio de pasado **avergonzado**

SINGULAR	PLURAL	SINGULAR	PLURAL
presente de indicativo		perfecto de indicativo	
avergüenz**o**	avergonz**amos**	**he** avergonzado	**hemos** avergonzado
avergüenz**as**	avergonz**áis**	**has** avergonzado	**habéis** avergonzado
avergüenz**a**	avergüenz**an**	**ha** avergonzado	**han** avergonzado
imperfecto de indicativo		pluscuamperfecto de indicativo	
avergonz**aba**	avergonz**ábamos**	**había** avergonzado	**habíamos** avergonzado
avergonz**abas**	avergonz**abais**	**habías** avergonzado	**habíais** avergonzado
avergonz**aba**	avergonz**aban**	**había** avergonzado	**habían** avergonzado
pretérito		pretérito anterior	
avergonc**é**	avergonz**amos**	**hube** avergonzado	**hubimos** avergonzado
avergonz**aste**	avergonz**asteis**	**hubiste** avergonzado	**hubisteis** avergonzado
avergonz**ó**	avergonz**aron**	**hubo** avergonzado	**hubieron** avergonzado
futuro		futuro perfecto	
avergonzar**é**	avergonzar**emos**	**habré** avergonzado	**habremos** avergonzado
avergonzar**ás**	avergonzar**éis**	**habrás** avergonzado	**habréis** avergonzado
avergonzar**á**	avergonzar**án**	**habrá** avergonzado	**habrán** avergonzado
condicional simple		condicional compuesto	
avergonzar**ía**	avergonzar**íamos**	**habría** avergonzado	**habríamos** avergonzado
avergonzar**ías**	avergonzar**íais**	**habrías** avergonzado	**habríais** avergonzado
avergonzar**ía**	avergonzar**ían**	**habría** avergonzado	**habrían** avergonzado
presente de subjuntivo		perfecto de subjuntivo	
avergüenc**e**	avergonc**emos**	**haya** avergonzado	**hayamos** avergonzado
avergüenc**es**	avergonc**éis**	**hayas** avergonzado	**hayáis** avergonzado
avergüenc**e**	avergüenc**en**	**haya** avergonzado	**hayan** avergonzado
imperfecto de subjuntivo		pluscuamperfecto de subjuntivo	
avergonzar**a**	avergonzár**amos**	**hubiera** avergonzado	**hubiéramos** avergonzado
avergonzar**as**	avergonzar**ais**	**hubieras** avergonzado	**hubierais** avergonzado
avergonzar**a**	avergonzar**an**	**hubiera** avergonzado	**hubieran** avergonzado
OR		OR	
avergonzas**e**	avergonzás**emos**	**hubiese** avergonzado	**hubiésemos** avergonzado
avergonzas**es**	avergonzas**eis**	**hubieses** avergonzado	**hubieseis** avergonzado
avergonzas**e**	avergonzas**en**	**hubiese** avergonzado	**hubiesen** avergonzado

imperativo	
—	avergoncemos
avergüenza;	avergonzad;
no avergüences	no avergoncéis
avergüence	avergüencen

to feel ashamed avergonzarse

gerundio **avergonzándose** participio de pasado **avergonzado**

presente de indicativo

SINGULAR	PLURAL
me avergüenz**o**	nos avergonz**amos**
te avergüenz**as**	os avergonz**áis**
se avergüenz**a**	se avergüenz**an**

imperfecto de indicativo

SINGULAR	PLURAL
me avergonz**aba**	nos avergonz**ábamos**
te avergonz**abas**	os avergonz**abais**
se avergonz**aba**	se avergonz**aban**

pretérito

SINGULAR	PLURAL
me avergonc**é**	nos avergonz**amos**
te avergonz**aste**	os avergonz**asteis**
se avergonz**ó**	se avergonz**aron**

futuro

SINGULAR	PLURAL
me avergonzar**é**	nos avergonzar**emos**
te avergonzar**ás**	os avergonzar**éis**
se avergonzar**á**	se avergonzar**án**

condicional simple

SINGULAR	PLURAL
me avergonzar**ía**	nos avergonzar**íamos**
te avergonzar**ías**	os avergonzar**íais**
se avergonzar**ía**	se avergonzar**ían**

presente de subjuntivo

SINGULAR	PLURAL
me avergüenc**e**	nos avergonc**emos**
te avergüenc**es**	os avergonc**éis**
se avergüenc**e**	se avergüenc**en**

imperfecto de subjuntivo

SINGULAR	PLURAL
me avergonzar**a**	nos avergonzár**amos**
te avergonzar**as**	os avergonzar**ais**
se avergonzar**a**	se avergonzar**an**
OR	
me avergonzas**e**	nos avergonzás**emos**
te avergonzas**es**	os avergonzas**eis**
se avergonzas**e**	se avergonzas**en**

imperativo

SINGULAR	PLURAL
—	avergoncémonos
avergüénzate; no te avergüences	avergonzaos; no os avergoncéis
avergüéncese	avergüéncense

perfecto de indicativo

SINGULAR	PLURAL
me he avergonzado	**nos hemos** avergonzado
te has avergonzado	**os habéis** avergonzado
se ha avergonzado	**se han** avergonzado

pluscuamperfecto de indicativo

SINGULAR	PLURAL
me había avergonzado	**nos habíamos** avergonzado
te habías avergonzado	**os habíais** avergonzado
se había avergonzado	**se habían** avergonzado

pretérito anterior

SINGULAR	PLURAL
me hube avergonzado	**nos hubimos** avergonzado
te hubiste avergonzado	**os hubisteis** avergonzado
se hubo avergonzado	**se hubieron** avergonzado

futuro perfecto

SINGULAR	PLURAL
me habré avergonzado	**nos habremos** avergonzado
te habrás avergonzado	**os habréis** avergonzado
se habrá avergonzado	**se habrán** avergonzado

condicional compuesto

SINGULAR	PLURAL
me habría avergonzado	**nos habríamos** avergonzado
te habrías avergonzado	**os habríais** avergonzado
se habría avergonzado	**se habrían** avergonzado

perfecto de subjuntivo

SINGULAR	PLURAL
me haya avergonzado	**nos hayamos** avergonzado
te hayas avergonzado	**os hayáis** avergonzado
se haya avergonzado	**se hayan** avergonzado

pluscuamperfecto de subjuntivo

SINGULAR	PLURAL
me hubiera avergonzado	**nos hubiéramos** avergonzado
te hubieras avergonzado	**os hubierai** avergonzado
se hubiera avergonzado	**se hubieran** avergonzado
OR	
me hubiese avergonzado	**nos hubiésemos** avergonzado
te hubieses avergonzado	**os hubieseis** avergonzado
se hubiese avergonzado	**se hubiesen** avergonzado

averiguar — to find out, to inquire

gerundio **averiguando** participio de pasado **averiguado**

SINGULAR	PLURAL
presente de indicativo	
averigu**o**	averigu**amos**
averigu**as**	averigu**áis**
averigu**a**	averigu**an**
imperfecto de indicativo	
averigu**aba**	averigu**ábamos**
averigu**abas**	averigu**abais**
averigu**aba**	averigu**aban**
pretérito	
averigü**é**	averigu**amos**
averigu**aste**	averigu**asteis**
averigu**ó**	averigu**aron**
futuro	
averiguar**é**	averiguar**emos**
averiguar**ás**	averiguar**éis**
averiguar**á**	averiguar**án**
condicional simple	
averiguar**ía**	averiguar**íamos**
averiguar**ías**	averiguar**íais**
averiguar**ía**	averiguar**ían**
presente de subjuntivo	
averigü**e**	averigü**emos**
averigü**es**	averigü**éis**
averigü**e**	averigü**en**
imperfecto de subjuntivo	
averiguar**a**	averiguár**amos**
averiguar**as**	averiguar**ais**
averiguar**a**	averiguar**an**
OR	
averiguas**e**	averiguás**emos**
averiguas**es**	averiguas**eis**
averiguas**e**	averiguas**en**
imperativo	
—	averigüemos
averigua; no averigües	averiguad; no averigüéis
averigüe	averigüen

SINGULAR	PLURAL
perfecto de indicativo	
he averiguado	**hemos** averiguado
has averiguado	**habéis** averiguado
ha averiguado	**han** averiguado
pluscuamperfecto de indicativo	
había averiguado	**habíamos** averiguado
habías averiguado	**habíais** averiguado
había averiguado	**habían** averiguado
pretérito anterior	
hube averiguado	**hubimos** averiguado
hubiste averiguado	**hubisteis** averiguado
hubo averiguado	**hubieron** averiguado
futuro perfecto	
habré averiguado	**habremos** averiguado
habrás averiguado	**habréis** averiguado
habrá averiguado	**habrán** averiguado
condicional compuesto	
habría averiguado	**habríamos** averiguado
habrías averiguado	**habríais** averiguado
habría averiguado	**habrían** averiguado
perfecto de subjuntivo	
haya averiguado	**hayamos** averiguado
hayas averiguado	**hayáis** averiguado
haya averiguado	**hayan** averiguado
pluscuamperfecto de subjuntivo	
hubiera averiguado	**hubiéramos** averiguado
hubieras averiguado	**hubierais** averiguado
hubiera averiguado	**hubieran** averiguado
OR	
hubiese averiguado	**hubiésemos** averiguado
hubieses averiguado	**hubieseis** averiguado
hubiese averiguado	**hubiesen** averiguado

to help **ayudar**

gerundio **ayudando** participio de pasado **ayudado**

SINGULAR	PLURAL	SINGULAR	PLURAL
presente de indicativo		perfecto de indicativo	
ayud**o**	ayud**amos**	**he** ayudado	**hemos** ayudado
ayud**as**	ayud**áis**	**has** ayudado	**habéis** ayudado
ayud**a**	ayud**an**	**ha** ayudado	**han** ayudado
imperfecto de indicativo		pluscuamperfecto de indicativo	
ayud**aba**	ayud**ábamos**	**había** ayudado	**habíamos** ayudado
ayud**abas**	ayud**abais**	**habías** ayudado	**habíais** ayudado
ayud**aba**	ayud**aban**	**había** ayudado	**habían** ayudado
pretérito		pretérito anterior	
ayud**é**	ayud**amos**	**hube** ayudado	**hubimos** ayudado
ayud**aste**	ayud**asteis**	**hubiste** ayudado	**hubisteis** ayudado
ayud**ó**	ayud**aron**	**hubo** ayudado	**hubieron** ayudado
futuro		futuro perfecto	
ayudar**é**	ayudar**emos**	**habré** ayudado	**habremos** ayudado
ayudar**ás**	ayudar**éis**	**habrás** ayudado	**habréis** ayudado
ayudar**á**	ayudar**án**	**habrá** ayudado	**habrán** ayudado
condicional simple		condicional compuesto	
ayudar**ía**	ayudar**íamos**	**habría** ayudado	**habríamos** ayudado
ayudar**ías**	ayudar**íais**	**habrías** ayudado	**habríais** ayudado
ayudar**ía**	ayudar**ían**	**habría** ayudado	**habrían** ayudado
presente de subjuntivo		perfecto de subjuntivo	
ayud**e**	ayud**emos**	**haya** ayudado	**hayamos** ayudado
ayud**es**	ayud**éis**	**hayas** ayudado	**hayáis** ayudado
ayud**e**	ayud**en**	**haya** ayudado	**hayan** ayudado
imperfecto de subjuntivo		pluscuamperfecto de subjuntivo	
ayudar**a**	ayudár**amos**	**hubiera** ayudado	**hubiéramos** ayudado
ayudar**as**	ayudar**ais**	**hubieras** ayudado	**hubierais** ayudado
ayudar**a**	ayudar**an**	**hubiera** ayudado	**hubieran** ayudado
OR		OR	
ayudas**e**	ayudás**emos**	**hubiese** ayudado	**hubiésemos** ayudado
ayudas**es**	ayudas**eis**	**hubieses** ayudado	**hubieseis** ayudado
ayudas**e**	ayudas**en**	**hubiese** ayudado	**hubiesen** ayudado

imperativo

—	ayudemos
ayuda; no ayudes	ayudad; no ayudéis
ayude	ayuden

bailar — to dance

gerundio **bailando** — participio de pasado **bailado**

SINGULAR	PLURAL
presente de indicativo	
bail**o**	bail**amos**
bail**as**	bail**áis**
bail**a**	bail**an**
imperfecto de indicativo	
bail**aba**	bail**ábamos**
bail**abas**	bail**abais**
bail**aba**	bail**aban**
pretérito	
bail**é**	bail**amos**
bail**aste**	bail**asteis**
bail**ó**	bail**aran**
futuro	
bailar**é**	bailar**emos**
bailar**ás**	bailar**éis**
bailar**á**	bailar**án**
condicional simple	
bailar**ía**	bailar**íamos**
bailar**ías**	bailar**íais**
bailar**ía**	bailar**ían**
presente de subjuntivo	
bail**e**	bail**emos**
bail**es**	bail**éis**
bail**e**	bail**en**
imperfecto de subjuntivo	
bailar**a**	bailár**amos**
bailar**as**	bailar**ais**
bailar**a**	bailar**an**
OR	
bailas**e**	bailás**emos**
bailas**es**	bailas**eis**
bailas**e**	bailas**en**
imperativo	
—	bailemos
baila; no bailes	bailad; no bailéis
baile	bailen

SINGULAR	PLURAL
perfecto de indicativo	
he bailado	**hemos** bailado
has bailado	**habéis** bailado
ha bailado	**han** bailado
pluscuamperfecto de indicativo	
había bailado	**habíamos** bailado
habías bailado	**habíais** bailado
había bailado	**habían** bailado
pretérito anterior	
hube bailado	**hubimos** bailado
hubiste bailado	**hubisteis** bailado
hubo bailado	**hubieron** bailado
futuro perfecto	
habré bailado	**habremos** bailado
habrás bailado	**habréis** bailado
habrá bailado	**habrán** bailado
condicional compuesto	
habría bailado	**habríamos** bailado
habrías bailado	**habríais** bailado
habría bailado	**habrían** bailado
perfecto de subjuntivo	
haya bailado	**hayamos** bailado
hayas bailado	**hayáis** bailado
haya bailado	**hayan** bailado
pluscuamperfecto de subjuntivo	
hubiera bailado	**hubiéramos** bailado
hubieras bailado	**hubierais** bailado
hubiera bailado	**hubieran** bailado
OR	
hubiese bailado	**hubiésemos** bailado
hubieses bailado	**hubieseis** bailado
hubiese bailado	**hubiesen** bailado

to go down, to reduce **bajar**

gerundio **bajando** participio de pasado **bajado**

SINGULAR	PLURAL	SINGULAR	PLURAL
presente de indicativo		perfecto de indicativo	
baj**o**	baj**amos**	**he** bajado	**hemos** bajado
baj**as**	baj**áis**	**has** bajado	**habéis** bajado
baj**a**	baj**an**	**ha** bajado	**han** bajado
imperfecto de indicativo		pluscuamperfecto de indicativo	
baj**aba**	baj**ábamos**	**había** bajado	**habíamos** bajado
baj**abas**	baj**abais**	**habías** bajado	**habíais** bajado
baj**aba**	baj**aban**	**había** bajado	**habían** bajado
pretérito		pretérito anterior	
baj**é**	baj**amos**	**hube** bajado	**hubimos** bajado
baj**aste**	baj**asteis**	**hubiste** bajado	**hubisteis** bajado
baj**ó**	baj**aron**	**hubo** bajado	**hubieron** bajado
futuro		futuro perfecto	
bajar**é**	bajar**emos**	**habré** bajado	**habremos** bajado
bajar**ás**	bajar**éis**	**habrás** bajado	**habréis** bajado
bajar**á**	bajar**án**	**habrá** bajado	**habrán** bajado
condicional simple		condicional compuesto	
bajar**ía**	bajar**íamos**	**habría** bajado	**habríamos** bajado
bajar**ías**	bajar**íais**	**habrías** bajado	**habríais** bajado
bajar**ía**	bajar**ían**	**habría** bajado	**habrían** bajado
presente de subjuntivo		perfecto de subjuntivo	
baj**e**	baj**emos**	**haya** bajado	**hayamos** bajado
baj**es**	baj**éis**	**hayas** bajado	**hayáis** bajado
baj**e**	baj**en**	**haya** bajado	**hayan** bajado
imperfecto de subjuntivo		pluscuamperfecto de subjuntivo	
bajar**a**	bajár**amos**	**hubiera** bajado	**hubiéramos** bajado
bajar**as**	bajar**ais**	**hubieras** bajado	**hubierais** bajado
bajar**a**	bajar**an**	**hubiera** bajado	**hubieran** bajado
OR		OR	
bajas**e**	bajás**emos**	**hubiese** bajado	**hubiésemos** bajado
bajas**es**	bajas**eis**	**hubieses** bajado	**hubieseis** bajado
bajas**e**	bajas**en**	**hubiese** bajado	**hubiesen** bajado

imperativo

—	bajemos
baja; no bajes	bajad; no bajéis
baje	bajen

balbucear — to stammer

gerundio **balbuceando** participio de pasado **balbuceado**

SINGULAR	PLURAL	SINGULAR	PLURAL
presente de indicativo		perfecto de indicativo	
balbuce**o**	balbuce**amos**	**he** balbuceado	**hemos** balbuceado
balbuce**as**	balbuce**áis**	**has** balbuceado	**habéis** balbuceado
balbuce**a**	balbuce**an**	**ha** balbuceado	**han** balbuceado
imperfecto de indicativo		pluscamperfecto de indicativo	
balbuce**aba**	balbuce**ábamos**	**había** balbuceado	**habíamos** balbuceado
balbuce**abas**	balbuce**abais**	**habías** balbuceado	**habíais** balbuceado
balbuce**aba**	balbuce**aban**	**había** balbuceado	**habían** balbuceado
pretérito		pretérito anterior	
balbuce**é**	balbuce**amos**	**hube** balbuceado	**hubimos** balbuceado
balbuce**aste**	balbuce**asteis**	**hubiste** balbuceado	**hubisteis** balbuceado
balbuce**ó**	balbuce**aron**	**hubo** balbuceado	**hubieron** balbuceado
futuro		futuro perfecto	
balbucear**é**	balbucear**emos**	**habré** balbuceado	**habremos** balbuceado
balbucear**ás**	balbucear**éis**	**habrás** balbuceado	**habréis** balbuceado
balbucear**á**	balbucear**án**	**habrá** balbuceado	**habrán** balbuceado
condicional simple		condicional compuesto	
balbucear**ía**	balbucear**íamos**	**habría** balbuceado	**habríamos** balbuceado
balbucear**ías**	balbucear**íais**	**habrías** balbuceado	**habríais** balbuceado
balbucear**ía**	balbucear**ían**	**habría** balbuceado	**habrían** balbuceado
presente de subjuntivo		perfecto de subjuntivo	
balbuce**e**	balbuce**emos**	**haya** balbuceado	**hayamos** balbuceado
balbuce**es**	balbuce**éis**	**hayas** balbuceado	**hayáis** balbuceado
balbuce**e**	balbuce**en**	**haya** balbuceado	**hayan** balbuceado
imperfecto de subjuntivo		pluscamperfecto de subjuntivo	
balbuceara**a**	balbuceár**amos**	**hubiera** balbuceado	**hubiéramos** balbuceado
balbucear**as**	balbucear**ais**	**hubieras** balbuceado	**hubierais** balbuceado
balbucear**a**	balbucear**an**	**hubiera** balbuceado	**hubieran** balbuceado
OR		OR	
balbucease**e**	balbuceás**emos**	**hubiese** balbuceado	**hubiésemos** balbuceado
balbuceas**es**	balbuceas**eis**	**hubieses** balbuceado	**hubieseis** balbuceado
balbuceas**e**	balbuceas**en**	**hubiese** balbuceado	**hubiesen** balbuceado

imperativo

—	balbuceemos
balbucea; no balbucees	balbucead; no balbuceéis
balbucee	balbuceen

to bathe — bañar

gerundio **bañando** participio de pasado **bañado**

SINGULAR	PLURAL
presente de indicativo	
bañ**o**	bañ**amos**
bañ**as**	bañ**áis**
bañ**a**	bañ**an**
imperfecto de indicativo	
bañ**aba**	bañ**ábamos**
bañ**abas**	bañ**abais**
bañ**aba**	bañ**aban**
pretérito	
bañ**é**	bañ**amos**
bañ**aste**	bañ**asteis**
bañ**ó**	bañ**aron**
futuro	
bañar**é**	bañar**emos**
bañar**ás**	bañar**éis**
bañar**á**	bañar**án**
condicional simple	
bañar**ía**	bañar**íamos**
bañar**ías**	bañar**íais**
bañar**ía**	bañar**ían**
presente de subjuntivo	
bañ**e**	bañ**emos**
bañ**es**	bañ**éis**
bañ**e**	bañ**en**
imperfecto de subjuntivo	
bañar**a**	bañár**amos**
bañar**as**	bañar**ais**
bañar**a**	bañar**an**
OR	
bañas**e**	bañás**emos**
bañas**es**	bañas**eis**
bañas**e**	bañas**en**
imperativo	
—	bañemos
baña; no bañes	bañad; no bañéis
bañe	bañen

SINGULAR	PLURAL
perfecto de indicativo	
he bañado	**hemos** bañado
has bañado	**habéis** bañado
ha bañado	**han** bañado
pluscuamperfecto de indicativo	
había bañado	**habíamos** bañado
habías bañado	**habíais** bañado
había bañado	**habían** bañado
pretérito anterior	
hube bañado	**hubimos** bañado
hubiste bañado	**hubisteis** bañado
hubo bañado	**hubieron** bañado
futuro perfecto	
habré bañado	**habremos** bañado
habrás bañado	**habréis** bañado
habrá bañado	**habrán** bañado
condicional compuesto	
habría bañado	**habríamos** bañado
habrías bañado	**habríais** bañado
habría bañado	**habrían** bañado
perfecto de subjuntivo	
haya bañado	**hayamos** bañado
hayas bañado	**hayáis** bañado
haya bañado	**hayan** bañado
pluscuamperfecto de subjuntivo	
hubiera bañado	**hubiéramos** bañado
hubieras bañado	**hubierais** bañado
hubiera bañado	**hubieran** bañado
OR	
hubiese bañado	**hubiésemos** bañado
hubieses bañado	**hubieseis** bañado
hubiese bañado	**hubiesen** bañado

B

barrer — to sweep, to whisk

gerundio **barriendo** participio de pasado **barrido**

presente de indicativo

SINGULAR	PLURAL
barr**o**	barr**emos**
barr**es**	barr**éis**
barr**e**	barr**en**

imperfecto de indicativo

SINGULAR	PLURAL
barr**ía**	barr**íamos**
barr**ías**	barr**íais**
barr**ía**	barr**ían**

pretérito

SINGULAR	PLURAL
barr**í**	barr**imos**
barr**iste**	barr**isteis**
barr**ió**	barr**ieron**

futuro

SINGULAR	PLURAL
barrer**é**	barrer**emos**
barrer**ás**	barrer**éis**
barrer**á**	barrer**án**

condicional simple

SINGULAR	PLURAL
barrer**ía**	barrer**íamos**
barrer**ías**	barrer**íais**
barrer**ía**	barrer**ían**

presente de subjuntivo

SINGULAR	PLURAL
barr**a**	barr**amos**
barr**as**	barr**áis**
barr**a**	barr**an**

imperfecto de subjuntivo

SINGULAR	PLURAL
barrier**a**	barriér**amos**
barrier**as**	barrier**ais**
barrier**a**	barrier**an**
OR	
barries**e**	barriés**emos**
barries**es**	barries**eis**
barries**e**	barries**en**

imperativo

SINGULAR	PLURAL
—	barramos
barre; no barras	barred; no barráis
barra	barran

perfecto de indicativo

SINGULAR	PLURAL
he barrido	**hemos** barrido
has barrido	**habéis** barrido
ha barrido	**han** barrido

pluscuamperfecto de indicativo

SINGULAR	PLURAL
había barrido	**habíamos** barrido
habías barrido	**habíais** barrido
había barrido	**habían** barrido

pretérito anterior

SINGULAR	PLURAL
hube barrido	**hubimos** barrido
hubiste barrido	**hubisteis** barrido
hubo barrido	**hubieron** barrido

futuro perfecto

SINGULAR	PLURAL
habré barrido	**habremos** barrido
habrás barrido	**habréis** barrido
habrá barrido	**habrán** barrido

condicional compuesto

SINGULAR	PLURAL
habría barrido	**habríamos** barrido
habrías barrido	**habríais** barrido
habría barrido	**habrían** barrido

perfecto de subjuntivo

SINGULAR	PLURAL
haya barrido	**hayamos** barrido
hayas barrido	**hayáis** barrido
haya barrido	**hayan** barrido

pluscuamperfecto de subjuntivo

SINGULAR	PLURAL
hubiera barrido	**hubiéramos** barrido
hubieras barrido	**hubierais** barrido
hubiera barrido	**hubieran** barrido
OR	
hubiese barrido	**hubiésemos** barrido
hubieses barrido	**hubieseis** barrido
hubiese barrido	**hubiesen** barrido

gerundio **bastando** participio de pasado **bastado**

SINGULAR	PLURAL
presente de indicativo	
bast**o**	bast**amos**
bast**as**	bast**áis**
bast**a**	bast**an**
imperfecto de indicativo	
bast**aba**	bast**ábamos**
bast**abas**	bast**abais**
bast**aba**	bast**aban**
pretérito	
bast**é**	bast**amos**
bast**aste**	bast**asteis**
bast**ó**	bast**aron**
futuro	
bastar**é**	bastar**emos**
bastar**ás**	bastar**éis**
bastar**á**	bastar**án**
condicional simple	
bastar**ía**	bastar**íamos**
bastar**ías**	bastar**íais**
bastar**ía**	bastar**ían**
presente de subjuntivo	
bast**e**	bast**emos**
bast**es**	bast**éis**
bast**e**	bast**en**
imperfecto de subjuntivo	
bastar**a**	bastár**amos**
bastar**as**	bastar**ais**
bastar**a**	bastar**an**
OR	
bastas**e**	bastás**emos**
bastas**es**	bastas**eis**
bastas**e**	bastas**en**
imperativo	
—	bastemos
basta; no bastes	bastad; no bastéis
baste	basten

SINGULAR	PLURAL
perfecto de indicativo	
he bastado	**hemos** bastado
has bastado	**habéis** bastado
ha bastado	**han** bastado
pluscuamperfecto de indicativo	
había bastado	**habíamos** bastado
habías bastado	**habíais** bastado
había bastado	**habían** bastado
pretérito anterior	
hube bastado	**hubimos** bastado
hubiste bastado	**hubisteis** bastado
hubo bastado	**hubieron** bastado
futuro perfecto	
habré bastado	**habremos** bastado
habrás bastado	**habréis** bastado
habrá bastado	**habrán** bastado
condicional compuesto	
habría bastado	**habríamos** bastado
habrías bastado	**habríais** bastado
habría bastado	**habrían** bastado
perfecto de subjuntivo	
haya bastado	**hayamos** bastado
hayas bastado	**hayáis** bastado
haya bastado	**hayan** bastado
pluscuamperfecto de subjuntivo	
hubiera bastado	**hubiéramos** bastado
hubieras bastado	**hubierais** bastado
hubiera bastado	**hubieran** bastado
OR	
hubiese bastado	**hubiésemos** bastado
hubieses bastado	**hubieseis** bastado
hubiese bastado	**hubiesen** bastado

batir — to beat

gerundio **batiendo** | participio de pasado **batido**

presente de indicativo

SINGULAR	PLURAL
bat**o**	bat**imos**
bat**es**	bat**ís**
bat**e**	bat**en**

imperfecto de indicativo

SINGULAR	PLURAL
bat**ía**	bat**íamos**
bat**ías**	bat**íais**
bat**ía**	bat**ían**

pretérito

SINGULAR	PLURAL
bat**í**	bat**imos**
bat**iste**	bat**isteis**
bati**ó**	bat**ieron**

futuro

SINGULAR	PLURAL
batir**é**	batir**emos**
batir**ás**	batir**éis**
batir**á**	batir**án**

condicional simple

SINGULAR	PLURAL
batir**ía**	batir**íamos**
batir**ías**	batir**íais**
batir**ía**	batir**ían**

presente de subjuntivo

SINGULAR	PLURAL
bat**a**	bat**amos**
bat**as**	bat**áis**
bat**a**	bat**an**

imperfecto de subjuntivo

SINGULAR	PLURAL
batier**a**	batiér**amos**
batier**as**	batier**ais**
batier**a**	batier**an**
OR	
baties**e**	batiés**emos**
baties**es**	baties**eis**
baties**e**	baties**en**

imperativo

SINGULAR	PLURAL
—	batamos
bate; no batas	batid; no batáis
bata	batan

perfecto de indicativo

SINGULAR	PLURAL
he batido	**hemos** batido
has batido	**habéis** batido
ha batido	**han** batido

pluscuamperfecto de indicativo

SINGULAR	PLURAL
había batido	**habíamos** batido
habías batido	**habíais** batido
había batido	**habían** batido

pretérito anterior

SINGULAR	PLURAL
hube batido	**hubimos** batido
hubiste batido	**hubisteis** batido
hubo batido	**hubieron** batido

futuro perfecto

SINGULAR	PLURAL
habré batido	**habremos** batido
habrás batido	**habréis** batido
habrá batido	**habrán** batido

condicional compuesto

SINGULAR	PLURAL
habría batido	**habríamos** batido
habrías batido	**habríais** batido
habría batido	**habrían** batido

perfecto de subjuntivo

SINGULAR	PLURAL
haya batido	**hayamos** batido
hayas batido	**hayáis** batido
haya batido	**hayan** batido

pluscuamperfecto de subjuntivo

SINGULAR	PLURAL
hubiera batido	**hubiéramos** batido
hubieras batido	**hubierais** batido
hubiera batido	**hubieran** batido
OR	
hubiese batido	**hubiésemos** batido
hubieses batido	**hubieseis** batido
hubiese batido	**hubiesen** batido

gerundio **bautizando** participio de pasado **bautizado**

SINGULAR	PLURAL	SINGULAR	PLURAL
presente de indicativo		perfecto de indicativo	
bautiz**o**	bautiz**amos**	**he** bautizado	**hemos** bautizado
bautiz**as**	bautiz**áis**	**has** bautizado	**habéis** bautizado
bautiz**a**	bautiz**an**	**ha** bautizado	**han** bautizado
imperfecto de indicativo		pluscuamperfecto de indicativo	
bautiz**aba**	bautiz**ábamos**	**había** bautizado	**habíamos** bautizado
bautiz**abas**	bautiz**abais**	**habías** bautizado	**habíais** bautizado
bautiz**aba**	bautiz**aban**	**había** bautizado	**habían** bautizado
pretérito		pretérito anterior	
bauti**cé**	bautiz**amos**	**hube** bautizado	**hubimos** bautizado
bautiz**aste**	bautiz**asteis**	**hubiste** bautizado	**hubisteis** bautizado
bautiz**ó**	bautiz**aron**	**hubo** bautizado	**hubieron** bautizado
futuro		futuro perfecto	
bautizar**é**	bautizar**emos**	**habré** bautizado	**habremos** bautizado
bautizar**ás**	bautizar**éis**	**habrás** bautizado	**habréis** bautizado
bautizar**á**	bautizar**án**	**habrá** bautizado	**habrán** bautizado
condicional simple		condicional compuesto	
bautizar**ía**	bautizar**íamos**	**habría** bautizado	**habríamos** bautizado
bautizar**ías**	bautizar**íais**	**habrías** bautizado	**habríais** bautizado
bautizar**ía**	bautizar**ían**	**habría** bautizado	**habrían** bautizado
presente de subjuntivo		perfecto de subjuntivo	
bautic**e**	bautic**emos**	**haya** bautizado	**hayamos** bautizado
bautic**es**	bautic**éis**	**hayas** bautizado	**hayáis** bautizado
bautic**e**	bautic**en**	**haya** bautizado	**hayan** bautizado
imperfecto de subjuntivo		pluscuamperfecto de subjuntivo	
bautizar**a**	bautizár**amos**	**hubiera** bautizado	**hubiéramos** bautizado
bautizar**as**	bautizar**ais**	**hubieras** bautizado	**hubierais** bautizado
bautizar**a**	bautizar**an**	**hubiera** bautizado	**hubieran** bautizado
OR		OR	
bautizas**e**	bautizás**emos**	**hubiese** bautizado	**hubiésemos** bautizado
bautizas**es**	bautizas**eis**	**hubieses** bautizado	**hubieseis** bautizado
bautizas**e**	bautizas**en**	**hubiese** bautizado	**hubiesen** bautizado

imperativo

—	bauticemos
bautiza; no bautices	bautizad; no bauticéis
bautice	bauticen

beber — to drink

gerundio **bebiendo** participio de pasado **bebido**

presente de indicativo

SINGULAR	PLURAL
beb**o**	beb**emos**
beb**es**	beb**éis**
beb**e**	beb**en**

imperfecto de indicativo

SINGULAR	PLURAL
beb**ía**	beb**íamos**
beb**ías**	beb**íais**
beb**ía**	beb**ían**

pretérito

SINGULAR	PLURAL
beb**í**	beb**imos**
beb**iste**	beb**isteis**
beb**ió**	beb**ieron**

futuro

SINGULAR	PLURAL
beber**é**	beber**emos**
beber**ás**	beber**éis**
beber**á**	beber**án**

condicional simple

SINGULAR	PLURAL
beber**ía**	beber**íamos**
beber**ías**	beber**íais**
beber**ía**	beber**ían**

presente de subjuntivo

SINGULAR	PLURAL
beb**a**	beb**amos**
beb**as**	beb**áis**
beb**a**	beb**an**

imperfecto de subjuntivo

SINGULAR	PLURAL
bebier**a**	bebiér**amos**
bebier**as**	bebier**ais**
bebier**a**	bebier**an**
OR	
bebies**e**	bebiés**emos**
bebies**es**	bebies**eis**
bebies**e**	bebies**en**

imperativo

SINGULAR	PLURAL
—	bebamos
bebe; no bebas	bebed; no bebáis
beba	beban

perfecto de indicativo

SINGULAR	PLURAL
he bebido	**hemos** bebido
has bebido	**habéis** bebido
ha bebido	**han** bebido

pluscuamperfecto de indicativo

SINGULAR	PLURAL
había bebido	**habíamos** bebido
habías bebido	**habíais** bebido
había bebido	**habían** bebido

pretérito anterior

SINGULAR	PLURAL
hube bebido	**hubimos** bebido
hubiste bebido	**hubisteis** bebido
hubo bebido	**hubieron** bebido

futuro perfecto

SINGULAR	PLURAL
habré bebido	**habremos** bebido
habrás bebido	**habréis** bebido
habrá bebido	**habrán** bebido

condicional compuesto

SINGULAR	PLURAL
habría bebido	**habríamos** bebido
habrías bebido	**habríais** bebido
habría bebido	**habrían** bebido

perfecto de subjuntivo

SINGULAR	PLURAL
haya bebido	**hayamos** bebido
hayas bebido	**hayáis** bebido
haya bebido	**hayan** bebido

pluscuamperfecto de subjuntivo

SINGULAR	PLURAL
hubiera bebido	**hubiéramos** bebido
hubieras bebido	**hubierais** bebido
hubiera bebido	**hubieran** bebido
OR	
hubiese bebido	**hubiésemos** bebido
hubieses bebido	**hubieseis** bebido
hubiese bebido	**hubiesen** bebido

gerundio **bendiciendo** participio de pasado **bendecido**

SINGULAR	PLURAL
presente de indicativo	
bendig**o**	bendec**imos**
bendic**es**	bendec**ís**
bendic**e**	bendic**en**
imperfecto de indicativo	
bendec**ía**	bendec**íamos**
bendec**ías**	bendec**íais**
bendec**ía**	bendec**ían**
pretérito	
bendij**e**	bendij**imos**
bendij**iste**	bendij**isteis**
bendij**o**	bendij**eron**
futuro	
bendecir**é**	bendecir**emos**
bendecir**ás**	bendecir**éis**
bendecir**á**	bendecir**án**
condicional simple	
bendecir**ía**	bendecir**íamos**
bendecir**ías**	bendecir**íais**
bendecir**ía**	bendecir**ían**
presente de subjuntivo	
bendig**a**	bendig**amos**
bendig**as**	bendig**áis**
bendig**a**	bendig**an**
imperfecto de subjuntivo	
bendijer**a**	bendijér**amos**
bendijer**as**	bendijer**ais**
bendijer**a**	bendijer**an**
OR	
bendijes**e**	bendijés**emos**
bendijes**es**	bendijes**eis**
bendijes**e**	bendijes**en**
imperativo	
—	bendigamos
bendice; no bendigas	bendecid; no bendigáis
bendiga	bendigan

SINGULAR	PLURAL
perfecto de indicativo	
he bendecido	**hemos** bendecido
has bendecido	**habéis** bendecido
ha bendecido	**han** bendecido
pluscuamperfecto de indicativo	
había bendecido	**habíamos** bendecido
habías bendecido	**habíais** bendecido
había bendecido	**habían** bendecido
pretérito anterior	
hube bendecido	**hubimos** bendecido
hubiste bendecido	**hubisteis** bendecido
hubo bendecido	**hubieron** bendecido
futuro perfecto	
habré bendecido	**habremos** bendecido
habrás bendecido	**habréis** bendecido
habrá bendecido	**habrán** bendecido
condicional compuesto	
habría bendecido	**habríamos** bendecido
habrías bendecido	**habríais** bendecido
habría bendecido	**habrían** bendecido
perfecto de subjuntivo	
haya bendecido	**hayamos** bendecido
hayas bendecido	**hayáis** bendecido
haya bendecido	**hayan** bendecido
pluscuamperfecto de subjuntivo	
hubiera bendecido	**hubiéramos** bendecido
hubieras bendecido	**hubierais** bendecido
hubiera bendecido	**hubieran** bendecido
OR	
hubiese bendecido	**hubiésemos** bendecido
hubieses bendecido	**hubieseis** bendecido
hubiese bendecido	**hubiesen** bendecido

beneficiar — to benefit

gerundio **beneficiando** participio de pasado **beneficiado**

SINGULAR	PLURAL
presente de indicativo	
benefici**o**	benefici**amos**
benefici**as**	benefici**áis**
benefici**a**	benefici**an**
imperfecto de indicativo	
benefici**aba**	benefici**ábamos**
benefici**abas**	benefici**abais**
benefici**aba**	benefici**aban**
pretérito	
benefici**é**	benefici**amos**
benefici**aste**	benefici**asteis**
benefici**ó**	benefici**aron**
futuro	
beneficiar**é**	beneficiar**emos**
beneficiar**ás**	beneficiar**éis**
beneficiar**á**	beneficiar**án**
condicional simple	
beneficiar**ía**	beneficiar**íamos**
beneficiar**ías**	beneficiar**íais**
beneficiar**ía**	beneficiar**ían**
presente de subjuntivo	
benefici**e**	benefici**emos**
benefici**es**	benefici**éis**
benefici**e**	benefici**en**
imperfecto de subjuntivo	
beneficiar**a**	beneficiár**amos**
beneficiar**as**	beneficiar**ais**
beneficiar**a**	beneficiar**an**
OR	
beneficias**e**	beneficiás**emos**
beneficias**es**	beneficias**eis**
beneficias**e**	beneficias**en**
imperativo	
—	beneficiemos
beneficia; no beneficies	beneficiad; no beneficiéis
beneficie	beneficien

SINGULAR	PLURAL
perfecto de indicativo	
he beneficiado	**hemos** beneficiado
has beneficiado	**habéis** beneficiado
ha beneficiado	**han** beneficiado
pluscuamperfecto de indicativo	
había beneficiado	**habíamos** beneficiado
habías beneficiado	**habíais** beneficiado
había beneficiado	**habían** beneficiado
pretérito anterior	
hube beneficiado	**hubimos** beneficiado
hubiste beneficiado	**hubisteis** beneficiado
hubo beneficiado	**hubieron** beneficiado
futuro perfecto	
habré beneficiado	**habremos** beneficiado
habrás beneficiado	**habréis** beneficiado
habrá beneficiado	**habrán** beneficiado
condicional compuesto	
habría beneficiado	**habríamos** beneficiado
habrías beneficiado	**habríais** beneficiado
habría beneficiado	**habrían** beneficiado
perfecto de subjuntivo	
haya beneficiado	**hayamos** beneficiado
hayas beneficiado	**hayáis** beneficiado
haya beneficiado	**hayan** beneficiado
pluscuamperfecto de subjuntivo	
hubiera beneficiado	**hubiéramos** beneficiado
hubieras beneficiado	**hubierais** beneficiado
hubiera beneficiado	**hubieran** beneficiado
OR	
hubiese beneficiado	**hubiésemos** beneficiado
hubieses beneficiado	**hubieseis** beneficiado
hubiese beneficiado	**hubiesen** beneficiado

gerundio **besando** participio de pasado **besado**

SINGULAR	PLURAL
presente de indicativo	
bes**o**	bes**amos**
bes**as**	bes**áis**
bes**a**	bes**an**
imperfecto de indicativo	
bes**aba**	bes**ábamos**
bes**abas**	bes**abais**
bes**aba**	bes**aban**
pretérito	
bes**é**	bes**amos**
bes**aste**	bes**asteis**
bes**ó**	bes**aron**
futuro	
besar**é**	besar**emos**
besar**ás**	besar**éis**
besar**á**	besar**án**
condicional simple	
besar**ía**	besar**íamos**
besar**ías**	besar**íais**
besar**ía**	besar**ían**
presente de subjuntivo	
bes**e**	bes**emos**
bes**es**	bes**éis**
bes**e**	bes**en**
imperfecto de subjuntivo	
besar**a**	besár**amos**
besar**as**	besar**ais**
besar**a**	besar**an**
OR	
besas**e**	besás**emos**
besas**es**	besas**eis**
besas**e**	besas**en**
imperativo	
—	besemos
besa; no beses	besad; no beséis
bese	besen

SINGULAR	PLURAL
perfecto de indicativo	
he besado	**hemos** besado
has besado	**habéis** besado
ha besado	**han** besado
pluscuamperfecto de indicativo	
había besado	**habíamos** besado
habías besado	**habíais** besado
había besado	**habían** besado
pretérito anterior	
hube besado	**hubimos** besado
hubiste besado	**hubisteis** besado
hubo besado	**hubieron** besado
futuro perfecto	
habré besado	**habremos** besado
habrás besado	**habréis** besado
habrá besado	**habrán** besado
condicional compuesto	
habría besado	**habríamos** besado
habrías besado	**habríais** besado
habría besado	**habrían** besado
perfecto de subjuntivo	
haya besado	**hayamos** besado
hayas besado	**hayáis** besado
haya besado	**hayan** besado
pluscuamperfecto de subjuntivo	
hubiera besado	**hubiéramos** besado
hubieras besado	**hubierais** besado
hubiera besado	**hubieran** besado
OR	
hubiese besado	**hubiésemos** besado
hubieses besado	**hubieseis** besado
hubiese besado	**hubiesen** besado

bisbisar — to mutter

gerundio **bisbisando** participio de pasado **bisbisado**

SINGULAR	PLURAL
presente de indicativo	
bisbis**o**	bisbis**amos**
bisbis**as**	bisbis**áis**
bisbis**a**	bisbis**an**
imperfecto de indicativo	
bisbis**aba**	bisbis**ábamos**
bisbis**abas**	bisbis**abais**
bisbis**aba**	bisbis**aban**
pretérito	
bisbis**é**	bisbis**amos**
bisbis**aste**	bisbis**asteis**
bisbis**ó**	bisbis**aron**
futuro	
bisbisar**é**	bisbisar**emos**
bisbisar**ás**	bisbisar**éis**
bisbisar**á**	bisbisar**án**
condicional simple	
bisbisar**ía**	bisbisar**íamos**
bisbisar**ías**	bisbisar**íais**
bisbisar**ía**	bisbisar**ían**
presente de subjuntivo	
bisbis**e**	bisbis**emos**
bisbis**es**	bisbis**éis**
bisbis**e**	bisbis**en**
imperfecto de subjuntivo	
bisbisar**a**	bisbisár**amos**
bisbisar**as**	bisbisar**ais**
bisbisar**a**	bisbisar**an**
OR	
bisbisas**e**	bisbisás**emos**
bisbisas**es**	bisbisas**eis**
bisbisas**e**	bisbisas**en**
imperativo	
—	bisbisemos
bisbisa; no bisbises	bisbisad; no bisbiséis
bisbise	bisbisen

SINGULAR	PLURAL
perfecto de indicativo	
he bisbisado	**hemos** bisbisado
has bisbisado	**habéis** bisbisado
ha bisbisado	**han** bisbisado
pluscuamperfecto de indicativo	
había bisbisado	**habíamos** bisbisado
habías bisbisado	**habíais** bisbisado
había bisbisado	**habían** bisbisado
pretérito anterior	
hube bisbisado	**hubimos** bisbisado
hubiste bisbisado	**hubisteis** bisbisado
hubo bisbisado	**hubieron** bisbisado
futuro perfecto	
habré bisbisado	**habremos** bisbisado
habrás bisbisado	**habréis** bisbisado
habrá bisbisado	**habrán** bisbisado
condicional compuesto	
habría bisbisado	**habríamos** bisbisado
habrías bisbisado	**habríais** bisbisado
habría bisbisado	**habrían** bisbisado
perfecto de subjuntivo	
haya bisbisado	**hayamos** bisbisado
hayas bisbisado	**hayáis** bisbisado
haya bisbisado	**hayan** bisbisado
pluscuamperfecto de subjuntivo	
hubiera bisbisado	**hubiéramos** bisbisado
hubieras bisbisado	**hubierais** bisbisado
hubiera bisbisado	**hubieran** bisbisado
OR	
hubiese bisbisado	**hubiésemos** bisbisado
hubieses bisbisado	**hubieseis** bisbisado
hubiese bisbisado	**hubiesen** bisbisado

to block — bloquear

gerundio **bloqueando** participio de pasado **bloqueado**

presente de indicativo

SINGULAR	PLURAL
bloque**o**	bloque**amos**
bloque**as**	bloque**áis**
bloque**a**	bloque**an**

imperfecto de indicativo

SINGULAR	PLURAL
bloque**aba**	bloque**ábamos**
bloque**abas**	bloque**abais**
bloque**aba**	bloque**aban**

pretérito

SINGULAR	PLURAL
bloque**é**	bloque**amos**
bloque**aste**	bloque**asteis**
bloque**ó**	bloque**aron**

futuro

SINGULAR	PLURAL
bloquear**é**	bloquear**emos**
bloquear**ás**	bloquear**éis**
bloquear**á**	bloquear**án**

condicional simple

SINGULAR	PLURAL
bloquear**ía**	bloquear**íamos**
bloquear**ías**	bloquear**íais**
bloquear**ía**	bloquear**ían**

presente de subjuntivo

SINGULAR	PLURAL
bloque**e**	bloque**emos**
bloque**es**	bloque**éis**
bloque**e**	bloque**en**

imperfecto de subjuntivo

SINGULAR	PLURAL
bloquear**a**	bloqueár**amos**
bloquear**as**	bloquear**ais**
bloquear**a**	bloquear**an**
OR	
bloquease**e**	bloqueás**emos**
bloqueas**es**	bloqueas**eis**
bloqueas**e**	bloqueas**en**

imperativo

SINGULAR	PLURAL
—	bloqueemos
bloquea; no bloquees	bloquead; no bloqueéis
bloquee	bloqueen

perfecto de indicativo

SINGULAR	PLURAL
he bloqueado	**hemos** bloqueado
has bloqueado	**habéis** bloqueado
ha bloqueado	**han** bloqueado

pluscuamperfecto de indicativo

SINGULAR	PLURAL
había bloqueado	**habíamos** bloqueado
habías bloqueado	**habíais** bloqueado
había bloqueado	**habían** bloqueado

pretérito anterior

SINGULAR	PLURAL
hube bloqueado	**hubimos** bloqueado
hubiste bloqueado	**hubisteis** bloqueado
hubo bloqueado	**hubieron** bloqueado

futuro perfecto

SINGULAR	PLURAL
habré bloqueado	**habremos** bloqueado
habrás bloqueado	**habréis** bloqueado
habrá bloqueado	**habrán** bloqueado

condicional compuesto

SINGULAR	PLURAL
habría bloqueado	**habríamos** bloqueado
habrías bloqueado	**habríais** bloqueado
habría bloqueado	**habrían** bloqueado

perfecto de subjuntivo

SINGULAR	PLURAL
haya bloqueado	**hayamos** bloqueado
hayas bloqueado	**hayáis** bloqueado
haya bloqueado	**hayan** bloqueado

pluscuamperfecto de subjuntivo

SINGULAR	PLURAL
hubiera bloqueado	**hubiéramos** bloqueado
hubieras bloqueado	**hubierais** bloqueado
hubiera bloqueado	**hubieran** bloqueado
OR	
hubiese bloqueado	**hubiésemos** bloqueado
hubieses bloqueado	**hubieseis** bloqueado
hubiese bloqueado	**hubiesen** bloqueado

bordear — to border, to go around

gerundio **bordeando** participio de pasado **bordeado**

SINGULAR	PLURAL	SINGULAR	PLURAL
presente de indicativo		perfecto de indicativo	
borde**o**	borde**amos**	**he** bordeado	**hemos** bordeado
borde**as**	borde**áis**	**has** bordeado	**habéis** bordeado
borde**a**	borde**an**	**ha** bordeado	**han** bordeado
imperfecto de indicativo		pluscuamperfecto de indicativo	
borde**aba**	borde**ábamos**	**había** bordeado	**habíamos** bordeado
borde**abas**	borde**abais**	**habías** bordeado	**habíais** bordeado
borde**aba**	borde**aban**	**había** bordeado	**habían** bordeado
pretérito		pretérito anterior	
borde**é**	borde**amos**	**hube** bordeado	**hubimos** bordeado
borde**aste**	borde**asteis**	**hubiste** bordeado	**hubisteis** bordeado
borde**ó**	borde**aron**	**hubo** bordeado	**hubieron** bordeado
futuro		futuro perfecto	
bordear**é**	bordear**emos**	**habré** bordeado	**habremos** bordeado
bordear**ás**	bordear**éis**	**habrás** bordeado	**habréis** bordeado
bordear**á**	bordear**án**	**habrá** bordeado	**habrán** bordeado
condicional simple		condicional compuesto	
bordear**ía**	bordear**íamos**	**habría** bordeado	**habríamos** bordeado
bordear**ías**	bordear**íais**	**habrías** bordeado	**habríais** bordeado
bordear**ía**	bordear**ían**	**habría** bordeado	**habrían** bordeado
presente de subjuntivo		perfecto de subjuntivo	
borde**e**	borde**emos**	**haya** bordeado	**hayamos** bordeado
borde**es**	borde**éis**	**hayas** bordeado	**hayáis** bordeado
borde**e**	borde**en**	**haya** bordeado	**hayan** bordeado
imperfecto de subjuntivo		pluscuamperfecto de subjuntivo	
bordear**a**	bordeár**amos**	**hubiera** bordeado	**hubiéramos** bordeado
bordear**as**	bordear**ais**	**hubieras** bordeado	**hubierais** bordeado
bordear**a**	bordear**an**	**hubiera** bordeado	**hubieran** bordeado
OR		OR	
bordeas**e**	bordeás**emos**	**hubiese** bordeado	**hubiésemos** bordeado
bordeas**es**	bordeas**eis**	**hubieses** bordeado	**hubieseis** bordeado
bordeas**e**	bordeas**en**	**hubiese** bordeado	**hubiesen** bordeado

imperativo

—	bordeemos
bordea; no bordees	bordead; no bordeéis
bordee	bordeen

to erase **borrar**

gerundio **borrando**   participio de pasado **borrado**

presente de indicativo

SINGULAR	PLURAL
borr**o**	borr**amos**
borr**as**	borr**áis**
borr**a**	borr**an**

imperfecto de indicativo

SINGULAR	PLURAL
borr**aba**	borr**ábamos**
borr**abas**	borr**abais**
borr**aba**	borr**aban**

pretérito

SINGULAR	PLURAL
borr**é**	borr**amos**
borr**aste**	borr**asteis**
borr**ó**	borr**aron**

futuro

SINGULAR	PLURAL
borrar**é**	borrar**emos**
borrar**ás**	borrar**éis**
borrar**á**	borrar**án**

condicional simple

SINGULAR	PLURAL
borrar**ía**	borrar**íamos**
borrar**ías**	borrar**íais**
borrar**ía**	borrar**ían**

presente de subjuntivo

SINGULAR	PLURAL
borr**e**	borr**emos**
borr**es**	borr**éis**
borr**e**	borr**en**

imperfecto de subjuntivo

SINGULAR	PLURAL
borrar**a**	borrár**amos**
borrar**as**	borrar**ais**
borrar**a**	borrar**an**
OR	
borras**e**	borrás**emos**
borras**es**	borras**eis**
borras**e**	borras**en**

imperativo

SINGULAR	PLURAL
—	borremos
borra; no borres	borrad; no borréis
borre	borren

perfecto de indicativo

SINGULAR	PLURAL
he borrado	**hemos** borrado
has borrado	**habéis** borrado
ha borrado	**han** borrado

pluscuamperfecto de indicativo

SINGULAR	PLURAL
había borrado	**habíamos** borrado
habías borrado	**habíais** borrado
había borrado	**habían** borrado

pretérito anterior

SINGULAR	PLURAL
hube borrado	**hubimos** borrado
hubiste borrado	**hubisteis** borrado
hubo borrado	**hubieron** borrado

futuro perfecto

SINGULAR	PLURAL
habré borrado	**habremos** borrado
habrás borrado	**habréis** borrado
habrá borrado	**habrán** borrado

condicional compuesto

SINGULAR	PLURAL
habría borrado	**habríamos** borrado
habrías borrado	**habríais** borrado
habría borrado	**habrían** borrado

perfecto de subjuntivo

SINGULAR	PLURAL
haya borrado	**hayamos** borrado
hayas borrado	**hayáis** borrado
haya borrado	**hayan** borrado

pluscuamperfecto de subjuntivo

SINGULAR	PLURAL
hubiera borrado	**hubiéramos** borrado
hubieras borrado	**hubierais** borrado
hubiera borrado	**hubieran** borrado
OR	
hubiese borrado	**hubiésemos** borrado
hubieses borrado	**hubieseis** borrado
hubiese borrado	**hubiesen** borrado

bostezar — to yawn, to gape

gerundio **bostezando** participio de pasado **bostezado**

SINGULAR	PLURAL	SINGULAR	PLURAL
presente de indicativo		perfecto de indicativo	
boste**zo**	boste**zamos**	**he** bostezado	**hemos** bostezado
boste**zas**	boste**záis**	**has** bostezado	**habéis** bostezado
boste**za**	boste**zan**	**ha** bostezado	**han** bostezado
imperfecto de indicativo		pluscamperfecto de indicativo	
bostez**aba**	bostez**ábamos**	**había** bostezado	**habíamos** bostezado
bostez**abas**	bostez**abais**	**habías** bostezado	**habíais** bostezado
bostez**aba**	bostez**aban**	**había** bostezado	**habían** bostezado
pretérito		pretérito anterior	
bostec**é**	bostez**amos**	**hube** bostezado	**hubimos** bostezado
bostez**aste**	bostez**asteis**	**hubiste** bostezado	**hubisteis** bostezado
bostez**ó**	bostez**aron**	**hubo** bostezado	**hubieron** bostezado
futuro		futuro perfecto	
bostezar**é**	bostezar**emos**	**habré** bostezado	**habremos** bostezado
bostezar**ás**	bostezar**éis**	**habrás** bostezado	**habréis** bostezado
bostezar**á**	bostezar**án**	**habrá** bostezado	**habrán** bostezado
condicional simple		condicional compuesto	
bostezar**ía**	bostezar**íamos**	**habría** bostezado	**habríamos** bostezado
bostezar**ías**	bostezar**íais**	**habrías** bostezado	**habríais** bostezado
bostezar**ía**	bostezar**ían**	**habría** bostezado	**habrían** bostezado
presente de subjuntivo		perfecto de subjuntivo	
bostec**e**	bostec**emos**	**haya** bostezado	**hayamos** bostezado
bostec**es**	bostec**éis**	**hayas** bostezado	**hayáis** bostezado
bostec**e**	bostec**en**	**haya** bostezado	**hayan** bostezado
imperfecto de subjuntivo		pluscamperfecto de subjuntivo	
bostezar**a**	bostezarár**amos**	**hubiera** bostezado	**hubiéramos** bostezado
bostezar**as**	bostezar**ais**	**hubieras** bostezado	**hubierais** bostezado
bostezar**a**	bostezar**an**	**hubiera** bostezado	**hubieran** bostezado
OR		OR	
bostezas**e**	bostezás**emos**	**hubiese** bostezado	**hubiésemos** bostezado
bostezas**es**	bostezas**eis**	**hubieses** bostezado	**hubieseis** bostezado
bostezas**e**	bostezas**en**	**hubiese** bostezado	**hubiesen** bostezado

imperativo

—	bostecemos
bosteza; no bosteces	bostezad; no bostecéis
bostece	bostecen

gerundio **botando** participio de pasado **botado**

SINGULAR	PLURAL	SINGULAR	PLURAL
presente de indicativo		perfecto de indicativo	
bot**o**	bot**amos**	**he** botado	**hemos** botado
bot**as**	bot**áis**	**has** botado	**habéis** botado
bot**a**	bot**an**	**ha** botado	**han** botado
imperfecto de indicativo		pluscuamperfecto de indicativo	
bot**aba**	bot**ábamos**	**había** botado	**habíamos** botado
bot**abas**	bot**abais**	**habías** botado	**habíais** botado
bot**aba**	bot**aban**	**había** botado	**habían** botado
pretérito		pretérito anterior	
bot**é**	bot**amos**	**hube** botado	**hubimos** botado
bot**aste**	bot**asteis**	**hubiste** botado	**hubisteis** botado
bot**ó**	bot**aron**	**hubo** botado	**hubieron** botado
futuro		futuro perfecto	
botar**é**	botar**emos**	**habré** botado	**habremos** botado
botar**ás**	botar**éis**	**habrás** botado	**habréis** botado
botar**á**	botar**án**	**habrá** botado	**habrán** botado
condicional simple		condicional compuesto	
botar**ía**	botar**íamos**	**habría** botado	**habríamos** botado
botar**ías**	botar**íais**	**habrías** botado	**habríais** botado
botar**ía**	botar**ían**	**habría** botado	**habrían** botado
presente de subjuntivo		perfecto de subjuntivo	
bot**e**	bot**emos**	**haya** botado	**hayamos** botado
bot**es**	bot**éis**	**hayas** botado	**hayáis** botado
bot**e**	bot**en**	**haya** botado	**hayan** botado
imperfecto de subjuntivo		pluscuamperfecto de subjuntivo	
botar**a**	botár**amos**	**hubiera** botado	**hubiéramos** botado
botar**as**	botar**ais**	**hubieras** botado	**hubierais** botado
botar**a**	botar**an**	**hubiera** botado	**hubieran** botado
OR		OR	
botas**e**	botás**emos**	**hubiese** botado	**hubiésemos** botado
botas**es**	botas**eis**	**hubieses** botado	**hubieseis** botado
botas**e**	botas**en**	**hubiese** botado	**hubiesen** botado

imperativo

—	botemos
bota; no botes	botad; no botéis
bote	boten

bregar — to toil, to deal with

gerundio **bregando** — participio de pasado **bregado**

SINGULAR	PLURAL
presente de indicativo	
brego	bregamos
bregas	bregáis
brega	bregan
imperfecto de indicativo	
bregaba	bregábamos
bregabas	bregabais
bregaba	bregaban
pretérito	
bregué	bregamos
bregaste	bregasteis
bregó	bregaron
futuro	
bregaré	bregaremos
bregarás	bregaréis
bregará	bregarán
condicional simple	
bregaría	bregaríamos
bregarías	bregaríais
bregaría	bregarían
presente de subjuntivo	
bregue	breguemos
bregues	breguéis
bregue	breguen
imperfecto de subjuntivo	
bregara	bregáramos
bregaras	bregarais
bregara	bregaran
OR	
bregase	bregásemos
bregases	bregaseis
bregase	bregasen
imperativo	
—	breguemos
brega; no bregues	bregad; no breguéis
bregue	breguen

SINGULAR	PLURAL
perfecto de indicativo	
he bregado	hemos bregado
has bregado	habéis bregado
ha bregado	han bregado
pluscuamperfecto de indicativo	
había bregado	habíamos bregado
habías bregado	habíais bregado
había bregado	habían bregado
pretérito anterior	
hube bregado	hubimos bregado
hubiste bregado	hubisteis bregado
hubo bregado	hubieron bregado
futuro perfecto	
habré bregado	habremos bregado
habrás bregado	habréis bregado
habrá bregado	habrán bregado
condicional compuesto	
habría bregado	habríamos bregado
habrías bregado	habríais bregado
habría bregado	habrían bregado
perfecto de subjuntivo	
haya bregado	hayamos bregado
hayas bregado	hayáis bregado
haya bregado	hayan bregado
pluscuamperfecto de subjuntivo	
hubiera bregado	hubiéramos bregado
hubieras bregado	hubierais bregado
hubiera bregado	hubieran bregado
OR	
hubiese bregado	hubiésemos bregado
hubieses bregado	hubieseis bregado
hubiese bregado	hubiesen bregado

to joke **bromear**

gerundio **bromeando** participio de pasado **bromeado**

SINGULAR	PLURAL
presente de indicativo	
brome**o**	brome**amos**
brome**as**	brome**áis**
brome**a**	brome**an**
imperfecto de indicativo	
brome**aba**	brome**ábamos**
brome**abas**	brome**abais**
brome**aba**	brome**aban**
pretérito	
brome**é**	brome**amos**
brome**aste**	brome**asteis**
brome**ó**	brome**aron**
futuro	
bromear**é**	bromear**emos**
bromear**ás**	bromear**éis**
bromear**á**	bromear**án**
condicional simple	
bromear**ía**	bromear**íamos**
bromear**ías**	bromear**íais**
bromear**ía**	bromear**ían**
presente de subjuntivo	
brome**e**	brome**emos**
brome**es**	brome**éis**
brome**e**	brome**en**
imperfecto de subjuntivo	
bromear**a**	bromeár**amos**
bromear**as**	bromear**ais**
bromear**a**	bromear**an**
OR	
bromease**e**	bromeás**emos**
bromeas**es**	bromeas**eis**
bromeas**e**	bromeas**en**
imperativo	
—	bromeemos
bromea; no bromees	bromead; no bromeéis
bromee	bromeen

SINGULAR	PLURAL
perfecto de indicativo	
he bromeado	**hemos** bromeado
has bromeado	**habéis** bromeado
ha bromeado	**han** bromeado
pluscuamperfecto de indicativo	
había bromeado	**habíamos** bromeado
habías bromeado	**habíais** bromeado
había bromeado	**habían** bromeado
pretérito anterior	
hube bromeado	**hubimos** bromeado
hubiste bromeado	**hubisteis** bromeado
hubo bromeado	**hubieron** bromeado
futuro perfecto	
habré bromeado	**habremos** bromeado
habrás bromeado	**habréis** bromeado
habrá bromeado	**habrán** bromeado
condicional compuesto	
habría bromeado	**habríamos** bromeado
habrías bromeado	**habríais** bromeado
habría bromeado	**habrían** bromeado
perfecto de subjuntivo	
haya bromeado	**hayamos** bromeado
hayas bromeado	**hayáis** bromeado
haya bromeado	**hayan** bromeado
pluscuamperfecto de subjuntivo	
hubiera bromeado	**hubiéramos** bromeado
hubieras bromeado	**hubierais** bromeado
hubiera bromeado	**hubieran** bromeado
OR	
hubiese bromeado	**hubiésemos** bromeado
hubieses bromeado	**hubieseis** bromeado
hubiese bromeado	**hubiesen** bromeado

broncear — to bronze, to tan

gerundio **bronceando** — participio de pasado **bronceado**

SINGULAR	PLURAL	SINGULAR	PLURAL
presente de indicativo		perfecto de indicativo	
bronce**o**	bronce**amos**	**he** bronceado	**hemos** bronceado
bronce**as**	bronce**áis**	**has** bronceado	**habéis** bronceado
bronce**a**	bronce**an**	**ha** bronceado	**han** bronceado
imperfecto de indicativo		pluscuamperfecto de indicativo	
bronce**aba**	bronce**ábamos**	**había** bronceado	**habíamos** bronceado
bronce**abas**	bronce**abais**	**habías** bronceado	**habíais** bronceado
bronce**aba**	bronce**aban**	**había** bronceado	**habían** bronceado
pretérito		pretérito anterior	
bronce**é**	bronce**amos**	**hube** bronceado	**hubimos** bronceado
bronce**aste**	bronce**asteis**	**hubiste** bronceado	**hubisteis** bronceado
bronce**ó**	bronce**aron**	**hubo** bronceado	**hubieron** bronceado
futuro		futuro perfecto	
broncear**é**	broncear**emos**	**habré** bronceado	**habremos** bronceado
broncear**ás**	broncear**éis**	**habrás** bronceado	**habréis** bronceado
broncear**á**	broncear**án**	**habrá** bronceado	**habrán** bronceado
condicional simple		condicional compuesto	
broncear**ía**	broncear**íamos**	**habría** bronceado	**habríamos** bronceado
broncear**ías**	broncear**íais**	**habrías** bronceado	**habríais** bronceado
broncear**ía**	broncear**ían**	**habría** bronceado	**habrían** bronceado
presente de subjuntivo		perfecto de subjuntivo	
bronce**e**	bronce**emos**	**haya** bronceado	**hayamos** bronceado
bronce**es**	bronce**éis**	**hayas** bronceado	**hayáis** bronceado
bronce**e**	bronce**en**	**haya** bronceado	**hayan** bronceado
imperfecto de subjuntivo		pluscuamperfecto de subjuntivo	
broncear**a**	bronceár**amos**	**hubiera** bronceado	**hubiéramos** bronceado
broncear**as**	broncear**ais**	**hubieras** bronceado	**hubierais** bronceado
broncear**a**	broncear**an**	**hubiera** bronceado	**hubieran** bronceado
OR		OR	
broncease**e**	bronceás**emos**	**hubiese** bronceado	**hubiésemos** bronceado
broncease**es**	bronceas**eis**	**hubieses** bronceado	**hubieseis** bronceado
broncease**e**	bronceas**en**	**hubiese** bronceado	**hubiesen** bronceado

imperativo

—	bronceemos
broncea; no broncees	broncead; no bronceéis
broncee	bronceen

gerundio **brotando** participio de pasado **brotado**

SINGULAR	PLURAL
presente de indicativo	
brot**o**	brot**amos**
brot**as**	brot**áis**
brot**a**	brot**an**
imperfecto de indicativo	
brot**aba**	brot**ábamos**
brot**abas**	brot**abais**
brot**aba**	brot**aban**
pretérito	
brot**é**	brot**amos**
brot**aste**	brot**asteis**
brot**ó**	brot**aron**
futuro	
brotar**é**	brotar**emos**
brotar**ás**	brotar**éis**
brotar**á**	brotar**án**
condicional simple	
brotar**ía**	brotar**íamos**
brotar**ías**	brotar**íais**
brotar**ía**	brotar**ían**
presente de subjuntivo	
brot**e**	brot**emos**
brot**es**	brot**éis**
brot**e**	brot**en**
imperfecto de subjuntivo	
brotar**a**	brotár**amos**
brotar**as**	brotar**ais**
brotar**a**	brotar**an**
OR	
brotas**e**	brotás**emos**
brotas**es**	brotas**eis**
brotas**e**	brotas**en**
imperativo	
—	brotemos
brota; no brotes	brotad; no brotéis
brote	broten

SINGULAR	PLURAL
perfecto de indicativo	
he brotado	**hemos** brotado
has brotado	**habéis** brotado
ha brotado	**han** brotado
pluscuamperfecto de indicativo	
había brotado	**habíamos** brotado
habías brotado	**habíais** brotado
había brotado	**habían** brotado
pretérito anterior	
hube brotado	**hubimos** brotado
hubiste brotado	**hubisteis** brotado
hubo brotado	**hubieron** brotado
futuro perfecto	
habré brotado	**habremos** brotado
habrás brotado	**habréis** brotado
habrá brotado	**habrán** brotado
condicional compuesto	
habría brotado	**habríamos** brotado
habrías brotado	**habríais** brotado
habría brotado	**habrían** brotado
perfecto de subjuntivo	
haya brotado	**hayamos** brotado
hayas brotado	**hayáis** brotado
haya brotado	**hayan** brotado
pluscuamperfecto de subjuntivo	
hubiera brotado	**hubiéramos** brotado
hubieras brotado	**hubierais** brotado
hubiera brotado	**hubieran** brotado
OR	
hubiese brotado	**hubiésemos** brotado
hubieses brotado	**hubieseis** brotado
hubiese brotado	**hubiesen** brotado

B

bullir

to seethe, to boil over

gerundio **bullendo** participio de pasado **bullido**

SINGULAR	PLURAL
presente de indicativo	
bull**o**	bull**imos**
bull**es**	bull**ís**
bull**e**	bull**en**
imperfecto de indicativo	
bull**ía**	bull**íamos**
bull**ías**	bull**íais**
bull**ía**	bull**ían**
pretérito	
bull**í**	bull**imos**
bull**iste**	bull**isteis**
bull**ó**	bull**eron**
futuro	
bullir**é**	bullir**emos**
bullir**ás**	bullir**éis**
bullir**á**	bullir**án**
condicional simple	
bullir**ía**	bullir**íamos**
bullir**ías**	bullir**íais**
bullir**ía**	bullir**ían**
presente de subjuntivo	
bull**a**	bull**amos**
bull**as**	bull**áis**
bull**a**	bull**an**
imperfecto de subjuntivo	
buller**a**	bullér**amos**
buller**as**	buller**ais**
buller**a**	buller**an**
OR	
bulles**e**	bullés**emos**
bulles**es**	bulles**eis**
bulles**e**	bulles**en**
imperativo	
—	bullamos
bulle; no bullas	bullid; no bulláis
bulla	bullan

SINGULAR	PLURAL
perfecto de indicativo	
he bullido	**hemos** bullido
has bullido	**habéis** bullido
ha bullido	**han** bullido
pluscuamperfecto de indicativo	
había bullido	**habíamos** bullido
habías bullido	**habíais** bullido
había bullido	**habían** bullido
pretérito anterior	
hube bullido	**hubimos** bullido
hubiste bullido	**hubisteis** bullido
hubo bullido	**hubieron** bullido
futuro perfecto	
habré bullido	**habremos** bullido
habrás bullido	**habréis** bullido
habrá bullido	**habrán** bullido
condicional compuesto	
habría bullido	**habríamos** bullido
habrías bullido	**habríais** bullido
habría bullido	**habrían** bullido
perfecto de subjuntivo	
haya bullido	**hayamos** bullido
hayas bullido	**hayáis** bullido
haya bullido	**hayan** bullido
pluscuamperfecto de subjuntivo	
hubiera bullido	**hubiéramos** bullido
hubieras bullido	**hubierais** bullido
hubiera bullido	**hubieran** bullido
OR	
hubiese bullido	**hubiésemos** bullido
hubieses bullido	**hubieseis** bullido
hubiese bullido	**hubiesen** bullido

gerundio **burlándose** participio de pasado **burlado**

SINGULAR	PLURAL	SINGULAR	PLURAL
presente de indicativo		perfecto de indicativo	
me burl**o**	nos burl**amos**	**me he** burlado	**nos hemos** burlado
te burl**as**	os burl**áis**	**te has** burlado	**os habéis** burlado
se burl**a**	se burl**an**	**se ha** burlado	**se han** burlado
imperfecto de indicativo		pluscuamperfecto de indicativo	
me burl**aba**	nos burl**ábamos**	**me había** burlado	**nos habíamos** burlado
te burl**abas**	os burl**abais**	**te habías** burlado	**os habíais** burlado
se burl**aba**	se burl**aban**	**se había** burlado	**se habían** burlado
pretérito		pretérito anterior	
me burl**é**	nos burl**amos**	**me hube** burlado	**nos hubimos** burlado
te burl**aste**	os burl**asteis**	**te hubiste** burlado	**os hubisteis** burlado
se burl**ó**	se burl**aron**	**se hubo** burlado	**se hubieron** burlado
futuro		futuro perfecto	
me burlar**é**	nos burlar**emos**	**me habré** burlado	**nos habremos** burlado
te burlar**ás**	os burlar**éis**	**te habrás** burlado	**os habréis** burlado
se burlar**á**	se burlar**án**	**se habrá** burlado	**se habrán** burlado
condicional simple		condicional compuesto	
me burlar**ía**	nos burlar**íamos**	**me habría** burlado	**nos habríamos** burlado
te burlar**ías**	os burlar**íais**	**te habrías** burlado	**os habríais** burlado
se burlar**ía**	se burlar**ían**	**se habría** burlado	**se habrían** burlado
presente de subjuntivo		perfecto de subjuntivo	
me burl**e**	nos burl**emos**	**me haya** burlado	**nos hayamos** burlado
te burl**es**	os burl**éis**	**te hayas** burlado	**os hayáis** burlado
se burl**e**	se burl**en**	**se haya** burlado	**se hayan** burlado
imperfecto de subjuntivo		pluscuamperfecto de subjuntivo	
me burlar**a**	nos burlár**amos**	**me hubiera** burlado	**nos hubiéramos** burlado
te burlar**as**	os burlar**ais**	**te hubieras** burlado	**os hubierais** burlado
se burlar**a**	se burlar**an**	**se hubiera** burlado	**se hubieran** burlado
OR		OR	
me burlas**e**	nos burlás**emos**	**me hubiese** burlado	**nos hubiésemos** burlado
te burlas**es**	os burlas**eis**	**te hubieses** burlado	**os hubieseis** burlado
se burlas**e**	se burlas**en**	**se hubiese** burlado	**se hubiesen** burlado

imperativo

—	burlémonos
búrlate; no te burles	burlaos; no os burléis
búrlese	búrlense

B

buscar — to search for

gerundio **buscando** participio de pasado **buscado**

SINGULAR	PLURAL	SINGULAR	PLURAL
presente de indicativo		perfecto de indicativo	
busc**o**	busc**amos**	**he** buscado	**hemos** buscado
busc**as**	busc**áis**	**has** buscado	**habéis** buscado
busc**a**	busc**an**	**ha** buscado	**han** buscado
imperfecto de indicativo		pluscuamperfecto de indicativo	
busc**aba**	busc**ábamos**	**había** buscado	**habíamos** buscado
busc**abas**	busc**abais**	**habías** buscado	**habíais** buscado
busc**aba**	busc**aban**	**había** buscado	**habían** buscado
pretérito		pretérito anterior	
busqu**é**	busc**amos**	**hube** buscado	**hubimos** buscado
busc**aste**	busc**asteis**	**hubiste** buscado	**hubisteis** buscado
busc**ó**	busc**aron**	**hubo** buscado	**hubieron** buscado
futuro		futuro perfecto	
buscar**é**	buscar**emos**	**habré** buscado	**habremos** buscado
buscar**ás**	buscar**éis**	**habrás** buscado	**habréis** buscado
buscar**á**	buscar**án**	**habrá** buscado	**habrán** buscado
condicional simple		condicional compuesto	
buscar**ía**	buscar**íamos**	**habría** buscado	**habríamos** buscado
buscar**ías**	buscar**íais**	**habrías** buscado	**habríais** buscado
buscar**ía**	buscar**ían**	**habría** buscado	**habrían** buscado
presente de subjuntivo		perfecto de subjuntivo	
busqu**e**	busqu**emos**	**haya** buscado	**hayamos** buscado
busqu**es**	busqu**éis**	**hayas** buscado	**hayáis** buscado
busqu**e**	busqu**en**	**haya** buscado	**hayan** buscado
imperfecto de subjuntivo		pluscuamperfecto de subjuntivo	
buscar**a**	buscár**amos**	**hubiera** buscado	**hubiéramos** buscado
buscar**as**	buscar**ais**	**hubieras** buscado	**hubierais** buscado
buscar**a**	buscar**an**	**hubiera** buscado	**hubieran** buscado
OR		OR	
busca**se**	buscás**emos**	**hubiese** buscado	**hubiésemos** buscado
busca**ses**	busca**seis**	**hubieses** buscado	**hubieseis** buscado
busca**se**	busca**sen**	**hubiese** buscado	**hubiesen** buscado

imperativo

SINGULAR	PLURAL
—	busquemos
busca; no busques	buscad; no busquéis
busque	busquen

to fit **caber**

gerundio **cabiendo** participio de pasado **cabido**

presente de indicativo

SINGULAR	PLURAL
quep**o**	cab**emos**
cab**es**	cab**éis**
cab**e**	cab**en**

imperfecto de indicativo

SINGULAR	PLURAL
cab**ía**	cab**íamos**
cab**ías**	cab**íais**
cab**ía**	cab**ían**

pretérito

SINGULAR	PLURAL
cup**e**	cup**imos**
cup**iste**	cup**isteis**
cup**o**	cup**ieron**

futuro

SINGULAR	PLURAL
cabr**é**	cabr**emos**
cabr**ás**	cabr**éis**
cabr**á**	cabr**án**

condicional simple

SINGULAR	PLURAL
cabr**ía**	cabr**íamos**
cabr**ías**	cabr**íais**
cabr**ía**	cabr**ían**

presente de subjuntivo

SINGULAR	PLURAL
quep**a**	quep**amos**
quep**as**	quep**áis**
quep**a**	quep**an**

imperfecto de subjuntivo

SINGULAR	PLURAL
cupier**a**	cupiér**amos**
cupier**as**	cupier**ais**
cupier**a**	cupier**an**
OR	
cupies**e**	cupiés**emos**
cupies**es**	cupies**eis**
cupies**e**	cupies**en**

imperativo

SINGULAR	PLURAL
—	quepamos
cabe; no quepas	cabed; no quepáis
quepa	quepan

perfecto de indicativo

SINGULAR	PLURAL
he cabido	**hemos** cabido
has cabido	**habéis** cabido
ha cabido	**han** cabido

pluscuamperfecto de indicativo

SINGULAR	PLURAL
había cabido	**habíamos** cabido
habías cabido	**habíais** cabido
había cabido	**habían** cabido

pretérito anterior

SINGULAR	PLURAL
hube cabido	**hubimos** cabido
hubiste cabido	**hubisteis** cabido
hubo cabido	**hubieron** cabido

futuro perfecto

SINGULAR	PLURAL
habré cabido	**habremos** cabido
habrás cabido	**habréis** cabido
habrá cabido	**habrán** cabido

condicional compuesto

SINGULAR	PLURAL
habría cabido	**habríamos** cabido
habrías cabido	**habríais** cabido
habría cabido	**habrían** cabido

perfecto de subjuntivo

SINGULAR	PLURAL
haya cabido	**hayamos** cabido
hayas cabido	**hayáis** cabido
haya cabido	**hayan** cabido

pluscuamperfecto de subjuntivo

SINGULAR	PLURAL
hubiera cabido	**hubiéramos** cabido
hubieras cabido	**hubierais** cabido
hubiera cabido	**hubieran** cabido
OR	
hubiese cabido	**hubiésemos** cabido
hubieses cabido	**hubieseis** cabido
hubiese cabido	**hubiesen** cabido

gerundio **cayendo** participio de pasado **caído**

SINGULAR	PLURAL	SINGULAR	PLURAL
presente de indicativo		perfecto de indicativo	
caig**o**	ca**emos**	**he** caído	**hemos** caído
ca**es**	ca**éis**	**has** caído	**habéis** caído
ca**e**	ca**en**	**ha** caído	**han** caído
imperfecto de indicativo		pluscuamperfecto de indicativo	
ca**ía**	ca**íamos**	**había** caído	**habíamos** caído
ca**ías**	ca**íais**	**habías** caído	**habíais** caído
ca**ía**	ca**ían**	**había** caído	**habían** caído
pretérito		pretérito anterior	
ca**í**	caí**mos**	**hube** caído	**hubimos** caído
caí**ste**	caí**steis**	**hubiste** caído	**hubisteis** caído
cay**ó**	cay**eron**	**hubo** caído	**hubieron** caído
futuro		futuro perfecto	
caer**é**	caer**emos**	**habré** caído	**habremos** caído
caer**ás**	caer**éis**	**habrás** caído	**habréis** caído
caer**á**	caer**án**	**habrá** caído	**habrán** caído
condicional simple		condicional compuesto	
caer**ía**	caer**íamos**	**habría** caído	**habríamos** caído
caer**ías**	caer**íais**	**habrías** caído	**habríais** caído
caer**ía**	caer**ían**	**habría** caído	**habrían** caído
presente de subjuntivo		perfecto de subjuntivo	
caig**a**	caig**amos**	**haya** caído	**hayamos** caído
caig**as**	caig**áis**	**hayas** caído	**hayáis** caído
caig**a**	caig**an**	**haya** caído	**hayan** caído
imperfecto de subjuntivo		pluscuamperfecto de subjuntivo	
cayer**a**	cayér**amos**	**hubiera** caído	**hubiéramos** caído
cayer**as**	cayer**ais**	**hubieras** caído	**hubierais** caído
cayer**a**	cayer**an**	**hubiera** caído	**hubieran** caído
OR		OR	
cayes**e**	cayés**emos**	**hubiese** caído	**hubiésemos** caído
cayes**es**	cayes**eis**	**hubieses** caído	**hubieseis** caído
cayes**e**	cayes**en**	**hubiese** caído	**hubiesen** caído

imperativo

—	caigamos
cae; no caigas	caed; no caigáis
caiga	caigan

to fall **caerse**

gerundio **cayéndose** participio de pasado **caído**

SINGULAR	PLURAL	SINGULAR	PLURAL
presente de indicativo		perfecto de indicativo	
me caig**o**	nos ca**emos**	**me he** caído	**nos hemos** caído
te ca**es**	os ca**éis**	**te has** caído	**os habéis** caído
se ca**e**	se ca**en**	**se ha** caído	**se han** caído
imperfecto de indicativo		pluscuamperfecto de indicativo	
me caí**a**	nos caí**amos**	**me había** caído	**nos habíamos** caído
te caí**as**	os caí**ais**	**te habías** caído	**os habíais** caído
se caí**a**	se caí**an**	**se había** caído	**se habían** caído
pretérito		pretérito anterior	
me ca**í**	nos caí**mos**	**me hube** caído	**nos hubimos** caído
te caí**ste**	os caí**steis**	**te hubiste** caído	**os hubisteis** caído
se cay**ó**	se cay**eron**	**se hubo** caído	**se hubieron** caído
futuro		futuro perfecto	
me caer**é**	nos caer**emos**	**me habré** caído	**nos habremos** caído
te caer**ás**	os caer**éis**	**te habrás** caído	**os habréis** caído
se caer**á**	se caer**án**	**se habrá** caído	**se habrán** caído
condicional simple		condicional compuesto	
me caer**ía**	nos caer**íamos**	**me habría** caído	**nos habríamos** caído
te caer**ías**	os caer**íais**	**te habrías** caído	**os habríais** caído
se caer**ía**	se caer**ían**	**se habría** caído	**se habrían** caído
presente de subjuntivo		perfecto de subjuntivo	
me caig**a**	nos caig**amos**	**me haya** caído	**nos hayamos** caído
te caig**as**	os caig**áis**	**te hayas** caído	**os hayáis** caído
se caig**a**	se caig**an**	**se haya** caído	**se hayan** caído
imperfecto de subjuntivo		pluscuamperfecto de subjuntivo	
me cayer**a**	nos cayér**amos**	**me hubiera** caído	**nos hubiéramos** caído
te cayer**as**	os cayer**ais**	**te hubieras** caído	**os hubierais** caído
se cayer**a**	se cayer**an**	**se hubiera** caído	**se hubieran** caído
OR		OR	
me cayes**e**	nos cayés**emos**	**me hubiese** caído	**nos hubiésemos** caído
te cayes**es**	os cayes**eis**	**te hubieses** caído	**os hubieseis** caído
se cayes**e**	se cayes**en**	**se hubiese** caído	**se hubiesen** caído

imperativo

—	caigámonos
cáete; no te caigas	caeos; no os caigáis
caígase	caíganse

calentar

to heat up, to warm up

gerundio **calentando**

participio de pasado **calentado**

presente de indicativo

SINGULAR	PLURAL
calient**o**	calent**amos**
calient**as**	calent**áis**
calient**a**	calient**an**

imperfecto de indicativo

SINGULAR	PLURAL
calent**aba**	calent**ábamos**
calent**abas**	calent**abais**
calent**aba**	calent**aban**

pretérito

SINGULAR	PLURAL
calent**é**	calent**amos**
calent**aste**	calent**asteis**
calent**ó**	calent**aron**

futuro

SINGULAR	PLURAL
calentar**é**	calentar**emos**
calentar**ás**	calentar**éis**
calentar**á**	calentar**án**

condicional simple

SINGULAR	PLURAL
calentar**ía**	calentar**íamos**
calentar**ías**	calentar**íais**
calentar**ía**	calentar**ían**

presente de subjuntivo

SINGULAR	PLURAL
calient**e**	calent**emos**
calient**es**	calent**éis**
calient**e**	calient**en**

imperfecto de subjuntivo

SINGULAR	PLURAL
calentar**a**	calentár**amos**
calentar**as**	calentar**ais**
calentar**a**	calentar**an**
OR	
calentas**e**	calentás**emos**
calentas**es**	calentas**eis**
calentas**e**	calentas**en**

imperativo

SINGULAR	PLURAL
—	calentemos
calienta; no calientes	calentad; no calentéis
caliente	calienten

perfecto de indicativo

SINGULAR	PLURAL
he calentado	**hemos** calentado
has calentado	**habéis** calentado
ha calentado	**han** calentado

pluscuamperfecto de indicativo

SINGULAR	PLURAL
había calentado	**habíamos** calentado
habías calentado	**habíais** calentado
había calentado	**habían** calentado

pretérito anterior

SINGULAR	PLURAL
hube calentado	**hubimos** calentado
hubiste calentado	**hubisteis** calentado
hubo calentado	**hubieron** calentado

futuro perfecto

SINGULAR	PLURAL
habré calentado	**habremos** calentado
habrás calentado	**habréis** calentado
habrá calentado	**habrán** calentado

condicional compuesto

SINGULAR	PLURAL
habría calentado	**habríamos** calentado
habrías calentado	**habríais** calentado
habría calentado	**habrían** calentado

perfecto de subjuntivo

SINGULAR	PLURAL
haya calentado	**hayamos** calentado
hayas calentado	**hayáis** calentado
haya calentado	**hayan** calentado

pluscuamperfecto de subjuntivo

SINGULAR	PLURAL
hubiera calentado	**hubiéramos** calentado
hubieras calentado	**hubierais** calentado
hubiera calentado	**hubieran** calentado
OR	
hubiese calentado	**hubiésemos** calentado
hubieses calentado	**hubieseis** calentado
hubiese calentado	**hubiesen** calentado

to be silent, to be quiet **callarse**

gerundio **callándose** participio de pasado **callado**

SINGULAR	PLURAL	SINGULAR	PLURAL
presente de indicativo		perfecto de indicativo	
me call**o**	nos call**amos**	**me he** callado	**nos hemos** callado
te call**as**	os call**áis**	**te has** callado	**os habéis** callado
se call**a**	se call**an**	**se ha** callado	**se han** callado
imperfecto de indicativo		pluscuamperfecto de indicativo	
me call**aba**	nos call**ábamos**	**me había** callado	**nos habíamos** callado
te call**abas**	os call**abais**	**te habías** callado	**os habíais** callado
se call**aba**	se call**aban**	**se había** callado	**se habían** callado
pretérito		pretérito anterior	
me call**é**	nos call**amos**	**me hube** callado	**nos hubimos** callado
te call**aste**	os call**asteis**	**te hubiste** callado	**os hubisteis** callado
se call**ó**	se call**aron**	**se hubo** callado	**se hubieron** callado
futuro		futuro perfecto	
me callar**é**	nos callar**emos**	**me habré** callado	**nos habremos** callado
te callar**ás**	os callar**éis**	**te habrás** callado	**os habréis** callado
se callar**á**	se callar**án**	**se habrá** callado	**se habrán** callado
condicional simple		condicional compuesto	
me callar**ía**	nos callar**íamos**	**me habría** callado	**nos habríamos** callado
te callar**ías**	os callar**íais**	**te habrías** callado	**os habríais** callado
se callar**ía**	se callar**ían**	**se habría** callado	**se habrían** callado
presente de subjuntivo		perfecto de subjuntivo	
me call**e**	nos call**emos**	**me haya** callado	**nos hayamos** callado
te call**es**	os call**éis**	**te hayas** callado	**os hayáis** callado
se call**e**	se call**en**	**se haya** callado	**se hayan** callado
imperfecto de subjuntivo		pluscuamperfecto de subjuntivo	
me callar**a**	nos callár**amos**	**me hubiera** callado	**nos hubiéramos** callado
te callar**as**	os callar**ais**	**te hubieras** callado	**os hubierais** callado
se callar**a**	se callar**an**	**se hubiera** callado	**se hubieran** callado
OR		OR	
me callas**e**	nos callás**emos**	**me hubiese** callado	**nos hubiésemos** callado
te callas**es**	os callas**eis**	**te hubieses** callado	**os hubieseis** callado
se callas**e**	se callas**en**	**se hubiese** callado	**se hubiesen** callado

imperativo

—	callémonos; no nos callemos
cállate; no te calles	callaos; no os calléis
cállese; no se calle	cállense; no se callen

calzar — to wear or put on shoes

gerundio **calzando** — participio de pasado **calzado**

SINGULAR	PLURAL
presente de indicativo	
calz**o**	calz**amos**
calz**as**	calz**áis**
calz**a**	calz**an**
imperfecto de indicativo	
calz**aba**	calz**ábamos**
calz**abas**	calz**abais**
calz**aba**	calz**aban**
pretérito	
calc**é**	calz**amos**
calz**aste**	calz**asteis**
calz**ó**	calz**aron**
futuro	
calzar**é**	calzar**emos**
calzar**ás**	calzar**éis**
calzar**á**	calzar**án**
condicional simple	
calzar**ía**	calzar**íamos**
calzar**ías**	calzar**íais**
calzar**ía**	calzar**ían**
presente de subjuntivo	
calc**e**	calc**emos**
calc**es**	calc**éis**
calc**e**	calc**en**
imperfecto de subjuntivo	
calzar**a**	calzár**amos**
calzar**as**	calzar**ais**
calzar**a**	calzar**an**
OR	
calzas**e**	calzás**emos**
calzas**es**	calzas**eis**
calzas**e**	calzas**en**
imperativo	
—	calcemos
calza; no calces	calzad; no calcéis
calce	calcen

SINGULAR	PLURAL
perfecto de indicativo	
he calzado	**hemos** calzado
has calzado	**habéis** calzado
ha calzado	**han** calzado
pluscuamperfecto de indicativo	
había calzado	**habíamos** calzado
habías calzado	**habíais** calzado
había calzado	**habían** calzado
pretérito anterior	
hube calzado	**hubimos** calzado
hubiste calzado	**hubisteis** calzado
hubo calzado	**hubieron** calzado
futuro perfecto	
habré calzado	**habremos** calzado
habrás calzado	**habréis** calzado
habrá calzado	**habrán** calzado
condicional compuesto	
habría calzado	**habríamos** calzado
habrías calzado	**habríais** calzado
habría calzado	**habrían** calzado
perfecto de subjuntivo	
haya calzado	**hayamos** calzado
hayas calzado	**hayáis** calzado
haya calzado	**hayan** calzado
pluscuamperfecto de subjuntivo	
hubiera calzado	**hubiéramos** calzado
hubieras calzado	**hubierais** calzado
hubiera calzado	**hubieran** calzado
OR	
hubiese calzado	**hubiésemos** calzado
hubieses calzado	**hubieseis** calzado
hubiese calzado	**hubiesen** calzado

to change — cambiar

gerundio **cambiando** participio de pasado **cambiado**

SINGULAR	PLURAL
presente de indicativo	
cambi**o**	cambi**amos**
cambi**as**	cambi**áis**
cambi**a**	cambi**an**
imperfecto de indicativo	
cambi**aba**	cambi**ábamos**
cambi**abas**	cambi**abais**
cambi**aba**	cambi**aban**
pretérito	
cambi**é**	cambi**amos**
cambi**aste**	cambi**asteis**
cambi**ó**	cambi**aron**
futuro	
cambiar**é**	cambiar**emos**
cambiar**ás**	cambiar**éis**
cambiar**á**	cambiar**án**
condicional simple	
cambiar**ía**	cambiar**íamos**
cambiar**ías**	cambiar**íais**
cambiar**ía**	cambiar**ían**
presente de subjuntivo	
cambi**e**	cambi**emos**
cambi**es**	cambi**éis**
cambi**e**	cambi**en**
imperfecto de subjuntivo	
cambiar**a**	cambiár**amos**
cambiar**as**	cambiar**ais**
cambiar**a**	cambiar**an**
OR	
cambias**e**	cambiás**emos**
cambias**es**	cambias**eis**
cambias**e**	cambias**en**
imperativo	
—	cambiemos
cambia; no cambies	cambiad; no cambiéis
cambie	cambien

SINGULAR	PLURAL
perfecto de indicativo	
he cambiado	**hemos** cambiado
has cambiado	**habéis** cambiado
ha cambiado	**han** cambiado
pluscuamperfecto de indicativo	
había cambiado	**habíamos** cambiado
habías cambiado	**habíais** cambiado
había cambiado	**habían** cambiado
pretérito anterior	
hube cambiado	**hubimos** cambiado
hubiste cambiado	**hubisteis** cambiado
hubo cambiado	**hubieron** cambiado
futuro perfecto	
habré cambiado	**habremos** cambiado
habrás cambiado	**habréis** cambiado
habrá cambiado	**habrán** cambiado
condicional compuesto	
habría cambiado	**habríamos** cambiado
habrías cambiado	**habríais** cambiado
habría cambiado	**habrían** cambiado
perfecto de subjuntivo	
haya cambiado	**hayamos** cambiado
hayas cambiado	**hayáis** cambiado
haya cambiado	**hayan** cambiado
pluscuamperfecto de subjuntivo	
hubiera cambiado	**hubiéramos** cambiado
hubieras cambiado	**hubierais** cambiado
hubiera cambiado	**hubieran** cambiado
OR	
hubiese cambiado	**hubiésemos** cambiado
hubieses cambiado	**hubieseis** cambiado
hubiese cambiado	**hubiesen** cambiado

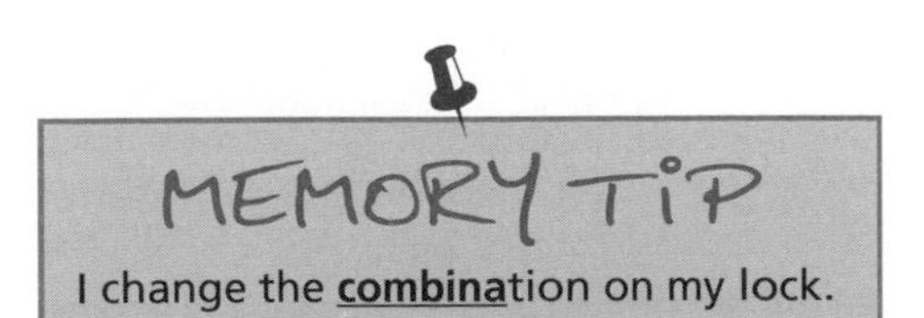

caminar — to walk

gerundio **caminando** — participio de pasado **caminado**

presente de indicativo

SINGULAR	PLURAL
camin**o**	camin**amos**
camin**as**	camin**áis**
camin**a**	camin**an**

imperfecto de indicativo

SINGULAR	PLURAL
camin**aba**	camin**ábamos**
camin**abas**	camin**abais**
camin**aba**	camin**aban**

pretérito

SINGULAR	PLURAL
camin**é**	camin**amos**
camin**aste**	camin**asteis**
camin**ó**	camin**aron**

futuro

SINGULAR	PLURAL
caminar**é**	caminar**emos**
caminar**ás**	caminar**éis**
caminar**á**	caminar**án**

condicional simple

SINGULAR	PLURAL
caminar**ía**	caminar**íamos**
caminar**ías**	caminar**íais**
caminar**ía**	caminar**ían**

presente de subjuntivo

SINGULAR	PLURAL
camin**e**	camin**emos**
camin**es**	camin**éis**
camin**e**	camin**en**

imperfecto de subjuntivo

SINGULAR	PLURAL
caminar**a**	caminár**amos**
caminar**as**	caminar**ais**
caminar**a**	caminar**an**
OR	
caminas**e**	caminás**emos**
caminas**es**	caminas**eis**
caminas**e**	caminas**en**

imperativo

SINGULAR	PLURAL
—	caminemos
camina; no camines	caminad; no caminéis
camine	caminen

perfecto de indicativo

SINGULAR	PLURAL
he caminado	**hemos** caminado
has caminado	**habéis** caminado
ha caminado	**han** caminado

pluscuamperfecto de indicativo

SINGULAR	PLURAL
había caminado	**habíamos** caminado
habías caminado	**habíais** caminado
había caminado	**habían** caminado

pretérito anterior

SINGULAR	PLURAL
hube caminado	**hubimos** caminado
hubiste caminado	**hubisteis** caminado
hubo caminado	**hubieron** caminado

futuro perfecto

SINGULAR	PLURAL
habré caminado	**habremos** caminado
habrás caminado	**habréis** caminado
habrá caminado	**habrán** caminado

condicional compuesto

SINGULAR	PLURAL
habría caminado	**habríamos** caminado
habrías caminado	**habríais** caminado
habría caminado	**habrían** caminado

perfecto de subjuntivo

SINGULAR	PLURAL
haya caminado	**hayamos** caminado
hayas caminado	**hayáis** caminado
haya caminado	**hayan** caminado

pluscuamperfecto de subjuntivo

SINGULAR	PLURAL
hubiera caminado	**hubiéramos** caminado
hubieras caminado	**hubierais** caminado
hubiera caminado	**hubieran** caminado
OR	
hubiese caminado	**hubiésemos** caminado
hubieses caminado	**hubieseis** caminado
hubiese caminado	**hubiesen** caminado

gerundio **cansándose** participio de pasado **cansado**

SINGULAR	PLURAL	SINGULAR	PLURAL
presente de indicativo		perfecto de indicativo	
me cans**o**	nos cans**amos**	**me he** cansado	**nos hemos** cansado
te cans**as**	os cans**áis**	**te has** cansado	**os habéis** cansado
se cans**a**	se cans**an**	**se ha** cansado	**se han** cansado
imperfecto de indicativo		pluscuamperfecto de indicativo	
me cans**aba**	nos cans**ábamos**	**me había** cansado	**nos habíamos** cansado
te cans**abas**	os cans**abais**	**te habías** cansado	**os habíais** cansado
se cans**aba**	se cans**aban**	**se había** cansado	**se habían** cansado
pretérito		pretérito anterior	
me cans**é**	nos cans**amos**	**me hube** cansado	**nos hubimos** cansado
te cans**aste**	os cans**asteis**	**te hubiste** cansado	**os hubisteis** cansado
se cans**ó**	se cans**aron**	**se hubo** cansado	**se hubieron** cansado
futuro		futuro perfecto	
me cansar**é**	nos cansar**emos**	**me habré** cansado	**nos habremos** cansado
te cansar**ás**	os cansar**éis**	**te habrás** cansado	**os habréis** cansado
se cansar**á**	se cansar**án**	**se habrá** cansado	**se habrán** cansado
condicional simple		condicional compuesto	
me cansar**ía**	nos cansar**íamos**	**me habría** cansado	**nos habríamos** cansado
te cansar**ías**	os cansar**íais**	**te habrías** cansado	**os habríais** cansado
se cansar**ía**	se cansar**ían**	**se habría** cansado	**se habrían** cansado
presente de subjuntivo		perfecto de subjuntivo	
me cans**e**	nos cans**emos**	**me haya** cansado	**nos hayamos** cansado
te cans**es**	os cans**éis**	**te hayas** cansado	**os hayáis** cansado
se cans**e**	se cans**en**	**se haya** cansado	**se hayan** cansado
imperfecto de subjuntivo		pluscuamperfecto de subjuntivo	
me cansar**a**	nos cansár**amos**	**me hubiera** cansado	**nos hubiéramos** cansado
te cansar**as**	os cansar**ais**	**te hubieras** cansado	**os hubierais** cansado
se cansar**a**	se cansar**an**	**se hubiera** cansado	**se hubieran** cansado
OR		OR	
me cansas**e**	nos cansás**emos**	**me hubiese** cansado	**nos hubiésemos** cansado
te cansas**es**	os cansas**eis**	**te hubieses** cansado	**os hubieseis** cansado
se cansas**e**	se cansas**en**	**se hubiese** cansado	**se hubiesen** cansado

imperativo

—	cansémonos; no nos cansemos
cánsate; no te canses	cansaos; no os canséis
cánsese; no se canse	cánsense; no se cansen

cantar — to sing

gerundio **cantando** participio de pasado **cantado**

SINGULAR	PLURAL
presente de indicativo	
cant**o**	cant**amos**
cant**as**	cant**áis**
cant**a**	cant**an**
imperfecto de indicativo	
cant**aba**	cant**ábamos**
cant**abas**	cant**abais**
cant**aba**	cant**aban**
pretérito	
cant**é**	cant**amos**
cant**aste**	cant**asteis**
cant**ó**	cant**aron**
futuro	
cantar**é**	cantar**emos**
cantar**ás**	cantar**éis**
cantar**á**	cantar**án**
condicional simple	
cantar**ía**	cantar**íamos**
cantar**ías**	cantar**íais**
cantar**ía**	cantar**ían**
presente de subjuntivo	
cant**e**	cant**emos**
cant**es**	cant**éis**
cant**e**	cant**en**
imperfecto de subjuntivo	
cantar**a**	cantár**amos**
cantar**as**	cantar**ais**
cantar**a**	cantar**an**
OR	
cantas**e**	cantás**emos**
cantas**es**	cantas**eis**
cantas**e**	cantas**en**
imperativo	
—	cantemos
canta; no cantes	cantad; no cantéis
cante	canten

SINGULAR	PLURAL
perfecto de indicativo	
he cantado	**hemos** cantado
has cantado	**habéis** cantado
ha cantado	**han** cantado
pluscuamperfecto de indicativo	
había cantado	**habíamos** cantado
habías cantado	**habíais** cantado
había cantado	**habían** cantado
pretérito anterior	
hube cantado	**hubimos** cantado
hubiste cantado	**hubisteis** cantado
hubo cantado	**hubieron** cantado
futuro perfecto	
habré cantado	**habremos** cantado
habrás cantado	**habréis** cantado
habrá cantado	**habrán** cantado
condicional compuesto	
habría cantado	**habríamos** cantado
habrías cantado	**habríais** cantado
habría cantado	**habrían** cantado
perfecto de subjuntivo	
haya cantado	**hayamos** cantado
hayas cantado	**hayáis** cantado
haya cantado	**hayan** cantado
pluscuamperfecto de subjuntivo	
hubiera cantado	**hubiéramos** cantado
hubieras cantado	**hubierais** cantado
hubiera cantado	**hubieran** cantado
OR	
hubiese cantado	**hubiésemos** cantado
hubieses cantado	**hubieseis** cantado
hubiese cantado	**hubiesen** cantado

to characterize — caracterizar

gerundio **caracterizando** participio de pasado **caracterizado**

SINGULAR	PLURAL	SINGULAR	PLURAL
presente de indicativo		perfecto de indicativo	
caracteriz**o**	caracteriz**amos**	**he** caracterizado	**hemos** caracterizado
caracteriz**as**	caracteriz**áis**	**has** caracterizado	**habéis** caracterizado
caracteriz**a**	caracteriz**an**	**ha** caracterizado	**han** caracterizado
imperfecto de indicativo		pluscuamperfecto de indicativo	
caracteriz**aba**	caracteriz**ábamos**	**había** caracterizado	**habíamos** caracterizado
caracteriz**abas**	caracteriz**abais**	**habías** caracterizado	**habíais** caracterizado
caracteriz**aba**	caracteriz**aban**	**había** caracterizado	**habían** caracterizado
pretérito		pretérito anterior	
caracteri**cé**	caracteriz**amos**	**hube** caracterizado	**hubimos** caracterizado
caracteriz**aste**	caracteriz**asteis**	**hubiste** caracterizado	**hubisteis** caracterizado
caracteriz**ó**	caracteriz**aron**	**hubo** caracterizado	**hubieron** caracterizado
futuro		futuro perfecto	
caracterizar**é**	caracterizar**emos**	**habré** caracterizado	**habremos** caracterizado
caracterizar**ás**	caracterizar**éis**	**habrás** caracterizado	**habréis** caracterizado
caracterizar**á**	caracterizar**án**	**habrá** caracterizado	**habrán** caracterizado
condicional simple		condicional compuesto	
caracterizar**ía**	caracterizar**íamos**	**habría** caracterizado	**habríamos** caracterizado
caracterizar**ías**	caracterizar**íais**	**habrías** caracterizado	**habríais** caracterizado
caracterizar**ía**	caracterizar**ían**	**habría** caracterizado	**habrían** caracterizado
presente de subjuntivo		perfecto de subjuntivo	
caracteric**e**	caracteric**emos**	**haya** caracterizado	**hayamos** caracterizado
caracteric**es**	caracteric**éis**	**hayas** caracterizado	**hayáis** caracterizado
caracteric**e**	caracteric**en**	**haya** caracterizado	**hayan** caracterizado
imperfecto de subjuntivo		pluscuamperfecto de subjuntivo	
caracterizar**a**	caracterizár**amos**	**hubiera** caracterizado	**hubiéramos** caracterizado
caracterizar**as**	caracterizar**ais**	**hubieras** caracterizado	**hubierais** caracterizado
caracterizar**a**	caracterizar**an**	**hubiera** caracterizado	**hubieran** caracterizado
OR		OR	
caracterizas**e**	caracterizás**emos**	**hubiese** caracterizado	**hubiésemos** caracterizado
caracterizas**es**	caracterizas**eis**	**hubieses** caracterizado	**hubieseis** caracterizado
caracterizas**e**	caracterizas**en**	**hubiese** caracterizado	**hubiesen** caracterizado

imperativo

—	caractericemos
caracteriza; no caracterices	caracterizad; no caractericéis
caracterice	caractericen

carecer — to lack

gerundio **careciendo** participio de pasado **carecido**

SINGULAR	PLURAL	SINGULAR	PLURAL
presente de indicativo		perfecto de indicativo	
carezc**o**	carec**emos**	**he** carecido	**hemos** carecido
carec**es**	carec**éis**	**has** carecido	**habéis** carecido
carec**e**	carec**en**	**ha** carecido	**han** carecido
imperfecto de indicativo		pluscuamperfecto de indicativo	
carec**ía**	carec**íamos**	**había** carecido	**habíamos** carecido
carec**ías**	carec**íais**	**habías** carecido	**habíais** carecido
carec**ía**	carec**ían**	**había** carecido	**habían** carecido
pretérito		pretérito anterior	
carec**í**	carec**imos**	**hube** carecido	**hubimos** carecido
carec**iste**	carec**isteis**	**hubiste** carecido	**hubisteis** carecido
careci**ó**	carec**ieron**	**hubo** carecido	**hubieron** carecido
futuro		futuro perfecto	
carecer**é**	carecer**emos**	**habré** carecido	**habremos** carecido
carecer**ás**	carecer**éis**	**habrás** carecido	**habréis** carecido
carecer**á**	carecer**án**	**habrá** carecido	**habrán** carecido
condicional simple		condicional compuesto	
carecer**ía**	carecer**íamos**	**habría** carecido	**habríamos** carecido
carecer**ías**	carecer**íais**	**habrías** carecido	**habríais** carecido
carecer**ía**	carecer**ían**	**habría** carecido	**habrían** carecido
presente de subjuntivo		perfecto de subjuntivo	
carezc**a**	carezc**amos**	**haya** carecido	**hayamos** carecido
carezc**as**	carezc**áis**	**hayas** carecido	**hayáis** carecido
carezc**a**	carezc**an**	**haya** carecido	**hayan** carecido
imperfecto de subjuntivo		pluscuamperfecto de subjuntivo	
careciera	careciér**amos**	**hubiera** carecido	**hubiéramos** carecido
careci**eras**	careci**erais**	**hubieras** carecido	**hubierais** carecido
careci**era**	careci**eran**	**hubiera** carecido	**hubieran** carecido
OR		OR	
careci**ese**	careciés**emos**	**hubiese** carecido	**hubiésemos** carecido
careci**eses**	careci**eseis**	**hubieses** carecido	**hubieseis** carecido
careci**ese**	careci**esen**	**hubiese** carecido	**hubiesen** carecido

imperativo

—	carezcamos
carece; no carezcas	careced; no carezcáis
carezca	carezcan

to load, to carry — cargar

gerundio **cargando** — participio de pasado **cargado**

presente de indicativo

SINGULAR	PLURAL
carg**o**	carg**amos**
carg**as**	carg**áis**
carg**a**	carg**an**

imperfecto de indicativo

SINGULAR	PLURAL
carg**aba**	carg**ábamos**
carg**abas**	carg**abais**
carg**aba**	carg**aban**

pretérito

SINGULAR	PLURAL
cargu**é**	carg**amos**
carg**aste**	carg**asteis**
carg**ó**	carg**aron**

futuro

SINGULAR	PLURAL
cargar**é**	cargar**emos**
cargar**ás**	cargar**éis**
cargar**á**	cargar**án**

condicional simple

SINGULAR	PLURAL
cargar**ía**	cargar**íamos**
cargar**ías**	cargar**íais**
cargar**ía**	cargar**ían**

presente de subjuntivo

SINGULAR	PLURAL
cargu**e**	cargu**emos**
cargu**es**	cargu**éis**
cargu**e**	cargu**en**

imperfecto de subjuntivo

SINGULAR	PLURAL
cargar**a**	cargár**amos**
cargar**as**	cargar**ais**
cargar**a**	cargar**an**
OR	
cargas**e**	cargás**emos**
cargas**es**	cargas**eis**
cargas**e**	cargas**en**

imperativo

SINGULAR	PLURAL
—	carguemos
carga; no cargues	cargad; no carguéis
cargue	carguen

perfecto de indicativo

SINGULAR	PLURAL
he cargado	**hemos** cargado
has cargado	**habéis** cargado
ha cargado	**han** cargado

pluscuamperfecto de indicativo

SINGULAR	PLURAL
había cargado	**habíamos** cargado
habías cargado	**habíais** cargado
había cargado	**habían** cargado

pretérito anterior

SINGULAR	PLURAL
hube cargado	**hubimos** cargado
hubiste cargado	**hubisteis** cargado
hubo cargado	**hubieron** cargado

futuro perfecto

SINGULAR	PLURAL
habré cargado	**habremos** cargado
habrás cargado	**habréis** cargado
habrá cargado	**habrán** cargado

condicional compuesto

SINGULAR	PLURAL
habría cargado	**habríamos** cargado
habrías cargado	**habríais** cargado
habría cargado	**habrían** cargado

perfecto de subjuntivo

SINGULAR	PLURAL
haya cargado	**hayamos** cargado
hayas cargado	**hayáis** cargado
haya cargado	**hayan** cargado

pluscuamperfecto de subjuntivo

SINGULAR	PLURAL
hubiera cargado	**hubiéramos** cargado
hubieras argado	**hubierais** cargado
hubiera argado	**hubieran** cargado
OR	
hubiese cargado	**hubiésemos** cargado
hubieses cargado	**hubieseis** cargado
hubiese argado	**hubiesen** argado

casarse — to get married, to marry

gerundio **casándose** participio de pasado **casado**

SINGULAR	PLURAL

presente de indicativo

SINGULAR	PLURAL
me cas**o**	nos cas**amos**
te cas**as**	os cas**áis**
se cas**a**	se cas**an**

imperfecto de indicativo

SINGULAR	PLURAL
me cas**aba**	nos cas**ábamos**
te cas**abas**	os cas**abais**
se cas**aba**	se cas**aban**

pretérito

SINGULAR	PLURAL
me cas**é**	nos cas**amos**
te cas**aste**	os cas**asteis**
se cas**ó**	se cas**aron**

futuro

SINGULAR	PLURAL
me casar**é**	nos casar**emos**
te casar**ás**	os casar**éis**
se casar**á**	se casar**án**

condicional simple

SINGULAR	PLURAL
me casar**ía**	nos casar**íamos**
te casar**ías**	os casar**íais**
se casar**ía**	se casar**ían**

presente de subjuntivo

SINGULAR	PLURAL
me cas**e**	nos cas**emos**
te cas**es**	os cas**éis**
se cas**e**	se cas**en**

imperfecto de subjuntivo

SINGULAR	PLURAL
me casar**a**	nos casár**amos**
te casar**as**	os casar**ais**
se casar**a**	se casar**an**
OR	
me casas**e**	nos casás**emos**
te casas**es**	os casas**eis**
se casas**e**	se casas**en**

imperativo

SINGULAR	PLURAL
—	casémonosno nos casemos
cásate; no te cases	casaos; no os caséis
cásese; no se case	cásense; no se casen

SINGULAR	PLURAL

perfecto de indicativo

SINGULAR	PLURAL
me he casado	**nos hemos** casado
te has casado	**os habéis** casado
se ha casado	**se han** casado

pluscuamperfecto de indicativo

SINGULAR	PLURAL
me había casado	**nos habíamos** casado
te habías casado	**os habíais** casado
se había casado	**se habían** casado

pretérito anterior

SINGULAR	PLURAL
me hube casado	**nos hubimos** casado
te hubiste casado	**os hubisteis** casado
se hubo casado	**se hubieron** casado

futuro perfecto

SINGULAR	PLURAL
me habré casado	**nos habremos** casado
te habrás casado	**os habréis** casado
se habrá casado	**se habrán** casado

condicional compuesto

SINGULAR	PLURAL
me habría casado	**nos habríamos** casado
te habrías casado	**os habríais** casado
se habría casado	**se habrían** casado

perfecto de subjuntivo

SINGULAR	PLURAL
me haya casado	**nos hayamos** casado
te hayas casado	**os hayáis** casado
se haya casado	**se hayan** casado

pluscuamperfecto de subjuntivo

SINGULAR	PLURAL
me hubiera casado	**nos hubiéramos** casado
te hubieras casado	**os hubierais** casado
se hubiera casado	**se hubieran** casado
OR	
me hubiese casado	**nos hubiésemos** casado
te hubieses casado	**os hubieseis** casado
se hubiese casado	**se hubiesen** casado

to blind — cegar

gerundio **cegando** participio de pasado **cegado**

SINGULAR	PLURAL	SINGULAR	PLURAL
presente de indicativo		perfecto de indicativo	
ciego	cegamos	he cegado	hemos cegado
ciegas	cegáis	has cegado	habéis cegado
ciega	ciegan	ha cegado	han cegado
imperfecto de indicativo		pluscuamperfecto de indicativo	
cegaba	cegábamos	había cegado	habíamos cegado
cegabas	cegabais	habías cegado	habíais cegado
cegaba	cegaban	había cegado	habían cegado
pretérito		pretérito anterior	
cegué	cegamos	hube cegado	hubimos cegado
cegaste	cegasteis	hubiste cegado	hubisteis cegado
cegó	cegaron	hubo cegado	hubieron cegado
futuro		futuro perfecto	
cegaré	cegaremos	habré cegado	habremos cegado
cegarás	cegaréis	habrás cegado	habréis cegado
cegará	cegarán	habrá cegado	habrán cegado
condicional simple		condicional compuesto	
cegaría	cegaríamos	habría cegado	habríamos cegado
cegarías	cegaríais	habrías cegado	habríais cegado
cegaría	cegarían	habría cegado	habrían cegado
presente de subjuntivo		perfecto de subjuntivo	
ciegue	ceguemos	haya cegado	hayamos cegado
ciegues	ceguéis	hayas cegado	hayáis cegado
ciegue	cieguen	haya cegado	hayan cegado
imperfecto de subjuntivo		pluscuamperfecto de subjuntivo	
cegara	cegáramos	hubiera cegado	hubiéramos cegado
cegaras	cegarais	hubieras cegado	hubierais cegado
cegara	cegaran	hubiera cegado	hubieran cegado
OR		OR	
cegase	cegásemos	hubiese cegado	hubiésemos cegado
cegases	cegaseis	hubieses cegado	hubieseis cegado
cegase	cegasen	hubiese cegado	hubiesen cegado

imperativo

—	ceguemos
ciega; no ciegues	cegad; no ceguéis
ciegue	cieguen

celebrar — to celebrate

gerundio **celebrando** participio de pasado **celebrado**

SINGULAR	PLURAL	SINGULAR	PLURAL
presente de indicativo		**perfecto de indicativo**	
celebr**o**	celebr**amos**	**he** celebrado	**hemos** celebrado
celebr**as**	celebr**áis**	**has** celebrado	**habéis** celebrado
celebr**a**	celebr**an**	**ha** celebrado	**han** celebrado
imperfecto de indicativo		**pluscuamperfecto de indicativo**	
celebr**aba**	celebr**ábamos**	**había** celebrado	**habíamos** celebrado
celebr**abas**	celebr**abais**	**habías** celebrado	**habíais** celebrado
celebr**aba**	celebr**aban**	**había** celebrado	**habían** celebrado
pretérito		**pretérito anterior**	
celebr**é**	celebr**amos**	**hube** celebrado	**hubimos** celebrado
celebr**aste**	celebr**asteis**	**hubiste** celebrado	**hubisteis** celebrado
celebr**ó**	celebr**aron**	**hubo** celebrado	**hubieron** celebrado
futuro		**futuro perfecto**	
celebrar**é**	celebrar**emos**	**habré** celebrado	**habremos** celebrado
celebrar**ás**	celebrar**éis**	**habrás** celebrado	**habréis** celebrado
celebrar**á**	celebrar**án**	**habrá** celebrado	**habrán** celebrado
condicional simple		**condicional compuesto**	
celebrar**ía**	celebrar**íamos**	**habría** celebrado	**habríamos** celebrado
celebrar**ías**	celebrar**íais**	**habrías** celebrado	**habríais** celebrado
celebrar**ía**	celebrar**ían**	**habría** celebrado	**habrían** celebrado
presente de subjuntivo		**perfecto de subjuntivo**	
celebr**e**	celebr**emos**	**haya** celebrado	**hayamos** celebrado
celebr**es**	celebr**éis**	**hayas** celebrado	**hayáis** celebrado
celebr**e**	celebr**en**	**haya** celebrado	**hayan** celebrado
imperfecto de subjuntivo		**pluscuamperfecto de subjuntivo**	
celebrar**a**	celebrár**amos**	**hubiera** celebrado	**hubiéramos** celebrado
celebrar**as**	celebrar**ais**	**hubieras** celebrado	**hubierais** celebrado
celebrar**a**	celebrar**an**	**hubiera** celebrado	**hubieran** celebrado
OR		OR	
celebras**e**	celebrás**emos**	**hubiese** celebrado	**hubiésemos** celebrado
celebras**es**	celebras**eis**	**hubieses** celebrado	**hubieseis** celebrado
celebras**e**	celebras**en**	**hubiese** celebrado	**hubiesen** celebrado

imperativo

—	celebremos
celebra; no celebres	celebrad; no celebréis
celebre	celebren

gerundio **cenando** participio de pasado **cenado**

SINGULAR	PLURAL	SINGULAR	PLURAL
presente de indicativo		perfecto de indicativo	
cen**o**	cen**amos**	**he** cenado	**hemos** cenado
cen**as**	cen**áis**	**has** cenado	**habéis** cenado
cen**a**	cen**an**	**ha** cenado	**han** cenado
imperfecto de indicativo		pluscuamperfecto de indicativo	
cen**aba**	cen**ábamos**	**había** cenado	**habíamos** cenado
cen**abas**	cen**abais**	**habías** cenado	**habíais** cenado
cen**aba**	cen**aban**	**había** cenado	**habían** cenado
pretérito		pretérito anterior	
cen**é**	cen**amos**	**hube** cenado	**hubimos** cenado
cen**aste**	cen**asteis**	**hubiste** cenado	**hubisteis** cenado
cen**ó**	cen**aron**	**hubo** cenado	**hubieron** cenado
futuro		futuro perfecto	
cenar**é**	cenar**emos**	**habré** cenado	**habremos** cenado
cenar**ás**	cenar**éis**	**habrás** cenado	**habréis** cenado
cenar**á**	cenar**án**	**habrá** cenado	**habrán** cenado
condicional simple		condicional compuesto	
cenar**ía**	cenar**íamos**	**habría** cenado	**habríamos** cenado
cenar**ías**	cenar**íais**	**habrías** cenado	**habríais** cenado
cenar**ía**	cenar**ían**	**habría** cenado	**habrían** cenado
presente de subjuntivo		perfecto de subjuntivo	
cen**e**	cen**emos**	**haya** cenado	**hayamos** cenado
cen**es**	cen**éis**	**hayas** cenado	**hayáis** cenado
cen**e**	cen**en**	**haya** cenado	**hayan** cenado
imperfecto de subjuntivo		pluscuamperfecto de subjuntivo	
cenar**a**	cenár**amos**	**hubiera** cenado	**hubiéramos** cenado
cenar**as**	cenar**ais**	**hubieras** cenado	**hubierais** cenado
cenar**a**	cenar**an**	**hubiera** cenado	**hubieran** cenado
OR		OR	
cenas**e**	cenás**emos**	**hubiese** cenado	**hubiésemos** cenado
cenas**es**	cenas**eis**	**hubieses** cenado	**hubieseis** cenado
cenas**e**	cenas**en**	**hubiese** cenado	**hubiesen** cenado

imperativo

—	cenemos
cena; no cenes	cenad; no cenéis
cene	cenen

cepillar — to brush

gerundio **cepillando** — participio de pasado **cepillado**

SINGULAR	PLURAL
presente de indicativo	
cepill**o**	cepill**amos**
cepill**as**	cepill**áis**
cepill**a**	cepill**an**
imperfecto de indicativo	
cepill**aba**	cepill**ábamos**
cepill**abas**	cepill**abais**
cepill**aba**	cepill**aban**
pretérito	
cepill**é**	cepill**amos**
cepill**aste**	cepill**asteis**
cepill**ó**	cepill**aron**
futuro	
cepillar**é**	cepillar**emos**
cepillar**ás**	cepillar**éis**
cepillar**á**	cepillar**án**
condicional simple	
cepillar**ía**	cepillar**íamos**
cepillar**ías**	cepillar**íais**
cepillar**ía**	cepillar**ían**
presente de subjuntivo	
cepill**e**	cepill**emos**
cepill**es**	cepill**éis**
cepill**e**	cepill**en**
imperfecto de subjuntivo	
cepillar**a**	cepillár**amos**
cepillar**as**	cepillar**ais**
cepillar**a**	cepillar**an**
OR	
cepillas**e**	cepillás**emos**
cepillas**es**	cepillas**eis**
cepillas**e**	cepillas**en**
imperativo	
—	cepillemos
cepilla; no cepilles	cepillad; no cepilléis
cepille	cepillen

SINGULAR	PLURAL
perfecto de indicativo	
he cepillado	**hemos** cepillado
has cepillado	**habéis** cepillado
ha cepillado	**han** cepillado
pluscuamperfecto de indicativo	
había cepillado	**habíamos** cepillado
habías cepillado	**habíais** cepillado
había cepillado	**habían** cepillado
pretérito anterior	
hube cepillado	**hubimos** cepillado
hubiste cepillado	**hubisteis** cepillado
hubo cepillado	**hubieron** cepillado
futuro perfecto	
habré cepillado	**habremos** cepillado
habrás cepillado	**habréis** cepillado
habrá cepillado	**habrán** cepillado
condicional compuesto	
habría cepillado	**habríamos** cepillado
habrías cepillado	**habríais** cepillado
habría cepillado	**habrían** cepillado
perfecto de subjuntivo	
haya cepillado	**hayamos** cepillado
hayas cepillado	**hayáis** cepillado
haya cepillado	**hayan** cepillado
pluscuamperfecto de subjuntivo	
hubiera cepillado	**hubiéramos** cepillado
hubieras cepillado	**hubierais** cepillado
hubiera cepillado	**hubieran** cepillado
OR	
hubiese cepillado	**hubiésemos** cepillado
hubieses cepillado	**hubieseis** cepillado
hubiese cepillado	**hubiesen** cepillado

to close **cerrar**

gerundio **cerrando** participio de pasado **cerrado**

SINGULAR	PLURAL	SINGULAR	PLURAL
presente de indicativo		perfecto de indicativo	
cierr**o**	cerr**amos**	**he** cerrado	**hemos** cerrado
cierr**as**	cerr**áis**	**has** cerrado	**habéis** cerrado
cierr**a**	cierr**an**	**ha** cerrado	**han** cerrado
imperfecto de indicativo		pluscuamperfecto de indicativo	
cerr**aba**	cerr**ábamos**	**había** cerrado	**habíamos** cerrado
cerr**abas**	cerr**abais**	**habías** cerrado	**habíais** cerrado
cerr**aba**	cerr**aban**	**había** cerrado	**habían** cerrado
pretérito		pretérito anterior	
cerr**é**	cerr**amos**	**hube** cerrado	**hubimos** cerrado
cerr**aste**	cerr**asteis**	**hubiste** cerrado	**hubisteis** cerrado
cerr**ó**	cerr**aron**	**hubo** cerrado	**hubieron** cerrado
futuro		futuro perfecto	
cerrar**é**	cerrar**emos**	**habré** cerrado	**habremos** cerrado
cerrar**ás**	cerrar**éis**	**habrás** cerrado	**habréis** cerrado
cerrar**á**	cerrar**án**	**habrá** cerrado	**habrán** cerrado
condicional simple		condicional compuesto	
cerrar**ía**	cerrar**íamos**	**habría** cerrado	**habríamos** cerrado
cerrar**ías**	cerrar**íais**	**habrías** cerrado	**habríais** cerrado
cerrar**ía**	cerrar**ían**	**habría** cerrado	**habrían** cerrado
presente de subjuntivo		perfecto de subjuntivo	
cierr**e**	cerr**emos**	**haya** cerrado	**hayamos** cerrado
cierr**es**	cerr**éis**	**hayas** cerrado	**hayáis** cerrado
cierr**e**	cierr**en**	**haya** cerrado	**hayan** cerrado
imperfecto de subjuntivo		pluscuamperfecto de subjuntivo	
cerrar**a**	cerrár**amos**	**hubiera** cerrado	**hubiéramos** cerrado
cerrar**as**	cerrar**ais**	**hubieras** cerrado	**hubierais** cerrado
cerrar**a**	cerrar**an**	**hubiera** cerrado	**hubieran** cerrado
OR		OR	
cerras**e**	cerrás**emos**	**hubiese** cerrado	**hubiésemos** cerrado
cerras**es**	cerras**eis**	**hubieses** cerrado	**hubieseis** cerrado
cerras**e**	cerras**en**	**hubiese** cerrado	**hubiesen** cerrado

imperativo

—	cerremos
cierra; no cierres	cerrad; no cerréis
cierre	cierren

C

certificar — to certify

gerundio **certificando** | participio de pasado **certificado**

SINGULAR	PLURAL	SINGULAR	PLURAL
presente de indicativo		perfecto de indicativo	
certific**o**	certific**amos**	**he** certificado	**hemos** certificado
certific**as**	certific**áis**	**has** certificado	**habéis** certificado
certific**a**	certific**an**	**ha** certificado	**han** certificado
imperfecto de indicativo		pluscuamperfecto de indicativo	
certific**aba**	certific**ábamos**	**había** certificado	**habíamos** certificado
certific**abas**	certific**abais**	**habías** certificado	**habíais** certificado
certific**aba**	certific**aban**	**había** certificado	**habían** certificado
pretérito		pretérito anterior	
certifiqu**é**	certific**amos**	**hube** certificado	**hubimos** certificado
certific**aste**	certific**asteis**	**hubiste** certificado	**hubisteis** certificado
certific**ó**	certific**aron**	**hubo** certificado	**hubieron** certificado
futuro		futuro perfecto	
certificar**é**	certificar**emos**	**habré** certificado	**habremos** certificado
certificar**ás**	certificar**éis**	**habrás** certificado	**habréis** certificado
certificar**á**	certificar**án**	**habrá** certificado	**habrán** certificado
condicional simple		condicional compuesto	
certificar**ía**	certificar**íamos**	**habría** certificado	**habríamos** certificado
certificar**ías**	certificar**íais**	**habrías** certificado	**habríais** certificado
certificar**ía**	certificar**ían**	**habría** certificado	**habrían** certificado
presente de subjuntivo		perfecto de subjuntivo	
certifiqu**e**	certifiqu**emos**	**haya** certificado	**hayamos** certificado
certifiqu**es**	certifiqu**éis**	**hayas** certificado	**hayáis** certificado
certifiqu**e**	certifiqu**en**	**haya** certificado	**hayan** certificado
imperfecto de subjuntivo		pluscuamperfecto de subjuntivo	
certificar**a**	certificár**amos**	**hubiera** certificado	**hubiéramos** certificado
certificar**as**	certificar**ais**	**hubieras** certificado	**hubierais** certificado
certificar**a**	certificar**an**	**hubiera** certificado	**hubieran** certificado
OR		OR	
certificas**e**	certificás**emos**	**hubiese** certificado	**hubiésemos** certificado
certificas**es**	certificas**eis**	**hubieses** certificado	**hubieseis** certificado
certificas**e**	certificas**en**	**hubiese** certificado	**hubiesen** certificado

imperativo

—	certifiquemos
certifica; no certifiques	certificad; no certifiquéis
certifique	certifiquen

to chat, to talk — charlar

gerundio **charlando** participio de pasado **charlado**

SINGULAR	PLURAL

presente de indicativo

charl**o**	charl**amos**
charl**as**	charl**áis**
charl**a**	charl**an**

imperfecto de indicativo

charl**aba**	charl**ábamos**
charl**abas**	charl**abais**
charl**aba**	charl**aban**

pretérito

charl**é**	charl**amos**
charl**aste**	charl**asteis**
charl**ó**	charl**aron**

futuro

charlar**é**	charlar**emos**
charlar**ás**	charlar**éis**
charlar**á**	charlar**án**

condicional simple

charlar**ía**	charlar**íamos**
charlar**ías**	charlar**íais**
charlar**ía**	charlar**ían**

presente de subjuntivo

charl**e**	charl**emos**
charl**es**	charl**éis**
charl**e**	charl**en**

imperfecto de subjuntivo

charlar**a**	charlár**amos**
charlar**as**	charlar**ais**
charlar**a**	charlar**an**
OR	
charlas**e**	charlás**emos**
charlas**es**	charlas**eis**
charlas**e**	charlas**en**

imperativo

—	charlemos
charla; no charles	charlad; no charléis
charle	charlen

SINGULAR	PLURAL

perfecto de indicativo

he charlado	**hemos** charlado
has charlado	**habéis** charlado
ha charlado	**han** charlado

pluscuamperfecto de indicativo

había charlado	**habíamos** charlado
habías charlado	**habíais** charlado
había charlado	**habían** charlado

pretérito anterior

hube charlado	**hubimos** charlado
hubiste charlado	**hubisteis** charlado
hubo charlado	**hubieron** charlado

futuro perfecto

habré charlado	**habremos** charlado
habrás charlado	**habréis** charlado
habrá charlado	**habrán** charlado

condicional compuesto

habría charlado	**habríamos** charlado
habrías charlado	**habríais** charlado
habría charlado	**habrían** charlado

perfecto de subjuntivo

haya charlado	**hayamos** charlado
hayas charlado	**hayáis** charlado
haya charlado	**hayan** charlado

pluscuamperfecto de subjuntivo

hubiera charlado	**hubiéramos** charlado
hubieras charlado	**hubierais** charlado
hubiera charlado	**hubieran** charlado
OR	
hubiese charlado	**hubiésemos** charlado
hubieses charlado	**hubieseis** charlado
hubiese charlado	**hubiesen** charlado

chistar — to mumble

gerundio **chistando** participio de pasado **chistado**

SINGULAR	PLURAL
presente de indicativo	
chist**o**	chist**amos**
chist**as**	chist**áis**
chist**a**	chist**an**
imperfecto de indicativo	
chist**aba**	chist**ábamos**
chist**abas**	chist**abais**
chist**aba**	chist**aban**
pretérito	
chist**é**	chist**amos**
chist**aste**	chist**asteis**
chist**ó**	chist**aron**
futuro	
chistar**é**	chistar**emos**
chistar**ás**	chistar**éis**
chistar**á**	chistar**án**
condicional simple	
chistar**ía**	chistar**íamos**
chistar**ías**	chistar**íais**
chistar**ía**	chistar**ían**
presente de subjuntivo	
chist**e**	chist**emos**
chist**es**	chist**éis**
chist**e**	chist**en**
imperfecto de subjuntivo	
chistar**a**	chistár**amos**
chistar**as**	chistar**ais**
chistar**a**	chistar**an**
OR	
chistas**e**	chistás**emos**
chistas**es**	chistas**eis**
chistas**e**	chistas**en**
imperativo	
—	chistemos
chista; no chistes	chistad; no chistéis
chiste	chisten

SINGULAR	PLURAL
perfecto de indicativo	
he chistado	**hemos** chistado
has chistado	**habéis** chistado
ha chistado	**han** chistado
pluscuamperfecto de indicativo	
había chistado	**habíamos** chistado
habías chistado	**habíais** chistado
había chistado	**habían** chistado
pretérito anterior	
hube chistado	**hubimos** chistado
hubiste chistado	**hubisteis** chistado
hubo chistado	**hubieron** chistado
futuro perfecto	
habré chistado	**habremos** chistado
habrás chistado	**habréis** chistado
habrá chistado	**habrán** chistado
condicional compuesto	
habría chistado	**habríamos** chistado
habrías chistado	**habríais** chistado
habría chistado	**habrían** chistado
perfecto de subjuntivo	
haya chistado	**hayamos** chistado
hayas chistado	**hayáis** chistado
haya chistado	**hayan** chistado
pluscuamperfecto de subjuntivo	
hubiera chistado	**hubiéramos** chistado
hubieras chistado	**hubierais** chistado
hubiera chistado	**hubieran** chistado
OR	
hubiese chistado	**hubiésemos** chistado
hubieses chistado	**hubieseis** chistado
hubiese chistado	**hubiesen** chistado

gerundio **chocando** participio de pasado **chocado**

SINGULAR	PLURAL
presente de indicativo	
choc**o**	choc**amos**
choc**as**	choc**áis**
choc**a**	choc**an**
imperfecto de indicativo	
choc**aba**	choc**ábamos**
choc**abas**	choc**abais**
choc**aba**	choc**aban**
pretérito	
choqu**é**	choc**amos**
choc**aste**	choc**asteis**
choc**ó**	choc**aron**
futuro	
chocar**é**	chocar**emos**
chocar**ás**	chocar**éis**
chocar**á**	chocar**án**
condicional simple	
chocar**ía**	chocar**íamos**
chocar**ías**	chocar**íais**
chocar**ía**	chocar**ían**
presente de subjuntivo	
choqu**e**	choqu**emos**
choqu**es**	choqu**éis**
choqu**e**	choqu**en**
imperfecto de subjuntivo	
chocar**a**	chocár**amos**
chocar**as**	chocar**ais**
chocar**a**	chocar**an**
OR	
chocas**e**	chocás**emos**
chocas**es**	chocas**eis**
chocas**e**	chocas**en**
imperativo	
—	choquemos
choca; no choques	chocad; no choquéis
choque	choquen

SINGULAR	PLURAL
perfecto de indicativo	
he chocado	**hemos** chocado
has chocado	**habéis** chocado
ha chocado	**han** chocado
pluscuamperfecto de indicativo	
había chocado	**habíamos** chocado
habías chocado	**habíais** chocado
había chocado	**habían** chocado
pretérito anterior	
hube chocado	**hubimos** chocado
hubiste chocado	**hubisteis** chocado
hubo chocado	**hubieron** chocado
futuro perfecto	
habré chocado	**habremos** chocado
habrás chocado	**habréis** chocado
habrá chocado	**habrán** chocado
condicional compuesto	
habría chocado	**habríamos** chocado
habrías chocado	**habríais** chocado
habría chocado	**habrían** chocado
perfecto de subjuntivo	
haya chocado	**hayamos** chocado
hayas chocado	**hayáis** chocado
haya chocado	**hayan** chocado
pluscuamperfecto de subjuntivo	
hubiera chocado	**hubiéramos** chocado
hubieras chocado	**hubierais** chocado
hubiera chocado	**hubieran** chocado
OR	
hubiese chocado	**hubiésemos** chocado
hubieses chocado	**hubieseis** chocado
hubiese chocado	**hubiesen** chocado

chupar — to suck

gerundio **chupando** — participio de pasado **chupado**

SINGULAR	PLURAL
presente de indicativo	
chup**o**	chup**amos**
chup**as**	chup**áis**
chup**a**	chup**an**
imperfecto de indicativo	
chup**aba**	chup**ábamos**
chup**abas**	chup**abais**
chup**aba**	chup**aban**
pretérito	
chup**é**	chup**amos**
chup**aste**	chup**asteis**
chup**ó**	chup**aron**
futuro	
chupar**é**	chupar**emos**
chupar**ás**	chupar**éis**
chupar**á**	chupar**án**
condicional simple	
chupar**ía**	chupar**íamos**
chupar**ías**	chupar**íais**
chupar**ía**	chupar**ían**
presente de subjuntivo	
chup**e**	chup**emos**
chup**es**	chup**éis**
chup**e**	chup**en**
imperfecto de subjuntivo	
chupar**a**	chupár**amos**
chupar**as**	chupar**ais**
chupar**a**	chupar**an**
OR	
chupas**e**	chupás**emos**
chupas**es**	chupas**eis**
chupas**e**	chupas**en**
imperativo	
—	chupemos
chupa; no chupes	chupad; no chupéis
chupe	chupen

SINGULAR	PLURAL
perfecto de indicativo	
he chupado	**hemos** chupado
has chupado	**habéis** chupado
ha chupado	**han** chupado
pluscuamperfecto de indicativo	
había chupado	**habíamos** chupado
habías chupado	**habíais** chupado
había chupado	**habían** chupado
pretérito anterior	
hube chupado	**hubimos** chupado
hubiste chupado	**hubisteis** chupado
hubo chupado	**hubieron** chupado
futuro perfecto	
habré chupado	**habremos** chupado
habrás chupado	**habréis** chupado
habrá chupado	**habrán** chupado
condicional compuesto	
habría chupado	**habríamos** chupado
habrías chupado	**habríais** chupado
habría chupado	**habrían** chupado
perfecto de subjuntivo	
haya chupado	**hayamos** chupado
hayas chupado	**hayáis** chupado
haya chupado	**hayan** chupado
pluscuamperfecto de subjuntivo	
hubiera chupado	**hubiéramos** chupado
hubieras chupado	**hubierais** chupado
hubiera chupado	**hubieran** chupado
OR	
hubiese chupado	**hubiésemos** chupado
hubieses chupado	**hubieseis** chupado
hubiese chupado	**hubiesen** chupado

gerundio **citando** participio de pasado **citado**

SINGULAR	PLURAL
presente de indicativo	
cit**o**	cit**amos**
cit**as**	cit**áis**
cit**a**	cit**an**
imperfecto de indicativo	
cit**aba**	cit**ábamos**
cit**abas**	cit**abais**
cit**aba**	cit**aban**
pretérito	
cit**é**	cit**amos**
cit**aste**	cit**asteis**
cit**ó**	cit**aron**
futuro	
citar**é**	citar**emos**
citar**ás**	citar**éis**
citar**á**	citar**án**
condicional simple	
citar**ía**	citar**íamos**
citar**ías**	citar**íais**
citar**ía**	citar**ían**
presente de subjuntivo	
cit**e**	cit**emos**
cit**es**	cit**éis**
cit**e**	cit**en**
imperfecto de subjuntivo	
citar**a**	citár**amos**
citar**as**	citar**ais**
citar**a**	citar**an**
OR	
citas**e**	citás**emos**
citas**es**	citas**eis**
citas**e**	citas**en**
imperativo	
—	citemos
cita; no cites	citad; no citéis
cite	citen

SINGULAR	PLURAL
perfecto de indicativo	
he citado	**hemos** citado
has citado	**habéis** citado
ha citado	**han** citado
pluscuamperfecto de indicativo	
había citado	**habíamos** citado
habías citado	**habíais** citado
había citado	**habían** citado
pretérito anterior	
hube citado	**hubimos** citado
hubiste citado	**hubisteis** citado
hubo citado	**hubieron** citado
futuro perfecto	
habré citado	**habremos** citado
habrás citado	**habréis** citado
habrá citado	**habrán** citado
condicional compuesto	
habría citado	**habríamos** citado
habrías citado	**habríais** citado
habría citado	**habrían** citado
perfecto de subjuntivo	
haya citado	**hayamos** citado
hayas citado	**hayáis** citado
haya citado	**hayan** citado
pluscuamperfecto de subjuntivo	
hubiera citado	**hubiéramos** citado
hubieras citado	**hubierais** citado
hubiera citado	**hubieran** citado
OR	
hubiese citado	**hubiésemos** citado
hubieses citado	**hubieseis** citado
hubiese citado	**hubiesen** citado

gerundio **cobrando** — participio de pasado **cobrado**

SINGULAR	PLURAL	SINGULAR	PLURAL
presente de indicativo		perfecto de indicativo	
cobr**o**	cobr**amos**	**he** cobrado	**hemos** cobrado
cobr**as**	cobr**áis**	**has** cobrado	**habéis** cobrado
cobr**a**	cobr**an**	**ha** cobrado	**han** cobrado
imperfecto de indicativo		pluscuamperfecto de indicativo	
cobr**aba**	cobr**ábamos**	**había** cobrado	**habíamos** cobrado
cobr**abas**	cobr**abais**	**habías** cobrado	**habíais** cobrado
cobr**aba**	cobr**aban**	**había** cobrado	**habían** cobrado
pretérito		pretérito anterior	
cobr**é**	cobr**amos**	**hube** cobrado	**hubimos** cobrado
cobr**aste**	cobr**asteis**	**hubiste** cobrado	**hubisteis** cobrado
cobr**ó**	cobr**aron**	**hubo** cobrado	**hubieron** cobrado
futuro		futuro perfecto	
cobrar**é**	cobrar**emos**	**habré** cobrado	**habremos** cobrado
cobrar**ás**	cobrar**éis**	**habrás** cobrado	**habréis** cobrado
cobrar**á**	cobrar**án**	**habrá** cobrado	**habrán** cobrado
condicional simple		condicional compuesto	
cobrar**ía**	cobrar**íamos**	**habría** cobrado	**habríamos** cobrado
cobrar**ías**	cobrar**íais**	**habrías** cobrado	**habríais** cobrado
cobrar**ía**	cobrar**ían**	**habría** cobrado	**habrían** cobrado
presente de subjuntivo		perfecto de subjuntivo	
cobr**e**	cobr**emos**	**haya** cobrado	**hayamos** cobrado
cobr**es**	cobr**éis**	**hayas** cobrado	**hayáis** cobrado
cobr**e**	cobr**en**	**haya** cobrado	**hayan** cobrado
imperfecto de subjuntivo		pluscuamperfecto de subjuntivo	
cobrar**a**	cobrár**amos**	**hubiera** cobrado	**hubiéramos** cobrado
cobrar**as**	cobrar**ais**	**hubieras** cobrado	**hubierais** cobrado
cobrar**a**	cobrar**an**	**hubiera** cobrado	**hubieran** cobrado
OR		OR	
cobras**e**	cobrás**emos**	**hubiese** cobrado	**hubiésemos** cobrado
cobras**es**	cobras**eis**	**hubieses** cobrado	**hubieseis** cobrado
cobras**e**	cobras**en**	**hubiese** cobrado	**hubiesen** cobrado

imperativo

—	cobremos
cobra; no cobres	cobrad; no cobréis
cobre	cobren

to cook **cocinar**

gerundio **cocinando** participio de pasado **cocinado**

SINGULAR	PLURAL
presente de indicativo	
cocin**o**	cocin**amos**
cocin**as**	cocin**áis**
cocin**a**	cocin**an**
imperfecto de indicativo	
cocin**aba**	cocin**ábamos**
cocin**abas**	cocin**abais**
cocin**aba**	cocin**aban**
pretérito	
cocin**é**	cocin**amos**
cocin**aste**	cocin**asteis**
cocin**ó**	cocin**aron**
futuro	
cocinar**é**	cocinar**emos**
cocinar**ás**	cocinar**éis**
cocinar**á**	cocinar**án**
condicional simple	
cocinar**ía**	cocinar**íamos**
cocinar**ías**	cocinar**íais**
cocinar**ía**	cocinar**ían**
presente de subjuntivo	
cocin**e**	cocin**emos**
cocin**es**	cocin**éis**
cocin**e**	cocin**en**
imperfecto de subjuntivo	
cocinar**a**	cocinár**amos**
cocinar**as**	cocinar**ais**
cocinar**a**	cocinar**an**
OR	
cocinas**e**	cocinás**emos**
cocinas**es**	cocinas**eis**
cocinas**e**	cocinas**en**
imperativo	
—	cocinemos
cocina; no cocines	cocinad; no cocinéis
cocine	cocinen

SINGULAR	PLURAL
perfecto de indicativo	
he cocinado	**hemos** cocinado
has cocinado	**habéis** cocinado
ha cocinado	**han** cocinado
pluscuamperfecto de indicativo	
había cocinado	**habíamos** cocinado
habías cocinado	**habíais** cocinado
había cocinado	**habían** cocinado
pretérito anterior	
hube cocinado	**hubimos** cocinado
hubiste cocinado	**hubisteis** cocinado
hubo cocinado	**hubieron** cocinado
futuro perfecto	
habré cocinado	**habremos** cocinado
habrás cocinado	**habréis** cocinado
habrá cocinado	**habrán** cocinado
condicional compuesto	
habría cocinado	**habríamos** cocinado
habrías cocinado	**habríais** cocinado
habría cocinado	**habrían** cocinado
perfecto de subjuntivo	
haya cocinado	**hayamos** cocinado
hayas cocinado	**hayáis** cocinado
haya cocinado	**hayan** cocinado
pluscuamperfecto de subjuntivo	
hubiera cocinado	**hubiéramos** cocinado
hubieras cocinado	**hubierais** cocinado
hubiera cocinado	**hubieran** cocinado
OR	
hubiese cocinado	**hubiésemos** cocinado
hubieses cocinado	**hubieseis** cocinado
hubiese cocinado	**hubiesen** cocinado

coger — to take, to grab*

gerundio **cogiendo** — participio de pasado **cogido**

SINGULAR	PLURAL
presente de indicativo	
coj**o**	cog**emos**
cog**es**	cog**éis**
cog**e**	cog**en**
imperfecto de indicativo	
cog**ía**	cog**íamos**
cog**ías**	cog**íais**
cog**ía**	cog**ían**
pretérito	
cog**í**	cog**imos**
cog**iste**	cog**isteis**
cog**ió**	cog**ieron**
futuro	
coger**é**	coger**emos**
coger**ás**	coger**éis**
coger**á**	coger**án**
condicional simple	
coger**ía**	coger**íamos**
coger**ías**	coger**íais**
coger**ía**	coger**ían**
presente de subjuntivo	
coj**a**	coj**amos**
coj**as**	coj**áis**
coj**a**	coj**an**
imperfecto de subjuntivo	
cogier**a**	cogiér**amos**
cogier**as**	cogier**ais**
cogier**a**	cogier**an**
OR	
cogies**e**	cogiés**emos**
cogies**es**	cogies**eis**
cogies**e**	cogies**en**
imperativo	
—	cojamos
coge; no cojas	coged; no cojáis
coja	cojan

SINGULAR	PLURAL
perfecto de indicativo	
he cogido	**hemos** cogido
has cogido	**habéis** cogido
ha cogido	**han** cogido
pluscuamperfecto de indicativo	
había cogido	**habíamos** cogido
habías cogido	**habíais** cogido
había cogido	**habían** cogido
pretérito anterior	
hube cogido	**hubimos** cogido
hubiste cogido	**hubisteis** cogido
hubo cogido	**hubieron** cogido
futuro perfecto	
habré cogido	**habremos** cogido
habrás cogido	**habréis** cogido
habrá cogido	**habrán** cogido
condicional compuesto	
habría cogido	**habríamos** cogido
habrías cogido	**habríais** cogido
habría cogido	**habrían** cogido
perfecto de subjuntivo	
haya cogido	**hayamos** cogido
hayas cogido	**hayáis** cogido
haya cogido	**hayan** cogido
pluscuamperfecto de subjuntivo	
hubiera cogido	**hubiéramos** cogido
hubieras cogido	**hubierais** cogido
hubiera cogido	**hubieran** cogido
OR	
hubiese cogido	**hubiésemos** cogido
hubieses cogido	**hubieseis** cogido
hubiese cogido	**hubiesen** cogido

*Note: In some countries **coger** has a vulgar meaning. The verbs **tomar** and **agarrar** are used instead.

gerundio **coligiendo** participio de pasado **colegido**

SINGULAR	PLURAL
presente de indicativo	
colij**o**	coleg**imos**
colig**es**	coleg**ís**
colig**e**	colig**en**
imperfecto de indicativo	
coleg**ía**	coleg**íamos**
coleg**ías**	coleg**íais**
coleg**ía**	coleg**ían**
pretérito	
coleg**í**	coleg**imos**
coleg**iste**	coleg**isteis**
colig**ió**	colig**ieron**
futuro	
colegir**é**	colegir**emos**
colegir**ás**	colegir**éis**
colegir**á**	colegir**án**
condicional simple	
colegir**ía**	colegir**íamos**
colegir**ías**	colegir**íais**
colegir**ía**	colegir**ían**
presente de subjuntivo	
colij**a**	colij**amos**
colij**as**	colij**áis**
colij**a**	colij**an**
imperfecto de subjuntivo	
coligier**a**	coligiér**amos**
coligier**as**	coligier**ais**
coligier**a**	coligier**an**
OR	
coligies**e**	coligiés**emos**
coligies**es**	coligies**eis**
coligies**e**	coligies**en**
imperativo	
—	colijamos
colige; no colijas	colegid; no colijáis
colija	colijan

SINGULAR	PLURAL
perfecto de indicativo	
he colegido	**hemos** colegido
has colegido	**habéis** colegido
ha colegido	**han** colegido
pluscuamperfecto de indicativo	
había colegido	**habíamos** colegido
habías colegido	**habíais** colegido
había colegido	**habían** colegido
pretérito anterior	
hube colegido	**hubimos** colegido
hubiste colegido	**hubisteis** colegido
hubo colegido	**hubieron** colegido
futuro perfecto	
habré colegido	**habremos** colegido
habrás colegido	**habréis** colegido
habrá colegido	**habrán** colegido
condicional compuesto	
habría colegido	**habríamos** colegido
habrías colegido	**habríais** colegido
habría colegido	**habrían** colegido
perfecto de subjuntivo	
haya colegido	**hayamos** colegido
hayas colegido	**hayáis** colegido
haya colegido	**hayan** colegido
pluscuamperfecto de subjuntivo	
hubiera colegido	**hubiéramos** colegido
hubieras colegido	**hubierais** colegido
hubiera colegido	**hubieran** colegido
OR	
hubiese colegido	**hubiésemos** colegido
hubieses colegido	**hubieseis** colegido
hubiese colegido	**hubiesen** colegido

colgar — to hang up

gerundio **colgando** — participio de pasado **colgado**

SINGULAR	PLURAL	SINGULAR	PLURAL
presente de indicativo		perfecto de indicativo	
cuelg**o**	colg**amos**	**he** colgado	**hemos** colgado
cuelg**as**	colg**áis**	**has** colgado	**habéis** colgado
cuelg**a**	cuelg**an**	**ha** colgado	**han** colgado
imperfecto de indicativo		pluscuamperfecto de indicativo	
colg**aba**	colg**ábamos**	**había** colgado	**habíamos** colgado
colg**abas**	colg**abais**	**habías** colgado	**habíais** colgado
colg**aba**	colg**aban**	**había** colgado	**habían** colgado
pretérito		pretérito anterior	
colgu**é**	colg**amos**	**hube** colgado	**hubimos** colgado
colg**aste**	colg**asteis**	**hubiste** colgado	**hubisteis** colgado
colg**ó**	colg**aron**	**hubo** colgado	**hubieron** colgado
futuro		futuro perfecto	
colgar**é**	colgar**emos**	**habré** colgado	**habremos** colgado
colgar**ás**	colgar**éis**	**habrás** colgado	**habréis** colgado
colgar**á**	colgar**án**	**habrá** colgado	**habrán** colgado
condicional simple		condicional compuesto	
colgar**ía**	colgar**íamos**	**habría** colgado	**habríamos** colgado
colgar**ías**	colgar**íais**	**habrías** colgado	**habríais** colgado
colgar**ía**	colgar**ían**	**habría** colgado	**habrían** colgado
presente de subjuntivo		perfecto de subjuntivo	
cuelgu**e**	colgu**emos**	**haya** colgado	**hayamos** colgado
cuelgu**es**	colgu**éis**	**hayas** colgado	**hayáis** colgado
cuelgu**e**	cuelgu**en**	**haya** colgado	**hayan** colgado
imperfecto de subjuntivo		pluscuamperfecto de subjuntivo	
colgar**a**	colgár**amos**	**hubiera** colgado	**hubiéramos** colgado
colgar**as**	colgar**ais**	**hubieras** colgado	**hubierais** colgado
colgar**a**	colgar**an**	**hubiera** colgado	**hubieran** colgado
OR		OR	
colgas**e**	colgás**emos**	**hubiese** colgado	**hubiésemos** colgado
colgas**es**	colgas**eis**	**hubieses** colgado	**hubieseis** colgado
colgas**e**	colgas**en**	**hubiese** colgado	**hubiesen** colgado

imperativo

—	colguemos
cuelga; no cuelgues	colgad; no colguéis
cuelgue	cuelguen

gerundio **colocando** — participio de pasado **colocado**

SINGULAR	PLURAL	SINGULAR	PLURAL
presente de indicativo		perfecto de indicativo	
coloc**o**	coloc**amos**	**he** colocado	**hemos** colocado
coloc**as**	coloc**áis**	**has** colocado	**habéis** colocado
coloc**a**	coloc**an**	**ha** colocado	**han** colocado
imperfecto de indicativo		pluscuamperfecto de indicativo	
coloc**aba**	coloc**ábamos**	**había** colocado	**habíamos** colocado
coloc**abas**	coloc**abais**	**habías** colocado	**habíais** colocado
coloc**aba**	coloc**aban**	**había** colocado	**habían** colocado
pretérito		pretérito anterior	
coloqu**é**	coloc**amos**	**hube** colocado	**hubimos** colocado
coloc**aste**	coloc**asteis**	**hubiste** colocado	**hubisteis** colocado
coloc**ó**	coloc**aron**	**hubo** colocado	**hubieron** colocado
futuro		futuro perfecto	
colocar**é**	colocar**emos**	**habré** colocado	**habremos** colocado
colocar**ás**	colocar**éis**	**habrás** colocado	**habréis** colocado
colocar**á**	colocar**án**	**habrá** colocado	**habrán** colocado
condicional simple		condicional compuesto	
colocar**ía**	colocar**íamos**	**habría** colocado	**habríamos** colocado
colocar**ías**	colocar**íais**	**habrías** colocado	**habríais** colocado
colocar**ía**	colocar**ían**	**habría** colocado	**habrían** colocado
presente de subjuntivo		perfecto de subjuntivo	
coloqu**e**	coloqu**emos**	**haya** colocado	**hayamos** colocado
coloqu**es**	coloqu**éis**	**hayas** colocado	**hayáis** colocado
coloqu**e**	coloqu**en**	**haya** colocado	**hayan** colocado
imperfecto de subjuntivo		pluscuamperfecto de subjuntivo	
colocar**a**	colocár**amos**	**hubiera** colocado	**hubiéramos** colocado
colocar**as**	colocar**ais**	**hubieras** colocado	**hubierais** colocado
colocar**a**	colocar**an**	**hubiera** colocado	**hubieran** colocado
OR		OR	
colocas**e**	colocás**emos**	**hubiese** colocado	**hubiésemos** colocado
colocas**es**	colocas**eis**	**hubieses** colocado	**hubieseis** colocado
colocas**e**	colocas**en**	**hubiese** colocado	**hubiesen** colocado

imperativo

—	coloquemos
coloca; no coloques	colocad; no coloquéis
coloque	coloquen

comenzar — to begin, to start

gerundio **comenzando** participio de pasado **comenzado**

SINGULAR	PLURAL	SINGULAR	PLURAL
presente de indicativo		perfecto de indicativo	
comienz**o**	comenz**amos**	**he** comenzado	**hemos** comenzado
comienz**as**	comenz**áis**	**has** comenzado	**habéis** comenzado
comienz**a**	comienz**an**	**ha** comenzado	**han** comenzado
imperfecto de indicativo		pluscuamperfecto de indicativo	
comenz**aba**	comenz**ábamos**	**había** comenzado	**habíamos** comenzado
comenz**abas**	comenz**abais**	**habías** comenzado	**habíais** comenzado
comenz**aba**	comenz**aban**	**había** comenzado	**habían** comenzado
pretérito		pretérito anterior	
comenc**é**	comenz**amos**	**hube** comenzado	**hubimos** comenzado
comenz**aste**	comenz**asteis**	**hubiste** comenzado	**hubisteis** comenzado
comenz**ó**	comenz**aron**	**hubo** comenzado	**hubieron** comenzado
futuro		futuro perfecto	
comenzar**é**	comenzar**emos**	**habré** comenzado	**habremos** comenzado
comenzar**ás**	comenzar**éis**	**habrás** comenzado	**habréis** comenzado
comenzar**á**	comenzar**án**	**habrá** comenzado	**habrán** comenzado
condicional simple		condicional compuesto	
comenzar**ía**	comenzar**íamos**	**habría** comenzado	**habríamos** comenzado
comenzar**ías**	comenzar**íais**	**habrías** comenzado	**habríais** comenzado
comenzar**ía**	comenzar**ían**	**habría** comenzado	**habrían** comenzado
presente de subjuntivo		perfecto de subjuntivo	
comienc**e**	comenc**emos**	**haya** comenzado	**hayamos** comenzado
comienc**es**	comenc**éis**	**hayas** comenzado	**hayáis** comenzado
comienc**e**	comienc**en**	**haya** comenzado	**hayan** comenzado
imperfecto de subjuntivo		pluscuamperfecto de subjuntivo	
comenzar**a**	comenzár**amos**	**hubiera** comenzado	**hubiéramos** comenzado
comenzar**as**	comenzar**ais**	**hubieras** comenzado	**hubierais** comenzado
comenzar**a**	comenzar**an**	**hubiera** comenzado	**hubieran** comenzado
OR		OR	
comenzas**e**	comenzás**emos**	**hubiese** comenzado	**hubiésemos** comenzado
comenzas**es**	comenzas**eis**	**hubieses** comenzado	**hubieseis** comenzado
comenzas**e**	comenzas**en**	**hubiese** comenzado	**hubiesen** comenzado

imperativo

—	comencemos
comienza; no comiences	comenzad; no comencéis
comience	comiencen

MUST KNOW VERB

to eat — comer

gerundio **comiendo** participio de pasado **comido**

presente de indicativo

SINGULAR	PLURAL
com**o**	com**emos**
com**es**	com**éis**
com**e**	com**en**

imperfecto de indicativo

SINGULAR	PLURAL
com**ía**	com**íamos**
com**ías**	com**íais**
com**ía**	com**ían**

pretérito

SINGULAR	PLURAL
com**í**	com**imos**
com**iste**	com**isteis**
com**ió**	com**ieron**

futuro

SINGULAR	PLURAL
comer**é**	comer**emos**
comer**ás**	comer**éis**
comer**á**	comer**án**

condicional simple

SINGULAR	PLURAL
comer**ía**	comer**íamos**
comer**ías**	comer**íais**
comer**ía**	comer**ían**

presente de subjuntivo

SINGULAR	PLURAL
com**a**	com**amos**
com**as**	com**áis**
com**a**	com**an**

imperfecto de subjuntivo

SINGULAR	PLURAL
comier**a**	comiér**amos**
comier**as**	comier**ais**
comier**a**	comier**an**
OR	
comies**e**	comiés**emos**
comies**es**	comies**eis**
comies**e**	comies**en**

imperativo

SINGULAR	PLURAL
—	comamos
come; no comas	comed; no comáis
coma	coman

perfecto de indicativo

SINGULAR	PLURAL
he comido	**hemos** comido
has comido	**habéis** comido
ha comido	**han** comido

pluscuamperfecto de indicativo

SINGULAR	PLURAL
había comido	**habíamos** comido
habías comido	**habíais** comido
había comido	**habían** comido

pretérito anterior

SINGULAR	PLURAL
hube comido	**hubimos** comido
hubiste comido	**hubisteis** comido
hubo comido	**hubieron** comido

futuro perfecto

SINGULAR	PLURAL
habré comido	**habremos** comido
habrás comido	**habréis** comido
habrá comido	**habrán** comido

condicional compuesto

SINGULAR	PLURAL
habría comido	**habríamos** comido
habrías comido	**habríais** comido
habría comido	**habrían** comido

perfecto de subjuntivo

SINGULAR	PLURAL
haya comido	**hayamos** comido
hayas comido	**hayáis** comido
haya comido	**hayan** comido

pluscuamperfecto de subjuntivo

SINGULAR	PLURAL
hubiera comido	**hubiéramos** comido
hubieras comido	**hubierais** comido
hubiera comido	**hubieran** comido
OR	
hubiese comido	**hubiésemos** comido
hubieses comido	**hubieseis** comido
hubiese comido	**hubiesen** comido

compartir — to share

gerundio **compartiendo** participio de pasado **compartido**

presente de indicativo

SINGULAR	PLURAL
compart**o**	compart**imos**
compart**es**	compart**ís**
compart**e**	compart**en**

imperfecto de indicativo

SINGULAR	PLURAL
compart**ía**	compart**íamos**
compart**ías**	compart**íais**
compañ**ía**	compart**ían**

pretérito

SINGULAR	PLURAL
compart**í**	compart**imos**
compart**iste**	compart**isteis**
companí**ó**	compart**ieron**

futuro

SINGULAR	PLURAL
compartir**é**	compartir**emos**
compartir**ás**	compartir**éis**
compartir**á**	compartir**án**

condicional simple

SINGULAR	PLURAL
compartir**ía**	compartir**íamos**
compartir**ías**	compartir**íais**
compartir**ía**	compartir**ían**

presente de subjuntivo

SINGULAR	PLURAL
compan**a**	compart**amos**
compan**as**	compart**áis**
compart**a**	compart**an**

imperfecto de subjuntivo

SINGULAR	PLURAL
compartier**a**	compartiér**amos**
compartier**as**	compartier**ais**
compartier**a**	compartier**an**
OR	
comparties**e**	compartiés**emos**
compartier**es**	compartier**eis**
compartier**e**	compartier**en**

imperativo

SINGULAR	PLURAL
—	compartamos
comparte; no compartas	compartid; no compartáis
comparta	compartan

perfecto de indicativo

SINGULAR	PLURAL
he compartido	**hemos** compartido
has compartido	**habéis** compartido
ha compartido	**han** compartido

pluscuamperfecto de indicativo

SINGULAR	PLURAL
había cumpartido	**habíamos** compartido
habías compartido	**habíais** compartido
había compartido	**habían** compartido

pretérito anterior

SINGULAR	PLURAL
hube compartido	**hubimos** compartido
hubiste compartido	**hubisteis** compartido
hubo compartido	**hubieron** compartido

futuro perfecto

SINGULAR	PLURAL
habré compartido	**habremos** compartido
habrás compartido	**habréis** compartido
habrá compartido	**habrán** compartido

condicional compuesto

SINGULAR	PLURAL
habría compartido	**habríamos** compartido
habrías compartido	**habríais** compartido
habría compartido	**habrían** compartido

perfecto de subjuntivo

SINGULAR	PLURAL
haya compartido	**hayamos** compartido
hayas compartido	**hayáis** compartido
haya compartido	**hayan** compartido

pluscuamperfecto de subjuntivo

SINGULAR	PLURAL
hubiera compartido	**hubiéramos** compartido
hubieras compartido	**hubierais** compartido
hubiera compartido	**hubieran** compartido
OR	
hubiese compartido	**hubiésemos** compartido
hubieses compartido	**hubieseis** compartido
hubiese compartido	**hubiesen** compartido

to compose — componer

gerundio **componiendo** participio de pasado **compuesto**

SINGULAR	PLURAL

presente de indicativo

compong**o**	compon**emos**
compon**es**	compon**éis**
compon**e**	compon**en**

imperfecto de indicativo

compon**ía**	compon**íamos**
compon**ías**	compon**íais**
compon**ía**	compon**ían**

pretérito

compus**e**	compus**imos**
compus**iste**	compus**isteis**
compus**o**	compus**ieron**

futuro

compondr**é**	compondr**emos**
compondr**ás**	compondr**éis**
compondr**á**	compondr**án**

condicional simple

compondr**ía**	compondr**íamos**
compondr**ías**	compondr**íais**
compondr**ía**	compondr**ían**

presente de subjuntivo

compong**a**	compong**amos**
compong**as**	compong**áis**
compong**a**	compong**an**

imperfecto de subjuntivo

compusier**a**	compusiér**amos**
compusier**as**	compusier**ais**
compusier**a**	compusier**an**
OR	
compusies**e**	compusiés**emos**
compusies**es**	compusies**eis**
compusies**e**	compusies**en**

imperativo

—	compongamos
compon; no compongas	componed; no compongáis
componga	compongan

SINGULAR	PLURAL

perfecto de indicativo

he compuesto	**hemos** compuesto
has compuesto	**habéis** compuesto
ha compuesto	**han** compuesto

pluscuamperfecto de indicativo

había compuesto	**habíamos** compuesto
habías compuesto	**habíais** compuesto
había compuesto	**habían** compuesto

pretérito anterior

hube compuesto	**hubimos** compuesto
hubiste compuesto	**hubisteis** compuesto
hubo compuesto	**hubieron** compuesto

futuro perfecto

habré compuesto	**habremos** compuesto
habrás compuesto	**habréis** compuesto
habrá compuesto	**habrán** compuesto

condicional compuesto

habría compuesto	**habríamos** compuesto
habrías compuesto	**habríais** compuesto
habría compuesto	**habrían** compuesto

perfecto de subjuntivo

haya compuesto	**hayamos** compuesto
hayas compuesto	**hayáis** compuesto
haya compuesto	**hayan** compuesto

pluscuamperfecto de subjuntivo

hubiera compuesto	**hubiéramos** compuesto
hubieras compuesto	**hubierais** compuesto
hubiera compuesto	**hubieran** compuesto
OR	
hubiese compuesto	**hubiésemos** compuesto
hubieses compuesto	**hubieseis** compuesto
hubiese compuesto	**hubiesen** compuesto

comprar — to buy, to purchase

gerundio **comprando** participio de pasado **comprado**

SINGULAR	PLURAL
presente de indicativo	
compr**o**	compr**amos**
compr**as**	compr**áis**
compr**a**	compr**an**
imperfecto de indicativo	
compr**aba**	compr**ábamos**
compr**abas**	compr**abais**
compr**aba**	compr**aban**
pretérito	
compr**é**	compr**amos**
compr**aste**	compr**asteis**
compr**ó**	compr**aron**
futuro	
comprar**é**	comprar**emos**
comprar**ás**	comprar**éis**
comprar**á**	comprar**án**
condicional simple	
comprar**ía**	comprar**íamos**
comprar**ías**	comprar**íais**
comprar**ía**	comprar**ían**
presente de subjuntivo	
compr**e**	compr**emos**
compr**es**	compr**éis**
compr**e**	compr**en**
imperfecto de subjuntivo	
comprar**a**	comprár**amos**
comprar**as**	comprar**ais**
comprar**a**	comprar**an**
OR	
compras**e**	comprás**emos**
comprás**es**	compras**eis**
comprás**e**	compras**en**
imperativo	
—	compremos
compra; no compres	comprad; no compréis
compre	compren

SINGULAR	PLURAL
perfecto de indicativo	
he comprado	**hemos** comprado
has comprado	**habéis** comprado
ha comprado	**han** comprado
pluscuamperfecto de indicativo	
había comprado	**habíamos** comprado
habías comprado	**habíais** comprado
había comprado	**habían** comprado
pretérito anterior	
hube comprado	**hubimos** comprado
hubiste comprado	**hubisteis** comprado
hubo comprado	**hubieron** comprado
futuro perfecto	
habré comprado	**habremos** comprado
habrás comprado	**habréis** comprado
habrá comprado	**habrán** comprado
condicional compuesto	
habría comprado	**habríamos** comprado
habrías comprado	**habríais** comprado
habría comprado	**habrían** comprado
perfecto de subjuntivo	
haya comprado	**hayamos** comprado
hayas comprado	**hayáis** comprado
haya comprado	**hayan** comprado
pluscuamperfecto de subjuntivo	
hubiera comprado	**hubiéramos** comprado
hubieras comprado	**hubierais** comprado
hubiera comprado	**hubieran** comprado
OR	
hubiese comprado	**hubiésemos** comprado
hubieses comprado	**hubieseis** comprado
hubiese comprado	**hubiesen** comprado

gerundio **comprendiendo** participio de pasado **comprendido**

SINGULAR	PLURAL	SINGULAR	PLURAL
presente de indicativo		perfecto de indicativo	
comprend**o**	comprend**emos**	**he** comprendido	**hemos** comprendido
comprend**es**	comprend**éis**	**has** comprendido	**habéis** comprendido
comprend**e**	comprend**en**	**ha** comprendido	**han** comprendido
imperfecto de indicativo		pluscuamperfecto de indicativo	
comprend**ía**	comprend**íamos**	**había** comprendido	**habíamos** comprendido
comprend**ías**	comprend**íais**	**habías** comprendido	**habíais** comprendido
comprend**ía**	comprend**ían**	**había** comprendido	**habían** comprendido
pretérito		pretérito anterior	
comprend**í**	comprend**imos**	**hube** comprendido	**hubimos** comprendido
comprend**iste**	comprend**isteis**	**hubiste** comprendido	**hubisteis** comprendido
comprend**ió**	comprend**ieron**	**hubo** comprendido	**hubieron** comprendido
futuro		futuro perfecto	
comprender**é**	comprender**emos**	**habré** comprendido	**habremos** comprendido
comprender**ás**	comprender**éis**	**habrás** comprendido	**habréis** comprendido
comprender**á**	comprender**án**	**habrá** comprendido	**habrán** comprendido
condicional simple		condicional compuesto	
comprender**ía**	comprender**íamos**	**habría** comprendido	**habríamos** comprendido
comprender**ías**	comprender**íais**	**habrías** comprendido	**habríais** comprendido
comprender**ía**	comprender**ían**	**habría** comprendido	**habrían** comprendido
presente de subjuntivo		perfecto de subjuntivo	
comprend**a**	comprend**amos**	**haya** comprendido	**hayamos** comprendido
comprend**as**	comprend**áis**	**hayas** comprendido	**hayáis** comprendido
comprend**a**	comprend**an**	**haya** comprendido	**hayan** comprendido
imperfecto de subjuntivo		pluscuamperfecto de subjuntivo	
comprendier**a**	comprendiér**amos**	**hubiera** comprendido	**hubiéramos** comprendido
comprendier**as**	comprendier**ais**	**hubieras** comprendido	**hubierais** comprendido
comprendier**a**	comprendier**an**	**hubiera** comprendido	**hubieran** comprendido
OR		OR	
comprendies**e**	comprendiés**emos**	**hubiese** comprendido	**hubiésemos** comprendido
comprendies**es**	comprendies**eis**	**hubieses** comprendido	**hubieseis** comprendido
comprendies**e**	comprendies**en**	**hubiese** comprendido	**hubiesen** comprendido
imperativo			
—	comprendamos		
comprende; no comprendas	comprended; no comprendáis		
comprenda	comprendan		

C

conducir — to drive, to lead

gerundio **conduciendo** — participio de pasado **conducido**

presente de indicativo

SINGULAR	PLURAL
conduzc**o**	conduc**imos**
conduc**es**	conduc**ís**
conduc**e**	conduc**en**

imperfecto de indicativo

SINGULAR	PLURAL
conduc**ía**	conduc**íamos**
conduc**ías**	conduc**íais**
conduc**ía**	conduc**ían**

pretérito

SINGULAR	PLURAL
conduj**e**	conduj**imos**
conduj**iste**	conduj**isteis**
conduj**o**	conduj**eron**

futuro

SINGULAR	PLURAL
conducir**é**	conducir**emos**
conducir**ás**	conducir**éis**
conducir**á**	conducir**án**

condicional simple

SINGULAR	PLURAL
conducir**ía**	conducir**íamos**
conducir**ías**	conducir**íais**
conducir**ía**	conducir**ían**

presente de subjuntivo

SINGULAR	PLURAL
conduzc**a**	conduzc**amos**
conduzc**as**	conduzc**áis**
conduzc**a**	conduzc**an**

imperfecto de subjuntivo

SINGULAR	PLURAL
conduje**ra**	condujé**ramos**
conduje**ras**	conduje**rais**
conduje**ra**	conduje**ran**
OR	
condujes**e**	condujés**emos**
condujes**es**	condujes**eis**
condujes**e**	condujes**en**

imperativo

SINGULAR	PLURAL
—	conduzcamos
conduce; no conduzcas	conducid; no conduzcáis
conduzca	conduzcan

perfecto de indicativo

SINGULAR	PLURAL
he conducido	**hemos** conducido
has conducido	**habéis** conducido
ha conducido	**han** conducido

pluscuamperfecto de indicativo

SINGULAR	PLURAL
había conducido	**habíamos** conducido
habías conducido	**habíais** conducido
había conducido	**habían** conducido

pretérito anterior

SINGULAR	PLURAL
hube conducido	**hubimos** conducido
hubiste conducido	**hubisteis** conducido
hubo conducido	**hubieron** conducido

futuro perfecto

SINGULAR	PLURAL
habré conducido	**habremos** conducido
habrás conducido	**habréis** conducido
habrá conducido	**habrán** conducido

condicional compuesto

SINGULAR	PLURAL
habría conducido	**habríamos** conducido
habrías conducido	**habríais** conducido
habría conducido	**habrían** conducido

perfecto de subjuntivo

SINGULAR	PLURAL
haya conducido	**hayamos** conducido
hayas conducido	**hayáis** conducido
haya conducido	**hayan** conducido

pluscuamperfecto de subjuntivo

SINGULAR	PLURAL
hubiera conducido	**hubiéramos** conducido
hubieras conducido	**hubierais** conducido
hubiera conducido	**hubieran** conducido
OR	
hubiese conducido	**hubiésemos** conducido
hubieses conducido	**hubieseis** conducido
hubiese conducido	**hubiesen** conducido

gerundio **confesando** participio de pasado **confesado**

SINGULAR	PLURAL	SINGULAR	PLURAL
presente de indicativo		perfecto de indicativo	
confies**o**	confes**amos**	**he** confesado	**hemos** confesado
confies**as**	confes**áis**	**has** confesado	**habéis** confesado
confies**a**	confies**an**	**ha** confesado	**han** confesado
imperfecto de indicativo		pluscuamperfecto de indicativo	
confes**aba**	confes**ábamos**	**había** confesado	**habíamos** confesado
confes**abas**	confes**abais**	**habías** confesado	**habíais** confesado
confes**aba**	confes**aban**	**había** confesado	**habían** confesado
pretérito		pretérito anterior	
confes**é**	confes**amos**	**hube** confesado	**hubimos** confesado
confes**aste**	confes**asteis**	**hubiste** confesado	**hubisteis** confesado
confes**ó**	confes**aron**	**hubo** confesado	**hubieron** confesado
futuro		futuro perfecto	
confesar**é**	confesar**emos**	**habré** confesado	**habremos** confesado
confesar**ás**	confesar**éis**	**habrás** confesado	**habréis** confesado
confesar**á**	confesar**án**	**habrá** confesado	**habrán** confesado
condicional simple		condicional compuesto	
confesar**ía**	confesar**íamos**	**habría** confesado	**habríamos** confesado
confesar**ías**	confesar**íais**	**habrías** confesado	**habríais** confesado
confesar**ía**	confesar**ían**	**habría** confesado	**habrían** confesado
presente de subjuntivo		perfecto de subjuntivo	
confies**e**	confes**emos**	**haya** confesado	**hayamos** confesado
confies**es**	confes**éis**	**hayas** confesado	**hayáis** confesado
confies**e**	confies**en**	**haya** confesado	**hayan** confesado
imperfecto de subjuntivo		pluscuamperfecto de subjuntivo	
confesar**a**	confesár**amos**	**hubiera** confesado	**hubiéramos** confesado
confesar**as**	confesar**ais**	**hubieras** confesado	**hubierais** confesado
confesar**a**	confesar**an**	**hubiera** confesado	**hubieran** confesado
OR		OR	
confesas**e**	confesás**emos**	**hubiese** confesado	**hubiésemos** confesado
confesas**es**	confesas**eis**	**hubieses** confesado	**hubieseis** confesado
confesas**e**	confesas**en**	**hubiese** confesado	**hubiesen** confesado

imperativo

—	confesemos
confiesa;	confesad;
no confieses	no confeséis
confiese	confiesen

conocer — to know, to be acquainted with

gerundio **conociendo** participio de pasado **conocido**

presente de indicativo

SINGULAR	PLURAL
conozc**o**	conoc**emos**
conoc**es**	conoc**éis**
conoc**e**	conoc**en**

perfecto de indicativo

SINGULAR	PLURAL
he conocido	**hemos** conocido
has conocido	**habéis** conocido
ha conocido	**han** conocido

imperfecto de indicativo

SINGULAR	PLURAL
conoc**ía**	conoc**íamos**
conoc**ías**	conoc**íais**
conoc**ía**	conoc**ían**

pluscuamperfecto de indicativo

SINGULAR	PLURAL
había conocido	**habíamos** conocido
habías conocido	**habíais** conocido
había conocido	**habían** conocido

pretérito

SINGULAR	PLURAL
conoc**í**	conoc**imos**
conoc**iste**	conoc**isteis**
conoc**ió**	conoc**ieron**

pretérito anterior

SINGULAR	PLURAL
hube conocido	**hubimos** conocido
hubiste conocido	**hubisteis** conocido
hubo conocido	**hubieron** conocido

futuro

SINGULAR	PLURAL
conocer**é**	conocer**emos**
conocer**ás**	conocer**éis**
conocer**á**	conocer**án**

futuro perfecto

SINGULAR	PLURAL
habré conocido	**habremos** conocido
habrás conocido	**habréis** conocido
habrá conocido	**habrán** conocido

condicional simple

SINGULAR	PLURAL
conocer**ía**	conocer**íamos**
conocer**ías**	conocer**íais**
conocer**ía**	conocer**ían**

condicional compuesto

SINGULAR	PLURAL
habría conocido	**habríamos** conocido
habrías conocido	**habríais** conocido
habría conocido	**habrían** conocido

presente de subjuntivo

SINGULAR	PLURAL
conozc**a**	conozc**amos**
conozc**as**	conozc**áis**
conozc**a**	conozc**an**

perfecto de subjuntivo

SINGULAR	PLURAL
haya conocido	**hayamos** conocido
hayas conocido	**hayáis** conocido
haya conocido	**hayan** conocido

imperfecto de subjuntivo

SINGULAR	PLURAL
conocier**a**	conociér**amos**
conocier**as**	conocier**ais**
conocier**a**	conocier**an**
OR	
conocies**e**	conociés**emos**
conocies**es**	conocies**eis**
conocies**e**	conocies**en**

pluscuamperfecto de subjuntivo

SINGULAR	PLURAL
hubiera conocido	**hubiéramos** conocido
hubieras conocido	**hubierais** conocido
hubiera conocido	**hubieran** conocido
OR	
hubiese conocido	**hubiésemos** conocido
hubieses conocido	**hubieseis** conocido
hubiese conocido	**hubiesen** conocido

imperativo

SINGULAR	PLURAL
—	conozcamos
conoce; no conozcas	conoced; no conozcáis
conozca	conozcan

gerundio **consiguiendo** participio de pasado **conseguido**

SINGULAR	PLURAL
presente de indicativo	
consig**o**	consegu**imos**
consigu**es**	consegu**ís**
consigu**e**	consigu**en**
imperfecto de indicativo	
consegu**ía**	consegu**íamos**
consegu**ías**	consegu**íais**
consegu**ía**	consegu**ían**
pretérito	
consegu**í**	consegu**imos**
consegu**iste**	consegu**isteis**
consigui**ó**	consigu**ieron**
futuro	
consegui**ré**	consegui**remos**
consegui**rás**	consegui**réis**
consegui**rá**	consegui**rán**
condicional simple	
consegui**ría**	consegui**ríamos**
consegui**rías**	consegui**ríais**
consegui**ría**	consegui**rían**
presente de subjuntivo	
consig**a**	consig**amos**
consig**as**	consig**áis**
consig**a**	consig**an**
imperfecto de subjuntivo	
consiguier**a**	consiguiér**amos**
consiguier**as**	consiguier**ais**
consiguier**a**	consiguier**an**
OR	
consiguies**e**	consiguié**semos**
consiguies**es**	consiguies**eis**
consiguies**e**	consiguies**en**
imperativo	
—	consigamos
consigue; no consigas	conseguid; no consigáis
consiga	consigan

SINGULAR	PLURAL
perfecto de indicativo	
he conseguido	**hemos** conseguido
has conseguido	**habéis** conseguido
ha conseguido	**han** conseguido
pluscuamperfecto de indicativo	
había conseguido	**habíamos** conseguido
habías conseguido	**habíais** conseguido
había conseguido	**habían** conseguido
pretérito anterior	
hube conseguido	**hubimos** conseguido
hubiste conseguido	**hubisteis** conseguido
hubo conseguido	**hubieron** conseguido
futuro perfecto	
habré conseguido	**habremos** conseguido
habrás conseguido	**habréis** conseguido
habrá conseguido	**habrán** conseguido
condicional compuesto	
habría conseguido	**habríamos** conseguido
habrías conseguido	**habríais** conseguido
habría conseguido	**habrían** conseguido
perfecto de subjuntivo	
haya conseguido	**hayamos** conseguido
hayas conseguido	**hayáis** conseguido
haya conseguido	**hayan** conseguido
pluscuamperfecto de subjuntivo	
hubiera conseguido	**hubiéramos** conseguido
hubieras conseguido	**hubierais** conseguido
hubiera conseguido	**hubieran** conseguido
OR	
hubiese conseguido	**hubiésemos** conseguido
hubieses conseguido	**hubieseis** conseguido
hubiese conseguido	**hubiesen** conseguido

constituir — to constitute

gerundio **constituyendo** — participio de pasado **constituido**

presente de indicativo

SINGULAR	PLURAL
constituy**o**	constitu**imos**
constituy**es**	constitu**ís**
constituy**e**	constituy**en**

imperfecto de indicativo

SINGULAR	PLURAL
constitu**ía**	constitu**íamos**
constitu**ías**	constitu**íais**
constitu**ía**	constitu**ían**

pretérito

SINGULAR	PLURAL
constitu**í**	constitu**imos**
constitu**iste**	constitu**isteis**
constituy**ó**	constituy**eron**

futuro

SINGULAR	PLURAL
constituir**é**	constituir**emos**
constituir**ás**	constituir**éis**
constituir**á**	constituir**án**

condicional simple

SINGULAR	PLURAL
constituir**ía**	constituir**íamos**
constituir**ías**	constituir**íais**
constituir**ía**	constituir**ían**

presente de subjuntivo

SINGULAR	PLURAL
constituy**a**	constituy**amos**
constituy**as**	constituy**áis**
constituy**a**	constituy**an**

imperfecto de subjuntivo

SINGULAR	PLURAL
constituyer**a**	constituyér**amos**
constituyer**as**	constituyer**ais**
constituyer**a**	constituyer**an**
OR	
constituyes**e**	constituyés**emos**
constituyes**es**	constituyes**eis**
constituyes**e**	constituyes**en**

imperativo

SINGULAR	PLURAL
—	constituyamos
constituye; no constituyas	constituid; no constituyáis
constituya	constituyan

perfecto de indicativo

SINGULAR	PLURAL
he constituido	**hemos** constituido
has constituido	**habéis** constituido
ha constituido	**han** constituido

pluscuamperfecto de indicativo

SINGULAR	PLURAL
había constituido	**habíamos** constituido
habías constituido	**habíais** constituido
había constituido	**habían** constituido

pretérito anterior

SINGULAR	PLURAL
hube constituido	**hubimos** constituido
hubiste constituido	**hubisteis** constituido
hubo constituido	**hubieron** constituido

futuro perfecto

SINGULAR	PLURAL
habré constituido	**habremos** constituido
habrás constituido	**habréis** constituido
habrá constituido	**habrán** constituido

condicional compuesto

SINGULAR	PLURAL
habría constituido	**habríamos** constituido
habrías constituido	**habríais** constituido
habría constituido	**habrían** constituido

perfecto de subjuntivo

SINGULAR	PLURAL
haya constituido	**hayamos** constituido
hayas constituido	**hayáis** constituido
haya constituido	**hayan** constituido

pluscuamperfecto de subjuntivo

SINGULAR	PLURAL
hubiera constituido	**hubiéramos** constituido
hubieras constituido	**hubierais** constituido
hubiera constituido	**hubieran** constituido
OR	
hubiese constituido	**hubiésemos** constituido
hubieses constituido	**hubieseis** constituido
hubiese constituido	**hubiesen** constituido

gerundio **construyendo** participio de pasado **construido**

SINGULAR	PLURAL
presente de indicativo	
construy**o**	constru**imos**
construy**es**	constru**ís**
construy**e**	construy**en**
imperfecto de indicativo	
constru**ía**	constru**íamos**
constru**ías**	constru**íais**
constru**ía**	constru**ían**
pretérito	
constru**í**	constru**imos**
constru**iste**	constru**isteis**
construy**ó**	construy**eron**
futuro	
construir**é**	construir**emos**
construir**ás**	construir**éis**
construir**á**	construir**án**
condicional simple	
construir**ía**	construir**íamos**
construir**ías**	construir**íais**
construir**ía**	construir**ían**
presente de subjuntivo	
construy**a**	construy**amos**
construy**as**	construy**áis**
construy**a**	construy**an**
imperfecto de subjuntivo	
construyer**a**	construyér**amos**
construyer**as**	construyer**ais**
construyer**a**	construyer**an**
OR	
construyes**e**	construyés**emos**
construyes**es**	construyes**eis**
construyes**e**	construyes**en**
imperativo	
—	construyamos
construye; no construyas	construid; no construyáis
construya	construyan

SINGULAR	PLURAL
perfecto de indicativo	
he construido	**hemos** construido
has construido	**habéis** construido
ha construido	**han** construido
pluscuamperfecto de indicativo	
había construido	**habíamos** construido
habías construido	**habíais** construido
había construido	**habían** construido
pretérito anterior	
hube construido	**hubimos** construido
hubiste construido	**hubisteis** construido
hubo construido	**hubieron** construido
futuro perfecto	
habré construido	**habremos** construido
habrás construido	**habréis** construido
habrá construido	**habrán** construido
condicional compuesto	
habría construido	**habríamos** construido
habrías construido	**habríais** construido
habría construido	**habrían** construido
perfecto de subjuntivo	
haya construido	**hayamos** construido
hayas construido	**hayáis** construido
haya construido	**hayan** construido
pluscuamperfecto de subjuntivo	
hubiera construido	**hubiéramos** construido
hubieras construido	**hubierais** construido
hubiera construido	**hubieran** construido
OR	
hubiese construido	**hubiésemos** construido
hubieses construido	**hubieseis** construido
hubiese construido	**hubiesen** construido

contar — to tell, to count

gerundio **contando** — participio de pasado **contado**

presente de indicativo

SINGULAR	PLURAL
cuent**o**	cont**amos**
cuent**as**	cont**áis**
cuent**a**	cuent**an**

imperfecto de indicativo

SINGULAR	PLURAL
cont**aba**	cont**ábamos**
cont**abas**	cont**abais**
cont**aba**	cont**aban**

pretérito

SINGULAR	PLURAL
cont**é**	cont**amos**
cont**aste**	cont**asteis**
cont**ó**	cont**aron**

futuro

SINGULAR	PLURAL
contar**é**	contar**emos**
contar**ás**	contar**éis**
contar**á**	contar**án**

condicional simple

SINGULAR	PLURAL
contar**ía**	contar**íamos**
contar**ías**	contar**íais**
contar**ía**	contar**ían**

presente de subjuntivo

SINGULAR	PLURAL
cuent**e**	cont**emos**
cuent**es**	cont**éis**
cuent**e**	cuent**en**

imperfecto de subjuntivo

SINGULAR	PLURAL
contar**a**	contár**amos**
contar**as**	contar**ais**
contar**a**	contar**an**
OR	
contas**e**	contás**emos**
contas**es**	contas**eis**
contas**e**	contas**en**

imperativo

SINGULAR	PLURAL
—	contemos
cuenta; no cuentes	contad; no contéis
cuente	cuenten

perfecto de indicativo

SINGULAR	PLURAL
he contado	**hemos** contado
has contado	**habéis** contado
ha contado	**han** contado

pluscuamperfecto de indicativo

SINGULAR	PLURAL
había contado	**habíamos** contado
habías contado	**habíais** contado
había contado	**habían** contado

pretérito anterior

SINGULAR	PLURAL
hube contado	**hubimos** contado
hubiste contado	**hubisteis** contado
hubo contado	**hubieron** contado

futuro perfecto

SINGULAR	PLURAL
habré contado	**habremos** contado
habrás contado	**habréis** contado
habrá contado	**habrán** contado

condicional compuesto

SINGULAR	PLURAL
habría contado	**habríamos** contado
habrías contado	**habríais** contado
habría contado	**habrían** contado

perfecto de subjuntivo

SINGULAR	PLURAL
haya contado	**hayamos** contado
hayas contado	**hayáis** contado
haya contado	**hayan** contado

pluscuamperfecto de subjuntivo

SINGULAR	PLURAL
hubiera contado	**hubiéramos** contado
hubieras contado	**hubierais** contado
hubiera contado	**hubieran** contado
OR	
hubiese contado	**hubiésemos** contado
hubieses contado	**hubieseis** contado
hubiese contado	**hubiesen** contado

to hold, to restrain **contener**

gerundio **conteniendo** participio de pasado **contenido**

presente de indicativo

SINGULAR	PLURAL
conteng**o**	conten**emos**
contien**es**	conten**éis**
contien**e**	contien**en**

imperfecto de indicativo

SINGULAR	PLURAL
conten**ía**	conten**íamos**
conten**ías**	conten**íais**
conten**ía**	conten**ían**

pretérito

SINGULAR	PLURAL
contuv**e**	contuv**imos**
contuv**iste**	contuv**isteis**
contuv**o**	contuv**ieron**

futuro

SINGULAR	PLURAL
contendr**é**	contendr**emos**
contendr**ás**	contendr**éis**
contendr**á**	contendr**án**

condicional simple

SINGULAR	PLURAL
contendr**ía**	contendr**íamos**
contendr**ías**	contendr**íais**
contendr**ía**	contendr**ían**

presente de subjuntivo

SINGULAR	PLURAL
conteng**a**	conteng**amos**
conteng**as**	conteg**áis**
conteng**a**	conteng**an**

imperfecto de subjuntivo

SINGULAR	PLURAL
contuvier**a**	contuvié**ramos**
contuvier**as**	contuvier**ais**
contuvier**a**	contuvier**an**
OR	
contuvies**e**	contuvié**semos**
contuvies**es**	contuvies**eis**
contuvies**e**	contuvies**en**

imperativo

SINGULAR	PLURAL
—	contengamos
conten;	contened;
no contengas	no contegáis
contenga	contengan

perfecto de indicativo

SINGULAR	PLURAL
he contenido	**hemos** contenido
has contenido	**habéis** contenido
ha contenido	**han** contenido

pluscuamperfecto de indicativo

SINGULAR	PLURAL
había contenido	**habíamos** contenido
habías contenido	**habíais** contenido
había contenido	**habían** contenido

pretérito anterior

SINGULAR	PLURAL
hube contenido	**hubimos** contenido
hubiste contenido	**hubisteis** contenido
hubo contenido	**hubieron** contenido

futuro perfecto

SINGULAR	PLURAL
habré contenido	**habremos** contenido
habrás contenido	**habréis** contenido
habrá contenido	**habrán** contenido

condicional compuesto

SINGULAR	PLURAL
habría contenido	**habríamos** contenido
habrías contenido	**habríais** contenido
habría contenido	**habrían** contenido

perfecto de subjuntivo

SINGULAR	PLURAL
haya contenido	**hayamos** contenido
hayas contenido	**hayáis** contenido
haya contenido	**hayan** contenido

pluscuamperfecto de subjuntivo

SINGULAR	PLURAL
hubiera contenido	**hubiéramos** contenido
hubieras contenido	**hubierais** contenido
hubiera contenido	**hubieran** contenido
OR	
hubiese contenido	**hubiésemos** contenido
hubieses contenido	**hubieseis** contenido
hubiese contenido	**hubiesen** contenido

contestar — to answer, to reply

gerundio **contestando** participio de pasado **contestado**

presente de indicativo

SINGULAR	PLURAL
contest**o**	contest**amos**
contest**as**	contest**áis**
contest**a**	contest**an**

imperfecto de indicativo

SINGULAR	PLURAL
contest**aba**	contest**ábamos**
contest**abas**	contest**abais**
contest**aba**	contest**aban**

pretérito

SINGULAR	PLURAL
contest**é**	contest**amos**
contest**aste**	contest**asteis**
contest**ó**	contest**aron**

futuro

SINGULAR	PLURAL
contestar**é**	contestar**emos**
contestar**ás**	contestar**éis**
contestar**á**	contestar**án**

condicional simple

SINGULAR	PLURAL
contestar**ía**	contestar**íamos**
contestar**ías**	contestar**íais**
contestar**ía**	contestar**ían**

presente de subjuntivo

SINGULAR	PLURAL
contest**e**	contest**emos**
contest**es**	contest**éis**
contest**e**	contest**en**

imperfecto de subjuntivo

SINGULAR	PLURAL
contestar**a**	contestár**amos**
contestar**as**	contestar**ais**
contestar**a**	contestar**an**
OR	
contestas**e**	contestás**emos**
contestas**es**	contestas**eis**
contestas**e**	contestas**en**

imperativo

SINGULAR	PLURAL
—	contestemos
contesta; no contestes	contestad; no contestéis
conteste	contesten

perfecto de indicativo

SINGULAR	PLURAL
he contestado	**hemos** contestado
has contestado	**habéis** contestado
ha contestado	**han** contestado

pluscuamperfecto de indicativo

SINGULAR	PLURAL
había contestado	**habíamos** contestado
habías contestado	**habíais** contestado
había contestado	**habían** contestado

pretérito anterior

SINGULAR	PLURAL
hube contestado	**hubimos** contestado
hubiste contestado	**hubisteis** contestado
hubo contestado	**hubieron** contestado

futuro perfecto

SINGULAR	PLURAL
habré contestado	**habremos** contestado
habrás contestado	**habréis** contestado
habrá contestado	**habrán** contestado

condicional compuesto

SINGULAR	PLURAL
habría contestado	**habríamos** contestado
habrías contestado	**habríais** contestado
habría contestado	**habrían** contestado

perfecto de subjuntivo

SINGULAR	PLURAL
haya contestado	**hayamos** contestado
hayas contestado	**hayáis** contestado
haya contestado	**hayan** contestado

pluscuamperfecto de subjuntivo

SINGULAR	PLURAL
hubiera contestado	**hubiéramos** contestado
hubieras contestado	**hubierais** contestado
hubiera contestado	**hubieran** contestado
OR	
hubiese contestado	**hubiésemos** contestado
hubieses contestado	**hubieseis** contestado
hubiese contestado	**hubiesen** contestado

gerundio **continuando** participio de pasado **continuado**

SINGULAR	PLURAL	SINGULAR	PLURAL
presente de indicativo		perfecto de indicativo	
continú**o**	continu**amos**	**he** continuado	**hemos** continuado
continú**as**	continu**áis**	**has** continuado	**habéis** continuado
continú**a**	continú**an**	**ha** continuado	**han** continuado
imperfecto de indicativo		pluscuamperfecto de indicativo	
continu**aba**	continu**ábamos**	**había** continuado	**habíamos** continuado
continu**abas**	continu**abais**	**habías** continuado	**habíais** continuado
continu**aba**	continu**aban**	**había** continuado	**habían** continuado
pretérito		pretérito anterior	
continu**é**	continu**amos**	**hube** continuado	**hubimos** continuado
continu**aste**	continu**asteis**	**hubiste** continuado	**hubisteis** continuado
continu**ó**	continu**aron**	**hubo** continuado	**hubieron** continuado
futuro		futuro perfecto	
continuar**é**	continuar**emos**	**habré** continuado	**habremos** continuado
continuar**ás**	continuar**éis**	**habrás** continuado	**habréis** continuado
continuar**á**	continuar**án**	**habrá** continuado	**habrán** continuado
condicional simple		condicional compuesto	
continuar**ía**	continuar**íamos**	**habría** continuado	**habríamos** continuado
continuar**ías**	continuar**íais**	**habrías** continuado	**habríais** continuado
continuar**ía**	continuar**ían**	**habría** continuado	**habrían** continuado
presente de subjuntivo		perfecto de subjuntivo	
contin**úe**	continu**emos**	**haya** continuado	**hayamos** continuado
contin**úes**	continu**éis**	**hayas** continuado	**hayáis** continuado
contin**úe**	contin**úen**	**haya** continuado	**hayan** continuado
imperfecto de subjuntivo		pluscuamperfecto de subjuntivo	
continuar**a**	continuár**amos**	**hubiera** continuado	**hubiéramos** continuado
continuar**as**	continuar**ais**	**hubieras** continuado	**hubierais** continuado
continuar**a**	continuar**an**	**hubiera** continuado	**hubieran** continuado
OR		OR	
continuas**e**	continuás**emos**	**hubiese** continuado	**hubiésemos** continuado
continuas**es**	continuas**eis**	**hubieses** continuado	**hubieseis** continuado
continuas**e**	continuas**en**	**hubiese** continuado	**hubiesen** continuado

imperativo

—	continuemos
continúa;	continuad;
no continúes	no continuéis
continúe	continúen

contribuir — to contribute

gerundio **contribuyendo** participio de pasado **contribuido**

SINGULAR	PLURAL	SINGULAR	PLURAL
presente de indicativo		perfecto de indicativo	
contribuy**o**	contribu**imos**	**he** contribuido	**hemos** contribuido
contribuy**es**	contribu**ís**	**has** contribuido	**habéis** contribuido
contribuy**e**	contribuy**en**	**ha** contribuido	**han** contribuido
imperfecto de indicativo		pluscuamperfecto de indicativo	
contribu**ía**	contribu**íamos**	**había** contribuido	**habíamos** contribuido
contribu**ías**	contribu**íais**	**habías** contribuido	**habíais** contribuido
contribu**ía**	contribu**ían**	**había** contribuido	**habían** contribuido
pretérito		pretérito anterior	
contribu**í**	contribu**imos**	**hube** contribuido	**hubimos** contribuido
contribu**íste**	contribu**ísteis**	**hubiste** contribuido	**hubisteis** contribuido
contribuy**ó**	contribuy**eron**	**hubo** contribuido	**hubieron** contribuido
futuro		futuro perfecto	
contribuir**é**	contribuir**emos**	**habré** contribuido	**habremos** contribuido
contribuir**ás**	contribuir**éis**	**habrás** contribuido	**habréis** contribuido
contribuir**á**	contribuir**án**	**habrá** contribuido	**habrán** contribuido
condicional simple		condicional compuesto	
contribuir**ía**	contribuir**íamos**	**habría** contribuido	**habríamos** contribuido
contribuir**ías**	contribuir**íais**	**habrías** contribuido	**habríais** contribuido
contribuir**ía**	contribuir**ían**	**habría** contribuido	**habrían** contribuido
presente de subjuntivo		perfecto de subjuntivo	
contribuy**a**	contribuy**amos**	**haya** contribuido	**hayamos** contribuido
contribuy**as**	contribuy**áis**	**hayas** contribuido	**hayáis** contribuido
contribuy**a**	contribuy**an**	**haya** contribuido	**hayan** contribuido
imperfecto de subjuntivo		pluscuamperfecto de subjuntivo	
contribuyer**a**	contribuyér**amos**	**hubiera** contribuido	**hubiéramos** contribuido
contribuyer**as**	contribuyer**ais**	**hubieras** contribuido	**hubierais** contribuido
contribuyer**a**	contribuyer**an**	**hubiera** contribuido	**hubieran** contribuido
OR		OR	
contribuyes**e**	contribuyés**emos**	**hubiese** contribuido	**hubiésemos** contribuido
contribuyes**es**	contribuyes**eis**	**hubieses** contribuido	**hubieseis** contribuido
contribuyes**e**	contribuyes**en**	**hubiese** contribuido	**hubiesen** contribuido

imperativo

—	contribuyamos
contribuye;	contribuid;
no contribuyas	no contribuyáis
contribuya	contribuyan

gerundio **convenciendo** participio de pasado **convencido**

SINGULAR	PLURAL
presente de indicativo	
convenz**o**	convenc**emos**
convenc**es**	convenc**éis**
convenc**e**	convenc**en**
imperfecto de indicativo	
convenc**ía**	convenc**íamos**
convenc**ías**	convenc**íais**
convenc**ía**	convenc**ían**
pretérito	
convenc**í**	convenc**imos**
convenc**iste**	convenc**isteis**
convenc**ió**	convenc**ieron**
futuro	
convencer**é**	convencer**emos**
convencer**ás**	convencer**éis**
convencer**á**	convencer**án**
condicional simple	
convencer**ía**	convencer**íamos**
convencer**ías**	convencer**íais**
convencer**ía**	convencer**ían**
presente de subjuntivo	
convenz**a**	convenz**amos**
convenz**as**	convenz**áis**
convenz**a**	convenz**an**
imperfecto de subjuntivo	
convencier**a**	convenciér**amos**
convencier**as**	convencier**ais**
convencier**a**	convencier**an**
OR	
conviencies**e**	convenciés**emos**
conviencies**es**	convencies**eis**
convencies**e**	convencies**en**
imperativo	
—	convenzamos
convence; no convenzas	convenced; no convenzáis
convenza	convenzan

SINGULAR	PLURAL
perfecto de indicativo	
he convencido	**hemos** convencido
has convencido	**habéis** convencido
ha convencido	**han** convencido
pluscuamperfecto de indicativo	
había convencido	**habíamos** convencido
habías convencido	**habíais** convencido
había convencido	**habían** convencido
pretérito anterior	
hube convencido	**hubimos** convencido
hubiste convencido	**hubisteis** convencido
hubo convencido	**hubieron** convencido
futuro perfecto	
habré convencido	**habremos** convencido
habrás convencido	**habréis** convencido
habrá convencido	**habrán** convencido
condicional compuesto	
habría convencido	**habríamos** convencido
habrías convencido	**habríais** convencido
habría convencido	**habrían** convencido
perfecto de subjuntivo	
haya convencido	**hayamos** convencido
hayas convencido	**hayáis** convencido
haya convencido	**hayan** convencido
pluscuamperfecto de subjuntivo	
hubiera convencido	**hubiéramos** convencido
hubieras convencido	**hubierais** convencido
hubiera convencido	**hubieran** convencido
OR	
hubiese convencido	**hubiésemos** convencido
hubieses convencido	**hubieseis** convencido
hubiese convencido	**hubiesen** convencido

convenir

to convene, to agree

gerundio **conviniendo** participio de pasado **convenido**

SINGULAR	PLURAL
presente de indicativo	
conveng**o**	conven**imos**
convien**es**	conven**ís**
convien**e**	convien**en**
imperfecto de indicativo	
conven**ía**	conven**íamos**
conven**ías**	conven**íais**
conven**ía**	conven**ían**
pretérito	
convin**e**	convin**imos**
convin**iste**	convin**isteis**
convin**o**	convin**ieron**
futuro	
convendr**é**	convendr**emos**
convendr**ás**	convendr**éis**
convendr**á**	convendr**án**
condicional simple	
convendr**ía**	convendr**íamos**
convendr**ías**	convendr**íais**
convendr**ía**	convendr**ían**
presente de subjuntivo	
conveng**a**	conveng**amos**
conveng**as**	conveng**áis**
conveng**a**	conveng**an**
imperfecto de subjuntivo	
convinier**a**	conviniér**amos**
convinier**as**	convinier**ais**
convinier**a**	convinier**an**
OR	
convinies**e**	conviniés**emos**
convinies**es**	convinies**eis**
convinies**e**	convinies**en**
imperativo	
—	convengamos
conven;	convenid;
no convengas	no convengáis
convenga	convengan

SINGULAR	PLURAL
perfecto de indicativo	
he convenido	**hemos** convenido
has convenido	**habéis** convenido
ha convenido	**han** convenido
pluscuamperfecto de indicativo	
había convenido	**habíamos** convenido
habías convenido	**habíais** convenido
había convenido	**habían** convenido
pretérito anterior	
hube convenido	**hubimos** convenido
hubiste convenido	**hubisteis** convenido
hubo convenido	**hubieron** convenido
futuro perfecto	
habré convenido	**habremos** convenido
habrás convenido	**habréis** convenido
habrá convenido	**habrán** convenido
condicional compuesto	
habría convenido	**habríamos** convenido
habrías convenido	**habríais** convenido
habría convenido	**habrían** convenido
perfecto de subjuntivo	
haya convenido	**hayamos** convenido
hayas convenido	**hayáis** convenido
haya convenido	**hayan** convenido
pluscuamperfecto de subjuntivo	
hubiera convenido	**hubiéramos** convenido
hubieras convenido	**hubierais** convenido
hubiera convenido	**hubieran** convenido
OR	
hubiese convenido	**hubiésemos** convenido
hubieses convenido	**hubieseis** convenido
hubiese convenido	**hubiesen** convenido

gerundio **convirtiendo** participio de pasado **convertido**

SINGULAR	PLURAL
presente de indicativo	
convierto	convertimos
conviertes	convertís
convierte	convierten
imperfecto de indicativo	
convertía	convertíamos
convertías	convertíais
convertía	convertían
pretérito	
convertí	convertimos
convertiste	convertisteis
convirtió	convirtieron
futuro	
convertiré	convertiremos
convertirás	convertiréis
convertirá	convertirán
condicional simple	
convertiría	convertiríamos
convertirías	convertiríais
convertiría	convertirían
presente de subjuntivo	
convierta	convirtamos
conviertas	convirtáis
convierta	conviertan
imperfecto de subjuntivo	
convirtiera	convirtiéramos
convirtieras	convirtierais
convirtiera	convirtieran
OR	
convirtiese	convirtiésemos
convirtieses	convirtieseis
convirtiese	convirtiesen
imperativo	
—	convirtamos
convierte; no conviertas	convertid; no convirtáis
convierta	conviertan

SINGULAR	PLURAL
perfecto de indicativo	
he convertido	hemos convertido
has convertido	habéis convertido
ha convertido	han convertido
pluscuamperfecto de indicativo	
había convertido	habíamos convertido
habías convertido	habíais convertido
había convertido	habían convertido
pretérito anterior	
hube convertido	hubimos convertido
hubiste convertido	hubisteis convertido
hubo convertido	hubieron convertido
futuro perfecto	
habré convertido	habremos convertido
habrás convertido	habréis convertido
habrá convertido	habrán convertido
condicional compuesto	
habría convertido	habríamos convertido
habrías convertido	habríais convertido
habría convertido	habrían convertido
perfecto de subjuntivo	
haya convertido	hayamos convertido
hayas convertido	hayáis convertido
haya convertido	hayan convertido
pluscuamperfecto de subjuntivo	
hubiera convertido	hubiéramos convertido
hubieras convertido	hubierais convertido
hubiera convertido	hubieran convertido
OR	
hubiese convertido	hubiésemos convertido
hubieses convertido	hubieseis convertido
hubiese convertido	hubiesen convertido

convocar — to convene, to call together

gerundio **convocando** — participio de pasado **convocado**

SINGULAR	PLURAL	SINGULAR	PLURAL
presente de indicativo		perfecto de indicativo	
convoc**o**	convoc**amos**	**he** convocado	**hemos** convocado
convoc**as**	convoc**áis**	**has** convocado	**habéis** convocado
convoc**a**	convoc**an**	**ha** convocado	**han** convocado
imperfecto de indicativo		pluscuamperfecto de indicativo	
convoc**aba**	convoc**ábamos**	**había** convocado	**habíamos** convocado
convoc**abas**	convoc**abais**	**habías** convocado	**habíais** convocado
convoc**aba**	convoc**aban**	**había** convocado	**habían** convocado
pretérito		pretérito anterior	
convoqu**é**	convoc**amos**	**hube** convocado	**hubimos** convocado
convoc**aste**	convoc**asteis**	**hubiste** convocado	**hubisteis** convocado
convoc**ó**	convoc**aron**	**hubo** convocado	**hubieron** convocado
futuro		futuro perfecto	
convocar**é**	convocar**emos**	**habré** convocado	**habremos** convocado
convocar**ás**	convocar**éis**	**habrás** convocado	**habréis** convocado
convocar**á**	convocar**án**	**habrá** convocado	**habrán** convocado
condicional simple		condicional compuesto	
convocar**ía**	convocar**íamos**	**habría** convocado	**habríamos** convocado
convocar**ías**	convocar**íais**	**habrías** convocado	**habríais** convocado
convocar**ía**	convocar**ían**	**habría** convocado	**habrían** convocado
presente de subjuntivo		perfecto de subjuntivo	
convoqu**e**	convoqu**emos**	**haya** convocado	**hayamos** convocado
convoqu**es**	convoqu**éis**	**hayas** convocado	**hayáis** convocado
convoqu**e**	convoqu**en**	**haya** convocado	**hayan** convocado
imperfecto de subjuntivo		pluscuamperfecto de subjuntivo	
convocar**a**	convocár**amos**	**hubiera** convocado	**hubiéramos** convocado
convocar**as**	copnvocar**ais**	**hubieras** convocado	**hubierais** convocado
convocar**a**	convocar**an**	**hubiera** convocado	**hubieran** convocado
OR		OR	
convocas**e**	convocás**emos**	**hubiese** convocado	**hubiésemos** convocado
convocas**es**	convocas**eis**	**hubieses** convocado	**hubieseis** convocado
convocas**e**	convocas**en**	**hubiese** convocado	**hubiesen** convocado

imperativo

—	convoquemos
convoca;	convocad;
no convoques	no convoquéis
convoque	convoquen

to correct **corregir**

gerundio **corrigiendo**

participio de pasado **corregido**

SINGULAR	PLURAL
presente de indicativo	
corrij**o**	corregi**mos**
corrig**es**	corregí**s**
corrig**e**	corrig**en**
imperfecto de indicativo	
correg**ía**	correg**íamos**
correg**ías**	correg**íais**
correg**ía**	correg**ían**
pretérito	
correg**í**	correg**imos**
correg**iste**	correg**isteis**
corrig**ió**	corrig**ieron**
futuro	
corregir**é**	corregir**emos**
corregir**ás**	corregir**éis**
corregir**á**	corregir**án**
condicional simple	
corregir**ía**	corregir**íamos**
corregir**ías**	corregir**íais**
corregir**ía**	corregir**ían**
presente de subjuntivo	
corrij**a**	corrij**amos**
corrij**as**	corrij**áis**
corrij**a**	corrij**an**
imperfecto de subjuntivo	
corrigier**a**	corrigiér**amos**
corrigier**as**	corrigier**ais**
corrigier**a**	corrigier**an**
OR	
corrigies**e**	corrigiés**emos**
corrigies**es**	corrigies**eis**
corrigies**e**	corrigies**en**
imperativo	
—	corrijamos
corrige; no corrijas	corregid; no corrijáis
corrija	corrijan

SINGULAR	PLURAL
perfecto de indicativo	
he corregido	**hemos** corregido
has corregido	**habéis** corregido
ha corregido	**han** corregido
pluscuamperfecto de indicativo	
había corregido	**habíamos** corregido
habías corregido	**habíais** corregido
había corregido	**habían** corregido
pretérito anterior	
hube corregido	**hubimos** corregido
hubiste corregido	**hubisteis** corregido
hubo corregido	**hubieron** corregido
futuro perfecto	
habré corregido	**habremos** corregido
habrás corregido	**habréis** corregido
habrá corregido	**habrán** corregido
condicional compuesto	
habría corregido	**habríamos** corregido
habrías corregido	**habríais** corregido
habría corregido	**habrían** corregido
perfecto de subjuntivo	
haya corregido	**hayamos** corregido
hayas corregido	**hayáis** corregido
haya corregido	**hayan** corregido
pluscuamperfecto de subjuntivo	
hubiera corregido	**hubiéramos** corregido
hubieras corregido	**hubierais** corregido
hubiera corregido	**hubieran** corregido
OR	
hubiese corregido	**hubiésemos** corregido
hubieses corregido	**hubieseis** corregido
hubiese corregido	**hubiesen** corregido

correr — to run, to race

gerundio **corriendo** participio de pasado **corrido**

SINGULAR	PLURAL	SINGULAR	PLURAL
presente de indicativo		perfecto de indicativo	
corr**o**	corr**emos**	**he** corrido	**hemos** corrido
corr**es**	corr**éis**	**has** corrido	**habéis** corrido
corr**e**	corr**en**	**ha** corrido	**han** corrido
imperfecto de indicativo		pluscuamperfecto de indicativo	
corr**ía**	corr**íamos**	**había** corrido	**habíamos** corrido
corr**ías**	corr**íais**	**habías** corrido	**habíais** corrido
corr**ía**	corr**ían**	**había** corrido	**habían** corrido
pretérito		pretérito anterior	
corr**í**	corr**imos**	**hube** corrido	**hubimos** corrido
corr**iste**	corr**isteis**	**hubiste** corrido	**hubisteis** corrido
corr**ió**	corr**ieron**	**hubo** corrido	**hubieron** corrido
futuro		futuro perfecto	
correr**é**	correr**emos**	**habré** corrido	**habremos** corrido
correr**ás**	correr**éis**	**habrás** corrido	**habréis** corrido
correr**á**	correr**án**	**habrá** corrido	**habrán** corrido
condicional simple		condicional compuesto	
correr**ía**	correr**íamos**	**habría** corrido	**habríamos** corrido
correr**ías**	correr**íais**	**habrías** corrido	**habríais** corrido
correr**ía**	correr**ían**	**habría** corrido	**habrían** corrido
presente de subjuntivo		perfecto de subjuntivo	
corr**a**	corr**amos**	**haya** corrido	**hayamos** corrido
corr**as**	corr**áis**	**hayas** corrido	**hayáis** corrido
corr**a**	corr**an**	**haya** corrido	**hayan** corrido
imperfecto de subjuntivo		pluscuamperfecto de subjuntivo	
corrier**a**	corriér**amos**	**hubiera** corrido	**hubiéramos** corrido
corrier**as**	corrier**ais**	**hubieras** corrido	**hubierais** corrido
corrier**a**	corrier**an**	**hubiera** corrido	**hubieran** corrido
OR		OR	
corries**e**	corriés**emos**	**hubiese** corrido	**hubiésemos** corrido
corries**es**	corries**eis**	**hubieses** corrido	**hubieseis** corrido
corries**e**	corries**en**	**hubiese** corrido	**hubiesen** corrido

imperativo

—	corramos
corre; no corras	corred; no corráis
corra	corran

MEMORY TIP

Don't run in the corridors!

gerundio **cortando** participio de pasado **cortado**

SINGULAR	PLURAL	SINGULAR	PLURAL
presente de indicativo		perfecto de indicativo	
cort**o**	cort**amos**	**he** cortado	**hemos** cortado
cort**as**	cort**áis**	**has** cortado	**habéis** cortado
cort**a**	cort**an**	**ha** cortado	**han** cortado
imperfecto de indicativo		pluscuamperfecto de indicativo	
cort**aba**	cort**ábamos**	**había** cortado	**habíamos** cortado
cort**abas**	cort**abais**	**habías** cortado	**habíais** cortado
cort**aba**	cort**aban**	**había** cortado	**habían** cortado
pretérito		pretérito anterior	
cort**é**	cort**amos**	**hube** cortado	**hubimos** cortado
cort**aste**	cort**asteis**	**hubiste** cortado	**hubisteis** cortado
cort**ó**	cort**aron**	**hubo** cortado	**hubieron** cortado
futuro		futuro perfecto	
cortar**é**	cortar**emos**	**habré** cortado	**habremos** cortado
cortar**ás**	cortar**éis**	**habrás** cortado	**habréis** cortado
cortar**á**	cortar**án**	**habrá** cortado	**habrán** cortado
condicional simple		condicional compuesto	
cortar**ía**	cortar**íamos**	**habría** cortado	**habríamos** cortado
cortar**ías**	cortar**íais**	**habrías** cortado	**habríais** cortado
cortar**ía**	cortar**ían**	**habría** cortado	**habrían** cortado
presente de subjuntivo		perfecto de subjuntivo	
cort**e**	cort**emos**	**haya** cortado	**hayamos** cortado
cort**es**	cort**éis**	**hayas** cortado	**hayáis** cortado
cort**e**	cort**en**	**haya** cortado	**hayan** cortado
imperfecto de subjuntivo		pluscuamperfecto de subjuntivo	
cortar**a**	cortár**amos**	**hubiera** cortado	**hubiéramos** cortado
cortar**as**	cortar**ais**	**hubieras** cortado	**hubierais** cortado
cortar**a**	cortar**an**	**hubiera** cortado	**hubieran** cortado
OR		OR	
cortas**e**	cortás**emos**	**hubiese** cortado	**hubiésemos** cortado
cortas**es**	cortas**eis**	**hubieses** cortado	**hubieseis** cortado
cortas**e**	cortas**en**	**hubiese** cortado	**hubiesen** cortado

imperativo

—	cortemos
corta; no cortes	cortad; no cortéis
corte	corten

costar — to cost

gerundio **costando** — participio de pasado **costado**

SINGULAR	PLURAL	SINGULAR	PLURAL
presente de indicativo		perfecto de indicativo	
cuest**a**	cuest**an**	**ha** costado	**han** costado
imperfecto de indicativo		pluscuamperfecto de indicativo	
cost**aba**	cost**aban**	**había** costado	**habían** costado
pretérito		pretérito anterior	
cost**ó**	cost**aron**	**hubo** costado	**hubieron** costado
futuro		futuro perfecto	
costar**á**	costar**án**	**habrá** costado	**habrán** costado
condicional simple		condicional compuesto	
costar**ía**	costar**ían**	**habría** costado	**habrían** costado
presente de subjuntivo		perfecto de subjuntivo	
cuest**e**	cuest**en**	**haya** costado	**hayan** costado
imperfecto de subjuntivo		pluscuamperfecto de subjuntivo	
costar**a**	costar**an**	**hubiera** costado	**hubieran** costado
OR		OR	
costas**e**	costas**en**	**hubiese** costado	**hubiesen** costado

imperativo

¡Que cueste!	¡Que cuesten!

to create **crear**

gerundio **creando** participio de pasado **creado**

SINGULAR	PLURAL

presente de indicativo

cre**o**	cre**amos**
cre**as**	cre**áis**
cre**a**	cre**an**

imperfecto de indicativo

cre**aba**	cre**ábamos**
cre**abas**	cre**abais**
cre**aba**	cre**aban**

pretérito

cre**é**	cre**amos**
cre**aste**	cre**asteis**
cre**ó**	cre**aron**

futuro

crear**é**	crear**emos**
crear**ás**	crear**éis**
crear**á**	crear**án**

condicional simple

crear**ía**	crear**íamos**
crear**ías**	crear**íais**
crear**ía**	crear**ían**

presente de subjuntivo

cre**e**	cre**emos**
cre**es**	cre**éis**
cre**e**	cre**en**

imperfecto de subjuntivo

creara**a**	creár**amos**
crear**as**	crear**ais**
crear**a**	crear**an**
OR	
creas**e**	creás**emos**
creas**es**	creas**eis**
creas**e**	creas**en**

imperativo

—	creemos
crea; no crees	cread; no creéis
cree	creen

SINGULAR	PLURAL

perfecto de indicativo

he creado	**hemos** creado
has creado	**habéis** creado
ha creado	**han** creado

pluscuamperfecto de indicativo

había creado	**habíamos** creado
habías creado	**habíais** creado
había creado	**habían** creado

pretérito anterior

hube creado	**hubimos** creado
hubiste creado	**hubisteis** creado
hubo creado	**hubieron** creado

futuro perfecto

habré creado	**habremos** creado
habrás creado	**habréis** creado
habrá creado	**habrán** creado

condicional compuesto

habría creado	**habríamos** creado
habrías creado	**habríais** creado
habría creado	**habrían** creado

perfecto de subjuntivo

haya creado	**hayamos** creado
hayas creado	**hayáis** creado
haya creado	**hayan** creado

pluscuamperfecto de subjuntivo

hubiera creado	**hubiéramos** creado
hubieras creado	**hubierais** creado
hubiera creado	**hubieran** creado
OR	
hubiese creado	**hubiésemos** creado
hubieses creado	**hubieseis** creado
hubiese creado	**hubiesen** creado

crecer — to grow

gerundio **creciendo** — participio de pasado **crecido**

SINGULAR	PLURAL
presente de indicativo	
crezc**o**	crec**emos**
crec**es**	crec**éis**
crec**e**	crec**en**
imperfecto de indicativo	
crec**ía**	crec**íamos**
crec**ías**	crec**íais**
crec**ía**	crec**ían**
pretérito	
crec**í**	crec**imos**
crec**iste**	crec**isteis**
crec**ió**	crec**ieron**
futuro	
crecer**é**	crecer**emos**
crecer**ás**	crecer**éis**
crecer**á**	crecer**án**
condicional simple	
crecer**ía**	crecer**íamos**
crecer**ías**	crecer**íais**
crecer**ía**	crecer**ían**
presente de subjuntivo	
crezc**a**	crezc**amos**
crezc**as**	crezc**áis**
crezc**a**	crezc**an**
imperfecto de subjuntivo	
crecier**a**	creciér**amos**
crecier**as**	crecier**ais**
crecier**a**	crecier**an**
OR	
creciese	creciés**emos**
crecies**es**	crecies**eis**
crecies**e**	crecies**en**
imperativo	
—	crezcamos
crece; no crezcas	creced; no crezcáis
crezca	crezcan

SINGULAR	PLURAL
perfecto de indicativo	
he crecido	**hemos** crecido
has crecido	**habéis** crecido
ha crecido	**han** crecido
pluscuamperfecto de indicativo	
había crecido	**habíamos** crecido
habías crecido	**habíais** crecido
había crecido	**habían** crecido
pretérito anterior	
hube crecido	**hubimos** crecido
hubiste crecido	**hubisteis** crecido
hubo crecido	**hubieron** crecido
futuro perfecto	
habré crecido	**habremos** crecido
habrás crecido	**habréis** crecido
habrá crecido	**habrán** crecido
condicional compuesto	
habría crecido	**habríamos** crecido
habrías crecido	**habríais** crecido
habría crecido	**habrían** crecido
perfecto de subjuntivo	
haya crecido	**hayamos** crecido
hayas crecido	**hayáis** crecido
haya crecido	**hayan** crecido
pluscuamperfecto de subjuntivo	
hubiera crecido	**hubiéramos** crecido
hubieras crecido	**hubierais** crecido
hubiera crecido	**hubieran** crecido
OR	
hubiese crecido	**hubiésemos** crecido
hubieses crecido	**hubieseis** crecido
hubiese crecido	**hubiesen** crecido

to believe **creer**

gerundio **creyendo** participio de pasado **creído**

SINGULAR	PLURAL	SINGULAR	PLURAL
presente de indicativo		perfecto de indicativo	
cre**o**	cre**emos**	**he** creído	**hemos** creído
cre**es**	cre**éis**	**has** creído	**habéis** creído
cre**e**	cre**en**	**ha** creído	**han** creído
imperfecto de indicativo		pluscuamperfecto de indicativo	
cre**ía**	cre**íamos**	**había** creído	**habíamos** creído
cre**ías**	cre**íais**	**habías** creído	**habíais** creído
cre**ía**	cre**ían**	**había** creído	**habían** creído
pretérito		pretérito anterior	
cre**í**	cre**ímos**	**hube** creído	**hubimos** creído
cre**íste**	cre**ísteis**	**hubiste** creído	**hubisteis** creído
crey**ó**	crey**eron**	**hubo** creído	**hubieron** creído
futuro		futuro perfecto	
creer**é**	creer**emos**	**habré** creído	**habremos** creído
creer**ás**	creer**éis**	**habrás** creído	**habréis** creído
creer**á**	creer**án**	**habrá** creído	**habrán** creído
condicional simple		condicional compuesto	
creer**ía**	creer**íamos**	**habría** creído	**habríamos** creído
creer**ía**	creer**íais**	**habrías** creído	**habríais** creído
creer**ía**	creer**ían**	**habría** creído	**habrían** creído
presente de subjuntivo		perfecto de subjuntivo	
cre**a**	cre**amos**	**haya** creído	**hayamos** creído
cre**as**	cre**áis**	**hayas** creído	**hayáis** creído
cre**a**	cre**an**	**haya** creído	**hayan** creído
imperfecto de subjuntivo		pluscuamperfecto de subjuntivo	
creyer**a**	creyér**amos**	**hubiera** creído	**hubiéramos** creído
creyer**as**	creyer**ais**	**hubieras** creído	**hubierais** creído
creyer**a**	creyer**an**	**hubiera** creído	**hubieran** creído
OR		OR	
creyes**e**	creyés**emos**	**hubiese** creído	**hubiésemos** creído
creyes**es**	creyes**eis**	**hubieses** creído	**hubieseis** creído
creyes**e**	creyes**en**	**hubiese** creído	**hubiesen** creído

imperativo

SINGULAR	PLURAL
—	creamos
cree; no creas	creed; no creáis
crea	crean

criar — to raise, to breed

gerundio **criando** — participio de pasado **criado**

SINGULAR	PLURAL	SINGULAR	PLURAL
presente de indicativo		perfecto de indicativo	
crí**o**	cri**amos**	**he** criado	**hemos** criado
crí**as**	cri**áis**	**has** criado	**habéis** criado
crí**a**	crí**an**	**ha** criado	**han** criado
imperfecto de indicativo		pluscuamperfecto de indicativo	
cri**aba**	cri**ábamos**	**había** criado	**habíamos** criado
cri**abas**	cri**abais**	**habías** criado	**habíais** criado
cri**aba**	cri**aban**	**había** criado	**habían** criado
pretérito		pretérito anterior	
cri**é**	cri**amos**	**hube** criado	**hubimos** criado
cri**aste**	cri**asteis**	**hubiste** criado	**hubisteis** criado
cri**ó**	cri**aron**	**hubo** criado	**hubieron** criado
futuro		futuro perfecto	
criar**é**	criar**emos**	**habré** criado	**habremos** criado
criar**ás**	criar**éis**	**habrás** criado	**habréis** criado
criar**á**	criar**án**	**habrá** criado	**habrán** criado
condicional simple		condicional compuesto	
criar**ía**	criar**íamos**	**habría** criado	**habríamos** criado
criar**ías**	criar**íais**	**habrías** criado	**habríais** criado
criar**ía**	criar**ían**	**habría** criado	**habrían** criado
presente de subjuntivo		perfecto de subjuntivo	
crí**e**	cri**emos**	**haya** criado	**hayamos** criado
crí**es**	cri**éis**	**hayas** criado	**hayáis** criado
crí**e**	crí**en**	**haya** criado	**hayan** criado
imperfecto de subjuntivo		pluscuamperfecto de subjuntivo	
criar**a**	criár**amos**	**hubiera** criado	**hubiéramos** criado
criar**as**	criar**ais**	**hubieras** criado	**hubierais** criado
criar**a**	criar**an**	**hubiera** criado	**hubieran** criado
OR		OR	
cria**se**	criá**semos**	**hubiese** criado	**hubiésemos** criado
cria**ses**	cria**seis**	**hubieses** criado	**hubieseis** criado
cria**se**	cria**sen**	**hubiese** criado	**hubiesen** criado

imperativo

—	criemos
cría; no críes	criad; no criéis
críe	críen

gerundio cruzando — **participio de pasado** cruzado

SINGULAR	PLURAL
presente de indicativo	
cruz**o**	cruz**amos**
cruz**as**	cruz**áis**
cruz**a**	cruz**an**
imperfecto de indicativo	
cruz**aba**	cruz**ábamos**
cruz**abas**	cruz**abais**
cruz**aba**	cruz**aban**
pretérito	
cruc**é**	cruz**amos**
cruz**aste**	cruz**asteis**
cruz**ó**	cruz**aron**
futuro	
cruzar**é**	cruzar**emos**
cruzar**ás**	cruzar**éis**
cruzar**á**	cruzar**án**
condicional simple	
cruzar**ía**	cruzar**íamos**
cruzar**ías**	cruzar**íais**
cruzar**ía**	cruzar**ían**
presente de subjuntivo	
cruc**e**	cruc**emos**
cruc**es**	cruc**éis**
cruc**e**	cruc**en**
imperfecto de subjuntivo	
cruzar**a**	cruzár**amos**
cruzar**as**	cruzar**ais**
cruzar**a**	cruzar**an**
OR	
cruzas**e**	cruzás**emos**
cruzas**es**	cruzas**eis**
cruzas**e**	cruzas**en**
imperativo	
—	crucemos
cruza; no cruces	cruzad; no crucéis
cruce	crucen

SINGULAR	PLURAL
perfecto de indicativo	
he cruzado	**hemos** cruzado
has cruzado	**habéis** cruzado
ha cruzado	**han** cruzado
pluscuamperfecto de indicativo	
había cruzado	**habíamos** cruzado
habías cruzado	**habíais** cruzado
había cruzado	**habían** cruzado
pretérito anterior	
hube cruzado	**hubimos** cruzado
hubiste cruzado	**hubisteis** cruzado
hubo cruzado	**hubieron** cruzado
futuro perfecto	
habré cruzado	**habremos** cruzado
habrás cruzado	**habréis** cruzado
habrá cruzado	**habrán** cruzado
condicional compuesto	
habría cruzado	**habríamos** cruzado
habrías cruzado	**habríais** cruzado
habría cruzado	**habrían** cruzado
perfecto de subjuntivo	
haya cruzado	**hayamos** cruzado
hayas cruzado	**hayáis** cruzado
haya cruzado	**hayan** cruzado
pluscuamperfecto de subjuntivo	
hubiera cruzado	**hubiéramos** cruzado
hubieras cruzado	**hubierais** cruzado
hubiera cruzado	**hubieran** cruzado
OR	
hubiese cruzado	**hubiésemos** cruzado
hubieses cruzado	**hubieseis** cruzado
hubiese cruzado	**hubiesen** cruzado

gerundio **cubriendo** participio de pasado **cubierto**

SINGULAR	PLURAL	SINGULAR	PLURAL
presente de indicativo		perfecto de indicativo	
cubr**o**	cubr**imos**	**he** cubierto	**hemos** cubierto
cubr**es**	cubr**ís**	**has** cubierto	**habéis** cubierto
cubr**e**	cubr**en**	**ha** cubierto	**han** cubierto
imperfecto de indicativo		pluscuamperfecto de indicativo	
cubr**ía**	cubr**íamos**	**había** cubierto	**habíamos** cubierto
cubr**ías**	cubr**íais**	**habías** cubierto	**habíais** cubierto
cubr**ía**	cubr**ían**	**había** cubierto	**habían** cubierto
pretérito		pretérito anterior	
cubr**í**	cubr**imos**	**hube** cubierto	**hubimos** cubierto
cubr**iste**	cubr**isteis**	**hubiste** cubierto	**hubisteis** cubierto
cubr**ió**	cubr**ieron**	**hubo** cubierto	**hubieron** cubierto
futuro		futuro perfecto	
cubrir**é**	cubrir**emos**	**habré** cubierto	**habremos** cubierto
cubrir**ás**	cubrir**éis**	**habrás** cubierto	**habréis** cubierto
cubrir**á**	cubrir**án**	**habrá** cubierto	**habrán** cubierto
condicional simple		condicional compuesto	
cubrir**ía**	cubrir**íamos**	**habría** cubierto	**habríamos** cubierto
cubrir**ías**	cubrir**íais**	**habrías** cubierto	**habríais** cubierto
cubrir**ía**	cubrir**ían**	**habría** cubierto	**habrían** cubierto
presente de subjuntivo		perfecto de subjuntivo	
cubr**a**	cubr**amos**	**haya** cubierto	**hayamos** cubierto
cubr**as**	cubr**áis**	**hayas** cubierto	**hayáis** cubierto
cubr**a**	cubr**an**	**haya** cubierto	**hayan** cubierto
imperfecto de subjuntivo		pluscuamperfecto de subjuntivo	
cubrier**a**	cubriér**amos**	**hubiera** cubierto	**hubiéramos** cubierto
cubrier**as**	cubrier**ais**	**hubieras** cubierto	**hubierais** cubierto
cubrier**a**	cubrier**an**	**hubiera** cubierto	**hubieran** cubierto
OR		OR	
cubries**e**	cubriés**emos**	**hubiese** cubierto	**hubiésemos** cubierto
cubries**es**	cubries**eis**	**hubieses** cubierto	**hubieseis** cubierto
cubries**e**	cubries**en**	**hubiese** cubierto	**hubiesen** cubierto

imperativo

—	cubramos
cubre; no cubras	cubrid; no cubráis
cubra	cubran

gerundio **cuidandose** participio de pasado **cuidado**

SINGULAR	PLURAL	SINGULAR	PLURAL
presente de indicativo		perfecto de indicativo	
me cuid**o**	nos cuid**amos**	**me he** cuidado	**nos hemos** cuidado
te cuid**as**	os cuid**áis**	**te has** cuidado	**os habéis** cuidado
se cuid**a**	se cuid**an**	**se ha** cuidado	**se han** cuidado
imperfecto de indicativo		pluscuamperfecto de indicativo	
me cuid**aba**	nos cuid**ábamos**	**me había** cuidado	**nos habíamos** cuidado
te cuid**abas**	os cuid**abais**	**te habías** cuidado	**os habíais** cuidado
se cuid**aba**	se cuid**aban**	**se había** cuidado	**se habían** cuidado
pretérito		pretérito anterior	
me cuid**é**	nos cuid**amos**	**me hube** cuidado	**nos hubimos** cuidado
te cuid**aste**	os cuid**asteis**	**te hubiste** cuidado	**os hubisteis** cuidado
se cuid**ó**	se cuid**aron**	**se hubo** cuidado	**se hubieron** cuidado
futuro		futuro perfecto	
me cuidar**é**	nos cuidar**emos**	**me habré** cuidado	**nos habremos** cuidado
te cuidar**ás**	os cuidar**éis**	**te habrás** cuidado	**os habréis** cuidado
se cuidar**á**	se cuidar**án**	**se habrá** cuidado	**se habrán** cuidado
condicional simple		condicional compuesto	
me cuidar**ía**	nos cuidar**íamos**	**me habría** cuidado	**nos habríamos** cuidado
te cuidar**ías**	os cuidar**íais**	**te habrías** cuidado	**os habríais** cuidado
se cuidar**ía**	se cuidar**ían**	**se habría** cuidado	**se habrían** cuidado
presente de subjuntivo		perfecto de subjuntivo	
me cuid**e**	nos cuid**emos**	**me haya** cuidado	**nos hayamos** cuidado
te cuid**es**	os cuid**éis**	**te hayas** cuidado	**os hayáis** cuidado
se cuid**e**	se cuid**en**	**se haya** cuidado	**se hayan** cuidado
imperfecto de subjuntivo		pluscuamperfecto de subjuntivo	
me cuidar**a**	nos cuidár**amos**	**me hubiera** cuidado	**nos hubiéramos** cuidado
te cuidar**as**	os cuidar**ais**	**te hubieras** cuidado	**os hubierais** cuidado
se cuidar**a**	se cuidar**an**	**se hubiera** cuidado	**se hubieran** cuidado
OR		OR	
me cuidas**e**	nos cuidás**emos**	**me hubiese** cuidado	**nos hubiésemos** cuidado
te cuidas**es**	os cuidas**eis**	**te hubieses** cuidado	**os hubieseis** cuidado
se cuidas**e**	se cuidas**en**	**se hubiese** cuidado	**se hubiesen** cuidado

imperativo

—	cuidémonos; no nos cuidemos
cuídate; no te cuides	cuidaos; no os cuidéis
cuídese; no se cuide	cuídense; no se cuiden

C

cumplir — to fulfill, to keep a promise

gerundio **cumpliendo** — participio de pasado **cumplido**

SINGULAR	PLURAL	SINGULAR	PLURAL
presente de indicativo		perfecto de indicativo	
cumpl**o**	cumpl**imos**	**he** cumplido	**hemos** cumplido
cumpl**es**	cumpl**ís**	**has** cumplido	**habéis** cumplido
cumpl**e**	cumpl**en**	**ha** cumplido	**han** cumplido
imperfecto de indicativo		pluscuamperfecto de indicativo	
cumpl**ía**	cumpl**íamos**	**había** cumplido	**habíamos** cumplido
cumpl**ías**	cumpl**íais**	**habías** cumplido	**habíais** cumplido
cumpl**ía**	cumpl**ían**	**había** cumplido	**habían** cumplido
pretérito		pretérito anterior	
cumpl**í**	cumpl**imos**	**hube** cumplido	**hubimos** cumplido
cumpl**iste**	cumpl**isteis**	**hubiste** cumplido	**hubisteis** cumplido
cumpl**ió**	cumpl**ieron**	**hubo** cumplido	**hubieron** cumplido
futuro		futuro perfecto	
cumplir**é**	cumplir**emos**	**habré** cumplido	**habremos** cumplido
cumplir**ás**	cumplir**éis**	**habrás** cumplido	**habréis** cumplido
cumplir**á**	cumplir**án**	**habrá** cumplido	**habrán** cumplido
condicional simple		condicional compuesto	
cumplir**ía**	cumplir**íamos**	**habría** cumplido	**habríamos** cumplido
cumplir**ías**	cumplir**íais**	**habrías** cumplido	**habríais** cumplido
cumplir**ía**	cumplir**ían**	**habría** cumplido	**habrían** cumplido
presente de subjuntivo		perfecto de subjuntivo	
cumpl**a**	cumpl**amos**	**haya** cumplido	**hayamos** cumplido
cumpl**as**	cumpl**áis**	**hayas** cumplido	**hayáis** cumplido
cumpl**a**	cumpl**an**	**haya** cumplido	**hayan** cumplido
imperfecto de subjuntivo		pluscuamperfecto de subjuntivo	
cumplier**a**	cumpliér**amos**	**hubiera** cumplido	**hubiéramos** cumplido
cumplier**as**	cumplier**ais**	**hubieras** cumplido	**hubierais** cumplido
cumplier**a**	cumplier**an**	**hubiera** cumplido	**hubieran** cumplido
OR		OR	
cumplies**e**	cumpliés**emos**	**hubiese** cumplido	**hubiésemos** cumplido
cumplies**es**	cumplies**eis**	**hubieses** cumplido	**hubieseis** cumplido
cumplies**e**	cumplies**en**	**hubiese** cumplido	**hubiesen** cumplido

imperativo

—	cumplamos
cumple; no cumplas	cumplid; no cumpláis
cumpla	cumplan

gerundio **dando** participio de pasado **dado**

SINGULAR	PLURAL	SINGULAR	PLURAL
presente de indicativo		perfecto de indicativo	
d**oy**	d**amos**	**he** dado	**hemos** dado
d**as**	d**ais**	**has** dado	**habéis** dado
d**a**	d**an**	**ha** dado	**han** dado
imperfecto de indicativo		pluscuamperfecto de indicativo	
d**aba**	d**ábamos**	**había** dado	**habíamos** dado
d**abas**	d**abais**	**habías** dado	**habíais** dado
d**aba**	d**aban**	**había** dado	**habían** dado
pretérito		pretérito anterior	
d**i**	d**imos**	**hube** dado	**hubimos** dado
d**iste**	d**isteis**	**hubiste** dado	**hubisteis** dado
di**o**	d**ieron**	**hubo** dado	**hubieron** dado
futuro		futuro perfecto	
dar**é**	dar**emos**	**habré** dado	**habremos** dado
dar**ás**	dar**éis**	**habrás** dado	**habréis** dado
dar**á**	dar**án**	**habrá** dado	**habrán** dado
condicional simple		condicional compuesto	
dar**ía**	dar**íamos**	**habría** dado	**habríamos** dado
dar**ías**	dar**íais**	**habrías** dado	**habríais** dado
dar**ía**	dar**ían**	**habría** dado	**habrían** dado
presente de subjuntivo		perfecto de subjuntivo	
d**é**	d**emos**	**haya** dado	**hayamos** dado
d**es**	d**eis**	**hayas** dado	**hayáis** dado
d**é**	d**en**	**haya** dado	**hayan** dado
imperfecto de subjuntivo		pluscuamperfecto de subjuntivo	
dier**a**	diér**amos**	**hubiera** dado	**hubiéramos** dado
dier**as**	dier**ais**	**hubieras** dado	**hubierais** dado
dier**a**	dier**an**	**hubiera** dado	**hubieran** dado
OR		OR	
dies**e**	diés**emos**	**hubiese** dado	**hubiésemos** dado
dies**es**	dies**eis**	**hubieses** dado	**hubieseis** dado
dies**e**	dies**en**	**hubiese** dado	**hubiesen** dado

imperativo

—	demos
da; no des	dad; no deis
dé	den

deber — to owe, to have to

gerundio **debiendo** participio de pasado **debido**

SINGULAR	PLURAL
presente de indicativo	
deb**o**	deb**emos**
deb**es**	deb**éis**
deb**e**	deb**en**
imperfecto de indicativo	
deb**ía**	deb**íamos**
deb**ías**	deb**íais**
deb**ía**	deb**ían**
pretérito	
deb**í**	deb**imos**
deb**iste**	deb**isteis**
deb**ió**	deb**ieron**
futuro	
deber**é**	deber**emos**
deber**ás**	deber**éis**
deber**á**	deber**án**
condicional simple	
deber**ía**	deber**íamos**
deber**ías**	deber**íais**
deber**ía**	deber**ían**
presente de subjuntivo	
deb**a**	deb**amos**
deb**as**	deb**áis**
deb**a**	deb**an**
imperfecto de subjuntivo	
debier**a**	debiér**amos**
debier**as**	debier**ais**
debier**a**	debier**an**
OR	
debies**e**	debiés**emos**
debies**es**	debies**eis**
debies**e**	debies**en**
imperativo	
—	debamos
debe; no debas	debed; no debáis
deba	deban

SINGULAR	PLURAL
perfecto de indicativo	
he debido	**hemos** debido
has debido	**habéis** debido
ha debido	**han** debido
pluscuamperfecto de indicativo	
había debido	**habíamos** debido
habías debido	**habíais** debido
había debido	**habían** debido
pretérito anterior	
hube debido	**hubimos** debido
hubiste debido	**hubisteis** debido
hubo debido	**hubieron** debido
futuro perfecto	
habré debido	**habremos** debido
habrás debido	**habréis** debido
habrá debido	**habrán** debido
condicional compuesto	
habría debido	**habríamos** debido
habrías debido	**habríais** debido
habría debido	**habrían** debido
perfecto de subjuntivo	
haya debido	**hayamos** debido
hayas debido	**hayáis** debido
haya debido	**hayan** debido
pluscuamperfecto de subjuntivo	
hubiera debido	**hubiéramos** debido
hubieras debido	**hubierais** debido
hubiera debido	**hubieran** debido
OR	
hubiese debido	**hubiésemos** debido
hubieses debido	**hubieseis** debido
hubiese debido	**hubiesen** debido

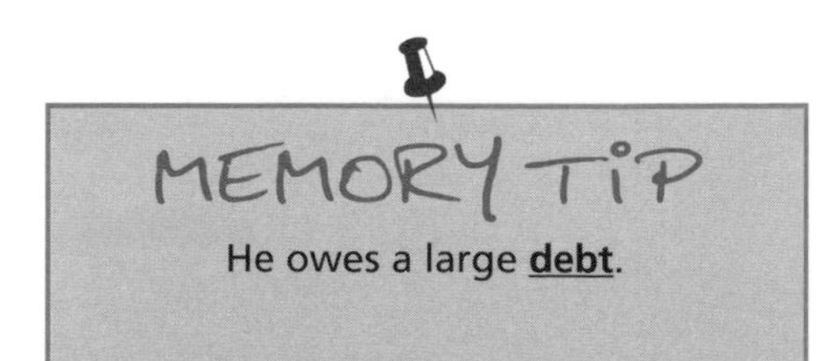

gerundio **decidiendo** participio de pasado **decidido**

SINGULAR	PLURAL	SINGULAR	PLURAL
presente de indicativo		perfecto de indicativo	
decid**o**	decid**imos**	**he** decidido	**hemos** decidido
decid**es**	decid**ís**	**has** decidido	**habéis** decidido
decid**e**	decid**en**	**ha** decidido	**han** decidido
imperfecto de indicativo		pluscuamperfecto de indicativo	
decid**ía**	decid**íamos**	**había** decidido	**habíamos** decidido
decid**ías**	decid**íais**	**habías** decidido	**habíais** decidido
decid**ía**	decid**ían**	**había** decidido	**habían** decidido
pretérito		pretérito anterior	
decid**í**	decid**imos**	**hube** decidido	**hubimos** decidido
decid**iste**	decid**isteis**	**hubiste** decidido	**hubisteis** decidido
decid**ió**	decid**ieron**	**hubo** decidido	**hubieron** decidido
futuro		futuro perfecto	
decidir**é**	decidir**emos**	**habré** decidido	**habremos** decidido
decidir**ás**	decidir**éis**	**habrás** decidido	**habréis** decidido
decidir**á**	decidir**án**	**habrá** decidido	**habrán** decidido
condicional simple		condicional compuesto	
decidir**ía**	decidir**íamos**	**habría** decidido	**habríamos** decidido
decidir**ías**	decidir**íais**	**habrías** decidido	**habríais** decidido
decidir**ía**	decidir**ían**	**habría** decidido	**habrían** decidido
presente de subjuntivo		perfecto de subjuntivo	
decid**a**	decid**amos**	**haya** decidido	**hayamos** decidido
decid**as**	decid**áis**	**hayas** decidido	**hayáis** decidido
decid**a**	decid**an**	**haya** decidido	**hayan** decidido
imperfecto de subjuntivo		pluscuamperfecto de subjuntivo	
decidier**a**	decidiér**amos**	**hubiera** decidido	**hubiéramos** decidido
decidier**as**	decidier**ais**	**hubieras** decidido	**hubierais** decidido
decidier**a**	decidier**an**	**hubiera** decidido	**hubieran** decidido
OR		OR	
decidies**e**	decidiés**emos**	**hubiese** decidido	**hubiésemos** decidido
decidies**es**	decidies**eis**	**hubieses** decidido	**hubieseis** decidido
decidies**e**	decidies**en**	**hubiese** decidido	**hubiesen** decidido

imperativo

—	decidamos
decide; no decidas	decidid; no decidáis
decida	decidan

decir

to tell, to say

gerundio **diciendo**   participio de pasado **dicho**

SINGULAR	PLURAL
presente de indicativo	
dig**o**	dec**imos**
dic**es**	dec**ís**
dic**e**	dic**en**
imperfecto de indicativo	
dec**ía**	dec**íamos**
dec**ías**	dec**íais**
dec**ía**	dec**ían**
pretérito	
dij**e**	dij**imos**
dij**iste**	dij**isteis**
dij**o**	dij**eron**
futuro	
dir**é**	dir**emos**
dir**ás**	dir**éis**
dir**á**	dir**án**
condicional simple	
dir**ía**	dir**íamos**
dir**ías**	dir**íais**
dir**ía**	dir**ían**
presente de subjuntivo	
dig**a**	dig**amos**
dig**as**	dig**áis**
dig**a**	dig**an**
imperfecto de subjuntivo	
dijer**a**	dijér**amos**
dijer**as**	dijer**ais**
dijer**a**	dijer**an**
OR	
dijes**e**	dijés**emos**
dijes**es**	dijes**eis**
dijes**e**	dijes**en**
imperativo	
—	digamos
di; no digas	decid; no digáis
diga	digan

SINGULAR	PLURAL
perfecto de indicativo	
he dicho	**hemos** dicho
has dicho	**habéis** dicho
ha dicho	**han** dicho
pluscuamperfecto de indicativo	
había dicho	**habíamos** dicho
habías dicho	**habíais** dicho
había dicho	**habían** dicho
pretérito anterior	
hube dicho	**hubimos** dicho
hubiste dicho	**hubisteis** dicho
hubo dicho	**hubieron** dicho
futuro perfecto	
habré dicho	**habremos** dicho
habrás dicho	**habréis** dicho
habrá dicho	**habrán** dicho
condicional compuesto	
habría dicho	**habríamos** dicho
habrías dicho	**habríais** dicho
habría dicho	**habrían** dicho
perfecto de subjuntivo	
haya dicho	**hayamos** dicho
hayas dicho	**hayáis** dicho
haya dicho	**hayan** dicho
pluscuamperfecto de subjuntivo	
hubiera dicho	**hubiéramos** dicho
hubieras dicho	**hubierais** dicho
hubiera dicho	**hubieran** dicho
OR	
hubiese dicho	**hubiésemos** dicho
hubieses dicho	**hubieseis** dicho
hubiese dicho	**hubiesen** dicho

gerundio **declarando** participio de pasado **declarado**

SINGULAR	PLURAL	SINGULAR	PLURAL
presente de indicativo		perfecto de indicativo	
declar**o**	declar**amos**	**he** declarado	**hemos** declarado
declar**as**	declar**áis**	**has** declarado	**habéis** declarado
declar**a**	declar**an**	**ha** declarado	**han** declarado
imperfecto de indicativo		pluscuamperfecto de indicativo	
declar**aba**	declar**ábamos**	**había** declarado	**habíamos** declarado
declar**abas**	declar**abais**	**habías** declarado	**habíais** declarado
declar**aba**	declar**aban**	**había** declarado	**habían** declarado
pretérito		pretérito anterior	
declar**é**	declar**amos**	**hube** declarado	**hubimos** declarado
declar**aste**	declar**asteis**	**hubiste** declarado	**hubisteis** declarado
declar**ó**	declar**aron**	**hubo** declarado	**hubieron** declarado
futuro		futuro perfecto	
declarar**é**	declarar**emos**	**habré** declarado	**habremos** declarado
declarar**ás**	declarar**éis**	**habrás** declarado	**habréis** declarado
declarar**á**	declarar**án**	**habrá** declarado	**habrán** declarado
condicional simple		condicional compuesto	
declarar**ía**	declarar**íamos**	**habría** declarado	**habríamos** declarado
declarar**ías**	declarar**íais**	**habrías** declarado	**habríais** declarado
declarar**ía**	declarar**ían**	**habría** declarado	**habrían** declarado
presente de subjuntivo		perfecto de subjuntivo	
declar**e**	declar**emos**	**haya** declarado	**hayamos** declarado
declar**es**	declar**éis**	**hayas** declarado	**hayáis** declarado
declar**e**	declar**en**	**haya** declarado	**hayan** declarado
imperfecto de subjuntivo		pluscuamperfecto de subjuntivo	
declarar**a**	declarár**amos**	**hubiera** declarado	**hubiéramos** declarado
declarar**as**	declarar**ais**	**hubieras** declarado	**hubierais** declarado
declarar**a**	declarar**an**	**hubiera** declarado	**hubieran** declarado
OR		OR	
declaras**e**	declarás**emos**	**hubiese** declarado	**hubiésemos** declarado
declaras**es**	declaras**eis**	**hubieses** declarado	**hubieseis** declarado
declaras**e**	declaras**en**	**hubiese** declarado	**hubiesen** declarado

imperativo

—	declaremos
declara; no declares	declarad; no declaréis
declare	declaren

D

dedicar — to dedicate

gerundio **dedicando** participio de pasado **dedicado**

SINGULAR	PLURAL
presente de indicativo	
dedic**o**	dedic**amos**
dedic**as**	dedic**áis**
dedic**a**	dedic**an**
imperfecto de indicativo	
dedic**aba**	dedic**ábamos**
dedic**abas**	dedic**abais**
dedic**aba**	dedic**aban**
pretérito	
dediqu**é**	dedic**amos**
dedic**aste**	dedic**asteis**
dedic**ó**	dedic**aron**
futuro	
dedicar**é**	dedicar**emos**
dedicar**ás**	dedicar**éis**
dedicar**á**	dedicar**án**
condicional simple	
dedicar**ía**	dedicar**íamos**
dedicar**ías**	dedicar**íais**
dedicar**ía**	dedicar**ían**
presente de subjuntivo	
dediqu**e**	dediqu**emos**
dediqu**es**	dediqu**éis**
dediqu**e**	dediqu**en**
imperfecto de subjuntivo	
dedicar**a**	dedicár**amos**
dedicar**as**	dedicar**ais**
dedicar**a**	dedicar**an**
OR	
dedicas**e**	dedicás**emos**
dedicas**es**	dedicas**eis**
dedicas**e**	dedicas**en**
imperativo	
—	dediquemos
dedica; no dediques	dedicad; no dediquéis
dedique	dediquen

SINGULAR	PLURAL
perfecto de indicativo	
he dedicado	**hemos** dedicado
has dedicado	**habéis** dedicado
ha dedicado	**han** dedicado
pluscuamperfecto de indicativo	
había dedicado	**habíamos** dedicado
habías dedicado	**habíais** dedicado
había dedicado	**habían** dedicado
pretérito anterior	
hube dedicado	**hubimos** dedicado
hubiste dedicado	**hubisteis** dedicado
hubo dedicado	**hubieron** dedicado
futuro perfecto	
habré dedicado	**habremos** dedicado
habrás dedicado	**habréis** dedicado
habrá dedicado	**habrán** dedicado
condicional compuesto	
habría dedicado	**habríamos** dedicado
habrías dedicado	**habríais** dedicado
habría dedicado	**habrían** dedicado
perfecto de subjuntivo	
haya dedicado	**hayamos** dedicado
hayas dedicado	**hayáis** dedicado
haya dedicado	**hayan** dedicado
pluscuamperfecto de subjuntivo	
hubiera dedicado	**hubiéramos** dedicado
hubieras dedicado	**hubierais** dedicado
hubiera dedicado	**hubieran** dedicado
OR	
hubiese dedicado	**hubiésemos** dedicado
hubieses dedicado	**hubieseis** dedicado
hubiese dedicado	**hubiesen** dedicado

to devote oneself **dedicarse**

gerundio **dedicándose** participio de pasado **dedicado**

SINGULAR	PLURAL	SINGULAR	PLURAL
presente de indicativo		perfecto de indicativo	
me dedic**o**	nos dedic**amos**	**me he** dedicado	**nos hemos** dedicado
te dedic**as**	os dedic**áis**	**te has** dedicado	**os habéis** dedicado
se dedic**a**	se dedic**an**	**se ha** dedicado	**se han** dedicado
imperfecto de indicativo		pluscuamperfecto de indicativo	
me dedic**aba**	nos dedic**ábamos**	**me había** dedicado	**nos habíamos** dedicado
te dedic**abas**	os dedic**abais**	**te habías** dedicado	**os habíais** dedicado
se dedic**aba**	se dedic**aban**	**se había** dedicado	**se habían** dedicado
pretérito		pretérito anterior	
me dediqu**é**	nos dedic**amos**	**me hube** dedicado	**nos hubimos** dedicado
te dedic**aste**	os dedic**asteis**	**te hubiste** dedicado	**os hubisteis** dedicado
se dedic**ó**	se dedic**aron**	**se hubo** dedicado	**se hubieron** dedicado
futuro		futuro perfecto	
me dedicar**é**	nos dedicar**emos**	**me habré** dedicado	**nos habremos** dedicado
te dedicar**ás**	os dedicar**éis**	**te habrás** dedicado	**os habréis** dedicado
se dedicar**á**	se dedicar**án**	**se habrá** dedicado	**se habrán** dedicado
condicional simple		condicional compuesto	
me dedicar**ía**	nos dedicar**íamos**	**me habría** dedicado	**nos habríamos** dedicado
te dedicar**ías**	os dedicar**íais**	**te habrías** dedicado	**os habríais** dedicado
se dedicar**ía**	se dedicar**ían**	**se habría** dedicado	**se habrían** dedicado
presente de subjuntivo		perfecto de subjuntivo	
me dediqu**e**	nos dediqu**emos**	**me haya** dedicado	**nos hayamos** dedicado
te dediqu**es**	os dediqu**éis**	**te hayas** dedicado	**os hayáis** dedicado
se dediqu**e**	se dediqu**en**	**se haya** dedicado	**se hayan** dedicado
imperfecto de subjuntivo		pluscuamperfecto de subjuntivo	
me dedicar**a**	nos dedicár**amos**	**me hubiera** dedicado	**nos hubiéramos** dedicado
te dedicar**as**	os dedicar**ais**	**te hubieras** dedicado	**os hubierais** dedicado
se dedicar**a**	se dedicar**an**	**se hubiera** dedicado	**se hubieran** dedicado
OR		OR	
me dedicas**e**	nos dedicás**emos**	**me hubiese** dedicado	**nos hubiésemos** dedicado
te dedicas**es**	os dedicas**eis**	**te hubieses** dedicado	**os hubieseis** dedicado
se dedicas**e**	se dedicas**en**	**se hubiese** dedicado	**se hubiesen** dedicado

imperativo

SINGULAR	PLURAL
—	dediquémonos
dedícate; no te dediques	dedicaos; no os dediquéis
dedíquese	dedíquense

deducir — to deduce, to infer, to assume

gerundio **deduciendo** participio de pasado **deducido**

SINGULAR	PLURAL
presente de indicativo	
deduzc**o**	deduc**imos**
deduc**es**	deduc**ís**
deduc**e**	deduc**en**
imperfecto de indicativo	
deduc**ía**	deduc**íamos**
deduc**ías**	deduc**íais**
deduc**ía**	deduc**ían**
pretérito	
deduj**e**	deduj**imos**
deduj**iste**	deduj**isteis**
deduj**o**	deduj**eron**
futuro	
deducir**é**	deducir**emos**
deducir**ás**	deducir**éis**
deducir**á**	deducir**án**
condicional simple	
deducir**ía**	deducir**íamos**
deducir**ías**	deducir**íais**
deducir**ía**	deducir**ían**
presente de subjuntivo	
deduzc**a**	deduzc**amos**
deduzc**as**	deduzc**áis**
deduzc**a**	deduzc**an**
imperfecto de subjuntivo	
dedujer**a**	dedujér**amos**
dedujer**as**	dedujer**ais**
dedujer**a**	dedujer**an**
OR	
dedujes**e**	dedujés**emos**
dedujes**es**	dedujes**eis**
dedujes**e**	dedujes**en**
imperativo	
—	deduzcamos
deduce; no deduzcas	deducid; no deduzcáis
deduzca	deduzcan

SINGULAR	PLURAL
perfecto de indicativo	
he deducido	**hemos** deducido
has deducido	**habéis** deducido
ha deducido	**han** deducido
pluscuamperfecto de indicativo	
había deducido	**habíamos** deducido
habías deducido	**habíais** deducido
había deducido	**habían** deducido
pretérito anterior	
hube deducido	**hubimos** deducido
hubiste deducido	**hubisteis** deducido
hubo deducido	**hubieron** deducido
futuro perfecto	
habré deducido	**habremos** deducido
habrás deducido	**habréis** deducido
habrá deducido	**habrán** deducido
condicional compuesto	
habría deducido	**habríamos** deducido
habrías deducido	**habríais** deducido
habría deducido	**habrían** deducido
perfecto de subjuntivo	
haya deducido	**hayamos** deducido
hayas deducido	**hayáis** deducido
haya deducido	**hayan** deducido
pluscuamperfecto de subjuntivo	
hubiera deducido	**hubiéramos** deducido
hubieras deducido	**hubierais** deducido
hubiera deducido	**hubieran** deducido
OR	
hubiese deducido	**hubiésemos** deducido
hubieses deducido	**hubieseis** deducido
hubiese deducido	**hubiesen** deducido

gerundio **defendiendo** participio de pasado **defendido**

SINGULAR	PLURAL
presente de indicativo	
defiend**o**	defend**emos**
defiend**es**	defend**éis**
defiend**e**	defiend**en**
imperfecto de indicativo	
defend**ía**	defend**íamos**
defend**ías**	defend**íais**
defend**ía**	defend**ían**
pretérito	
defend**í**	defend**imos**
defend**iste**	defend**isteis**
defend**ió**	defend**ieron**
futuro	
defender**é**	defender**emos**
defender**ás**	defender**éis**
defender**á**	defender**án**
condicional simple	
defender**ía**	defender**íamos**
defender**ías**	defender**íais**
defender**ía**	defender**ían**
presente de subjuntivo	
defiend**a**	defend**amos**
defiend**as**	defend**áis**
defiend**a**	defiend**an**
imperfecto de subjuntivo	
defendier**a**	defendiér**amos**
defendier**as**	defendier**ais**
defendier**a**	defendier**an**
OR	
defendies**e**	defendiés**emos**
defendies**es**	defendies**eis**
defendies**e**	defendies**en**
imperativo	
—	defendamos
defiende; no defiendas	defended; no defendáis
defienda	defiendan

SINGULAR	PLURAL
perfecto de indicativo	
he defendido	**hemos** defendido
has defendido	**habéis** defendido
ha defendido	**han** defendido
pluscuamperfecto de indicativo	
había defendido	**habíamos** defendido
habías defendido	**habíais** defendido
había defendido	**habían** defendido
pretérito anterior	
hube defendido	**hubimos** defendido
hubiste defendido	**hubisteis** defendido
hubo defendido	**hubieron** defendido
futuro perfecto	
habré defendido	**habremos** defendido
habrás defendido	**habréis** defendido
habrá defendido	**habrán** defendido
condicional compuesto	
habría defendido	**habríamos** defendido
habrías defendido	**habríais** defendido
habría defendido	**habrían** defendido
perfecto de subjuntivo	
haya defendido	**hayamos** defendido
hayas defendido	**hayáis** defendido
haya defendido	**hayan** defendido
pluscuamperfecto de subjuntivo	
hubiera defendido	**hubiéramos** defendido
hubieras defendido	**hubierais** defendido
hubiera defendido	**hubieran** defendido
OR	
hubiese defendido	**hubiésemos** defendido
hubieses defendido	**hubieseis** defendido
hubiese defendido	**hubiesen** defendido

defraudar — to defraud

gerundio **defraudando** participio de pasado **defraudado**

SINGULAR	PLURAL	SINGULAR	PLURAL
presente de indicativo		perfecto de indicativo	
defraud**o**	defraud**amos**	**he** defraudado	**hemos** defraudado
defraud**as**	defraud**áis**	**has** defraudado	**habéis** defraudado
defraud**a**	defraud**an**	**ha** defraudado	**han** defraudado
imperfecto de indicativo		pluscuamperfecto de indicativo	
defraud**aba**	defraud**ábamos**	**había** defraudado	**habíamos** defraudado
defraud**abas**	defraud**abais**	**habías** defraudado	**habíais** defraudado
defraud**aba**	defraud**aban**	**había** defraudado	**habían** defraudado
pretérito		pretérito anterior	
defraud**é**	defraud**amos**	**hube** defraudado	**hubimos** defraudado
defraud**aste**	defraud**asteis**	**hubiste** defraudado	**hubisteis** defraudado
defraud**ó**	defraud**aron**	**hubo** defraudado	**hubieron** defraudado
futuro		futuro perfecto	
defraudar**é**	defraudar**emos**	**habré** defraudado	**habremos** defraudado
defraudar**ás**	defraudar**éis**	**habrás** defraudado	**habréis** defraudado
defraudar**á**	defraudar**án**	**habrá** defraudado	**habrán** defraudado
condicional simple		condicional compuesto	
defraudar**ía**	defraudar**íamos**	**habría** defraudado	**habríamos** defraudado
defraudar**ías**	defraudar**íais**	**habrías** defraudado	**habríais** defraudado
defraudar**ía**	defraudar**ían**	**habría** defraudado	**habrían** defraudado
presente de subjuntivo		perfecto de subjuntivo	
defraud**e**	defraud**emos**	**haya** defraudado	**hayamos** defraudado
defraud**es**	defraud**éis**	**hayas** defraudado	**hayáis** defraudado
defraud**e**	defraud**en**	**haya** defraudado	**hayan** defraudado
imperfecto de subjuntivo		pluscuamperfecto de subjuntivo	
defraudar**a**	defraudár**amos**	**hubiera** defraudado	**hubiéramos** defraudado
defraudar**as**	defraudar**ais**	**hubieras** defraudado	**hubierais** defraudado
defraudar**a**	defraudar**an**	**hubiera** defraudado	**hubieran** defraudado
OR		OR	
defraudas**e**	defraudás**emos**	**hubiese** defraudado	**hubiésemos** defraudado
defraudas**es**	defraudas**eis**	**hubieses** defraudado	**hubieseis** defraudado
defraudas**e**	defraudas**en**	**hubiese** defraudado	**hubiesen** defraudado

imperativo

—	defraudemos
defrauda; no defraudes	defraudad; no defraudéis
defraude	defrauden

to allow, to leave behind **dejar**

gerundio **dejando** participio de pasado **dejado**

SINGULAR	PLURAL
presente de indicativo	
dej**o**	dej**amos**
dej**as**	dej**áis**
dej**a**	dej**an**
imperfecto de indicativo	
dej**aba**	dej**ábamos**
dej**abas**	dej**abais**
dej**aba**	dej**aban**
pretérito	
dej**é**	dej**amos**
dej**aste**	dej**asteis**
dej**ó**	dej**aron**
futuro	
dejar**é**	dejar**emos**
dejar**ás**	dejar**éis**
dejar**á**	dejar**án**
condicional simple	
dejar**ía**	dejar**íamos**
dejar**ías**	dejar**íais**
dejar**ía**	dejar**ían**
presente de subjuntivo	
dej**e**	dej**emos**
dej**es**	dej**éis**
dej**e**	dej**en**
imperfecto de subjuntivo	
dejar**a**	dejár**amos**
dejar**as**	dejar**ais**
dejar**a**	dejar**an**
OR	
dejas**e**	dejás**emos**
dejas**es**	dejas**eis**
dejas**e**	dejas**en**
imperativo	
—	dejemos
deja; no dejes	dejad; no dejéis
deje	dejen

SINGULAR	PLURAL
perfecto de indicativo	
he dejado	**hemos** dejado
has dejado	**habéis** dejado
ha dejado	**han** dejado
pluscuamperfecto de indicativo	
había dejado	**habíamos** dejado
habías dejado	**habíais** dejado
había dejado	**habían** dejado
pretérito anterior	
hube dejado	**hubimos** dejado
hubiste dejado	**hubisteis** dejado
hubo dejado	**hubieron** dejado
futuro perfecto	
habré dejado	**habremos** dejado
habrás dejado	**habréis** dejado
habrá dejado	**habrán** dejado
condicional compuesto	
habría dejado	**habríamos** dejado
habrías dejado	**habríais** dejado
habría dejado	**habrían** dejado
perfecto de subjuntivo	
haya dejado	**hayamos** dejado
hayas dejado	**hayáis** dejado
haya dejado	**hayan** dejado
pluscuamperfecto de subjuntivo	
hubiera dejado	**hubiéramos** dejado
hubieras dejado	**hubierais** dejado
hubiera dejado	**hubieran** dejado
OR	
hubiese dejado	**hubiésemos** dejado
hubieses dejado	**hubieseis** dejado
hubiese dejado	**hubiesen** dejado

delinquir to be delinquent, to violate the law

gerundio **delinquiendo** participio de pasado **delinquido**

SINGULAR	PLURAL	SINGULAR	PLURAL
presente de indicativo		perfecto de indicativo	
delinc**o**	delinqu**imos**	**he** delinquido	**hemos** delinquido
delinqu**es**	delinqu**ís**	**has** delinquido	**habéis** delinquido
delinqu**e**	delinqu**en**	**ha** delinquido	**han** delinquido
imperfecto de indicativo		pluscuamperfecto de indicativo	
delinqu**ía**	delinqu**íamos**	**había** delinquido	**habíamos** delinquido
delinqu**ías**	delinqu**íais**	**habías** delinquido	**habíais** delinquido
delinqu**ía**	delinqu**ían**	**había** delinquido	**habían** delinquido
pretérito		pretérito anterior	
delinqu**í**	delinqu**imos**	**hube** delinquido	**hubimos** delinquido
delinqu**iste**	delinqu**isteis**	**hubiste** delinquido	**hubisteis** delinquido
delinqui**ó**	delinqu**ieron**	**hubo** delinquido	**hubieron** delinquido
futuro		futuro perfecto	
delinquir**é**	delinquir**emos**	**habré** delinquido	**habremos** delinquido
delinquir**ás**	delinquir**éis**	**habrás** delinquido	**habréis** delinquido
delinquir**á**	delinquir**án**	**habrá** delinquido	**habrán** delinquido
condicional simple		condicional compuesto	
delinquir**ía**	delinquir**íamos**	**habría** delinquido	**habríamos** delinquido
delinquir**ías**	delinquir**íais**	**habrías** delinquido	**habríais** delinquido
delinquir**ía**	delinquir**ían**	**habría** delinquido	**habrían** delinquido
presente de subjuntivo		perfecto de subjuntivo	
delinc**a**	delinc**amos**	**haya** delinquido	**hayamos** delinquido
delinc**as**	delinc**áis**	**hayas** delinquido	**hayáis** delinquido
delinc**a**	delinc**an**	**haya** delinquido	**hayan** delinquido
imperfecto de subjuntivo		pluscuamperfecto de subjuntivo	
delinquier**a**	delinquiér**amos**	**hubiera** delinquido	**hubiéramos** delinquido
delinquier**as**	delinquier**ais**	**hubieras** delinquido	**hubierais** delinquido
delinquier**a**	delinquier**an**	**hubiera** delinquido	**hubieran** delinquido
OR		OR	
delinquies**e**	delinquiés**emos**	**hubiese** delinquido	**hubiésemos** delinquida
delinquies**es**	delinquies**e**	**hubieses** delinquido	**hubieseis** delinquido
delinquies**eis**	delinquies**en**	**hubiese** delinquido	**hubiesen** delinquido

imperativo

—	delincamos
delinque; no delincas	delinquid; no delincáis
delinca	delincan

gerundio **demostrando** participio de pasado **demostrado**

SINGULAR	PLURAL	SINGULAR	PLURAL
presente de indicativo		perfecto de indicativo	
demuestr**o**	demostr**amos**	**he** demostrado	**hemos** demostrado
demuestr**as**	demostr**áis**	**has** demostrado	**habéis** demostrado
demuestr**a**	demuestr**an**	**ha** demostrado	**han** demostrado
imperfecto de indicativo		pluscuamperfecto de indicativo	
demostr**aba**	demostr**ábamos**	**había** demostrado	**habíamos** demostrado
demostr**abas**	demostr**abais**	**habías** demostrado	**habíais** demostrado
demostr**aba**	demostr**aban**	**había** demostrado	**habían** demostrado
pretérito		pretérito anterior	
demostr**é**	demostr**amos**	**hube** demostrado	**hubimos** demostrado
demostr**aste**	demostr**asteis**	**hubiste** demostrado	**hubisteis** demostrado
demostr**ó**	demostr**aron**	**hubo** demostrado	**hubieron** demostrado
futuro		futuro perfecto	
demostrar**é**	demostrar**emos**	**habré** demostrado	**habremos** demostrado
demostrar**ás**	demostrar**éis**	**habrás** demostrado	**habréis** demostrado
demostrar**á**	demostrar**án**	**habrá** demostrado	**habrán** demostrado
condicional simple		condicional compuesto	
demostrar**ía**	demostrar**íamos**	**habría** demostrado	**habríamos** demostrado
demostrar**ías**	demostrar**íais**	**habrías** demostrado	**habríais** demostrado
demostrar**ía**	demostrar**ían**	**habría** demostrado	**habrían** demostrado
presente de subjuntivo		perfecto de subjuntivo	
demuestr**e**	demostr**emos**	**haya** demostrado	**hayamos** demostrado
demuestr**es**	demostr**éis**	**hayas** demostrado	**hayáis** demostrado
demuestr**e**	demuestr**en**	**haya** demostrado	**hayan** demostrado
imperfecto de subjuntivo		pluscuamperfecto de subjuntivo	
demostrar**a**	demostrár**amos**	**hubiera** demostrado	**hubiéramos** demostrado
demostrar**as**	demostrar**ais**	**hubieras** demostrado	**hubierais** demostrado
demostrar**a**	demostrar**an**	**hubiera** demostrado	**hubieran** demostrado
OR		OR	
demostras**e**	demostrás**emos**	**hubiese** demostrado	**hubiésemos** demostrado
demostras**es**	demostras**eis**	**hubieses** demostrado	**hubieseis** demostrado
demostras**e**	demostras**en**	**hubiese** demostrado	**hubiesen** demostrado

imperativo

—	demostremos
demuestra;	demostrad;
no demuestres	no demostréis
demuestre	demuestren

D

denegar — to refuse

gerundio **denegando** participio de pasado **denegado**

SINGULAR	PLURAL	SINGULAR	PLURAL
presente de indicativo		perfecto de indicativo	
denieg**o**	deneg**amos**	**he** denegado	**hemos** denegado
denieg**as**	deneg**áis**	**has** denegado	**habéis** denegado
denieg**a**	denieg**an**	**ha** denegado	**han** denegado
imperfecto de indicativo		pluscuamperfecto de indicativo	
deneg**aba**	deneg**ábamos**	**había** denegado	**habíamos** denegado
deneg**abas**	deneg**abais**	**habías** denegado	**habíais** denegado
deneg**aba**	deneg**aban**	**había** denegado	**habían** denegado
pretérito		pretérito anterior	
denegu**é**	deneg**amos**	**hube** denegado	**hubimos** denegado
deneg**aste**	deneg**asteis**	**hubiste** denegado	**hubisteis** denegado
deneg**ó**	deneg**aron**	**hubo** denegado	**hubieron** denegado
futuro		futuro perfecto	
denegar**é**	denegar**emos**	**habré** denegado	**habremos** denegado
denegar**ás**	denegar**éis**	**habrás** denegado	**habréis** denegado
denegar**á**	denegar**án**	**habrá** denegado	**habrán** denegado
condicional simple		condicional compuesto	
denegar**ía**	denegar**íamos**	**habría** denegado	**habríamos** denegado
denegar**ías**	denegar**íais**	**habrías** denegado	**habríais** denegado
denegar**ía**	denegar**ían**	**habría** denegado	**habrían** denegado
presente de subjuntivo		perfecto de subjuntivo	
deniegu**e**	denegu**emos**	**haya** denegado	**hayamos** denegado
deniegu**es**	denegu**éis**	**hayas** denegado	**hayáis** denegado
deniegu**e**	deniegu**en**	**haya** denegado	**hayan** denegado
imperfecto de subjuntivo		pluscuamperfecto de subjuntivo	
denegar**a**	denegár**amos**	**hubiera** denegado	**hubiéramos** denegado
denegar**as**	denegar**ais**	**hubieras** denegado	**hubierais** denegado
denegar**a**	denegar**an**	**hubiera** denegado	**hubieran** denegado
OR		OR	
denegas**e**	denegás**emos**	**hubiese** denegado	**hubiésemos** denegado
denegas**es**	denegas**eis**	**hubieses** denegado	**hubieseis** denegado
denegas**e**	denegas**en**	**hubiese** denegado	**hubiesen** denegado

imperativo

—	deneguemos
deniega; no deniegues	denegad; no deneguéis
deniegue	denieguen

gerundio **denunciando** participio de pasado **denunciado**

SINGULAR	PLURAL
presente de indicativo	
denunci**o**	denunci**amos**
denunci**as**	denunci**áis**
denunci**a**	denunci**an**
imperfecto de indicativo	
denunci**aba**	denunci**ábamos**
denunci**abas**	denunci**abais**
denunci**aba**	denunci**aban**
pretérito	
denunci**é**	denunci**amos**
denunci**aste**	denunci**asteis**
denunci**ó**	denunci**aron**
futuro	
denunciar**é**	denunciar**emos**
denunciar**ás**	denunciar**éis**
denunciar**á**	denunciar**án**
condicional simple	
denunciar**ía**	denunciar**íamos**
denunciar**ías**	denunciar**íais**
denunciar**ía**	denunciar**ían**
presente de subjuntivo	
denunci**e**	denunci**emos**
denunci**es**	denunci**éis**
denunci**e**	denunci**en**
imperfecto de subjuntivo	
denunciar**a**	denunciár**amos**
denunciar**as**	denunciar**ais**
denunciar**a**	denunciar**an**
OR	
denuncías**e**	denunciás**emos**
denuncias**es**	denuncias**eis**
denuncias**e**	denuncias**en**
imperativo	
—	denunciemos
denuncia; no denuncies	denunciad; no denunciéis
denuncie	denuncien

SINGULAR	PLURAL
perfecto de indicativo	
he denunciado	**hemos** denunciado
has denunciado	**habéis** denunciado
ha denunciado	**han** denunciado
pluscuamperfecto de indicativo	
había denunciado	**habíamos** denunciado
habías denunciado	**habíais** denunciado
había denunciado	**habían** denunciado
pretérito anterior	
hube denunciado	**hubimos** denunciado
hubiste denunciado	**hubisteis** denunciado
hubo denunciado	**hubieron** denunciado
futuro perfecto	
habré denunciado	**habremos** denunciado
habrás denunciado	**habréis** denunciado
habrá denunciado	**habrán** denunciado
condicional compuesto	
habría denunciado	**habríamos** denunciado
habrías denunciado	**habríais** denunciado
habría denunciado	**habrían** denunciado
perfecto de subjuntivo	
haya denunciado	**hayamos** denunciado
hayas denunciado	**hayáis** denunciado
haya denunciado	**hayan** denunciado
pluscuamperfecto de subjuntivo	
hubiera denunciado	**hubiéramos** denunciado
hubieras denunciado	**hubierais** denunciado
hubiera denunciado	**hubieran** denunciado
OR	
hubiese denunciado	**hubiésemos** denunciado
hubieses denunciado	**hubieseis** denunciado
hubiese denunciado	**hubiesen** denunciado

D

depender — to depend on

gerundio **dependiendo** — participio de pasado **dependido**

SINGULAR	PLURAL
presente de indicativo	
depend**o**	depend**emos**
depend**es**	depend**éis**
depend**e**	depend**en**
imperfecto de indicativo	
depend**ía**	depend**íamos**
depend**ías**	depend**íais**
depend**ía**	depend**ían**
pretérito	
depend**í**	depend**imos**
depend**iste**	depend**isteis**
depend**ió**	depend**ieron**
futuro	
depender**é**	depender**emos**
depender**ás**	depender**éis**
depender**á**	depender**án**
condicional simple	
depender**ía**	depender**íamos**
depender**ías**	depender**íais**
depender**ía**	depender**ían**
presente de subjuntivo	
depend**a**	depend**amos**
depend**as**	depend**áis**
depend**a**	depend**an**
imperfecto de subjuntivo	
dependier**a**	dependiér**amos**
dependier**as**	dependier**ais**
dependier**a**	dependier**an**
OR	
dependies**e**	dependiés**emos**
dependies**es**	dependies**eis**
dependies**e**	dependies**en**
imperativo	
—	dependamos
depende; no dependas	depended; no dependáis
dependa	dependan

SINGULAR	PLURAL
perfecto de indicativo	
he dependido	**hemos** dependido
has dependido	**habéis** dependido
ha dependido	**han** dependido
pluscuamperfecto de indicativo	
había dependido	**habíamos** dependido
habías dependido	**habíais** dependido
había dependido	**habían** dependido
pretérito anterior	
hube dependido	**hubimos** dependido
hubiste dependido	**hubisteis** dependido
hubo dependido	**hubieron** dependido
futuro perfecto	
habré dependido	**habremos** dependido
habrás dependido	**habréis** dependido
habrá dependido	**habrán** dependido
condicional compuesto	
habría dependido	**habríamos** dependido
habrías dependido	**habríais** dependido
habría dependido	**habrían** dependido
perfecto de subjuntivo	
haya dependido	**hayamos** dependido
hayas dependido	**hayáis** dependido
haya dependido	**hayan** dependido
pluscuamperfecto de subjuntivo	
hubiera dependido	**hubiéramos** dependido
hubieras dependido	**hubierais** dependido
hubiera dependido	**hubieran** dependido
OR	
hubiese dependido	**hubiésemos** dependido
hubieses dependido	**hubieseis** dependido
hubiese dependido	**hubiesen** dependido

gerundio **deponiendo** — participio de pasado **depuesto**

SINGULAR	PLURAL	SINGULAR	PLURAL
presente de indicativo		perfecto de indicativo	
depong**o**	depon**emos**	**he** depuesto	**hemos** depuesto
depon**es**	depon**éis**	**has** depuesto	**habéis** depuesto
depon**e**	depon**en**	**ha** depuesto	**han** depuesto
imperfecto de indicativo		pluscuamperfecto de indicativo	
depon**ía**	depon**íamos**	**había** depuesto	**habíamos** depuesto
depon**ías**	depon**íais**	**habías** depuesto	**habíais** depuesto
depon**ía**	depon**ían**	**había** depuesto	**habían** depuesto
pretérito		pretérito anterior	
depus**e**	depus**imos**	**hube** depuesto	**hubimos** depuesto
depus**iste**	depus**isteis**	**hubiste** depuesto	**hubisteis** depuesto
depus**o**	depus**ieron**	**hubo** depuesto	**hubieron** depuesto
futuro		futuro perfecto	
depondr**é**	depondr**emos**	**habré** depuesto	**habremos** depuesto
depondr**ás**	depondr**éis**	**habrás** depuesto	**habréis** depuesto
depondr**á**	depondr**án**	**habrá** depuesto	**habrán** depuesto
condicional simple		condicional compuesto	
depondr**ía**	depondr**íamos**	**habría** depuesto	**habríamos** depuesto
depondr**ías**	depondr**íais**	**habrías** depuesto	**habríais** depuesto
depondr**ía**	depondr**ían**	**habría** depuesto	**habrían** depuesto
presente de subjuntivo		perfecto de subjuntivo	
depong**a**	depong**amos**	**haya** depuesto	**hayamos** depuesto
depong**as**	depong**áis**	**hayas** depuesto	**hayáis** depuesto
depong**a**	depong**an**	**haya** depuesto	**hayan** depuesto
imperfecto de subjuntivo		pluscuamperfecto de subjuntivo	
depusier**a**	depusiér**amos**	**hubiera** depuesto	**hubiéramos** depuesto
depusier**as**	depusier**ais**	**hubieras** depuesto	**hubierais** depuesto
depusier**a**	depusier**an**	**hubiera** depuesto	**hubieran** depuesto
OR		OR	
depusies**e**	depusiés**emos**	**hubiese** depuesto	**hubiésemos** depuesto
depusies**es**	depusies**eis**	**hubieses** depuesto	**hubieseis** depuesto
depusies**e**	depusies**en**	**hubiese** depuesto	**hubiesen** depuesto

imperativo

—	depongamos
depone; no depongas	deponed; no depongáis
deponga	depongan

deportar — to deport

gerundio **deportando** participio de pasado **deportado**

SINGULAR	PLURAL
presente de indicativo	
deport**o**	deport**amos**
deport**as**	deport**áis**
deport**a**	deport**an**
imperfecto de indicativo	
deport**aba**	deport**ábamos**
deport**abas**	deport**abais**
deport**aba**	deport**aban**
pretérito	
deport**é**	deport**amos**
deport**aste**	deport**asteis**
deport**ó**	deport**aron**
futuro	
deportar**é**	deportar**emos**
deportar**ás**	deportar**éis**
deportar**á**	deportar**án**
condicional simple	
deportar**ía**	deportar**íamos**
deportar**ías**	deportar**íais**
deportar**ía**	deportar**ían**
presente de subjuntivo	
deport**e**	deport**emos**
deport**es**	deport**éis**
deport**e**	deport**en**
imperfecto de subjuntivo	
deportar**a**	deportár**amos**
deportar**as**	deportar**ais**
deportar**a**	deportar**an**
OR	
deportas**e**	deportás**emos**
deportas**es**	deportas**eis**
deportas**e**	deportas**en**
imperativo	
—	deportemos
deporta; no deportes	deportad; no deportéis
deporte	deporten

SINGULAR	PLURAL
perfecto de indicativo	
he deportado	**hemos** deportado
has deportado	**habéis** deportado
ha deportado	**han** deportado
pluscuamperfecto de indicativo	
había deportado	**habíamos** deportado
habías deportado	**habíais** deportado
había deportado	**habían** deportado
pretérito anterior	
hube deportado	**hubimos** deportado
hubiste deportado	**hubisteis** deportado
hubo deportado	**hubieron** deportado
futuro perfecto	
habré deportado	**habremos** deportado
habrás deportado	**habréis** deportado
habrá deportado	**habrán** deportado
condicional compuesto	
habría deportado	**habríamos** deportado
habrías deportado	**habríais** deportado
habría deportado	**habrían** deportado
perfecto de subjuntivo	
haya deportado	**hayamos** deportado
hayas deportado	**hayáis** deportado
haya deportado	**hayan** deportado
pluscuamperfecto de subjuntivo	
hubiera deportado	**hubiéramos** deportado
hubieras deportado	**hubierais** deportado
hubiera deportado	**hubieran** deportado
OR	
hubiese deportado	**hubiésemos** deportado
hubieses deportado	**hubieseis** deportado
hubiese deportado	**hubiesen** deportado

gerundio **derivando** participio de pasado **derivado**

SINGULAR	PLURAL
presente de indicativo	
derivo	derivamos
derivas	deriváis
deriva	derivan
imperfecto de indicativo	
derivaba	derivábamos
derivabas	derivabais
derivaba	derivaban
pretérito	
derivé	derivamos
derivaste	derivasteis
derivó	derivaron
futuro	
derivaré	derivaremos
derivarás	derivaréis
derivará	derivarán
condicional simple	
derivaría	derivaríamos
derivarías	derivaríais
derivaría	derivarían
presente de subjuntivo	
derive	derivemos
derives	derivéis
derive	deriven
imperfecto de subjuntivo	
derivara	deriváramos
derivaras	derivarais
derivara	derivaran
OR	
derivase	derivásemos
derivases	derivaseis
derivase	derivasen
imperativo	
—	derivemos
deriva; no derives	derivad; no derivéis
derive	deriven

SINGULAR	PLURAL
perfecto de indicativo	
he derivado	hemos derivado
has derivado	habéis derivado
ha derivado	han derivado
pluscuamperfecto de indicativo	
había derivado	habíamos derivado
habías derivado	habíais derivado
había derivado	habían derivado
pretérito anterior	
hube derivado	hubimos derivado
hubiste derivado	hubisteis derivado
hubo derivado	hubieron derivado
futuro perfecto	
habré derivado	habremos derivado
habrás derivado	habréis derivado
habrá derivado	habrán derivado
condicional compuesto	
habría derivado	habríamos derivado
habrías derivado	habríais derivado
habría derivado	habrían derivado
perfecto de subjuntivo	
haya derivado	hayamos derivado
hayas derivado	hayáis derivado
haya derivado	hayan derivado
pluscuamperfecto de subjuntivo	
hubiera derivado	hubiéramos derivado
hubieras derivado	hubierais derivado
hubiera derivado	hubieran derivado
OR	
hubiese derivado	hubiésemos derivado
hubieses derivado	hubieseis derivado
hubiese derivado	hubiesen derivado

derribar — to demolish, to overthrow

gerundio **derribando** — participio de pasado **derribado**

SINGULAR	PLURAL	SINGULAR	PLURAL
presente de indicativo		**perfecto de indicativo**	
derrib**o**	derrib**amos**	**he** derribado	**hemos** derribado
derrib**as**	derrib**áis**	**has** derribado	**habéis** derribado
derrib**a**	derrib**an**	**ha** derribado	**han** derribado
imperfecto de indicativo		**pluscuamperfecto de indicativo**	
derrib**aba**	derrib**ábamos**	**había** derribado	**habíamos** derribado
derrib**abas**	derrib**abais**	**habías** derribado	**habíais** derribado
derrib**aba**	derrib**aban**	**había** derribado	**habían** derribado
pretérito		**pretérito anterior**	
derrib**é**	derrib**amos**	**hube** derribado	**hubimos** derribado
derrib**aste**	derrib**asteis**	**hubiste** derribado	**hubisteis** derribado
derrib**ó**	derrib**aron**	**hubo** derribado	**hubieron** derribado
futuro		**futuro perfecto**	
derribar**é**	derribar**emos**	**habré** derribado	**habremos** derribado
derribar**ás**	derribar**éis**	**habrás** derribado	**habréis** derribado
derribar**á**	derribar**án**	**habrá** derribado	**habrán** derribado
condicional simple		**condicional compuesto**	
derribar**ía**	derribar**íamos**	**habría** derribado	**habríamos** derribado
derribar**ías**	derribar**íais**	**habrías** derribado	**habríais** derribado
derribar**ía**	derribar**ían**	**habría** derribado	**habrían** derribado
presente de subjuntivo		**perfecto de subjuntivo**	
derrib**e**	derrib**emos**	**haya** derribado	**hayamos** derribado
derrib**es**	derrib**éis**	**hayas** derribado	**hayáis** derribado
derrib**e**	derrib**en**	**haya** derribado	**hayan** derribado
imperfecto de subjuntivo		**pluscuamperfecto de subjuntivo**	
derribar**a**	derribár**amos**	**hubiera** derribado	**hubiéramos** derribado
derribar**as**	derribar**ais**	**hubieras** derribado	**hubierais** derribado
derribar**a**	derribar**an**	**hubiera** derribado	**hubieran** derribado
OR		OR	
derribas**e**	derribás**emos**	**hubiese** derribado	**hubiésemos** derribado
derribas**es**	derribas**eis**	**hubieses** derribado	**hubieseis** derribado
derribas**e**	derribas**en**	**hubiese** derribado	**hubiesen** derribado

imperativo

SINGULAR	PLURAL
—	derribemos
derriba; no derribes	derribad; no derribéis
derribe	derriben

to defy, to challenge — desafiar

gerundio **desafiando** participio de pasado **desafiado**

SINGULAR	PLURAL

presente de indicativo

desafí**o**	desafi**amos**
desafí**as**	desafi**áis**
desafí**a**	desafí**an**

imperfecto de indicativo

desafi**aba**	desafi**ábamos**
desafi**abas**	desafi**abais**
desafi**aba**	desafi**aban**

pretérito

desafi**é**	desafi**amos**
desafi**aste**	desafi**asteis**
desafi**ó**	desafi**aron**

futuro

desafiar**é**	desafiar**emos**
desafiar**ás**	desafiar**éis**
desafiar**á**	desafiar**án**

condicional simple

desafiar**ía**	desafiar**íamos**
desafiar**ías**	desafiar**íais**
desafiar**ía**	desafiar**ían**

presente de subjuntivo

desafí**e**	desafi**emos**
desafí**es**	desafi**éis**
desafí**e**	desafí**en**

imperfecto de subjuntivo

desafiar**a**	desafiár**amos**
desafiar**as**	desafiar**ais**
desafiar**a**	desafiar**an**
OR	
desafias**e**	desafiás**emos**
desafias**es**	desafias**eis**
desafias**e**	desafias**en**

imperativo

—	desafiemos
desafía; no desafíes	desafiad; no desafiéis
desafíe	desafíen

SINGULAR	PLURAL

perfecto de indicativo

he desafiado	**hemos** desafiado
has desafiado	**habéis** desafiado
ha desafiado	**han** desafiado

pluscuamperfecto de indicativo

había desafiado	**habíamos** desafiado
habías desafiado	**habíais** desafiado
había desafiado	**habían** desafiado

pretérito anterior

hube desafiado	**hubimos** desafiado
hubiste desafiado	**hubisteis** desafiado
hubo desafiado	**hubieron** desafiado

futuro perfecto

habré desafiado	**habremos** desafiado
habrás desafiado	**habréis** desafiado
habrá desafiado	**habrán** desafiado

condicional compuesto

habría desafiado	**habríamos** desafiado
habrías desafiado	**habríais** desafiado
habría desafiado	**habrían** desafiado

perfecto de subjuntivo

haya desafiado	**hayamos** desafiado
hayas desafiado	**hayáis** desafiado
haya desafiado	**hayan** desafiado

pluscuamperfecto de subjuntivo

hubiera desafiado	**hubiéramos** desafiado
hubieras desafiado	**hubierais** desafiado
hubiera desafiado	**hubieran** desafiado
OR	
hubiese desafiado	**hubiésemos** desafiado
hubieses desafiado	**hubieseis** desafiado
hubiese desafiado	**hubiesen** desafiado

desamparar — to abandon

gerundio **desamparando** participio de pasado **desamparado**

SINGULAR	PLURAL	SINGULAR	PLURAL
presente de indicativo		perfecto de indicativo	
desampar**o**	desampar**amos**	**he** desamparado	**hemos** desamparado
desampar**as**	desampar**áis**	**has** desamparado	**habéis** desamparado
desampar**a**	desampar**an**	**ha** desamparado	**han** desamparado
imperfecto de indicativo		pluscuamperfecto de indicativo	
desampar**aba**	desampar**ábamos**	**había** desamparado	**habíamos** desamparado
desampar**abas**	desampar**abais**	**habías** desamparado	**habíais** desamparado
desampar**aba**	desampar**aban**	**había** desamparado	**habían** desamparado
pretérito		pretérito anterior	
desampar**é**	desampar**amos**	**hube** desamparado	**hubimos** desamparado
desampar**aste**	desampar**asteis**	**hubiste** desamparado	**hubisteis** desamparado
desampar**ó**	desampar**aron**	**hubo** desamparado	**hubieron** desamparado
futuro		futuro perfecto	
desamparar**é**	desamparar**emos**	**habré** desamparado	**habremos** desamparado
desamparar**ás**	desamparar**éis**	**habrás** desamparado	**habréis** desamparado
desamparar**á**	desamparar**án**	**habrá** desamparado	**habrán** desamparado
condicional simple		condicional compuesto	
desamparar**ía**	desamparar**íamos**	**habría** desamparado	**habríamos** desamparado
desamparar**ías**	desamparar**íais**	**habrías** desamparado	**habríais** desamparado
desamparar**ía**	desamparar**ían**	**habría** desamparado	**habrían** desamparado
presente de subjuntivo		perfecto de subjuntivo	
desampar**e**	desampar**emos**	**haya** desamparado	**hayamos** desamparado
desampar**es**	desampar**éis**	**hayas** desamparado	**hayáis** desamparado
desampar**e**	desampar**en**	**haya** desamparado	**hayan** desamparado
imperfecto de subjuntivo		pluscuamperfecto de subjuntivo	
desamparar**a**	desamparár**amos**	**hubiera** desamparado	**hubiéramos** desamparado
desamparar**as**	desamparar**ais**	**hubieras** desamparado	**hubierais** desamparado
desamparar**a**	desamparar**an**	**hubiera** desamparado	**hubieran** desamparado
OR		OR	
desamparas**e**	desamparás**emos**	**hubiese** desamparado	**hubiésemos** desamparado
desamparas**es**	desamparas**eis**	**hubieses** desamparado	**hubieseis** desamparado
desamparas**e**	desamparas**en**	**hubiese** desamparado	**hubiesen** desamparado

imperativo

—	desamparemos
desampara;	desamparad;
no desampares	no desamparéis
desampare	desamparen

to disappear **desaparecer**

gerundio **desapareciendo** participio de pasado **desaparecido**

SINGULAR	PLURAL
presente de indicativo	
desaparezc**o**	desaparec**emos**
desaparec**es**	desaparec**éis**
desaparec**e**	desaparec**en**
imperfecto de indicativo	
desaparec**ía**	desaparec**íamos**
desaparec**ías**	desaparec**íais**
desaparec**ía**	desaparec**ían**
pretérito	
desaparec**í**	desaparec**imos**
desaparec**iste**	desaparec**isteis**
desaparec**ió**	desaparec**ieron**
futuro	
desaparecer**é**	desaparecer**emos**
desaparecer**ás**	desaparecer**éis**
desaparecer**á**	desaparecer**án**
condicional simple	
desaparecer**ía**	desaparecer**íamos**
desaparecer**ías**	desaparecer**íais**
desaparecer**ía**	desaparecer**ían**
presente de subjuntivo	
desaparezc**a**	desaparezc**amos**
desaparezc**as**	desaparezc**áis**
desaparezc**a**	desaparezc**an**
imperfecto de subjuntivo	
desapareci**era**	desapareci**éramos**
desapareci**eras**	desapareci**erais**
desapareci**era**	desapareci**eran**
OR	
desapareci**ese**	desapareci**ésemos**
desapareci**eses**	desapareci**eseis**
desapareci**ese**	desapareci**esen**
imperativo	
—	desaparezcamos
desaparece; no desaparezcas	desapareced; no desaparezcáis
desaparezca	desaparezcan

SINGULAR	PLURAL
perfecto de indicativo	
he desaparecido	**hemos** desaparecido
has desaparecido	**habéis** desaparecido
ha desaparecido	**han** desaparecido
pluscuamperfecto de indicativo	
había desaparecido	**habíamos** desaparecido
habías desaparecido	**habíais** desaparecido
había desaparecido	**habían** desaparecido
pretérito anterior	
hube desaparecido	**hubimos** desaparecido
hubiste desaparecido	**hubisteis** desaparecido
hubo desaparecido	**hubieron** desaparecido
futuro perfecto	
habré desaparecido	**habremos** desaparecido
habrás desaparecido	**habréis** desaparecido
habrá desaparecido	**habrán** desaparecido
condicional compuesto	
habría desaparecido	**habríamos** desaparecido
habrías desaparecido	**habríais** desaparecido
habría desaparecido	**habrían** desaparecido
perfecto de subjuntivo	
haya desaparecido	**hayamos** desaparecido
hayas desaparecido	**hayáis** desaparecido
haya desaparecido	**hayan** desaparecido
pluscuamperfecto de subjuntivo	
hubiera desaparecido	**hubiéramos** desaparecido
hubieras desaparecido	**hubierais** desaparecido
hubiera desaparecido	**hubieran** desaparecido
OR	
hubiese desaparecido	**hubiésemos** desaparecido
hubieses desaparecido	**hubieseis** desaparecido
hubiese desaparecido	**hubiesen** desaparecido

desayunarse — to have breakfast

gerundio **desayunándose** participio de pasado **desayunado**

presente de indicativo

SINGULAR	PLURAL
me desayun**o**	nos desayun**amos**
te desayun**as**	os desayun**áis**
se desayun**a**	se desayun**an**

imperfecto de indicativo

SINGULAR	PLURAL
me desayun**aba**	nos desayun**ábamos**
te desayun**abas**	os desayun**abais**
se desayun**aba**	se desayun**aban**

pretérito

SINGULAR	PLURAL
me desayun**é**	nos desayun**amos**
te desayun**aste**	os desayun**asteis**
se desayun**ó**	se desayun**aron**

futuro

SINGULAR	PLURAL
me desayunar**é**	nos desayunar**emos**
te desayunar**ás**	os desayunar**éis**
se desayunar**á**	se desayunar**án**

condicional simple

SINGULAR	PLURAL
me desayunar**ía**	nos desayunar**íamos**
te desayunar**ías**	os desayunar**íais**
se desayunar**ía**	se desayunar**ían**

presente de subjuntivo

SINGULAR	PLURAL
me desayun**e**	nos desayun**emos**
te desayun**es**	os desayun**éis**
se desayun**e**	se desayun**en**

imperfecto de subjuntivo

SINGULAR	PLURAL
me desayunar**a**	nos desayunár**amos**
te desayunar**as**	os desayunar**ais**
se desayunar**a**	se desayunar**an**
OR	
me desayunas**e**	nos desayunás**emos**
te desayunas**es**	os desayunas**eis**
se desayunas**e**	se desayunas**en**

imperativo

SINGULAR	PLURAL
—	desayunémonos
desayúnate;	desayunaos;
no te desayunes	no os desayunéis
desayúnese	desayúnense

perfecto de indicativo

SINGULAR	PLURAL
me he desayunado	**nos hemos** desayunado
te has desayunado	**os habéis** desayunado
se ha desayunado	**se han** desayunado

pluscuamperfecto de indicativo

SINGULAR	PLURAL
me había desayunado	**nos habíamos** desayunado
te habías desayunado	**os habíais** desayunado
se había desayunado	**se habían** desayunado

pretérito anterior

SINGULAR	PLURAL
me hube desayunado	**nos hubimos** desayunado
te hubiste desayunado	**os hubisteis** desayunado
se hubo desayunado	**se hubieron** desayunado

futuro perfecto

SINGULAR	PLURAL
me habré desayunado	**nos habremos** desayunado
te habrás desayunado	**os habréis** desayunado
se habrá desayunado	**se habrán** desayunado

condicional compuesto

SINGULAR	PLURAL
me habría desayunado	**nos habríamos** desayunado
te habrías desayunado	**os habríais** desayunado
se habría desayunado	**se habrían** desayunado

perfecto de subjuntivo

SINGULAR	PLURAL
me haya desayunado	**nos hayamos** desayunado
te hayas desayunado	**os hayáis** desayunado
se haya desayunado	**se hayan** desayunado

pluscuamperfecto de subjuntivo

SINGULAR	PLURAL
me hubiera desayunado	**nos hubiéramos** desayunado
te hubieras desayunado	**os hubierais** desayunado
se hubiera desayunado	**se hubieran** desayunado
OR	
me hubiese desayunado	**nos hubiésemos** desayunado
te hubieses desayunado	**os hubieseis** desayunado
se hubiese desayunado	**se hubiesen** desayunado

to rest — descansar

gerundio **descansando** participio de pasado **descansado**

presente de indicativo

SINGULAR	PLURAL
descans**o**	descans**amos**
descans**as**	descans**áis**
descans**a**	descans**an**

imperfecto de indicativo

SINGULAR	PLURAL
descans**aba**	descans**ábamos**
descans**abas**	descans**abais**
descans**aba**	descans**aban**

pretérito

SINGULAR	PLURAL
descans**é**	descans**amos**
descans**aste**	descans**asteis**
descans**ó**	descans**aron**

futuro

SINGULAR	PLURAL
descansar**é**	descansar**emos**
descansar**ás**	descansar**éis**
descansar**á**	descansar**án**

condicional simple

SINGULAR	PLURAL
descansar**ía**	descansar**íamos**
descansar**ías**	descansar**íais**
descansar**ía**	descansar**ían**

presente de subjuntivo

SINGULAR	PLURAL
descans**e**	descans**emos**
descans**es**	descans**éis**
descans**e**	descans**en**

imperfecto de subjuntivo

SINGULAR	PLURAL
descansar**a**	descansár**amos**
descansar**as**	descansar**ais**
descansar**a**	descansar**an**
OR	
descansas**e**	descansás**emos**
descansas**es**	descansas**eis**
descansas**e**	descansas**en**

imperativo

SINGULAR	PLURAL
—	descansemos
descansa; no descanses	descansad; no descanséis
descanse	descansen

perfecto de indicativo

SINGULAR	PLURAL
he descansado	**hemos** descansado
has descansado	**habéis** descansado
ha descansado	**han** descansado

pluscuamperfecto de indicativo

SINGULAR	PLURAL
había descansado	**habíamos** descansado
habías descansado	**habíais** descansado
había descansado	**habían** descansado

pretérito anterior

SINGULAR	PLURAL
hube descansado	**hubimos** descansado
hubiste descansado	**hubisteis** descansado
hubo descansado	**hubieron** descansado

futuro perfecto

SINGULAR	PLURAL
habré descansado	**habremos** descansado
habrás descansado	**habréis** descansado
habrá descansado	**habrán** descansado

condicional compuesto

SINGULAR	PLURAL
habría descansado	**habríamos** descansado
habrías descansado	**habríais** descansado
habría descansado	**habrían** descansado

perfecto de subjuntivo

SINGULAR	PLURAL
haya descansado	**hayamos** descansado
hayas descansado	**hayáis** descansado
haya descansado	**hayan** descansado

pluscuamperfecto de subjuntivo

SINGULAR	PLURAL
hubiera descansado	**hubiéramos** descansado
hubieras descansado	**hubierais** descansado
hubiera descansado	**hubieran** descansado
OR	
hubiese descansado	**hubiésemos** descansado
hubieses descansado	**hubieseis** descansado
hubiese descansado	**hubiesen** descansado

describir — to describe, to delineate

gerundio **describiendo** — participio de pasado **descrito**

SINGULAR	PLURAL
presente de indicativo	
describ**o**	describ**imos**
describ**es**	describ**ís**
describ**e**	describ**en**
imperfecto de indicativo	
describ**ía**	describ**íamos**
describ**ías**	describ**íais**
describ**ía**	describ**ían**
pretérito	
describ**í**	describ**imos**
describ**iste**	describ**isteis**
describ**ió**	describ**ieron**
futuro	
describir**é**	describir**emos**
describir**ás**	describir**éis**
describir**á**	describir**án**
condicional simple	
describir**ía**	describir**íamos**
describir**ías**	describir**íais**
describir**ía**	describir**ían**
presente de subjuntivo	
describ**a**	describ**amos**
describ**as**	describ**áis**
describ**a**	describ**an**
imperfecto de subjuntivo	
describier**a**	describiér**amos**
describier**as**	describier**ais**
describier**a**	describier**an**
OR	
describies**e**	describiés**emos**
describies**es**	describies**eis**
describies**e**	describies**en**
imperativo	
—	describamos
describe; no describas	describid; no describáis
describa	describan

SINGULAR	PLURAL
perfecto de indicativo	
he descrito	**hemos** descrito
has descrito	**habéis** descrito
ha descrito	**han** descrito
pluscuamperfecto de indicativo	
había descrito	**habíamos** descrito
habías descrito	**habíais** descrito
había descrito	**habían** descrito
pretérito anterior	
hube descrito	**hubimos** descrito
hubiste descrito	**hubisteis** descrito
hubo descrito	**hubieron** descrito
futuro perfecto	
habré descrito	**habremos** descrito
habrás descrito	**habréis** descrito
habrá descrito	**habrán** descrito
condicional compuesto	
habría descrito	**habríamos** descrito
habrías descrito	**habríais** descrito
habría descrito	**habrían** descrito
perfecto de subjuntivo	
haya descrito	**hayamos** descrito
hayas descrito	**hayáis** descrito
haya descrito	**hayan** descrito
pluscuamperfecto de subjuntivo	
hubiera descrito	**hubiéramos** descrito
hubieras descrito	**hubierais** descrito
hubiera descrito	**hubieran** descrito
OR	
hubiese descrito	**hubiésemos** descrito
hubieses descrito	**hubieseis** descrito
hubiese descrito	**hubiesen** descrito

to discover, to uncover **descubrir**

gerundio **descubriendo** participio de pasado **descubierto**

SINGULAR	PLURAL
presente de indicativo	
descubr**o**	descubr**imos**
descubr**es**	descubr**ís**
descubr**e**	descubr**en**
imperfecto de indicativo	
descubr**ía**	descubr**íamos**
descubr**ías**	descubr**íais**
descubr**ía**	descubr**ían**
pretérito	
descubr**í**	descubr**imos**
descubr**iste**	descubr**isteis**
descubri**ó**	descubr**ieron**
futuro	
descubrir**é**	descubrir**emos**
descubrir**ás**	descubrir**éis**
descubrir**á**	descubrir**án**
condicional simple	
descubrir**ía**	descubrir**íamos**
descubrir**ías**	descubrir**íais**
descubrir**ía**	descubrir**ían**
presente de subjuntivo	
descubr**a**	descubr**amos**
descubr**as**	descubr**áis**
descubr**a**	descubr**an**
imperfecto de subjuntivo	
descubrier**a**	descubriér**amos**
descubrier**as**	descubrier**ais**
descubrier**a**	descubrier**an**
OR	
descubries**e**	descubriés**emos**
descubries**es**	descubries**eis**
descubries**e**	descubries**en**
imperativo	
—	descubramos
descubre; no descubras	descubrid; no descubráis
descubra	descubran

SINGULAR	PLURAL
perfecto de indicativo	
he descubierto	**hemos** descubierto
has descubierto	**habéis** descubierto
ha descubierto	**han** descubierto
pluscuamperfecto de indicativo	
había descubierto	**habíamos** descubierto
habías descubierto	**habíais** descubierto
había descubierto	**habían** descubierto
pretérito anterior	
hube descubierto	**hubimos** descubierto
hubiste descubierto	**hubisteis** descubierto
hubo descubierto	**hubieron** descubierto
futuro perfecto	
habré descubierto	**habremos** descubierto
habrás descubierto	**habréis** descubierto
habrá descubierto	**habrán** descubierto
condicional compuesto	
habría descubierto	**habríamos** descubierto
habrías descubierto	**habríais** descubierto
habría descubierto	**habrían** descubierto
perfecto de subjuntivo	
haya descubierto	**hayamos** descubierto
hayas descubierto	**hayáis** descubierto
haya descubierto	**hayan** descubierto
pluscuamperfecto de subjuntivo	
hubiera descubierto	**hubiéramos** descubierto
hubieras descubierto	**hubierais** descubierto
hubiera descubierto	**hubieran** descubierto
OR	
hubiese descubierto	**hubiésemos** descubierto
hubieses descubierto	**hubieseis** descubierto
hubiese descubierto	**hubiesen** descubierto

destacar — to emphasize, to stand out

gerundio **destacando** — participio de pasado **destacado**

SINGULAR	PLURAL

presente de indicativo

destac**o**	destac**amos**
destac**as**	destac**áis**
destac**a**	destac**an**

imperfecto de indicativo

destac**aba**	destac**ábamos**
destac**abas**	destac**abais**
destac**aba**	destac**aban**

pretérito

destaqu**é**	destac**amos**
destac**aste**	destac**asteis**
destac**ó**	destac**aron**

futuro

destacar**é**	destacar**emos**
destacar**ás**	destacar**éis**
destacar**á**	destacar**án**

condicional simple

destacar**ía**	destacar**íamos**
destacar**ías**	destacar**íais**
destacar**ía**	destacar**ían**

presente de subjuntivo

destaqu**e**	destaqu**emos**
destaqu**es**	destaqu**éis**
destaqu**e**	destaqu**en**

imperfecto de subjuntivo

destacar**a**	destacár**amos**
destacar**as**	destacar**ais**
destacar**a**	destacar**an**
OR	
destacas**e**	destacás**emos**
destacas**es**	destacas**eis**
destacas**e**	destacas**en**

imperativo

—	destaquemos
destaca;	destacad;
no destaques	no destaquéis
destaque	destaquen

SINGULAR	PLURAL

perfecto de indicativo

he destacado	**hemos** destacado
has destacado	**habéis** destacado
ha destacado	**han** destacado

pluscuamperfecto de indicativo

había destacado	**habíamos** destacado
habías destacado	**habíais** destacado
había destacado	**habían** destacado

pretérito anterior

hube destacado	**hubimos** destacado
hubiste destacado	**hubisteis** destacado
hubo destacado	**hubieron** destacado

futuro perfecto

habré destacado	**habremos** destacado
habrás destacado	**habréis** destacado
habrá destacado	**habrán** destacado

condicional compuesto

habría destacado	**habríamos** destacado
habrías destacado	**habríais** destacado
habría destacado	**habrían** destacado

perfecto de subjuntivo

haya destacado	**hayamos** destacado
hayas destacado	**hayáis** destacado
haya destacado	**hayan** destacado

pluscuamperfecto de subjuntivo

hubiera destacado	**hubiéramos** destacado
hubieras destacado	**hubierais** destacado
hubiera destacado	**hubieran** destacado
OR	
hubiese destacado	**hubiésemos** destacado
hubieses destacado	**hubieseis** destacado
hubiese destacado	**hubiesen** destacado

gerundio **desterrando** participio de pasado **desterrado**

SINGULAR	PLURAL
presente de indicativo	
destierr**o**	desterr**amos**
destierr**as**	desterr**áis**
destierr**a**	destierr**an**
imperfecto de indicativo	
desterr**aba**	desterr**ábamos**
desterr**abas**	desterr**abais**
desterr**aba**	desterr**aban**
pretérito	
desterr**é**	desterr**amos**
desterr**aste**	desterr**asteis**
desterr**ó**	desterr**aron**
futuro	
desterrar**é**	desterrar**emos**
desterrar**ás**	desterrar**éis**
desterrar**á**	desterrar**án**
condicional simple	
desterrar**ía**	desterrar**íamos**
desterrar**ías**	desterrar**íais**
desterrar**ía**	desterrar**ían**
presente de subjuntivo	
destierr**e**	desterr**emos**
destierr**es**	desterr**éis**
destierr**e**	destierr**en**
imperfecto de subjuntivo	
desterrar**a**	desterrár**amos**
desterrar**as**	desterrar**ais**
desterrar**a**	desterrar**an**
OR	
desterras**e**	desterrás**emos**
desterras**es**	desterras**eis**
desterras**e**	desterras**en**
imperativo	
—	desterremos
destierra; no destierres	desterrad; no desterréis
destierre	destierren

SINGULAR	PLURAL
perfecto de indicativo	
he desterrado	**hemos** desterrado
has desterrado	**habéis** desterrado
ha desterrado	**han** desterrado
pluscuamperfecto de indicativo	
había desterrado	**habíamos** desterrado
habías desterrado	**habíais** desterrado
había desterrado	**habían** desterrado
pretérito anterior	
hube desterrado	**hubimos** desterrado
hubiste desterrado	**hubisteis** desterrado
hubo desterrado	**hubieron** desterrado
futuro perfecto	
habré desterrado	**habremos** desterrado
habrás desterrado	**habréis** desterrado
habrá desterrado	**habrán** desterrado
condicional compuesto	
habría desterrado	**habríamos** desterrado
habrías desterrado	**habríais** desterrado
habría desterrado	**habrían** desterrado
perfecto de subjuntivo	
haya desterrado	**hayamos** desterrado
hayas desterrado	**hayáis** desterrado
haya desterrado	**hayan** desterrado
pluscuamperfecto de subjuntivo	
hubiera desterrado	**hubiéramos** desterrado
hubieras desterrado	**hubierais** desterrado
hubiera desterrado	**hubieran** desterrado
OR	
hubiese desterrado	**hubiésemos** desterrado
hubieses desterrado	**hubieseis** desterrado
hubiese desterrado	**hubiesen** desterrado

gerundio **destituyendo** participio de pasado **destituido**

SINGULAR	PLURAL
presente de indicativo	
destituy**o**	destitu**imos**
destituy**es**	destitu**ís**
destituy**e**	destituy**en**
imperfecto de indicativo	
destitu**ía**	destitu**íamos**
destitu**ías**	destitu**íais**
destitu**ía**	destitu**ían**
pretérito	
destitu**í**	destitu**imos**
destitu**iste**	destitu**isteis**
destituy**ó**	destituy**eron**
futuro	
destituir**é**	destituir**emos**
destituir**ás**	destituir**éis**
destituir**á**	destituir**án**
condicional simple	
destituir**ía**	destituir**íamos**
destituir**ías**	destituir**íais**
destituir**ía**	destituir**ían**
presente de subjuntivo	
destituy**a**	destituy**amos**
destituy**as**	destituy**áis**
destituy**a**	destituy**an**
imperfecto de subjuntivo	
destituyer**a**	destituyér**amos**
destituyer**as**	destituyer**ais**
destituyer**a**	destituyer**an**
OR	
destituyes**e**	destituyés**emos**
destituyes**es**	destituyes**eis**
destituyes**e**	destituyes**en**
imperativo	
—	destituyamos
destituye; no destituyas	destituid; no destituyáis
destituya	destituyan

SINGULAR	PLURAL
perfecto de indicativo	
he destituido	**hemos** destituido
has destituido	**habéis** destituido
ha destituido	**han** destituido
pluscuamperfecto de indicativo	
había destituido	**habíamos** destituido
habías destituido	**habíais** destituido
había destituido	**habían** destituido
pretérito anterior	
hube destituido	**hubimos** destituido
hubiste destituido	**hubisteis** destituido
hubo destituido	**hubieron** destituido
futuro perfecto	
habré destituido	**habremos** destituido
habrás destituido	**habréis** destituido
habrá destituido	**habrán** destituido
condicional compuesto	
habría destituido	**habríamos** destituido
habrías destituido	**habríais** destituido
habría destituido	**habrían** destituido
perfecto de subjuntivo	
haya destituido	**hayamos** destituido
hayas destituido	**hayáis** destituido
haya destituido	**hayan** destituido
pluscuamperfecto de subjuntivo	
hubiera destituido	**hubiéramos** destituido
hubieras destituido	**hubierais** destituido
hubiera destituido	**hubieran** destituido
OR	
hubiese destituido	**hubiésemos** destituido
hubieses destituido	**hubieseis** destituido
hubiese destituido	**hubiesen** destituido

to undress oneself — desvestirse

gerundio **desvistiéndose** participio de pasado **desvestido**

presente de indicativo

SINGULAR	PLURAL
me desvist**o**	nos desvest**imos**
te desvist**es**	os desvest**ís**
se desvist**e**	se desvist**en**

imperfecto de indicativo

SINGULAR	PLURAL
me desvest**ía**	nos desvest**íamos**
te desvest**ías**	os desvest**íais**
se desvest**ía**	se desvest**ían**

pretérito

SINGULAR	PLURAL
me desvest**í**	nos desvest**imos**
te desvest**iste**	os desvest**ísteis**
se desvist**ió**	se desvist**ieron**

futuro

SINGULAR	PLURAL
me desvestir**é**	nos desvestir**emos**
te desvestir**ás**	os desvestir**éis**
se desvestir**á**	se desvestir**án**

condicional simple

SINGULAR	PLURAL
me desvestir**ía**	nos desvestir**íamos**
te desvestir**ías**	os desvestir**íais**
se desvestir**ía**	se desvestir**ían**

presente de subjuntivo

SINGULAR	PLURAL
me desvist**a**	nos desvist**amos**
te desvist**as**	os desvist**áis**
se desvist**a**	se desvist**an**

imperfecto de subjuntivo

SINGULAR	PLURAL
me desvistier**a**	nos desvistiér**amos**
te desvistier**as**	os desvistier**ais**
se desvistier**a**	se desvistier**an**
OR	
me desvisties**e**	nos desvistiés**emos**
te desvisties**es**	os desvisties**eis**
se desvisties**e**	se desvisties**en**

imperativo

SINGULAR	PLURAL
—	desvistámonos
desvístete; no te desvistas	desvestios; no os desvistáis
desvístase	desvístanse

perfecto de indicativo

SINGULAR	PLURAL
me he desvestido	**nos hemos** desvestido
te has desvestido	**os habéis** desvestido
se ha desvestido	**se han** desvestido

pluscuamperfecto de indicativo

SINGULAR	PLURAL
me había desvestido	**nos habíamos** desvestido
te habías desvestido	**os habíais** desvestido
se había desvestido	**se habían** desvestido

pretérito anterior

SINGULAR	PLURAL
me hube desvestido	**nos hubimos** desvestido
te hubiste desvestido	**os hubisteis** desvestido
se hubo desvestido	**se hubieron** desvestido

futuro perfecto

SINGULAR	PLURAL
me habré desvestido	**nos habremos** desvestido
te habrás desvestido	**os habréis** desvestido
se habrá desvestido	**se habrán** desvestido

condicional compuesto

SINGULAR	PLURAL
me habría desvestido	**nos habríamos** desvestido
te habrías desvestido	**os habríais** desvestido
se habría desvestido	**se habrían** desvestido

perfecto de subjuntivo

SINGULAR	PLURAL
me haya desvestido	**nos hayamos** desvestido
te hayas desvestido	**os hayáis** desvestido
se haya desvestido	**se hayan** desvestido

pluscuamperfecto de subjuntivo

SINGULAR	PLURAL
me hubiera desvestido	**nos hubiéramos** desvestido
te hubieras desvestido	**os hubierais** desvestido
se hubiera desvestido	**se hubieran** desvestido
OR	
me hubiese desvestido	**nos hubiésemos** desvestido
te hubieses desvestido	**os hubieseis** desvestido
se hubiese desvestido	**se hubiesen** desvestido

detener — to arrest

gerundio **deteniendo** participio de pasado **detenido**

SINGULAR	PLURAL
presente de indicativo	
deteng**o**	deten**emos**
detien**es**	deten**éis**
detien**e**	detien**en**
imperfecto de indicativo	
deten**ía**	deten**íamos**
deten**ías**	deten**íais**
deten**ía**	deten**ían**
pretérito	
detuv**e**	detuv**imos**
detuv**iste**	detuv**isteis**
detuv**o**	detuv**ieron**
futuro	
detendr**é**	detendr**emos**
detendr**ás**	detendr**éis**
detendr**á**	detendr**án**
condicional simple	
detendr**ía**	detendr**íamos**
detendr**ías**	detendr**íais**
detendr**ía**	detendr**ían**
presente de subjuntivo	
desaparezc**a**	desaparezc**amos**
desaparezc**as**	desaparezc**áis**
desaparezc**a**	desaparezc**an**
imperfecto de subjuntivo	
detuvier**a**	detuviér**amos**
detuvier**as**	detuvier**ais**
detuvier**a**	detuvier**an**
OR	
detuvies**e**	detuviés**emos**
detuvies**es**	detuvies**eis**
detuvies**e**	detuvies**en**
imperativo	
—	detengamos
detén; no detengas	detened; no detengáis
detenga	detengan

SINGULAR	PLURAL
perfecto de indicativo	
he detenido	**hemos** detenido
has detenido	**habéis** detenido
ha detenido	**han** detenido
pluscuamperfecto de indicativo	
había detenido	**habíamos** detenido
habías detenido	**habíais** detenido
había detenido	**habían** detenido
pretérito anterior	
hube detenido	**hubimos** detenido
hubiste detenido	**hubisteis** detenido
hubo detenido	**hubieron** detenido
futuro perfecto	
habré detenido	**habremos** detenido
habrás detenido	**habréis** detenido
habrá detenido	**habrán** detenido
condicional compuesto	
habría detenido	**habríamos** detenido
habrías detenido	**habríais** detenido
habría detenido	**habrían** detenido
perfecto de subjuntivo	
haya detenido	**hayamos** detenido
hayas detenido	**hayáis** detenido
haya detenido	**hayan** detenido
pluscuamperfecto de subjuntivo	
hubiera detenido	**hubiéramos** detenido
hubieras detenido	**hubierais** detenido
hubiera detenido	**hubieran** detenido
OR	
hubiese detenido	**hubiésemos** detenido
hubieses detenido	**hubieseis** detenido
hubiese detenido	**hubiesen** detenido

to give back an object — devolver

gerundio **devolviendo** participio de pasado **devuelto**

SINGULAR	PLURAL
presente de indicativo	
devuelv**o**	devolv**emos**
devuelv**es**	devolv**éis**
devuelv**e**	devuelv**en**
imperfecto de indicativo	
devolv**ía**	devolv**íamos**
devolv**ías**	devolv**íais**
devolv**ía**	devolv**ían**
pretérito	
devolv**í**	devolv**imos**
devolv**iste**	devolv**isteis**
devolv**ió**	devolv**ieron**
futuro	
devolver**é**	devolver**emos**
devolver**ás**	devolver**éis**
devolver**á**	devolver**án**
condicional simple	
devolver**ía**	devolver**íamos**
devolver**ías**	devolver**íais**
devolver**ía**	devolver**ían**
presente de subjuntivo	
devuelv**a**	devolv**amos**
devuelv**as**	devolv**áis**
devuelv**a**	devuelv**an**
imperfecto de subjuntivo	
devolvier**a**	devolviér**amos**
devolvier**as**	devolvier**ais**
devolvier**a**	devolvier**an**
OR	
devolvies**e**	devolviés**emos**
devolvies**es**	devolvies**eis**
devolvies**e**	devolvies**en**
imperativo	
—	devolvamos
devuelve; no devuelvas	devolved; no devolváis
devuelva	devuelvan

SINGULAR	PLURAL
perfecto de indicativo	
he devuelto	**hemos** devuelto
has devuelto	**habéis** devuelto
ha devuelto	**han** devuelto
pluscuamperfecto de indicativo	
había devuelto	**habíamos** devuelto
habías devuelto	**habíais** devuelto
había devuelto	**habían** devuelto
pretérito anterior	
hube devuelto	**hubimos** devuelto
hubiste devuelto	**hubisteis** devuelto
hubo devuelto	**hubieron** devuelto
futuro perfecto	
habré devuelto	**habremos** devuelto
habrás devuelto	**habréis** devuelto
habrá devuelto	**habrán** devuelto
condicional compuesto	
habría devuelto	**habríamos** devuelto
habrías devuelto	**habríais** devuelto
habría devuelto	**habrían** devuelto
perfecto de subjuntivo	
haya devuelto	**hayamos** devuelto
hayas devuelto	**hayáis** devuelto
haya devuelto	**hayan** devuelto
pluscuamperfecto de subjuntivo	
hubiera devuelto	**hubiéramos** devuelto
hubieras devuelto	**hubierais** devuelto
hubiera devuelto	**hubieran** devuelto
OR	
hubiese devuelto	**hubiésemos** devuelto
hubieses devuelto	**hubieseis** devuelto
hubiese devuelto	**hubiesen** devuelto

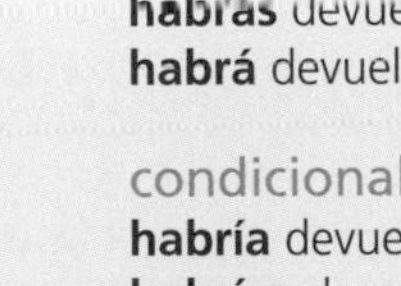

D

dibujar

to draw, to sketch

gerundio **dibujando** participio de pasado **dibujado**

SINGULAR	PLURAL	SINGULAR	PLURAL
presente de indicativo		perfecto de indicativo	
dibuj**o**	dibuj**amos**	**he** dibujado	**hemos** dibujado
dibuj**as**	dibuj**áis**	**has** dibujado	**habéis** dibujado
dibuj**a**	dibuj**an**	**ha** dibujado	**han** dibujado
imperfecto de indicativo		pluscuamperfecto de indicativo	
dibuj**aba**	dibuj**ábamos**	**había** dibujado	**habíamos** dibujado
dibuj**abas**	dibuj**abais**	**habías** dibujado	**habíais** dibujado
dibuj**aba**	dibuj**aban**	**había** dibujado	**habían** dibujado
pretérito		pretérito anterior	
dibuj**é**	dibuj**amos**	**hube** dibujado	**hubimos** dibujado
dibuj**aste**	dibuj**asteis**	**hubiste** dibujado	**hubisteis** dibujado
dibuj**ó**	dibuj**aron**	**hubo** dibujado	**hubieron** dibujado
futuro		futuro perfecto	
dibujar**é**	dibujar**emos**	**habré** dibujado	**habremos** dibujado
dibujar**ás**	dibujar**éis**	**habrás** dibujado	**habréis** dibujado
dibujar**á**	dibujar**án**	**habrá** dibujado	**habrán** dibujado
condicional simple		condicional compuesto	
dibujar**ía**	dibujar**íamos**	**habría** dibujado	**habríamos** dibujado
dibujar**ías**	dibujar**íais**	**habrías** dibujado	**habríais** dibujado
dibujar**ía**	dibujar**ían**	**habría** dibujado	**habrían** dibujado
presente de subjuntivo		perfecto de subjuntivo	
dibuj**e**	dibuj**emos**	**haya** dibujado	**hayamos** dibujado
dibuj**es**	dibuj**éis**	**hayas** dibujado	**hayáis** dibujado
dibuj**e**	dibuj**en**	**haya** dibujado	**hayan** dibujado
imperfecto de subjuntivo		pluscuamperfecto de subjuntivo	
dibujar**a**	dibujár**amos**	**hubiera** dibujado	**hubiéramos** dibujado
dibujar**as**	dibujar**ais**	**hubieras** dibujado	**hubierais** dibujado
dibujar**a**	dibujar**an**	**hubiera** dibujado	**hubieran** dibujado
OR		OR	
dibujas**e**	dibujás**emos**	**hubiese** dibujado	**hubiésemos** dibujado
dibujas**es**	dibujas**eis**	**hubieses** dibujado	**hubieseis** dibujado
dibujas**e**	dibujas**en**	**hubiese** dibujado	**hubiesen** dibujado

imperativo

—	dibujemos
dibuja; no dibujes	dibujad; no dibujéis
dibuje	dibujen

gerundio **dirigiendo** participio de pasado **dirigido**

SINGULAR	PLURAL
presente de indicativo	
dirij**o**	dirig**imos**
dirig**es**	dirig**ís**
dirig**e**	dirig**en**
imperfecto de indicativo	
dirig**ía**	dirig**íamos**
dirig**ías**	dirig**íais**
dirig**ía**	dirig**ían**
pretérito	
dirig**í**	dirig**imos**
dirig**iste**	dirig**isteis**
dirig**ió**	dirig**ieron**
futuro	
dirigir**é**	dirigir**emos**
dirigir**ás**	dirigir**éis**
dirigir**á**	dirigir**án**
condicional simple	
dirigir**ía**	dirigir**íamos**
dirigir**ías**	dirigir**íais**
dirigir**ía**	dirigir**ían**
presente de subjuntivo	
dirij**a**	dirij**amos**
dirij**as**	dirij**áis**
dirij**a**	dirij**an**
imperfecto de subjuntivo	
dirigier**a**	dirigiér**amos**
dirigier**as**	dirigier**ais**
dirigier**a**	dirigier**an**
OR	
dirigies**e**	dirigiés**emos**
dirigies**es**	dirigies**eis**
dirigies**e**	dirigies**en**
imperativo	
—	dirijamos
dirige; no dirijas	dirigid; no dirijáis
dirija	dirijan

SINGULAR	PLURAL
perfecto de indicativo	
he dirigido	**hemos** dirigido
has dirigido	**habéis** dirigido
ha dirigido	**han** dirigido
pluscuamperfecto de indicativo	
había dirigido	**habíamos** dirigido
habías dirigido	**habíais** dirigido
había dirigido	**habían** dirigido
pretérito anterior	
hube dirigido	**hubimos** dirigido
hubiste dirigido	**hubisteis** dirigido
hubo dirigido	**hubieron** dirigido
futuro perfecto	
habré dirigido	**habremos** dirigido
habrás dirigido	**habréis** dirigido
habrá dirigido	**habrán** dirigido
condicional compuesto	
habría dirigido	**habríamos** dirigido
habrías dirigido	**habríais** dirigido
habría dirigido	**habrían** dirigido
perfecto de subjuntivo	
haya dirigido	**hayamos** dirigido
hayas dirigido	**hayáis** dirigido
haya dirigido	**hayan** dirigido
pluscuamperfecto de subjuntivo	
hubiera dirigido	**hubiéramos** dirigido
hubieras dirigido	**hubierais** dirigido
hubiera dirigido	**hubieran** dirigido
OR	
hubiese dirigido	**hubiésemos** dirigido
hubieses dirigido	**hubieseis** dirigido
hubiese dirigido	**hubiesen** dirigido

disculparse to apologize, to excuse oneself

gerundio **disculpándose** participio de pasado **disculpado**

SINGULAR	PLURAL	SINGULAR	PLURAL
presente de indicativo		perfecto de indicativo	
me disculp**o**	nos disculp**amos**	**me he** disculpado	**nos hemos** disculpado
te disculp**as**	os disculp**áis**	**te has** disculpado	**os habéis** disculpado
se disculp**a**	se disculp**an**	**se ha** disculpado	**se han** disculpado
imperfecto de indicativo		pluscuamperfecto de indicativo	
me disculp**aba**	nos disculp**ábamos**	**me había** disculpado	**nos habíamos** disculpado
te disculp**abas**	os disculp**abais**	**te habías** disculpado	**os habíais** disculpado
se disculp**aba**	se disculp**aban**	**se había** disculpado	**se habían** disculpado
pretérito		pretérito anterior	
me disculp**é**	nos disculp**amos**	**me hube** disculpado	**nos hubimos** disculpado
te disculp**aste**	os disculp**asteis**	**te hubiste** disculpado	**os hubisteis** disculpado
se disculp**ó**	se disculp**aron**	**se hubo** disculpado	**se hubieron** disculpado
futuro		futuro perfecto	
me disculpar**é**	nos disculpar**emos**	**me habré** disculpado	**nos habremos** disculpado
te disculpar**ás**	os disculpar**éis**	**te habrás** disculpado	**os habréis** disculpado
se disculpar**á**	se disculpar**án**	**se habrá** disculpado	**se habrán** disculpado
condicional simple		condicional compuesto	
me disculpar**ía**	nos disculpar**íamos**	**me habría** disculpado	**nos habríamos** disculpado
te disculpar**ías**	os disculpar**íais**	**te habrías** disculpado	**os habríais** disculpado
se disculpar**ía**	se disculpar**ían**	**se habría** disculpado	**se habrían** disculpado
presente de subjuntivo		perfecto de subjuntivo	
me disculp**e**	nos disculp**emos**	**me haya** disculpado	**nos hayamos** disculpado
te disculp**es**	os disculp**éis**	**te hayas** disculpado	**os hayáis** disculpado
se disculp**e**	se disculp**en**	**se haya** disculpado	**se hayan** disculpado
imperfecto de subjuntivo		pluscuamperfecto de subjuntivo	
me disculpar**a**	nos disculpár**amos**	**me hubiera** disculpado	**nos hubiéramos** disculpado
te disculpar**as**	os disculpar**ais**	**te hubieras** disculpado	**os hubierais** disculpado
se disculpar**a**	se disculpar**an**	**se hubiera** disculpado	**se hubieran** disculpado
OR		OR	
me disculpas**e**	nos disculpás**emos**	**me hubiese** disculpado	**nos hubiésemos** disculpado
te disculpas**es**	os disculpas**eis**	**te hubieses** disculpado	**os hubieseis** disculpado
se disculpas**e**	se disculpas**en**	**se hubiese** disculpado	**se hubiesen** disculpado

imperativo

—	disculpémonos
discúlpate;	disculpaos;
no te disculpes	no os disculpéis
discúlpese	discúlpense

presente de indicativo

SINGULAR	PLURAL
discut**o**	discut**imos**
discut**es**	discut**ís**
discut**e**	discut**en**

imperfecto de indicativo

SINGULAR	PLURAL
discut**ía**	discut**íamos**
discut**ías**	discut**íais**
discut**ía**	discut**ían**

pretérito

SINGULAR	PLURAL
discut**í**	discut**imos**
discut**iste**	discut**isteis**
discut**ió**	discut**ieron**

futuro

SINGULAR	PLURAL
discutir**é**	discutir**emos**
discutir**ás**	discutir**éis**
discutir**á**	discutir**án**

condicional simple

SINGULAR	PLURAL
discutir**ía**	discutir**íamos**
discutir**ías**	discutir**íais**
discutir**ía**	discutir**ían**

presente de subjuntivo

SINGULAR	PLURAL
discut**a**	discut**amos**
discut**as**	discut**áis**
discut**a**	discut**an**

imperfecto de subjuntivo

SINGULAR	PLURAL
discutier**a**	discutiér**amos**
discutier**as**	discutier**ais**
discutier**a**	discutier**an**
OR	
discuties**e**	discutiés**emos**
discuties**es**	discuties**eis**
discuties**e**	discuties**en**

imperativo

SINGULAR	PLURAL
—	discutamos
discute; no discutas	discutid; no discutáis
discuta	discutan

perfecto de indicativo

SINGULAR	PLURAL
he discutido	**hemos** discutido
has discutido	**habéis** discutido
ha discutido	**han** discutido

pluscuamperfecto de indicativo

SINGULAR	PLURAL
había discutido	**habíamos** discutido
habías discutido	**habíais** discutido
había discutido	**habían** discutido

pretérito anterior

SINGULAR	PLURAL
hube discutido	**hubimos** discutido
hubiste discutido	**hubisteis** discutido
hubo discutido	**hubieron** discutido

futuro perfecto

SINGULAR	PLURAL
habré discutido	**habremos** discutido
habrás discutido	**habréis** discutido
habrá discutido	**habrán** discutido

condicional compuesto

SINGULAR	PLURAL
habría discutido	**habríamos** discutido
habrías discutido	**habríais** discutido
habría discutido	**habrían** discutido

perfecto de subjuntivo

SINGULAR	PLURAL
haya discutido	**hayamos** discutido
hayas discutido	**hayáis** discutido
haya discutido	**hayan** discutido

pluscuamperfecto de subjuntivo

SINGULAR	PLURAL
hubiera discutido	**hubiéramos** discutido
hubieras discutido	**hubierais** discutido
hubiera discutido	**hubieran** discutido
OR	
hubiese discutido	**hubiésemos** discutido
hubieses discutido	**hubieseis** discutido
hubiese discutido	**hubiesen** discutido

diseñar — to design

gerundio **diseñando** — participio de pasado **diseñado**

SINGULAR	PLURAL	SINGULAR	PLURAL
presente de indicativo		**perfecto de indicativo**	
diseñ**o**	diseñ**amos**	**he** diseñado	**hemos** diseñado
diseñ**as**	diseñ**áis**	**has** diseñado	**habéis** diseñado
diseñ**a**	diseñ**an**	**ha** diseñado	**han** diseñado
imperfecto de indicativo		**pluscuamperfecto de indicativo**	
diseñ**aba**	diseñ**ábamos**	**había** diseñado	**habíamos** diseñado
diseñ**abas**	diseñ**abais**	**habías** diseñado	**habíais** diseñado
diseñ**aba**	diseñ**aban**	**había** diseñado	**habían** diseñado
pretérito		**pretérito anterior**	
diseñ**é**	diseñ**amos**	**hube** diseñado	**hubimos** diseñado
diseñ**aste**	diseñ**asteis**	**hubiste** diseñado	**hubisteis** diseñado
diseñ**ó**	diseñ**aron**	**hubo** diseñado	**hubieron** diseñado
futuro		**futuro perfecto**	
diseñar**é**	diseñar**emos**	**habré** diseñado	**habremos** diseñado
diseñar**ás**	diseñar**éis**	**habrás** diseñado	**habréis** diseñado
diseñar**á**	diseñar**án**	**habrá** diseñado	**habrán** diseñado
condicional simple		**condicional compuesto**	
diseñar**ía**	diseñar**íamos**	**habría** diseñado	**habríamos** diseñado
diseñar**ías**	diseñar**íais**	**habrías** diseñado	**habríais** diseñado
diseñar**ía**	diseñar**ían**	**habría** diseñado	**habrían** diseñado
presente de subjuntivo		**perfecto de subjuntivo**	
diseñ**e**	diseñ**emos**	**haya** diseñado	**hayamos** diseñado
diseñ**es**	diseñ**éis**	**hayas** diseñado	**hayáis** diseñado
diseñ**e**	diseñ**en**	**haya** diseñado	**hayan** diseñado
imperfecto de subjuntivo		**pluscuamperfecto de subjuntivo**	
diseñar**a**	diseñár**amos**	**hubiera** diseñado	**hubiéramos** diseñado
diseñar**as**	diseñar**ais**	**hubieras** diseñado	**hubierais** diseñado
diseñar**a**	diseñar**an**	**hubiera** diseñado	**hubieran** diseñado
OR		OR	
diseñas**e**	diseñás**emos**	**hubiese** diseñado	**hubiésemos** diseñado
diseñas**es**	diseñas**eis**	**hubieses** diseñado	**hubieseis** diseñado
diseñas**e**	diseñas**en**	**hubiese** diseñado	**hubiesen** diseñado

imperativo

—	diseñemos
diseña; no diseñes	diseñad; no diseñéis
diseñe	diseñen

gerundio **disfrutando** participio de pasado **disfrutado**

SINGULAR	PLURAL	SINGULAR	PLURAL
presente de indicativo		perfecto de indicativo	
disfrut**o**	disfrut**amos**	**he** disfrutado	**hemos** disfrutado
disfrut**as**	disfrut**áis**	**has** disfrutado	**habéis** disfrutado
disfrut**a**	disfrut**an**	**ha** disfrutado	**han** disfrutado
imperfecto de indicativo		pluscuamperfecto de indicativo	
disfrut**aba**	disfrut**ábamos**	**había** disfrutado	**habíamos** disfrutado
disfrut**abas**	disfrut**abais**	**habías** disfrutado	**habíais** disfrutado
disfrut**aba**	disfrut**aban**	**había** disfrutado	**habían** disfrutado
pretérito		pretérito anterior	
disfrut**é**	disfrut**amos**	**hube** disfrutado	**hubimos** disfrutado
disfrut**aste**	disfrut**asteis**	**hubiste** disfrutado	**hubisteis** disfrutado
disfrut**ó**	disfrut**aron**	**hubo** disfrutado	**hubieron** disfrutado
futuro		futuro perfecto	
disfrutar**é**	disfrutar**emos**	**habré** disfrutado	**habremos** disfrutado
disfrutar**ás**	disfrutar**éis**	**habrás** disfrutado	**habréis** disfrutado
disfrutar**á**	disfrutar**án**	**habrá** disfrutado	**habrán** disfrutado
condicional simple		condicional compuesto	
disfrutar**ía**	disfrutar**íamos**	**habría** disfrutado	**habríamos** disfrutado
disfrutar**ías**	disfrutar**íais**	**habrías** disfrutado	**habríais** disfrutado
disfrutar**ía**	disfrutar**ían**	**habría** disfrutado	**habrían** disfrutado
presente de subjuntivo		perfecto de subjuntivo	
disfrut**e**	disfrut**emos**	**haya** disfrutado	**hayamos** disfrutado
disfrut**es**	disfrut**éis**	**hayas** disfrutado	**hayáis** disfrutado
disfrut**e**	disfrut**en**	**haya** disfrutado	**hayan** disfrutado
imperfecto de subjuntivo		pluscuamperfecto de subjuntivo	
disfrutar**a**	disfrutár**amos**	**hubiera** disfrutado	**hubiéramos** disfrutado
disfrutar**as**	disfrutar**ais**	**hubieras** disfrutado	**hubierais** disfrutado
disfrutar**a**	disfrutar**an**	**hubiera** disfrutado	**hubieran** disfrutado
OR		OR	
disfrutas**e**	disfrutás**emos**	**hubiese** disfrutado	**hubiésemos** disfrutado
disfrutas**es**	disfrutas**eis**	**hubieses** disfrutado	**hubieseis** disfrutado
disfrutas**e**	disfrutas**en**	**hubiese** disfrutado	**hubiesen** disfrutado

imperativo

—	disfrutemos
disfruta; no disfrutes	disfrutad; no disfrutéis
disfrute	disfruten

dispensar

to dispense, to excuse

gerundio **dispensando** participio de pasado **dispensado**

SINGULAR	PLURAL
presente de indicativo	
dispens**o**	dispens**amos**
dispens**as**	dispens**áis**
dispens**a**	dispens**an**
imperfecto de indicativo	
dispens**aba**	dispens**ábamos**
dispens**abas**	dispens**abais**
dispens**aba**	dispens**aban**
pretérito	
dispens**é**	dispens**amos**
dispens**aste**	dispens**asteis**
dispens**ó**	dispens**aron**
futuro	
dispensar**é**	dispensar**emos**
dispensar**ás**	dispensar**éis**
dispensar**á**	dispensar**án**
condicional simple	
dispensar**ía**	dispensar**íamos**
dispensar**ías**	dispensar**íais**
dispensar**ía**	dispensar**ían**
presente de subjuntivo	
dispens**e**	dispens**emos**
dispens**es**	dispens**éis**
dispens**e**	dispens**en**
imperfecto de subjuntivo	
dispensar**a**	dispensár**amos**
dispensar**as**	dispensar**ais**
dispensar**a**	dispensar**an**
OR	
dispensas**e**	dispensás**emos**
dispensas**es**	dispensas**eis**
dispensas**e**	dispensas**en**
imperativo	
—	dispensemos
dispensa; no dispenses	dispensad; no dispenséis
dispense	dispensen

SINGULAR	PLURAL
perfecto de indicativo	
he dispensado	**hemos** dispensado
has dispensado	**habéis** dispensado
ha dispensado	**han** dispensado
pluscuamperfecto de indicativo	
había dispensado	**habíamos** dispensado
habías dispensado	**habíais** dispensado
había dispensado	**habían** dispensado
pretérito anterior	
hube dispensado	**hubimos** dispensado
hubiste dispensado	**hubisteis** dispensado
hubo dispensado	**hubieron** dispensado
futuro perfecto	
habré dispensado	**habremos** dispensado
habrás dispensado	**habréis** dispensado
habrá dispensado	**habrán** dispensado
condicional compuesto	
habría dispensado	**habríamos** dispensado
habrías dispensado	**habríais** dispensado
habría dispensado	**habrían** dispensado
perfecto de subjuntivo	
haya dispensado	**hayamos** dispensado
hayas dispensado	**hayáis** dispensado
haya dispensado	**hayan** dispensado
pluscuamperfecto de subjuntivo	
hubiera dispensado	**hubiéramos** dispensado
hubieras dispensado	**hubierais** dispensado
hubiera dispensado	**hubieran** dispensado
OR	
hubiese dispensado	**hubiésemos** dispensado
hubieses dispensado	**hubieseis** dispensado
hubiese dispensado	**hubiesen** dispensado

gerundio **dispersando** participio de pasado **dispersado**

SINGULAR	PLURAL	SINGULAR	PLURAL
presente de indicativo		perfecto de indicativo	
dispers**o**	dispers**amos**	**he** dispersado	**hemos** dispersado
dispers**as**	dispers**áis**	**has** dispersado	**habéis** dispersado
dispers**a**	dispers**an**	**ha** dispersado	**han** dispersado
imperfecto de indicativo		pluscuamperfecto de indicativo	
dispers**aba**	dispers**ábamos**	**había** dispersado	**habíamos** dispersado
dispers**abas**	dispers**abais**	**habías** dispersado	**habíais** dispersado
dispers**aba**	dispers**aban**	**había** dispersado	**habían** dispersado
pretérito		pretérito anterior	
dispers**é**	dispers**amos**	**hube** dispersado	**hubimos** dispersado
dispers**aste**	dispers**asteis**	**hubiste** dispersado	**hubisteis** dispersado
dispers**ó**	dispers**aron**	**hubo** dispersado	**hubieron** dispersado
futuro		futuro perfecto	
dispersar**é**	dispersar**emos**	**habré** dispersado	**habremos** dispersado
dispersar**ás**	dispersar**éis**	**habrás** dispersado	**habréis** dispersado
dispersar**á**	dispersar**án**	**habrá** dispersado	**habrán** dispersado
condicional simple		condicional compuesto	
dispersar**ía**	dispersar**íamos**	**habría** dispersado	**habríamos** dispersado
dispersar**ías**	dispersar**íais**	**habrías** dispersado	**habríais** dispersado
dispersar**ía**	dispersar**ían**	**habría** dispersado	**habrían** dispersado
presente de subjuntivo		perfecto de subjuntivo	
disperse**e**	disper**semos**	**haya** dispersado	**hayamos** dispersado
dispers**es**	dispers**éis**	**hayas** dispersado	**hayáis** dispersado
dispers**e**	dispers**en**	**haya** dispersado	**hayan** dispersado
imperfecto de subjuntivo		pluscuamperfecto de subjuntivo	
dispersar**a**	dispersár**amos**	**hubiera** dispersado	**hubiéramos** dispersado
dispersar**as**	dispersar**ais**	**hubieras** dispersado	**hubierais** dispersado
dispersar**a**	dispersar**an**	**hubiera** dispersado	**hubieran** dispersado
OR		OR	
dispersas**e**	dispersás**emos**	**hubiese** dispersado	**hubiésemos** dispersado
dispersas**es**	dispersas**eis**	**hubieses** dispersado	**hubieseis** dispersado
dispersas**e**	dispersas**en**	**hubiese** dispersado	**hubiesen** dispersado

imperativo

—	dispersemos
dispersa; no disperses	dispersad; no disperséis
disperse	dispersen

distinguir — to distinguish

gerundio **distinguiendo** — participio de pasado **distinguido**

SINGULAR	PLURAL

presente de indicativo

SINGULAR	PLURAL
disting**o**	distingu**imos**
distingu**es**	distingu**ís**
distingu**e**	distingu**en**

imperfecto de indicativo

SINGULAR	PLURAL
distingu**ía**	distingu**íamos**
distingu**ías**	distingu**íais**
distingu**ía**	distingu**ían**

pretérito

SINGULAR	PLURAL
distingu**í**	distingu**imos**
distingu**iste**	distingu**isteis**
distingu**ió**	distingu**ieron**

futuro

SINGULAR	PLURAL
distinguir**é**	distinguir**emos**
distinguir**ás**	distinguir**éis**
distinguir**á**	distinguir**án**

condicional simple

SINGULAR	PLURAL
distinguir**ía**	distinguir**íamos**
distinguir**ías**	distinguir**íais**
distinguir**ía**	distinguir**ían**

presente de subjuntivo

SINGULAR	PLURAL
disting**a**	disting**amos**
disting**as**	disting**áis**
disting**a**	disting**an**

imperfecto de subjuntivo

SINGULAR	PLURAL
distinguier**a**	distinguiér**amos**
distinguier**as**	distinguier**ais**
distinguier**a**	distinguier**an**
OR	
distinguies**e**	distinguiés**emos**
distinguies**es**	distinguies**eis**
distinguies**e**	distinguies**en**

imperativo

SINGULAR	PLURAL
—	distingamos
distingue; no distingas	distinguid; no distingáis
distinga	distingan

perfecto de indicativo

SINGULAR	PLURAL
he distinguido	**hemos** distinguido
has distinguido	**habéis** distinguido
ha distinguido	**han** distinguido

pluscuamperfecto de indicativo

SINGULAR	PLURAL
había distinguido	**habíamos** distinguido
habías distinguido	**habíais** distinguido
había distinguido	**habían** distinguido

pretérito anterior

SINGULAR	PLURAL
hube distinguido	**hubimos** distinguido
hubiste distinguido	**hubisteis** distinguido
hubo distinguido	**hubieron** distinguido

futuro perfecto

SINGULAR	PLURAL
habré distinguido	**habremos** distinguido
habrás distinguido	**habréis** distinguido
habrá distinguido	**habrán** distinguido

condicional compuesto

SINGULAR	PLURAL
habría distinguido	**habríamos** distinguido
habrías distinguido	**habríais** distinguido
habría distinguido	**habrían** distinguido

perfecto de subjuntivo

SINGULAR	PLURAL
haya distinguido	**hayamos** distinguido
hayas distinguido	**hayáis** distinguido
haya distinguido	**hayan** distinguido

pluscuamperfecto de subjuntivo

SINGULAR	PLURAL
hubiera distinguido	**hubiéramos** distinguido
hubieras distinguido	**hubierais** distinguido
hubiera distinguido	**hubieran** distinguido
OR	
hubiese distinguido	**hubiésemos** distinguido
hubieses distinguido	**hubieseis** distinguido
hubiese distinguido	**hubiesen** distinguido

gerundio **distribuyendo** participio de pasado **distribuido**

SINGULAR	PLURAL
presente de indicativo	
distribuy**o**	distribu**imos**
distribuy**es**	distribu**ís**
distribuy**e**	distribuy**en**
imperfecto de indicativo	
distribu**ía**	distribu**íamos**
distribu**ías**	distribu**íais**
distribu**ía**	distribu**ían**
pretérito	
distribu**í**	distribu**imos**
distribu**iste**	distribu**isteis**
distribuy**ó**	distribuy**eron**
futuro	
distribuir**é**	distribuir**emos**
distribuir**ás**	distribuir**éis**
distribuir**á**	distribuir**án**
condicional simple	
distribuir**ía**	distribuir**íamos**
distribuir**ías**	distribuir**íais**
distribuir**ía**	distribuir**ían**
presente de subjuntivo	
distribuy**a**	distribuy**amos**
distribuy**as**	distribuy**áis**
distribuy**a**	distribuy**an**
imperfecto de subjuntivo	
distribuyer**a**	distribuyér**amos**
distribuyer**as**	distribuyer**ais**
distribuyer**a**	distribuyer**an**
OR	
distribuyes**e**	distribuyés**emos**
distribuyes**es**	distribuyes**eis**
distribuyes**e**	distribuyes**en**
imperativo	
—	distribuyamos
distribuye; no distribuyas	distribuid; no distribuyáis
distribuya	distribuyan

SINGULAR	PLURAL
perfecto de indicativo	
he distribuido	**hemos** distribuido
has distribuido	**habéis** distribuido
ha distribuido	**han** distribuido
pluscuamperfecto de indicativo	
había distribuido	**habíamos** distribuido
habías distribuido	**habíais** distribuido
había distribuido	**habían** distribuido
pretérito anterior	
hube distribuido	**hubimos** distribuido
hubiste distribuido	**hubisteis** distribuido
hubo distribuido	**hubieron** distribuido
futuro perfecto	
habré distribuido	**habremos** distribuido
habrás distribuido	**habréis** distribuido
habrá distribuido	**habrán** distribuido
condicional compuesto	
habría distribuido	**habríamos** distribuido
habrías distribuido	**habríais** distribuido
habría distribuido	**habrían** distribuido
perfecto de subjuntivo	
haya distribuido	**hayamos** distribuido
hayas distribuido	**hayáis** distribuido
haya distribuido	**hayan** distribuido
pluscuamperfecto de subjuntivo	
hubiera distribuido	**hubiéramos** distribuido
hubieras distribuido	**hubierais** distribuido
hubiera distribuido	**hubieran** distribuido
OR	
hubiese distribuido	**hubiésemos** distribuido
hubieses distribuido	**hubieseis** distribuido
hubiese distribuido	**hubiesen** distribuido

divertir — to entertain

gerundio **divirtiendo** — participio de pasado **divertido**

presente de indicativo

SINGULAR	PLURAL
diviert**o**	divert**imos**
diviert**es**	divert**ís**
diviert**e**	diviert**en**

imperfecto de indicativo

SINGULAR	PLURAL
divert**ía**	divert**íamos**
divert**ías**	divert**íais**
divert**ía**	divert**ían**

pretérito

SINGULAR	PLURAL
divert**í**	divert**imos**
divert**iste**	divert**isteis**
divirti**ó**	divirt**ieron**

futuro

SINGULAR	PLURAL
divertir**é**	divertir**emos**
divertir**ás**	divertir**éis**
divertir**á**	divertir**án**

condicional simple

SINGULAR	PLURAL
divertir**ía**	divertir**íamos**
divertir**ías**	divertir**íais**
divertir**ía**	divertir**ían**

presente de subjuntivo

SINGULAR	PLURAL
diviert**a**	divirt**amos**
diviert**as**	divirt**áis**
diviert**a**	diviert**an**

imperfecto de subjuntivo

SINGULAR	PLURAL
divirtier**a**	divirtiér**amos**
divirtier**as**	divirtier**ais**
divirtier**a**	divirtier**an**
OR	
divirties**e**	divirtiés**emos**
divirties**es**	divirties**eis**
divirties**e**	divirties**en**

imperativo

SINGULAR	PLURAL
—	divirtamos
divierte; no diviertas	divertid; no divirtáis
divierta	diviertan

perfecto de indicativo

SINGULAR	PLURAL
he divertido	**hemos** divertido
has divertido	**habéis** divertido
ha divertido	**han** divertido

pluscuamperfecto de indicativo

SINGULAR	PLURAL
había divertido	**habíamos** divertido
habías divertido	**habíais** divertido
había divertido	**habían** divertido

pretérito anterior

SINGULAR	PLURAL
hube divertido	**hubimos** divertido
hubiste divertido	**hubisteis** divertido
hubo divertido	**hubieron** divertido

futuro perfecto

SINGULAR	PLURAL
habré divertido	**habremos** divertido
habrás divertido	**habréis** divertido
habrá divertido	**habrán** divertido

condicional compuesto

SINGULAR	PLURAL
habría divertido	**habríamos** divertido
habrías divertido	**habríais** divertido
habría divertido	**habrían** divertido

perfecto de subjuntivo

SINGULAR	PLURAL
haya divertido	**hayamos** divertido
hayas divertido	**hayáis** divertido
haya divertido	**hayan** divertido

pluscuamperfecto de subjuntivo

SINGULAR	PLURAL
hubiera divertido	**hubiéramos** divertido
hubieras divertido	**hubierais** divertido
hubiera divertido	**hubieran** divertido
OR	
hubiese divertido	**hubiésemos** divertido
hubieses divertido	**hubieseis** divertido
hubiese divertido	**hubiesen** divertido

to have a good time **divertirse**

gerundio **divirtiéndose** participio de pasado **divertido**

presente de indicativo

SINGULAR	PLURAL
me diviert**o**	nos divert**imos**
te diviert**es**	os divert**ís**
se diviert**e**	se diviert**en**

imperfecto de indicativo

SINGULAR	PLURAL
me divert**ía**	nos divert**íamos**
te divert**ías**	os divert**íais**
se divert**ía**	se divert**ían**

pretérito

SINGULAR	PLURAL
me divert**í**	nos divert**imos**
te divert**iste**	os divert**isteis**
se divirti**ó**	se divirt**ieron**

futuro

SINGULAR	PLURAL
me divertir**é**	nos divertir**emos**
te divertir**ás**	os divertir**éis**
se divertir**á**	se divertir**án**

condicional simple

SINGULAR	PLURAL
me divertir**ía**	nos divertir**íamos**
te divertir**ías**	os divertir**íais**
se divertir**ía**	se divertir**ían**

presente de subjuntivo

SINGULAR	PLURAL
me diviert**a**	nos divirt**amos**
te diviert**as**	os divirt**áis**
se diviert**a**	se diviert**an**

imperfecto de subjuntivo

SINGULAR	PLURAL
me divirtier**a**	nos divirtiér**amos**
te divirtier**as**	os divirtier**ais**
se divirtier**a**	se divirtier**an**
OR	
me divirties**e**	nos divirtiés**emos**
te divirties**es**	os divirties**eis**
se divirties**e**	se divirties**en**

imperativo

SINGULAR	PLURAL
—	divirtámonos; no nos divirtamos
diviértete; no te diviertas	divertíos; no os divirtáis
diviértase; no se divierta	diviértanse; no se diviertan

perfecto de indicativo

SINGULAR	PLURAL
me he divertido	**nos hemos** divertido
te has divertido	**os habéis** divertido
se ha divertido	**se han** divertido

pluscuamperfecto de indicativo

SINGULAR	PLURAL
me había divertido	**nos habíamos** divertido
te habías divertido	**os habíais** divertido
se había divertido	**se habían** divertido

pretérito anterior

SINGULAR	PLURAL
me hube divertido	**nos hubimos** divertido
te hubiste divertido	**os hubisteis** divertido
se hubo divertido	**se hubieron** divertido

futuro perfecto

SINGULAR	PLURAL
me habré divertido	**nos habremos** divertido
te habrás divertido	**os habréis** divertido
se habrá divertido	**se habrán** divertido

condicional compuesto

SINGULAR	PLURAL
me habría divertido	**nos habríamos** divertido
te habrías divertido	**os habríais** divertido
se habría divertido	**se habrían** divertido

perfecto de subjuntivo

SINGULAR	PLURAL
me haya divertido	**nos hayamos** divertido
te hayas divertido	**os hayáis** divertido
se haya divertido	**se hayan** divertido

pluscuamperfecto de subjuntivo

SINGULAR	PLURAL
me hubiera divertido	**nos hubiéramos** divertido
te hubieras divertido	**os hubierais** divertido
se hubiera divertido	**se hubieran** divertido
OR	
me hubiese divertido	**nos hubiésemos** divertido
te hubieses divertido	**os hubieseis** divertido
se hubiese divertido	**se hubiesen** divertido

divorciarse — to be (get) divorced

gerundio **divorciándose** participio de pasado **divorciado**

SINGULAR	PLURAL	SINGULAR	PLURAL
presente de indicativo		perfecto de indicativo	
me divorci**o**	nos divorci**amos**	**me he** divorciado	**nos hemos** divorciado
te divorci**as**	os divorci**áis**	**te has** divorciado	**os habéis** divorciado
se divorci**a**	se divorci**an**	**se ha** divorciado	**se han** divorciado
imperfecto de indicativo		pluscuamperfecto de indicativo	
me divorci**aba**	nos divorci**ábamos**	**me había** divorciado	**nos habíamos** divorciado
te divorci**abas**	os divorci**abais**	**te habías** divorciado	**os habíais** divorciado
se divorci**aba**	se divorci**aban**	**se había** divorciado	**se habían** divorciado
pretérito		pretérito anterior	
me divorci**é**	nos divorci**amos**	**me hube** divorciado	**nos hubimos** divorciado
te divorci**aste**	os divorci**asteis**	**te hubiste** divorciado	**os hubisteis** divorciado
se divorci**ó**	se divorci**aron**	**se hubo** divorciado	**se hubieron** divorciado
futuro		futuro perfecto	
me divorciar**é**	nos divorciar**emos**	**me habré** divorciado	**nos habremos** divorciado
te divorciar**ás**	os divorciar**éis**	**te habrás** divorciado	**os habréis** divorciado
se divoricar**á**	se divorciar**án**	**se habrá** divorciado	**se habrán** divorciado
condicional simple		condicional compuesto	
me divorciar**ía**	nos divorciar**íamos**	**me habría** divorciado	**nos habríamos** divorciado
te divorciar**ías**	os divorciar**íais**	**te habrías** divorciado	**os habríais** divorciado
se divoricar**ía**	se divorciar**ían**	**se habría** divorciado	**se habrían** divorciado
presente de subjuntivo		perfecto de subjuntivo	
me divorci**e**	nos divorci**emos**	**me haya** divorciado	**nos hayamos** divorciado
te divorci**es**	os divorci**éis**	**te hayas** divorciado	**os hayáis** divorciado
se divorci**e**	se divorci**en**	**se haya** divorciado	**se hayan** divorciado
imperfecto de subjuntivo		pluscuamperfecto de subjuntivo	
me divorciar**a**	nos divorciár**amos**	**me hubiera** divorciado	**nos hubiéramos** divorciado
fe divorciar**as**	os divorciar**ais**	**te hubieras** divorciado	**os hubierais** divorciado
se divorciar**a**	se divorciar**an**	**se hubiera** divorciado	**se hubieran** divorciado
OR		OR	
me divorcias**e**	nos divorciás**emos**	**me hubiese** divorciado	**nos hubiésemos** divorciado
te divorcias**es**	os divorcias**eis**	**te hubieses** divorciado	**os hubieseis** divorciado
se divorcias**e**	se divorcias**en**	**se hubiese** divorciado	**se hubiesen** divorciado

imperativo

—	divorciémonos
divórciate;	divorciaos;
no te divorcies	no os divorciéis
divórciese	divórciense

gerundio **doliendo** participio de pasado **dolido**

	SINGULAR	PLURAL
presente de indicativo	duel**o**	dol**emos**
	duel**es**	dol**éis**
	duel**e**	duel**en**
imperfecto de indicativo	dol**ía**	dol**íamos**
	dol**ías**	dol**íais**
	dol**ía**	dol**ían**
pretérito	dol**í**	dol**imos**
	dol**iste**	dol**isteis**
	dol**ió**	dol**ieron**
futuro	doler**é**	doler**emos**
	doler**ás**	doler**éis**
	doler**á**	doler**án**
condicional simple	doler**ía**	doler**íamos**
	doler**ías**	doler**íais**
	doler**ía**	doler**ían**
presente de subjuntivo	duel**a**	dol**amos**
	duel**as**	dol**áis**
	duel**a**	duel**an**
imperfecto de subjuntivo	dolier**a**	doliér**amos**
	dolier**as**	dolier**ais**
	dolier**a**	dolier**an**
	OR	
	doliese	doliés**emos**
	dolies**es**	dolies**eis**
	dolies**e**	dolies**en**
imperativo	—	dolamos
	duele; no duelas	doled; no doléis
	duela	duelan

	SINGULAR	PLURAL
perfecto de indicativo	**he** dolido	**hemos** dolido
	has dolido	**habéis** dolido
	ha dolido	**han** dolido
pluscuamperfecto de indicativo	**había** dolido	**habíamos** dolido
	habías dolido	**habíais** dolido
	había dolido	**habían** dolido
pretérito anterior	**hube** dolido	**hubimos** dolido
	hubiste dolido	**hubisteis** dolido
	hubo dolido	**hubieron** dolido
futuro perfecto	**habré** dolido	**habremos** dolido
	habrás dolido	**habréis** dolido
	habrá dolido	**habrán** dolido
condicional compuesto	**habría** dolido	**habríamos** dolido
	habrías dolido	**habríais** dolido
	habría dolido	**habrían** dolido
perfecto de subjuntivo	**haya** dolido	**hayamos** dolido
	hayas dolido	**hayáis** dolido
	haya dolido	**hayan** dolido
pluscuamperfecto de subjuntivo	**hubiera** dolido	**hubiéramos** dolido
	hubieras dolido	**hubierais** dolido
	hubiera dolido	**hubieran** dolido
	OR	
	hubiese dolido	**hubiésemos** dolido
	hubieses dolido	**hubieseis** dolido
	hubiese dolido	**hubiesen** dolido

dormir — to sleep

gerundio **durmiendo** | participio de pasado **dormido**

SINGULAR	PLURAL
presente de indicativo	
duerm**o**	dorm**imos**
duerm**es**	dorm**ís**
duerm**e**	duerm**en**
imperfecto de indicativo	
dorm**ía**	dorm**íamos**
dorm**ías**	dorm**íais**
dorm**ía**	dorm**ían**
pretérito	
dorm**í**	dorm**imos**
dorm**iste**	dorm**isteis**
durm**ió**	durm**ieron**
futuro	
dormir**é**	dormir**emos**
dormir**ás**	dormir**éis**
dormir**á**	dormir**án**
condicional simple	
dormir**ía**	dormir**íamos**
dormir**ías**	dormir**íais**
dormir**ía**	dormir**ían**
presente de subjuntivo	
duerm**a**	durm**amos**
duerm**as**	durm**áis**
duerm**a**	duerm**an**
imperfecto de subjuntivo	
durmier**a**	durmiér**amos**
durmier**as**	durmier**ais**
durmier**a**	durmier**an**
OR	
durmies**e**	durmiés**emos**
durmies**es**	durmies**eis**
durmies**e**	durmies**en**
imperativo	
—	durmamos
duerme; no duermas	dormid; no durmáis
duerma	duerman

SINGULAR	PLURAL
perfecto de indicativo	
he dormido	**hemos** dormido
has dormido	**habéis** dormido
ha dormido	**han** dormido
pluscuamperfecto de indicativo	
había dormido	**habíamos** dormido
habías dormido	**habíais** dormido
había dormido	**habían** dormido
pretérito anterior	
hube dormido	**hubimos** dormido
hubiste dormido	**hubisteis** dormido
hubo dormido	**hubieron** dormido
futuro perfecto	
habré dormido	**habremos** dormido
habrás dormido	**habréis** dormido
habrá dormido	**habrán** dormido
condicional compuesto	
habría dormido	**habríamos** dormido
habrías dormido	**habríais** dormido
habría dormido	**habrían** dormido
perfecto de subjuntivo	
haya dormido	**hayamos** dormido
hayas dormido	**hayáis** dormido
haya dormido	**hayan** dormido
pluscuamperfecto de subjuntivo	
hubiera dormido	**hubiéramos** dormido
hubieras dormido	**hubierais** dormido
hubiera dormido	**hubieran** dormido
OR	
hubiese dormido	**hubiésemos** dormido
hubieses dormido	**hubieseis** dormido
hubiese dormido	**hubiesen** dormido

MEMORY TIP

Norm sleeps in the dorm.

gerundio **dotando** participio de pasado **dotado**

SINGULAR	PLURAL
presente de indicativo	
dot**o**	dot**amos**
dot**as**	dot**áis**
dot**a**	dot**an**
imperfecto de indicativo	
dot**aba**	dot**ábamos**
dot**abas**	dot**abais**
dot**aba**	dot**aban**
pretérito	
dot**é**	dot**amos**
dot**aste**	dot**asteis**
dot**ó**	dot**aron**
futuro	
dotar**é**	dotar**emos**
dotar**ás**	dotar**éis**
dotar**á**	dotar**án**
condicional simple	
dotar**ía**	dotar**íamos**
dotar**ías**	dotar**íais**
dotar**ía**	dotar**ían**
presente de subjuntivo	
dot**e**	dot**emos**
dot**es**	dot**éis**
dot**e**	dot**en**
imperfecto de subjuntivo	
dotar**a**	dotár**amos**
dotar**as**	dotar**ais**
dotar**a**	dotar**an**
OR	
dotas**e**	dotás**emos**
dotas**es**	dotas**eis**
dotas**e**	dotas**en**
imperativo	
—	dotemos
dota; no dotes	dotad; no dotéis
dote	doten

SINGULAR	PLURAL
perfecto de indicativo	
he dotado	**hemos** dotado
has dotado	**habéis** dotado
ha dotado	**han** dotado
pluscuamperfecto de indicativo	
había dotado	**habíamos** dotado
habías dotado	**habíais** dotado
había dotado	**habían** dotado
pretérito anterior	
hube dotado	**hubimos** dotado
hubiste dotado	**hubisteis** dotado
hubo dotado	**hubieron** dotado
futuro perfecto	
habré dotado	**habremos** dotado
habrás dotado	**habréis** dotado
habrá dotado	**habrán** dotado
condicional compuesto	
habría dotado	**habríamos** dotado
habrías dotado	**habríais** dotado
habría dotado	**habrían** dotado
perfecto de subjuntivo	
haya dotado	**hayamos** dotado
hayas dotado	**hayáis** dotado
haya dotado	**hayan** dotado
pluscuamperfecto de subjuntivo	
hubiera dotado	**hubiéramos** dotado
hubieras dotado	**hubierais** dotado
hubiera dotado	**hubieran** dotado
OR	
hubiese dotado	**hubiésemos** dotado
hubieses dotado	**hubieseis** dotado
hubiese dotado	**hubiesen** dotado

ducharse to take a shower, to shower oneself

gerundio **duchándose** participio de pasado **duchado**

SINGULAR	PLURAL	SINGULAR	PLURAL
presente de indicativo		perfecto de indicativo	
me duch**o**	nos duch**amos**	**me he** duchado	**nos hemos** duchado
te duch**as**	os duch**áis**	**te has** duchado	**os habéis** duchado
se duch**a**	se duch**an**	**se ha** duchado	**se han** duchado
imperfecto de indicativo		pluscuamperfecto de indicativo	
me duch**aba**	nos duch**ábamos**	**me había** duchado	**nos habíamos** duchado
te duch**abas**	os duch**abais**	**te habías** duchado	**os habíais** duchado
se duch**aba**	se duch**aban**	**se había** duchado	**se habían** duchado
pretérito		pretérito anterior	
me duch**é**	nos duch**amos**	**me hube** duchado	**nos hubimos** duchado
te duch**aste**	os duch**asteis**	**te hubiste** duchado	**os hubisteis** duchado
se duch**ó**	se duch**aron**	**se hubo** duchado	**se hubieron** duchado
futuro		futuro perfecto	
me duchar**é**	nos duchar**emos**	**me habré** duchado	**nos habremos** duchado
te duchar**ás**	os duchar**éis**	**te habrás** duchado	**os habréis** duchado
se duchar**á**	se duchar**án**	**se habrá** duchado	**se habrán** duchado
condicional simple		condicional compuesto	
me duchar**ía**	nos duchar**íamos**	**me habría** duchado	**nos habríamos** duchado
te duchar**ías**	os duchar**íais**	**te habrías** duchado	**os habríais** duchado
se duchar**ía**	se duchar**ían**	**se habría** duchado	**se habrían** duchado
presente de subjuntivo		perfecto de subjuntivo	
me duch**e**	nos duch**emos**	**me haya** duchado	**nos hayamos** duchado
te duch**es**	os duch**éis**	**te hayas** duchado	**os hayáis** duchado
se duch**e**	se duch**en**	**se haya** duchado	**se hayan** duchado
imperfecto de subjuntivo		pluscuamperfecto de subjuntivo	
me duchar**a**	nos duchár**amos**	**me hubiera** duchado	**nos hubiéramos** duchado
te duchar**as**	os duchar**ais**	**te hubieras** duchado	**os hubierais** duchado
se duchar**a**	se duchar**an**	**se hubiera** duchado	**se hubieran** duchado
OR		OR	
me duchas**e**	nos duchás**emos**	**me hubiese** duchado	**nos hubiésemos** duchado
te duchas**es**	os duchas**eis**	**te hubieses** duchado	**os hubieseis** duchado
se duchas**e**	se duchas**en**	**se hubiese** duchado	**se hubiesen** duchado

imperativo

—	duchémonos
dúchate;	duchaos;
no te duches	no os duchéis
dúchese	dúchense

MUST KNOW VERB

gerundio **dudando** participio de pasado **dudado**

SINGULAR	PLURAL
presente de indicativo	
dud**o**	dud**amos**
dud**as**	dud**áis**
dud**a**	dud**an**
imperfecto de indicativo	
dud**aba**	dud**ábamos**
dud**abas**	dud**abais**
dud**aba**	dud**aban**
pretérito	
dud**é**	dud**amos**
dud**aste**	dud**asteis**
dud**ó**	dud**aron**
futuro	
dudar**é**	dudar**emos**
dudar**ás**	dudar**éis**
dudar**á**	dudar**án**
condicional simple	
dudar**ía**	dudar**íamos**
dudar**ías**	dudar**íais**
dudar**ía**	dudar**ían**
presente de subjuntivo	
dud**e**	dud**emos**
dud**es**	dud**éis**
dud**e**	dud**en**
imperfecto de subjuntivo	
dudar**a**	dudár**amos**
dudar**as**	dudar**ais**
dudar**a**	dudar**an**
OR	
dudas**e**	dudás**emos**
dudas**es**	dudas**eis**
dudas**e**	dudas**en**
imperativo	
—	dudemos
duda; no dudes	dudad; no dudéis
dude	duden

SINGULAR	PLURAL
perfecto de indicativo	
he dudado	**hemos** dudado
has dudado	**habéis** dudado
ha dudado	**han** dudado
pluscuamperfecto de indicativo	
había dudado	**habíamos** dudado
habías dudado	**habíais** dudado
había dudado	**habían** dudado
pretérito anterior	
hube dudado	**hubimos** dudado
hubiste dudado	**hubisteis** dudado
hubo dudado	**hubieron** dudado
futuro perfecto	
habré dudado	**habremos** dudado
habrás dudado	**habréis** dudado
habrá dudado	**habrán** dudado
condicional compuesto	
habría dudado	**habríamos** dudado
habrías dudado	**habríais** dudado
habría dudado	**habrían** dudado
perfecto de subjuntivo	
haya dudado	**hayamos** dudado
hayas dudado	**hayáis** dudado
haya dudado	**hayan** dudado
pluscuamperfecto de subjuntivo	
hubiera dudado	**hubiéramos** dudado
hubieras dudado	**hubierais** dudado
hubiera dudado	**hubieran** dudado
OR	
hubiese dudado	**hubiésemos** dudado
hubieses dudado	**hubieseis** dudado
hubiese dudado	**hubiesen** dudado

echar — to throw

gerundio **echando** participio de pasado **echado**

SINGULAR	PLURAL	SINGULAR	PLURAL
presente de indicativo		perfecto de indicativo	
ech**o**	ech**amos**	**he** echado	**hemos** echado
ech**as**	ech**áis**	**has** echado	**habéis** echado
ech**a**	ech**an**	**ha** echado	**han** echado
imperfecto de indicativo		pluscuamperfecto de indicativo	
ech**aba**	ech**ábamos**	**había** echado	**habíamos** echado
ech**abas**	ech**abais**	**habías** echado	**habíais** echado
ech**aba**	ech**aban**	**había** echado	**habían** echado
pretérito		pretérito anterior	
ech**é**	ech**amos**	**hube** echado	**hubimos** echado
ech**aste**	ech**asteis**	**hubiste** echado	**hubisteis** echado
ech**ó**	ech**aron**	**hubo** echado	**hubieron** echado
futuro		futuro perfecto	
echar**é**	echar**emos**	**habré** echado	**habremos** echado
echar**ás**	echar**éis**	**habrás** echado	**habréis** echado
echar**á**	echar**án**	**habrá** echado	**habrán** echado
condicional simple		condicional compuesto	
echar**ía**	echar**íamos**	**habría** echado	**habríamos** echado
echar**ías**	echar**íais**	**habrías** echado	**habríais** echado
echar**ía**	echar**ían**	**habría** echado	**habrían** echado
presente de subjuntivo		perfecto de subjuntivo	
ech**e**	ech**emos**	**haya** echado	**hayamos** echado
ech**es**	ech**éis**	**hayas** echado	**hayáis** echado
ech**e**	ech**en**	**haya** echado	**hayan** echado
imperfecto de subjuntivo		pluscuamperfecto de subjuntivo	
echar**a**	echár**amos**	**hubiera** echado	**hubiéramos** echado
echar**as**	echar**ais**	**hubieras** echado	**hubierais** echado
echar**a**	echar**an**	**hubiera** echado	**hubieran** echado
OR		OR	
echas**e**	echás**emos**	**hubiese** echado	**hubiésemos** echado
echas**es**	echas**eis**	**hubieses** echado	**hubieseis** echado
echas**e**	echas**en**	**hubiese** echado	**hubiesen** echado

imperativo

—	echemos
echa; no eches	echad; no echeis
eche	echen

to carry out, to execute **ejecutar**

gerundio **ejecutando** participio de pasado **ejecutado**

SINGULAR	PLURAL
presente de indicativo	
ejecut**o**	ejecut**amos**
ejecut**as**	ejecut**áis**
ejecut**a**	ejecut**an**
imperfecto de indicativo	
ejecut**aba**	ejecut**ábamos**
ejecut**abas**	ejecut**abais**
ejecut**aba**	ejecut**aban**
pretérito	
ejecut**é**	ejecut**amos**
ejecut**aste**	ejecut**asteis**
ejecut**ó**	ejecut**aron**
futuro	
ejecutar**é**	ejecutar**emos**
ejecutar**ás**	ejecutar**éis**
ejecutar**á**	ejecutar**án**
condicional simple	
ejecutar**ía**	ejecutar**íamos**
ejecutar**ías**	ejecutar**íais**
ejecutar**ía**	ejecutar**ían**
presente de subjuntivo	
ejecut**e**	ejecut**emos**
ejecut**es**	ejecut**éis**
ejecut**e**	ejecut**en**
imperfecto de subjuntivo	
ejecutar**a**	ejecutár**amos**
ejecutar**as**	ejecutar**ais**
ejecutar**a**	ejecutar**an**
OR	
ejecutas**e**	ejecutás**emos**
ejecutas**es**	ejecutas**eis**
ejecutas**e**	ejecutas**en**
imperativo	
—	ejecutemos
ejecuta; no ejecutes	ejecutad; no ejecutéis
ejecute	ejecuten

SINGULAR	PLURAL
perfecto de indicativo	
he ejecutado	**hemos** ejecutado
has ejecutado	**habéis** ejecutado
ha ejecutado	**han** ejecutado
pluscuamperfecto de indicativo	
había ejecutado	**habíamos** ejecutado
habías ejecutado	**habíais** ejecutado
había ejecutado	**habían** ejecutado
pretérito anterior	
hube ejecutado	**hubimos** ejecutado
hubiste ejecutado	**hubisteis** ejecutado
hubo ejecutado	**hubieron** ejecutado
futuro perfecto	
habré ejecutado	**habremos** ejecutado
habrás ejecutado	**habréis** ejecutado
habrá ejecutado	**habrán** ejecutado
condicional compuesto	
habría ejecutado	**habríamos** ejecutado
habrías ejecutado	**habríais** ejecutado
habría ejecutado	**habrían** ejecutado
perfecto de subjuntivo	
haya ejecutado	**hayamos** ejecutado
hayas ejecutado	**hayáis** ejecutado
haya ejecutado	**hayan** ejecutado
pluscuamperfecto de subjuntivo	
hubiera ejecutado	**hubiéramos** ejecutado
hubieras ejecutado	**hubierais** ejecutado
hubiera ejecutado	**hubieran** ejecutado
OR	
hubiese ejecutado	**hubiésemos** ejecutado
hubieses ejecutado	**hubieseis** ejecutado
hubiese ejecutado	**hubiesen** ejecutado

elegir — to choose

gerundio **eligiendo**   participio de pasado **eligido**

SINGULAR	PLURAL
presente de indicativo	
elij**o**	eleg**imos**
elig**es**	eleg**ís**
elig**e**	elig**en**
imperfecto de indicativo	
eleg**ía**	eleg**íamos**
eleg**ías**	eleg**íais**
eleg**ía**	eleg**ían**
pretérito	
eleg**í**	eleg**imos**
eleg**iste**	eleg**isteis**
elig**ió**	elig**ieron**
futuro	
elegir**é**	elegir**emos**
elegir**ás**	elegir**éis**
elegir**á**	elegir**án**
condicional simple	
elegir**ía**	elegir**íamos**
elegir**ías**	elegir**íais**
elegir**ía**	elegir**ían**
presente de subjuntivo	
elij**a**	elij**amos**
elij**as**	elij**áis**
elij**a**	elij**an**
imperfecto de subjuntivo	
eligier**a**	eligiér**amos**
eligier**as**	eligier**ais**
eligier**a**	eligier**an**
OR	
eligies**e**	eligiés**emos**
eligies**es**	eligies**eis**
eligies**e**	eligies**en**
imperativo	
—	elijamos
elige; no elijas	elegid; no elijáis
elija	elijan

SINGULAR	PLURAL
perfecto de indicativo	
he elegido	**hemos** elegido
has elegido	**habéis** elegido
ha elegido	**han** elegido
pluscuamperfecto de indicativo	
había elegido	**habíamos** elegido
habías elegido	**habíais** elegido
había elegido	**habían** elegido
pretérito anterior	
hube elegido	**hubimos** elegido
hubiste elegido	**hubisteis** elegido
hubo elegido	**hubieron** elegido
futuro perfecto	
habré elegido	**habremos** elegido
habrás elegido	**habréis** elegido
habrá elegido	**habrán** elegido
condicional compuesto	
habría elegido	**habríamos** elegido
habrías elegido	**habríais** elegido
habría elegido	**habrían** elegido
perfecto de subjuntivo	
haya elegido	**hayamos** elegido
hayas elegido	**hayáis** elegido
haya elegido	**hayan** elegido
pluscuamperfecto de subjuntivo	
hubiera elegido	**hubiéramos** elegido
hubieras elegido	**hubierais** elegido
hubiera elegido	**hubieran** elegido
OR	
hubiese elegido	**hubiésemos** elegido
hubieses elegido	**hubieseis** elegido
hubiese elegido	**hubiesen** elegido

gerundio **embebiendo** participio de pasado **embebido**

SINGULAR	PLURAL	SINGULAR	PLURAL
presente de indicativo		perfecto de indicativo	
embeb**o**	embeb**emos**	**he** embebido	**hemos** embebido
embeb**es**	embeb**éis**	**has** embebido	**habéis** embebido
embeb**e**	embeb**en**	**ha** embebido	**han** embebido
imperfecto de indicativo		pluscuamperfecto de indicativo	
embeb**ía**	embeb**íamos**	**había** embebido	**habíamos** embebido
embeb**ías**	embeb**íais**	**habías** embebido	**habíais** embebido
embeb**ía**	embeb**ían**	**había** embebido	**habían** embebido
pretérito		pretérito anterior	
embeb**í**	embeb**imos**	**hube** embebido	**hubimos** embebido
embeb**iste**	embeb**isteis**	**hubiste** embebido	**hubisteis** embebido
embeb**ió**	embeb**ieron**	**hubo** embebido	**hubieron** embebido
futuro		futuro perfecto	
embeber**é**	embeber**emos**	**habré** embebido	**habremos** embebido
embeber**ás**	embeber**éis**	**habrás** embebido	**habréis** embebido
embeber**á**	embeber**án**	**habrá** embebido	**habrán** embebido
condicional simple		condicional compuesto	
embeber**ía**	embeber**íamos**	**habría** embebido	**habríamos** embebido
embeber**ías**	embeber**íais**	**habrías** embebido	**habríais** embebido
embeber**ía**	embeber**ían**	**habría** embebido	**habrían** embebido
presente de subjuntivo		perfecto de subjuntivo	
embeb**a**	embeb**amos**	**haya** embebido	**hayamos** embebido
embeb**as**	embeb**áis**	**hayas** embebido	**hayáis** embebido
embeb**a**	embeb**an**	**haya** embebido	**hayan** embebido
imperfecto de subjuntivo		pluscuamperfecto de subjuntivo	
embebier**a**	embebiér**amos**	**hubiera** embebido	**hubiéramos** embebido
embebier**as**	embebier**ais**	**hubieras** embebido	**hubierais** embebido
embebier**a**	embebier**an**	**hubiera** embebido	**hubieran** embebido
OR		OR	
embebies**e**	embebiés**emos**	**hubiese** embebido	**hubiésemos** embebido
embebies**es**	embebies**eis**	**hubieses** embebido	**hubieseis** embebido
embebies**e**	embebies**en**	**hubiese** embebido	**hubiesen** embebido

imperativo

—	embebamos
embebe; no embebas	embebed; no embebáis
embeba	embeban

empezar — to start

gerundio **empezando** participio de pasado **empezado**

presente de indicativo

SINGULAR	PLURAL
empiez**o**	empez**amos**
empiez**as**	empez**áis**
empiez**a**	empiez**an**

imperfecto de indicativo

SINGULAR	PLURAL
empez**aba**	empez**ábamos**
empez**abas**	empez**abais**
empez**aba**	empez**aban**

pretérito

SINGULAR	PLURAL
empec**é**	empez**amos**
empez**aste**	empez**asteis**
empez**ó**	empez**aron**

futuro

SINGULAR	PLURAL
empezar**é**	empezar**emos**
empezar**ás**	empezar**éis**
empezar**á**	empezar**án**

condicional simple

SINGULAR	PLURAL
empezar**ía**	empezar**íamos**
empezar**ías**	empezar**íais**
empezar**ía**	empezar**ían**

presente de subjuntivo

SINGULAR	PLURAL
empiec**e**	empec**emos**
empiec**es**	empec**éis**
empiec**e**	empiec**en**

imperfecto de subjuntivo

SINGULAR	PLURAL
empezar**a**	empezár**amos**
empezar**as**	empezar**ais**
empezar**a**	empezar**an**
OR	
empezas**e**	empezás**emos**
empezas**es**	empezas**eis**
empezas**e**	empezas**en**

imperativo

SINGULAR	PLURAL
—	empecemos
empieza; no empieces	empezad; no empecéis
empiece	empiecen

perfecto de indicativo

SINGULAR	PLURAL
he empezado	**hemos** empezado
has empezado	**habéis** empezado
ha empezado	**han** empezado

pluscuamperfecto de indicativo

SINGULAR	PLURAL
había empezado	**habíamos** empezado
habías empezado	**habíais** empezado
había empezado	**habían** empezado

pretérito anterior

SINGULAR	PLURAL
hube empezado	**hubimos** empezado
hubiste empezado	**hubisteis** empezado
hubo empezado	**hubieron** empezado

futuro perfecto

SINGULAR	PLURAL
habré empezado	**habremos** empezado
habrás empezado	**habréis** empezado
habrá empezado	**habrán** empezado

condicional compuesto

SINGULAR	PLURAL
habría empezado	**habríamos** empezado
habrías empezado	**habríais** empezado
habría empezado	**habrían** empezado

perfecto de subjuntivo

SINGULAR	PLURAL
haya empezado	**hayamos** empezado
hayas empezado	**hayáis** empezado
haya empezado	**hayan** empezado

pluscuamperfecto de subjuntivo

SINGULAR	PLURAL
hubiera empezado	**hubiéramos** empezado
hubieras empezado	**hubierais** empezado
hubiera empezado	**hubieran** empezado
OR	
hubiese empezado	**hubiésemos** empezado
hubieses empezado	**hubieseis** empezado
hubiese empezado	**hubiesen** empezado

gerundio **empleando** participio de pasado **empleado**

SINGULAR	PLURAL	SINGULAR	PLURAL
presente de indicativo		perfecto de indicativo	
emple**o**	emple**amos**	**he** empleado	**hemos** empleado
emple**as**	emple**áis**	**has** empleado	**habéis** empleado
emple**a**	emple**an**	**ha** empleado	**han** empleado
imperfecto de indicativo		pluscuamperfecto de indicativo	
emple**aba**	emple**ábamos**	**había** empleado	**habíamos** empleado
emple**abas**	emple**abais**	**habías** empleado	**habíais** empleado
emple**aba**	emple**aban**	**había** empleado	**habían** empleado
pretérito		pretérito anterior	
emple**é**	emple**amos**	**hube** empleado	**hubimos** empleado
emple**aste**	emple**asteis**	**hubiste** empleado	**hubisteis** empleado
emple**ó**	emple**aron**	**hubo** empleado	**hubieron** empleado
futuro		futuro perfecto	
emplear**é**	emplear**emos**	**habré** empleado	**habremos** empleado
emplear**ás**	emplear**éis**	**habrás** empleado	**habréis** empleado
emplear**á**	emplear**án**	**habrá** empleado	**habrán** empleado
condicional simple		condicional compuesto	
emplear**ía**	emplear**íamos**	**habría** empleado	**habríamos** empleado
emplear**ías**	emplear**íais**	**habrías** empleado	**habríais** empleado
emplear**ía**	emplear**ían**	**habría** empleado	**habrían** empleado
presente de subjuntivo		perfecto de subjuntivo	
emple**e**	emple**emos**	**haya** empleado	**hayamos** empleado
emple**es**	emple**éis**	**hayas** empleado	**hayáis** empleado
emple**e**	emple**en**	**haya** empleado	**hayan** empleado
imperfecto de subjuntivo		pluscuamperfecto de subjuntivo	
emplear**a**	empleár**amos**	**hubiera** empleado	**hubiéramos** empleado
emplear**as**	emplear**ais**	**hubieras** empleado	**hubierais** empleado
emplear**a**	emplear**an**	**hubiera** empleado	**hubieran** empleado
OR		OR	
emplease	empleás**emos**	**hubiese** empleado	**hubiésemos** empleado
emplease**s**	emplease**is**	**hubieses** empleado	**hubieseis** empleado
emplease	emplease**n**	**hubiese** empleado	**hubiesen** empleado

imperativo

—	empleemos
emplea; no emplees	emplead, no empleéis
emplee	empleen

E

encender — to turn on, to light

gerundio **encendiendo** participio de pasado **encendido**

SINGULAR	PLURAL	SINGULAR	PLURAL
presente de indicativo		perfecto de indicativo	
enciend**o**	encend**emos**	**he** encendido	**hemos** encendido
enciend**es**	encend**éis**	**has** encendido	**habéis** encendido
enciend**e**	enciend**en**	**ha** encendido	**han** encendido
imperfecto de indicativo		pluscuamperfecto de indicativo	
encend**ía**	encend**íamos**	**había** encendido	**habíamos** encendido
encend**ías**	encend**íais**	**habías** encendido	**habíais** encendido
encend**ía**	encend**ían**	**había** encendido	**habían** encendido
pretérito		pretérito anterior	
encend**í**	encend**imos**	**hube** encendido	**hubimos** encendido
encend**iste**	encend**isteis**	**hubiste** encendido	**hubisteis** encendido
encend**ió**	encend**ieron**	**hubo** encendido	**hubieron** encendido
futuro		futuro perfecto	
encender**é**	encender**emos**	**habré** encendido	**habremos** encendido
encender**ás**	encender**éis**	**habrás** encendido	**habréis** encendido
encender**á**	encender**án**	**habrá** encendido	**habrán** encendido
condicional simple		condicional compuesto	
encender**ía**	encender**íamos**	**habría** encendido	**habríamos** encendido
encender**ías**	encender**íais**	**habrías** encendido	**habríais** encendido
encender**ía**	encender**ían**	**habría** encendido	**habrían** encendido
presente de subjuntivo		perfecto de subjuntivo	
enciend**a**	encend**amos**	**haya** encendido	**hayamos** encendido
enciend**as**	encend**áis**	**hayas** encendido	**hayáis** encendido
enciend**a**	enciend**an**	**haya** encendido	**hayan** encendido
imperfecto de subjuntivo		pluscuamperfecto de subjuntivo	
encendier**a**	encendiér**amos**	**hubiera** encendido	**hubiéramos** encendido
encendier**as**	encendier**ais**	**hubieras** encendido	**hubierais** encendido
encendier**a**	encendier**an**	**hubiera** encendido	**hubieran** encendido
OR		OR	
encendies**e**	encendiés**emos**	**hubiese** encendido	**hubiésemos** encendido
encendies**es**	encendies**eis**	**hubieses** encendido	**hubieseis** encendido
encendies**e**	encendies**en**	**hubiese** encendido	**hubiesen** encendido

imperativo

—	encendamos
enciende;	encended;
no enciendas	no encendáis
encienda	enciendan

gerundio **encerrando** participio de pasado **encerrado**

SINGULAR	PLURAL	SINGULAR	PLURAL
presente de indicativo		perfecto de indicativo	
encierr**o**	encerr**amos**	**he** encerrado	**hemos** encerrado
encierr**as**	encerr**áis**	**has** encerrado	**habéis** encerrado
encierr**a**	encierr**an**	**ha** encerrado	**han** encerrado
imperfecto de indicativo		pluscuamperfecto de indicativo	
encerr**aba**	encerr**ábamos**	**había** encerrado	**habíamos** encerrado
encerr**abas**	encerr**abais**	**habías** encerrado	**habíais** encerrado
encerr**aba**	encerr**aban**	**había** encerrado	**habían** encerrado
pretérito		pretérito anterior	
encerr**é**	encerr**amos**	**hube** encerrado	**hubimos** encerrado
encerr**aste**	encerr**asteis**	**hubiste** encerrado	**hubisteis** encerrado
encerr**ó**	encerr**aron**	**hubo** encerrado	**hubieron** encerrado
futuro		futuro perfecto	
encerrar**é**	encerrar**emos**	**habré** encerrado	**habremos** encerrado
encerrar**ás**	encerrar**éis**	**habrás** encerrado	**habréis** encerrado
encerrar**á**	encerrar**án**	**habrá** encerrado	**habrán** encerrado
condicional simple		condicional compuesto	
encerrar**ía**	encerrar**íamos**	**habría** encerrado	**habríamos** encerrado
encerrar**ías**	encerrar**íais**	**habrías** encerrado	**habríais** encerrado
encerrar**ía**	encerrar**ían**	**habría** encerrado	**habrían** encerrado
presente de subjuntivo		perfecto de subjuntivo	
encierr**e**	encerr**emos**	**haya** encerrado	**hayamos** encerrado
encierr**es**	encerr**éis**	**hayas** encerrado	**hayáis** encerrado
encierr**e**	encierr**en**	**haya** encerrado	**hayan** encerrado
imperfecto de subjuntivo		pluscuamperfecto de subjuntivo	
encerrar**a**	encerrár**amos**	**hubiera** encerrado	**hubiéramos** encerrado
encerrar**as**	encerrar**ais**	**hubieras** encerrado	**hubierais** encerrado
encerrar**a**	encerrar**an**	**hubiera** encerrado	**hubieran** encerrado
OR		OR	
encerras**e**	encerrás**emos**	**hubiese** encerrado	**hubiésemos** encerrado
encerras**es**	encerras**eis**	**hubieses** encerrado	**hubieseis** encerrado
encerras**e**	encerras**en**	**hubiese** encerrado	**hubiesen** encerrado

imperativo

—	encerremos
encierra; no encierres	encerrad; no encerréis
encierre	encierren

encontrar — to find, to encounter

gerundio **encontrando** participio de pasado **encontrado**

SINGULAR	PLURAL	SINGULAR	PLURAL
presente de indicativo		perfecto de indicativo	
encuentr**o**	encontr**amos**	**he** encontrado	**hemos** encontrado
encuentr**as**	encontr**áis**	**has** encontrado	**habéis** encontrado
encuentr**a**	encuentr**an**	**ha** encontrado	**han** encontrado
imperfecto de indicativo		pluscuamperfecto de indicativo	
encontr**aba**	encontr**ábamos**	**había** encontrado	**habíamos** encontrado
encontr**abas**	encontr**abais**	**habías** encontrado	**habíais** encontrado
encontr**aba**	encontr**aban**	**había** encontrado	**habían** encontrado
pretérito		pretérito anterior	
encontr**é**	encontr**amos**	**hube** encontrado	**hubimos** encontrado
encontr**aste**	encontr**asteis**	**hubiste** encontrado	**hubisteis** encontrado
encontr**ó**	encontr**aron**	**hubo** encontrado	**hubieron** encontrado
futuro		futuro perfecto	
encontrar**é**	encontrar**emos**	**habré** encontrado	**habremos** encontrado
encontrar**ás**	encontrar**éis**	**habrás** encontrado	**habréis** encontrado
encontrar**á**	encontrar**án**	**habrá** encontrado	**habrán** encontrado
condicional simple		condicional compuesto	
encontrar**ía**	encontrar**íamos**	**habría** encontrado	**habríamos** encontrado
encontrar**ías**	encontrar**íais**	**habrías** encontrado	**habríais** encontrado
encontrar**ía**	encontrar**ían**	**habría** encontrado	**habrían** encontrado
presente de subjuntivo		perfecto de subjuntivo	
encuentr**e**	encontr**emos**	**haya** encontrado	**hayamos** encontrado
encuentr**es**	encontr**éis**	**hayas** encontrado	**hayáis** encontrado
encuentr**e**	encuentr**en**	**haya** encontrado	**hayan** encontrado
imperfecto de subjuntivo		pluscuamperfecto de subjuntivo	
encontrar**a**	encontrár**amos**	**hubiera** encontrado	**hubiéramos** encontrado
encontrar**as**	encontrar**ais**	**hubieras** encontrado	**hubierais** encontrado
encontrar**a**	encontrar**an**	**hubiera** encontrado	**hubieran** encontrado
OR		OR	
encontras**e**	encontrás**emos**	**hubiese** encontrado	**hubiésemos** encontrado
encontras**es**	encontras**eis**	**hubieses** encontrado	**hubieseis** encontrado
encontras**e**	encontras**en**	**hubiese** encontrado	**hubiesen** encontrado

imperativo

—	encontremos
encuentra; no encuentres	encontrad; no encontréis
encuentre	encuentren

gerundio **enfadando** participio de pasado **enfadado**

SINGULAR	PLURAL
presente de indicativo	
enfad**o**	enfad**amos**
enfad**as**	enfad**áis**
enfad**a**	enfad**an**
imperfecto de indicativo	
enfad**aba**	enfad**ábamos**
enfad**abas**	enfad**abais**
enfad**aba**	enfad**aban**
pretérito	
enfad**é**	enfad**amos**
enfad**aste**	enfad**asteis**
enfad**ó**	enfad**aron**
futuro	
enfadar**é**	enfadar**emos**
enfadar**ás**	enfadar**éis**
enfadar**á**	enfadar**án**
condicional simple	
enfadar**ía**	enfadar**íamos**
enfadar**ías**	enfadar**íais**
enfadar**ía**	enfadar**ían**
presente de subjuntivo	
enfad**e**	enfad**emos**
enfad**es**	enfad**éis**
enfad**e**	enfad**en**
imperfecto de subjuntivo	
enfadar**a**	enfadár**amos**
enfadar**as**	enfadar**ais**
enfadar**a**	enfadar**an**
OR	
enfadas**e**	enfadás**emos**
enfadas**es**	enfadas**eis**
enfadas**e**	enfadas**en**
imperativo	
—	enfademos
enfada; no enfades	enfadad; no enfadéis
enfade	enfaden

SINGULAR	PLURAL
perfecto de indicativo	
he enfadado	**hemos** enfadado
has enfadado	**habéis** enfadado
ha enfadado	**han** enfadado
pluscuamperfecto de indicativo	
había enfadado	**habíamos** enfadado
habías enfadado	**habíais** enfadado
había enfadado	**habían** enfadado
pretérito anterior	
hube enfadado	**hubimos** enfadado
hubiste enfadado	**hubisteis** enfadado
hubo enfadado	**hubieron** enfadado
futuro perfecto	
habré enfadado	**habremos** enfadado
habrás enfadado	**habréis** enfadado
habrá enfadado	**habrán** enfadado
condicional compuesto	
habría enfadado	**habríamos** enfadado
habrías enfadado	**habríais** enfadado
habría enfadado	**habrían** enfadado
perfecto de subjuntivo	
haya enfadado	**hayamos** enfadado
hayas enfadado	**hayáis** enfadado
haya enfadado	**hayan** enfadado
pluscuamperfecto de subjuntivo	
hubiera enfadado	**hubiéramos** enfadado
hubieras enfadado	**hubierais** enfadado
hubiera enfadado	**hubieran** enfadado
OR	
hubiese enfadado	**hubiésemos** enfadado
hubieses enfadado	**hubieseis** enfadado
hubiese enfadado	**hubiesen** enfadado

enfadarse — to get annoyed, angry

gerundio **enfadándose** participio de pasado **enfadado**

SINGULAR	PLURAL	SINGULAR	PLURAL
presente de indicativo		**perfecto de indicativo**	
me enfad**o**	nos enfad**amos**	**me he** enfadado	**nos hemos** enfadado
te enfad**as**	os enfad**áis**	**te has** enfadado	**os habéis** enfadado
se enfad**a**	se enfad**an**	**se ha** enfadado	**se han** enfadado
imperfecto de indicativo		**pluscuamperfecto de indicativo**	
me enfad**aba**	nos enfad**ábamos**	**me había** enfadado	**nos habíamos** enfadado
te enfad**abas**	os enfad**abais**	**te habías** enfadado	**os habíais** enfadado
se enfad**aba**	se enfad**aban**	**se había** enfadado	**se habían** enfadado
pretérito		**pretérito anterior**	
me enfad**é**	nos enfad**amos**	**me hube** enfadado	**nos hubimos** enfadado
te enfad**aste**	os enfad**asteis**	**te hubiste** enfadado	**os hubisteis** enfadado
se enfad**ó**	se enfad**aron**	**se hubo** enfadado	**se hubieron** enfadado
futuro		**futuro perfecto**	
me enfadar**é**	nos enfadar**emos**	**me habré** enfadado	**nos habremos** enfadado
te enfadar**ás**	os enfadar**éis**	**te habrás** enfadado	**os habréis** enfadado
se enfadar**á**	se enfadar**án**	**se habrá** enfadado	**se habrán** enfadado
condicional simple		**condicional compuesto**	
me enfadar**ía**	nos enfadar**íamos**	**me habría** enfadado	**nos habríamos** enfadado
te enfadar**ías**	os enfadar**íais**	**te habrías** enfadado	**os habríais** enfadado
se enfadar**ía**	se enfadar**ían**	**se habría** enfadado	**se habrían** enfadado
presente de subjuntivo		**perfecto de subjuntivo**	
me enfad**e**	nos enfad**emos**	**me haya** enfadado	**nos hayamos** enfadado
te enfad**es**	os enfad**éis**	**te hayas** enfadado	**os hayáis** enfadado
se enfad**e**	se enfad**en**	**se haya** enfadado	**se hayan** enfadado
imperfecto de subjuntivo		**pluscuamperfecto de subjuntivo**	
me enfadar**a**	nos enfadár**amos**	**me hubiera** enfadado	**nos hubiéramos** enfadado
te enfadar**as**	os enfadar**ais**	**te hubieras** enfadado	**os hubierais** enfadado
se enfadar**a**	se enfadar**an**	**se hubiera** enfadado	**se hubieran** enfadado
OR		OR	
me enfadas**e**	nos enfadás**emos**	**me hubiese** enfadado	**nos hubiésemos** enfadado
te enfadas**es**	os enfadas**eis**	**te hubieses** enfadado	**os hubieseis** enfadado
se enfadas**e**	se enfadas**en**	**se hubiese** enfadado	**se hubiesen** enfadado

imperativo

SINGULAR	PLURAL
—	enfadémonos; no nos enfademos
enfádate; no te enfades	enfadaos; no os enfadéis
enfádese; no se enfade	enfádense; no se enfaden

to become sick — enfermarse

gerundio enfermándose — **participio de pasado** enfermado

SINGULAR	PLURAL
presente de indicativo	
me enfermo	nos enfermamos
te enfermas	os enfermáis
se enferma	se enferman
imperfecto de indicativo	
me enfermaba	nos enfermábamos
te enfermabas	os enfermabais
se enfermaba	se enfermaban
pretérito	
me enfermé	nos enfermamos
te enfermaste	os enfermasteis
se enfermó	se enfermaron
futuro	
me enfermaré	nos enfermaremos
te enfermarás	os enfermaréis
se enfermará	se enfermarán
condicional simple	
me enfermaría	nos enfermaríamos
te enfermarías	os enfermaríais
se enfermaría	se enfermarían
presente de subjuntivo	
me enferme	nos enfermemos
te enfermes	os enferméis
se enferme	se enfermen
imperfecto de subjuntivo	
me enfermara	nos enfermáramos
te enfermaras	os enfermarais
se enfermara	se enfermaran
OR	
me enfermase	nos enfermásemos
te enfermases	os enfermaseis
se enfermase	se enfermasen

SINGULAR	PLURAL
perfecto de indicativo	
me he enfermado	nos hemos enfermado
te has enfermado	os habéis enfermado
se ha enfermado	se han enfermado
pluscuamperfecto de indicativo	
me había enfermado	nos habíamos enfermado
te habías enfermado	os habíais enfermado
se había enfermado	se habían enfermado
pretérito anterior	
me hube enfermado	nos hubimos enfermado
te hubiste enfermado	os hubisteis enfermado
se hubo enfermado	se hubieron enfermado
futuro perfecto	
me habré enfermado	nos habremos enfermado
te habrás enfermado	os habréis enfermado
se habrá enfermado	se habrán enfermado
condicional compuesto	
me habría enfermado	nos habríamos enfermado
te habrías enfermado	os habríais enfermado
se habría enfermado	se habrían enfermado
perfecto de subjuntivo	
me haya enfermado	nos hayamos enfermado
te hayas enfermado	os hayáis enfermado
se haya enfermado	se hayan enfermado
pluscuamperfecto de subjuntivo	
me hubiera enfermado	nos hubiéramos enfermado
te hubieras enfermado	os hubierais enfermado
se hubiera enfermado	se hubieran enfermado
OR	
me hubiese enfermado	nos hubiésemos enfermado
te hubieses enfermado	os hubieseis enfermado
se hubiese enfermado	se hubiesen enfermado

imperativo

—	enfermémonos; no nos enfermemos
enfermáte; no te enfermes	enfermaos; no os enferméis
enférmese; no se enferme	enférmense; no se enfermen

enojarse — to become angry

gerundio **enojándose** participio de pasado **enojado**

SINGULAR	PLURAL	SINGULAR	PLURAL
presente de indicativo		perfecto de indicativo	
me enoj**o**	nos enoj**amos**	**me he** enojado	**nos hemos** enojado
te enoj**as**	os enoj**áis**	**te has** enojado	**os habéis** enojado
se enoj**a**	se enoj**an**	**se ha** enojado	**se han** enojado
imperfecto de indicativo		pluscuamperfecto de indicativo	
me enoj**aba**	nos enoj**ábamos**	**me había** enojado	**nos habíamos** enojado
te enoj**abas**	os enoj**abais**	**te habías** enojado	**os habíais** enojado
se enoj**aba**	se enoj**aban**	**se había** enojado	**se habían** enojado
pretérito		pretérito anterior	
me enoj**é**	nos enoj**amos**	**me hube** enojado	**nos hubimos** enojado
te enoj**aste**	os enoj**asteis**	**te hubiste** enojado	**os hubisteis** enojado
se enoj**ó**	se enoj**aron**	**se hubo** enojado	**se hubieron** enojado
futuro		futuro perfecto	
me enojar**é**	nos enojar**emos**	**me habré** enojado	**nos habremos** enojado
te enojar**ás**	os enojar**éis**	**te habrás** enojado	**os habréis** enojado
se enojar**á**	se enojar**án**	**se habrá** enojado	**se habrán** enojado
condicional simple		condicional compuesto	
me enojar**ía**	nos enojar**íamos**	**me habría** enojado	**nos habríamos** enojado
te enojar**ías**	os enojar**íais**	**te habrías** enojado	**os habríais** enojado
se enojar**ía**	se enojar**ían**	**se habría** enojado	**se habrían** enojado
presente de subjuntivo		perfecto de subjuntivo	
me enoj**e**	nos enoj**emos**	**me haya** enojado	**nos hayamos** enojado
te enoj**es**	os enoj**éis**	**te hayas** enojado	**os hayáis** enojado
se enoj**e**	se enoj**en**	**se haya** enojado	**se hayan** enojado
imperfecto de subjuntivo		pluscuamperfecto de subjuntivo	
me enojar**a**	nos enojár**amos**	**me hubiera** enojado	**nos hubiéramos** enojado
te enojar**as**	os enojar**ais**	**te hubieras** enojado	**os hubierais** enojado
se enojar**a**	se enojar**an**	**se hubiera** enojado	**se hubieran** enojado
OR		OR	
me enojas**e**	nos enojás**emos**	**me hubiese** enojado	**nos hubiésemos** enojado
te enojas**es**	os enojas**eis**	**te hubieses** enojado	**os hubieseis** enojado
se enojas**e**	se enojas**en**	**se hubiese** enojado	**se hubiesen** enojado

imperativo

—	enojémonos; no nos enojemos
enójate; no te enojes	enojaos; no os enojáis
enójese; no se enoje	enójense; no se enojen

to teach **enseñar**

gerundio **enseñando** participio de pasado **enseñado**

presente de indicativo

SINGULAR	PLURAL
enseñ**o**	enseñ**amos**
enseñ**as**	enseñ**áis**
enseñ**a**	enseñ**an**

imperfecto de indicativo

SINGULAR	PLURAL
enseñ**aba**	enseñ**ábamos**
enseñ**abas**	enseñ**abais**
enseñ**aba**	enseñ**aban**

pretérito

SINGULAR	PLURAL
enseñ**é**	enseñ**amos**
enseñ**aste**	enseñ**asteis**
enseñ**ó**	enseñ**aron**

futuro

SINGULAR	PLURAL
enseñar**é**	enseñar**emos**
enseñar**ás**	enseñar**éis**
enseñar**á**	enseñar**án**

condicional simple

SINGULAR	PLURAL
enseñar**ía**	enseñar**íamos**
enseñar**ías**	enseñar**íais**
enseñar**ía**	enseñar**ían**

presente de subjuntivo

SINGULAR	PLURAL
enseñ**e**	enseñ**emos**
enseñ**es**	enseñ**éis**
enseñ**e**	enseñ**en**

imperfecto de subjuntivo

SINGULAR	PLURAL
enseñar**a**	enseñár**amos**
enseñar**as**	enseñar**ais**
enseñar**a**	enseñar**an**
OR	
enseñas**e**	enseñás**emos**
enseñas**es**	enseñas**eis**
enseñas**e**	enseñas**en**

imperativo

SINGULAR	PLURAL
—	enseñemos
enseña; no enseñes	enseñad; no enseñéis
enseñe	enseñen

perfecto de indicativo

SINGULAR	PLURAL
he enseñado	**hemos** enseñado
has enseñado	**habéis** enseñado
ha enseñado	**han** enseñado

pluscuamperfecto de indicativo

SINGULAR	PLURAL
había enseñado	**habíamos** enseñado
habías enseñado	**habíais** enseñado
había enseñado	**habían** enseñado

pretérito anterior

SINGULAR	PLURAL
hube enseñado	**hubimos** enseñado
hubiste enseñado	**hubisteis** enseñado
hubo enseñado	**hubieron** enseñado

futuro perfecto

SINGULAR	PLURAL
habré enseñado	**habremos** enseñado
habrás enseñado	**habréis** enseñado
habrá enseñado	**habrán** enseñado

condicional compuesto

SINGULAR	PLURAL
habría enseñado	**habríamos** enseñado
habrías enseñado	**habríais** enseñado
habría enseñado	**habrían** enseñado

perfecto de subjuntivo

SINGULAR	PLURAL
haya enseñado	**hayamos** enseñado
hayas enseñado	**hayáis** enseñado
haya enseñado	**hayan** enseñado

pluscuamperfecto de subjuntivo

SINGULAR	PLURAL
hubiera enseñado	**hubiéramos** enseñado
hubieras enseñado	**hubierais** enseñado
hubiera enseñado	**hubieran** enseñado
OR	
hubiese enseñado	**hubiésemos** enseñado
hubieses enseñado	**hubieseis** enseñado
hubiese enseñado	**hubiesen** enseñado

ensuciarse — to get dirty

gerundio **ensuciándose** participio de pasado **ensuciado**

SINGULAR	PLURAL	SINGULAR	PLURAL
presente de indicativo		perfecto de indicativo	
me ensuci**o**	nos ensuci**amos**	**me he** ensuciado	**nos hemos** ensuciado
te ensuci**as**	os ensuci**áis**	**te has** ensuciado	**os habéis** ensuciado
se ensuci**a**	se ensuci**an**	**se ha** ensuciado	**se han** ensuciado
imperfecto de indicativo		pluscuamperfecto de indicativo	
me ensuci**aba**	nos ensuci**ábamos**	**me había** ensuciado	**nos habíamos** ensuciado
te ensuci**abas**	os ensuci**abais**	**te habías** ensuciado	**os habíais** ensuciado
se ensuci**aba**	se ensuci**aban**	**se había** ensuciado	**se habían** ensuciado
pretérito		pretérito anterior	
me ensuci**é**	nos ensuci**amos**	**me hube** ensuciado	**nos hubimos** ensuciado
te ensuci**aste**	os ensuci**asteis**	**te hubiste** ensuciado	**os hubisteis** ensuciado
se ensuci**ó**	se ensuci**aron**	**se hubo** ensuciado	**se hubieron** ensuciado
futuro		futuro perfecto	
me ensuciar**é**	nos ensuciar**emos**	**me habré** ensuciado	**nos habremos** ensuciado
te ensuciar**ás**	os ensuciar**éis**	**te habrás** ensuciado	**os habréis** ensuciado
se ensuciar**á**	se ensuciar**án**	**se habrá** ensuciado	**se habrán** ensuciado
condicional simple		condicional compuesto	
me ensuciar**ía**	nos ensuciar**íamos**	**me habría** ensuciado	**nos habríamos** ensuciado
te ensuciar**ías**	os ensuciar**íais**	**te habrías** ensuciado	**os habríais** ensuciado
se ensuciar**ía**	se ensuciar**ían**	**se habría** ensuciado	**se habrían** ensuciado
presente de subjuntivo		perfecto de subjuntivo	
me ensuci**e**	nos ensuci**emos**	**me haya** ensuciado	**nos hayamos** ensuciado
te ensuci**es**	os ensuci**éis**	**te hayas** ensuciado	**os hayáis** ensuciado
se ensuci**e**	se ensuci**en**	**se haya** ensuciado	**se hayan** ensuciado
imperfecto de subjuntivo		pluscuamperfecto de subjuntivo	
me ensuciar**a**	nos ensuciár**amos**	**me hubiera** ensuciado	**nos hubiéramos** ensuciado
te ensuciar**as**	os ensuciar**ais**	**te hubieras** ensuciado	**os hubierais** ensuciado
se ensuciar**a**	se ensuciar**an**	**se hubiera** ensuciado	**se hubieran** ensuciado
OR		OR	
me ensucias**e**	nos ensuciás**emos**	**me hubiese** ensuciado	**nos hubiésemos** ensuciado
te ensucias**es**	os ensucias**eis**	**te hubieses** ensuciado	**os hubieseis** ensuciado
se ensucias**e**	se ensucias**en**	**se hubiese** ensuciado	**se hubiesen** ensuciado

imperativo

—	ensuciémonos
ensúciate;	ensuciaos;
no te ensucies	no os ensuciéis
ensúciese	ensúciense

gerundio **entendiendo** participio de pasado **entendido**

SINGULAR	PLURAL	SINGULAR	PLURAL
presente de indicativo		perfecto de indicativo	
entiend**o**	entend**emos**	**he** entendido	**hemos** entendido
entiend**es**	entend**éis**	**has** entendido	**habéis** entendido
entiend**e**	entiend**en**	**ha** entendido	**han** entendido
imperfecto de indicativo		pluscuamperfecto de indicativo	
entend**ía**	entend**íamos**	**había** entendido	**habíamos** entendido
entend**ías**	entend**íais**	**habías** entendido	**habíais** entendido
entend**ía**	entend**ían**	**había** entendido	**habían** entendido
pretérito		pretérito anterior	
entend**í**	entend**imos**	**hube** entendido	**hubimos** entendido
entend**iste**	entend**isteis**	**hubiste** entendido	**hubisteis** entendido
entend**ió**	entend**ieron**	**hubo** entendido	**hubieron** entendido
futuro		futuro perfecto	
entender**é**	entender**emos**	**habré** entendido	**habremos** entendido
entender**ás**	entender**éis**	**habrás** entendido	**habréis** entendido
entender**á**	entender**án**	**habrá** entendido	**habrán** entendido
condicional simple		condicional compuesto	
entender**ía**	entender**íamos**	**habría** entendido	**habríamos** entendido
entender**ías**	entender**íais**	**habrías** entendido	**habríais** entendido
entender**ía**	entender**ían**	**habría** entendido	**habrían** entendido
presente de subjuntivo		perfecto de subjuntivo	
entiend**a**	entend**amos**	**haya** entendido	**hayamos** entendido
entiend**as**	entend**áis**	**hayas** entendido	**hayáis** entendido
entiend**a**	entiend**an**	**haya** entendido	**hayan** entendido
imperfecto de subjuntivo		pluscuamperfecto de subjuntivo	
entendier**a**	entendiér**amos**	**hubiera** entendido	**hubiéramos** entendido
entendier**as**	entendier**ais**	**hubieras** entendido	**hubierais** entendido
entendier**a**	entendier**an**	**hubiera** entendido	**hubieran** entendido
OR		OR	
entendies**e**	entendiés**emos**	**hubiese** entendido	**hubiésemos** entendido
entendies**es**	entendies**eis**	**hubieses** entendido	**hubieseis** entendido
entendies**e**	entendies**en**	**hubiese** entendido	**hubiesen** entendido

imperativo

—	entendamos
entiende; no entiendas	entended; no entendáis
entienda	entiendan

enterarse — to find out

gerundio **enterándose** participio de pasado **enterado**

SINGULAR	PLURAL
presente de indicativo	
me enter**o**	nos enter**amos**
te enter**as**	os enter**áis**
se enter**a**	se enter**an**
imperfecto de indicativo	
me enter**aba**	nos enter**ábamos**
te enter**abas**	os enter**abais**
se enter**aba**	se enter**aban**
pretérito	
me enter**é**	nos enter**amos**
te enter**aste**	os enter**asteis**
se enter**ó**	se enter**aron**
futuro	
me enterar**é**	nos enterar**emos**
te enterar**ás**	os enterar**éis**
se enterar**á**	se enterar**án**
condicional simple	
me enterar**ía**	nos enterar**íamos**
te enterar**ías**	os enterar**íais**
se enterar**ía**	se enterar**ían**
presente de subjuntivo	
me enter**e**	nos enter**emos**
te enter**es**	os enter**éis**
se enter**e**	se enter**en**
imperfecto de subjuntivo	
me enterar**a**	nos enterár**amos**
te enterar**as**	os enterar**ais**
se enterar**a**	se enterar**an**
OR	
me enteras**e**	nos enterás**emos**
te enteras**es**	os enteras**eis**
se enteras**e**	se enteras**en**
imperativo	
—	enterémonos
entérate;	enteraos;
no te enteres	no os enteréis
entérese	entérense

SINGULAR	PLURAL
perfecto de indicativo	
me he enterado	**nos hemos** enterado
te has enterado	**os habéis** enterado
se ha enterado	**se han** enterado
pluscuamperfecto de indicativo	
me había enterado	**nos habíamos** enterado
te habías enterado	**os habíais** enterado
se había enterado	**se habían** enterado
pretérito anterior	
me hube enterado	**nos hubimos** enterado
te hubiste enterado	**os hubisteis** enterado
se hubo enterado	**se hubieron** enterado
futuro perfecto	
me habré enterado	**nos habremos** enterado
te habrás enterado	**os habréis** enterado
se habrá enterado	**se habrán** enterado
condicional compuesto	
me habría enterado	**nos habríamos** enterado
te habrías enterado	**os habríais** enterado
se habría enterado	**se habrían** enterado
perfecto de subjuntivo	
me haya enterado	**nos hayamos** enterado
te hayas enterado	**os hayáis** enterado
se haya enterado	**se hayan** enterado
pluscuamperfecto de subjuntivo	
me hubiera enterado	**nos hubiéramos** enterado
te hubieras enterado	**os hubierais** enterado
se hubiera enterado	**se hubieran** enterado
OR	
me hubiese enterado	**nos hubiésemos** enterado
te hubieses enterado	**os hubieseis** enterado
se hubiese enterado	**se hubiesen** enterado

to enter **entrar**

gerundio **entrando** participio de pasado **entrado**

SINGULAR	PLURAL
presente de indicativo	
entr**o**	entr**amos**
entr**as**	entr**áis**
entr**a**	entr**an**
imperfecto de indicativo	
entr**aba**	entr**ábamos**
entr**abas**	entr**abais**
entr**aba**	entr**aban**
pretérito	
entr**é**	entr**amos**
entr**aste**	entr**asteis**
entr**ó**	entr**aron**
futuro	
entrar**é**	entrar**emos**
entrar**ás**	entrar**éis**
entrar**á**	entrar**án**
condicional simple	
entrar**ía**	entrar**íamos**
entrar**ías**	entrar**íais**
entrar**ía**	entrar**ían**
presente de subjuntivo	
entr**e**	entr**emos**
entr**es**	entr**éis**
entr**e**	entr**en**
imperfecto de subjuntivo	
entrar**a**	entrár**amos**
entrar**as**	entrar**ais**
entrar**a**	entrar**an**
OR	
entras**e**	entrás**emos**
entras**es**	entras**eis**
entras**e**	entras**en**
imperativo	
—	entremos
entra; no entres	entrad; no entréis
entre	entren

SINGULAR	PLURAL
perfecto de indicativo	
he entrado	**hemos** entrado
has entrado	**habéis** entrado
ha entrado	**han** entrado
pluscuamperfecto de indicativo	
había entrado	**habíamos** entrado
habías entrado	**habíais** entrado
había entrado	**habían** entrado
pretérito anterior	
hube entrado	**hubimos** entrado
hubiste entrado	**hubisteis** entrado
hubo entrado	**hubieron** entrado
futuro perfecto	
habré entrado	**habremos** entrado
habrás entrado	**habréis** entrado
habrá entrado	**habrán** entrado
condicional compuesto	
habría entrado	**habríamos** entrado
habrías entrado	**habríais** entrado
habría entrado	**habrían** entrado
perfecto de subjuntivo	
haya entrado	**hayamos** entrado
hayas entrado	**hayáis** entrado
haya entrado	**hayan** entrado
pluscuamperfecto de subjuntivo	
hubiera entrado	**hubiéramos** entrado
hubieras entrado	**hubierais** entrado
hubiera entrado	**hubieran** entrado
OR	
hubiese entrado	**hubiésemos** entrado
hubieses entrado	**hubieseis** entrado
hubiese entrado	**hubiesen** entrado

gerundio **entregando** — participio de pasado **entregado**

SINGULAR	PLURAL	SINGULAR	PLURAL
presente de indicativo		perfecto de indicativo	
entreg**o**	entreg**amos**	**he** entregado	**hemos** entregado
entreg**as**	entreg**áis**	**has** entregado	**habéis** entregado
entreg**a**	entreg**an**	**ha** entregado	**han** entregado
imperfecto de indicativo		pluscuamperfecto de indicativo	
entreg**aba**	entreg**ábamos**	**había** entregado	**habíamos** entregado
entreg**abas**	entreg**abais**	**habías** entregado	**habíais** entregado
entreg**aba**	entreg**aban**	**había** entregado	**habían** entregado
pretérito		pretérito anterior	
entregu**é**	entreg**amos**	**hube** entregado	**hubimos** entregado
entreg**aste**	entreg**asteis**	**hubiste** entregado	**hubisteis** entregado
entreg**ó**	entreg**aron**	**hubo** entregado	**hubieron** entregado
futuro		futuro perfecto	
entregar**é**	entregar**emos**	**habré** entregado	**habremos** entregado
entregar**ás**	entregar**éis**	**habrás** entregado	**habréis** entregado
entregar**á**	entregar**án**	**habrá** entregado	**habrán** entregado
condicional simple		condicional compuesto	
entregar**ía**	entregar**íamos**	**habría** entregado	**habríamos** entregado
entregar**ías**	entregar**íais**	**habrías** entregado	**habríais** entregado
entregar**ía**	entregar**ían**	**habría** entregado	**habrían** entregado
presente de subjuntivo		perfecto de subjuntivo	
entregu**e**	entregu**emos**	**haya** entregado	**hayamos** entregado
entregu**es**	entregu**éis**	**hayas** entregado	**hayáis** entregado
entregu**e**	entregu**en**	**haya** entregado	**hayan** entregado
imperfecto de subjuntivo		pluscuamperfecto de subjuntivo	
entregar**a**	entregár**amos**	**hubiera** entregado	**hubiéramos** entregado
entregar**as**	entregar**ais**	**hubieras** entregado	**hubierais** entregado
entregar**a**	entregar**an**	**hubiera** entregado	**hubieran** entregado
OR		OR	
entregas**e**	entregás**emos**	**hubiese** entregado	**hubiésemos** entregado
entregas**es**	entregas**eis**	**hubieses** entregado	**hubieseis** entregado
entregas**e**	entregas**en**	**hubiese** entregado	**hubiesen** entregado

imperativo

—	entreguemos
entrega;	entregad;
no entregues	no entreguéis
entregue	entreguen

gerundio **enunciando** participio de pasado **enunciado**

SINGULAR	PLURAL	SINGULAR	PLURAL
presente de indicativo		perfecto de indicativo	
enunci**o**	enunci**amos**	**he** enunciado	**hemos** enunciado
enunci**as**	enunci**áis**	**has** enunciado	**habéis** enunciado
enunci**a**	enunci**an**	**ha** enunciado	**han** enunciado
imperfecto de indicativo		pluscuamperfecto de indicativo	
enunci**aba**	enunci**ábamos**	**había** enunciado	**habíamos** enunciado
enunci**abas**	enunci**abais**	**habías** enunciado	**habíais** enunciado
enunci**aba**	enunci**aban**	**había** enunciado	**habían** enunciado
pretérito		pretérito anterior	
enunci**é**	enunci**amos**	**hube** enunciado	**hubimos** enunciado
enunci**aste**	enunci**asteis**	**hubiste** enunciado	**hubisteis** enunciado
enunci**ó**	enunci**aron**	**hubo** enunciado	**hubieron** enunciado
futuro		futuro perfecto	
enunciar**é**	enunciar**emos**	**habré** enunciado	**habremos** enunciado
enunciar**ás**	enunciar**éis**	**habrás** enunciado	**habréis** enunciado
enunciar**á**	enunciar**án**	**habrá** enunciado	**habrán** enunciado
condicional simple		condicional compuesto	
enunciar**ía**	enunciar**íamos**	**habría** enunciado	**habríamos** enunciado
enunciar**ías**	enunciar**íais**	**habrías** enunciado	**habríais** enunciado
enunciar**ía**	enunciar**ían**	**habría** enunciado	**habrían** enunciado
presente de subjuntivo		perfecto de subjuntivo	
enunci**e**	enunci**emos**	**haya** enunciado	**hayamos** enunciado
enunci**es**	enunci**éis**	**hayas** enunciado	**hayáis** enunciado
enunci**e**	enunci**en**	**haya** enunciado	**hayan** enunciado
imperfecto de subjuntivo		pluscuamperfecto de subjuntivo	
enunciar**a**	enunciár**amos**	**hubiera** enunciado	**hubiéramos** enunciado
enunciar**as**	enunciar**ais**	**hubieras** enunciado	**hubierais** enunciado
enunciar**a**	enunciar**an**	**hubiera** enunciado	**hubieran** enunciado
OR		OR	
enuncias**e**	enunciás**emos**	**hubiese** enunciado	**hubiésemos** enunciado
enuncias**es**	enuncias**eis**	**hubieses** enunciado	**hubieseis** enunciado
enuncias**e**	enuncias**en**	**hubiese** enunciado	**hubiesen** enunciado

imperativo

—	enunciemos
enuncia; no enuncies	enunciad; no enunciéis
enuncie	enuncien

E

envejecer

to grow old, to age

gerundio **envejeciendo** participio de pasado **envejecido**

SINGULAR	PLURAL
presente de indicativo	
envejezc**o**	envejec**emos**
envejec**es**	envejec**éis**
envejec**e**	envejec**en**
imperfecto de indicativo	
envejec**ía**	envejec**íamos**
envejec**ías**	envejec**íais**
envejec**ía**	envejec**ían**
pretérito	
envejec**í**	envejec**imos**
envejec**iste**	envejec**isteis**
envejec**ió**	envejec**ieron**
futuro	
envejecer**é**	envejecer**emos**
envejecer**ás**	envejecer**éis**
envejecer**á**	envejecer**án**
condicional simple	
envejecer**ía**	envejecer**íamos**
envejecer**ías**	envejecer**íais**
envejecer**ía**	envejecer**ían**
presente de subjuntivo	
envejezc**a**	envejezc**amos**
envejezc**as**	envejezc**áis**
envejezc**a**	envejezc**an**
imperfecto de subjuntivo	
envejecier**a**	envejeciér**amos**
envejecier**as**	envejecier**ais**
envejecier**a**	envejecier**an**
OR	
envejecies**e**	envejeciés**emos**
envejecies**es**	envejecies**eis**
envejecies**e**	envejecies**en**
imperativo	
—	envejezcamos
envejece; no envejezcas	envejeced; no envejezcáis
envejezca	envejezcan

SINGULAR	PLURAL
perfecto de indicativo	
he envejecido	**hemos** envejecido
has envejecido	**habéis** envejecido
ha envejecido	**han** envejecido
pluscuamperfecto de indicativo	
había envejecido	**habíamos** envejecido
habías envejecido	**habíais** envejecido
había envejecido	**habían** envejecido
pretérito anterior	
hube envejecido	**hubimos** envejecido
hubiste envejecido	**hubisteis** envejecido
hubo envejecido	**hubieron** envejecido
futuro perfecto	
habré envejecido	**habremos** envejecido
habrás envejecido	**habréis** envejecido
habrá envejecido	**habrán** envejecido
condicional compuesto	
habría envejecido	**habríamos** envejecido
habrías envejecido	**habríais** envejecido
habría envejecido	**habrían** envejecido
perfecto de subjuntivo	
haya envejecido	**hayamos** envejecido
hayas envejecido	**hayáis** envejecido
haya envejecido	**hayan** envejecido
pluscuamperfecto de subjuntivo	
hubiera envejecido	**hubiéramos** envejecido
hubieras envejecido	**hubierais** envejecido
hubiera envejecido	**hubieran** envejecido
OR	
hubiese envejecido	**hubiésemos** envejecido
hubieses envejecido	**hubieseis** envejecido
hubiese envejecido	**hubiesen** envejecido

gerundio **enviando** participio de pasado **enviado**

SINGULAR	PLURAL
presente de indicativo	
envío	enviamos
envías	enviáis
envía	envían
imperfecto de indicativo	
enviaba	enviábamos
enviabas	enviabais
enviaba	enviaban
pretérito	
envié	enviamos
enviaste	enviasteis
envió	enviaron
futuro	
enviaré	enviaremos
enviarás	enviaréis
enviará	enviarán
condicional simple	
enviaría	enviaríamos
enviarías	enviaríais
enviaría	enviarían
presente de subjuntivo	
envíe	enviemos
envíes	enviéis
envíe	envíen
imperfecto de subjuntivo	
enviara	enviáramos
enviaras	enviarais
enviara	enviaran
OR	
enviase	enviásemos
enviases	enviaseis
enviase	enviasen
imperativo	
—	enviemos
envía; no envíes	enviad; no enviéis
envíe	envíen

SINGULAR	PLURAL
perfecto de indicativo	
he enviado	hemos enviado
has enviado	habéis enviado
ha enviado	han enviado
pluscuamperfecto de indicativo	
había enviado	habíamos enviado
habías enviado	habíais enviado
había enviado	habían enviado
pretérito anterior	
hube enviado	hubimos enviado
hubiste enviado	hubisteis enviado
hubo enviado	hubieron enviado
futuro perfecto	
habré enviado	habremos enviado
habrás enviado	habréis enviado
habrá enviado	habrán enviado
condicional compuesto	
habría enviado	habríamos enviado
habrías enviado	habríais enviado
habría enviado	habrían enviado
perfecto de subjuntivo	
haya enviado	hayamos enviado
hayas enviado	hayáis enviado
haya enviado	hayan enviado
pluscuamperfecto de subjuntivo	
hubiera enviado	hubiéramos enviado
hubieras enviado	hubierais enviado
hubiera enviado	hubieran enviado
OR	
hubiese enviado	hubiésemos enviado
hubieses enviado	hubieseis enviado
hubiese enviado	hubiesen enviado

equivocarse — to be mistaken

gerundio **equivocándose** participio de pasado **equivocado**

presente de indicativo

SINGULAR	PLURAL
me equivoc**o**	nos equivoc**amos**
te equivoc**as**	os equivoc**áis**
se equivoc**a**	se equivoc**an**

imperfecto de indicativo

SINGULAR	PLURAL
me equivoc**aba**	nos equivoc**ábamos**
te equivoc**abas**	os equivoc**abais**
se equivoc**aba**	se equivoc**aban**

pretérito

SINGULAR	PLURAL
me equivoqu**é**	nos equivoc**amos**
te equivoc**aste**	os equivoc**asteis**
se equivoc**ó**	se equivoc**aron**

futuro

SINGULAR	PLURAL
me equivocar**é**	nos equivocar**emos**
te equivocar**ás**	os equivocar**éis**
se equivocar**á**	se equivocar**án**

condicional simple

SINGULAR	PLURAL
me equivocar**ía**	nos equivocar**íamos**
te equivocar**ías**	os equivocar**íais**
se equivocar**ía**	se equivocar**ían**

presente de subjuntivo

SINGULAR	PLURAL
me equivoqu**e**	nos equivoqu**emos**
te equivoqu**es**	os equivoqu**éis**
se equivoqu**e**	se equivoqu**en**

imperfecto de subjuntivo

SINGULAR	PLURAL
me equivocar**a**	nos equivocár**amos**
te equivocar**as**	os equivocar**ais**
se equivocar**a**	se equivocar**an**
OR	
me equivocas**e**	nos equivocás**emos**
te equivocas**es**	os equivocas**eis**
se equivocas**e**	se equivocas**en**

imperativo

SINGULAR	PLURAL
—	equivoquemonos; no nos equivoquemos
equivócate; no te equivoques	equivocaos; no os equivoquéis
equivóquese; no se equivoque	equivóquense; no se equivoquen

perfecto de indicativo

SINGULAR	PLURAL
me he equivocado	**nos hemos** equivocado
te has equivocado	**os habéis** equivocado
se ha equivocado	**se han** equivocado

pluscuamperfecto de indicativo

SINGULAR	PLURAL
me había equivocado	**nos habíamos** equivocado
te habías equivocado	**os habíais** equivocado
se había equivocado	**se habían** equivocado

pretérito anterior

SINGULAR	PLURAL
me hube equivocado	**nos hubimos** equivocado
te hubiste equivocado	**os hubisteis** equivocado
se hubo equivocado	**se hubieron** equivocado

futuro perfecto

SINGULAR	PLURAL
me habré equivocado	**nos habremos** equivocado
te habrás equivocado	**os habréis** equivocado
se habrá equivocado	**se habrán** equivocado

condicional compuesto

SINGULAR	PLURAL
me habría equivocado	**nos habríamos** equivocado
te habrías equivocado	**os habríais** equivocado
se habría equivocado	**se habrían** equivocado

perfecto de subjuntivo

SINGULAR	PLURAL
me haya equivocado	**nos hayamos** equivocado
te hayas equivocado	**os hayáis** equivocado
se haya equivocado	**se hayan** equivocado

pluscuamperfecto de subjuntivo

SINGULAR	PLURAL
me hubiera equivocado	**nos hubiéramos** equivocado
te hubieras equivocado	**os hubierais** equivocado
se hubiera equivocado	**se hubieran** equivocado
OR	
me hubiese equivocado	**nos hubiésemos** equivocado
te hubieses equivocado	**os hubieseis** equivocado
se hubiese equivocado	**se hubiesen** equivocado

gerundio **irguiendo** participio de pasado **erguido**

SINGULAR	PLURAL
presente de indicativo	
irg**o** (yerg**o**)	ergu**imos**
irgu**es** (yergu**es**)	ergu**ís**
irgu**e** (yergu**e**)	irgu**en** (yergu**en**)
imperfecto de indicativo	
ergu**ía**	ergu**íamos**
ergu**ías**	ergu**íais**
ergu**ía**	ergu**ían**
pretérito	
ergu**í**	ergu**imos**
ergu**iste**	ergu**isteis**
irgu**ió**	irgu**ieron**
futuro	
erguir**é**	erguir**emos**
erguir**ás**	erguir**éis**
erguir**á**	erguir**án**
condicional simple	
erguir**ía**	erguir**íamos**
erguir**ías**	erguir**íais**
erguir**ía**	erguir**ían**
presente de subjuntivo	
irg**a** (yerg**a**)	irg**amos** (yerg**amos**)
irg**as** (yerg**as**)	irg**áis** (yerg**áis**)
irg**a** (yerg**a**)	irg**an** (yerg**an**)
imperfecto de subjuntivo	
irguier**a**	irguiér**amos**
irguier**as**	irguier**ais**
irguier**a**	irguier**an**
OR	
irguies**e**	irguiés**emos**
irguies**es**	irguies**eis**
irguies**e**	irguies**en**
imperativo	
—	irgamos (yergamos)
irgue (yergue); no irgas (yergas)	erguid; no irgáis (no yergáis)
irga (yerga)	irgan (yergan)

SINGULAR	PLURAL
perfecto de indicativo	
he erguido	**hemos** erguido
has erguido	**habéis** erguido
ha erguido	**han** erguido
pluscuamperfecto de indicativo	
había erguido	**habíamos** erguido
habías erguido	**habíais** erguido
había erguido	**habían** erguido
pretérito anterior	
hube erguido	**hubimos** erguido
hubiste erguido	**hubisteis** erguido
hubo erguido	**hubieron** erguido
futuro perfecto	
habré erguido	**habremos** erguido
habrás erguido	**habréis** erguido
habrá erguido	**habrán** erguido
condicional compuesto	
habría erguido	**habríamos** erguido
habrías erguido	**habríais** erguido
habría erguido	**habrían** erguido
perfecto de subjuntivo	
haya erguido	**hayamos** erguido
hayas erguido	**hayáis** erguido
haya erguido	**hayan** erguido
pluscuamperfecto de subjuntivo	
hubiera erguido	**hubiéramos** erguido
hubieras erguido	**hubierais** erguido
hubiera erguido	**hubieran** erguido
OR	
hubiese erguido	**hubiésemos** erguido
hubieses erguido	**hubieseis** erguido
hubiese erguido	**hubiesen** erguido

erigir — to erect

gerundio **erigiendo** participio de pasado **erigido**

SINGULAR	PLURAL	SINGULAR	PLURAL
presente de indicativo		perfecto de indicativo	
erij**o**	erig**imos**	**he** erigido	**hemos** erigido
erig**es**	erig**ís**	**has** erigido	**habéis** erigido
erig**e**	erig**en**	**ha** erigido	**han** erigido
imperfecto de indicativo		pluscuamperfecto de indicativo	
erig**ía**	erig**íamos**	**había** erigido	**habíamos** erigido
erig**ías**	erig**íais**	**habías** erigido	**habíais** erigido
erig**ía**	erig**ían**	**había** erigido	**habían** erigido
pretérito		pretérito anterior	
erig**í**	erig**imos**	**hube** erigido	**hubimos** erigido
erig**iste**	erig**isteis**	**hubiste** erigido	**hubisteis** erigido
erig**ió**	erig**ieron**	**hubo** erigido	**hubieron** erigido
futuro		futuro perfecto	
erigir**é**	erigir**emos**	**habré** erigido	**habremos** erigido
erigir**ás**	erigir**éis**	**habrás** erigido	**habréis** erigido
erigir**á**	erigir**án**	**habrá** erigido	**habrán** erigido
condicional simple		condicional compuesto	
erigir**ía**	erigir**íamos**	**habría** erigido	**habríamos** erigido
erigir**ías**	erigir**íais**	**habrías** erigido	**habríais** erigido
erigir**ía**	erigir**ían**	**habría** erigido	**habrían** erigido
presente de subjuntivo		perfecto de subjuntivo	
erij**a**	erij**amos**	**haya** erigido	**hayamos** erigido
erij**as**	erij**áis**	**hayas** erigido	**hayáis** erigido
erij**a**	erij**an**	**haya** erigido	**hayan** erigido
imperfecto de subjuntivo		pluscuamperfecto de subjuntivo	
erigier**a**	erigiér**amos**	**hubiera** erigido	**hubiéramos** erigido
erigier**as**	erigier**ais**	**hubieras** erigido	**hubierais** erigido
erigier**a**	erigier**an**	**hubiera** erigido	**hubieran** erigido
OR		OR	
erigies**e**	erigiés**emos**	**hubiese** erigido	**hubiésemos** erigido
erigies**es**	erigies**eis**	**hubieses** erigido	**hubieseis** erigido
erigies**e**	erigies**en**	**hubiese** erigido	**hubiesen** erigido

imperativo

—	erijamos
erige; no erijas	erigid; no erijáis
erija	erijan

gerundio **errando** participio de pasado **errado**

SINGULAR	PLURAL	SINGULAR	PLURAL
presente de indicativo		perfecto de indicativo	
yerr**o**	err**amos**	**he** errado	**hemos** errado
yerr**as**	err**áis**	**has** errado	**habéis** errado
yerr**a**	yerr**an**	**ha** errado	**han** errado
imperfecto de indicativo		pluscuamperfecto de indicativo	
err**aba**	err**ábamos**	**había** errado	**habíamos** errado
err**abas**	err**abais**	**habías** errado	**habíais** errado
err**aba**	err**aban**	**había** errado	**habían** errado
pretérito		pretérito anterior	
err**é**	err**amos**	**hube** errado	**hubimos** errado
err**aste**	err**asteis**	**hubiste** errado	**hubisteis** errado
err**ó**	err**aron**	**hubo** errado	**hubieron** errado
futuro		futuro perfecto	
errar**é**	errar**emos**	**habré** errado	**habremos** errado
errar**ás**	errar**éis**	**habrás** errado	**habréis** errado
errar**á**	errar**án**	**habrá** errado	**habrán** errado
condicional simple		condicional compuesto	
errar**ía**	errar**íamos**	**habría** errado	**habríamos** errado
errar**ías**	errar**íais**	**habrías** errado	**habríais** errado
errar**ía**	errar**ían**	**habría** errado	**habrían** errado
presente de subjuntivo		perfecto de subjuntivo	
yerr**e**	err**emos**	**haya** errado	**hayamos** errado
yerr**es**	err**éis**	**hayas** errado	**hayáis** errado
yerr**e**	yerr**en**	**haya** errado	**hayan** errado
imperfecto de subjuntivo		pluscuamperfecto de subjuntivo	
errar**a**	errár**amos**	**hubiera** errado	**hubiéramos** errado
errar**as**	errar**ais**	**hubieras** errado	**hubierais** errado
errar**a**	errar**an**	**hubiera** errado	**hubieran** errado
OR		OR	
erras**e**	errás**emos**	**hubiese** errado	**hubiésemos** errado
erras**es**	erras**eis**	**hubieses** errado	**hubieseis** errado
erras**e**	erras**en**	**hubiese** errado	**hubiesen** errado

imperativo

—	erremos
yerra; no yerres	errad; no erréis
yerre	yerren

E

escoger — to choose, to select

gerundio **escogiendo** — participio de pasado **escogido**

SINGULAR	PLURAL
presente de indicativo	
escoj**o**	escog**emos**
escog**es**	escog**éis**
escog**e**	escog**en**
imperfecto de indicativo	
escog**ía**	escog**íamos**
escog**ías**	escog**íais**
escog**ía**	escog**ían**
pretérito	
escog**í**	escog**imos**
escog**iste**	escog**isteis**
escog**ió**	escog**ieron**
futuro	
escoger**é**	escoger**emos**
escoger**ás**	escoger**éis**
escoger**á**	escoger**án**
condicional simple	
escoger**ía**	escoger**íamos**
escoger**ías**	escoger**íais**
escoger**ía**	escoger**ían**
presente de subjuntivo	
escoj**a**	escoj**amos**
escoj**as**	escoj**áis**
escoj**a**	escoj**an**
imperfecto de subjuntivo	
escogier**a**	escogiér**amos**
escogier**as**	escogier**ais**
escogier**a**	escogier**an**
OR	
escogies**e**	escogiés**emos**
escogies**es**	escogies**eis**
escogies**e**	escogies**en**
imperativo	
—	escojamos
escoge; no escojas	escoged; no escojáis
escoja	escojan

SINGULAR	PLURAL
perfecto de indicativo	
he escogido	**hemos** escogido
has escogido	**habéis** escogido
ha escogido	**han** escogido
pluscuamperfecto de indicativo	
había escogido	**habíamos** escogido
habías escogido	**habíais** escogido
había escogido	**habían** escogido
pretérito anterior	
hube escogido	**hubimos** escogido
hubiste escogido	**hubisteis** escogido
hubo escogido	**hubieron** escogido
futuro perfecto	
habré escogido	**habremos** escogido
habrás escogido	**habréis** escogido
habrá escogido	**habrán** escogido
condicional compuesto	
habría escogido	**habríamos** escogido
habrías escogido	**habríais** escogido
habría escogido	**habrían** escogido
perfecto de subjuntivo	
haya escogido	**hayamos** escogido
hayas escogido	**hayáis** escogido
haya escogido	**hayan** escogido
pluscuamperfecto de subjuntivo	
hubiera escogido	**hubiéramos** escogido
hubieras escogido	**hubierais** escogido
hubiera escogido	**hubieran** escogido
OR	
hubiese escogido	**hubiésemos** escogido
hubieses escogido	**hubieseis** escogido
hubiese escogido	**hubiesen** escogido

to write — escribir

gerundio **escribiendo** participio de pasado **escrito**

presente de indicativo

SINGULAR	PLURAL
escrib**o**	escrib**imos**
escrib**es**	escrib**ís**
escrib**e**	escrib**en**

imperfecto de indicativo

SINGULAR	PLURAL
escrib**ía**	escrib**íamos**
escrib**ías**	escrib**íais**
escrib**ía**	escrib**ían**

pretérito

SINGULAR	PLURAL
escrib**í**	escrib**imos**
escrib**iste**	escrib**isteis**
escrib**ió**	escrib**ieron**

futuro

SINGULAR	PLURAL
escribir**é**	escribir**emos**
escribir**ás**	escribir**éis**
escribir**á**	escribir**án**

condicional simple

SINGULAR	PLURAL
escribir**ía**	escribir**íamos**
escribir**ías**	escribir**íais**
escribir**ía**	escribir**ían**

presente de subjuntivo

SINGULAR	PLURAL
escrib**a**	escrib**amos**
escrib**as**	escrib**áis**
escrib**a**	escrib**an**

imperfecto de subjuntivo

SINGULAR	PLURAL
escribier**a**	escribiér**amos**
escribier**as**	escribier**ais**
escribier**a**	escribier**an**
OR	
escribies**e**	escribiés**emos**
escribies**es**	escribies**eis**
escribies**e**	escribies**en**

imperativo

SINGULAR	PLURAL
—	escribamos
escribe; no escribas	escribid; no escribáis
escriba	escriban

perfecto de indicativo

SINGULAR	PLURAL
he escrito	**hemos** escrito
has escrito	**habéis** escrito
ha escrito	**han** escrito

pluscuamperfecto de indicativo

SINGULAR	PLURAL
había escrito	**habíamos** escrito
habías escrito	**habíais** escrito
había escrito	**habían** escrito

pretérito anterior

SINGULAR	PLURAL
hube escrito	**hubimos** escrito
hubiste escrito	**hubisteis** escrito
hubo escrito	**hubieron** escrito

futuro perfecto

SINGULAR	PLURAL
habré escrito	**habremos** escrito
habrás escrito	**habréis** escrito
habrá escrito	**habrán** escrito

condicional compuesto

SINGULAR	PLURAL
habría escrito	**habríamos** escrito
habrías escrito	**habríais** escrito
habría escrito	**habrían** escrito

perfecto de subjuntivo

SINGULAR	PLURAL
haya escrito	**hayamos** escrito
hayas escrito	**hayáis** escrito
haya escrito	**hayan** escrito

pluscuamperfecto de subjuntivo

SINGULAR	PLURAL
hubiera escrito	**hubiéramos** escrito
hubieras escrito	**hubierais** escrito
hubiera escrito	**hubieran** escrito
OR	
hubiese escrito	**hubiésemos** escrito
hubieses escrito	**hubieseis** escrito
hubiese escrito	**hubiesen** escrito

escuchar — to listen to

gerundio **escuchando** — participio de pasado **escuchado**

presente de indicativo

SINGULAR	PLURAL
escuch**o**	escuch**amos**
escuch**as**	escuch**áis**
escuch**a**	escuch**an**

imperfecto de indicativo

SINGULAR	PLURAL
escuch**aba**	escuch**ábamos**
escuch**abas**	escuch**abais**
escuch**aba**	escuch**aban**

pretérito

SINGULAR	PLURAL
escuch**é**	escuch**amos**
escuch**aste**	escuch**asteis**
escuch**ó**	escuch**aron**

futuro

SINGULAR	PLURAL
escuchar**é**	escuchar**emos**
escuchar**ás**	escuchar**éis**
escuchar**á**	escuchar**án**

condicional simple

SINGULAR	PLURAL
escuchar**ía**	escuchar**íamos**
escuchar**ías**	escuchar**íais**
escuchar**ía**	escuchar**ían**

presente de subjuntivo

SINGULAR	PLURAL
escuch**e**	escuch**emos**
escuch**es**	escuch**éis**
escuch**e**	escuch**en**

imperfecto de subjuntivo

SINGULAR	PLURAL
escuchar**a**	escuchár**amos**
escuchar**as**	escuchar**ais**
escuchar**a**	escuchar**an**
OR	
escuchas**e**	escuchás**emos**
escuchas**es**	escuchas**eis**
escuchas**e**	escuchas**en**

imperativo

SINGULAR	PLURAL
—	escuchemos
escucha; no escuches	escuchad; no escuchéis
escuche	escuchen

perfecto de indicativo

SINGULAR	PLURAL
he escuchado	**hemos** escuchado
has escuchado	**habéis** escuchado
ha escuchado	**han** escuchado

pluscuamperfecto de indicativo

SINGULAR	PLURAL
había escuchado	**habíamos** escuchado
habías escuchado	**habíais** escuchado
había escuchado	**habían** escuchado

pretérito anterior

SINGULAR	PLURAL
hube escuchado	**hubimos** escuchado
hubiste escuchado	**hubisteis** escuchado
hubo escuchado	**hubieron** escuchado

futuro perfecto

SINGULAR	PLURAL
habré escuchado	**habremos** escuchado
habrás escuchado	**habréis** escuchado
habrá escuchado	**habrán** escuchado

condicional compuesto

SINGULAR	PLURAL
habría escuchado	**habríamos** escuchado
habrías escuchado	**habríais** escuchado
habría escuchado	**habrían** escuchado

perfecto de subjuntivo

SINGULAR	PLURAL
haya escuchado	**hayamos** escuchado
hayas escuchado	**hayáis** escuchado
haya escuchado	**hayan** escuchado

pluscuamperfecto de subjuntivo

SINGULAR	PLURAL
hubiera escuchado	**hubiéramos** escuchado
hubieras escuchado	**hubierais** escuchado
hubiera escuchado	**hubieran** escuchado
OR	
hubiese escuchado	**hubiésemos** escuchado
hubieses escuchado	**hubieseis** escuchado
hubiese escuchado	**hubiesen** escuchado

gerundio **esparciendo** participio de pasado **esparcido**

SINGULAR	PLURAL
presente de indicativo	
esparz**o**	esparc**emos**
esparc**es**	esparc**éis**
esparc**e**	esparc**en**
imperfecto de indicativo	
esparc**ía**	esparc**íamos**
esparc**ías**	esparc**íais**
esparc**ía**	esparc**ían**
pretérito	
esparc**í**	esparc**imos**
esparc**iste**	esparc**isteis**
esparc**ió**	esparc**ieron**
futuro	
esparcir**é**	esparcir**emos**
esparcir**ás**	esparcir**éis**
esparcir**á**	esparcir**án**
condicional simple	
esparcir**ía**	esparcir**íamos**
esparcir**ías**	esparcir**íais**
esparcir**ía**	esparcir**ían**
presente de subjuntivo	
esparz**a**	esparz**amos**
esparz**as**	esparz**áis**
esparz**a**	esparz**an**
imperfecto de subjuntivo	
esparcier**a**	esparciér**amos**
esparcier**as**	esparcier**ais**
esparcier**a**	esparcier**an**
OR	
esparcies**e**	esparciés**emos**
esparcies**es**	esparcies**eis**
esparcies**e**	esparcies**en**
imperativo	
—	esparzamos
esparce; no esparzas	esparcid; no esparzáis
esparza	esparzan

SINGULAR	PLURAL
perfecto de indicativo	
he esparcido	**hemos** esparcido
has esparcido	**habéis** esparcido
ha esparcido	**han** esparcido
pluscuamperfecto de indicativo	
había esparcido	**habíamos** esparcido
habías esparcido	**habíais** esparcido
había esparcido	**habían** esparcido
pretérito anterior	
hube esparcido	**hubimos** esparcido
hubiste esparcido	**hubisteis** esparcido
hubo esparcido	**hubieron** esparcido
futuro perfecto	
habré esparcido	**habremos** esparcido
habrás esparcido	**habréis** esparcido
habrá esparcido	**habrán** esparcido
condicional compuesto	
habría esparcido	**habríamos** esparcido
habrías esparcido	**habríais** esparcido
habría esparcido	**habrían** esparcido
perfecto de subjuntivo	
haya esparcido	**hayamos** esparcido
hayas esparcido	**hayáis** esparcido
haya esparcido	**hayan** esparcido
pluscuamperfecto de subjuntivo	
hubiera esparcido	**hubiéramos** esparcido
hubieras esparcido	**hubierais** esparcido
hubiera esparcido	**hubieran** esparcido
OR	
hubiese esparcido	**hubiésemos** esparcido
hubieses esparcido	**hubieseis** esparcido
hubiese esparcido	**hubiesen** esparcido

esperar — to wait for, to hope

gerundio **esperando** participio de pasado **esperado**

SINGULAR	PLURAL	SINGULAR	PLURAL
presente de indicativo		perfecto de indicativo	
esper**o**	esper**amos**	**he** esperado	**hemos** esperado
esper**as**	esper**áis**	**has** esperado	**habéis** esperado
esper**a**	esper**an**	**ha** esperado	**han** esperado
imperfecto de indicativo		pluscuamperfecto de indicativo	
esper**aba**	esper**ábamos**	**había** esperado	**habíamos** esperado
esper**abas**	esper**abais**	**habías** esperado	**habíais** esperado
esper**aba**	esper**aban**	**había** esperado	**habían** esperado
pretérito		pretérito anterior	
esper**é**	esper**amos**	**hube** esperado	**hubimos** esperado
esper**aste**	esper**asteis**	**hubiste** esperado	**hubisteis** esperado
esper**ó**	esper**aron**	**hubo** esperado	**hubieron** esperado
futuro		futuro perfecto	
esperar**é**	esperar**emos**	**habré** esperado	**habremos** esperado
esperar**ás**	esperar**éis**	**habrás** esperado	**habréis** esperado
esperar**á**	esperar**án**	**habrá** esperado	**habrán** esperado
condicional simple		condicional compuesto	
esperar**ía**	esperar**íamos**	**habría** esperado	**habríamos** esperado
esperar**ías**	esperar**íais**	**habrías** esperado	**habríais** esperado
esperar**ía**	esperar**ían**	**habría** esperado	**habrían** esperado
presente de subjuntivo		perfecto de subjuntivo	
esper**e**	esper**emos**	**haya** esperado	**hayamos** esperado
esper**es**	esper**éis**	**hayas** esperado	**hayáis** esperado
esper**e**	esper**en**	**haya** esperado	**hayan** esperado
imperfecto de subjuntivo		pluscuamperfecto de subjuntivo	
esperar**a**	esperár**amos**	**hubiera** esperado	**hubiéramos** esperado
esperar**as**	esperar**ais**	**hubieras** esperado	**hubierais** esperado
esperar**a**	esperar**an**	**hubiera** esperado	**hubieran** esperado
OR		OR	
esperas**e**	esperás**emos**	**hubiese** esperado	**hubiésemos** esperado
esperas**es**	esperas**eis**	**hubieses** esperado	**hubieseis** esperado
esperas**e**	esperas**en**	**hubiese** esperado	**hubiesen** esperado

imperativo

—	esperemos
espera; no esperes	esperad; no esperéis
espere	esperen

to ski — esquiar

gerundio **esquiando** participio de pasado **esquiado**

presente de indicativo

SINGULAR	PLURAL
esquí**o**	esqui**amos**
esquí**as**	esqui**áis**
esquí**a**	esquí**an**

imperfecto de indicativo

SINGULAR	PLURAL
esqui**aba**	esqui**ábamos**
esqui**abas**	esqui**abais**
esqui**aba**	esqui**aban**

pretérito

SINGULAR	PLURAL
esqui**é**	esqui**amos**
esqui**aste**	esqui**asteis**
esqui**ó**	esqui**aron**

futuro

SINGULAR	PLURAL
esquiar**é**	esquiar**emos**
esquiar**ás**	esquiar**éis**
esquiar**á**	esquiar**án**

condicional simple

SINGULAR	PLURAL
esquiar**ía**	esquiar**íamos**
esquiar**ías**	esquiar**íais**
esquiar**ía**	esquiar**ían**

presente de subjuntivo

SINGULAR	PLURAL
esquí**e**	esqui**emos**
esquí**es**	esqui**éis**
esquí**e**	esquí**en**

imperfecto de subjuntivo

SINGULAR	PLURAL
esquiar**a**	esquiár**amos**
esquiar**as**	esquiar**ais**
esquiar**a**	esquar**an**
OR	
esquias**e**	esquiás**emos**
esquias**es**	esquias**eis**
esquias**e**	esquias**en**

imperativo

SINGULAR	PLURAL
—	esquiemos
esquía; no esquíes	esquiad; no esquiéis
esquíe	esquíen

perfecto de indicativo

SINGULAR	PLURAL
he esquiado	**hemos** esquiado
has esquiado	**habéis** esquiado
ha esquiado	**han** esquiado

pluscuamperfecto de indicativo

SINGULAR	PLURAL
había esquiado	**habíamos** esquiado
habías esquiado	**habíais** esquiado
había esquiado	**habían** esquiado

pretérito anterior

SINGULAR	PLURAL
hube esquiado	**hubimos** esquiado
hubiste esquiado	**hubisteis** esquiado
hubo esquiado	**hubieron** esquiado

futuro perfecto

SINGULAR	PLURAL
habré esquiado	**habremos** esquiado
habrás esquiado	**habréis** esquiado
habrá esquiado	**habrán** esquiado

condicional compuesto

SINGULAR	PLURAL
habría esquiado	**habríamos** esquiado
habrías esquiado	**habríais** esquiado
habría esquiado	**habrían** esquiado

perfecto de subjuntivo

SINGULAR	PLURAL
haya esquiado	**hayamos** esquiado
hayas esquiado	**hayáis** esquiado
haya esquiado	**hayan** esquiado

pluscuamperfecto de subjuntivo

SINGULAR	PLURAL
hubiera esquiado	**hubiéramos** esquiado
hubieras esquiado	**hubierais** esquiado
hubiera esquiado	**hubieran** esquiado
OR	
hubiese esquiado	**hubiésemos** esquiado
hubieses esquiado	**hubieseis** esquiado
hubiese esquiado	**hubiesen** esquiado

gerundio **estando** participio de pasado **estado**

SINGULAR	PLURAL
presente de indicativo	
est**oy**	est**amos**
est**ás**	est**áis**
est**á**	est**án**
imperfecto de indicativo	
est**aba**	est**ábamos**
est**abas**	est**abais**
est**aba**	est**aban**
pretérito	
estuv**e**	estuv**imos**
estuv**iste**	estuv**isteis**
estuv**o**	estuv**ieron**
futuro	
estar**é**	estar**emos**
estar**ás**	estar**éis**
estar**á**	estar**án**
condicional simple	
estar**ía**	estar**íamos**
estar**ías**	estar**íais**
estar**ía**	estar**ían**
presente de subjuntivo	
est**é**	est**emos**
est**és**	est**éis**
est**é**	est**én**
imperfecto de subjuntivo	
estuvier**a**	estuviér**amos**
estuvier**as**	estuvier**ais**
estuvier**a**	estuvier**an**
OR	
estuvies**e**	estuviés**emos**
estuvies**es**	estuvies**eis**
estuvies**e**	estuvies**en**
imperativo	
—	estemos
está; no estés	estad; no estéis
esté	estén

SINGULAR	PLURAL
perfecto de indicativo	
he estado	**hemos** estado
has estado	**habéis** estado
ha estado	**han** estado
pluscuamperfecto de indicativo	
había estado	**habíamos** estado
habías estado	**habíais** estado
había estado	**habían** estado
pretérito anterior	
hube estado	**hubimos** estado
hubiste estado	**hubisteis** estado
hubo estado	**hubieron** estado
futuro perfecto	
habré estado	**habremos** estado
habrás estado	**habréis** estado
habrá estado	**habrán** estado
condicional compuesto	
habría estado	**habríamos** estado
habrías estado	**habríais** estado
habría estado	**habrían** estado
perfecto de subjuntivo	
haya estado	**hayamos** estado
hayas estado	**hayáis** estado
haya estado	**hayan** estado
pluscuamperfecto de subjuntivo	
hubiera estado	**hubiéramos** estado
hubieras estado	**hubierais** estado
hubiera estado	**hubieran** estado
OR	
hubiese estado	**hubiésemos** estado
hubieses estado	**hubieseis** estado
hubiese estado	**hubiesen** estado

MUST KNOW VERB

SINGULAR	PLURAL
presente de indicativo	
estudi**o**	estudi**amos**
estudi**as**	estudi**áis**
estudi**a**	estudi**an**
imperfecto de indicativo	
estudi**aba**	estudi**ábamos**
estudi**abas**	estudi**abais**
estudi**aba**	estudi**aban**
pretérito	
estudi**é**	estudi**amos**
estudi**aste**	estudi**asteis**
estudi**ó**	estudi**aron**
futuro	
estudiar**é**	estudiar**emos**
estudiar**ás**	estudiar**éis**
estudiar**á**	estudiar**án**
condicional simple	
estudiar**ía**	estudiar**íamos**
estudiar**ías**	estudiar**íais**
estudiar**ía**	estudiar**ían**
presente de subjuntivo	
estudi**e**	estudi**emos**
estudi**es**	estudi**éis**
estudi**e**	estudi**en**
imperfecto de subjuntivo	
estudiar**a**	estudiár**amos**
estudiar**as**	estudiar**ais**
estudiar**a**	estudiar**an**
OR	
estudias**e**	estudiás**emos**
estudias**es**	estudias**eis**
estudias**e**	estudias**en**
imperativo	
—	estudiemos
estudia; no estudies	estudiad; no estudiéis
estudie	estudien

SINGULAR	PLURAL
perfecto de indicativo	
he estudiado	**hemos** estudiado
has estudiado	**habéis** estudiado
ha estudiado	**han** estudiado
pluscuamperfecto de indicativo	
había estudiado	**habíamos** estudiado
habías estudiado	**habíais** estudiado
había estudiado	**habían** estudiado
pretérito anterior	
hube estudiado	**hubimos** estudiado
hubiste estudiado	**hubisteis** estudiado
hubo estudiado	**hubieron** estudiado
futuro perfecto	
habré estudiado	**habremos** estudiado
habrás estudiado	**habréis** estudiado
habrá estudiado	**habrán** estudiado
condicional compuesto	
habría estudiado	**habríamos** estudiado
habrías estudiado	**habríais** estudiado
habría estudiado	**habrían** estudiado
perfecto de subjuntivo	
haya estudiado	**hayamos** estudiado
hayas estudiado	**hayáis** estudiado
haya estudiado	**hayan** estudiado
pluscuamperfecto de subjuntivo	
hubiera estudiado	**hubiéramos** estudiado
hubieras estudiado	**hubierais** estudiado
hubiera estudiado	**hubieran** estudiado
OR	
hubiese estudiado	**hubiésemos** estudiado
hubieses estudiado	**hubieseis** estudiado
hubiese estudiado	**hubiesen** estudiado

evaluar — to evaluate

gerundio **evaluando** — participio de pasado **evaluado**

presente de indicativo

SINGULAR	PLURAL
evalú**o**	evalu**amos**
evalú**as**	evalu**áis**
evalú**a**	evalú**an**

imperfecto de indicativo

SINGULAR	PLURAL
evalu**aba**	evalu**ábamos**
evalu**abas**	evalu**abais**
evalu**aba**	evalu**aban**

pretérito

SINGULAR	PLURAL
evalu**é**	evalu**amos**
evalu**aste**	evalu**asteis**
evalu**ó**	evalu**aron**

futuro

SINGULAR	PLURAL
evaluar**é**	evaluar**emos**
evaluar**ás**	evaluar**éis**
evaluar**á**	evaluar**án**

condicional simple

SINGULAR	PLURAL
evaluar**ía**	evaluar**íamos**
evaluar**ías**	evaluar**íais**
evaluar**ía**	evaluar**ían**

presente de subjuntivo

SINGULAR	PLURAL
evalú**e**	evalu**emos**
evalú**es**	evalu**éis**
evalú**e**	evalú**en**

imperfecto de subjuntivo

SINGULAR	PLURAL
evaluar**a**	evaluár**amos**
evaluar**as**	evaluar**ais**
evaluar**a**	evaluar**an**
OR	
evaluas**e**	evaluás**emos**
evaluas**es**	evaluas**eis**
evaluas**e**	evaluas**en**

imperativo

SINGULAR	PLURAL
—	evaluemos
evalúa; no evalúes	evaluad; no evaluéis
evalúe	evalúen

perfecto de indicativo

SINGULAR	PLURAL
he evaluado	**hemos** evaluado
has evaluado	**habéis** evaluado
ha evaluado	**han** evaluado

pluscuamperfecto de indicativo

SINGULAR	PLURAL
había evaluado	**habíamos** evaluado
habías evaluado	**habíais** evaluado
había evaluado	**habían** evaluado

pretérito anterior

SINGULAR	PLURAL
hube evaluado	**hubimos** evaluado
hubiste evaluado	**hubisteis** evaluado
hubo evaluado	**hubieron** evaluado

futuro perfecto

SINGULAR	PLURAL
habré evaluado	**habremos** evaluado
habrás evaluado	**habréis** evaluado
habrá evaluado	**habrán** evaluado

condicional compuesto

SINGULAR	PLURAL
habría evaluado	**habríamos** evaluado
habrías evaluado	**habríais** evaluado
habría evaluado	**habrían** evaluado

perfecto de subjuntivo

SINGULAR	PLURAL
haya evaluado	**hayamos** evaluado
hayas evaluado	**hayáis** evaluado
haya evaluado	**hayan** evaluado

pluscuamperfecto de subjuntivo

SINGULAR	PLURAL
hubiera evaluado	**hubiéramos** evaluado
hubieras evaluado	**hubierais** evaluado
hubiera evaluado	**hubieran** evaluado
OR	
hubiese evaluado	**hubiésemos** evaluado
hubieses evaluado	**hubieseis** evaluado
hubiese evaluado	**hubiesen** evaluado

gerundio **exigiendo** participio de pasado **exigido**

SINGULAR	PLURAL	SINGULAR	PLURAL
presente de indicativo		perfecto de indicativo	
exij**o**	exig**imos**	**he** exigido	**hemos** exigido
exig**es**	exig**ís**	**has** exigido	**habéis** exigido
exig**e**	exig**en**	**ha** exigido	**han** exigido
imperfecto de indicativo		pluscuamperfecto de indicativo	
exig**ía**	exig**íamos**	**había** exigido	**habíamos** exigido
exig**ías**	exig**íais**	**habías** exigido	**habíais** exigido
exig**ía**	exig**ían**	**había** exigido	**habían** exigido
pretérito		pretérito anterior	
exig**í**	exig**imos**	**hube** exigido	**hubimos** exigido
exig**iste**	exig**isteis**	**hubiste** exigido	**hubisteis** exigido
exig**ió**	exig**ieron**	**hubo** exigido	**hubieron** exigido
futuro		futuro perfecto	
exigir**é**	exigir**emos**	**habré** exigido	**habremos** exigido
exigir**ás**	exigir**éis**	**habrás** exigido	**habréis** exigido
exigir**á**	exigir**án**	**habrá** exigido	**habrán** exigido
condicional simple		condicional compuesto	
exigir**ía**	exigir**íamos**	**habría** exigido	**habríamos** exigido
exigir**ías**	exigir**íais**	**habrías** exigido	**habríais** exigido
exigir**ía**	exigir**ían**	**habría** exigido	**habrían** exigido
presente de subjuntivo		perfecto de subjuntivo	
exij**a**	exij**amos**	**haya** exigido	**hayamos** exigido
exij**as**	exij**áis**	**hayas** exigido	**hayáis** exigido
exij**a**	exij**an**	**haya** exigido	**hayan** exigido
imperfecto de subjuntivo		pluscuamperfecto de subjuntivo	
exigier**a**	exigiér**amos**	**hubiera** exigido	**hubiéramos** exigido
exigier**as**	exigier**ais**	**hubieras** exigido	**hubierais** exigido
exigier**a**	exigier**an**	**hubiera** exigido	**hubieran** exigido
OR		OR	
exigies**e**	exigiés**emos**	**hubiese** exigido	**hubiésemos** exigido
exigies**es**	exigies**eis**	**hubieses** exigido	**hubieseis** exigido
exigies**e**	exigies**en**	**hubiese** exigido	**hubiesen** exigido

imperativo

—	exijamos
exige; no exijas	exigid; no exijáis
exija	exijan

fabricar — to fabricate, to manufacture

gerundio **fabricando** participio de pasado **fabricado**

SINGULAR	PLURAL	SINGULAR	PLURAL
presente de indicativo		perfecto de indicativo	
fabric**o**	fabric**amos**	**he** fabricado	**hemos** fabricado
fabric**as**	fabric**áis**	**has** fabricado	**habéis** fabricado
fabric**a**	fabric**an**	**ha** fabricado	**han** fabricado
imperfecto de indicativo		pluscuamperfecto de indicativo	
fabric**aba**	fabric**ábamos**	**había** fabricado	**habíamos** fabricado
fabric**abas**	fabric**abais**	**habías** fabricado	**habíais** fabricado
fabric**aba**	fabric**aban**	**había** fabricado	**habían** fabricado
pretérito		pretérito anterior	
fabriqu**é**	fabric**amos**	**hube** fabricado	**hubimos** fabricado
fabric**aste**	fabric**asteis**	**hubiste** fabricado	**hubisteis** fabricado
fabric**ó**	fabric**aron**	**hubo** fabricado	**hubieron** fabricado
futuro		futuro perfecto	
fabricar**é**	fabricar**emos**	**habré** fabricado	**habremos** fabricado
fabricar**ás**	fabricar**éis**	**habrás** fabricado	**habréis** fabricado
fabricar**á**	fabricar**án**	**habrá** fabricado	**habrán** fabricado
condicional simple		condicional compuesto	
fabricar**ía**	fabricar**íamos**	**habría** fabricado	**habríamos** fabricado
fabricar**ías**	fabricar**íais**	**habrías** fabricado	**habríais** fabricado
fabricar**ía**	fabricar**ían**	**habría** fabricado	**habrían** fabricado
presente de subjuntivo		perfecto de subjuntivo	
fabriqu**e**	fabriqu**emos**	**haya** fabricado	**hayamos** fabricado
fabriqu**es**	fabriqu**éis**	**hayas** fabricado	**hayáis** fabricado
fabriqu**e**	fabriqu**en**	**haya** fabricado	**hayan** fabricado
imperfecto de subjuntivo		pluscuamperfecto de subjuntivo	
fabricar**a**	fabricár**amos**	**hubiera** fabricado	**hubiéramos** fabricado
fabricar**as**	fabricar**ais**	**hubieras** fabricado	**hubierais** fabricado
fabricar**a**	fabricar**an**	**hubiera** fabricado	**hubieran** fabricado
OR		OR	
fabricas**e**	fabricás**emos**	**hubiese** fabricado	**hubiésemos** fabricado
fabricas**es**	fabricas**eis**	**hubieses** fabricado	**hubieseis** fabricado
fabricas**e**	fabricas**en**	**hubiese** fabricado	**hubiesen** fabricado

imperativo

—	fabriquemos
fabrica; no fabriques	fabricad; no fabriquéis
fabrique	fabriquen

to lack, to miss **faltar**

gerundio **faltando** participio de pasado **faltado**

SINGULAR	PLURAL
presente de indicativo	
falt**o**	falt**amos**
falt**as**	falt**iás**
falt**a**	falt**an**
imperfecto de indicativo	
falt**aba**	falt**ábamos**
falt**abas**	falt**abais**
falt**aba**	falt**aban**
pretérito	
falt**é**	falt**amos**
falt**aste**	falt**asteis**
falt**ó**	falt**aron**
futuro	
faltar**é**	faltar**emos**
faltar**ás**	faltar**éis**
faltar**á**	faltar**án**
condicional simple	
faltar**ía**	faltar**íamos**
faltar**ías**	faltar**íais**
faltar**ía**	faltar**ían**
presente de subjuntivo	
falt**e**	falt**emos**
falt**es**	falt**éis**
falt**e**	falt**en**
imperfecto de subjuntivo	
faltar**a**	faltár**amos**
faltar**as**	faltar**ais**
faltar**a**	faltar**an**
OR	
faltas**e**	faltás**emos**
faltas**es**	faltas**eis**
faltas**e**	faltas**en**
imperativo	
—	faltemos
falta; no faltes	faltad; no faltéis
falte	falten

SINGULAR	PLURAL
perfecto de indicativo	
he faltado	**hemos** faltado
has faltado	**habéis** faltado
ha faltado	**han** faltado
pluscuamperfecto de indicativo	
había faltado	**habíamos** faltado
habías faltado	**habíais** faltado
había faltado	**habían** faltado
pretérito anterior	
hube faltado	**hubimos** faltado
hubiste faltado	**hubisteis** faltado
hubo faltado	**hubieron** faltado
futuro perfecto	
habré faltado	**habremos** faltado
habrás faltado	**habréis** faltado
habrá faltado	**habrán** faltado
condicional compuesto	
habría faltado	**habríamos** faltado
habrías faltado	**habríais** faltado
habría faltado	**habrían** faltado
perfecto de subjuntivo	
haya faltado	**hayamos** faltado
hayas faltado	**hayáis** faltado
haya faltado	**hayan** faltado
pluscuamperfecto de subjuntivo	
hubiera faltado	**hubiéramos** faltado
hubieras faltado	**hubierais** faltado
hubiera faltado	**hubieran** faltado
OR	
hubiese faltado	**hubiésemos** faltado
hubieses faltado	**hubieseis** faltado
hubiese faltado	**hubiesen** faltado

favorecer — to favor

gerundio **favoreciendo** — participio de pasado **favorecido**

SINGULAR	PLURAL
presente de indicativo	
favorezc**o**	favorec**emos**
favorec**es**	favorec**éis**
favorec**e**	favorec**en**
imperfecto de indicativo	
favorec**ía**	favorec**íamos**
favorec**ías**	favorec**íais**
favorec**ía**	favorec**ían**
pretérito	
favorec**í**	favorec**imos**
favorec**iste**	favorec**isteis**
favorec**ió**	favorec**ieron**
futuro	
favorecer**é**	favorecer**emos**
favorecer**ás**	favorecer**éis**
favorecer**á**	favorecer**án**
condicional simple	
favorecer**ía**	favorecer**íamos**
favorecer**ías**	favorecer**íais**
favorecer**ía**	favorecer**ían**
presente de subjuntivo	
favorezc**a**	favorezc**amos**
favorezc**as**	favorezc**áis**
favorezc**a**	favorezc**an**
imperfecto de subjuntivo	
favorecier**a**	favoreciér**amos**
favorecier**as**	favorecier**ais**
favorecier**a**	favorecier**an**
OR	
favoreciese**e**	favoreciés**emos**
favorecies**es**	favorecies**eis**
favorecies**e**	favorecies**en**
imperativo	
—	favorezcamos
favorece;	favoreced;
no favorezcas	no favorezcáis
favorezca	favorezcan

SINGULAR	PLURAL
perfecto de indicativo	
he favorecido	**hemos** favorecido
has favorecido	**habéis** favorecido
ha favorecido	**han** favorecido
pluscuamperfecto de indicativo	
había favorecido	**habíamos** favorecido
habías favorecido	**habíais** favorecido
había favorecido	**habían** favorecido
pretérito anterior	
hube favorecido	**hubimos** favorecido
hubiste favorecido	**hubisteis** favorecido
hubo favorecido	**hubieron** favorecido
futuro perfecto	
habré favorecido	**habremos** favorecido
habrás favorecido	**habréis** favorecido
habrá favorecido	**habrán** favorecido
condicional compuesto	
habría favorecido	**habríamos** favorecido
habrías favorecido	**habríais** favorecido
habría favorecido	**habrían** favorecido
perfecto de subjuntivo	
haya favorecido	**hayamos** favorecido
hayas favorecido	**hayáis** favorecido
haya favorecido	**hayan** favorecido
pluscuamperfecto de subjuntivo	
hubiera favorecido	**hubiéramos** favorecido
hubieras favorecido	**hubierais** favorecido
hubiera favorecido	**hubieran** favorecido
OR	
hubiese favorecido	**hubiésemos** favorecido
hubieses favorecido	**hubieseis** favorecido
hubiese favorecido	**hubiesen** favorecido

gerundio **felicitando** participio de pasado **felicitado**

SINGULAR	PLURAL
presente de indicativo	
felicit**o**	felicit**amos**
felicit**as**	felicit**áis**
felicit**a**	felicit**an**
imperfecto de indicativo	
felicit**aba**	felicit**ábamos**
felicit**abas**	felicit**abais**
felicit**aba**	felicit**aban**
pretérito	
felicit**é**	felicit**amos**
felicit**aste**	felicit**asteis**
felicit**ó**	felicit**aron**
futuro	
felicitar**é**	felicitar**emos**
felicitar**ás**	felicitar**éis**
felicitar**á**	felicitar**án**
condicional simple	
felicitar**ía**	felicitar**íamos**
felicitar**ías**	felicitar**íais**
felicitar**ía**	felicitar**ían**
presente de subjuntivo	
felicit**e**	felicit**emos**
felicit**es**	felicit**éis**
felicit**e**	felicit**en**
imperfecto de subjuntivo	
felicitar**a**	felicitár**amos**
felicitar**as**	felicitar**ais**
felicitar**a**	felicitar**an**
OR	
felicitas**e**	felicitás**emos**
felicitas**es**	felicitas**eis**
felicitas**e**	felicitas**en**
imperativo	
—	felicitemos
felicita; no felicites	felicitad; no felicitéis
felicite	feliciten

SINGULAR	PLURAL
perfecto de indicativo	
he felicitado	**hemos** felicitado
has felicitado	**habéis** felicitado
ha felicitado	**han** felicitado
pluscuamperfecto de indicativo	
había felicitado	**habíamos** felicitado
habías felicitado	**habíais** felicitado
había felicitado	**habían** felicitado
pretérito anterior	
hube felicitado	**hubimos** felicitado
hubiste felicitado	**hubisteis** felicitado
hubo felicitado	**hubieron** felicitado
futuro perfecto	
habré felicitado	**habremos** felicitado
habrás felicitado	**habréis** felicitado
habrá felicitado	**habrán** felicitado
condicional compuesto	
habría felicitado	**habríamos** felicitado
habrías felicitado	**habríais** felicitado
habría felicitado	**habrían** felicitado
perfecto de subjuntivo	
haya felicitado	**hayamos** felicitado
hayas felicitado	**hayáis** felicitado
haya felicitado	**hayan** felicitado
pluscuamperfecto de subjuntivo	
hubiera felicitado	**hubiéramos** felicitado
hubieras felicitado	**hubierais** felicitado
hubiera felicitado	**hubieran** felicitado
OR	
hubiese felicitado	**hubiésemos** felicitado
hubieses felicitado	**hubieseis** felicitado
hubiese felicitado	**hubiesen** felicitado

festejar — to celebrate

gerundio **festejando** participio de pasado **festejado**

SINGULAR	PLURAL	SINGULAR	PLURAL
presente de indicativo		perfecto de indicativo	
festej**o**	festej**amos**	**he** festejado	**hemos** festejado
festej**as**	festej**áis**	**has** festejado	**habéis** festejado
festej**a**	festej**an**	**ha** festejado	**han** festejado
imperfecto de indicativo		pluscuamperfecto de indicativo	
festej**aba**	festej**ábamos**	**había** festejado	**habíamos** festejado
festej**abas**	festej**abais**	**habías** festejado	**habíais** festejado
fetsej**aba**	festej**aban**	**había** festejado	**habían** festejado
pretérito		pretérito anterior	
festej**é**	festej**amos**	**hube** festejado	**hubimos** festejado
festej**aste**	festej**asteis**	**hubiste** festejado	**hubisteis** festejado
festej**ó**	festej**aron**	**hubo** festejado	**hubieron** festejado
futuro		futuro perfecto	
festejar**é**	festejar**emos**	**habré** festejado	**habremos** festejado
festejar**ás**	festejar**éis**	**habrás** festejado	**habréis** festejado
festejar**á**	festejar**án**	**habrá** festejado	**habrán** festejado
condicional simple		condicional compuesto	
festejar**ía**	festejar**íamos**	**habría** festejado	**habríamos** festejado
festejar**ías**	festejar**íais**	**habrías** festejado	**habríais** festejado
festejar**ía**	festejar**ían**	**habría** festejado	**habrían** festejado
presente de subjuntivo		perfecto de subjuntivo	
festej**e**	festej**emos**	**haya** festejado	**hayamos** festejado
festej**es**	festej**éis**	**hayas** festejado	**hayáis** festejado
festej**e**	festej**en**	**haya** festejado	**hayan** festejado
imperfecto de subjuntivo		pluscuamperfecto de subjuntivo	
festejar**a**	festejár**amos**	**hubiera** festejado	**hubiéramos** festejado
festejar**as**	festejar**ais**	**hubieras** festejado	**hubierais** festejado
festejar**a**	festejar**an**	**hubiera** festejado	**hubieran** festejado
OR		OR	
festejas**e**	festejás**emos**	**hubiese** festejado	**hubiésemos** festejado
festejas**es**	festejas**eis**	**hubieses** festejado	**hubieseis** festejado
festejas**e**	festejas**en**	**hubiese** festejado	**hubiesen** festejado

imperativo

—	festejemos
festeja; no festejes	festejad; no festejéis
festeje	festejen

gerundio **fiando** participio de pasado **fiado**

SINGULAR	PLURAL	SINGULAR	PLURAL
presente de indicativo		perfecto de indicativo	
fí**o**	fi**amos**	**he** fiado	**hemos** fiado
fí**as**	fi**áis**	**has** fiado	**habéis** fiado
fí**a**	fí**an**	**ha** fiado	**han** fiado
imperfecto de indicativo		pluscuamperfecto de indicativo	
fi**aba**	fi**ábamos**	**había** fiado	**habíamos** fiado
fi**abas**	fi**abais**	**habías** fiado	**habíais** fiado
fi**aba**	fi**aban**	**había** fiado	**habían** fiado
pretérito		pretérito anterior	
fi**é**	fi**amos**	**hube** fiado	**hubimos** fiado
fi**aste**	fi**asteis**	**hubiste** fiado	**hubisteis** fiado
fi**ó**	fi**aron**	**hubo** fiado	**hubieron** fiado
futuro		futuro perfecto	
fiar**é**	fiar**emos**	**habré** fiado	**habremos** fiado
fiar**ás**	fiar**éis**	**habrás** fiado	**habréis** fiado
fiar**á**	fiar**án**	**habrá** fiado	**habrán** fiado
condicional simple		condicional compuesto	
fiar**ía**	fiar**íamos**	**habría** fiado	**habríamos** fiado
fiar**ías**	fiar**íais**	**habrías** fiado	**habríais** fiado
fiar**ía**	fiar**ían**	**habría** fiado	**habrían** fiado
presente de subjuntivo		perfecto de subjuntivo	
fí**e**	fi**emos**	**haya** fiado	**hayamos** fiado
fí**es**	fi**éis**	**hayas** fiado	**hayáis** fiado
fí**e**	fí**en**	**haya** fiado	**hayan** fiado
imperfecto de subjuntivo		pluscuamperfecto de subjuntivo	
fiar**a**	fiár**amos**	**hubiera** fiado	**hubiéramos** fiado
fiar**as**	fiar**ais**	**hubieras** fiado	**hubierais** fiado
fiar**a**	fiar**an**	**hubiera** fiado	**hubieran** fiado
OR		OR	
fias**e**	fiás**emos**	**hubiese** fiado	**hubiésemos** fiado
fias**es**	fias**eis**	**hubieses** fiado	**hubieseis** fiado
fias**e**	fias**en**	**hubiese** fiado	**hubiesen** fiado

imperativo

—	fiemos
fía; no fíes	fiad; no fiéis
fíe	fíen

fiarse — to trust

gerundio **fiándose** — participio de pasado **fiado**

SINGULAR	PLURAL
presente de indicativo	
me fí**o**	nos fi**amos**
te fí**as**	os fi**áis**
se fí**a**	se fí**an**
imperfecto de indicativo	
me fi**aba**	nos fi**ábamos**
te fi**abas**	os fi**abais**
se fi**aba**	se fi**aban**
pretérito	
me fi**é**	nos fi**amos**
te fi**aste**	os fi**asteis**
se fi**ó**	se fi**aron**
futuro	
me fiar**é**	nos fiar**emos**
te fiar**ás**	os fiar**éis**
se fiar**á**	se fiar**án**
condicional simple	
me fiar**ía**	nos fiar**íamos**
te fiar**ías**	os fiar**íais**
se fiar**ía**	se fiar**ían**
presente de subjuntivo	
me fí**e**	nos fi**emos**
te fí**es**	os fi**éis**
se fí**e**	se fí**en**
imperfecto de subjuntivo	
me fiar**a**	nos fiár**amos**
te fiar**as**	os fiar**ais**
se fiar**a**	se fiar**an**
OR	
me fias**e**	nos fiás**emos**
te fias**es**	os fias**eis**
se fias**e**	se fias**en**
imperativo	
—	fiémonos
fíate; no te fíes	fiaos; no os fiéis
fíese	fíense

SINGULAR	PLURAL
perfecto de indicativo	
me he fiado	**nos hemos** fiado
te has fiado	**os habéis** fiado
se ha fiado	**se han** fiado
pluscuamperfecto de indicativo	
me había fiado	**nos habíamos** fiado
te habías fiado	**os habíais** fiado
se había fiado	**se habían** fiado
pretérito anterior	
me hube fiado	**nos hubimos** fiado
te hubiste fiado	**os hubisteis** fiado
se hubo fiado	**se hubieron** fiado
futuro perfecto	
me habré fiado	**nos habremos** fiado
te habrás fiado	**os habréis** fiado
se habrá fiado	**se habrán** fiado
condicional compuesto	
me habría fiado	**nos habríamos** fiado
te habrías fiado	**os habríais** fiado
se habría fiado	**se habrían** fiado
perfecto de subjuntivo	
me haya fiado	**nos hayamos** fiado
te hayas fiado	**os hayáis** fiado
se haya fiado	**se hayan** fiado
pluscuamperfecto de subjuntivo	
me hubiera fiado	**nos hubiéramos** fiado
te hubieras fiado	**os hubierais** fiado
se hubiera fiado	**se hubieran** fiado
OR	
me hubiese fiado	**nos hubiésemos** fiado
te hubieses fiado	**os hubieseis** fiado
se hubiese fiado	**se hubiesen** fiado

gerundio **fijándose** participio de pasado **fijado**

SINGULAR	PLURAL
presente de indicativo	
me fij**o**	nos fij**amos**
te fij**as**	os fij**áis**
se fij**a**	se fij**an**
imperfecto de indicativo	
me fij**aba**	nos fij**ábamos**
te fij**abas**	os fij**abais**
se fij**aba**	se fij**aban**
pretérito	
me fij**é**	nos fij**amos**
te fij**aste**	os fij**asteis**
se fij**ó**	se fij**aron**
futuro	
me fijar**é**	nos fijar**emos**
te fijar**ás**	os fijar**éis**
se fijar**á**	se fijar**án**
condicional simple	
me fijar**ía**	nos fijar**íamos**
te fijar**ías**	os fijar**íais**
se fijar**ía**	se fijar**ían**
presente de subjuntivo	
me fij**e**	nos fij**emos**
te fij**es**	os fij**éis**
se fij**e**	se fij**en**
imperfecto de subjuntivo	
me fijar**a**	nos fijár**amos**
te fijar**as**	os fijar**ais**
se fijar**a**	se fijar**an**
OR	
me fijas**e**	nos fijás**emos**
te fijas**es**	os fijas**eis**
se fijas**e**	se fijas**en**
imperativo	
—	fijémonos
fíjate; no te fijes	fijaos; no os fijéis
fíjese	fíjense

SINGULAR	PLURAL
perfecto de indicativo	
me he fijado	**nos hemos** fijado
te has fijado	**os habéis** fijado
se ha fijado	**se han** fijado
pluscuamperfecto de indicativo	
me había fijado	**nos habíamos** fijado
te habías fijado	**os habíais** fijado
se había fijado	**se habían** fijado
pretérito anterior	
me hube fijado	**nos hubimos** fijado
te hubiste fijado	**os hubisteis** fijado
se hubo fijado	**se hubieron** fijado
futuro perfecto	
me habré fijado	**nos habremos** fijado
te habrás fijado	**os habréis** fijado
se habrá fijado	**se habrán** fijado
condicional compuesto	
me habría fijado	**nos habríamos** fijado
te habrías fijado	**os habríais** fijado
se habría fijado	**se habrían** fijado
perfecto de subjuntivo	
me haya fijado	**nos hayamos** fijado
te hayas fijado	**os hayáis** fijado
se haya fijado	**se hayan** fijado
pluscuamperfecto de subjuntivo	
me hubiera fijado	**nos hubiéramos** fijado
te hubieras fijado	**os hubierais** fijado
se hubiera fijado	**se hubieran** fijado
OR	
me hubiese fijado	**nos hubiésemos** fijado
te hubieses fijado	**os hubieseis** fijado
se hubiese fijado	**se hubiesen** fijado

finalizar — to finish, to end

gerundio **finalizando** participio de pasado **finalizado**

SINGULAR	PLURAL	SINGULAR	PLURAL
presente de indicativo		perfecto de indicativo	
finaliz**o**	finaliz**amos**	**he** finalizado	**hemos** finalizado
finaliz**as**	finaliz**áis**	**has** finalizado	**habéis** finalizado
finaliz**a**	finaliz**an**	**ha** finalizado	**han** finalizado
imperfecto de indicativo		pluscuamperfecto de indicativo	
finaliz**aba**	finaliz**ábamos**	**había** finalizado	**habíamos** finalizado
finaliz**abas**	finaliz**abais**	**habías** finalizado	**habíais** finalizado
finaliz**aba**	finaliz**aban**	**había** finalizado	**habían** finalizado
pretérito		pretérito anterior	
finalic**é**	finaliz**amos**	**hube** finalizado	**hubimos** finalizado
finaliz**aste**	finaliz**asteis**	**hubiste** finalizado	**hubisteis** finalizado
finaliz**ó**	finaliz**aron**	**hubo** finalizado	**hubieron** finalizado
futuro		futuro perfecto	
finalizar**é**	finalizar**emos**	**habré** finalizado	**habremos** finalizado
finalizar**ás**	finalizar**éis**	**habrás** finalizado	**habréis** finalizado
finalizar**á**	finalizar**án**	**habrá** finalizado	**habrán** finalizado
condicional simple		condicional compuesto	
finalizar**ía**	finalizar**íamos**	**habría** finalizado	**habríamos** finalizado
finalizar**ías**	finalizar**íais**	**habrías** finalizado	**habríais** finalizado
finalizar**ía**	finalizar**ían**	**habría** finalizado	**habrían** finalizado
presente de subjuntivo		perfecto de subjuntivo	
finalic**e**	finalic**emos**	**haya** finalizado	**hayamos** finalizado
finalic**es**	finalic**éis**	**hayas** finalizado	**hayáis** finalizado
finalic**e**	finalic**en**	**haya** finalizado	**hayan** finalizado
imperfecto de subjuntivo		pluscuamperfecto de subjuntivo	
finalizar**a**	finalizár**amos**	**hubiera** finalizado	**hubiéramos** finalizado
finalizar**as**	finalizar**ais**	**hubieras** finalizado	**hubierais** finalizado
finalizar**a**	finalizar**an**	**hubiera** finalizado	**hubieran** finalizado
OR		OR	
finalizas**e**	finalizás**emos**	**hubiese** finalizado	**hubiésemos** finalizado
finalizas**es**	finalizas**eis**	**hubieses** finalizado	**hubieseis** finalizado
finalizas**e**	finalizas**en**	**hubiese** finalizado	**hubiesen** finalizado

imperativo

—	finalicemos
finaliza; no finalices	finalizad; no finalicéis
finalice	finalicen

gerundio **fingiendo** — participio de pasado **fingido**

SINGULAR	PLURAL
presente de indicativo	
fin**jo**	fing**imos**
fing**es**	fing**ís**
fing**e**	fing**en**
imperfecto de indicativo	
fing**ía**	fing**íamos**
fing**ías**	fing**íais**
fing**ía**	fing**ían**
pretérito	
fing**í**	fing**imos**
fing**iste**	fing**isteis**
fing**ió**	fing**ieron**
futuro	
fingir**é**	fingir**emos**
fingir**ás**	fingir**éis**
fingir**á**	fingir**án**
condicional simple	
fingir**ía**	fingir**íamos**
fingir**ías**	fingir**íais**
fingir**ía**	fingir**ían**
presente de subjuntivo	
finj**a**	finj**amos**
finj**as**	finj**áis**
finj**a**	finj**an**
imperfecto de subjuntivo	
fingier**a**	fingiér**amos**
fingier**as**	fingier**ais**
fingier**a**	fingier**an**
OR	
fingies**e**	fingiés**emos**
fingies**es**	fingies**eis**
fingies**e**	fingies**en**
imperativo	
—	finjamos
finge; no finjas	fingid; no finjáis
finja	finjan

SINGULAR	PLURAL
perfecto de indicativo	
he fingido	**hemos** fingido
has fingido	**habéis** fingido
ha fingido	**han** fingido
pluscuamperfecto de indicativo	
había fingido	**habíamos** fingido
habías fingido	**habíais** fingido
había fingido	**habían** fingido
pretérito anterior	
hube fingido	**hubimos** fingido
hubiste fingido	**hubisteis** fingido
hubo fingido	**hubieron** fingido
futuro perfecto	
habré fingido	**habremos** fingido
habrás fingido	**habréis** fingido
habrá fingido	**habrán** fingido
condicional compuesto	
habría fingido	**habríamos** fingido
habrías fingido	**habríais** fingido
habría fingido	**habrían** fingido
perfecto de subjuntivo	
haya fingido	**hayamos** fingido
hayas fingido	**hayáis** fingido
haya fingido	**hayan** fingido
pluscuamperfecto de subjuntivo	
hubiera fingido	**hubiéramos** fingido
hubieras fingido	**hubierais** fingido
hubiera fingido	**hubieran** fingido
OR	
hubiese fingido	**hubiésemos** fingido
hubieses fingido	**hubieseis** fingido
hubiese fingido	**hubiesen** fingido

firmar — to sign

gerundio **firmando** participio de pasado **firmado**

SINGULAR	PLURAL
presente de indicativo	
firm**o**	firm**amos**
firm**as**	firm**áis**
firm**a**	firm**an**
imperfecto de indicativo	
firm**aba**	firm**ábamos**
firm**abas**	firm**abais**
firm**aba**	firm**aban**
pretérito	
firm**é**	firm**amos**
firm**aste**	firm**asteis**
firm**ó**	firm**aron**
futuro	
firmar**é**	firmar**emos**
firmar**ás**	firmar**éis**
firmar**á**	firmar**án**
condicional simple	
firmar**ía**	firmar**íamos**
firmar**ías**	firmar**íais**
firmar**ía**	firmar**ían**
presente de subjuntivo	
firm**e**	firm**emos**
firm**es**	firm**éis**
firm**e**	firm**en**
imperfecto de subjuntivo	
firmar**a**	firmár**amos**
firmar**as**	firmar**ais**
firmar**a**	firmar**an**
OR	
firmas**e**	firmás**emos**
firmas**es**	firmas**eis**
firmas**e**	firmas**en**
imperativo	
—	firmemos
firma; no firmes	firmad; no firméis
firme	firmen

SINGULAR	PLURAL
perfecto de indicativo	
he firmado	**hemos** firmado
has firmado	**habéis** firmado
ha firmado	**han** firmado
pluscuamperfecto de indicativo	
había firmado	**habíamos** firmado
habías firmado	**habíais** firmado
había firmado	**habían** firmado
pretérito anterior	
hube firmado	**hubimos** firmado
hubiste firmado	**hubisteis** firmado
hubo firmado	**hubieron** firmado
futuro perfecto	
habré firmado	**habremos** firmado
habrás firmado	**habréis** firmado
habrá firmado	**habrán** firmado
condicional compuesto	
habría firmado	**habríamos** firmado
habrías firmado	**habríais** firmado
habría firmado	**habrían** firmado
perfecto de subjuntivo	
haya firmado	**hayamos** firmado
hayas firmado	**hayáis** firmado
haya firmado	**hayan** firmado
pluscuamperfecto de subjuntivo	
hubiera firmado	**hubiéramos** firmado
hubieras firmado	**hubierais** firmado
hubiera firmado	**hubieran** firmado
OR	
hubiese firmado	**hubiésemos** firmado
hubieses firmado	**hubieseis** firmado
hubiese firmado	**hubiesen** firmado

to form, to shape — formar

gerundio **formando** participio de pasado **formado**

presente de indicativo

SINGULAR	PLURAL
form**o**	form**amos**
form**as**	form**áis**
form**a**	form**an**

imperfecto de indicativo

SINGULAR	PLURAL
form**aba**	form**ábamos**
form**abas**	form**abais**
form**aba**	form**aban**

pretérito

SINGULAR	PLURAL
form**é**	form**amos**
form**aste**	form**asteis**
form**ó**	form**aron**

futuro

SINGULAR	PLURAL
formar**é**	formar**emos**
formar**ás**	formar**éis**
formar**á**	formar**án**

condicional simple

SINGULAR	PLURAL
formar**ía**	formar**íamos**
formar**ías**	formar**íais**
formar**ía**	formar**ían**

presente de subjuntivo

SINGULAR	PLURAL
form**e**	form**emos**
form**es**	form**éis**
form**e**	form**en**

imperfecto de subjuntivo

SINGULAR	PLURAL
formar**a**	formár**amos**
formar**as**	formar**ais**
formar**a**	formar**an**
OR	
formas**e**	formás**emos**
formas**es**	formas**eis**
formas**e**	formas**en**

imperativo

SINGULAR	PLURAL
—	formemos
forma; no formes	formad; no forméis
forme	formen

perfecto de indicativo

SINGULAR	PLURAL
he formado	**hemos** formado
has formado	**habéis** formado
ha formado	**han** formado

pluscuamperfecto de indicativo

SINGULAR	PLURAL
había formado	**habíamos** formado
habías formado	**habíais** formado
había formado	**habían** formado

pretérito anterior

SINGULAR	PLURAL
hube formado	**hubimos** formado
hubiste formado	**hubisteis** formado
hubo formado	**hubieron** formado

futuro perfecto

SINGULAR	PLURAL
habré formado	**habremos** formado
habrás formado	**habréis** formado
habrá formado	**habrán** formado

condicional compuesto

SINGULAR	PLURAL
habría formado	**habríamos** formado
habrías formado	**habríais** formado
habría formado	**habrían** formado

perfecto de subjuntivo

SINGULAR	PLURAL
haya formado	**hayamos** formado
hayas formado	**hayáis** formado
haya formado	**hayan** formado

pluscuamperfecto de subjuntivo

SINGULAR	PLURAL
hubiera formado	**hubiéramos** formado
hubieras formado	**hubierais** formado
hubiera formado	**hubieran** formado
OR	
hubiese formado	**hubiésemos** formado
hubieses formado	**hubieseis** formado
hubiese formado	**hubiesen** formado

forzar — to force, to strain

gerundio **forzando** participio de pasado **forzado**

SINGULAR	PLURAL
presente de indicativo	
fuerz**o**	forz**amos**
fuerz**as**	forz**áis**
fuerz**a**	fuerz**an**
imperfecto de indicativo	
forz**aba**	forz**ábamos**
forz**abas**	forz**abais**
forz**aba**	forz**aban**
pretérito	
forc**é**	forz**amos**
forz**aste**	forz**asteis**
forz**ó**	forz**aron**
futuro	
forzar**é**	forzar**emos**
forzar**ás**	forzar**éis**
forzar**á**	forzar**án**
condicional simple	
forzar**ía**	forzar**íamos**
forzar**ías**	forzar**íais**
forzar**ía**	forzar**ían**
presente de subjuntivo	
fuerc**e**	forc**emos**
fuerc**es**	forc**éis**
fuerc**e**	fuerc**en**
imperfecto de subjuntivo	
forzar**a**	forzár**amos**
forzar**as**	forzar**ais**
forzar**a**	forzar**an**
OR	
forzas**e**	forzás**emos**
forzas**es**	forzas**eis**
forzas**e**	forzas**en**
imperativo	
—	forcemos
fuerza; no fuerces	forzad; no forcéis
fuerce	fuercen

SINGULAR	PLURAL
perfecto de indicativo	
he forzado	**hemos** forzado
has forzado	**habéis** forzado
ha forzado	**han** forzado
pluscuamperfecto de indicativo	
había forzado	**habíamos** forzado
habías forzado	**habíais** forzado
había forzado	**habían** forzado
pretérito anterior	
hube forzado	**hubimos** forzado
hubiste forzado	**hubisteis** forzado
hubo forzado	**hubieron** forzado
futuro perfecto	
habré forzado	**habremos** forzado
habrás forzado	**habréis** forzado
habrá forzado	**habrán** forzado
condicional compuesto	
habría forzado	**habríamos** forzado
habrías forzado	**habríais** forzado
habría forzado	**habrían** forzado
perfecto de subjuntivo	
haya forzado	**hayamos** forzado
hayas forzado	**hayáis** forzado
haya forzado	**hayan** forzado
pluscuamperfecto de subjuntivo	
hubiera forzado	**hubiéramos** forzado
hubieras forzado	**hubierais** forzado
hubiera forzado	**hubieran** forzado
OR	
hubiese forzado	**hubiésemos** forzado
hubieses forzado	**hubieseis** forzado
hubiese forzado	**hubiesen** forzado

to wash dishes, to scrub — fregar

gerundio **fregando** participio de pasado **fregado**

SINGULAR	PLURAL
presente de indicativo	
frieg**o**	freg**amos**
frieg**as**	freg**áis**
frieg**a**	frieg**an**
imperfecto de indicativo	
freg**aba**	freg**ábamos**
freg**abas**	freg**abais**
freg**aba**	freg**aban**
pretérito	
fregu**é**	freg**amos**
freg**aste**	freg**asteis**
freg**ó**	freg**aron**
futuro	
fregar**é**	fregar**emos**
fregar**ás**	fregar**éis**
fregar**á**	fregar**án**
condicional simple	
fregar**ía**	fregar**íamos**
fregar**ías**	fregar**íais**
fregar**ía**	fregar**ían**
presente de subjuntivo	
friegu**e**	fregu**emos**
friegu**es**	fregu**éis**
friegu**e**	friegu**en**
imperfecto de subjuntivo	
fregar**a**	fregár**amos**
fregar**as**	fregar**ais**
fregar**a**	fregar**an**
OR	
fregas**e**	fregás**emos**
fregas**es**	fregas**eis**
fregas**e**	fregas**en**
imperativo	
—	freguemos
friega; no friegues	fregad; no freguéis
friegue	frieguen

SINGULAR	PLURAL
perfecto de indicativo	
he fregado	**hemos** fregado
has fregado	**habéis** fregado
ha fregado	**han** fregado
pluscuamperfecto de indicativo	
había fregado	**habíamos** fregado
habías fregado	**habíais** fregado
había fregado	**habían** fregado
pretérito anterior	
hube fregado	**hubimos** fregado
hubiste fregado	**hubisteis** fregado
hubo fregado	**hubieron** fregado
futuro perfecto	
habré fregado	**habremos** fregado
habrás fregado	**habréis** fregado
habrá fregado	**habrán** fregado
condicional compuesto	
habría fregado	**habríamos** fregado
habrías fregado	**habríais** fregado
habría fregado	**habrían** fregado
perfecto de subjuntivo	
haya fregado	**hayamos** fregado
hayas fregado	**hayáis** fregado
haya fregado	**hayan** fregado
pluscuamperfecto de subjuntivo	
hubiera fregado	**hubiéramos** fregado
hubieras fregado	**hubierais** fregado
hubiera fregado	**hubieran** fregado
OR	
hubiese fregado	**hubiésemos** fregado
hubieses fregado	**hubieseis** fregado
hubiese fregado	**hubiesen** fregado

freír

to fry

gerundio **friendo** participio de pasado **frito** *or* **freído**

SINGULAR	PLURAL
presente de indicativo	
frí**o**	fre**ímos**
frí**es**	fre**ís**
frí**e**	frí**en**
imperfecto de indicativo	
fre**ía**	fre**íamos**
fre**ías**	fre**íais**
fre**ía**	fre**ían**
pretérito	
fre**í**	fre**ímos**
fre**iste**	fre**isteis**
fri**ó**	fri**eron**
futuro	
freir**é**	freir**emos**
freir**ás**	freir**éis**
freir**á**	freir**án**
condicional simple	
freir**ía**	freir**íamos**
freir**ías**	freir**íais**
freir**ía**	freir**ían**
presente de subjuntivo	
frí**a**	fri**amos**
frí**as**	fri**áis**
frí**a**	frí**an**
imperfecto de subjuntivo	
frier**a**	friér**amos**
frier**as**	frier**ais**
frier**a**	frier**an**
OR	
fries**e**	friés**emos**
fries**es**	fries**eis**
fries**e**	fries**en**
imperativo	
—	friamos
fríe; no frías	freíd; no friáis
fría	frían

SINGULAR	PLURAL
perfecto de indicativo	
he frito	**hemos** frito
has frito	**habéis** frito
ha frito	**han** frito
pluscuamperfecto de indicativo	
había frito	**habíamos** frito
habías frito	**habíais** frito
había frito	**habían** frito
pretérito anterior	
hube frito	**hubimos** frito
hubiste frito	**hubisteis** frito
hubo frito	**hubieron** frito
futuro perfecto	
habré frito	**habremos** frito
habrás frito	**habréis** frito
habrá frito	**habrán** frito
condicional compuesto	
habría frito	**habríamos** frito
habrías frito	**habríais** frito
habría frito	**habrían** frito
perfecto de subjuntivo	
haya frito	**hayamos** frito
hayas frito	**hayáis** frito
haya frito	**hayan** frito
pluscuamperfecto de subjuntivo	
hubiera frito	**hubiéramos** frito
hubieras frito	**hubierais** frito
hubiera frito	**hubieran** frito
OR	
hubiese frito	**hubiésemos** frito
hubieses frito	**hubieseis** frito
hubiese frito	**hubiesen** frito

gerundio **fumando** participio de pasado **fumado**

SINGULAR	PLURAL	SINGULAR	PLURAL
presente de indicativo		perfecto de indicativo	
fum**o**	fum**amos**	**he** fumado	**hemos** fumado
fum**as**	fum**áis**	**has** fumado	**habéis** fumado
fum**a**	fum**an**	**ha** fumado	**han** fumado
imperfecto de indicativo		pluscuamperfecto de indicativo	
fum**aba**	fum**ábamos**	**había** fumado	**habíamos** fumado
fum**abas**	fum**abais**	**habías** fumado	**habíais** fumado
fum**aba**	fum**aban**	**había** fumado	**habían** fumado
pretérito		pretérito anterior	
fum**é**	fum**amos**	**hube** fumado	**hubimos** fumado
fum**aste**	fum**asteis**	**hubiste** fumado	**hubisteis** fumado
fum**ó**	fum**aron**	**hubo** fumado	**hubieron** fumado
futuro		futuro perfecto	
fumar**é**	fumar**emos**	**habré** fumado	**habremos** fumado
fumar**ás**	fumar**éis**	**habrás** fumado	**habréis** fumado
fumar**á**	fumar**án**	**habrá** fumado	**habrán** fumado
condicional simple		condicional compuesto	
fumar**ía**	fumar**íamos**	**habría** fumado	**habríamos** fumado
fumar**ías**	fumar**íais**	**habrías** fumado	**habríais** fumado
fumar**ía**	fumar**ían**	**habría** fumado	**habrían** fumado
presente de subjuntivo		perfecto de subjuntivo	
fum**e**	fum**emos**	**haya** fumado	**hayamos** fumado
fum**es**	fum**éis**	**hayas** fumado	**hayáis** fumado
fum**e**	fum**en**	**haya** fumado	**hayan** fumado
imperfecto de subjuntivo		pluscuamperfecto de subjuntivo	
fumar**a**	fumár**amos**	**hubiera** fumado	**hubiéramos** fumado
fumar**ás**	fumar**ais**	**hubieras** fumado	**hubierais** fumado
fumar**a**	fumar**an**	**hubiera** fumado	**hubieran** fumado
OR		OR	
fumas**e**	fumás**emos**	**hubiese** fumado	**hubiésemos** fumado
fumas**es**	fumas**eis**	**hubieses** fumado	**hubieseis** fumado
fumas**e**	fumas**en**	**hubiese** fumado	**hubiesen** fumado

imperativo

—	fumemos
fuma; no fumes	fumad; no fuméis
fume	fumen

funcionar — to function

gerundio **funcionando** participio de pasado **funcionado**

SINGULAR	PLURAL	SINGULAR	PLURAL
presente de indicativo		perfecto de indicativo	
funcion**o**	funcion**amos**	**he** funcionado	**hemos** funcionado
funcion**as**	funcion**áis**	**has** funcionado	**habéis** funcionado
funcion**a**	funcion**an**	**ha** funcionado	**han** funcionado
imperfecto de indicativo		pluscuamperfecto de indicativo	
funcion**aba**	funcion**ábamos**	**había** funcionado	**habíamos** funcionado
funcion**abas**	funcion**abais**	**habías** funcionado	**habíais** funcionado
funcion**aba**	funcion**aban**	**había** funcionado	**habían** funcionado
pretérito		pretérito anterior	
funcion**é**	funcion**amos**	**hube** funcionado	**hubimos** funcionado
funcion**aste**	funcion**asteis**	**hubiste** funcionado	**hubisteis** funcionado
funcion**ó**	funcion**aron**	**hubo** funcionado	**hubieron** funcionado
futuro		futuro perfecto	
funcionar**é**	funcionar**emos**	**habré** funcionado	**habremos** funcionado
funcionar**ás**	funcionar**éis**	**habrás** funcionado	**habréis** funcionado
funcionar**á**	funcionar**án**	**habrá** funcionado	**habrán** funcionado
condicional simple		condicional compuesto	
funcionar**ía**	funcionar**íamos**	**habría** funcionado	**habríamos** funcionado
funcionar**ías**	funcionar**íais**	**habrías** funcionado	**habríais** funcionado
funcionar**ía**	funcionar**ían**	**habría** funcionado	**habrían** funcionado
presente de subjuntivo		perfecto de subjuntivo	
funcion**e**	funcion**emos**	**haya** funcionado	**hayamos** funcionado
funcion**es**	funcion**éis**	**hayas** funcionado	**hayáis** funcionado
funcion**e**	funcion**en**	**haya** funcionado	**hayan** funcionado
imperfecto de subjuntivo		pluscuamperfecto de subjuntivo	
funcionar**a**	funcionár**amos**	**hubiera** funcionado	**hubiéramos** funcionado
funcionar**as**	funcionar**ais**	**hubieras** funcionado	**hubierais** funcionado
funcionar**a**	funcionar**an**	**hubiera** funcionado	**hubieran** funcionado
OR		OR	
funcionas**e**	funcionás**emos**	**hubiese** funcionado	**hubiésemos** funcionado
funcionas**es**	funionas**eis**	**hubieses** funcionado	**hubieseis** funcionado
funcionas**e**	funcionas**en**	**hubiese** funcionado	**hubiesen** funcionado

imperativo

—	funcionemos
funciona;	funcionad;
no funciones	no funcionéis
funcione	funcionen

SINGULAR	PLURAL	SINGULAR	PLURAL
presente de indicativo		perfecto de indicativo	
gan**o**	gan**amos**	**he** ganado	**hemos** ganado
gan**as**	gan**áis**	**has** ganado	**habéis** ganado
gan**a**	gan**an**	**ha** ganado	**han** ganado
imperfecto de indicativo		pluscuamperfecto de indicativo	
gan**aba**	gan**ábamos**	**había** ganado	**habíamos** ganado
gan**abas**	gan**abais**	**habías** ganado	**habíais** ganado
gan**aba**	gan**aban**	**había** ganado	**habían** ganado
pretérito		pretérito anterior	
gan**é**	gan**amos**	**hube** ganado	**hubimos** ganado
gan**aste**	gan**asteis**	**hubiste** ganado	**hubisteis** ganado
gan**ó**	gan**aron**	**hubo** ganado	**hubieron** ganado
futuro		futuro perfecto	
ganar**é**	ganar**emos**	**habré** ganado	**habremos** ganado
ganar**ás**	ganar**éis**	**habrás** ganado	**habréis** ganado
ganar**á**	ganar**án**	**habrá** ganado	**habrán** ganado
condicional simple		condicional compuesto	
ganar**ía**	ganar**íamos**	**habría** ganado	**habríamos** ganado
ganar**ías**	ganar**íais**	**habrías** ganado	**habríais** ganado
ganar**ía**	ganar**ían**	**habría** ganado	**habrían** ganado
presente de subjuntivo		perfecto de subjuntivo	
gan**e**	gan**emos**	**haya** ganado	**hayamos** ganado
gan**es**	gan**éis**	**hayas** ganado	**hayáis** ganado
gan**e**	gan**en**	**haya** ganado	**hayan** ganado
imperfecto de subjuntivo		pluscuamperfecto de subjuntivo	
ganar**a**	ganár**amos**	**hubiera** ganado	**hubiéramos** ganado
ganar**as**	ganar**ais**	**hubieras** ganado	**hubierais** ganado
ganar**a**	ganar**an**	**hubiera** ganado	**hubieran** ganado
OR		OR	
ganas**e**	ganás**emos**	**hubiese** ganado	**hubiésemos** ganado
ganas**es**	ganas**eis**	**hubieses** ganado	**hubieseis** ganado
ganas**e**	ganas**en**	**hubiese** ganado	**hubiesen** ganado

imperativo

—	ganemos
gana; no ganes	ganad; no ganéis
gane	ganen

garantizar — to guarantee

gerundio **garantizando** participio de pasado **garantizado**

presente de indicativo

SINGULAR	PLURAL
garantiz**o**	garantiz**amos**
garantiz**as**	garantiz**áis**
garantiz**a**	garantiz**an**

imperfecto de indicativo

SINGULAR	PLURAL
garantiz**aba**	garantiz**ábamos**
garantiz**abas**	garantiz**abais**
garantiz**aba**	garantiz**aban**

pretérito

SINGULAR	PLURAL
garantic**é**	garantiz**amos**
garantiz**aste**	garantiz**asteis**
garantiz**ó**	garantiz**aron**

futuro

SINGULAR	PLURAL
garantizar**é**	garantizar**emos**
garantizar**ás**	garantizar**éis**
garantizar**á**	garantizar**án**

condicional simple

SINGULAR	PLURAL
garantizar**ía**	garantizar**íamos**
garantizar**ías**	garantizar**íais**
garantizar**ía**	garantizar**ían**

presente de subjuntivo

SINGULAR	PLURAL
garantic**e**	garantic**emos**
garantic**es**	garantic**éis**
garantic**e**	garantic**en**

imperfecto de subjuntivo

SINGULAR	PLURAL
garantizar**a**	garantizár**amos**
garantizar**as**	garantizar**ais**
garantizar**a**	garantizar**an**
OR	
garantizas**e**	garantizás**emos**
garantizas**es**	garantizas**eis**
garantizas**e**	garantizas**en**

imperativo

SINGULAR	PLURAL
—	garanticemos
garantiza; no garantices	garantizad; no garanticéis
garantice	garanticen

perfecto de indicativo

SINGULAR	PLURAL
he garantizado	**hemos** garantizado
has garantizado	**habéis** garantizado
ha garantizado	**han** garantizado

pluscuamperfecto de indicativo

SINGULAR	PLURAL
había garantizado	**habíamos** garantizado
habías garantizado	**habíais** garantizado
había garantizado	**habían** garantizado

pretérito anterior

SINGULAR	PLURAL
hube garantizado	**hubimos** garantizado
hubiste garantizado	**hubisteis** garantizado
hubo garantizado	**hubieron** garantizado

futuro perfecto

SINGULAR	PLURAL
habré garantizado	**habremos** garantizado
habrás garantizado	**habréis** garantizado
habrá garantizado	**habrán** garantizado

condicional computeso

SINGULAR	PLURAL
habría garantizado	**habríamos** garantizado
habrías garantizado	**habríais** garantizado
habría garantizado	**habrían** garantizado

perpecto de subjuntivo

SINGULAR	PLURAL
haya garantizado	**hayamos** garantizado
hayas garantizado	**hayáis** garantizado
haya garantizado	**hayan** garantizado

pluscuamperfecto de subjuntivo

SINGULAR	PLURAL
hubiera garantizado	**hubiéramos** garantizado
hubieras garantizado	**hubierais** garantizado
hubiera garantizado	**hubieran** garantizado
OR	
hubiese garantizado	**hubiésemos** garantizado
hubieses garantizado	**hubieseis** garantizado
hubiese garantizado	**hubiesen** garantizado

to spend money, to waste **gastar**

gerundio **gastando** participio de pasado **gastado**

SINGULAR	PLURAL
presente de indicativo	
gast**o**	gast**amos**
gast**as**	gast**áis**
gast**a**	gast**an**
imperfecto de indicativo	
gast**aba**	gast**ábamos**
gast**abas**	gast**abais**
gast**aba**	gast**aban**
pretérito	
gast**é**	gast**amos**
gast**aste**	gast**asteis**
gast**ó**	gast**aron**
futuro	
gastar**é**	gastar**emos**
gastar**ás**	gastar**éis**
gastar**á**	gastar**án**
condicional simple	
gastar**ía**	gastar**íamos**
gastar**ías**	gastar**íais**
gastar**ía**	gastar**ían**
presente de subjuntivo	
gast**e**	gast**emos**
gast**es**	gast**éis**
gast**e**	gast**en**
imperfecto de subjuntivo	
gastar**a**	gastár**amos**
gastar**as**	gastar**ais**
gastar**a**	gastar**an**
OR	
gastas**e**	gastás**emos**
gastas**es**	gastas**eis**
gastas**e**	gastas**en**
imperativo	
—	gastemos
gasta; no gastes	gastad; no gastéis
gaste	gasten

SINGULAR	PLURAL
perfecto de indicativo	
he gastado	**hemos** gastado
has gastado	**habéis** gastado
ha gastado	**han** gastado
pluscuamperfecto de indicativo	
había gastado	**habíamos** gastado
habías gastado	**habíais** gastado
había gastado	**habían** gastado
pretérito anterior	
hube gastado	**hubimos** gastado
hubiste gastado	**hubisteis** gastado
hubo gastado	**hubieron** gastado
futuro perfecto	
habré gastado	**habremos** gastado
habrás gastado	**habréis** gastado
habrá gastado	**habrán** gastado
condicional compuesto	
habría gastado	**habríamos** gastado
habrías gastado	**habríais** gastado
habría gastado	**habrían** gastado
perfecto de subjuntivo	
haya gastado	**hayamos** gastado
hayas gastado	**hayáis** gastado
haya gastado	**hayan** gastado
pluscuamperfecto de subjuntivo	
hubiera gastado	**hubiéramos** gastado
hubieras gastado	**hubierais** gastado
hubiera gastado	**hubieran** gastado
OR	
hubiese gastado	**hubiésemos** gastado
hubieses gastado	**hubieseis** gastado
hubiese gastado	**hubiesen** gastado

MEMORY TIP

I spend a lot on gas!

G

gerundio **gimiendo** participio de pasado **gemido**

SINGULAR	PLURAL
presente de indicativo	
gim**o**	gem**imos**
gim**es**	gem**ís**
gim**e**	gim**en**
imperfecto de indicativo	
gem**ía**	gem**íamos**
gem**ías**	gem**íais**
gem**ía**	gem**ían**
pretérito	
gem**í**	gem**imos**
gem**iste**	gem**isteis**
gimi**ó**	gim**ieron**
futuro	
gemir**é**	gemir**emos**
gemir**ás**	gemir**éis**
gemir**á**	gemir**án**
condicional simple	
gemir**ía**	gemir**íamos**
gemir**ías**	gemir**íais**
gemir**ía**	gemir**ían**
presente de subjuntivo	
gim**a**	gim**amos**
gim**as**	gim**áis**
gim**a**	gim**an**
imperfecto de subjuntivo	
gimier**a**	gimiér**amos**
gimier**as**	gimier**ais**
gimier**a**	gimier**an**
OR	
gimies**e**	gimiés**emos**
gimies**es**	gimies**eis**
gimies**e**	gimies**en**
imperativo	
—	gimamos
gime; no gimas	gemid; no gimáis
gima	giman

SINGULAR	PLURAL
perfecto de indicativo	
he gemido	**hemos** gemido
has gemido	**habéis** gemido
ha gemido	**han** gemido
pluscuamperfecto de indicativo	
había gemido	**habíamos** gemido
habías gemido	**habíais** gemido
había gemido	**habían** gemido
pretérito anterior	
hube gemido	**hubimos** gemido
hubiste gemido	**hubisteis** gemido
hubo gemido	**hubieron** gemido
futuro perfecto	
habré gemido	**habremos** gemido
habrás gemido	**habréis** gemido
habrá gemido	**habrán** gemido
condicional compuesto	
habría gemido	**habríamos** gemido
habrías gemido	**habríais** gemido
habría gemido	**habrían** gemido
perfecto de subjuntivo	
haya gemido	**hayamos** gemido
hayas gemido	**hayáis** gemido
haya gemido	**hayan** gemido
pluscuamperfecto de subjuntivo	
hubiera gemido	**hubiéramos** gemido
hubieras gemido	**hubierais** gemido
hubiera gemido	**hubieran** gemido
OR	
hubiese gemido	**hubiésemos** gemido
hubieses gemido	**hubieseis** gemido
hubiese gemido	**hubiesen** gemido

to govern — gobernar

gerundio **gobernando** participio de pasado **gobernado**

SINGULAR	PLURAL
presente de indicativo	
gobiern**o**	gobern**amos**
gobiern**as**	gobern**áis**
gobiern**a**	gobiern**an**
imperfecto de indicativo	
gobern**aba**	gobern**ábamos**
gobern**abas**	gobern**abais**
gobern**aba**	gobern**aban**
pretérito	
gobern**é**	gobern**amos**
gobern**aste**	gobern**asteis**
gobern**ó**	gobern**aron**
futuro	
gobernar**é**	gobernar**emos**
gobernar**ás**	gobernar**éis**
gobernar**á**	gobernar**án**
condicional simple	
gobernar**ía**	gobernar**íamos**
gobernar**ías**	gobernar**íais**
gobernar**ía**	gobernar**ían**
presente de subjuntivo	
gobiern**e**	gobern**emos**
gobiern**es**	gobern**éis**
gobiern**e**	gobiern**en**
imperfecto de subjuntivo	
gobernar**a**	gobernár**amos**
gobernar**as**	gobernar**ais**
gobernar**a**	gobernar**an**
OR	
gobernas**e**	gobernás**emos**
gobernas**es**	gobernas**eis**
gobernas**e**	gobernas**en**
imperativo	
—	gobernemos
gobierna; no gobiernes	gobernad; no gobernéis
gobierne	gobiernen

SINGULAR	PLURAL
perfecto de indicativo	
he gobernado	**hemos** gobernado
has gobernado	**habéis** gobernado
ha gobernado	**han** gobernado
pluscuamperfecto de indicativo	
había gobernado	**habíamos** gobernado
habías gobernado	**habíais** gobernado
había gobernado	**habían** gobernado
pretérito anterior	
hube gobernado	**hubimos** gobernado
hubiste gobernado	**hubisteis** gobernado
hubo gobernado	**hubieron** gobernado
futuro perfecto	
habré gobernado	**habremos** gobernado
habrás gobernado	**habréis** gobernado
habrá gobernado	**habrán** gobernado
condicional compuesto	
habría gobernado	**habríamos** gobernado
habrías gobernado	**habríais** gobernado
habría gobernado	**habrían** gobernado
perfecto de subjuntivo	
haya gobernado	**hayamos** gobernado
hayas gobernado	**hayáis** gobernado
haya gobernado	**hayan** gobernado
pluscuamperfecto de subjuntivo	
hubiera gobernado	**hubiéramos** gobernado
hubieras gobernado	**hubierais** gobernado
hubiera gobernado	**hubieran** gobernado
OR	
hubiese gobernado	**hubiésemos** gobernado
hubieses gobernado	**hubieseis** gobernado
hubiese gobernado	**hubiesen** gobernado

to hit, to strike

gerundio **golpeando** participio de pasado **golpeado**

SINGULAR	PLURAL
presente de indicativo	
golpe**o**	golpe**amos**
golpe**as**	golpe**áis**
golpe**a**	golpe**an**
imperfecto de indicativo	
golpe**aba**	golpe**ábamos**
golpe**abas**	golpe**abais**
golpe**aba**	golpe**aban**
pretérito	
golpe**é**	golpe**amos**
golpe**aste**	golpe**asteis**
golpe**ó**	golpe**aron**
futuro	
golpear**é**	golpear**emos**
golpear**ás**	golpear**éis**
golpear**á**	golpear**án**
condicional simple	
golpear**ía**	golpear**íamos**
golpear**ías**	golpear**íais**
golpear**ía**	golpear**ían**
presente de subjuntivo	
golpe**e**	golpe**emos**
golpe**es**	golpe**éis**
golpe**e**	golpe**en**
imperfecto de subjuntivo	
golpear**a**	golpeár**amos**
golpear**as**	golpear**ais**
golpear**a**	golpear**an**
OR	
golpeas**e**	golpeás**emos**
golpeas**es**	golpeas**eis**
golpeas**e**	golpeas**en**
imperativo	
—	golpeemos
golpea; no golpees	golpead; no golpeéis
golpee	golpeen

SINGULAR	PLURAL
perfecto de indicativo	
he golpeado	**hemos** golpeado
has golpeado	**habéis** golpeado
ha golpeado	**han** golpeado
pluscuamperfecto de indicativo	
había golpeado	**habíamos** golpeado
habías golpeado	**habíais** golpeado
había golpeado	**habían** golpeado
pretérito anterior	
hube golpeado	**hubimos** golpeado
hubiste golpeado	**hubisteis** golpeado
hubo golpeado	**hubieron** golpeado
futuro perfecto	
habré golpeado	**habremos** golpeado
habrás golpeado	**habréis** golpeado
habrá golpeado	**habrán** golpeado
condicional compuesto	
habría golpeado	**habríamos** golpeado
habrías golpeado	**habríais** golpeado
habría golpeado	**habrían** golpeado
perfecto de subjuntivo	
haya golpeado	**hayamos** golpeado
hayas golpeado	**hayáis** golpeado
haya golpeado	**hayan** golpeado
pluscuamperfecto de subjuntivo	
hubiera golpeado	**hubiéramos** golpeado
hubieras golpeado	**hubierais** golpeado
hubiera golpeado	**hubieran** golpeado
OR	
hubiese golpeado	**hubiésemos** golpeado
hubieses golpeado	**hubieseis** golpeado
hubiese golpeado	**hubiesen** golpeado

to enjoy **gozar**

gerundio **gozando** participio de pasado **gozado**

SINGULAR	PLURAL	SINGULAR	PLURAL
presente de indicativo		perfecto de indicativo	
goz**o**	goz**amos**	**he** gozado	**hemos** gozado
goz**as**	goz**áis**	**has** gozado	**habéis** gozado
goz**a**	goz**an**	**ha** gozado	**han** gozado
imperfecto de indicativo		pluscuamperfecto de indicativo	
goz**aba**	goz**ábamos**	**había** gozado	**habíamos** gozado
goz**abas**	goz**abais**	**habías** gozado	**habíais** gozado
goz**aba**	goz**aban**	**había** gozado	**habían** gozado
pretérito		pretérito anterior	
goc**é**	goz**amos**	**hube** gozado	**hubimos** gozado
goz**aste**	goz**asteis**	**hubiste** gozado	**hubisteis** gozado
goz**ó**	goz**aron**	**hubo** gozado	**hubieron** gozado
futuro		futuro perfecto	
gozar**é**	gozar**emos**	**habré** gozado	**habremos** gozado
gozar**ás**	gozar**éis**	**habrás** gozado	**habréis** gozado
gozar**á**	gozar**án**	**habrá** gozado	**habrán** gozado
condicional simple		condicional compuesto	
gozar**ía**	gozar**íamos**	**habría** gozado	**habríamos** gozado
gozar**ías**	gozar**íais**	**habrías** gozado	**habríais** gozado
gozar**ía**	gozar**ían**	**habría** gozado	**habrían** gozado
presente de subjuntivo		perfecto de subjuntivo	
goc**e**	goc**emos**	**haya** gozado	**hayamos** gozado
goc**es**	goc**éis**	**hayas** gozado	**hayáis** gozado
goc**e**	goc**en**	**haya** gozado	**hayan** gozado
imperfecto de subjuntivo		pluscuamperfecto de subjuntivo	
gozar**a**	gozár**amos**	**hubiera** gozado	**hubiéramos** gozado
gozar**as**	gozar**ais**	**hubieras** gozado	**hubierais** gozado
gozar**a**	gozar**an**	**hubiera** gozado	**hubieran** gozado
OR		OR	
gozas**e**	gozás**emos**	**hubiese** gozado	**hubiésemos** gozado
gozas**es**	gozas**eis**	**hubieses** gozado	**hubieseis** gozado
gozas**e**	gozas**en**	**hubiese** gozado	**hubiesen** gozado

imperativo

—	gocemos
goza; no goces	gozad; no gocéis
goce	gocen

G

grabar — to record

gerundio **grabando** — participio de pasado **grabado**

SINGULAR	PLURAL	SINGULAR	PLURAL
presente de indicativo		perfecto de indicativo	
grab**o**	grab**amos**	**he** grabado	**hemos** grabado
grab**as**	grab**áis**	**has** grabado	**habéis** grabado
grab**a**	grab**an**	**ha** grabado	**han** grabado
imperfecto de indicativo		pluscuamperfecto de indicativo	
grab**aba**	grab**ábamos**	**había** grabado	**habíamos** grabado
grab**abas**	grab**abais**	**habías** grabado	**habíais** grabado
grab**aba**	grab**aban**	**había** grabado	**habían** grabado
pretérito		pretérito anterior	
grab**é**	grab**amos**	**hube** grabado	**hubimos** grabado
grab**aste**	grab**asteis**	**hubiste** grabado	**hubisteis** grabado
grab**ó**	grab**aron**	**hubo** grabado	**hubieron** grabado
futuro		futuro perfecto	
grabar**é**	grabar**emos**	**habré** grabado	**habremos** grabado
grabar**ás**	grabar**éis**	**habrás** grabado	**habréis** grabado
grabar**á**	grabar**án**	**habrá** grabado	**habrán** grabado
condicional simple		condicional compuesto	
grabar**ía**	grabar**íamos**	**habría** grabado	**habríamos** grabado
grabar**ías**	grabar**íais**	**habrías** grabado	**habríais** grabado
grabar**ía**	grabar**ían**	**habría** grabado	**habrían** grabado
presente de subjuntivo		perfecto de subjuntivo	
grab**e**	grab**emos**	**haya** grabado	**hayamos** grabado
grab**es**	grab**éis**	**hayas** grabado	**hayáis** grabado
grab**e**	grab**en**	**haya** grabado	**hayan** grabado
imperfecto de subjuntivo		pluscuamperfecto de subjuntivo	
grabar**a**	grabár**amos**	**hubiera** grabado	**hubiéramos** grabado
grabar**as**	grabar**ais**	**hubieras** grabado	**hubierais** grabado
grabar**a**	grabar**an**	**hubiera** grabado	**hubieran** grabado
OR		OR	
grabas**e**	grabás**emos**	**hubiese** grabado	**hubiésemos** grabado
grabas**es**	grabas**eis**	**hubieses** grabado	**hubieseis** grabado
grabas**e**	grabas**en**	**hubiese** grabado	**hubiesen** grabado

imperativo

—	grabemos
graba; no grabes	grabad; no grabéis
grabe	graben

to graduate — graduar

gerundio graduando **participio de pasado** graduado

presente de indicativo

SINGULAR	PLURAL
gradú**o**	gradu**amos**
gradú**as**	gradu**áis**
gradú**a**	gradú**an**

imperfecto de indicativo

SINGULAR	PLURAL
gradu**aba**	gradu**ábamos**
gradu**abas**	gradu**abais**
gradu**aba**	gradu**aban**

pretérito

SINGULAR	PLURAL
gradu**é**	gradu**amos**
gradu**aste**	gradu**asteis**
gradu**ó**	gradu**aron**

futuro

SINGULAR	PLURAL
graduar**é**	graduar**emos**
graduar**ás**	graduar**éis**
graduar**á**	graduar**án**

condicional simple

SINGULAR	PLURAL
graduar**ía**	graduar**íamos**
graduar**ías**	graduar**íais**
graduar**ía**	graduar**ían**

presente de subjuntivo

SINGULAR	PLURAL
gradú**e**	gradu**emos**
gradú**es**	gradu**éis**
gradú**e**	gradú**en**

imperfecto de subjuntivo

SINGULAR	PLURAL
gradua**ra**	graduá**ramos**
gradua**ras**	gradua**rais**
gradua**ra**	gradua**ran**
OR	
gradua**se**	graduá**semos**
gradua**ses**	gradua**seis**
gradua**se**	gradua**sen**

imperativo

SINGULAR	PLURAL
—	graduemos
gradúa; no gradúes	graduad; no graduéis
gradúe	gradúen

perfecto de indicativo

SINGULAR	PLURAL
he graduado	**hemos** graduado
has graduado	**habéis** graduado
ha graduado	**han** graduado

pluscuamperfecto de indicativo

SINGULAR	PLURAL
había graduado	**habíamos** graduado
habías graduado	**habíais** graduado
había graduado	**habían** graduado

pretérito anterior

SINGULAR	PLURAL
hube graduado	**hubimos** graduado
hubiste graduado	**hubisteis** graduado
hubo graduado	**hubieron** graduado

futuro perfecto

SINGULAR	PLURAL
habré graduado	**habremos** graduado
habrás graduado	**habréis** graduado
habrá graduado	**habrán** graduado

condicional compuesto

SINGULAR	PLURAL
habría graduado	**habríamos** graduado
habrías graduado	**habríais** graduado
habría graduado	**habrían** graduado

perfecto de subjuntivo

SINGULAR	PLURAL
haya graduado	**hayamos** graduado
hayas graduado	**hayáis** graduado
haya graduado	**hayan** graduado

pluscuamperfecto de subjuntivo

SINGULAR	PLURAL
hubiera graduado	**hubiéramos** graduado
hubieras graduado	**hubierais** graduado
hubiera graduado	**hubieran** graduado
OR	
hubiese graduado	**hubiésemos** graduado
hubieses graduado	**hubieseis** graduado
hubiese graduado	**hubiesen** graduado

gritar — to shout, to scream

gerundio **gritando** — participio de pasado **gritado**

SINGULAR	PLURAL
presente de indicativo	
grit**o**	grit**amos**
grit**as**	grit**áis**
grit**a**	grit**an**
imperfecto de indicativo	
grit**aba**	grit**ábamos**
grit**abas**	grit**abais**
grit**aba**	grit**aban**
pretérito	
grit**é**	grit**amos**
grit**aste**	grit**asteis**
grit**ó**	grit**aron**
futuro	
gritar**é**	gritar**emos**
gritar**ás**	gritar**éis**
gritar**á**	gritar**án**
condicional simple	
gritar**ía**	gritar**íamos**
gritar**ías**	gritar**íais**
gritar**ía**	gritar**ían**
presente de subjuntivo	
grit**e**	grit**emos**
grit**es**	grit**éis**
grit**e**	grit**en**
imperfecto de subjuntivo	
gritar**a**	gritár**amos**
gritar**as**	gritar**ais**
gritar**a**	gritar**an**
OR	
gritas**e**	gritás**emos**
gritas**es**	gritas**eis**
gritas**e**	gritas**en**
imperativo	
—	gritemos
grita; no grites	gritad; no gritéis
grite	griten

SINGULAR	PLURAL
perfecto de indicativo	
he gritado	**hemos** gritado
has gritado	**habéis** gritado
ha gritado	**han** gritado
pluscuamperfecto de indicativo	
había gritado	**habíamos** gritado
habías gritado	**habíais** gritado
había gritado	**habían** gritado
pretérito anterior	
hube gritado	**hubimos** gritado
hubiste gritado	**hubisteis** gritado
hubo gritado	**hubieron** gritado
futuro perfecto	
habré gritado	**habremos** gritado
habrás gritado	**habréis** gritado
habrá gritado	**habrán** gritado
condicional compuesto	
habría gritado	**habríamos** gritado
habrías gritado	**habríais** gritado
habría gritado	**habrían** gritado
perfecto de subjuntivo	
haya gritado	**hayamos** gritado
hayas gritado	**hayáis** gritado
haya gritado	**hayan** gritado
pluscuamperfecto de subjuntivo	
hubiera gritado	**hubiéramos** gritado
hubieras gritado	**hubierais** gritado
hubiera gritado	**hubieran** gritado
OR	
hubiese gritado	**hubiésemos** gritado
hubieses gritado	**hubieseis** gritado
hubiese gritado	**hubiesen** gritado

to grumble, to growl **gruñir**

gerundio **gruñendo** participio de pasado **gruñido**

presente de indicativo

SINGULAR	PLURAL
gruñ**o**	gruñ**imos**
gruñ**es**	gruñ**ís**
gruñ**e**	gruñ**en**

imperfecto de indicativo

SINGULAR	PLURAL
gruñ**ía**	gruñ**íamos**
gruñ**ías**	gruñ**íais**
gruñ**ía**	gruñ**ían**

pretérito

SINGULAR	PLURAL
gruñ**í**	gruñ**imos**
gruñ**iste**	gruñ**ísteis**
gruñ**o**	gruñ**eron**

futuro

SINGULAR	PLURAL
gruñir**é**	gruñir**emos**
gruñis**te**	gruñir**éis**
gruñir**á**	gruñir**án**

condicional simple

SINGULAR	PLURAL
gruñir**ía**	gruñir**íamos**
gruñir**ías**	gruñir**íais**
gruñir**ía**	gruñir**ían**

presente de subjuntivo

SINGULAR	PLURAL
gruñ**a**	gruñ**amos**
gruñ**as**	gruñ**áis**
gruñ**a**	gruñ**an**

imperfecto de subjuntivo

SINGULAR	PLURAL
gruñer**a**	gruñér**amos**
gruñer**as**	gruñer**ais**
gruñer**a**	gruñer**an**
OR	
gruñes**e**	gruñés**emos**
gruñes**es**	gruñes**eis**
gruñes**e**	gruñes**en**

imperativo

SINGULAR	PLURAL
—	gruñamos
gruñe; no gruñas	gruñid; no gruñáis
gruña	gruñan

perfecto de indicativo

SINGULAR	PLURAL
he gruñido	**hemos** gruñido
has gruñido	**habéis** gruñido
ha gruñido	**han** gruñido

pluscuamperfecto de indicativo

SINGULAR	PLURAL
había gruñido	**habíamos** gruñido
habías gruñido	**habíais** gruñido
había gruñido	**habían** gruñido

pretérito anterior

SINGULAR	PLURAL
hube gruñido	**hubimos** gruñido
hubiste gruñido	**hubisteis** gruñido
hubo gruñido	**hubieron** gruñido

futuro perfecto

SINGULAR	PLURAL
habré gruñido	**habremos** gruñido
habrás gruñido	**habréis** gruñido
habrá gruñido	**habrán** gruñido

condicional compuesto

SINGULAR	PLURAL
habría gruñido	**habríamos** gruñido
habrías gruñido	**habríais** gruñido
habría gruñido	**habrían** gruñido

perfecto de subjuntivo

SINGULAR	PLURAL
haya gruñido	**hayamos** gruñido
hayas gruñido	**hayáis** gruñido
haya gruñido	**hayan** gruñido

pluscuamperfecto de subjuntivo

SINGULAR	PLURAL
hubiera gruñido	**hubiéramos** gruñido
hubieras gruñido	**hubierais** gruñido
hubiera gruñido	**hubieran** gruñido
OR	
hubiese gruñido	**hubiésemos** gruñido
hubieses gruñido	**hubieseis** gruñido
hubiese gruñido	**hubiesen** gruñido

guiar — to guide, to lead

gerundio **guiando** participio de pasado **guiado**

SINGULAR	PLURAL
presente de indicativo	
guí**o**	gui**amos**
guí**as**	gui**áis**
guí**a**	guí**an**
imperfecto de indicativo	
gui**aba**	gui**ábamos**
gui**abas**	gui**abais**
gui**aba**	gui**aban**
pretérito	
gui**é**	gui**amos**
gui**aste**	gui**asteis**
gui**ó**	gui**aron**
futuro	
guiar**é**	guiar**emos**
guiar**ás**	guiar**éis**
guiar**á**	guiar**án**
condicional simple	
guiar**ía**	guiar**íamos**
guiar**ías**	guiar**íais**
guiar**ía**	guiar**ían**
presente de subjuntivo	
guí**e**	gui**emos**
guí**es**	gui**éis**
guí**e**	guí**en**
imperfecto de subjuntivo	
guiar**a**	guiár**amos**
guiar**as**	guiar**ais**
guiar**a**	guiar**an**
OR	
guias**e**	guiás**emos**
guias**es**	guias**eis**
guias**e**	guias**en**
imperativo	
—	guiemos
guía; no guíes	guiad; no guiéis
guíe	guíen

SINGULAR	PLURAL
perfecto de indicativo	
he guiado	**hemos** guiado
has guiado	**habéis** guiado
ha guiado	**han** guiado
pluscuamperfecto de indicativo	
había guiado	**habíamos** guiado
habías guiado	**habíais** guiado
había guiado	**habían** guiado
pretérito anterior	
hube guiado	**hubimos** guiado
hubiste guiado	**hubisteis** guiado
hubo guiado	**hubieron** guiado
futuro perfecto	
habré guiado	**habremos** guiado
habrás guiado	**habréis** guiado
habrá guiado	**habrán** guiado
condicional compuesto	
habría guiado	**habríamos** guiado
habrías guiado	**habríais** guiado
habría guiado	**habrían** guiado
perfecto de subjuntivo	
haya guiado	**hayamos** guiado
hayas guiado	**hayáis** guiado
haya guiado	**hayan** guiado
pluscuamperfecto de subjuntivo	
hubiera guiado	**hubiéramos** guiado
hubieras guiado	**hubierais** guiado
hubiera guiado	**hubieran** guiado
OR	
hubiese guiado	**hubiésemos** guiado
hubieses guiado	**hubieseis** guiado
hubiese guiado	**hubiesen** guiado

to like, to be pleasing to **gustar**

gerundio **gustando** participio de pasado **gustado**

SINGULAR	PLURAL
presente de indicativo	
gust**a**	gust**an**
imperfecto de indicativo	
gust**aba**	gust**aban**
pretérito	
gust**o**	gust**aron**
futuro	
gustar**á**	gustar**án**
condicional simple	
gustar**ía**	gustar**ían**
presente de subjuntivo	
gust**e**	gust**en**
imperfecto de subjuntivo	
gustar**a**	gustar**an**
OR	
gustas**e**	gustas**en**
imperativo	
¡Que guste!	¡Que gusten!

SINGULAR	PLURAL
perfecto de indicativo	
ha gustado	**han** gustado
pluscuamperfecto de indicativo	
había gustado	**habían** gustado
pretérito anterior	
hubo gustado	**hubieron** gustado
futuro perfecto	
habrá gustado	**habrán** gustado
condicional computeso	
habría gustado	**habrían** gustado
perfecto de subjuntivo	
haya gustado	**hayan** gustado
pluscuamperfecto de subjuntivo	
hubiera gustado	**hubieran** gustado
OR	
hubiese gustado	**hubiesen** gustado

haber — to have (helping verb)

gerundio **habiendo** participio de pasado **habido**

SINGULAR	PLURAL	SINGULAR	PLURAL
presente de indicativo		perfecto de indicativo	
h**e**	h**emos**	**he** habido	**hemos** habido
h**as**	h**abéis**	**has** habido	**habéis** habido
h**a**	h**an**	**ha** habido	**han** habido
imperfecto de indicativo		pluscuamperfecto de indicativo	
hab**ía**	hab**íamos**	**había** habido	**habíamos** habido
hab**ías**	hab**íais**	**habías** habido	**habíais** habido
hab**ía**	hab**ían**	**había** habido	**habían** habido
pretérito		pretérito anterior	
hub**e**	hub**imos**	**hube** habido	**hubimos** habido
hub**iste**	hub**isteis**	**hubiste** habido	**hubisteis** habido
hub**o**	hub**ieron**	**hubo** habido	**hubieron** habido
futuro		futuro perfecto	
habr**é**	habr**emos**	**habré** habido	**habremos** habido
habr**ás**	habr**éis**	**habrás** habido	**habréis** habido
habr**á**	habr**án**	**habrá** habido	**habrán** habido
condicional simple		condicional compuesto	
habr**ía**	habr**íamos**	**habría** habido	**habríamos** habido
habr**ías**	habr**íais**	**habrías** habido	**habríais** habido
habr**ía**	habr**ían**	**habría** habido	**habrían** habido
presente de subjuntivo		perfecto de subjuntivo	
hay**a**	hay**amos**	**haya** habido	**hayamos** habido
hay**as**	hay**áis**	**hayas** habido	**hayáis** habido
hay**a**	hay**an**	**haya** habido	**hayan** habido
imperfecto de subjuntivo		pluscuamperfecto de subjuntivo	
hubier**a**	hubiér**amos**	**hubiera** habido	**hubiéramos** habido
hubier**as**	hubier**ais**	**hubieras** habido	**hubierais** habido
hubier**a**	hubier**an**	**hubiera** habido	**hubieran** habido
OR		OR	
hubies**e**	hubiés**emos**	**hubiese** habido	**hubiésemos** habido
hubies**es**	hubies**eis**	**hubieses** habido	**hubieseis** habido
hubies**e**	hubies**en**	**hubiese** habido	**hubiesen** habido

imperativo

—	hayamos
he; no hayas	habed; no hayáis
haya	hayan

to speak, to talk **hablar**

gerundio **hablando** participio de pasado **hablado**

SINGULAR	PLURAL
presente de indicativo	
habl**o**	habl**amos**
habl**as**	habl**áis**
habl**a**	habl**an**
imperfecto de indicativo	
habl**aba**	habl**ábamos**
habl**abas**	habl**abais**
habl**aba**	habl**aban**
pretérito	
habl**é**	habl**amos**
habl**aste**	habl**asteis**
habl**ó**	habl**aron**
futuro	
hablar**é**	hablar**emos**
hablar**ás**	hablar**éis**
hablar**á**	hablar**án**
condicional simple	
hablar**ía**	hablar**íamos**
hablar**ías**	hablar**íais**
hablar**ía**	hablar**ían**
presente de subjuntivo	
habl**e**	habl**emos**
habl**es**	habl**éis**
habl**e**	habl**en**
imperfecto de subjuntivo	
hablar**a**	hablár**amos**
hablar**as**	hablar**ais**
hablar**a**	hablar**an**
OR	
habla**se**	hablás**emos**
hablas**es**	hablas**eis**
hablas**e**	hablas**en**
imperativo	
—	hablemos
habla; no hables	hablad; no habléis
hable	hablen

SINGULAR	PLURAL
perfecto de indicativo	
he hablado	**hemos** hablado
has hablado	**habéis** hablado
ha hablado	**han** hablado
pluscuamperfecto de indicativo	
había hablado	**habíamos** hablado
habías hablado	**habíais** hablado
había hablado	**habían** hablado
pretérito anterior	
hube hablado	**hubimos** hablado
hubiste hablado	**hubisteis** hablado
hubo hablado	**hubieron** hablado
futuro perfecto	
habré hablado	**habremos** hablado
habrás hablado	**habréis** hablado
habrá hablado	**habrán** hablado
condicional compuesto	
habría hablado	**habríamos** hablado
habrías hablado	**habríais** hablado
habría hablado	**habrían** hablado
perfecto de subjuntivo	
haya hablado	**hayamos** hablado
hayas hablado	**hayáis** hablado
haya hablado	**hayan** hablado
pluscuamperfecto de subjuntivo	
hubiera hablado	**hubiéramos** hablado
hubieras hablado	**hubierais** hablado
hubiera hablado	**hubieran** hablado
OR	
hubiese hablado	**hubiésemos** hablado
hubieses hablado	**hubieseis** hablado
hubiese hablado	**hubiesen** hablado

hacer — to do, to make

gerundio **haciendo** — participio de pasado **hecho**

presente de indicativo

SINGULAR	PLURAL
hag**o**	hac**emos**
hac**es**	hac**éis**
hac**e**	hac**en**

imperfecto de indicativo

SINGULAR	PLURAL
hac**ía**	hac**íamos**
hac**ías**	hac**íais**
hac**ía**	hac**ían**

pretérito

SINGULAR	PLURAL
hic**e**	hic**imos**
hic**iste**	hic**isteis**
hiz**o**	hic**ieron**

futuro

SINGULAR	PLURAL
har**é**	har**emos**
har**ás**	har**éis**
har**á**	har**án**

condicional simple

SINGULAR	PLURAL
har**ía**	har**íamos**
har**ías**	har**íais**
har**ía**	har**ían**

presente de subjuntivo

SINGULAR	PLURAL
hag**a**	hag**amos**
hag**as**	hag**áis**
hag**a**	hag**an**

imperfecto de subjuntivo

SINGULAR	PLURAL
hicier**a**	hicié**ramos**
hicier**as**	hicier**ais**
hicier**a**	hicier**an**
OR	
hicies**e**	hicié**semos**
hicies**es**	hicies**eis**
hicies**e**	hicies**en**

imperativo

SINGULAR	PLURAL
—	hagamos
haz; no hagas	haced; no hagáis
haga	hagan

perfecto de indicativo

SINGULAR	PLURAL
he hecho	**hemos** hecho
has hecho	**habéis** hecho
ha hecho	**han** hecho

pluscuamperfecto de indicativo

SINGULAR	PLURAL
había hecho	**habíamos** hecho
habías hecho	**habíais** hecho
había hecho	**habían** hecho

pretérito anterior

SINGULAR	PLURAL
hube hecho	**hubimos** hecho
hubiste hecho	**hubisteis** hecho
hubo hecho	**hubieron** hecho

futuro perfecto

SINGULAR	PLURAL
habré hecho	**habremos** hecho
habrás hecho	**habréis** hecho
habrá hecho	**habrán** hecho

condicional compuesto

SINGULAR	PLURAL
habría hecho	**habríamos** hecho
habrías hecho	**habríais** hecho
habría hecho	**habrían** hecho

perfecto de subjuntivo

SINGULAR	PLURAL
haya hecho	**hayamos** hecho
hayas hecho	**hayáis** hecho
haya hecho	**hayan** hecho

pluscuamperfecto de subjuntivo

SINGULAR	PLURAL
hubiera hecho	**hubiéramos** hecho
hubieras hecho	**hubierais** hecho
hubiera hecho	**hubieran** hecho
OR	
hubiese hecho	**hubiésemos** hecho
hubieses hecho	**hubieseis** hecho
hubiese hecho	**hubiesen** hecho

gerundio **hallando** participio de pasado **hallado**

SINGULAR	PLURAL
presente de indicativo	
hall**o**	hall**amos**
hall**as**	hall**áis**
hall**a**	hall**an**
imperfecto de indicativo	
hall**aba**	hall**ábamos**
hall**abas**	hall**abais**
hall**aba**	hall**aban**
pretérito	
hall**é**	hall**amos**
hall**aste**	hall**asteis**
hall**ó**	hall**aron**
futuro	
hallar**é**	hallar**emos**
hallar**ás**	hallar**éis**
hallar**á**	hallar**án**
condicional simple	
hallar**ía**	hallar**íamos**
hallar**ías**	hallar**íais**
hallar**ía**	hallar**ían**
presente de subjuntivo	
hall**e**	hall**emos**
hall**es**	hall**éis**
hall**e**	hall**en**
imperfecto de subjuntivo	
hallar**a**	hallár**amos**
hallar**as**	hallar**ais**
hallar**a**	hallar**an**
OR	
halls**e**	hallás**emos**
hallas**es**	hallas**eis**
hallas**e**	hallas**en**
imperativo	
—	hallemos
halla; no halles	hallad; no halléis
halle	hallen

SINGULAR	PLURAL
perfecto de indicativo	
he hallado	**hemos** hallado
has hallado	**habéis** hallado
ha hallado	**han** hallado
pluscuamperfecto de indicativo	
había hallado	**habíamos** hallado
habías hallado	**habíais** hallado
había hallado	**habían** hallado
pretérito anterior	
hube hallado	**hubimos** hallado
hubiste hallado	**hubisteis** hallado
hubo hallado	**hubieron** hallado
futuro perfecto	
habré hallado	**habremos** hallado
habrás hallado	**habréis** hallado
habrá hallado	**habrán** hallado
condicional compuesto	
habría hallado	**habríamos** hallado
habrías hallado	**habríais** hallado
habría hallado	**habrían** hallado
perfecto de subjuntivo	
haya hallado	**hayamos** hallado
hayas hallado	**hayáis** hallado
haya hallado	**hayan** hallado
pluscuamperfecto de subjuntivo	
hubiera hallado	**hubiéramos** hallado
hubieras hallado	**hubierais** hallado
hubiera hallado	**hubieran** hallado
OR	
hubiese hallado	**hubiésemos** hallado
hubieses hallado	**hubieseis** hallado
hubiese hallado	**hubiesen** hallado

gerundio **heredando** participio de pasado **heredado**

SINGULAR	PLURAL	SINGULAR	PLURAL
presente de indicativo		perfecto de indicativo	
hered**o**	hered**amos**	**he** heredado	**hemos** heredado
hered**as**	hered**áis**	**has** heredado	**habéis** heredado
hered**a**	hered**an**	**ha** heredado	**han** heredado
imperfecto de indicativo		pluscuamperfecto de indicativo	
hered**aba**	hered**ábamos**	**había** heredado	**habíamos** heredado
hered**abas**	hered**abais**	**habías** heredado	**habíais** heredado
hered**aba**	hered**aban**	**había** heredado	**habían** heredado
pretérito		pretérito anterior	
hered**é**	hered**amos**	**hube** heredado	**hubimos** heredado
hered**aste**	hered**asteis**	**hubiste** heredado	**hubisteis** heredado
hered**ó**	hered**aron**	**hubo** heredado	**hubieron** heredado
futuro		futuro perfecto	
heredar**é**	heredar**emos**	**habré** heredado	**habremos** heredado
heredar**ás**	heredar**éis**	**habrás** heredado	**habréis** heredado
heredar**á**	heredar**án**	**habrá** heredado	**habrán** heredado
condicional simple		condicional compuesto	
heredar**ía**	heredar**íamos**	**habría** heredado	**habríamos** heredado
heredar**ías**	heredar**íais**	**habrías** heredado	**habríais** heredado
heredar**ía**	heredar**ían**	**habría** heredado	**habrían** heredado
presente de subjuntivo		perfecto de subjuntivo	
hered**e**	hered**emos**	**haya** heredado	**hayamos** heredado
hered**es**	hered**éis**	**hayas** heredado	**hayáis** heredado
hered**e**	hered**en**	**haya** heredado	**hayan** heredado
imperfecto de subjuntivo		pluscuamperfecto de subjuntivo	
heredar**a**	heredár**amos**	**hubiera** heredado	**hubiéramos** heredado
heredar**as**	heredar**ais**	**hubieras** heredado	**hubierais** heredado
heredar**a**	heredar**an**	**hubiera** heredado	**hubieran** heredado
OR		OR	
heredas**e**	heredás**emos**	**hubiese** heredado	**hubiésemos** heredado
heredas**es**	heredas**eis**	**hubieses** heredado	**hubieseis** heredado
heredas**e**	heredas**en**	**hubiese** heredado	**hubiesen** heredado

imperativo

—	heredemos
hereda; no heredes	heredad; no heredéis
herede	hereden

to wound, to hurt — herir

gerundio **hiriendo** | participio de pasado **herido**

SINGULAR	PLURAL
presente de indicativo	
hier**o**	her**imos**
hier**es**	her**ís**
hier**e**	hier**en**
imperfecto de indicativo	
her**ía**	her**íamos**
her**ías**	her**íais**
her**ía**	her**ían**
pretérito	
her**í**	her**imos**
her**iste**	her**isteis**
hir**ió**	hir**ieron**
futuro	
herir**é**	herir**emos**
herir**ás**	herir**éis**
herir**á**	herir**án**
condicional simple	
herir**ía**	herir**íamos**
herir**ías**	herir**íais**
herir**ía**	herir**ían**
presente de subjuntivo	
hier**a**	hir**amos**
hier**as**	hir**áis**
hier**a**	hier**an**
imperfecto de subjuntivo	
hirier**a**	hirier**amos**
hirier**as**	hirier**ais**
hirier**a**	hirier**an**
OR	
hiries**e**	hiriés**emos**
hiries**es**	hiries**eis**
hiries**e**	hiries**en**
imperativo	
—	hiramos
hiere; no hieras	herid; no hiráis
hiera	hieran

SINGULAR	PLURAL
perfecto de indicativo	
he herido	**hemos** herido
has herido	**habéis** herido
ha herido	**han** herido
pluscuamperfecto de indicativo	
había herido	**habíamos** herido
habías herido	**habíais** herido
había herido	**habían** herido
pretérito anterior	
hube herido	**hubimos** herido
hubiste herido	**hubisteis** herido
hubo herido	**hubieron** herido
futuro perfecto	
habré herido	**habremos** herido
habrás herido	**habréis** herido
habrá herido	**habrán** herido
condicional compuesto	
habría herido	**habríamos** herido
habrías herido	**habríais** herido
habría herido	**habrían** herido
perfecto de subjuntivo	
haya herido	**hayamos** herido
hayas herido	**hayáis** herido
haya herido	**hayan** herido
pluscuamperfecto de subjuntivo	
hubiera herido	**hubiéramos** herido
hubieras herido	**hubierais** herido
hubiera herido	**hubieran** herido
OR	
hubiese herido	**hubiésemos** herido
hubieses herido	**hubieseis** herido
hubiese herido	**hubiesen** herido

huir — to flee, to escape

gerundio **huyendo** participio de pasado **huido**

SINGULAR	PLURAL
presente de indicativo	
huy**o**	hu**imos**
huy**es**	hu**ís**
huy**e**	huy**en**
imperfecto de indicativo	
hu**ía**	hu**íamos**
hu**ías**	hu**íais**
hu**ía**	hu**ían**
pretérito	
hu**í**	hu**imos**
hu**iste**	hu**isteis**
huy**ó**	huy**eron**
futuro	
huir**é**	huir**emos**
huir**ás**	huir**éis**
huir**á**	huir**án**
condicional simple	
huir**ía**	huir**íamos**
huir**ías**	huir**íais**
huir**ía**	huir**ían**
presente de subjuntivo	
huy**a**	huy**amos**
huy**as**	huy**áis**
huy**a**	huy**an**
imperfecto de subjuntivo	
huyer**a**	huyér**amos**
huyer**as**	huyer**ais**
huyer**a**	huyer**an**
OR	
huyes**e**	huyés**emos**
huyes**es**	huyes**eis**
huyes**e**	huyes**en**
imperativo	
—	huyamos
huye; no huyas	huid; no huyáis
huya	huyan

SINGULAR	PLURAL
perfecto de indicativo	
he huido	**hemos** huido
has huido	**habéis** huido
ha huido	**han** huido
pluscuamperfecto de indicativo	
había huido	**habíamos** huido
habías huido	**habíais** huido
había huido	**habían** huido
pretérito anterior	
hube huido	**hubimos** huido
hubiste huido	**hubisteis** huido
hubo huido	**hubieron** huido
futuro perfecto	
habré huido	**habremos** huido
habrás huido	**habréis** huido
habrá huido	**habrán** huido
condicional compuesto	
habría huido	**habríamos** huido
habrías huido	**habríais** huido
habría huido	**habrían** huido
perfecto de subjuntivo	
haya huido	**hayamos** huido
hayas huido	**hayáis** huido
haya huido	**hayan** huido
pluscuamperfecto de subjuntivo	
hubiera huido	**hubiéramos** huido
hubieras huido	**hubierais** huido
hubiera huido	**hubieran** huido
OR	
hubiese huido	**hubiésemos** huido
hubieses huido	**hubieseis** huido
hubiese huido	**hubiesen** huido

gerundio **identificando** participio de pasado **identificado**

SINGULAR	PLURAL	SINGULAR	PLURAL
presente de indicativo		perfecto de indicativo	
identific**o**	identific**amos**	**he** identificado	**hemos** identificado
identific**as**	identific**áis**	**has** identificado	**habéis** identificado
identific**a**	identific**an**	**ha** identificado	**han** identificado
imperfecto de indicativo		pluscuamperfecto de indicativo	
identific**aba**	identific**ábamos**	**había** identificado	**habíamos** identificado
identific**abas**	identific**abais**	**habías** identificado	**habíais** identificado
identific**aba**	identific**aban**	**había** identificado	**habían** identificado
pretérito		pretérito anterior	
identifiqu**é**	identific**amos**	**hube** identificado	**hubimos** identificado
identific**aste**	identific**asteis**	**hubiste** identificado	**hubisteis** identificado
identific**ó**	identific**aron**	**hubo** identificado	**hubieron** identificado
futuro		futuro perfecto	
identificar**é**	identificar**emos**	**habré** identificado	**habremos** identificado
identificar**ás**	identificar**éis**	**habrás** identificado	**habréis** identificado
identificar**á**	identificar**án**	**habrá** identificado	**habrán** identificado
condicional simple		condicional compuesto	
identificar**ía**	identificar**íamos**	**habría** identificado	**habríamos** identificado
identificar**ías**	identificar**íais**	**habrías** identificado	**habríais** identificado
identificar**ía**	identificar**ían**	**habría** identificado	**habrían** identificado
presente de subjuntivo		perfecto de subjuntivo	
identifiqu**e**	identifiqu**emos**	**haya** identificado	**hayamos** identificado
identifiqu**es**	identifiqu**éis**	**hayas** identificado	**hayáis** identificado
identifiqu**e**	identifiqu**en**	**haya** identificado	**hayan** identificado
imperfecto de subjuntivo		pluscuamperfecto de subjuntivo	
identificar**a**	identificár**amos**	**hubiera** identificado	**hubiéramos** identificado
identificar**as**	identificar**ais**	**hubieras** identificado	**hubierais** identificado
identificar**a**	identificar**an**	**hubiera** identificado	**hubieran** identificado
OR		OR	
identificas**e**	identificás**emos**	**hubiese** identificado	**hubiésemos** identificado
identificas**es**	identificas**eis**	**hubieses** identificado	**hubieseis** identificado
identificas**e**	identificas**en**	**hubiese** identificado	**hubiesen** identificado

imperativo

—	identifiquemos
identifica; no identifiques	identificad; no identifiquéis
identifique	identifiquen

I

ignorar — to ignore

gerundio **ignorando** participio de pasado **ignorado**

presente de indicativo

SINGULAR	PLURAL
ignor**o**	ignor**amos**
ignor**as**	ignor**áis**
ignor**a**	ignor**an**

imperfecto de indicativo

SINGULAR	PLURAL
ignor**aba**	ignor**ábamos**
ignor**abas**	ignor**abais**
ignor**aba**	ignor**aban**

pretérito

SINGULAR	PLURAL
ignor**é**	ignor**amos**
ignor**aste**	ignor**asteis**
ignor**ó**	ignor**aron**

futuro

SINGULAR	PLURAL
ignorar**é**	ignorár**emos**
ignorar**ás**	ignorar**éis**
ignorar**á**	ignorar**án**

condicional simple

SINGULAR	PLURAL
ignoarar**ía**	ignorar**íamos**
ignóarar**ías**	ignorar**íais**
ignorar**ía**	ignorar**ían**

presente de subjuntivo

SINGULAR	PLURAL
ignor**e**	ignor**emos**
ignor**es**	ignor**éis**
ignor**e**	ignor**en**

imperfecto de subjuntivo

SINGULAR	PLURAL
ignorar**a**	ignorár**amos**
ignorar**as**	ignorar**ais**
ignorar**a**	ignorar**an**
OR	
ignoras**e**	ignorás**emos**
ignoras**es**	ignoras**eis**
ignoras**e**	ignoras**en**

perfecto de indicativo

SINGULAR	PLURAL
he ignorado	**hemos** ignorado
has ignorado	**habéis** ignorado
ha ignorado	**han** ignorado

pluscuamperfecto de indicativo

SINGULAR	PLURAL
había ignorado	**habíamos** ignorado
habías ignorado	**habíais** ignorado
había ignorado	**habían** ignorado

pretérito anterior

SINGULAR	PLURAL
hube ignorado	**hubimos** ignorado
hubiste ignorado	**hubisteis** ignorado
hubo ignorado	**hubieron** ignorado

futuro perfecto

SINGULAR	PLURAL
habré ignorado	**habremos** ignorado
habrás ignorado	**habréis** ignorado
habrá ignorado	**habrán** ignorado

condicional compuesto

SINGULAR	PLURAL
habría ignorado	**habríamos** ignorado
habrías ignorado	**habríais** ignorado
habría ignorado	**habrían** ignorado

perfecto de subjuntivo

SINGULAR	PLURAL
haya ignorado	**hayamos** ignorado
hayas ignorado	**hayáis** ignorado
haya ignorado	**hayan** ignorado

pluscuamperfecto de subjuntivo

SINGULAR	PLURAL
hubiera ignorado	**hubiéramos** ignorado
hubieras ignorado	**hubierais** ignorado
hubiera ignorado	**hubieran** ignorado
OR	
hubiese ignorado	**hubiésemos** ignorado
hubieses ignorado	**hubieseis** ignorado
hubiese ignorado	**hubiesen** ignorado

imperativo

SINGULAR	PLURAL
—	ignoremos
ignora; no ignores	ignorad; no ignoréis
ignore	ignoren

to make illegal — ilegalizar

gerundio **ilegalizando** — participio de pasado **ilegalizado**

SINGULAR	PLURAL
presente de indicativo	
ilegaliz**o**	ilegaliz**amos**
ilegaliz**as**	ilegaliz**áis**
ilegaliz**a**	ilegaliz**an**
imperfecto de indicativo	
ilegaliz**aba**	ilegaliz**ábamos**
ilegaliz**abas**	ilegaliz**abais**
ilegaliz**aba**	ilegaliz**aban**
pretérito	
ilegalic**é**	ilegaliz**amos**
ilegaliz**aste**	ilegaliz**asteis**
ilegaliz**ó**	ilegaliz**aron**
futuro	
ilegalizar**é**	ilegalizar**emos**
ilegalizar**ás**	ilegalizar**éis**
ilegalizar**á**	ilegalizar**án**
condicional simple	
ilegalizar**ía**	ilegalizar**íamos**
ilegalizar**ías**	ilegalizar**íais**
ilegalizar**ía**	ilegalizar**ían**
presente de subjuntivo	
ilegalic**e**	ilegalic**emos**
ilegalic**es**	ilegalic**éis**
ilegalic**e**	ilegalic**en**
imperfecto de subjuntivo	
ilegalizar**a**	ilegalizár**amos**
ilegalizar**as**	ilegalizar**ais**
ilegalizar**a**	ilegalizar**an**
OR	
ilegalizas**e**	ilegalizás**emos**
ilegalizas**es**	ilegalizas**eis**
ilegalizas**e**	ilegalizas**en**
imperativo	
—	ilegalicemos
ilegaliza; no ilegalices	ilegalizad; no ilegalicéis
ilegalice	ilegalicen

SINGULAR	PLURAL
perfecto de indicativo	
he ilegalizado	**hemos** ilegalizado
has ilegalizado	**habéis** ilegalizado
ha ilegalizado	**han** ilegalizado
pluscuamperfecto de indicativo	
había ilegalizado	**habíamos** ilegalizado
habías ilegalizado	**habíais** ilegalizado
había ilegalizado	**habían** ilegalizado
pretérito anterior	
hube ilegalizado	**hubimos** ilegalizado
hubiste ilegalizado	**hubisteis** ilegalizado
hubo ilegalizado	**hubieron** ilegalizado
futuro perfecto	
habré ilegalizado	**habremos** ilegalizado
habrás ilegalizado	**habréis** ilegalizado
habrá ilegalizado	**habrán** ilegalizado
condicional compuesto	
habría ilegalizado	**habríamos** ilegalizado
habrías ilegalizado	**habríais** ilegalizado
habría ilegalizado	**habrían** ilegalizado
perfecto de subjuntivo	
haya ilegalizado	**hayamos** ilegalizado
hayas ilegalizado	**hayáis** ilegalizado
haya ilegalizado	**hayan** ilegalizado
pluscuamperfecto de subjuntivo	
hubiera ilegalizado	**hubiéramos** ilegalizado
hubieras ilegalizado	**hubierais** ilegalizado
hubiera ilegalizado	**hubieran** ilegalizado
OR	
hubiese ilegalizado	**hubiésemos** ilegalizado
hubieses ilegalizado	**hubieseis** ilegalizado
hubiese ilegalizado	**hubiesen** ilegalizado

imitar — to imitate

gerundio **imitando** participio de pasado **imitado**

SINGULAR	PLURAL	SINGULAR	PLURAL
presente de indicativo		perfecto de indicativo	
imit**o**	imit**amos**	**he** imitado	**hemos** imitado
imit**as**	imit**áis**	**has** imitado	**habéis** imitado
imit**a**	imit**an**	**ha** imitado	**han** imitado
imperfecto de indicativo		pluscuamperfecto de indicativo	
imit**aba**	imit**ábamos**	**había** imitado	**habíamos** imitado
imit**abas**	imit**abais**	**habías** imitado	**habíais** imitado
imit**aba**	imit**aban**	**había** imitado	**habían** imitado
pretérito		pretérito anterior	
imit**é**	imit**amos**	**hube** imitado	**hubimos** imitado
imit**aste**	imit**asteis**	**hubiste** imitado	**hubisteis** imitado
imit**ó**	imit**aron**	**hubo** imitado	**hubieron** imitado
futuro		futuro perfecto	
imitar**é**	imitar**emos**	**habré** imitado	**habremos** imitado
imitar**ás**	imitar**éis**	**habrás** imitado	**habréis** imitado
imitar**á**	imitar**án**	**habrá** imitado	**habrán** imitado
condicional simple		condicional compuesto	
imitar**ía**	imitar**íamos**	**habría** imitado	**habríamos** imitado
imitar**ías**	imitar**íais**	**habrías** imitado	**habríais** imitado
imitar**ía**	imitar**ían**	**habría** imitado	**habrían** imitado
presente de subjuntivo		perfecto de subjuntivo	
imit**e**	imit**emos**	**haya** imitado	**hayamos** imitado
imit**es**	imit**éis**	**hayas** imitado	**hayáis** imitado
imit**e**	imit**en**	**haya** imitado	**hayan** imitado
imperfecto de subjuntivo		pluscuamperfecto de subjuntivo	
imitar**a**	imitár**amos**	**hubiera** imitado	**hubiéramos** imitado
imitar**as**	imitar**ais**	**hubieras** imitado	**hubierais** imitado
imitar**a**	imitar**an**	**hubiera** imitado	**hubieran** imitado
OR		OR	
imitas**e**	imitás**emos**	**hubiese** imitado	**hubiésemos** imitado
imitas**es**	imitas**eis**	**hubieses** imitado	**hubieseis** imitado
imitas**e**	imitas**en**	**hubiese** imitado	**hubiesen** imitado

imperativo

—	imitemos
imita; no imites	imitad; no imitéis
imite	imiten

gerundio **implementando** participio de pasado **implementado**

SINGULAR	PLURAL
presente de indicativo	
implement**o**	implement**amos**
implement**as**	implement**áis**
implement**a**	implement**an**
imperfecto de indicativo	
implement**aba**	implement**ábamos**
implement**abas**	implement**abais**
implement**aba**	implement**aban**
pretérito	
implement**é**	implement**amos**
implement**aste**	implement**asteis**
implement**ó**	implement**aron**
futuro	
implementar**é**	implementar**emos**
implementar**ás**	implementar**éis**
implementar**á**	implementar**án**
condicional simple	
implementar**ía**	implementar**íamos**
implementar**ías**	implementar**íais**
implementar**ía**	implementar**ían**
presente de subjuntivo	
implement**e**	implement**emos**
implement**es**	implement**éis**
implement**e**	implement**en**
imperfecto de subjuntivo	
implementar**a**	implementár**amos**
implementar**as**	implementar**ais**
implementar**a**	implementar**an**
OR	
implementas**e**	implementás**emos**
implementas**es**	implementas**eis**
implementas**e**	implementas**en**
imperativo	
—	implementemos
implementa; no implementes	implementad; no implementéis
implemente	implementen

SINGULAR	PLURAL
perfecto de indicativo	
he implementado	**hemos** implementado
has implementado	**habéis** implementado
ha implementado	**han** implementado
pluscuamperfecto de indicativo	
había implementado	**habíamos** implementado
habías implementado	**habíais** implementado
había implementado	**habían** implementado
pretérito anterior	
hube implementado	**hubimos** implementado
hubiste implementado	**hubisteis** implementado
hubo implementado	**hubieron** implementado
futuro perfecto	
habré implementado	**habremos** implementado
habrás implementado	**habréis** implementado
habrá implementado	**habrán** implementado
condicional compuesto	
habría implementado	**habríamos** implementado
habrías implementado	**habríais** implementado
habría implementado	**habrían** implementado
perfecto de subjuntivo	
haya implementado	**hayamos** implementado
hayas implementado	**hayáis** implementado
haya implementado	**hayan** implementado
pluscuamperfecto de subjuntivo	
hubiera implementado	**hubiéramos** implementado
hubieras implementado	**hubierais** implementado
hubiera implementado	**hubieran** implementado
OR	
hubiese implementado	**hubiésemos** implementado
hubieses implementado	**hubieseis** implementado
hubiese implementado	**hubiesen** implementado

implicar

to implicate, to involve

gerundio **implicando**

participio de pasado **implicado**

SINGULAR	PLURAL
presente de indicativo	
implic**o**	implic**amos**
implic**as**	implic**áis**
implic**a**	implic**an**
imperfecto de indicativo	
implic**aba**	implic**ábamos**
implic**abas**	implic**abais**
implic**aba**	implic**aban**
pretérito	
impliqu**é**	implic**amos**
implic**aste**	implic**asteis**
implic**ó**	implic**aron**
futuro	
implicar**é**	implicar**emos**
implicar**ás**	implicar**éis**
implicar**á**	implicar**án**
condicional simple	
implicar**ía**	implicar**íamos**
implicar**ías**	implicar**íais**
implicar**ía**	implicar**ían**
presente de subjuntivo	
impliqu**e**	impliqu**emos**
impliqu**es**	impliqu**éis**
impliqu**e**	impliqu**en**
imperfecto de subjuntivo	
implicar**a**	implicár**amos**
implicar**as**	implicar**ais**
implicar**a**	implicar**an**
OR	
implicas**e**	implicás**emos**
implicas**es**	implicas**eis**
implicas**e**	implicas**en**
imperativo	
—	impliquemos
implica; no impliques	implicad; no impliquéis
implique	impliquen

SINGULAR	PLURAL
perfecto de indicativo	
he implicado	**hemos** implicado
has implicado	**habéis** implicado
ha implicado	**han** implicado
pluscuamperfecto de indicativo	
había implicado	**habíamos** implicado
habías implicado	**habíais** implicado
había implicado	**habían** implicado
pretérito anterior	
hube implicado	**hubimos** implicado
hubiste implicado	**hubisteis** implicado
hubo implicado	**hubieron** implicado
futuro perfecto	
habré implicado	**habremos** implicado
habrás implicado	**habréis** implicado
habrá implicado	**habrán** implicado
condicional compuesto	
habría implicado	**habríamos** implicado
habrías implicado	**habríais** implicado
habría implicado	**habrían** implicado
perfecto de subjuntivo	
haya implicado	**hayamos** implicado
hayas implicado	**hayáis** implicado
haya implicado	**hayan** implicado
pluscuamperfecto de subjuntivo	
hubiera implicado	**hubiéramos** implicado
hubieras implicado	**hubierais** implicado
hubiera implicado	**hubieran** implicado
OR	
hubiese implicado	**hubiésemos** implicado
hubieses implicado	**hubieseis** implicado
hubiese implicado	**hubiesen** implicado

gerundio **imponiendo** participio de pasado **impuesto**

SINGULAR	PLURAL	SINGULAR	PLURAL
presente de indicativo		perfecto de indicativo	
impong**o**	impon**emos**	**he** impuesto	**hemos** impuesto
impon**es**	impon**éis**	**has** impuesto	**habéis** impuesto
impon**e**	impon**en**	**ha** impuesto	**han** impuesto
imperfecto de indicativo		pluscuamperfecto de indicativo	
impon**ía**	impon**íamos**	**había** impuesto	**habíamos** impuesto
impon**ías**	impon**íais**	**habías** impuesto	**habíais** impuesto
impon**ía**	impon**ían**	**había** impuesto	**habían** impuesto
pretérito		pretérito anterior	
impus**e**	impus**imos**	**hube** impuesto	**hubimos** impuesto
impus**iste**	impus**isteis**	**hubiste** impuesto	**hubisteis** impuesto
impus**o**	impus**ieron**	**hubo** impuesto	**hubieron** impuesto
futuro		futuro perfecto	
impondr**é**	impondr**emos**	**habré** impuesto	**habremos** impuesto
impondr**ás**	impondr**éis**	**habrás** impuesto	**habréis** impuesto
impondr**á**	impondr**án**	**habrá** impuesto	**habrán** impuesto
condicional simple		condicional compuesto	
impondr**ía**	impondr**íamos**	**habría** impuesto	**habríamos** impuesto
impondr**ías**	impondr**íais**	**habrías** impuesto	**habríais** impuesto
impondr**ía**	impondr**ían**	**habría** impuesto	**habrían** impuesto
presente de subjuntivo		perfecto de subjuntivo	
impong**a**	impong**amos**	**haya** impuesto	**hayamos** impuesto
impong**as**	impong**áis**	**hayas** impuesto	**hayáis** impuesto
impong**a**	impong**an**	**haya** impuesto	**hayan** impuesto
imperfecto de subjuntivo		pluscuamperfecto de subjuntivo	
impusier**a**	impusiér**amos**	**hubiera** impuesto	**hubiéramos** impuesto
impusier**as**	impusier**ais**	**hubieras** impuesto	**hubierais** impuesto
impusier**a**	impusier**an**	**hubiera** impuesto	**hubieran** impuesto
OR		OR	
impusies**e**	impusiés**emos**	**hubiese** impuesto	**hubiésemos** impuesto
impusies**es**	impusies**eis**	**hubieses** impuesto	**hubieseis** impuesto
impusies**e**	impusies**en**	**hubiese** impuesto	**hubiesen** impuesto

imperativo

—	impongamos
impón; no impongas	imponed; no impongáis
imponga	impongan

imprimir — to print

gerundio **imprimiendo** — participio de pasado **imprimido**

SINGULAR	PLURAL
presente de indicativo	
imprim**o**	imprim**imos**
imprim**es**	imprim**ís**
imprim**e**	imprim**en**
imperfecto de indicativo	
imprim**ía**	imprim**íamos**
imprim**ías**	imprim**íais**
imprim**ía**	imprim**ían**
pretérito	
imprim**í**	imprim**imos**
imprim**iste**	imprim**isteis**
imprim**ió**	imprim**ieron**
futuro	
imprimir**é**	imprimir**emos**
imprimir**ás**	imprimir**éis**
imprimir**á**	imprimir**án**
condicional simple	
imprimir**ía**	imprimir**íamos**
imprimir**ías**	imprimir**íais**
imprimir**ía**	imprimir**ían**
presente de subjuntivo	
imprim**a**	imprim**amos**
imprim**as**	imprim**áis**
imprim**a**	imprim**an**
imperfecto de subjuntivo	
imprimier**a**	imprimiér**amos**
imprimier**as**	imprimier**ais**
imprimier**a**	imprimier**an**
OR	
imprimies**e**	imprimiés**emos**
imprimies**es**	imprimies**eis**
imprimies**e**	imprimies**en**
imperativo	
—	imprimamos
imprime; no imprimas	imprimid; no imprimáis
imprima	impriman

SINGULAR	PLURAL
perfecto de indicativo	
he imprimido	**hemos** imprimido
has imprimido	**habéis** imprimido
ha imprimido	**han** imprimido
pluscuamperfecto de indicativo	
había imprimido	**habíamos** imprimido
habías imprimido	**habíais** imprimido
había imprimido	**habían** imprimido
pretérito anterior	
hube imprimido	**hubimos** imprimido
hubiste imprimido	**hubisteis** imprimido
hubo imprimido	**hubieron** imprimido
futuro perfecto	
habré imprimido	**habremos** imprimido
habrás imprimido	**habréis** imprimido
habrá imprimido	**habrán** imprimido
condicional compuesto	
habría imprimido	**habríamos** imprimido
habrías imprimido	**habríais** imprimido
habría imprimido	**habrían** imprimido
perfecto de subjuntivo	
haya imprimido	**hayamos** imprimido
hayas imprimido	**hayáis** imprimido
haya imprimido	**hayan** imprimido
pluscuamperfecto de subjuntivo	
hubiera imprimido	**hubiéramos** imprimido
hubieras imprimido	**hubierais** imprimido
hubiera imprimido	**hubieran** imprimido
OR	
hubiese imprimido	**hubiésemos** imprimido
hubieses imprimido	**hubieseis** imprimido
hubiese imprimido	**hubiesen** imprimido

to include — incluir

gerundio **incluyendo** participio de pasado **incluido**

SINGULAR	PLURAL
presente de indicativo	
incluy**o**	inclu**imos**
incluy**es**	inclu**ís**
incluy**e**	incluy**en**
imperfecto de indicativo	
inclu**ía**	inclu**íamos**
inclu**ías**	inclu**íais**
inclu**ía**	inclu**ían**
pretérito	
inclu**í**	inclu**imos**
inclu**iste**	inclu**isteis**
incluy**ó**	incluy**eron**
futuro	
incluir**é**	incluir**emos**
incluir**ás**	incluir**éis**
incluir**á**	incluir**án**
condicional simple	
incluir**ía**	incluir**íamos**
incluir**ías**	incluir**íais**
incluir**ía**	incluir**ían**
presente de subjuntivo	
incluy**a**	incluy**amos**
incluy**as**	incluy**áis**
incluy**a**	incluy**an**
imperfecto de subjuntivo	
incluyer**a**	incluyér**amos**
incluyer**as**	incluyer**ais**
incluyer**a**	incluyer**an**
OR	
incluyes**e**	incluyés**emos**
incluyes**es**	incluyes**eis**
incluyes**e**	incluyes**en**
imperativo	
—	incluyamos
incluye; no incluyas	incluid; no incluyáis
incluya	incluyan

SINGULAR	PLURAL
perfecto de indicativo	
he incluido	**hemos** incluido
has incluido	**habéis** incluido
ha incluido	**han** incluido
pluscuamperfecto de indicativo	
había incluido	**habíamos** incluido
habías incluido	**habíais** incluido
había incluido	**habían** incluido
pretérito anterior	
hube incluido	**hubimos** incluido
hubiste incluido	**hubisteis** incluido
hubo incluido	**hubieron** incluido
futuro perfecto	
habré incluido	**habremos** incluido
habrás incluido	**habréis** incluido
habrá incluido	**habrán** incluido
condicional compuesto	
habría incluido	**habríamos** incluido
habrías incluido	**habríais** incluido
habría incluido	**habrían** incluido
perfecto de subjuntivo	
haya incluido	**hayamos** incluido
hayas incluido	**hayáis** incluido
haya incluido	**hayan** incluido
pluscuamperfecto de subjuntivo	
hubiera incluido	**hubiéramos** incluido
hubieras incluido	**hubierais** incluido
hubiera incluido	**hubieran** incluido
OR	
hubiese incluido	**hubiésemos** incluido
hubieses incluido	**hubieseis** incluido
hubiese incluido	**hubiesen** incluido

incorporar — to incorporate

gerundio **incorporando** participio de pasado **incorporado**

SINGULAR	PLURAL	SINGULAR	PLURAL
presente de indicativo		perfecto de indicativo	
incorpor**o**	incorpor**amos**	**he** incorporado	**hemos** incorporado
incorpor**as**	incorpor**áis**	**has** incorporado	**habéis** incorporado
incorpor**a**	incorpor**an**	**ha** incorporado	**han** incorporado
imperfecto de indicativo		pluscuamperfecto de indicativo	
incorpor**aba**	incorpor**ábamos**	**había** incorporado	**habíamos** incorporado
incorpor**abas**	incorpor**abais**	**habías** incorporado	**habíais** incorporado
incorpor**aba**	incorpor**aban**	**había** incorporado	**habían** incorporado
pretérito		pretérito anterior	
incorpor**é**	incorpor**amos**	**hube** incorporado	**hubimos** incorporado
incorpor**aste**	incorpor**asteis**	**hubiste** incorporado	**hubisteis** incorporado
incorpor**ó**	incorpor**aron**	**hubo** incorporado	**hubieron** incorporado
futuro		futuro perfecto	
incorporar**é**	incorporar**emos**	**habré** incorporado	**habremos** incorporado
incorporar**ás**	incorporar**éis**	**habrás** incorporado	**habréis** incorporado
incorporar**á**	incorporar**án**	**habrá** incorporado	**habrán** incorporado
condicional simple		condicional compuesto	
incorporar**ía**	incorporar**íamos**	**habría** incorporado	**habríamos** incorporado
incorporar**ías**	incorporar**íais**	**habrías** incorporado	**habríais** incorporado
incorporar**ía**	incorporar**ían**	**habría** incorporado	**habrían** incorporado
presente de subjuntivo		perfecto de subjuntivo	
incorpor**e**	incorpor**emos**	**haya** incorporado	**hayamos** incorporado
incorpor**es**	incorpor**éis**	**hayas** incorporado	**hayáis** incorporado
incorpor**e**	incorpor**en**	**haya** incorporado	**hayan** incorporado
imperfecto de subjuntivo		pluscuamperfecto de subjuntivo	
incorporar**a**	incorporár**amos**	**hubiera** incorporado	**hubiéramos** incorporado
incorporar**as**	incorporar**ais**	**hubieras** incorporado	**hubierais** incorporado
incorporar**a**	incorporar**an**	**hubiera** incorporado	**hubieran** incorporado
OR		OR	
incorporas**e**	incorporás**emos**	**hubiese** incorporado	**hubiésemos** incorporado
incorporas**es**	incorporas**eis**	**hubieses** incorporado	**hubieseis** incorporado
incorporas**e**	incorporas**en**	**hubiese** incorporado	**hubiesen** incorporado

imperativo

—	incorporemos
incorpora; no incorpores	incorporad; no incorporéis
incorpore	incorporen

gerundio **indicando** participio de pasado **indicado**

SINGULAR	PLURAL	SINGULAR	PLURAL
presente de indicativo		perfecto de indicativo	
indic**o**	indic**amos**	**he** indicado	**hemos** indicado
indic**as**	indic**áis**	**has** indicado	**habéis** indicado
indic**a**	indic**an**	**ha** indicado	**han** indicado
imperfecto de indicativo		pluscuamperfecto de indicativo	
indic**aba**	indic**ábamos**	**había** indicado	**habíamos** indicado
indic**abas**	indic**abais**	**habías** indicado	**habíais** indicado
indic**aba**	indic**aban**	**había** indicado	**habían** indicado
pretérito		pretérito anterior	
indiqu**é**	indic**amos**	**hube** indicado	**hubimos** indicado
indic**aste**	indic**asteis**	**hubiste** indicado	**hubisteis** indicado
indic**ó**	indic**aron**	**hubo** indicado	**hubieron** indicado
futuro		futuro perfecto	
indicar**é**	indicar**emos**	**habré** indicado	**habremos** indicado
indicar**ás**	indicar**éis**	**habrás** indicado	**habréis** indicado
indicar**á**	indicar**án**	**habrá** indicado	**habrán** indicado
condicional simple		condicional compuesto	
indicar**ía**	indicar**íamos**	**habría** indicado	**habríamos** indicado
indicar**ías**	indicar**íais**	**habrías** indicado	**habríais** indicado
indicar**ía**	indicar**ían**	**habría** indicado	**habrían** indicado
presente de subjuntivo		perfecto de subjuntivo	
indiqu**e**	indiqu**emos**	**haya** indicado	**hayamos** indicado
indiqu**es**	indiqu**éis**	**hayas** indicado	**hayáis** indicado
indiqu**e**	indiqu**en**	**haya** indicado	**hayan** indicado
imperfecto de subjuntivo		pluscuamperfecto de subjuntivo	
indicar**a**	indicár**amos**	**hubiera** indicado	**hubiéramos** indicado
indicar**as**	indicar**ais**	**hubieras** indicado	**hubierais** indicado
indicar**a**	indicar**an**	**hubiera** indicado	**hubieran** indicado
OR		OR	
indicas**e**	indicás**emos**	**hubiese** indicado	**hubiésemos** indicado
indicas**es**	indicas**eis**	**hubieses** indicado	**hubieseis** indicado
indicas**e**	indicas**en**	**hubiese** indicado	**hubiesen** indicado

imperativo

—	indiquemos
indica; no indiques	indicad; no indiquéis
indique	indiquen

inducir — to induce, to influence

gerundio **inducir**iendo — participio de pasado **inducido**

SINGULAR	PLURAL	SINGULAR	PLURAL
presente de indicativo		perfecto de indicativo	
induzc**o**	induc**imos**	**he** inducido	**hemos** inducido
induc**es**	induc**ís**	**has** inducido	**habéis** inducido
induc**e**	induc**en**	**ha** inducido	**han** inducido
imperfecto de indicativo		pluscuamperfecto de indicativo	
induc**ía**	induc**íamos**	**había** inducido	**habíamos** inducido
induc**ías**	induc**íais**	**habías** inducido	**habíais** inducido
induc**ía**	induc**ían**	**había** inducido	**habían** inducido
pretérito		pretérito anterior	
induj**e**	induj**imos**	**hube** inducido	**hubimos** inducido
induj**iste**	induj**isteis**	**hubiste** inducido	**hubisteis** inducido
induj**o**	induj**eron**	**hubo** inducido	**hubieron** inducido
futuro		futuro perfecto	
induciré	induciremos	**habré** inducido	**habremos** inducido
inducir**ás**	inducir**éis**	**habrás** inducido	**habréis** inducido
inducir**á**	inducir**án**	**habrá** inducido	**habrán** inducido
condicional simple		condicional compuesto	
inducir**ía**	inducir**íamos**	**habría** inducido	**habríamos** inducido
inducir**ías**	inducir**íais**	**habrías** inducido	**habríais** inducido
inducir**ía**	inducir**ían**	**habría** inducido	**habrían** inducido
presente de subjuntivo		perfecto de subjuntivo	
induzc**a**	induzc**amos**	**haya** inducido	**hayamos** inducido
induzc**as**	induzc**áis**	**hayas** inducido	**hayáis** inducido
induzc**a**	induzc**an**	**haya** inducido	**hayan** inducido
imperfecto de subjuntivo		pluscuamperfecto de subjuntivo	
indujer**a**	indujér**amos**	**hubiera** inducido	**hubiéramos** inducido
indujer**as**	indujer**ais**	**hubieras** inducido	**hubierais** inducido
indujer**a**	indujer**an**	**hubiera** inducido	**hubieran** inducido
OR		OR	
indujes**e**	indujés**emos**	**hubiese** inducido	**hubiésemos** inducido
indujes**es**	indujes**eis**	**hubieses** inducido	**hubieseis** inducido
indujes**e**	indujes**en**	**hubiese** inducido	**hubiesen** inducido

imperativo

—	induzcamos
induce; no induzcas	inducid; no induzcáis
induzca	induzcan

to infer — inferir

gerundio **infiriendo** participio de pasado **inferido**

SINGULAR	PLURAL	SINGULAR	PLURAL
presente de indicativo		perfecto de indicativo	
infier**o**	infer**imos**	**he** inferido	**hemos** inferido
infier**es**	infer**ís**	**has** inferido	**habéis** inferido
infier**e**	infier**en**	**ha** inferido	**han** inferido
imperfecto de indicativo		pluscuamperfecto de indicativo	
infer**ía**	infer**íamos**	**había** inferido	**habíamos** inferido
infer**ías**	infer**íais**	**habías** inferido	**habíais** inferido
infer**ía**	infer**ían**	**había** inferido	**habían** inferido
pretérito		pretérito anterior	
infer**í**	infer**imos**	**hube** inferido	**hubimos** inferido
infer**iste**	infer**isteis**	**hubiste** inferido	**hubisteis** inferido
infiri**ó**	infir**ieron**	**hubo** inferido	**hubieron** inferido
futuro		futuro perfecto	
inferir**é**	inferir**emos**	**habré** inferido	**habremos** inferido
inferir**ás**	inferir**éis**	**habrás** inferido	**habréis** inferido
inferir**á**	inferir**án**	**habrá** inferido	**habrán** inferido
condicional simple		condicional compuesto	
inferir**ía**	inferir**íamos**	**habría** inferido	**habríamos** inferido
inferir**ías**	inferir**íais**	**habrías** inferido	**habríais** inferido
inferir**ía**	inferir**ían**	**habría** inferido	**habrían** inferido
presente de subjuntivo		perfecto de subjuntivo	
infier**a**	infir**amos**	**haya** inferido	**hayamos** inferido
infier**as**	infir**áis**	**hayas** inferido	**hayáis** inferido
infier**a**	infier**an**	**haya** inferido	**hayan** inferido
imperfecto de subjuntivo		pluscuamperfecto de subjuntivo	
infirier**a**	infiriér**amos**	**hubiera** inferido	**hubiéramos** inferido
infirier**as**	infirier**ais**	**hubieras** inferido	**hubierais** inferido
infirier**a**	infirier**an**	**hubiera** inferido	**hubieran** inferido
OR		OR	
infiries**e**	infiriés**emos**	**hubiese** inferido	**hubiésemos** inferido
infiries**es**	infiries**eis**	**hubieses** inferido	**hubieseis** inferido
infiries**e**	infiries**en**	**hubiese** inferido	**hubiesen** inferido

imperativo

—	infiramos
infiere; no infieras	inferid; no infiráis
infiera	infieran

I

infligir — to inflict

gerundio **infligiendo** participio de pasado **infligido**

SINGULAR	PLURAL
presente de indicativo	
inflij**o**	infligi**mos**
inflig**es**	inflig**ís**
inflig**e**	inflig**en**
imperfecto de indicativo	
inflig**ía**	inflig**íamos**
inflig**ías**	inflig**íais**
inflig**ía**	inflig**ían**
pretérito	
inflig**í**	inflig**imos**
inflig**iste**	inflig**isteis**
inflig**ió**	inflig**ieron**
futuro	
infligir**é**	infligir**emos**
infligir**ás**	infligir**éis**
infligir**á**	infligir**án**
condicional simple	
infligir**ía**	infligir**íamos**
infligir**ías**	infligir**íais**
infligir**ía**	infligir**ían**
presente de subjuntivo	
inflij**a**	inflij**amos**
inflij**as**	inflij**áis**
inflij**a**	inflij**an**
imperfecto de subjuntivo	
infligier**a**	infligiér**amos**
infligier**as**	infligier**ais**
infligier**a**	infligier**an**
OR	
infligies**e**	infligiés**emos**
infligies**es**	infligies**eis**
infligies**e**	infligies**en**
imperativo	
—	inflijamos
inflige; no inflijas	infligid; no inflijáis
inflija	inflijan

SINGULAR	PLURAL
perfecto de indicativo	
he infligido	**hemos** infligido
has infligido	**habéis** infligido
ha infligido	**han** infligido
pluscuamperfecto de indicativo	
había infligido	**habíamos** infligido
habías infligido	**habíais** infligido
había infligido	**habían** infligido
pretérito anterior	
hube infligido	**hubimos** infligido
hubiste infligido	**hubisteis** infligido
hubo infligido	**hubieron** infligido
futuro perfecto	
habré infligido	**habremos** infligido
habrás infligido	**habréis** infligido
habrá infligido	**habrán** infligido
condicional compuesto	
habría infligido	**habríamos** infligido
habrías infligido	**habríais** infligido
habría infligido	**habrían** infligido
perfecto de subjuntivo	
haya infligido	**hayamos** infligido
hayas infligido	**hayáis** infligido
haya infligido	**hayan** infligido
pluscuamperfecto de subjuntivo	
hubiera infligido	**hubiéramos** infligido
hubieras infligido	**hubierais** infligido
hubiera infligido	**hubieran** infligido
OR	
hubiese infligido	**hubiésemos** infligido
hubieses infligido	**hubieseis** infligido
hubiese infligido	**hubiesen** infligido

to influence — influir

gerundio **influyendo** — participio de pasado **influido**

presente de indicativo

SINGULAR	PLURAL
influy**o**	influ**imos**
influy**es**	influ**ís**
influy**e**	influy**en**

imperfecto de indicativo

SINGULAR	PLURAL
influ**ía**	influ**íamos**
influ**ías**	influ**íais**
influ**ía**	influ**ían**

pretérito

SINGULAR	PLURAL
influ**í**	influ**imos**
influ**iste**	influ**isteis**
influy**ó**	influy**eron**

futuro

SINGULAR	PLURAL
influir**é**	influir**emos**
influir**ás**	influir**éis**
influir**á**	influir**án**

condicional simple

SINGULAR	PLURAL
influir**ía**	influir**íamos**
influir**ías**	influir**íais**
influir**ía**	influir**ían**

presente de subjuntivo

SINGULAR	PLURAL
influy**a**	influy**amos**
influy**as**	influy**áis**
influy**a**	influy**an**

imperfecto de subjuntivo

SINGULAR	PLURAL
influyer**a**	influyér**amos**
influyer**as**	influyer**ais**
influyer**a**	influyer**an**
OR	
influyes**e**	influyés**emos**
influyes**es**	influyes**eis**
influyes**e**	influyes**en**

imperativo

SINGULAR	PLURAL
—	influyamos
influye; no influyas	influid; no influyáis
influya	influyan

perfecto de indicativo

SINGULAR	PLURAL
he influido	**hemos** influido
has influido	**habéis** influido
ha influido	**han** influido

pluscuamperfecto de indicativo

SINGULAR	PLURAL
había influido	**habíamos** influido
habías influido	**habíais** influido
había influido	**habían** influido

pretérito anterior

SINGULAR	PLURAL
hube influido	**hubimos** influido
hubiste influido	**hubisteis** influido
hubo influido	**hubieron** influido

futuro perfecto

SINGULAR	PLURAL
habré influido	**habremos** influido
habrás influido	**habréis** influido
habrá influido	**habrán** influido

condicional compuesto

SINGULAR	PLURAL
habría influido	**habríamos** influido
habrías influido	**habríais** influido
habría influido	**habrían** influido

perfecto de subjuntivo

SINGULAR	PLURAL
haya influido	**hayamos** influido
hayas influido	**hayáis** influido
haya influido	**hayan** influido

pluscuamperfecto de subjuntivo

SINGULAR	PLURAL
hubiera influido	**hubiéramos** influido
hubieras influido	**hubierais** influido
hubiera influido	**hubieran** influido
OR	
hubiese influido	**hubiésemos** influido
hubieses influido	**hubieseis** influido
hubiese influido	**hubiesen** influido

informar — to inform

gerundio **informando** participio de pasado **informado**

presente de indicativo

SINGULAR	PLURAL
inform**o**	inform**amos**
inform**as**	inform**áis**
inform**a**	inform**an**

imperfecto de indicativo

SINGULAR	PLURAL
inform**aba**	inform**ábamos**
inform**abas**	inform**abais**
inform**aba**	inform**aban**

pretérito

SINGULAR	PLURAL
inform**é**	inform**amos**
inform**aste**	inform**asteis**
inform**ó**	inform**aron**

futuro

SINGULAR	PLURAL
informar**é**	informar**emos**
informar**ás**	informar**éis**
informar**á**	informar**án**

condicional simple

SINGULAR	PLURAL
informar**ía**	informar**íamos**
informar**ías**	informar**íais**
informar**ía**	informar**ían**

presente de subjuntivo

SINGULAR	PLURAL
inform**e**	inform**emos**
inform**es**	inform**éis**
inform**e**	inform**en**

imperfecto de subjuntivo

SINGULAR	PLURAL
informar**a**	informár**amos**
informar**as**	informar**ais**
informar**a**	informar**an**
OR	
informas**e**	informás**emos**
informas**es**	informas**eis**
informas**e**	informas**en**

imperativo

SINGULAR	PLURAL
—	informemos
informa; no informes	informad; no informéis
informe	informen

perfecto de indicativo

SINGULAR	PLURAL
he informado	**hemos** informado
has informado	**habéis** informado
ha informado	**han** informado

pluscuamperfecto de indicativo

SINGULAR	PLURAL
había informado	**habíamos** informado
habías informado	**habíais** informado
había informado	**habían** informado

pretérito anterior

SINGULAR	PLURAL
hube informado	**hubimos** informado
hubiste informado	**hubisteis** informado
hubo informado	**hubieron** informado

futuro perfecto

SINGULAR	PLURAL
habré informado	**habremos** informado
habrás informado	**habréis** informado
habrá informado	**habrán** informado

condicional compuesto

SINGULAR	PLURAL
habría informado	**habríamos** informado
habrías informado	**habríais** informado
habría informado	**habrían** informado

perfecto de subjuntivo

SINGULAR	PLURAL
haya informado	**hayamos** informado
hayas informado	**hayáis** informado
haya informado	**hayan** informado

pluscuamperfecto de subjuntivo

SINGULAR	PLURAL
hubiera informado	**hubiéramos** informado
hubieras informado	**hubierais** informado
hubiera informado	**hubieran** informado
OR	
hubiese informado	**hubiésemos** informado
hubieses informado	**hubieseis** informado
hubiese informado	**hubiesen** informado

gerundio **ingresando** participio de pasado **ingresado**

SINGULAR	PLURAL
presente de indicativo	
ingres**o**	ingres**amos**
ingres**as**	ingres**áis**
ingres**a**	ingres**an**
imperfecto de indicativo	
ingres**aba**	ingres**ábamos**
ingres**abas**	ingres**abais**
ingres**aba**	ingres**aban**
pretérito	
ingres**é**	ingres**amos**
ingres**aste**	ingres**asteis**
ingres**ó**	ingres**aron**
futuro	
ingresar**é**	ingresar**emos**
ingresar**ás**	ingresar**éis**
ingresar**á**	ingresar**án**
condicional simple	
ingresar**ía**	ingresar**íamos**
ingresar**ías**	ingresar**íais**
ingresar**ía**	ingresar**ían**
presente de subjuntivo	
ingres**e**	ingres**emos**
ingres**es**	ingres**éis**
ingres**e**	ingres**en**
imperfecto de subjuntivo	
ingresar**a**	ingresár**amos**
ingresar**as**	ingresar**ais**
ingresar**a**	ingresar**an**
OR	
ingresas**e**	ingresás**emos**
ingresas**es**	ingresas**eis**
ingresas**e**	ingresas**en**
imperativo	
—	ingresemos
ingresa; no ingreses	ingresad; no ingreséis
ingrese	ingresen

SINGULAR	PLURAL
perfecto de indicativo	
he ingresado	**hemos** ingresado
has ingresado	**habéis** ingresado
ha ingresado	**han** ingresado
pluscuamperfecto de indicativo	
había ingresado	**habíamos** ingresado
habías ingresado	**habíais** ingresado
había ingresado	**habían** ingresado
pretérito anterior	
hube ingresado	**hubimos** ingresado
hubiste ingresado	**hubisteis** ingresado
hubo ingresado	**hubieron** ingresado
futuro perfecto	
habré ingresado	**habremos** ingresado
habrás ingresado	**habréis** ingresado
habrá ingresado	**habrán** ingresado
condicional compuesto	
habría ingresado	**habríamos** ingresado
habrías ingresado	**habríais** ingresado
habría ingresado	**habrían** ingresado
perfecto de subjuntivo	
haya ingresado	**hayamos** ingresado
hayas ingresado	**hayáis** ingresado
haya ingresado	**hayan** ingresado
pluscuamperfecto de subjuntivo	
hubiera ingresado	**hubiéramos** ingresado
hubieras ingresado	**hubierais** ingresado
hubiera ingresado	**hubieran** ingresado
OR	
hubiese ingresado	**hubiésemos** ingresado
hubieses ingresado	**hubieseis** ingresado
hubiese ingresado	**hubiesen** ingresado

iniciar — to initiate

gerundio **iniciando** — participio de pasado **iniciado**

SINGULAR	PLURAL
presente de indicativo	
inici**o**	inici**amos**
inici**as**	inici**áis**
inici**a**	inici**an**
imperfecto de indicativo	
inici**aba**	inici**ábamos**
inici**abas**	inici**abais**
inici**aba**	inici**aban**
pretérito	
inici**é**	inici**amos**
inici**aste**	inici**asteis**
inici**ó**	inici**aron**
futuro	
iniciar**é**	iniciar**emos**
iniciar**ás**	iniciar**éis**
iniciar**á**	iniciar**án**
condicional simple	
iniciar**ía**	iniciar**íamos**
iniciar**ías**	iniciar**íais**
iniciar**ía**	iniciar**ían**
presente de subjuntivo	
inici**e**	inici**emos**
inici**es**	inici**éis**
inici**e**	inici**en**
imperfecto de subjuntivo	
iniciar**a**	iniciár**amos**
iniciar**as**	iniciar**ais**
iniciar**a**	iniciar**an**
OR	
inicias**e**	iniciás**emos**
inicias**es**	inicias**eis**
inicias**e**	inicias**en**
imperativo	
—	iniciemos
inicia; no inicies	iniciad; no iniciéis
inicie	inicien

SINGULAR	PLURAL
perfecto de indicativo	
he iniciado	**hemos** iniciado
has iniciado	**habéis** iniciado
ha iniciado	**han** iniciado
pluscuamperfecto de indicativo	
había iniciado	**habíamos** iniciado
habías iniciado	**habíais** iniciado
había iniciado	**habían** iniciado
pretérito anterior	
hube iniciado	**hubimos** iniciado
hubiste iniciado	**hubisteis** iniciado
hubo iniciado	**hubieron** iniciado
futuro perfecto	
habré iniciado	**habremos** iniciado
habrás iniciado	**habréis** iniciado
habrá iniciado	**habrán** iniciado
condicional compuesto	
habría iniciado	**habríamos** iniciado
habrías iniciado	**habríais** iniciado
habría iniciado	**habrían** iniciado
perfecto de subjuntivo	
haya iniciado	**hayamos** iniciado
hayas iniciado	**hayáis** iniciado
haya iniciado	**hayan** iniciado
pluscuamperfecto de subjuntivo	
hubiera iniciado	**hubiéramos** iniciado
hubieras iniciado	**hubierais** iniciado
hubiera iniciado	**hubieran** iniciado
OR	
hubiese iniciado	**hubiésemos** iniciado
hubieses iniciado	**hubieseis** iniciado
hubiese iniciado	**hubiesen** iniciado

gerundio **inmigrando** participio de pasado **inmigrado**

SINGULAR	PLURAL
presente de indicativo	
inmigr**o**	inmigr**amos**
inmigr**as**	inmigr**áis**
inmigr**a**	inmigr**an**
imperfecto de indicativo	
inmigr**aba**	inmigr**ábamos**
inmigr**abas**	inmigr**abais**
inmigr**aba**	inmigr**aban**
pretérito	
inmigr**é**	inmigr**amos**
inmigr**aste**	inmigr**asteis**
inmigr**ó**	inmigr**aron**
futuro	
inmigrar**é**	inmigrar**emos**
inmigrar**ás**	inmigrar**éis**
inmigrar**á**	inmigrar**án**
condicional simple	
inmigrar**ía**	inmigrar**íamos**
inmigrar**ías**	inmigrar**íais**
inmigrar**ía**	inmigrar**ían**
presente de subjuntivo	
inmigr**e**	inmigr**emos**
inmigr**es**	inmigr**éis**
inmigr**e**	inmigr**en**
imperfecto de subjuntivo	
inmigrar**a**	inmigrár**amos**
inmigrar**as**	inmigrar**ais**
inmigrar**a**	inmigrar**an**
OR	
inmigras**e**	inmigrás**emos**
inmigras**es**	inmigras**eis**
inmigras**e**	inmigras**en**

SINGULAR	PLURAL
perfecto de indicativo	
he inmigrado	**hemos** inmigrado
has inmigrado	**habéis** inmigrado
ha inmigrado	**han** inmigrado
pluscuamperfecto de indicativo	
había inmigrado	**habíamos** inmigrado
habías inmigrado	**habíais** inmigrado
había inmigrado	**habían** inmigrado
pretérito anterior	
hube inmigrado	**hubimos** inmigrado
hubiste inmigrado	**hubisteis** inmigrado
hubo inmigrado	**hubieron** inmigrado
futuro perfecto	
habré inmigrado	**habremos** inmigrado
habrás inmigrado	**habréis** inmigrado
habrá inmigrado	**habrán** inmigrado
condicional compuesto	
habría inmigrado	**habríamos** inmigrado
habrías inmigrado	**habríais** inmigrado
habría inmigrado	**habrían** inmigrado
perfecto de subjuntivo	
haya inmigrado	**hayamos** inmigrado
hayas inmigrado	**hayáis** inmigrado
haya inmigrado	**hayan** inmigrado
pluscuamperfecto de subjuntivo	
hubiera inmigrado	**hubiéramos** inmigrado
hubieras inmigrado	**hubierais** inmigrado
hubiera inmigrado	**hubieran** inmigrado
OR	
hubiese inmigrado	**hubiésemos** inmigrado
hubieses inmigrado	**hubieseis** inmigrado
hubiese inmigrado	**hubiesen** inmigrado

imperativo

—	inmigremos
inmigra; no inmigres	inmigrad; no inmigréis
inmigre	inmigren

inscribir to enroll, to register, to engrave

gerundio **inscribiendo** participio de pasado **inscrito**

SINGULAR	PLURAL	SINGULAR	PLURAL
presente de indicativo		perfecto de indicativo	
inscrib**o**	inscrib**imos**	**he** inscrito	**hemos** inscrito
inscrib**es**	inscrib**ís**	**has** inscrito	**habéis** inscrito
inscrib**e**	inscrib**en**	**ha** inscrito	**han** inscrito
imperfecto de indicativo		pluscuamperfecto de indicativo	
inscrib**ía**	inscrib**íamos**	**había** inscrito	**habíamos** inscrito
inscrib**ías**	inscrib**íais**	**habías** inscrito	**habíais** inscrito
inscrib**ía**	inscrib**ían**	**había** inscrito	**habían** inscrito
pretérito		pretérito anterior	
inscrib**í**	inscrib**imos**	**hube** inscrito	**hubimos** inscrito
inscrib**iste**	inscrib**isteis**	**hubiste** inscrito	**hubisteis** inscrito
inscrib**ió**	inscrib**ieron**	**hubo** inscrito	**hubieron** inscrito
futuro		futuro perfecto	
inscribir**é**	inscribir**emos**	**habré** inscrito	**habremos** inscrito
inscribir**ás**	inscribir**éis**	**habrás** inscrito	**habréis** inscrito
inscribir**á**	inscribir**án**	**habrá** inscrito	**habrán** inscrito
condicional simple		condicional compuesto	
inscribir**ía**	inscribir**íamos**	**habría** inscrito	**habríamos** inscrito
inscribir**ías**	inscribir**íais**	**habrías** inscrito	**habríais** inscrito
inscribir**ía**	inscribir**ían**	**habría** inscrito	**habrían** inscrito
presente de subjuntivo		perfecto de subjuntivo	
inscrib**a**	inscrib**amos**	**haya** inscrito	**hayamos** inscrito
inscrib**as**	inscrib**áis**	**hayas** inscrito	**hayáis** inscrito
inscrib**a**	inscrib**an**	**haya** inscrito	**hayan** inscrito
imperfecto de subjuntivo		pluscuamperfecto de subjuntivo	
inscribier**a**	inscribiér**amos**	**hubiera** inscrito	**hubiéramos** inscrito
inscribier**as**	inscribier**ais**	**hubieras** inscrito	**hubierais** inscrito
inscribier**a**	inscribier**an**	**hubiera** inscrito	**hubieran** inscrito
OR		OR	
inscribies**e**	inscribiés**emos**	**hubiese** inscrito	**hubiésemos** inscrito
inscribies**es**	inscribies**eis**	**hubieses** inscrito	**hubieseis** inscrito
inscribies**e**	inscribies**en**	**hubiese** inscrito	**hubiesen** inscrito

imperativo

—	inscribamos
inscribe; no inscribas	inscribid; no inscribáis
inscriba	inscriban

to enroll, to register, to sign up **inscribirse**

gerundio **inscribiéndose** participio de pasado **inscrito**

SINGULAR	PLURAL	SINGULAR	PLURAL
presente de indicativo		perfecto de indicativo	
me inscrib**o**	nos inscrib**imos**	**me he** inscrito	**nos hemos** inscrito
te inscrib**es**	os inscrib**ís**	**te has** inscrito	**os habéis** inscrito
se inscrib**e**	se inscrib**en**	**se ha** inscrito	**se han** inscrito
imperfecto de indicativo		pluscuamperfecto de indicativo	
me inscrib**ía**	nos inscrib**íamos**	**me había** inscrito	**nos habíamos** inscrito
te inscrib**ías**	os inscrib**íais**	**te habías** inscrito	**os habíais** inscrito
se inscrib**ía**	se inscrib**ían**	**se había** inscrito	**se habían** inscrito
pretérito		pretérito anterior	
me inscrib**í**	nos inscrib**imos**	**me hube** inscrito	**nos hubimos** inscrito
te inscrib**iste**	os inscrib**isteis**	**te hubiste** inscrito	**os hubisteis** inscrito
se inscrib**ió**	se inscrib**ieron**	**se hubo** inscrito	**se hubieron** inscrito
futuro		futuro perfecto	
me inscribir**é**	nos inscribir**emos**	**me habré** inscrito	**nos habremos** inscrito
te inscribir**ás**	os inscribir**éis**	**te habrás** inscrito	**os habréis** inscrito
se inscribir**á**	se inscribir**án**	**se habrá** inscrito	**se habrán** inscrito
condicional simple		condicional compuesto	
me inscribir**ía**	nos inscribir**íamos**	**me habría** inscrito	**nos habríamos** inscrito
te inscribir**ías**	os inscribir**íais**	**te habrías** inscrito	**os habríais** inscrito
se inscribir**ía**	se inscribir**ían**	**se habría** inscrito	**se habrían** inscrito
presente de subjuntivo		perfecto de subjuntivo	
me inscrib**a**	nos inscrib**amos**	**me haya** inscrito	**nos hayamos** inscrito
te inscrib**as**	os inscrib**áis**	**te hayas** inscrito	**os hayáis** inscrito
se inscrib**a**	se inscrib**an**	**se haya** inscrito	**se hayan** inscrito
imperfecto de subjuntivo		pluscuamperfecto de subjuntivo	
me inscribier**a**	nos inscribiér**amos**	**me hubiera** inscrito	**nos hubiéramos** inscrito
te inscribier**as**	os inscribier**ais**	**te hubieras** inscrito	**os hubierais** inscrito
se inscribier**a**	se inscribier**an**	**se hubiera** inscrito	**se hubieran** inscrito
OR		OR	
me inscribies**e**	nos inscribiés**emos**	**me hubiese** inscrito	**nos hubiésemos** inscrito
te inscribies**es**	os inscribies**eis**	**te hubieses** inscrito	**os hubieseis** inscrito
se inscribies**e**	se inscribies**en**	**se hubiese** inscrito	**se hubiesen** inscrito

imperativo

—	inscribámonos
inscríbete;	inscribios;
no te inscribas	no os inscribáis
inscríbase	inscríbanse

I

gerundio **insistiendo** participio de pasado **insistido**

SINGULAR	PLURAL
presente de indicativo	
insist**o**	insist**imos**
insist**es**	insist**ís**
insist**e**	insist**en**
imperfecto de indicativo	
insist**ía**	insist**íamos**
insist**ías**	insist**íais**
insist**ía**	insist**ían**
pretérito	
insist**í**	insist**imos**
insist**iste**	insist**isteis**
insist**ió**	insist**ieron**
futuro	
insistir**é**	insistir**emos**
insistir**ás**	insistir**éis**
insistir**á**	insistir**án**
condicional simple	
insistir**ía**	insistir**íamos**
insistir**ías**	insistir**íais**
insistir**ía**	insistir**ían**
presente de subjuntivo	
insist**a**	insist**amos**
insist**as**	insist**áis**
insist**a**	insist**an**
imperfecto de subjuntivo	
insistier**a**	insistiér**amos**
insistier**as**	insistier**ais**
insistier**a**	insistier**an**
OR	
insisties**e**	insistiés**emos**
insisties**es**	insisties**eis**
insisties**e**	insisties**en**
imperativo	
—	insistamos
insiste; no insistas	insistid; no insistáis
insista	insistan

SINGULAR	PLURAL
perfecto de indicativo	
he insistido	**hemos** insistido
has insistido	**habéis** insistido
ha insistido	**han** insistido
pluscuamperfecto de indicativo	
había insistido	**habíamos** insistido
habías insistido	**habíais** insistido
había insistido	**habían** insistido
pretérito anterior	
hube insistido	**hubimos** insistido
hubiste insistido	**hubisteis** insistido
hubo insistido	**hubieron** insistido
futuro perfecto	
habré insistido	**habremos** insistido
habrás insistido	**habréis** insistido
habrá insistido	**habrán** insistido
condicional compuesto	
habría insistido	**habríamos** insistido
habrías insistido	**habríais** insistido
habría insistido	**habrían** insistido
perfecto de subjuntivo	
haya insistido	**hayamos** insistido
hayas insistido	**hayáis** insistido
haya insistido	**hayan** insistido
pluscuamperfecto de subjuntivo	
hubiera insistido	**hubiéramos** insistido
hubieras insistido	**hubierais** insistido
hubiera insistido	**hubieran** insistido
OR	
hubiese insistido	**hubiésemos** insistido
hubieses insistido	**hubieseis** insistido
hubiese insistido	**hubiesen** insistido

gerundio **inspeccionando** participio de pasado **inspeccionado**

SINGULAR	PLURAL	SINGULAR	PLURAL
presente de indicativo		perfecto de indicativo	
inspeccion**o**	inspeccion**amos**	**he** inspeccionado	**hemos** inspeccionado
inspeccion**as**	inspeccion**áis**	**has** inspeccionado	**habéis** inspeccionado
inspeccion**a**	inspeccion**an**	**ha** inspeccionado	**han** inspeccionado
imperfecto de indicativo		pluscuamperfecto de indicativo	
inspeccion**aba**	inspeccion**ábamos**	**había** inspeccionado	**habíamos** inspeccionado
inspeccion**abas**	inspeccion**abais**	**habías** inspeccionado	**habíais** inspeccionado
inspeccion**aba**	inspeccion**aban**	**había** inspeccionado	**habían** inspeccionado
pretérito		pretérito anterior	
inspeccion**é**	inspeccion**amos**	**hube** inspeccionado	**hubimos** inspeccionado
inspeccion**aste**	inspeccion**asteis**	**hubiste** inspeccionado	**hubisteis** inspeccionado
inspeccion**ó**	inspeccion**aron**	**hubo** inspeccionado	**hubieron** inspeccionado
futuro		futuro perfecto	
inspeccionar**é**	inspeccionar**emos**	**habré** inspeccionado	**habremos** inspeccionado
inspeccionar**ás**	inspeccionar**éis**	**habrás** inspeccionado	**habréis** inspeccionado
inspeccionar**á**	inspeccionar**án**	**habrá** inspeccionado	**habrán** inspeccionado
condicional simple		condicional compuesto	
inspeccionar**ía**	inspeccionar**íamos**	**habría** inspeccionado	**habríamos** inspeccionado
inspeccionar**ías**	inspeccionar**íais**	**habrías** inspeccionado	**habríais** inspeccionado
inspeccionar**ía**	inspeccionar**ían**	**habría** inspeccionado	**habrían** inspeccionado
presente de subjuntivo		perfecto de subjuntivo	
inspeccion**e**	inspeccion**emos**	**haya** inspeccionado	**hayamos** inspeccionado
inspeccion**es**	inspeccion**éis**	**hayas** inspeccionado	**hayáis** inspeccionado
inspeccion**e**	inspeccion**en**	**haya** inspeccionado	**hayan** inspeccionado
imperfecto de subjuntivo		pluscuamperfecto de subjuntivo	
inspeccionar**a**	inspeccionár**amos**	**hubiera** inspeccionado	**hubiéramos** inspeccionado
inspeccionar**as**	inspeccionar**ais**	**hubieras** inspeccionado	**hubierais** inspeccionado
inspeccionar**a**	inspeccionar**an**	**hubiera** inspeccionado	**hubieran** inspeccionado
OR		OR	
inspeccionas**e**	inspeccionás**emos**	**hubiese** inspeccionado	**hubiésemos** inspeccionado
inspeccionas**es**	inspeccionas**eis**	**hubieses** inspeccionado	**hubieseis** inspeccionado
inspeccionas**e**	inspeccionas**en**	**hubiese** inspeccionado	**hubiesen** inspeccionado
imperativo			
—	inspeccionemos		
inspecciona;	inspeccionad;		
no inspecciones	no inspeccionéis		
inspeccione	inspeccionen		

gerundio **inspirando** participio de pasado **inspirado**

SINGULAR	PLURAL
presente de indicativo	
inspir**o**	inspir**amos**
inspir**as**	inspir**áis**
inspir**a**	inspir**an**
imperfecto de indicativo	
inspir**aba**	inspir**ábamos**
inspir**abas**	inspir**abais**
inspir**aba**	inspir**aban**
pretérito	
inspir**é**	inspir**amos**
inspir**aste**	inspir**asteis**
inspir**ó**	inspir**aron**
futuro	
inspirar**é**	inspirar**emos**
inspirar**ás**	inspirar**éis**
inspirar**á**	inspirar**án**
condicional simple	
inspirar**ía**	inspirar**íamos**
inspirar**ías**	inspirar**íais**
inspirar**ía**	inspirar**ían**
presente de subjuntivo	
inspir**e**	inspir**emos**
inspir**es**	inspir**éis**
inspir**e**	inspir**en**
imperfecto de subjuntivo	
inspirar**a**	inspirár**amos**
inspirar**as**	inspirar**ais**
inspirar**a**	inspirar**an**
OR	
inspiras**e**	inspirás**emos**
inspiras**es**	inspiras**eis**
inspiras**e**	inspiras**en**
imperativo	
—	inspiremos
inspira; no inspires	inspirad; no inspiréis
inspire	inspiren

SINGULAR	PLURAL
perfecto de indicativo	
he inspirado	**hemos** inspirado
has inspirado	**habéis** inspirado
ha inspirado	**han** inspirado
pluscuamperfecto de indicativo	
había inspirado	**habíamos** inspirado
habías inspirado	**habíais** inspirado
había inspirado	**habían** inspirado
pretérito anterior	
hube inspirado	**hubimos** inspirado
hubiste inspirado	**hubisteis** inspirado
hubo inspirado	**hubieron** inspirado
futuro perfecto	
habré inspirado	**habremos** inspirado
habrás inspirado	**habréis** inspirado
habrá inspirado	**habrán** inspirado
condicional compuesto	
habría inspirado	**habríamos** inspirado
habrías inspirado	**habríais** inspirado
habría inspirado	**habrían** inspirado
perfecto de subjuntivo	
haya inspirado	**hayamos** inspirado
hayas inspirado	**hayáis** inspirado
haya inspirado	**hayan** inspirado
pluscuamperfecto de subjuntivo	
hubiera inspirado	**hubiéramos** inspirado
hubieras inspirado	**hubierais** inspirado
hubiera inspirado	**hubieran** inspirado
OR	
hubiese inspirado	**hubiésemos** inspirado
hubieses inspirado	**hubieseis** inspirado
hubiese inspirado	**hubiesen** inspirado

gerundio **instituyendo** participio de pasado **instituido**

SINGULAR	PLURAL
presente de indicativo	
instituy**o**	institu**imos**
instituy**es**	institu**ís**
instituy**e**	instituy**en**
imperfecto de indicativo	
institu**ía**	institu**íamos**
institu**ías**	institu**íais**
institu**ía**	institu**ían**
pretérito	
institu**í**	institu**imos**
institu**iste**	institu**isteis**
instituy**ó**	instituy**eron**
futuro	
instituir**é**	instituir**emos**
instituir**ás**	instituir**éis**
instituir**á**	instituir**án**
condicional simple	
instituir**ía**	instituir**íamos**
instituir**ías**	instituir**íais**
instituir**ía**	instituir**ían**
presente de subjuntivo	
instituy**a**	instituy**amos**
instituy**as**	instituy**áis**
instituy**a**	instituy**an**
imperfecto de subjuntivo	
instituyer**a**	instituyér**amos**
instituyer**as**	instituyer**ais**
instituyer**a**	instituyer**an**
OR	
instituyes**e**	instituyés**emos**
instituyes**es**	instituyes**eis**
instituyes**e**	instituyes**en**
imperativo	
—	instituyamos
instituye; no instituyas	instituid; no instituyáis
instituya	instituyan

SINGULAR	PLURAL
perfecto de indicativo	
he instituido	**hemos** instituido
has instituido	**habéis** instituido
ha instituido	**han** instituido
pluscuamperfecto de indicativo	
había instituido	**habíamos** instituido
habías instituido	**habíais** instituido
había instituido	**habían** instituido
pretérito anterior	
hube instituido	**hubimos** instituido
hubiste instituido	**hubisteis** instituido
hubo instituido	**hubieron** instituido
futuro perfecto	
habré instituido	**habremos** instituido
habrás instituido	**habréis** instituido
habrá instituido	**habrán** instituido
condicional compuesto	
habría instituido	**habríamos** instituido
habrías instituido	**habríais** instituido
habría instituido	**habrían** instituido
perfecto de subjuntivo	
haya instituido	**hayamos** instituido
hayas instituido	**hayáis** instituido
haya instituido	**hayan** instituido
pluscuamperfecto de subjuntivo	
hubiera instituido	**hubiéramos** instituido
hubieras instituido	**hubierais** instituido
hubiera instituido	**hubieran** instituido
OR	
hubiese instituido	**hubiésemos** instituido
hubieses instituido	**hubieseis** instituido
hubiese instituido	**hubiesen** instituido

insultar — to insult

gerundio **insultando** — participio de pasado **insultado**

SINGULAR	PLURAL	SINGULAR	PLURAL
presente de indicativo		perfecto de indicativo	
insult**o**	insult**amos**	**he** insultado	**hemos** insultado
insult**as**	insult**áis**	**has** insultado	**habéis** insultado
insult**a**	insult**an**	**ha** insultado	**han** insultado
imperfecto de indicativo		pluscuamperfecto de indicativo	
insult**aba**	insult**ábamos**	**había** insultado	**habíamos** insultado
insult**abas**	insult**abais**	**habías** insultado	**habíais** insultado
insult**aba**	insult**aban**	**había** insultado	**habían** insultado
pretérito		pretérito anterior	
insult**é**	insult**amos**	**hube** insultado	**hubimos** insultado
insult**aste**	insult**asteis**	**hubiste** insultado	**hubisteis** insultado
insult**ó**	insult**aron**	**hubo** insultado	**hubieron** insultado
futuro		futuro perfecto	
insultar**é**	insultar**emos**	**habré** insultado	**habremos** insultado
insultar**ás**	insultar**éis**	**habrás** insultado	**habréis** insultado
insultar**á**	insultar**án**	**habrá** insultado	**habrán** insultado
condicional simple		condicional compuesto	
insultar**ía**	insultar**íamos**	**habría** insultado	**habríamos** insultado
insultar**ías**	insultar**íais**	**habrías** insultado	**habríais** insultado
insultar**ía**	insultar**ían**	**habría** insultado	**habrían** insultado
presente de subjuntivo		perfecto de subjuntivo	
insult**e**	insult**emos**	**haya** insultado	**hayamos** insultado
insult**es**	insult**éis**	**hayas** insultado	**hayáis** insultado
insult**e**	insult**en**	**haya** insultado	**hayan** insultado
imperfecto de subjuntivo		pluscuamperfecto de subjuntivo	
insultar**a**	insultár**amos**	**hubiera** insultado	**hubiéramos** insultado
insultar**as**	insultar**ais**	**hubieras** insultado	**hubierais** insultado
insultar**a**	insultar**an**	**hubiera** insultado	**hubieran** insultado
OR		OR	
insultas**e**	insultás**emos**	**hubiese** insultado	**hubiésemos** insultado
insultas**es**	insultas**eis**	**hubieses** insultado	**hubieseis** insultado
insultas**e**	insultas**en**	**hubiese** insultado	**hubiesen** insultado

imperativo

—	insultemos
insulta; no insultes	insultad; no insultéis
insulte	insulten

gerundio **intentando** participio de pasado **intentado**

SINGULAR	PLURAL
presente de indicativo	
intent**o**	intent**amos**
intent**as**	intent**áis**
intent**a**	intent**an**
imperfecto de indicativo	
intent**aba**	intent**ábamos**
intent**abas**	intent**abais**
intent**aba**	intent**aban**
pretérito	
intent**é**	intent**amos**
intent**aste**	intent**asteis**
intent**ó**	intent**aron**
futuro	
intentar**é**	intentar**emos**
intentar**ás**	intentar**éis**
intentar**á**	intentar**án**
condicional simple	
intentar**ía**	intentar**íamos**
intentar**ías**	intentar**íais**
intentar**ía**	intentar**ían**
presente de subjuntivo	
intent**e**	intent**emos**
intent**es**	intent**éis**
intent**e**	intent**en**
imperfecto de subjuntivo	
intentar**a**	intentár**amos**
intentar**as**	intentar**ais**
intentar**a**	intentar**an**
OR	
intentas**e**	intentás**emos**
intentas**es**	intentas**eis**
intentas**e**	intentas**en**
imperativo	
—	intentemos
intenta; no intentes	intentad; no intentéis
intente	intenten

SINGULAR	PLURAL
perfecto de indicativo	
he intentado	**hemos** intentado
has intentado	**habéis** intentado
ha intentado	**han** intentado
pluscuamperfecto de indicativo	
había intentado	**habíamos** intentado
habías intentado	**habíais** intentado
había intentado	**habían** intentado
pretérito anterior	
hube intentado	**hubimos** intentado
hubiste intentado	**hubisteis** intentado
hubo intentado	**hubieron** intentado
futuro perfecto	
habré intentado	**habremos** intentado
habrás intentado	**habréis** intentado
habrá intentado	**habrán** intentado
condicional compuesto	
habría intentado	**habríamos** intentado
habrías intentado	**habríais** intentado
habría intentado	**habrían** intentado
perfecto de subjuntivo	
haya intentado	**hayamos** intentado
hayas intentado	**hayáis** intentado
haya intentado	**hayan** intentado
pluscuamperfecto de subjuntivo	
hubiera intentado	**hubiéramos** intentado
hubieras intentado	**hubierais** intentado
hubiera intentado	**hubieran** intentado
OR	
hubiese intentado	**hubiésemos** intentado
hubieses intentado	**hubieseis** intentado
hubiese intentado	**hubiesen** intentado

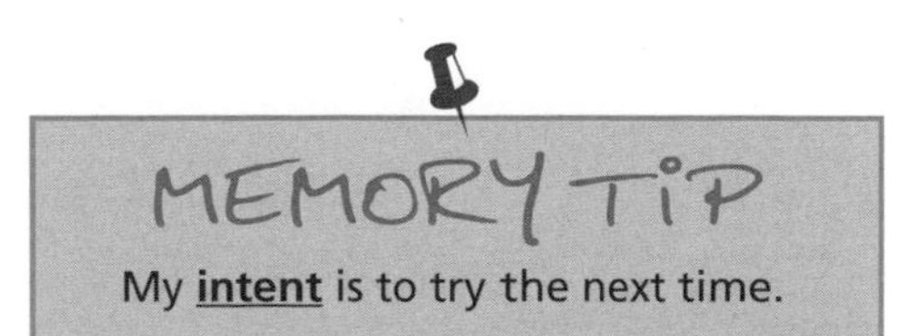

interesarse — to be interested in

gerundio **interesándose** — participio de pasado **interesado**

SINGULAR	PLURAL	SINGULAR	PLURAL
presente de indicativo		perfecto de indicativo	
me intereso	nos interesamos	me he interesado	nos hemos interesado
te interesas	os interesáis	te has interesado	os habéis interesado
se interesa	se interesan	se ha interesado	se han interesado
imperfecto de indicativo		pluscuamperfecto de indicativo	
me interesaba	nos interesábamos	me había interesado	nos habíamos interesado
te interesabas	os interesabais	te habías interesado	os habíais interesado
se interesaba	se interesaban	se había interesado	se habían interesado
pretérito		pretérito anterior	
me interesé	nos interesamos	me hube interesado	nos hubimos interesado
te interesaste	os interesasteis	te hubiste interesado	os hubisteis interesado
se interesó	se interesaron	se hubo interesado	se hubieron interesado
futuro		futuro perfecto	
me interesaré	nos interesaremos	me habré interesado	nos habremos interesado
te interesarás	os interesaréis	te habrás interesado	os habréis interesado
se interesará	se interesarán	se habrá interesado	se habrán interesado
condicional simple		condicional compuesto	
me interesaría	nos interesaríamos	me habría interesado	nos habríamos interesado
te interesarías	os interesaríais	te habrías interesado	os habríais interesado
se interesaría	se interesarían	se habría interesado	se habrían interesado
presente de subjuntivo		perfecto de subjuntivo	
me interese	nos interesemos	me haya interesado	nos hayamos interesado
te intereses	os intereséis	te hayas interesado	os hayáis interesado
se interese	se interesen	se haya interesado	se hayan interesado
imperfecto de subjuntivo		pluscuamperfecto de subjuntivo	
me interesara	nos interesáramos	me hubiera interesado	nos hubiéramos interesado
te interesaras	os interesarais	te hubieras interesado	os hubierais interesado
se interesara	se interesaran	se hubiera interesado	se hubieran interesado
OR		OR	
me interesase	nos interesásemos	me hubiese interesado	nos hubiésemos interesado
te interesases	os interesaseis	te hubieses interesado	os hubieseis interesado
se interesase	se interesasen	se hubiese interesado	se hubiesen interesado

imperativo

—	interesémonos
interésate;	interesaos;
no te intereses	no os intereséis
interésese	interésense

gerundio **interpretando** participio de pasado **interpretado**

SINGULAR	PLURAL	SINGULAR	PLURAL
presente de indicativo		perfecto de indicativo	
interpret**o**	interpret**amos**	**he** interpretado	**hemos** interpretado
interpret**as**	interpret**áis**	**has** interpretado	**habéis** interpretado
interpret**a**	interpret**an**	**ha** interpretado	**han** interpretado
imperfecto de indicativo		pluscuamperfecto de indicativo	
interpret**aba**	interpret**ábamos**	**había** interpretado	**habíamos** interpretado
interpret**abas**	interpret**abais**	**habías** interpretado	**habíais** interpretado
interpret**aba**	interpret**aban**	**había** interpretado	**habían** interpretado
pretérito		pretérito anterior	
interpret**é**	interpret**amos**	**hube** interpretado	**hubimos** interpretado
interpret**aste**	interpret**asteis**	**hubiste** interpretado	**hubisteis** interpretado
interpret**ó**	interpret**aron**	**hubo** interpretado	**hubieron** interpretado
futuro		futuro perfecto	
interpretar**é**	interpretar**emos**	**habré** interpretado	**habremos** interpretado
interpretar**ás**	interpretar**éis**	**habrás** interpretado	**habréis** interpretado
interpretar**á**	interpretar**án**	**habrá** interpretado	**habrán** interpretado
condicional simple		condicional compuesto	
interpretar**ía**	interpretar**íamos**	**habría** interpretado	**habríamos** interpretado
interpretar**ías**	interpretar**íais**	**habrías** interpretado	**habríais** interpretado
interpretar**ía**	interpretar**ían**	**habría** interpretado	**habrían** interpretado
presente de subjuntivo		perfecto de subjuntivo	
interpret**e**	interpret**emos**	**haya** interpretado	**hayamos** interpretado
interpret**es**	interpret**éis**	**hayas** interpretado	**hayáis** interpretado
interpret**e**	interpret**en**	**haya** interpretado	**hayan** interpretado
imperfecto de subjuntivo		pluscuamperfecto de subjuntivo	
interpretar**a**	interpretár**amos**	**hubiera** interpretado	**hubiéramos** interpretado
interpretar**as**	interpretar**ais**	**hubieras** interpretado	**hubierais** interpretado
interpretar**a**	interpretar**an**	**hubiera** interpretado	**hubieran** interpretado
OR		OR	
interpretas**e**	interpretás**emos**	**hubiese** interpretado	**hubiésemos** interpretado
interpretas**es**	interpretas**eis**	**hubieses** interpretado	**hubieseis** interpretado
interpretas**e**	interpretas**en**	**hubiese** interpretado	**hubiesen** interpretado

imperativo

—	interpretemos
interpreta; no interpretes	interpretad; no interpretéis
interprete	interpreten

interrumpir — to interrupt

gerundio **interrumpiendo** — participio de pasado **interrumpido**

SINGULAR	PLURAL
presente de indicativo	
interrump**o**	interrump**imos**
interrump**es**	interrump**ís**
interrump**e**	interrump**en**
imperfecto de indicativo	
interrump**ía**	interrump**íamos**
interrump**ías**	interrump**íais**
interrump**ía**	interrump**ían**
pretérito	
interrump**í**	interrump**imos**
interrump**iste**	interrump**isteis**
interrump**ió**	interrump**ieron**
futuro	
interrumpir**é**	interrumpir**emos**
interrumpir**ás**	interrumpir**éis**
interrumpir**á**	interrumpir**án**
condicional simple	
interrumpir**ía**	interrumpir**íamos**
interrumpir**ías**	interrumpir**íais**
interrumpir**ía**	interrumpir**ían**
presente de subjuntivo	
interrump**a**	interrump**amos**
interrump**as**	interrump**áis**
interrump**a**	interrump**an**
imperfecto de subjuntivo	
interrumpier**a**	interrumpiér**amos**
interrumpier**as**	interrumpier**ais**
interrumpier**a**	interrumpier**an**
OR	
interrumpies**e**	interrumpiés**emos**
interrumpies**es**	interrumpies**eis**
interrumpies**e**	interrumpies**en**
imperativo	
—	interrumpamos
interrumpe; no interrumpas	interrumpid; no interrumpáis
interrumpa	interrumpan

SINGULAR	PLURAL
perfecto de indicativo	
he interrumpido	**hemos** interrumpido
has interrumpido	**habéis** interrumpido
ha interrumpido	**han** interrumpido
pluscuamperfecto de indicativo	
había interrumpido	**habíamos** interrumpido
habías interrumpido	**habíais** interrumpido
había interrumpido	**habían** interrumpido
pretérito anterior	
hube interrumpido	**hubimos** interrumpido
hubiste interrumpido	**hubisteis** interrumpido
hubo interrumpido	**hubieron** interrumpido
futuro perfecto	
habré interrumpido	**habremos** interrumpido
habrás interrumpido	**habréis** interrumpido
habrá interrumpido	**habrán** interrumpido
condicional compuesto	
habría interrumpido	**habríamos** interrumpido
habrías interrumpido	**habríais** interrumpido
habría interrumpido	**habrían** interrumpido
perfecto de subjuntivo	
haya interrumpido	**hayamos** interrumpido
hayas interrumpido	**hayáis** interrumpido
haya interrumpido	**hayan** interrumpido
pluscuamperfecto de subjuntivo	
hubiera interrumpido	**hubiéramos** interrumpido
hubieras interrumpido	**hubierais** interrumpido
hubiera interrumpido	**hubieran** interrumpido
OR	
hubiese interrumpido	**hubiésemos** interrumpido
hubieses interrumpido	**hubieseis** interrumpido
hubiese interrumpido	**hubiesen** interrumpido

gerundio **interviniendo** participio de pasado **intervenido**

SINGULAR	PLURAL
presente de indicativo	
interveng**o**	interven**imos**
intervien**es**	interven**ís**
intervien**e**	intervien**en**
imperfecto de indicativo	
interven**ía**	interven**íamos**
interven**ías**	interven**íais**
interven**ía**	interven**ían**
pretérito	
intervin**e**	intervin**imos**
intervin**iste**	intervin**isteis**
intervin**o**	intervin**ieron**
futuro	
intervendr**é**	intervendr**emos**
intervendr**ás**	intervendr**éis**
intervendr**á**	intervendr**án**
condicional simple	
intervendr**ía**	intervendr**íamos**
intervendr**ías**	intervendr**íais**
intervendr**ía**	intervendr**ían**
presente de subjuntivo	
interveng**a**	interveng**amos**
interveng**as**	interveng**áis**
interveng**a**	interveng**an**
imperfecto de subjuntivo	
intervinier**a**	interviniér**amos**
intervinier**as**	intervinier**ais**
intervinier**a**	intervinier**an**
OR	
intervinies**e**	interviniés**emos**
intervinies**es**	intervinies**eis**
intervinies**e**	intervinies**en**
imperativo	
—	intervengamos
intervén; no intervengas	intervenid; no intervengáis
intervenga	intervengan

SINGULAR	PLURAL
perfecto de indicativo	
he intervenido	**hemos** intervenido
has intervenido	**habéis** intervenido
ha intervenido	**han** intervenido
pluscuamperfecto de indicativo	
había intervenido	**habíamos** intervenido
habías intervenido	**habíais** intervenido
había intervenido	**habían** intervenido
pretérito anterior	
hube intervenido	**hubimos** intervenido
hubiste intervenido	**hubisteis** intervenido
hubo intervenido	**hubieron** intervenido
futuro perfecto	
habré intervenido	**habremos** intervenido
habrás intervenido	**habréis** intervenido
habrá intervenido	**habrán** intervenido
condicional compuesto	
habría intervenido	**habríamos** intervenido
habrías intervenido	**habríais** intervenido
habría intervenido	**habrían** intervenido
perfecto de subjuntivo	
haya intervenido	**hayamos** intervenido
hayas intervenido	**hayáis** intervenido
haya intervenido	**hayan** intervenido
pluscuamperfecto de subjuntivo	
hubiera intervenido	**hubiéramos** intervenido
hubieras intervenido	**hubierais** intervenido
hubiera intervenido	**hubieran** intervenido
OR	
hubiese intervenido	**hubiésemos** intervenido
hubieses intervenido	**hubieseis** intervenido
hubiese intervenido	**hubiesen** intervenido

introducir — to insert, to introduce

gerundio **introduciendo** participio de pasado **introducido**

SINGULAR	PLURAL	SINGULAR	PLURAL
presente de indicativo		perfecto de indicativo	
introduzc**o**	introduc**imos**	**he** introducido	**hemos** introducido
introduc**es**	introduc**ís**	**has** introducido	**habéis** introducido
introduc**e**	introduc**en**	**ha** introducido	**han** introducido
imperfecto de indicativo		pluscuamperfecto de indicativo	
introduc**ía**	introduc**íamos**	**había** introducido	**habíamos** introducido
introduc**ías**	introduc**íais**	**habías** introducido	**habíais** introducido
introduc**ía**	introduc**ían**	**había** introducido	**habían** introducido
pretérito		pretérito anterior	
introduj**e**	introduj**imos**	**hube** introducido	**hubimos** introducido
introduj**iste**	introduj**isteis**	**hubiste** introducido	**hubisteis** introducido
introduj**o**	introduj**eron**	**hubo** introducido	**hubieron** introducido
futuro		futuro perfecto	
introducir**é**	introducir**emos**	**habré** introducido	**habremos** introducido
introducir**ás**	introducir**éis**	**habrás** introducido	**habréis** introducido
introducir**á**	introducir**án**	**habrá** introducido	**habrán** introducido
condicional simple		condicional compuesto	
introducir**ía**	introducir**íamos**	**habría** introducido	**habríamos** introducido
introducir**ías**	introducir**íais**	**habrías** introducido	**habríais** introducido
introducir**ía**	introducir**ían**	**habría** introducido	**habrían** introducido
presente de subjuntivo		perfecto de subjuntivo	
introduzc**a**	introduzc**amos**	**haya** introducido	**hayamos** introducido
introduzc**as**	introduzc**áis**	**hayas** introducido	**hayáis** introducido
introduzc**a**	introduzc**an**	**haya** introducido	**hayan** introducido
imperfecto de subjuntivo		pluscuamperfecto de subjuntivo	
introdujer**a**	introdujér**amos**	**hubiera** introducido	**hubiéramos** introducido
introdujer**as**	introdujer**ais**	**hubieras** introducido	**hubierais** introducido
introdujer**a**	introdujer**an**	**hubiera** introducido	**hubieran** introducido
OR		OR	
introdujes**e**	introdujés**emos**	**hubiese** introducido	**hubiésemos** introducido
introdujes**es**	introdujes**eis**	**hubieses** introducido	**hubieseis** introducido
introdujes**e**	introdujes**en**	**hubiese** introducido	**hubiesen** introducido

imperativo

—	introduzcamos
introduce; no introduzcas	introducid; no introduzcáis
introduzca	introduzcan

gerundio **inventando** participio de pasado **inventado**

SINGULAR	PLURAL
presente de indicativo	
invent**o**	invent**amos**
invent**as**	invent**áis**
invent**a**	invent**an**
imperfecto de indicativo	
invent**aba**	invent**ábamos**
invent**abas**	invent**abais**
invent**aba**	invent**aban**
pretérito	
invent**é**	invent**amos**
invent**aste**	invent**asteis**
invent**ó**	invent**aron**
futuro	
inventar**é**	inventar**emos**
inventar**ás**	inventar**éis**
inventar**á**	inventar**án**
condicional simple	
inventar**ía**	inventar**íamos**
inventar**ías**	inventar**íais**
inventar**ía**	inventar**ían**
presente de subjuntivo	
invent**e**	invent**emos**
invent**es**	invent**éis**
invent**e**	invent**en**
imperfecto de subjuntivo	
inventar**a**	inventár**amos**
inventar**as**	inventar**ais**
inventar**a**	inventar**an**
OR	
inventas**e**	inventás**emos**
inventas**es**	inventas**eis**
inventas**e**	inventas**en**
imperativo	
—	inventemos
inventa; no inventes	inventad; no inventéis
invente	inventen

SINGULAR	PLURAL
perfecto de indicativo	
he inventado	**hemos** inventado
has inventado	**habéis** inventado
ha inventado	**han** inventado
pluscuamperfecto de indicativo	
había inventado	**habíamos** inventado
habías inventado	**habíais** inventado
había inventado	**habían** inventado
pretérito anterior	
hube inventado	**hubimos** inventado
hubiste inventado	**hubisteis** inventado
hubo inventado	**hubieron** inventado
futuro perfecto	
habré inventado	**habremos** inventado
habrás inventado	**habréis** inventado
habrá inventado	**habrán** inventado
condicional compuesto	
habría inventado	**habríamos** inventado
habrías inventado	**habríais** inventado
habría inventado	**habrían** inventado
perfecto de subjuntivo	
haya inventado	**hayamos** inventado
hayas inventado	**hayáis** inventado
haya inventado	**hayan** inventado
pluscuamperfecto de subjuntivo	
hubiera inventado	**hubiéramos** inventado
hubieras inventado	**hubierais** inventado
hubiera inventado	**hubieran** inventado
OR	
hubiese inventado	**hubiésemos** inventado
hubieses inventado	**hubieseis** inventado
hubiese inventado	**hubiesen** inventado

invertir — to invest

gerundio **inviritendo** participio de pasado **invertido**

SINGULAR	PLURAL	SINGULAR	PLURAL
presente de indicativo		perfecto de indicativo	
inviert**o**	invert**imos**	**he** invertido	**hemos** invertido
inviert**es**	invert**ís**	**has** invertido	**habéis** invertido
inviert**e**	inviert**en**	**ha** invertido	**han** invertido
imperfecto de indicativo		pluscuamperfecto de indicativo	
invert**ía**	invert**íamos**	**había** invertido	**habíamos** invertido
invert**ías**	invert**íais**	**habías** invertido	**habíais** invertido
invert**ía**	invert**ían**	**había** invertido	**habían** invertido
pretérito		pretérito anterior	
invert**í**	invert**imos**	**hube** invertido	**hubimos** invertido
invert**iste**	invert**isteis**	**hubiste** invertido	**hubisteis** invertido
invirti**ó**	invirt**ieron**	**hubo** invertido	**hubieron** invertido
futuro		futuro perfecto	
invertir**é**	invertir**emos**	**habré** invertido	**habremos** invertido
invertir**ás**	invertir**éis**	**habrás** invertido	**habréis** invertido
invertir**á**	invertir**án**	**habrá** invertido	**habrán** invertido
condicional simple		condicional compuesto	
invertir**ía**	invertir**íamos**	**habría** invertido	**habríamos** invertido
invertir**ías**	invertir**íais**	**habrías** invertido	**habríais** invertido
invertir**ía**	invertir**ían**	**habría** invertido	**habrían** invertido
presente de subjuntivo		perfecto de subjuntivo	
inviert**a**	invirt**amos**	**haya** invertido	**hayamos** invertido
inviert**as**	invirt**áis**	**hayas** invertido	**hayáis** invertido
inviert**a**	inviert**an**	**haya** invertido	**hayan** invertido
imperfecto de subjuntivo		pluscuamperfecto de subjuntivo	
invirtier**a**	invirtiér**amos**	**hubiera** invertido	**hubiéramos** invertido
invirtier**as**	invirtier**ais**	**hubieras** invertido	**hubierais** invertido
invirtier**a**	invirtier**an**	**hubiera** invertido	**hubieran** invertido
OR		OR	
invirties**e**	invirtiés**emos**	**hubiese** invertido	**hubiésemos** invertido
invirties**es**	invirties**eis**	**hubieses** invertido	**hubieseis** invertido
invirties**e**	invirties**en**	**hubiese** invertido	**hubiesen** invertido

imperativo

—	invirtamos
invierte; no inviertas	invertid; no invirtáis
invierta	inviertan

gerundio **investigando** participio de pasado **investigado**

SINGULAR	PLURAL
presente de indicativo	
investig**o**	investig**amos**
investig**as**	investig**áis**
investig**a**	investig**an**
imperfecto de indicativo	
investig**aba**	investig**ábamos**
investig**abas**	investig**abais**
investig**aba**	investig**aban**
pretérito	
investigu**é**	investig**amos**
investig**aste**	investig**asteis**
investig**ó**	investig**aron**
futuro	
investigar**é**	investigar**emos**
investigar**ás**	investigar**éis**
investigar**á**	investigar**án**
condicional simple	
investigar**ía**	investigar**íamos**
investigar**ías**	investigar**íais**
investigar**ía**	investigar**ían**
presente de subjuntivo	
investigu**e**	investigu**emos**
investigu**es**	investigu**éis**
investigu**e**	investigu**en**
imperfecto de subjuntivo	
investigar**a**	investigár**amos**
investigar**as**	investigar**ais**
investigar**a**	investigar**an**
OR	
investigas**e**	investigás**emos**
investigas**es**	investigas**eis**
investigas**e**	investigas**en**
imperativo	
—	investiguemos
investiga; no investigues	investigad; no investiguéis
investigue	investiguen

SINGULAR	PLURAL
perfecto de indicativo	
he investigado	**hemos** investigado
has investigado	**habéis** investigado
ha investigado	**han** investigado
pluscuamperfecto de indicativo	
había investigado	**habíamos** investigado
habías investigado	**habíais** investigado
había investigado	**habían** investigado
pretérito anterior	
hube investigado	**hubimos** investigado
hubiste investigado	**hubisteis** investigado
hubo investigado	**hubieron** investigado
futuro perfecto	
habré investigado	**habremos** investigado
habrás investigado	**habréis** investigado
habrá investigado	**habrán** investigado
condicional compuesto	
habría investigado	**habríamos** investigado
habrías investigado	**habríais** investigado
habría investigado	**habrían** investigado
perfecto de subjuntivo	
haya investigado	**hayamos** investigado
hayas investigado	**hayáis** investigado
haya investigado	**hayan** investigado
pluscuamperfecto de subjuntivo	
hubiera investigado	**hubiéramos** investigado
hubieras investigado	**hubierais** investigado
hubiera investigado	**hubieran** investigado
OR	
hubiese investigado	**hubiésemos** investigado
hubieses investigado	**hubieseis** investigado
hubiese investigado	**hubiesen** investigado

invitar — to invite

gerundio **invitando**

participio de pasado **invitado**

presente de indicativo

SINGULAR	PLURAL
invit**o**	invit**amos**
invit**as**	invit**áis**
invit**a**	invit**an**

imperfecto de indicativo

SINGULAR	PLURAL
invit**aba**	invit**ábamos**
invit**abas**	invit**abais**
invit**aba**	invit**aban**

pretérito

SINGULAR	PLURAL
invit**é**	invit**amos**
invit**aste**	invit**asteis**
invit**ó**	invit**aron**

futuro

SINGULAR	PLURAL
invitar**é**	invitar**emos**
invitar**ás**	invitar**éis**
invitar**á**	invitar**án**

condicional simple

SINGULAR	PLURAL
invitar**ía**	invitar**íamos**
invitar**ías**	invitar**íais**
invitar**ía**	invitar**ían**

presente de subjuntivo

SINGULAR	PLURAL
invit**e**	invit**emos**
invit**es**	invit**éis**
invit**e**	invit**en**

imperfecto de subjuntivo

SINGULAR	PLURAL
invitar**a**	invitár**amos**
invitar**as**	invitar**ais**
invitar**a**	invitar**an**
OR	
invitas**e**	invitás**emos**
invitas**es**	invitas**eis**
invitas**e**	invitas**en**

imperativo

SINGULAR	PLURAL
—	invitemos
invita; no invites	invitad; no invitéis
invite	inviten

perfecto de indicativo

SINGULAR	PLURAL
he invitado	**hemos** invitado
has invitado	**habéis** invitado
ha invitado	**han** invitado

pluscuamperfecto de indicativo

SINGULAR	PLURAL
había invitado	**habíamos** invitado
habías invitado	**habíais** invitado
había invitado	**habían** invitado

pretérito anterior

SINGULAR	PLURAL
hube invitado	**hubimos** invitado
hubiste invitado	**hubisteis** invitado
hubo invitado	**hubieron** invitado

futuro perfecto

SINGULAR	PLURAL
habré invitado	**habremos** invitado
habrás invitado	**habréis** invitado
habrá invitado	**habrán** invitado

condicional compuesto

SINGULAR	PLURAL
habría invitado	**habríamos** invitado
habrías invitado	**habríais** invitado
habría invitado	**habrían** invitado

perfecto de subjuntivo

SINGULAR	PLURAL
haya invitado	**hayamos** invitado
hayas invitado	**hayáis** invitado
haya invitado	**hayan** invitado

pluscuamperfecto de subjuntivo

SINGULAR	PLURAL
hubiera invitado	**hubiéramos** invitado
hubieras invitado	**hubierais** invitado
hubiera invitado	**hubieran** invitado
OR	
hubiese invitado	**hubiésemos** invitado
hubieses invitado	**hubieseis** invitado
hubiese invitado	**hubiesen** invitado

to inject — inyectar

gerundio **inyectando** — participio de pasado **inyectado**

SINGULAR	PLURAL	SINGULAR	PLURAL
presente de indicativo		perfecto de indicativo	
inyect**o**	inyect**amos**	**he** inyectado	**hemos** inyectado
inyect**as**	inyect**áis**	**has** inyectado	**habéis** inyectado
inyect**a**	inyect**an**	**ha** inyectado	**han** inyectado
imperfecto de indicativo		pluscuamperfecto de indicativo	
inyect**aba**	inyect**ábamos**	**había** inyectado	**habíamos** inyectado
inyect**abas**	inyect**abais**	**habías** inyectado	**habíais** inyectado
inyect**aba**	inyect**aban**	**había** inyectado	**habían** inyectado
pretérito		pretérito anterior	
inyect**é**	inyect**amos**	**hube** inyectado	**hubimos** inyectado
inyect**aste**	inyect**asteis**	**hubiste** inyectado	**hubisteis** inyectado
inyect**ó**	inyect**aron**	**hubo** inyectado	**hubieron** inyectado
futuro		futuro perfecto	
inyectar**é**	inyectar**emos**	**habré** inyectado	**habremos** inyectado
inyectar**ás**	inyectar**éis**	**habrás** inyectado	**habréis** inyectado
inyectar**á**	inyectar**án**	**habrá** inyectado	**habrán** inyectado
condicional simple		condicional compuesto	
inyectar**ía**	inyectar**íamos**	**habría** inyectado	**habríamos** inyectado
inyectar**ías**	inyectar**íais**	**habrías** inyectado	**habríais** inyectado
inyectar**ía**	inyectar**ían**	**habría** inyectado	**habrían** inyectado
presente de subjuntivo		perfecto de subjuntivo	
inyect**e**	inyect**emos**	**haya** inyectado	**hayamos** inyectado
inyect**es**	inyect**éis**	**hayas** inyectado	**hayáis** inyectado
inyect**e**	inyect**en**	**haya** inyectado	**hayan** inyectado
imperfecto de subjuntivo		pluscuamperfecto de subjuntivo	
inyectar**a**	inyectár**amos**	**hubiera** inyectado	**hubiéramos** inyectado
inyectar**as**	inyectar**ais**	**hubieras** inyectado	**hubierais** inyectado
inyectar**a**	inyectar**an**	**hubiera** inyectado	**hubieran** inyectado
OR		OR	
inyectas**e**	inyectás**emos**	**hubiese** inyectado	**hubiésemos** inyectado
inyectas**es**	inyectas**eis**	**hubieses** inyectado	**hubieseis** inyectado
inyectas**e**	inyectas**en**	**hubiese** inyectado	**hubiesen** inyectado

imperativo

—	inyectemos
inyecta; no inyectes	inyectad; no inyectéis
inyecte	inyecten

I

gerundio **yendo** participio de pasado **ido**

presente de indicativo

SINGULAR	PLURAL
v**oy**	v**amos**
v**as**	v**ais**
v**a**	v**an**

imperfecto de indicativo

SINGULAR	PLURAL
ib**a**	íb**amos**
ib**as**	ib**ais**
ib**a**	ib**an**

pretérito

SINGULAR	PLURAL
fu**i**	fu**imos**
fu**iste**	fu**isteis**
fu**e**	fu**eron**

futuro

SINGULAR	PLURAL
ir**é**	ir**emos**
ir**ás**	ir**éis**
ir**á**	ir**án**

condicional simple

SINGULAR	PLURAL
ir**ía**	ir**íamos**
ir**ías**	ir**íais**
ir**ía**	ir**ían**

presente de subjuntivo

SINGULAR	PLURAL
vay**a**	vay**amos**
vay**as**	vay**áis**
vay**a**	vay**an**

imperfecto de subjuntivo

SINGULAR	PLURAL
fuer**a**	fuér**amos**
fuer**as**	fuer**ais**
fuer**a**	fuer**an**
OR	
fues**e**	fués**emos**
fues**es**	fues**eis**
fues**e**	fues**en**

imperativo

SINGULAR	PLURAL
—	vamos (no vayamos)
ve; no vayas	id; no vayáis
vava	vayan

perfecto de indicativo

SINGULAR	PLURAL
he ido	**hemos** ido
has ido	**habéis** ido
ha ido	**han** ido

pluscuamperfecto de indicativo

SINGULAR	PLURAL
había ido	**habíamos** ido
habías ido	**habíais** ido
había ido	**habían** ido

pretérito anterior

SINGULAR	PLURAL
hube ido	**hubimos** ido
hubiste ido	**hubisteis** ido
hubo ido	**hubieron** ido

futuro perfecto

SINGULAR	PLURAL
habré ido	**habremos** ido
habrás ido	**habréis** ido
habrá ido	**habrán** ido

condicional compuesto

SINGULAR	PLURAL
habría ido	**habríamos** ido
habrías ido	**habríais** ido
habría ido	**habrían** ido

perfecto de subjuntivo

SINGULAR	PLURAL
haya ido	**hayamos** ido
hayas ido	**hayáis** ido
haya ido	**hayan** ido

pluscuamperfecto de subjuntivo

SINGULAR	PLURAL
hubiera ido	**hubiéramos** ido
hubieras ido	**hubierais** ido
hubiera ido	**hubieran** ido
OR	
hubiese ido	**hubiésemos** ido
hubieses ido	**hubieseis** ido
hubiese ido	**hubiesen** ido

to go away **irse**

gerundio **yéndose** participio de pasado **ido**

SINGULAR	PLURAL
presente de indicativo	
me v**oy**	nos v**amos**
te v**as**	os v**ais**
se v**a**	se v**an**
imperfecto de indicativo	
me **iba**	nos **íbamos**
te **ibas**	os **ibais**
se **iba**	se **iban**
pretérito	
me fu**i**	nos fu**imos**
te fu**iste**	os fu**isteis**
se fu**e**	se fu**eron**
futuro	
me ir**é**	nos ir**emos**
te ir**ás**	os ir**éis**
se ir**á**	se ir**án**
condicional simple	
me ir**ía**	nos ir**íamos**
te ir**ías**	os ir**íais**
se ir**ía**	se ir**ían**
presente de subjuntivo	
me vay**a**	nos vay**amos**
te vay**as**	os vay**áis**
se vay**a**	se vay**an**
imperfecto de subjuntivo	
me fuer**a**	nos fuér**amos**
te fuer**as**	os fuer**ais**
se fuer**a**	se fuer**an**
OR	
me fues**e**	nos fués**emos**
te fues**es**	os fues**eis**
se fues**e**	se fues**en**
imperativo	
—	vámonos; no nos vayamos
vete; no te vayas	idos; no os vayáis
váyase; no se vaya	váyanse; no se vayan

SINGULAR	PLURAL
perfecto de indicativo	
me he ido	**nos hemos** ido
te has ido	**os habéis** ido
se ha ido	**se han** ido
pluscuamperfecto de indicativo	
me había ido	**nos habíamos** ido
te habías ido	**os habíais** ido
se había ido	**se habían** ido
pretérito anterior	
me hube ido	**nos hubimos** ido
te hubiste ido	**os hubisteis** ido
se hubo ido	**se hubieron** ido
futuro perfecto	
me habré ido	**nos habremos** ido
te habrás ido	**os habréis** ido
se habrá ido	**se habrán** ido
condicional compuesto	
me habría ido	**nos habríamos** ido
te habrías ido	**os habríais** ido
se habría ido	**se habrían** ido
perfecto de subjuntivo	
me haya ido	**nos hayamos** ido
te hayas ido	**os hayáis** ido
se haya ido	**se hayan** ido
pluscuamperfecto de subjuntivo	
me hubiera ido	**nos hubiéramos** ido
te hubieras ido	**os hubierais** ido
se hubiera ido	**se hubieran** ido
OR	
me hubiese ido	**nos hubiésemos** ido
te hubieses ido	**os hubieseis** ido
se hubiese ido	**se hubiesen** ido

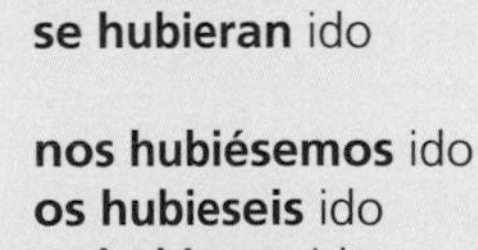

jugar — to play

gerundio **jugando** — participio de pasado **jugado**

SINGULAR	PLURAL
presente de indicativo	
jueg**o**	jug**amos**
jueg**as**	jug**áis**
jueg**a**	jueg**an**
imperfecto de indicativo	
jug**aba**	jug**ábamos**
jug**abas**	jug**abais**
jug**aba**	jug**aban**
pretérito	
jug**ué**	jug**amos**
jug**aste**	jug**asteis**
jug**ó**	jug**aron**
futuro	
jugar**é**	jugar**emos**
jugar**ás**	jugar**éis**
jugar**á**	jugar**án**
condicional simple	
jugar**ía**	jugar**íamos**
jugar**ías**	jugar**íais**
jugar**ía**	jugar**ían**
presente de subjuntivo	
juegu**e**	jugu**emos**
juegu**es**	jugu**éis**
juegu**e**	juegu**en**
imperfecto de subjuntivo	
jugar**a**	jugár**amos**
jugar**as**	jugar**ais**
jugar**a**	jugar**an**
OR	
jugas**e**	jugás**emos**
jugas**es**	jugas**eis**
jugas**e**	jugas**en**
imperativo	
—	juguemos
juega; no juegues	jugad; no juguéis
juegue	jueguen

SINGULAR	PLURAL
perfecto de indicativo	
he jugado	**hemos** jugado
has jugado	**habéis** jugado
ha jugado	**han** jugado
pluscuamperfecto de indicativo	
había jugado	**habíamos** jugado
habías jugado	**habíais** jugado
había jugado	**habían** jugado
pretérito anterior	
hube jugado	**hubimos** jugado
hubiste jugado	**hubisteis** jugado
hubo jugado	**hubieron** jugado
futuro perfecto	
habré jugado	**habremos** jugado
habrás jugado	**habréis** jugado
habrá jugado	**habrán** jugado
condicional compuesto	
habría jugado	**habríamos** jugado
habrías jugado	**habríais** jugado
habría jugado	**habrían** jugado
perfecto de subjuntivo	
haya jugado	**hayamos** jugado
hayas jugado	**hayáis** jugado
haya jugado	**hayan** jugado
pluscuamperfecto de subjuntivo	
hubiera jugado	**hubiéramos** jugado
hubieras jugado	**hubierais** jugado
hubiera jugado	**hubieran** jugado
OR	
hubiese jugado	**hubiésemos** jugado
hubieses jugado	**hubieseis** jugado
hubiese jugado	**hubiesen** jugado

to join, to unite, to connect **juntar**

gerundio **juntando** participio de pasado **juntado**

SINGULAR	PLURAL	SINGULAR	PLURAL
presente de indicativo		perfecto de indicativo	
junt**o**	junt**amos**	**he** juntado	**hemos** juntado
junt**as**	junt**áis**	**has** juntado	**habéis** juntado
junt**a**	junt**an**	**ha** juntado	**han** juntado
imperfecto de indicativo		pluscuamperfecto de indicativo	
junt**aba**	junt**ábamos**	**había** juntado	**habíamos** juntado
junt**abas**	junt**abais**	**habías** juntado	**habíais** juntado
junt**aba**	junt**aban**	**había** juntado	**habían** juntado
pretérito		pretérito anterior	
junt**é**	junt**amos**	**hube** juntado	**hubimos** juntado
junt**aste**	junt**asteis**	**hubiste** juntado	**hubisteis** juntado
junt**ó**	junt**aron**	**hubo** juntado	**hubieron** juntado
futuro		futuro perfecto	
juntar**é**	juntar**emos**	**habré** juntado	**habremos** juntado
juntar**ás**	juntar**éis**	**habrás** juntado	**habréis** juntado
juntar**á**	juntar**án**	**habrá** juntado	**habrán** juntado
condicional simple		condicional compuesto	
juntar**ía**	juntar**íamos**	**habría** juntado	**habríamos** juntado
juntar**ías**	juntar**íais**	**habrías** juntado	**habríais** juntado
juntar**ía**	juntar**ían**	**habría** juntado	**habrían** juntado
presente de subjuntivo		perfecto de subjuntivo	
junt**e**	junt**emos**	**haya** juntado	**hayamos** juntado
junt**es**	junt**éis**	**hayas** juntado	**hayáis** juntado
junt**e**	junt**en**	**haya** juntado	**hayan** juntado
imperfecto de subjuntivo		pluscuamperfecto de subjuntivo	
juntar**a**	juntár**amos**	**hubiera** juntado	**hubiéramos** juntado
juntar**as**	juntar**ais**	**hubieras** juntado	**hubierais** juntado
juntar**a**	juntar**an**	**hubiera** juntado	**hubieran** juntado
OR		OR	
juntas**e**	juntás**emos**	**hubiese** juntado	**hubiésemos** juntado
juntas**es**	juntas**eis**	**hubieses** juntado	**hubieseis** juntado
juntas**e**	juntas**en**	**hubiese** juntado	**hubiesen** juntado

imperativo

—	juntemos
junta; no juntes	juntad; no juntéis
junte	junten

J

jurar — to swear, to take an oath

gerundio **jurando** participio de pasado **jurado**

SINGULAR	PLURAL	SINGULAR	PLURAL
presente de indicativo		perfecto de indicativo	
jur**o**	jur**amos**	**he** jurado	**hemos** jurado
jur**as**	jur**áis**	**has** jurado	**habéis** jurado
jur**a**	jur**an**	**ha** jurado	**han** jurado
imperfecto de indicativo		pluscuamperfecto de indicativo	
jur**aba**	jur**ábamos**	**había** jurado	**habíamos** jurado
jur**abas**	jur**abais**	**habías** jurado	**habíais** jurado
jur**aba**	jur**aban**	**había** jurado	**habían** jurado
pretérito		pretérito anterior	
jur**é**	jur**amos**	**hube** jurado	**hubimos** jurado
jur**aste**	jur**asteis**	**hubiste** jurado	**hubisteis** jurado
jur**ó**	jur**aron**	**hubo** jurado	**hubieron** jurado
futuro		futuro perfecto	
jurar**é**	jurar**emos**	**habré** jurado	**habremos** jurado
jurar**ás**	jurar**éis**	**habrás** jurado	**habréis** jurado
jurar**á**	jurar**án**	**habrá** jurado	**habrán** jurado
condicional simple		condicional compuesto	
jurar**ía**	jurar**íamos**	**habría** jurado	**habríamos** jurado
jurar**ías**	jurar**íais**	**habrías** jurado	**habríais** jurado
jurar**ía**	jurar**ían**	**habría** jurado	**habrían** jurado
presente de subjuntivo		perfecto de subjuntivo	
jur**e**	jur**emos**	**haya** jurado	**hayamos** jurado
jur**es**	jur**éis**	**hayas** jurado	**hayáis** jurado
jur**e**	jur**en**	**haya** jurado	**hayan** jurado
imperfecto de subjuntivo		pluscuamperfecto de subjuntivo	
jurar**a**	jurár**amos**	**hubiera** jurado	**hubiéramos** jurado
jurar**as**	jurar**ais**	**hubieras** jurado	**hubierais** jurado
jurar**a**	jurar**an**	**hubiera** jurado	**hubieran** jurado
OR		OR	
juras**e**	jurás**emos**	**hubiese** jurado	**hubiésemos** jurado
juras**es**	juras**eis**	**hubieses** jurado	**hubieseis** jurado
juras**e**	juras**en**	**hubiese** jurado	**hubiesen** jurado

imperativo

—	juremos
jura; no jures	jurad; no juréis
jure	juren

gerundio **justificando** participio de pasado **justificado**

SINGULAR	PLURAL	SINGULAR	PLURAL
presente de indicativo		perfecto de indicativo	
justific**o**	justific**amos**	**he** justificado	**hemos** justificado
justific**as**	justific**áis**	**has** justificado	**habéis** justificado
justific**a**	justific**an**	**ha** justificado	**han** justificado
imperfecto de indicativo		pluscuamperfecto de indicativo	
justific**aba**	justific**ábamos**	**había** justificado	**habíamos** justificado
justific**abas**	justific**abais**	**habías** justificado	**habíais** justificado
justific**aba**	justific**aban**	**había** justificado	**habían** justificado
pretérito		pretérito anterior	
justifiqu**é**	justific**amos**	**hube** justificado	**hubimos** justificado
justific**aste**	justific**asteis**	**hubiste** justificado	**hubisteis** justificado
justific**ó**	justific**aron**	**hubo** justificado	**hubieron** justificado
futuro		futuro perfecto	
justificar**é**	justificar**emos**	**habré** justificado	**habremos** justificado
justificar**ás**	justificar**éis**	**habrás** justificado	**habréis** justificado
justificar**á**	justificar**án**	**habrá** justificado	**habrán** justificado
condicional simple		condicional compuesto	
justificar**ía**	justificar**íamos**	**habría** justificado	**habríamos** justificado
justificar**ías**	justificar**íais**	**habrías** justificado	**habríais** justificado
justificar**ía**	justificar**ían**	**habría** justificado	**habrían** justificado
presente de subjuntivo		perfecto de subjuntivo	
justifiqu**e**	justifiqu**emos**	**haya** justificado	**hayamos** justificado
justifiqu**es**	justifiqu**éis**	**hayas** justificado	**hayáis** justificado
justifiqu**e**	justifiqu**en**	**haya** justificado	**hayan** justificado
imperfecto de subjuntivo		pluscuamperfecto de subjuntivo	
justificar**a**	justificár**amos**	**hubiera** justificado	**hubiéramos** justificado
justificar**as**	justificar**ais**	**hubieras** justificado	**hubierais** justificado
justificar**a**	justificar**an**	**hubiera** justificado	**hubieran** justificado
OR		OR	
justificas**e**	justificás**emos**	**hubiese** justificado	**hubiésemos** justificado
justificas**es**	justificas**eis**	**hubieses** justificado	**hubieseis** justificado
justificas**e**	justificas**en**	**hubiese** justificado	**hubiesen** justificado

imperativo

—	justifiquemos
justifica;	justificad;
no justifiques	no justifiquéis
justifique	justifiquen

juzgar — to judge

gerundio **juzgando** participio de pasado **juzgado**

SINGULAR	PLURAL	SINGULAR	PLURAL
presente de indicativo		perfecto de indicativo	
juzg**o**	juzg**amos**	**he** juzgado	**hemos** juzgado
juzg**as**	juzg**áis**	**has** juzgado	**habéis** juzgado
juzg**a**	juzg**an**	**ha** juzgado	**han** juzgado
imperfecto de indicativo		pluscuamperfecto de indicativo	
juzg**aba**	juzg**ábamos**	**había** juzgado	**habíamos** juzgado
juzg**abas**	juzg**abais**	**habías** juzgado	**habíais** juzgado
juzg**aba**	juzg**aban**	**había** juzgado	**habían** juzgado
pretérito		pretérito anterior	
juzgu**é**	juzg**amos**	**hube** juzgado	**hubimos** juzgado
juzg**aste**	juzg**asteis**	**hubiste** juzgado	**hubisteis** juzgado
juzg**ó**	juzg**aron**	**hubo** juzgado	**hubieron** juzgado
futuro		futuro perfecto	
juzgar**é**	juzgar**emos**	**habré** juzgado	**habremos** juzgado
juzgar**ás**	juzgar**éis**	**habrás** juzgado	**habréis** juzgado
juzgar**á**	juzgar**án**	**habrá** juzgado	**habrán** juzgado
condicional simple		condicional compuesto	
juzgar**ía**	juzgar**íamos**	**habría** juzgado	**habríamos** juzgado
juzgar**ías**	juzgar**íais**	**habrías** juzgado	**habríais** juzgado
juzgar**ía**	juzgar**ían**	**habría** juzgado	**habrían** juzgado
presente de subjuntivo		perfecto de subjuntivo	
juzgu**e**	juzgu**emos**	**haya** juzgado	**hayamos** juzgado
juzgu**es**	juzgu**éis**	**hayas** juzgado	**hayáis** juzgado
juzgu**e**	juzgu**en**	**haya** juzgado	**hayan** juzgado
imperfecto de subjuntivo		pluscuamperfecto de subjuntivo	
juzgar**a**	juzgár**amos**	**hubiera** juzgado	**hubiéramos** juzgado
juzgar**as**	juzgar**ais**	**hubieras** juzgado	**hubierais** juzgado
juzgar**a**	juzgar**an**	**hubiera** juzgado	**hubieran** juzgado
OR		OR	
juzgas**e**	juzgás**emos**	**hubiese** juzgado	**hubiésemos** juzgado
juzgas**es**	juzgas**eis**	**hubieses** juzgado	**hubieseis** juzgado
juzgas**e**	juzgas**en**	**hubiese** juzgado	**hubiesen** juzgado

imperativo

—	juzguemos
juzga; no juzgues	juzgad; no juzguéis
juzgue	juzguen

to throw, to launch **lanzar**

gerundio **lanzando** participio de pasado **lanzado**

SINGULAR	PLURAL
presente de indicativo	
lanz**o**	lanz**amos**
lanz**as**	lanz**áis**
lanz**a**	lanz**an**
imperfecto de indicativo	
lanz**aba**	lanz**ábamos**
lanz**abas**	lanz**abais**
lanz**aba**	lanz**aban**
pretérito	
lanc**é**	lanz**amos**
lanz**aste**	lanz**asteis**
lanz**ó**	lanz**aron**
futuro	
lanzar**é**	lanzar**emos**
lanzar**ás**	lanzar**éis**
lanzar**á**	lanzar**án**
condicional simple	
lanzar**ía**	lanzar**íamos**
lanzar**ías**	lanzar**íais**
lanzar**ía**	lanzar**ían**
presente de subjuntivo	
lanc**e**	lanc**emos**
lanc**es**	lanc**éis**
lanc**e**	lanc**en**
imperfecto de subjuntivo	
lanzar**a**	lanzár**amos**
lanzar**as**	lanzar**ais**
lanzar**a**	lanzar**an**
OR	
lanzas**e**	lanzás**emos**
lanzas**es**	lanzas**eis**
lanzas**e**	lanzas**en**
imperativo	
—	lancemos
lanza; no lances	lanzad; no lancéis
lance	lancen

SINGULAR	PLURAL
perfecto de indicativo	
he lanzado	**hemos** lanzado
has lanzado	**habéis** lanzado
ha lanzado	**han** lanzado
pluscuamperfecto de indicativo	
había lanzado	**habíamos** lanzado
habías lanzado	**habíais** lanzado
había lanzado	**habían** lanzado
pretérito anterior	
hube lanzado	**hubimos** lanzado
hubiste lanzado	**hubisteis** lanzado
hubo lanzado	**hubieron** lanzado
futuro perfecto	
habré lanzado	**habremos** lanzado
habrás lanzado	**habréis** lanzado
habrá lanzado	**habrán** lanzado
condicional compuesto	
habría lanzado	**habríamos** lanzado
habrías lanzado	**habríais** lanzado
habría lanzado	**habrían** lanzado
perfecto de subjuntivo	
haya lanzado	**hayamos** lanzado
hayas lanzado	**hayáis** lanzado
haya lanzado	**hayan** lanzado
pluscuamperfecto de subjuntivo	
hubiera lanzado	**hubiéramos** lanzado
hubieras lanzado	**hubierais** lanzado
hubiera lanzado	**hubieran** lanzado
OR	
hubiese lanzado	**hubiésemos** lanzado
hubieses lanzado	**hubieseis** lanzado
hubiese lanzado	**hubiesen** lanzado

lavar — to wash

gerundio **lavando** — participio de pasado **lavado**

SINGULAR	PLURAL	SINGULAR	PLURAL
presente de indicativo		perfecto de indicativo	
lav**o**	lav**amos**	**he** lavado	**hemos** lavado
lav**as**	lav**áis**	**has** lavado	**habéis** lavado
lav**a**	lav**an**	**ha** lavado	**han** lavado
imperfecto de indicativo		pluscuamperfecto de indicativo	
lav**aba**	lav**ábamos**	**había** lavado	**habíamos** lavado
lav**abas**	lav**abais**	**habías** lavado	**habíais** lavado
lav**aba**	lav**aban**	**había** lavado	**habían** lavado
pretérito		pretérito anterior	
lav**é**	lav**amos**	**hube** lavado	**hubimos** lavado
lav**aste**	lav**asteis**	**hubiste** lavado	**hubisteis** lavado
lav**ó**	lav**aron**	**hubo** lavado	**hubieron** lavado
futuro		futuro perfecto	
lavar**é**	lavar**emos**	**habré** lavado	**habremos** lavado
lavar**ás**	lavar**éis**	**habrás** lavado	**habréis** lavado
lavar**á**	lavar**án**	**habrá** lavado	**habrán** lavado
condicional simple		condicional compuesto	
lavar**ía**	lavar**íamos**	**habría** lavado	**habríamos** lavado
lavar**ías**	lavar**íais**	**habrías** lavado	**habríais** lavado
lavar**ía**	lavar**ían**	**habría** lavado	**habrían** lavado
presente de subjuntivo		perfecto de subjuntivo	
lav**e**	lav**emos**	**haya** lavado	**hayamos** lavado
lav**es**	lav**éis**	**hayas** lavado	**hayáis** lavado
lav**e**	lav**en**	**haya** lavado	**hayan** lavado
imperfecto de subjuntivo		pluscuamperfecto de subjuntivo	
lavar**a**	lavár**amos**	**hubiera** lavado	**hubiéramos** lavado
lavar**as**	lavar**ais**	**hubieras** lavado	**hubierais** lavado
lavar**a**	lavar**an**	**hubiera** lavado	**hubieran** lavado
OR		OR	
lavas**e**	lavás**emos**	**hubiese** lavado	**hubiésemos** lavado
lavas**es**	lavas**eis**	**hubieses** lavado	**hubieseis** lavado
lavas**e**	lavas**en**	**hubiese** lavado	**hubiesen** lavado

imperativo

—	lavemos
lava; no laves	lavad; no lavéis
lave	laven

to read **leer**

gerundio **leyendo** participio de pasado **leído**

presente de indicativo

SINGULAR	PLURAL
le**o**	le**emos**
le**es**	le**éis**
le**e**	le**en**

imperfecto de indicativo

SINGULAR	PLURAL
le**ía**	le**íamos**
le**ías**	le**íais**
le**ía**	le**ían**

pretérito

SINGULAR	PLURAL
le**í**	le**ímos**
le**íste**	le**ísteis**
ley**ó**	ley**eron**

futuro

SINGULAR	PLURAL
leer**é**	leer**emos**
leer**ás**	leer**éis**
leer**á**	leer**án**

condicional simple

SINGULAR	PLURAL
leer**ía**	leer**íamos**
leer**ías**	leer**íais**
leer**ía**	leer**ían**

presente de subjuntivo

SINGULAR	PLURAL
le**a**	le**amos**
le**as**	le**áis**
le**a**	le**an**

imperfecto de subjuntivo

SINGULAR	PLURAL
leyer**a**	leyér**amos**
leyer**as**	leyer**ais**
leyer**a**	leyer**an**
OR	
leyes**e**	leyés**emos**
leyes**es**	leyes**eis**
leyes**e**	leyes**en**

imperativo

SINGULAR	PLURAL
—	leamos
lee; no leas	leed; no leáis
lea	lean

perfecto de indicativo

SINGULAR	PLURAL
he leído	**hemos** leído
has leído	**habéis** leído
ha leído	**han** leído

pluscuamperfecto de indicativo

SINGULAR	PLURAL
había leído	**habíamos** leído
habías leído	**habíais** leído
había leído	**habían** leído

pretérito anterior

SINGULAR	PLURAL
hube leído	**hubimos** leído
hubiste leído	**hubisteis** leído
hubo leído	**hubieron** leído

futuro perfecto

SINGULAR	PLURAL
habré leído	**habremos** leído
habrás leído	**habréis** leído
habrá leído	**habrán** leído

condicional compuesto

SINGULAR	PLURAL
habría leído	**habríamos** leído
habrías leído	**habríais** leído
habría leído	**habrían** leído

perfecto de subjuntivo

SINGULAR	PLURAL
haya leído	**hayamos** leído
hayas leído	**hayáis** leído
haya leído	**hayan** leído

pluscuamperfecto de subjuntivo

SINGULAR	PLURAL
hubiera leído	**hubiéramos** leído
hubieras leído	**hubierais** leído
hubiera leído	**hubieran** leído
OR	
hubiese leído	**hubiésemos** leído
hubieses leído	**hubieseis** leído
hubiese leído	**hubiesen** leído

levantar — to lift, to raise

gerundio **levantando** | participio de pasado **levantado**

SINGULAR	PLURAL	SINGULAR	PLURAL
presente de indicativo		perfecto de indicativo	
levant**o**	levant**amos**	**he** levantado	**hemos** levantado
levant**as**	levant**áis**	**has** levantado	**habéis** levantado
levant**a**	levant**an**	**ha** levantado	**han** levantado
imperfecto de indicativo		pluscuamperfecto de indicativo	
levant**aba**	levant**ábamos**	**había** levantado	**habíamos** levantado
levant**abas**	levant**abais**	**habías** levantado	**habíais** levantado
levant**aba**	levant**aban**	**había** levantado	**habían** levantado
pretérito		pretérito anterior	
levant**é**	levant**amos**	**hube** levantado	**hubimos** levantado
levant**aste**	levant**asteis**	**hubiste** levantado	**hubisteis** levantado
levant**ó**	levant**aron**	**hubo** levantado	**hubieron** levantado
futuro		futuro perfecto	
levantar**é**	levantar**emos**	**habré** levantado	**habremos** levantado
levantar**ás**	levantar**éis**	**habrás** levantado	**habréis** levantado
levantar**á**	levantar**án**	**habrá** levantado	**habrán** levantado
condicional simple		condicional compuesto	
levantar**ía**	levantar**íamos**	**habría** levantado	**habríamos** levantado
levantar**ías**	levantar**íais**	**habrías** levantado	**habríais** levantado
levantar**ía**	levantar**ían**	**habría** levantado	**habrían** levantado
presente de subjuntivo		perfecto de subjuntivo	
levant**e**	levant**emos**	**haya** levantado	**hayamos** levantado
levant**es**	levant**éis**	**hayas** levantado	**hayáis** levantado
levant**e**	levant**en**	**haya** levantado	**hayan** levantado
imperfecto de subjuntivo		pluscuamperfecto de subjuntivo	
levantar**a**	levantár**amos**	**hubiera** levantado	**hubiéramos** levantado
levantar**as**	levantar**ais**	**hubieras** levantado	**hubierais** levantado
levantar**a**	levantar**an**	**hubiera** levantado	**hubieran** levantado
OR		OR	
levantas**e**	levantás**emos**	**hubiese** levantado	**hubiésemos** levantado
levantas**es**	levantas**eis**	**hubieses** levantado	**hubieseis** levantado
levantas**e**	levantas**en**	**hubiese** levantado	**hubiesen** levantado

imperativo

—	levantemos
levanta; no levantes	levantad; no levantéis
levante	levanten

to clean **limpiar**

gerundio **limpiando** participio de pasado **limpiado**

SINGULAR	PLURAL
presente de indicativo	
limpi**o**	limpi**amos**
limpi**as**	limpi**áis**
limpi**a**	limpi**an**
imperfecto de indicativo	
limpi**aba**	limpi**ábamos**
limpi**abas**	limpi**abais**
limpi**aba**	limpi**aban**
pretérito	
limpi**é**	limpi**amos**
limpi**aste**	limpi**asteis**
limpi**ó**	limpi**aron**
futuro	
limpiar**é**	limpi**aremos**
limpiar**ás**	limpi**aréis**
llimpiar**á**	limpi**arán**
condicional simple	
limpiar**ía**	limpiar**íamos**
limpiar**ías**	limpiar**íais**
limpiar**ía**	limpiar**ían**
presente de subjuntivo	
limpi**e**	limpi**emos**
limpi**es**	limpi**éis**
limpi**e**	limpi**en**
imperfecto de subjuntivo	
limpiar**a**	limiár**amos**
limpiar**as**	limpiar**ais**
limpiar**a**	limpiar**an**
OR	
limpias**e**	limpiás**emos**
limpias**es**	limpias**eis**
limpias**e**	limpias**en**
imperativo	
—	limpiemos
limpia; no limpies	limpiad; no limpiéis
limpie	limpien

SINGULAR	PLURAL
perfecto de indicativo	
he limpiado	**hemos** limpiado
has limpiado	**habéis** limpiado
ha limpiado	**han** limpiado
pluscuamperfecto de indicativo	
había limpiado	**habíamos** limpiado
habías limpiado	**habíais** limpiado
había limpiado	**habían** limpiado
pretérito anterior	
hube limpiado	**hubimos** limpiado
hubiste limpiado	**hubisteis** limpiado
hubo limpiado	**hubieron** limpiado
futuro perfecto	
habré limpiado	**habremos** limpiado
habrás limpiado	**habréis** limpiado
habrá limpiado	**habrán** limpiado
condicional compuesto	
habría limpiado	**habríamos** limpiado
habrías limpiado	**habríais** limpiado
habría limpiado	**habrían** limpiado
perfecto de subjuntivo	
haya limpiado	**hayamos** limpiado
hayas limpiado	**hayáis** limpiado
haya limpiado	**hayan** limpiado
pluscuamperfecto de subjuntivo	
hubiera limpiado	**hubiéramos** limpiado
hubieras limpiado	**hubierais** limpiado
hubiera limpiado	**hubieran** limpiado
OR	
hubiese limpiado	**hubiésemos** limpiado
hubieses limpiado	**hubieseis** limpiado
hubiese limpiado	**hubiesen** limpiado

llamar — to call, to name

gerundio **llamando** participio de pasado **llamado**

SINGULAR	PLURAL	SINGULAR	PLURAL
presente de indicativo		*perfecto de indicativo*	
llam**o**	llam**amos**	**he** llamado	**hemos** llamado
llam**as**	llam**áis**	**has** llamado	**habéis** llamado
llam**a**	llam**an**	**ha** llamado	**han** llamado
imperfecto de indicativo		*pluscuamperfecto de indicativo*	
llam**aba**	llam**ábamos**	**había** llamado	**habíamos** llamado
llam**abas**	llam**abais**	**habías** llamado	**habíais** llamado
llam**aba**	llam**aban**	**había** llamado	**habían** llamado
pretérito		*pretérito anterior*	
llam**é**	llam**amos**	**hube** llamado	**hubimos** llamado
llam**aste**	llam**asteis**	**hubiste** llamado	**hubisteis** llamado
llam**ó**	llam**aron**	**hubo** llamado	**hubieron** llamado
futuro		*futuro perfecto*	
llamar**é**	llamar**emos**	**habré** llamado	**habremos** llamado
llamar**ás**	llamar**éis**	**habrás** llamado	**habréis** llamado
llamar**á**	llamar**án**	**habrá** llamado	**habrán** llamado
condicional simple		*condicional compuesto*	
llamar**ía**	llamar**íamos**	**habría** llamado	**habríamos** llamado
llamar**ías**	llamar**íais**	**habrías** llamado	**habríais** llamado
llamar**ía**	llamar**ían**	**habría** llamado	**habrían** llamado
presente de subjuntivo		*perfecto de subjuntivo*	
llam**e**	llam**emos**	**haya** llamado	**hayamos** llamado
llam**es**	llam**éis**	**hayas** llamado	**hayáis** llamado
llam**e**	llam**en**	**haya** llamado	**hayan** llamado
imperfecto de subjuntivo		*pluscuamperfecto de subjuntivo*	
llamar**a**	llamár**amos**	**hubiera** llamado	**hubiéramos** llamado
llamar**as**	llamar**ais**	**hubieras** llamado	**hubierais** llamado
llamar**a**	llamar**an**	**hubiera** llamado	**hubieran** llamado
OR		OR	
llamas**e**	llamás**emos**	**hubiese** llamado	**hubiésemos** llamado
llamas**es**	llamas**eis**	**hubieses** llamado	**hubieseis** llamado
llamas**e**	llamas**en**	**hubiese** llamado	**hubiesen** llamado

imperativo

—	llamemos
llama; no llames	llamad; no llaméis
llame	llamen

gerundio **llegando** participio de pasado **llegado**

SINGULAR	PLURAL
presente de indicativo	
lleg**o**	lleg**amos**
lleg**as**	lleg**áis**
lleg**a**	lleg**an**
imperfecto de indicativo	
lleg**aba**	lleg**ábamos**
lleg**abas**	lleg**abais**
lleg**aba**	lleg**aban**
pretérito	
llegu**é**	lleg**amos**
lleg**aste**	lleg**asteis**
lleg**ó**	lleg**aron**
futuro	
llegar**é**	llegar**emos**
llegar**ás**	llegar**éis**
llegar**á**	llegar**án**
condicional simple	
llegar**ía**	llegar**íamos**
llegar**ías**	llegar**íais**
llegar**ía**	llegar**ían**
presente de subjuntivo	
llegu**e**	llegu**emos**
llegu**es**	llegu**éis**
llegu**e**	llegu**en**
imperfecto de subjuntivo	
llegar**a**	llegár**amos**
llegar**as**	llegar**ais**
llegar**a**	llegar**an**
OR	
llegas**e**	llegás**emos**
llegas**es**	llegas**eis**
llegas**e**	llegas**en**
imperativo	
—	lleguemos
llega; no llegues	llegad; no lleguéis
llegue	lleguen

SINGULAR	PLURAL
perfecto de indicativo	
he llegado	**hemos** llegado
has llegado	**habéis** llegado
ha llegado	**han** llegado
pluscuamperfecto de indicativo	
había llegado	**habíamos** llegado
habías llegado	**habíais** llegado
había llegado	**habían** llegado
pretérito anterior	
hube llegado	**hubimos** llegado
hubiste llegado	**hubisteis** llegado
hubo llegado	**hubieron** llegado
futuro perfecto	
habré llegado	**habremos** llegado
habrás llegado	**habréis** llegado
habrá llegado	**habrán** llegado
condicional compuesto	
habría llegado	**habríamos** llegado
habrías llegado	**habríais** llegado
habría llegado	**habrían** llegado
perfecto de subjuntivo	
haya llegado	**hayamos** llegado
hayas llegado	**hayáis** llegado
haya llegado	**hayan** llegado
pluscuamperfecto de subjuntivo	
hubiera llegado	**hubiéramos** llegado
hubieras llegado	**hubierais** llegado
hubiera llegado	**hubieran** llegado
OR	
hubiese llegado	**hubiésemos** llegado
hubieses llegado	**hubieseis** llegado
hubiese llegado	**hubiesen** llegado

llenar — to fill

gerundio **llenando** participio de pasado **llenado**

SINGULAR	PLURAL	SINGULAR	PLURAL
presente de indicativo		perfecto de indicativo	
llen**o**	llen**amos**	**he** llenado	**hemos** llenado
llen**as**	llen**áis**	**has** llenado	**habéis** llenado
llen**a**	llen**an**	**ha** llenado	**han** llenado
imperfecto de indicativo		pluscuamperfecto de indicativo	
llen**aba**	llen**ábamos**	**había** llenado	**habíamos** llenado
llen**abas**	llen**abais**	**habías** llenado	**habíais** llenado
llen**aba**	llen**aban**	**había** llenado	**habían** llenado
pretérito		pretérito anterior	
llen**é**	llen**amos**	**hube** llenado	**hubimos** llenado
llen**aste**	llen**asteis**	**hubiste** llenado	**hubisteis** llenado
llen**ó**	llen**aron**	**hubo** llenado	**hubieron** llenado
futuro		futuro perfecto	
llenar**é**	llenar**emos**	**habré** llenado	**habremos** llenado
llenar**ás**	llenar**éis**	**habrás** llenado	**habréis** llenado
llenar**á**	llenar**án**	**habrá** llenado	**habrán** llenado
condicional simple		condicional compuesto	
llenar**ía**	llenar**íamos**	**habría** llenado	**habríamos** llenado
llenar**ías**	llenar**íais**	**habrías** llenado	**habríais** llenado
llenar**ía**	llenar**ían**	**habría** llenado	**habrían** llenado
presente de subjuntivo		perfecto de subjuntivo	
llen**e**	llen**emos**	**haya** llenado	**hayamos** llenado
llen**es**	llen**éis**	**hayas** llenado	**hayáis** llenado
llen**e**	llen**en**	**haya** llenado	**hayan** llenado
imperfecto de subjuntivo		pluscuamperfecto de subjuntivo	
llenar**a**	llenár**amos**	**hubiera** llenado	**hubiéramos** llenado
llenar**as**	llenar**ais**	**hubieras** llenado	**hubierais** llenado
llenar**a**	llenar**an**	**hubiera** llenado	**hubieran** llenado
OR		OR	
llenas**e**	llenás**emos**	**hubiese** llenado	**hubiésemos** llenado
llenas**es**	llenas**eis**	**hubieses** llenado	**hubieseis** llenado
llenas**e**	llenas**en**	**hubiese** llenado	**hubiesen** llenado

imperativo

—	llenemos
llena; no llenes	llenad; no llenéis
llene	llenen

gerundio **llevando** participio de pasado **llevado**

SINGULAR	PLURAL	SINGULAR	PLURAL
presente de indicativo		perfecto de indicativo	
llev**o**	llev**amos**	**he** llevado	**hemos** llevado
llev**as**	llev**áis**	**has** llevado	**habéis** llevado
llev**a**	llev**an**	**ha** llevado	**han** llevado
imperfecto de indicativo		pluscuamperfecto de indicativo	
llev**aba**	llev**ábamos**	**había** llevado	**habíamos** llevado
llev**abas**	llev**abais**	**habías** llevado	**habíais** llevado
llev**aba**	llev**aban**	**había** llevado	**habían** llevado
pretérito		pretérito anterior	
llev**é**	llev**amos**	**hube** llevado	**hubimos** llevado
llev**aste**	llev**asteis**	**hubiste** llevado	**hubisteis** llevado
llev**ó**	llev**aron**	**hubo** llevado	**hubieron** llevado
futuro		futuro perfecto	
llevar**é**	llevar**emos**	**habré** llevado	**habremos** llevado
llevar**ás**	llevar**éis**	**habrás** llevado	**habréis** llevado
llevar**á**	llevar**án**	**habrá** llevado	**habrán** llevado
condicional simple		condicional compuesto	
llevar**ía**	llevar**íamos**	**habría** llevado	**habríamos** llevado
llevar**ías**	llevar**íais**	**habrías** llevado	**habríais** llevado
llevar**ía**	llevar**ían**	**habría** llevado	**habrían** llevado
presente de subjuntivo		perfecto de subjuntivo	
llev**e**	llev**emos**	**haya** llevado	**hayamos** llevado
llev**es**	llev**éis**	**hayas** llevado	**hayáis** llevado
llev**e**	llev**en**	**haya** llevado	**hayan** llevado
imperfecto de subjuntivo		pluscuamperfecto de subjuntivo	
llevar**a**	llevár**amos**	**hubiera** llevado	**hubiéramos** llevado
llevar**as**	llevar**ais**	**hubieras** llevado	**hubierais** llevado
llevar**a**	llevar**an**	**hubiera** llevado	**hubieran** llevado
OR		OR	
llevas**e**	llevás**emos**	**hubiese** llevado	**hubiésemos** llevado
llevas**es**	llevas**eis**	**hubieses** llevado	**hubieseis** llevado
llevas**e**	llevas**en**	**hubiese** llevado	**hubiesen** llevado

imperativo

—	llevemos
lleva; no lleves	llevad; no llevéis
lleve	lleven

llorar — to cry

gerundio **llorando** participio de pasado **llorado**

SINGULAR	PLURAL	SINGULAR	PLURAL
presente de indicativo		perfecto de indicativo	
llor**o**	llor**amos**	**he** llorado	**hemos** llorado
llor**as**	llor**áis**	**has** llorado	**habéis** llorado
llor**a**	llor**an**	**ha** llorado	**han** llorado
imperfecto de indicativo		pluscuamperfecto de indicativo	
llor**aba**	llor**ábamos**	**había** llorado	**habíamos** llorado
llor**abas**	llor**abais**	**habías** llorado	**habíais** llorado
llor**aba**	llor**aban**	**había** llorado	**habían** llorado
pretérito		pretérito anterior	
llor**é**	llor**amos**	**hube** llorado	**hubimos** llorado
llor**aste**	llor**asteis**	**hubiste** llorado	**hubisteis** llorado
llor**ó**	llor**aron**	**hubo** llorado	**hubieron** llorado
futuro		futuro perfecto	
llorar**é**	llorar**emos**	**habré** llorado	**habremos** llorado
llorar**ás**	llorar**éis**	**habrás** llorado	**habréis** llorado
llorar**á**	llorar**án**	**habrá** llorado	**habrán** llorado
condicional simple		condicional compuesto	
llorar**ía**	llorar**íamos**	**habría** llorado	**habríamos** llorado
llorar**ías**	llorar**íais**	**habrías** llorado	**habríais** llorado
llorar**ía**	llorar**ían**	**habría** llorado	**habrían** llorado
presente de subjuntivo		perfecto de subjuntivo	
llor**e**	llor**emos**	**haya** llorado	**hayamos** llorado
llor**es**	llor**éis**	**hayas** llorado	**hayáis** llorado
llor**e**	llor**en**	**haya** llorado	**hayan** llorado
imperfecto de subjuntivo		pluscuamperfecto de subjuntivo	
llorar**a**	llorár**amos**	**hubiera** llorado	**hubiéramos** llorado
llorar**as**	llorar**ais**	**hubieras** llorado	**hubierais** llorado
llorar**a**	llorar**an**	**hubiera** llorado	**hubieran** llorado
OR		OR	
lloras**e**	llorás**emos**	**hubiese** llorado	**hubiésemos** llorado
lloras**es**	lloras**eis**	**hubieses** llorado	**hubieseis** llorado
lloras**e**	lloras**en**	**hubiese** llorado	**hubiesen** llorado

imperativo

—	lloremos
llora; no llores	llorad; no lloréis
llore	lloren

gerundio **luchando** participio de pasado **luchado**

SINGULAR	PLURAL	SINGULAR	PLURAL
presente de indicativo		perfecto de indicativo	
luch**o**	luch**amos**	**he** luchado	**hemos** luchado
luch**as**	luch**áis**	**has** luchado	**habéis** luchado
luch**a**	luch**an**	**ha** luchado	**han** luchado
imperfecto de indicativo		pluscuamperfecto de indicativo	
luch**aba**	luch**ábamos**	**había** luchado	**habíamos** luchado
luch**abas**	luch**abais**	**habías** luchado	**habíais** luchado
luch**aba**	luch**aban**	**había** luchado	**habían** luchado
pretérito		pretérito anterior	
luch**é**	luch**amos**	**hube** luchado	**hubimos** luchado
luch**aste**	luch**asteis**	**hubiste** luchado	**hubisteis** luchado
luch**ó**	luch**aron**	**hubo** luchado	**hubieron** luchado
futuro		futuro perfecto	
luchar**é**	luchar**emos**	**habré** luchado	**habremos** luchado
luchar**ás**	luchar**éis**	**habrás** luchado	**habréis** luchado
luchar**á**	luchar**án**	**habrá** luchado	**habrán** luchado
condicional simple		condicional compuesto	
luchar**ía**	luchar**íamos**	**habría** luchado	**habríamos** luchado
luchar**ías**	luchar**íais**	**habrías** luchado	**habríais** luchado
luchar**ía**	luchar**ían**	**habría** luchado	**habrían** luchado
presente de subjuntivo		perfecto de subjuntivo	
luch**e**	luch**emos**	**haya** luchado	**hayamos** luchado
luch**es**	luch**éis**	**hayas** luchado	**hayáis** luchado
luch**e**	luch**en**	**haya** luchado	**hayan** luchado
imperfecto de subjuntivo		pluscuamperfecto de subjuntivo	
luchar**a**	luchár**amos**	**hubiera** luchado	**hubiéramos** luchado
luchar**as**	luchar**ais**	**hubieras** luchado	**hubierais** luchado
luchar**a**	luchar**an**	**hubiera** luchado	**hubieran** luchado
OR		OR	
luchas**e**	luchás**emos**	**hubiese** luchado	**hubiésemos** luchado
luchas**es**	luchas**eis**	**hubieses** luchado	**hubieseis** luchado
luchas**e**	luchas**en**	**hubiese** luchado	**hubiesen** luchado

imperativo

SINGULAR	PLURAL
—	luchemos
lucha; no luches	luchad; no luchéis
luche	luchen

L

madurar — to mature, to ripen

gerundio **madurando** — participio de pasado **madurado**

SINGULAR	PLURAL	SINGULAR	PLURAL
presente de indicativo		**perfecto de indicativo**	
maduro	maduramos	he madurado	hemos madurado
maduras	maduráis	has madurado	habéis madurado
madura	maduran	ha madurado	han madurado
imperfecto de indicativo		**pluscuamperfecto de indicativo**	
maduraba	madurábamos	había madurado	habíamos madurado
madurabas	madurabais	habías madurado	habíais madurado
maduraba	maduraban	había madurado	habían madurado
pretérito		**pretérito anterior**	
maduré	maduramos	hube madurado	hubimos madurado
maduraste	madurasteis	hubiste madurado	hubisteis madurado
maduró	maduraron	hubo madurado	hubieron madurado
futuro		**futuro perfecto**	
maduraré	maduraremos	habré madurado	habremos madurado
madurarás	maduraréis	habrás madurado	habréis madurado
madurará	madurarán	habrá madurado	habrán madurado
condicional simple		**condicional compuesto**	
maduraría	maduraríamos	habría madurado	habríamos madurado
madurarías	maduraríais	habrías madurado	habríais madurado
maduraría	madurarían	habría madurado	habrían madurado
presente de subjuntivo		**perfecto de subjuntivo**	
madure	maduremos	haya madurado	hayamos madurado
madures	maduréis	hayas madurado	hayáis madurado
madure	maduren	haya madurado	hayan madurado
imperfecto de subjuntivo		**pluscuamperfecto de subjuntivo**	
madurara	maduráramos	hubiera madurado	hubiéramos madurado
maduraras	madurarais	hubieras madurado	hubierais madurado
madurara	maduraran	hubiera madurado	hubieran madurado
OR		OR	
madurase	madurásemos	hubiese madurado	hubiésemos madurado
madurases	maduraseis	hubieses madurado	hubieseis madurado
madurase	madurasen	hubiese madurado	hubiesen madurado

imperativo

SINGULAR	PLURAL
—	maduremos
madura; no madures	madurad; no maduréis
madure	maduren

to curse — maldecir

gerundio **maldiciendo** participio de pasado **maldecido**

presente de indicativo

SINGULAR	PLURAL
maldig**o**	maldec**imos**
maldic**es**	maldec**ís**
maldic**e**	maldic**en**

imperfecto de indicativo

SINGULAR	PLURAL
maldec**ía**	maldec**íamos**
maldec**ías**	maldec**íais**
maldec**ía**	maldec**ían**

pretérito

SINGULAR	PLURAL
maldij**e**	maldij**imos**
maldij**iste**	maldij**isteis**
maldij**o**	maldij**eron**

futuro

SINGULAR	PLURAL
maldecir**é**	maldecir**emos**
maldecir**ás**	maldecir**éis**
maldecir**á**	maldecir**án**

condicional simple

SINGULAR	PLURAL
maldecir**ía**	maldecir**íamos**
maldecir**ías**	maldecir**íais**
maldecir**ía**	maldecir**ían**

presente de subjuntivo

SINGULAR	PLURAL
maldig**a**	maldig**amos**
maldig**as**	maldig**áis**
maldig**a**	maldig**an**

imperfecto de subjuntivo

SINGULAR	PLURAL
maldijer**a**	maldijér**amos**
maldijer**as**	maldijer**ais**
maldijer**a**	maldijer**an**
OR	
maldijes**e**	maldijés**emos**
maldijes**es**	maldijes**eis**
maldijes**e**	maldijes**en**

imperativo

SINGULAR	PLURAL
—	maldigamos
maldice; no maldigas	maldecid; no maldigáis
maldiga	maldigan

perfecto de indicativo

SINGULAR	PLURAL
he maldecido	**hemos** maldecido
has maldecido	**habéis** maldecido
ha maldecido	**han** maldecido

pluscuamperfecto de indicativo

SINGULAR	PLURAL
había maldecido	**habíamos** maldecido
habías maldecido	**habíais** maldecido
había maldecido	**habían** maldecido

pretérito anterior

SINGULAR	PLURAL
hube maldecido	**hubimos** maldecido
hubiste maldecido	**hubisteis** maldecido
hubo maldecido	**hubieron** maldecido

futuro perfecto

SINGULAR	PLURAL
habré maldecido	**habremos** maldecido
habrás maldecido	**habréis** maldecido
habrá maldecido	**habrán** maldecido

condicional compuesto

SINGULAR	PLURAL
habría maldecido	**habríamos** maldecido
habrías maldecido	**habríais** maldecido
habría maldecido	**habrían** maldecido

perfecto de subjuntivo

SINGULAR	PLURAL
haya maldecido	**hayamos** maldecido
hayas maldecido	**hayáis** maldecido
haya maldecido	**hayan** maldecido

pluscuamperfecto de subjuntivo

SINGULAR	PLURAL
hubiera maldecido	**hubiéramos** maldecido
hubieras maldecido	**hubierais** maldecido
hubiera maldecido	**hubieran** maldecido
OR	
hubiese maldecido	**hubiésemos** maldecido
hubieses maldecido	**hubieseis** maldecido
hubiese maldecido	**hubiesen** maldecido

maltratar — to mistreat, to abuse

gerundio **maltratando** participio de pasado **maltratado**

SINGULAR	PLURAL	SINGULAR	PLURAL
presente de indicativo		perfecto de indicativo	
maltrat**o**	maltrat**amos**	**he** maltratado	**hemos** maltratado
maltrat**as**	maltrat**áis**	**has** maltratado	**habéis** maltratado
maltrat**a**	maltrat**an**	**ha** maltratado	**han** maltratado
imperfecto de indicativo		pluscuamperfecto de indicativo	
maltrat**aba**	maltrat**ábamos**	**había** maltratado	**habíamos** maltratado
maltrat**abas**	maltrat**abais**	**habías** maltratado	**habíais** maltratado
maltrat**aba**	maltrat**aban**	**había** maltratado	**habían** maltratado
pretérito		pretérito anterior	
maltrat**é**	maltrat**amos**	**hube** maltratado	**hubimos** maltratado
maltrat**aste**	maltrat**asteis**	**hubiste** maltratado	**hubisteis** maltratado
maltrat**ó**	maltrat**aron**	**hubo** maltratado	**hubieron** maltratado
futuro		futuro perfecto	
maltratar**é**	maltratar**emos**	**habré** maltratado	**habremos** maltratado
maltratar**ás**	maltratar**éis**	**habrás** maltratado	**habréis** maltratado
maltratar**á**	maltratar**án**	**habrá** maltratado	**habrán** maltratado
condicional simple		condicional compuesto	
maltratar**ía**	maltratar**íamos**	**habría** maltratado	**habríamos** maltratado
maltratar**ías**	maltratar**íais**	**habrías** maltratado	**habríais** maltratado
maltratar**ía**	maltratar**ían**	**habría** maltratado	**habrían** maltratado
presente de subjuntivo		perfecto de subjuntivo	
maltrat**e**	maltrat**emos**	**haya** maltratado	**hayamos** maltratado
maltrat**es**	maltrat**éis**	**hayas** maltratado	**hayáis** maltratado
maltrat**e**	maltrat**en**	**haya** maltratado	**hayan** maltratado
imperfecto de subjuntivo		pluscuamperfecto de subjuntivo	
maltratar**a**	maltratár**amos**	**hubiera** maltratado	**hubiéramos** maltratado
maltratar**as**	maltratar**ais**	**hubieras** maltratado	**hubierais** maltratado
maltratar**a**	maltratar**an**	**hubiera** maltratado	**hubieran** maltratado
OR		OR	
maltratas**e**	maltratás**emos**	**hubiese** maltratado	**hubiésemos** maltratado
maltratas**es**	maltratas**eis**	**hubieses** maltratado	**hubieseis** maltratado
maltratas**e**	maltratas**en**	**hubiese** maltratado	**hubiesen** maltratado

imperativo

—	maltratemos
maltrata; no maltrates	maltratad; no maltratéis
maltrate	maltraten

gerundio **mandando** participio de pasado **mandado**

presente de indicativo

SINGULAR	PLURAL
mand**o**	mand**amos**
mand**as**	mand**áis**
mand**a**	mand**an**

imperfecto de indicativo

SINGULAR	PLURAL
mand**aba**	mand**ábamos**
mand**abas**	mand**abais**
mand**aba**	mand**aban**

pretérito

SINGULAR	PLURAL
mand**é**	mand**amos**
mand**aste**	mand**asteis**
mand**ó**	mand**aron**

futuro

SINGULAR	PLURAL
mandar**é**	mandar**emos**
mandar**ás**	mandar**éis**
mandar**á**	mandar**án**

condicional simple

SINGULAR	PLURAL
mandar**ía**	mandar**íamos**
mandar**ías**	mandar**íais**
mandar**ía**	mandar**ían**

presente de subjuntivo

SINGULAR	PLURAL
mand**e**	mand**emos**
mand**es**	mand**éis**
mand**e**	mand**en**

imperfecto de subjuntivo

SINGULAR	PLURAL
mandar**a**	mandár**amos**
mandar**as**	mandar**ais**
mandar**a**	mandar**an**
OR	
mandas**e**	mandás**emos**
mandas**es**	mandas**eis**
mandas**e**	mandas**en**

imperativo

SINGULAR	PLURAL
—	mandemos
manda; no mandes	mandad; no mandéis
mande	manden

perfecto de indicativo

SINGULAR	PLURAL
he mandado	**hemos** mandado
has mandado	**habéis** mandado
ha mandado	**han** mandado

pluscuamperfecto de indicativo

SINGULAR	PLURAL
había mandado	**habíamos** mandado
habías mandado	**habíais** mandado
había mandado	**habían** mandado

pretérito anterior

SINGULAR	PLURAL
hube mandado	**hubimos** mandado
hubiste mandado	**hubisteis** mandado
hubo mandado	**hubieron** mandado

futuro perfecto

SINGULAR	PLURAL
habré mandado	**habremos** mandado
habrás mandado	**habréis** mandado
habrá mandado	**habrán** mandado

condicional compuesto

SINGULAR	PLURAL
habría mandado	**habríamos** mandado
habrías mandado	**habríais** mandado
habría mandado	**habrían** mandado

perfecto de subjuntivo

SINGULAR	PLURAL
haya mandado	**hayamos** mandado
hayas mandado	**hayáis** mandado
haya mandado	**hayan** mandado

pluscuamperfecto de subjuntivo

SINGULAR	PLURAL
hubiera mandado	**hubiéramos** mandado
hubieras mandado	**hubierais** mandado
hubiera mandado	**hubieran** mandado
OR	
hubiese mandado	**hubiésemos** mandado
hubieses mandado	**hubieseis** mandado
hubiese mandado	**hubiesen** mandado

manejar — to manage, to handle

gerundio **manejando** — participio de pasado **manejado**

SINGULAR	PLURAL	SINGULAR	PLURAL
presente de indicativo		perfecto de indicativo	
manej**o**	manej**amos**	**he** manejado	**hemos** manejado
manej**as**	manej**áis**	**has** manejado	**habéis** manejado
manej**a**	manej**an**	**ha** manejado	**han** manejado
imperfecto de indicativo		pluscuamperfecto de indicativo	
manej**aba**	manej**ábamos**	**había** manejado	**habíamos** manejado
manej**abas**	manej**abais**	**habías** manejado	**habíais** manejado
manej**aba**	manej**aban**	**había** manejado	**habían** manejado
pretérito		pretérito anterior	
manej**é**	manej**amos**	**hube** manejado	**hubimos** manejado
manej**aste**	manej**asteis**	**hubiste** manejado	**hubisteis** manejado
manej**ó**	manej**aron**	**hubo** manejado	**hubieron** manejado
futuro		futuro perfecto	
manejar**é**	manejar**emos**	**habré** manejado	**habremos** manejado
manejar**ás**	manejar**éis**	**habrás** manejado	**habréis** manejado
manejar**á**	manejar**án**	**habrá** manejado	**habrán** manejado
condicional simple		condicional compuesto	
manejar**ía**	manejar**íamos**	**habría** manejado	**habríamos** manejado
manejar**ías**	manejar**íais**	**habrías** manejado	**habríais** manejado
manejar**ía**	manejar**ían**	**habría** manejado	**habrían** manejado
presente de subjuntivo		perfecto de subjuntivo	
manej**e**	manej**emos**	**haya** manejado	**hayamos** manejado
manej**es**	manej**éis**	**hayas** manejado	**hayáis** manejado
manej**e**	manej**en**	**haya** manejado	**hayan** manejado
imperfecto de subjuntivo		pluscuamperfecto de subjuntivo	
manejar**a**	manejár**amos**	**hubiera** manejado	**hubiéramos** manejado
manejar**as**	manejar**ais**	**hubieras** manejado	**hubierais** manejado
manejar**a**	manejar**an**	**hubiera** manejado	**hubieran** manejado
OR		OR	
manejas**e**	manejás**emos**	**hubiese** manejado	**hubiésemos** manejado
manejas**es**	manejas**eis**	**hubieses** manejado	**hubieseis** manejado
manejas**e**	manejas**en**	**hubiese** manejado	**hubiesen** manejado

imperativo

—	manejemos
maneja; no manejes	manejad; no manejéis
maneje	manejen

gerundio **manifestando** participio de pasado **manifestado**

SINGULAR	PLURAL	SINGULAR	PLURAL
presente de indicativo		perfecto de indicativo	
manifiest**o**	manifest**amos**	**he** manifestado	**hemos** manifestado
manifiest**as**	manifest**áis**	**has** manifestado	**habéis** manifestado
manifiest**a**	manifiest**an**	**ha** manifestado	**han** manifestado
imperfecto de indicativo		pluscuamperfecto de indicativo	
manifest**aba**	manifest**ábamos**	**había** manifestado	**habíamos** manifestado
manifest**abas**	manifest**abais**	**habías** manifestado	**habíais** manifestado
manifest**aba**	manifest**aban**	**había** manifestado	**habían** manifestado
pretérito		pretérito anterior	
manifest**é**	manifest**amos**	**hube** manifestado	**hubimos** manifestado
manifest**aste**	manifest**asteis**	**hubiste** manifestado	**hubisteis** manifestado
manifest**ó**	manifest**aron**	**hubo** manifestado	**hubieron** manifestado
futuro		futuro perfecto	
manifestar**é**	manifestar**emos**	**habré** manifestado	**habremos** manifestado
manifestar**ás**	manifestar**éis**	**habrás** manifestado	**habréis** manifestado
manifestar**á**	manifestar**án**	**habrá** manifestado	**habrán** manifestado
condicional simple		condicional compuesto	
manifestar**ía**	manifestar**íamos**	**habría** manifestado	**habríamos** manifestado
manifestar**ías**	manifestar**íais**	**habrías** manifestado	**habríais** manifestado
manifestar**ía**	manifestar**ían**	**habría** manifestado	**habrían** manifestado
presente de subjuntivo		perfecto de subjuntivo	
manifiest**e**	manifest**emos**	**haya** manifestado	**hayamos** manifestado
manifiest**es**	manifest**éis**	**hayas** manifestado	**hayáis** manifestado
manifiest**e**	manifiest**en**	**haya** manifestado	**hayan** manifestado
imperfecto de subjuntivo		pluscuamperfecto de subjuntivo	
manifestar**a**	manifestár**amos**	**hubiera** manifestado	**hubiéramos** manifestado
manifestar**as**	manifestar**ais**	**hubieras** manifestado	**hubierais** manifestado
manifestar**a**	manifestar**an**	**hubiera** manifestado	**hubieran** manifestado
OR		OR	
manifestas**e**	manifestás**emos**	**hubiese** manifestado	**hubiésemos** manifestado
manifestas**es**	manifestas**eis**	**hubieses** manifestado	**hubieseis** manifestado
manifestas**e**	manifestas**en**	**hubiese** manifestado	**hubiesen** manifestado

imperativo

—	manifestemos
manifiesta; no manifiestes	manifestad; no manifestéis
manifieste	manifiesten

M

manipular — to manipulate

gerundio **manipulando** participio de pasado **manipulado**

SINGULAR	PLURAL
presente de indicativo	
manipul**o**	manipul**amos**
manipul**as**	manipul**áis**
manipul**a**	manipul**an**
imperfecto de indicativo	
manipul**aba**	manipul**ábamos**
manipul**abas**	manipul**abais**
manipul**aba**	manipul**aban**
pretérito	
manipul**é**	manipul**amos**
manipul**aste**	manipul**asteis**
manipul**ó**	manipul**aron**
futuro	
manipular**é**	manipular**emos**
manipular**ás**	manipular**éis**
manipular**á**	manipular**án**
condicional simple	
manipular**ía**	manipular**íamos**
manipular**ías**	manipular**íais**
manipular**ía**	manipular**ían**
presente de subjuntivo	
manipul**e**	manipul**emos**
manipul**es**	manipul**éis**
manipul**e**	manipul**en**
imperfecto de subjuntivo	
manipular**a**	manipulár**amos**
manipular**as**	manipular**ais**
manipular**a**	manipular**an**
OR	
manipulas**e**	manipulás**emos**
manipulas**es**	manipulas**eis**
manipulas**e**	manipulas**en**
imperativo	
—	manipulemos
manipula; no manipules	manipulad; no manipuléis
manipule	manipulen

SINGULAR	PLURAL
perfecto de indicativo	
he manipulado	**hemos** manipulado
has manipulado	**habéis** manipulado
ha manipulado	**han** manipulado
pluscuamperfecto de indicativo	
había manipulado	**habíamos** manipulado
habías manipulado	**habíais** manipulado
había manipulado	**habían** manipulado
pretérito anterior	
hube manipulado	**hubimos** manipulado
hubiste manipulado	**hubisteis** manipulado
hubo manipulado	**hubieron** manipulado
futuro perfecto	
habré manipulado	**habremos** manipulado
habrás manipulado	**habréis** manipulado
habrá manipulado	**habrán** manipulado
condicional compuesto	
habría manipulado	**habríamos** manipulado
habrías manipulado	**habríais** manipulado
habría manipulado	**habrían** manipulado
perfecto de subjuntivo	
haya manipulado	**hayamos** manipulado
hayas manipulado	**hayáis** manipulado
haya manipulado	**hayan** manipulado
pluscuamperfecto de subjuntivo	
hubiera manipulado	**hubiéramos** manipulado
hubieras manipulado	**hubierais** manipulado
hubiera manipulado	**hubieran** manipulado
OR	
hubiese manipulado	**hubiésemos** manipulado
hubieses manipulado	**hubieseis** manipulado
hubiese manipulado	**hubiesen** manipulado

gerundio **manteniendo** participio de pasado **mantenido**

SINGULAR	PLURAL	SINGULAR	PLURAL
presente de indicativo		perfecto de indicativo	
manteng**o**	manten**emos**	**he** mantenido	**hemos** mantenido
mantien**es**	manten**éis**	**has** mantenido	**habéis** mantenido
mantien**e**	mantien**en**	**ha** mantenido	**han** mantenido
imperfecto de indicativo		pluscuamperfecto de indicativo	
manten**ía**	manten**íamos**	**había** mantenido	**habíamos** mantenido
manten**ías**	manten**íais**	**habías** mantenido	**habíais** mantenido
manten**ía**	manten**ían**	**había** mantenido	**habían** mantenido
pretérito		pretérito anterior	
mantuv**e**	mantuv**imos**	**hube** mantenido	**hubimos** mantenido
mantuv**iste**	mantuv**isteis**	**hubiste** mantenido	**hubisteis** mantenido
mantuv**o**	mantuv**ieron**	**hubo** mantenido	**hubieron** mantenido
futuro		futuro perfecto	
mantendr**é**	mantendr**emos**	**habré** mantenido	**habremos** mantenido
mantendr**ás**	mantendr**éis**	**habrás** mantenido	**habréis** mantenido
mantendr**á**	mantendr**án**	**habrá** mantenido	**habrán** mantenido
condicional simple		condicional compuesto	
mantendr**ía**	mantendr**íamos**	**habría** mantenido	**habríamos** mantenido
mantendr**ías**	mantendr**íais**	**habrías** mantenido	**habríais** mantenido
mantendr**ía**	mantendr**ían**	**habría** mantenido	**habrían** mantenido
presente de subjuntivo		perfecto de subjuntivo	
manteng**a**	manteng**amos**	**haya** mantenido	**hayamos** mantenido
manteng**as**	manteng**áis**	**hayas** mantenido	**hayáis** mantenido
manteng**a**	manteng**an**	**haya** mantenido	**hayan** mantenido
imperfecto de subjuntivo		pluscuamperfecto de subjuntivo	
mantuvier**a**	mantuvié**ramos**	**hubiera** mantenido	**hubiéramos** mantenido
mantuvier**as**	mantuvier**ais**	**hubieras** mantenido	**hubierais** mantenido
mantuvier**a**	mantuvier**an**	**hubiera** mantenido	**hubieran** mantenido
OR		OR	
mantuvies**e**	mantuvié**semos**	**hubiese** mantenido	**hubiésemos** mantenido
mantuvies**es**	mantuvies**eis**	**hubieses** mantenido	**hubieseis** mantenido
mantuvies**e**	mantuvies**en**	**hubiese** mantenido	**hubiesen** mantenido

imperativo

—	mantengamos
manten; no mantengas	mantened; no mantengáis
mantenga	mantengan

marcar — to mark, to note, to observe

gerundio **marcando** — participio de pasado **marcado**

SINGULAR	PLURAL
presente de indicativo	
marc**o**	marc**amos**
marc**as**	marc**áis**
marc**a**	marc**an**
imperfecto de indicativo	
marc**aba**	marc**ábamos**
marc**abas**	marc**abais**
marc**aba**	marc**aban**
pretérito	
marqu**é**	marc**amos**
marc**aste**	marc**asteis**
marc**ó**	marc**aron**
futuro	
marcar**é**	marcar**emos**
marcar**ás**	marcar**éis**
marcar**á**	marcar**án**
condicional simple	
marcar**ía**	marcar**íamos**
marcar**ías**	marcar**íais**
marcar**ía**	marcar**ían**
presente de subjuntivo	
marqu**e**	marqu**emos**
marqu**es**	marqu**éis**
marqu**e**	marqu**en**
imperfecto de subjuntivo	
marcar**a**	marcár**amos**
marcar**as**	marcar**ais**
marcar**a**	marcar**an**
OR	
marcas**e**	marcás**emos**
marcas**es**	marcas**eis**
marcas**e**	marcas**en**
imperativo	
—	marquemos
marca; no marques	marcad; no marquéis
marque	marquen

SINGULAR	PLURAL
perfecto de indicativo	
he marcado	**hemos** marcado
has marcado	**habéis** marcado
ha marcado	**han** marcado
pluscuamperfecto de indicativo	
había marcado	**habíamos** marcado
habías marcado	**habíais** marcado
había marcado	**habían** marcado
pretérito anterior	
hube marcado	**hubimos** marcado
hubiste marcado	**hubisteis** marcado
hubo marcado	**hubieron** marcado
futuro perfecto	
habré marcado	**habremos** marcado
habrás marcado	**habréis** marcado
habrá marcado	**habrán** marcado
condicional compuesto	
habría marcado	**habríamos** marcado
habrías marcado	**habríais** marcado
habría marcado	**habrían** marcado
perfecto de subjuntivo	
haya marcado	**hayamos** marcado
hayas marcado	**hayáis** marcado
haya marcado	**hayan** marcado
pluscuamperfecto de subjuntivo	
hubiera marcado	**hubiéramos** marcado
hubieras marcado	**hubierais** marcado
hubiera marcado	**hubieran** marcado
OR	
hubiese marcado	**hubiésemos** marcado
hubieses marcado	**hubieseis** marcado
hubiese marcado	**hubiesen** marcado

gerundio **marchando** participio de pasado **marchado**

SINGULAR	PLURAL	SINGULAR	PLURAL
presente de indicativo		perfecto de indicativo	
march**o**	march**amos**	**he** marchado	**hemos** marchado
march**as**	march**áis**	**has** marchado	**habéis** marchado
march**a**	march**an**	**ha** marchado	**han** marchado
imperfecto de indicativo		pluscuamperfecto de indicativo	
march**aba**	march**ábamos**	**había** marchado	**habíamos** marchado
march**abas**	march**abais**	**habías** marchado	**habíais** marchado
march**aba**	march**aban**	**había** marchado	**habían** marchado
pretérito		pretérito anterior	
march**é**	march**amos**	**hube** marchado	**hubimos** marchado
march**aste**	march**asteis**	**hubiste** marchado	**hubisteis** marchado
march**ó**	march**aron**	**hubo** marchado	**hubieron** marchado
futuro		futuro perfecto	
marchar**é**	marchar**emos**	**habré** marchado	**habremos** marchado
marchar**ás**	marchar**éis**	**habrás** marchado	**habréis** marchado
marchar**á**	marchar**án**	**habrá** marchado	**habrán** marchado
condicional simple		condicional compuesto	
marchar**ía**	marchar**íamos**	**habría** marchado	**habríamos** marchado
marchar**ías**	marchar**íais**	**habrías** marchado	**habríais** marchado
marchar**ía**	marchar**ían**	**habría** marchado	**habrían** marchado
presente de subjuntivo		perfecto de subjuntivo	
march**e**	march**emos**	**haya** marchado	**hayamos** marchado
march**es**	march**éis**	**hayas** marchado	**hayáis** marchado
march**e**	march**en**	**haya** marchado	**hayan** marchado
imperfecto de subjuntivo		pluscuamperfecto de subjuntivo	
marchar**a**	marchár**amos**	**hubiera** marchado	**hubiéramos** marchado
marchar**as**	marchar**ais**	**hubieras** marchado	**hubierais** marchado
marchar**a**	marchar**an**	**hubiera** marchado	**hubieran** marchado
OR		OR	
marchas**e**	marchás**emos**	**hubiese** marchado	**hubiésemos** marchado
marchas**es**	marchas**eis**	**hubieses** marchado	**hubieseis** marchado
marchas**e**	marchas**en**	**hubiese** marchado	**hubiesen** marchado

imperativo

—	marchemos
marcha;	marchad;
no marches	no marchéis
marche	marchen

M

marcharse — to go away, to leave

gerundio **marchándose** participio de pasado **marchado**

SINGULAR	PLURAL	SINGULAR	PLURAL
presente de indicativo		perfecto de indicativo	
me march**o**	nos march**amos**	**me he** marchado	**nos hemos** marchado
te march**as**	os march**áis**	**te has** marchado	**os habéis** marchado
se march**a**	se march**an**	**se ha** marchado	**se han** marchado
imperfecto de indicativo		pluscuamperfecto de indicativo	
me march**aba**	nos march**ábamos**	**me había** marchado	**nos habíamos** marchado
te march**abas**	os march**abais**	**te habías** marchado	**os habíais** marchado
se march**aba**	se march**aban**	**se había** marchado	**se habían** marchado
pretérito		pretérito anterior	
me march**é**	nos march**amos**	**me hube** marchado	**nos hubimos** marchado
te march**aste**	os march**asteis**	**te hubiste** marchado	**os hubisteis** marchado
se march**ó**	se march**aron**	**se hubo** marchado	**se hubieron** marchado
futuro		futuro perfecto	
me marchar**é**	nos marchar**emos**	**me habré** marchado	**nos habremos** marchado
te marchar**ás**	os marchar**éis**	**te habrás** marchado	**os habréis** marchado
se marchar**á**	se marchar**án**	**se habrá** marchado	**se habrán** marchado
condicional simple		condicional compuesto	
me marchar**ía**	nos marchar**íamos**	**me habría** marchado	**nos habríamos** marchado
te marchar**ías**	os marchar**íais**	**te habrías** marchado	**os habríais** marchado
se marchar**ían**	se marchar**ían**	**se habría** marchado	**se habrían** marchado
presente de subjuntivo		perfecto de subjuntivo	
me march**e**	nos march**emos**	**me haya** marchado	**nos hayamos** marchado
te march**es**	os march**éis**	**te hayas** marchado	**os hayáis** marchado
se march**e**	se march**en**	**se haya** marchado	**se hayan** marchado
imperfecto de subjuntivo		pluscuamperfecto de subjuntivo	
me marchar**a**	nos marchár**amos**	**me hubiera** marchado	**nos hubiéramos** marchado
te marchar**as**	os marchar**ais**	**te hubieras** marchado	**os hubierais** marchado
se marchar**a**	se marchar**an**	**se hubiera** marchado	**se hubieran** marchado
OR		OR	
me marchas**e**	nos marchás**emos**	**me hubiese** marchado	**nos hubiésemos** marchado
te marchas**es**	os marchas**eis**	**te hubieses** marchado	**os hubieseis** marchado
se marchas**e**	se marchas**en**	**se hubiese** marchado	**se hubiesen** marchado

imperativo

—	marchémonos
márchate; no te marches	marchaos; no os marchéis
márchese	márchense

gerundio **matando** participio de pasado **matado**

SINGULAR	PLURAL
presente de indicativo	
mat**o**	mat**amos**
mat**as**	mat**áis**
mat**a**	mat**an**
imperfecto de indicativo	
mat**aba**	mat**ábamos**
mat**abas**	mat**abais**
mat**aba**	mat**aban**
pretérito	
mat**é**	mat**amos**
mat**aste**	mat**asteis**
mat**ó**	mat**aron**
futuro	
matar**é**	matar**emos**
matar**ás**	matar**éis**
matar**á**	matar**án**
condicional simple	
matar**ía**	matar**íamos**
matar**ías**	matar**íais**
matar**ía**	matar**ían**
presente de subjuntivo	
mat**e**	mat**emos**
mat**es**	mat**éis**
mat**e**	mat**en**
imperfecto de subjuntivo	
matar**a**	matár**amos**
matar**as**	matar**ais**
matar**a**	matar**an**
OR	
matas**e**	matás**emos**
matas**es**	matas**eis**
matas**e**	matas**en**
imperativo	
—	matemos
mata; no mates	matad; no matéis
mate	maten

SINGULAR	PLURAL
perfecto de indicativo	
he matado	**hemos** matado
has matado	**habéis** matado
ha matado	**han** matado
pluscuamperfecto de indicativo	
había matado	**habíamos** matado
habías matado	**habíais** matado
había matado	**habían** matado
pretérito anterior	
hube matado	**hubimos** matado
hubiste matado	**hubisteis** matado
hubo matado	**hubieron** matado
futuro perfecto	
habré matado	**habremos** matado
habrás matado	**habréis** matado
habrá matado	**habrán** matado
condicional compuesto	
habría matado	**habríamos** matado
habrías matado	**habríais** matado
habría matado	**habrían** matado
perfecto de subjuntivo	
haya matado	**hayamos** matado
hayas matado	**hayáis** matado
haya matado	**hayan** matado
pluscuamperfecto de subjuntivo	
hubiera matado	**hubiéramos** matado
hubieras matado	**hubierais** matado
hubiera matado	**hubieran** matado
OR	
hubiese matado	**hubiésemos** matado
hubieses matado	**hubieseis** matado
hubiese matado	**hubiesen** matado

medir

to measure

gerundio **midiendo** participio de pasado **medido**

SINGULAR	PLURAL
presente de indicativo	
mid**o**	med**imos**
mid**es**	med**ís**
mid**e**	mid**en**
imperfecto de indicativo	
med**ía**	med**íamos**
med**ías**	med**íais**
med**ía**	med**ían**
pretérito	
med**í**	med**imos**
med**iste**	med**isteis**
midi**ó**	mid**ieron**
futuro	
medir**é**	medir**emos**
medir**ás**	medir**éis**
medir**á**	medir**án**
condicional simple	
medir**ía**	medir**íamos**
medir**ías**	medir**íais**
medir**ía**	medir**ían**
presente de subjuntivo	
mid**a**	mid**amos**
mid**as**	mid**áis**
mid**a**	mid**an**
imperfecto de subjuntivo	
midier**a**	midiér**amos**
midier**as**	midier**ais**
midier**a**	midier**an**
OR	
midies**e**	midiés**emos**
midies**es**	midies**eis**
midies**e**	midies**en**
imperativo	
—	midamos
mide;	medid;
no midas	no midáis
mida	midan

SINGULAR	PLURAL
perfecto de indicativo	
he medido	**hemos** medido
has medido	**habéis** medido
ha medido	**han** medido
pluscuamperfecto de indicativo	
había medido	**habíamos** medido
habías medido	**habíais** medido
había medido	**habían** medido
pretérito anterior	
hube medido	**hubimos** medido
hubiste medido	**hubisteis** medido
hubo medido	**hubieron** medido
futuro perfecto	
habré medido	**habremos** medido
habrás medido	**habréis** medido
habrá medido	**habrán** medido
condicional compuesto	
habría medido	**habríamos** medido
habrías medido	**habríais** medido
habría medido	**habrían** medido
perfecto de subjuntivo	
haya medido	**hayamos** medido
hayas medido	**hayáis** medido
haya medido	**hayan** medido
pluscuamperfecto de subjuntivo	
hubiera medido	**hubiéramos** medido
hubieras medido	**hubierais** medido
hubiera medido	**hubieran** medido
OR	
hubiese medido	**hubiésemos** medido
hubieses medido	**hubieseis** medido
hubiese medido	**hubiesen** medido

to make better, to get better **mejorar**

gerundio **aprendiendo** participio de pasado **endiendo**

presente de indicativo

SINGULAR	PLURAL
mejor**o**	mejor**amos**
mejor**as**	mejor**áis**
mejor**a**	mejor**an**

imperfecto de indicativo

SINGULAR	PLURAL
mejor**aba**	mejor**ábamos**
mejor**abas**	mejor**abais**
mejor**aba**	mejor**aban**

pretérito

SINGULAR	PLURAL
mejor**é**	mejor**amos**
mejor**aste**	mejor**asteis**
mejor**ó**	mejor**aron**

futuro

SINGULAR	PLURAL
mejorar**é**	mejorar**emos**
mejorar**ás**	mejorar**éis**
mejorar**á**	mejorar**án**

condicional simple

SINGULAR	PLURAL
mejorar**ía**	mejorar**íamos**
mejorar**ías**	mejorar**íais**
mejorar**ía**	mejorar**ían**

presente de subjuntivo

SINGULAR	PLURAL
mejor**e**	mejor**emos**
mejor**es**	mejor**éis**
mejor**e**	mejor**en**

imperfecto de subjuntivo

SINGULAR	PLURAL
mejorar**a**	mejorár**amos**
mejorar**as**	mejorar**ais**
mejorar**a**	mejorar**an**
OR	
mejoras**e**	mejorás**emos**
mejoras**es**	mejoras**eis**
mejoras**e**	mejoras**en**

imperativo

SINGULAR	PLURAL
—	mejoremos
mejora; no mejores	mejorad; no mejoréis
mejore	mejoren

perfecto de indicativo

SINGULAR	PLURAL
he mejorado	**hemos** mejorado
has mejorado	**habéis** mejorado
ha mejorado	**han** mejorado

pluscuamperfecto de indicativo

SINGULAR	PLURAL
había mejorado	**habíamos** mejorado
habías mejorado	**habíais** mejorado
había mejorado	**habían** mejorado

pretérito anterior

SINGULAR	PLURAL
hube mejorado	**hubimos** mejorado
hubiste mejorado	**hubisteis** mejorado
hubo mejorado	**hubieron** mejorado

futuro perfecto

SINGULAR	PLURAL
habré mejorado	**habremos** mejorado
habrás mejorado	**habréis** mejorado
habrá mejorado	**habrán** mejorado

condicional compuesto

SINGULAR	PLURAL
habría mejorado	**habríamos** mejorado
habrías mejorado	**habríais** mejorado
habría mejorado	**habrían** mejorado

perfecto de subjuntivo

SINGULAR	PLURAL
haya mejorado	**hayamos** mejorado
hayas mejorado	**hayáis** mejorado
haya mejorado	**hayan** mejorado

pluscuamperfecto de subjuntivo

SINGULAR	PLURAL
hubiera mejorado	**hubiéramos** mejorado
hubieras mejorado	**hubierais** mejorado
hubiera mejorado	**hubieran** mejorado
OR	
hubiese mejorado	**hubiésemos** mejorado
hubieses mejorado	**hubieseis** mejorado
hubiese mejorado	**hubiesen** mejorado

mencionar — to mention

gerundio **mencionando** participio de pasado **mencionado**

SINGULAR	PLURAL	SINGULAR	PLURAL
presente de indicativo		perfecto de indicativo	
mencion**o**	mencion**amos**	**he** mencionado	**hemos** mencionado
mencion**as**	mencion**áis**	**has** mencionado	**habéis** mencionado
mencion**a**	mencion**an**	**ha** mencionado	**han** mencionado
imperfecto de indicativo		pluscuamperfecto de indicativo	
mencion**aba**	mencion**ábamos**	**había** mencionado	**habíamos** mencionado
mencion**abas**	mencion**abais**	**habías** mencionado	**habíais** mencionado
mencion**aba**	mencion**aban**	**había** mencionado	**habían** mencionado
pretérito		pretérito anterior	
mencion**é**	mencion**amos**	**hube** mencionado	**hubimos** mencionado
mencion**aste**	mencion**asteis**	**hubiste** mencionado	**hubisteis** mencionado
mencion**ó**	mencion**aron**	**hubo** mencionado	**hubieron** mencionado
futuro		futuro perfecto	
mencionar**é**	mencionar**emos**	**habré** mencionado	**habremos** mencionado
mencionar**ás**	mencionar**éis**	**habrás** mencionado	**habréis** mencionado
mencionar**á**	mencionar**án**	**habrá** mencionado	**habrán** mencionado
condicional simple		condicional compuesto	
mencionar**ía**	mencionar**íamos**	**habría** mencionado	**habríamos** mencionado
mencionar**ías**	mencionar**íais**	**habrías** mencionado	**habríais** mencionado
mencionar**ía**	mencionar**ían**	**habría** mencionado	**habrían** mencionado
presente de subjuntivo		perfecto de subjuntivo	
mencion**e**	mencion**emos**	**haya** mencionado	**hayamos** mencionado
mencion**es**	mencion**éis**	**hayas** mencionado	**hayáis** mencionado
mencion**e**	mencion**en**	**haya** mencionado	**hayan** mencionado
imperfecto de subjuntivo		pluscuamperfecto de subjuntivo	
mencionar**a**	mencionár**amos**	**hubiera** mencionado	**hubiéramos** mencionado
mencionar**as**	mencionar**ais**	**hubieras** mencionado	**hubierais** mencionado
mencionar**a**	mencionar**an**	**hubiera** mencionado	**hubieran** mencionado
OR		OR	
mencionas**e**	mencionás**emos**	**hubiese** mencionado	**hubiésemos** mencionado
mencionas**es**	mencionas**eis**	**hubieses** mencionado	**hubieseis** mencionado
mencionas**e**	mencionas**en**	**hubiese** mencionado	**hubiesen** mencionado

imperativo

—	mencionemos
menciona; no menciones	mencionad; no mencionéis
mencione	mencionen

to lie — mentir

gerundio **mintiendo** participio de pasado **mentido**

SINGULAR	PLURAL
presente de indicativo	
mient**o**	ment**imos**
mient**es**	ment**ís**
mient**e**	mient**en**
imperfecto de indicativo	
ment**ía**	ment**íamos**
ment**ías**	ment**íais**
ment**ía**	ment**ían**
pretérito	
ment**í**	ment**imos**
ment**iste**	ment**isteis**
mint**ió**	mint**ieron**
futuro	
mentir**é**	mentir**emos**
mentir**ás**	mentir**éis**
mentir**á**	mentir**án**
condicional simple	
mentir**ía**	mentir**íamos**
mentir**ías**	mentir**íais**
mentir**ía**	mentir**ían**
presente de subjuntivo	
mient**a**	mint**amos**
mient**as**	mint**áis**
mient**a**	mient**an**
imperfecto de subjuntivo	
mintier**a**	mintiér**amos**
mintier**as**	mintier**ais**
mintier**a**	mintier**an**
OR	
mienties**e**	mintiés**emos**
minties**es**	minties**eis**
minties**e**	minties**en**
imperativo	
—	mintamos
miente; no mientas	mentid; no mintáis
mienta	mientan

SINGULAR	PLURAL
perfecto de indicativo	
he mentido	**hemos** mentido
has mentido	**habéis** mentido
ha mentido	**han** mentido
pluscuamperfecto de indicativo	
había mentido	**habíamos** mentido
habías mentido	**habíais** mentido
había mentido	**habían** mentido
pretérito anterior	
hube mentido	**hubimos** mentido
hubiste mentido	**hubisteis** mentido
hubo mentido	**hubieron** mentido
futuro perfecto	
habré mentido	**habremos** mentido
habrás mentido	**habréis** mentido
habrá mentido	**habrán** mentido
condicional compuesto	
habría mentido	**habríamos** mentido
habrías mentido	**habríais** mentido
habría mentido	**habrían** mentido
perfecto de subjuntivo	
haya mentido	**hayamos** mentido
hayas mentido	**hayáis** mentido
haya mentido	**hayan** mentido
pluscuamperfecto de subjuntivo	
hubiera mentido	**hubiéramos** mentido
hubieras mentido	**hubierais** mentido
hubiera mentido	**hubieran** mentido
OR	
hubiese mentido	**hubiésemos** mentido
hubieses mentido	**hubieseis** mentido
hubiese mentido	**hubiesen** mentido

merecer — to deserve, to earn

gerundio **mereciendo** participio de pasado **merecido**

SINGULAR	PLURAL
presente de indicativo	
merezc**o**	merec**emos**
merec**es**	merec**éis**
merec**e**	merec**en**
imperfecto de indicativo	
merec**ía**	merec**íamos**
merec**ías**	merec**íais**
merec**ía**	merec**ían**
pretérito	
merec**í**	merec**imos**
merec**iste**	merec**isteis**
merec**ió**	merec**ieron**
futuro	
merecer**é**	merecer**emos**
merecer**ás**	merecer**éis**
merecer**á**	merecer**án**
condicional simple	
merecer**ía**	merecer**íamos**
merecer**ías**	merecer**íais**
merecer**ía**	merecer**ían**
presente de subjuntivo	
merezc**a**	merezc**amos**
merezc**as**	merezc**áis**
merezc**a**	merezc**an**
imperfecto de subjuntivo	
merecier**a**	mereciér**amos**
merecier**as**	merecier**ais**
merecier**a**	merecier**an**
OR	
merecies**e**	mereciés**emos**
merecies**es**	merecies**eis**
merecies**e**	merecies**en**
imperativo	
—	merezcamos
merece; no merezcas	mereced; no merezcáis
merezca	merezcan

SINGULAR	PLURAL
perfecto de indicativo	
he merecido	**hemos** merecido
has merecido	**habéis** merecido
ha merecido	**han** merecido
pluscuamperfecto de indicativo	
había merecido	**habíamos** merecido
habías merecido	**habíais** merecido
había merecido	**habían** merecido
pretérito anterior	
hube merecido	**hubimos** merecido
hubiste merecido	**hubisteis** merecido
hubo merecido	**hubieron** merecido
futuro perfecto	
habré merecido	**habremos** merecido
habrás merecido	**habréis** merecido
habrá merecido	**habrán** merecido
condicional compuesto	
habría merecido	**habríamos** merecido
habrías merecido	**habríais** merecido
habría merecido	**habrían** merecido
perfecto de subjuntivo	
haya merecido	**hayamos** merecido
hayas merecido	**hayáis** merecido
haya merecido	**hayan** merecido
pluscuamperfecto de subjuntivo	
hubiera merecido	**hubiéramos** merecido
hubieras merecido	**hubierais** merecido
hubiera merecido	**hubieran** merecido
OR	
hubiese merecido	**hubiésemos** merecido
hubieses merecido	**hubieseis** merecido
hubiese merecido	**hubiesen** merecido

gerundio **metiendo** participio de pasado **metido**

SINGULAR	PLURAL
presente de indicativo	
met**o**	met**emos**
met**es**	met**éis**
met**e**	met**en**
imperfecto de indicativo	
met**ía**	met**íamos**
met**ías**	met**íais**
met**ía**	met**ían**
pretérito	
met**í**	met**imos**
met**iste**	met**isteis**
met**ió**	met**ieron**
futuro	
meter**é**	meter**emos**
meter**ás**	meter**éis**
meter**á**	meter**án**
condicional simple	
meter**ía**	meter**íamos**
meter**ías**	meter**íais**
meter**ía**	meter**ían**
presente de subjuntivo	
met**a**	met**amos**
met**as**	met**áis**
met**a**	met**an**
imperfecto de subjuntivo	
metier**a**	metiér**amos**
metier**as**	metier**ais**
metier**a**	metier**an**
OR	
meties**e**	metiés**emos**
meties**es**	meties**eis**
meties**e**	meties**en**
imperativo	
—	metamos
mete; no metas	meted; no metáis
meta	metan

SINGULAR	PLURAL
perfecto de indicativo	
he metido	**hemos** metido
has metido	**habéis** metido
ha metido	**han** metido
pluscuamperfecto de indicativo	
había metido	**habíamos** metido
habías metido	**habíais** metido
había metido	**habían** metido
pretérito anterior	
hube metido	**hubimos** metido
hubiste metido	**hubisteis** metido
hubo metido	**hubieron** metido
futuro perfecto	
habré metido	**habremos** metido
habrás metido	**habréis** metido
habrá metido	**habrán** metido
condicional compuesto	
habría metido	**habríamos** metido
habrías metido	**habríais** metido
habría metido	**habrían** metido
perfecto de subjuntivo	
haya metido	**hayamos** metido
hayas metido	**hayáis** metido
haya metido	**hayan** metido
pluscuamperfecto de subjuntivo	
hubiera metido	**hubiéramos** metido
hubieras metido	**hubierais** metido
hubiera metido	**hubieran** metido
OR	
hubiese metido	**hubiésemos** metido
hubieses metido	**hubieseis** metido
hubiese metido	**hubiesen** metido

mirar — to look, to watch

gerundio **mirando** — participio de pasado **mirado**

	SINGULAR	PLURAL
presente de indicativo		
	mir**o**	mir**amos**
	mir**as**	mir**áis**
	mir**a**	mir**an**
imperfecto de indicativo		
	mir**aba**	mir**ábamos**
	mir**abas**	mir**abais**
	mir**aba**	mir**aban**
pretérito		
	mir**é**	mir**amos**
	mir**aste**	mir**asteis**
	mir**ó**	mir**aron**
futuro		
	mirar**é**	mirar**emos**
	mirar**ás**	mirar**éis**
	mirar**á**	mirar**án**
condicional simple		
	mirar**ía**	mirar**íamos**
	mirar**ías**	mirar**íais**
	mirar**ía**	mirar**ían**
presente de subjuntivo		
	mir**e**	mir**emos**
	mir**es**	mir**éis**
	mir**e**	mir**en**
imperfecto de subjuntivo		
	mirar**a**	mirár**amos**
	mirar**as**	mirar**ais**
	mirar**a**	mirar**an**
	OR	
	miras**e**	mirás**emos**
	miras**es**	miras**eis**
	miras**e**	miras**en**
imperativo		
	—	miremos
	mira; no mires	mirad; no miréis
	mire	miren

	SINGULAR	PLURAL
perfecto de indicativo		
	he mirado	**hemos** mirado
	has mirado	**habéis** mirado
	ha mirado	**han** mirado
pluscuamperfecto de indicativo		
	había mirado	**habíamos** mirado
	habías mirado	**habíais** mirado
	había mirado	**habían** mirado
pretérito anterior		
	hube mirado	**hubimos** mirado
	hubiste mirado	**hubisteis** mirado
	hubo mirado	**hubieron** mirado
futuro perfecto		
	habré mirado	**habremos** mirado
	habrás mirado	**habréis** mirado
	habrá mirado	**habrán** mirado
condicional compuesto		
	habría mirado	**habríamos** mirado
	habrías mirado	**habríais** mirado
	habría mirado	**habrían** mirado
perfecto de subjuntivo		
	haya mirado	**hayamos** mirado
	hayas mirado	**hayáis** mirado
	haya mirado	**hayan** mirado
pluscuamperfecto de subjuntivo		
	hubiera mirado	**hubiéramos** mirado
	hubieras mirado	**hubierais** mirado
	hubiera mirado	**hubieran** mirado
	OR	
	hubiese mirado	**hubiésemos** mirado
	hubieses mirado	**hubieseis** mirado
	hubiese mirado	**hubiesen** mirado

Johnny looks at himself in the **mirror**.

to look at oneself **mirarse**

gerundio **mirándose** participio de pasado **mirado**

presente de indicativo

SINGULAR	PLURAL
me mir**o**	nos mir**amos**
te mir**as**	os mir**áis**
se mir**a**	se mir**an**

imperfecto de indicativo

SINGULAR	PLURAL
me mir**aba**	nos mir**ábamos**
te mir**abas**	os mir**abais**
se mir**aba**	se mir**aban**

pretérito

SINGULAR	PLURAL
me mir**é**	nos mir**amos**
te mir**aste**	os mir**asteis**
se mir**ó**	se mir**aron**

futuro

SINGULAR	PLURAL
me mirar**é**	nos mirar**emos**
te mirar**ás**	os mirar**éis**
se mirar**á**	se mirar**án**

condicional simple

SINGULAR	PLURAL
me mirar**ía**	nos mirar**íamos**
te mirar**ías**	os mirar**íais**
se mirar**ía**	se mirar**ían**

presente de subjuntivo

SINGULAR	PLURAL
me mir**e**	nos mir**emos**
te mir**es**	os mir**éis**
se mir**e**	se mir**en**

imperfecto de subjuntivo

SINGULAR	PLURAL
me mirar**a**	nos mirár**amos**
te mirar**as**	os mirar**ais**
se mirar**a**	se mirar**an**
OR	
me miras**e**	nos mirás**emos**
te miras**es**	os miras**eis**
se miras**e**	se miras**en**

imperativo

SINGULAR	PLURAL
—	mirémonos
mírate; no te mires	miraos; no os miréis
mírese	mírense

perfecto de indicativo

SINGULAR	PLURAL
me he mirado	**nos hemos** mirado
te has mirado	**os habéis** mirado
se ha mirado	**se han** mirado

pluscuamperfecto de indicativo

SINGULAR	PLURAL
me había mirado	**nos habíamos** mirado
te habías mirado	**os habíais** mirado
se había mirado	**se habían** mirado

pretérito anterior

SINGULAR	PLURAL
me hube mirado	**nos hubimos** mirado
te hubiste mirado	**os hubisteis** mirado
se hubo mirado	**se hubieron** mirado

futuro perfecto

SINGULAR	PLURAL
me habré mirado	**nos habremos** mirado
te habrás mirado	**os habréis** mirado
se habrá mirado	**se habrán** mirado

condicional compuesto

SINGULAR	PLURAL
me habría mirado	**nos habríamos** mirado
te habrías mirado	**os habríais** mirado
se habría mirado	**se habrían** mirado

perfecto de subjuntivo

SINGULAR	PLURAL
me haya mirado	**nos hayamos** mirado
te hayas mirado	**os hayáis** mirado
se haya mirado	**se hayan** mirado

pluscuamperfecto de subjuntivo

SINGULAR	PLURAL
me hubiera mirado	**nos hubiéramos** mirado
te hubieras mirado	**os hubierais** mirado
se hubiera mirado	**se hubieran** mirado
OR	
me hubiese mirado	**nos hubiésemos** mirado
te hubieses mirado	**os hubieseis** mirado
se hubiese mirado	**se hubiesen** mirado

mojarse — to get wet

gerundio **mojándose** — participio de pasado **mojado**

SINGULAR	PLURAL	SINGULAR	PLURAL
presente de indicativo		perfecto de indicativo	
me moj**o**	nos moj**amos**	**me he** mojado	**nos hemos** mojado
te moj**as**	os moj**áis**	**te has** mojado	**os habéis** mojado
se moj**a**	se moj**an**	**se ha** mojado	**se han** mojado
imperfecto de indicativo		pluscuamperfecto de indicativo	
me moj**aba**	nos moj**ábamos**	**me había** mojado	**nos habíamos** mojado
te moj**abas**	os moj**abais**	**te habías** mojado	**os habíais** mojado
se moj**aba**	se moj**aban**	**se había** mojado	**se habían** mojado
pretérito		pretérito anterior	
me moj**é**	nos moj**amos**	**me hube** mojado	**nos hubimos** mojado
te moj**aste**	os moj**asteis**	**te hubiste** mojado	**os hubisteis** mojado
se moj**ó**	se moj**aron**	**se hubo** mojado	**se hubieron** mojado
futuro		futuro perfecto	
me mojar**é**	nos mojar**emos**	**me habré** mojado	**nos habremos** mojado
te mojar**ás**	os mojar**éis**	**te habrás** mojado	**os habréis** mojado
se mojar**á**	se mojar**án**	**se habrá** mojado	**se habrán** mojado
condicional simple		condicional compuesto	
me mojar**ía**	nos mojar**íamos**	**me habría** mojado	**nos habríamos** mojado
te mojar**ías**	os mojar**íais**	**te habrías** mojado	**os habríais** mojado
se mojar**ía**	se mojar**ían**	**se habría** mojado	**se habrían** mojado
presente de subjuntivo		perfecto de subjuntivo	
me moj**e**	nos moj**emos**	**me haya** mojado	**nos hayamos** mojado
te moj**es**	os moj**éis**	**te hayas** mojado	**os hayáis** mojado
se moj**e**	se moj**en**	**se haya** mojado	**se hayan** mojado
imperfecto de subjuntivo		pluscuamperfecto de subjuntivo	
me mojar**a**	nos mojár**amos**	**me hubiera** mojado	**nos hubiéramos** mojado
te mojar**as**	os mojar**ais**	**te hubieras** mojado	**os hubierais** mojado
se mojar**a**	se mojar**an**	**se hubiera** mojado	**se hubieran** mojado
OR		OR	
me mojas**e**	nos mojás**emos**	**me hubiese** mojado	**nos hubiésemos** mojado
te mojas**es**	os mojas**eis**	**te hubieses** mojado	**os hubieseis** mojado
se mojas**e**	se mojas**en**	**se hubiese** mojado	**se hubiesen** mojado

imperativo

—	mojémonos
mójate; no te mojes	mojaos; no os mojéis
mójese	mójense

gerundio **molestando** participio de pasado **molestado**

SINGULAR	PLURAL
presente de indicativo	
molest**o**	molest**amos**
molest**as**	molest**áis**
molest**a**	molest**an**
imperfecto de indicativo	
molest**aba**	molest**ábamos**
molest**abas**	molest**abais**
molest**aba**	molest**aban**
pretérito	
molest**é**	molest**amos**
molest**aste**	molest**asteis**
molest**ó**	molest**aron**
futuro	
molestar**é**	molestar**emos**
molestar**ás**	molestar**éis**
molestar**á**	molestar**án**
condicional simple	
molestar**ía**	molestar**íamos**
molestar**ías**	molestar**íais**
molestar**ía**	molestar**ían**
presente de subjuntivo	
molest**e**	molest**emos**
molest**es**	molest**éis**
molest**e**	molest**en**
imperfecto de subjuntivo	
molestar**a**	molestár**amos**
molestar**as**	molestar**ais**
molestar**a**	molestar**an**
OR	
molestas**e**	molestás**emos**
molestas**es**	molestas**eis**
molestas**e**	molestas**en**
imperativo	
—	molestemos
molesta; no molestes	molestad; no molestéis
moleste	molesten

SINGULAR	PLURAL
perfecto de indicativo	
he molestado	**hemos** molestado
has molestado	**habéis** molestado
ha molestado	**han** molestado
pluscuamperfecto de indicativo	
había molestado	**habíamos** molestado
habías molestado	**habíais** molestado
había molestado	**habían** molestado
pretérito anterior	
hube molestado	**hubimos** molestado
hubiste molestado	**hubisteis** molestado
hubo molestado	**hubieron** molestado
futuro perfecto	
habré molestado	**habremos** molestado
habrás molestado	**habréis** molestado
habrá molestado	**habrán** molestado
condicional compuesto	
habría molestado	**habríamos** molestado
habrías molestado	**habríais** molestado
habría molestado	**habrían** molestado
perfecto de subjuntivo	
haya molestado	**hayamos** molestado
hayas molestado	**hayáis** molestado
haya molestado	**hayan** molestado
pluscuamperfecto de subjuntivo	
hubiera molestado	**hubiéramos** molestado
hubieras molestado	**hubierais** molestado
hubiera molestado	**hubieran** molestado
OR	
hubiese molestado	**hubiésemos** molestado
hubieses molestado	**hubieseis** molestado
hubiese molestado	**hubiesen** molestado

montar — to mount, to ride

gerundio **montando** participio de pasado **montado**

SINGULAR	PLURAL
presente de indicativo	
mont**o**	mont**amos**
mont**as**	mont**áis**
mont**a**	mont**an**
imperfecto de indicativo	
mont**aba**	mont**ábamos**
mont**abas**	mont**abais**
mont**aba**	mont**aban**
pretérito	
mont**é**	mont**amos**
mont**aste**	mont**asteis**
mont**ó**	mont**aron**
futuro	
montar**é**	montar**emos**
montar**ás**	montar**éis**
montar**á**	montar**án**
condicional simple	
montar**ía**	montar**íamos**
montar**ías**	montar**íais**
montar**ía**	montar**ían**
presente de subjuntivo	
mont**e**	mont**emos**
mont**es**	mont**éis**
mont**e**	mont**en**
imperfecto de subjuntivo	
montar**a**	montár**amos**
montar**as**	montar**ais**
montar**a**	montar**an**
OR	
montas**e**	montás**emos**
montas**es**	montas**eis**
montas**e**	montas**en**
imperativo	
—	montemos
monta; no montes	montad; no montéis
monte	monten

SINGULAR	PLURAL
perfecto de indicativo	
he montado	**hemos** montado
has montado	**habéis** montado
ha montado	**han** montado
pluscuamperfecto de indicativo	
había montado	**habíamos** montado
habías montado	**habíais** montado
había montado	**habían** montado
pretérito anterior	
hube montado	**hubimos** montado
hubiste montado	**hubisteis** montado
hubo montado	**hubieron** montado
futuro perfecto	
habré montado	**habremos** montado
habrás montado	**habréis** montado
habrá montado	**habrán** montado
condicional compuesto	
habría montado	**habríamos** montado
habrías montado	**habríais** montado
habría montado	**habrían** montado
perfecto de subjuntivo	
haya montado	**hayamos** montado
hayas montado	**hayáis** montado
haya montado	**hayan** montado
pluscuamperfecto de subjuntivo	
hubiera montado	**hubiéramos** montado
hubieras montado	**hubierais** montado
hubiera montado	**hubieran** montado
OR	
hubiese montado	**hubiésemos** montado
hubieses montado	**hubieseis** montado
hubiese montado	**hubiesen** montado

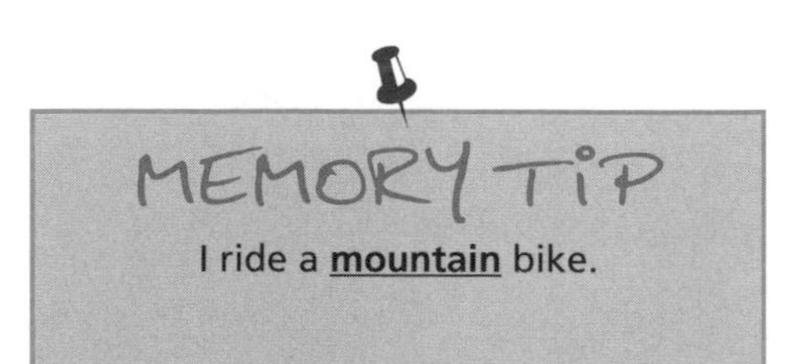

to bite — morder

gerundio **mordiendo** participio de pasado **mordido**

SINGULAR	PLURAL
presente de indicativo	
muerd**o**	mord**emos**
muerd**es**	mord**éis**
muerd**e**	muerd**en**
imperfecto de indicativo	
mord**ía**	mord**íamos**
mord**ías**	mord**íais**
mord**ía**	mord**ían**
pretérito	
mord**í**	mord**imos**
mord**iste**	mord**isteis**
mord**ió**	mord**ieron**
futuro	
morder**é**	morder**emos**
morder**ás**	morder**éis**
morder**á**	morder**án**
condicional simple	
morder**ía**	morder**íamos**
morder**ías**	morder**íais**
morder**ía**	morder**ían**
presente de subjuntivo	
muerd**a**	mord**amos**
muerd**as**	mord**áis**
muerd**a**	muerd**an**
imperfecto de subjuntivo	
mordier**a**	mordiér**amos**
mordier**as**	mordier**ais**
mordier**a**	mordier**an**
OR	
mordies**e**	mordiés**emos**
mordies**es**	mordies**eis**
mordies**e**	mordies**en**
imperativo	
—	mordamos
muerde; no muerdas	morded; no mordáis
muerda	muerdan

SINGULAR	PLURAL
perfecto de indicativo	
he mordido	**hemos** mordido
has mordido	**habéis** mordido
ha mordido	**han** mordido
pluscuamperfecto de indicativo	
había mordido	**habíamos** mordido
habías mordido	**habíais** mordido
había mordido	**habían** mordido
pretérito anterior	
hube mordido	**hubimos** mordido
hubiste mordido	**hubisteis** mordido
hubo mordido	**hubieron** mordido
futuro perfecto	
habré mordido	**habremos** mordido
habrás mordido	**habréis** mordido
habrá mordido	**habrán** mordido
condicional compuesto	
habría mordido	**habríamos** mordido
habrías mordido	**habríais** mordido
habría mordido	**habrían** mordido
perfecto de subjuntivo	
haya mordido	**hayamos** mordido
hayas mordido	**hayáis** mordido
haya mordido	**hayan** mordido
pluscuamperfecto de subjuntivo	
hubiera mordido	**hubiéramos** mordido
hubieras mordido	**hubierais** mordido
hubiera mordido	**hubieran** mordido
OR	
hubiese mordido	**hubiésemos** mordido
hubieses mordido	**hubieseis** mordido
hubiese mordido	**hubiesen** mordido

morir — to die

gerundio **muriendo** — participio de pasado **muerto**

SINGULAR	PLURAL
presente de indicativo	
muer**o**	mor**imos**
muer**es**	mor**ís**
muer**e**	muer**en**
imperfecto de indicativo	
mor**ía**	mor**íamos**
mor**ías**	mor**íais**
mor**ía**	mor**ían**
pretérito	
mor**í**	mor**imos**
mor**iste**	mor**isteis**
mur**ió**	mur**ieron**
futuro	
morir**é**	morir**emos**
morir**ás**	morir**éis**
morir**á**	morir**án**
condicional simple	
morir**ía**	morir**íamos**
morir**ías**	morir**íais**
morir**ía**	morir**ían**
presente de subjuntivo	
muer**a**	mur**amos**
muer**as**	mur**áis**
muer**a**	muer**an**
imperfecto de subjuntivo	
murier**a**	muriér**amos**
murier**as**	murier**ais**
murier**a**	murier**an**
OR	
muries**e**	muriés**emos**
muries**es**	muries**eis**
muries**e**	muries**en**
imperativo	
—	muramos
muere;	morid;
no mueras	no muráis
muera	mueran

SINGULAR	PLURAL
perfecto de indicativo	
he muerto	**hemos** muerto
has muerto	**habéis** muerto
ha muerto	**han** muerto
pluscuamperfecto de indicativo	
había muerto	**habíamos** muerto
habías muerto	**habíais** muerto
había muerto	**habían** muerto
pretérito anterior	
hube muerto	**hubimos** muerto
hubiste muerto	**hubisteis** muerto
hubo muerto	**hubieron** muerto
futuro perfecto	
habré muerto	**habremos** muerto
habrás muerto	**habréis** muerto
habrá muerto	**habrán** muerto
condicional compuesto	
habría muerto	**habríamos** muerto
habrías muerto	**habríais** muerto
habría muerto	**habrían** muerto
perfecto de subjuntivo	
haya muerto	**hayamos** muerto
hayas muerto	**hayáis** muerto
haya muerto	**hayan** muerto
pluscuamperfecto de subjuntivo	
hubiera muerto	**hubiéramos** muerto
hubieras muerto	**hubierais** muerto
hubiera muerto	**hubieran** muerto
OR	
hubiese muerto	**hubiésemos** muerto
hubieses muerto	**hubieseis** muerto
hubiese muerto	**hubiesen** muerto

gerundio **mostrando** participio de pasado **mostrado**

SINGULAR	PLURAL	SINGULAR	PLURAL
presente de indicativo		perfecto de indicativo	
muestr**o**	mostr**amos**	**he** mostrado	**hemos** mostrado
muestr**as**	mostr**áis**	**has** mostrado	**habéis** mostrado
muestr**a**	muestr**an**	**ha** mostrado	**han** mostrado
imperfecto de indicativo		pluscuamperfecto de indicativo	
mostr**aba**	mostr**ábamos**	**había** mostrado	**habíamos** mostrado
mostr**abas**	mostr**abais**	**habías** mostrado	**habíais** mostrado
mostr**aba**	mostr**aban**	**había** mostrado	**habían** mostrado
pretérito		pretérito anterior	
mostr**é**	mostr**amos**	**hube** mostrado	**hubimos** mostrado
mostr**aste**	mostr**asteis**	**hubiste** mostrado	**hubisteis** mostrado
mostr**ó**	mostr**aron**	**hubo** mostrado	**hubieron** mostrado
futuro		futuro perfecto	
mostrar**é**	mostrar**emos**	**habré** mostrado	**habremos** mostrado
mostrar**ás**	mostrar**éis**	**habrás** mostrado	**habréis** mostrado
mostrar**á**	mostrar**án**	**habrá** mostrado	**habrán** mostrado
condicional simple		condicional compuesto	
mostrar**ía**	mostrar**íamos**	**habría** mostrado	**habríamos** mostrado
mostrar**ías**	mostrar**íais**	**habrías** mostrado	**habríais** mostrado
mostrar**ía**	mostrar**ían**	**habría** mostrado	**habrían** mostrado
presente de subjuntivo		perfecto de subjuntivo	
muestr**e**	mostr**emos**	**haya** mostrado	**hayamos** mostrado
muestr**es**	mostr**éis**	**hayas** mostrado	**hayáis** mostrado
muestr**e**	muestr**en**	**haya** mostrado	**hayan** mostrado
imperfecto de subjuntivo		pluscuamperfecto de subjuntivo	
mostrar**a**	mostrár**amos**	**hubiera** mostrado	**hubiéramos** mostrado
mostrar**as**	mostrar**ais**	**hubieras** mostrado	**hubierais** mostrado
mostrar**a**	mostrar**an**	**hubiera** mostrado	**hubieran** mostrado
OR		OR	
mostras**e**	mostrás**emos**	**hubiese** mostrado	**hubiésemos** mostrado
mostras**es**	mostras**eis**	**hubieses** mostrado	**hubieseis** mostrado
mostras**e**	mostras**en**	**hubiese** mostrado	**hubiesen** mostrado

imperativo	
—	mostremos
muestra; no muestres	mostrad; no mostréis
muestre	muestren

M

mover — to move, to excite

gerundio **moviendo** participio de pasado **movido**

presente de indicativo

SINGULAR	PLURAL
muev**o**	mov**emos**
muev**es**	mov**éis**
muev**e**	muev**en**

imperfecto de indicativo

SINGULAR	PLURAL
mov**ía**	mov**íamos**
mov**ías**	mov**íais**
mov**ía**	mov**ían**

pretérito

SINGULAR	PLURAL
mov**í**	mov**imos**
mov**iste**	mov**isteis**
mov**ió**	mov**ieron**

futuro

SINGULAR	PLURAL
mover**é**	mover**emos**
mover**ás**	mover**éis**
mover**á**	mover**án**

condicional simple

SINGULAR	PLURAL
mover**ía**	mover**íamos**
mover**ías**	mover**íais**
mover**ía**	mover**ían**

presente de subjuntivo

SINGULAR	PLURAL
muev**a**	mov**amos**
muev**as**	mov**áis**
muev**a**	muev**an**

imperfecto de subjuntivo

SINGULAR	PLURAL
movier**a**	moviér**amos**
movier**as**	movier**ais**
movier**a**	movier**an**
OR	
movies**e**	moviés**emos**
movies**es**	movies**eis**
movies**e**	movies**en**

imperativo

SINGULAR	PLURAL
—	movamos
mueve; no muevas	moved; no mováis
mueva	muevan

perfecto de indicativo

SINGULAR	PLURAL
he movido	**hemos** movido
has movido	**habéis** movido
ha movido	**han** movido

pluscuamperfecto de indicativo

SINGULAR	PLURAL
había movido	**habíamos** movido
habías movido	**habíais** movido
había movido	**habían** movido

pretérito anterior

SINGULAR	PLURAL
hube movido	**hubimos** movido
hubiste movido	**hubisteis** movido
hubo movido	**hubieron** movido

futuro perfecto

SINGULAR	PLURAL
habré movido	**habremos** movido
habrás movido	**habréis** movido
habrá movido	**habrán** movido

condicional compuesto

SINGULAR	PLURAL
habría movido	**habríamos** movido
habrías movido	**habríais** movido
habría movido	**habrían** movido

perfecto de subjuntivo

SINGULAR	PLURAL
haya movido	**hayamos** movido
hayas movido	**hayáis** movido
haya movido	**hayan** movido

pluscuamperfecto de subjuntivo

SINGULAR	PLURAL
hubiera movido	**hubiéramos** movido
hubieras movido	**hubierais** movido
hubiera movido	**hubieran** movido
OR	
hubiese movido	**hubiésemos** movido
hubieses movido	**hubieseis** movido
hubiese movido	**hubiesen** movido

gerundio **mudándose** participio de pasado **mudado**

SINGULAR	PLURAL	SINGULAR	PLURAL
presente de indicativo		perfecto de indicativo	
me mud**o**	nos mud**amos**	**me he** mudado	**nos hemos** mudado
te mud**as**	os mud**áis**	**te has** mudado	**os habéis** mudado
se mud**a**	se mud**an**	**se ha** mudado	**se han** mudado
imperfecto de indicativo		pluscuamperfecto de indicativo	
me mud**aba**	nos mud**ábamos**	**me había** mudado	**nos habíamos** mudado
te mud**abas**	os mud**abais**	**te habías** mudado	**os habíais** mudado
se mud**aba**	se mud**aban**	**se había** mudado	**se habían** mudado
pretérito		pretérito anterior	
me mud**é**	nos mud**amos**	**me hube** mudado	**nos hubimos** mudado
te mud**aste**	os mud**asteis**	**te hubiste** mudado	**os hubisteis** mudado
se mud**ó**	se mud**aron**	**se hubo** mudado	**se hubieron** mudado
futuro		futuro perfecto	
me mudar**é**	nos mudar**emos**	**me habré** mudado	**nos habremos** mudado
te mudar**ás**	os mudar**éis**	**te habrás** mudado	**os habréis** mudado
se mudar**á**	se mudar**án**	**se habrá** mudado	**se habrán** mudado
condicional simple		condicional compuesto	
me mudar**ía**	nos mudar**íamos**	**me habría** mudado	**nos habríamos** mudado
te mudar**ías**	os mudar**íais**	**te habrías** mudado	**os habríais** mudado
se mudar**ía**	se mudar**ían**	**se habría** mudado	**se habrían** mudado
presente de subjuntivo		perfecto de subjuntivo	
me mud**e**	nos mud**emos**	**me haya** mudado	**nos hayamos** mudado
te mud**es**	os mud**éis**	**te hayas** mudado	**os hayáis** mudado
se mud**e**	se mud**en**	**se haya** mudado	**se hayan** mudado
imperfecto de subjuntivo		pluscuamperfecto de subjuntivo	
me mudar**a**	nos mudár**amos**	**me hubiera** mudado	**nos hubiéramos** mudado
te mudar**as**	os mudar**ais**	**te hubieras** mudado	**os hubierais** mudado
se mudar**a**	se mudar**an**	**se hubiera** mudado	**se hubieran** mudado
OR		OR	
me muda**sen**	nos mudás**emos**	**me hubiese** mudado	**nos hubiésemos** mudado
te muda**ses**	os muda**seis**	**te hubieses** mudado	**os hubieseis** mudado
se muda**se**	se muda**sen**	**se hubiese** mudado	**se hubiesen** mudado

imperativo

—	mudémonos
múdate; no te mudes	mudaos; no os mudéis
múdese	múdense

M

nacer — to be born

gerundio **naciendo** — participio de pasado **nacido**

SINGULAR	PLURAL	SINGULAR	PLURAL
presente de indicativo		perfecto de indicativo	
nazc**o**	nac**emos**	**he** nacido	**hemos** nacido
nac**es**	nac**éis**	**has** nacido	**habéis** nacido
nac**e**	nac**en**	**ha** nacido	**han** nacido
imperfecto de indicativo		pluscuamperfecto de indicativo	
nac**ía**	nac**íamos**	**había** nacido	**habíamos** nacido
nac**ías**	nac**íais**	**habías** nacido	**habíais** nacido
nac**ía**	nac**ían**	**había** nacido	**habían** nacido
pretérito		pretérito anterior	
nac**í**	nac**imos**	**hube** nacido	**hubimos** nacido
nac**iste**	nac**isteis**	**hubiste** nacido	**hubisteis** nacido
naci**ó**	nac**ieron**	**hubo** nacido	**hubieron** nacido
futuro		futuro perfecto	
nacer**é**	nacer**emos**	**habré** nacido	**habremos** nacido
nacer**ás**	nacer**éis**	**habrás** nacido	**habréis** nacido
nacer**á**	nacer**án**	**habrá** nacido	**habrán** nacido
condicional simple		condicional compuesto	
nacer**ía**	nacer**íamos**	**habría** nacido	**habríamos** nacido
nacer**ías**	nacer**íais**	**habrías** nacido	**habríais** nacido
nacer**ía**	nacer**ían**	**habría** nacido	**habrían** nacido
presente de subjuntivo		perfecto de subjuntivo	
nazc**a**	nazc**amos**	**haya** nacido	**hayamos** nacido
nazc**as**	nazc**áis**	**hayas** nacido	**hayáis** nacido
nazc**a**	nazc**an**	**haya** nacido	**hayan** nacido
imperfecto de subjuntivo		pluscuamperfecto de subjuntivo	
nacier**a**	naciér**amos**	**hubiera** nacido	**hubiéramos** nacido
nacier**as**	nacier**ais**	**hubieras** nacido	**hubierais** nacido
nacier**a**	nacier**an**	**hubiera** nacido	**hubieran** nacido
OR		OR	
nacies**e**	naciés**emos**	**hubiese** nacido	**hubiésemos** nacido
nacies**es**	nacies**eis**	**hubieses** nacido	**hubieseis** nacido
nacies**e**	nacies**en**	**hubiese** nacido	**hubiesen** nacido

imperativo

—	nazcamos
nace; no nazcas	naced; no nazcáis
nazca	nazcan

to swim **nadar**

gerundio **nadando** participio de pasado **nadado**

SINGULAR	PLURAL	SINGULAR	PLURAL
presente de indicativo		perfecto de indicativo	
nad**o**	nad**amos**	**he** nadado	**hemos** nadado
nad**as**	nad**áis**	**has** nadado	**habéis** nadado
nad**a**	nad**an**	**ha** nadado	**han** nadado
imperfecto de indicativo		pluscuamperfecto de indicativo	
nad**aba**	nad**ábamos**	**había** nadado	**habíamos** nadado
nad**abas**	nad**abais**	**habías** nadado	**habíais** nadado
nad**aba**	nad**aban**	**había** nadado	**habían** nadado
pretérito		pretérito anterior	
nad**é**	nad**amos**	**hube** nadado	**hubimos** nadado
nad**aste**	nad**asteis**	**hubiste** nadado	**hubisteis** nadado
nad**ó**	nad**aron**	**hubo** nadado	**hubieron** nadado
futuro		futuro perfecto	
nadar**é**	nadar**emos**	**habré** nadado	**habremos** nadado
nadar**ás**	nadar**éis**	**habrás** nadado	**habréis** nadado
nadar**á**	nadar**án**	**habrá** nadado	**habrán** nadado
condicional simple		condicional compuesto	
nadar**ía**	nadar**íamos**	**habría** nadado	**habríamos** nadado
nadar**ías**	nadar**íais**	**habrías** nadado	**habríais** nadado
nadar**ía**	nadar**ían**	**habría** nadado	**habrían** nadado
presente de subjuntivo		perfecto de subjuntivo	
nad**e**	nad**emos**	**haya** nadado	**hayamos** nadado
nad**es**	nad**éis**	**hayas** nadado	**hayáis** nadado
nad**e**	nad**en**	**haya** nadado	**hayan** nadado
imperfecto de subjuntivo		pluscuamperfecto de subjuntivo	
nadar**a**	nadár**amos**	**hubiera** nadado	**hubiéramos** nadado
nadar**as**	nadar**ais**	**hubieras** nadado	**hubierais** nadado
nadar**a**	nadar**an**	**hubiera** nadado	**hubieran** nadado
OR		OR	
nadas**e**	nadás**emos**	**hubiese** nadado	**hubiésemos** nadado
nadas**es**	nadas**eis**	**hubieses** nadado	**hubieseis** nadado
nadas**e**	nadas**en**	**hubiese** nadado	**hubiesen** nadado

imperativo

—	nademos
nada; no nades	nadad; no nadéis
nade	naden

N

naturalizar — to naturalize

gerundio **naturalizando** participio de pasado **naturalizado**

SINGULAR	PLURAL
presente de indicativo	
naturaliz**o**	naturaliz**amos**
naturaliz**as**	naturaliz**áis**
naturaliz**a**	naturaliz**an**
imperfecto de indicativo	
naturaliz**aba**	naturaliz**ábamos**
naturaliz**abas**	naturaliz**abais**
naturaliz**aba**	naturaliz**aban**
pretérito	
naturalic**é**	naturaliz**amos**
naturaliz**aste**	naturaliz**asteis**
naturaliz**ó**	naturaliz**aron**
futuro	
naturalizar**é**	naturalizar**emos**
naturalizar**ás**	naturalizar**éis**
naturalizar**á**	naturalizar**án**
condicional simple	
naturalizar**ía**	naturalizar**íamos**
naturalizar**ías**	naturalizar**íais**
naturalizar**ía**	naturalizar**ían**
presente de subjuntivo	
naturalic**e**	naturalic**emos**
naturalic**es**	naturalic**éis**
naturalic**e**	naturalic**en**
imperfecto de subjuntivo	
naturalizar**a**	naturalizár**amos**
naturalizar**as**	naturalizar**ais**
naturalizar**a**	naturalizar**an**
OR	
naturalizas**e**	naturalizás**emos**
naturalizas**es**	naturalizas**eis**
naturalizas**e**	naturalizas**en**
imperativo	
—	naturalicemos
naturaliza; no naturalices	naturalizad; no naturalicéis
naturalice	naturalicen

SINGULAR	PLURAL
perfecto de indicativo	
he naturalizado	**hemos** naturalizado
has naturalizado	**habéis** naturalizado
ha naturalizado	**han** naturalizado
pluscuamperfecto de indicativo	
había naturalizado	**habíamos** naturalizado
habías naturalizado	**habíais** naturalizado
había naturalizado	**habían** naturalizado
pretérito anterior	
hube naturalizado	**hubimos** naturalizado
hubiste naturalizado	**hubisteis** naturalizado
hubo naturalizado	**hubieron** naturalizado
futuro perfecto	
habré naturalizado	**habremos** naturalizado
habrás naturalizado	**habréis** naturalizado
habrá naturalizado	**habrán** naturalizado
condicional compuesto	
habría naturalizado	**habríamos** naturalizado
habrías naturalizado	**habríais** naturalizado
habría naturalizado	**habrían** naturalizado
perfecto de subjuntivo	
haya naturalizado	**hayamos** naturalizado
hayas naturalizado	**hayáis** naturalizado
haya naturalizado	**hayan** naturalizado
pluscuamperfecto de subjuntivo	
hubiera naturalizado	**hubiéramos** naturalizado
hubieras naturalizado	**hubierais** naturalizado
hubiera naturalizado	**hubieran** naturalizado
OR	
hubiese naturalizado	**hubiésemos** naturalizado
hubieses naturalizado	**hubieseis** naturalizado
hubiese naturalizado	**hubiesen** naturalizado

to navigate, to sail **navegar**

gerundio **navegando** participio de pasado **navegado**

SINGULAR	PLURAL	SINGULAR	PLURAL
presente de indicativo		perfecto de indicativo	
naveg**o**	naveg**amos**	**he** navegado	**hemos** navegado
naveg**as**	naveg**áis**	**has** navegado	**habéis** navegado
naveg**a**	naveg**an**	**ha** navegado	**han** navegado
imperfecto de indicativo		pluscuamperfecto de indicativo	
naveg**aba**	naveg**ábamos**	**había** navegado	**habíamos** navegado
naveg**abas**	naveg**abais**	**habías** navegado	**habíais** navegado
naveg**aba**	naveg**aban**	**había** navegado	**habían** navegado
pretérito		pretérito anterior	
navegu**é**	naveg**amos**	**hube** navegado	**hubimos** navegado
naveg**aste**	naveg**asteis**	**hubiste** navegado	**hubisteis** navegado
naveg**ó**	naveg**aron**	**hubo** navegado	**hubieron** navegado
futuro		futuro perfecto	
navegar**é**	navegar**emos**	**habré** navegado	**habremos** navegado
navegar**ás**	navegar**éis**	**habrás** navegado	**habréis** navegado
navegar**á**	navegar**án**	**habrá** navegado	**habrán** navegado
condicional simple		condicional compuesto	
navegar**ía**	navegar**íamos**	**habría** navegado	**habríamos** navegado
navegar**ías**	navegar**íais**	**habrías** navegado	**habríais** navegado
navegar**ía**	navegar**ían**	**habría** navegado	**habrían** navegado
presente de subjuntivo		perfecto de subjuntivo	
navegu**e**	navegu**emos**	**haya** navegado	**hayamos** navegado
navegu**es**	navegu**éis**	**hayas** navegado	**hayáis** navegado
navegu**e**	navegu**en**	**haya** navegado	**hayan** navegado
imperfecto de subjuntivo		pluscuamperfecto de subjuntivo	
navegar**a**	navegár**amos**	**hubiera** navegado	**hubiéramos** navegado
navegar**as**	navegar**ais**	**hubieras** navegado	**hubierais** navegado
navegar**a**	navegar**an**	**hubiera** navegado	**hubieran** navegado
OR		OR	
navegas**e**	navegás**emos**	**hubiese** navegado	**hubiésemos** navegado
navegas**es**	navegas**eis**	**hubieses** navegado	**hubieseis** navegado
navegas**e**	navegas**en**	**hubiese** navegado	**hubiesen** navegado

imperativo

—	naveguemos
navega; no navegues	navegad; no naveguéis
navegue	naveguen

N

necesitar — to need

gerundio **necesitando** — participio de pasado **necesitado**

SINGULAR	PLURAL
presente de indicativo	
necesit**o**	necesit**amos**
necesit**as**	necesit**áis**
necesit**a**	necesit**an**
imperfecto de indicativo	
necesit**aba**	necesit**ábamos**
necesit**abas**	necesit**abais**
necesit**aba**	necesit**aban**
pretérito	
necesit**é**	necesit**amos**
necesit**aste**	necesit**asteis**
necesit**ó**	necesit**aron**
futuro	
necesitar**é**	necesitar**emos**
necesitar**ás**	necesitar**éis**
necesitar**á**	necesitar**án**
condicional simple	
necesitar**ía**	necesitar**íamos**
necesitar**ías**	necesitar**íais**
necesitar**ía**	necesitar**ían**
presente de subjuntivo	
necesit**e**	necesit**emos**
necesit**es**	necesit**éis**
necesit**e**	necesit**en**
imperfecto de subjuntivo	
necesitar**a**	necesitár**amos**
necesitar**as**	necesitar**ais**
necesitar**a**	necesitar**an**
OR	
necesitas**e**	necesitás**emos**
necesitas**es**	necesitas**eis**
necesitas**e**	necesitas**en**
imperativo	
—	necesitemos
necesita; no necesites	necesitad; no necesitéis
necesite	necesiten

SINGULAR	PLURAL
perfecto de indicativo	
he necesitado	**hemos** necesitado
has necesitado	**habéis** necesitado
ha necesitado	**han** necesitado
pluscuamperfecto de indicativo	
había necesitado	**habíamos** necesitado
habías necesitado	**habíais** necesitado
había necesitado	**habían** necesitado
pretérito anterior	
hube necesitado	**hubimos** necesitado
hubiste necesitado	**hubisteis** necesitado
hubo necesitado	**hubieron** necesitado
futuro perfecto	
habré necesitado	**habremos** necesitado
habrás necesitado	**habréis** necesitado
habrá necesitado	**habrán** necesitado
condicional compuesto	
habría necesitado	**habríamos** necesitado
habrías necesitado	**habríais** necesitado
habría necesitado	**habrían** necesitado
perfecto de subjuntivo	
haya necesitado	**hayamos** necesitado
hayas necesitado	**hayáis** necesitado
haya necesitado	**hayan** necesitado
pluscuamperfecto de subjuntivo	
hubiera necesitado	**hubiéramos** necesitado
hubieras necesitado	**hubierais** necesitado
hubiera necesitado	**hubieran** necesitado
OR	
hubiese necesitado	**hubiésemos** necesitado
hubieses necesitado	**hubieseis** necesitado
hubiese necesitado	**hubiesen** necesitado

gerundio **negando** participio de pasado **negado**

SINGULAR	PLURAL	SINGULAR	PLURAL
presente de indicativo		perfecto de indicativo	
nieg**o**	neg**amos**	**he** negado	**hemos** negado
nieg**as**	neg**áis**	**has** negado	**habéis** negado
nieg**a**	nieg**an**	**ha** negado	**han** negado
imperfecto de indicativo		pluscuamperfecto de indicativo	
neg**aba**	neg**ábamos**	**había** negado	**habíamos** negado
neg**abas**	neg**abais**	**habías** negado	**habíais** negado
neg**aba**	neg**aban**	**había** negado	**habían** negado
pretérito		pretérito anterior	
negu**é**	neg**amos**	**hube** negado	**hubimos** negado
neg**aste**	neg**asteis**	**hubiste** negado	**hubisteis** negado
neg**ó**	neg**aron**	**hubo** negado	**hubieron** negado
futuro		futuro perfecto	
negar**é**	negar**emos**	**habré** negado	**habremos** negado
negar**ás**	negar**éis**	**habrás** negado	**habréis** negado
negar**á**	negar**án**	**habrá** negado	**habrán** negado
condicional simple		condicional compuesto	
negar**ía**	negar**íamos**	**habría** negado	**habríamos** negado
negar**ías**	negar**íais**	**habrías** negado	**habríais** negado
negar**ía**	negar**ían**	**habría** negado	**habrían** negado
presente de subjuntivo		perfecto de subjuntivo	
niegu**e**	negu**emos**	**haya** negado	**hayamos** negado
niegu**es**	negu**éis**	**hayas** negado	**hayáis** negado
niegu**e**	niegu**en**	**haya** negado	**hayan** negado
imperfecto de subjuntivo		pluscuamperfecto de subjuntivo	
negar**a**	negár**amos**	**hubiera** negado	**hubiéramos** negado
negar**as**	negar**ais**	**hubieras** negado	**hubierais** negado
negar**a**	negar**an**	**hubiera** negado	**hubieran** negado
OR		OR	
negas**e**	negás**emos**	**hubiese** negado	**hubiésemos** negado
negas**es**	negas**eis**	**hubieses** negado	**hubieseis** negado
negas**e**	negas**en**	**hubiese** negado	**hubiesen** negado

imperativo

—	neguemos
niega; no niegues	negad; no neguéis
niegue	nieguen

nevar — to snow

gerundio **nevando** — participio de pasado **nevado**

SINGULAR	PLURAL
presente de indicativo	
nieva	nievan
imperfecto de indicativo	
nevaba	nevaban
pretérito	
nevó	nevaron
futuro	
nevará	nevarán
condicional simple	
nevaría	nevarían
presente de subjuntivo	
nieve	nieven
imperfecto de subjuntivo	
nevara	nevaran
OR	
nevase	nevasen
imperativo	
¡Qué nieve!	¡Que no nieve!

SINGULAR	PLURAL
perfecto de indicativo	
ha nevado	han nevado
pluscuamperfecto de indicativo	
había nevado	habían nevado
pretérito anterior	
hube nevado	hubimos nevado
hubiste nevado	hubisteis nevado
hubo nevado	hubieron nevado
futuro perfecto	
habrá nevado	habrán nevado
condicional compuesto	
habría nevado	habrían nevado
perfecto de subjuntivo	
haya nevado	hayan nevado
pluscuamperfecto de subjuntivo	
hubiera nevado	hubieran nevado
OR	
hubiese nevado	hubiesen nevado

to obey **obedecer**

gerundio **obedeciendo**

participio de pasado **obedecido**

SINGULAR	PLURAL

presente de indicativo

SINGULAR	PLURAL
obedezc**o**	obedec**emos**
obedec**es**	obedec**éis**
obedec**e**	obedec**en**

imperfecto de indicativo

SINGULAR	PLURAL
obedec**ía**	obedec**íamos**
obedec**ías**	obedec**íais**
obedec**ía**	obedec**ían**

pretérito

SINGULAR	PLURAL
obedec**í**	obedec**imos**
obedec**iste**	obedec**isteis**
obedec**ió**	obedec**ieron**

futuro

SINGULAR	PLURAL
obedecer**é**	obedecer**emos**
obedecer**ás**	obedecer**éis**
obedecer**á**	obedecer**án**

condicional simple

SINGULAR	PLURAL
obedecer**ía**	obedecer**íamos**
obedecer**ías**	obedecer**íais**
obedecer**ía**	obedecer**ían**

presente de subjuntivo

SINGULAR	PLURAL
obedezc**a**	obedezc**amos**
obedezc**as**	obedezc**áis**
obedezc**a**	obedezc**an**

imperfecto de subjuntivo

SINGULAR	PLURAL
obedecier**a**	obedeciér**amos**
obedecier**as**	obedecier**ais**
obedecier**a**	obedecier**an**
OR	
obedecies**e**	obediecies**emos**
obedecies**es**	obedecies**eis**
obedecies**e**	obedecies**en**

imperativo

SINGULAR	PLURAL
—	obedezcamos
obedece; no obedezcas	obedeced; no obedezcáis
obedezca	obedezcan

perfecto de indicativo

SINGULAR	PLURAL
he obedecido	**hemos** obedecido
has obedecido	**habéis** obedecido
ha obedecido	**han** obedecido

pluscuamperfecto de indicativo

SINGULAR	PLURAL
había obedecido	**habíamos** obedecido
habías obedecido	**habíais** obedecido
había obedecido	**habían** obedecido

pretérito anterior

SINGULAR	PLURAL
hube obedecido	**hubimos** obedecido
hubiste obedecido	**hubisteis** obedecido
hubo obedecido	**hubieron** obedecido

futuro perfecto

SINGULAR	PLURAL
habré obedecido	**habremos** obedecido
habrás obedecido	**habréis** obedecido
habrá obedecido	**habrán** obedecido

condicional compuesto

SINGULAR	PLURAL
habría obedecido	**habríamos** obedecido
habrías obedecido	**habríais** obedecido
habría obedecido	**habrían** obedecido

perfecto de subjuntivo

SINGULAR	PLURAL
haya obedecido	**hayamos** obedecido
hayas obedecido	**hayáis** obedecido
haya obedecido	**hayan** obedecido

pluscuamperfecto de subjuntivo

SINGULAR	PLURAL
hubiera obedecido	**hubiéramos** obedecido
hubieras obedecido	**hubierais** obedecido
hubiera obedecido	**hubieran** obedecido
OR	
hubiese obedecido	**hubiésemos** obedecido
hubieses obedecido	**hubieseis** obedecido
hubiese obedecido	**hubiesen** obedecido

obligar — to oblige, to force

gerundio **obligando** — participio de pasado **obligado**

SINGULAR	PLURAL	SINGULAR	PLURAL
presente de indicativo		perfecto de indicativo	
oblig**o**	oblig**amos**	**he** obligado	**hemos** obligado
oblig**as**	oblig**áis**	**has** obligado	**habéis** obligado
oblig**a**	oblig**an**	**ha** obligado	**han** obligado
imperfecto de indicativo		pluscuamperfecto de indicativo	
oblig**aba**	oblig**ábamos**	**había** obligado	**habíamos** obligado
oblig**abas**	oblig**abais**	**habías** obligado	**habíais** obligado
oblig**aba**	oblig**aban**	**había** obligado	**habían** obligado
pretérito		pretérito anterior	
obligu**é**	oblig**amos**	**hube** obligado	**hubimos** obligado
oblig**aste**	oblig**asteis**	**hubiste** obligado	**hubisteis** obligado
oblig**ó**	oblig**aron**	**hubo** obligado	**hubieron** obligado
futuro		futuro perfecto	
obligar**é**	obligar**emos**	**habré** obligado	**habremos** obligado
obligar**ás**	obligar**éis**	**habrás** obligado	**habréis** obligado
obligar**á**	obligar**án**	**habrá** obligado	**habrán** obligado
condicional simple		condicional compuesto	
obligar**ía**	obligar**íamos**	**habría** obligado	**habríamos** obligado
obligar**ías**	obligar**íais**	**habrías** obligado	**habríais** obligado
obligar**ía**	obligar**ían**	**habría** obligado	**habrían** obligado
presente de subjuntivo		perfecto de subjuntivo	
obligu**e**	obligu**emos**	**haya** obligado	**hayamos** obligado
obligu**es**	obligu**éis**	**hayas** obligado	**hayáis** obligado
obligu**e**	obligu**en**	**haya** obligado	**hayan** obligado
imperfecto de subjuntivo		pluscuamperfecto de subjuntivo	
obligar**a**	obligár**amos**	**hubiera** obligado	**hubiéramos** obligado
obligar**as**	obligar**ais**	**hubieras** obligado	**hubierais** obligado
obligar**a**	obligar**an**	**hubiera** obligado	**hubieran** obligado
OR		OR	
obligas**e**	obligás**emos**	**hubiese** obligado	**hubiésemos** obligado
obligas**es**	obligas**eis**	**hubieses** obligado	**hubieseis** obligado
obligas**e**	obligas**en**	**hubiese** obligado	**hubiesen** obligado

imperativo

—	obliguemos
obliga; no obligues	obligad; no obliguéis
obligue	obliguen

gerundio **obsequiando** participio de pasado **obsequiado**

SINGULAR	PLURAL	SINGULAR	PLURAL
presente de indicativo		perfecto de indicativo	
obsequí**o**	obsequi**amos**	**he** obsequiado	**hemos** obsequiado
obsequí**as**	obsequi**áis**	**has** obsequiado	**habéis** obsequiado
obsequí**a**	obsequí**an**	**ha** obsequiado	**han** obsequiado
imperfecto de indicativo		pluscuamperfecto de indicativo	
obsequi**aba**	obsequi**ábamos**	**había** obsequiado	**habíamos** obsequiado
obsequi**abas**	obsequi**abais**	**habías** obsequiado	**habíais** obsequiado
obsequi**aba**	obsequi**aban**	**había** obsequiado	**habían** obsequiado
pretérito		pretérito anterior	
obsequi**é**	obsequi**amos**	**hube** obsequiado	**hubimos** obsequiado
obsequi**aste**	obsequi**asteis**	**hubiste** obsequiado	**hubisteis** obsequiado
obsequi**ó**	obsequi**aron**	**hubo** obsequiado	**hubieron** obsequiado
futuro		futuro perfecto	
obsequiar**é**	obsequiar**emos**	**habré** obsequiado	**habremos** obsequiado
obsequiar**ás**	obsequiar**éis**	**habrás** obsequiado	**habréis** obsequiado
obsequiar**á**	obsequiar**án**	**habrá** obsequiado	**habrán** obsequiado
condicional simple		condicional compuesto	
obsequiar**ía**	obsequiar**íamos**	**habría** obsequiado	**habríamos** obsequiado
obsequiar**ías**	obsequiar**íais**	**habrías** obsequiado	**habríais** obsequiado
obsequiar**ía**	obsequiar**ían**	**habría** obsequiado	**habrían** obsequiado
presente de subjuntivo		perfecto de subjuntivo	
obsequí**e**	obsequi**emos**	**haya** obsequiado	**hayamos** obsequiado
obsequí**es**	obsequi**éis**	**hayas** obsequiado	**hayáis** obsequiado
obsequí**e**	obsequí**en**	**haya** obsequiado	**hayan** obsequiado
imperfecto de subjuntivo		pluscuamperfecto de subjuntivo	
obsequiar**a**	obsequiár**amos**	**hubiera** obsequiado	**hubiéramos** obsequiado
obsequiar**as**	obsequiar**ais**	**hubieras** obsequiado	**hubierais** obsequiado
obsequiar**a**	obsequiar**an**	**hubiera** obsequiado	**hubieran** obsequiado
OR		OR	
obsequias**e**	obsequiás**emos**	**hubiese** obsequiado	**hubiésemos** obsequiado
obsequias**es**	obsequias**eis**	**hubieses** obsequiado	**hubieseis** obsequiado
obsequias**e**	obsequias**en**	**hubiese** obsequiado	**hubiesen** obsequiado

imperativo

—	obsequiemos
obsequía; no obsequíes	obsequiad; no obsequiéis
obsequíe	obsequíen

O

obstar — to hinder

gerundio **obstando** — participio de pasado **obstado**

SINGULAR	PLURAL	SINGULAR	PLURAL
presente de indicativo		perfecto de indicativo	
obst**o**	obst**amos**	**he** obstado	**hemos** obstado
obst**as**	obst**áis**	**has** obstado	**habéis** obstado
obst**a**	obst**an**	**ha** obstado	**han** obstado
imperfecto de indicativo		pluscuamperfecto de indicativo	
obst**aba**	obst**ábamos**	**había** obstado	**habíamos** obstado
obst**abas**	obst**abais**	**habías** obstado	**habíais** obstado
obst**aba**	obst**aban**	**había** obstado	**habían** obstado
pretérito		pretérito anterior	
obst**é**	obst**amos**	**hube** obstado	**hubimos** obstado
obst**aste**	obst**asteis**	**hubiste** obstado	**hubisteis** obstado
obst**ó**	obst**aron**	**hubo** obstado	**hubieron** obstado
futuro		futuro perfecto	
obstar**é**	obstar**emos**	**habré** obstado	**habremos** obstado
obstar**ás**	obstar**éis**	**habrás** obstado	**habréis** obstado
obstar**á**	obstar**án**	**habrá** obstado	**habrán** obstado
condicional simple		condicional compuesto	
obstar**ía**	obstar**íamos**	**habría** obstado	**habríamos** obstado
obstar**ías**	obstar**íais**	**habrías** obstado	**habríais** obstado
obstar**ía**	obstar**ían**	**habría** obstado	**habrían** obstado
presente de subjuntivo		perfecto de subjuntivo	
obst**e**	obst**emos**	**haya** obstado	**hayamos** obstado
obst**es**	obst**éis**	**hayas** obstado	**hayáis** obstado
obst**e**	obst**en**	**haya** obstado	**hayan** obstado
imperfecto de subjuntivo		pluscuamperfecto de subjuntivo	
obstar**a**	obstár**amos**	**hubiera** obstado	**hubiéramos** obstado
obstar**as**	obstar**ais**	**hubieras** obstado	**hubierais** obstado
obstar**a**	obstar**an**	**hubiera** obstado	**hubieran** obstado
OR		OR	
obstas**e**	obstás**emos**	**hubiese** obstado	**hubiésemos** obstado
obstas**es**	obstas**eis**	**hubieses** obstado	**hubieseis** obstado
obstas**e**	obstas**en**	**hubiese** obstado	**hubiesen** obstado

imperativo

—	obstemos
obsta; no obstes	obsta; no obstéis
obste	obsten

gerundio **ocultando** participio de pasado **ocultado**

SINGULAR	PLURAL
presente de indicativo	
oculto	ocultamos
ocultas	ocultáis
oculta	ocultan
imperfecto de indicativo	
ocultaba	ocultábamos
ocultabas	ocultabais
ocultaba	ocultaban
pretérito	
oculté	ocultamos
ocultaste	ocultasteis
ocultó	ocultaron
futuro	
ocultaré	ocultaremos
ocultarás	ocultaréis
ocultará	ocultarán
condicional simple	
ocultaría	ocultaríamos
ocultarías	ocultaríais
ocultaría	ocultarían
presente de subjuntivo	
oculte	ocultemos
ocultes	ocultéis
oculte	oculten
imperfecto de subjuntivo	
ocultara	ocultáramos
ocultaras	ocultarais
ocultara	ocultaran
OR	
ocultase	ocultásemos
ocultases	ocultaseis
ocultase	ocultasen
imperativo	
—	ocultemos
oculta; no ocultes	ocultad; no ocultéis
oculte	oculten

SINGULAR	PLURAL
perfecto de indicativo	
he ocultado	hemos ocultado
has ocultado	habéis ocultado
ha ocultado	han ocultado
pluscuamperfecto de indicativo	
había ocultado	habíamos ocultado
habías ocultado	habíais ocultado
había ocultado	habían ocultado
pretérito anterior	
hube ocultado	hubimos ocultado
hubiste ocultado	hubisteis ocultado
hubo ocultado	hubieron ocultado
futuro perfecto	
habré ocultado	habremos ocultado
habrás ocultado	habréis ocultado
habrá ocultado	habrán ocultado
condicional compuesto	
habría ocultado	habríamos ocultado
habrías ocultado	habríais ocultado
habría ocultado	habrían ocultado
perfecto de subjuntivo	
haya ocultado	hayamos ocultado
hayas ocultado	hayáis ocultado
haya ocultado	hayan ocultado
pluscuamperfecto de subjuntivo	
hubiera ocultado	hubiéramos ocultado
hubieras ocultado	hubierais ocultado
hubiera ocultado	hubieran ocultado
OR	
hubiese ocultado	hubiésemos ocultado
hubieses ocultado	hubieseis ocultado
hubiese ocultado	hubiesen ocultado

gerundio **ocultándose** participio de pasado **ocultado**

SINGULAR	PLURAL	SINGULAR	PLURAL
presente de indicativo		perfecto de indicativo	
me ocult**o**	nos ocult**amos**	**me he** ocultado	**nos hemos** ocultado
te ocult**as**	os ocult**áis**	**te has** ocultado	**os habéis** ocultado
se ocult**a**	se ocult**an**	**se ha** ocultado	**se han** ocultado
imperfecto de indicativo		pluscuamperfecto de indicativo	
me ocult**aba**	nos ocult**ábamos**	**me había** ocultado	**nos habíamos** ocultado
te ocult**abas**	os ocult**abais**	**te habías** ocultado	**os habíais** ocultado
se ocult**aba**	se ocult**aban**	**se había** ocultado	**se habían** ocultado
pretérito		pretérito anterior	
me ocult**é**	nos ocult**amos**	**me hube** ocultado	**nos hubimos** ocultado
te ocult**aste**	os ocult**asteis**	**te hubiste** ocultado	**os hubisteis** ocultado
se ocult**ó**	se ocult**aron**	**se hubo** ocultado	**se hubieron** ocultado
futuro		futuro perfecto	
me ocultar**é**	nos ocultar**emos**	**me habré** ocultado	**nos habremos** ocultado
te ocultar**ás**	os ocultar**éis**	**te habrás** ocultado	**os habréis** ocultado
se ocultar**á**	se ocultar**án**	**se habrá** ocultado	**se habrán** ocultado
condicional simple		condicional compuesto	
me ocultar**ía**	nos ocultar**íamos**	**me habría** ocultado	**nos habríamos** ocultado
te ocultar**ías**	os ocultar**íais**	**te habrías** ocultado	**os habríais** ocultado
se ocultar**ía**	se ocultar**ían**	**se habría** ocultado	**se habrían** ocultado
presente de subjuntivo		perfecto de subjuntivo	
me ocult**e**	nos ocult**emos**	**me haya** ocultado	**nos hayamos** ocultado
te ocult**es**	os ocult**éis**	**te hayas** ocultado	**os hayáis** ocultado
se ocult**e**	se ocult**en**	**se haya** ocultado	**se hayan** ocultado
imperfecto de subjuntivo		pluscuamperfecto de subjuntivo	
me ocultar**a**	nos ocultár**amos**	**me hubiera** ocultado	**nos hubiéramos** ocultado
te ocultar**as**	os ocultar**ais**	**te hubieras** ocultado	**os hubierais** ocultado
se ocultar**a**	se ocultar**an**	**se hubiera** ocultado	**se hubieran** ocultado
OR		OR	
me ocultas**e**	nos ocultás**emos**	**me hubiese** ocultado	**nos hubiésemos** ocultado
te ocultas**es**	os ocultas**eis**	**te hubieses** ocultado	**os hubieseis** ocultado
se ocultas**e**	se ocultas**en**	**se hubiese** ocultado	**se hubiesen** ocultado

imperativo

—	ocultémonos
ocúltate;	ocultaos;
no te ocultes	no os ocultéis
ocúltese	ocúltense

gerundio **ocupando** participio de pasado **ocupado**

SINGULAR	PLURAL	SINGULAR	PLURAL
presente de indicativo		perfecto de indicativo	
ocup**o**	ocup**amos**	**he** ocupado	**hemos** ocupado
ocup**as**	ocup**áis**	**has** ocupado	**habéis** ocupado
ocup**a**	ocup**an**	**ha** ocupado	**han** ocupado
imperfecto de indicativo		pluscuamperfecto de indicativo	
ocup**aba**	ocup**ábamos**	**había** ocupado	**habíamos** ocupado
ocup**abas**	ocup**abais**	**habías** ocupado	**habíais** ocupado
ocup**aba**	ocup**aban**	**había** ocupado	**habían** ocupado
pretérito		pretérito anterior	
ocup**é**	ocup**amos**	**hube** ocupado	**hubimos** ocupado
ocup**aste**	ocup**asteis**	**hubiste** ocupado	**hubisteis** ocupado
ocup**ó**	ocup**aron**	**hubo** ocupado	**hubieron** ocupado
futuro		futuro perfecto	
ocupar**é**	ocupar**emos**	**habré** ocupado	**habremos** ocupado
ocupar**ás**	ocupar**éis**	**habrás** ocupado	**habréis** ocupado
ocupar**á**	ocupar**án**	**habrá** ocupado	**habrán** ocupado
condicional simple		condicional compuesto	
ocupar**ía**	ocupar**íamos**	**habría** ocupado	**habríamos** ocupado
ocupar**ías**	ocupar**íais**	**habrías** ocupado	**habríais** ocupado
ocupar**ía**	ocupar**ían**	**habría** ocupado	**habrían** ocupado
presente de subjuntivo		perfecto de subjuntivo	
ocup**e**	ocup**emos**	**haya** ocupado	**hayamos** ocupado
ocup**es**	ocup**éis**	**hayas** ocupado	**hayáis** ocupado
ocup**e**	ocup**en**	**haya** ocupado	**hayan** ocupado
imperfecto de subjuntivo		pluscuamperfecto de subjuntivo	
ocupar**a**	ocupár**amos**	**hubiera** ocupado	**hubiéramos** ocupado
ocupar**as**	ocupar**ais**	**hubieras** ocupado	**hubierais** ocupado
ocupar**a**	ocupar**an**	**hubiera** ocupado	**hubieran** ocupado
OR		OR	
ocupas**e**	ocupas**emos**	**hubiese** ocupado	**hubiésemos** ocupado
ocupas**es**	ocupas**eis**	**hubieses** ocupado	**hubieseis** ocupado
ocupas**e**	ocupas**en**	**hubiese** ocupado	**hubiesen** ocupado

imperativo

—	ocupemos
ocupa; no ocupes	ocupad; no ocupéis
ocupe	ocupen

ocurrir — to happen

gerundio **ocurriendo** participio de pasado **ocurrido**

SINGULAR	PLURAL	SINGULAR	PLURAL
presente de indicativo		perfecto de indicativo	
ocurr**o**	ocurr**imos**	**he** ocurrido	**hemos** ocurrido
ocurr**es**	ocurr**ís**	**has** ocurrido	**habéis** ocurrido
ocurr**e**	ocurr**en**	**ha** ocurrido	**han** ocurrido
imperfecto de indicativo		pluscuamperfecto de indicativo	
ocurr**ía**	ocurr**íamos**	**había** ocurrido	**habíamos** ocurrido
ocurr**ías**	ocurr**íais**	**habías** ocurrido	**habíais** ocurrido
ocurr**ía**	ocurr**ían**	**había** ocurrido	**habían** ocurrido
pretérito		pretérito anterior	
ocurr**í**	ocurr**imos**	**hube** ocurrido	**hubimos** ocurrido
ocurr**iste**	ocurr**isteis**	**hubiste** ocurrido	**hubisteis** ocurrido
ocurri**ó**	ocurr**ieron**	**hubo** ocurrido	**hubieron** ocurrido
futuro		futuro perfecto	
ocurrir**é**	ocurrir**emos**	**habré** ocurrido	**habremos** ocurrido
ocurrir**ás**	ocurrir**éis**	**habrás** ocurrido	**habréis** ocurrido
ocurrir**á**	ocurrir**án**	**habrá** ocurrido	**habrán** ocurrido
condicional simple		condicional compuesto	
ocurrir**ía**	ocurrir**íamos**	**habría** ocurrido	**habríamos** ocurrido
ocurrir**ías**	ocurrir**íais**	**habrías** ocurrido	**habríais** ocurrido
ocurrir**ía**	ocurrir**ían**	**habría** ocurrido	**habrían** ocurrido
presente de subjuntivo		perfecto de subjuntivo	
ocurr**a**	ocurr**amos**	**haya** ocurrido	**hayamos** ocurrido
ocurr**as**	ocurr**áis**	**hayas** ocurrido	**hayáis** ocurrido
ocurr**a**	ocurr**an**	**haya** ocurrido	**hayan** ocurrido
imperfecto de subjuntivo		pluscuamperfecto de subjuntivo	
ocurrier**a**	ocurriér**amos**	**hubiera** ocurrido	**hubiéramos** ocurrido
ocurrier**as**	ocurrier**ais**	**hubieras** ocurrido	**hubierais** ocurrido
ocurrier**a**	ocurrier**an**	**hubiera** ocurrido	**hubieran** ocurrido
OR		OR	
ocurries**e**	ocurriés**emos**	**hubiese** ocurrido	**hubiésemos** ocurrido
ocurries**es**	ocurries**eis**	**hubieses** ocurrido	**hubieseis** ocurrido
ocurries**e**	ocurries**en**	**hubiese** ocurrido	**hubiesen** ocurrido

imperativo

—	ocurramos
ocurre; no ocurras	ocurrid; no ocurráis
ocurra	ocurran

to hate **odiar**

gerundio **odiando** participio de pasado **odiado**

SINGULAR	PLURAL
presente de indicativo	
odi**o**	odi**amos**
odi**as**	odi**áis**
odi**a**	odi**an**
imperfecto de indicativo	
odi**aba**	odi**ábamos**
odi**abas**	odi**abais**
odi**aba**	odi**aban**
pretérito	
odi**é**	odi**amos**
odi**aste**	odi**asteis**
odi**ó**	odi**aron**
futuro	
odiar**é**	odiar**emos**
odiar**ás**	odiar**éis**
odiar**á**	odiar**án**
condicional simple	
odiar**ía**	odiar**íamos**
odiar**ías**	odiar**íais**
odiar**ía**	odiar**ían**
presente de subjuntivo	
odi**e**	odi**emos**
odi**es**	odi**éis**
odi**e**	odi**en**
imperfecto de subjuntivo	
odiar**a**	odiár**amos**
odiar**as**	odiar**ais**
odiar**a**	odiar**an**
OR	
odias**e**	odiás**emos**
odias**es**	odias**eis**
odias**e**	odias**en**
imperativo	
—	odiemos
odia; no odies	odiad; no odiéis
odie	odien

SINGULAR	PLURAL
perfecto de indicativo	
he odiado	**hemos** odiado
has odiado	**habéis** odiado
ha odiado	**han** odiado
pluscuamperfecto de indicativo	
había odiado	**habíamos** odiado
habías odiado	**habíais** odiado
había odiado	**habían** odiado
pretérito anterior	
hube odiado	**hubimos** odiado
hubiste odiado	**hubisteis** odiado
hubo odiado	**hubieron** odiado
futuro perfecto	
habré odiado	**habremos** odiado
habrás odiado	**habréis** odiado
habrá odiado	**habrán** odiado
condicional compuesto	
habría odiado	**habríamos** odiado
habrías odiado	**habríais** odiado
habría odiado	**habrían** odiado
perfecto de subjuntivo	
haya odiado	**hayamos** odiado
hayas odiado	**hayáis** odiado
haya odiado	**hayan** odiado
pluscuamperfecto de subjuntivo	
hubiera odiado	**hubiéramos** odiado
hubieras odiado	**hubierais** odiado
hubiera odiado	**hubieran** odiado
OR	
hubiese odiado	**hubiésemos** odiado
hubieses odiado	**hubieseis** odiado
hubiese odiado	**hubiesen** odiado

gerundio **ofreciendo** participio de pasado **ofrecido**

SINGULAR	PLURAL
presente de indicativo	
ofrezc**o**	ofrec**emos**
ofrec**es**	ofrec**éis**
ofrec**e**	ofrec**en**
imperfecto de indicativo	
ofrec**ía**	ofrec**íamos**
ofrec**ías**	ofrec**íais**
ofrec**ía**	ofrec**ían**
pretérito	
ofrec**í**	ofrec**imos**
ofrec**iste**	ofrec**isteis**
ofrec**ió**	ofrec**ieron**
futuro	
ofrecer**é**	ofrecer**emos**
ofrecer**ás**	ofrecer**éis**
ofrecer**á**	ofrecer**án**
condicional simple	
ofrecer**ía**	ofrecer**íamos**
ofrecer**ías**	ofrecer**íais**
ofrecer**ía**	ofrecer**ían**
presente de subjuntivo	
ofrezc**a**	ofrezc**amos**
ofrezc**as**	ofrezc**áis**
ofrezc**a**	ofrezc**an**
imperfecto de subjuntivo	
ofrecier**a**	ofreciér**amos**
ofrecier**as**	ofrecier**ais**
ofrecier**a**	ofrecier**an**
OR	
ofrecies**e**	ofreciés**emos**
ofrecies**es**	ofrecies**eis**
ofrecies**e**	ofrecies**en**
imperativo	
—	ofrezcamos
ofrece; no ofrezcas	ofreced; no ofrezcáis
ofrezca	ofrezcan

SINGULAR	PLURAL
perfecto de indicativo	
he ofrecido	**hemos** ofrecido
has ofrecido	**habéis** ofrecido
ha ofrecido	**han** ofrecido
pluscuamperfecto de indicativo	
había ofrecido	**habíamos** ofrecido
habías ofrecido	**habíais** ofrecido
había ofrecido	**habían** ofrecido
pretérito anterior	
hube ofrecido	**hubimos** ofrecido
hubiste ofrecido	**hubisteis** ofrecido
hubo ofrecido	**hubieron** ofrecido
futuro perfecto	
habré ofrecido	**habremos** ofrecido
habrás ofrecido	**habréis** ofrecido
habrá ofrecido	**habrán** ofrecido
condicional compuesto	
habría ofrecido	**habríamos** ofrecido
habrías ofrecido	**habríais** ofrecido
habría ofrecido	**habrían** ofrecido
perfecto de subjuntivo	
haya ofrecido	**hayamos** ofrecido
hayas ofrecido	**hayáis** ofrecido
haya ofrecido	**hayan** ofrecido
pluscuamperfecto de subjuntivo	
hubiera ofrecido	**hubiéramos** ofrecido
hubieras ofrecido	**hubierais** ofrecido
hubiera ofrecido	**hubieran** ofrecido
OR	
hubiese ofrecido	**hubiésemos** ofrecido
hubieses ofrecido	**hubieseis** ofrecido
hubiese ofrecido	**hubiesen** ofrecido

to hear **oír**

gerundio **oyendo** participio de pasado **oído**

SINGULAR	PLURAL
presente de indicativo	
oig**o**	o**ímos**
oy**es**	o**ís**
oy**e**	oy**en**
imperfecto de indicativo	
o**ía**	o**íamos**
o**ías**	o**íais**
o**ía**	o**ían**
pretérito	
o**í**	o**ímos**
o**íste**	o**ísteis**
oy**ó**	oy**eron**
futuro	
oir**é**	oir**emos**
oir**ás**	oir**éis**
oir**á**	oir**án**
condicional simple	
oir**ía**	oir**íamos**
oir**ías**	oir**íais**
oir**ía**	oir**ían**
presente de subjuntivo	
oig**a**	oig**amos**
oig**as**	oig**áis**
oig**a**	oig**an**
imperfecto de subjuntivo	
oyer**a**	oyér**amos**
oyer**as**	oyer**ais**
oyer**a**	oyer**an**
OR	
oyes**e**	oyés**emos**
oyes**es**	oyes**eis**
oyes**e**	oyes**en**
imperativo	
—	oigamos
oye; no oigas	oíd; no oigáis
oiga	oigan

SINGULAR	PLURAL
perfecto de indicativo	
he oído	**hemos** oído
has oído	**habéis** oído
ha oído	**han** oído
pluscuamperfecto de indicativo	
había oído	**habíamos** oído
habías oído	**habíais** oído
había oído	**habían** oído
pretérito anterior	
hube oído	**hubimos** oído
hubiste oído	**hubisteis** oído
hubo oído	**hubieron** oído
futuro perfecto	
habré oído	**habremos** oído
habrás oído	**habréis** oído
habrá oído	**habrán** oído
condicional compuesto	
habría oído	**habríamos** oído
habrías oído	**habríais** oído
habría oído	**habrían** oído
perfecto de subjuntivo	
haya oído	**hayamos** oído
hayas oído	**hayáis** oído
haya oído	**hayan** oído
pluscuamperfecto de subjuntivo	
hubiera oído	**hubiéramos** oído
hubieras oído	**hubierais** oído
hubiera oído	**hubieran** oído
OR	
hubiese oído	**hubiésemos** oído
hubieses oído	**hubieseis** oído
hubiese oído	**hubiesen** oído

oler — to smell

gerundio **oliendo** participio de pasado **olido**

SINGULAR	PLURAL	SINGULAR	PLURAL
presente de indicativo		perfecto de indicativo	
huel**o**	ol**emos**	**he** olido	**hemos** olido
huel**es**	ol**éis**	**has** olido	**habéis** olido
huel**e**	huel**en**	**ha** olido	**han** olido
imperfecto de indicativo		pluscuamperfecto de indicativo	
ol**ía**	ol**íamos**	**había** olido	**habíamos** olido
ol**ías**	ol**íais**	**habías** olido	**habíais** olido
ol**ía**	ol**ían**	**había** olido	**habían** olido
pretérito		pretérito anterior	
ol**í**	ol**imos**	**hube** olido	**hubimos** olido
ol**iste**	ol**isteis**	**hubiste** olido	**hubisteis** olido
ol**ió**	ol**ieron**	**hubo** olido	**hubieron** olido
futuro		futuro perfecto	
oler**é**	oler**emos**	**habré** olido	**habremos** olido
oler**ás**	oler**éis**	**habrás** olido	**habréis** olido
oler**á**	oler**án**	**habrá** olido	**habrán** olido
condicional simple		condicional compuesto	
oler**ía**	oler**íamos**	**habría** olido	**habríamos** olido
oler**ías**	oler**íais**	**habrías** olido	**habríais** olido
oler**ía**	oler**ían**	**habría** olido	**habrían** olido
presente de subjuntivo		perfecto de subjuntivo	
huel**a**	ol**amos**	**haya** olido	**hayamos** olido
huel**as**	ol**áis**	**hayas** olido	**hayáis** olido
huel**a**	huel**an**	**haya** olido	**hayan** olido
imperfecto de subjuntivo		pluscuamperfecto de subjuntivo	
olier**a**	oliér**amos**	**hubiera** olido	**hubiéramos** olido
olier**as**	olier**ais**	**hubieras** olido	**hubierais** olido
olier**a**	olier**an**	**hubiera** olido	**hubieran** olido
OR		OR	
olies**e**	oliés**emos**	**hubiese** olido	**hubiésemos** olido
olies**es**	olies**eis**	**hubieses** olido	**hubieseis** olido
olies**e**	olies**en**	**hubiese** olido	**hubiesen** olido

imperativo

—	olamos
huele; no huelas	oled; no oláis
huela	huelan

gerundio **olvidando** participio de pasado **olvidado**

SINGULAR	PLURAL
presente de indicativo	
olvid**o**	olvid**amos**
olvid**as**	olvid**áis**
olvid**a**	olvid**an**
imperfecto de indicativo	
olvid**aba**	olvid**ábamos**
olvid**abas**	olvid**abais**
olvid**aba**	olvid**aban**
pretérito	
olvid**é**	olvid**amos**
olvid**aste**	olvid**asteis**
olvid**ó**	olvid**aron**
futuro	
olvidar**é**	olvidar**emos**
olvidar**ás**	olvidar**éis**
olvidar**á**	olvidar**án**
condicional simple	
olvidar**ía**	olvidar**íamos**
olvidar**ías**	olvidar**íais**
olvidar**ía**	olvidar**ían**
presente de subjuntivo	
olvid**e**	olvid**emos**
olvid**es**	olvid**éis**
olvid**e**	olvid**en**
imperfecto de subjuntivo	
olvidar**a**	olvidár**amos**
olvidar**as**	olvidar**ais**
olvidar**a**	olvidar**an**
OR	
olvidas**e**	olvidás**emos**
olvidas**es**	olvidas**eis**
olvidas**e**	olvidas**en**
imperativo	
—	olvidemos
olvida; no olvides	olvidad; no olvidéis
olvide	olviden

SINGULAR	PLURAL
perfecto de indicativo	
he olvidado	**hemos** olvidado
has olvidado	**habéis** olvidado
ha olvidado	**han** olvidado
pluscuamperfecto de indicativo	
había olvidado	**habíamos** olvidado
habías olvidado	**habíais** olvidado
había olvidado	**habían** olvidado
pretérito anterior	
hube olvidado	**hubimos** olvidado
hubiste olvidado	**hubisteis** olvidado
hubo olvidado	**hubieron** olvidado
futuro perfecto	
habré olvidado	**habremos** olvidado
habrás olvidado	**habréis** olvidado
habrá olvidado	**habrán** olvidado
condicional compuesto	
habría olvidado	**habríamos** olvidado
habrías olvidado	**habríais** olvidado
habría olvidado	**habrían** olvidado
perfecto de subjuntivo	
haya olvidado	**hayamos** olvidado
hayas olvidado	**hayáis** olvidado
haya olvidado	**hayan** olvidado
pluscuamperfecto de subjuntivo	
hubiera olvidado	**hubiéramos** olvidado
hubieras olvidado	**hubierais** olvidado
hubiera olvidado	**hubieran** olvidado
OR	
hubiese olvidado	**hubiésemos** olvidado
hubieses olvidado	**hubieseis** olvidado
hubiese olvidado	**hubiesen** olvidado

omitir

to omit

gerundio **omitiendo** participio de pasado **omitido**

SINGULAR	PLURAL
presente de indicativo	
omit**o**	omit**imos**
omit**es**	omit**ís**
omit**e**	omit**en**
imperfecto de indicativo	
omit**ía**	omit**íamos**
omit**ías**	omit**íais**
omit**ía**	omit**ían**
pretérito	
omit**í**	omit**imos**
omit**iste**	omit**isteis**
omit**ió**	omit**ieron**
futuro	
omitir**é**	omitir**emos**
omitir**ás**	omitir**éis**
omitir**á**	omitir**án**
condicional simple	
omitir**ía**	omitir**íamos**
omitir**ías**	omitir**íais**
omitir**ía**	omitir**ían**
presente de subjuntivo	
omit**a**	omit**amos**
omit**as**	omit**áis**
omit**a**	omit**an**
imperfecto de subjuntivo	
omitier**a**	omitiér**amos**
omitier**as**	omitier**ais**
omitier**a**	omitier**an**
OR	
omities**e**	omitiés**emos**
omities**es**	omities**eis**
omities**e**	omities**en**
imperativo	
—	omitamos
omite; no omitas	omitid; no omitáis
omita	omitan

SINGULAR	PLURAL
perfecto de indicativo	
he omitido	**hemos** omitido
has omitido	**habéis** omitido
ha omitido	**han** omitido
pluscuamperfecto de indicativo	
había omitido	**habíamos** omitido
habías omitido	**habíais** omitido
había omitido	**habían** omitido
pretérito anterior	
hube omitido	**hubimos** omitido
hubiste omitido	**hubisteis** omitido
hubo omitido	**hubieron** omitido
futuro perfecto	
habré omitido	**habremos** omitido
habrás omitido	**habréis** omitido
habrá omitido	**habrán** omitido
condicional compuesto	
habría omitido	**habríamos** omitido
habrías omitido	**habríais** omitido
habría omitido	**habrían** omitido
perfecto de subjuntivo	
haya omitido	**hayamos** omitido
hayas omitido	**hayáis** omitido
haya omitido	**hayan** omitido
pluscuamperfecto de subjuntivo	
hubiera omitido	**hubiéramos** omitido
hubieras omitido	**hubierais** omitido
hubiera omitido	**hubieran** omitido
OR	
hubiese omitido	**hubiésemos** omitido
hubieses omitido	**hubieseis** omitido
hubiese omitido	**hubiesen** omitido

to operate — operar

gerundio **operando**

participio de pasado **operado**

presente de indicativo

SINGULAR	PLURAL
oper**o**	oper**amos**
oper**as**	oper**áis**
oper**a**	oper**an**

imperfecto de indicativo

SINGULAR	PLURAL
oper**aba**	oper**ábamos**
oper**abas**	oper**abais**
oper**aba**	oper**aban**

pretérito

SINGULAR	PLURAL
oper**é**	oper**amos**
oper**aste**	oper**asteis**
oper**ó**	oper**aron**

futuro

SINGULAR	PLURAL
operar**é**	operar**emos**
operar**ás**	operar**éis**
operar**á**	operar**án**

condicional simple

SINGULAR	PLURAL
operar**ía**	operar**íamos**
operar**ías**	operar**íais**
operar**ía**	operar**ían**

presente de subjuntivo

SINGULAR	PLURAL
oper**e**	oper**emos**
oper**es**	oper**éis**
oper**e**	oper**en**

imperfecto de subjuntivo

SINGULAR	PLURAL
operar**a**	operár**amos**
operar**as**	operar**ais**
operar**a**	operar**an**
OR	
operas**e**	operás**emos**
operas**es**	operas**eis**
operas**e**	operas**en**

imperativo

SINGULAR	PLURAL
—	operemos
opera; no operes	operad; no operéis
opere	operen

perfecto de indicativo

SINGULAR	PLURAL
he operado	**hemos** operado
has operado	**habéis** operado
ha operado	**han** operado

pluscuamperfecto de indicativo

SINGULAR	PLURAL
había operado	**habíamos** operado
habías operado	**habíais** operado
había operado	**habían** operado

pretérito anterior

SINGULAR	PLURAL
hube operado	**hubimos** operado
hubiste operado	**hubisteis** operado
hubo operado	**hubieron** operado

futuro perfecto

SINGULAR	PLURAL
habré operado	**habremos** operado
habrás operado	**habréis** operado
habrá operado	**habrán** operado

condicional compuesto

SINGULAR	PLURAL
habría operado	**habríamos** operado
habrías operado	**habríais** operado
habría operado	**habrían** operado

perfecto de subjuntivo

SINGULAR	PLURAL
haya operado	**hayamos** operado
hayas operado	**hayáis** operado
haya operado	**hayan** operado

pluscuamperfecto de subjuntivo

SINGULAR	PLURAL
hubiera operado	**hubiéramos** operado
hubieras operado	**hubierais** operado
hubiera operado	**hubieran** operado
OR	
hubiese operado	**hubiésemos** operado
hubieses operado	**hubieseis** operado
hubiese operado	**hubiesen** operado

oponer — to oppose

gerundio **oponiendo** participio de pasado **opuesto**

SINGULAR	PLURAL	SINGULAR	PLURAL
presente de indicativo		perfecto de indicativo	
opong**o**	opon**emos**	**he** opuesto	**hemos** opuesto
opon**es**	opon**éis**	**has** opuesto	**habéis** opuesto
opon**e**	opon**en**	**ha** opuesto	**han** opuesto
imperfecto de indicativo		pluscuamperfecto de indicativo	
opon**ía**	opon**íamos**	**había** opuesto	**habíamos** opuesto
opon**ías**	opon**íais**	**habías** opuesto	**habíais** opuesto
opon**ía**	opon**ían**	**había** opuesto	**habían** opuesto
pretérito		pretérito anterior	
opus**e**	opus**imos**	**hube** opuesto	**hubimos** opuesto
opus**iste**	opus**isteis**	**hubiste** opuesto	**hubisteis** opuesto
opus**o**	opus**ieron**	**hubo** opuesto	**hubieron** opuesto
futuro		futuro perfecto	
opondr**é**	opondr**emos**	**habré** opuesto	**habremos** opuesto
opondr**ás**	opondr**éis**	**habrás** opuesto	**habréis** opuesto
opondr**á**	opondr**án**	**habrá** opuesto	**habrán** opuesto
condicional simple		condicional compuesto	
opondr**ía**	opondr**íamos**	**habría** opuesto	**habríamos** opuesto
opondr**ías**	opondr**íais**	**habrías** opuesto	**habríais** opuesto
opondr**ía**	opondr**ían**	**habría** opuesto	**habrían** opuesto
presente de subjuntivo		perfecto de subjuntivo	
oponga**a**	opong**amos**	**haya** opuesto	**hayamos** opuesto
opong**as**	opong**áis**	**hayas** opuesto	**hayáis** opuesto
opong**a**	opong**an**	**haya** opuesto	**hayan** opuesto
imperfecto de subjuntivo		pluscuamperfecto de subjuntivo	
opusier**a**	opusiér**amos**	**hubiera** opuesto	**hubiéramos** opuesto
opusier**as**	opusier**ais**	**hubieras** opuesto	**hubierais** opuesto
opusier**a**	opusier**an**	**hubiera** opuesto	**hubieran** opuesto
OR		OR	
opusies**e**	opusiés**emos**	**hubiese** opuesto	**hubiésemos** opuesto
opusies**es**	opusies**eis**	**hubieses** opuesto	**hubieseis** opuesto
opusies**e**	opusies**en**	**hubiese** opuesto	**hubiesen** opuesto

imperativo

—	opongamos
opón; no opongas	oponed; no opongáis
oponga	opongan

gerundio **optando** participio de pasado **optado**

SINGULAR	PLURAL
presente de indicativo	
opt**o**	opt**amos**
opt**as**	opt**áis**
opt**a**	opt**an**
imperfecto de indicativo	
opt**aba**	opt**ábamos**
opt**abas**	opt**abais**
opt**aba**	opt**aban**
pretérito	
opt**é**	opt**amos**
opt**aste**	opt**asteis**
opt**ó**	opt**aron**
futuro	
optar**é**	optar**emos**
optar**ás**	optar**éis**
optar**á**	optar**án**
condicional simple	
optar**ía**	optar**íamos**
optar**ías**	optar**íais**
optar**ía**	optar**ían**
presente de subjuntivo	
opt**e**	opt**emos**
opt**es**	opt**éis**
opt**e**	opt**en**
imperfecto de subjuntivo	
optar**a**	optár**amos**
optar**as**	optar**ais**
optar**a**	optar**an**
OR	
optas**e**	optás**emos**
optas**es**	optas**eis**
optas**e**	optas**en**
imperativo	
—	optemos
opta; no optes	optad; no optéis
opte	opten

SINGULAR	PLURAL
perfecto de indicativo	
he optado	**hemos** optado
has optado	**habéis** optado
ha optado	**han** optado
pluscuamperfecto de indicativo	
había optado	**habíamos** optado
habías optado	**habíais** optado
había optado	**habían** optado
pretérito anterior	
hube optado	**hubimos** optado
hubiste optado	**hubisteis** optado
hubo optado	**hubieron** optado
futuro perfecto	
habré optado	**habremos** optado
habrás optado	**habréis** optado
habrá optado	**habrán** optado
condicional compuesto	
habría optado	**habríamos** optado
habrías optado	**habríais** optado
habría optado	**habrían** optado
perfecto de subjuntivo	
haya optado	**hayamos** optado
hayas optado	**hayáis** optado
haya optado	**hayan** optado
pluscuamperfecto de subjuntivo	
hubiera optado	**hubiéramos** optado
hubieras optado	**hubierais** optado
hubiera optado	**hubieran** optado
OR	
hubiese optado	**hubiésemos** optado
hubieses optado	**hubieseis** optado
hubiese optado	**hubiesen** optado

orar — to pray

gerundio **orando** participio de pasado **orado**

SINGULAR	PLURAL	SINGULAR	PLURAL
presente de indicativo		perfecto de indicativo	
or**o**	or**amos**	**he** orado	**hemos** orado
or**as**	or**áis**	**has** orado	**habéis** orado
or**a**	or**an**	**ha** orado	**han** orado
imperfecto de indicativo		pluscuamperfecto de indicativo	
or**aba**	or**ábamos**	**había** orado	**habíamos** orado
or**abas**	or**abais**	**habías** orado	**habíais** orado
or**aba**	or**aban**	**había** orado	**habían** orado
pretérito		pretérito anterior	
or**é**	or**amos**	**hube** orado	**hubimos** orado
or**aste**	or**asteis**	**hubiste** orado	**hubisteis** orado
or**ó**	or**aron**	**hubo** orado	**hubieron** orado
futuro		futuro perfecto	
orar**é**	orar**emos**	**habré** orado	**habremos** orado
orar**ás**	orar**éis**	**habrás** orado	**habréis** orado
orar**á**	orar**án**	**habrá** orado	**habrán** orado
condicional simple		condicional compuesto	
orar**ía**	orar**íamos**	**habría** orado	**habríamos** orado
orar**ías**	orar**íais**	**habrías** orado	**habríais** orado
orar**ía**	orar**ían**	**habría** orado	**habrían** orado
presente de subjuntivo		perfecto de subjuntivo	
or**e**	or**emos**	**haya** orado	**hayamos** orado
or**es**	or**éis**	**hayas** orado	**hayáis** orado
or**e**	or**en**	**haya** orado	**hayan** orado
imperfecto de subjuntivo		pluscuamperfecto de subjuntivo	
orar**a**	orár**amos**	**hubiera** orado	**hubiéramos** orado
orar**as**	orar**ais**	**hubieras** orado	**hubierais** orado
orar**a**	orar**an**	**hubiera** orado	**hubieran** orado
OR		OR	
oras**e**	orás**emos**	**hubiese** orado	**hubiésemos** orado
oras**es**	oras**eis**	**hubieses** orado	**hubieseis** orado
oras**e**	oras**en**	**hubiese** orado	**hubiesen** orado

imperativo

—	oremos
ora; no ores	orad; no oréis
ore	oren

gerundio **ordenando** participio de pasado **ordenado**

SINGULAR	PLURAL	SINGULAR	PLURAL
presente de indicativo		perfecto de indicativo	
orden**o**	orden**amos**	**he** ordenado	**hemos** ordenado
orden**as**	orden**áis**	**has** ordenado	**habéis** ordenado
orden**a**	orden**an**	**ha** ordenado	**han** ordenado
imperfecto de indicativo		pluscuamperfecto de indicativo	
orden**aba**	orden**ábamos**	**había** ordenado	**habíamos** ordenado
orden**abas**	orden**abais**	**habías** ordenado	**habíais** ordenado
orden**aba**	orden**aban**	**había** ordenado	**habían** ordenado
pretérito		pretérito anterior	
orden**é**	orden**amos**	**hube** ordenado	**hubimos** ordenado
orden**aste**	orden**asteis**	**hubiste** ordenado	**hubisteis** ordenado
orden**ó**	orden**aron**	**hubo** ordenado	**hubieron** ordenado
futuro		futuro perfecto	
ordenar**é**	ordenar**emos**	**habré** ordenado	**habremos** ordenado
ordenar**ás**	ordenar**éis**	**habrás** ordenado	**habréis** ordenado
ordenar**á**	ordenar**án**	**habrá** ordenado	**habrán** ordenado
condicional simple		condicional compuesto	
ordenar**ía**	ordenar**íamos**	**habría** ordenado	**habríamos** ordenado
ordenar**ías**	ordenar**íais**	**habrías** ordenado	**habríais** ordenado
ordenar**ía**	ordenar**ían**	**habría** ordenado	**habrían** ordenado
presente de subjuntivo		perfecto de subjuntivo	
orden**e**	orden**emos**	**haya** ordenado	**hayamos** ordenado
orden**es**	orden**éis**	**hayas** ordenado	**hayáis** ordenado
orden**e**	orden**en**	**haya** ordenado	**hayan** ordenado
imperfecto de subjuntivo		pluscuamperfecto de subjuntivo	
ordenar**a**	ordenár**amos**	**hubiera** ordenado	**hubiéramos** ordenado
ordenar**as**	ordenar**ais**	**hubieras** ordenado	**hubierais** ordenado
ordenar**a**	ordenar**an**	**hubiera** ordenado	**hubieran** ordenado
OR		OR	
ordenas**e**	ordenás**emos**	**hubiese** ordenado	**hubiésemos** ordenado
ordenas**es**	ordenas**eis**	**hubieses** ordenado	**hubieseis** ordenado
ordenas**e**	ordenas**en**	**hubiese** ordenado	**hubiesen** ordenado

imperativo

—	ordenemos
ordena; no ordenes	ordenad; no ordenéis
ordene	ordenen

O

organizar — to organize

gerundio **organizando** participio de pasado **organizado**

SINGULAR	PLURAL
presente de indicativo	
organiz**o**	organiz**amos**
organiz**as**	organiz**áis**
organiz**a**	organiz**an**
imperfecto de indicativo	
organiz**aba**	organiz**ábamos**
organiz**abas**	organiz**abais**
organiz**aba**	organiz**aban**
pretérito	
organic**é**	organiz**amos**
organiz**aste**	organiz**asteis**
organiz**ó**	organiz**aron**
futuro	
organizar**é**	organizar**emos**
organizar**ás**	organizar**éis**
organizar**á**	organizar**án**
condicional simple	
organizar**ía**	organizar**íamos**
organizar**ías**	organizar**íais**
organizar**ía**	organizar**ían**
presente de subjuntivo	
organic**e**	organic**emos**
organic**es**	organic**éis**
organic**e**	organic**en**
imperfecto de subjuntivo	
organizar**a**	organizár**amos**
organizar**as**	organizar**ais**
organizar**a**	organizar**an**
OR	
organizas**e**	organizás**emos**
organizas**es**	organizas**eis**
organizas**e**	organizas**en**
imperativo	
—	organicemos
organiza; no organices	organizad; no organicéis
organice	organicen

SINGULAR	PLURAL
perfecto de indicativo	
he organizado	**hemos** organizado
has organizado	**habéis** organizado
ha organizado	**han** organizado
pluscuamperfecto de indicativo	
había organizado	**habíamos** organizado
habías organizado	**habíais** organizado
había organizado	**habían** organizado
pretérito anterior	
hube organizado	**hubimos** organizado
hubiste organizado	**hubisteis** organizado
hubo organizado	**hubieron** organizado
futuro perfecto	
habré organizado	**habremos** organizado
habrás organizado	**habréis** organizado
habrá organizado	**habrán** organizado
condicional compuesto	
habría organizado	**habríamos** organizado
habrías organizado	**habríais** organizado
habría organizado	**habrían** organizado
perfecto de subjuntivo	
haya organizado	**hayamos** organizado
hayas organizado	**hayáis** organizado
haya organizado	**hayan** organizado
pluscuamperfecto de subjuntivo	
hubiera organizado	**hubiéramos** organizado
hubieras organizado	**hubierais** organizado
hubiera organizado	**hubieran** organizado
OR	
hubiese organizado	**hubiésemos** organizado
hubieses organizado	**hubieseis** organizado
hubiese organizado	**hubiesen** organizado

to dare, to venture — osar

gerundio **osando** participio de pasado **osado**

SINGULAR	PLURAL
presente de indicativo	
os**o**	os**amos**
os**as**	os**áis**
os**a**	os**an**
imperfecto de indicativo	
os**aba**	os**ábamos**
os**abas**	os**abais**
os**aba**	os**aban**
pretérito	
os**é**	os**amos**
os**aste**	os**asteis**
os**ó**	os**aron**
futuro	
osar**é**	osar**emos**
osar**ás**	osar**éis**
osar**á**	osar**án**
condicional simple	
osar**ía**	osar**íamos**
osar**ías**	osar**íais**
osar**ía**	osar**ían**
presente de subjuntivo	
os**e**	os**emos**
os**es**	os**éis**
os**e**	os**en**
imperfecto de subjuntivo	
osar**a**	osár**amos**
osar**as**	osar**ais**
osar**a**	osar**an**
OR	
osas**e**	osás**emos**
osas**es**	osas**eis**
osas**e**	osas**en**
imperativo	
—	osemos
osa; no oses	osad; no oséis
ose	osen

SINGULAR	PLURAL
perfecto de indicativo	
he osado	**hemos** osado
has osado	**habéis** osado
ha osado	**han** osado
pluscuamperfecto de indicativo	
había osado	**habíamos** osado
habías osado	**habíais** osado
había osado	**habían** osado
pretérito anterior	
hube osado	**hubimos** osado
hubiste osado	**hubisteis** osado
hubo osado	**hubieron** osado
futuro perfecto	
habré osado	**habremos** osado
habrás osado	**habréis** osado
habrá osado	**habrán** osado
condicional compuesto	
habría osado	**habríamos** osado
habrías osado	**habríais** osado
habría osado	**habrían** osado
perfecto de subjuntivo	
haya osado	**hayamos** osado
hayas osado	**hayáis** osado
haya osado	**hayan** osado
pluscuamperfecto de subjuntivo	
hubiera osado	**hubiéramos** osado
hubieras osado	**hubierais** osado
hubiera osado	**hubieran** osado
OR	
hubiese osado	**hubiésemos** osado
hubieses osado	**hubieseis** osado
hubiese osado	**hubiesen** osado

ostentar — to flaunt

gerundio **ostentando** — participio de pasado **ostentado**

SINGULAR	PLURAL	SINGULAR	PLURAL
presente de indicativo		perfecto de indicativo	
ostent**o**	ostent**amos**	**he** ostentado	**hemos** ostentado
ostent**as**	ostent**áis**	**has** ostentado	**habéis** ostentado
ostent**a**	ostent**an**	**ha** ostentado	**han** ostentado
imperfecto de indicativo		pluscuamperfecto de indicativo	
ostent**aba**	ostent**ábamos**	**había** ostentado	**habíamos** ostentado
ostent**abas**	ostent**abais**	**habías** ostentado	**habíais** ostentado
ostent**aba**	ostent**aban**	**había** ostentado	**habían** ostentado
pretérito		pretérito anterior	
ostent**é**	ostent**amos**	**hube** ostentado	**hubimos** ostentado
ostent**aste**	ostent**asteis**	**hubiste** ostentado	**hubisteis** ostentado
ostent**ó**	ostent**aron**	**hubo** ostentado	**hubieron** ostentado
futuro		futuro perfecto	
ostentar**é**	ostentar**emos**	**habré** ostentado	**habremos** ostentado
ostentar**ás**	ostentar**éis**	**habrás** ostentado	**habréis** ostentado
ostentar**á**	ostentar**án**	**habrá** ostentado	**habrán** ostentado
condicional simple		condicional compuesto	
ostentar**ía**	ostentar**íamos**	**habría** ostentado	**habríamos** ostentado
ostentar**ías**	ostentar**íais**	**habrías** ostentado	**habríais** ostentado
ostentar**ía**	ostentar**ían**	**habría** ostentado	**habrían** ostentado
presente de subjuntivo		perfecto de subjuntivo	
ostent**e**	ostent**emos**	**haya** ostentado	**hayamos** ostentado
ostent**es**	ostent**éis**	**hayas** ostentado	**hayáis** ostentado
ostent**e**	ostent**en**	**haya** ostentado	**hayan** ostentado
imperfecto de subjuntivo		pluscuamperfecto de subjuntivo	
ostentar**a**	ostentár**amos**	**hubiera** ostentado	**hubiéramos** ostentado
ostentar**as**	ostentar**ais**	**hubieras** ostentado	**hubierais** ostentado
ostentar**a**	ostentar**an**	**hubiera** ostentado	**hubieran** ostentado
OR		OR	
ostentas**e**	ostentás**emos**	**hubiese** ostentado	**hubiésemos** ostentado
ostentas**es**	ostentas**eis**	**hubieses** ostentado	**hubieseis** ostentado
ostentas**e**	ostentas**en**	**hubiese** ostentado	**hubiesen** ostentado

imperativo

—	ostentemos
ostenta; no ostentes	ostentad; no ostentéis
ostente	ostenten

to grant, to award — otorgar

gerundio **otorgando** participio de pasado **otorgado**

SINGULAR	PLURAL
presente de indicativo	
otorg**o**	otorg**amos**
otorg**as**	otorg**áis**
otorg**a**	otorg**an**
imperfecto de indicativo	
otorg**aba**	otorg**ábamos**
otorg**abas**	otorg**abais**
otorg**aba**	otorg**aban**
pretérito	
otorgu**é**	otorg**amos**
otorg**aste**	otorg**asteis**
otorg**ó**	otorg**aron**
futuro	
otorgar**é**	otorgar**emos**
otorgar**ás**	otorgar**éis**
otorgar**á**	otorgar**án**
condicional simple	
otorgar**ía**	otorgar**íamos**
otorgar**ías**	otorgar**íais**
otorgar**ía**	otorgar**ían**
presente de subjuntivo	
otorgu**e**	otorgu**emos**
otorgu**es**	otorgu**éis**
otorgu**e**	otorgu**en**
imperfecto de subjuntivo	
otorgar**a**	otorgár**amos**
otorgar**as**	otorgar**ais**
otorgar**a**	otorgar**an**
OR	
otorgas**e**	otorgás**emos**
otorgas**es**	otorgas**eis**
otorgas**e**	otorgas**en**
imperativo	
—	otorguemos
otorga; no otorgues	otorgad; no otorguéis
otorgue	otorguen

SINGULAR	PLURAL
perfecto de indicativo	
he otorgado	**hemos** otorgado
has otorgado	**habéis** otorgado
ha otorgado	**han** otorgado
pluscuamperfecto de indicativo	
había otorgado	**habíamos** otorgado
habías otorgado	**habíais** otorgado
había otorgado	**habían** otorgado
pretérito anterior	
hube otorgado	**hubimos** otorgado
hubiste otorgado	**hubisteis** otorgado
hubo otorgado	**hubieron** otorgado
futuro perfecto	
habré otorgado	**habremos** otorgado
habrás otorgado	**habréis** otorgado
habrá otorgado	**habrán** otorgado
condicional compuesto	
habría otorgado	**habríamos** otorgado
habrías otorgado	**habríais** otorgado
habría otorgado	**habrían** otorgado
perfecto de subjuntivo	
haya otorgado	**hayamos** otorgado
hayas otorgado	**hayáis** otorgado
haya otorgado	**hayan** otorgado
pluscuamperfecto de subjuntivo	
hubiera otorgado	**hubiéramos** otorgado
hubieras otorgado	**hubierais** otorgado
hubiera otorgado	**hubieran** otorgado
OR	
hubiese otorgado	**hubiésemos** otorgado
hubieses otorgado	**hubieseis** otorgado
hubiese otorgado	**hubiesen** otorgado

pagar — to pay for

gerundio **pagando** — participio de pasado **pagado**

SINGULAR	PLURAL	SINGULAR	PLURAL
presente de indicativo		perfecto de indicativo	
pag**o**	pag**amos**	**he** pagado	**hemos** pagado
pag**as**	pag**áis**	**has** pagado	**habéis** pagado
pag**a**	pag**an**	**ha** pagado	**han** pagado
imperfecto de indicativo		pluscuamperfecto de indicativo	
pag**aba**	pag**ábamos**	**había** pagado	**habíamos** pagado
pag**abas**	pag**abais**	**habías** pagado	**habíais** pagado
pag**aba**	pag**aban**	**había** pagado	**habían** pagado
pretérito		pretérito anterior	
pagu**é**	pag**amos**	**hube** pagado	**hubimos** pagado
pag**aste**	pag**asteis**	**hubiste** pagado	**hubisteis** pagado
pag**ó**	pag**aron**	**hubo** pagado	**hubieron** pagado
futuro		futuro perfecto	
pagar**é**	pagar**emos**	**habré** pagado	**habremos** pagado
pagar**ás**	pagar**éis**	**habrás** pagado	**habréis** pagado
pagar**á**	pagar**án**	**habrá** pagado	**habrán** pagado
condicional simple		condicional compuesto	
pagar**ía**	pagar**íamos**	**habría** pagado	**habríamos** pagado
pagar**ías**	pagar**íais**	**habrías** pagado	**habríais** pagado
pagar**ía**	pagar**ían**	**habría** pagado	**habrían** pagado
presente de subjuntivo		perfecto de subjuntivo	
pagu**e**	pagu**emos**	**haya** pagado	**hayamos** pagado
pagu**es**	pagu**éis**	**hayas** pagado	**hayáis** pagado
pagu**e**	pagu**en**	**haya** pagado	**hayan** pagado
imperfecto de subjuntivo		pluscuamperfecto de subjuntivo	
pagar**a**	pagár**amos**	**hubiera** pagado	**hubiéramos** pagado
pagar**as**	pagar**ais**	**hubieras** pagado	**hubierais** pagado
pagar**a**	pagar**an**	**hubiera** pagado	**hubieran** pagado
OR		OR	
pagas**e**	pagás**emos**	**hubiese** pagado	**hubiésemos** pagado
pagas**es**	pagas**eis**	**hubieses** pagado	**hubieseis** pagado
pagas**e**	pagas**en**	**hubiese** pagado	**hubiesen** pagado

imperativo

—	paguemos
paga; no pagues	pagad; no paguéis
pague	paguen

MUST KNOW VERB

to stop someone or something, to stand **parar**

gerundio **parando** participio de pasado **parado**

SINGULAR	PLURAL
presente de indicativo	
par**o**	par**amos**
par**as**	par**áis**
par**a**	par**an**
imperfecto de indicativo	
par**aba**	par**ábamos**
par**abas**	par**abais**
par**aba**	par**aban**
pretérito	
par**é**	par**amos**
par**aste**	par**asteis**
par**ó**	par**aron**
futuro	
parar**é**	parar**emos**
parar**ás**	parar**éis**
parar**á**	parar**án**
condicional simple	
parar**ía**	parar**íamos**
parar**ías**	parar**íais**
parar**ía**	parar**ían**
presente de subjuntivo	
par**e**	par**emos**
par**es**	par**éis**
par**e**	par**en**
imperfecto de subjuntivo	
parar**a**	parár**amos**
parar**as**	parar**ais**
parar**a**	parar**an**
OR	
paras**e**	parás**emos**
paras**es**	paras**eis**
paras**e**	paras**en**
imperativo	
—	paremos
para; no pares	parad; no paréis
pare	paren

SINGULAR	PLURAL
perfecto de indicativo	
he parado	**hemos** parado
has parado	**habéis** parado
ha parado	**han** parado
pluscuamperfecto de indicativo	
había parado	**habíamos** parado
habías parado	**habíais** parado
había parado	**habían** parado
pretérito anterior	
hube parado	**hubimos** parado
hubiste parado	**hubisteis** parado
hubo parado	**hubieron** parado
futuro perfecto	
habré parado	**habremos** parado
habrás parado	**habréis** parado
habrá parado	**habrán** parado
condicional compuesto	
habría parado	**habríamos** parado
habrías parado	**habríais** parado
habría parado	**habrían** parado
perfecto de subjuntivo	
haya parado	**hayamos** parado
hayas parado	**hayáis** parado
haya parado	**hayan** parado
pluscuamperfecto de subjuntivo	
hubiera parado	**hubiéramos** parado
hubieras parado	**hubierais** parado
hubiera parado	**hubieran** parado
OR	
hubiese parado	**hubiésemos** parado
hubieses parado	**hubieseis** parado
hubiese parado	**hubiesen** parado

pararse — to stop oneself, to stand

gerundio **parándose** participio de pasado **parado**

SINGULAR	PLURAL	SINGULAR	PLURAL
presente de indicativo		perfecto de indicativo	
me par**o**	nos par**amos**	**me he** parado	**nos hemos** parado
te par**as**	os par**áis**	**te has** parado	**os habéis** parado
se par**a**	se par**an**	**se ha** parado	**se han** parado
imperfecto de indicativo		pluscuamperfecto de indicativo	
me par**aba**	nos par**ábamos**	**me había** parado	**nos habíamos** parado
te par**abas**	os par**abais**	**te habías** parado	**os habíais** parado
se par**aba**	se par**aban**	**se había** parado	**se habían** parado
pretérito		pretérito anterior	
me par**é**	nos par**amos**	**me hube** parado	**nos hubimos** parado
te par**aste**	os par**asteis**	**te hubiste** parado	**os hubisteis** parado
se par**ó**	se par**aron**	**se hubo** parado	**se hubieron** parado
futuro		futuro perfecto	
me parar**é**	nos parar**emos**	**me habré** parado	**nos habremos** parado
te parar**ás**	os parar**éis**	**te habrás** parado	**os habréis** parado
se parar**á**	se parar**án**	**se habrá** parado	**se habrán** parado
condicional simple		condicional compuesto	
me parar**ía**	nos parar**íamos**	**me habría** parado	**nos habríamos** parado
te parar**ías**	os parar**íais**	**te habrías** parado	**os habríais** parado
se parar**ía**	se parar**ían**	**se habría** parado	**se habrían** parado
presente de subjuntivo		perfecto de subjuntivo	
me par**e**	nos par**emos**	**me haya** parado	**nos hayamos** parado
te par**es**	os par**éis**	**te hayas** parado	**os hayáis** parado
se par**e**	se par**en**	**se haya** parado	**se hayan** parado
imperfecto de subjuntivo		pluscuamperfecto de subjuntivo	
me parar**a**	nos parár**amos**	**me hubiera** parado	**nos hubiéramos** parado
te parar**as**	os parar**ais**	**te hubieras** parado	**os hubierais** parado
se parar**a**	se parar**an**	**se hubiera** parado	**se hubieran** parado
OR		OR	
me paras**e**	nos parás**emos**	**me hubiese** parado	**nos hubiésemos** parado
te paras**es**	os paras**eis**	**te hubieses** parado	**os hubieseis** parado
se paras**e**	se paras**en**	**se hubiese** parado	**se hubiesen** parado

imperativo

—	parémonos
párate; no te pares	paraos; no os paréis
párese	párense

gerundio **pareciendo** participio de pasado **parecido**

SINGULAR	PLURAL
presente de indicativo	
parezc**o**	parec**emos**
parec**es**	parec**éis**
parec**e**	parec**en**
imperfecto de indicativo	
parec**ía**	parec**íamos**
parec**ías**	parec**íais**
parec**ía**	parec**ían**
pretérito	
parec**í**	parec**imos**
parec**iste**	parec**isteis**
parec**ió**	parec**ieron**
futuro	
parecer**é**	parecer**emos**
parecer**ás**	parecer**éis**
parecer**á**	parecer**án**
condicional simple	
parecer**ía**	parecer**íamos**
parecer**ías**	parecer**íais**
parecer**ía**	parecer**ían**
presente de subjuntivo	
parezc**a**	parezc**amos**
parezc**as**	parezc**áis**
parezc**a**	parezc**an**
imperfecto de subjuntivo	
parecier**a**	pareciér**amos**
parecier**as**	parecier**ais**
parecier**a**	parecier**an**
OR	
parecies**e**	pareciés**emos**
parecies**es**	parecies**eis**
parecies**e**	parecies**en**
imperativo	
—	parezcamos
parece; no parezcas	pareced; no parezcáis
parezca	parezcan

SINGULAR	PLURAL
perfecto de indicativo	
he parecido	**hemos** parecido
has parecido	**habéis** parecido
ha parecido	**han** parecido
pluscuamperfecto de indicativo	
había parecido	**habíamos** parecido
habías parecido	**habíais** parecido
había parecido	**habían** parecido
pretérito anterior	
hube parecido	**hubimos** parecido
hubiste parecido	**hubisteis** parecido
hubo parecido	**hubieron** parecido
futuro perfecto	
habré parecido	**habremos** parecido
habrás parecido	**habréis** parecido
habrá parecido	**habrán** parecido
condicional compuesto	
habría parecido	**habríamos** parecido
habrías parecido	**habríais** parecido
habría parecido	**habrían** parecido
perfecto de subjuntivo	
haya parecido	**hayamos** parecido
hayas parecido	**hayáis** parecido
haya parecido	**hayan** parecido
pluscuamperfecto de subjuntivo	
hubiera parecido	**hubiéramos** parecido
hubieras parecido	**hubierais** parecido
hubiera parecido	**hubieran** parecido
OR	
hubiese parecido	**hubiésemos** parecido
hubieses parecido	**hubieseis** parecido
hubiese parecido	**hubiesen** parecido

parecerse — to resemble each other

gerundio **pareciéndose** participio de pasado **parecido**

presente de indicativo

SINGULAR	PLURAL
me parezc**o**	nos parec**emos**
te parec**es**	os parec**éis**
se parec**e**	se parec**en**

imperfecto de indicativo

SINGULAR	PLURAL
me parec**ía**	nos parec**íamos**
te parec**ías**	os parec**íais**
se parec**ía**	se parec**ían**

pretérito

SINGULAR	PLURAL
me parec**í**	nos parec**imos**
te parec**iste**	os parec**isteis**
se parec**ió**	se parec**ieron**

futuro

SINGULAR	PLURAL
me parecer**é**	nos parecer**emos**
te parecer**ás**	os parecer**éis**
se parecer**á**	se parecer**án**

condicional simple

SINGULAR	PLURAL
me parecer**ía**	nos parecer**íamos**
te parecer**ías**	os parecer**íais**
se parecer**ía**	se parecer**ían**

presente de subjuntivo

SINGULAR	PLURAL
me parezc**a**	nos parezc**amos**
te parezc**as**	os parezc**áis**
se parezc**a**	se parezc**an**

imperfecto de subjuntivo

SINGULAR	PLURAL
me parecier**a**	nos pareciér**amos**
te parecier**as**	os parecier**ais**
se parecier**a**	se parecier**an**
OR	
me parecies**e**	nos pareciés**emos**
te parecies**es**	os parecies**eis**
se parecies**e**	se parecies**en**

imperativo

SINGULAR	PLURAL
—	parezcámonos
parécete; no te parezcas	pareceos; no os parezcáis
parézcase	parézcanse

perfecto de indicativo

SINGULAR	PLURAL
me he parecido	**nos hemos** parecido
te has parecido	**os habéis** parecido
se ha parecido	**se han** parecido

pluscuamperfecto de indicativo

SINGULAR	PLURAL
me había parecido	**nos habíamos** parecido
te habías parecido	**os habíais** parecido
se había parecido	**se habían** parecido

pretérito anterior

SINGULAR	PLURAL
me hube parecido	**nos hubimos** parecido
te hubiste parecido	**os hubisteis** parecido
se hubo parecido	**se hubieron** parecido

futuro perfecto

SINGULAR	PLURAL
me habré parecido	**nos habremos** parecido
te habrás parecido	**os habréis** parecido
se habrá parecido	**se habrán** parecido

condicional compuesto

SINGULAR	PLURAL
me habría parecido	**nos habríamos** parecido
te habrías parecido	**os habríais** parecido
se habría parecido	**se habrían** parecido

perfecto de subjuntivo

SINGULAR	PLURAL
me haya parecido	**nos hayamos** parecido
te hayas parecido	**os hayáis** parecido
se haya parecido	**se hayan** parecido

pluscuamperfecto de subjuntivo

SINGULAR	PLURAL
me hubiera parecido	**nos hubiéramos** parecido
te hubieras parecido	**os hubierais** parecido
se hubiera parecido	**se hubieran** parecido
OR	
me hubiese parecido	**nos hubiésemos** parecido
te hubieses parecido	**os hubieseis** parecido
se hubiese parecido	**se hubiesen** parecido

to leave, to divide

partir

gerundio **partiendo** participio de pasado **partido**

SINGULAR	PLURAL	SINGULAR	PLURAL
presente de indicativo		perfecto de indicativo	
part**o**	part**imos**	**he** partido	**hemos** partido
part**es**	part**ís**	**has** partido	**habéis** partido
part**e**	part**en**	**ha** partido	**han** partido
imperfecto de indicativo		pluscuamperfecto de indicativo	
part**ía**	part**íamos**	**había** partido	**habíamos** partido
part**ías**	part**íais**	**habías** partido	**habíais** partido
part**ía**	part**ían**	**había** partido	**habían** partido
pretérito		pretérito anterior	
part**í**	part**imos**	**hube** partido	**hubimos** partido
part**iste**	part**isteis**	**hubiste** partido	**hubisteis** partido
part**ió**	part**ieron**	**hubo** partido	**hubieron** partido
futuro		futuro perfecto	
partir**é**	partir**emos**	**habré** partido	**habremos** partido
partir**ás**	partir**éis**	**habrás** partido	**habréis** partido
partir**á**	partir**án**	**habrá** partido	**habrán** partido
condicional simple		condicional compuesto	
partir**ía**	partir**íamos**	**habría** partido	**habríamos** partido
partir**ías**	partir**íais**	**habrías** partido	**habríais** partido
partir**ía**	partir**ían**	**habría** partido	**habrían** partido
presente de subjuntivo		perfecto de subjuntivo	
part**a**	part**amos**	**haya** partido	**hayamos** partido
part**as**	part**áis**	**hayas** partido	**hayáis** partido
part**a**	part**an**	**haya** partido	**hayan** partido
imperfecto de subjuntivo		pluscuamperfecto de subjuntivo	
partier**a**	partiér**amos**	**hubiera** partido	**hubiéramos** partido
partier**as**	partier**ais**	**hubieras** partido	**hubierais** partido
partier**a**	partier**an**	**hubiera** partido	**hubieran** partido
OR		OR	
parties**e**	partiés**emos**	**hubiese** partido	**hubiésemos** partido
partie**ses**	parties**eis**	**hubieses** partido	**hubieseis** partido
parties**e**	parties**en**	**hubiese** partido	**hubiesen** partido

imperativo

—	partamos
parte; no partas	partid; no partáis
parta	partan

P

gerundio **pasando** participio de pasado **pasado**

SINGULAR	PLURAL
presente de indicativo	
pas**o**	pas**amos**
pas**as**	pas**áis**
pas**a**	pas**an**
imperfecto de indicativo	
pas**aba**	pas**ábamos**
pas**abas**	pas**abais**
pas**aba**	pas**aban**
pretérito	
pas**é**	pas**amos**
pas**aste**	pas**asteis**
pas**ó**	pas**aron**
futuro	
pasar**é**	pasar**emos**
pasar**ás**	pasar**éis**
pasar**á**	pasar**án**
condicional simple	
pasar**ía**	pasar**íamos**
pasar**ías**	pasar**íais**
pasar**ía**	pasar**ían**
presente de subjuntivo	
pas**e**	pas**emos**
pas**es**	pas**éis**
pas**e**	pas**en**
imperfecto de subjuntivo	
pasar**a**	pasár**amos**
pasar**as**	pasar**ais**
pasar**a**	pasar**an**
OR	
pase**e**	pasás**emos**
pasas**es**	pasas**eis**
pasas**e**	pasas**en**
imperativo	
—	pasemos
pasa; no pases	pasad; no paséis
pase	pasen

SINGULAR	PLURAL
perfecto de indicativo	
he pasado	**hemos** pasado
has pasado	**habéis** pasado
ha pasado	**han** pasado
pluscuamperfecto de indicativo	
había pasado	**habíamos** pasado
habías pasado	**habíais** pasado
había pasado	**habían** pasado
pretérito anterior	
hube pasado	**hubimos** pasado
hubiste pasado	**hubisteis** pasado
hubo pasado	**hubieron** pasado
futuro perfecto	
habré pasado	**habremos** pasado
habrás pasado	**habréis** pasado
habrá pasado	**habrán** pasado
condicional compuesto	
habría pasado	**habríamos** pasado
habrías pasado	**habríais** pasado
habría pasado	**habrían** pasado
perfecto de subjuntivo	
haya pasado	**hayamos** pasado
hayas pasado	**hayáis** pasado
haya pasado	**hayan** pasado
pluscuamperfecto de subjuntivo	
hubiera pasado	**hubiéramos** pasado
hubieras pasado	**hubierais** pasado
hubiera pasado	**hubieran** pasado
OR	
hubiese pasado	**hubiésemos** pasado
hubieses pasado	**hubieseis** pasado
hubiese pasado	**hubiesen** pasado

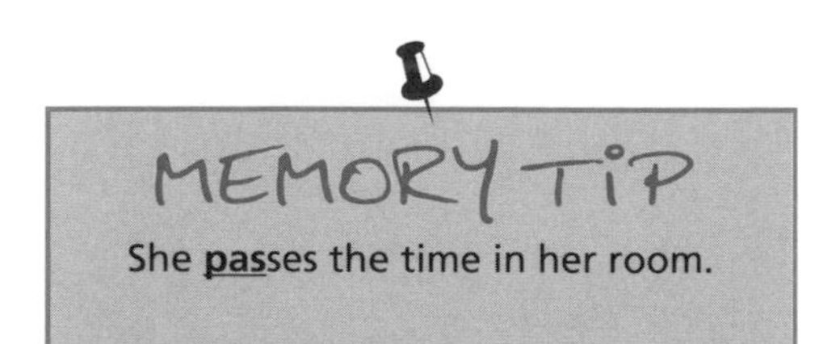

gerundio **paseándose** participio de pasado **paseado**

SINGULAR	PLURAL	SINGULAR	PLURAL
presente de indicativo		perfecto de indicativo	
me pase**o**	nos pase**amos**	**me he** paseado	**nos hemos** paseado
te pase**as**	os pase**áis**	**te has** paseado	**os habéis** paseado
se pase**a**	se pase**an**	**se ha** paseado	**se han** paseado
imperfecto de indicativo		pluscuamperfecto de indicativo	
me pase**aba**	nos pase**ábamos**	**me había** paseado	**nos habíamos** paseado
te pase**abas**	os pase**abais**	**te habías** paseado	**os habíais** paseado
se pase**aba**	se pase**aban**	**se había** paseado	**se habían** paseado
pretérito		pretérito anterior	
me pase**é**	nos pase**amos**	**me hube** paseado	**nos hubimos** paseado
te pase**aste**	os pase**asteis**	**te hubiste** paseado	**os hubisteis** paseado
se pase**ó**	se pase**aron**	**se hubo** paseado	**se hubieron** paseado
futuro		futuro perfecto	
me pasear**é**	nos pasear**emos**	**me habré** paseado	**nos habremos** paseado
te pasear**ás**	os pasear**éis**	**te habrás** paseado	**os habréis** paseado
se pasear**á**	se pasear**án**	**se habrá** paseado	**se habrán** paseado
condicional simple		condicional compuesto	
me pasear**ía**	nos pasear**íamos**	**me habría** paseado	**nos habríamos** paseado
te pasear**ías**	os pasear**íais**	**te habrías** paseado	**os habríais** paseado
se pasear**ía**	se pasear**ían**	**se habría** paseado	**se habrían** paseado
presente de subjuntivo		perfecto de subjuntivo	
me pase**e**	nos pase**emos**	**me haya** paseado	**nos hayamos** paseado
te pase**es**	os pase**éis**	**te hayas** paseado	**os hayáis** paseado
se pase**e**	se pase**en**	**se haya** paseado	**se hayan** paseado
imperfecto de subjuntivo		pluscuamperfecto de subjuntivo	
me pasear**a**	nos paseár**amos**	**me hubiera** paseado	**nos hubiéramos** paseado
te pasear**as**	os pasear**ais**	**te hubieras** paseado	**os hubierais** paseado
se pasear**a**	se pasear**an**	**se hubiera** paseado	**se hubieran** paseado
OR		OR	
me pasease**e**	nos paseás**emos**	**me hubiese** paseado	**nos hubiésemos** paseado
te pasease**es**	os pasease**is**	**te hubieses** paseado	**os hubieseis** paseado
se pasease**e**	se pasease**en**	**se hubiese** paseado	**se hubiesen** paseado

imperativo

—	paseémonos
paséate; no te pasees	paseaos; no os paseéis
paséese	paséense

gerundio **pidiendo** participio de pasado **pedido**

SINGULAR	PLURAL	SINGULAR	PLURAL
presente de indicativo		perfecto de indicativo	
pid**o**	ped**imos**	**he** pedido	**hemos** pedido
pid**es**	ped**ís**	**has** pedido	**habéis** pedido
pid**e**	pid**en**	**ha** pedido	**han** pedido
imperfecto de indicativo		pluscuamperfecto de indicativo	
ped**ía**	ped**íamos**	**había** pedido	**habíamos** pedido
ped**ías**	ped**íais**	**habías** pedido	**habíais** pedido
ped**ía**	ped**ían**	**había** pedido	**habían** pedido
pretérito		pretérito anterior	
ped**í**	ped**imos**	**hube** pedido	**hubimos** pedido
ped**iste**	ped**isteis**	**hubiste** pedido	**hubisteis** pedido
pidi**ó**	pid**ieron**	**hubo** pedido	**hubieron** pedido
futuro		futuro perfecto	
pedir**é**	pedir**emos**	**habré** pedido	**habremos** pedido
pedir**ás**	pedir**éis**	**habrás** pedido	**habréis** pedido
pedir**á**	pedir**án**	**habrá** pedido	**habrán** pedido
condicional simple		condicional compuesto	
pedir**ía**	pedir**íamos**	**habría** pedido	**habríamos** pedido
pedir**ías**	pedir**íais**	**habrías** pedido	**habríais** pedido
pedir**ía**	pedir**ían**	**habría** pedido	**habrían** pedido
presente de subjuntivo		perfecto de subjuntivo	
pid**a**	pid**amos**	**haya** pedido	**hayamos** pedido
pid**as**	pid**áis**	**hayas** pedido	**hayáis** pedido
pid**a**	pid**an**	**haya** pedido	**hayan** pedido
imperfecto de subjuntivo		pluscuamperfecto de subjuntivo	
pidier**a**	pidiér**amos**	**hubiera** pedido	**hubiéramos** pedido
pidier**as**	pidier**ais**	**hubieras** pedido	**hubierais** pedido
pidier**a**	pidier**an**	**hubiera** pedido	**hubieran** pedido
OR		OR	
pidies**e**	pidiés**emos**	**hubiese** pedido	**hubiésemos** pedido
pidies**es**	pidies**eis**	**hubieses** pedido	**hubieseis** pedido
pidies**e**	pidies**en**	**hubiese** pedido	**hubiesen** pedido

imperativo

—	pidamos
pide; no pidas	pedid; no pidáis
pida	pidan

to hit, to slap, to stick **pegar**

gerundio **pegando** participio de pasado **pegado**

SINGULAR	PLURAL
presente de indicativo	
peg**o**	peg**amos**
peg**as**	peg**áis**
peg**a**	peg**an**
imperfecto de indicativo	
peg**aba**	peb**ábamos**
peg**abas**	peg**abais**
peg**aba**	peg**aban**
pretérito	
pegu**é**	peg**amos**
peg**aste**	pesg**asteis**
peg**ó**	peg**aron**
futuro	
pegar**é**	pegar**emos**
pegar**ás**	pegar**éis**
pegar**á**	pegar**án**
condicional simple	
pegar**ía**	pegar**íamos**
pegar**ías**	pegar**íais**
pegar**ía**	pegar**ían**
presente de subjuntivo	
pegu**e**	pegu**emos**
pegu**es**	pegu**éis**
pegu**e**	pegu**en**
imperfecto de subjuntivo	
pegar**a**	pegár**amos**
pegar**as**	pegar**ais**
pegar**a**	pegar**an**
OR	
pegas**e**	pegás**emos**
pegas**es**	pegas**eis**
pegas**e**	pegas**en**
imperativo	
—	peguemos
pega; no pegues	pegad; no peguéis
pegue	peguen

SINGULAR	PLURAL
perfecto de indicativo	
he pegado	**hemos** pegado
has pegado	**habéis** pegado
ha pegado	**han** pegado
pluscuamperfecto de indicativo	
había pegado	**habíamos** pegado
habías pegado	**habíais** pegado
había pegado	**habían** pegado
pretérito anterior	
hube pegado	**hubimos** pegado
hubiste pegado	**hubisteis** pegado
hubo pegado	**hubieron** pegado
futuro perfecto	
habré pegado	**habremos** pegado
habrás pegado	**habréis** pegado
habrá pegado	**habrán** pegado
condicional compuesto	
habría pegado	**habríamos** pegado
habrías pegado	**habríais** pegado
habría pegado	**habrían** pegado
perfecto de subjuntivo	
haya pegado	**hayamos** pegado
hayas pegado	**hayáis** pegado
haya pegado	**hayan** pegado
pluscuamperfecto de subjuntivo	
hubiera pegado	**hubiéramos** pegado
hubieras pegado	**hubierais** pegado
hubiera pegado	**hubieran** pegado
OR	
hubiese pegado	**hubiésemos** pegado
hubieses pegado	**hubieseis** pegado
hubiese pegado	**hubiesen** pegado

peinarse — to comb one's hair

gerundio **peinándose** participio de pasado **peinado**

SINGULAR	PLURAL	SINGULAR	PLURAL
presente de indicativo		perfecto de indicativo	
me pein**o**	nos pein**amos**	**me he** peinado	**nos hemos** peinado
te pein**as**	os pein**áis**	**te has** peinado	**os habéis** peinado
se pein**a**	se pein**an**	**se ha** peinado	**se han** peinado
imperfecto de indicativo		pluscuamperfecto de indicativo	
me pein**aba**	nos pein**ábamos**	**me había** peinado	**nos habíamos** peinado
te pein**abas**	os pein**abais**	**te habías** peinado	**os habíais** peinado
se pein**aba**	se pein**aban**	**se había** peinado	**se habían** peinado
pretérito		pretérito anterior	
me pein**é**	nos pein**amos**	**me hube** peinado	**nos hubimos** peinado
te pein**aste**	os pein**asteis**	**te hubiste** peinado	**os hubisteis** peinado
se pein**ó**	se pein**aron**	**se hubo** peinado	**se hubieron** peinado
futuro		futuro perfecto	
me peinar**é**	nos peinar**emos**	**me habré** peinado	**nos habremos** peinado
te peinar**ás**	os peinar**éis**	**te habrás** peinado	**os habréis** peinado
se peinar**á**	se peinar**án**	**se habrá** peinado	**se habrán** peinado
condicional simple		condicional compuesto	
me peinar**ía**	nos peinar**íamos**	**me habría** peinado	**nos habríamos** peinado
te peinar**ías**	os peinar**íais**	**te habrías** peinado	**os habríais** peinado
se peinar**ía**	se peinar**ían**	**se habría** peinado	**se habrían** peinado
presente de subjuntivo		perfecto de subjuntivo	
me pein**e**	nos pein**emos**	**me haya** peinado	**nos hayamos** peinado
te pein**es**	os pein**éis**	**te hayas** peinado	**os hayáis** peinado
se pein**e**	se pein**en**	**se haya** peinado	**se hayan** peinado
imperfecto de subjuntivo		pluscuamperfecto de subjuntivo	
me peinar**a**	nos peinár**amos**	**me hubiera** peinado	**nos hubiéramos** peinado
te peinar**as**	os peinar**ais**	**te hubieras** peinado	**os hubierais** peinado
se peinar**a**	se peinar**an**	**se hubiera** peinado	**se hubieran** peinado
OR		OR	
me peinas**e**	nos peinás**emos**	**me hubiese** peinado	**nos hubiésemos** peinado
te peinas**es**	os peinas**eis**	**te hubieses** peinado	**os hubieseis** peinado
se peinas**e**	se peinas**en**	**se hubiese** peinado	**se hubiesen** peinado

imperativo

—	peinémonos
peínate; no te peines	peinaos; no os peinéis
peínese	peínense

to think **pensar**

gerundio **pensando** participio de pasado **pensado**

SINGULAR	PLURAL	SINGULAR	PLURAL
presente de indicativo		perfecto de indicativo	
piens**o**	pens**amos**	**he** pensado	**hemos** pensado
piens**as**	pens**áis**	**has** pensado	**habéis** pensado
piens**a**	piens**an**	**ha** pensado	**han** pensado
imperfecto de indicativo		pluscuamperfecto de indicativo	
pens**aba**	pens**ábamos**	**había** pensado	**habíamos** pensado
pens**abas**	pens**abais**	**habías** pensado	**habíais** pensado
pens**aba**	pens**aban**	**había** pensado	**habían** pensado
pretérito		pretérito anterior	
pens**é**	pens**amos**	**hube** pensado	**hubimos** pensado
pens**aste**	pens**asteis**	**hubiste** pensado	**hubisteis** pensado
pens**ó**	pens**aron**	**hubo** pensado	**hubieron** pensado
futuro		futuro perfecto	
pensar**é**	pensar**emos**	**habré** pensado	**habremos** pensado
pensar**ás**	pensar**éis**	**habrás** pensado	**habréis** pensado
pensar**á**	pensar**án**	**habrá** pensado	**habrán** pensado
condicional simple		condicional compuesto	
pensar**ía**	pensar**íamos**	**habría** pensado	**habríamos** pensado
pensar**ías**	pensar**íais**	**habrías** pensado	**habríais** pensado
pensar**ía**	pensar**ían**	**habría** pensado	**habrían** pensado
presente de subjuntivo		perfecto de subjuntivo	
piens**e**	pens**emos**	**haya** pensado	**hayamos** pensado
piens**es**	pens**éis**	**hayas** pensado	**hayáis** pensado
piens**e**	piens**en**	**haya** pensado	**hayan** pensado
imperfecto de subjuntivo		pluscuamperfecto de subjuntivo	
pensar**a**	pensár**amos**	**hubiera** pensado	**hubiéramos** pensado
pensar**as**	pensar**ais**	**hubieras** pensado	**hubierais** pensado
pensar**a**	pensar**an**	**hubiera** pensado	**hubieran** pensado
OR		OR	
pensas**e**	pensás**emos**	**hubiese** pensado	**hubiésemos** pensado
pensas**es**	pensas**eis**	**hubieses** pensado	**hubieseis** pensado
pensas**e**	pensas**en**	**hubiese** pensado	**hubiesen** pensado

imperativo

—	pensemos
piensa; no pienses	pensad; no penséis
piense	piensen

percibir — to perceive

gerundio **percibiendo** — participio de pasado **percibido**

SINGULAR	PLURAL	SINGULAR	PLURAL
presente de indicativo		perfecto de indicativo	
percib**o**	percib**imos**	**he** percibido	**hemos** percibido
percib**es**	percib**ís**	**has** percibido	**habéis** percibido
percib**e**	percib**en**	**ha** percibido	**han** percibido
imperfecto de indicativo		pluscuamperfecto de indicativo	
percib**ía**	percib**íamos**	**había** percibido	**habíamos** percibido
percib**ías**	percib**íais**	**habías** percibido	**habíais** percibido
percib**ía**	percib**ían**	**había** percibido	**habían** percibido
pretérito		pretérito anterior	
percib**í**	percib**imos**	**hube** percibido	**hubimos** percibido
percib**iste**	percib**isteis**	**hubiste** percibido	**hubisteis** percibido
percibi**ó**	percib**ieron**	**hubo** percibido	**hubieron** percibido
futuro		futuro perfecto	
percibir**é**	percibir**emos**	**habré** percibido	**habremos** percibido
percibir**ás**	percibir**éis**	**habrás** percibido	**habréis** percibido
percibir**á**	percibir**án**	**habrá** percibido	**habrán** percibido
condicional simple		condicional compuesto	
percibir**ía**	percibir**íamos**	**habría** percibido	**habríamos** percibido
percibir**ías**	percibir**íais**	**habrías** percibido	**habríais** percibido
percibir**ía**	percibir**ían**	**habría** percibido	**habrían** percibido
presente de subjuntivo		perfecto de subjuntivo	
percib**a**	percib**amos**	**haya** percibido	**hayamos** percibido
percib**as**	percib**áis**	**hayas** percibido	**hayáis** percibido
percib**a**	percib**an**	**haya** percibido	**hayan** percibido
imperfecto de subjuntivo		pluscuamperfecto de subjuntivo	
percibier**a**	percibiér**amos**	**hubiera** percibido	**hubiéramos** percibido
percibier**as**	percibier**ais**	**hubieras** percibido	**hubierais** percibido
percibier**a**	percibier**an**	**hubiera** percibido	**hubieran** percibido
OR		OR	
percibies**e**	percibiés**emos**	**hubiese** percibido	**hubiésemos** percibido
percibies**es**	percibies**eis**	**hubieses** percibido	**hubieseis** percibido
percibies**e**	percibies**en**	**hubiese** percibido	**hubiesen** percibido

imperativo

—	percibamos
percibe; no percibas	percibid; no percibáis
perciba	perciban

to lose **perder**

gerundio **perdiendo** participio de pasado **perdido**

SINGULAR	PLURAL
presente de indicativo	
pierd**o**	perd**emos**
pierd**es**	perd**éis**
pierd**e**	pierd**en**
imperfecto de indicativo	
perd**ía**	perd**íamos**
perd**ías**	perd**íais**
perd**ía**	perd**ían**
pretérito	
perd**í**	perd**imos**
perd**iste**	perd**isteis**
perd**ió**	perd**ieron**
futuro	
perder**é**	perder**emos**
perder**ás**	perder**éis**
perder**á**	perder**án**
condicional simple	
perder**ía**	perder**íamos**
perder**ías**	perder**íais**
perder**ía**	perder**ían**
presente de subjuntivo	
pierd**a**	perd**amos**
pierd**as**	perd**áis**
pierd**a**	pierd**an**
imperfecto de subjuntivo	
perdier**a**	perdiér**amos**
perdier**as**	perdier**ais**
perdier**a**	perdier**an**
OR	
perdies**e**	perdiés**emos**
perdies**es**	perdies**eis**
perdies**e**	perdies**en**
imperativo	
—	perdamos
pierde; no pierdas	perded; no perdáis
pierda	pierdan

SINGULAR	PLURAL
perfecto de indicativo	
he perdido	**hemos** perdido
has perdido	**habéis** perdido
ha perdido	**han** perdido
pluscuamperfecto de indicativo	
había perdido	**habíamos** perdido
habías perdido	**habíais** perdido
había perdido	**habían** perdido
pretérito anterior	
hube perdido	**hubimos** perdido
hubiste perdido	**hubisteis** perdido
hubo perdido	**hubieron** perdido
futuro perfecto	
habré perdido	**habremos** perdido
habrás perdido	**habréis** perdido
habrá perdido	**habrán** perdido
condicional compuesto	
habría perdido	**habríamos** perdido
habrías perdido	**habríais** perdido
habría perdido	**habrían** perdido
perfecto de subjuntivo	
haya perdido	**hayamos** perdido
hayas perdido	**hayáis** perdido
haya perdido	**hayan** perdido
pluscuamperfecto de subjuntivo	
hubiera perdido	**hubiéramos** perdido
hubieras perdido	**hubierais** perdido
hubiera perdido	**hubieran** perdido
OR	
hubiese perdido	**hubiésemos** perdido
hubieses perdido	**hubieseis** perdido
hubiese perdido	**hubiesen** perdido

perdonar to pardon, to forgive, to excuse

gerundio **perdonando** participio de pasado **perdonado**

SINGULAR	PLURAL	SINGULAR	PLURAL
presente de indicativo		perfecto de indicativo	
perdon**o**	perdon**amos**	**he** perdonado	**hemos** perdonado
perdon**as**	perdon**áis**	**has** perdonado	**habéis** perdonado
perdon**a**	perdon**an**	**ha** perdonado	**han** perdonado
imperfecto de indicativo		pluscuamperfecto de indicativo	
perdon**aba**	perdon**ábamos**	**había** perdonado	**habíamos** perdonado
perdon**abas**	perdon**abais**	**habías** perdonado	**habíais** perdonado
perdon**aba**	perdon**aban**	**había** perdonado	**habían** perdonado
pretérito		pretérito anterior	
perdon**é**	perdon**amos**	**hube** perdonado	**hubimos** perdonado
perdon**aste**	perdon**asteis**	**hubiste** perdonado	**hubisteis** perdonado
perdon**ó**	perdon**aron**	**hubo** perdonado	**hubieron** perdonado
futuro		futuro perfecto	
perdonar**é**	perdonar**emos**	**habré** perdonado	**habremos** perdonado
perdonar**ás**	perdonar**éis**	**habrás** perdonado	**habréis** perdonado
perdonar**á**	perdonar**án**	**habrá** perdonado	**habrán** perdonado
condicional simple		condicional compuesto	
perdonar**ía**	perdonar**íamos**	**habría** perdonado	**habríamos** perdonado
perdonar**ías**	perdonar**íais**	**habrías** perdonado	**habríais** perdonado
perdonar**ía**	perdonar**ían**	**habría** perdonado	**habrían** perdonado
presente de subjuntivo		perfecto de subjuntivo	
perdon**e**	perdon**emos**	**haya** perdonado	**hayamos** perdonado
perdon**es**	perdon**éis**	**hayas** perdonado	**hayáis** perdonado
perdon**e**	perdon**en**	**haya** perdonado	**hayan** perdonado
imperfecto de subjuntivo		pluscuamperfecto de subjuntivo	
perdonar**a**	perdonár**amos**	**hubiera** perdonado	**hubiéramos** perdonado
perdonar**as**	perdonar**ais**	**hubieras** perdonado	**hubierais** perdonado
perdonar**a**	perdonar**an**	**hubiera** perdonado	**hubieran** perdonado
OR		OR	
perdonas**e**	perdonás**emos**	**hubiese** perdonado	**hubiésemos** perdonado
perdonas**es**	perdonas**eis**	**hubieses** perdonado	**hubieseis** perdonado
perdonas**e**	perdonas**en**	**hubiese** perdonado	**hubiesen** perdonado

imperativo

—	perdonemos
perdona;	perdonad;
no perdones	no perdonéis
perdone	perdonen

gerundio **permaneciendo** participio de pasado **permanecido**

SINGULAR	PLURAL	SINGULAR	PLURAL
presente de indicativo		perfecto de indicativo	
permanezc**o**	permanec**emos**	**he** permanecido	**hemos** permanecido
permanec**es**	permanec**éis**	**has** permanecido	**habéis** permanecido
permanec**e**	permanec**en**	**ha** permanecido	**han** permanecido
imperfecto de indicativo		pluscuamperfecto de indicativo	
permanec**ía**	permanec**íamos**	**había** permanecido	**habíamos** permanecido
permanec**ías**	permanec**íais**	**habías** permanecido	**habíais** permanecido
permanec**ía**	permanec**ían**	**había** permanecido	**habían** permanecido
pretérito		pretérito anterior	
permanec**í**	permanec**imos**	**hube** permanecido	**hubimos** permanecido
permanec**iste**	permanec**isteis**	**hubiste** permanecido	**hubisteis** permanecido
permanec**ió**	permanec**ieron**	**hubo** permanecido	**hubieron** permanecido
futuro		futuro perfecto	
permanecer**é**	permanecer**emos**	**habré** permanecido	**habremos** permanecido
permanecer**ás**	permanecer**éis**	**habrás** permanecido	**habréis** permanecido
permanecer**á**	permanecer**án**	**habrá** permanecido	**habrán** permanecido
condicional simple		condicional compuesto	
permanecer**ía**	permanecer**íamos**	**habría** permanecido	**habríamos** permanecido
permanecer**ías**	permanecer**íais**	**habrías** permanecido	**habríais** permanecido
permanecer**ía**	permanecer**ían**	**habría** permanecido	**habrían** permanecido
presente de subjuntivo		perfecto de subjuntivo	
permanezc**a**	permanezc**amos**	**haya** permanecido	**hayamos** permanecido
permanezc**as**	permanezc**áis**	**hayas** permanecido	**hayáis** permanecido
permanezc**a**	permanezc**an**	**haya** permanecido	**hayan** permanecido
imperfecto de subjuntivo		pluscuamperfecto de subjuntivo	
permanecier**a**	permaneciér**amos**	**hubiera** permanecido	**hubiéramos** permanecido
permanecier**as**	permanecier**ais**	**hubieras** permanecido	**hubierais** permanecido
permanecier**a**	permanecier**an**	**hubiera** permanecido	**hubieran** permanecido
OR		OR	
permaneci**ese**	permaneciés**emos**	**hubiese** permanecido	**hubiésemos** permanecido
permanecies**es**	permanecies**eis**	**hubieses** permanecido	**hubieseis** permanecido
permanecies**e**	permanecies**en**	**hubiese** permanecido	**hubiesen** permanecido

imperativo

—	permanezcamos
permanece;	permaneced;
no permanezcas	no permanezcáis
permanezca	permanezcan

permitir — to permit, to allow

gerundio **permitiendo** participio de pasado **permitido**

SINGULAR	PLURAL	SINGULAR	PLURAL
presente de indicativo		perfecto de indicativo	
permit**o**	permit**imos**	**he** permitido	**hemos** permitido
permit**es**	permit**ís**	**has** permitido	**habéis** permitido
permit**e**	permit**en**	**ha** permitido	**han** permitido
imperfecto de indicativo		pluscuamperfecto de indicativo	
permit**ía**	permit**íamos**	**había** permitido	**habíamos** permitido
permit**ías**	permit**íais**	**habías** permitido	**habíais** permitido
permit**ía**	permit**ían**	**había** permitido	**habían** permitido
pretérito		pretérito anterior	
permit**í**	permit**imos**	**hube** permitido	**hubimos** permitido
permit**iste**	permit**isteis**	**hubiste** permitido	**hubisteis** permitido
permit**ió**	permit**ieron**	**hubo** permitido	**hubieron** permitido
futuro		futuro perfecto	
permitir**é**	permitir**emos**	**habré** permitido	**habremos** permitido
permitir**ás**	permitir**éis**	**habrás** permitido	**habréis** permitido
permitir**á**	permitir**án**	**habrá** permitido	**habrán** permitido
condicional simple		condicional compuesto	
permitir**ía**	permitir**íamos**	**habría** permitido	**habríamos** permitido
permitir**ías**	permitir**íais**	**habrías** permitido	**habríais** permitido
permitir**ía**	permitir**ían**	**habría** permitido	**habrían** permitido
presente de subjuntivo		perfecto de subjuntivo	
permit**a**	permit**amos**	**haya** permitido	**hayamos** permitido
permit**as**	permit**áis**	**hayas** permitido	**hayáis** permitido
permit**a**	permit**an**	**haya** permitido	**hayan** permitido
imperfecto de subjuntivo		pluscuamperfecto de subjuntivo	
permitier**a**	permitiér**amos**	**hubiera** permitido	**hubiéramos** permitido
permitier**as**	permitier**ais**	**hubieras** permitido	**hubierais** permitido
permitier**a**	permitier**an**	**hubiera** permitido	**hubieran** permitido
OR		OR	
permities**e**	permitiés**emos**	**hubiese** permitido	**hubiésemos** permitido
permities**es**	permities**eis**	**hubieses** permitido	**hubieseis** permitido
permities**e**	permities**en**	**hubiese** permitido	**hubiesen** permitido

imperativo

—	permitamos
permite; no permitas	permitid; no permitáis
permita	permitan

gerundio **persiguiendo** participio de pasado **perseguido**

SINGULAR	PLURAL
presente de indicativo	
persig**o**	persegu**imos**
persigu**es**	persegu**ís**
persigu**e**	persigu**en**
imperfecto de indicativo	
persegu**ía**	persegu**íamos**
persegu**ías**	persegu**íais**
persegu**ía**	persegu**ían**
pretérito	
persegu**í**	persegu**imos**
persegu**iste**	persegu**isteis**
persigu**ió**	persigu**ieron**
futuro	
perseguir**é**	perseguir**emos**
perseguir**ás**	perseguir**éis**
perseguir**á**	perseguir**án**
condicional simple	
perseguir**ía**	perseguir**íamos**
perseguir**ías**	perseguir**íais**
perseguir**ía**	perseguir**ían**
presente de subjuntivo	
persig**a**	persig**amos**
persig**as**	persig**áis**
persig**a**	persig**an**
imperfecto de subjuntivo	
persiguier**a**	persiguiér**amos**
persiguier**as**	persiguier**ais**
persiguier**a**	persiguier**an**
OR	
persiguies**e**	persiguiés**emos**
persiguies**es**	persiguies**eis**
persiguies**e**	persiguies**en**

SINGULAR	PLURAL
perfecto de indicativo	
he perseguido	**hemos** perseguido
has perseguido	**habéis** perseguido
ha perseguido	**han** perseguido
pluscuamperfecto de indicativo	
había perseguido	**habíamos** perseguido
habías perseguido	**habíais** perseguido
había perseguido	**habían** perseguido
pretérito anterior	
hube perseguido	**hubimos** perseguido
hubiste perseguido	**hubisteis** perseguido
hubo perseguido	**hubieron** perseguido
futuro perfecto	
habré perseguido	**habremos** perseguido
habrás perseguido	**habréis** perseguido
habrá perseguido	**habrán** perseguido
condicional compuesto	
habría perseguido	**habríamos** perseguido
habrías perseguido	**habríais** perseguido
habría perseguido	**habrían** perseguido
perfecto de subjuntivo	
haya perseguido	**hayamos** perseguido
hayas perseguido	**hayáis** perseguido
haya perseguido	**hayan** perseguido
pluscuamperfecto de subjuntivo	
hubiera perseguido	**hubiéramos** perseguido
hubieras perseguido	**hubierais** perseguido
hubiera perseguido	**hubieran** perseguido
OR	
hubiese perseguido	**hubiésemos** perseguido
hubieses perseguido	**hubieseis** perseguido
hubiese perseguido	**hubiesen** perseguido

imperativo

—	persigamos
persigue; no persigas	perseguid; no persigáis
persiga	persigan

pertenecer — to pertain

gerundio **perteneciendo** participio de pasado **pertenecido**

SINGULAR	PLURAL	SINGULAR	PLURAL
presente de indicativo		perfecto de indicativo	
pertenezc**o**	pertenec**emos**	**he** pertenecido	**hemos** pertenecido
pertenec**es**	pertenec**éis**	**has** pertenecido	**habéis** pertenecido
pertenec**e**	pertenec**en**	**ha** pertenecido	**han** pertenecido
imperfecto de indicativo		pluscuamperfecto de indicativo	
pertenec**ía**	pertenec**íamos**	**había** pertenecido	**habíamos** pertenecido
pertenec**ías**	pertenec**íais**	**habías** pertenecido	**habíais** pertenecido
pertenec**ía**	pertenec**ían**	**había** pertenecido	**habían** pertenecido
pretérito		pretérito anterior	
pertenec**í**	pertenec**imos**	**hube** pertenecido	**hubimos** pertenecido
pertenec**iste**	pertenec**isteis**	**hubiste** pertenecido	**hubisteis** pertenecido
pertenec**ió**	pertenec**ieron**	**hubo** pertenecido	**hubieron** pertenecido
futuro		futuro perfecto	
pertenecer**é**	pertenecer**emos**	**habré** pertenecido	**habremos** pertenecido
pertenecer**ás**	pertenecer**éis**	**habrás** pertenecido	**habréis** pertenecido
pertenecer**á**	pertenecer**án**	**habrá** pertenecido	**habrán** pertenecido
condicional simple		condicional compuesto	
pertenecer**ía**	pertenecer**íamos**	**habría** pertenecido	**habríamos** pertenecido
pertenecer**ías**	pertenecer**íais**	**habrías** pertenecido	**habríais** pertenecido
pertenecer**ía**	pertenecer**ían**	**habría** pertenecido	**habrían** pertenecido
presente de subjuntivo		perfecto de subjuntivo	
pertenezc**a**	pertenezc**amos**	**haya** pertenecido	**hayamos** pertenecido
pertenezc**as**	pertenezc**áis**	**hayas** pertenecido	**hayáis** pertenecido
pertenezc**a**	pertenezc**an**	**haya** pertenecido	**hayan** pertenecido
imperfecto de subjuntivo		pluscuamperfecto de subjuntivo	
pertenecier**a**	perteneciér**amos**	**hubiera** pertenecido	**hubiéramos** pertenecido
pertenecier**as**	pertenecier**ais**	**hubieras** pertenecido	**hubierais** pertenecido
pertenecier**a**	pertenecier**an**	**hubiera** pertenecido	**hubieran** pertenecido
OR		OR	
pertenecies**e**	perteneciés**emos**	**hubiese** pertenecido	**hubiésemos** pertenecido
pertenecies**es**	pertenecies**eis**	**hubieses** pertenecido	**hubieseis** pertenecido
pertenecies**e**	pertenecies**en**	**hubiese** pertenecido	**hubiesen** pertenecido

imperativo

—	pertenezcamos
pertenece;	perteneced;
no pertenezcas	no pertenezcáis
pertenezca	pertenezcan

gerundio **pintando** participio de pasado **pintado**

SINGULAR	PLURAL
presente de indicativo	
pint**o**	pint**amos**
pint**as**	pint**áis**
pint**a**	pint**an**
imperfecto de indicativo	
pint**aba**	pint**ábamos**
pint**abas**	pint**abais**
pint**aba**	pint**aban**
pretérito	
pint**é**	pint**amos**
pint**aste**	pint**asteis**
pint**ó**	pint**aron**
futuro	
pintar**é**	pintar**emos**
pintar**ás**	pintar**éis**
pintar**á**	pintar**án**
condicional simple	
pintar**ía**	pintar**íamos**
pintar**ías**	pintar**íais**
pintar**ía**	pintar**ían**
presente de subjuntivo	
pint**e**	pint**emos**
pint**es**	pint**éis**
pint**e**	pint**en**
imperfecto de subjuntivo	
pintar**a**	pintár**amos**
pintar**as**	pintar**ais**
pintar**a**	pintar**an**
OR	
pintas**e**	pintás**emos**
pintas**es**	pintas**eis**
pintas**e**	pintas**en**
imperativo	
—	pintemos
pinta; no pintes	pintad; no pintéis
pinte	pinten

SINGULAR	PLURAL
perfecto de indicativo	
he pintado	**hemos** pintado
has pintado	**habéis** pintado
ha pintado	**han** pintado
pluscuamperfecto de indicativo	
había pintado	**habíamos** pintado
habías pintado	**habíais** pintado
había pintado	**habían** pintado
pretérito anterior	
hube pintado	**hubimos** pintado
hubiste pintado	**hubisteis** pintado
hubo pintado	**hubieron** pintado
futuro perfecto	
habré pintado	**habremos** pintado
habrás pintado	**habréis** pintado
habrá pintado	**habrán** pintado
condicional compuesto	
habría pintado	**habríamos** pintado
habrías pintado	**habríais** pintado
habría pintado	**habrían** pintado
perfecto de subjuntivo	
haya pintado	**hayamos** pintado
hayas pintado	**hayáis** pintado
haya pintado	**hayan** pintado
pluscuamperfecto de subjuntivo	
hubiera pintado	**hubiéramos** pintado
hubieras pintado	**hubierais** pintado
hubiera pintado	**hubieran** pintado
OR	
hubiese pintado	**hubiésemos** pintado
hubieses pintado	**hubieseis** pintado
hubiese pintado	**hubiesen** pintado

pintarse — to make up one's face

gerundio **pintándose** participio de pasado **pintado**

SINGULAR	PLURAL	SINGULAR	PLURAL
presente de indicativo		perfecto de indicativo	
me pint**o**	nos pint**amos**	**me he** pintado	**nos hemos** pintado
te pint**as**	os pint**áis**	**te has** pintado	**os habéis** pintado
se pint**a**	se pint**an**	**se ha** pintado	**se han** pintado
imperfecto de indicativo		pluscuamperfecto de indicativo	
me pint**aba**	nos pint**ábamos**	**me había** pintado	**nos habíamos** pintado
te pint**abas**	os pint**abais**	**te habías** pintado	**os habíais** pintado
se pint**aba**	se pint**aban**	**se había** pintado	**se habían** pintado
pretérito		pretérito anterior	
me pint**é**	nos pint**amos**	**me hube** pintado	**nos hubimos** pintado
te pint**aste**	os pint**asteis**	**te hubiste** pintado	**os hubisteis** pintado
se pint**ó**	se pint**aron**	**se hubo** pintado	**se hubieron** pintado
futuro		futuro perfecto	
me pintar**é**	nos pintar**emos**	**me habré** pintado	**nos habremos** pintado
te pintar**ás**	os pintar**éis**	**te habrás** pintado	**os habréis** pintado
se pintar**á**	se pintar**án**	**se habrá** pintado	**se habrán** pintado
condicional simple		condicional compuesto	
me pintar**ía**	nos pintar**íamos**	**me habría** pintado	**nos habríamos** pintado
te pintar**ías**	os pintar**íais**	**te habrías** pintado	**os habríais** pintado
se pintar**ía**	se pintar**ían**	**se habría** pintado	**se habrían** pintado
presente de subjuntivo		perfecto de subjuntivo	
me pint**e**	nos pint**emos**	**me haya** pintado	**nos hayamos** pintado
te pint**es**	os pint**éis**	**te hayas** pintado	**os hayáis** pintado
se pint**e**	se pint**en**	**se haya** pintado	**se hayan** pintado
imperfecto de subjuntivo		pluscuamperfecto de subjuntivo	
me pintar**a**	nos pintár**amos**	**me hubiera** pintado	**nos hubiéramos** pintado
te pintar**as**	os pintar**ais**	**te hubieras** pintado	**os hubierais** pintado
se pintar**a**	se pintar**an**	**se hubiera** pintado	**se hubieran** pintado
OR		OR	
me pintas**e**	nos pintás**emos**	**me hubiese** pintado	**nos hubiésemos** pintado
te pintas**es**	os pintas**eis**	**te hubieses** pintado	**os hubieseis** pintado
se pintas**e**	se pintas**en**	**se hubiese** pintado	**se hubiesen** pintado

imperativo

—	pintémonos
píntate; no te pintes	pintaos; no os pintéis
píntese	píntense

SINGULAR	PLURAL	SINGULAR	PLURAL
presente de indicativo		perfecto de indicativo	
pis**o**	pis**amos**	**he** pisado	**hemos** pisado
pis**as**	pis**áis**	**has** pisado	**habéis** pisado
pis**a**	pis**an**	**ha** pisado	**han** pisado
imperfecto de indicativo		pluscuamperfecto de indicativo	
pis**aba**	pis**ábamos**	**había** pisado	**habíamos** pisado
pis**abas**	pis**abais**	**habías** pisado	**habíais** pisado
pis**aba**	pis**aban**	**había** pisado	**habían** pisado
pretérito		pretérito anterior	
pis**é**	pis**amos**	**hube** pisado	**hubimos** pisado
pis**aste**	pis**asteis**	**hubiste** pisado	**hubisteis** pisado
pis**ó**	pis**aron**	**hubo** pisado	**hubieron** pisado
futuro		futuro perfecto	
pisar**é**	pisar**emos**	**habré** pisado	**habremos** pisado
pisar**ás**	pisar**éis**	**habrás** pisado	**habréis** pisado
pisar**á**	pisar**án**	**habrá** pisado	**habrán** pisado
condicional simple		condicional compuesto	
pisar**ía**	pisar**íamos**	**habría** pisado	**habríamos** pisado
pisar**ías**	pisar**íais**	**habrías** pisado	**habríais** pisado
pisar**ía**	pisar**ían**	**habría** pisado	**habrían** pisado
presente de subjuntivo		perfecto de subjuntivo	
pis**e**	pis**emos**	**haya** pisado	**hayamos** pisado
pis**es**	pis**éis**	**hayas** pisado	**hayáis** pisado
pis**e**	pis**en**	**haya** pisado	**hayan** pisado
imperfecto de subjuntivo		pluscuamperfecto de subjuntivo	
pisar**a**	pisár**amos**	**hubiera** pisado	**hubiéramos** pisado
pisar**as**	pisar**ais**	**hubieras** pisado	**hubierais** pisado
pisar**a**	pisar**an**	**hubiera** pisado	**hubieran** pisado
OR		OR	
pisas**e**	pisás**emos**	**hubiese** pisado	**hubiésemos** pisado
pisas**es**	pisas**eis**	**hubieses** pisado	**hubieseis** pisado
pisas**e**	pisas**en**	**hubiese** pisado	**hubiesen** pisado

imperativo

—	pisemos
pisa; no pises	pisad; no piséis
pise	pisen

placer — to gratify, to humor, to please

gerundio **placiendo** participio de pasado **placido**

SINGULAR	PLURAL	SINGULAR	PLURAL
presente de indicativo		perfecto de indicativo	
plazc**o**	plac**emos**	**he** placido	**hemos** placido
plac**es**	plac**éis**	**has** placido	**habéis** placido
plac**e**	plac**en**	**ha** placido	**han** placido
imperfecto de indicativo		pluscuamperfecto de indicativo	
plac**ía**	plac**íamos**	**había** placido	**habíamos** placido
plac**ías**	plac**íais**	**habías** placido	**habíais** placido
plac**ía**	plac**ían**	**había** placido	**habían** placido
pretérito		pretérito anterior	
plac**í**	plac**imos**	**hube** placido	**hubimos** placido
plac**iste**	plac**isteis**	**hubiste** placido	**hubisteis** placido
plac**ió**	plac**ieron**	**hubo** placido	**hubieron** placido
futuro		futuro perfecto	
placer**é**	placer**emos**	**habré** placido	**habremos** placido
placer**ás**	placer**éis**	**habrás** placido	**habréis** placido
placer**á**	placer**án**	**habrá** placido	**habrán** placido
condicional simple		condicional compuesto	
placer**ía**	placer**íamos**	**habría** placido	**habríamos** placido
placer**ías**	placer**íais**	**habrías** placido	**habríais** placido
placer**ía**	placer**ían**	**habría** placido	**habrían** placido
presente de subjuntivo		perfecto de subjuntivo	
plazc**a**	plazc**amos**	**haya** placido	**hayamos** placido
plazc**as**	plazc**áis**	**hayas** placido	**hayáis** placido
plazc**a**	plazc**an**	**haya** placido	**hayan** placido
imperfecto de subjuntivo		pluscuamperfecto de subjuntivo	
placier**a**	placiér**amos**	**hubiera** placido	**hubiéramos** placido
placier**as**	placier**ais**	**hubieras** placido	**hubierais** placido
placier**a**	placier**an**	**hubiera** placido	**hubieran** placido
OR		OR	
placies**e**	placiés**emos**	**hubiese** placido	**hubiésemos** placido
placies**es**	placies**eis**	**hubieses** placido	**hubieseis** placido
placies**e**	placies**en**	**hubiese** placido	**hubiesen** placido

imperativo

—	plazcamos
place; no plazcas	placed; no plazcáis
plazca	plazcan

gerundio **platicando** participio de pasado **platicado**

SINGULAR	PLURAL	SINGULAR	PLURAL
presente de indicativo		perfecto de indicativo	
platic**o**	platic**amos**	**he** platicado	**hemos** platicado
platic**as**	platic**áis**	**has** platicado	**habéis** platicado
platic**a**	platic**an**	**ha** platicado	**han** platicado
imperfecto de indicativo		pluscuamperfecto de indicativo	
platic**aba**	platic**ábamos**	**había** platicado	**habíamos** platicado
platic**abas**	platic**abais**	**habías** platicado	**habíais** platicado
platic**aba**	platic**aban**	**había** platicado	**habían** platicado
pretérito		pretérito anterior	
platiqu**é**	platic**amos**	**hube** platicado	**hubimos** platicado
platic**aste**	platic**asteis**	**hubiste** platicado	**hubisteis** platicado
platic**ó**	platic**aron**	**hubo** platicado	**hubieron** platicado
futuro		futuro perfecto	
platicar**é**	platicar**emos**	**habré** platicado	**habremos** platicado
platicar**ás**	platicar**éis**	**habrás** platicado	**habréis** platicado
platicar**á**	platicar**án**	**habrá** platicado	**habrán** platicado
condicional simple		condicional compuesto	
platicar**ía**	platicar**íamos**	**habría** platicado	**habríamos** platicado
platicar**ías**	platicar**íais**	**habrías** platicado	**habríais** platicado
platicar**ía**	platicar**ían**	**habría** platicado	**habrían** platicado
presente de subjuntivo		perfecto de subjuntivo	
platiqu**e**	platiqu**emos**	**haya** platicado	**hayamos** platicado
platiqu**es**	platiqu**éis**	**hayas** platicado	**hayáis** platicado
platiqu**e**	platiqu**en**	**haya** platicado	**hayan** platicado
imperfecto de subjuntivo		pluscuamperfecto de subjuntivo	
platicar**a**	platicár**amos**	**hubiera** platicado	**hubiéramos** platicado
platicar**as**	platicar**ais**	**hubieras** platicado	**hubierais** platicado
platicar**a**	platicar**an**	**hubiera** platicado	**hubieran** platicado
OR		OR	
platicas**e**	platicás**emos**	**hubiese** platicado	**hubiésemos** platicado
platicas**es**	platicas**eis**	**hubieses** platicado	**hubieseis** platicado
platicas**e**	platicas**en**	**hubiese** platicado	**hubiesen** platicado

imperativo

—	platiquemos
platica; no platiques	platicad; no platiquéis
platique	platiquen

poder — to be able, can

gerundio **pudiendo** participio de pasado **podido**

SINGULAR	PLURAL	SINGULAR	PLURAL
presente de indicativo		perfecto de indicativo	
pued**o**	pod**emos**	**he** podido	**hemos** podido
pued**es**	pod**éis**	**has** podido	**habéis** podido
pued**e**	pued**en**	**ha** podido	**han** podido
imperfecto de indicativo		pluscuamperfecto de indicativo	
pod**ía**	pod**íamos**	**había** podido	**habíamos** podido
pod**ías**	pod**íais**	**habías** podido	**habíais** podido
pod**ía**	pod**ían**	**había** podido	**habían** podido
pretérito		pretérito anterior	
pud**e**	pud**imos**	**hube** podido	**hubimos** podido
pud**iste**	pud**isteis**	**hubiste** podido	**hubisteis** podido
pud**o**	pud**ieron**	**hubo** podido	**hubieron** podido
futuro		futuro perfecto	
podr**é**	podr**emos**	**habré** podido	**habremos** podido
podr**ás**	podr**éis**	**habrás** podido	**habréis** podido
podr**á**	podr**án**	**habrá** podido	**habrán** podido
condicional simple		condicional compuesto	
podr**ía**	podr**íamos**	**habría** podido	**habríamos** podido
podr**ías**	podr**íais**	**habrías** podido	**habríais** podido
podr**ía**	podr**ían**	**habría** podido	**habrían** podido
presente de subjuntivo		perfecto de subjuntivo	
pued**a**	pod**amos**	**haya** podido	**hayamos** podido
pued**as**	pod**áis**	**hayas** podido	**hayáis** podido
pued**a**	pued**an**	**haya** podido	**hayan** podido
imperfecto de subjuntivo		pluscuamperfecto de subjuntivo	
pudier**a**	pudiér**amos**	**hubiera** podido	**hubiéramos** podido
pudier**as**	pudier**ais**	**hubieras** podido	**hubierais** podido
pudier**a**	pudier**an**	**hubiera** podido	**hubieran** podido
OR		OR	
pudies**e**	pudiés**emos**	**hubiese** podido	**hubiésemos** podido
pudies**es**	pudies**eis**	**hubieses** podido	**hubieseis** podido
pudies**e**	pudies**en**	**hubiese** podido	**hubiesen** podido
imperativo			
—	podamos		
puede; no puedas	poded; no podáis		
pueda	puedan		

to put, to turn on TV, radio **poner**

gerundio **poniendo** participio de pasado **puesto**

SINGULAR	PLURAL	SINGULAR	PLURAL
presente de indicativo		perfecto de indicativo	
pong**o**	pon**emos**	**he** puesto	**hemos** puesto
pon**es**	pon**éis**	**has** puesto	**habéis** puesto
pon**e**	pon**en**	**ha** puesto	**han** puesto
imperfecto de indicativo		pluscuamperfecto de indicativo	
pon**ía**	pon**íamos**	**había** puesto	**habíamos** puesto
pon**ías**	pon**íais**	**habías** puesto	**habíais** puesto
pon**ía**	pon**ían**	**había** puesto	**habían** puesto
pretérito		pretérito anterior	
pus**e**	pus**imos**	**hube** puesto	**hubimos** puesto
pus**iste**	pus**isteis**	**hubiste** puesto	**hubisteis** puesto
pus**o**	pus**ieron**	**hubo** puesto	**hubieron** puesto
futuro		futuro perfecto	
pondr**é**	pondr**emos**	**habré** puesto	**habremos** puesto
pondr**ás**	pondr**éis**	**habrás** puesto	**habréis** puesto
pondr**á**	pondr**án**	**habrá** puesto	**habrán** puesto
condicional simple		condicional compuesto	
pondr**ía**	pondr**íamos**	**habría** puesto	**habríamos** puesto
pondr**ías**	pondr**íais**	**habrías** puesto	**habríais** puesto
pondr**ía**	pondr**ían**	**habría** puesto	**habrían** puesto
presente de subjuntivo		perfecto de subjuntivo	
pong**a**	pong**amos**	**haya** puesto	**hayamos** puesto
pong**as**	pong**áis**	**hayas** puesto	**hayáis** puesto
pong**a**	pong**an**	**haya** puesto	**hayan** puesto
imperfecto de subjuntivo		pluscuamperfecto de subjuntivo	
pusier**a**	pusié**ramos**	**hubiera** puesto	**hubiéramos** puesto
pusier**as**	pusier**ais**	**hubieras** puesto	**hubierais** puesto
pusier**a**	pusier**an**	**hubiera** puesto	**hubieran** puesto
OR		OR	
pusies**e**	pusié**semos**	**hubiese** puesto	**hubiésemos** puesto
pusies**es**	pusies**eis**	**hubieses** puesto	**hubieseis** puesto
pusies**e**	pusies**en**	**hubiese** puesto	**hubiesen** puesto

imperativo

SINGULAR	PLURAL
—	pongamos
pon; no pongas	poned; no pongáis
ponga	pongan

ponerse — to put on clothing, to become

gerundio **poniéndose** — participio de pasado **puesto**

SINGULAR	PLURAL	SINGULAR	PLURAL
presente de indicativo		*perfecto de indicativo*	
me pong**o**	nos pon**emos**	**me he** puesto	**nos hemos** puesto
te pon**es**	os pon**éis**	**te has** puesto	**os habéis** puesto
se pon**e**	se pon**en**	**se ha** puesto	**se han** puesto
imperfecto de indicativo		*pluscuamperfecto de indicativo*	
me pon**ía**	nos pon**íamos**	**me había** puesto	**nos habíamos** puesto
te pon**ías**	os pon**íais**	**te habías** puesto	**os habíais** puesto
se pon**ía**	se pon**ían**	**se había** puesto	**se habían** puesto
pretérito		*pretérito anterior*	
me pus**e**	nos pus**imos**	**me hube** puesto	**nos hubimos** puesto
te pus**iste**	os pus**isteis**	**te hubiste** puesto	**os hubisteis** puesto
se pus**o**	se pus**ieron**	**se hubo** puesto	**se hubieron** puesto
futuro		*futuro perfecto*	
me pondr**é**	nos pondr**emos**	**me habré** puesto	**nos habremos** puesto
te pondr**ás**	os pondr**éis**	**te habrás** puesto	**os habréis** puesto
se pondr**á**	se pondr**án**	**se habrá** puesto	**se habrán** puesto
condicional simple		*condicional compuesto*	
me pondr**ía**	nos pondr**íamos**	**me habría** puesto	**nos habríamos** puesto
te pondr**ías**	os pondr**íais**	**te habrías** puesto	**os habríais** puesto
se pondr**ía**	se pondr**ían**	**se habría** puesto	**se habrían** puesto
presente de subjuntivo		*perfecto de subjuntivo*	
me pong**a**	nos pong**amos**	**me haya** puesto	**nos hayamos** puesto
te pong**as**	os pong**áis**	**te hayas** puesto	**os hayáis** puesto
se pong**a**	se pong**an**	**se haya** puesto	**se hayan** puesto
imperfecto de subjuntivo		*pluscuamperfecto de subjuntivo*	
me pusier**a**	nos pusiér**amos**	**me hubiera** puesto	**nos hubiéramos** puesto
te pusier**as**	os pusier**ais**	**te hubieras** puesto	**os hubierais** puesto
se pusier**a**	se pusier**an**	**se hubiera** puesto	**se hubieran** puesto
OR		OR	
me pusies**e**	nos pusiés**emos**	**me hubiese** puesto	**nos hubiésemos** puesto
te pusies**es**	os pusies**eis**	**te hubieses** puesto	**os hubieseis** puesto
se pusies**e**	se pusies**en**	**se hubiese** puesto	**se hubiesen** puesto

imperativo

—	pongámonos
ponte; no te pongas	poneos; no os pongáis
póngase	pónganse

gerundio **poseyendo** participio de pasado **poseído**

SINGULAR	PLURAL
presente de indicativo	
pose**o**	pose**emos**
pose**es**	pose**éis**
pose**e**	pose**en**
imperfecto de indicativo	
pose**ía**	pose**íamos**
pose**ías**	pose**íais**
pose**ía**	pose**ían**
pretérito	
pose**í**	pose**ímos**
pose**íste**	pose**ísteis**
pose**yó**	pose**yeron**
futuro	
poseer**é**	poseer**emos**
poseer**ás**	poseer**éis**
poseer**á**	poseer**án**
condicional simple	
poseer**ía**	poseer**íamos**
poseer**ías**	poseer**íais**
poseer**ía**	poseer**ían**
presente de subjuntivo	
pose**a**	pose**amos**
pose**as**	pose**áis**
pose**a**	pose**an**
imperfecto de subjuntivo	
poseyer**a**	poseyér**amos**
poseyer**as**	poseyer**ais**
poseyer**a**	poseyer**an**
OR	
poseyes**e**	poseyés**emos**
poseyes**es**	poseyes**eis**
poseyes**e**	poseyes**en**
imperativo	
—	poseamos
posee; no poseas	poseed; no poseáis
posea	posean

SINGULAR	PLURAL
perfecto de indicativo	
he poseído	**hemos** poseído
has poseído	**habéis** poseído
ha poseído	**han** poseído
pluscuamperfecto de indicativo	
había poseído	**habíamos** poseído
habías poseído	**habíais** poseído
había poseído	**habían** poseído
pretérito anterior	
hube poseído	**hubimos** poseído
hubiste poseído	**hubisteis** poseído
hubo poseído	**hubieron** poseído
futuro perfecto	
habré poseído	**habremos** poseído
habrás poseído	**habréis** poseído
habrá poseído	**habrán** poseído
condicional compuesto	
habría poseído	**habríamos** poseído
habrías poseído	**habríais** poseído
habría poseído	**habrían** poseído
perfecto de subjuntivo	
haya poseído	**hayamos** poseído
hayas poseído	**hayáis** poseído
haya poseído	**hayan** poseído
pluscuamperfecto de subjuntivo	
hubiera poseído	**hubiéramos** poseído
hubieras poseído	**hubierais** poseído
hubiera poseído	**hubieran** poseído
OR	
hubiese poseído	**hubiésemos** poseído
hubieses poseído	**hubieseis** poseído
hubiese poseído	**hubiesen** poseído

practicar — to practice

gerundio **practicando** participio de pasado **practicado**

SINGULAR	PLURAL
presente de indicativo	
practic**o**	practic**amos**
practic**as**	practic**áis**
practic**a**	practic**an**
imperfecto de indicativo	
practic**aba**	practic**ábamos**
practic**abas**	practic**abais**
practic**aba**	practic**aban**
pretérito	
practiqu**é**	practic**amos**
practic**aste**	practic**asteis**
practic**ó**	practic**aron**
futuro	
practicar**é**	practicar**emos**
practicar**ás**	practicar**éis**
practicar**á**	practicar**án**
condicional simple	
practicar**ía**	practicar**íamos**
practicar**ías**	practicar**íais**
practicar**ía**	practicar**ían**
presente de subjuntivo	
practiqu**e**	practiqu**emos**
practiqu**es**	practiqu**éis**
practiqu**e**	practiqu**en**
imperfecto de subjuntivo	
practicar**a**	practicár**amos**
practicar**as**	practicar**ais**
practicar**a**	practicar**an**
OR	
practicas**e**	practicás**emos**
practicas**es**	practicas**eis**
practicas**e**	practicas**en**
imperativo	
—	practiquemos
practica; no practiques	practicad; no practiquéis
practique	practiquen

SINGULAR	PLURAL
perfecto de indicativo	
he practicado	**hemos** practicado
has practicado	**habéis** practicado
ha practicado	**han** practicado
pluscuamperfecto de indicativo	
había practicado	**habíamos** practicado
habías practicado	**habíais** practicado
había practicado	**habían** practicado
pretérito anterior	
hube practicado	**hubimos** practicado
hubiste practicado	**hubisteis** practicado
hubo practicado	**hubieron** practicado
futuro perfecto	
habré practicado	**habremos** practicado
habrás practicado	**habréis** practicado
habrá practicado	**habrán** practicado
condicional compuesto	
habría practicado	**habríamos** practicado
habrías practicado	**habríais** practicado
habría practicado	**habrían** practicado
perfecto de subjuntivo	
haya practicado	**hayamos** practicado
hayas practicado	**hayáis** practicado
haya practicado	**hayan** practicado
pluscuamperfecto de subjuntivo	
hubiera practicado	**hubiéramos** practicado
hubieras practicado	**hubierais** practicado
hubiera practicado	**hubieran** practicado
OR	
hubiese practicado	**hubiésemos** practicado
hubieses practicado	**hubieseis** practicado
hubiese practicado	**hubiesen** practicado

gerundio **prediciendo** participio de pasado **predicho**

SINGULAR	PLURAL	SINGULAR	PLURAL
presente de indicativo		perfecto de indicativo	
predig**o**	predec**imos**	**he** predicho	**hemos** predicho
predic**es**	predec**ís**	**has** predicho	**habéis** predicho
predic**e**	predic**en**	**ha** predicho	**han** predicho
imperfecto de indicativo		pluscuamperfecto de indicativo	
predec**ía**	predec**íamos**	**había** predicho	**habíamos** predicho
predec**ías**	predec**íais**	**habías** predicho	**habíais** predicho
predec**ía**	predec**ían**	**había** predicho	**habían** predicho
pretérito		pretérito anterior	
predij**e**	predij**imos**	**hube** predicho	**hubimos** predicho
predij**iste**	predij**isteis**	**hubiste** predicho	**hubisteis** predicho
predij**o**	predij**eron**	**hubo** predicho	**hubieron** predicho
futuro		futuro perfecto	
predecir**é**	predecir**emos**	**habré** predicho	**habremos** predicho
predecir**ás**	predecir**éis**	**habrás** predicho	**habréis** predicho
predecir**á**	predecir**án**	**habrá** predicho	**habrán** predicho
condicional simple		condicional compuesto	
predecir**ía**	predecir**íamos**	**habría** predicho	**habríamos** predicho
predecir**ías**	predecir**íais**	**habrías** predicho	**habríais** predicho
predecir**ía**	predecir**ían**	**habría** predicho	**habrían** predicho
presente de subjuntivo		perfecto de subjuntivo	
predig**a**	predig**amos**	**haya** predicho	**hayamos** predicho
predig**as**	predig**áis**	**hayas** predicho	**hayáis** predicho
predig**a**	predig**an**	**haya** predicho	**hayan** predicho
imperfecto de subjuntivo		pluscuamperfecto de subjuntivo	
predijer**a**	predijér**amos**	**hubiera** predicho	**hubiéramos** predicho
predijer**as**	predijer**ais**	**hubieras** predicho	**hubierais** predicho
predijer**a**	predijer**an**	**hubiera** predicho	**hubieran** predicho
OR		OR	
predijes**e**	predijés**emos**	**hubiese** predicho	**hubiésemos** predicho
predijes**es**	predijes**eis**	**hubieses** predicho	**hubieseis** predicho
predijes**e**	predijes**en**	**hubiese** predicho	**hubiesen** predicho

imperativo

—	predigamos
predice; no predigas	predecid; no predigáis
prediga	predigan

predicar — to preach

gerundio **predicando** participio de pasado **predicado**

SINGULAR	PLURAL
presente de indicativo	
predic**o**	predic**amos**
predic**as**	predic**áis**
predic**a**	predic**an**
imperfecto de indicativo	
predic**aba**	predic**ábamos**
predic**abas**	predic**abais**
predic**aba**	predic**aban**
pretérito	
prediqu**é**	predic**amos**
predic**aste**	predic**asteis**
predic**ó**	predic**aron**
futuro	
predicar**é**	predicar**emos**
predicar**ás**	predicar**éis**
predicar**á**	predicar**án**
condicional simple	
predicar**ía**	predicar**íamos**
predicar**ías**	predicar**íais**
predicar**ía**	predicar**ían**
presente de subjuntivo	
prediqu**e**	prediqu**emos**
prediqu**es**	prediqu**éis**
prediqu**e**	prediqu**en**
imperfecto de subjuntivo	
predicar**a**	predicár**amos**
predicar**as**	predicar**ais**
predicar**a**	predicar**an**
OR	
predicas**e**	predicás**emos**
predicas**es**	predicas**eis**
predicas**e**	predicas**en**
imperativo	
—	prediquemos
predica; no prediques	predicad; no prediquéis
predique	prediquen

SINGULAR	PLURAL
perfecto de indicativo	
he predicado	**hemos** predicado
has predicado	**habéis** predicado
ha predicado	**han** predicado
pluscuamperfecto de indicativo	
había predicado	**habíamos** predicado
habías predicado	**habíais** predicado
había predicado	**habían** predicado
pretérito anterior	
hube predicado	**hubimos** predicado
hubiste predicado	**hubisteis** predicado
hubo predicado	**hubieron** predicado
futuro perfecto	
habré predicado	**habremos** predicado
habrás predicado	**habréis** predicado
habrá predicado	**habrán** predicado
condicional compuesto	
habría predicado	**habríamos** predicado
habrías predicado	**habríais** predicado
habría predicado	**habrían** predicado
perfecto de subjuntivo	
haya predicado	**hayamos** predicado
hayas predicado	**hayáis** predicado
haya predicado	**hayan** predicado
pluscuamperfecto de subjuntivo	
hubiera predicado	**hubiéramos** predicado
hubieras predicado	**hubierais** predicado
hubiera predicado	**hubieran** predicado
OR	
hubiese predicado	**hubiésemos** predicado
hubieses predicado	**hubieseis** predicado
hubiese predicado	**hubiesen** predicado

gerundio **prefiriendo** participio de pasado **preferido**

SINGULAR	PLURAL
presente de indicativo	
prefier**o**	prefer**imos**
prefier**es**	prefer**ís**
prefier**e**	prefier**en**
imperfecto de indicativo	
prefer**ía**	prefer**íamos**
prefer**ías**	prefer**íais**
prefer**ía**	prefer**ían**
pretérito	
prefer**í**	prefer**imos**
prefer**iste**	prefer**isteis**
prefir**ió**	prefir**ieron**
futuro	
preferir**é**	preferir**emos**
preferir**ás**	preferir**éis**
preferir**á**	preferir**án**
condicional simple	
preferir**ía**	preferir**íamos**
preferir**ías**	preferir**íais**
preferir**ía**	preferir**ían**
presente de subjuntivo	
prefier**a**	prefir**amos**
prefier**as**	prefir**áis**
prefier**a**	prefier**an**
imperfecto de subjuntivo	
prefirier**a**	prefiriér**amos**
prefirier**as**	prefirier**ais**
prefirier**a**	prefirier**an**
OR	
prefiries**e**	prefiriés**emos**
prefiries**es**	prefiries**eis**
prefiries**e**	prefiries**en**
imperativo	
—	prefiramos
prefiere; no prefieras	preferid; no prefiráis
prefiera	prefieran

SINGULAR	PLURAL
perfecto de indicativo	
he preferido	**hemos** preferido
has preferido	**habéis** preferido
ha preferido	**han** preferido
pluscuamperfecto de indicativo	
había preferido	**habíamos** preferido
habías preferido	**habíais** preferido
había preferido	**habían** preferido
pretérito anterior	
hube preferido	**hubimos** preferido
hubiste preferido	**hubisteis** preferido
hubo preferido	**hubieron** preferido
futuro perfecto	
habré preferido	**habremos** preferido
habrás preferido	**habréis** preferido
habrá preferido	**habrán** preferido
condicional compuesto	
habría preferido	**habríamos** preferido
habrías preferido	**habríais** preferido
habría preferido	**habrían** preferido
perfecto de subjuntivo	
haya preferido	**hayamos** preferido
hayas preferido	**hayáis** preferido
haya preferido	**hayan** preferido
pluscuamperfecto de subjuntivo	
hubiera preferido	**hubiéramos** preferido
hubieras preferido	**hubierais** preferido
hubiera preferido	**hubieran** preferido
OR	
hubiese preferido	**hubiésemos** preferido
hubieses preferido	**hubieseis** preferido
hubiese preferido	**hubiesen** preferido

preguntar — to ask

gerundio **preguntando** participio de pasado **preguntado**

SINGULAR	PLURAL	SINGULAR	PLURAL
presente de indicativo		perfecto de indicativo	
pregunt**o**	pregunt**amos**	**he** preguntado	**hemos** preguntado
pregunt**as**	pregunt**áis**	**has** preguntado	**habéis** preguntado
pregunt**a**	pregunt**an**	**ha** preguntado	**han** preguntado
imperfecto de indicativo		pluscuamperfecto de indicativo	
pregunt**aba**	pregunt**ábamos**	**había** preguntado	**habíamos** preguntado
pregunt**abas**	pregunt**abais**	**habías** preguntado	**habíais** preguntado
pregunt**aba**	pregunt**aban**	**había** preguntado	**habían** preguntado
pretérito		pretérito anterior	
pregunt**é**	pregunt**amos**	**hube** preguntado	**hubimos** preguntado
pregunt**aste**	pregunt**asteis**	**hubiste** preguntado	**hubisteis** preguntado
pregunt**ó**	pregunt**aron**	**hubo** preguntado	**hubieron** preguntado
futuro		futuro perfecto	
preguntar**é**	preguntar**emos**	**habré** preguntado	**habremos** preguntado
preguntar**ás**	preguntar**éis**	**habrás** preguntado	**habréis** preguntado
preguntar**á**	preguntar**án**	**habrá** preguntado	**habrán** preguntado
condicional simple		condicional compuesto	
preguntar**ía**	preguntar**íamos**	**habría** preguntado	**habríamos** preguntado
preguntar**ías**	preguntar**íais**	**habrías** preguntado	**habríais** preguntado
preguntar**ía**	preguntar**ían**	**habría** preguntado	**habrían** preguntado
presente de subjuntivo		perfecto de subjuntivo	
pregunt**e**	pregunt**emos**	**haya** preguntado	**hayamos** preguntado
pregunt**es**	pregunt**éis**	**hayas** preguntado	**hayáis** preguntado
pregunt**e**	pregunt**en**	**haya** preguntado	**hayan** preguntado
imperfecto de subjuntivo		pluscuamperfecto de subjuntivo	
preguntar**a**	preguntár**amos**	**hubiera** preguntado	**hubiéramos** preguntado
preguntar**as**	preguntar**ais**	**hubieras** preguntado	**hubierais** preguntado
preguntar**a**	preguntar**an**	**hubiera** preguntado	**hubieran** preguntado
OR		OR	
preguntas**e**	preguntás**emos**	**hubiese** preguntado	**hubiésemos** preguntado
preguntas**es**	preguntas**eis**	**hubieses** preguntado	**hubieseis** preguntado
preguntas**e**	preguntas**en**	**hubiese** preguntado	**hubiesen** preguntado

imperativo

—	preguntemos
pregunta; no preguntes	preguntad; no preguntéis
pregunte	pregunten

MUST KNOW VERB

gerundio **preocupándose** participio de pasado **preocupado**

SINGULAR	PLURAL	SINGULAR	PLURAL
presente de indicativo		perfecto de indicativo	
me preocup**o**	nos preocup**amos**	**me he** preocupado	**nos hemos** preocupado
te preocup**as**	os preocup**áis**	**te has** preocupado	**os habéis** preocupado
se preocup**a**	se preocup**an**	**se ha** preocupado	**se han** preocupado
imperfecto de indicativo		pluscuamperfecto de indicativo	
me preocup**aba**	nos preocup**ábamos**	**me había** preocupado	**nos habíamos** preocupado
te preocup**abas**	os preocup**abais**	**te habías** preocupado	**os habíais** preocupado
se preocup**aba**	se preocup**aban**	**se había** preocupado	**se habían** preocupado
pretérito		pretérito anterior	
me preocup**é**	nos preocup**amos**	**me hube** preocupado	**nos hubimos** preocupado
te preocup**aste**	os preocup**asteis**	**te hubiste** preocupado	**os hubisteis** preocupado
se preocup**ó**	se preocup**aron**	**se hubo** preocupado	**se hubieron** preocupado
futuro		futuro perfecto	
me preocup**aré**	nos preocup**aremos**	**me habré** preocupado	**nos habremos** preocupado
te preocup**arás**	os preocup**aréis**	**te habrás** preocupado	**os habréis** preocupado
se preocup**ará**	se preocup**arán**	**se habrá** preocupado	**se habrán** preocupado
condicional simple		condicional compuesto	
me preocupar**ía**	nos preocupar**íamos**	**me habría** preocupado	**nos habríamos** preocupado
te preocupar**ías**	os preocupar**íais**	**te habrías** preocupado	**os habríais** preocupado
se preocupar**ía**	se preocupar**ían**	**se habría** preocupado	**se habrían** preocupado
presente de subjuntivo		perfecto de subjuntivo	
me preocup**e**	nos preocup**emos**	**me haya** preocupado	**nos hayamos** preocupado
te preocup**es**	os preocup**éis**	**te hayas** preocupado	**os hayáis** preocupado
se preocup**e**	se preocup**en**	**se haya** preocupado	**se hayan** preocupado
imperfecto de subjuntivo		pluscuamperfecto de subjuntivo	
me preocupar**a**	nos preocupár**amos**	**me hubiera** preocupado	**nos hubiéramos** preocupado
te preocupar**as**	os preocupar**ais**	**te hubieras** preocupado	**os hubierais** preocupado
se preocupar**a**	se preocupar**an**	**se hubiera** preocupado	**se hubieran** preocupado
OR		OR	
me preocupas**e**	nos preocupás**emos**	**me hubiese** preocupado	**nos hubiésemos** preocupado
te preocupas**es**	os preocupas**eis**	**te hubieses** preocupado	**os hubieseis** preocupado
se preocupas**e**	se preocupas**en**	**se hubiese** preocupado	**se hubiesen** preocupado

imperativo

—	preocupémonos
preocúpate;	preocupaos;
no te preocupes	no os preocupéis
preocúpese	preocúpense

preparar — to prepare

gerundio **preparando** — participio de pasado **preparado**

SINGULAR	PLURAL
presente de indicativo	
prepar**o**	prepar**amos**
prepar**as**	prepar**áis**
prepar**a**	prepar**an**
imperfecto de indicativo	
prepar**aba**	prepar**ábamos**
prepar**abas**	prepar**abais**
prepar**aba**	prepar**aban**
pretérito	
prepar**é**	prepar**amos**
prepar**aste**	prepar**asteis**
prepar**ó**	prepar**aron**
futuro	
preparar**é**	preparar**emos**
preparar**ás**	preparar**éis**
preparar**á**	preparar**án**
condicional simple	
preparar**ía**	preparar**íamos**
preparar**ías**	preparar**íais**
preparar**ía**	preparar**ían**
presente de subjuntivo	
prepar**e**	prepar**emos**
prepar**es**	prepar**éis**
prepar**e**	prepar**en**
imperfecto de subjuntivo	
preparar**a**	preparár**amos**
preparar**as**	preparar**ais**
preparar**a**	preparar**an**
OR	
preparas**e**	preparás**emos**
preparas**es**	preparas**eis**
preparas**e**	preparas**en**
imperativo	
—	preparemos
prepara; no prepares	preparad; no preparéis
prepare	preparen

SINGULAR	PLURAL
perfecto de indicativo	
he preparado	**hemos** preparado
has preparado	**habéis** preparado
ha preparado	**han** preparado
pluscuamperfecto de indicativo	
había preparado	**habíamos** preparado
habías preparado	**habíais** preparado
había preparado	**habían** preparado
pretérito anterior	
hube preparado	**hubimos** preparado
hubiste preparado	**hubisteis** preparado
hubo preparado	**hubieron** preparado
futuro perfecto	
habré preparado	**habremos** preparado
habrás preparado	**habréis** preparado
habrá preparado	**habrán** preparado
condicional compuesto	
habría preparado	**habríamos** preparado
habrías preparado	**habríais** preparado
habría preparado	**habrían** preparado
perfecto de subjuntivo	
haya preparado	**hayamos** preparado
hayas preparado	**hayáis** preparado
haya preparado	**hayan** preparado
pluscuamperfecto de subjuntivo	
hubiera preparado	**hubiéramos** preparado
hubieras preparado	**hubierais** preparado
hubiera preparado	**hubieran** preparado
OR	
hubiese preparado	**hubiésemos** preparado
hubieses preparado	**hubieseis** preparado
hubiese preparado	**hubiesen** preparado

to be prepared, to get ready **preparerse**

gerundio **preparándose** participio de pasado **preparado**

SINGULAR	PLURAL	SINGULAR	PLURAL
presente de indicativo		perfecto de indicativo	
me prepar**o**	nos prepar**amos**	**me he** preparado	**nos hemos** preparado
te prepar**as**	os prepar**áis**	**te has** preparado	**os habéis** preparado
se prepar**a**	se prepar**an**	**se ha** preparado	**se han** preparado
imperfecto de indicativo		pluscuamperfecto de indicativo	
me prepar**aba**	nos prepar**ábamos**	**me había** preparado	**nos habíamos** preparado
te prepar**abas**	os prepar**abais**	**te habías** preparado	**os habíais** preparado
se prepar**aba**	se prepar**aban**	**se había** preparado	**se habían** preparado
pretérito		pretérito anterior	
me prepar**é**	nos prepar**amos**	**me hube** preparado	**nos hubimos** preparado
te prepar**aste**	os prepar**asteis**	**te hubiste** preparado	**os hubisteis** preparado
se prepar**ó**	se prepar**aron**	**se hubo** preparado	**se hubieron** preparado
futuro		futuro perfecto	
me preparar**é**	nos preparar**emos**	**me habré** preparado	**nos habremos** preparado
te preparar**ás**	os preparar**éis**	**te habrás** preparado	**os habréis** preparado
se preparar**á**	se preparar**án**	**se habrá** preparado	**se habrán** preparado
condicional simple		condicional compuesto	
me preparar**ía**	nos preparar**íamos**	**me habría** preparado	**nos habríamos** preparado
te preparar**ías**	os preparar**íais**	**te habrías** preparado	**os habríais** preparado
se preparar**ía**	se preparar**ían**	**se habría** preparado	**se habrían** preparado
presente de subjuntivo		perfecto de subjuntivo	
me prepar**e**	nos prepar**emos**	**me haya** preparado	**nos hayamos** preparado
te prepar**es**	os prepar**éis**	**te hayas** preparado	**os hayáis** preparado
se prepar**e**	se prepar**en**	**se haya** preparado	**se hayan** preparado
imperfecto de subjuntivo		pluscuamperfecto de subjuntivo	
me preparar**a**	nos preparár**amos**	**me hubiera** preparado	**nos hubiéramos** preparado
te preparar**as**	os preparar**ais**	**te hubieras** preparado	**os hubierais** preparado
se preparar**a**	se preparar**an**	**se hubiera** preparado	**se hubieran** preparado
OR		OR	
me prepara**se**	nos preparás**emos**	**me hubiese** preparado	**nos hubiésemos** preparado
te prepara**ses**	os prepara**seis**	**te hubieses** preparado	**os hubieseis** preparado
se prepara**se**	se prepara**sen**	**se hubiese** preparado	**se hubiesen** preparado

imperativo

—	preparémonos
prepárate; no te prepares	preparaos; no os preparéis
prepárese	prepárense

P

presentar — to present

gerundio **presentando** — participio de pasado **presentado**

SINGULAR	PLURAL
presente de indicativo	
present**o**	present**amos**
present**as**	present**áis**
present**a**	present**an**
imperfecto de indicativo	
present**aba**	present**ábamos**
present**abas**	present**abais**
present**aba**	present**aban**
pretérito	
present**é**	present**amos**
present**aste**	present**asteis**
present**ó**	present**aron**
futuro	
presentar**é**	presentar**emos**
presentar**ás**	presentar**éis**
presentar**á**	presentar**án**
condicional simple	
presentar**ía**	presentar**íamos**
presentar**ías**	presentar**íais**
presentar**ía**	presentar**ían**
presente de subjuntivo	
present**e**	present**emos**
present**es**	present**éis**
present**e**	present**en**
imperfecto de subjuntivo	
presentar**a**	presentár**amos**
presentar**as**	presentar**ais**
presentar**a**	presentar**an**
OR	
presentas**e**	presentás**emos**
presentas**es**	presentas**eis**
presentas**e**	presentas**en**
imperativo	
—	presentemos
presenta; no presentes	presentad; no presentéis
presente	presenten

SINGULAR	PLURAL
perfecto de indicativo	
he presentado	**hemos** presentado
has presentado	**habéis** presentado
ha presentado	**han** presentado
pluscuamperfecto de indicativo	
había presentado	**habíamos** presentado
habías presentado	**habíais** presentado
había presentado	**habían** presentado
pretérito anterior	
hube presentado	**hubimos** presentado
hubiste presentado	**hubisteis** presentado
hubo presentado	**hubieron** presentado
futuro perfecto	
habré presentado	**habremos** presentado
habrás presentado	**habréis** presentado
habrá presentado	**habrán** presentado
condicional compuesto	
habría presentado	**habríamos** presentado
habrías presentado	**habríais** presentado
habría presentado	**habrían** presentado
perfecto de subjuntivo	
haya presentado	**hayamos** presentado
hayas presentado	**hayáis** presentado
haya presentado	**hayan** presentado
pluscuamperfecto de subjuntivo	
hubiera presentado	**hubiéramos** presentado
hubieras presentado	**hubierais** presentado
hubiera presentado	**hubieran** presentado
OR	
hubiese presentado	**hubiésemos** presentado
hubieses presentado	**hubieseis** presentado
hubiese presentado	**hubiesen** presentado

gerundio **prestando** participio de pasado **prestado**

SINGULAR	PLURAL	SINGULAR	PLURAL
presente de indicativo		perfecto de indicativo	
prest**o**	prest**amos**	**he** prestado	**hemos** prestado
prest**as**	prest**áis**	**has** prestado	**habéis** prestado
prest**a**	prest**an**	**ha** prestado	**han** prestado
imperfecto de indicativo		pluscuamperfecto de indicativo	
prest**aba**	prest**ábamos**	**había** prestado	**habíamos** prestado
prest**abas**	prest**abais**	**habías** prestado	**habíais** prestado
prest**aba**	prest**aban**	**había** prestado	**habían** prestado
pretérito		pretérito anterior	
prest**é**	prest**amos**	**hube** prestado	**hubimos** prestado
prest**aste**	prest**asteis**	**hubiste** prestado	**hubisteis** prestado
prest**ó**	prest**aron**	**hubo** prestado	**hubieron** prestado
futuro		futuro perfecto	
prestar**é**	prestar**emos**	**habré** prestado	**habremos** prestado
prestar**ás**	prestar**éis**	**habrás** prestado	**habréis** prestado
prestar**á**	prestar**án**	**habrá** prestado	**habrán** prestado
condicional simple		condicional compuesto	
prestar**ía**	prestar**íamos**	**habría** prestado	**habríamos** prestado
prestar**ías**	prestar**íais**	**habrías** prestado	**habríais** prestado
prestar**ía**	prestar**ían**	**habría** prestado	**habrían** prestado
presente de subjuntivo		perfecto de subjuntivo	
prest**e**	prest**emos**	**haya** prestado	**hayamos** prestado
prest**es**	prest**éis**	**hayas** prestado	**hayáis** prestado
prest**e**	prest**en**	**haya** prestado	**hayan** prestado
imperfecto de subjuntivo		pluscuamperfecto de subjuntivo	
prestar**a**	prestár**amos**	**hubiera** prestado	**hubiéramos** prestado
prestar**as**	prestar**ais**	**hubieras** prestado	**hubierais** prestado
prestar**a**	prestar**an**	**hubiera** prestado	**hubieran** prestado
OR		OR	
presta**se**	prestás**emos**	**hubiese** prestado	**hubiésemos** prestado
presta**ses**	presta**seis**	**hubieses** prestado	**hubieseis** prestado
presta**se**	presta**sen**	**hubiese** prestado	**hubiesen** prestado

imperativo

—	prestemos
presta; no prestes	prestad; no prestéis
preste	presten

principiar — to begin

gerundio **principiando** participio de pasado **principiado**

SINGULAR	PLURAL	SINGULAR	PLURAL
presente de indicativo		perfecto de indicativo	
principi**o**	principi**amos**	**he** principiado	**hemos** principiado
principi**as**	principi**áis**	**has** principiado	**habéis** principiado
principi**a**	principi**an**	**ha** principiado	**han** principiado
imperfecto de indicativo		pluscuamperfecto de indicativo	
principi**aba**	principi**ábamos**	**había** principiado	**habíamos** principiado
principi**abas**	principi**abais**	**habías** principiado	**habíais** principiado
principi**aba**	principi**aban**	**había** principiado	**habían** principiado
pretérito		pretérito anterior	
principi**é**	principi**amos**	**hube** principiado	**hubimos** principiado
principi**aste**	principi**asteis**	**hubiste** principiado	**hubisteis** principiado
principi**ó**	principi**aron**	**hubo** principiado	**hubieron** principiado
futuro		futuro perfecto	
principiar**é**	principiar**emos**	**habré** principiado	**habremos** principiado
principiar**ás**	principiar**éis**	**habrás** principiado	**habréis** principiado
principiar**á**	principiar**án**	**habrá** principiado	**habrán** principiado
condicional simple		condicional compuesto	
principiar**ía**	principiar**íamos**	**habría** principiado	**habríamos** principiado
principiar**ías**	principiar**íais**	**habrías** principiado	**habríais** principiado
principiar**ía**	principiar**ían**	**habría** principiado	**habrían** principiado
presente de subjuntivo		perfecto de subjuntivo	
principi**e**	principi**emos**	**haya** principiado	**hayamos** principiado
principi**es**	principi**éis**	**hayas** principiado	**hayáis** principiado
principi**e**	principi**en**	**haya** principiado	**hayan** principiado
imperfecto de subjuntivo		pluscuamperfecto de subjuntivo	
principiar**a**	principiár**amos**	**hubiera** principiado	**hubiéramos** principiado
principiar**as**	principiar**ais**	**hubieras** principiado	**hubierais** principiado
principiar**a**	principiar**an**	**hubiera** principiado	**hubieran** principiado
OR		OR	
principias**e**	principiás**emos**	**hubiese** principiado	**hubiésemos** principiado
principias**es**	principias**eis**	**hubieses** principiado	**hubieseis** principiado
principias**e**	principias**en**	**hubiese** principiado	**hubiesen** principiado

imperativo

—	
principia	principiemos
no principies	principiad; no principiéis
principie	principien

to try, to test, to prove **probar**

gerundio **probando** participio de pasado **probado**

SINGULAR	PLURAL	SINGULAR	PLURAL
presente de indicativo		perfecto de indicativo	
prueb**o**	prob**amos**	**he** probado	**hemos** probado
prueb**as**	prob**áis**	**has** probado	**habéis** probado
prueb**a**	prueb**an**	**ha** probado	**han** probado
imperfecto de indicativo		pluscuamperfecto de indicativo	
prob**aba**	prob**ábamos**	**había** probado	**habíamos** probado
prob**abas**	prob**abais**	**habías** probado	**habíais** probado
prob**aba**	prob**aban**	**había** probado	**habían** probado
pretérito		pretérito anterior	
prob**é**	prob**amos**	**hube** probado	**hubimos** probado
prob**aste**	prob**asteis**	**hubiste** probado	**hubisteis** probado
prob**ó**	prob**aron**	**hubo** probado	**hubieron** probado
futuro		futuro perfecto	
probar**é**	probar**emos**	**habré** probado	**habremos** probado
probar**ás**	probar**éis**	**habrás** probado	**habréis** probado
probar**á**	probar**án**	**habrá** probado	**habrán** probado
condicional simple		condicional compuesto	
probar**ía**	probar**íamos**	**habría** probado	**habríamos** probado
probar**ías**	probar**íais**	**habrías** probado	**habríais** probado
probar**ía**	probar**ían**	**habría** probado	**habrían** probado
presente de subjuntivo		perfecto de subjuntivo	
prueb**e**	prob**emos**	**haya** probado	**hayamos** probado
prueb**es**	prob**éis**	**hayas** probado	**hayáis** probado
prueb**e**	prueb**en**	**haya** probado	**hayan** probado
imperfecto de subjuntivo		pluscuamperfecto de subjuntivo	
probar**a**	probár**amos**	**hubiera** probado	**hubiéramos** probado
probar**as**	probar**ais**	**hubieras** probado	**hubierais** probado
probar**a**	probar**an**	**hubiera** probado	**hubieran** probado
OR		OR	
probas**e**	probás**emos**	**hubiese** probado	**hubiésemos** probado
probas**es**	probas**eis**	**hubieses** probado	**hubieseis** probado
probas**e**	probas**en**	**hubiese** probado	**hubiesen**

imperativo

—	probemos
prueba; no pruebes	probad; no probéis
pruebe	prueben

P

probarse — to try on clothes

gerundio **probándose** participio de pasado **probado**

SINGULAR	PLURAL	SINGULAR	PLURAL
presente de indicativo		perfecto de indicativo	
me prueb**o**	nos prob**amos**	**me he** probado	**nos hemos** probado
te prueb**as**	os prob**áis**	**te has** probado	**os habéis** probado
se prueb**a**	se prueb**an**	**se ha** probado	**se han** probado
imperfecto de indicativo		pluscuamperfecto de indicativo	
me prob**aba**	nos prob**ábamos**	**me había** probado	**nos habíamos** probado
te prob**abas**	os prob**abais**	**te habías** probado	**os habíais** probado
se prob**aba**	se prob**aban**	**se había** probado	**se habían** probado
pretérito		pretérito anterior	
me prob**é**	nos prob**amos**	**me hube** probado	**nos hubimos** probado
te prob**aste**	os prob**asteis**	**te hubiste** probado	**os hubisteis** probado
se prob**ó**	se prob**aron**	**se hubo** probado	**se hubieron** probado
futuro		futuro perfecto	
me probar**é**	nos probar**emos**	**me habré** probado	**nos habremos** probado
te probar**ás**	os probar**éis**	**te habrás** probado	**os habréis** probado
se probar**á**	se probar**án**	**se habrá** probado	**se habrán** probado
condicional simple		condicional compuesto	
me probar**ía**	nos probar**íamos**	**me habría** probado	**nos habríamos** probado
te probar**ías**	os probar**íais**	**te habrías** probado	**os habríais** probado
se probar**ía**	se probar**ían**	**se habría** probado	**se habrían** probado
presente de subjuntivo		perfecto de subjuntivo	
me prueb**e**	nos prob**emos**	**me haya** probado	**nos hayamos** probado
te prueb**es**	os prob**éis**	**te hayas** probado	**os hayáis** probado
se prueb**e**	se prueb**en**	**se haya** probado	**se hayan** probado
imperfecto de subjuntivo		pluscuamperfecto de subjuntivo	
me probar**a**	nos probár**amos**	**me hubiera** probado	**nos hubiéramos** probado
te probar**as**	os probar**ais**	**te hubieras** probado	**os hubierais** probado
se probar**a**	se probar**an**	**se hubiera** probado	**se hubieran** probado
OR		OR	
me probas**e**	nos probás**emos**	**me hubiese** probado	**nos hubiésemos** probado
te probas**es**	os probas**eis**	**te hubieses** probado	**os hubieseis** probado
se probas**e**	se probas**en**	**se hubiese** probado	**se hubiesen** probado

imperativo

—	probémonos
pruébate;	probaos;
no te pruebes	no os probéis
pruébese	pruébense

gerundio **proclamando** participio de pasado **proclamado**

SINGULAR	PLURAL	SINGULAR	PLURAL
presente de indicativo		perfecto de indicativo	
proclam**o**	proclam**amos**	**he** proclamado	**hemos** proclamado
proclam**as**	proclam**áis**	**has** proclamado	**habéis** proclamado
proclam**a**	proclam**an**	**ha** proclamado	**han** proclamado
imperfecto de indicativo		pluscuamperfecto de indicativo	
proclam**aba**	proclam**ábamos**	**había** proclamado	**habíamos** proclamado
proclam**abas**	proclam**abais**	**habías** proclamado	**habíais** proclamado
proclam**aba**	proclam**aban**	**había** proclamado	**habían** proclamado
pretérito		pretérito anterior	
proclam**é**	proclam**amos**	**hube** proclamado	**hubimos** proclamado
proclam**aste**	proclam**asteis**	**hubiste** proclamado	**hubisteis** proclamado
proclam**ó**	proclam**aron**	**hubo** proclamado	**hubieron** proclamado
futuro		futuro perfecto	
proclamar**é**	proclamar**emos**	**habré** proclamado	**habremos** proclamado
proclamar**ás**	proclamar**éis**	**habrás** proclamado	**habréis** proclamado
proclamar**á**	proclamar**án**	**habrá** proclamado	**habrán** proclamado
condicional simple		condicional compuesto	
proclamar**ía**	proclamar**íamos**	**habría** proclamado	**habríamos** proclamado
proclamar**ías**	proclamar**íais**	**habrías** proclamado	**habríais** proclamado
proclamar**ía**	proclamar**ían**	**habría** proclamado	**habrían** proclamado
presente de subjuntivo		perfecto de subjuntivo	
proclam**e**	proclam**emos**	**haya** proclamado	**hayamos** proclamado
proclam**es**	proclam**éis**	**hayas** proclamado	**hayáis** proclamado
proclam**e**	proclam**en**	**haya** proclamado	**hayan** proclamado
imperfecto de subjuntivo		pluscuamperfecto de subjuntivo	
proclamar**a**	proclamár**amos**	**hubiera** proclamado	**hubiéramos** proclamado
proclamar**as**	proclamar**ais**	**hubieras** proclamado	**hubierais** proclamado
proclamar**a**	proclamar**an**	**hubiera** proclamado	**hubieran** proclamado
OR		OR	
proclamas**e**	proclamás**emos**	**hubiese** proclamado	**hubiésemos** proclamado
proclamas**es**	proclamas**eis**	**hubieses** proclamado	**hubieseis** proclamado
proclamas**e**	proclamas**en**	**hubiese** proclamado	**hubiesen** proclamado

imperativo

—	proclamemos
proclama;	proclamad;
no proclames	no proclaméis
proclame	proclamen

producir — to produce, to cause

gerundio **producIendo**

participio de pasado **producido**

presente de indicativo

SINGULAR	PLURAL
produzc**o**	produc**imos**
produc**es**	produc**ís**
produc**e**	produc**en**

imperfecto de indicativo

SINGULAR	PLURAL
produc**ía**	produc**íamos**
produc**ías**	produc**íais**
produc**ía**	produc**ían**

pretérito

SINGULAR	PLURAL
produj**e**	produj**imos**
produj**iste**	produj**isteis**
produj**o**	produj**eron**

futuro

SINGULAR	PLURAL
producir**é**	producir**emos**
producir**ás**	producir**éis**
producir**á**	producir**án**

condicional simple

SINGULAR	PLURAL
producir**ía**	producir**íamos**
producir**ías**	producir**íais**
producir**ía**	producir**ían**

presente de subjuntivo

SINGULAR	PLURAL
produzc**a**	produzc**amos**
produzc**as**	produzc**áis**
produzc**a**	produzc**an**

imperfecto de subjuntivo

SINGULAR	PLURAL
produjer**a**	produjér**amos**
produjer**as**	produjer**ais**
produjer**a**	produjer**an**
OR	
produjes**e**	produjés**emos**
produjes**es**	produjes**eis**
produjes**e**	produjes**en**

imperativo

SINGULAR	PLURAL
—	produzcamos
produce; no produzcas	producid; no produzcáis
produzca	produzcan

perfecto de indicativo

SINGULAR	PLURAL
he producido	**hemos** producido
has producido	**habéis** producido
ha producido	**han** producido

pluscuamperfecto de indicativo

SINGULAR	PLURAL
había producido	**habíamos** producido
habías producido	**habíais** producido
había producido	**habían** producido

pretérito anterior

SINGULAR	PLURAL
hube producido	**hubimos** producido
hubiste producido	**hubisteis** producido
hubo producido	**hubieron** producido

futuro perfecto

SINGULAR	PLURAL
habré producido	**habremos** producido
habrás producido	**habréis** producido
habrá producido	**habrán** producido

condicional compuesto

SINGULAR	PLURAL
habría producido	**habríamos** producido
habrías producido	**habríais** producido
habría producido	**habrían** producido

perfecto de subjuntivo

SINGULAR	PLURAL
haya producido	**hayamos** producido
hayas producido	**hayáis** producido
haya producido	**hayan** producido

pluscuamperfecto de subjuntivo

SINGULAR	PLURAL
hubiera producido	**hubiéramos** producido
hubieras producido	**hubierais** produddo
hubiera producido	**hubieran** producido
OR	
hubiese producido	**hubiésemos** producido
hubieses producido	**hubieseis** producido
hubiese producido	**hubiesen** producido

to prohibit, to forbid — prohibir

gerundio **prohibiendo** participio de pasado **prohibido**

SINGULAR	PLURAL

presente de indicativo

prohib**o**	prohib**imos**
prohib**es**	prohib**ís**
prohib**e**	prohib**en**

imperfecto de indicativo

prohib**ía**	prohib**íamos**
prohib**ías**	prohib**íais**
prohib**ía**	prohib**ían**

pretérito

prohib**í**	prohib**imos**
prohib**iste**	prohib**isteis**
prohib**ió**	prohib**ieron**

futuro

prohibir**é**	prohibir**emos**
prohibir**ás**	prohibir**éis**
prohibir**á**	prohibir**án**

condicional simple

prohibir**á**	prohibir**íamos**
prohibir**ías**	prohibir**íais**
prohibir**ía**	prohibir**ían**

presente de subjuntivo

prohib**a**	prohib**amos**
prohib**as**	prohib**áis**
prohib**a**	prohib**an**

imperfecto de subjuntivo

prohibier**a**	prohibiér**amos**
prohibier**as**	prohibier**ais**
prohibier**a**	prohibier**an**
OR	
prohibies**e**	prohibiés**emos**
prohibies**es**	prohibies**eis**
prohibies**e**	prohibies**en**

imperativo

—	prohibamos
prohibe; no prohibas	prohibid; no prohibáis
prohiba	prohiban

SINGULAR	PLURAL

perfecto de indicativo

he prohibido	**hemos** prohibido
has prohibido	**habéis** prohibido
ha prohibido	**han** prohibido

pluscuamperfecto de indicativo

había prohibido	**habíamos** prohibido
habías prohibido	**habíais** prohibido
había prohibido	**habían** prohibido

pretérito anterior

hube prohibido	**hubimos** prohibido
hubiste prohibido	**hubisteis** prohibido
hubo prohibido	**hubieron** prohibido

futuro perfecto

habré prohibido	**habremos** prohibido
habrás prohibido	**habréis** prohibido
habrá prohibido	**habrán** prohibido

condicional compuesto

habría prohibido	**habríamos** prohibido
habrías prohibido	**habríais** prohibido
habría prohibido	**habrían** prohibido

perfecto de subjuntivo

haya prohibido	**hayamos** prohibido
hayas prohibido	**hayáis** prohibido
haya prohibido	**hayan** prohibido

pluscuamperfecto de subjuntivo

hubiera prohibido	**hubiéramos** prohibido
hubieras prohibido	**hubierais** prohibido
hubiera prohibido	**hubieran** prohibido
OR	
hubiese prohibido	**hubiésemos** prohibido
hubieses prohibido	**hubieseis** prohibido
hubiese prohibido	**hubiesen** prohibido

pronunciar — to pronounce

gerundio **pronunciando** participio de pasado **pronunciado**

SINGULAR	PLURAL	SINGULAR	PLURAL
presente de indicativo		perfecto de indicativo	
pronunci**o**	pronunci**amos**	**he** pronunciado	**hemos** pronunciado
pronunci**as**	pronunci**áis**	**has** pronunciado	**habéis** pronunciado
pronunci**a**	pronunci**an**	**ha** pronunciado	**han** pronunciado
imperfecto de indicativo		pluscuamperfecto de indicativo	
pronunci**aba**	pronunci**ábamos**	**había** pronunciado	**habíamos** pronunciado
pronunci**abas**	pronunci**abais**	**habías** pronunciado	**habíais** pronunciado
pronunci**aba**	pronunci**aban**	**había** pronunciado	**habían** pronunciado
pretérito		pretérito anterior	
pronunci**é**	pronunci**amos**	**hube** pronunciado	**hubimos** pronunciado
pronunci**aste**	pronunci**asteis**	**hubiste** pronunciado	**hubisteis** pronunciado
pronunci**ó**	pronunci**aron**	**hubo** pronunciado	**hubieron** pronunciado
futuro		futuro perfecto	
pronunciar**é**	pronunciar**emos**	**habré** pronunciado	**habremos** pronunciado
pronunciar**ás**	pronunciar**éis**	**habrás** pronunciado	**habréis** pronunciado
pronunciar**á**	pronunciar**án**	**habrá** pronunciado	**habrán** pronunciado
condicional simple		condicional compuesto	
pronunciar**ía**	pronunciar**íamos**	**habría** pronunciado	**habríamos** pronunciado
pronunciar**ías**	pronunciar**íais**	**habrías** pronunciado	**habríais** pronunciado
pronunciar**ía**	pronunciar**ían**	**habría** pronunciado	**habrían** pronunciado
presente de subjuntivo		perfecto de subjuntivo	
pronunci**e**	pronunci**emos**	**haya** pronunciado	**hayamos** pronunciado
pronunci**es**	pronunci**éis**	**hayas** pronunciado	**hayáis** pronunciado
pronunci**e**	pronunci**en**	**haya** pronunciado	**hayan** pronunciado
imperfecto de subjuntivo		pluscuamperfecto de subjuntivo	
pronunciar**a**	pronunciár**amos**	**hubiera** pronunciado	**hubiéramos** pronunciado
pronunciar**as**	pronunciar**ais**	**hubieras** pronunciado	**hubierais** pronunciado
pronunciar**a**	pronunciar**an**	**hubiera** pronunciado	**hubieran** pronunciado
OR		OR	
pronuncias**e**	pronunciás**emos**	**hubiese** pronunciado	**hubiésemos** pronunciado
pronuncias**es**	pronuncias**eis**	**hubieses** pronunciado	**hubieseis** pronunciado
pronuncias**e**	pronuncias**en**	**hubiese** pronunciado	**hubiesen** pronunciado
imperativo			
—	pronunciemos		
pronuncia; no pronuncies	pronunciad; no pronunciéis		
pronuncie	pronuncien		

gerundio **proporcionando** participio de pasado **proporcionado**

SINGULAR	PLURAL	SINGULAR	PLURAL
presente de indicativo		perfecto de indicativo	
proporciono	proporcionamos	he proporcionado	hemos proporcionado
proporcionas	proporcionáis	has proporcionado	habéis proporcionado
proporciona	proporcionan	ha proporcionado	han proporcionado
imperfecto de indicativo		pluscuamperfecto de indicativo	
proporcionaba	proporcionábamos	había proporcionado	habíamos proporcionado
proporcionabas	proporcionabais	habías proporcionado	habíais proporcionado
proporcionaba	proporcionaban	había proporcionado	habían proporcionado
pretérito		pretérito anterior	
proporcioné	proporcionamos	hube proporcionado	hubimos proporcionado
proporcionaste	proporcionasteis	hubiste proporcionado	hubisteis proporcionado
proporcionó	proporcionaron	hubo proporcionado	hubieron proporcionado
futuro		futuro perfecto	
proporcionaré	proporcionaremos	habré proporcionado	habremos proporcionado
proporcionarás	proporcionaréis	habrás proporcionado	habréis proporcionado
proporcionará	proporcionarán	habrá proporcionado	habrán proporcionado
condicional simple		condicional compuesto	
proporcionaría	proporcionaríamos	habría proporcionado	habríamos proporcionado
proporcionarías	proporcionaríais	habrías proporcionado	habríais proporcionado
proporcionaría	proporcionarían	habría proporcionado	habrían proporcionado
presente de subjuntivo		perfecto de subjuntivo	
proporcione	proporcionemos	haya proporcionado	hayamos proporcionado
proporciones	proporcionéis	hayas proporcionado	hayáis proporcionado
proporcione	proporcionen	haya proporcionado	hayan proporcionado
imperfecto de subjuntivo		pluscuamperfecto de subjuntivo	
proporcionara	proporcionáramos	hubiera proporcionado	hubiéramos proporcionado
proporcionaras	proporcionarais	hubieras proporcionado	hubierais proporcionado
proporcionara	proporcionaran	hubiera proporcionado	hubieran proporcionado
OR		OR	
proporcionase	proporcionásemos	hubiese proporcionado	hubiésemos proporcionado
proporcionases	proporcionaseis	hubieses proporcionado	hubieseis proporcionado
proporcionase	proporcionasen	hubiese proporcionado	hubiesen proporcionado

imperativo

—	proporcionemos
proporciona;	proporcionad;
no proporciones	no proporcionéis
proporcione	proporcionen

proteger — to protect

gerundio **protegiendo** — participio de pasado **protegido**

SINGULAR	PLURAL	SINGULAR	PLURAL
presente de indicativo		perfecto de indicativo	
protej**o**	proteg**emos**	**he** protegido	**hemos** protegido
proteg**es**	proteg**éis**	**has** protegido	**habéis** protegido
proteg**e**	proteg**en**	**ha** protegido	**han** protegido
imperfecto de indicativo		pluscuamperfecto de indicativo	
proteg**ía**	proteg**íamos**	**había** protegido	**habíamos** protegido
proteg**ías**	proteg**íais**	**habías** protegido	**habíais** protegido
proteg**ía**	proteg**ían**	**había** protegido	**habían** protegido
pretérito		pretérito anterior	
proteg**í**	proteg**imos**	**hube** protegido	**hubimos** protegido
proteg**iste**	proteg**isteis**	**hubiste** protegido	**hubisteis** protegido
proteg**ió**	proteg**ieron**	**hubo** protegido	**hubieron** protegido
futuro		futuro perfecto	
proteger**é**	proteger**emos**	**habré** protegido	**habremos** protegido
proteger**ás**	proteger**éis**	**habrás** protegido	**habréis** protegido
proteger**á**	proteger**án**	**habrá** protegido	**habrán** protegido
condicional simple		condicional compuesto	
proteger**ía**	proteger**íamos**	**habría** protegido	**habríamos** protegido
proteger**ías**	proteger**íais**	**habrías** protegido	**habríais** protegido
proteger**ía**	proteger**ían**	**habría** protegido	**habrían** protegido
presente de subjuntivo		perfecto de subjuntivo	
protej**a**	protej**amos**	**haya** protegido	**hayamos** protegido
protej**as**	protej**áis**	**hayas** protegido	**hayáis** protegido
protej**a**	protej**an**	**haya** protegido	**hayan** protegido
imperfecto de subjuntivo		pluscuamperfecto de subjuntivo	
protegier**a**	protegiér**amos**	**hubiera** protegido	**hubiéramos** protegido
protegier**as**	protegier**ais**	**hubieras** protegido	**hubierais** protegido
protegier**a**	protegier**an**	**hubiera** protegido	**hubieran** protegido
OR		OR	
protegies**e**	protegiés**emos**	**hubiese** protegido	**hubiésemos** protegido
protegies**es**	protegies**eis**	**hubieses** protegido	**hubieseis** protegido
protegies**e**	protegies**en**	**hubiese** protegido	**hubiesen** protegido

imperativo

—	protejamos
protege; no protejas	proteged; no protejáis
proteja	protejan

gerundio **pudriendo** participio de pasado **podrido**

SINGULAR	PLURAL
presente de indicativo	
pudr**o**	pudr**imos**
pudr**es**	pudr**ís**
pudr**e**	pudr**en**
imperfecto de indicativo	
pudr**ía**	pudr**íamos**
pudr**ías**	pudr**íais**
pudr**ía**	pudr**ían**
pretérito	
pudr**í** or podr**í**	pudr**imos**
pudr**iste**	pudr**isteis**
pudr**ió**	pudr**ieron**
futuro	
pudrir**é** or podrir**é**	pudrir**emos**
pudrir**ás**	pudrir**éis**
pudrir**á**	pudrir**án**
condicional simple	
pudrir**ía** or podrir**ía**	pudrir**íamos**
pudrir**ías**	pudrir**íais**
pudrir**ía**	pudrir**ían**
presente de subjuntivo	
pudr**a**	pudr**amos**
pudr**as**	pudr**áis**
pudr**a**	pudr**an**
imperfecto de subjuntivo	
pudrier**a**	pudriér**amos**
pudrier**as**	pudrier**ais**
pudrier**a**	pudrier**an**
OR	
pudries**e**	pudriés**emos**
pudries**es**	pudries**eis**
pudries**e**	pudries**en**
imperativo	
—	pudramos
pudre; no pudras	pudrid; no pudráis
pudra	pudran

SINGULAR	PLURAL
perfecto de indicativo	
he podrido	**hemos** podrido
has podrido	**habéis** podrido
ha podrido	**han** podrido
pluscuamperfecto de indicativo	
había podrido	**habíamos** podrido
habías podrido	**habíais** podrido
había podrido	**habían** podrido
pretérito anterior	
hube podrido	**hubimos** podrido
hubiste podrido	**hubisteis** podrido
hubo podrido	**hubieron** podrido
futuro perfecto	
habré podrido	**habremos** podrido
habrás podrido	**habréis** podrido
habrá podrido	**habrán** podrido
condicional compuesto	
habría podrido	**habríamos** podrido
habrías podrido	**habríais** podrido
habría podrido	**habrían** podrido
perfecto de subjuntivo	
haya podrido	**hayamos** podrido
hayas podrido	**hayáis** podrido
haya podrido	**hayan** podrido
pluscuamperfecto de subjuntivo	
hubiera podrido	**hubiéramos** podrido
hubieras podrido	**hubierais** podrido
hubiera podrido	**hubieran** podrido
OR	
hubiese podrido	**hubiésemos** podrido
hubieses podrido	**hubieseis** podrido
hubiese podrido	**hubiesen** podrido

pulir — to polish

gerundio **puliendo** — participio de pasado **pulido**

SINGULAR	PLURAL
presente de indicativo	
pul**o**	pul**imos**
pul**es**	pul**ís**
pul**e**	pul**en**
imperfecto de indicativo	
pul**ía**	pul**íamos**
pul**ías**	pul**íais**
pul**ía**	pul**ían**
pretérito	
pul**í**	pul**imos**
pul**iste**	pul**isteis**
pul**ió**	pul**ieron**
futuro	
pulir**é**	pulir**emos**
pulir**ás**	pulir**éis**
pulir**á**	pulir**án**
condicional simple	
pulir**ía**	pulir**íamos**
pulir**ías**	pulir**íais**
pulir**ía**	pulir**ían**
presente de subjuntivo	
pul**a**	pul**amos**
pul**as**	pul**áis**
pul**a**	pul**an**
imperfecto de subjuntivo	
puliera	puliér**amos**
pulier**as**	pulier**ais**
puliera	pulier**an**
OR	
pulies**e**	puliés**emos**
pulies**es**	pulies**eis**
pulies**e**	pulies**en**
imperativo	
—	pulamos
pule; no pulas	pulid; no puláis
pula	pulan

SINGULAR	PLURAL
perfecto de indicativo	
he pulido	**hemos** pulido
has pulido	**habéis** pulido
ha pulido	**han** pulido
pluscuamperfecto de indicativo	
había pulido	**habíamos** pulido
habías pulido	**habíais** pulido
había pulido	**habían** pulido
pretérito anterior	
hube pulido	**hubimos** pulido
hubiste pulido	**hubisteis** pulido
hubo pulido	**hubieron** pulido
futuro perfecto	
habré pulido	**habremos** pulido
habrás pulido	**habréis** pulido
habrá pulido	**habrán** pulido
condicional compuesto	
habría pulido	**habríamos** pulido
habrías pulido	**habríais** pulido
habría pulido	**habrían** pulido
perfecto de subjuntivo	
haya pulido	**hayamos** pulido
hayas pulido	**hayáis** pulido
haya pulido	**hayan** pulido
pluscuamperfecto de subjuntivo	
hubiera pulido	**hubiéramos** pulido
hubieras pulido	**hubierais** pulido
hubiera pulido	**hubieran** pulido
OR	
hubiese pulido	**hubiésemos** pulido
hubieses pulido	**hubieseis** pulido
hubiese pulido	**hubiesen** pulido

to stay, to remain **quedarse**

gerundio **quedándose** participio de pasado **quedado**

SINGULAR	PLURAL	SINGULAR	PLURAL
presente de indicativo		perfecto de indicativo	
me qued**o**	nos qued**amos**	**me he** quedado	**nos hemos** quedado
te queda**s**	os qued**áis**	**te has** quedado	**os habéis** quedado
se qued**a**	se qued**an**	**se ha** quedado	**se han** quedado
imperfecto de indicativo		pluscuamperfecto de indicativo	
me qued**aba**	nos qued**ábamos**	**me había** quedado	**nos habíamos** quedado
te qued**abas**	os qued**abais**	**te habías** quedado	**os habíais** quedado
se qued**aba**	se qued**aban**	**se había** quedado	**se habían** quedado
pretérito		pretérito anterior	
me qued**é**	nos qued**amos**	**me hube** quedado	**nos hubimos** quedado
te qued**aste**	os qued**asteis**	**te hubiste** quedado	**os hubisteis** quedado
se qued**ó**	se qued**aron**	**se hubo** quedado	**se hubieron** quedado
futuro		futuro perfecto	
me quedar**é**	nos quedar**emos**	**me habré** quedado	**nos habremos** quedado
te quedar**ás**	os quedar**éis**	**te habrás** quedado	**os habréis** quedado
se quedar**á**	se quedar**án**	**se habrá** quedado	**se habrán** quedado
condicional simple		condicional compuesto	
me quedar**ía**	nos quedar**íamos**	**me habría** quedado	**nos habríamos** quedado
te quedar**ías**	os quedar**íais**	**te habrías** quedado	**os habríais** quedado
se quedar**ía**	se quedar**ían**	**se habría** quedado	**se habrían** quedado
presente de subjuntivo		perfecto de subjuntivo	
me qued**e**	nos qued**emos**	**me haya** quedado	**nos hayamos** quedado
te qued**es**	os qued**éis**	**te hayas** quedado	**os hayáis** quedado
se qued**e**	se qued**en**	**se haya** quedado	**se hayan** quedado
imperfecto de subjuntivo		pluscuamperfecto de subjuntivo	
me quedar**a**	nos quedár**amos**	**me hubiera** quedado	**nos hubiéramos** quedado
te quedar**as**	os quedar**ais**	**te hubieras** quedado	**os hubierais** quedado
se quedar**a**	se quedar**an**	**se hubiera** quedado	**se hubieran** quedado
OR		OR	
me quedas**e**	nos quedás**emos**	**me hubiese** quedado	**nos hubiésemos** quedado
te quedas**es**	os quedas**eis**	**te hubieses** quedado	**os hubieseis** quedado
se quedas**e**	se quedas**en**	**se hubiese** quedado	**se hubiesen** quedado

imperativo

—	quedémonos
quédate;	quedaos;
no te quedes	no os quedéis
quédese	quédense

quejarse — to complain, to grumble

gerundio **quejándose** — participio de pasado **quejado**

SINGULAR	PLURAL	SINGULAR	PLURAL
presente de indicativo		perfecto de indicativo	
me quej**o**	nos quej**amos**	**me he** quejado	**nos hemos** quejado
te quej**as**	os quej**áis**	**te has** quejado	**os habéis** quejado
se quej**a**	se quej**an**	**se ha** quejado	**se han** quejado
imperfecto de indicativo		pluscuamperfecto de indicativo	
me quej**aba**	nos quej**ábamos**	**me había** quejado	**nos habíamos** quejado
te quej**abas**	os quej**abais**	**te habías** quejado	**os habíais** quejado
se quej**aba**	se quej**aban**	**se había** quejado	**se habían** quejado
pretérito		pretérito anterior	
me quej**é**	nos quej**amos**	**me hube** quejado	**nos hubimos** quejado
te quej**aste**	os quej**asteis**	**te hubiste** quejado	**os hubisteis** quejado
se quej**ó**	se quej**aron**	**se hubo** quejado	**se hubieron** quejado
futuro		futuro perfecto	
me quejar**é**	nos quejar**emos**	**me habré** quejado	**nos habremos** quejado
te quejar**ás**	os quejar**éis**	**te habrás** quejado	**os habréis** quejado
se quejar**á**	se quejar**án**	**se habrá** quejado	**se habrán** quejado
condicional simple		condicional compuesto	
me quejar**ía**	nos quejar**íamos**	**me habría** quejado	**nos habríamos** quejado
te quejar**ías**	os quejar**íais**	**te habrías** quejado	**os habríais** quejado
se quejar**ía**	se quejar**ían**	**se habría** quejado	**se habrían** quejado
presente de subjuntivo		perfecto de subjuntivo	
me quej**e**	nos quej**emos**	**me haya** quejado	**nos hayamos** quejado
te quej**es**	os quej**éis**	**te hayas** quejado	**os hayáis** quejado
se quej**e**	se quej**en**	**se haya** quejado	**se hayan** quejado
imperfecto de subjuntivo		pluscuamperfecto de subjuntivo	
me quejar**a**	nos quejár**amos**	**me hubiera** quejado	**nos hubiéramos** quejado
te quejara**s**	os quejar**ais**	**te hubieras** quejado	**os hubierais** quejado
se quejar**a**	se quejar**an**	**se hubiera** quejado	**se hubieran** quejado
OR		OR	
me quejas**e**	nos quejás**emos**	**me hubiese** quejado	**nos hubiésemos** quejado
te quejas**es**	os quejas**eis**	**te hubieses** quejado	**os hubieseis** quejado
se quejas**e**	se quejas**en**	**se hubiese** quejado	**se hubiesen** quejado

imperativo

—	quejémonos
quéjate; no te quejes	quejaos; no os quejéis
quéjese	quéjense

gerundio **quemando** participio de pasado **quemado**

SINGULAR	PLURAL	SINGULAR	PLURAL
presente de indicativo		perfecto de indicativo	
quem**o**	quem**amos**	**he** quemado	**hemos** quemado
quem**as**	quem**áis**	**has** quemado	**habéis** quemado
quem**a**	quem**an**	**ha** quemado	**han** quemado
imperfecto de indicativo		pluscuamperfecto de indicativo	
quem**aba**	quem**ábamos**	**había** quemado	**habíamos** quemado
quem**abas**	quem**abais**	**habías** quemado	**habíais** quemado
quem**aba**	quem**aban**	**había** quemado	**habían** quemado
pretérito		pretérito anterior	
quem**é**	quem**amos**	**hube** quemado	**hubimos** quemado
quem**aste**	quem**asteis**	**hubiste** quemado	**hubisteis** quemado
quem**ó**	quem**aron**	**hubo** quemado	**hubieron** quemado
futuro		futuro perfecto	
quemar**é**	quemar**emos**	**habré** quemado	**habremos** quemado
quemar**ás**	quemar**éis**	**habrás** quemado	**habréis** quemado
quemar**á**	quemar**án**	**habrá** quemado	**habrán** quemado
condicional simple		condicional compuesto	
quemar**ía**	quemar**íamos**	**habría** quemado	**habríamos** quemado
quemar**ías**	quemar**íais**	**habrías** quemado	**habríais** quemado
quemar**ía**	quemar**ían**	**habría** quemado	**habrían** quemado
presente de subjuntivo		perfecto de subjuntivo	
quem**e**	quem**emos**	**haya** quemado	**hayamos** quemado
quem**es**	quem**éis**	**hayas** quemado	**hayáis** quemado
quem**e**	quem**en**	**haya** quemado	**hayan** quemado
imperfecto de subjuntivo		pluscuamperfecto de subjuntivo	
quemar**a**	quemár**amos**	**hubiera** quemado	**hubiéramos** quemado
quemar**as**	quemar**ais**	**hubieras** quemado	**hubierais** quemado
quemar**a**	quemar**an**	**hubiera** quemado	**hubieran** quemado
OR		OR	
quemas**e**	quemás**emos**	**hubiese** quemado	**hubiésemos** quemado
quemas**es**	quemas**eis**	**hubieses** quemado	**hubieseis** quemado
quemas**e**	quemas**en**	**hubiese** quemado	**hubiesen** quemado

imperativo

—	quememos
quema; no quemes	quemad; no queméis
queme	quemen

Q

querer — to want, to wish

gerundio **queriendo** | participio de pasado **querido**

SINGULAR	PLURAL	SINGULAR	PLURAL
presente de indicativo		perfecto de indicativo	
quier**o**	quer**emos**	**he** querido	**hemos** querido
quier**es**	quer**éis**	**has** querido	**habéis** querido
quier**e**	quier**en**	**ha** querido	**han** querido
imperfecto de indicativo		pluscuamperfecto de indicativo	
quer**ía**	quer**íamos**	**había** querido	**habíamos** querido
quer**ías**	quer**íais**	**habías** querido	**habíais** querido
quer**ía**	quer**ían**	**había** querido	**habían** querido
pretérito		pretérito anterior	
quis**e**	quis**imos**	**hube** querido	**hubimos** querido
quis**iste**	quis**isteis**	**hubiste** querido	**hubisteis** querido
quis**o**	quis**ieron**	**hubo** querido	**hubieron** querido
futuro		futuro perfecto	
querr**é**	querr**emos**	**habré** querido	**habremos** querido
querr**ás**	querr**éis**	**habrás** querido	**habréis** querido
querr**á**	querr**án**	**habrá** querido	**habrán** querido
condicional simple		condicional compuesto	
querr**ía**	querr**íamos**	**habría** querido	**habríamos** querido
querr**ías**	querr**íais**	**habrías** querido	**habríais** querido
querr**ía**	querr**ían**	**habría** querido	**habrían** querido
presente de subjuntivo		perfecto de subjuntivo	
quier**a**	quer**amos**	**haya** querido	**hayamos** querido
quier**as**	quer**áis**	**hayas** querido	**hayáis** querido
quier**a**	quier**an**	**haya** querido	**hayan** querido
imperfecto de subjuntivo		pluscuamperfecto de subjuntivo	
quisier**a**	quisiér**amos**	**hubiera** querido	**hubiéramos** querido
quisier**as**	quisier**ais**	**hubieras** querido	**hubierais** querido
quisier**a**	quisier**an**	**hubiera** querido	**hubieran** querido
OR		OR	
quisies**e**	quisiés**emos**	**hubiese** querido	**hubiésemos** querido
quisies**es**	quisies**eis**	**hubieses** querido	**hubieseis** querido
quisies**e**	quisies**en**	**hubiese** querido	**hubiesen** querido

imperativo

—	queramos
quiere; no quieras	quered; no queráis
quiera	quieran

gerundio **quitándose** participio de pasado **quitado**

SINGULAR	PLURAL	SINGULAR	PLURAL
presente de indicativo		perfecto de indicativo	
me quit**o**	nos quit**amos**	**me he** quitado	**nos hemos** quitado
te quit**as**	os quit**áis**	**te has** quitado	**os habéis** quitado
se quit**a**	se quit**an**	**se ha** quitado	**se han** quitado
imperfecto de indicativo		pluscuamperfecto de indicativo	
me quit**aba**	nos quit**ábamos**	**me había** quitado	**nos habíamos** quitado
te quit**abas**	os quit**abais**	**te habías** quitado	**os habíais** quitado
se quit**aba**	se quit**aban**	**se había** quitado	**se habían** quitado
pretérito		pretérito anterior	
me quit**é**	nos quit**amos**	**me hube** quitado	**nos hubimos** quitado
te quit**aste**	os quit**asteis**	**te hubiste** quitado	**os hubisteis** quitado
se quit**ó**	se quit**aron**	**se hubo** quitado	**se hubieron** quitado
futuro		futuro perfecto	
me quitar**é**	nos quitar**emos**	**me habré** quitado	**nos habremos** quitado
te quitar**ás**	os quitar**éis**	**te habrás** quitado	**os habréis** quitado
se quitar**á**	se quitar**án**	**se habrá** quitado	**se habrán** quitado
condicional simple		condicional compuesto	
me quitar**ía**	nos quitar**íamos**	**me habría** quitado	**nos habríamos** quitado
te quitar**ías**	os quitar**íais**	**te habrías** quitado	**os habríais** quitado
se quitar**ía**	se quitar**ían**	**se habría** quitado	**se habrían** quitado
presente de subjuntivo		perfecto de subjuntivo	
me quit**e**	nos quit**emos**	**me haya** quitado	**nos hayamos** quitado
te quit**es**	os quit**éis**	**te hayas** quitado	**os hayáis** quitado
se quit**e**	se quit**en**	**se haya** quitado	**se hayan** quitado
imperfecto de subjuntivo		pluscuamperfecto de subjuntivo	
me quitar**a**	nos quitár**amos**	**me hubiera** quitado	**nos hubiéramos** quitado
te quitar**as**	os quitar**ais**	**te hubieras** quitado	**os hubierais** quitado
se quitar**a**	se quitar**an**	**se hubiera** quitado	**se hubieran** quitado
OR		OR	
me quitas**e**	nos quitás**emos**	**me hubiese** quitado	**nos hubiésemos** quitado
te quitas**es**	os quitas**eis**	**te hubieses** quitado	**os hubieseis** quitado
se quitas**e**	se quitas**en**	**se hubiese** quitado	**se hubiesen** quitado

imperativo

—	quitémonos
quítate; no te quites	quitaos; no os quitéis
quítese	quítense

raer — to scrape off

gerundio **rayendo** — participio de pasado **raído**

SINGULAR	PLURAL

presente de indicativo

raig**o**	ra**emos**
ra**es**	ra**éis**
ra**e**	ra**en**

imperfecto de indicativo

ra**ía**	ra**íamos**
ra**ías**	ra**íais**
ra**ía**	ra**ían**

pretérito

ra**í**	ra**ímos**
ra**íste**	ra**ísteis**
ray**ó**	ray**eron**

futuro

raer**é**	raer**emos**
raer**ás**	raer**éis**
raer**á**	raer**án**

condicional simple

raer**ía**	raer**íamos**
raer**ías**	raer**íais**
raer**ía**	raer**ían**

presente de subjuntivo

raig**a**	raig**amos**
raig**as**	raig**áis**
raig**a**	raig**an**

imperfecto de subjuntivo

rayer**a**	rayér**amos**
rayer**as**	rayer**ais**
rayer**a**	rayer**an**
OR	
rayes**e**	rayés**emos**
rayes**es**	rayes**eis**
rayes**e**	rayes**en**

imperativo

—	raigamos
rae; no raigas	raed; no raigáis
raiga	raigan

SINGULAR	PLURAL

perfecto de indicativo

he raído	**hemos** raído
has raído	**habéis** raído
ha raído	**han** raído

pluscuamperfecto de indicativo

había raído	**habíamos** raído
habías raído	**habíais** raído
había raído	**habían** raído

pretérito anterior

hube raído	**hubimos** raído
hubiste raído	**hubisteis** raído
hubo raído	**hubieron** raído

futuro perfecto

habré raído	**habremos** raído
habrás raído	**habréis** raído
habrá raído	**habrán** raído

condicional compuesto

habría raído	**habríamos** raído
habrías raído	**habríais** raído
habría raído	**habrían** raído

perfecto de subjuntivo

haya raído	**hayamos** raído
hayas raído	**hayáis** raído
haya raído	**hayan** raído

pluscuamperfecto de subjuntivo

hubiera raído	**hubiéramos** raído
hubieras raído	**hubierais** raído
hubiera raído	**hubieran** raído
OR	
hubiese raído	**hubiésemos** raído
hubieses raído	**hubieseis** raído
hubiese raído	**hubiesen** raído

to scratch — rascar

gerundio **rascando** participio de pasado **rascado**

SINGULAR	PLURAL
presente de indicativo	
rasc**o**	rasc**amos**
rasc**as**	rasc**áis**
rasc**a**	rasc**an**
imperfecto de indicativo	
rasc**aba**	rasc**ábamos**
rasc**abas**	rasc**abais**
rasc**aba**	rasc**aban**
pretérito	
rasqu**é**	rasc**amos**
rasc**aste**	rasc**asteis**
rasc**ó**	rasc**aron**
futuro	
rascar**é**	rascar**emos**
rascar**ás**	rascar**éis**
rascar**á**	rascar**án**
condicional simple	
rascar**ía**	rascar**íamos**
rascar**ías**	rascar**íais**
rascar**ía**	rascar**ían**
presente de subjuntivo	
rasqu**e**	rasqu**emos**
rasqu**es**	rasqu**éis**
rasqu**e**	rasqu**en**
imperfecto de subjuntivo	
rascar**a**	rascár**amos**
rascar**as**	rascar**ais**
rascar**a**	rascar**an**
OR	
rascas**e**	rascás**emos**
rascas**es**	rascas**eis**
rascas**e**	rascas**en**
imperativo	
—	rasquemos
rasca;	rascad;
no rasques	no rasquéis
rasque	rasquen

SINGULAR	PLURAL
perfecto de indicativo	
he rascado	**hemos** rascado
has rascado	**habéis** rascado
ha rascado	**han** rascado
pluscuamperfecto de indicativo	
había rascado	**habíamos** rascado
habías rascado	**habíais** rascado
había rascado	**habían** rascado
pretérito anterior	
hube rascado	**hubimos** rascado
hubiste rascado	**hubisteis** rascado
hubo rascado	**hubieron** rascado
futuro perfecto	
habré rascado	**habremos** rascado
habrás rascado	**habréis** rascado
habrá rascado	**habrán** rascado
condicional compuesto	
habría rascado	**habríamos** rascado
habrías rascado	**habríais** rascado
habría rascado	**habrían** rascado
perfecto de subjuntivo	
haya rascado	**hayamos** rascado
hayas rascado	**hayáis** rascado
haya rascado	**hayan** rascado
pluscuamperfecto de subjuntivo	
hubiera rascado	**hubiéramos** rascado
hubieras rascado	**hubierais** rascado
hubiera rascado	**hubieran** rascado
OR	
hubiese rascado	**hubiésemos** rascado
hubieses rascado	**hubieseis** rascado
hubiese rascado	**hubiesen** rascado

realizar — to realize, to carry out, to fulfill

gerundio **realizando** participio de pasado **realizado**

SINGULAR	PLURAL	SINGULAR	PLURAL
presente de indicativo		perfecto de indicativo	
realiz**o**	realiz**amos**	**he** realizado	**hemos** realizado
realiz**as**	realiz**áis**	**has** realizado	**habéis** realizado
realiz**a**	realiz**an**	**ha** realizado	**han** realizado
imperfecto de indicativo		pluscuamperfecto de indicativo	
realiz**aba**	realiz**ábamos**	**había** realizado	**habíamos** realizado
realiz**abas**	realiz**abais**	**habías** realizado	**habíais** realizado
realiz**aba**	realiz**aban**	**había** realizado	**habían** realizado
pretérito		pretérito anterior	
realic**é**	realiz**amos**	**hube** realizado	**hubimos** realizado
realiz**aste**	realiz**asteis**	**hubiste** realizado	**hubisteis** realizado
realiz**ó**	realiz**aron**	**hubo** realizado	**hubieron** realizado
futuro		futuro perfecto	
realizar**é**	realizar**emos**	**habré** realizado	**habremos** realizado
realizar**ás**	realizar**éis**	**habrás** realizado	**habréis** realizado
realizar**á**	realizar**án**	**habrá** realizado	**habrán** realizado
condicional simple		condicional compuesto	
realizar**ía**	realizar**íamos**	**habría** realizado	**habríamos** realizado
realizar**ías**	realizar**íais**	**habrías** realizado	**habríais** realizado
realizar**ía**	realizar**ían**	**habría** realizado	**habrían** realizado
presente de subjuntivo		perfecto de subjuntivo	
realic**e**	realic**emos**	**haya** realizado	**hayamos** realizado
realic**es**	realic**éis**	**hayas** realizado	**hayáis** realizado
realic**e**	realic**en**	**haya** realizado	**hayan** realizado
imperfecto de subjuntivo		pluscuamperfecto de subjuntivo	
realizar**a**	realizár**amos**	**hubiera** realizado	**hubiéramos** realizado
realizar**as**	realizar**ais**	**hubieras** realizado	**hubierais** realizado
realizar**a**	realizar**an**	**hubiera** realizado	**hubieran** realizado
OR		OR	
realizas**e**	realizás**emos**	**hubiese** realizado	**hubiésemos** realizado
realizas**es**	realizas**eis**	**hubieses** realizado	**hubieseis** realizado
realizas**e**	realizas**en**	**hubiese** realizado	**hubiesen** realizado

imperativo

—	realicemos
realiza; no realices	realizad; no realicéis
realice	realicen

gerundio **recibiendo** participio de pasado **recibido**

SINGULAR	PLURAL	SINGULAR	PLURAL
presente de indicativo		perfecto de indicativo	
recib**o**	recib**imos**	**he** recibido	**hemos** recibido
recib**es**	recib**ís**	**has** recibido	**habéis** recibido
recib**e**	recib**en**	**ha** recibido	**han** recibido
imperfecto de indicativo		pluscuamperfecto de indicativo	
recib**ía**	recib**íamos**	**había** recibido	**habíamos** recibido
recib**ías**	recib**íais**	**habías** recibido	**habíais** recibido
recib**ía**	recib**ían**	**había** recibido	**habían** recibido
pretérito		pretérito anterior	
recib**í**	recib**imos**	**hube** recibido	**hubimos** recibido
recib**iste**	recib**isteis**	**hubiste** recibido	**hubisteis** recibido
recib**ió**	recib**ieron**	**hubo** recibido	**hubieron** recibido
futuro		futuro perfecto	
recibir**é**	recibir**emos**	**habré** recibido	**habremos** recibido
recibir**ás**	recibir**éis**	**habrás** recibido	**habréis** recibido
recibir**á**	recibir**án**	**habrá** recibido	**habrán** recibido
condicional simple		condicional compuesto	
recibir**ía**	recibir**íamos**	**habría** recibido	**habríamos** recibido
recibir**ías**	recibir**íais**	**habrías** recibido	**habríais** recibido
recibir**ía**	recibir**ían**	**habría** recibido	**habrían** recibido
presente de subjuntivo		perfecto de subjuntivo	
recib**a**	recib**amos**	**haya** recibido	**hayamos** recibido
recib**as**	recib**áis**	**hayas** recibido	**hayáis** recibido
recib**a**	recib**an**	**haya** recibido	**hayan** recibido
imperfecto de subjuntivo		pluscuamperfecto de subjuntivo	
recibier**a**	recibiér**amos**	**hubiera** recibido	**hubiéramos** recibido
recibier**as**	recibier**ais**	**hubieras** recibido	**hubierais** recibido
recibier**a**	recibier**an**	**hubiera** recibido	**hubieran** recibido
OR		OR	
recibies**e**	recibiés**emos**	**hubiese** recibido	**hubiésemos** recibido
recibies**es**	recibies**eis**	**hubieses** recibido	**hubieseis** recibido
recibies**e**	recibies**en**	**hubiese** recibido	**hubiesen** recibido

imperativo

—	recibamos
recibe; no recibas	recibid; no recibáis
reciba	reciban

R

recoger — to pick up, to gather

gerundio **recogiendo** — participio de pasado **recogido**

SINGULAR	PLURAL	SINGULAR	PLURAL
presente de indicativo		perfecto de indicativo	
recoj**o**	recog**emos**	**he** recogido	**hemos** recogido
recog**es**	recog**éis**	**has** recogido	**habéis** recogido
recog**e**	recog**en**	**ha** recogido	**han** recogido
imperfecto de indicativo		pluscuamperfecto de indicativo	
recog**ía**	recog**íamos**	**había** recogido	**habíamos** recogido
recog**ías**	recog**íais**	**habías** recogido	**habíais** recogido
recog**ía**	recog**ían**	**había** recogido	**habían** recogido
pretérito		pretérito anterior	
recog**í**	recog**imos**	**hube** recogido	**hubimos** recogido
recog**iste**	recog**isteis**	**hubiste** recogido	**hubisteis** recogido
recogi**ó**	recog**ieron**	**hubo** recogido	**hubieron** recogido
futuro		futuro perfecto	
recoger**é**	recoger**emos**	**habré** recogido	**habremos** recogido
recoger**ás**	recoger**éis**	**habrás** recogido	**habréis** recogido
recoger**á**	recoger**án**	**habrá** recogido	**habrán** recogido
condicional simple		condicional compuesto	
recoger**ía**	recoger**íamos**	**habría** recogido	**habríamos** recogido
recoger**ías**	recoger**íais**	**habrías** recogido	**habríais** recogido
recoger**ía**	recoger**ían**	**habría** recogido	**habrían** recogido
presente de subjuntivo		perfecto de subjuntivo	
recoj**a**	recoj**amos**	**haya** recogido	**hayamos** recogido
recoj**as**	recoj**áis**	**hayas** recogido	**hayáis** recogido
recoj**a**	recoj**an**	**haya** recogido	**hayan** recogido
imperfecto de subjuntivo		pluscuamperfecto de subjuntivo	
recogier**a**	recogiér**amos**	**hubiera** recogido	**hubiéramos** recogido
recogier**as**	recogier**ais**	**hubieras** recogido	**hubierais** recogido
recogier**a**	recogier**an**	**hubiera** recogido	**hubieran** recogido
OR		OR	
recogies**e**	recogiés**emos**	**hubiese** recogido	**hubiésemos** recogido
recogies**es**	recogies**eis**	**hubieses** recogido	**hubieseis** recogido
recogies**e**	recogies**en**	**hubiese** recogido	**hubiesen** recogido

imperativo

—	recojamos
recoge;	recoged;
no recojas	no recojáis
recoja	recojan

gerundio **recomendando** participio de pasado **recomendado**

SINGULAR	PLURAL	SINGULAR	PLURAL
presente de indicativo		perfecto de indicativo	
recomiend**o**	recomend**amos**	**he** recomendado	**hemos** recomendado
recomiend**as**	recomend**áis**	**has** recomendado	**habéis** recomendado
recomiend**a**	recomiend**an**	**ha** recomendado	**han** recomendado
imperfecto de indicativo		pluscuamperfecto de indicativo	
recomend**aba**	recomend**ábamos**	**había** recomendado	**habíamos** recomendado
recomend**abas**	recomend**abais**	**habías** recomendado	**habíais** recomendado
recomend**aba**	recomend**aban**	**había** recomendado	**habían** recomendado
pretérito		pretérito anterior	
recomend**é**	recomend**amos**	**hube** recomendado	**hubimos** recomendado
recomend**aste**	recomend**asteis**	**hubiste** recomendado	**hubisteis** recomendado
recomend**ó**	recomend**aron**	**hubo** recomendado	**hubieron** recomendado
futuro		futuro perfecto	
recomendar**é**	recomendar**emos**	**habré** recomendado	**habremos** recomendado
recomendar**ás**	recomendar**éis**	**habrás** recomendado	**habréis** recomendado
recomendar**á**	recomendar**án**	**habrá** recomendado	**habrán** recomendado
condicional simple		condicional compuesto	
recomendar**ía**	recomendar**íamos**	**habría** recomendado	**habríamos** recomendado
recomendar**ías**	recomendar**íais**	**habrías** recomendado	**habríais** recomendado
recomendar**ía**	recomendar**ían**	**habría** recomendado	**habrían** recomendado
presente de subjuntivo		perfecto de subjuntivo	
recomiend**e**	recomend**emos**	**haya** recomendado	**hayamos** recomendado
recomiend**es**	recomend**éis**	**hayas** recomendado	**hayáis** recomendado
recomiend**e**	recomiend**en**	**haya** recomendado	**hayan** recomendado
imperfecto de subjuntivo		pluscuamperfecto de subjuntivo	
recomendar**a**	recomendár**amos**	**hubiera** recomendado	**hubiéramos** recomendado
recomendar**as**	recomendar**ais**	**hubieras** recomendado	**hubierais** recomendado
recomendar**a**	recomendar**an**	**hubiera** recomendado	**hubieran** recomendado
OR		OR	
recomendas**e**	recomendás**emos**	**hubiese** recomendado	**hubiésemos** recomendado
recomendas**es**	recomendas**eis**	**hubieses** recomendado	**hubieseis** recomendado
recomendas**e**	recomendas**en**	**hubiese** recomendado	**hubiesen** recomendado

imperativo

—	recomendemos
recomienda; no recomiendes	recomendad; no recomendéis
recomiende	recomienden

R

recopilar — to compile

gerundio **recopilando** participio de pasado **recopilado**

SINGULAR	PLURAL	SINGULAR	PLURAL
presente de indicativo		perfecto de indicativo	
recopil**o**	recopil**amos**	**he** recopilado	**hemos** recopilado
recopil**as**	recopil**áis**	**has** recopilado	**habéis** recopilado
recopil**a**	recopil**an**	**ha** recopilado	**han** recopilado
imperfecto de indicativo		pluscuamperfecto de indicativo	
recopil**aba**	recopil**ábamos**	**había** recopilado	**habíamos** recopilado
recopil**abas**	recopil**abais**	**habías** recopilado	**habíais** recopilado
recopil**aba**	recopil**aban**	**había** recopilado	**habían** recopilado
pretérito		pretérito anterior	
recopil**é**	recopil**amos**	**hube** recopilado	**hubimos** recopilado
recopil**aste**	recopil**asteis**	**hubiste** recopilado	**hubisteis** recopilado
recopil**ó**	recopil**aron**	**hubo** recopilado	**hubieron** recopilado
futuro		futuro perfecto	
recopilar**é**	recopilar**emos**	**habré** recopilado	**habremos** recopilado
recopilar**ás**	recopilar**éis**	**habrás** recopilado	**habréis** recopilado
recopilar**á**	recopilar**án**	**habrá** recopilado	**habrán** recopilado
condicional simple		condicional compuesto	
recopilar**ía**	recopilar**íamos**	**habría** recopilado	**habríamos** recopilado
recopilar**ías**	recopilar**íais**	**habrías** recopilado	**habríais** recopilado
recopilar**ía**	recopilar**ían**	**habría** recopilado	**habrían** recopilado
presente de subjuntivo		perfecto de subjuntivo	
recopil**e**	recopil**emos**	**haya** recopilado	**hayamos** recopilado
recopil**es**	recopil**éis**	**hayas** recopilado	**hayáis** recopilado
recopil**e**	recopil**en**	**haya** recopilado	**hayan** recopilado
imperfecto de subjuntivo		pluscuamperfecto de subjuntivo	
recopilar**a**	recopilár**amos**	**hubiera** recopilado	**hubiéramos** recopilado
recopilar**as**	recopilar**ais**	**hubieras** recopilado	**hubierais** recopilado
recopilar**a**	recopilar**an**	**hubiera** recopilado	**hubieran** recopilado
OR		OR	
recopilas**e**	recopilás**emos**	**hubiese** recopilado	**hubiésemos** recopilado
recopilas**es**	recopilas**eis**	**hubieses** recopilado	**hubieseis** recopilado
recopilas**e**	recopilas**en**	**hubiese** recopilado	**hubiesen** recopilado

imperativo

—	recopilemos
recopila;	recopilad;
no recopiles	no recopiléis
recopile	recopilen

to remember, to remind **recordar**

gerundio **recordando** participio de pasado **recordado**

SINGULAR	PLURAL
presente de indicativo	
recuerd**o**	record**amos**
recuerd**as**	record**áis**
recuerd**a**	recuerd**an**
imperfecto de indicativo	
record**aba**	record**ábamos**
record**abas**	record**abais**
record**aba**	record**aban**
pretérito	
record**é**	record**amos**
record**aste**	record**asteis**
record**ó**	record**aron**
futuro	
recordar**é**	recordar**emos**
recordar**ás**	recordar**éis**
recordar**á**	recordar**án**
condicional simple	
recordar**ía**	recordar**íamos**
recordar**ías**	recordar**íais**
recordar**ía**	recordar**ían**
presente de subjuntivo	
recuerd**e**	record**emos**
recuerd**es**	record**éis**
recuerd**e**	recuerd**en**
imperfecto de subjuntivo	
recordar**a**	recordár**amos**
recordar**as**	recordar**ais**
recordar**a**	recordar**an**
OR	
recordas**e**	recordás**emos**
recordas**es**	recordas**eis**
recordas**e**	recordas**en**
imperativo	
—	recordemos
recuerda; no recuerdes	recordad; no recordéis
recuerde	recuerden

SINGULAR	PLURAL
perfecto de indicativo	
he recordado	**hemos** recordado
has recordado	**habéis** recordado
ha recordado	**han** recordado
pluscuamperfecto de indicativo	
había recordado	**habíamos** recordado
habías recordado	**habíais** recordado
había recordado	**habían** recordado
pretérito anterior	
hube recordado	**hubimos** recordado
hubiste recordado	**hubisteis** recordado
hubo recordado	**hubieron** recordado
futuro perfecto	
habré recordado	**habremos** recordado
habrás recordado	**habréis** recordado
habrá recordado	**habrán** recordado
condicional compuesto	
habría recordado	**habríamos** recordado
habrías recordado	**habríais** recordado
habría recordado	**habrían** recordado
perfecto de subjuntivo	
haya recordado	**hayamos** recordado
hayas recordado	**hayáis** recordado
haya recordado	**hayan** recordado
pluscuamperfecto de subjuntivo	
hubiera recordado	**hubiéramos** recordado
hubieras recordado	**hubierais** recordado
hubiera recordado	**hubieran** recordado
OR	
hubiese recordado	**hubiésemos** recordado
hubieses recordado	**hubieseis** recordado
hubiese recordado	**hubiesen** recordado

reducir — to reduce, to diminish

gerundio **reduciendo** — participio de pasado **reducido**

SINGULAR	PLURAL
presente de indicativo	
reduzc**o**	reduc**imos**
reduc**es**	reduc**ís**
reduc**e**	reduc**en**
imperfecto de indicativo	
reduc**ía**	reduc**íamos**
reduc**ías**	reduc**íais**
reduc**ía**	reduc**ían**
pretérito	
reduj**e**	reduj**imos**
reduj**iste**	reduj**isteis**
reduj**o**	reduj**eron**
futuro	
reducir**é**	reducir**emos**
reducir**ás**	reducir**éis**
reducir**á**	reducir**án**
condicional simple	
reducir**ía**	reducir**íamos**
reducir**ías**	reducir**íais**
reducir**ía**	reducir**ían**
presente de subjuntivo	
reduzc**a**	reduzc**amos**
reduzc**as**	reduzc**áis**
reduzc**a**	reduzc**an**
imperfecto de subjuntivo	
reduj**era**	reduj**éramos**
reduj**eras**	reduj**erais**
reduj**era**	reduj**eran**
OR	
reduj**ese**	reduj**ésemos**
reduj**eses**	reduj**eseis**
reduj**ese**	reduj**esen**
imperativo	
—	reduzcamos
reduce; no reduzcas	reducid; no reduzcáis
reduzca	reduzcan

SINGULAR	PLURAL
perfecto de indicativo	
he reducido	**hemos** reducido
has reducido	**habéis** reducido
ha reducido	**han** reducido
pluscuamperfecto de indicativo	
había reducido	**habíamos** reducido
habías reducido	**habíais** reducido
había reducido	**habían** reducido
pretérito anterior	
hube reducido	**hubimos** reducido
hubiste reducido	**hubisteis** reducido
hubo reducido	**hubieron** reducido
futuro perfecto	
habré reducido	**habremos** reducido
habrás reducido	**habréis** reducido
habrá reducido	**habrán** reducido
condicional compuesto	
habría reducido	**habríamos** reducido
habrías reducido	**habríais** reducido
habría reducido	**habrían** reducido
perfecto de subjuntivo	
haya reducido	**hayamos** reducido
hayas reducido	**hayáis** reducido
haya reducido	**hayan** reducido
pluscuamperfecto de subjuntivo	
hubiera reducido	**hubiéramos** reducido
hubieras reducido	**hubierais** reducido
hubiera reducido	**hubieran** reducido
OR	
hubiese reducido	**hubiésemos** reducido
hubieses reducido	**hubieseis** reducido
hubiese reducido	**hubiesen** reducido

gerundio **refiriendo** participio de pasado **referido**

SINGULAR	PLURAL	SINGULAR	PLURAL
presente de indicativo		perfecto de indicativo	
refier**o**	refer**imos**	**he** referido	**hemos** referido
refier**es**	refer**ís**	**has** referido	**habéis** referido
refier**e**	refier**en**	**ha** referido	**han** referido
imperfecto de indicativo		pluscuamperfecto de indicativo	
refer**ía**	refer**íamos**	**había** referido	**habíamos** referido
refer**ías**	refer**íais**	**habías** referido	**habíais** referido
refer**ía**	refer**ían**	**había** referido	**habían** referido
pretérito		pretérito anterior	
refer**í**	refer**imos**	**hube** referido	**hubimos** referido
refer**iste**	refer**isteis**	**hubiste** referido	**hubisteis** referido
refir**ió**	refir**ieron**	**hubo** referido	**hubieron** referido
futuro		futuro perfecto	
referir**é**	referir**emos**	**habré** referido	**habremos** referido
referir**ás**	referir**éis**	**habrás** referido	**habréis** referido
referir**á**	referir**án**	**habrá** referido	**habrán** referido
condicional simple		condicional compuesto	
referir**ía**	referir**íamos**	**habría** referido	**habríamos** referido
referir**ías**	referir**íais**	**habrías** referido	**habríais** referido
referir**ía**	referir**ían**	**habría** referido	**habrían** referido
presente de subjuntivo		perfecto de subjuntivo	
refier**a**	refir**amos**	**haya** referido	**hayamos** referido
refier**as**	refir**áis**	**hayas** referido	**hayáis** referido
refier**a**	refier**an**	**haya** referido	**hayan** referido
imperfecto de subjuntivo		pluscuamperfecto de subjuntivo	
refirier**a**	refiriér**amos**	**hubiera** referido	**hubiéramos** referido
refirier**as**	refirier**ais**	**hubieras** referido	**hubierais** referido
refirier**a**	refirier**an**	**hubiera** referido	**hubieran** referido
OR		OR	
refiries**e**	refiriés**emos**	**hubiese** referido	**hubiésemos** referido
refiries**es**	refiries**eis**	**hubieses** referido	**hubieseis** referido
refiries**e**	refiries**en**	**hubiese** referido	**hubiesen** referido

imperativo

—	refiramos
refiere; no refieras	referid; no refiráis
refiera	refieran

R

regañar

to scold, to tell off

gerundio **regañando**

participio de pasado **regañado**

SINGULAR	PLURAL
presente de indicativo	
regañ**o**	regañ**amos**
regañ**as**	regañ**áis**
regañ**a**	regañ**an**
imperfecto de indicativo	
regañ**aba**	regañ**ábamos**
regañ**abas**	regañ**abais**
regañ**aba**	regañ**aban**
pretérito	
regañ**é**	regañ**amos**
regañ**aste**	regañ**asteis**
regañ**ó**	regañ**aron**
futuro	
regañar**é**	regañar**emos**
regañar**ás**	regañar**éis**
regañar**á**	regañar**án**
condicional simple	
regañar**ía**	regañar**íamos**
regañar**ías**	regañar**íais**
regañar**ía**	regañar**ían**
presente de subjuntivo	
regañ**e**	regañ**emos**
regañ**es**	regañ**éis**
regañ**e**	regañ**en**
imperfecto de subjuntivo	
regañar**a**	regañár**amos**
regañar**as**	regañar**ais**
regañar**a**	regañar**an**
OR	
regañas**e**	regañás**emos**
regañas**es**	regañas**eis**
regañas**e**	regañas**en**
imperativo	
—	regañemos
regaña; no regañes	regañad; no regañéis
regañe	regañen

SINGULAR	PLURAL
perfecto de indicativo	
he regañado	**hemos** regañado
has regañado	**habéis** regañado
ha regañado	**han** regañado
pluscuamperfecto de indicativo	
había regañado	**habíamos** regañado
habías regañado	**habíais** regañado
había regañado	**habían** regañado
pretérito anterior	
hube regañado	**hubimos** regañado
hubiste regañado	**hubisteis** regañado
hubo regañado	**hubieron** regañado
futuro perfecto	
habré regañado	**habremos** regañado
habrás regañado	**habréis** regañado
habrá regañado	**habrán** regañado
condicional compuesto	
habría regañado	**habríamos** regañado
habrías regañado	**habríais** regañado
habría regañado	**habrían** regañado
perfecto de subjuntivo	
haya regañado	**hayamos** regañado
hayas regañado	**hayáis** regañado
haya regañado	**hayan** regañado
pluscuamperfecto de subjuntivo	
hubiera regañado	**hubiéramos** regañado
hubieras regañado	**hubierais** regañado
hubiera regañado	**hubieran** regañado
OR	
hubiese regañado	**hubiésemos** regañado
hubieses regañado	**hubieseis** regañado
hubiese regañado	**hubiesen** regañado

to water, to sprinkle — regar

gerundio **regando** participio de pasado **regado**

SINGULAR	PLURAL	SINGULAR	PLURAL
presente de indicativo		**perfecto de indicativo**	
rieg**o**	reg**amos**	**he** regado	**hemos** regado
rieg**as**	reg**áis**	**has** regado	**habéis** regado
rieg**a**	rieg**an**	**ha** regado	**han** regado
imperfecto de indicativo		**pluscuamperfecto de indicativo**	
reg**aba**	reg**ábamos**	**había** regado	**habíamos** regado
reg**abas**	reg**abais**	**habías** regado	**habíais** regado
reg**aba**	reg**aban**	**había** regado	**habían** regado
pretérito		**pretérito anterior**	
regu**é**	reg**amos**	**hube** regado	**hubimos** regado
reg**aste**	reg**asteis**	**hubiste** regado	**hubisteis** regado
reg**ó**	reg**aron**	**hubo** regado	**hubieron** regado
futuro		**futuro perfecto**	
regar**é**	regar**emos**	**habré** regado	**habremos** regado
regar**ás**	regar**éis**	**habrás** regado	**habréis** regado
regar**á**	regar**án**	**habrá** regado	**habrán** regado
condicional simple		**condicional compuesto**	
regar**ía**	regar**íamos**	**habría** regado	**habríamos** regado
regar**ías**	regar**íais**	**habrías** regado	**habríais** regado
regar**ía**	regar**ían**	**habría** regado	**habrían** regado
presente de subjuntivo		**perfecto de subjuntivo**	
riegu**e**	regu**emos**	**haya** regado	**hayamos** regado
riegu**es**	regu**éis**	**hayas** regado	**hayáis** regado
riegu**e**	riegu**en**	**haya** regado	**hayan** regado
imperfecto de subjuntivo		**pluscuamperfecto de subjuntivo**	
regar**a**	regár**amos**	**hubiera** regado	**hubiéramos** regado
regar**as**	regar**ais**	**hubieras** regado	**hubierais** regado
regar**a**	regar**an**	**hubiera** regado	**hubieran** regado
OR		OR	
regas**e**	regás**emos**	**hubiese** regado	**hubiésemos** regado
regas**es**	regas**eis**	**hubieses** regado	**hubieseis** regado
regas**e**	regas**en**	**hubiese** regado	**hubiesen** regado

imperativo

SINGULAR	PLURAL
—	reguemos
riega; no riegues	regad; no reguéis
riegue	rieguen

R

regatear — to bargain, to haggle

gerundio **regateando** — participio de pasado **regateado**

SINGULAR	PLURAL	SINGULAR	PLURAL
presente de indicativo		perfecto de indicativo	
regate**o**	regate**amos**	**he** regateado	**hemos** regateado
regate**as**	regate**áis**	**has** regateado	**habéis** regateado
regate**a**	regate**an**	**ha** regateado	**han** regateado
imperfecto de indicativo		pluscuamperfecto de indicativo	
regate**aba**	regate**ábamos**	**había** regateado	**habíamos** regateado
regate**abas**	regate**abais**	**habías** regateado	**habíais** regateado
regate**aba**	regate**aban**	**había** regateado	**habían** regateado
pretérito		pretérito anterior	
regate**é**	regate**amos**	**hube** regateado	**hubimos** regateado
regate**aste**	regate**asteis**	**hubiste** regateado	**hubisteis** regateado
regate**ó**	regate**aron**	**hubo** regateado	**hubieron** regateado
futuro		futuro perfecto	
regatear**é**	regatear**emos**	**habré** regateado	**habremos** regateado
regatear**ás**	regatear**éis**	**habrás** regateado	**habréis** regateado
regatear**á**	regatear**án**	**habrá** regateado	**habrán** regateado
condicional simple		condicional compuesto	
regatear**ía**	regatear**íamos**	**habría** regateado	**habríamos** regateado
regatear**ías**	regatear**íais**	**habrías** regateado	**habríais** regateado
regatear**ía**	regatear**ían**	**habría** regateado	**habrían** regateado
presente de subjuntivo		perfecto de subjuntivo	
regate**e**	regate**emos**	**haya** regateado	**hayamos** regateado
regate**es**	regate**éis**	**hayas** regateado	**hayáis** regateado
regate**e**	regate**en**	**haya** regateado	**hayan** regateado
imperfecto de subjuntivo		pluscuamperfecto de subjuntivo	
regatear**a**	regateár**amos**	**hubiera** regateado	**hubiéramos** regateado
regatear**as**	regatear**ais**	**hubieras** regateado	**hubierais** regateado
regatear**a**	regatear**an**	**hubiera** regateado	**hubieran** regateado
OR		OR	
regatease**e**	regateás**emos**	**hubiese** regateado	**hubiésemos** regateado
regateas**es**	regateas**eis**	**hubieses** regateado	**hubieseis** regateado
regateas**e**	regateas**en**	**hubiese** regateado	**hubiesen** regateado

imperativo

—	regateemos
regatea; no regatees	regatead; no regateéis
regatee	regateen

gerundio **regresando** participio de pasado **regresado**

SINGULAR	PLURAL	SINGULAR	PLURAL
presente de indicativo		perfecto de indicativo	
regres**o**	regres**amos**	**he** regresado	**hemos** regresado
regres**as**	regres**áis**	**has** regresado	**habéis** regresado
regres**a**	regres**an**	**ha** regresado	**han** regresado
imperfecto de indicativo		pluscuamperfecto de indicativo	
regres**aba**	regres**ábamos**	**había** regresado	**habíamos** regresado
regres**abas**	regres**abais**	**habías** regresado	**habíais** regresado
regres**aba**	regres**aban**	**había** regresado	**habían** regresado
pretérito		pretérito anterior	
regres**é**	regres**amos**	**hube** regresado	**hubimos** regresado
regres**aste**	regres**asteis**	**hubiste** regresado	**hubisteis** regresado
regres**ó**	regres**aron**	**hubo** regresado	**hubieron** regresado
futuro		futuro perfecto	
regresar**é**	regresar**emos**	**habré** regresado	**habremos** regresado
regresar**ás**	regresar**éis**	**habrás** regresado	**habréis** regresado
regresar**á**	regresar**án**	**habrá** regresado	**habrán** regresado
condicional simple		condicional compuesto	
regresar**ía**	regresar**íamos**	**habría** regresado	**habríamos** regresado
regresar**ías**	regresar**íais**	**habrías** regresado	**habríais** regresado
regresar**ía**	regresar**ían**	**habría** regresado	**habrían** regresado
presente de subjuntivo		perfecto de subjuntivo	
regres**e**	regres**emos**	**haya** regresado	**hayamos** regresado
regres**es**	regres**éis**	**hayas** regresado	**hayáis** regresado
regres**e**	regres**en**	**haya** regresado	**hayan** regresado
imperfecto de subjuntivo		pluscuamperfecto de subjuntivo	
regresar**a**	regresár**amos**	**hubiera** regresado	**hubiéramos** regresado
regresar**as**	regresar**ais**	**hubieras** regresado	**hubierais** regresado
regresar**a**	regresar**an**	**hubiera** regresado	**hubieran** regresado
OR		OR	
regresas**e**	regresás**emos**	**hubiese** regresado	**hubiésemos** regresado
regresas**es**	regresas**eis**	**hubieses** regresado	**hubieseis** regresado
regresas**e**	regresas**en**	**hubiese** regresado	**hubiesen** regresado

imperativo

—	regresemos
regresa; no regreses	regresad; no regreséis
regrese	regresen

reír — to laugh

gerundio **riendo** — participio de pasado **reído**

SINGULAR	PLURAL
presente de indicativo	
rí**o**	re**ímos**
rí**es**	re**ís**
rí**e**	rí**en**
imperfecto de indicativo	
re**ía**	re**íamos**
re**ías**	re**íais**
re**ía**	re**ían**
pretérito	
re**í**	re**ímos**
re**íste**	re**ísteis**
ri**ó**	ri**eron**
futuro	
reir**é**	reir**emos**
reir**ás**	reir**éis**
reir**á**	reir**án**
condicional simple	
reir**ía**	reir**íamos**
reir**ías**	reir**íais**
reir**ía**	reir**ían**
presente de subjuntivo	
rí**a**	ri**amos**
rí**as**	ri**áis**
rí**a**	rí**an**
imperfecto de subjuntivo	
rier**a**	riér**amos**
rier**as**	rier**ais**
rier**a**	rier**an**
OR	
ries**e**	riés**emos**
ries**es**	ries**eis**
ries**e**	ries**en**
imperativo	
—	riamos
ríe;	reíd;
no rías	no riáis
ría	rían

SINGULAR	PLURAL
perfecto de indicativo	
he reído	**hemos** reído
has reído	**habéis** reído
ha reído	**han** reído
pluscuamperfecto de indicativo	
había reído	**habíamos** reído
habías reído	**habíais** reído
había reído	**habían** reído
pretérito anterior	
hube reído	**hubimos** reído
hubiste reído	**hubisteis** reído
hubo reído	**hubieron** reído
futuro perfecto	
habré reído	**habremos** reído
habrás reído	**habréis** reído
habrá reído	**habrán** reído
condicional compuesto	
habría reído	**habríamos** reído
habrías reído	**habríais** reído
habría reído	**habrían** reído
perfecto de subjuntivo	
haya reído	**hayamos** reído
hayas reído	**hayáis** reído
haya reído	**hayan** reído
pluscuamperfecto de subjuntivo	
hubiera reído	**hubiéramos** reído
hubieras reído	**hubierais** reído
hubiera reído	**hubieran** reído
OR	
hubiese reído	**hubiésemos** reído
hubieses reído	**hubieseis** reído
hubiese reído	**hubiesen** reído

gerundio **riñendo** participio de pasado **reñido**

SINGULAR	PLURAL	SINGULAR	PLURAL
presente de indicativo		perfecto de indicativo	
riñ**o**	reñ**imos**	**he** reñido	**hemos** reñido
riñ**es**	reñ**ís**	**has** reñido	**habéis** reñido
riñ**e**	riñ**en**	**ha** reñido	**han** reñido
imperfecto de indicativo		pluscuamperfecto de indicativo	
reñ**ía**	reñ**íamos**	**había** reñido	**habíamos** reñido
reñ**ías**	reñ**íais**	**habías** reñido	**habíais** reñido
reñ**ía**	reñ**ían**	**había** reñido	**habían** reñido
pretérito		pretérito anterior	
reñ**í**	reñ**imos**	**hube** reñido	**hubimos** reñido
reñ**iste**	reñ**isteis**	**hubiste** reñido	**hubisteis** reñido
riñ**ó**	riñ**eron**	**hubo** reñido	**hubieron** reñido
futuro		futuro perfecto	
reñir**é**	reñir**emos**	**habré** reñido	**habremos** reñido
reñir**ás**	reñir**éis**	**habrás** reñido	**habréis** reñido
reñir**á**	reñir**án**	**habrá** reñido	**habrán** reñido
condicional simple		condicional compuesto	
reñir**ía**	reñir**íamos**	**habría** reñido	**habríamos** reñido
reñir**ías**	reñir**íais**	**habrías** reñido	**habríais** reñido
reñir**ía**	reñir**ían**	**habría** reñido	**habrían** reñido
presente de subjuntivo		perfecto de subjuntivo	
riñ**a**	riñ**amos**	**haya** reñido	**hayamos** reñido
riñ**as**	riñ**áis**	**hayas** reñido	**hayáis** reñido
riñ**a**	riñ**an**	**haya** reñido	**hayan** reñido
imperfecto de subjuntivo		pluscuamperfecto de subjuntivo	
riñer**a**	riñér**amos**	**hubiera** reñido	**hubiéramos** reñido
riñer**as**	riñer**ais**	**hubieras** reñido	**hubierais** reñido
riñer**a**	riñer**an**	**hubiera** reñido	**hubieran** reñido
OR		OR	
riñes**e**	riñés**emos**	**hubiese** reñido	**hubiésemos** reñido
riñes**es**	riñes**eis**	**hubieses** reñido	**hubieseis** reñido
riñes**e**	riñes**en**	**hubiese** reñido	**hubiesen** reñido

imperativo

—	riñamos
riñe;	reñid;
no riñas	no riñáis
riña	riñan

reparar — to repair, to fix

gerundio **reparando** | participio de pasado **reparado**

presente de indicativo

SINGULAR	PLURAL
repar**o**	repar**amos**
repar**as**	repar**áis**
repar**a**	repar**an**

imperfecto de indicativo

SINGULAR	PLURAL
repar**aba**	repar**ábamos**
repar**abas**	repar**abais**
repar**aba**	repar**aban**

pretérito

SINGULAR	PLURAL
repar**é**	repar**amos**
repar**aste**	repar**asteis**
repar**ó**	repar**aron**

futuro

SINGULAR	PLURAL
reparar**é**	reparar**emos**
reparar**ás**	reparar**éis**
reparar**á**	reparar**án**

condicional simple

SINGULAR	PLURAL
reparar**ía**	reparar**íamos**
reparar**ías**	reparar**íais**
reparar**ía**	reparar**ían**

presente de subjuntivo

SINGULAR	PLURAL
repar**e**	repar**emos**
repar**es**	repar**éis**
repar**e**	repar**en**

imperfecto de subjuntivo

SINGULAR	PLURAL
reparar**a**	reparár**amos**
reparar**as**	reparar**ais**
reparar**a**	reparar**an**
OR	
reparas**e**	reparás**emos**
reparas**es**	reparas**eis**
reparas**e**	reparas**en**

imperativo

SINGULAR	PLURAL
—	reparemos
repara;	reparad;
no repares	no reparéis
repare	reparen

perfecto de indicativo

SINGULAR	PLURAL
he reparado	**hemos** reparado
has reparado	**habéis** reparado
ha reparado	**han** reparado

pluscuamperfecto de indicativo

SINGULAR	PLURAL
había reparado	**habíamos** reparado
habías reparado	**habíais** reparado
había reparado	**habían** reparado

pretérito anterior

SINGULAR	PLURAL
hube reparado	**hubimos** reparado
hubiste reparado	**hubisteis** reparado
hubo reparado	**hubieron** reparado

futuro perfecto

SINGULAR	PLURAL
habré reparado	**habremos** reparado
habrás reparado	**habréis** reparado
habrá reparado	**habrán** reparado

condicional compuesto

SINGULAR	PLURAL
habría reparado	**habríamos** reparado
habrías reparado	**habríais** reparado
habría reparado	**habrían** reparado

perfecto de subjuntivo

SINGULAR	PLURAL
haya reparado	**hayamos** reparado
hayas reparado	**hayáis** reparado
haya reparado	**hayan** reparado

pluscuamperfecto de subjuntivo

SINGULAR	PLURAL
hubiera reparado	**hubiéramos** reparado
hubieras reparado	**hubierais** reparado
hubiera reparado	**hubieran** reparado
OR	
hubiese reparado	**hubiésemos** reparado
hubieses reparado	**hubieseis** reparado
hubiese reparado	**hubiesen** reparado

gerundio **resfriando** participio de pasado **resfriado**

SINGULAR	PLURAL	SINGULAR	PLURAL
presente de indicativo		perfecto de indicativo	
resfrí**o**	resfri**amos**	**he** resfriado	**hemos** resfriado
resfrí**as**	resfri**áis**	**has** resfriado	**habéis** resfriado
resfrí**a**	resfrí**an**	**ha** resfriado	**han** resfriado
imperfecto de indicativo		pluscuamperfecto de indicativo	
resfri**aba**	resfri**ábamos**	**había** resfriado	**habíamos** resfriado
resfri**abas**	resfri**abais**	**habías** resfriado	**habíais** resfriado
resfri**aba**	resfri**aban**	**había** resfriado	**habían** resfriado
pretérito		pretérito anterior	
resfri**é**	resfri**amos**	**hube** resfriado	**hubimos** resfriado
resfri**aste**	resfri**asteis**	**hubiste** resfriado	**hubisteis** resfriado
resfri**ó**	resfri**aron**	**hubo** resfriado	**hubieron** resfriado
futuro		futuro perfecto	
resfriar**é**	resfriar**emos**	**habré** resfriado	**habremos** resfriado
resfriar**ás**	resfriar**éis**	**habrás** resfriado	**habréis** resfriado
resfriar**á**	resfriar**án**	**habrá** resfriado	**habrán** resfriado
condicional simple		condicional compuesto	
resfriar**ía**	resfriar**íamos**	**habría** resfriado	**habríamos** resfriado
resfriar**ías**	resfriar**íais**	**habrías** resfriado	**habríais** resfriado
resfriar**ía**	resfriar**ían**	**habría** resfriado	**habrían** resfriado
presente de subjuntivo		perfecto de subjuntivo	
resfrí**e**	resfri**emos**	**haya** resfriado	**hayamos** resfriado
resfrí**es**	resfri**éis**	**hayas** resfriado	**hayáis** resfriado
resfrí**e**	resfrí**en**	**haya** resfriado	**hayan** resfriado
imperfecto de subjuntivo		pluscuamperfecto de subjuntivo	
resfriar**a**	resfriár**amos**	**hubiera** resfriado	**hubiéramos** resfriado
resfriar**as**	resfriar**ais**	**hubieras** resfriado	**hubierais** resfriado
resfriar**a**	resfriar**an**	**hubiera** resfriado	**hubieran** resfriado
OR		OR	
resfrias**e**	resfriás**emos**	**hubiese** resfriado	**hubiésemos** resfriado
resfrias**es**	resfrias**eis**	**hubieses** resfriado	**hubieseis** resfriado
resfrias**e**	resfrias**en**	**hubiese** resfriado	**hubiesen** resfriado

imperativo

—	resfriemos
resfría;	resfriad;
no resfríes	no resfriéis
resfríe	resfríen

R

resolver to solve

gerundio **resolviendo** participio de pasado **resuelto**

SINGULAR	PLURAL	SINGULAR	PLURAL
presente de indicativo		perfecto de indicativo	
resuelv**o**	resolv**emos**	**he** resuelto	**hemos** resuelto
resuelv**es**	resolv**éis**	**has** resuelto	**habéis** resuelto
resuelv**e**	resuelv**en**	**ha** resuelto	**han** resuelto
imperfecto de indicativo		pluscuamperfecto de indicativo	
resolv**ía**	resolv**íamos**	**había** resuelto	**habíamos** resuelto
resolv**ías**	resolv**íais**	**habías** resuelto	**habíais** resuelto
resolv**ía**	resolv**ían**	**había** resuelto	**habían** resuelto
pretérito		pretérito anterior	
resolv**í**	resolv**imos**	**hube** resuelto	**hubimos** resuelto
resolv**iste**	resolv**isteis**	**hubiste** resuelto	**hubisteis** resuelto
resolv**ió**	resolv**ieron**	**hubo** resuelto	**hubieron** resuelto
futuro		futuro perfecto	
resolver**é**	resolver**emos**	**habré** resuelto	**habremos** resuelto
resolver**ás**	resolver**éis**	**habrás** resuelto	**habréis** resuelto
resolver**á**	resolver**án**	**habrá** resuelto	**habrán** resuelto
condicional simple		condicional compuesto	
resolver**ía**	resolver**íamos**	**habría** resuelto	**habríamos** resuelto
resolver**ías**	resolver**íais**	**habrías** resuelto	**habríais** resuelto
resolver**ía**	resolver**ían**	**habría** resuelto	**habrían** resuelto
presente de subjuntivo		perfecto de subjuntivo	
resuelv**a**	resolv**amos**	**haya** resuelto	**hayamos** resuelto
resuelv**as**	resolv**áis**	**hayas** resuelto	**hayáis** resuelto
resuelv**a**	resuelv**an**	**haya** resuelto	**hayan** resuelto
imperfecto de subjuntivo		pluscuamperfecto de subjuntivo	
resolvier**a**	resolviér**amos**	**hubiera** resuelto	**hubiéramos** resuelto
resolvier**as**	resolvier**ais**	**hubieras** resuelto	**hubierais** resuelto
resolvier**a**	resolvier**an**	**hubiera** resuelto	**hubieran** resuelto
OR		OR	
resolvies**e**	resolviés**emos**	**hubiese** resuelto	**hubiésemos** resuelto
resolvies**es**	resolvies**eis**	**hubieses** resuelto	**hubieseis** resuelto
resolvies**e**	resolvies**en**	**hubiese** resuelto	**hubiesen** resuelto

imperativo

—	resolvamos
resuelve; no resuelvas	resolved; no resolváis
resuelva	resuelvan

to respect **respetar**

gerundio **respetando** participio de pasado **respetado**

presente de indicativo

SINGULAR	PLURAL
respet**o**	respet**amos**
respet**as**	respet**áis**
respet**a**	respet**an**

imperfecto de indicativo

SINGULAR	PLURAL
respet**aba**	respet**ábamos**
respet**abas**	respet**abais**
respet**aba**	respet**aban**

pretérito

SINGULAR	PLURAL
respet**é**	respet**amos**
respet**aste**	respet**asteis**
respet**ó**	respet**aron**

futuro

SINGULAR	PLURAL
respetar**é**	respetar**emos**
respetar**ás**	respetar**éis**
respetar**á**	respetar**án**

condicional simple

SINGULAR	PLURAL
respetar**ía**	respetar**íamos**
respetar**ías**	respetar**íais**
respetar**ía**	respetar**ían**

presente de subjuntivo

SINGULAR	PLURAL
respet**e**	respet**emos**
respet**es**	respet**éis**
respet**e**	respet**en**

imperfecto de subjuntivo

SINGULAR	PLURAL
respetar**a**	respetár**amos**
respetar**as**	respetar**ais**
respetar**a**	respetar**an**
OR	
respetas**e**	respetás**emos**
respetas**es**	respetas**eis**
respetas**e**	respetas**en**

imperativo

SINGULAR	PLURAL
—	respetemos
respeta; no respetes	respetad; no respetéis
respete	respeten

perfecto de indicativo

SINGULAR	PLURAL
he respetado	**hemos** respetado
has respetado	**habéis** respetado
ha respetado	**han** respetado

pluscuamperfecto de indicativo

SINGULAR	PLURAL
había respetado	**habíamos** respetado
habías respetado	**habíais** respetado
había respetado	**habían** respetado

pretérito anterior

SINGULAR	PLURAL
hube respetado	**hubimos** respetado
hubiste respetado	**hubisteis** respetado
hubo respetado	**hubieron** respetado

futuro perfecto

SINGULAR	PLURAL
habré respetado	**habremos** respetado
habrás respetado	**habréis** respetado
habrá respetado	**habrán** respetado

condicional compuesto

SINGULAR	PLURAL
habría respetado	**habríamos** respetado
habrías respetado	**habríais** respetado
habría respetado	**habrían** respetado

perfecto de subjuntivo

SINGULAR	PLURAL
haya respetado	**hayamos** respetado
hayas respetado	**hayáis** respetado
haya respetado	**hayan** respetado

pluscuamperfecto de subjuntivo

SINGULAR	PLURAL
hubiera respetado	**hubiéramos** respetado
hubieras respetado	**hubierais** respetado
hubiera respetado	**hubieran** respetado
OR	
hubiese respetado	**hubiésemos** respetado
hubieses respetado	**hubieseis** respetado
hubiese respetado	**hubiesen** respetado

responder — to answer, to respond

gerundio **respondiendo** participio de pasado **respondido**

SINGULAR	PLURAL	SINGULAR	PLURAL
presente de indicativo		perfecto de indicativo	
respond**o**	respond**emos**	**he** respondido	**hemos** respondido
respond**es**	respond**éis**	**has** respondido	**habéis** respondido
respond**e**	respond**en**	**ha** respondido	**han** respondido
imperfecto de indicativo		pluscuamperfecto de indicativo	
respond**ía**	respond**íamos**	**había** respondido	**habíamos** respondido
respond**ías**	respond**íais**	**habías** respondido	**habíais** respondido
respond**ía**	respond**ían**	**había** respondido	**habían** respondido
pretérito		pretérito anterior	
respond**í**	respond**imos**	**hube** respondido	**hubimos** respondido
respond**iste**	respond**isteis**	**hubiste** respondido	**hubisteis** respondido
respond**ió**	respond**ieron**	**hubo** respondido	**hubieron** respondido
futuro		futuro perfecto	
responder**é**	responder**emos**	**habré** respondido	**habremos** respondido
responder**ás**	responder**éis**	**habrás** respondido	**habréis** respondido
responder**á**	responder**án**	**habrá** respondido	**habrán** respondido
condicional simple		condicional compuesto	
responder**ía**	responder**íamos**	**habría** respondido	**habríamos** respondido
responder**ías**	responder**íais**	**habrías** respondido	**habríais** respondido
responder**ía**	responder**ían**	**habría** respondido	**habrían** respondido
presente de subjuntivo		perfecto de subjuntivo	
respond**a**	respond**amos**	**haya** respondido	**hayamos** respondido
respond**as**	respond**áis**	**hayas** respondido	**hayáis** respondido
respond**a**	respond**an**	**haya** respondido	**hayan** respondido
imperfecto de subjuntivo		pluscuamperfecto de subjuntivo	
respondier**a**	respondiér**amos**	**hubiera** respondido	**hubiéramos** respondido
respondier**as**	respondier**ais**	**hubieras** respondido	**hubierais** respondido
respondier**a**	respondier**an**	**hubiera** respondido	**hubieran** respondido
OR		OR	
respondies**e**	respondiés**emos**	**hubiese** respondido	**hubiésemos** respondido
respondies**es**	respondies**eis**	**hubieses** respondido	**hubieseis** respondido
respondies**e**	respondies**en**	**hubiese** respondido	**hubiesen** respondido

imperativo

SINGULAR	PLURAL
—	respondamos
responde; no respondas	responded; no respondáis
responda	respondan

gerundio **restituyendo** participio de pasado **restituido**

SINGULAR	PLURAL	SINGULAR	PLURAL
presente de indicativo		perfecto de indicativo	
restituy**o**	restitu**imos**	**he** restituido	**hemos** restituido
restituy**es**	restitu**ís**	**has** restituido	**habéis** restituido
restituy**e**	restituy**en**	**ha** restituido	**han** restituido
imperfecto de indicativo		pluscuamperfecto de indicativo	
restitu**ía**	restitu**íamos**	**había** restituido	**habíamos** restituido
restitu**ías**	restitu**íais**	**habías** restituido	**habíais** restituido
restitu**ía**	restitu**ían**	**había** restituido	**habían** restituido
pretérito		pretérito anterior	
restitu**í**	restitu**imos**	**hube** restituido	**hubimos** restituido
restitu**iste**	restitu**ísteis**	**hubiste** restituido	**hubisteis** restituido
restituy**ó**	restituy**eron**	**hubo** restituido	**hubieron** restituido
futuro		futuro perfecto	
restituir**é**	restituir**emos**	**habré** restituido	**habremos** restituido
restituir**ás**	restituir**éis**	**habrás** restituido	**habréis** restituido
restituir**á**	restituir**án**	**habrá** restituido	**habrán** restituido
condicional simple		condicional compuesto	
restituir**ía**	restituir**íamos**	**habría** restituido	**habríamos** restituido
restituir**ías**	restituir**íais**	**habrías** restituido	**habríais** restituido
restituir**ía**	restituir**ían**	**habría** restituido	**habrían** restituido
presente de subjuntivo		perfecto de subjuntivo	
restituy**a**	restituy**amos**	**haya** restituido	**hayamos** restituido
restituy**as**	restituy**áis**	**hayas** restituido	**hayáis** restituido
restituy**a**	restituy**an**	**haya** restituido	**hayan** restituido
imperfecto de subjuntivo		pluscuamperfecto de subjuntivo	
restituyer**a**	restituyér**amos**	**hubiera** restituido	**hubiéramos** restituido
restituyer**as**	restituyer**ais**	**hubieras** restituido	**hubierais** restituido
restituyer**a**	restituyer**an**	**hubiera** restituido	**hubieran** restituido
OR		OR	
restituyes**e**	restituyés**emos**	**hubiese** restituido	**hubiésemos** restituido
restituyes**es**	restituyes**eis**	**hubieses** restituido	**hubieseis** restituido
restituyes**e**	restituyes**en**	**hubiese** restituido	**hubiesen** restituido

imperativo

—	restituyamos
restituye;	restituid;
no restituyas	no restituyáis
restituya	restituyan

resumir — to summarize

gerundio **resumiendo** — participio de pasado **resumido**

SINGULAR	PLURAL	SINGULAR	PLURAL
presente de indicativo		perfecto de indicativo	
resum**o**	resum**imos**	**he** resumido	**hemos** resumido
resum**es**	resum**ís**	**has** resumido	**habéis** resumido
resum**e**	resum**en**	**ha** resumido	**han** resumido
imperfecto de indicativo		pluscuamperfecto de indicativo	
resum**ía**	resum**íamos**	**había** resumido	**habíamos** resumido
resum**ías**	resum**íais**	**habías** resumido	**habíais** resumido
resum**ía**	resum**ían**	**había** resumido	**habían** resumido
pretérito		pretérito anterior	
resum**í**	resum**imos**	**hube** resumido	**hubimos** resumido
resum**iste**	resum**isteis**	**hubiste** resumido	**hubisteis** resumido
resumi**ó**	resum**ieron**	**hubo** resumido	**hubieron** resumido
futuro		futuro perfecto	
resumir**é**	resumir**emos**	**habré** resumido	**habremos** resumido
resumir**ás**	resumir**éis**	**habrás** resumido	**habréis** resumido
resumir**á**	resumir**án**	**habrá** resumido	**habrán** resumido
condicional simple		condicional compuesto	
resumir**ía**	resumir**íamos**	**habría** resumido	**habríamos** resumido
resumir**ías**	resumir**íais**	**habrías** resumido	**habríais** resumido
resumir**ía**	resumir**ían**	**habría** resumido	**habrían** resumido
presente de subjuntivo		perfecto de subjuntivo	
resum**a**	resum**amos**	**haya** resumido	**hayamos** resumido
resum**as**	resum**áis**	**hayas** resumido	**hayáis** resumido
resum**a**	resum**an**	**haya** resumido	**hayan** resumido
imperfecto de subjuntivo		pluscuamperfecto de subjuntivo	
resumier**a**	resumiér**amos**	**hubiera** resumido	**hubiéramos** resumido
resumier**as**	resumier**ais**	**hubieras** resumido	**hubierais** resumido
resumier**a**	resumier**an**	**hubiera** resumido	**hubieran** resumido
OR		OR	
resumies**e**	resumiés**emos**	**hubiese** resumido	**hubiésemos** resumido
resumies**es**	resumies**eis**	**hubieses** resumido	**hubieseis** resumido
resumies**e**	resumies**en**	**hubiese** resumido	**hubiesen** resumido

imperativo

—	resumamos
resume;	resumid;
no resumas	no resumáis
resuma	resuman

gerundio **retirando** participio de pasado **retirado**

SINGULAR	PLURAL	SINGULAR	PLURAL
presente de indicativo		perfecto de indicativo	
retir**o**	retir**amos**	**he** retirado	**hemos** retirado
retir**as**	retir**áis**	**has** retirado	**habéis** retirado
retir**a**	retir**an**	**ha** retirado	**han** retirado
imperfecto de indicativo		pluscuamperfecto de indicativo	
retir**aba**	retir**ábamos**	**había** retirado	**habíamos** retirado
retir**abas**	retir**abais**	**habías** retirado	**habíais** retirado
retir**aba**	retir**aban**	**había** retirado	**habían** retirado
pretérito		pretérito anterior	
retir**é**	retir**amos**	**hube** retirado	**hubimos** retirado
retir**aste**	retir**asteis**	**hubiste** retirado	**hubisteis** retirado
retir**o**	retir**aron**	**hubo** retirado	**hubieron** retirado
futuro		futuro perfecto	
retirar**é**	retirar**emos**	**habré** retirado	**habremos** retirado
retirar**ás**	retirar**éis**	**habrás** retirado	**habréis** retirado
retirar**á**	retirar**án**	**habrá** retirado	**habrán** retirado
condicional simple		condicional compuesto	
retirar**ía**	retirar**íamos**	**habría** retirado	**habríamos** retirado
retirar**ías**	retirar**íais**	**habrías** retirado	**habríais** retirado
retirar**ía**	retirar**ían**	**habría** retirado	**habrían** retirado
presente de subjuntivo		perfecto de subjuntivo	
retir**e**	retir**emos**	**haya** retirado	**hayamos** retirado
retir**es**	retir**éis**	**hayas** retirado	**hayáis** retirado
retir**e**	retir**en**	**haya** retirado	**hayan** retirado
imperfecto de subjuntivo		pluscuamperfecto de subjuntivo	
retirar**a**	retirár**amos**	**hubiera** retirado	**hubiéramos** retirado
retirar**as**	retirar**ais**	**hubieras** retirado	**hubierais** retirado
retirar**a**	retirar**an**	**hubiera** retirado	**hubieran** retirado
OR		OR	
retiras**e**	retirás**emos**	**hubiese** retirado	**hubiésemos** retirado
retiras**es**	retiras**eis**	**hubieses** retirado	**hubieseis** retirado
retiras**e**	retiras**en**	**hubiese** retirado	**hubiesen** retirado

imperativo

—	retiremos
retira; no retires	retirad; no retiréis
retire	retiren

R

gerundio **retrasando** participio de pasado **retrasado**

SINGULAR	PLURAL	SINGULAR	PLURAL
presente de indicativo		perfecto de indicativo	
retras**o**	retras**amos**	**he** retrasado	**hemos** retrasado
retras**as**	retras**áis**	**has** retrasado	**habéis** retrasado
retras**a**	retras**an**	**ha** retrasado	**han** retrasado
imperfecto de indicativo		pluscuamperfecto de indicativo	
retras**aba**	retras**ábamos**	**había** retrasado	**habíamos** retrasado
retras**abas**	retras**abais**	**habías** retrasado	**habíais** retrasado
retras**aba**	retras**aban**	**había** retrasado	**habían** retrasado
pretérito		pretérito anterior	
retras**é**	retras**amos**	**hube** retrasado	**hubimos** retrasado
retras**aste**	retras**asteis**	**hubiste** retrasado	**hubisteis** retrasado
retras**ó**	retras**aron**	**hubo** retrasado	**hubieron** retrasado
futuro		futuro perfecto	
retrasar**é**	retrasar**emos**	**habré** retrasado	**habremos** retrasado
retrasar**ás**	retrasar**éis**	**habrás** retrasado	**habréis** retrasado
retrasar**á**	retrasar**án**	**habrá** retrasado	**habrán** retrasado
condicional simple		condicional compuesto	
retrasar**ía**	retrasar**íamos**	**habría** retrasado	**habríamos** retrasado
retrasar**ías**	retrasar**íais**	**habrías** retrasado	**habríais** retrasado
retrasar**ía**	retrasar**ían**	**habría** retrasado	**habrían** retrasado
presente de subjuntivo		perfecto de subjuntivo	
retras**e**	retras**emos**	**haya** retrasado	**hayamos** retrasado
retras**es**	retras**éis**	**hayas** retrasado	**hayáis** retrasado
retras**e**	retras**en**	**haya** retrasado	**hayan** retrasado
imperfecto de subjuntivo		pluscuamperfecto de subjuntivo	
retrasar**a**	retrasár**amos**	**hubiera** retrasado	**hubiéramos** retrasado
retrasar**as**	retrasar**ais**	**hubieras** retrasado	**hubierais** retrasado
retrasar**a**	retrasar**an**	**hubiera** retrasado	**hubieran** retrasado
OR		OR	
retrasas**e**	retrasás**emos**	**hubiese** retrasado	**hubiésemos** retrasado
retrasas**es**	retrasas**eis**	**hubieses** retrasado	**hubieseis** retrasado
retrasas**e**	retrasas**en**	**hubiese** retrasado	**hubiesen** retrasado

imperativo

—	retrasemos
retrasa; no retrases	retrasad; no retraséis
retrase	retrasen

gerundio **reuniéndose** participio de pasado **reunido**

SINGULAR	PLURAL	SINGULAR	PLURAL
presente de indicativo		perfecto de indicativo	
me reún**o**	nos reun**imos**	**me he** reunido	**nos hemos** reunido
te reún**es**	os reun**ís**	**te has** reunido	**os habéis** reunido
se reún**e**	se reún**en**	**se ha** reunido	**se han** reunido
imperfecto de indicativo		pluscuamperfecto de indicativo	
me reun**ía**	nos reun**íamos**	**me había** reunido	**nos habíamos** reunido
te reun**ías**	os reun**íais**	**te habías** reunido	**os habíais** reunido
se reun**ía**	se reun**ían**	**se había** reunido	**se habían** reunido
pretérito		pretérito anterior	
me reun**í**	nos reun**imos**	**me hube** reunido	**nos hubimos** reunido
te reun**iste**	os reun**isteis**	**te hubiste** reunido	**os hubisteis** reunido
se reun**ió**	se reun**ieron**	**se hubo** reunido	**se hubieron** reunido
futuro		futuro perfecto	
me reunir**é**	nos reunir**emos**	**me habré** reunido	**nos habremos** reunido
te reunir**ás**	os reunir**éis**	**te habrás** reunido	**os habréis** reunido
se reunir**á**	se reunir**án**	**se habrá** reunido	**se habrán** reunido
condicional simple		condicional compuesto	
me reunir**ía**	nos reunir**íamos**	**me habría** reunido	**nos habríamos** reunido
te reunir**ías**	os reunir**íais**	**te habrías** reunido	**os habríais** reunido
se reunir**ía**	se reunir**ían**	**se habría** reunido	**se habrían** reunido
presente de subjuntivo		perfecto de subjuntivo	
me reún**a**	nos reun**amos**	**me haya** reunido	**nos hayamos** reunido
te reún**as**	os reun**áis**	**te hayas** reunido	**os hayáis** reunido
se reún**a**	se reún**an**	**se haya** reunido	**se hayan** reunido
imperfecto de subjuntivo		pluscuamperfecto de subjuntivo	
me reunier**a**	nos reuniér**amos**	**me hubiera** reunido	**nos hubiéramos** reunido
te reunier**as**	os reunier**ais**	**te hubieras** reunido	**os hubierais** reunido
se reunier**a**	se reunier**an**	**se hubiera** reunido	**se hubieran** reunido
OR		OR	
me reunies**e**	nos reuniés**emos**	**me hubiese** reunido	**nos hubiésemos** reunido
te reunies**es**	os reunies**eis**	**te hubieses** reunido	**os hubieseis** reunido
se reunies**e**	se reunies**en**	**se hubiese** reunido	**se hubiesen** reunido

imperativo

—	reunámonos
reúnete;	reunios;
no te reúnas	no os reunáis
reúnase	reúnanse

MEMORY TIP

Everyone gets together at the **reunion**.

gerundio **revocando** participio de pasado **revocado**

SINGULAR	PLURAL	SINGULAR	PLURAL
presente de indicativo		perfecto de indicativo	
revoc**o**	revoc**amos**	**he** revocado	**hemos** revocado
revoc**as**	revoc**áis**	**has** revocado	**habéis** revocado
revoc**a**	revoc**an**	**ha** revocado	**han** revocado
imperfecto de indicativo		pluscuamperfecto de indicativo	
revoc**aba**	revoc**ábamos**	**había** revocado	**habíamos** revocado
revoc**abas**	revoc**abais**	**habías** revocado	**habíais** revocado
revoc**aba**	revoc**aban**	**había** revocado	**habían** revocado
pretérito		pretérito anterior	
revoqu**é**	revoc**amos**	**hube** revocado	**hubimos** revocado
revoc**aste**	revoc**asteis**	**hubiste** revocado	**hubisteis** revocado
revoc**ó**	revoc**aron**	**hubo** revocado	**hubieron** revocado
futuro		futuro perfecto	
revocar**é**	revocar**emos**	**habré** revocado	**habremos** revocado
revocar**ás**	revocar**éis**	**habrás** revocado	**habréis** revocado
revocar**á**	revocar**án**	**habrá** revocado	**habrán** revocado
condicional simple		condicional compuesto	
revocar**ía**	revocar**íamos**	**habría** revocado	**habríamos** revocado
revocar**ías**	revocar**íais**	**habrías** revocado	**habríais** revocado
revocar**ía**	revocar**ían**	**habría** revocado	**habrían** revocado
presente de subjuntivo		perfecto de subjuntivo	
revoqu**e**	revoqu**emos**	**haya** revocado	**hayamos** revocado
revoqu**es**	revoqu**éis**	**hayas** revocado	**hayáis** revocado
revoqu**e**	revoqu**en**	**haya** revocado	**hayan** revocado
imperfecto de subjuntivo		pluscuamperfecto de subjuntivo	
revocar**a**	revocár**amos**	**hubiera** revocado	**hubiéramos** revocado
revocar**as**	revocar**ais**	**hubieras** revocado	**hubierais** revocado
revocar**a**	revocar**an**	**hubiera** revocado	**hubieran** revocado
OR		OR	
revocas**e**	revocás**emos**	**hubiese** revocado	**hubiésemos** revocador
revocas**es**	revocas**eis**	**hubieses** revocado	**hubieseis** revocado
revocas**e**	revocas**en**	**hubiese** revocado	**hubiesen** revocado

imperativo

—	revoquemos
revoca; no revoques	revocad; no revoquéis
revoque	revoquen

gerundio **revolviendo** participio de pasado **revuelto**

SINGULAR	PLURAL
presente de indicativo	
revuelv**o**	revolv**emos**
revuelv**es**	revolv**éis**
revuelv**e**	revuelv**en**
imperfecto de indicativo	
revolv**ía**	revolv**íamos**
revolv**ías**	revolv**íais**
revolv**ía**	revolv**ían**
pretérito	
revolv**í**	revolv**imos**
revolv**iste**	revolv**isteis**
revolv**ió**	revolv**ieron**
futuro	
revolver**é**	revolver**emos**
revolver**ás**	revolver**éis**
revolver**á**	revolver**án**
condicional simple	
revolver**ía**	revolver**íamos**
revolver**ías**	revolver**íais**
revolver**ía**	revolver**ían**
presente de subjuntivo	
revuelv**a**	revolv**amos**
revuelv**as**	revolv**áis**
revuelv**a**	revuelv**an**
imperfecto de subjuntivo	
revolvier**a**	revolviér**amos**
revolvier**as**	revolvier**ais**
revolvier**a**	revolvier**an**
OR	
revolvies**e**	revolviés**emos**
revolvies**es**	revolvies**eis**
revolvies**e**	revolvies**en**
imperativo	
—	revolvamos
revuelve; no revuelvas	revolved; no revolváis
revuelva	revuelvan

SINGULAR	PLURAL
perfecto de indicativo	
he revuelto	**hemos** revuelto
has revuelto	**habéis** revuelto
ha revuelto	**han** revuelto
pluscuamperfecto de indicativo	
había revuelto	**habíamos** revuelto
habías revuelto	**habíais** revuelto
había revuelto	**habían** revuelto
pretérito anterior	
hube revuelto	**hubimos** revuelto
hubiste revuelto	**hubisteis** revuelto
hubo revuelto	**hubieron** revuelto
futuro perfecto	
habré revuelto	**habremos** revuelto
habrás revuelto	**habréis** revuelto
habrá revuelto	**habrán** revuelto
condicional compuesto	
habría revuelto	**habríamos** revuelto
habrías revuelto	**habríais** revuelto
habría revuelto	**habrían** revuelto
perfecto de subjuntivo	
haya revuelto	**hayamos** revuelto
hayas revuelto	**hayáis** revuelto
haya revuelto	**hayan** revuelto
pluscuamperfecto de subjuntivo	
hubiera revuelto	**hubiéramos** revuelto
hubieras revuelto	**hubierais** revuelto
hubiera revuelto	**hubieran** revuelto
OR	
hubiese revuelto	**hubiésemos** revuelto
hubieses revuelto	**hubieseis** revuelto
hubiese revuelto	**hubiesen** revuelto

rezar — to pray

gerundio **rezando** participio de pasado **rezado**

SINGULAR	PLURAL	SINGULAR	PLURAL
presente de indicativo		perfecto de indicativo	
rez**o**	rez**amos**	**he** rezado	**hemos** rezado
rez**as**	rez**áis**	**has** rezado	**habéis** rezado
rez**a**	rez**an**	**ha** rezado	**han** rezado
imperfecto de indicativo		pluscuamperfecto de indicativo	
rez**aba**	rez**ábamos**	**había** rezado	**habíamos** rezado
rez**abas**	rez**abais**	**habías** rezado	**habíais** rezado
rez**aba**	rez**aban**	**había** rezado	**habían** rezado
pretérito		pretérito anterior	
rec**é**	rez**amos**	**hube** rezado	**hubimos** rezado
rez**aste**	rez**asteis**	**hubiste** rezado	**hubisteis** rezado
rez**ó**	rez**aron**	**hubo** rezado	**hubieron** rezado
futuro		futuro perfecto	
rezar**é**	rezar**emos**	**habré** rezado	**habremos** rezado
rezar**ás**	rezar**éis**	**habrás** rezado	**habréis** rezado
rezar**á**	rezar**án**	**habrá** rezado	**habrán** rezado
condicional simple		condicional compuesto	
rezar**ía**	rezar**íamos**	**habría** rezado	**habríamos** rezado
rezar**ías**	rezar**íais**	**habrías** rezado	**habríais** rezado
rezar**ía**	rezar**ían**	**habría** rezado	**habrían** rezado
presente de subjuntivo		perfecto de subjuntivo	
rec**e**	rec**emos**	**haya** rezado	**hayamos** rezado
rec**es**	rec**éis**	**hayas** rezado	**hayáis** rezado
rec**e**	rec**en**	**haya** rezado	**hayan** rezado
imperfecto de subjuntivo		pluscuamperfecto de subjuntivo	
rezar**a**	rezár**amos**	**hubiera** rezado	**hubiéramos** rezado
rezar**as**	rezar**ais**	**hubieras** rezado	**hubierais** rezado
rezar**a**	rezar**an**	**hubiera** rezado	**hubieran** rezado
OR		OR	
rezas**e**	rezás**emos**	**hubiese** rezado	**hubiésemos** rezado
rezas**es**	rezas**eis**	**hubieses** rezado	**hubieseis** rezado
rezas**e**	rezas**en**	**hubiese** rezado	**hubiesen** rezado

imperativo

SINGULAR	PLURAL
—	recemos
reza; no reces	rezad; no recéis
rece	recen

to steal, to rob **robar**

gerundio **robando** participio de pasado **robado**

SINGULAR	PLURAL
presente de indicativo	
rob**o**	rob**amos**
rob**as**	rob**áis**
rob**a**	rob**an**
imperfecto de indicativo	
rob**aba**	rob**ábamos**
rob**abas**	rob**abais**
rob**aba**	rob**aban**
pretérito	
rob**é**	rob**amos**
rob**aste**	rob**asteis**
rob**ó**	rob**aron**
futuro	
robar**é**	robar**emos**
robar**ás**	robar**éis**
robar**á**	robar**án**
condicional simple	
robar**ía**	robar**íamos**
robar**ías**	robar**íais**
robar**ía**	robar**ían**
presente de subjuntivo	
rob**e**	rob**emos**
rob**es**	rob**éis**
rob**e**	rob**en**
imperfecto de subjuntivo	
robar**a**	robár**amos**
robar**as**	robar**ais**
robar**a**	robar**an**
OR	
robas**e**	robás**emos**
robas**es**	robas**eis**
robas**e**	robas**en**
imperativo	
—	robemos
roba; no robes	robad; no robéis
robe	roben

SINGULAR	PLURAL
perfecto de indicativo	
he robado	**hemos** robado
has robado	**habéis** robado
ha robado	**han** robado
pluscuamperfecto de indicativo	
había robado	**habíamos** robado
habías robado	**habíais** robado
había robado	**habían** robado
pretérito anterior	
hube robado	**hubimos** robado
hubiste robado	**hubisteis** robado
hubo robado	**hubieron** robado
futuro perfecto	
habré robado	**habremos** robado
habrás robado	**habréis** robado
habrá robado	**habrán** robado
condicional compuesto	
habría robado	**habríamos** robado
habrías robado	**habríais** robado
habría robado	**habrían** robado
perfecto de subjuntivo	
haya robado	**hayamos** robado
hayas robado	**hayáis** robado
haya robado	**hayan** robado
pluscuamperfecto de subjuntivo	
hubiera robado	**hubiéramos** robado
hubieras robado	**hubierais** robado
hubiera robado	**hubieran** robado
OR	
hubiese robado	**hubiésemos** robado
hubieses robado	**hubieseis** robado
hubiese robado	**hubiesen** robado

gerundio **rociando** — participio de pasado **rociado**

SINGULAR	PLURAL
presente de indicativo	
rocí**o**	roci**amos**
rocí**as**	roci**áis**
rocí**a**	rocí**an**
imperfecto de indicativo	
roci**aba**	roci**ábamos**
roci**abas**	roci**abais**
roci**aba**	roci**aban**
pretérito	
roci**é**	roci**amos**
roci**aste**	roci**asteis**
roci**ó**	roci**aron**
futuro	
rociar**é**	rociar**emos**
rociar**ás**	rociar**éis**
rociar**á**	rociar**án**
condicional simple	
rociar**ía**	rociar**íamos**
rociar**ías**	rociar**íais**
rociar**ía**	rociar**ían**
presente de subjuntivo	
rocí**e**	roci**emos**
rocí**es**	roci**éis**
rocí**e**	rocí**en**
imperfecto de subjuntivo	
rociar**a**	rociár**amos**
rociar**as**	rociar**ais**
rociar**a**	rociar**an**
OR	
rocias**e**	rociás**emos**
rocias**es**	rocias**eis**
rocias**e**	rocias**en**
imperativo	
—	rociemos
rocía; no rocíes	rociad; no rociéis
rocíe	rocíen

SINGULAR	PLURAL
perfecto de indicativo	
he rociado	**hemos** rociado
has rociado	**habéis** rociado
ha rociado	**han** rociado
pluscuamperfecto de indicativo	
había rociado	**habíamos** rociado
habías rociado	**habíais** rociado
había rociado	**habían** rociado
pretérito anterior	
hube rociado	**hubimos** rociado
hubiste rociado	**hubisteis** rociado
hubo rociado	**hubieron** rociado
futuro perfecto	
habré rociado	**habremos** rociado
habrás rociado	**habréis** rociado
habrá rociado	**habrán** rociado
condicional compuesto	
habría rociado	**habríamos** rociado
habrías rociado	**habríais** rociado
habría rociado	**habrían** rociado
perfecto de subjuntivo	
haya rociado	**hayamos** rociado
hayas rociado	**hayáis** rociado
haya rociado	**hayan** rociado
pluscuamperfecto de subjuntivo	
hubiera rociado	**hubiéramos** rociado
hubieras rociado	**hubierais** rociado
hubiera rociado	**hubieran** rociado
OR	
hubiese rociado	**hubiésemos** rociado
hubieses rociado	**hubieseis** rociado
hubiese rociado	**hubiesen** rociado

to gnaw **roer**

gerundio **royendo**

participio de pasado **roído**

presente de indicativo

SINGULAR	PLURAL
roig**o**	ro**emos**
ro**es**	ro**éis**
ro**e**	ro**en**

imperfecto de indicativo

SINGULAR	PLURAL
ro**ía**	ro**íamos**
ro**ías**	ro**íais**
ro**ía**	ro**ían**

pretérito

SINGULAR	PLURAL
ro**í**	ro**ímos**
ro**iste**	ro**ísteis**
roy**ó**	roy**eron**

futuro

SINGULAR	PLURAL
roer**é**	roer**emos**
roer**ás**	roer**éis**
roer**á**	roer**án**

condicional simple

SINGULAR	PLURAL
roer**ía**	roer**íamos**
roer**ías**	roer**íais**
roer**ía**	roer**ían**

presente de subjuntivo

SINGULAR	PLURAL
roig**a**	roig**amos**
roy**a**	roy**amos**
roig**as**	roig**áis**
roig**a**	roig**an**

imperfecto de subjuntivo

SINGULAR	PLURAL
royer**a**	royér**amos**
royer**as**	royer**ais**
royer**a**	royer**an**
OR	
royes**e**	royés**emos**
royes**es**	royes**eis**
royes**e**	royes**en**

imperativo

SINGULAR	PLURAL
—	roigamos
roe; no roigas	roed; no roigáis
roiga	roigan

perfecto de indicativo

SINGULAR	PLURAL
he roído	**hemos** roído
has roído	**habéis** roído
ha roído	**han** roído

pluscuamperfecto de indicativo

SINGULAR	PLURAL
había roído	**habíamos** roído
habías roído	**habíais** roído
había roído	**habían** roído

pretérito anterior

SINGULAR	PLURAL
hube roído	**hubimos** roído
hubiste roído	**hubisteis** roído
hubo roído	**hubieron** roído

futuro perfecto

SINGULAR	PLURAL
habré roído	**habremos** roído
habrás roído	**habréis** roído
habrá roído	**habrán** roído

condicional compuesto

SINGULAR	PLURAL
habría roído	**habríamos** roído
habrías roído	**habríais** roído
habría roído	**habrían** roído

perfecto de subjuntivo

SINGULAR	PLURAL
haya roído	**hayamos** roído
hayas roído	**hayáis** roído
haya roído	**hayan** roído

pluscuamperfecto de subjuntivo

SINGULAR	PLURAL
hubiera roído	**hubiéramos** roído
hubieras roido	**hubierais** roído
hubiera roído	**hubieran** roído
OR	
hubiese roído	**hubiésemos** roído
hubieses roído	**hubieseis** roído
hubiese roído	**hubiesen** roído

rogar — to beg for, to ask

gerundio **rogando** participio de pasado **rogado**

presente de indicativo

SINGULAR	PLURAL
rueg**o**	rog**amos**
rueg**as**	rog**áis**
rueg**a**	rueg**an**

imperfecto de indicativo

SINGULAR	PLURAL
rog**aba**	rog**ábamos**
rog**abas**	rog**abais**
rog**aba**	rog**aban**

pretérito

SINGULAR	PLURAL
rogu**é**	rog**amos**
rog**aste**	rog**asteis**
rog**ó**	rog**aron**

futuro

SINGULAR	PLURAL
rogar**é**	rogar**emos**
rogar**ás**	rogar**éis**
rogar**á**	rogar**án**

condicional simple

SINGULAR	PLURAL
rogar**ía**	rogar**íamos**
rogar**ías**	rogar**íais**
rogar**ía**	rogar**ían**

presente de subjuntivo

SINGULAR	PLURAL
ruegu**e**	rogu**emos**
ruegu**es**	rogu**éis**
ruegu**e**	ruegu**en**

imperfecto de subjuntivo

SINGULAR	PLURAL
rogar**a**	rogár**amos**
rogar**as**	rogar**ais**
rogar**a**	rogar**an**
OR	
rogas**e**	rogás**emos**
rogas**es**	rogas**eis**
rogas**e**	rogas**en**

imperativo

SINGULAR	PLURAL
—	reguemos
ruega; no ruegues	rogad; no roguéis
ruegue	rueguen

perfecto de indicativo

SINGULAR	PLURAL
he rogado	**hemos** rogado
has rogado	**habéis** rogado
ha rogado	**han** rogado

pluscuamperfecto de indicativo

SINGULAR	PLURAL
había rogado	**habíamos** rogado
habías rogado	**habíais** rogado
había rogado	**habían** rogado

pretérito anterior

SINGULAR	PLURAL
hube rogado	**hubimos** rogado
hubiste rogado	**hubisteis** rogado
hubo rogado	**hubieron** rogado

futuro perfecto

SINGULAR	PLURAL
habré rogado	**habremos** rogado
habrás rogado	**habréis** rogado
habrá rogado	**habrán** rogado

condicional compuesto

SINGULAR	PLURAL
habría rogado	**habríamos** rogado
habrías rogado	**habríais** rogado
habría rogado	**habrían** rogado

perfecto de subjuntivo

SINGULAR	PLURAL
haya rogado	**hayamos** rogado
hayas rogado	**hayáis** rogado
haya rogado	**hayan** rogado

pluscuamperfecto de subjuntivo

SINGULAR	PLURAL
hubiera rogado	**hubiéramos** rogado
hubieras rogado	**hubierais** rogado
hubiera rogado	**hubieran** rogado
OR	
hubiese rogado	**hubiésemos** rogado
hubieses rogado	**hubieseis** rogado
hubiese rogado	**hubiesen** rogado

to break **romper**

gerundio **rompiendo** participio de pasado **roto**

SINGULAR	PLURAL
presente de indicativo	
romp**o**	romp**emos**
romp**es**	romp**éis**
romp**e**	romp**en**
imperfecto de indicativo	
romp**ía**	romp**íamos**
romp**ías**	romp**íais**
romp**ía**	romp**ían**
pretérito	
romp**í**	romp**imos**
romp**iste**	romp**isteis**
romp**ió**	romp**ieron**
futuro	
romper**é**	romper**emos**
romper**ás**	romper**éis**
romper**á**	romper**án**
condicional simple	
romper**ía**	romper**íamos**
romper**ías**	romper**íais**
romper**ía**	romper**ían**
presente de subjuntivo	
romp**a**	romp**amos**
romp**as**	romp**áis**
romp**a**	romp**an**
imperfecto de subjuntivo	
rompier**a**	rompiér**amos**
rompier**as**	rompier**ais**
rompier**a**	rompier**an**
OR	
rompies**e**	rompiés**emos**
rompies**es**	rompies**eis**
rompies**e**	rompies**en**
imperativo	
—	rompamos
rompe; no rompas	romped; no rompáis
rompa	rompan

SINGULAR	PLURAL
perfecto de indicativo	
he roto	**hemos** roto
has roto	**habéis** roto
ha roto	**han** roto
pluscuamperfecto de indicativo	
había roto	**habíamos** roto
habías roto	**habíais** roto
había roto	**habían** roto
pretérito anterior	
hube roto	**hubimos** roto
hubiste roto	**hubisteis** roto
hubo roto	**hubieron** roto
futuro perfecto	
habré roto	**habremos** roto
habrás roto	**habréis** roto
habrá roto	**habrán** roto
condicional compuesto	
habría roto	**habríamos** roto
habrías roto	**habríais** roto
habría roto	**habrían** roto
perfecto de subjuntivo	
haya roto	**hayamos** roto
hayas roto	**hayáis** roto
haya roto	**hayan** roto
pluscuamperfecto de subjuntivo	
hubiera roto	**hubiéramos** roto
hubieras roto	**hubierais** roto
hubiera roto	**hubieran** roto
OR	
hubiese roto	**hubiésemos** roto
hubieses roto	**hubieseis** roto
hubiese roto	**hubiesen** roto

roncar — to snore

gerundio **roncando** — participio de pasado **roncado**

SINGULAR	PLURAL
presente de indicativo	
ronc**o**	ronc**amos**
ronc**as**	ronc**áis**
ronc**a**	ronc**an**
imperfecto de indicativo	
ronc**aba**	ronc**ábamos**
ronc**abas**	ronc**abais**
ronc**aba**	ronc**aban**
pretérito	
ronqu**é**	ronc**amos**
ronc**aste**	ronc**asteis**
ronc**ó**	ronc**aron**
futuro	
roncar**é**	roncar**emos**
roncar**ás**	roncar**éis**
roncar**á**	roncar**án**
condicional simple	
roncar**ía**	roncar**íamos**
roncar**ías**	roncar**íais**
roncar**ía**	roncar**ían**
presente de subjuntivo	
ronqu**e**	ronqu**emos**
ronqu**es**	ronqu**éis**
ronqu**e**	ronqu**en**
imperfecto de subjuntivo	
roncar**a**	roncár**amos**
roncar**as**	roncar**ais**
roncar**a**	roncar**an**
OR	
roncas**e**	roncás**emos**
roncas**es**	roncas**eis**
roncas**e**	roncas**en**
imperativo	
—	ronquemos
ronca;	roncad;
no ronques	no ronquéis
ronque	ronquen

SINGULAR	PLURAL
perfecto de indicativo	
he roncado	**hemos** roncado
has roncado	**habéis** roncado
ha roncado	**han** roncado
pluscuamperfecto de indicativo	
había roncado	**habíamos** roncado
habías roncado	**habíais** roncado
había roncado	**habían** roncado
pretérito anterior	
hube roncado	**hubimos** roncado
hubiste roncado	**hubisteis** roncado
hubo roncado	**hubieron** roncado
futuro perfecto	
habré roncado	**habremos** roncado
habrás roncado	**habréis** roncado
habrá roncado	**habrán** roncado
condicional compuesto	
habría roncado	**habríamos** roncado
habrías roncado	**habríais** roncado
habría roncado	**habrían** roncado
perfecto de subjuntivo	
haya roncado	**hayamos** roncado
hayas roncado	**hayáis** roncado
haya roncado	**hayan** roncado
pluscuamperfecto de subjuntivo	
hubiera roncado	**hubiéramos** roncado
hubieras roncado	**hubierais** roncado
hubiera roncado	**hubieran** roncado
OR	
hubiese roncado	**hubiésemos** roncado
hubieses roncado	**hubieseis** roncado
hubiese roncado	**hubiesen** roncado

to roar — rugir

gerundio **rugiendo** participio de pasado **rugido**

presente de indicativo

SINGULAR	PLURAL
ruj**o**	rug**imos**
rug**es**	rug**ís**
rug**e**	rug**en**

imperfecto de indicativo

SINGULAR	PLURAL
rug**ía**	rug**íamos**
rug**ías**	rug**íais**
rug**ía**	rug**ían**

pretérito

SINGULAR	PLURAL
rug**í**	rug**imos**
rug**iste**	rug**isteis**
rug**ió**	rug**ieron**

futuro

SINGULAR	PLURAL
rugir**é**	rugir**emos**
rugir**ás**	rugir**éis**
rugir**á**	rugir**án**

condicional simple

SINGULAR	PLURAL
rugir**ía**	rugir**íamos**
rugir**ías**	rugir**íais**
rugir**ía**	rugir**ían**

presente de subjuntivo

SINGULAR	PLURAL
ruj**a**	ruj**amos**
ruj**as**	ruj**áis**
ruj**a**	ruj**an**

imperfecto de subjuntivo

SINGULAR	PLURAL
rugier**a**	rugiér**amos**
rugier**as**	rugier**ais**
rugier**a**	rugier**an**
OR	
rugies**e**	rugiés**emos**
rugies**es**	rugies**eis**
rugies**e**	rugies**en**

imperativo

SINGULAR	PLURAL
—	rujamos
ruge; no rujas	rugid; no rujáis
ruja	rujan

perfecto de indicativo

SINGULAR	PLURAL
he rugido	**hemos** rugido
has rugido	**habéis** rugido
habéis rugido	**han** rugido

pluscuamperfecto de indicativo

SINGULAR	PLURAL
había rugido	**habíamos** rugido
habías rugido	**habíais** rugido
había rugido	**habían** rugido

pretérito anterior

SINGULAR	PLURAL
hube rugido	**hubimos** rugido
hubiste rugido	**hubisteis** rugido
hubo rugido	**hubieron** rugido

futuro perfecto

SINGULAR	PLURAL
habré rugido	**habremos** rugido
habrás rugido	**habréis** rugido
habrá rugido	**habrán** rugido

condicional compuesto

SINGULAR	PLURAL
habría rugido	**habríamos** rugido
habrías rugido	**habríais** rugido
habría rugido	**habrían** rugido

perfecto de subjuntivo

SINGULAR	PLURAL
haya rugido	**hayamos** rugido
hayas rugido	**hayáis** rugido
haya rugido	**hayan** rugido

pluscuamperfecto de subjuntivo

SINGULAR	PLURAL
hubiera rugido	**hubiéramos** rugido
hubieras rugido	**hubierais** rugido
hubiera rugido	**hubieran** rugido
OR	
hubiese rugido	**hubiésemos** rugido
hubieses rugido	**hubieseis** rugido
hubiese rugido	**hubiesen** rugido

saber — to know, to know how

gerundio **sabiendo** — participio de pasado **sabido**

SINGULAR	PLURAL
presente de indicativo	
s**é**	sab**emos**
sab**es**	sab**éis**
sab**e**	sab**en**
imperfecto de indicativo	
sab**ia**	sab**íamos**
sab**ías**	sab**íais**
sab**ía**	sab**ían**
pretérito	
sup**e**	sup**imos**
sup**iste**	sup**isteis**
sup**o**	sup**ieron**
futuro	
sabr**é**	sabr**emos**
sabr**ás**	sabr**éis**
sabr**á**	sabr**án**
condicional simple	
sabr**ía**	sabr**íamos**
sabr**ías**	sabr**íais**
sabr**ía**	sabr**ían**
presente de subjuntivo	
sep**a**	sep**amos**
sep**as**	sep**áis**
sep**a**	sep**an**
imperfecto de subjuntivo	
supier**a**	supiér**amos**
supier**as**	supier**ais**
supier**a**	supier**an**
OR	
supies**e**	supiés**emos**
supies**es**	supies**eis**
supies**e**	supies**en**
imperativo	
—	sepamos
sabe; no sepas	sabed; no sepáis
sepa	sepan

SINGULAR	PLURAL
perfecto de indicativo	
he sabido	**hemos** sabido
has sabido	**habéis** sabido
ha sabido	**han** sabido
pluscuamperfecto de indicativo	
había sabido	**habíamos** sabido
habías sabido	**habíais** sabido
había sabido	**habían** sabido
pretérito anterior	
hube sabido	**hubimos** sabido
hubiste sabido	**hubisteis** sabido
hubo sabido	**hubieron** sabido
futuro perfecto	
habré sabido	**habremos** sabido
habrás sabido	**habréis** sabido
habrá sabido	**habrán** sabido
condicional compuesto	
habría sabido	**habríamos** sabido
habrías sabido	**habríais** sabido
habría sabido	**habrían** sabido
perfecto de subjuntivo	
haya sabido	**hayamos** sabido
hayas sabido	**hayáis** sabido
haya sabido	**hayan** sabido
pluscuamperfecto de subjuntivo	
hubiera sabido	**hubiéramos** sabido
hubieras sabido	**hubierais** sabido
hubiera sabido	**hubieran** sabido
OR	
hubiese sabido	**hubiésemos** sabido
hubieses sabido	**hubieseis** sabido
hubiese sabido	**hubiesen** sabido

gerundio **sacando** participio de pasado **sacado**

SINGULAR	PLURAL	SINGULAR	PLURAL
presente de indicativo		perfecto de indicativo	
sac**o**	sac**amos**	**he** sacado	**hemos** sacado
sac**as**	sac**áis**	**has** sacado	**habéis** sacado
sac**a**	sac**an**	**ha** sacado	**han** sacado
imperfecto de indicativo		pluscuamperfecto de indicativo	
sac**aba**	sac**ábamos**	**había** sacado	**habíamos** sacado
sac**abas**	sac**abais**	**habías** sacado	**habíais** sacado
sac**aba**	sac**aban**	**había** sacado	**habían** sacado
pretérito		pretérito anterior	
saqu**é**	sac**amos**	**hube** sacado	**hubimos** sacado
sac**aste**	sac**asteis**	**hubiste** sacado	**hubisteis** sacado
sac**ó**	sac**aron**	**hubo** sacado	**hubieron** sacado
futuro		futuro perfecto	
sacar**é**	sacar**emos**	**habré** sacado	**habremos** sacado
sacar**ás**	sacar**éis**	**habrás** sacado	**habréis** sacado
sacar**á**	sacar**án**	**habrá** sacado	**habrán** sacado
condicional simple		condicional compuesto	
sacar**ía**	sacar**íamos**	**habría** sacado	**habríamos** sacado
sacar**ías**	sacar**íais**	**habrías** sacado	**habríais** sacado
sacar**ía**	sacar**ían**	**habría** sacado	**habrían** sacado
presente de subjuntivo		perfecto de subjuntivo	
saqu**e**	saqu**emos**	**haya** sacado	**hayamos** sacado
saqu**es**	saqu**éis**	**hayas** sacado	**hayáis** sacado
saqu**e**	saqu**en**	**haya** sacado	**hayan** sacado
imperfecto de subjuntivo		pluscuamperfecto de subjuntivo	
sacar**a**	sacár**amos**	**hubiera** sacado	**hubiéramos** sacado
sacar**as**	sacar**ais**	**hubieras** sacado	**hubierais** sacado
sacar**a**	sacar**an**	**hubiera** sacado	**hubieran** sacado
OR		OR	
sacas**e**	sacás**emos**	**hubiese** sacado	**hubiésemos** sacado
sacas**es**	sacas**eis**	**hubieses** sacado	**hubieseis** sacado
sacas**e**	sacas**en**	**hubiese** sacado	**hubiesen** sacado

imperativo

—	saquemos
saca; no saques	sacad; no saquéis
saque	saquen

S

sacudir — to shake, to jolt

gerundio **sacudiendo** — participio de pasado **sacudido**

SINGULAR	PLURAL	SINGULAR	PLURAL
presente de indicativo		perfecto de indicativo	
sacud**o**	sacudi**mos**	**he** sacudido	**hemos** sacudido
sacud**es**	sacud**ís**	**has** sacudido	**habéis** sacudido
sacud**e**	sacud**en**	**ha** sacudido	**han** sacudido
imperfecto de indicativo		pluscuamperfecto de indicativo	
sacud**ía**	sacud**íamos**	**había** sacudido	**habíamos** sacudido
sacud**ías**	sacud**íais**	**habías** sacudido	**habíais** sacudido
sacud**ía**	sacud**ían**	**había** sacudido	**habían** sacudido
pretérito		pretérito anterior	
sacud**í**	sacud**imos**	**hube** sacudido	**hubimos** sacudido
sacud**iste**	sacud**isteis**	**hubiste** sacudido	**hubisteis** sacudido
sacud**ió**	sacud**ieron**	**hubo** sacudido	**hubieron** sacudido
futuro		futuro perfecto	
sacudir**é**	sacudir**emos**	**habré** sacudido	**habremos** sacudido
sacudir**ás**	sacudir**éis**	**habrás** sacudido	**habréis** sacudido
sacudir**á**	sacudir**án**	**habrá** sacudido	**habrán** sacudido
condicional simple		condicional compuesto	
sacudir**ía**	sacudir**íamos**	**habría** sacudido	**habríamos** sacudido
sacudir**ías**	sacudir**íais**	**habrías** sacudido	**habríais** sacudido
sacudir**ía**	sacudir**ían**	**habría** sacudido	**habrían** sacudido
presente de subjuntivo		perfecto de subjuntivo	
sacud**a**	sacud**amos**	**haya** sacudido	**hayamos** sacudido
sacud**as**	sacud**áis**	**hayas** sacudido	**hayáis** sacudido
sacud**a**	sacud**an**	**haya** sacudido	**hayan** sacudido
imperfecto de subjuntivo		pluscuamperfecto de subjuntivo	
sacudier**a**	sacudiér**amos**	**hubiera** sacudido	**hubiéramos** sacudido
sacudier**as**	sacudier**ais**	**hubieras** sacudido	**hubierais** sacudido
sacudier**a**	sacudier**an**	**hubiera** sacudido	**hubieran** sacudido
OR		OR	
sacudies**e**	sacudiés**emos**	**hubiese** sacudido	**hubiésemos** sacudido
sacudies**es**	sacudies**eis**	**hubieses** sacudido	**hubieseis** sacudido
sacudies**e**	sacudies**en**	**hubiese** sacudido	**hubiesen** sacudido

imperativo

—	sacudamos
sacude; no sacudas	sacudid; no sacudáis
sacuda	sacudan

gerundio **saliendo** participio de pasado **salido**

SINGULAR	PLURAL
presente de indicativo	
salg**o**	sal**imos**
sal**es**	sal**ís**
sal**e**	sal**en**
imperfecto de indicativo	
sal**ía**	sal**íamos**
sal**ías**	sal**íais**
sal**ía**	sal**ían**
pretérito	
sal**í**	sal**imos**
sal**iste**	sal**isteis**
sal**ió**	sal**ieron**
futuro	
saldr**é**	saldr**emos**
saldr**ás**	saldr**éis**
saldr**á**	saldr**án**
condicional simple	
saldr**ía**	saldr**íamos**
saldr**ías**	saldr**íais**
saldr**ía**	saldr**ían**
presente de subjuntivo	
saig**a**	salg**amos**
salg**as**	salg**áis**
salg**a**	salg**an**
imperfecto de subjuntivo	
salier**a**	saliér**amos**
salier**as**	salier**ais**
salier**a**	salier**an**
OR	
salies**e**	saliés**emos**
salies**es**	salies**eis**
salies**e**	salies**en**
imperativo	
—	salgamos
sal; no salgas	salid; no salgáis
salga	salgan

SINGULAR	PLURAL
perfecto de indicativo	
he salido	**hemos** salido
has salido	**habéis** salido
ha salido	**han** salido
pluscuamperfecto de indicativo	
había salido	**habíamos** salido
habías salido	**habíais** salido
había salido	**habían** salido
pretérito anterior	
hube salido	**hubimos** salido
hubiste salido	**hubisteis** salido
hubo salido	**hubieron** salido
futuro perfecto	
habré salido	**habremos** salido
habrás salido	**habréis** salido
habrá salido	**habrán** salido
condicional compuesto	
habría salido	**habríamos** salido
habrías salido	**habríais** salido
habría salido	**habrían** salido
perfecto de subjuntivo	
haya salido	**hayamos** salido
hayas salido	**hayáis** salido
haya salido	**hayan** salido
pluscuamperfecto de subjuntivo	
hubiera salido	**hubiéramos** salido
hubieras salido	**hubierais** salido
hubiera salido	**hubieran** salido
OR	
hubiese salido	**hubiésemos** salido
hubieses salido	**hubieseis** salido
hubiese salido	**hubiesen** salido

saltar — to jump

gerundio **saltando** — participio de pasado **saltado**

SINGULAR	PLURAL	SINGULAR	PLURAL
presente de indicativo		perfecto de indicativo	
salt**o**	salt**amos**	**he** saltado	**hemos** saltado
salt**as**	salt**áis**	**has** saltado	**habéis** saltado
salt**a**	salt**an**	**ha** saltado	**han** saltado
imperfecto de indicativo		pluscuamperfecto de indicativo	
salt**aba**	salt**ábamos**	**había** saltado	**habíamos** saltado
salt**abas**	salt**abais**	**habías** saltado	**habíais** saltado
salt**aba**	salt**aban**	**había** saltado	**habían** saltado
pretérito		pretérito anterior	
salt**é**	salt**amos**	**hube** saltado	**hubimos** saltado
salt**aste**	salt**asteis**	**hubiste** saltado	**hubisteis** saltado
salt**ó**	salt**aron**	**hubo** saltado	**hubieron** saltado
futuro		futuro perfecto	
saltar**é**	saltar**emos**	**habré** saltado	**habremos** saltado
saltar**ás**	saltar**éis**	**habrás** saltado	**habréis** saltado
saltar**á**	saltar**án**	**habrá** saltado	**habrán** saltado
condicional simple		condicional compuesto	
saltar**ía**	saltar**íamos**	**habría** saltado	**habríamos** saltado
saltar**ías**	saltar**íais**	**habrías** saltado	**habríais** saltado
saltar**ía**	saltar**ían**	**habría** saltado	**habrían** saltado
presente de subjuntivo		perfecto de subjuntivo	
salt**e**	salt**emos**	**haya** saltado	**hayamos** saltado
salt**es**	salt**éis**	**hayas** saltado	**hayáis** saltado
salt**e**	salt**en**	**haya** saltado	**hayan** saltado
imperfecto de subjuntivo		pluscuamperfecto de subjuntivo	
saltar**a**	saltár**amos**	**hubiera** saltado	**hubiéramos** saltado
saltar**as**	saltar**ais**	**hubieras** saltado	**hubierais** saltado
saltar**a**	saltar**an**	**hubiera** saltado	**hubieran** saltado
OR		OR	
saltas**e**	saltás**emos**	**hubiese** saltado	**hubiésemos** saltado
saltas**es**	saltas**eis**	**hubieses** saltado	**hubieseis** saltado
saltas**e**	saltas**en**	**hubiese** saltado	**hubiesen** saltado

imperativo

—	saltemos
salta; no saltes	saltad; no saltéis
salte	salten

gerundio **saludando** participio de pasado **saludado**

SINGULAR	PLURAL
presente de indicativo	
salud**o**	salud**amos**
salud**as**	salud**áis**
salud**a**	salud**an**
imperfecto de indicativo	
salud**aba**	salud**ábamos**
salud**abas**	salud**abais**
salud**aba**	salud**aban**
pretérito	
salud**é**	salud**amos**
salud**aste**	salud**asteis**
salud**ó**	salud**aron**
futuro	
saludar**é**	saludar**emos**
saludar**ás**	saludar**éis**
saludar**á**	saludar**án**
condicional simple	
saludar**ía**	saludar**íamos**
saludar**ías**	saludar**íais**
saludar**ía**	saludar**ían**
presente de subjuntivo	
salud**e**	salud**emos**
salud**es**	salud**éis**
salud**e**	salud**en**
imperfecto de subjuntivo	
saludar**a**	saludár**amos**
saludar**as**	saludar**ais**
saludar**a**	saludar**an**
OR	
saludas**e**	saludás**emos**
saludas**es**	saludas**eis**
saludas**e**	saludas**en**
imperativo	
—	saludemos
saluda; no saludes	saludad; no saludéis
salude	saluden

SINGULAR	PLURAL
perfecto de indicativo	
he saludado	**hemos** saludado
has saludado	**habéis** saludado
ha saludado	**han** saludado
pluscuamperfecto de indicativo	
había saludado	**habíamos** saludado
habías saludado	**habíais** saludado
había saludado	**habían** saludado
pretérito anterior	
hube saludado	**hubimos** saludado
hubiste saludado	**hubisteis** saludado
hubo saludado	**hubieron** saludado
futuro perfecto	
habré saludado	**habremos** saludado
habrás saludado	**habréis** saludado
habrá saludado	**habrán** saludado
condicional compuesto	
habría saludado	**habríamos** saludado
habrías saludado	**habríais** saludado
habría saludado	**habrían** saludado
perfecto de subjuntivo	
haya saludado	**hayamos** saludado
hayas saludado	**hayáis** saludado
haya saludado	**hayan** saludado
pluscuamperfecto de subjuntivo	
hubiera saludado	**hubiéramos** saludado
hubieras saludado	**hubierais** saludado
hubiera saludado	**hubieran** saludado
OR	
hubiese saludado	**hubiésemos** saludado
hubieses saludado	**hubieseis** saludado
hubiese saludado	**hubiesen** saludado

secarse — to dry oneself

gerundio **secándose** — participio de pasado **secado**

SINGULAR	PLURAL	SINGULAR	PLURAL
presente de indicativo		perfecto de indicativo	
me sec**o**	nos sec**amos**	**me he** secado	**nos hemos** secado
te sec**as**	os sec**áis**	**te has** secado	**os habéis** secado
se sec**a**	se sec**an**	**se ha** secado	**se han** secado
imperfecto de indicativo		pluscuamperfecto de indicativo	
me sec**aba**	nos sec**ábamos**	**me había** secado	**nos habíamos** secado
te sec**abas**	os sec**abais**	**te habías** secado	**os habíais** secado
se sec**aba**	se sec**aban**	**se había** secado	**se habían** secado
pretérito		pretérito anterior	
me sequ**é**	nos sec**amos**	**me hube** secado	**nos hubimos** secado
te sec**aste**	os sec**asteis**	**te hubiste** secado	**os hubisteis** secado
se sec**ó**	se sec**aron**	**se hubo** secado	**se hubieron** secado
futuro		futuro perfecto	
me secar**é**	nos secar**emos**	**me habré** secado	**nos habremos** secado
te secar**ás**	os secar**éis**	**te habrás** secado	**os habréis** secado
se secar**á**	se secar**án**	**se habrá** secado	**se habrán** secado
condicional simple		condicional compuesto	
me secar**ía**	nos secar**íamos**	**me habría** secado	**nos habríamos** secado
te secar**ías**	os secar**íais**	**te habrías** secado	**os habríais** secado
se secar**ía**	se secar**ían**	**se habría** secado	**se habrían** secado
presente de subjuntivo		perfecto de subjuntivo	
me sequ**e**	nos sequ**emos**	**me haya** secado	**nos hayamos** secado
te sequ**es**	os sequ**éis**	**te hayas** secado	**os hayáis** secado
se sequ**e**	se sequ**en**	**se haya** secado	**se hayan** secado
imperfecto de subjuntivo		pluscuamperfecto de subjuntivo	
me secar**a**	nos secár**amos**	**me hubiera** secado	**nos hubiéramos** secado
te secar**as**	os secar**ais**	**te hubieras** secado	**os hubierais** secado
se secar**a**	se secar**an**	**se hubiera** secado	**se hubieran** secado
OR		OR	
me secas**e**	nos secás**emos**	**me hubiese** secado	**nos hubiésemos** secado
te secas**es**	os secas**eis**	**te hubieses** secado	**os hubieseis** secado
se secas**e**	se seca s**en**	**se hubiese** secado	**se hubiesen** secado

imperativo

—	sequémonos; no nos sequemos
sécate; no te seques	secaos; no sequéis
sequése; no se seque	sequénse; no se sequen

to follow, to pursue, to continue **seguir**

gerundio **siguiendo** participio de pasado **seguido**

presente de indicativo

SINGULAR	PLURAL
sig**o**	segu**imos**
sigu**es**	segu**ís**
sigu**e**	sigu**en**

imperfecto de indicativo

SINGULAR	PLURAL
segu**ía**	segu**íamos**
segu**ías**	segu**íais**
ségu**ía**	segu**ían**

pretérito

SINGULAR	PLURAL
segu**í**	segu**imos**
segu**iste**	segu**isteis**
sigu**ió**	sigu**ieron**

futuro

SINGULAR	PLURAL
seguir**é**	seguir**emos**
seguir**ás**	seguir**éis**
seguir**á**	seguir**án**

condicional simple

SINGULAR	PLURAL
seguir**ía**	seguir**íamos**
seguir**ías**	seguir**íais**
seguir**ía**	seguir**ían**

presente de subjuntivo

SINGULAR	PLURAL
sig**a**	sig**amos**
sig**as**	sig**áis**
sig**a**	sig**an**

imperfecto de subjuntivo

SINGULAR	PLURAL
siguier**a**	siguiér**amos**
siguier**as**	siguier**ais**
siguier**a**	siguier**an**
OR	
siguies**e**	siguiés**emos**
siguies**es**	siguies**eis**
siguies**e**	siguies**en**

imperativo

SINGULAR	PLURAL
—	sigamos
sigue; no sigas	seguid; no sigáis
siga	sigan

perfecto de indicativo

SINGULAR	PLURAL
he seguido	**hemos** seguido
has seguido	**habéis** seguido
ha seguido	**han** seguido

pluscuamperfecto de indicativo

SINGULAR	PLURAL
había seguido	**habíamos** seguido
habías seguido	**habíais** seguido
había seguido	**habían** seguido

pretérito anterior

SINGULAR	PLURAL
hube seguido	**hubimos** seguido
hubiste seguido	**hubisteis** seguido
hubo seguido	**hubieron** seguido

futuro perfecto

SINGULAR	PLURAL
habré seguido	**habremos** seguido
habrás seguido	**habréis** seguido
habrá seguido	**habrán** seguido

condicional compuesto

SINGULAR	PLURAL
habría seguido	**habríamos** seguido
habrías seguido	**habríais** seguido
habría seguido	**habrían** seguido

perfecto de subjuntivo

SINGULAR	PLURAL
haya seguido	**hayamos** seguido
hayas seguido	**hayáis** seguido
haya seguido	**hayan** seguido

pluscuamperfecto de subjuntivo

SINGULAR	PLURAL
hubiera seguido	**hubiéramos** seguido
hubieras seguido	**hubierais** seguido
hubiera seguido	**hubieran** seguido
OR	
hubiese seguido	**hubiésemos** seguido
hubieses seguido	**hubieseis** seguido
hubiese seguido	**hubiesen** seguido

señalar — to signal, to indicate

gerundio **señalando** participio de pasado **señalado**

presente de indicativo

SINGULAR	PLURAL
señal**o**	señal**amos**
señal**as**	señal**áis**
señal**a**	señal**an**

imperfecto de indicativo

SINGULAR	PLURAL
señal**aba**	señal**ábamos**
señal**abas**	señal**abais**
señal**aba**	señal**aban**

pretérito

SINGULAR	PLURAL
señal**é**	señal**amos**
señal**aste**	señal**asteis**
señal**ó**	señal**aron**

futuro

SINGULAR	PLURAL
señalar**é**	señalar**emos**
señalar**ás**	señalar**éis**
señalar**á**	señalar**án**

condicional simple

SINGULAR	PLURAL
señalar**ía**	señalar**íamos**
señalar**ías**	señalar**íais**
señalar**ía**	señalar**ían**

presente de subjuntivo

SINGULAR	PLURAL
señal**e**	señal**emos**
señal**es**	señal**éis**
señal**e**	señal**en**

imperfecto de subjuntivo

SINGULAR	PLURAL
señalar**a**	señalár**amos**
señalar**as**	señalar**ais**
señalar**a**	señalar**an**
OR	
señalas**e**	señalás**emos**
señalas**es**	señalas**eis**
señalas**e**	señalas**en**

imperativo

SINGULAR	PLURAL
—	señalemos
señala; no señales	señalad; no señaléis
señale	señalen

perfecto de indicativo

SINGULAR	PLURAL
he señalado	**hemos** señalado
has señalado	**habéis** señalado
ha señalado	**han** señalado

pluscuamperfecto de indicativo

SINGULAR	PLURAL
había señalado	**habíamos** señalado
habías señalado	**habíais** señalado
había señalado	**habían** señalado

pretérito anterior

SINGULAR	PLURAL
hube señalado	**hubimos** señalado
hubiste señalado	**hubisteis** señalado
hubo señalado	**hubieron** señalado

futuro perfecto

SINGULAR	PLURAL
habré señalado	**habremos** señalado
habrás señalado	**habréis** señalado
habrá señalado	**habrán** señalado

condicional compuesto

SINGULAR	PLURAL
habría señalado	**habríamos** señalado
habrías señalado	**habríais** señalado
habría señalado	**habrían** señalado

perfecto de subjuntivo

SINGULAR	PLURAL
haya señalado	**hayamos** señalado
hayas señalado	**hayáis** señalado
haya señalado	**hayan** señalado

pluscuamperfecto de subjuntivo

SINGULAR	PLURAL
hubiera señalado	**hubiéramos** señalado
hubieras señalado	**hubierais** señalado
hubiera señalado	**hubieran** señalado
OR	
hubiese señalado	**hubiésemos** señalado
hubieses señalado	**hubieseis** señalado
hubiese señalado	**hubiesen** señalado

gerundio **sentándose** participio de pasado **sentado**

SINGULAR	PLURAL	SINGULAR	PLURAL
presente de indicativo		perfecto de indicativo	
me sient**o**	nos sent**amos**	**me he** sentado	**nos hemos** sentado
te sient**as**	os sent**áis**	**te has** sentado	**os habéis** sentado
se sient**a**	se sient**an**	**se ha** sentado	**se han** sentado
imperfecto de indicativo		pluscuamperfecto de indicativo	
me sent**aba**	nos sent**ábamos**	**me había** sentado	**nos habíamos** sentado
te sent**abas**	os sent**abais**	**te habías** sentado	**os habíais** sentado
se sent**aba**	se sent**aban**	**se había** sentado	**se habían** sentado
pretérito		pretérito anterior	
me sent**é**	nos sent**amos**	**me hube** sentado	**nos hubimos** sentado
te sent**aste**	os sent**asteis**	**te hubiste** sentado	**os hubisteis** sentado
se sent**ó**	se sent**aron**	**se hubo** sentado	**se hubieron** sentado
futuro		futuro perfecto	
me sentar**é**	nos sentar**emos**	**me habré** sentado	**nos habremos** sentado
te sentar**ás**	os sentar**éis**	**te habrás** sentado	**os habréis** sentado
se sentar**á**	se sentar**án**	**se habrá** sentado	**se habrán** sentado
condicional simple		condicional compuesto	
me sentar**ía**	nos sentar**íamos**	**me habría** sentado	**nos habríamos** sentado
te sentar**ías**	os sentar**íais**	**te habrías** sentado	**os habríais** sentado
se sentar**ía**	se sentar**ían**	**se habría** sentado	**se habrían** sentado
presente de subjuntivo		perfecto de subjuntivo	
me sient**e**	nos sent**emos**	**me haya** sentado	**nos hayamos** sentado
te sient**es**	os sent**éis**	**te hayas** sentado	**os hayáis** sentado
se sient**e**	se sient**en**	**se haya** sentado	**se hayan** sentado
imperfecto de subjuntivo		pluscuamperfecto de subjuntivo	
me sentar**a**	nos sentár**amos**	**me hubiera** sentado	**nos hubiéramos** sentado
te sentar**as**	os sentar**ais**	**te hubieras** sentado	**os hubierais** sentado
se sentar**a**	se sentar**an**	**se hubiera** sentado	**se hubieran** sentado
OR		OR	
me sentas**e**	nos sentás**emos**	**me hubiese** sentado	**nos hubiésemos** sentado
te sentas**es**	os sentas**eis**	**te hubieses** sentado	**os hubieseis** sentado
se sentas**e**	se sentas**en**	**se hubiese** sentado	**se hubiesen** sentado

imperativo

—	sentémonos; no nos sentemos
siéntate; no te sientes	sentaos; no os sentéis
siéntese; no se siente	siéntense; no se sienten

S

sentir — to feel, to regret

gerundio **sintiendo** — participio de pasado **sentido**

SINGULAR	PLURAL
presente de indicativo	
sient**o**	sent**imos**
sient**es**	sent**ís**
sient**e**	sient**en**
imperfecto de indicativo	
sent**ía**	sent**íamos**
sent**ías**	sent**íais**
sent**ía**	sent**ían**
pretérito	
sent**í**	sent**imos**
sent**iste**	sent**isteis**
sinti**ó**	sint**ieron**
futuro	
sentir**é**	sentir**emos**
sentir**ás**	sentir**éis**
sentir**á**	sentir**án**
condicional simple	
sentir**ía**	sentir**íamos**
sentir**ías**	sentir**íais**
sentir**ía**	sentir**ían**
presente de subjuntivo	
sient**a**	sint**amos**
sient**as**	sint**áis**
sient**a**	sient**an**
imperfecto de subjuntivo	
sintier**a**	sintié**ramos**
sintier**as**	sintier**ais**
sintier**a**	sintier**an**
OR	
sinties**e**	sintié**semos**
sinties**es**	sinties**eis**
sinties**e**	sinties**en**

imperativo

SINGULAR	PLURAL
—	sintamos
siente; no sientas	sentid; no sintáis
sienta	sientan

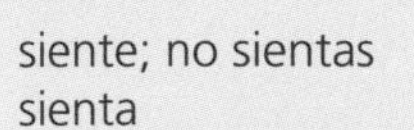

SINGULAR	PLURAL
perfecto de indicativo	
he sentido	**hemos** sentido
has sentido	**habéis** sentido
ha sentido	**han** sentido
pluscuamperfecto de indicativo	
había sentido	**habíamos** sentido
habías sentido	**habíais** sentido
había sentido	**habían** sentido
pretérito anterior	
hube sentido	**hubimos** sentido
hubiste sentido	**hubisteis** sentido
hubo sentido	**hubieron** sentido
futuro perfecto	
habré sentido	**habremos** sentido
habrás sentido	**habréis** sentido
habrá sentido	**habrán** sentido
condicional compuesto	
habría sentido	**habríamos** sentido
habrías sentido	**habríais** sentido
habría sentido	**habrían** sentido
perfecto de subjuntivo	
haya sentido	**hayamos** sentido
hayas sentido	**hayáis** sentido
haya sentido	**hayan** sentido
pluscuamperfecto de subjuntivo	
hubiera sentido	**hubiéramos** sentido
hubieras sentido	**hubierais** sentido
hubiera sentido	**hubieran** sentido
OR	
hubiese sentido	**hubiésemos** sentido
hubieses sentido	**hubieseis** sentido
hubiese sentido	**hubiesen** sentido

to feel (well, ill) sentirse

gerundio **sintiéndose** participio de pasado **sentido**

SINGULAR	PLURAL
presente de indicativo	
me sient**o**	nos sent**imos**
te sient**es**	os sent**ís**
se sient**e**	se sient**en**
imperfecto de indicativo	
me sent**ía**	nos sent**íamos**
te sent**ías**	os sent**íais**
se sent**ía**	se sent**ían**
pretérito	
me sent**í**	nos sent**imos**
te sent**iste**	os sent**isteis**
se sint**ió**	se sint**ieron**
futuro	
me sentir**é**	nos sentir**emos**
te sentir**ás**	os sentir**éis**
se sentir**á**	se sentir**án**
condicional simple	
me sentir**ía**	nos sentir**íamos**
te sentir**ías**	os sentir**íais**
se sentir**ía**	se sentir**ían**
presente de subjuntivo	
me sient**a**	nos sint**amos**
te sient**as**	os sint**áis**
se sient**a**	se sient**an**
imperfecto de subjuntivo	
me sintier**a**	nos sintiér**amos**
te sintier**as**	os sintier**ais**
se sintier**a**	se sintier**an**
OR	
me sinties**e**	nos sintiés**emos**
te sinties**es**	os sinties**eis**
se sinties**e**	se sinties**en**
imperativo	
—	sintámonos
siéntete; no te sientas	sentios; no os sintáis
siéntase	siéntanse

SINGULAR	PLURAL
perfecto de indicativo	
me he sentido	**nos hemos** sentido
te has sentido	**os habéis** sentido
se ha sentido	**se han** sentido
pluscuamperfecto de indicativo	
me había sentido	**nos habíamos** sentido
te habías sentido	**os habíais** sentido
se había sentido	**se habían** sentido
pretérito anterior	
me hube sentido	**nos hubimos** sentido
te hubiste sentido	**os hubisteis** sentido
se hubo sentido	**se hubieron** sentido
futuro perfecto	
me habré sentido	**nos habremos** sentido
te habrás sentido	**os habréis** sentido
se habrá sentido	**se habrán** sentido
condicional compuesto	
me habría sentido	**nos habríamos** sentido
te habrías sentido	**os habríais** sentido
se habría sentido	**se habrían** sentido
perfecto de subjuntivo	
me haya sentido	**nos hayamos** sentido
te hayas sentido	**os hayáis** sentido
se haya sentido	**se hayan** sentido
pluscuamperfecto de subjuntivo	
me hubiera sentido	**nos hubiéramos** sentido
te hubieras sentido	**os hubierais** sentido
se hubiera sentido	**se hubieran** sentido
OR	
me hubiese sentido	**nos hubiésemos** sentido
te hubieses sentido	**os hubieseis** sentido
se hubiese sentido	**se hubiesen** sentido

separar — to separate

gerundio **separando** — participio de pasado **separado**

SINGULAR	PLURAL	SINGULAR	PLURAL
presente de indicativo		perfecto de indicativo	
separ**o**	separ**amos**	**he** separado	**hemos** separado
separ**as**	separ**áis**	**has** separado	**habéis** separado
separ**a**	separ**an**	**ha** separado	**han** separado
imperfecto de indicativo		pluscuamperfecto de indicativo	
separ**aba**	separ**ábamos**	**había** separado	**habíamos** separado
separ**abas**	separ**abais**	**habías** separado	**habíais** separado
separ**aba**	separ**aban**	**había** separado	**habían** separado
pretérito		pretérito anterior	
separ**é**	separ**amos**	**hube** separado	**hubimos** separado
separ**aste**	separ**asteis**	**hubiste** separado	**hubisteis** separado
separ**ó**	separ**aron**	**hubo** separado	**hubieron** separado
futuro		futuro perfecto	
separar**é**	separar**emos**	**habré** separado	**habremos** separado
separar**ás**	separar**éis**	**habrás** separado	**habréis** separado
separar**á**	separar**án**	**habrá** separado	**habrán** separado
condicional simple		condicional compuesto	
separar**ía**	separar**íamos**	**habría** separado	**habríamos** separado
separar**ías**	separar**íais**	**habrías** separado	**habríais** separado
separar**ía**	separar**ían**	**habría** separado	**habrían** separado
presente de subjuntivo		perfecto de subjuntivo	
separ**e**	separ**emos**	**haya** separado	**hayamos** separado
separ**es**	separ**éis**	**hayas** separado	**hayáis** separado
separ**e**	separ**en**	**haya** separado	**hayan** separado
imperfecto de subjuntivo		pluscuamperfecto de subjuntivo	
separar**a**	separár**amos**	**hubiera** separado	**hubiéramos** separado
separar**as**	separar**ais**	**hubieras** separado	**hubierais** separado
separar**a**	separar**an**	**hubiera** separado	**hubieran** separado
OR		OR	
separas**e**	separás**emos**	**hubiese** separado	**hubiésemos** separado
separas**es**	separas**eis**	**hubieses** separado	**hubieseis** separado
separas**e**	separas**en**	**hubiese** separado	**hubiesen** separado

imperativo

—	separemos
separa; no separes	separad; no separéis
separe	separen

gerundio **siendo**

participio de pasado **sido**

presente de indicativo

SINGULAR	PLURAL
s**oy**	s**omos**
er**es**	s**ois**
es	s**on**

imperfecto de indicativo

SINGULAR	PLURAL
er**a**	ér**amos**
er**as**	er**ais**
er**a**	er**an**

pretérito

SINGULAR	PLURAL
fu**i**	fu**imos**
fu**iste**	fu**isteis**
fu**e**	fu**eron**

futuro

SINGULAR	PLURAL
ser**é**	ser**emos**
ser**ás**	ser**éis**
ser**á**	ser**án**

condicional simple

SINGULAR	PLURAL
ser**ía**	ser**íamos**
ser**ías**	ser**íais**
ser**ía**	ser**ían**

presente de subjuntivo

SINGULAR	PLURAL
se**a**	se**amos**
se**as**	se**áis**
se**a**	se**an**

imperfecto de subjuntivo

SINGULAR	PLURAL
fuer**a**	fuér**amos**
fuer**as**	fuer**ais**
fuer**a**	fuer**an**
OR	
fues**e**	fués**emos**
fues**es**	fues**eis**
fues**e**	fues**en**

imperativo

SINGULAR	PLURAL
—	seamos
sé; no seas	sed; no seáis
sea	sean

perfecto de indicativo

SINGULAR	PLURAL
he sido	**hemos** sido
has sido	**habéis** sido
ha sido	**han** sido

pluscuamperfecto de indicativo

SINGULAR	PLURAL
había sido	**habíamos** sido
habías sido	**habíais** sido
había sido	**habían** sido

pretérito anterior

SINGULAR	PLURAL
hube sido	**hubimos** sido
hubiste sido	**hubisteis** sido
hubo sido	**hubieron** sido

futuro perfecto

SINGULAR	PLURAL
habré sido	**habremos** sido
habrás sido	**habréis** sido
habrá sido	**habrán** sido

condicional compuesto

SINGULAR	PLURAL
habría sido	**habríamos** sido
habrías sido	**habríais** sido
habría sido	**habrían** sido

perfecto de subjuntivo

SINGULAR	PLURAL
haya sido	**hayamos** sido
hayas sido	**hayáis** sido
haya sido	**hayan** sido

pluscuamperfecto de subjuntivo

SINGULAR	PLURAL
hubiera sido	**hubiéramos** sido
hubieras sido	**hubierais** sido
hubiera sido	**hubieran** sido
OR	
hubiese sido	**hubiésemos** sido
hubieses sido	**hubieseis** sido
hubiese sido	**hubiesen** sido

servir — to serve

gerundio **sirviendo** participio de pasado **servido**

presente de indicativo

SINGULAR	PLURAL
sirv**o**	serv**imos**
sirv**es**	serv**ís**
sirv**e**	sirv**en**

imperfecto de indicativo

SINGULAR	PLURAL
serv**ía**	serv**íamos**
serv**ías**	serv**íais**
serv**ía**	serv**ían**

pretérito

SINGULAR	PLURAL
serv**í**	serv**imos**
serv**iste**	serv**ísteis**
sirv**ió**	sirv**ieron**

futuro

SINGULAR	PLURAL
servir**é**	servir**emos**
servir**ás**	servir**éis**
servir**á**	servir**án**

condicional simple

SINGULAR	PLURAL
servir**ía**	servir**íamos**
servir**ías**	servir**íais**
servir**ía**	servir**ían**

presente de subjuntivo

SINGULAR	PLURAL
sirv**a**	sirv**amos**
sirv**as**	sirv**áis**
sirv**a**	sirv**an**

imperfecto de subjuntivo

SINGULAR	PLURAL
sirvier**a**	sirviér**amos**
sirvier**as**	sirvier**ais**
sirvier**a**	sirvier**an**
OR	
sirvies**e**	sirviés**emos**
sirvies**es**	sirvies**eis**
sirvies**e**	sirvies**en**

imperativo

SINGULAR	PLURAL
—	sirvamos
sirve; no sirvas	servid; no sirváis
sirva	sirvan

perfecto de indicativo

SINGULAR	PLURAL
he servido	**hemos** servido
has servido	**habéis** servido
ha servido	**han** servido

pluscuamperfecto de indicativo

SINGULAR	PLURAL
había servido	**habíamos** servido
habías servido	**habíais** servido
había servido	**habían** servido

pretérito anterior

SINGULAR	PLURAL
hube servido	**hubimos** servido
hubiste servido	**hubisteis** servido
hubo servido	**hubieron** servido

futuro perfecto

SINGULAR	PLURAL
habré servido	**habremos** servido
habrás servido	**habréis** servido
habrá servido	**habrán** servido

condicional compuesto

SINGULAR	PLURAL
habría servido	**habríamos** servido
habrías servido	**habríais** servido
habría servido	**habrían** servido

perfecto de subjuntivo

SINGULAR	PLURAL
haya servido	**hayamos** servido
hayas servido	**hayáis** servido
haya servido	**hayan** servido

pluscuamperfecto de subjuntivo

SINGULAR	PLURAL
hubiera servido	**hubiéramos** servido
hubieras servido	**hubierais** servido
hubiera servido	**hubieran** servido
OR	
hubiese servido	**hubiésemos** servido
hubieses servido	**hubieseis** servido
hubiese servido	**hubiesen** servido

gerundio **sofocando** participio de pasado **sofocado**

SINGULAR	PLURAL	SINGULAR	PLURAL
presente de indicativo		perfecto de indicativo	
sofoc**o**	sofoc**amos**	**he** sofocado	**hemos** sofocado
sofoc**as**	sofoc**áis**	**has** sofocado	**habéis** sofocado
sofoc**a**	sofoc**an**	**ha** sofocado	**han** sofocado
imperfecto de indicativo		pluscuamperfecto de indicativo	
sofoc**aba**	sofoc**ábamos**	**había** sofocado	**habíamos** sofocado
sofoc**abas**	sofoc**abais**	**habías** sofocado	**habíais** sofocado
sofoc**aba**	sofoc**aban**	**había** sofocado	**habían** sofocado
pretérito		pretérito anterior	
sofoqu**é**	sofoc**amos**	**hube** sofocado	**hubimos** sofocado
sofoc**aste**	sofoc**asteis**	**hubiste** sofocado	**hubisteis** sofocado
sofoc**ó**	sofoc**aron**	**hubo** sofocado	**hubieron** sofocado
futuro		futuro perfecto	
sofocar**é**	sofocar**emos**	**habré** sofocado	**habremos** sofocado
sofocar**ás**	sofocar**éis**	**habrás** sofocado	**habréis** sofocado
sofocar**á**	sofocar**án**	**habrá** sofocado	**habrán** sofocado
condicional simple		condicional compuesto	
sofocar**ía**	sofocar**íamos**	**habría** sofocado	**habríamos** sofocado
sofocar**ías**	sofocar**íais**	**habrías** sofocado	**habríais** sofocado
sofocar**ía**	sofocar**ían**	**habría** sofocado	**habrían** sofocado
presente de subjuntivo		perfecto de subjuntivo	
sofoqu**e**	sofoqu**emos**	**haya** sofocado	**hayamos** sofocado
sofoqu**es**	sofoqu**éis**	**hayas** sofocado	**hayáis** sofocado
sofoqu**e**	sofoqu**en**	**haya** sofocado	**hayan** sofocado
imperfecto de subjuntivo		pluscuamperfecto de subjuntivo	
sofocar**a**	sofocár**amos**	**hubiera** sofocado	**hubiéramos** sofocado
sofocar**as**	sofocar**ais**	**hubieras** sofocado	**hubierais** sofocado
sofocar**a**	sofocar**an**	**hubiera** sofocado	**hubieran** sofocado
OR		OR	
sofocas**e**	sofocás**emos**	**hubiese** sofocado	**hubiésemos** sofocado
sofocas**es**	sofocas**eis**	**hubieses** sofocado	**hubieseis** sofocado
sofocas**e**	sofocas**en**	**hubiese** sofocado	**hubiesen** sofocado

imperativo

—	sofoquemos
sofoca; no sofoques	sofocad; no sofoquéis
sofoque	sofoquen

soler*

to be in the habit of

gerundio **soliendo**

participio de pasado **solido**

SINGULAR	PLURAL
presente de indicativo	
suel**o**	sol**emos**
suel**es**	sol**éis**
suel**e**	suel**en**
imperfecto de indicativo	
sol**ía**	sol**íamos**
sol**ías**	sol**íais**
sol**ía**	sol**ían**
presente de subjuntivo	
suel**a**	sol**amos**
suel**as**	sol**áis**
suel**a**	suel**an**
imperativo	
—	

SINGULAR	PLURAL
perfecto de indicativo	
he solido	**hemos** solido
has solido	**habéis** solido
ha solido	**han** solido

*The verb **soler** is always followed by an infinitive.

to sob, to whimper — sollozar

gerundio **sollozando** | participio de pasado **sollozado**

presente de indicativo

SINGULAR	PLURAL
solloz**o**	solloz**amos**
solloz**as**	solloz**áis**
solloz**a**	solloz**an**

imperfecto de indicativo

SINGULAR	PLURAL
solloz**aba**	solloz**ábamos**
solloz**abas**	solloz**abais**
solloz**aba**	solloz**aban**

pretérito

SINGULAR	PLURAL
sollo**cé**	solloz**amos**
solloz**aste**	solloz**asteis**
solloz**ó**	solloz**aron**

futuro

SINGULAR	PLURAL
sollozar**é**	sollozar**emos**
sollozar**ás**	sollozar**éis**
sollozar**á**	sollozar**án**

condicional simple

SINGULAR	PLURAL
sollozar**ía**	sollozar**íamos**
sollozar**ías**	sollozar**íais**
sollozar**ía**	sollozar**ían**

presente de subjuntivo

SINGULAR	PLURAL
solloc**e**	solloc**emos**
solloc**es**	solloc**éis**
solloc**e**	solloc**en**

imperfecto de subjuntivo

SINGULAR	PLURAL
sollozar**a**	sollozár**amos**
sollozar**as**	sollozar**ais**
sollozar**a**	sollozar**an**
OR	
sollozas**e**	sollozás**emos**
sollozas**es**	sollozas**eis**
sollozas**e**	sollozas**en**

imperativo

SINGULAR	PLURAL
—	sollecemos
solloza; no solloces	sollozad; no sollocéis
solloce	sollocen

perfecto de indicativo

SINGULAR	PLURAL
he sollozado	**hemos** sollozado
has sollozado	**habéis** sollozado
ha sollozado	**han** sollozado

pluscuamperfecto de indicativo

SINGULAR	PLURAL
había sollozado	**habíamos** sollozado
habías sollozado	**habíais** sollozado
había sollozado	**habían** sollozado

pretérito anterior

SINGULAR	PLURAL
hube sollozado	**hubimos** sollozado
hubiste sollozado	**hubisteis** sollozado
hubo sollozado	**hubieron** sollozado

futuro perfecto

SINGULAR	PLURAL
habré sollozado	**habremos** sollozado
habrás sollozado	**habréis** sollozado
habrá sollozado	**habrán** sollozado

condicional compuesto

SINGULAR	PLURAL
habría sollozado	**habríamos** sollozado
habrías sollozado	**habríais** sollozado
habría sollozado	**habrían** sollozado

perfecto de subjuntivo

SINGULAR	PLURAL
haya sollozado	**hayamos** sollozado
hayas sollozado	**hayáis** sollozado
haya sollozado	**hayan** sollozado

pluscuamperfecto de subjuntivo

SINGULAR	PLURAL
hubiera sollozado	**hubiéramos** sollozado
hubieras sollozado	**hubierais** sollozado
hubiera sollozado	**hubieran** sollozado
OR	
hubiese sollozado	**hubiésemos** sollozado
hubieses sollozado	**hubieseis** sollozado
hubiese sollozado	**hubiesen** sollozado

someter — to subdue, to subject

gerundio **sometiendo** participio de pasado **sometido**

SINGULAR	PLURAL
presente de indicativo	
somet**o**	somet**emos**
somet**es**	somet**éis**
somet**e**	somet**en**
imperfecto de indicativo	
somet**ía**	somet**íamos**
somet**ías**	somet**íais**
somet**ía**	somet**ían**
pretérito	
somet**í**	somet**imos**
somet**iste**	somet**isteis**
somet**ió**	somet**ieron**
futuro	
someter**é**	someter**emos**
someter**ás**	someter**éis**
someter**á**	someter**án**
condicional simple	
someter**ía**	someter**íamos**
someter**ías**	someter**íais**
someter**ía**	someter**ían**
presente de subjuntivo	
somet**a**	somet**amos**
somet**as**	somet**áis**
somet**a**	somet**an**
imperfecto de subjuntivo	
sometier**a**	sometiér**amos**
sometier**as**	sometier**ais**
sometier**a**	sometier**an**
OR	
someties**e**	sometiés**emos**
someties**es**	someties**eis**
someties**e**	someties**en**
imperativo	
—	sometamos
somete; no sometas	someted; no sometáis
someta	sometan

SINGULAR	PLURAL
perfecto de indicativo	
he sometido	**hemos** sometido
has sometido	**habéis** sometido
ha sometido	**han** sometido
pluscuamperfecto de indicativo	
había sometido	**habíamos** sometido
habías sometido	**habíais** sometido
había sometido	**habían** sometido
pretérito anterior	
hube sometido	**hubimos** sometido
hubiste sometido	**hubisteis** sometido
hubo sometido	**hubieron** sometido
futuro perfecto	
habré sometido	**habremos** sometido
habrás sometido	**habréis** sometido
habrá sometido	**habrán** sometido
condicional compuesto	
habría sometido	**habríamos** sometido
habrías sometido	**habríais** sometido
habría sometido	**habrían** sometido
perfecto de subjuntivo	
haya sometido	**hayamos** sometido
hayas sometido	**hayáis** sometido
haya sometido	**hayan** sometido
pluscuamperfecto de subjuntivo	
hubiera sometido	**hubiéramos** sometido
hubieras sometido	**hubierais** sometido
hubiera sometido	**hubieran** sometido
OR	
hubiese sometido	**hubiésemos** sometido
hubieses sometido	**hubieseis** sometido
hubiese sometido	**hubiesen** sometido

gerundio **sonando** participio de pasado **sonado**

SINGULAR	PLURAL	SINGULAR	PLURAL
presente de indicativo		perfecto de indicativo	
sueno	sonamos	**he** sonado	**hemos** sonado
suenas	sonáis	**has** sonado	**habéis** sonado
suena	suenan	**ha** sonado	**han** sonado
imperfecto de indicativo		pluscuamperfecto de indicativo	
sonaba	sonábamos	**había** sonado	**habíamos** sonado
sonabas	sonabais	**habías** sonado	**habíais** sonado
sonaba	sonaban	**había** sonado	**habían** sonado
pretérito		pretérito anterior	
soné	sonamos	**hube** sonado	**hubimos** sonado
sonaste	sonasteis	**hubiste** sonado	**hubisteis** sonado
sonó	sonaron	**hubo** sonado	**hubieron** sonado
futuro		futuro perfecto	
sonaré	sonaremos	**habré** sonado	**habremos** sonado
sonarás	sonaréis	**habrás** sonado	**habréis** sonado
sonará	sonarán	**habrá** sonado	**habrán** sonado
condicional simple		condicional compuesto	
sonaría	sonaríamos	**habría** sonado	**habríamos** sonado
sonarías	sonaríais	**habrías** sonado	**habríais** sonado
sonaría	sonarían	**habría** sonado	**habrían** sonado
presente de subjuntivo		perfecto de subjuntivo	
suene	sonemos	**haya** sonado	**hayamos** sonado
suenes	sonéis	**hayas** sonado	**hayáis** sonado
suene	suenen	**haya** sonado	**hayan** sonado
imperfecto de subjuntivo		pluscuamperfecto de subjuntivo	
sonara	sonáramos	**hubiera** sonado	**hubiéramos** sonado
sonaras	sonarais	**hubieras** sonado	**hubierais** sonado
sonara	sonaran	**hubiera** sonado	**hubieran** sonado
OR		OR	
sonase	sonásemos	**hubiese** sonado	**hubiésemos** sonado
sonases	sonaseis	**hubieses** sonado	**hubieseis** sonado
sonase	sonasen	**hubiese** sonado	**hubiesen** sonado

imperativo

—	sonemos
suena; no suenes	sonad; no sonéis
suene	suenen

soñar — to dream

gerundio **soñando** — participio de pasado **soñado**

SINGULAR	PLURAL
presente de indicativo	
sueñ**o**	soñ**amos**
sueñ**as**	soñ**áis**
sueñ**a**	sueñ**an**
imperfecto de indicativo	
soñ**aba**	soñ**ábamos**
soñ**abas**	soñ**abais**
soñ**aba**	soñ**aban**
pretérito	
soñ**é**	soñ**amos**
soñ**aste**	soñ**asteis**
soñ**ó**	soñ**aron**
futuro	
soñar**é**	soñar**emos**
soñar**ás**	soñar**éis**
soñar**á**	soñar**án**
condicional simple	
soñar**ía**	soñar**íamos**
soñar**ías**	soñar**íais**
soñar**ía**	soñar**ían**
presente de subjuntivo	
sueñ**e**	soñ**emos**
sueñ**es**	soñ**éis**
sueñ**e**	sueñ**en**
imperfecto de subjuntivo	
soñar**a**	soñár**amos**
soñar**as**	soñar**ais**
soñar**a**	soñar**an**
OR	
soñas**e**	soñás**emos**
soñas**es**	soñas**eis**
soñas**e**	soñas**en**
imperativo	
—	soñemos
sueña; no sueñes	soñad; no soñéis
sueñe	sueñen

SINGULAR	PLURAL
perfecto de indicativo	
he soñado	**hemos** soñado
has soñado	**habéis** soñado
ha soñado	**han** soñado
pluscuamperfecto de indicativo	
había soñado	**habíamos** soñado
habías soñado	**habíais** soñado
había soñado	**habían** soñado
pretérito anterior	
hube soñado	**hubimos** soñado
hubiste soñado	**hubisteis** soñado
hubo soñado	**hubieron** soñado
futuro perfecto	
habré soñado	**habremos** soñado
habrás soñado	**habréis** soñado
habrá soñado	**habrán** soñado
condicional compuesto	
habría soñado	**habríamos** soñado
habrías soñado	**habríais** soñado
habría soñado	**habrían** soñado
perfecto de subjuntivo	
haya soñado	**hayamos** soñado
hayas soñado	**hayáis** soñado
haya soñado	**hayan** soñado
pluscuamperfecto de subjuntivo	
hubiera soñado	**hubiéramos** soñado
hubieras soñado	**hubierais** soñado
hubiera soñado	**hubieran** soñado
OR	
hubiese soñado	**hubiésemos** soñado
hubieses soñado	**hubieseis** soñado
hubiese soñado	**hubiesen** soñado

gerundio **sonriendo** participio de pasado **sonreído**

SINGULAR	PLURAL	SINGULAR	PLURAL
presente de indicativo		perfecto de indicativo	
sonrí**o**	sonreí**mos**	**he** sonreído	**hemos** sonreído
sonrí**es**	sonre**ís**	**has** sonreído	**habéis** sonreído
sonrí**e**	sonrí**en**	**ha** sonreído	**han** sonreído
imperfecto de indicativo		pluscuamperfecto de indicativo	
sonre**ía**	sonre**íamos**	**había** sonreído	**habíamos** sonreído
sonre**ías**	sonre**íais**	**habías** sonreído	**habíais** sonreído
sonre**ía**	sonre**ían**	**había** sonreído	**habían** sonreído
pretérito		pretérito anterior	
sonre**í**	sonre**ímos**	**hube** sonreído	**hubimos** sonreído
sonre**íste**	sonre**ísteis**	**hubiste** sonreído	**hubisteis** sonreído
sonri**ó**	sonr**ieron**	**hubo** sonreído	**hubieron** sonreído
futuro		futuro perfecto	
sonreir**é**	sonreir**emos**	**habré** sonreído	**habremos** sonreído
sonreir**ás**	sonreir**éis**	**habrás** sonreído	**habréis** sonreído
sonreir**á**	sonreir**án**	**habrá** sonreído	**habrán** sonreído
condicional simple		condicional compuesto	
sonreir**ía**	sonreir**íamos**	**habría** sonreído	**habríamos** sonreído
sonreir**ías**	sonreir**íais**	**habrías** sonreído	**habríais** sonreído
sonreir**ía**	sonreir**ían**	**habría** sonreído	**habrían** sonreído
presente de subjuntivo		perfecto de subjuntivo	
sonrí**a**	sonri**amos**	**haya** sonreído	**hayamos** sonreído
sonrí**as**	sonri**áis**	**hayas** sonreído	**hayáis** sonreído
sonrí**a**	sonrí**an**	**haya** sonreído	**hayan** sonreído
imperfecto de subjuntivo		pluscuamperfecto de subjuntivo	
sonrier**a**	sonriér**amos**	**hubiera** sonreído	**hubiéramos** sonreído
sonrier**as**	sonrier**ais**	**hubieras** sonreído	**hubierais** sonreído
sonrier**a**	sonrier**an**	**hubiera** sonreído	**hubieran** sonreído
OR		OR	
sonries**e**	sonriés**emos**	**hubiese** sonreído	**hubiésemos** sonreído
sonries**es**	sonries**eis**	**hubieses** sonreído	**hubieseis** sonreído
sonries**e**	sonries**en**	**hubiese** sonreído	**hubiesen** sonreído

imperativo

—	sonriamos
sonríe; no sonrías	sonreíd; no sonriáis
sonría	sonrían

gerundio **soplando** — participio de pasado **soplado**

SINGULAR	PLURAL	SINGULAR	PLURAL
presente de indicativo		perfecto de indicativo	
sopl**o**	sopl**amos**	**he** soplado	**hemos** soplado
sopl**as**	sopl**áis**	**has** soplado	**habéis** soplado
sopl**a**	sopl**an**	**ha** soplado	**han** soplado
imperfecto de indicativo		pluscuamperfecto de indicativo	
sopl**aba**	sopl**ábamos**	**había** soplado	**habíamos** soplado
sopl**abas**	sopl**abais**	**habías** soplado	**habíais** soplado
sopl**aba**	sopl**aban**	**había** soplado	**habían** soplado
pretérito		pretérito anterior	
sopl**é**	sopl**amos**	**hube** soplado	**hubimos** soplado
sopl**aste**	sopl**asteis**	**hubiste** soplado	**hubisteis** soplado
sopl**ó**	sopl**aron**	**hubo** soplado	**hubieron** soplado
futuro		futuro perfecto	
soplar**é**	soplar**emos**	**habré** soplado	**habremos** soplado
soplar**ás**	soplar**éis**	**habrás** soplado	**habréis** soplado
soplar**á**	soplar**án**	**habrá** soplado	**habrán** soplado
condicional simple		condicional compuesto	
soplar**ía**	soplar**íamos**	**habría** soplado	**habríamos** soplado
soplar**ías**	soplar**íais**	**habrías** soplado	**habríais** soplado
soplar**ía**	soplar**ían**	**habría** soplado	**habrían** soplado
presente de subjuntivo		perfecto de subjuntivo	
sopl**e**	sopl**emos**	**haya** soplado	**hayamos** soplado
sopl**es**	sopl**éis**	**hayas** soplado	**hayáis** soplado
sopl**e**	sopl**en**	**haya** soplado	**hayan** soplado
imperfecto de subjuntivo		pluscuamperfecto de subjuntivo	
soplar**a**	sopl**áramos**	**hubiera** soplado	**hubiéramos** soplado
soplar**as**	soplar**ais**	**hubieras** soplado	**hubierais** soplado
soplar**a**	soplar**an**	**hubiera** soplado	**hubieran** soplado
OR		OR	
soplas**e**	soplás**emos**	**hubiese** soplado	**hubiésemos** soplado
soplas**es**	soplas**eis**	**hubieses** soplado	**hubieseis** soplado
soplas**e**	soplas**en**	**hubiese** soplado	**hubiesen** soplado

imperativo

—	soplemos
sopla; no soples	soplad; no sopléis
sople	soplen

to surprise, to astonish sorprender

gerundio **sorprendiendo** participio de pasado **sorprendido**

SINGULAR	PLURAL
presente de indicativo	
sorprend**o**	sorprend**emos**
sorprend**es**	sorprend**éis**
sorprend**e**	sorprend**en**
imperfecto de indicativo	
sorprend**ía**	sorprend**íamos**
sorprend**ías**	sorprend**íais**
sorprend**ía**	sorprend**ían**
pretérito	
sorprend**í**	sorprend**imos**
sorprend**iste**	sorprend**isteis**
sorprend**ió**	sorprend**ieron**
futuro	
sorprender**é**	sorprender**emos**
sorprender**ás**	sorprender**éis**
sorprender**á**	sorprender**án**
condicional simple	
sorprender**ía**	sorprender**íamos**
sorprender**ías**	sorprender**íais**
sorprender**ía**	sorprender**ían**
presente de subjuntivo	
sorprend**a**	sorprend**amos**
sorprend**as**	sorprend**áis**
sorprend**a**	sorprend**an**
imperfecto de subjuntivo	
sorprendier**a**	sorprendiér**amos**
sorprendier**as**	sorprendier**ais**
sorprendier**a**	sorprendier**an**
OR	
sorprendies**e**	sorprendiés**emos**
sorprendies**es**	sorprendies**eis**
sorprendies**e**	sorprendies**en**
imperativo	
—	sorprendamos
sorprende; no sorprendas	sorprended; no sorprendáis
sorprenda	sorprendan

SINGULAR	PLURAL
perfecto de indicativo	
he sorprendido	**hemos** sorprendido
has sorprendido	**habéis** sorprendido
ha sorprendido	**han** sorprendido
pluscuamperfecto de indicativo	
había sorprendido	**habíamos** sorprendido
habías sorprendido	**habíais** sorprendido
había sorprendido	**habían** sorprendido
pretérito anterior	
hube sorprendido	**hubimos** sorprendido
hubiste sorprendido	**hubisteis** sorprendido
hubo sorprendido	**hubieron** sorprendido
futuro perfecto	
habré sorprendido	**habremos** sorprendido
habrás sorprendido	**habréis** sorprendido
habrá sorprendido	**habrán** sorprendido
condicional compuesto	
habría sorprendido	**habríamos** sorprendido
habrías sorprendido	**habríais** sorprendido
habría sorprendido	**habrían** sorprendido
perfecto de subjuntivo	
haya sorprendido	**hayamos** sorprendido
hayas sorprendido	**hayáis** sorprendido
haya sorprendido	**hayan** sorprendido
pluscuamperfecto de subjuntivo	
hubiera sorprendido	**hubiéramos** sorprendido
hubieras sorprendido	**hubierais** sorprendido
hubiera sorprendido	**hubieran** sorprendido
OR	
hubiese sorprendido	**hubiésemos** sorprendido
hubieses sorprendido	**hubieseis** sorprendido
hubiese sorprendido	**hubiesen** sorprendido

sospechar — to suspect

gerundio **sospechando** participio de pasado **sospechado**

SINGULAR	PLURAL
presente de indicativo	
sospech**o**	sospech**amos**
sospech**as**	sospech**áis**
sospech**a**	sospech**an**
imperfecto de indicativo	
sospech**aba**	sospech**ábamos**
sospech**abas**	sospech**abais**
sospech**aba**	sospech**aban**
pretérito	
sospech**é**	sospech**amos**
sospech**aste**	sospech**asteis**
sospech**ó**	sospech**aron**
futuro	
sospechar**é**	sospechar**emos**
sospechar**ás**	sospechar**éis**
sospechar**á**	sospechar**án**
condicional simple	
sospechar**ía**	sospechar**íamos**
sospechar**ías**	sospechar**íais**
sospechar**ía**	sospechar**ían**
presente de subjuntivo	
sospech**e**	sospech**emos**
sospech**es**	sospech**éis**
sospech**e**	sospech**en**
imperfecto de subjuntivo	
sospechar**a**	sospechár**amos**
sospechar**as**	sospechar**ais**
sospechar**a**	sospechar**an**
OR	
sospechas**e**	sospechás**emos**
sospechas**es**	sospechas**eis**
sospechas**e**	sospechas**en**
imperativo	
—	sospechemos
sospecha; no sospeches	sospechad; no sospechéis
sospeche	sospechen

SINGULAR	PLURAL
perfecto de indicativo	
he sospechado	**hemos** sospechado
has sospechado	**habéis** sospechado
ha sospechado	**han** sospechado
pluscuamperfecto de indicativo	
había sospechado	**habíamos** sospechado
habías sospechado	**habíais** sospechado
había sospechado	**habían** sospechado
pretérito anterior	
hube sospechado	**hubimos** sospechado
hubiste sospechado	**hubisteis** sospechado
hubo sospechado	**hubieron** sospechado
futuro perfecto	
habré sospechado	**habremos** sospechado
habrás sospechado	**habréis** sospechado
habrá sospechado	**habrán** sospechado
condicional compuesto	
habría sospechado	**habríamos** sospechado
habrías sospechado	**habríais** sospechado
habría sospechado	**habrían** sospechado
perfecto de subjuntivo	
haya sospechado	**hayamos** sospechado
hayas sospechado	**hayáis** sospechado
haya sospechado	**hayan** sospechado
pluscuamperfecto de subjuntivo	
hubiera sospechado	**hubiéramos** sospechado
hubieras sospechado	**hubierais** sospechado
hubiera sospechado	**hubieran** sospechado
OR	
hubiese sospechado	**hubiésemos** sospechado
hubieses sospechado	**hubieseis** sospechado
hubiese sospechado	**hubiesen** sospechado

SINGULAR	PLURAL	SINGULAR	PLURAL
presente de indicativo		perfecto de indicativo	
sosteng**o**	sosten**emos**	**he** sostenido	**hemos** sostenido
sostien**es**	sosten**éis**	**has** sostenido	**habéis** sostenido
sostien**e**	sostien**en**	**ha** sostenido	**han** sostenido
imperfecto de indicativo		pluscuamperfecto de indicativo	
sosten**ía**	sosten**íamos**	**había** sostenido	**habíamos** sostenido
sosten**ías**	sosten**íais**	**habías** sostenido	**habíais** sostenido
sosten**ía**	sosten**ían**	**había** sostenido	**habían** sostenido
pretérito		pretérito anterior	
sostuv**e**	sostuv**imos**	**hube** sostenido	**hubimos** sostenido
sostuv**iste**	sostuv**isteis**	**hubiste** sostenido	**hubisteis** sostenido
sostuv**o**	sostuv**ieron**	**hubo** sostenido	**hubieron** sostenido
futuro		futuro perfecto	
sostendr**é**	sostendr**emos**	**habré** sostenido	**habremos** sostenido
sostendr**ás**	sostendr**éis**	**habrás** sostenido	**habréis** sostenido
sostendr**á**	sostendr**án**	**habrá** sostenido	**habrán** sostenido
condicional simple		condicional compuesto	
sostendr**ía**	sostendr**íamos**	**habría** sostenido	**habríamos** sostenido
sostendr**ías**	sostendr**íais**	**habrías** sostenido	**habríais** sostenido
sostendr**ía**	sostendr**ían**	**habría** sostenido	**habrían** sostenido
presente de subjuntivo		perfecto de subjuntivo	
sosteng**a**	sosteng**amos**	**haya** sostenido	**hayamos** sostenido
sosteng**as**	sosteng**áis**	**hayas** sostenido	**hayáis** sostenido
sosteng**a**	sosteng**an**	**haya** sostenido	**hayan** sostenido
imperfecto de subjuntivo		pluscuamperfecto de subjuntivo	
sostuvier**a**	sostuviér**amos**	**hubiera** sostenido	**hubiéramos** sostenido
sostuvier**as**	sostuvier**ais**	**hubieras** sostenido	**hubierais** sostenido
sostuvier**a**	sostuvier**an**	**hubiera** sostenido	**hubieran** sostenido
OR		OR	
sostuvies**e**	sostuviés**emos**	**hubiese** sostenido	**hubiésemos** sostenido
sostuvies**es**	sostuvies**eis**	**hubieses** sostenido	**hubieseis** sostenido
sostuvies**e**	sostuvies**en**	**hubiese** sostenido	**hubiesen** sostenido

imperativo

—	sostengamos
sostén; no sostengas	sostened; no sostengáis
sostenga	sostengan

subestimar — to underestimate

gerundio **subestimando** participio de pasado **subestimado**

SINGULAR	PLURAL
presente de indicativo	
subestim**o**	subestim**amos**
subestim**as**	subestim**áis**
subestim**a**	subestim**an**
imperfecto de indicativo	
subestim**aba**	subestim**ábamos**
subestim**abas**	subestim**abais**
subestim**aba**	subestim**aban**
pretérito	
subestim**é**	subestim**amos**
subestim**aste**	subestim**asteis**
subestim**ó**	subestim**aron**
futuro	
subestimar**é**	subestimar**emos**
subestimar**ás**	subestimar**éis**
subestimar**á**	subestimar**án**
condicional simple	
subestimar**ía**	subestimar**íamos**
subestimar**ías**	subestimar**íais**
subestimar**ía**	subestimar**ían**
presente de subjuntivo	
subestim**e**	subestim**emos**
subestim**es**	subestim**éis**
subestim**e**	subestim**en**
imperfecto de subjuntivo	
subestimar**a**	subestimár**amos**
subestimar**as**	subestimar**ais**
subestimar**a**	subestimar**an**
OR	
subestimas**e**	subestimás**emos**
subestimas**es**	subestimas**eis**
subestimas**e**	subestimas**en**
imperativo	
—	subestimemos
subestima; no subestimes	subestimad; no subestiméis
subestime	subestimen

SINGULAR	PLURAL
perfecto de indicativo	
he subestimado	**hemos** subestimado
has subestimado	**habéis** subestimado
ha subestimado	**han** subestimado
pluscuamperfecto de indicativo	
había subestimado	**habíamos** subestimado
habías subestimado	**habíais** subestimado
había subestimado	**habían** subestimado
pretérito anterior	
hube subestimado	**hubimos** subestimado
hubiste subestimado	**hubisteis** subestimado
hubo subestimado	**hubieron** subestimado
futuro perfecto	
habré subestimado	**habremos** subestimado
habrás subestimado	**habréis** subestimado
habrá subestimado	**habrán** subestimado
condicional compuesto	
habría subestimado	**habríamos** subestimado
habrías subestimado	**habríais** subestimado
habría subestimado	**habrían** subestimado
perfecto de subjuntivo	
haya subestimado	**hayamos** subestimado
hayas subestimado	**hayáis** subestimado
haya subestimado	**hayan** subestimado
pluscuamperfecto de subjuntivo	
hubiera subestimado	**hubiéramos** subestimado
hubieras subestimado	**hubierais** subestimado
hubiera subestimado	**hubieran** subestimado
OR	
hubiese subestimado	**hubiésemos** subestimado
hubieses subestimado	**hubieseis** subestimado
hubiese subestimado	**hubiesen** subestimado

to climb, to go up **subir**

gerundio **subiendo** participio de pasado **subido**

SINGULAR	PLURAL
presente de indicativo	
sub**o**	sub**imos**
sub**es**	sub**ís**
sub**e**	sub**en**
imperfecto de indicativo	
sub**ía**	sub**íamos**
sub**ías**	sub**íais**
sub**ía**	sub**ían**
pretérito	
sub**í**	sub**imos**
sub**iste**	sub**isteis**
sub**ió**	sub**ieron**
futuro	
subir**é**	subir**emos**
subir**ás**	subir**éis**
subir**á**	subir**án**
condicional simple	
subir**ía**	subir**íamos**
subir**ías**	subir**íais**
subir**ía**	subir**ían**
presente de subjuntivo	
sub**a**	sub**amos**
sub**as**	sub**áis**
sub**a**	sub**an**
imperfecto de subjuntivo	
subier**a**	subiér**amos**
subier**as**	subier**ais**
subier**a**	subier**an**
OR	
subies**e**	subiés**emos**
subies**es**	subies**eis**
subies**e**	subies**en**
imperativo	
—	subamos
sube; no subas	subid; no subáis
suba	suban

SINGULAR	PLURAL
perfecto de indicativo	
he subido	**hemos** subido
has subido	**habéis** subido
ha subido	**han** subido
pluscuamperfecto de indicativo	
había subido	**habíamos** subido
habías subido	**habíais** subido
había subido	**habían** subido
pretérito anterior	
hube subido	**hubimos** subido
hubiste subido	**hubisteis** subido
hubo subido	**hubieron** subido
futuro perfecto	
habré subido	**habremos** subido
habrás subido	**habréis** subido
habrá subido	**habrán** subido
condicional compuesto	
habría subido	**habríamos** subido
habrías subido	**habríais** subido
habría subido	**habrían** subido
perfecto de subjuntivo	
haya subido	**hayamos** subido
hayas subido	**hayáis** subido
haya subido	**hayan** subido
pluscuamperfecto de subjuntivo	
hubiera subido	**hubiéramos** subido
hubieras subido	**hubierais** subido
hubiera subido	**hubieran** subido
OR	
hubiese subido	**hubiésemos** subido
hubieses subido	**hubieseis** subido
hubiese subido	**hubiesen** subido

subscribir — to subscribe, to agree

gerundio **subscribiendo** — participio de pasado **subscrito**

presente de indicativo

SINGULAR	PLURAL
subscrib**o**	subscrib**imos**
subscrib**es**	subscrib**ís**
subscrib**e**	subscrib**en**

imperfecto de indicativo

SINGULAR	PLURAL
subscrib**ía**	subscnb**iamos**
subscrib**ías**	subscrib**íais**
subscrib**ía**	subscrib**ían**

pretérito

SINGULAR	PLURAL
subscrib**í**	subscrib**imos**
subscrib**iste**	subscrib**isteis**
subscrib**ió**	subscrib**ieron**

futuro

SINGULAR	PLURAL
subscribir**é**	subscribir**emos**
subscribir**ás**	subscribir**éis**
subscribir**ó**	subscribir**án**

condicional simple

SINGULAR	PLURAL
subscribir**ía**	subscribir**íamos**
subscribir**ías**	subscribir**íais**
subscribir**ía**	subscribir**ían**

presente de subjuntivo

SINGULAR	PLURAL
subscrib**a**	subscrib**amos**
subscrib**as**	subscrib**áis**
subscrib**a**	subscrib**an**

imperfecto de subjuntivo

SINGULAR	PLURAL
subscribier**a**	subscribiér**amos**
subscribier**as**	subscribier**ais**
subscribier**a**	subscribier**an**
OR	
subscribies**e**	subscribiés**emos**
subscribies**es**	subscribies**eis**
subscribies**e**	subscribies**en**

imperativo

SINGULAR	PLURAL
—	subscribamos
subscribe; no subscribas	subscribid; no subscribáis
subscriba	subscriban

perfecto de indicativo

SINGULAR	PLURAL
he subscrito	**hemos** subscrito
has subscrito	**habéis** subscrito
ha subscrito	**han** subscrito

pluscuamperfecto de indicativo

SINGULAR	PLURAL
había subscrito	**habíamos** subscrito
habías subscrito	**habíais** subscrito
había subscrito	**habían** subscrito

pretérito anterior

SINGULAR	PLURAL
hube subscrito	**hubimos** subscrito
hubiste subscrito	**hubisteis** subscrito
hubo subscrito	**hubieron** subscrito

futuro perfecto

SINGULAR	PLURAL
habré subscrito	**habremos** subscrito
habrás subscrito	**habréis** subscrito
habrá subscrito	**habrán** subscrito

condicional compuesto

SINGULAR	PLURAL
habría subscrito	**habríamos** subscrito
habrías subscrito	**habríais** subscrito
habría subscrito	**habrían** subscrito

perfecto de subjuntivo

SINGULAR	PLURAL
haya subscrito	**hayamos** subscrito
hayas subscrito	**hayáis** subscrito
haya subscrito	**hayan** subscrito

pluscuamperfecto de subjuntivo

SINGULAR	PLURAL
hubiera subscrito	**hubiéramos** subscrito
hubieras subscrito	**hubierais** subscrito
hubiera subscrito	**hubieran** subscrito
OR	
hubiese subscrito	**hubiésemos** subscrito
hubieses subscrito	**hubieseis** subscrito
hubiese subscrito	**hubiesen** subscrito

gerundio **sufriendo** participio de pasado **sufrido**

SINGULAR	PLURAL
presente de indicativo	
sufr**o**	sufr**imos**
sufr**es**	sufr**ís**
sufr**e**	sufr**en**
imperfecto de indicativo	
sufr**ía**	sufr**íamos**
sufr**ías**	sufr**íais**
sufr**ía**	sufr**ían**
pretérito	
sufr**í**	sufr**imos**
sufr**iste**	sufr**isteis**
sufr**ió**	sufr**ieron**
futuro	
sufrir**é**	sufrir**emos**
sufrir**ás**	sufrir**éis**
sufrir**á**	sufrir**án**
condicional simple	
sufrir**ía**	sufrir**íamos**
sufrir**ías**	sufrir**íais**
sufrir**ía**	sufrir**ían**
presente de subjuntivo	
sufr**a**	sufr**amos**
sufr**as**	sufr**áis**
sufr**a**	sufr**an**
imperfecto de subjuntivo	
sufrier**a**	sufriér**amos**
sufrier**as**	sufrier**ais**
sufrier**a**	sufrier**an**
OR	
sufries**e**	sufriés**emos**
sufries**es**	sufries**eis**
sufries**e**	sufries**en**
imperativo	
—	suframos
sufre; no sufras	sufrid; no sufráis
sufra	sufran

SINGULAR	PLURAL
perfecto de indicativo	
he sufrido	**hemos** sufrido
has sufrido	**habéis** sufrido
ha sufrido	**han** sufrido
pluscuamperfecto de indicativo	
había sufrido	**habíamos** sufrido
habías sufrido	**habíais** sufrido
había sufrido	**habían** sufrido
pretérito anterior	
hube sufrido	**hubimos** sufrido
hubiste sufrido	**hubisteis** sufrido
hubo sufrido	**hubieron** sufrido
futuro perfecto	
habré sufrido	**habremos** sufrido
habrás sufrido	**habréis** sufrido
habrá sufrido	**habrán** sufrido
condicional compuesto	
habría sufrido	**habríamos** sufrido
habrías sufrido	**habríais** sufrido
habría sufrido	**habrían** sufrido
perfecto de subjuntivo	
haya sufrido	**hayamos** sufrido
hayas sufrido	**hayáis** sufrido
haya sufrido	**hayan** sufrido
pluscuamperfecto de subjuntivo	
hubiera sufrido	**hubiéramos** sufrido
hubieras sufrido	**hubierais** sufrido
hubiera sufrido	**hubieran** sufrido
OR	
hubiese sufrido	**hubiésemos** sufrido
hubieses sufrido	**hubieseis** sufrido
hubiese sufrido	**hubiesen** sufrido

sugerir — to suggest, to hint

gerundio **sugiriendo** participio de pasado **sugerido**

presente de indicativo

SINGULAR	PLURAL
sugier**o**	suger**imos**
sugier**es**	suger**ís**
sugier**e**	sugier**en**

imperfecto de indicativo

SINGULAR	PLURAL
suger**ía**	suger**íamos**
suger**ías**	suger**íais**
suger**ía**	suger**ían**

pretérito

SINGULAR	PLURAL
suger**í**	suger**imos**
suger**iste**	suger**isteis**
sugiri**ó**	sugir**ieron**

futuro

SINGULAR	PLURAL
sugerir**é**	sugerir**emos**
sugerir**ás**	sugerir**éis**
sugerir**á**	sugerir**án**

condicional simple

SINGULAR	PLURAL
sugerir**ía**	sugerir**íamos**
sugerir**ías**	sugerir**íais**
sugerir**ía**	sugerir**ían**

presente de subjuntivo

SINGULAR	PLURAL
sugier**a**	sugir**amos**
sugier**as**	sugir**áis**
sugier**a**	sugier**an**

imperfecto de subjuntivo

SINGULAR	PLURAL
sugirier**a**	sugiriér**amos**
sugirier**as**	sugirier**ais**
sugirier**a**	sugirier**an**
OR	
sugiries**e**	sugiriés**emos**
sugiries**es**	sugiries**eis**
sugiries**e**	sugiries**en**

imperativo

SINGULAR	PLURAL
—	sugiramos
sugiere; no sugieras	sugerid; no sugiráis
sugiera	sugieran

perfecto de indicativo

SINGULAR	PLURAL
he sugerido	**hemos** sugerido
has sugerido	**habéis** sugerido
ha sugerido	**han** sugerido

pluscuamperfecto de indicativo

SINGULAR	PLURAL
había sugerido	**habíamos** sugerido
habías sugerido	**habíais** sugerido
había sugerido	**habían** sugerido

pretérito anterior

SINGULAR	PLURAL
hube sugerido	**hubimos** sugerido
hubiste sugerido	**hubisteis** sugerido
hubo sugerido	**hubieron** sugerido

futuro perfecto

SINGULAR	PLURAL
habré sugerido	**habremos** sugerido
habrás sugerido	**habréis** sugerido
habrá sugerido	**habrán** sugerido

condicional compuesto

SINGULAR	PLURAL
habría sugerido	**habríamos** sugerido
habrías sugerido	**habríais** sugerido
habría sugerido	**habrían** sugerido

perfecto de subjuntivo

SINGULAR	PLURAL
haya sugerido	**hayamos** sugerido
hayas sugerido	**hayáis** sugerido
haya sugerido	**hayan** sugerido

pluscuamperfecto de subjuntivo

SINGULAR	PLURAL
hubiera sugerido	**hubiéramos** sugerido
hubieras sugerido	**hubierais** sugerido
hubiera sugerido	**hubieran** sugerido
OR	
hubiese sugerido	**hubiésemos** sugerido
hubieses sugerido	**hubieseis** sugerido
hubiese sugerido	**hubiesen** sugerido

gerundio **sumergiendo** participio de pasado **sumergido**

SINGULAR	PLURAL	SINGULAR	PLURAL
presente de indicativo		perfecto de indicativo	
sumerj**o**	sumerg**imos**	**he** sumergido	**hemos** sumergido
sumerg**es**	sumerg**ís**	**has** sumergido	**habéis** sumergido
sumerg**e**	sumerg**en**	**ha** sumergido	**han** sumergido
imperfecto de indicativo		pluscuamperfecto de indicativo	
sumerg**ía**	sumerg**íamos**	**había** sumergido	**habíamos** sumergido
sumerg**ías**	sumerg**íais**	**habías** sumergido	**habíais** sumergido
sumerg**ía**	sumerg**ían**	**había** sumergido	**habían** sumergido
pretérito		pretérito anterior	
sumerg**í**	sumerg**imos**	**hube** sumergido	**hubimos** sumergido
sumerg**iste**	sumerg**isteis**	**hubiste** sumergido	**hubisteis** sumergido
sumerg**ió**	sumerg**ieron**	**hubo** sumergido	**hubieron** sumergido
futuro		futuro perfecto	
sumergir**é**	sumergir**emos**	**habré** sumergido	**habremos** sumergido
sumergir**ás**	sumergir**éis**	**habrás** sumergido	**habréis** sumergido
sumergir**á**	sumergir**án**	**habrá** sumergido	**habrán** sumergido
condicional simple		condicional compuesto	
sumergir**ía**	sumergir**íamos**	**habría** sumergido	**habríamos** sumergido
sumergir**ías**	sumergir**íais**	**habrías** sumergido	**habríais** sumergido
sumergir**ía**	sumergir**ían**	**habría** sumergido	**habrían** sumergido
presente de subjuntivo		perfecto de subjuntivo	
sumerj**a**	sumerj**amos**	**haya** sumergido	**hayamos** sumergido
sumerj**as**	sumerj**áis**	**hayas** sumergido	**hayáis** sumergido
sumerj**a**	sumerj**an**	**haya** sumergido	**hayan** sumergido
imperfecto de subjuntivo		pluscuamperfecto de subjuntivo	
sumergier**a**	sumergiér**amos**	**hubiera** sumergido	**hubiéramos** sumergido
sumergier**as**	sumergier**ais**	**hubieras** sumergido	**hubierais** sumergido
sumergier**a**	sumergier**an**	**hubiera** sumergido	**hubieran** sumergido
OR		OR	
sumergies**e**	sumergiés**emos**	**hubiese** sumergido	**hubiésemos** sumergido
sumergies**es**	sumergies**eis**	**hubieses** sumergido	**hubieseis** sumergido
sumergies**e**	sumergies**en**	**hubiese** sumergido	**hubiesen** sumergido

imperativo

—	sumerjamos
sumerge;	sumergid;
no sumerjas	no sumerjáis
sumerja	sumerjan

suponer

to suppose, to assume

gerundio **suponiendo**

participio de pasado **supuesto**

SINGULAR	PLURAL
presente de indicativo	
supong**o**	supon**emos**
supon**es**	supon**éis**
supon**e**	supon**en**
imperfecto de indicativo	
supon**ía**	supon**íamos**
supon**ías**	supon**íais**
supon**ía**	supon**ían**
pretérito	
supus**e**	sup**imos**
sup**iste**	sup**isteis**
sup**o**	sup**ieron**
futuro	
supondr**é**	supondr**emos**
supondr**ás**	supondr**éis**
supondr**á**	supondr**án**
condicional simple	
supondr**ía**	supondr**íamos**
supondr**ías**	supondr**íais**
supondr**ía**	supondr**ían**
presente de subjuntivo	
supong**a**	supong**amos**
supong**as**	supong**áis**
supong**a**	supong**an**
imperfecto de subjuntivo	
supusier**a**	supusiér**amos**
supusier**as**	supusier**ais**
supusier**a**	supusier**an**
OR	
supusies**e**	supusiés**emos**
supusies**es**	supusies**eis**
supusies**e**	supusies**en**
imperativo	
—	supongamos
supón; no supongas	suponed; no supongáis
suponga	supongan

SINGULAR	PLURAL
perfecto de indicativo	
he supuesto	**hemos** supuesto
has supuesto	**habéis** supuesto
ha supuesto	**han** supuesto
pluscuamperfecto de indicativo	
había supuesto	**habíamos** supuesto
habías supuesto	**habíais** supuesto
había supuesto	**habían** supuesto
pretérito anterior	
hube supuesto	**hubimos** supuesto
hubiste supuesto	**hubisteis** supuesto
hubo supuesto	**hubieron** supuesto
futuro perfecto	
habré supuesto	**habremos** supuesto
habrás supuesto	**habréis** supuesto
habrá supuesto	**habrán** supuesto
condicional compuesto	
habría supuesto	**habríamos** supuesto
habrías supuesto	**habríais** supuesto
habría supuesto	**habrían** supuesto
perfecto de subjuntivo	
haya supuesto	**hayamos** supuesto
hayas supuesto	**hayáis** supuesto
haya supuesto	**hayan** supuesto
pluscuamperfecto de subjuntivo	
hubiera supuesto	**hubiéramos** supuesto
hubieras supuesto	**hubierais** supuesto
hubiera supuesto	**hubieran** supuesto
OR	
hubiese supuesto	**hubiésemos** supuesto
hubieses supuesto	**hubieseis** supuesto
hubiese supuesto	**hubiesen** supuesto

to emerge — surgir

gerundio **surgiendo** participio de pasado **surgido**

SINGULAR	PLURAL
presente de indicativo	
surj**o**	surg**imos**
surg**es**	surg**ís**
surg**e**	surg**en**
imperfecto de indicativo	
surg**ía**	surg**íamos**
surg**ías**	surg**íais**
surg**ía**	surg**ían**
pretérito	
surg**í**	surg**imos**
surg**iste**	surg**isteis**
surg**io**	surg**ieron**
futuro	
surgir**é**	surgir**emos**
surgir**ás**	surgir**éis**
surgir**á**	surgir**án**
condicional simple	
surgir**ía**	surgir**íamos**
surgir**ías**	surgir**íais**
surgir**ía**	surgir**ían**
presente de subjuntivo	
surj**a**	surj**amos**
surj**as**	surj**áis**
surj**a**	surj**an**
imperfecto de subjuntivo	
surgier**a**	surgiér**amos**
surgier**as**	surgier**ais**
surgier**a**	surgier**an**
OR	
surgies**e**	surgiés**emos**
surgies**es**	surgies**eis**
surgies**e**	surgies**en**
imperativo	
—	surjamos
surge; no surjas	surgid; no surjáis
surja	surjan

SINGULAR	PLURAL
perfecto de indicativo	
he surgido	**hemos** surgido
has surgido	**habéis** surgido
ha surgido	**han** surgido
pluscuamperfecto de indicativo	
había surgido	**habíamos** surgido
habías surgido	**habíais** surgido
había surgido	**habían** surgido
pretérito anterior	
hube surgido	**hubimos** surgido
hubiste surgido	**hubisteis** surgido
hubo surgido	**hubieron** surgido
futuro perfecto	
habré surgido	**habremos** surgido
habrás surgido	**habréis** surgido
habrá surgido	**habrán** surgido
condicional compuesto	
habría surgido	**habríamos** surgido
habrías surgido	**habríais** surgido
habría surgido	**habrían** surgido
perfecto de subjuntivo	
haya surgido	**hayamos** surgido
hayas surgido	**hayáis** surgido
haya surgido	**hayan** surgido
pluscuamperfecto de subjuntivo	
hubiera surgido	**hubiéramos** surgido
hubieras surgido	**hubierais** surgido
hubiera surgido	**hubieran** surgido
OR	
hubiese surgido	**hubiésemos** surgido
hubieses surgido	**hubieseis** surgido
hubiese surgido	**hubiesen** surgido

suspirar — to sigh

gerundio **suspirando** participio de pasado **suspirado**

SINGULAR	PLURAL
presente de indicativo	
suspir**o**	suspir**amos**
suspir**as**	suspir**áis**
suspir**a**	suspir**an**
imperfecto de indicativo	
suspir**aba**	suspir**ábamos**
suspir**abas**	suspir**abais**
suspir**aba**	suspir**aban**
pretérito	
suspir**é**	suspir**amos**
suspir**aste**	suspir**asteis**
suspir**ó**	suspir**aron**
futuro	
suspirar**é**	suspirar**emos**
suspirar**ás**	suspirar**éis**
suspirar**á**	suspirar**án**
condicional simple	
suspirar**ía**	suspirar**íamos**
suspirar**ías**	suspirar**íais**
suspirar**ía**	suspirar**ían**
presente de subjuntivo	
suspir**e**	suspir**emos**
suspir**es**	suspir**éis**
suspir**e**	suspir**en**
imperfecto de subjuntivo	
suspirar**a**	suspirár**amos**
suspirar**as**	suspirar**ais**
suspirar**a**	suspirar**an**
OR	
suspiras**e**	suspirás**emos**
suspiras**es**	suspiras**eis**
suspiras**e**	suspiras**en**
imperativo	
—	suspiremos
suspira; no suspires	suspirad; no suspiréis
suspire	suspiren

SINGULAR	PLURAL
perfecto de indicativo	
he suspirado	**hemos** suspirado
has suspirado	**habéis** suspirado
ha suspirado	**han** suspirado
pluscuamperfecto de indicativo	
había suspirado	**habíamos** suspirado
habías suspirado	**habíais** suspirado
había suspirado	**habían** suspirado
pretérito anterior	
hube suspirado	**hubimos** suspirado
hubiste suspirado	**hubisteis** suspirado
hubo suspirado	**hubieron** suspirado
futuro perfecto	
habré suspirado	**habremos** suspirado
habrás suspirado	**habréis** suspirado
habrá suspirado	**habrán** suspirado
condicional compuesto	
habría suspirado	**habríamos** suspirado
habrías suspirado	**habríais** suspirado
habría suspirado	**habrían** suspirado
perfecto de subjuntivo	
haya suspirado	**hayamos** suspirado
hayas suspirado	**hayáis** suspirado
haya suspirado	**hayan** suspirado
pluscuamperfecto de subjuntivo	
hubiera suspirado	**hubiéramos** suspirado
hubieras suspirado	**hubierais** suspirado
hubiera suspirado	**hubieran** suspirado
OR	
hubiese suspirado	**hubiésemos** suspirado
hubieses suspirado	**hubieseis** suspirado
hubiese suspirado	**hubiesen** suspirado

to pluck, to play a stringed instrument **tañer**

gerundio **tañendo** participio de pasado **tañido**

SINGULAR	PLURAL
presente de indicativo	
tañ**o**	tañ**emos**
tañ**es**	tañ**éis**
tañ**e**	tañ**en**
imperfecto de indicativo	
tañ**ía**	tañ**íamos**
tañ**ías**	tañ**íais**
tañ**ía**	tañ**ían**
pretérito	
tañ**í**	tañ**imos**
tan**iste**	tañ**isteis**
tañ**ó**	tañ**eron**
futuro	
tañer**é**	tañer**emos**
tañer**ás**	tañer**éis**
tañer**á**	tañer**án**
condicional simple	
tañer**ía**	tañer**íamos**
tañer**ías**	tañer**íais**
tañer**ía**	tañer**ían**
presente de subjuntivo	
tañ**a**	tañ**amos**
tañ**as**	tañ**áis**
tañ**a**	tañ**an**
imperfecto de subjuntivo	
tañer**a**	tañér**amos**
tañer**as**	tañer**ais**
tañer**a**	tañer**an**
OR	
tañes**e**	tañés**emos**
tañes**es**	tañes**eis**
tañes**e**	tañes**en**
imperativo	
—	tañamos
tañe; no tañas	tañed; no tañáis
taña	tañan

SINGULAR	PLURAL
perfecto de indicativo	
he tañido	**hemos** tañido
has tañido	**habéis** tañido
ha tañido	**han** tañido
pluscuamperfecto de indicativo	
había tañido	**habíamos** tañido
habías tañido	**habíais** tañido
había tañido	**habían** tañido
pretérito anterior	
hube tañido	**hubimos** tañido
hubiste tañido	**hubisteis** tañido
hubo tañido	**hubieron** tañido
futuro perfecto	
habré tañido	**habremos** tañido
habrás tañido	**habréis** tañido
habrá tañido	**habrán** tañido
condicional compuesto	
habría tañido	**habríamos** tañido
habrías tañido	**habríais** tañido
habría tañido	**habrían** tañido
perfecto de subjuntivo	
haya tañido	**hayamos** tañido
hayas tañido	**hayáis** tañido
haya tañido	**hayan** tañido
pluscuamperfecto de subjuntivo	
hubiera tañido	**hubiéramos** tañido
hubieras tañido	**hubierais** tañido
hubiera tañido	**hubieran** tañido
OR	
hubiese tañido	**hubiésemos** tañido
hubieses tañido	**hubieseis** tañido
hubiese tañido	**hubiesen** tañido

tardar — to delay, to be delayed

gerundio **tardando** — participio de pasado **tardado**

SINGULAR	PLURAL	SINGULAR	PLURAL
presente de indicativo		perfecto de indicativo	
tard**o**	tard**amos**	**he** tardado	**hemos** tardado
tard**as**	tard**áis**	**has** tardado	**habéis** tardado
tard**a**	tard**an**	**ha** tardado	**han** tardado
imperfecto de indicativo		pluscuamperfecto de indicativo	
tard**aba**	tard**ábamos**	**había** tardado	**habíamos** tardado
tard**abas**	tard**abais**	**habías** tardado	**habíais** tardado
tard**aba**	tard**aban**	**había** tardado	**habían** tardado
pretérito		pretérito anterior	
tard**é**	tard**amos**	**hube** tardado	**hubimos** tardado
tard**aste**	tard**asteis**	**hubiste** tardado	**hubisteis** tardado
tard**ó**	tard**aron**	**hubo** tardado	**hubieron** tardado
futuro		futuro perfecto	
tardar**é**	tardar**emos**	**habré** tardado	**habremos** tardado
tardar**ás**	tardar**éis**	**habrás** tardado	**habréis** tardado
tardar**á**	tardar**án**	**habrá** tardado	**habrán** tardado
condicional simple		condicional compuesto	
tardar**ía**	tardar**íamos**	**habría** tardado	**habríamos** tardado
tardar**ías**	tardar**íais**	**habrías** tardado	**habríais** tardado
tardar**ía**	tardar**ían**	**habría** tardado	**habrían** tardado
presente de subjuntivo		perfecto de subjuntivo	
tard**e**	tard**emos**	**haya** tardado	**hayamos** tardado
tard**es**	tard**éis**	**hayas** tardado	**hayáis** tardado
tard**e**	tard**en**	**haya** tardado	**hayan** tardado
imperfecto de subjuntivo		pluscuamperfecto de subjuntivo	
tardar**a**	tardár**amos**	**hubiera** tardado	**hubiéramos** tardado
tardar**as**	tardar**ais**	**hubieras** tardado	**hubierais** tardado
tardar**a**	tardar**an**	**hubiera** tardado	**hubieran** tardado
OR		OR	
tardas**e**	tardás**emos**	**hubiese** tardado	**hubiésemos** tardado
tardas**es**	tardas**eis**	**hubieses** tardado	**hubieseis** tardado
tardas**e**	tardas**en**	**hubiese** tardado	**hubiesen** tardado

imperativo

tarda	tardemos
no tardes	tardad; no tardéis
tarde	tarden

gerundio **temblando** participio de pasado **temblado**

SINGULAR	PLURAL	SINGULAR	PLURAL
presente de indicativo		perfecto de indicativo	
tiembl**o**	tembl**amos**	**he** temblado	**hemos** temblado
tiembl**as**	tembl**áis**	**has** temblado	**habéis** temblado
tiembl**a**	tiembl**an**	**ha** temblado	**han** temblado
imperfecto de indicativo		pluscuamperfecto de indicativo	
tembl**aba**	tembl**ábamos**	**había** temblado	**habíamos** temblado
tembl**abas**	tembl**abais**	**habías** temblado	**habíais** temblado
tembl**aba**	tembl**aban**	**había** temblado	**habían** temblado
pretérito		pretérito anterior	
tembl**é**	tembl**amos**	**hube** temblado	**hubimos** temblado
tembl**aste**	tembl**asteis**	**hubiste** temblado	**hubisteis** temblado
tembl**ó**	tembl**aron**	**hubo** temblado	**hubieron** temblado
futuro		futuro perfecto	
temblar**é**	temblar**emos**	**habré** temblado	**habremos** temblado
temblar**ás**	temblar**éis**	**habrás** temblado	**habréis** temblado
temblar**á**	temblar**án**	**habrá** temblado	**habrán** temblado
condicional simple		condicional compuesto	
temblar**ía**	temblar**íamos**	**habría** temblado	**habríamos** temblado
temblar**ías**	temblar**íais**	**habrías** temblado	**habríais** temblado
temblar**ía**	temblar**ían**	**habría** temblado	**habrían** temblado
presente de subjuntivo		perfecto de subjuntivo	
tiembl**e**	tembl**emos**	**haya** temblado	**hayamos** temblado
tiembl**es**	tembl**éis**	**hayas** temblado	**hayáis** temblado
tiembl**e**	tiembl**en**	**haya** temblado	**hayan** temblado
imperfecto de subjuntivo		pluscuamperfecto de subjuntivo	
temblar**a**	temblár**amos**	**hubiera** temblado	**hubiéramos** temblado
temblar**as**	temblar**ais**	**hubieras** temblado	**hubierais** temblado
temblar**a**	temblar**an**	**hubiera** temblado	**hubieran** temblado
OR		OR	
temblas**e**	temblás**emos**	**hubiese** temblado	**hubiésemos** temblado
temblas**es**	temblas**eis**	**hubieses** temblado	**hubieseis** temblado
temblas**e**	temblas**en**	**hubiese** temblado	**hubiesen** temblado

imperativo

—	temblemos
tiembla; no tiembles	temblad; no tembléis
tiemble	tiemblen

tener — to have

gerundio **teniendo** participio de pasado **tenido**

presente de indicativo

SINGULAR	PLURAL
teng**o**	ten**emos**
tien**es**	ten**éis**
tien**e**	tien**en**

imperfecto de indicativo

SINGULAR	PLURAL
ten**ía**	ten**íamos**
ten**ías**	ten**íais**
ten**ía**	ten**ían**

pretérito

SINGULAR	PLURAL
tuv**e**	tuv**imos**
tuv**iste**	tuv**isteis**
tuv**o**	tuv**ieron**

futuro

SINGULAR	PLURAL
tendr**é**	tendr**emos**
tendr**ás**	tendr**éis**
tendr**á**	tendr**án**

condicional simple

SINGULAR	PLURAL
tendr**ía**	tendr**íamos**
tendr**ías**	tendr**íais**
tendr**ía**	tendr**ían**

presente de subjuntivo

SINGULAR	PLURAL
teng**a**	teng**amos**
teng**as**	teng**áis**
teng**a**	teng**an**

imperfecto de subjuntivo

SINGULAR	PLURAL
tuvier**a**	tuvié**ramos**
tuvier**as**	tuvier**ais**
tuvier**a**	tuvier**an**
OR	
tuvies**e**	tuvié**semos**
tuvies**es**	tuvies**eis**
tuvies**e**	tuvies**en**

imperativo

SINGULAR	PLURAL
—	tengamos
ten; no tengas	tened; no tengáis
tenga	tengan

perfecto de indicativo

SINGULAR	PLURAL
he tenido	**hemos** tenido
has tenido	**habéis** tenido
ha tenido	**han** tenido

pluscuamperfecto de indicativo

SINGULAR	PLURAL
había tenido	**habíamos** tenido
habías tenido	**habíais** tenido
había tenido	**habían** tenido

pretérito anterior

SINGULAR	PLURAL
hube tenido	**hubimos** tenido
hubiste tenido	**hubisteis** tenido
hubo tenido	**hubieron** tenido

futuro perfecto

SINGULAR	PLURAL
habré tenido	**habremos** tenido
habrás tenido	**habréis** tenido
habrá tenido	**habrán** tenido

condicional compuesto

SINGULAR	PLURAL
habría tenido	**habríamos** tenido
habrías tenido	**habríais** tenido
habría tenido	**habrían** tenido

perfecto de subjuntivo

SINGULAR	PLURAL
haya tenido	**hayamos** tenido
hayas tenido	**hayáis** tenido
haya tenido	**hayan** tenido

pluscuamperfecto de subjuntivo

SINGULAR	PLURAL
hubiera tenido	**hubiéramos** tenido
hubieras tenido	**hubierais** tenido
hubiera tenido	**hubieran** tenido
OR	
hubiese tenido	**hubiésemos** tenido
hubieses tenido	**hubieseis** tenido
hubiese tenido	**hubiesen** tenido

MUST KNOW VERB

to tempt — tentar

gerundio **tentando** participio de pasado **tentado**

SINGULAR	PLURAL	SINGULAR	PLURAL
presente de indicativo		perfecto de indicativo	
tient**o**	tent**amos**	**he** tentado	**hemos** tentado
tient**as**	tent**áis**	**has** tentado	**habéis** tentado
tient**a**	tient**an**	**ha** tentado	**han** tentado
imperfecto de indicativo		pluscuamperfecto de indicativo	
tent**aba**	tent**ábamos**	**había** tentado	**habíamos** tentado
tent**abas**	tent**abais**	**habías** tentado	**habíais** tentado
tent**aba**	tent**aban**	**había** tentado	**habían** tentado
pretérito		pretérito anterior	
tent**é**	tent**amos**	**hube** tentado	**hubimos** tentado
tent**aste**	tent**asteis**	**hubiste** tentado	**hubisteis** tentado
tent**ó**	tent**aron**	**hubo** tentado	**hubieron** tentado
futuro		futuro perfecto	
tentar**é**	tentar**emos**	**habré** tentado	**habremos** tentado
tentar**ás**	tentar**éis**	**habrás** tentado	**habréis** tentado
tentar**á**	tentar**án**	**habrá** tentado	**habrán** tentado
condicional simple		condicional compuesto	
tentar**ía**	tentar**íamos**	**habría** tentado	**habríamos** tentado
tentar**ías**	tentar**íais**	**habrías** tentado	**habríais** tentado
tentar**ía**	tentar**ían**	**habría** tentado	**habrían** tentado
presente de subjuntivo		perfecto de subjuntivo	
tient**e**	tent**emos**	**haya** tentado	**hayamos** tentado
tient**es**	tent**éis**	**hayas** tentado	**hayáis** tentado
tient**e**	tient**en**	**haya** tentado	**hayan** tentado
imperfecto de subjuntivo		pluscuamperfecto de subjuntivo	
tentar**a**	tentár**amos**	**hubiera** tentado	**hubiéramos** tentado
tentar**as**	tentar**ais**	**hubieras** tentado	**hubierais** tentado
tentar**a**	tentar**an**	**hubiera** tentado	**hubieran** tentado
OR		OR	
tentas**e**	tentás**emos**	**hubiese** tentado	**hubiésemos** tentado
tentas**es**	tentas**eis**	**hubieses** tentado	**hubieseis** tentado
tentas**e**	tentas**en**	**hubiese** tentado	**hubiesen** tentado

imperativo

tienta	tentemos
no tientes	tentad; no tentéis
tiente	tienten

T

terminar — to terminate

gerundio **terminando** — participio de pasado **terminado**

SINGULAR	PLURAL	SINGULAR	PLURAL
presente de indicativo		perfecto de indicativo	
termin**o**	termin**amos**	**he** terminado	**hemos** terminado
termin**as**	termin**áis**	**has** terminado	**habéis** terminado
termin**a**	termin**an**	**ha** terminado	**han** terminado
imperfecto de indicativo		pluscuamperfecto de indicativo	
termin**aba**	termin**ábamos**	**había** terminado	**habíamos** terminado
termin**abas**	termin**abais**	**habías** terminado	**habíais** terminado
termin**aba**	termin**aban**	**había** terminado	**habían** terminado
pretérito		pretérito anterior	
termin**é**	termin**amos**	**hube** terminado	**hubimos** terminado
termin**aste**	termin**asteis**	**hubiste** terminado	**hubisteis** terminado
termin**ó**	termin**aron**	**hubo** terminado	**hubieron** terminado
futuro		futuro perfecto	
terminar**é**	terminar**emos**	**habré** terminado	**habremos** terminado
terminar**ás**	terminar**éis**	**habrás** terminado	**habréis** terminado
terminar**á**	terminar**án**	**habrá** terminado	**habrán** terminado
condicional simple		condicional compuesto	
terminar**ía**	terminar**íamos**	**habría** terminado	**habríamos** terminado
terminar**ías**	terminar**íais**	**habrías** terminado	**habríais** terminado
terminar**ía**	terminar**ían**	**habría** terminado	**habrían** terminado
presente de subjuntivo		perfecto de subjuntivo	
termin**e**	termin**emos**	**haya** terminado	**hayamos** terminado
termin**es**	termin**éis**	**hayas** terminado	**hayáis** terminado
termin**e**	termin**en**	**haya** terminado	**hayan** terminado
imperfecto de subjuntivo		pluscuamperfecto de subjuntivo	
terminar**a**	terminár**amos**	**hubiera** terminado	**hubiéramos** terminado
terminar**as**	terminar**ais**	**hubieras** terminado	**hubierais** terminado
terminar**a**	terminar**an**	**hubiera** terminado	**hubieran** terminado
OR		OR	
terminas**e**	terminás**emos**	**hubiese** terminado	**hubiésemos** terminado
terminas**es**	terminas**eis**	**hubieses** terminado	**hubieseis** terminado
terminas**e**	terminas**en**	**hubiese** terminado	**hubiesen** terminado

imperativo

termina	terminemos
no termines	terminad; no terminéis
termine	terminen

gerundio **testificando** participio de pasado **testificado**

SINGULAR	PLURAL	SINGULAR	PLURAL
presente de indicativo		perfecto de indicativo	
testific**o**	testific**amos**	**he** testificado	**hemos** testificado
testific**as**	testific**áis**	**has** testificado	**habéis** testificado
testific**a**	testific**an**	**ha** testificado	**han** testificado
imperfecto de indicativo		pluscuamperfecto de indicativo	
testific**aba**	testific**ábamos**	**había** testificado	**habíamos** testificado
testific**abas**	testific**abais**	**habías** testificado	**habíais** testificado
testific**aba**	testific**aban**	**había** testificado	**habían** testificado
pretérito		pretérito anterior	
testifiqu**é**	testific**amos**	**hube** testificado	**hubimos** testificado
testific**aste**	testific**asteis**	**hubiste** testificado	**hubisteis** testificado
testific**ó**	testific**aron**	**hubo** testificado	**hubieron** testificado
futuro		futuro perfecto	
testificar**é**	testificar**emos**	**habré** testificado	**habremos** testificado
testificar**ás**	testificar**éis**	**habrás** testificado	**habréis** testificado
testificar**á**	testificar**án**	**habrá** testificado	**habrán** testificado
condicional simple		condicional compuesto	
testificar**ía**	testificar**íamos**	**habría** testificado	**habríamos** testificado
testificar**ías**	testificar**íais**	**habrías** testificado	**habríais** testificado
testificar**ía**	testificar**ían**	**habría** testificado	**habrían** testificado
presente de subjuntivo		perfecto de subjuntivo	
testifiqu**e**	testifiqu**emos**	**haya** testificado	**hayamos** testificado
testifiqu**es**	testifiqu**éis**	**hayas** testificado	**hayáis** testificado
testifiqu**e**	testifiqu**en**	**haya** testificado	**hayan** testificado
imperfecto de subjuntivo		pluscuamperfecto de subjuntivo	
testificar**a**	testificár**amos**	**hubiera** testificado	**hubiéramos** testificado
testificar**as**	testificar**ais**	**hubieras** testificado	**hubierais** testificado
testificar**a**	testificar**an**	**hubiera** testificado	**hubieran** testificado
OR		OR	
testificas**e**	testificás**emos**	**hubiese** testificado	**hubiésemos** testificado
testificas**es**	testificas**eis**	**hubieses** testificado	**hubieseis** testificado
testificas**e**	testificas**en**	**hubiese** testificado	**hubiesen** testificado

imperativo

testifica	testifiquemos
no testifiques	testificad; no testifiquéis
testifique	testifiquen

gerundio **tipificando** participio de pasado **tipificado**

SINGULAR	PLURAL
presente de indicativo	
tipific**o**	tipific**amos**
tipific**as**	tipific**áis**
tipific**a**	tipific**an**
imperfecto de indicativo	
tipific**aba**	tipific**ábamos**
tipific**abas**	tipific**abais**
tipific**aba**	tipific**aban**
pretérito	
tipifiqu**é**	tipific**amos**
tipific**aste**	tipific**asteis**
tipific**ó**	tipific**aron**
futuro	
tipificar**é**	tipificar**emos**
tipificar**ás**	tipificar**éis**
tipificar**á**	tipificar**án**
condicional simple	
tipificar**ía**	tipificar**íamos**
tipificar**ías**	tipificar**íais**
tipificar**ía**	tipificar**ían**
presente de subjuntivo	
tipifiqu**e**	tipifiqu**emos**
tipifiqu**es**	tipifiqu**éis**
tipifiqu**e**	tipifiqu**en**
imperfecto de subjuntivo	
tipificar**a**	tipificár**amos**
tipificar**as**	tipificar**ais**
tipificar**a**	tipificar**an**
OR	
tipificas**e**	tipificás**emos**
tipificas**es**	tipificas**eis**
tipificas**e**	tipificas**en**
imperativo	
tipifica	tipifiquemos
no tipifiques	tipificad; no tipifiquéis
tipifique	tipifiquen

SINGULAR	PLURAL
perfecto de indicativo	
he tipificado	**hemos** tipificado
has tipificado	**habéis** tipificado
ha tipificado	**han** tipificado
pluscuamperfecto de indicativo	
había tipificado	**habíamos** tipificado
habías tipificado	**habíais** tipificado
había tipificado	**habían** tipificado
pretérito anterior	
hube tipificado	**hubimos** tipificado
hubiste tipificado	**hubisteis** tipificado
hubo tipificado	**hubieron** tipificado
futuro perfecto	
habré tipificado	**habremos** tipificado
habrás tipificado	**habréis** tipificado
habrá tipificado	**habrán** tipificado
condicional compuesto	
habría tipificado	**habríamos** tipificado
habrías tipificado	**habríais** tipificado
habría tipificado	**habrían** tipificado
perfecto de subjuntivo	
haya tipificado	**hayamos** tipificado
hayas tipificado	**hayáis** tipificado
haya tipificado	**hayan** tipificado
pluscuamperfecto de subjuntivo	
hubiera tipificado	**hubiéramos** tipificado
hubieras tipificado	**hubierais** tipificado
hubiera tipificado	**hubieran** tipificado
OR	
hubiese tipificado	**hubiésemos** tipificado
hubieses tipificado	**hubieseis** tipificado
hubiese tipificado	**hubiesen** tipificado

gerundio **tiranizando** — participio de pasado **tiranizado**

SINGULAR	PLURAL
presente de indicativo	
tiraniz**o**	tiraniz**amos**
tiraniz**as**	tiraniz**áis**
tiraniz**a**	tiraniz**an**
imperfecto de indicativo	
tiraniz**aba**	tiraniz**ábamos**
tiraniz**abas**	tiraniz**abais**
tiraniz**aba**	tiraniz**aban**
pretérito	
tiranic**é**	tiraniz**amos**
tiraniz**aste**	tiraniz**asteis**
tiraniz**ó**	tiraniz**aron**
futuro	
tiranizar**é**	tiranizar**emos**
tiranizar**ás**	tiranizar**éis**
tiranizar**á**	tiranizar**án**
condicional simple	
tiranizar**ía**	tiranizar**íamos**
tiranizar**ías**	tiranizar**íais**
tiranizar**ía**	tiranizar**ían**
presente de subjuntivo	
tiranic**e**	tiranic**emos**
tiranic**es**	tiranic**éis**
tiranic**e**	tiranic**en**
imperfecto de subjuntivo	
tiranizar**a**	tranizár**amos**
tiranizar**as**	tiranizar**ais**
tiranizar**a**	tiranizar**an**
OR	
tiranizas**e**	tiranizás**emos**
tiranizas**es**	tiranizas**eis**
tiranizas**e**	tiranizas**en**
imperativo	
tiraniza	tiranicemos
no tiranices	tiranizad; no tiranicéis
tiranice	tiranicen

SINGULAR	PLURAL
perfecto de indicativo	
he tiranizado	**hemos** tiranizado
has tiranizado	**habéis** tiranizado
ha tiranizado	**han** tiranizado
pluscuamperfecto de indicativo	
había tiranizado	**habíamos** tiranizado
habías tiranizado	**habíais** tiranizado
había tiranizado	**habían** tiranizado
pretérito anterior	
hube tiranizado	**hubimos** tiranizado
hubiste tiranizado	**hubisteis** tiranizado
hubo tiranizado	**hubieron** tiranizado
futuro perfecto	
habré tiranizado	**habremos** tiranizado
habrás tiranizado	**habréis** tiranizado
habrá tiranizado	**habrán** tiranizado
condicional compuesto	
habría tiranizado	**habríamos** tiranizado
habrías tiranizado	**habríais** tiranizado
habría tiranizado	**habrían** tiranizado
perfecto de subjuntivo	
haya tiranizado	**hayamos** tiranizado
hayas tiranizado	**hayáis** tiranizado
haya tiranizado	**hayan** tiranizado
pluscuamperfecto de subjuntivo	
hubiera tiranizado	**hubiéramos** tiranizado
hubieras tiranizado	**hubierais** tiranizado
hubiera tiranizado	**hubieran** tiranizado
OR	
hubiese tiranizado	**hubiésemos** tiranizado
hubieses tiranizado	**hubieseis** tiranizado
hubiese tiranizado	**hubiesen** tiranizado

tocar — to touch, to play an instrument

gerundio **tocando** participio de pasado **tocado**

SINGULAR	PLURAL	SINGULAR	PLURAL
presente de indicativo		perfecto de indicativo	
toc**o**	toc**amos**	**he** tocado	**hemos** tocado
toc**as**	toc**áis**	**has** tocado	**habéis** tocado
toc**a**	toc**an**	**ha** tocado	**han** tocado
imperfecto de indicativo		pluscuamperfecto de indicativo	
toca**ba**	toc**ábamos**	**había** tocado	**habíamos** tocado
toc**abas**	toc**abais**	**habías** tocado	**habíais** tocado
toc**aba**	toc**aban**	**había** tocado	**habían** tocado
pretérito		pretérito anterior	
toqu**é**	toc**amos**	**hube** tocado	**hubimos** tocado
toc**aste**	toc**asteis**	**hubiste** tocado	**hubisteis** tocado
toc**ó**	toc**aron**	**hubo** tocado	**hubieron** tocado
futuro		futuro perfecto	
tocar**é**	tocar**emos**	**habré** tocado	**habremos** tocado
tocar**ás**	tocar**éis**	**habrás** tocado	**habréis** tocado
tocar**á**	tocar**án**	**habrá** tocado	**habrán** tocado
condicional simple		condicional compuesto	
tocar**ía**	tocar**íamos**	**habría** tocado	**habríamos** tocado
tocar**ías**	tocar**íais**	**habrías** tocado	**habríais** tocado
tocar**ía**	tocar**ían**	**habría** tocado	**habrían** tocado
presente de subjuntivo		perfecto de subjuntivo	
toqu**e**	toqu**emos**	**haya** tocado	**hayamos** tocado
toqu**es**	toqu**éis**	**hayas** tocado	**hayáis** tocado
toqu**e**	toqu**en**	**haya** tocado	**hayan** tocado
imperfecto de subjuntivo		pluscuamperfecto de subjuntivo	
tocar**a**	tocár**amos**	**hubiera** tocado	**hubiéramos** tocado
tocar**as**	tocar**ais**	**hubieras** tocado	**hubierais** tocado
tocar**a**	tocar**an**	**hubiera** tocado	**hubieran** tocado
OR		OR	
tocas**e**	tocás**emos**	**hubiese** tocado	**hubiésemos** tocado
tocas**es**	tocas**eis**	**hubieses** tocado	**hubieseis** tocado
tocas**e**	tocas**en**	**hubiese** tocado	**hubiesen** tocado

imperativo

—	toquemos
toca; no toques	tocad; no toquéis
toque	toquen

to tolerate **tolerar**

gerundio **tolerando** participio de pasado **tolerado**

SINGULAR	PLURAL
presente de indicativo	
toler**o**	toler**amos**
toler**as**	toler**áis**
toler**a**	toler**an**
imperfecto de indicativo	
toler**aba**	toler**ábamos**
toler**abas**	toler**abais**
toler**aba**	toler**aban**
pretérito	
toler**é**	toler**amos**
toler**aste**	toler**asteis**
toler**ó**	toler**aron**
futuro	
tolerar**é**	tolerar**emos**
tolerar**ás**	tolerar**éis**
tolerar**á**	tolerar**án**
condicional simple	
tolerar**ía**	tolerar**íamos**
tolerar**ías**	tolerar**íais**
tolerar**ía**	tolerar**ían**
presente de subjuntivo	
toler**e**	toler**emos**
toler**es**	toler**éis**
toler**e**	toler**en**
imperfecto de subjuntivo	
tolerar**a**	toleráramos
tolerar**as**	tolerar**ais**
tolerar**a**	tolerar**an**
OR	
toleras**e**	tolerás**emos**
toleras**es**	toleras**eis**
toleras**e**	toleras**en**
imperativo	
tolera	toleremos
no toleres	tolerad; no toleréis
tolere	toleren

SINGULAR	PLURAL
perfecto de indicativo	
he tolerado	**hemos** tolerado
has tolerado	**habéis** tolerado
ha tolerado	**han** tolerado
pluscuamperfecto de indicativo	
había tolerado	**habíamos** tolerado
habías tolerado	**habíais** tolerado
había tolerado	**habían** tolerado
pretérito anterior	
hube tolerado	**hubimos** tolerado
hubiste tolerado	**hubisteis** tolerado
hubo tolerado	**hubieron** tolerado
futuro perfecto	
habré tolerado	**habremos** tolerado
habrás tolerado	**habréis** tolerado
habrá tolerado	**habrán** tolerado
condicional compuesto	
habría tolerado	**habríamos** tolerado
habrías tolerado	**habríais** tolerado
habría tolerado	**habrían** tolerado
perfecto de subjuntivo	
haya tolerado	**hayamos** tolerado
hayas tolerado	**hayáis** tolerado
haya tolerado	**hayan** tolerado
pluscuamperfecto de subjuntivo	
hubiera tolerado	**hubiéramos** tolerado
hubieras tolerado	**hubierais** tolerado
hubiera tolerado	**hubieran** tolerado
OR	
hubiese tolerado	**hubiésemos** tolerado
hubieses tolerado	**hubieseis** tolerado
hubiese tolerado	**hubiesen** tolerado

tomar — to take

gerundio **tomando** — participio de pasado **tomado**

SINGULAR	PLURAL	SINGULAR	PLURAL
presente de indicativo		perfecto de indicativo	
tom**o**	tom**amos**	**he** tomado	**hemos** tomado
tom**as**	tom**áis**	**has** tomado	**habéis** tomado
tom**a**	tom**an**	**ha** tomado	**han** tomado
imperfecto de indicativo		pluscuamperfecto de indicativo	
tom**aba**	tom**ábamos**	**había** tomado	**habíamos** tomado
tom**abas**	tom**abais**	**habías** tomado	**habíais** tomado
tom**aba**	tom**aban**	**había** tomado	**habían** tomado
pretérito		pretérito anterior	
tom**é**	tom**amos**	**hube** tomado	**hubimos** tomado
tom**aste**	tom**asteis**	**hubiste** tomado	**hubisteis** tomado
tom**ó**	tom**aron**	**hubo** tomado	**hubieron** tomado
futuro		futuro perfecto	
tomar**é**	tomar**emos**	**habré** tomado	**habremos** tomado
tomar**ás**	tomar**éis**	**habrás** tomado	**habréis** tomado
tomar**á**	tomar**án**	**habrá** tomado	**habrán** tomado
condicional simple		condicional compuesto	
tomar**ía**	tomar**íamos**	**habría** tomado	**habríamos** tomado
tomar**ías**	tomar**íais**	**habrías** tomado	**habríais** tomado
tomar**ía**	tomar**ían**	**habría** tomado	**habrían** tomado
presente de subjuntivo		perfecto de subjuntivo	
tom**e**	tom**emos**	**haya** tomado	**hayamos** tomado
tom**es**	tom**éis**	**hayas** tomado	**hayáis** tomado
tom**e**	tom**en**	**haya** tomado	**hayan** tomado
imperfecto de subjuntivo		pluscuamperfecto de subjuntivo	
tomar**a**	tomár**amos**	**hubiera** tomado	**hubiéramos** tomado
tomar**as**	tomar**ais**	**hubieras** tomado	**hubierais** tomado
tomar**a**	tomar**an**	**hubiera** tomado	**hubieran** tomado
OR		OR	
tomas**e**	tomás**emos**	**hubiese** tomado	**hubiésemos** tomado
tomas**es**	tomas**eis**	**hubieses** tomado	**hubieseis** tomado
tomas**e**	tomas**en**	**hubiese** tomado	**hubiesen** tomado

imperativo

—	tomemos
toma; no tomes	tomad; no toméis
tome	tomen

gerundio **torciendo** participio de pasado **torcido**

SINGULAR	PLURAL	SINGULAR	PLURAL
presente de indicativo		perfecto de indicativo	
tuerz**o**	torc**emos**	**he** torcido	**hemos** torcido
tierc**es**	torc**éis**	**has** torcido	**habéis** torcido
tuerc**e**	tuerc**en**	**ha** torcido	**han** torcido
imperfecto de indicativo		pluscuamperfecto de indicativo	
torc**ía**	torc**íamos**	**había** torcido	**habíamos** torcido
torc**ías**	torc**íais**	**habías** torcido	**habíais** torcido
torc**ía**	torc**ían**	**había** torcido	**habían** torcido
pretérito		pretérito anterior	
torc**í**	torc**imos**	**hube** torcido	**hubimos** torcido
torc**iste**	torc**isteis**	**hubiste** torcido	**hubisteis** torcido
torci**ó**	torc**ieron**	**hubo** torcido	**hubieron** torcido
futuro		futuro perfecto	
torcer**é**	torcer**emos**	**habré** torcido	**habremos** torcido
torcer**ás**	torcer**éis**	**habrás** torcido	**habréis** torcido
torcer**á**	torcer**án**	**habrá** torcido	**habrán** torcido
condicional simple		condicional compuesto	
torcer**ía**	torcer**íamos**	**habría** torcido	**habríamos** torcido
torcer**ías**	torcer**íais**	**habrías** torcido	**habríais** torcido
torcer**ía**	torcer**ían**	**habría** torcido	**habrían** torcido
presente de subjuntivo		perfecto de subjuntivo	
tuerz**a**	torz**amos**	**haya** torcido	**hayamos** torcido
tuerz**as**	torz**áis**	**hayas** torcido	**hayáis** torcido
tuerz**a**	tuerz**an**	**haya** torcido	**hayan** torcido
imperfecto de subjuntivo		pluscuamperfecto de subjuntivo	
torcier**a**	torciér**amos**	**hubiera** torcido	**hubiéramos** torcido
torcier**as**	torcier**ais**	**hubieras** torcido	**hubierais** torcido
torcier**a**	torcier**an**	**hubiera** torcido	**hubieran** torcido
OR		OR	
torcies**e**	torciés**emos**	**hubiese** torcido	**hubiésemos** torcido
torcies**es**	torcies**eis**	**hubieses** torcido	**hubieseis** torcido
torcies**e**	torcies**en**	**hubiese** torcido	**hubiesen** torcido

imperativo

—	torzamos
tuerce; no tuerzas	torced; no torzáis
tuerza	tuerzan

torear — to bullfight

gerundio **toreando** — participio de pasado **toreado**

SINGULAR	PLURAL
presente de indicativo	
tore**o**	tore**amos**
tore**as**	tore**áis**
tore**a**	tore**an**
imperfecto de indicativo	
tore**aba**	tore**ábamos**
tore**abas**	tore**abais**
tore**aba**	tore**aban**
pretérito	
tore**é**	tore**amos**
tore**aste**	tore**asteis**
tore**ó**	tore**aron**
futuro	
torear**é**	torear**emos**
torear**ás**	torear**éis**
torear**á**	torear**án**
condicional simple	
torear**ía**	torear**íamos**
torear**ías**	torear**íais**
torear**ía**	torear**ían**
presente de subjuntivo	
tore**e**	tore**emos**
tore**es**	tore**éis**
tore**e**	tore**en**
imperfecto de subjuntivo	
torear**a**	toreár**amos**
torear**as**	torear**ais**
torear**a**	torear**an**
OR	
torease**e**	toreás**emos**
toreas**es**	toreas**eis**
toreas**e**	toreas**en**
imperativo	
torea	toreemos
no torees	toread; no toreéis
toree	toreen

SINGULAR	PLURAL
perfecto de indicativo	
he toreado	**hemos** toreado
has toreado	**habéis** toreado
ha toreado	**han** toreado
pluscuamperfecto de indicativo	
había toreado	**habíamos** toreado
habías toreado	**habíais** toreado
había toreado	**habían** toreado
pretérito anterior	
hube toreado	**hubimos** toreado
hubiste toreado	**hubisteis** toreado
hubo toreado	**hubieron** toreado
futuro perfecto	
habré toreado	**habremos** toreado
habrás toreado	**habréis** toreado
habrá toreado	**habrán** toreado
condicional compuesto	
habría toreado	**habríamos** toreado
habrías toreado	**habríais** toreado
habría toreado	**habrían** toreado
perfecto de subjuntivo	
haya toreado	**hayamos** toreado
hayas toreado	**hayáis** toreado
haya toreado	**hayan** toreado
pluscuamperfecto de subjuntivo	
hubiera toreado	**hubiéramos** toreado
hubieras toreado	**hubierais** toreado
hubiera toreado	**hubieran** toreado
OR	
hubiese toreado	**hubiésemos** toreado
hubieses toreado	**hubieseis** toreado
hubiese toreado	**hubiesen** toreado

to cough — toser

gerundio **tosiendo** participio de pasado **tosido**

SINGULAR	PLURAL	SINGULAR	PLURAL
presente de indicativo		perfecto de indicativo	
tos**o**	tos**emos**	**he** tosido	**hemos** tosido
tos**es**	tos**éis**	**has** tosido	**habéis** tosido
tos**e**	tos**en**	**ha** tosido	**han** tosido
imperfecto de indicativo		pluscuamperfecto de indicativo	
tos**ía**	tos**íamos**	**había** tosido	**habíamos** tosido
tos**ías**	tos**íais**	**habías** tosido	**habíais** tosido
tos**ía**	tos**ían**	**había** tosido	**habían** tosido
pretérito		pretérito anterior	
tos**í**	tos**imos**	**hube** tosido	**hubimos** tosido
tos**iste**	tos**isteis**	**hubiste** tosido	**hubisteis** tosido
tos**ió**	tos**ieron**	**hubo** tosido	**hubieron** tosido
futuro		futuro perfecto	
toser**é**	toser**emos**	**habré** tosido	**habremos** tosido
toser**ás**	toser**éis**	**habrás** tosido	**habréis** tosido
toser**á**	toser**án**	**habrá** tosido	**habrán** tosido
condicional simple		condicional compuesto	
toser**ía**	toser**íamos**	**habría** tosido	**habríamos** tosido
toser**ías**	toser**íais**	**habrías** tosido	**habríais** tosido
toser**ía**	toser**ían**	**habría** tosido	**habrían** tosido
presente de subjuntivo		perfecto de subjuntivo	
tos**a**	tos**amos**	**haya** tosido	**hayamos** tosido
tos**as**	tos**áis**	**hayas** tosido	**hayáis** tosido
tos**a**	tos**an**	**haya** tosido	**hayan** tosido
imperfecto de subjuntivo		pluscuamperfecto de subjuntivo	
tosier**a**	tosiér**amos**	**hubiera** tosido	**hubiéramos** tosido
tosier**as**	tosier**ais**	**hubieras** tosido	**hubierais** tosido
tosier**a**	tosier**an**	**hubiera** tosido	**hubieran** tosido
OR		OR	
tosies**e**	tosiés**emos**	**hubiese** tosido	**hubiésemos** tosido
tosies**es**	tosies**eis**	**hubieses** tosido	**hubieseis** tosido
tosies**e**	tosies**en**	**hubiese** tosido	**hubiesen** tosido

imperativo

tose	tosamos
no tosas	tosed; no tosáis
tosa	tosan

T

gerundio **tostando** — participio de pasado **tostado**

SINGULAR	PLURAL
presente de indicativo	
tuest**o**	tost**amos**
tuest**as**	tost**áis**
tuest**a**	tuest**an**
imperfecto de indicativo	
tost**aba**	tost**ábamos**
tost**abas**	tost**abais**
tost**aba**	tost**aban**
pretérito	
tost**é**	tost**amos**
tost**aste**	tost**asteis**
tost**ó**	tost**aron**
futuro	
tostar**é**	tostar**emos**
tostar**ás**	tostar**éis**
tostar**á**	tostar**án**
condicional simple	
tostar**ía**	tostar**íamos**
tostar**ías**	tostar**íais**
tostar**ía**	tostar**ían**
presente de subjuntivo	
tuest**e**	tost**emos**
tuest**es**	tost**éis**
tuest**e**	tuest**en**
imperfecto de subjuntivo	
tostar**a**	tostár**amos**
tostar**as**	tostar**ais**
tostar**a**	tostar**an**
OR	
tostas**e**	tostás**emos**
tostas**es**	tostas**eis**
tostas**e**	tostas**en**
imperativo	
—	tostemos
tuesta; no tuestes	tostad; no tostéis
tueste	tuesten

SINGULAR	PLURAL
perfecto de indicativo	
he tostado	**hemos** tostado
has tostado	**habéis** tostado
ha tostado	**han** tostado
pluscuamperfecto de indicativo	
había tostado	**habíamos** tostado
habías tostado	**habíais** tostado
había tostado	**habían** tostado
pretérito anterior	
hube tostado	**hubimos** tostado
hubiste tostado	**hubisteis** tostado
hubo tostado	**hubieron** tostado
futuro perfecto	
habré tostado	**habremos** tostado
habrás tostado	**habréis** tostado
habrá tostado	**habrán** tostado
condicional compuesto	
habría tostado	**habríamos** tostado
habrías tostado	**habríais** tostado
habría tostado	**habrían** tostado
perfecto de subjuntivo	
haya tostado	**hayamos** tostado
hayas tostado	**hayáis** tostado
haya tostado	**hayan** tostado
pluscuamperfecto de subjuntivo	
hubiera tostado	**hubiéramos** tostado
hubieras tostado	**hubierais** tostado
hubiera tostado	**hubieran** tostado
OR	
hubiese tostado	**hubiésemos** tostado
hubieses tostado	**hubieseis** tostado
hubiese tostado	**hubiesen** tostado

gerundio **trabajando** participio de pasado **trabajado**

SINGULAR	PLURAL
presente de indicativo	
trabaj**o**	trabaj**amos**
trabaj**as**	trabaj**áis**
trabaj**a**	trabaj**an**
imperfecto de indicativo	
trabaj**aba**	trabaj**ábamos**
trabaj**abas**	trabaj**abais**
trabaj**aba**	trabaj**aban**
pretérito	
trabaj**é**	trabaj**amos**
trabaj**aste**	trabaj**asteis**
trabaj**ó**	trabaj**aron**
futuro	
trabajar**é**	trabajar**emos**
trabajar**ás**	trabajar**éis**
trabajar**á**	trabajar**án**
condicional simple	
trabajar**ía**	trabajar**íamos**
trabajar**ías**	trabajar**íais**
trabajar**ía**	trabajar**ían**
presente de subjuntivo	
trabaj**e**	trabaj**emos**
trabaj**es**	trabaj**éis**
trabaj**e**	trabaj**en**
imperfecto de subjuntivo	
trabajar**a**	trabajár**amos**
trabajar**as**	trabajar**ais**
trabajar**a**	trabajar**an**
OR	
trabajas**e**	trabajás**emos**
trabajas**es**	trabajas**eis**
trabajas**e**	trabajas**en**
imperativo	
—	trabajemos
trabaja; no trabajes	trabajad; no trabajéis
trabaje	trabajen

SINGULAR	PLURAL
perfecto de indicativo	
he trabajado	**hemos** trabajado
has trabajado	**habéis** trabajado
ha trabajado	**han** trabajado
pluscuamperfecto de indicativo	
había trabajado	**habíamos** trabajado
habías trabajado	**habíais** trabajado
había trabajado	**habían** trabajado
pretérito anterior	
hube trabajado	**hubimos** trabajado
hubiste trabajado	**hubisteis** trabajado
hubo trabajado	**hubieron** trabajado
futuro perfecto	
habré trabajado	**habremos** trabajado
habrás trabajado	**habréis** trabajado
habrá trabajado	**habrán** trabajado
condicional compuesto	
habría trabajado	**habríamos** trabajado
habrías trabajado	**habríais** trabajado
habría trabajado	**habrían** trabajado
perfecto de subjuntivo	
haya trabajado	**hayamos** trabajado
hayas trabajado	**hayáis** trabajado
haya trabajado	**hayan** trabajado
pluscuamperfecto de subjuntivo	
hubiera trabajado	**hubiéramos** trabajado
hubieras trabajado	**hubierais** trabajado
hubiera trabajado	**hubieran** trabajado
OR	
hubiese trabajado	**hubiésemos** trabajado
hubieses trabajado	**hubieseis** trabajado
hubiese trabajado	**hubiesen** trabajado

traducir to translate

gerundio **traduciendo** participio de pasado **traducido**

SINGULAR	PLURAL
presente de indicativo	
traduzc**o**	traduc**imos**
traduc**es**	traduc**ís**
traduc**e**	traduc**en**
imperfecto de indicativo	
traduc**ía**	traduc**íamos**
traduc**ías**	traduc**íais**
traduc**ía**	traduc**ían**
pretérito	
traduj**e**	traduj**imos**
traduj**iste**	traduj**isteis**
traduj**o**	traduej**eron**
futuro	
traducir**é**	traducir**emos**
traducir**ás**	traducir**éis**
traducir**á**	traducir**án**
condicional simple	
traducir**ía**	traducir**íamos**
traducir**ías**	traducir**íais**
traducir**ía**	traducir**ían**
presente de subjuntivo	
traduzc**a**	traduzc**amos**
traduzc**as**	traduzc**áis**
traduzc**a**	traduzc**an**
imperfecto de subjuntivo	
traduj**era**	traduj**éramos**
traduj**eras**	traduj**erais**
traduj**era**	traduj**eran**
OR	
traduj**ese**	traduj**ésemos**
traduj**eses**	traduj**eseis**
traduj**ese**	traduj**esen**
imperativo	
—	traduzcamos
traduce; no traduzcas	traducid; no traduzcáis
traduzca	traduzcan

SINGULAR	PLURAL
perfecto de indicativo	
he traducido	**hemos** traducido
has traducido	**habéis** traducido
ha traducido	**han** traducido
pluscuamperfecto de indicativo	
había traducido	**habíamos** traducido
habías traducido	**habíais** traducido
había traducido	**habían** traducido
pretérito anterior	
hube traducido	**hubimos** traducido
hubiste traducido	**hubisteis** traducido
hubo traducido	**hubieron** traducido
futuro perfecto	
habré traducido	**habremos** traducido
habrás traducido	**habréis** traducido
habrá traducido	**habrán** traducido
condicional compuesto	
habría traducido	**habríamos** traducido
habrías traducido	**habríais** traducido
habría traducido	**habrían** traducido
perfecto de subjuntivo	
haya traducido	**hayamos** traducido
hayas traducido	**hayáis** traducido
haya traducido	**hayan** traducido
pluscuamperfecto de subjuntivo	
hubiera traducido	**hubiéramos** traducido
hubieras traducido	**hubierais** traducido
hubiera traducido	**hubieran** traducido
OR	
hubiese traducido	**hubiésemos** traducido
hubieses traducido	**hubieseis** traducido
hubiese traducido	**hubiesen** traducido

to bring **traer**

gerundio **trayendo** participio de pasado **traído**

SINGULAR	PLURAL	SINGULAR	PLURAL
presente de indicativo		perfecto de indicativo	
traig**o**	tra**emos**	**he** traído	**hemos** traído
tra**es**	tra**éis**	**has** traído	**habéis** traído
tra**e**	tra**en**	**ha** traído	**han** traído
imperfecto de indicativo		pluscuamperfecto de indicativo	
traí**a**	traí**amos**	**había** traído	**habíamos** traído
traí**as**	traí**ais**	**habías** traído	**habíais** traído
traí**a**	traí**an**	**había** traído	**habían** traído
pretérito		pretérito anterior	
traj**e**	traj**imos**	**hube** traído	**hubimos** traído
traj**iste**	traj**isteis**	**hubiste** traído	**hubisteis** traído
traj**o**	traj**eron**	**hubo** traído	**hubieron** traído
futuro		futuro perfecto	
traer**é**	traer**emos**	**habré** traído	**habremos** traído
traer**ás**	traer**éis**	**habrás** traído	**habréis** traído
traer**á**	traer**án**	**habrá** traído	**habrán** traído
condicional simple		condicional compuesto	
traer**ía**	traer**íamos**	**habría** traído	**habríamos** traído
traer**ías**	traer**íais**	**habrías** traído	**habríais** traído
traer**ía**	traer**ían**	**habría** traído	**habrían** traído
presente de subjuntivo		perfecto de subjuntivo	
traig**a**	traig**amos**	**haya** traído	**hayamos** traído
traig**as**	traig**áis**	**hayas** traído	**hayáis** traído
traig**a**	traig**an**	**haya** traído	**hayan** traído
imperfecto de subjuntivo		pluscuamperfecto de subjuntivo	
trajer**a**	trajér**amos**	**hubiera** traído	**hubiéramos** traído
trajer**as**	trajer**ais**	**hubieras** traído	**hubierais** traído
trajer**a**	trajer**an**	**hubiera** traído	**hubieran** traído
OR		OR	
trajes**e**	trajés**emos**	**hubiese** traído	**hubiésemos** traído
trajes**es**	trajes**eis**	**hubieses** traído	**hubieseis** traído
trajes**e**	trajes**en**	**hubiese** traído	**hubiesen** traído

imperativo

—	traigamos
trae; no traigas	traed; no traigáis
traiga	traigan

traicionar — to betray

gerundio **traicionando** — participio de pasado **traicionado**

SINGULAR	PLURAL
presente de indicativo	
traicion**o**	traicion**amos**
traicion**as**	traicion**áis**
traicion**a**	traicion**an**
imperfecto de indicativo	
traicion**aba**	traicion**ábamos**
traicion**abas**	traicion**abais**
traicion**aba**	traicion**aban**
pretérito	
traicion**é**	traicion**amos**
traicion**aste**	traicion**asteis**
traicion**ó**	traicion**aron**
futuro	
traicionar**é**	traicionar**emos**
traicionar**ás**	traicionar**éis**
traicionar**á**	traicionar**án**
condicional simple	
traicionar**ía**	traicionar**íamos**
traicionar**ías**	traicionar**íais**
traicionar**ía**	traicionar**ían**
presente de subjuntivo	
traicion**e**	traicion**emos**
traicion**es**	traicion**éis**
traicion**e**	traicion**en**
imperfecto de subjuntivo	
traicionar**a**	traicionár**amos**
traicionar**as**	traicionar**ais**
traicionar**a**	traicionar**an**
OR	
traicionas**e**	traicionás**emos**
traicionas**es**	traicionas**eis**
traicionas**e**	traicionas**en**
imperativo	
—	traicionemos
traiciona; no traiciones	traicionad; no traicionéis
traicione	traicionen

SINGULAR	PLURAL
perfecto de indicativo	
he traicionado	**hemos** traicionado
has traicionado	**habéis** traicionado
ha traicionado	**han** traicionado
pluscuamperfecto de indicativo	
había traicionado	**habíamos** traicionado
habías traicionado	**habíais** traicionado
había traicionado	**habían** traicionado
pretérito anterior	
hube traicionado	**hubimos** traicionado
hubiste traicionado	**hubisteis** traicionado
hubo traicionado	**hubieron** traicionado
futuro perfecto	
habré traicionado	**habremos** traicionado
habrás traicionado	**habréis** traicionado
habrá traicionado	**habrán** traicionado
condicional compuesto	
habría traicionado	**habríamos** traicionado
habrías traicionado	**habríais** traicionado
habría traicionado	**habrían** traicionado
perfecto de subjuntivo	
haya traicionado	**hayamos** traicionado
hayas traicionado	**hayáis** traicionado
haya traicionado	**hayan** traicionado
pluscuamperfecto de subjuntivo	
hubiera traicionado	**hubiéramos** traicionado
hubieras traicionado	**hubierais** traicionado
hubiera traicionado	**hubieran** traicionado
OR	
hubiese traicionado	**hubiésemos** traicionado
hubieses traicionado	**hubieseis** traicionado
hubiese traicionado	**hubiesen** traicionado

to transcend **trascender**

gerundio **trascendiendo** participio de pasado **trascendido**

SINGULAR	PLURAL	SINGULAR	PLURAL
presente de indicativo		perfecto de indicativo	
trasciend**o**	trascend**emos**	**he** trascendido	**hemos** trascendido
trasciend**es**	trascend**éis**	**has** trascendido	**habéis** trascendido
trasciend**e**	trasciend**en**	**ha** trascendido	**han** trascendido
imperfecto de indicativo		pluscuamperfecto de indicativo	
trascend**ía**	trascend**íamos**	**había** trascendido	**habíamos** trascendido
trascend**ías**	trascend**íais**	**habías** trascendido	**habíais** trascendido
trascend**ía**	trascend**ían**	**había** trascendido	**habían** trascendido
pretérito		pretérito anterior	
trascend**í**	trascend**imos**	**hube** trascendido	**hubimos** trascendido
trascend**iste**	trascend**isteis**	**hubiste** trascendido	**hubisteis** trascendido
trascendi**ó**	trascend**ieron**	**hubo** trascendido	**hubieron** trascendido
futuro		futuro perfecto	
trascender**é**	trascender**emos**	**habré** trascendido	**habremos** trascendido
trascender**ás**	trascender**éis**	**habrás** trascendido	**habréis** trascendido
trascender**á**	trascender**án**	**habrá** trascendido	**habrán** trascendido
condicional simple		condicional compuesto	
trascender**ía**	trascender**íamos**	**habría** trascendido	**habríamos** trascendido
trascender**ías**	trascender**íais**	**habrías** trascendido	**habríais** trascendido
trascender**ía**	trascender**ían**	**habría** trascendido	**habrían** trascendido
presente de subjuntivo		perfecto de subjuntivo	
trasciend**a**	trascend**amos**	**haya** trascendido	**hayamos** trascendido
trasciend**as**	trascend**áis**	**hayas** trascendido	**hayáis** trascendido
trasciend**a**	trasciend**an**	**haya** trascendido	**hayan** trascendido
imperfecto de subjuntivo		pluscuamperfecto de subjuntivo	
trascendier**a**	trascendiér**amos**	**hubiera** trascendido	**hubiéramos** trascendido
trascendier**as**	trascendier**ais**	**hubieras** trascendido	**hubierais** trascendido
trascendier**a**	trascendier**an**	**hubiera** trascendido	**hubieran** trascendido
OR		OR	
trascendies**e**	trascendiés**emos**	**hubiese** trascendido	**hubiésemos** trascendido
trascendies**es**	trascendies**eis**	**hubieses** trascendido	**hubieseis** trascendido
trascendies**e**	trascendies**en**	**hubiese** trascendido	**hubiesen** trascendido

imperativo

—	trascendamos
trasciende; no trasciendas	trascended; no trascendáis
trascienda	trasciendan

T

tratar — to attempt, to try

gerundio **tratando** participio de pasado **tratado**

SINGULAR	PLURAL
presente de indicativo	
trat**o**	trat**amos**
trat**as**	trat**áis**
trat**a**	trat**an**
imperfecto de indicativo	
trat**aba**	trat**ábamos**
trat**abas**	trat**abais**
trat**aba**	trat**aban**
pretérito	
trat**é**	trat**amos**
trat**aste**	trat**asteis**
trat**ó**	trat**aron**
futuro	
tratar**é**	tratar**emos**
tratar**ás**	tratar**éis**
tratar**á**	tratar**án**
condicional simple	
tratar**ía**	tratar**íamos**
tratar**ías**	tratar**íais**
tratar**ía**	tratar**ían**
presente de subjuntivo	
trat**e**	trat**emos**
trat**es**	trat**éis**
trat**e**	trat**en**
imperfecto de subjuntivo	
tratar**a**	tratár**amos**
tratar**as**	tratar**ais**
tratar**a**	tratar**an**
OR	
tratas**e**	tratás**emos**
tratas**es**	tratas**eis**
tratas**e**	tratas**en**
imperativo	
—	tratemos
trata; no trates	tratad; no tratéis
trate	traten

SINGULAR	PLURAL
perfecto de indicativo	
he tratado	**hemos** tratado
has tratado	**habéis** tratado
ha tratado	**han** tratado
pluscuamperfecto de indicativo	
había tratado	**habíamos** tratado
habías tratado	**habíais** tratado
había tratado	**habían** tratado
pretérito anterior	
hube tratado	**hubimos** tratado
hubiste tratado	**hubisteis** tratado
hubo tratado	**hubieron** tratado
futuro perfecto	
habré tratado	**habremos** tratado
habrás tratado	**habréis** tratado
habrá tratado	**habrán** tratado
condicional compuesto	
habría tratado	**habríamos** tratado
habrías tratado	**habríais** tratado
habría tratado	**habrían** tratado
perfecto de subjuntivo	
haya tratado	**hayamos** tratado
hayas tratado	**hayáis** tratado
haya tratado	**hayan** tratado
pluscuamperfecto de subjuntivo	
hubiera tratado	**hubiéramos** tratado
hubieras tratado	**hubierais** tratado
hubiera tratado	**hubieran** tratado
OR	
hubiese tratado	**hubiésemos** tratado
hubieses tratado	**hubieseis** tratado
hubiese tratado	**hubiesen** tratado

gerundio **trepidando** participio de pasado **trepidado**

SINGULAR	PLURAL	SINGULAR	PLURAL
presente de indicativo		perfecto de indicativo	
trepid**o**	trepid**amos**	**he** trepidado	**hemos** trepidado
trepid**as**	trepid**áis**	**has** trepidado	**habéis** trepidado
trepid**a**	trepid**an**	**ha** trepidado	**han** trepidado
imperfecto de indicativo		pluscuamperfecto de indicativo	
trepid**aba**	trepid**ábamos**	**había** trepidado	**habíamos** trepidado
trepid**abas**	trepid**abais**	**habías** trepidado	**habíais** trepidado
trepid**aba**	trepid**aban**	**había** trepidado	**habían** trepidado
pretérito		pretérito anterior	
trepid**é**	trepid**amos**	**hube** trepidado	**hubimos** trepidado
trepid**aste**	trepid**asteis**	**hubiste** trepidado	**hubisteis** trepidado
trepid**ó**	trepid**aron**	**hubo** trepidado	**hubieron** trepidado
futuro		futuro perfecto	
trepidar**é**	trepidar**emos**	**habré** trepidado	**habremos** trepidado
trepidar**ás**	trepidar**éis**	**habrás** trepidado	**habréis** trepidado
trepidar**á**	trepidar**án**	**habrá** trepidado	**habrán** trepidado
condicional simple		condicional compuesto	
trepidar**ía**	trepidar**íamos**	**habría** trepidado	**habríamos** trepidado
trepidar**ías**	trepidar**íais**	**habrías** trepidado	**habríais** trepidado
trepidar**ía**	trepidar**ían**	**habría** trepidado	**habrían** trepidado
presente de subjuntivo		perfecto de subjuntivo	
trepid**e**	trepid**emos**	**haya** trepidado	**hayamos** trepidado
trepid**es**	trepid**éis**	**hayas** trepidado	**hayáis** trepidado
trepid**e**	trepid**en**	**haya** trepidado	**hayan** trepidado
imperfecto de subjuntivo		pluscuamperfecto de subjuntivo	
trepidar**a**	trepidár**amos**	**hubiera** trepidado	**hubiéramos** trepidado
trepidar**as**	trepidar**ais**	**hubieras** trepidado	**hubierais** trepidado
trepidar**a**	trepidar**an**	**hubiera** trepidado	**hubieran** trepidado
OR		OR	
trepidas**e**	trepidás**emos**	**hubiese** trepidado	**hubiésemos** trepidado
trepidas**es**	trepidas**eis**	**hubieses** trepidado	**hubieseis** trepidado
trepidas**e**	trepidas**en**	**hubiese** trepidado	**hubiesen** trepidado

imperativo

—	trepidemos
trepida; no trepides	trepidad; no trepidéis
trepide	trepiden

tronchar — to snap, to shatter

gerundio **tronchando** — participio de pasado **tronchado**

SINGULAR	PLURAL	SINGULAR	PLURAL
presente de indicativo		perfecto de indicativo	
tronch**o**	tronch**amos**	**he** tronchado	**hemos** tronchado
tronch**as**	tronch**áis**	**has** tronchado	**habéis** tronchado
tronch**a**	tronch**an**	**ha** tronchado	**han** tronchado
imperfecto de indicativo		pluscuamperfecto de indicativo	
tronch**aba**	tronch**ábamos**	**había** tronchado	**habíamos** tronchado
tronch**abas**	tronch**abais**	**habías** tronchado	**habíais** tronchado
tronch**aba**	tronch**aban**	**había** tronchado	**habían** tronchado
pretérito		pretérito anterior	
tronch**é**	tronch**amos**	**hube** tronchado	**hubimos** tronchado
tronch**aste**	tronch**asteis**	**hubiste** tronchado	**hubisteis** tronchado
tronch**ó**	tronch**aron**	**hubo** tronchado	**hubieron** tronchado
futuro		futuro perfecto	
tronchar**é**	tronchar**emos**	**habré** tronchado	**habremos** tronchado
tronchar**ás**	tronchar**éis**	**habrás** tronchado	**habréis** tronchado
tronchar**á**	tronchar**án**	**habrá** tronchado	**habrán** tronchado
condicional simple		condicional compuesto	
tronchar**ía**	tronchar**íamos**	**habría** tronchado	**habríamos** tronchado
tronchar**ías**	tronchar**íais**	**habrías** tronchado	**habríais** tronchado
tronchar**ía**	tronchar**ían**	**habría** tronchado	**habrían** tronchado
presente de subjuntivo		perfecto de subjuntivo	
tronch**e**	tronch**emos**	**haya** tronchado	**hayamos** tronchado
tronch**es**	tronch**éis**	**hayas** tronchado	**hayáis** tronchado
tronch**e**	tronch**en**	**haya** tronchado	**hayan** tronchado
imperfecto de subjuntivo		pluscuamperfecto de subjuntivo	
tronchar**a**	tronchár**amos**	**hubiera** tronchado	**hubiéramos** tronchado
tronchar**as**	tronchar**ais**	**hubieras** tronchado	**hubierais** tronchado
tronchar**a**	tronchar**an**	**hubiera** tronchado	**hubieran** tronchado
OR		OR	
tronchas**e**	tronchás**emos**	**hubiese** tronchado	**hubiésemos** tronchado
tronchas**es**	tronchas**eis**	**hubieses** tronchado	**hubieseis** tronchado
tronchas**e**	tronchas**en**	**hubiese** tronchado	**hubiesen** tronchado

imperativo

—	tronchemos
troncha; no tronches	tronchad; no tronchéis
tronche	tronchen

gerundio **tropezando** participio de pasado **tropezado**

SINGULAR	PLURAL
presente de indicativo	
tropiez**o**	tropez**amos**
tropiez**as**	tropez**áis**
tropiez**a**	tropiez**an**
imperfecto de indicativo	
tropez**aba**	tropez**ábamos**
tropez**abas**	tropez**abais**
tropez**aba**	tropez**aban**
pretérito	
tropec**é**	tropez**amos**
tropez**aste**	tropez**asteis**
tropez**ó**	tropez**aron**
futuro	
tropezar**é**	tropezar**emos**
tropezar**ás**	tropezar**éis**
tropezar**á**	tropezar**án**
condicional simple	
tropezar**ía**	tropezar**íamos**
tropezar**ías**	tropezar**íais**
tropezar**ía**	tropezar**ían**
presente de subjuntivo	
tropiec**e**	tropec**emos**
tropiec**es**	tropec**éis**
tropiec**e**	tropiec**en**
imperfecto de subjuntivo	
tropezar**a**	tropezár**amos**
tropezar**as**	tropezar**ais**
tropezar**a**	tropezar**an**
OR	
tropezas**e**	tropezás**emos**
tropezas**es**	tropezas**eis**
tropezas**e**	tropezas**en**
imperativo	
—	tropecemos
tropieza; no tropieces	tropezad; no tropecéis
tropiece	tropiecen

SINGULAR	PLURAL
perfecto de indicativo	
he tropezado	**hemos** tropezado
has tropezado	**habéis** tropezado
ha tropezado	**han** tropezado
pluscuamperfecto de indicativo	
había tropezado	**habíamos** tropezado
habías tropezado	**habíais** tropezado
había tropezado	**habían** tropezado
pretérito anterior	
hube tropezado	**hubimos** tropezado
hubiste tropezado	**hubisteis** tropezado
hubo tropezado	**hubieron** tropezado
futuro perfecto	
habré tropezado	**habremos** tropezado
habrás tropezado	**habréis** tropezado
habrá tropezado	**habrán** tropezado
condicional compuesto	
habría tropezado	**habríamos** tropezado
habrías tropezado	**habríais** tropezado
habría tropezado	**habrían** tropezado
perfecto de subjuntivo	
haya tropezado	**hayamos** tropezado
hayas tropezado	**hayáis** tropezado
haya tropezado	**hayan** tropezado
pluscuamperfecto de subjuntivo	
hubiera tropezado	**hubiéramos** tropezado
hubieras tropezado	**hubierais** tropezado
hubiera tropezado	**hubieran** tropezado
OR	
hubiese tropezado	**hubiésemos** tropezado
hubieses tropezado	**hubieseis** tropezado
hubiese tropezado	**hubiesen** tropezado

tumbar — to knock down

gerundio **tumbando** participio de pasado **tumbado**

SINGULAR	PLURAL
presente de indicativo	
tumb**o**	tumb**amos**
tumb**as**	tumb**áis**
tumb**a**	tumb**an**
imperfecto de indicativo	
tumb**aba**	tumb**ábamos**
tumb**abas**	tumb**abais**
tumb**aba**	tumb**aban**
pretérito	
tumb**é**	tumb**amos**
tumb**aste**	tumb**asteis**
tumb**ó**	tumb**aron**
futuro	
tumbar**é**	tumbar**emos**
tumbar**ás**	tumbar**éis**
tumbar**á**	tumbar**án**
condicional simple	
tumbar**ía**	tumbar**íamos**
tumbar**ías**	tumbar**íais**
tumbar**ía**	tumbar**ían**
presente de subjuntivo	
tumb**e**	tumb**emos**
tumb**es**	tumb**éis**
tumb**e**	tumb**en**
imperfecto de subjuntivo	
tumbar**a**	tumbár**amos**
tumbar**as**	tumbar**ais**
tumbar**a**	tumbar**an**
OR	
tumbas**e**	tumbás**emos**
tumbas**es**	tumbas**eis**
tumbas**e**	tumbas**en**
imperativo	
—	tumbemos
tumba; no tumbas	tumbad; no tumbéis
tumbe	tumben

SINGULAR	PLURAL
perfecto de indicativo	
he tumbado	**hemos** tumbado
has tumbado	**habéis** tumbado
ha tumbado	**han** tumbado
pluscuamperfecto de indicativo	
había tumbado	**habíamos** tumbado
habías tumbado	**habíais** tumbado
había tumbado	**habían** tumbado
pretérito anterior	
hube tumbado	**hubimos** tumbado
hubiste tumbado	**hubisteis** tumbado
hubo tumbado	**hubieron** tumbado
futuro perfecto	
habré tumbado	**habremos** tumbado
habrás tumbado	**habréis** tumbado
habrá tumbado	**habrán** tumbado
condicional compuesto	
habría tumbado	**habríamos** tumbado
habrías tumbado	**habríais** tumbado
habría tumbado	**habrían** tumbado
perfecto de subjuntivo	
haya tumbado	**hayamos** tumbado
hayas tumbado	**hayáis** tumbado
haya tumbado	**hayan** tumbado
pluscuamperfecto de subjuntivo	
hubiera tumbado	**hubiéramos** tumbado
hubieras tumbado	**hubierais** tumbado
hubiera tumbado	**hubieran** tumbado
OR	
hubiese tumbado	**hubiésemos** tumbado
hubieses tumbado	**hubieseis** tumbado
hubiese tumbado	**hubiesen** tumbado

tutear to address another informally, using tú

gerundio **tuteando** participio de pasado **tuteado**

SINGULAR	PLURAL	SINGULAR	PLURAL
presente de indicativo		perfecto de indicativo	
tute**o**	tute**amos**	**he** tuteado	**hemos** tuteado
tute**as**	tute**áis**	**has** tuteado	**habéis** tuteado
tute**a**	tute**an**	**ha** tuteado	**han** tuteado
imperfecto de indicativo		pluscuamperfecto de indicativo	
tute**aba**	tute**ábamos**	**había** tuteado	**habíamos** tuteado
tute**abas**	tute**abais**	**habías** tuteado	**habíais** tuteado
tute**aba**	tute**aban**	**había** tuteado	**habían** tuteado
pretérito		pretérito anterior	
tute**é**	tute**amos**	**hube** tuteado	**hubimos** tuteado
tute**aste**	tute**asteis**	**hubiste** tuteado	**hubisteis** tuteado
tute**ó**	tute**aron**	**hubo** tuteado	**hubieron** tuteado
futuro		futuro perfecto	
tutear**é**	tutear**emos**	**habré** tuteado	**habremos** tuteado
tutear**ás**	tutear**éis**	**habrás** tuteado	**habréis** tuteado
tutear**á**	tutear**án**	**habrá** tuteado	**habrán** tuteado
condicional simple		condicional compuesto	
tutear**ía**	tutear**íamos**	**habría** tuteado	**habríamos** tuteado
tutear**ías**	tutear**íais**	**habrías** tuteado	**habríais** tuteado
tutear**ía**	tutear**ían**	**habría** tuteado	**habrían** tuteado
presente de subjuntivo		perfecto de subjuntivo	
tute**e**	tute**emos**	**haya** tuteado	**hayamos** tuteado
tute**es**	tute**éis**	**hayas** tuteado	**hayáis** tuteado
tute**e**	tute**en**	**haya** tuteado	**hayan** tuteado
imperfecto de subjuntivo		pluscuamperfecto de subjuntivo	
tutear**a**	tuteár**amos**	**hubiera** tuteado	**hubiéramos** tuteado
tutear**as**	tutear**ais**	**hubieras** tuteado	**hubierais** tuteado
tutear**a**	tutear**an**	**hubiera** tuteado	**hubieran** tuteado
OR		OR	
tutease**e**	tuteás**emos**	**hubiese** tuteado	**hubiésemos** tuteado
teutease**es**	tuteas**eis**	**hubieses** tuteado	**hubieseis** tuteado
tutease**e**	tuteas**en**	**hubiese** tuteado	**hubiesen** tuteado

imperativo

—	tuteemos
tutea; no tutees	tutead; no tuteéis
tutee	tuteen

unir — to connect, to unite

gerundio **uniendo** participio de pasado **unido**

SINGULAR	PLURAL
presente de indicativo	
un**o**	un**imos**
un**es**	un**ís**
un**e**	un**en**
imperfecto de indicativo	
un**ía**	un**íamos**
un**ías**	un**íais**
un**ía**	un**ían**
pretérito	
un**í**	un**imos**
un**iste**	un**isteis**
un**ió**	un**ieron**
futuro	
unir**é**	unir**emos**
unir**ás**	unir**éis**
unir**á**	unir**án**
condicional simple	
unir**ía**	unir**íamos**
unir**ías**	unir**íais**
unir**ía**	unir**ían**
presente de subjuntivo	
un**a**	un**amos**
un**as**	un**áis**
un**a**	un**an**
imperfecto de subjuntivo	
unier**a**	uniér**amos**
unier**as**	unier**ais**
unier**a**	unier**an**
OR	
unies**e**	uniés**emos**
unies**es**	unies**eis**
unies**e**	unies**en**
imperativo	
—	unamos
une; no unas	unid; no unáis
una	unan

SINGULAR	PLURAL
perfecto de indicativo	
he unido	**hemos** unido
has unido	**habéis** unido
ha unido	**han** unido
pluscuamperfecto de indicativo	
había unido	**habíamos** unido
habías unido	**habíais** unido
había unido	**habían** unido
pretérito anterior	
hube unido	**hubimos** unido
hubiste unido	**hubisteis** unido
hubo unido	**hubieron** unido
futuro perfecto	
habré unido	**habremos** unido
habrás unido	**habréis** unido
habrá unido	**habrán** unido
condicional compuesto	
habría unido	**habríamos** unido
habrías unido	**habríais** unido
habría unido	**habrían** unido
perfecto de subjuntivo	
haya unido	**hayamos** unido
hayas unido	**hayáis** unido
haya unido	**hayan** unido
pluscuamperfecto de subjuntivo	
hubiera unido	**hubiéramos** unido
hubieras unido	**hubierais** unido
hubiera unido	**hubieran** unido
OR	
hubiese unido	**hubiésemos** unido
hubieses unido	**hubieseis** unido
hubiese unido	**hubiesen** unido

gerundio **untando** participio de pasado **untado**

SINGULAR	PLURAL	SINGULAR	PLURAL
presente de indicativo		perfecto de indicativo	
unt**o**	unt**amos**	**he** untado	**hemos** untado
unt**as**	unt**áis**	**has** untado	**habéis** untado
unt**a**	unt**an**	**ha** untado	**han** untado
imperfecto de indicativo		pluscuamperfecto de indicativo	
unt**aba**	unt**ábamos**	**había** untado	**habíamos** untado
unt**abas**	unt**abais**	**habías** untado	**habíais** untado
unt**aba**	unt**aban**	**había** untado	**habían** untado
pretérito		pretérito anterior	
unt**é**	unt**amos**	**hube** untado	**hubimos** untado
unt**aste**	unt**asteis**	**hubiste** untado	**hubisteis** untado
unt**ó**	unt**aron**	**hubo** untado	**hubieron** untado
futuro		futuro perfecto	
untar**é**	untar**emos**	**habré** untado	**habremos** untado
untar**ás**	untar**éis**	**habrás** untado	**habréis** untado
untar**á**	untar**án**	**habrá** untado	**habrán** untado
condicional simple		condicional compuesto	
untar**ía**	untar**íamos**	**habría** untado	**habríamos** untado
untar**ías**	untar**íais**	**habrías** untado	**habríais** untado
untar**ía**	untar**ían**	**habría** untado	**habrían** untado
presente de subjuntivo		perfecto de subjuntivo	
unt**e**	unt**emos**	**haya** untado	**hayamos** untado
unt**es**	unt**éis**	**hayas** untado	**hayáis** untado
unt**e**	unt**en**	**haya** untado	**hayan** untado
imperfecto de subjuntivo		pluscuamperfecto de subjuntivo	
untar**a**	untár**amos**	**hubiera** untado	**hubiéramos** untado
untar**as**	untar**ais**	**hubieras** untado	**hubierais** untado
untar**a**	untar**an**	**hubiera** untado	**hubieran** untado
OR		OR	
untas**e**	untás**emos**	**hubiese** untado	**hubiésemos** untado
untas**es**	untas**eis**	**hubieses** untado	**hubieseis** untado
untas**e**	untas**en**	**hubiese** untado	**hubiesen** untado

imperativo

—	untemos
unta; no untes	untad; no untéis
unte	unten

U

usar — to use

gerundio **usando** | participio de pasado **usado**

presente de indicativo

SINGULAR	PLURAL
us**o**	us**amos**
us**as**	us**áis**
us**a**	us**an**

imperfecto de indicativo

SINGULAR	PLURAL
us**aba**	us**ábamos**
us**abas**	us**abais**
us**aba**	us**aban**

pretérito

SINGULAR	PLURAL
us**é**	us**amos**
us**aste**	us**asteis**
us**ó**	us**aron**

futuro

SINGULAR	PLURAL
usar**é**	usar**emos**
usar**ás**	usar**éis**
usar**á**	usar**án**

condicional simple

SINGULAR	PLURAL
usar**ía**	usar**íamos**
usar**ías**	usar**íais**
usar**ía**	usar**ían**

presente de subjuntivo

SINGULAR	PLURAL
us**e**	us**emos**
us**es**	us**éis**
us**e**	us**en**

imperfecto de subjuntivo

SINGULAR	PLURAL
usar**a**	usár**amos**
usar**as**	usar**ais**
usar**a**	usar**an**
OR	
usas**e**	usás**emos**
usas**es**	usas**eis**
usas**e**	usas**en**

imperativo

SINGULAR	PLURAL
—	usemos
usa; no uses	usad; no uséis
use	usen

perfecto de indicativo

SINGULAR	PLURAL
he usado	**hemos** usado
has usado	**habéis** usado
ha usado	**han** usado

pluscuamperfecto de indicativo

SINGULAR	PLURAL
había usado	**habíamos** usado
habías usado	**habíais** usado
había usado	**habían** usado

pretérito anterior

SINGULAR	PLURAL
hube usado	**hubimos** usado
hubiste usado	**hubisteis** usado
hubo usado	**hubieron** usado

futuro perfecto

SINGULAR	PLURAL
habré usado	**habremos** usado
habrás usado	**habréis** usado
habrá usado	**habrán** usado

condicional compuesto

SINGULAR	PLURAL
habría usado	**habríamos** usado
habrías usado	**habríais** usado
habría usado	**habrían** usado

perfecto de subjuntivo

SINGULAR	PLURAL
haya usado	**hayamos** usado
hayas usado	**hayáis** usado
haya usado	**hayan** usado

pluscuamperfecto de subjuntivo

SINGULAR	PLURAL
hubiera usado	**hubiéramos** usado
hubieras usado	**hubierais** usado
hubiera usado	**hubieran** usado
OR	
hubiese usado	**hubiésemos** usado
hubieses usado	**hubieseis** usado
hubiese usado	**hubiesen** usado

to utilize utilizar

gerundio **utilizando** participio de pasado **utilizado**

SINGULAR	PLURAL
presente de indicativo	
utiliz**o**	utiliz**amos**
utiliz**as**	utiliz**áis**
utiliz**a**	utiliz**an**
imperfecto de indicativo	
utiliz**aba**	utiliz**ábamos**
utiliz**abas**	utiliz**abais**
utiliz**aba**	utiliz**aban**
pretérito	
utilic**é**	utiliz**amos**
utiliz**aste**	utiliz**asteis**
utiliz**ó**	utiliz**aron**
futuro	
utilizar**é**	utilizar**emos**
utilizar**ás**	utilizar**éis**
utilizar**á**	utilizar**án**
condicional simple	
utilizar**ía**	utilizar**íamos**
utilizar**ías**	utilizar**íais**
utilizar**ía**	utilizar**ían**
presente de subjuntivo	
utilic**e**	utilic**emos**
utilic**es**	utilic**éis**
utilic**e**	utilic**en**
imperfecto de subjuntivo	
utilizar**a**	utilizár**amos**
utilizar**as**	utilizar**ais**
utilizar**a**	utilizar**an**
OR	
utilizas**e**	utilizás**emos**
utilizas**es**	utilizas**eis**
utilizas**e**	utilizas**en**
imperativo	
—	utilicemos
utiliza; no utilices	utilizad; no utilicéis
utilice	utilicen

SINGULAR	PLURAL
perfecto de indicativo	
he utilizado	**hemos** utilizado
has utilizado	**habéis** utilizado
ha utilizado	**han** utilizado
pluscuamperfecto de indicativo	
había utilizado	**habíamos** utilizado
habías utilizado	**habíais** utilizado
había utilizado	**habían** utilizado
pretérito anterior	
hube utilizado	**hubimos** utilizado
hubiste utilizado	**hubisteis** utilizado
hubo utilizado	**hubieron** utilizado
futuro perfecto	
habré utilizado	**habremos** utilizado
habrás utilizado	**habréis** utilizado
habrá utilizado	**habrán** utilizado
condicional compuesto	
habría utilizado	**habríamos** utilizado
habrías utilizado	**habríais** utilizado
habría utilizado	**habrían** utilizado
perfecto de subjuntivo	
haya utilizado	**hayamos** utilizado
hayas utilizado	**hayáis** utilizado
haya utilizado	**hayan** utilizado
pluscuamperfecto de subjuntivo	
hubiera utilizado	**hubiéramos** utilizado
hubieras utilizado	**hubierais** utilizado
hubiera utilizado	**hubieran** utilizado
OR	
hubiese utilizado	**hubiésemos** utilizado
hubieses utilizado	**hubieseis** utilizado
hubiese utilizado	**hubiesen** utilizado

vaciar — to empty

gerundio **vaciando** participio de pasado **vaciado**

SINGULAR	PLURAL	SINGULAR	PLURAL
presente de indicativo		perfecto de indicativo	
vací**o**	vaci**amos**	**he** vaciado	**hemos** vaciado
vací**as**	vaci**áis**	**has** vaciado	**habéis** vaciado
vací**a**	vací**an**	**ha** vaciado	**han** vaciado
imperfecto de indicativo		pluscuamperfecto de indicativo	
vaci**aba**	vaci**ábamos**	**había** vaciado	**habíamos** vaciado
vaci**abas**	vaci**abais**	**habías** vaciado	**habíais** vaciado
vaci**aba**	vaci**aban**	**había** vaciado	**habían** vaciado
pretérito		pretérito anterior	
vaci**é**	vaci**amos**	**hube** vaciado	**hubimos** vaciado
vaci**aste**	vaci**asteis**	**hubiste** vaciado	**hubisteis** vaciado
vaci**ó**	vaci**aron**	**hubo** vaciado	**hubieron** vaciado
futuro		futuro perfecto	
vaciar**é**	vaciar**emos**	**habré** vaciado	**habremos** vaciado
vaciar**ás**	vaciar**éis**	**habrás** vaciado	**habréis** vaciado
vaciar**á**	vaciar**án**	**habrá** vaciado	**habrán** vaciado
condicional simple		condicional compuesto	
vaciar**ía**	vaciar**íamos**	**habría** vaciado	**habríamos** vaciado
vaciar**ías**	vaciar**íais**	**habrías** vaciado	**habríais** vaciado
vaciar**ía**	vaciar**ían**	**habría** vaciado	**habrían** vaciado
presente de subjuntivo		perfecto de subjuntivo	
vací**e**	vaci**emos**	**haya** vaciado	**hayamos** vaciado
vací**es**	vaci**éis**	**hayas** vaciado	**hayáis** vaciado
vací**e**	vací**en**	**haya** vaciado	**hayan** vaciado
imperfecto de subjuntivo		pluscuamperfecto de subjuntivo	
vaciar**a**	vaciár**amos**	**hubiera** vaciado	**hubiéramos** vaciado
vaciar**as**	vaciar**ais**	**hubieras** vaciado	**hubierais** vaciado
vaciar**a**	vaciar**an**	**hubiera** vaciado	**hubieran** vaciado
OR		OR	
vacias**e**	vaciás**emos**	**hubiese** vaciado	**hubiésemos** vaciado
vacias**es**	vacias**eis**	**hubieses** vaciado	**hubieseis** vaciado
vacias**e**	vacias**en**	**hubiese** vaciado	**hubiesen** vaciado

imperativo

—	vaciemos
vacía; no vacíes	vaciad; no vaciéis
vacíe	vacíen

to be worth and to cost **valer**

gerundio **valiendo** participio de pasado **valido**

presente de indicativo

SINGULAR	PLURAL
valg**o**	val**emos**
val**es**	val**éis**
val**e**	val**en**

imperfecto de indicativo

SINGULAR	PLURAL
val**ía**	val**íamos**
val**ías**	val**íais**
val**ía**	val**ían**

pretérito

SINGULAR	PLURAL
val**í**	val**imos**
val**iste**	val**isteis**
val**ió**	val**ieron**

futuro

SINGULAR	PLURAL
valdr**é**	valdr**emos**
valdr**ás**	valdr**éis**
valdr**á**	valdr**án**

condicional simple

SINGULAR	PLURAL
valdr**ía**	valdr**íamos**
valdr**ías**	valdr**íais**
valdr**ía**	valdr**ían**

presente de subjuntivo

SINGULAR	PLURAL
valg**a**	valg**amos**
valg**as**	valg**áis**
valg**a**	valg**an**

imperfecto de subjuntivo

SINGULAR	PLURAL
valier**a**	valiér**amos**
valier**as**	valier**ais**
valier**a**	valier**an**
OR	
valies**e**	valiés**emos**
valies**es**	valies**eis**
valies**e**	valies**en**

imperativo

SINGULAR	PLURAL
—	valgamos
val or vale;	valed;
no valgas	no valgáis
valga	valgan

perfecto de indicativo

SINGULAR	PLURAL
he valido	**hemos** valido
has valido	**habéis** valido
ha valido	**han** valido

pluscuamperfecto de indicativo

SINGULAR	PLURAL
había valido	**habíamos** valido
habías valido	**habíais** valido
había valido	**habían** valido

pretérito anterior

SINGULAR	PLURAL
hube valido	**hubimos** valido
hubiste valido	**hubisteis** valido
hubo valido	**hubieron** valido

futuro perfecto

SINGULAR	PLURAL
habré valido	**habremos** valido
habrás valido	**habréis** valido
habrá valido	**habrán** valido

condicional compuesto

SINGULAR	PLURAL
habría valido	**habríamos** valido
habrías valido	**habríais** valido
habría valido	**habrían** valido

perfecto de subjuntivo

SINGULAR	PLURAL
haya valido	**hayamos** valido
hayas valido	**hayáis** valido
haya valido	**hayan** valido

pluscuamperfecto de subjuntivo

SINGULAR	PLURAL
hubiera valido	**hubiéramos** valido
hubieras valido	**hubierais** valido
hubiera valido	**hubieran** valido
OR	
hubiese valido	**hubiésemos** valido
hubieses valido	**hubieseis** valido
hubiese valido	**hubiesen** valido

vedar — to prohibit

gerundio **vedando** — participio de pasado **vedado**

SINGULAR	PLURAL	SINGULAR	PLURAL
presente de indicativo		perfecto de indicativo	
ved**o**	ved**amos**	**he** vedado	**hemos** vedado
ved**as**	ved**áis**	**has** vedado	**habéis** vedado
ved**a**	ved**an**	**ha** vedado	**han** vedado
imperfecto de indicativo		pluscuamperfecto de indicativo	
ved**aba**	ved**ábamos**	**había** vedado	**habíamos** vedado
ved**abas**	ved**abais**	**habías** vedado	**habíais** vedado
ved**aba**	ved**aban**	**había** vedado	**habían** vedado
pretérito		pretérito anterior	
ved**é**	ved**amos**	**hube** vedado	**hubimos** vedado
ved**aste**	ved**asteis**	**hubiste** vedado	**hubisteis** vedado
ved**ó**	ved**aron**	**hubo** vedado	**hubieron** vedado
futuro		futuro perfecto	
vedar**é**	vedar**emos**	**habré** vedado	**habremos** vedado
vedar**ás**	vedar**éis**	**habrás** vedado	**habréis** vedado
vedar**á**	vedar**án**	**habrá** vedado	**habrán** vedado
condicional simple		condicional compuesto	
vedar**ía**	vedar**íamos**	**habría** vedado	**habríamos** vedado
vedar**ías**	vedar**íais**	**habrías** vedado	**habríais** vedado
vedar**ía**	vedar**ían**	**habría** vedado	**habrían** vedado
presente de subjuntivo		perfecto de subjuntivo	
ved**e**	ved**emos**	**haya** vedado	**hayamos** vedado
ved**es**	ved**éis**	**hayas** vedado	**hayáis** vedado
ved**e**	ved**en**	**haya** vedado	**hayan** vedado
imperfecto de subjuntivo		pluscuamperfecto de subjuntivo	
vedar**a**	vedár**amos**	**hubiera** vedado	**hubiéramos** vedado
vedar**as**	vedar**ais**	**hubieras** vedado	**hubierais** vedado
vedar**a**	vedar**an**	**hubiera** vedado	**hubieran** vedado
OR		OR	
vedas**e**	vedás**emos**	**hubiese** vedado	**hubiésemos** vedado
vedas**es**	vedas**eis**	**hubieses** vedado	**hubieseis** vedado
vedas**e**	vedas**en**	**hubiese** vedado	**hubiesen** vedado

imperativo

—	vedemos
veda; no vedes	vedad; no vedéis
vede	veden

gerundio **velando** participio de pasado **velado**

SINGULAR	PLURAL	SINGULAR	PLURAL
presente de indicativo		perfecto de indicativo	
vel**o**	vel**amos**	**he** velado	**hemos** velado
vel**as**	vel**áis**	**has** velado	**habéis** velado
vel**a**	vel**an**	**ha** velado	**han** velado
imperfecto de indicativo		pluscuamperfecto de indicativo	
vel**aba**	vel**ábamos**	**había** velado	**habíamos** velado
vel**abas**	vel**abais**	**habías** velado	**habíais** velado
vel**aba**	vel**aban**	**había** velado	**habían** velado
pretérito		pretérito anterior	
vel**é**	vel**amos**	**hube** velado	**hubimos** velado
vel**aste**	vel**asteis**	**hubiste** velado	**hubisteis** velado
vel**ó**	vel**aron**	**hubo** velado	**hubieron** velado
futuro		futuro perfecto	
velar**é**	velar**emos**	**habré** velado	**habremos** velado
velar**ás**	velar**éis**	**habrás** velado	**habréis** velado
velar**á**	velar**án**	**habrá** velado	**habrán** velado
condicional simple		condicional compuesto	
velar**ía**	velar**íamos**	**habría** velado	**habríamos** velado
velar**ías**	velar**íais**	**habrías** velado	**habríais** velado
velar**ía**	velar**ían**	**habría** velado	**habrían** velado
presente de subjuntivo		perfecto de subjuntivo	
vel**e**	vel**emos**	**haya** velado	**hayamos** velado
vel**es**	vel**éis**	**hayas** velado	**hayáis** velado
vel**e**	vel**en**	**haya** velado	**hayan** velado
imperfecto de subjuntivo		pluscuamperfecto de subjuntivo	
velar**a**	velár**amos**	**hubiera** velado	**hubiéramos** velado
velar**as**	velar**ais**	**hubieras** velado	**hubierais** velado
velar**a**	velar**an**	**hubiera** velado	**hubieran** velado
OR		OR	
velas**e**	velás**emos**	**hubiese** velado	**hubiésemos** velado
velas**es**	velas**eis**	**hubieses** velado	**hubieseis** velado
velas**e**	velas**en**	**hubiese** velado	**hubiesen** velado

imperativo

—	velemos
vela; no veles	velad; no veléis
vele	velen

V

vencer — to conquer, to overcome, to defeat

gerundio **venciendo** — participio de pasado **vencido**

SINGULAR	PLURAL
presente de indicativo	
venz**o**	venc**emos**
venc**es**	venc**éis**
venc**e**	venc**en**
imperfecto de indicativo	
venc**ía**	venc**íamos**
venc**ías**	venc**íais**
venc**ía**	venc**ían**
pretérito	
venc**í**	venc**imos**
venc**iste**	venc**isteis**
venc**ió**	venc**ieron**
futuro	
vencer**é**	vencer**emos**
vencer**ás**	vencer**éis**
vencer**á**	vencer**án**
condicional simple	
vencer**ía**	vencer**íamos**
vencer**ías**	vencer**íais**
vencer**ía**	vencer**ían**
presente de subjuntivo	
venz**a**	venz**amos**
venz**as**	venz**áis**
venz**a**	venz**an**
imperfecto de subjuntivo	
vencier**a**	venciér**amos**
vencier**as**	vencier**ais**
vencier**a**	vencier**an**
OR	
venciese**e**	venciés**emos**
venciese**s**	venciese**is**
venciese**e**	venciese**n**
imperativo	
—	venzamos
vence; no venzas	venced; no venzáis
venza	venzan

SINGULAR	PLURAL
perfecto de indicativo	
he vencido	**hemos** vencido
has vencido	**habéis** vencido
ha vencido	**han** vencido
pluscuamperfecto de indicativo	
había vencido	**habíamos** vencido
habías vencido	**habíais** vencido
había vencido	**habían** vencido
pretérito anterior	
hube vencido	**hubimos** vencido
hubiste vencido	**hubisteis** vencido
hubo vencido	**hubieron** vencido
futuro perfecto	
habré vencido	**habremos** vencido
habrás vencido	**habréis** vencido
habrá vencido	**habrán** vencido
condicional compuesto	
habría vencido	**habríamos** vencido
habrías vencido	**habríais** vencido
habría vencido	**habrían** vencido
perfecto de subjuntivo	
haya vencido	**hayamos** vencido
hayas vencido	**hayáis** vencido
haya vencido	**hayan** vencido
pluscuamperfecto de subjuntivo	
hubiera vencido	**hubiéramos** vencido
hubieras vencido	**hubierais** vencido
hubiera vencido	**hubieran** vencido
OR	
hubiese vencido	**hubiésemos** vencido
hubieses vencido	**hubieseis** vencido
hubiese vencido	**hubiesen** vencido

gerundio **vendiendo** participio de pasado **vendido**

SINGULAR	PLURAL	SINGULAR	PLURAL
presente de indicativo		perfecto de indicativo	
vend**o**	vend**emos**	**he** vendido	**hemos** vendido
vend**es**	vend**éis**	**has** vendido	**habéis** vendido
vend**e**	vend**en**	**ha** vendido	**han** vendido
imperfecto de indicativo		pluscuamperfecto de indicativo	
vend**ía**	vend**íamos**	**había** vendido	**habíamos** vendido
vend**ías**	vend**íais**	**habías** vendido	**habíais** vendido
vend**ía**	vend**ían**	**había** vendido	**habían** vendido
pretérito		pretérito anterior	
vend**í**	vend**imos**	**hube** vendido	**hubimos** vendido
vend**iste**	vend**isteis**	**hubiste** vendido	**hubisteis** vendido
vend**ió**	vend**ieron**	**hubo** vendido	**hubieron** vendido
futuro		futuro perfecto	
vender**é**	vender**emos**	**habré** vendido	**habremos** vendido
vender**ás**	vender**éis**	**habrás** vendido	**habréis** vendido
vender**á**	vender**án**	**habrá** vendido	**habrán** vendido
condicional simple		condicional compuesto	
vender**ía**	vender**íamos**	**habría** vendido	**habríamos** vendido
vender**ías**	vender**íais**	**habrías** vendido	**habríais** vendido
vender**ía**	vender**ían**	**habría** vendido	**habrían** vendido
presente de subjuntivo		perfecto de subjuntivo	
vend**a**	vend**amos**	**haya** vendido	**hayamos** vendido
vend**as**	vend**áis**	**hayas** vendido	**hayáis** vendido
vend**a**	vend**an**	**haya** vendido	**hayan** vendido
imperfecto de subjuntivo		pluscuamperfecto de subjuntivo	
vendier**a**	vendiér**amos**	**hubiera** vendido	**hubiéramos** vendido
vendier**as**	vendier**ais**	**hubieras** vendido	**hubierais** vendido
vendier**a**	vendier**an**	**hubiera** vendido	**hubieran** vendido
OR		OR	
vendies**e**	vendiés**emos**	**hubiese** vendido	**hubiésemos** vendido
vendies**es**	vendies**eis**	**hubieses** vendido	**hubieseis** vendido
vendies**e**	vendies**en**	**hubiese** vendido	**hubiesen** vendido

imperativo

—	vendamos
vende; no vendas	vended; no vendáis
venda	vendan

venir — to come

gerundio **viniendo** participio de pasado **venido**

presente de indicativo

SINGULAR	PLURAL
veng**o**	ven**imos**
vien**es**	ven**ís**
vien**e**	vien**en**

imperfecto de indicativo

SINGULAR	PLURAL
ven**ía**	ven**íamos**
ven**ías**	ven**íais**
ven**ía**	ven**ían**

pretérito

SINGULAR	PLURAL
vin**e**	vin**imos**
vin**iste**	vin**isteis**
vin**o**	vin**ieron**

futuro

SINGULAR	PLURAL
vendr**é**	vendr**emos**
vendr**ás**	vendr**éis**
vendr**á**	vendr**án**

condicional simple

SINGULAR	PLURAL
vendr**ía**	vendr**íamos**
vendr**ías**	vendr**íais**
vendr**ía**	vendr**ían**

presente de subjuntivo

SINGULAR	PLURAL
veng**a**	veng**amos**
veng**as**	veng**áis**
veng**a**	veng**an**

imperfecto de subjuntivo

SINGULAR	PLURAL
vinier**a**	viniér**amos**
vinier**as**	vinier**ais**
vinier**a**	vinier**an**
OR	
vinies**e**	viniés**emos**
vinies**es**	vinies**eis**
vinies**e**	vinies**en**

imperativo

SINGULAR	PLURAL
—	vengamos
ven; no vengas	venid; no vengáis
venga	vengan

perfecto de indicativo

SINGULAR	PLURAL
he venido	**hemos** venido
has venido	**habéis** venido
ha venido	**han** venido

pluscuamperfecto de indicativo

SINGULAR	PLURAL
había venido	**habíamos** venido
habías venido	**habíais** venido
había venido	**habían** venido

pretérito anterior

SINGULAR	PLURAL
hube venido	**hubimos** venido
hubiste venido	**hubisteis** venido
hubo venido	**hubieron** venido

futuro perfecto

SINGULAR	PLURAL
habré venido	**habremos** venido
habrás venido	**habréis** venido
habrá venido	**habrán** venido

condicional compuesto

SINGULAR	PLURAL
habría venido	**habríamos** venido
habrías venido	**habríais** venido
habría venido	**habrían** venido

perfecto de subjuntivo

SINGULAR	PLURAL
haya venido	**hayamos** venido
hayas venido	**hayáis** venido
haya venido	**hayan** venido

pluscuamperfecto de subjuntivo

SINGULAR	PLURAL
hubiera venido	**hubiéramos** venido
hubieras venido	**hubierais** venido
hubiera venido	**hubieran** venido
OR	
hubiese venido	**hubiésemos** venido
hubieses venido	**hubieseis** venido
hubiese venido	**hubiesen** venido

gerundio **viendo** participio de pasado **visto**

SINGULAR	PLURAL	SINGULAR	PLURAL
presente de indicativo		perfecto de indicativo	
ve**o**	v**emos**	**he** visto	**hemos** visto
v**es**	v**eis**	**has** visto	**habéis** visto
v**e**	v**en**	**ha** visto	**han** visto
imperfecto de indicativo		pluscuamperfecto de indicativo	
ve**ía**	ve**íamos**	**había** visto	**habíamos** visto
ve**ías**	ve**íais**	**habías** visto	**habíais** visto
ve**ía**	ve**ían**	**había** visto	**habían** visto
pretérito		pretérito anterior	
v**i**	v**imos**	**hube** visto	**hubimos** visto
v**iste**	v**isteis**	**hubiste** visto	**hubisteis** visto
v**io**	v**ieron**	**hubo** visto	**hubieron** visto
futuro		futuro perfecto	
ver**é**	ver**emos**	**habré** visto	**habremos** visto
ver**ás**	ver**éis**	**habrás** visto	**habréis** visto
ver**á**	ver**án**	**habrá** visto	**habrán** visto
condicional simple		condicional compuesto	
ver**ía**	ver**íamos**	**habría** visto	**habríamos** visto
ver**ías**	ver**íais**	**habrías** visto	**habríais** visto
ver**ía**	ver**ían**	**habría** visto	**habrían** visto
presente de subjuntivo		perfecto de subjuntivo	
ve**a**	ve**amos**	**haya** visto	**hayamos** visto
ve**as**	ve**áis**	**hayas** visto	**hayáis** visto
ve**a**	ve**an**	**haya** visto	**hayan** visto
imperfecto de subjuntivo		pluscuamperfecto de subjuntivo	
vier**a**	viér**amos**	**hubiera** visto	**hubiéramos** visto
vier**as**	vier**ais**	**hubieras** visto	**hubierais** visto
vier**a**	vier**an**	**hubiera** visto	**hubieran** visto
OR		OR	
vies**e**	viés**emos**	**hubiese** visto	**hubiésemos** visto
vies**es**	vies**eis**	**hubieses** visto	**hubieseis** visto
vies**e**	vies**en**	**hubiese** visto	**hubiesen** visto

imperativo

—	veamos
ve; no veas	ved; no veáis
vea	vean

V

veranear — to summer

gerundio **veraneando** participio de pasado **veraneado**

SINGULAR	PLURAL
presente de indicativo	
verane**o**	verane**amos**
verane**as**	verane**áis**
verane**a**	verane**an**
imperfecto de indicativo	
verane**aba**	verane**ábamos**
verane**abas**	verane**abais**
verane**aba**	verane**aban**
pretérito	
verane**é**	verane**amos**
verane**aste**	verane**asteis**
verane**ó**	verane**aron**
futuro	
veranear**é**	veranear**emos**
veranear**ás**	veranear**éis**
veranear**á**	veranear**án**
condicional simple	
veranear**ía**	veranear**íamos**
veranear**ías**	veranear**íais**
veranear**ía**	veranear**ían**
presente de subjuntivo	
verane**e**	verane**emos**
verane**es**	verane**éis**
verane**e**	verane**en**
imperfecto de subjuntivo	
veranear**a**	veraneár**amos**
veranear**as**	veranear**ais**
veranear**a**	veranear**an**
OR	
veranease**e**	veraneás**emos**
veraneas**es**	veraneas**eis**
veranease**e**	veraneas**en**
imperativo	
—	veraneemos
veranea; no veranees	veranead; no veraneéis
veranee	veraneen

SINGULAR	PLURAL
perfecto de indicativo	
he veraneado	**hemos** veraneado
has veraneado	**habéis** veraneado
ha veraneado	**han** veraneado
pluscuamperfecto de indicativo	
había veraneado	**habíamos** veraneado
habías veraneado	**habíais** veraneado
había veraneado	**habían** veraneado
pretérito anterior	
hube veraneado	**hubimos** veraneado
hubiste veraneado	**hubisteis** veraneado
hubo veraneado	**hubieron** veraneado
futuro perfecto	
habré veraneado	**habremos** veraneado
habrás veraneado	**habréis** veraneado
habrá veraneado	**habrán** veraneado
condicional compuesto	
habría veraneado	**habríamos** veraneado
habrías veraneado	**habríais** veraneado
habría veraneado	**habrían** veraneado
perfecto de subjuntivo	
haya veraneado	**hayamos** veraneado
hayas veraneado	**hayáis** veraneado
haya veraneado	**hayan** veraneado
pluscuamperfecto de subjuntivo	
hubiera veraneado	**hubiéramos** veraneado
hubieras veraneado	**hubierais** veraneado
hubiera veraneado	**hubieran** veraneado
OR	
hubiese veraneado	**hubiésemos** veraneado
hubieses veraneado	**hubieseis** veraneado
hubiese veraneado	**hubiesen** veraneado

to get dressed **vestirse**

gerundio **vistiéndose** participio de pasado **vestido**

SINGULAR	PLURAL
presente de indicativo	
me vist**o**	nos vest**imos**
te vist**es**	os vest**ís**
se vist**e**	se vist**en**
imperfecto de indicativo	
me vest**ía**	nos vest**íamos**
te vest**ías**	os vest**íais**
se vest**ía**	se vest**ían**
pretérito	
me vest**í**	nos vest**imos**
te vest**iste**	os vest**isteis**
se visti**ó**	se vist**ieron**
futuro	
me vestir**é**	nos vestir**emos**
te vestir**ás**	os vestir**éis**
se vestir**á**	se vestir**án**
condicional simple	
me vestir**ía**	nos vestir**íamos**
te vestir**ías**	os vestir**íais**
se vestir**ía**	se vestir**ían**
presente de subjuntivo	
me vist**a**	me vist**amos**
te vist**as**	os vist**áis**
se vist**a**	se vist**an**
imperfecto de subjuntivo	
me vistier**a**	nos vistiér**amos**
te vistier**as**	os vistier**ais**
se vistier**a**	se vistier**an**
OR	
me vistiese	nos vistiés**emos**
te visties**es**	os visties**eis**
se visties**e**	se visties**en**
imperativo	
—	vistámonos; no nos vistamos
vístete; no te vistas	vestíos; no os vistáis
vístase; no se vista	vístanse; no se vistan

SINGULAR	PLURAL
perfecto de indicativo	
me he vestido	**nos hemos** vestido
te has vestido	**os habéis** vestido
se ha vestido	**se han** vestido
pluscuamperfecto de indicativo	
me había vestido	**nos habíamos** vestido
te habías vestido	**os habíais** vestido
se había vestido	**se habían** vestido
pretérito anterior	
me hube vestido	**nos hubimos** vestido
te hubiste vestido	**os hubisteis** vestido
se hubo vestido	**se hubieron** vestido
futuro perfecto	
me habré vestido	**nos habremos** vestido
te habrás vestido	**os habréis** vestido
se habrá vestido	**se habrán** vestido
condicional compuesto	
me habría vestido	**nos habríamos** vestido
te habrías vestido	**os habríais** vestido
se habría vestido	**se habrían** vestido
perfecto de subjuntivo	
me haya vestido	**nos hayamos** vestido
te hayas vestido	**os hayáis** vestido
se haya vestido	**se hayan** vestido
pluscuamperfecto de subjuntivo	
me hubiera vestido	**nos hubiéramos** vestido
te hubieras vestido	**os hubierais** vestido
se hubiera vestido	**se hubieran** vestido
OR	
me hubiese vestido	**nos hubiésemos** vestido
te hubieses vestido	**os hubieseis** vestido
se hubiese vestido	**se hubiesen** vestido

viajar

to travel

gerundio **viajando** participio de pasado **viajado**

SINGULAR	PLURAL	SINGULAR	PLURAL
presente de indicativo		perfecto de indicativo	
viaj**o**	viaj**amos**	**he** viajado	**hemos** viajado
viaj**as**	viaj**áis**	**has** viajado	**habéis** viajado
viaj**a**	viaj**an**	**ha** viajado	**han** viajado
imperfecto de indicativo		pluscuamperfecto de indicativo	
viaj**aba**	viaj**ábamos**	**había** viajado	**habíamos** viajado
viaj**abas**	viaj**abais**	**habías** viajado	**habíais** viajado
viaj**aba**	viaj**aban**	**había** viajado	**habían** viajado
pretérito		pretérito anterior	
viaj**é**	viaj**amos**	**hube** viajado	**hubimos** viajado
viaj**aste**	viaj**asteis**	**hubiste** viajado	**hubisteis** viajado
viaj**ó**	viaj**aron**	**hubo** viajado	**hubieron** viajado
futuro		futuro perfecto	
viajar**é**	viajar**emos**	**habré** viajado	**habremos** viajado
viajar**ás**	viajar**éis**	**habrás** viajado	**habréis** viajado
viajar**á**	viajar**án**	**habrá** viajado	**habrán** viajado
condicional simple		condicional compuesto	
viajar**ía**	viajar**íamos**	**habría** viajado	**habríamos** viajado
viajar**ías**	viajar**íais**	**habrías** viajado	**habríais** viajado
viajar**ía**	viajar**ían**	**habría** viajado	**habrían** viajado
presente de subjuntivo		perfecto de subjuntivo	
viaj**e**	viaj**emos**	**haya** viajado	**hayamos** viajado
viaj**es**	viaj**éis**	**hayas** viajado	**hayáis** viajado
viaj**e**	viaj**en**	**haya** viajado	**hayan** viajado
imperfecto de subjuntivo		pluscuamperfecto de subjuntivo	
viajar**a**	viajár**amos**	**hubiera** viajado	**hubiéramos** viajado
viajar**as**	viajar**ais**	**hubieras** viajado	**hubierais** viajado
viajar**a**	viajar**an**	**hubiera** viajado	**hubieran** viajado
OR		OR	
viajas**e**	viajás**emos**	**hubiese** viajado	**hubiésemos** viajado
viajas**es**	viajas**eis**	**hubieses** viajado	**hubieseis** viajado
viajas**e**	viajas**en**	**hubiese** viajado	**hubiesen** viajado

imperativo

—	viajemos
viaja; no viajes	viajad; no viajéis
viaje	viajen

gerundio **vigilando** participio de pasado **vigilado**

SINGULAR	PLURAL	SINGULAR	PLURAL
presente de indicativo		perfecto de indicativo	
vigil**o**	vigil**amos**	**he** vigilado	**hemos** vigilado
vigil**as**	vigil**áis**	**has** vigilado	**habéis** vigilado
vigil**a**	vigil**an**	**ha** vigilado	**han** vigilado
imperfecto de indicativo		pluscuamperfecto de indicativo	
vigil**aba**	vigil**ábamos**	**había** vigilado	**habíamos** vigilado
vigil**abas**	vigil**abais**	**habías** vigilado	**habíais** vigilado
vigil**aba**	vigil**aban**	**había** vigilado	**habían** vigilado
pretérito		pretérito anterior	
vigil**é**	vigil**amos**	**hube** vigilado	**hubimos** vigilado
vigil**aste**	vigil**asteis**	**hubiste** vigilado	**hubisteis** vigilado
vigil**ó**	vigil**aron**	**hubo** vigilado	**hubieron** vigilado
futuro		futuro perfecto	
vigilar**é**	vigilar**emos**	**habré** vigilado	**habremos** vigilado
vigilar**ás**	vigilar**éis**	**habrás** vigilado	**habréis** vigilado
vigilar**á**	vigilar**án**	**habrá** vigilado	**habrán** vigilado
condicional simple		condicional compuesto	
vigilar**ía**	vigilar**íamos**	**habría** vigilado	**habríamos** vigilado
vigilar**ías**	vigilar**íais**	**habrías** vigilado	**habríais** vigilado
vigilar**ía**	vigilar**ían**	**habría** vigilado	**habrían** vigilado
presente de subjuntivo		perfecto de subjuntivo	
vigil**e**	vigil**emos**	**haya** vigilado	**hayamos** vigilado
vigil**es**	vigil**éis**	**hayas** vigilado	**hayáis** vigilado
vigil**e**	vigil**en**	**haya** vigilado	**hayan** vigilado
imperfecto de subjuntivo		pluscuamperfecto de subjuntivo	
vigilar**a**	vigilár**amos**	**hubiera** vigilado	**hubiéramos** vigilado
vigilar**as**	vigilar**ais**	**hubieras** vigilado	**hubierais** vigilado
vigilar**a**	vigilar**an**	**hubiera** vigilado	**hubieran** vigilado
OR		OR	
vigilas**e**	vigilás**emos**	**hubiese** vigilado	**hubiésemos** vigilado
vigilas**es**	vigilas**eis**	**hubieses** vigilado	**hubieseis** vigilado
vigilas**e**	vigilas**en**	**hubiese** vigilado	**hubiesen** vigilado

imperativo

—	vigilemos
vigila; no vigiles	vigilad; no vigiléis
vigile	vigilen

V

visitar — to visit

gerundio **visitando** | participio de pasado **visitado**

SINGULAR	PLURAL
presente de indicativo	
visit**o**	visit**amos**
visit**as**	visit**áis**
visit**a**	visit**an**
imperfecto de indicativo	
visit**aba**	visit**ábamos**
visit**abas**	visit**abais**
visit**aba**	visit**aban**
pretérito	
visit**é**	visit**amos**
visit**aste**	visit**asteis**
visit**ó**	visit**aron**
futuro	
visitar**é**	visitar**emos**
visitar**ás**	visitar**éis**
visitar**á**	visitar**án**
condicional simple	
visitar**ía**	visitar**íamos**
visitar**ías**	visitar**íais**
visitar**ía**	visitar**ían**
presente de subjuntivo	
visit**e**	visit**emos**
visit**es**	visit**éis**
visit**e**	visit**en**
imperfecto de subjuntivo	
visitar**a**	visitár**amos**
visitar**as**	visitar**ais**
visitar**a**	visitar**an**
OR	
visitas**e**	visitás**emos**
visitas**es**	visitas**eis**
visitas**e**	visitas**en**
imperativo	
—	visitemos
visita; no visites	visitad; no visitéis
visite	visiten

SINGULAR	PLURAL
perfecto de indicativo	
he visitado	**hemos** visitado
has visitado	**habéis** visitado
ha visitado	**han** visitado
pluscuamperfecto de indicativo	
había visitado	**habíamos** visitado
habías visitado	**habíais** visitado
había visitado	**habían** visitado
pretérito anterior	
hube visitado	**hubimos** visitado
hubiste visitado	**hubisteis** visitado
hubo visitado	**hubieron** visitado
futuro perfecto	
habré visitado	**habremos** visitado
habrás visitado	**habréis** visitado
habrá visitado	**habrán** visitado
condicional compuesto	
habría visitado	**habríamos** visitado
habrías visitado	**habríais** visitado
habría visitado	**habrían** visitado
perfecto de subjuntivo	
haya visitado	**hayamos** visitado
hayas visitado	**hayáis** visitado
haya visitado	**hayan** visitado
pluscuamperfecto de subjuntivo	
hubiera visitado	**hubiéramos** visitado
hubieras visitado	**hubierais** visitado
hubiera visitado	**hubieran** visitado
OR	
hubiese visitado	**hubiésemos** visitado
hubieses visitado	**hubieseis** visitado
hubiese visitado	**hubiesen** visitado

gerundio **viviendo** participio de pasado **vivido**

SINGULAR	PLURAL	SINGULAR	PLURAL
presente de indicativo		perfecto de indicativo	
viv**o**	viv**imos**	**he** vivido	**hemos** vivido
viv**es**	viv**ís**	**has** vivido	**habéis** vivido
viv**e**	viv**en**	**ha** vivido	**han** vivido
imperfecto de indicativo		pluscuamperfecto de indicativo	
viv**ía**	viv**íamos**	**había** vivido	**habíamos** vivido
viv**ías**	viv**íais**	**habías** vivido	**habíais** vivido
viv**ía**	viv**ían**	**había** vivido	**habían** vivido
pretérito		pretérito anterior	
viv**í**	viv**imos**	**hube** vivido	**hubimos** vivido
viv**iste**	viv**isteis**	**hubiste** vivido	**hubisteis** vivido
viv**ió**	viv**ieron**	**hubo** vivido	**hubieron** vivido
futuro		futuro perfecto	
vivir**é**	vivir**emos**	**habré** vivido	**habremos** vivido
vivir**ás**	vivir**éis**	**habrás** vivido	**habréis** vivido
vivir**á**	vivir**án**	**habrá** vivido	**habrán** vivido
condicional simple		condicional compuesto	
vivir**ía**	vivir**íamos**	**habría** vivido	**habríamos** vivido
vivir**ías**	vivir**íais**	**habrías** vivido	**habríais** vivido
vivir**ía**	vivir**ían**	**habría** vivido	**habrían** vivido
presente de subjuntivo		perfecto de subjuntivo	
viv**a**	viv**amos**	**haya** vivido	**hayamos** vivido
viv**as**	viv**áis**	**hayas** vivido	**hayáis** vivido
viv**a**	viv**an**	**haya** vivido	**hayan** vivido
imperfecto de subjuntivo		pluscuamperfecto de subjuntivo	
vivier**a**	viviér**amos**	**hubiera** vivido	**hubiéramos** vivido
vivier**as**	vivier**ais**	**hubieras** vivido	**hubierais** vivido
vivier**a**	vivier**an**	**hubiera** vivido	**hubieran** vivido
OR		OR	
vivies**e**	viviés**emos**	**hubiese** vivido	**hubiésemos** vivido
vivies**es**	vivies**eis**	**hubieses** vivido	**hubieseis** vivido
vivies**e**	vivies**en**	**hubiese** vivido	**hubiesen** vivido

imperativo

—	vivamos
vive; no vivas	vivid; no viváis
viva	vivan

volar — to fly

gerundio volando — **participio de pasado** volado

presente de indicativo

SINGULAR	PLURAL
vuel**o**	vol**amos**
vuel**as**	vol**áis**
vuel**a**	vuel**an**

imperfecto de indicativo

SINGULAR	PLURAL
vol**aba**	vol**ábamos**
vol**abas**	vol**abais**
vol**aba**	vol**aban**

pretérito

SINGULAR	PLURAL
vol**é**	vol**amos**
vol**aste**	vol**asteis**
vol**ó**	vol**aron**

futuro

SINGULAR	PLURAL
volar**é**	volar**emos**
volar**ás**	volar**éis**
volar**á**	volar**án**

condicional simple

SINGULAR	PLURAL
volar**ía**	volar**íamos**
volar**ías**	volar**íais**
volar**ía**	volar**ían**

presente de subjuntivo

SINGULAR	PLURAL
vuel**e**	vol**emos**
vuel**es**	vol**éis**
vuel**e**	vuel**en**

imperfecto de subjuntivo

SINGULAR	PLURAL
volar**a**	volár**amos**
volar**as**	volar**ais**
volar**a**	volar**an**
OR	
volas**e**	volás**emos**
volas**es**	volas**eis**
volas**e**	volas**en**

imperativo

SINGULAR	PLURAL
—	volemos
vuela; no vueles	volad; no voléis
vuele	vuelen

perfecto de indicativo

SINGULAR	PLURAL
he volado	**hemos** volado
has volado	**habéis** volado
ha volado	**han** volado

pluscuamperfecto de indicativo

SINGULAR	PLURAL
había volado	**habíamos** volado
habías volado	**habíais** volado
había volado	**habían** volado

pretérito anterior

SINGULAR	PLURAL
hube volado	**hubimos** volado
hubiste volado	**hubisteis** volado
hubo volado	**hubieron** volado

futuro perfecto

SINGULAR	PLURAL
habré volado	**habremos** volado
habrás volado	**habréis** volado
habrá volado	**habrán** volado

condicional compuesto

SINGULAR	PLURAL
habría volado	**habríamos** volado
habrías volado	**habríais** volado
habría volado	**habrían** volado

perfecto de subjuntivo

SINGULAR	PLURAL
haya volado	**hayamos** volado
hayas volado	**hayáis** volado
haya volado	**hayan** volado

pluscuamperfecto de subjuntivo

SINGULAR	PLURAL
hubiera volado	**hubiéramos** volado
hubieras volado	**hubierais** volado
hubiera volado	**hubieran** volado
OR	
hubiese volado	**hubiésemos** volado
hubieses volado	**hubieseis** volado
hubiese volado	**hubiesen** volado

gerundio **volviendo** participio de pasado **vuelto**

SINGULAR	PLURAL	SINGULAR	PLURAL
presente de indicativo		perfecto de indicativo	
vuelv**o**	volv**emos**	**he** vuelto	**hemos** vuelto
vuelv**es**	volv**éis**	**has** vuelto	**habéis** vuelto
vuelv**e**	vuelv**en**	**ha** vuelto	**han** vuelto
imperfecto de indicativo		pluscuamperfecto de indicativo	
volv**ía**	volv**íamos**	**había** vuelto	**habíamos** vuelto
volv**ías**	volv**íais**	**habías** vuelto	**habíais** vuelto
volv**ía**	volv**ían**	**había** vuelto	**habían** vuelto
pretérito		pretérito anterior	
volv**í**	volv**imos**	**hube** vuelto	**hubimos** vuelto
volv**iste**	volv**isteis**	**hubiste** vuelto	**hubisteis** vuelto
volv**ió**	volv**ieron**	**hubo** vuelto	**hubieron** vuelto
futuro		futuro perfecto	
volver**é**	volver**emos**	**habré** vuelto	**habremos** vuelto
volver**ás**	volver**éis**	**habrás** vuelto	**habréis** vuelto
volver**á**	volver**án**	**habrá** vuelto	**habrán** vuelto
condicional simple		condicional compuesto	
volver**ía**	volver**íamos**	**habría** vuelto	**habríamos** vuelto
volver**ías**	volver**íais**	**habrías** vuelto	**habríais** vuelto
volver**ía**	volver**ían**	**habría** vuelto	**habrían** vuelto
presente de subjuntivo		perfecto de subjuntivo	
vuelv**a**	volv**amos**	**haya** vuelto	**hayamos** vuelto
vuelv**as**	volv**áis**	**hayas** vuelto	**hayáis** vuelto
vuelv**a**	vuelv**an**	**haya** vuelto	**hayan** vuelto
imperfecto de subjuntivo		pluscuamperfecto de subjuntivo	
volvier**a**	volvié**ramos**	**hubiera** vuelto	**hubiéramos** vuelto
volvier**as**	volvier**ais**	**hubieras** vuelto	**hubierais** vuelto
volvier**a**	volvier**an**	**hubiera** vuelto	**hubieran** vuelto
OR		OR	
volvies**e**	volvié**semos**	**hubiese** vuelto	**hubiésemos** vuelto
volvies**es**	volvies**eis**	**hubieses** vuelto	**hubieseis** vuelto
volvies**e**	volvies**en**	**hubiese** vuelto	**hubiesen** vuelto

imperativo

—	volvamos
vuelve; no vuelvas	volved; no volváis
vuelva	vuelvan

votar — to vote

gerundio **votando** participio de pasado **votado**

SINGULAR	PLURAL	SINGULAR	PLURAL
presente de indicativo		perfecto de indicativo	
vot**o**	vot**amos**	**he** votado	**hemos** votado
vot**as**	vot**áis**	**has** votado	**habéis** votado
vot**a**	vot**an**	**ha** votado	**han** votado
imperfecto de indicativo		pluscuamperfecto de indicativo	
vot**aba**	vot**ábamos**	**había** votado	**habíamos** votado
vot**abas**	vot**abais**	**habías** votado	**habíais** votado
vot**aba**	vot**aban**	**había** votado	**habían** votado
pretérito		pretérito anterior	
vot**é**	vot**amos**	**hube** votado	**hubimos** votado
vot**aste**	vot**asteis**	**hubiste** votado	**hubisteis** votado
vot**ó**	vot**aron**	**hubo** votado	**hubieron** votado
futuro		futuro perfecto	
votar**é**	votar**emos**	**habré** votado	**habremos** votado
votar**ás**	votar**éis**	**habrás** votado	**habréis** votado
votar**á**	votar**án**	**habrá** votado	**habrán** votado
condicional simple		condicional compuesto	
votar**ía**	votar**íamos**	**habría** votado	**habríamos** votado
votar**ías**	votar**íais**	**habrías** votado	**habríais** votado
votar**ía**	votar**ían**	**habría** votado	**habrían** votado
presente de subjuntivo		perfecto de subjuntivo	
vot**e**	vot**emos**	**haya** votado	**hayamos** votado
vot**es**	vot**éis**	**hayas** votado	**hayáis** votado
vot**e**	vot**en**	**haya** votado	**hayan** votado
imperfecto de subjuntivo		pluscuamperfecto de subjuntivo	
votar**a**	votár**amos**	**hubiera** votado	**hubiéramos** votado
votar**as**	votar**ais**	**hubieras** votado	**hubierais** votado
votar**a**	votar**an**	**hubiera** votado	**hubieran** votado
OR		OR	
votas**e**	votás**emos**	**hubiese** votado	**hubiésemos** votado
votas**es**	votas**eis**	**hubieses** votado	**hubieseis** votado
votas**e**	votas**en**	**hubiese** votado	**hubiesen** votado

imperativo	
—	votemos
vota; no votes	votad; no votéis
vote	voten

gerundio **yaciendo** participio de pasado **yacido**

SINGULAR	PLURAL	SINGULAR	PLURAL
presente de indicativo		perfecto de indicativo	
yazc**o** (yazg**o**/yag**o**)	yac**emos**	**he** yacido	**hemos** yacido
yac**es**	yac**éis**	**has** yacido	**habéis** yacido
yac**e**	yac**en**	**ha** yacido	**han** yacido
imperfecto de indicativo		pluscuamperfecto de indicativo	
yac**ía**	yac**íamos**	**había** yacido	**habíamos** yacido
yac**ías**	yac**íais**	**habías** yacido	**habíais** yacido
yac**ía**	yac**ían**	**había** yacido	**habían** yacido
pretérito		pretérito anterior	
yac**í**	yac**imos**	**hube** yacido	**hubimos** yacido
yac**iste**	yac**isteis**	**hubiste** yacido	**hubisteis** yacido
yac**ió**	yac**ieron**	**hubo** yacido	**hubieron** yacido
futuro		futuro perfecto	
yacer**é**	yacer**emos**	**habré** yacido	**habremos** yacido
yacer**ás**	yacer**éis**	**habrás** yacido	**habréis** yacido
yacer**á**	yacer**án**	**habrá** yacido	**habrán** yacido
condicional simple		condicional compuesto	
yacer**ía**	yacer**íamos**	**habría** yacido	**habríamos** yacido
yacer**ías**	yacer**íais**	**habrías** yacido	**habríais** yacido
yacer**ía**	yacer**ían**	**habría** yacido	**habrían** yacido
presente de subjuntivo		perfecto de subjuntivo	
yazc**a**	yazc**amos**	**haya** yacido	**hayamos** yacido
yazc**as**	yazc**áis**	**hayas** yacido	**hayáis** yacido
yazc**a**	yazc**an**	**haya** yacido	**hayan** yacido
imperfecto de subjuntivo		pluscuamperfecto de subjuntivo	
yacier**a**	yaciér**amos**	**hubiera** yacido	**hubiéramos** yacido
yacier**as**	yacier**ais**	**hubieras** yacido	**hubierais** yacido
yacier**a**	yacier**an**	**hubiera** yacido	**hubieran** yacido
OR		OR	
yacies**e**	yaciés**emos**	**hubiese** yacido	**hubiésemos** yacido
yacies**es**	yacies**eis**	**hubieses** yacido	**hubieseis** yacido
yacies**e**	yacies**en**	**hubiese** yacido	**hubiesen** yacido

imperativo

—	yazcamos
	yazgamos
yace; no yazcas	yaced; no yazcáis
no yasgas	no yazgáis
yazca	yazcan

zumbar — to buzz, to hum

gerundio **zumbando** participio de pasado **zumbado**

SINGULAR	PLURAL	SINGULAR	PLURAL
presente de indicativo		perfecto de indicativo	
zumb**o**	zumb**amos**	**he** zumbado	**hemos** zumbado
zumb**as**	zumb**áis**	**has** zumbado	**habéis** zumbado
zumb**a**	zumb**an**	**ha** zumbado	**han** zumbado
imperfecto de indicativo		pluscuamperfecto de indicativo	
zumb**aba**	zumb**ábamos**	**había** zumbado	**habíamos** zumbado
zumb**abas**	zumb**abais**	**habías** zumbado	**habíais** zumbado
zumb**aba**	zumb**aban**	**había** zumbado	**habían** zumbado
pretérito		pretérito anterior	
zumb**é**	zumb**amos**	**hube** zumbado	**hubimos** zumbado
zumb**aste**	zumb**asteis**	**hubiste** zumbado	**hubisteis** zumbado
zumb**ó**	zumb**aron**	**hubo** zumbado	**hubieron** zumbado
futuro		futuro perfecto	
zumbar**é**	zumbar**emos**	**habré** zumbado	**habremos** zumbado
zumbar**ás**	zumbar**éis**	**habrás** zumbado	**habréis** zumbado
zumbar**á**	zumbar**án**	**habrá** zumbado	**habrán** zumbado
condicional simple		condicional compuesto	
zumbar**ía**	zumbar**íamos**	**habría** zumbado	**habríamos** zumbado
zumbar**ías**	zumbar**íais**	**habrías** zumbado	**habríais** zumbado
zumbar**ía**	zumbar**ían**	**habría** zumbado	**habrían** zumbado
presente de subjuntivo		perfecto de subjuntivo	
zumb**e**	zumb**emos**	**haya** zumbado	**hayamos** zumbado
zumb**es**	zumb**éis**	**hayas** zumbado	**hayáis** zumbado
zumb**e**	zumb**en**	**haya** zumbado	**hayan** zumbado
imperfecto de subjuntivo		pluscuamperfecto de subjuntivo	
zumbar**a**	zumbár**amos**	**hubiera** zumbado	**hubiéramos** zumbado
zumbar**as**	zumbar**ais**	**hubieras** zumbado	**hubierais** zumbado
zumbar**a**	zumbar**an**	**hubiera** zumbado	**hubieran** zumbado
OR		OR	
zumbas**e**	zumbás**emos**	**hubiese** zumbado	**hubiésemos** zumbado
zumbas**es**	zumbas**eis**	**hubieses** zumbado	**hubieseis** zumbado
zumbas**e**	zumbas**en**	**hubiese** zumbado	**hubiesen** zumbado

imperativo

—	zumbemos
zumba; no zumbes	zumbad; no zumbéis
zumbe	zumben

gerundio **zurciendo** participio de pasado **zurcido**

SINGULAR	PLURAL
presente de indicativo	
zurz**o**	zurc**imos**
zurc**es**	zurc**ís**
zurc**e**	zurc**en**
imperfecto de indicativo	
zurc**ía**	zurc**íamos**
zurc**ías**	zurc**íais**
zurc**ía**	zurc**ían**
pretérito	
zurc**í**	zurc**imos**
zurc**iste**	zurc**isteis**
zurc**ió**	zurc**ieron**
futuro	
zurcir**é**	zurcir**emos**
zurcir**ás**	zurcir**éis**
zurcir**á**	zurcir**án**
condicional simple	
zurcir**ía**	zurcir**íamos**
zurcir**ías**	zurcir**íais**
zurcir**ía**	zurcir**ían**
presente de subjuntivo	
zurz**a**	zurz**amos**
zurz**as**	zurz**áis**
zurz**a**	zurz**an**
imperfecto de subjuntivo	
zurcier**a**	zurciér**amos**
zurcier**as**	zurcier**ais**
zurcier**a**	zurcier**an**
OR	
zurcies**e**	zurciés**emos**
zurcies**es**	zurcies**eis**
zurcies**e**	zurcies**en**
imperativo	
—	zurzamos
zurce; no zurzas	zurcid; no zurzáis
zurza	zurzan

SINGULAR	PLURAL
perfecto de indicativo	
he zurcido	**hemos** zurcido
has zurcido	**habéis** zurcido
ha zurcido	**han** zurcido
pluscuamperfecto de indicativo	
había zurcido	**habíamos** zurcido
habías zurcido	**habíais** zurcido
había zurcido	**habían** zurcido
pretérito anterior	
hube zurcido	**hubimos** zurcido
hubiste zurcido	**hubisteis** zurcido
hubo zurcido	**hubieron** zurcido
futuro perfecto	
habré zurcido	**habremos** zurcido
habrás zurcido	**habréis** zurcido
habrá zurcido	**habrán** zurcido
condicional compuesto	
habría zurcido	**habríamos** zurcido
habrías zurcido	**habríais** zurcido
habría zurcido	**habrían** zurcido
perfecto de subjuntivo	
haya zurcido	**hayamos** zurcido
hayas zurcido	**hayáis** zurcido
haya zurcido	**hayan** zurcido
pluscuamperfecto de subjuntivo	
hubiera zurcido	**hubiéramos** zurcido
hubieras zurcido	**hubierais** zurcido
hubiera zurcido	**hubieran** zurcido
OR	
hubiese zurcido	**hubiésemos** zurcido
hubieses zurcido	**hubieseis** zurcido
hubiese zurcido	**hubiesen** zurcido

Exercise 1

Choose the form of the verb that corresponds to the subject in each sentence. The first one is done for you.

1. Los chicos ___correren___ en el parque todos los días.

   (A) corro
   (B) corren
   (C) corres
   (D) corremos
   (E) corre

2. Nosotros ______________ muchas tarjetas postales a los amigos.

   (A) escribo
   (B) escriben
   (C) escribes
   (D) escribe
   (E) escribimos

3. Mi mamá ______________ a una clase de ejercicios aeróbicos.

   (A) asistes
   (B) asiste
   (C) asisto
   (D) asistimos
   (E) asisten

4. ¿ ______________ tú muchas cartas de amor?

   (A) Recibo
   (B) Recibimos
   (C) Reciben
   (D) Recibes
   (E) Recibe

5. Los estudiantes ______________ un libro de William Shakespeare.

   (A) leo
   (B) leemos
   (C) leen
   (D) lee
   (E) lees

6. El chico ______________ los zapatos en el mercado.

   (A) vende
   (B) vendo
   (C) vendemos
   (D) venden
   (E) vendes

7. Ustedes ______________________ mucho en la clase de español.

   (A) aprenden
   (B) aprendes
   (C) aprende
   (D) aprendo
   (E) aprendemos

8. Yo ______________________ en la clase de arte.

   (A) dibuja
   (B) dibujo
   (C) dibujamos
   (D) dibujan
   (E) dibujas

Exercise 2

Fill in the spaces with the present form of the verb in parentheses. The first one is done for you.

1. Elisa y yo ______pedimos______ (pedir) comida rápida a veces.
2. Nadie ______________________ (recordar) la fecha.
3. Ellos ______________________ (divertirse) en el parque.
4. Yo ______________________ (devolver) el libro a la biblioteca.
5. Mi madre ______________________ (servir) sopa todos los días.
6. Tú ______________________ (conseguir) buenos regalos.

Exercise 3

Read each dialog below. Choose the verb in the correct tense from the selection of choices. The first one is done for you.

1. **Estudiante A:** Conocí al nuevo alumno en la clase de estudios sociales.
   Estudiante B: ¿De verdad? ¿Cuándo lo conociste?

   Estudiante A **replies:** Lo conocí ayer.
   (A) Lo conozco ayer.
   (B) Lo he conocido ayer.
   (C) Lo conocí ayer.
   (D) Lo voy a conocer ayer.

2. **Señora A:** ¿Te gustan las películas de amor?
   Señora B: No. No me gustan para nada.
   Señora A: ¿Por qué?

   Señora B **replies:**
   (A) ¡Me aburrieron!
   (B) ¡Me están aburriendo!
   (C) ¡Me aburren!
   (D) ¡Me hayan aburrido!

3. **Muchacho A:** ¿A qué país hispanohablante te interesaría visitar?

   Muchacho B **replies:**
   (A) Siempre quiero ver Argentina.
   (B) Siempre he querido ver Argentina.
   (C) Siempre quiera ver Argentina.
   (D) Siempre haya querido ver Argentina.

4. **Estudiante A:** ¿Para cuándo tienes que entregar esa tarea?
   Estudiante B: El profesor la quiere para mañana.
   Estudiante A: ¿La has comenzado?
   Estudiante B: Mejor que eso...

   Estudiante B **continues:**
   (A) ¡Ya la entregué!
   (B) ¡Ya la entregue!
   (C) ¡Ya la entregaría!
   (D) ¡Ya la entregaba!

Exercise 4

Fill in the spaces with the correct form of the imperfect verb in parentheses. The first one is done for you.

1. Él siempre ____seguía____ todas las reglas.

   (A) seguía
   (B) seguían
   (C) seguíamos
   (D) seguías

2. Yo les ________________ mucho trabajo.

   (A) exigíamos
   (B) exigían
   (C) exigía
   (D) exigías

3. Su éxito me ______________ mucho celos.

(A) provocaba
(B) provocabas
(C) provocaban
(D) provocábamos

4. Tú me ______________ tu calculadora.

(A) prestaba
(B) prestaban
(C) prestabas
(D) prestábamos

5. Él me ______________ todas las noches.

(A) llamaba
(B) llamábamos
(C) llamaban
(D) llamabas

6. Ustedes ______________ las tradiciones de la casa.

(A) mantenían
(B) mantenías
(C) manteníamos
(D) mantenía

7. Ella ______________ más dinero.

(A) merecías
(B) merecían
(C) merecía
(D) merecíamos

8. Nosotros ______________ los veranos juntos.

(A) pasábamos
(B) pasaban
(C) pasabas
(D) pasaba

Exercise 5

In each sentence, change the underlined term el otro día to a menudo. You must also change the verb from the preterite tense to the imperfect tense. The first one is done for you.

1. Mi amigo *vino* el otro día. → Mi amigo *venía* a menudo.
2. Marisol lo vio el otro día.
3. Tú me lo repetiste el otro día.
4. Almorzamos en un restaurante elegante el otro día.
5. Ustedes me regañaron el otro día.
6. Yo te busqué el otro día.
7. Nosotros nos reímos mucho el otro día.

Exercise 6

In each sentence, change the underlined term repetidamente to ayer. You must also change the verb from the imperfect tense to the preterite tense. The first one is done for you.

1. Él nos mentía repetidamente. → Él nos *mintió* ayer.
2. Ella llegaba tarde repetidamente. ____________
3. Yo iba allá repetidamente. ____________
4. Ellos me lo decían repetidamente. ____________
5. Tú cenabas en casa repetidamente. ____________
6. Usted ofrecía ayuda repetidamente. ____________
7. Ustedes enfrentaban muchos desafíos repetidamente. ____________

Exercise 7

Fill in the spaces with the preterite form of the verb in parentheses. The first one is done for you.

Querido Diario:

Ayer yo ___fui___ (ir) al parque de atracciones con mis amigos. Fue una experiencia interesante para todos.

¡Nosotros ____________ (montar) la montaña rusa más alta del país! A mí me ____________ (encantar) las montañas rusas y ____________ (aprovechar) del día en el parque para montar varias veces. No tuve miedo pero a algunos de mis amigos les dio mucho susto.

Por ejemplo, mi amiga Yesenia no ___________ (pasar) un día muy feliz. Ella se ___________ (enfermar). A lo mejor ella ___________ (comer) algo pesado para el desayuno que no le ___________ (caer) bien. ¡Qué lástima!

Para mí, ¡ ___________ (ser) un día inolvidable!

- Rafael

Exercise 8

Fill in the spaces with the imperfect form of the verb in parentheses. The first one is done for you.

Cuando yo ___era___ niño (ser), yo ___________ (conocer) a todos los niños de mi vecindario. Todos los días nos ___________ (encontrar) en la playa. Me ___________ (fascinar) jugar en la arena. Mi mejor amigo y yo ___________ (hacer) castillos y ___________ (nadar) en las olas. Me acuerdo que ___________ (comer) bocadillos y ___________ (tomar) jugo de piña. Mi mamá siempre ___________ (leer) el periódico y mi papá ___________ (descansar) en su silla. Los veranos de mi juventud ___________ (ser) unos veranos idílicos.

Exercise 9

Fill in the conversation with the correct form of the underlined verb in the preterite tense. The first one is done for you.

Estudiante A: ¿Hablas con la profesora en español?
Estudiante B: ¡Claro! Ayer, yo ___hablé___ con ella en español.
Estudiante A: ¿Siempre trabajas mucho en su clase?
Estudiante B: Ayer mi amigo y yo ___________ muchísimo.
Estudiante A: ¿No crees que recibimos mucha tarea en el texto?
Estudiante B: Sí, anoche nosotros ___________ demasiada tarea.
Estudiante A: ¿Haces la tarea todos los días?
Estudiante B: Bueno... ayer ___________ mi tarea, pero no lo hago siempre.
Estudiante A: ¿Tú crees que los estudiantes escuchan la lección?
Estudiante B: Ayer, todos ___________ la lección.

Exercise 10

Fill in the spaces with the correct form of the verb in parentheses. The first one is done for you.

1. Él ___venía___ aquí a menudo.

   (A) venía
   (B) vino

2. Yo le __________ con frecuencia.

   (A) hablé
   (B) hablaba

3. Carlos me lo __________ varias veces.

   (A) repetía
   (B) repitió

4. Anoche él __________ muchos regalos.

   (A) recibió
   (B) recibía

5. Él me __________ todas las noches.

   (A) llamaba
   (B) llamó

6. Uds. __________ atención en la clase ayer.

   (A) prestaron
   (B) prestaban

7. Ella __________ a su amiga el martes pasado.

   (A) ayudaba
   (B) ayudó

8. Yo __________ la clase ayer.

   (A) empezaba
   (B) empecé

Exercise 11

Fill in the spaces with the future form of the verb in parentheses. The first one is done for you.

1. (asistir) Mañana yo asistiré al concierto en el parque.
2. (tener) Beto ______ que estudiar para pasar esa clase tan difícil.
3. (poder) Rosa no ______ jugar tenis en el campeonato. Se lastimó la rodilla.
4. (convertir) Ellos ______ esa basura en una obra de arte.
5. (andar) Mis amigos y yo ______ por toda la cuidad la semana que viene.
6. (mantener) Ellos ______ la casa limpia mientras sus padres están de vacaciones.
7. (hacer) Ella ______ su tarea después de hacer sus quehaceres.
8. (decir) Usted ______ la verdad, como siempre.

Exercise 12

Fill in the conversations with the correct form of the verb in parentheses in the conditional tense. The first one is done for you.

1. **Estudiante A:** ¿Te gustaría ir al cuarto de computadoras? (gustar)
   Estudiante B: Sí, pero ______ que ir primero a mi gaveta. (tener)
   Estudiante A: Yo te ______, pero tengo que comenzar mi trabajo. ¿Te veo allá? (acompañar)
   Estudiante B: Vale. Te veo.

2. **Estudiante A:** ¿Cómo te ______ si tuvieras que irse de este país a vivir en otro? (sentir)
   Estudiante B: No sé qué emociones ______ (tendría). ¿Qué crees tú?
   Estudiante A: Creo que ______ al no estar cerca de mi familia. (sufrir)
   Estudiante B: Yo también. Pero también pienso que ______ una oportunidad para crecer. (ser)
   Estudiante A: Puede ser. De todos modos, ______ mucho para aprender el idioma del nuevo país. (estudiar)

Exercise 13

Read the dialog below. Fill in the blanks with the correct form of the verb in parentheses. The first one is done for you.

Situation: You are lost in Mexico City. You are trying to find the Palacio de Bellas Artes. You stop a woman on the street to ask for directions.

Tú: Perdón, Señora. ¿Me puedes ___decir___ (decir) dónde queda el Palacio de Bellas Artes?

Señora: A ver. ¿Dónde se ________ (encontrar)? ________ (haber) que mirar en el mapa.

Tú: Aquí tenemos uno. Yo ya ________ (buscar), pero no lo ________ (alcanzar) a ver.

Señora: Ah, sí. Ahora ________ (recordar). ________ (ir) al Zócalo, y ________ (seguir) derecho hasta el Parque Alameda. Esta en el lado este del parque.

Exercise 14

Choose the correct form of the verb to complete each sentence. The first one is done for you.

1. Llegué tarde, pero no perdí el examen. "Más ___vale___ tarde que nunca."

   (A) valdrá
   (B) valga
   (C) valió
   (D) vale

2. Mi mejor amiga no ha decidido todavía a qué universidad quiere asistir. Quiero que ________ la mía para estar juntos.

   (A) escoja
   (B) escoge
   (C) escogió
   (D) haya escogido

3. Martina y Juan van a viajar a Colombia este verano. Deben de ________ del viaje para visitar el Museo de Oro en Bogotá.

   (A) aprovechan
   (B) aprovecharían

(C) aprovechar
(D) aprovechen

4. A veces sueño con ganar la lotería. Si tuviera más dinero, __________ un viaje alrededor del mundo.

(A) haría
(B) está haciendo
(C) hizo
(D) hace

5. ¿No te gustan las verduras? Son sabrosas, y además, __________ muchas vitaminas.

(A) proveer
(B) proveen
(C) proveerían
(D) proveyeran

Exercise 15

Read this passage from the Puerto Rican folktale "*Juan Bobo y el caldero*". Fill in the blanks with the correct form of each verb. The first one is done for you.

Toda la gente del pueblo conocía a Juan Bobo. El era famoso por sus actos poco inteligentes y por su pereza. No le __gustaba__ trabajar y siempre se __________ cuando su mamá lo llamaba para ayudarle con algo.

Un día, la mamá de Juan Bobo quería hacer una sopa de gallina, que era su favorito. La mamá buscaba y buscaba por toda la cocina, pero no __________ un caldero sufiente grande para cocinar la sopa. Entonces, __________ a su hijo:

"Juan, ven acá. ¡Te necesito!", gritó ella, pero Juan no __________. Trató de nuevo. "Ven, Juan. ¡Juancito!", pero nada.

1.

(A) gustó
(B) gustaba
(C) gustaría
(D) gustaron

2.

(A) escondía
(B) escondió
(C) haya escondido
(D) ha escondió

3.

(A) encontraría
(B) encontró
(C) encuentra
(D) encontraría

4.

(A) llamó
(B) llamará
(C) llamaría
(D) ha llamado

5.

(A) aparecía
(B) apareció
(C) aparecería
(D) aparecerá

Exercise 16

Read this passage from the Mexican folktale "*El perezoso dichoso*". Fill in the blanks with the correct form of each verb. The first one is done for you.

En el mercado, el muchacho perezoso trató de vender su ceniza. Cuando una señora lo vio se 1. sorprendió y le dijo:

—"Mi'jo, nadie te va a comprar eso. 2. __________ esta.moneda ..me das pesar."

Satsifecho, el muchacho dejó su mercancía y 3. __________ en seguida de compras. Lo primero que vio fue una bonita máscara en la forma del Diablo y la 4. __________.

Contento con su compra, el muchacho fue al bosque y se hizo un fuego. Un grupo de ladrones, al ver las llamas, 5. __________ y decidió calentarse junto al fuego. Pronto se durmieron todos.

1.

(A) sorpenderá
(B) sorprendió
(C) ha sorprendido
(D) sorprendía

2.

(A) Tiene
(B) Ten
(C) Tenga
(D) Tenemos

3.

(A) fui
(B) fue
(C) fuiste
(D) fueron

4.

(A) compra
(B) compro
(C) compró
(D) compré

5.

(A) se acercaron
(B) se acerqué
(C) se acerca
(D) se acercó

Exercise 17

Read this passage from the Colombian folktale "*Cómo el sapo llegó a ser aplastado*". Fill in the blanks with the correct form of each verb. The first one is done for you.

Por todo el bosque, los animales 1. hablaban con mucha anticipación de la fiesta de los dioses. Todos iban a ir, vestidos en sus mejores trajes. Todos, menos el sapo.

—"¿Cómo 2. ____________ al Cielo?", pensaba. "Yo siempre quería ir para hablar con los dioses. Les tengo muchas cosas importantes que decir. Pero, ¿cómo puedo yo 3. ____________ al cielo como mis hermanos los pájaros?"

Día tras día el sapo 4. ____________ a los gavilanes volar por las nubes y les tenía celos.

1.

(A) hablaba
(B) hablaban
(C) hablabas
(D) hablabamos

2.

(A) llegué
(B) llegaba
(C) llegaría
(D) llegaré

3.

(A) subir
(B) subo
(C) subí
(D) subía

4.

(A) vio
(B) veía
(C) viste
(D) vieron

Exercise 18

Read this passage from the Argentinian folktale "*La costurera malvada*". Fill in the blanks with the correct form of each verb. The first one has been done for you.

Al día siguiente, se 1. despertó y vió el vestido colgado en el armario, ¡pero no era el vestido bonito de la señora! Era el viejo, él que creía que le 2. ____________ a la señora pobre.

Al contemplar el misterio, la costurera 3. ____________ muy raro. Tocó sus piernas y los sintió bien y puntudas. Cuando se 4. ____________ en el espejo de su dormitorio, vio una escena increíble: Como castigo por su maldad, ¡ella se 5. ____________ en unas tijeras!

1.

(A) despertó
(B) despertará
(C) despertaba
(D) despierta

2.

(A) dio
(B) daba
(C) ha dado
(D) había dado

3.

(A) se siente
(B) se sienta
(C) se sintió
(D) se ha sentado

4.

(A) mira
(B) miró
(C) mire
(D) mirará

5.

(A) convierte
(B) convirtió
(C) había convertido
(D) ha convertido

1. abrir
2. acabar
3. andar
4. aprender
5. ayudar
6. bajar
7. bañar
8. beber
9. botar
10. caber
11. caer/caerse
12. callarse
13. caminar
14. cantar
15. cenar
16. cerrar
17. cocinar
18. coger
19. comenzar
20. comer
21. comprar
22. conducir
23. conocer
24. construir
25. contar
26. convencer
27. creer
28. dar
29. deber
30. decir
31. dejar
32. devolver
33. dormir/dormirse
34. ducharse
35. encontrar
36. enfermarse
37. entender
38. entrar
39. escoger
40. escribir
41. estar
42. estudiar
43. gastar
44. gustar
45. haber
46. hablar
47. hacer
48. ir/irse
49. leer
50. limpiar
51. llamar
52. llevar
53. mirar/mirarse
54. oír
55. pagar
56. partir
57. pasar
58. pensar
59. perder
60. poder
61. poner/ponerse
62. preguntar
63. quedarse
64. querer
65. saber
66. salir
67. sentir/sentirse
68. ser
69. tener
70. tomar
71. traer
72. venir
73. ver
74. vivir
75. volver

1. acercarse
2. alcanzar
3. apoyar
4. aprovechar
5. aumentar
6. buscar
7. caber
8. comparar
9. confiar
10. conocer
11. contribuir
12. convertir
13. crear
14. crecer
15. dar
16. deber
17. decir
18. dejar
19. demostrar
20. doler
21. empezar
22. encontrar
23. enfrentar
24. escoger
25. esperar
26. estar
27. exigir
28. exisitir
29. fabricar
30. ganar
31. haber
32. hacer
33. introducir
34. ir
35. jugar
36. limpiar
37. llegar
38. llevar
39. llover
40. mandar
41. mantener
42. merecer
43. morirse
44. ofrecer
45. oir
46. olvidar
47. pasar
48. pedir
49. pensar
50. perder
51. poder
52. poner
53. prestar
54. proponer
55. protegerse
56. proveer
57. provocar
58. querer
59. realizar
60. reconstruir
61. recordar
62. reducir
63. reirse
64. requerir
65. revelar
66. saber
67. sacar
68. seguir
69. sentir
70. ser
71. sufrir
72. tener
73. valer
74. venir
75. ver

Tech **VERB** List

Useful tech verbs in *español.*

apply	**aplicar**
back up	**hacer copia de seguridad**
boldface	**poner en negrita**
cancel	**cancelar**
choose	**elegir**
clear	**borrar**
click	**hacer clic**
close	**cerrar**
copy	**copiar**
create shortcut	**crear acceso directo**
delete	**eliminar**

Tech VERB list

Useful tech verbs in *español*.

dock	**acoplar**
double-click	**hacer doble clic**
download (music)	**descargar (música)**
drag	**arrastrar**
drag-and-drop	**arrastrar y colocar**
edit	**editar, modificar**
exit	**salir**
explore	**explorar**
file	**archivar**
find	**buscar**
find next	**buscar siguiente**
finish	**finalizar**

Spanish TEXT messaging

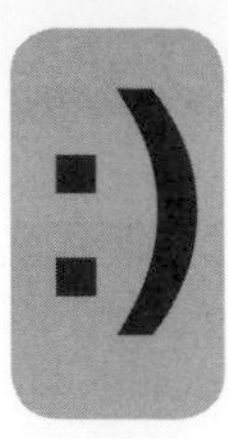

Text your friends in *español.*

110pre	siempre	*always*
a10, a2, bye, chao, chau, dew, dw	adiós	*goodbye*
ac	hace	*(form of hacer: to do)* *Ex: you are doing* *Ex: he/she is doing*
aki	aquí	*here*
amr	amor	*love*
aora	ahora	*now*
asdc	al salir de clase	*after class*
asias	gracias	*thanks*
b	bien	*good*
bb	bebé	*baby*
bbr	beber	*to drink*
bs, bss	beso(s)	*kiss(es)*
b7s	besitos	*kisses*
c	sé, se	*i know (reflexive pronoun)*
cam	cámara	*camera*
d	de	*from, of*
d2	dedos	*fingers*
dcr	decir	*to say*
dfcl	difícil	*difficult*
dim	dime	*tell me*
dnd	¿dónde?	*where?*
exo	hecho	*act*
ems	hemos	*we have*
ers	eres/¿eres?	*you are/are you?*
ers2	eres tú/¿eres tú?	*you are/are you?*
eys	ellos/as	*they (pl.)*
grrr	enfadado	*angry*
finde	fin de semana	*weekend*

Spanish **TEXT** messaging

:)

Text your friends in *español*.

fsta	fiesta	*party*
hl	hasta luego	*see you later*
hla	hola	*hello*
iwal	igual	*the same*
k	que, ¿qué?	*what, what?*
kbza	cabeza	*head*
kls	clase	*class*
kntm	cuéntame	*tell me*
kyat	cállate	*shut up*
km	como	*as, like*
m1ml	mándame un mensaje luego	*send me a message later*
mim	misión imposible	*mission impossible*
msj	mensaje	*message*
mxo	mucho	*a lot*
nph	no puedo hablar	*i can't talk now*
npn	no pasa nada	*nothing is happening*
pa	para, padre	*for, father*
pco	poco	*a little*
pdt	piérdete	*get lost*
pf, pls	por favor	*please*
pq	porque, ¿por qué?	*because, why?*
q	¿qué?	*what?*
q acs?	¿qué haces?	*what are you doing?*
qand, qando, cnd	cuando, ¿cuándo?	*when, when?*
qdms	quedamos	*we're staying*
q plomo!	¡qué plomo!	*what a drag!*
q qrs?	¿qué quieres?	*what do you want?*
q risa!	¡qué risa!	*what a laugh!*
q sea	que sea	*whatever*
q tal?	¿qué tal?	*what's up?*
sbs?	¿sabes?	*do you know?*
salu2	saludos	*hello, goodbye*

Spanish **TEXT** messaging

Text your friends in *español.*

sms	mensaje	*message*
spro	espero	*i hope*
tq	te quiero	*i love you*
tqi	tengo que irme	*i have to go*
tas OK?	¿estás bien?	*are you OK?*
tb	también	*also*
uni	universidad	*university, college*
vns?	¿vienes?	*are you coming?*
vos	vosotros	*you (p.)*
wpa	¡guapa!	*sweet!*
xdon	perdón	*sorry*
xfa	por favor	*please*
xo	pero	*but*
xq	porque, ¿por qué?	*because, why?*
ymam, ymm	llámame	*call me*
zzz	dormir	*to sleep*
+	más	*more*
:)	feliz, alegre	*happy*
:(	triste	*sad*
+o-	más o menos	*more or less*
-	menos	*less*
:p	sacar lengua	*tongue sticking out*
;)	guiño	*wink*
cm	cómo	*how*
cuant	¿cuánto(s)?	*how much?, how many?*
cn	con	*with*
cnt	contesta	*answer*
cox	coche	*car*
cda	cada	*each*
dl	del	*of, from*
dsd	desde	*from, since*
gent	gente	*people*
ay	hay	*is there?, there is...*

Spanish TEXT messaging

Text your friends in *español*

:)

kien	quién	*who*
ksa	casa	*house, home*
kdar	quedar	*to stay*
k+l	¿qué tal?	*what's up?*
l	él	*he*
ls	ellos/as	*they*
mñn	mañana	*tomorrow*
mx	mucho	*a lot*
mu	muy	*very*
na	nada	*nothing*
nox	noche	*night*
n	en, no	*in, no*
sta	esta	*this*
tng	tengo	*i have*
t	te	*you*
s	sí, si	*yes, if*
tkm	te quiero mucho	*i love you a lot*
vy	voy	*i am going*
kcs	¿qué haces?	*what are you doing?*
bin	bien	*good*
to2	todos	*all, everyone*
tb	también	*also*
KO	estoy muerto	*i'm in big trouble (lit. i'm dead)*

Taking a Spanish test or a quiz soon? Preparing for a test is not only about studying content such as Spanish verbs, reading, vocabulary, useful expressions or culture, it is also about practicing and using your learning skills.

The Berlitz author, review and editorial team would like to share with you some test-taking strategies that have worked for them. Many of these strategies may be familiar to you but it's always helpful to review them again. Remember that enhancing your learning skills will help you with all of your classes!

¡Buena suerte!

General Test Taking Tips: Before the Test

- Review test-taking strategies to help you get a head start on the test.
- Prepping for an exam really begins on your first day of class. Reading, reviewing and keeping up with your class work is the first step to test prep.
- Take good notes in class, especially when your teacher suggests that you write something down.
- Review your notes on a regular basis (at least twice a week).
- Review additional classroom assignments such as worksheets, in class activities, assignments or readings.
- Review previous quizzes, tests and any test preparation materials related to your class.
- Study with a partner or with a small group of classmates.
- If your teacher has a review session be sure that you attend the review session.
- During the review session be sure to ask questions, ask for clarification and for additional practice activities.
- Prepare a brief tip sheet for yourself in which you summarize important information, conjugation endings, vocabulary definitions and ideas so that you can review at a glance.
- Spend additional time on material that is more challenging for you and remember there is material that you do know and probably know quite well!
- Get a good night of sleep. Remember that "all nighters" deprive you of the sleep you need to perform well.
- Be sure to eat well before your test.

Test Taking Tips: During the Test

- Be sure to bring extra pencils, pens, paper, erasers or any other materials and resources that your teacher has allowed you to use for the test.
- Arrive early so that you are not stressed.
- Bring a watch to class so that you can manage your time.
- Scan the entire test before you begin so that you know what you will need to do to manage your time.
- Read instruction lines carefully. Be sure that you answer what you are being asked.
- Do the sections that you know well first so that you can move to the sections that are more challenging.
- Balance the amount of time that you spend on each question. If you find that you are spending too much time on one question, skip the question and come back to it later.
- Be sure that you save about 10 minutes at the end of the test to review. You may be able to catch your own mistakes.

Test Taking Tips: After the Test

- Review your test and see if you can identify your own mistakes. If you can't identify your mistakes, ask your teacher.
- Correct your test mistakes in your notebook for future reference.
- Review the test to see what sections you did well on and what sections you need to review again. Make a list so that you can begin to prepare for your next quiz or test.
- Keep your test for future reference and for review and practice.

Verb Activities Answer Key

Exercise 1

1. (B) corren
2. (E) escribimos
3. (B) asiste
4. (D) recibes
5. (C) leen
6. (A) vende
7. (A) aprenden
8. (B) dibujo

Exercise 2

1. pedimos
2. recuerda
3. se divierten
4. devuelvo
5. sirve
6. consigues

Exercise 3

1. (C) conocí
2. (C) aburren
3. (B) he querido
4. (A) entregué

Verb Activities Answer Key

Exercise 4

1. (A) seguia
2. (C) exigía
3. (A) provocaba
4. (C) prestabas
5. (A) llamaba
6. (A) mantenían
7. (C) merecía
8. (A) pasábamos

Exercise 5

1. Mi amigo *venía* a menudo.
2. Marisol lo veía a menudo.
3. Tú me lo repetías a menudo.
4. Almorzábamos en un restaurante elegante a menudo.
5. Ustedes me regañaban a menudo.
6. Yo te buscaba a menudo.
7. Nosotros nos reíamos a menudo.

Exercise 6

1. Él nos *mintió* ayer.
2. Ella llegó tarde ayer.
3. Yo fui a la playa ayer.
4. Ellos me lo dijeron ayer.
5. Tú cenaste en casa ayer.
6. Usted ofrecío ayuda ayer.
7. Ustedes enfrentaron muchos desafíos ayer.

Exercise 7

1. fui
2. montamos
3. encantaron
4. aproveché
5. pasó
6. enfermó
7. comió
8. cayó
9. Fue

Exercise 8

1. era
2. conocía
3. encontrábamos
4. fascinaba
5. hacíamos
6. nadábamos
7. comía
8. tomaba
9. leía
10. descansaba
11. eran

Exercise 9

1. hablé
2. trabajamos
3. recibimos
4. hice
5. escuchamos

Exercise 10

1. (A) venía
2. (B) hablaba
3. (A) repetía
4. (A) recibió

5. (A) llamaba
6. (A) prestaron
7. (B) ayudó
8. (B) empecé

Exercise 11

1. asistiré
2. tendá
3. podrá
4. convertirán
5. andaremos
6. mantendrán
7. hará
8. dirá

Exercise 12

1. gustaría, tendría, acompañaría
2. sentirías, tendría, sufriría, sería, estudiaría

Exercise 13

1. decir
2. encuentra
3. Hay
4. busqué
5. alcanzo
6. recuerdo
7. Ve
8. Sigue

Exercise 14

1. (D) vale
2. (A) escoja
3. (D) aprovechen
4. (A) haría
5. (B) proveen

Exercise 15

1. (B) gustaba
2. (A) escondía
3. (C) encontraba
4. (A) llamó
5. (A) aparecía

Exercise 16

1. (B) sorprendió
2. (B) Ten
3. (B) fue
4. (C) compró
5. (A) se acercaron

Exercise 17

1. (B) hablaban
2. (D) llegaré
3. (A) subir
4. (A) lleven
5. (B) veía

Exercise 18

1. (A) despertó

2. (D) había dado

3. (C) se sintió

4. (B) miró

5. (C) había convertido

Notes

Model Verbs

Below you will find a list of model verbs. We have included these verbs since most other Spanish verbs are conjugated like one of these model forms. We suggest that you study these model verbs; once you know their conjugations you will be able to conjugate most any verb!

On the following pages you will find an index of an additional 2500 verbs. Each verb is followed by an English translation. The English translation is followed by a number, for example: *abalanzar*, to balance, 67. The number 67 refers to the page number where you will find the conjugation of the verb *colgar*. The verb *abalanzar* is conjugated like the model verb colgar.

Index Of Over 2500 Spanish Verbs

A

B

C

E

F

H

I

N

O

P

Q

S

U

V

X

Y

Z